THE HOUSEHOLD ACCOUNTS OF LADY MARGARET BEAUFORT (1443–1509)

From the Archives of St John's College, Cambridge

Records of Social and Economic History is a British Academy Research Project.

The British Academy, established by Royal Charter in 1902, is the national academy for the humanities and social sciences, promoting, sustaining and representing advanced research. As an academy composed of senior scholars throughout the UK, it gives recognition to academic excellence and achievement, and plays a leadership role in representing the humanities and social sciences nationally and internationally. As a learned society, the British Academy facilitates the research of individuals and groups of scholars.

More information can be found at *www.thebritishacademy.ac.uk*

RECORDS OF SOCIAL AND ECONOMIC HISTORY
NEW SERIES 63

THE HOUSEHOLD ACCOUNTS OF LADY MARGARET BEAUFORT (1443–1509)

From the Archives of St John's College, Cambridge

EDITED BY
SUSAN POWELL

Published for THE BRITISH ACADEMY
by OXFORD UNIVERSITY PRESS

Oxford University Press, Great Clarendon Street, Oxford OX2 6DP

First edition published in 2022

British Library Cataloguing in Publication Data
Data available

Library of Congress Cataloging in Publication Data
Data available

Typeset by
New Leaf Design, Malton, North Yorkshire
Printed in Great Britain by
TJ Books, Padstow, Cornwall

ISBN 978–0–19–726704–2

FOREWORD

The richness of Lady Margaret Beaufort's life defies encapsulation. Married aged twelve to a man twice her age, she gave birth a year later to her only child, Henry Tudor. Her skilful plotting on his behalf bore the richest fruit possible with his triumph at Bosworth in 1485 in the Wars of the Roses and crowning as Henry VII. She did not return to the shadows after that triumph. She outlived her son, as she did three husbands, all from leading peerage families. In her final years she established two Cambridge colleges – Christ's and, posthumously, St John's. In sum, her life is testament to the profound inequalities and hierarchies of the time, including the power of dynastic politics and the critical role that women like Beaufort could play. We can see in her more than just the seeds of the determination, ambition and politicking that characterised the Tudor monarchs. She was buried in Westminster Abbey, with Bishop John Fisher, Chancellor of Cambridge University and a future cardinal, preaching in fulsome praise of an extraordinary life.

Professor Sue Powell has produced here a fine edition of many of the complex household accounts of Beaufort from the archives of St John's College. As a formidably rich leading landowner, her household was a large and intricate organization of relations, officials, advisers, servants and visitors. Its needs, both the everyday and the exceptional, were considerable. To meet them ensured that its wider influence was extensive, quite apart from Beaufort's patronage, piety and charity. The accounts help us to understand the management of this enterprise, and through records of its purchases and gifts some of its economic functions, social relations and cultural significance.

Committee member Professor Chris Woolgar gave freely of his time and expertise to Professor Powell as she prepared this edition, while Professor Harding, the general editor of the series, also provided invaluable guidance. Geetha Nair, Portia Taylor and their colleagues at the British Academy saw the volume through the press with great care and skill. I am very grateful to them all for their considerable efforts. Finally, the Committee wishes to thank St John's College Cambridge for its generous permission and help.

Julian Hoppit, Chair, Records of Social and Economic History Committee
August 2022

Contents

Acknowledgements x
Note On Archival References and the Edited Texts xi
Abbreviations xiv
Editorial Conventions xvi
List of Plates xix

Introduction 1
1 Lady Margaret Beaufort and her Household Accounts 2
1.1 The Accounts of Lady Margaret Beaufort 4
1.2 The Edited Accounts 5
1.2.1 D91.16 (William Bedell) 5
1.2.2 D102.10 (Henry Hornby) 5
1.2.3 D91.17, D91.20, D91.21, D91.19, D102.1 (James Clarell, Miles Worsley, Robert Fremingham) 6
1.2.4 D102.2, D102.6 (Roger Ormeston) 6
1.3 The Unedited Accounts 7
1.4 Accounts of Other Households 9

2 Lady Margaret Beaufort and her Officers and Household 13
2.1 The Personnel 13
2.1.1 The computus (D91.16) of William Bedell 13
2.1.2 The book of receipts and payments (D102.10) of Henry Hornby 14
2.1.3 The chamber accounts 15
2.1.3.1 The chamber accounts (D91.17) of James Clarell 15
2.1.3.2 The chamber accounts (D91.20, D91.21, D91.19) of Miles Worsley 15
2.1.3.3 The chamber accounts (D102.1) of Robert Fremingham 16
2.1.4 The accounts (D102.2, D102.6) of Sir Roger Ormeston 16
2.2 The Household 17

3 The Compilation of the Accounts 32
3.1 The Accountants 32
3.2 The Format of the Accounts 33
3.3 The Stages of Compilation of the Accounts 35

3.4 Checking the Accounts 38
3.5 The Audit 40
3.6 Accountant and Auditor 41

4 The Edited Accounts 46
4.1 The computus (D91.16) of William Bedell 46
4.2 The book of receipts and payments (D102.10) of Henry Hornby 51
4.3 The chamber accounts (D91.17, D91.20, D91.21, D91.19, D102.1) 55
4.3.1 The chamber accounts of James Clarell (D91.17) 55
4.3.2 The chamber accounts of Miles Worsley (D91.20, D91.21, D91.19) 57
4.3.3 The chamber accounts of Robert Fremingham (D102.1) 63
4.4 The accounts of Sir Roger Ormeston (D102.2, D102.6) 65

5 The Hands 67
5.1 The Summary Hand of the Audit 69
5.2 The 'Sprawling' Hand 70
5.3 The Auditors and Accountants 71
5.4 The Cursive Hands of the Accountants 74
5.4.1 The 'curly' hand 75
5.4.2 The hand of D91.16 76
5.4.3 The hand of D102.10 77
5.4.4 The hand of D91.17 79
5.4.5 The hand of D91.20, D91.21, D91.19 80
5.4.6 The hand of D102.1 82
5.4.7 The hand of D102.2 and D102.6 83
5.5 The Signature Hand 84

Edited Texts
D91.16 (SJLM/1/1/1/1) The Latin roll of William Bedell 1506–7 85
D102.10 (SJLM/1/1/6/1) Lady Margaret's Book of Receipts and Payments kept by Henry Hornby 1499–1509 137
D91.17 (SJLM/1/1/2/1) The Chamber Account of the Cofferer James Clarell 1498–9 207
D91.20 (SJLM/1/1/3/1) The Account of the Cofferer/Treasurer of the Chamber Miles Worsley 1502–5 247
D91.21 (SJLM/1/1/3/2) The Account of the Treasurer of the Chamber Miles Worsley 1505–7 389

D91.19 (SJLM/1/1/3/3) The Account of the Treasurer of the Chamber Miles Worsley 1507–9 499
D102.1 (SJLM/1/1/5/1) The Account of the Treasurer of the Chamber Robert Fremingham 1509 603
D102.2 and D102.6 (SJLM/1/1/4/1 and SJLM/1/1/4/2) The Account of the Chamberlain Roger Ormeston 1501–2 625
APPENDIX: D56.131 (SJLM/7/5/8) Rewards made to Lady Margaret's servants, 1509 647

Select Glossary 651
Index Of People 689
Index Of Places 739
General index 751
Select Bibliography 765

Cambridge, St John's College, Institutional Archives: Table of Equivalences 1 773
Cambridge, St John's College, Institutional Archives: Table of Equivalences 2 775

ACKNOWLEDGEMENTS

The research for this edition began in the autumn term of 2009, when the University of Salford granted me research leave which enabled me to spend the term at St John's College, Cambridge, where I transcribed the documents edited here. I am grateful to the University of Salford (of which I am now Emeritus Professor of Medieval Texts and Culture) and to the Master (then the late Christopher Dobson) and Fellows of St John's, who offered me accommodation close to the college and some dining rights (much to be desired at St John's, where the kitchen is exceptional). I am also grateful for the generosity of both Master and Fellows during my frequent subsequent visits. My first term at St John's coincided with the period during which Mark Nicholls was President, who was unfailingly kind to a newcomer. Since then, as Librarian, he has consistently supported and furthered my work, with the generous assistance of the Sub-Librarian, Kathryn McKee, and the present Archivist, Lynsey Darby.

However, my first debt is to Malcolm Underwood, the Archivist who welcomed me in my first forays into Lady Margaret's accounts in the mid–1990s. Sitting at a small table in the archivist's room (then in New Court), I learned much as I studied the documents and Malcolm answered my questions. His knowledge of Lady Margaret Beaufort is unparalleled, and his book, *The King's Mother*, co-edited with Michael K. Jones, has been my constant companion over the last decades. Indeed, I have two copies in two locations. I would not have reached this stage of my work if Malcolm had not been Archivist of St John's when I first became interested in Lady Margaret.

I have likewise learned much from Chris Woolgar, who has answered with patience a multitude of emails on both large and small matters. He has provided knowledgeable information in many areas in which I, as a non-historian, have been woefully ignorant, and his *Household Accounts from Medieval England* has been a frequent recourse. I am fortunate that he was appointed my mentor by the committee of the Records of Social and Economic History. Over the last twelve years he has commented carefully and thoughtfully on much of the material edited here, and he was my first reader for this edition. Any errors are undoubtedly due entirely to me. Likewise, I thank Vanessa Harding, who was my second reader.

Colleagues, friends, and family have helped in ways too numerous to mention, but, for particular services rendered, I would like to thank Veronica O'Mara, Gillian Sage and David Starkey. I have much enjoyed my time spent with Lady Margaret Beaufort and say goodbye, or possibly *au revoir*, with regret.

NOTE ON ARCHIVAL REFERENCES AND THE EDITED TEXTS

A preliminary note is necessary before the edited accounts are listed below. When Malcolm Underwood was appointed to the post of Archivist at St John's College, Cambridge in 1974, all the documents relating to Lady Margaret were housed in drawers. Up to that point they had been referred to in general terms, e.g. 'Lady Margaret's will' (of which there are several versions in the archives), 'various documents in folio, belonging to St John's college, bound together in red morocco in 1869, and lettered on the side; "Inventory of lady Margaret's wardrobe ..."', 'a little quarto volume of 37 pages of manuscript sewn together'.[1] All the documents were conserved between 1976 and 1978, and Underwood worked through them, providing paginations[2] and 'shelfmarks' based on the drawers (hence the 'Inventory' just mentioned became D91.24.1 and D91.24.2, and the 'little quarto volume' became D57.43). When my own work began in 2009, this was the system I worked with, and the references I used in my publications.[3] From the academic year 2014–15 the St John's archives have been in the process of being re-catalogued,[4] using AtoM (Access to Memory) software so that they might conform to international recognised standards and be added to databases such as the Archives Hub.

The re-cataloguing began when the bulk of my transcription and editing had been completed and affects the way in which the indexes and glossaries are referenced. The system employed here uses the original references for the edited texts, viz. **16/1** (SJCA D91.16, p. 1), **10/2** (SJCA D102.10, p. 2), **17/23** (SJCA D91.17, p. 23), **20/4** (SJCA D91.20, p. 4), **21/5** (SJCA D91.21, p. 5), **19/6** (SJCA D91.19, p. 6), **1/7** (SJCA D102.1, p. 7), **2/8** (SJCA D102.2, p. 8), **6/9** (SJCA D102.6, p. 9). In the introductory material to the edition the same system is used, but normally with the reference in full, e.g. D91.16/1, D102.10/2, etc. The new references for these documents are, respectively, SJLM/1/1/1/1; SJLM/1/1/6/1; SJLM/1/1/2/1/; SJLM/1/1/3/1; SJLM/1/1/3/2;

[1] C. H. Cooper (ed.), *Memoir of Margaret Countess of Richmond and Derby* (Cambridge: Cambridge University Press, 1874), pp. 129, 178; R. F. Scott, 'On a List (preserved in the Treasury of St John's College) of the Plate, Books and Vestments Bequeathed by the Lady Margaret to Christ's College', *Proceedings of the Cambridge Antiquarian Society* 9 (1896), 349–67 at 349.

[2] Only D102.1 was foliated, as Underwood became more familiar with archival processes.

[3] It was, of course, the system used in the seminal research of M. R. Jones and Malcolm G. Underwood, *The King's Mother: Lady Margaret Beaufort, Countess of Richmond and Derby* (Cambridge: Cambridge University Press, 1982).

[4] <https://www.sjcarchives.org.uk/institutional/index.php/the-records-of-lady-margaret-beaufort>

SJLM/1/1/3/3; SJLM/1/1/5/1; SJLM/1/1/4/1, SJLM/1/1/4/2. (For the full equivalences of the old and new references used in this edition see Cambridge, St John's College, Institutional Archives: Table Of Equivalences 1 and 2 at the end of this edition.)

The decision to prioritise the original, rather than the new, references has been taken out of a desire for clarity (cf. 16/1, i.e. D91.16, p. 1, with its alternative /1/1/1/1/1, or even 1/1/1/1, p. 1) and as being of the greatest use to those who are already familiar with the seminal scholarship which uses the original references. Any document edited here can be accessed on the SJC Archives website by typing in the original reference (which is noted as 'alternative identifier' at the foot of each document description). However, to this date (17.11.2021) not all the items relevant to Lady Margaret have been re-catalogued, e.g. D6.4, one of the four versions of an agreement to convert St John's Hospital into St John's College.

In the edition as a whole and in the indexes/glossaries, the documents edited here are arranged in the order below, an order based partly on language (Latin first), partly on chronology, and partly on generic type:

LATIN

Computus (roll) of the treasurer of the household, William Bedell

- **SJCA D91.16** (SJLM/1/1/1/1) 13 January 1506–13 January 1507

ENGLISH

Book of receipts and payments, kept principally by the secretary/dean of chapel, later chancellor, Henry Hornby

- **SJCA D102.10** (SJLM/1/1/6/1) 1 January 1499–3 October 1509

Accounts of the cofferer (from 14 January 1506 'treasurer of the chamber'): James Clarell, Miles Worsley, Robert Fremingham

- **SJCA D91.17** (SJLM/1/1/2/1) Clarell, 24 June 1498–12 January 1499
- **SJCA D91.20** (SJLM/1/1/3/1) Worsley, Collyweston, 2 February 1502–14 January 1505
- **SJCA D91.21** (SJLM/1/1/3/2) Worsley, Croydon, 14 January 1505–14 January 1507
- **SJCA D91.19** (SJLM/1/1/3/3) Worsley, Hatfield, 14 January 1507–14 January 1509

- **SJCA D102.1** (SJLM/1/1/5/1) Fremingham, Hatfield, 20 January 1509–29 June 1509

Accounts of the chamberlain, Sir Roger Ormeston
- **SJCA D102.2** (SJLM/1/1/4/1) 20 May–18 December 1501
- **SJCA D102.6** (SJLM/1/1/4/2) [9 January–11 February 1502]

Appendix: Rewards made to Lady Margaret's servants after her death, 1509
- **SJCA D56.131** (SJLM/7/5/8)

ABBREVIATIONS

BL	British Library, London
DMLBS	*Dictionary of Medieval Latin from British Sources*, ed. R. E. Latham, D. R. Howlett, and Richard Ashdowne, 17 fascicules in 3 vols (London: Oxford University Press for the British Academy, 1975–2013) [available at <https://logeion.uchicago.edu/>]
EETS	Early English Text Society (OS Original Series, ES Extra Series)
LCCP	Lexis of Cloth and Clothing Project (University of Manchester) [available at <http://lexisproject.arts.manchester.ac.uk/>]
ME	Middle English
MED	*Middle English Dictionary* [available at <https://quod.lib.umich.edu/m/middle-english-dictionary/dictionary>]
ODNB	*Oxford Dictionary of National Biography* [available to subscribers at <https://www.oxforddnb.com/>]
OED	*Oxford English Dictionary* [available to subscribers at <https://www.oed.com/>]
OF	Old French
STC	*A Short-Title Catalogue of Books Printed in England, Scotland and Ireland and of English Books Printed Abroad 1475–1640*, ed. A. W. Pollard and G. R. Redgrave, 2nd edn W. A. Jackson and F. S. Ferguson, completed Katharine F. Pantzer, 3 vols (London: The Bibliographical Society, 1986–91) [available in a revised but less reliable form at <http://estc.bl.uk/>]
TNA	The National Archives, Kew

ABBREVIATIONS FOR COINAGE, WEIGHTS, MEASURES

For terms relating to coinage, weights and measures see also the Glossaries passim.

(bus.) bussellus 'bushel', a unit of dry measure of 4 pecks/8 gallons

(C^{ma}) centum majus 'long hundred', i.e. 120; **(C^{mi}) centum minus** 'short hundred', i.e. 100 (both at D91.16/11) (*DMLBS* **centum** 1d)

(cwt) 'centum weight', hundredweight, i.e. 100 or 112 lb. (*DMLBS* **centum** 2; *OED* **hundredweight** *n.* (1543 ref.))

(d.) denarius 'penny'

(dd.) duodenarius 'dozen'

(di.) dimidium 'half'; ~ **quarter** one-eighth

(dol.) dolium tun, cask, a unit of measure of liquid or dry goods

(dwt) 'denarius weight', pennyweight, i.e. one-twentieth of an ounce (*DMLBS* **denarius** 10; *OED* **pennyweight** *n.* 1 (1552 ref.))

(lag.) lagena as a unit of liquid measure, one gallon (*DMLBS* 2); as a unit of dry measure, one-eighth of a bushel (*DMLBS* 3d)

(li.) libra 'pound' (£), one pound in currency (*DMLBS* 3, 4)

(lib.) libra 'pound' (lb.), one pound in dry weight, normally 16 ounces (but see *DMLBS* 1, 2)

(marc.) marca 'mark', two-thirds of a pound sterling (13s. 4d.)

(ob.) obolus 'halfpenny' (½d.)

(oz.) 'ounce', one-sixteenth of a pound (lb.) in weight

(pec.) pecca peck, one quarter of a bushel

(pet.) petra 'stone' in dry weight, normally 14lb. (but see Glossary and *DMLBS* 6)

(qua.) quadrans 'farthing'(¼d.) (*DMLBS* 2)

(qr.) quarterius 'quarter', a unit of dry measure, normally eight bushels (but see *DMLBS* **quartarius** 2)

(s.) solidus 'shilling' (s.)

(virg.) virga 'verge', a linear measure of one yard, i.e. three foot (*DMLBS* 6b)

EDITORIAL CONVENTIONS

Transcriptions of the documents use minimal modern punctuation (only full-stops); upper case is limited to names of people and places, e.g. ‘sir’, ‘master’, but ‘Roger’, ‘London’. The orthography of the original texts is preserved; expansions are italicised only for English text (Roman is used for expansions where material is otherwise italicised, e.g. left margins). <i>/<j>, <u>/<v> are normalised according to present-day spelling, e.g. ‘in’ but ‘juncture’ (ME ‘in’/‘iunctur’); ‘iii’ (ME ‘iij’); ‘unto’ and ‘velom’ (ME ‘vnto’/‘velom’); ‘love’ (ME ‘loue’). The ampersand is always transcribed ‘and’/‘et’ without italicisation. Numbers are regularised, e.g. ‘M’ even if written ‘m^{l}’, ‘CCCC’ even if written ‘IVC’ or ‘C^{iiii}’, e.g. MDCCCCxiii li. v s. iiii d. qua.’ (£1,913 5s. 4¼d.).[5] There are two archaic forms used in the English texts, the thorn <þ>, sometimes written in the shape of <y>, e.g. ‘þat’ (‘that’), and the yogh <ʒ>, used finally for /z/ (and so transcibed in this edition) but sometimes also used initially and medially for /j/, e.g. ‘ʒere’ (‘year’). ‘Ludeʒard’ (‘Lydiard’) and medially in place of <g>, e.g. ‘bowʒht’. The thorn is always transcribed <þ>; final yogh is transcribed <z> but initial or medial yogh is retained (‘ʒere’, ‘Lydeʒard’, ‘bowʒht’). Initial <ff> is normalised to <f> but retained medially and finally, e.g. ‘wyffe’ ‘off’.

In English text, genitive (i.e. possessive) and plural contractions are always expanded *-es* (except for ‘lad*ys*’ and other familiar spellings, e.g. ‘Harr*ys*’). Flourishes are normally expanded *–e* but *–y* is sometimes appropriate, e.g. ‘Januar*y*’ (MS ‘Januar’), ‘Henr*y*’ (MS ‘Henr’), ‘lectuary’ (MS ‘lectuar’).[6] The spellings ‘maister’/‘master’ are differentiated, since one hand (that of Miles Worsley) favours ‘maister’/‘maistres’ and it is a distinctive feature by which to identify his hand. Superscript letters are sometimes otiose, e.g. Fremyngh^{a}m’ and perhaps ‘serv^{a}nt’, cf. ‘servant(e)’ 10/1, 5, although sometimes ‘servaunt’ may be intended, cf. ‘s*er*vaunt*es*’ 10/132; in the edited text superscript <a> is not expanded and the more common spelling ‘ant’ is used.[7] However, ‘Will^{a}m’ clearly indicates omission of <i> and is here transcribed ‘Will*i*am’, e.g. 19/100.

[5] However, numbers above 4,000 (there are several high 1,000s in D91.16, for example) are indicated ‘VM’, ‘VIM’, etc. (5,000, 6,000); numbers above 400 are regularly represented with ‘D’ (i.e. 500), e.g. ‘DCCCC’ (even if written ‘ix^{C}’, e.g. D102.10/86). (The distinctive use of Arabic numerals (‘5C’, ‘9C’) at D102.10/4 is preserved.) ‘li.’ ‘s.’ ‘d.’ ‘qua.’ ‘ob.’ are not italicised. Differences between hands, e.g. ‘ls’/‘li’ are not noted.

[6] Flourishes are particularly common in D.102.2 and D102.6 (the account of Roger Ormeston).

[7] For example, sixteen examples of uncontracted ‘-ant’ and four of uncontracted ‘-aunt’ in D91.21.

Cancellations are recorded < >; entries above line \ /; « » indicates an annotation added later to the text; indecipherable material is recorded [...] when it encompasses no more than three potential letters, but [.....] when longer. Square brackets (with no footnote) are also used to indicate letter(s) missing from a word, e.g. 'bar[o]ne' (MS 'barne'); where a word is emended, the MS spelling is given in a footnote, e.g. 'M[a]xey' (MS 'Mixey'); where a letter is editorially omitted, this is indicated in a footnote, eg. 'wardrop' (MS 'wrardrop'), 'george' (MS 'geoorge'). Editorial intervention has been minimal, given the variation in dialect and spelling at the period.[8] Abbreviations are used for weights, measurements, etc. in Latin text (see Abbreviations above), but not in English text unless they are clearly Latin, e.g. 'unce' (not 'oz.'). Individual sums and/or unit prices are sometimes underlined in the original documents in order to give them prominence within the entry; this underlining is inconsistent but is replicated where it occurs in the texts edited here.

All material in the left margin is italicised, both headings and notes (expansions are in normal font). Left brackets linking entries, often with a marginal heading, and occasional right bracketes linking totals, are only footnoted. The italicised marginal note is normally placed just before the item to which it refers, on the same line, although minor marginal comments are placed as appropriate within the item. In the documents a line from an entry (e.g. D91.16, Plate 2), often with brackets to the right of an entry (e.g. D102/10, Plate 5), invariably leads to a sum which is aligned right;[9] in this edition three dots, preceded and followed by a space (distinct from the bracketed three or five dots mentioned above, which indicate an indecipherable reading), demarcate the entry from the sum (which may be accompanied by notes), e.g.

Item delyv*er*ed unto m*aister* Peksall for money send to m*aister* presydent for the wrytyng of a boke for my lad*ys* g*r*ace ... vi s. viii d.

My lady Jane. Item the ix day of the said moneth as money lent to my lady Jane ... <xx s.> «nichil hic quia postea inter arreragias huius anni»[10]

Double angle brackets (as above, after the single angle brackets used to indicate the cancellation of the sum) are used for those marginal annotations

[8] Care has been taken not to over-edit and lose potentially significant dialect or idiolect variation, e.g. 'Friste' (first), which occurs in the preliminary material to 1502–3 and 1504–5 (20/4, 192), or 'ad' (at), which occurs twice on one page in the end material for 1502–3 (20/65), are not emended.

[9] D91.16 often uses a line to demarcate from the rest of the text sums of money (Plate 1) or amounts (Plate 3). These are not aligned right in the original document but are nevertheless marked here with the same three dots (cf. also 'Totalis', 'Summa', etc. in all the documents); their actual position in the text is discernible from the fact that they occur within continuous text.

[10] Right-aligned notes are not strictly marginal and are not italicised here (the distinction between margin and body of text does not usually exist to the right of a page). However, their status is recorded in footnotes or by angle brackets, as here.

in the chamber accounts which appear to be by a member of the auditing team; these normally occur in the right margin, are never in the hand of the entry itself, and comment on the arithmetic or status of the entry. The end-of-page (sometimes mid-page) total sum is set to the right; it usually occurs after the word 'Summa (totalis/partis/pagine)'. Few further attempts are made to replicate the layout of the document text, although footnotes describe any relevant layout of material. Marks of notation occasionally indicate that checking has been carried out, e.g. a long-tailed <z> or a trefoil, or that items need to be checked or remembered, e.g. a cross.[11]

Each edited text is preceded by a Description and a Summary of the contents of the text. The Description details: material, page size (height x width in millimetres), quiring, pagination,[12] any unusual features of the manuscript (such as inserted slips or extended pages), binding, and boxing of the manuscript. The earliest stage of conservation took place 1976–8 under the then archivist, Malcolm Underwood; more recently (2014–15) the re-cataloguing of the St John's College archives has led to new conservation of some documents. For example, the roll, formerly cased in a waterproof buckram cylinder, is now in a rectangular grey box. Previous references have been cancelled on the manuscripts and their boxes (where they have such); the first stage of re-cataloguing led to the substitution of a slant for the full stop (e.g. D91/16); the new cataloguing has replaced these by the new reference (e.g. /1/1/1/1).[13] The Description of each document attempts to take account of these stages ('MGU' indicates the hand of the former archivist Malcolm G. Underwood, on whom and on the re-cataloguing see Note on Archival References and the Edited Texts above).

[11] These are noted in the Descriptions of each text but only the long-tailed <z> is reproduced (in the edited text of D91.16).

[12] Only D102.1 is foliated.

[13] Previous references to SJCA (St John's College Archives) are now replaced by SJLM (St John's Lady Margaret).

LIST OF PLATES

D91.16 (SJLM/1/1/1/1)
1. D91.16, sheet 16
2. D91.16, sheet 25
3. D91.16, sheet 9d
4. D91.16, sheet 21d

D102.10 (SJLM/1/1/6/1)
5. D102.10, p. 67
6. D102.10, p. 113
7. D102.10, pp. 126–7

D91.17 (SJLM /1/1/2/1)
8. D91.17, p. 19
9. D91.17, p. 66

D91.20 (SJLM/1/1/3/1)
10. D91.20, p. 4
11. D91.20, p. 134
12. D91.20, extension to p. 134

D91.21 (SJLM/1/1/3/2)
13. D91.21, p. 1
14. D91.21, p. 22

D91.19 (SJLM/1/1/3/3)
15. D91.19, pp. 50–1
16. D91.p. 73

D102.1 (SJLM /1/1/5/1)
17. D102.1, f. 4r

D102.2 (SJLM /1/1/4/1)
18. D102.2, pp. 2–3

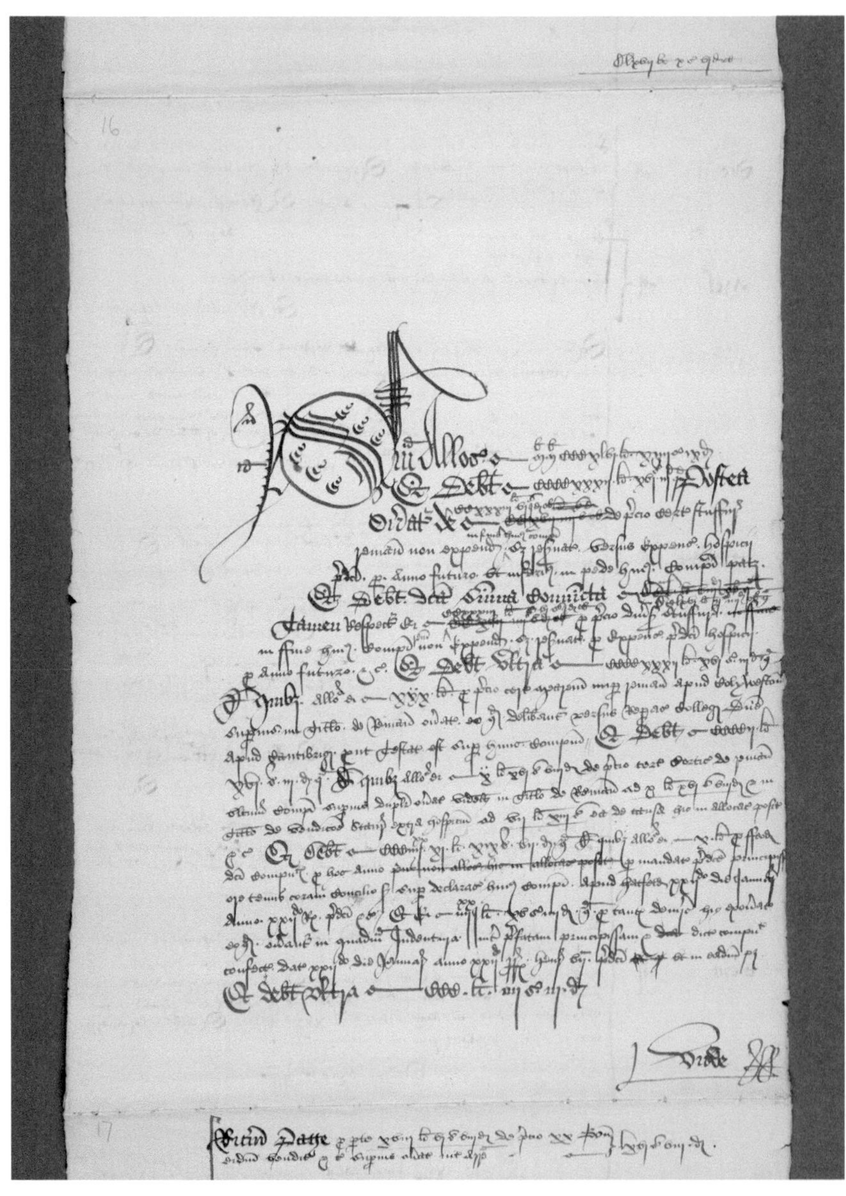

Plate 1 D91.16 (SJLM/1/1/1/1), sheet 16

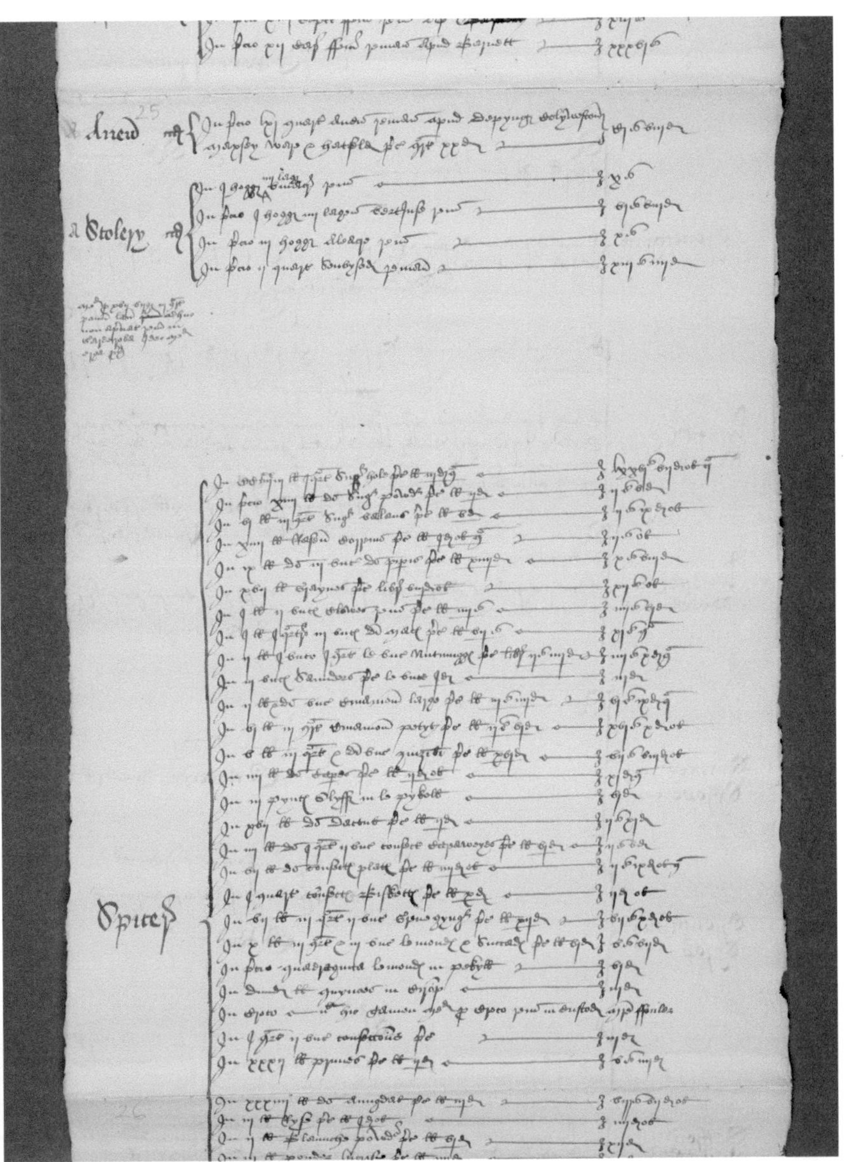

Plate 2 D91.16 (SJLM/1/1/1/1), sheet 25

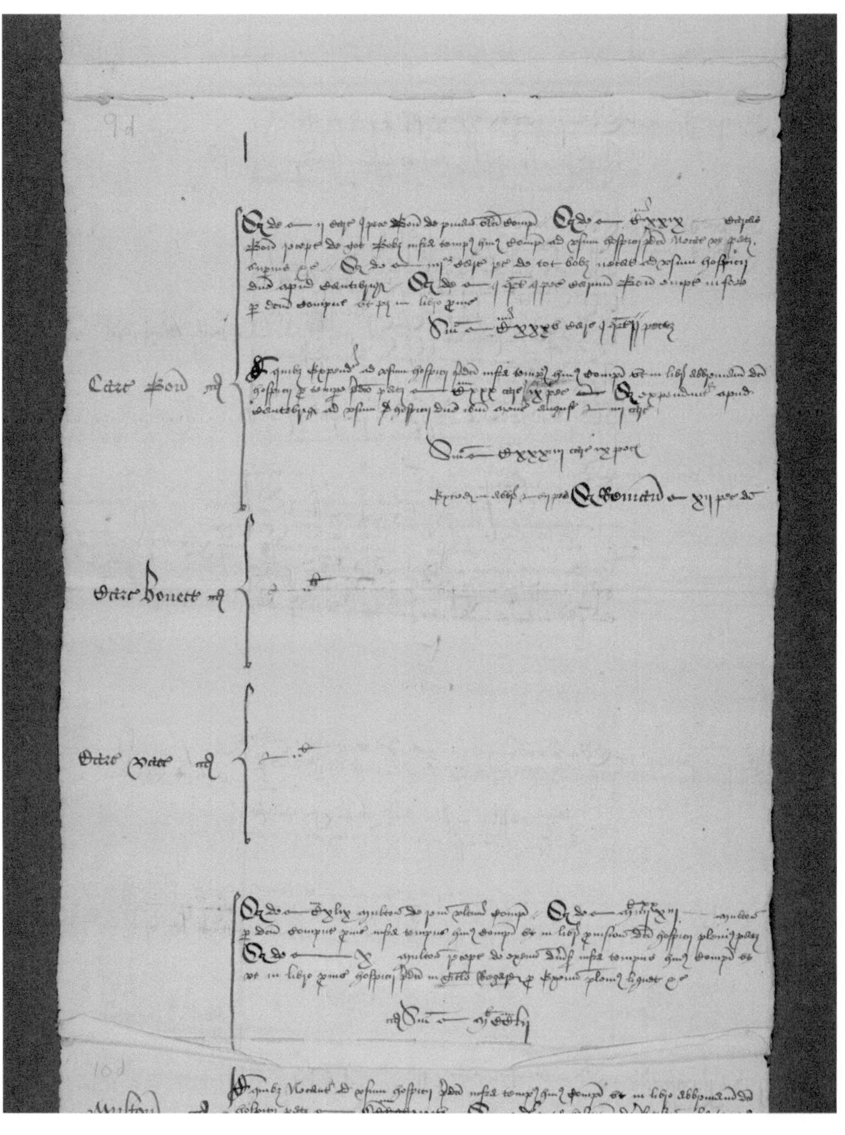

Plate 3 D91.16 (SJLM/1/1/1/1), sheet 9d

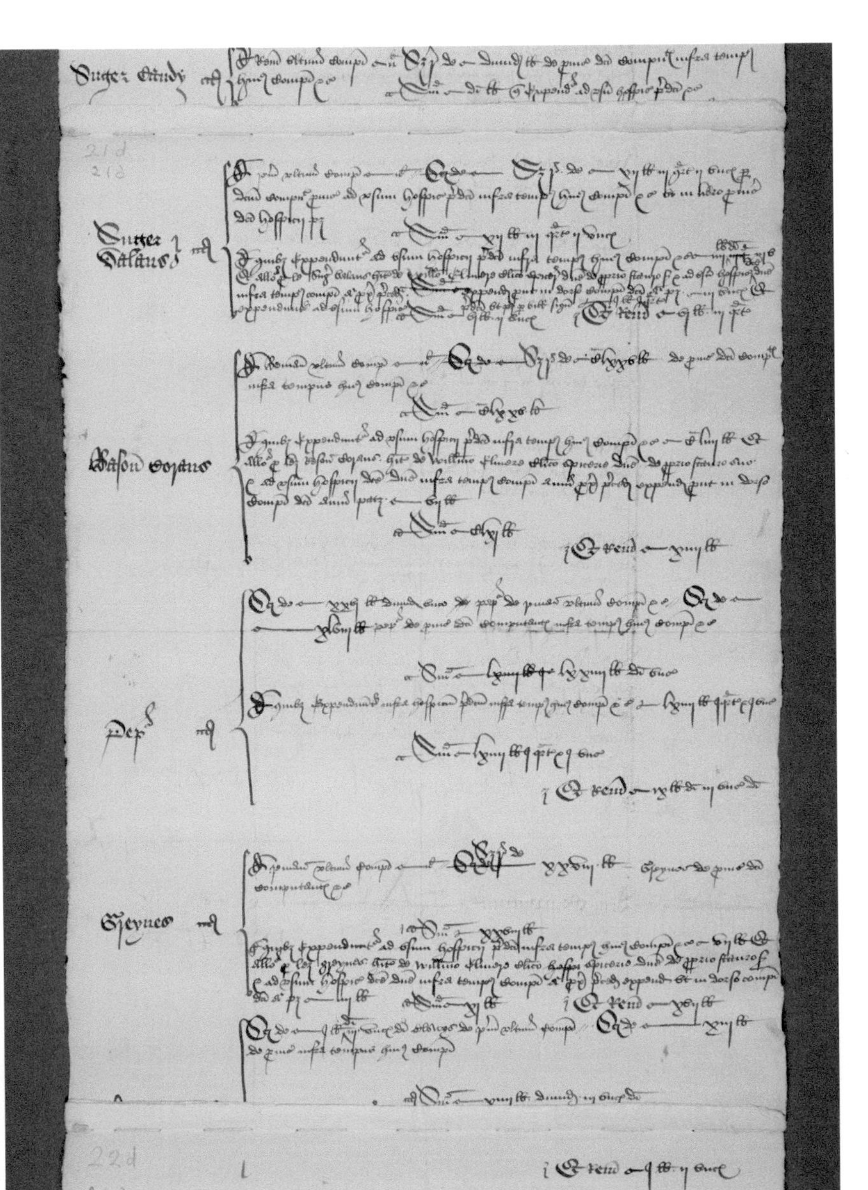

Plate 4 D91.16 (SJLM/1/1/1/1), sheet 21d

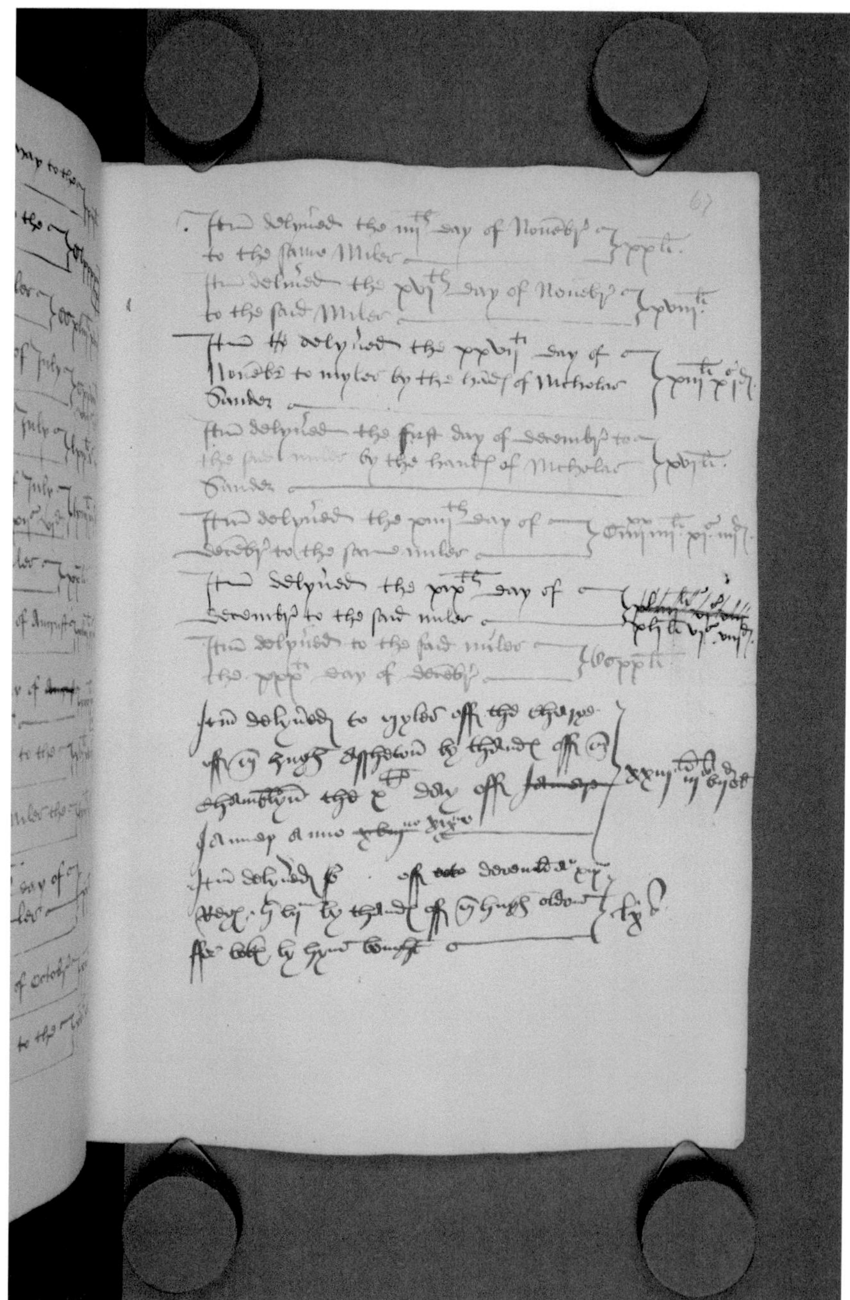

Plate 5 D102.10 (SJLM/1/1/6/1), p. 67

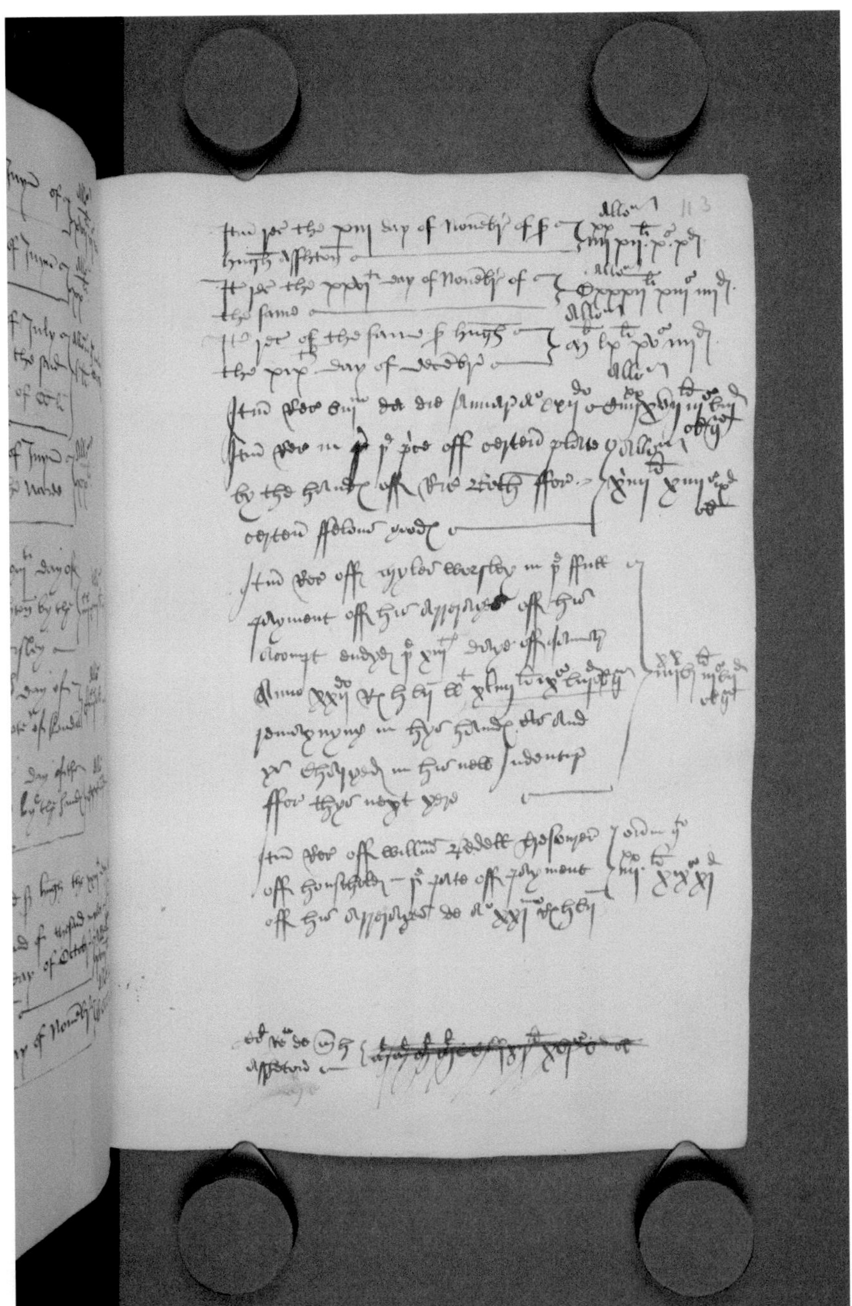

Plate 6 D102.10 (SJLM/1/1/6/1), p. 113

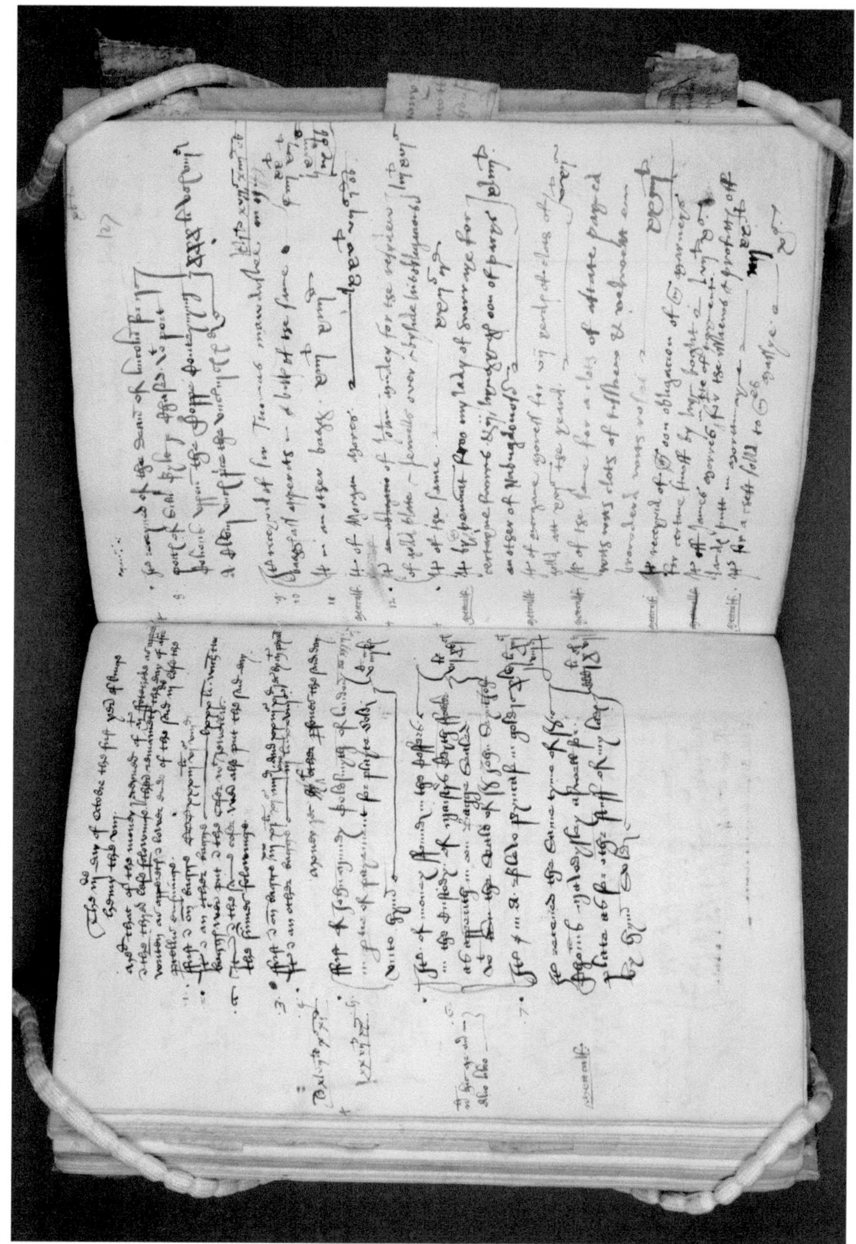

Plate 7 D102.10 (SJLM/1/1/6/1), pp. 126-7

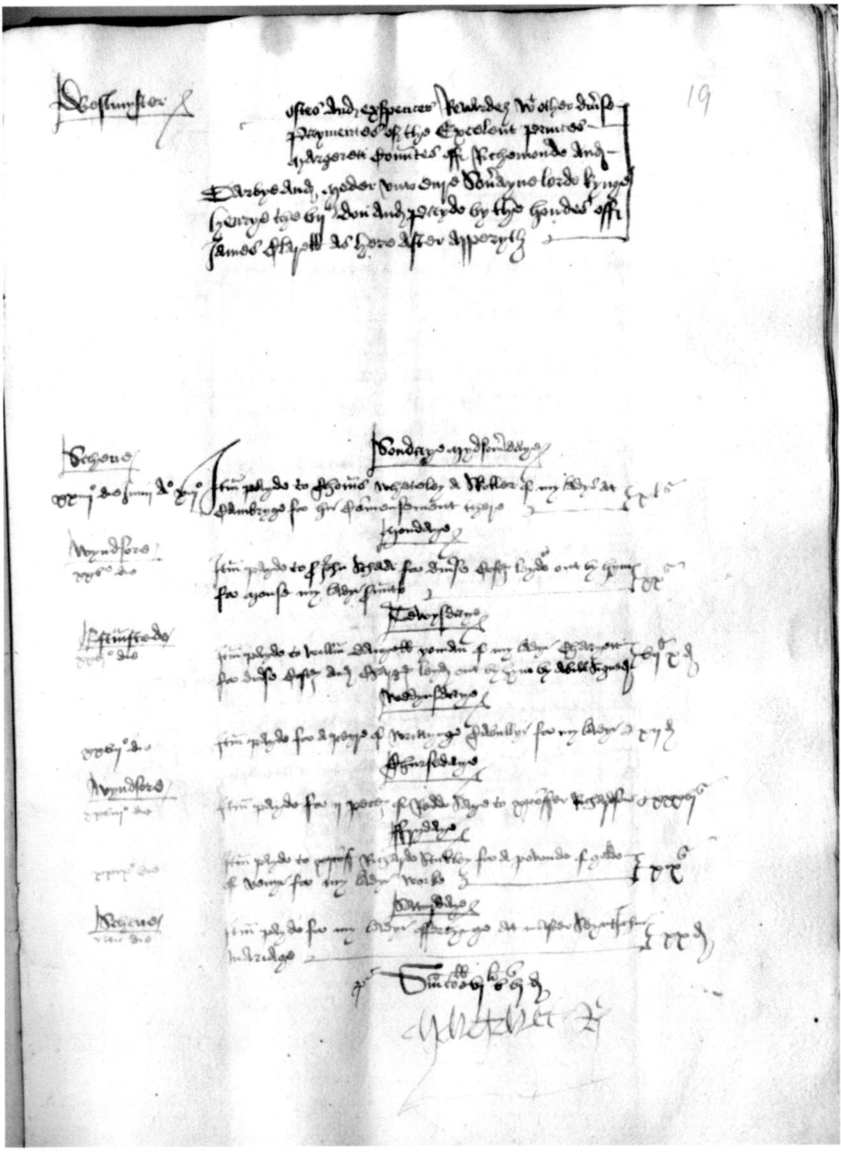

Plate 8 D91.17 (SJLM/1/1/2/1), p. 19

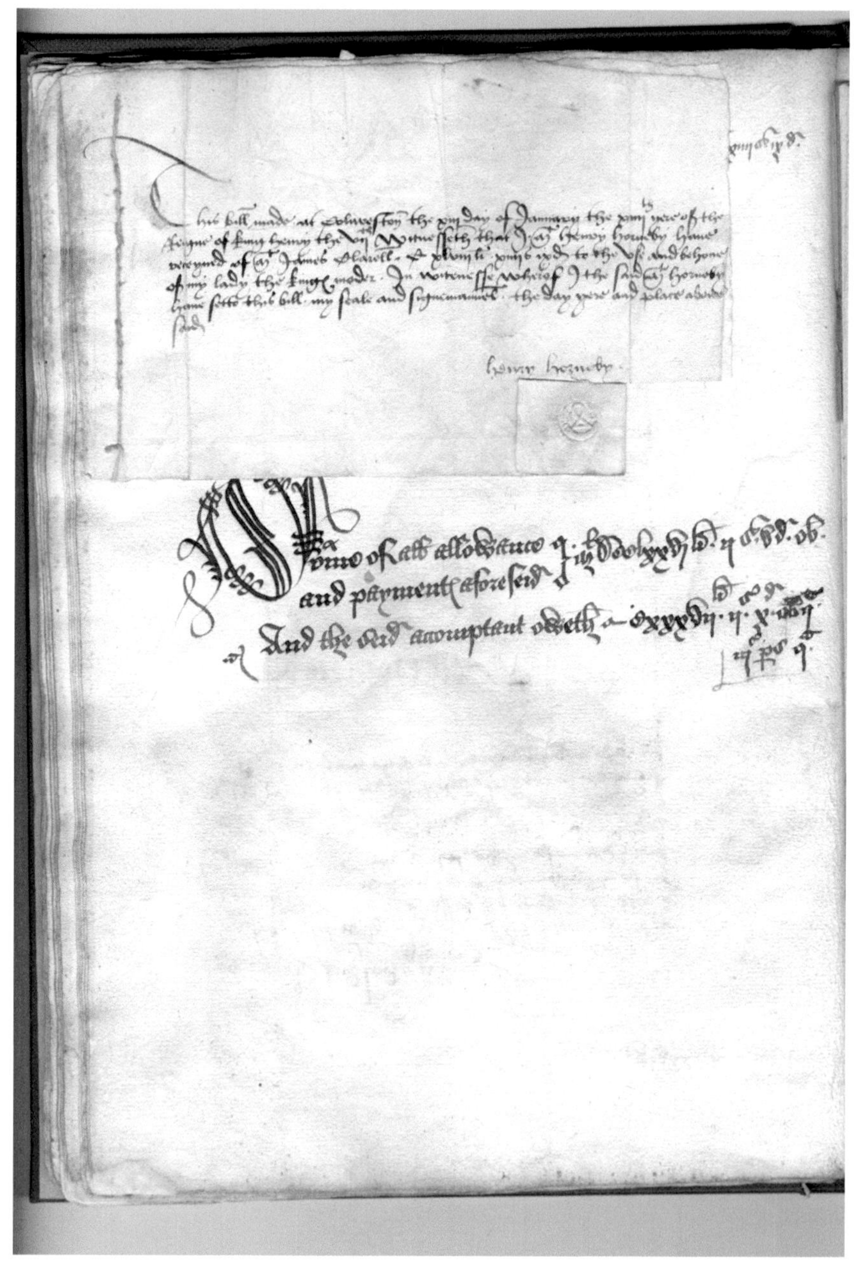

Plate 9 D91.17 (SJLM/1/1/2/1), p. 66

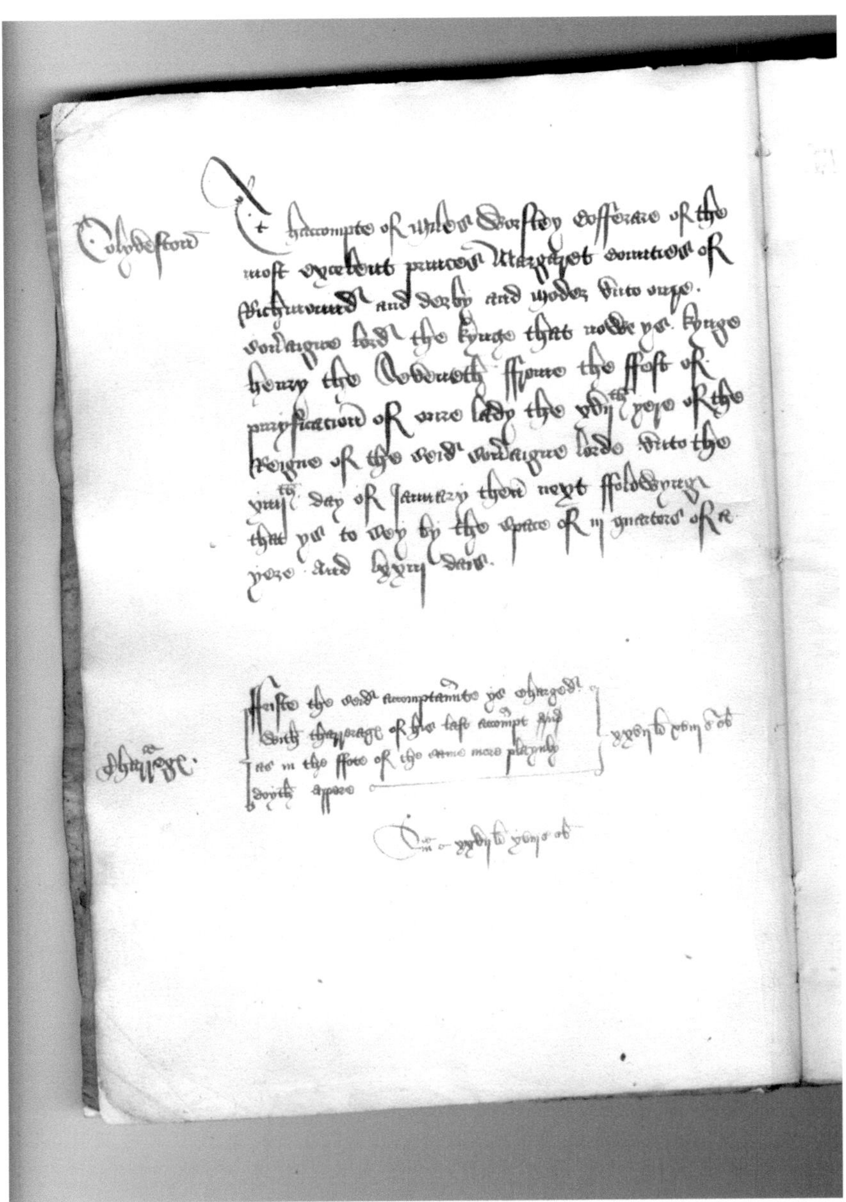

Plate 10 D91.20 (SJLM/1/1/3/1), p. 4

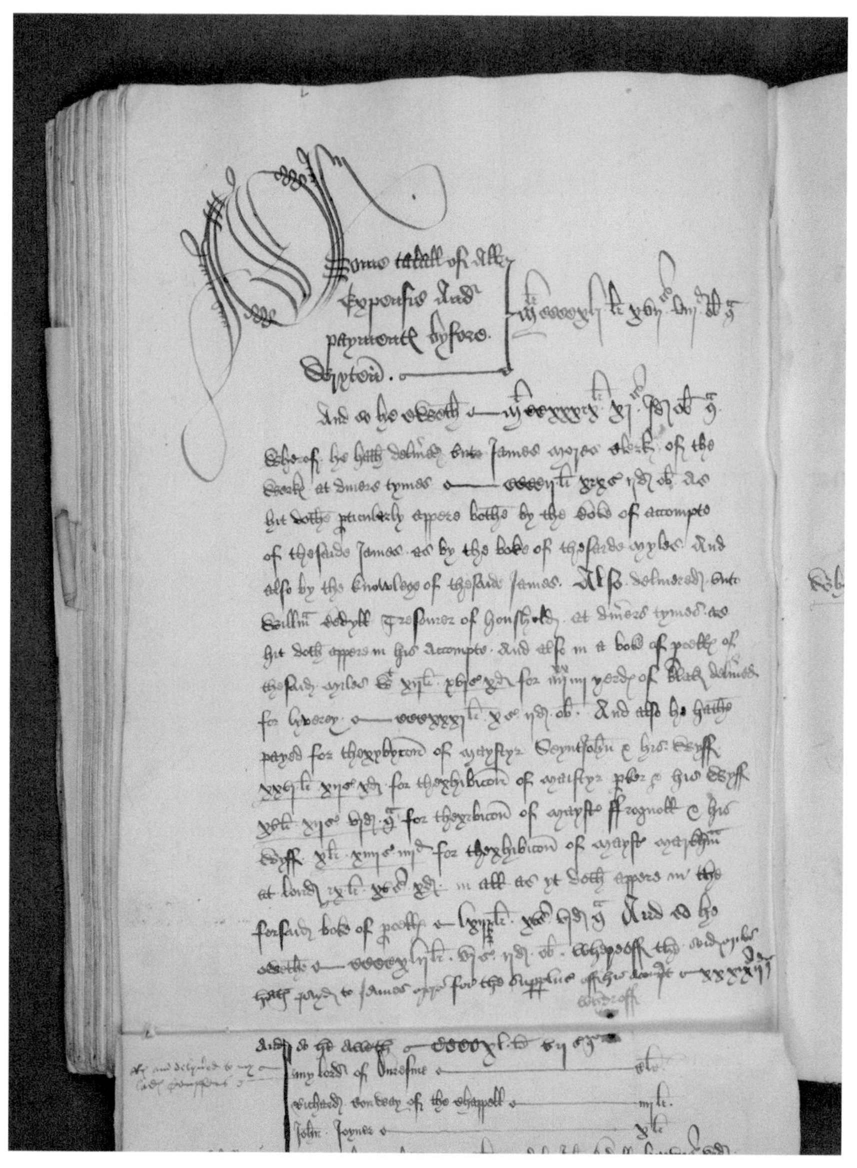

Plate 11 D91.20 (SJLM/1/1/3/1), p. 134

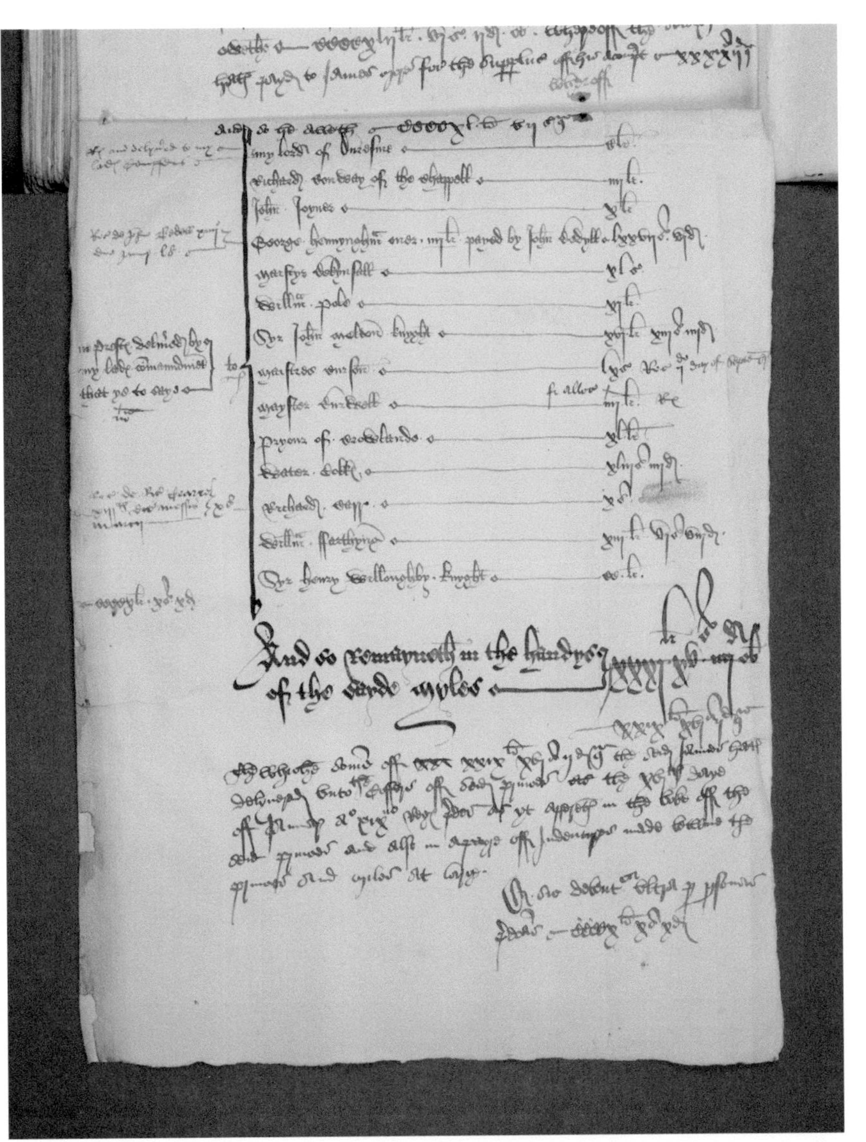

Plate 12 D91.20 (SJLM/1/1/3/1), extension to p. 134

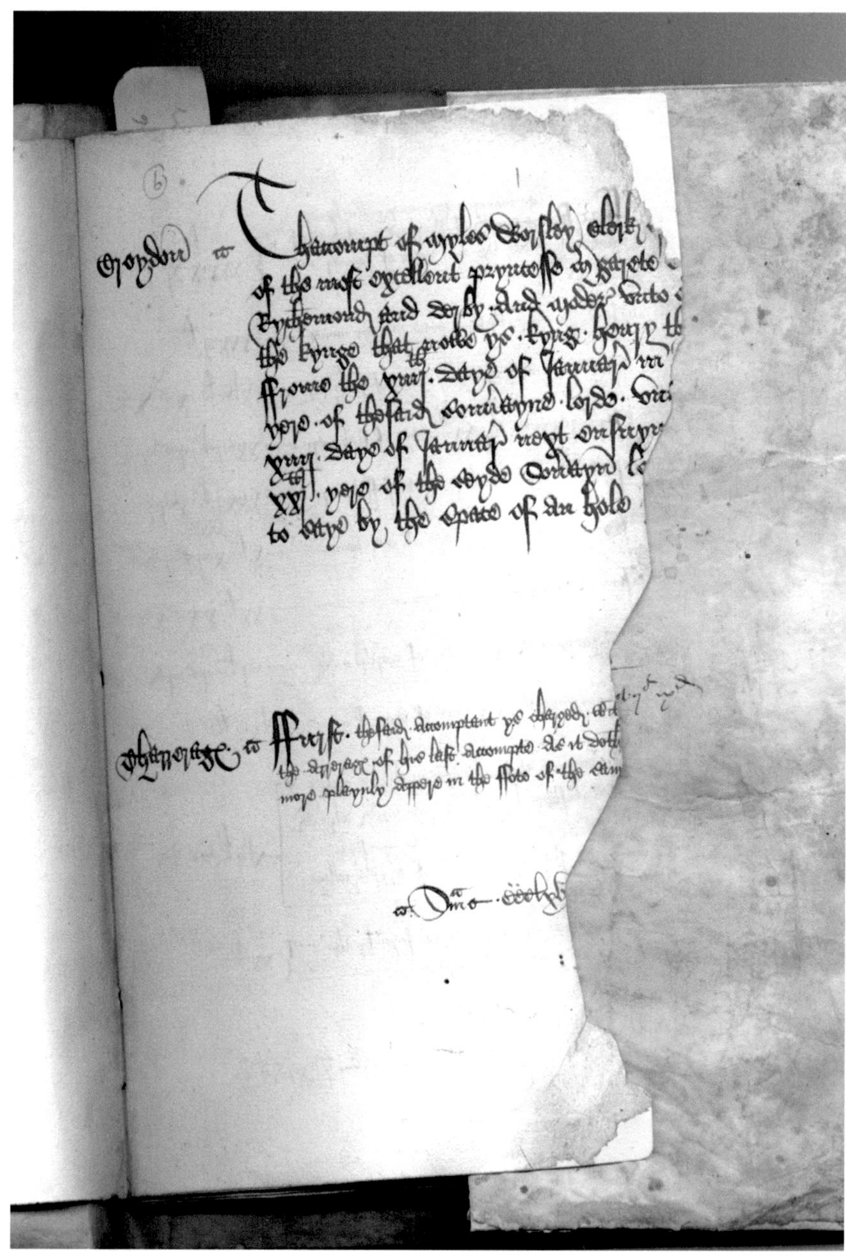

Plate 13 D91.21 (SJLM/1/1/3/2), p. 1

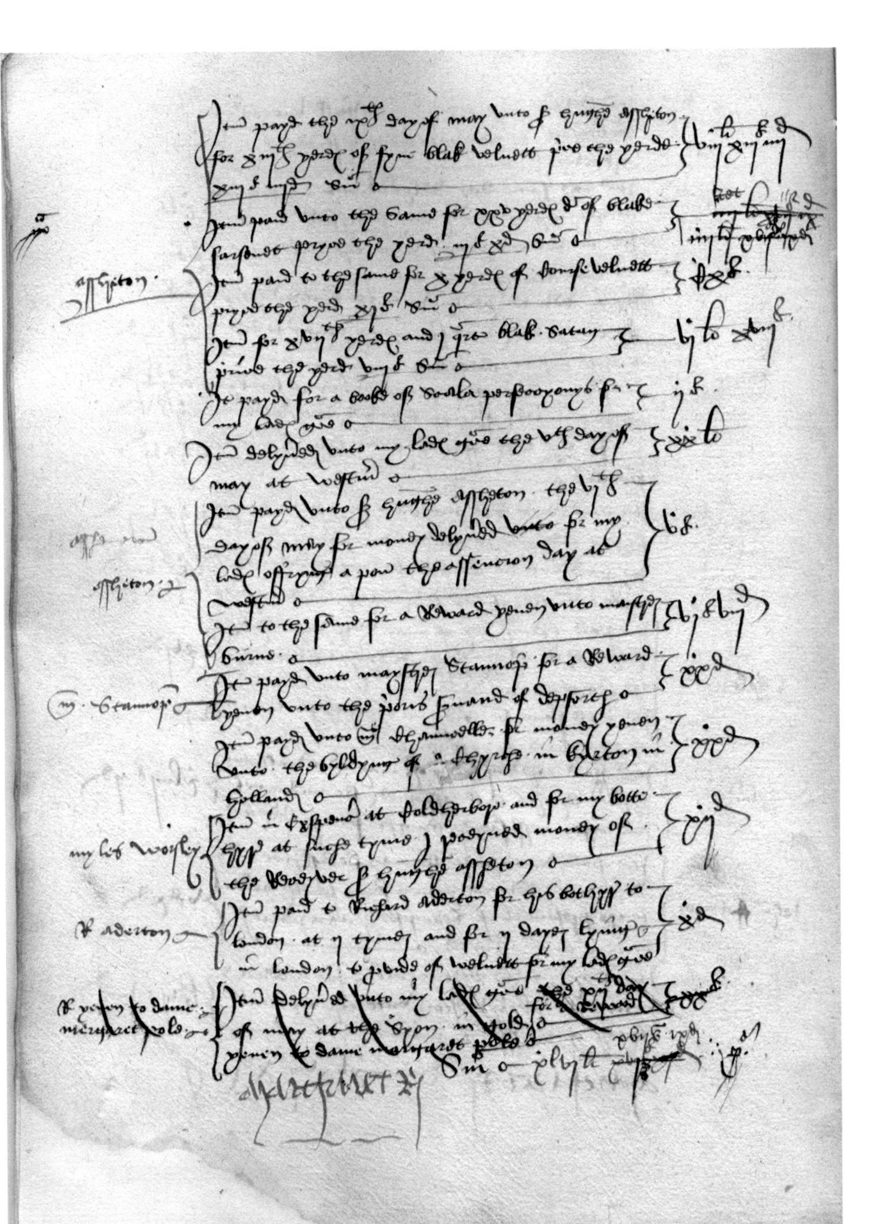

Plate 14 D91.21 (SJLM/1/1/3/2), p. 22

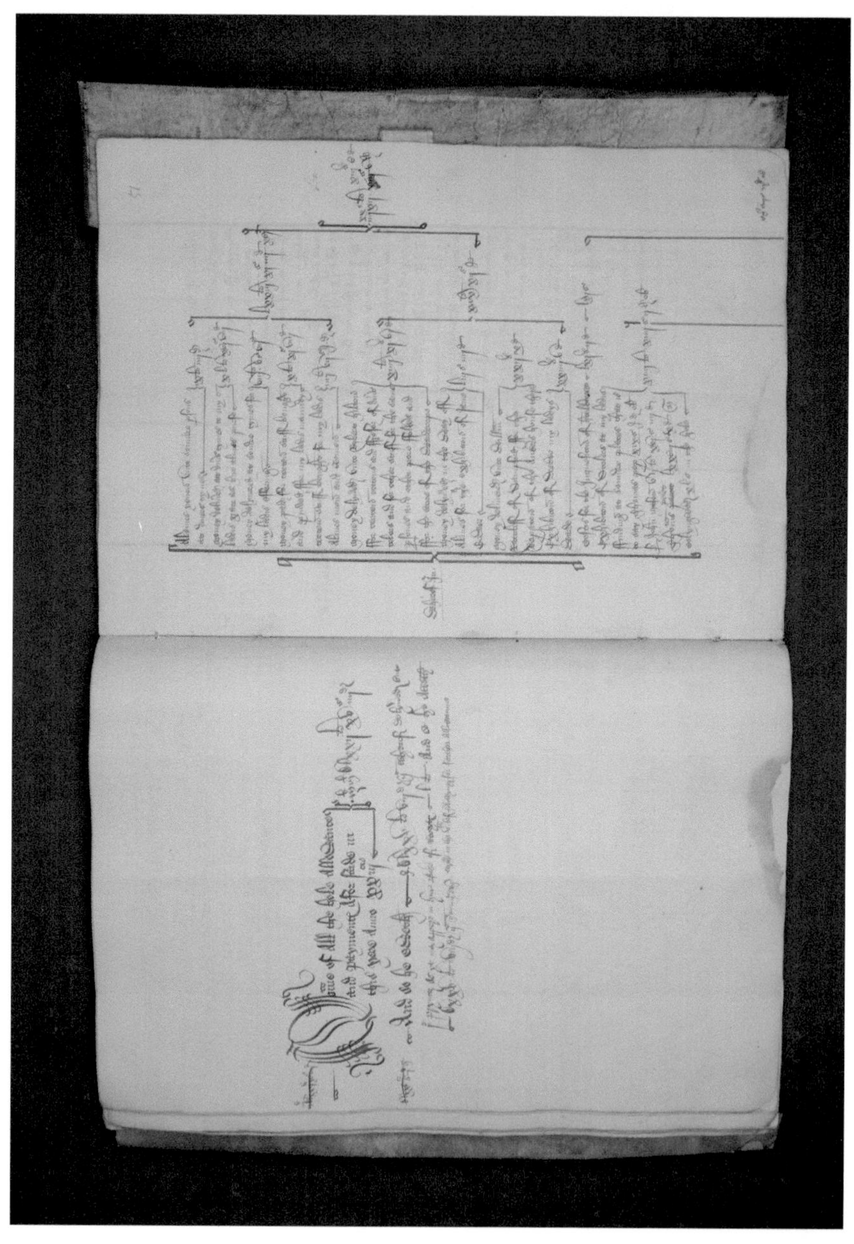

Plate 15 D91.19 (SJLM/1/1/3/3), pp. 50–1

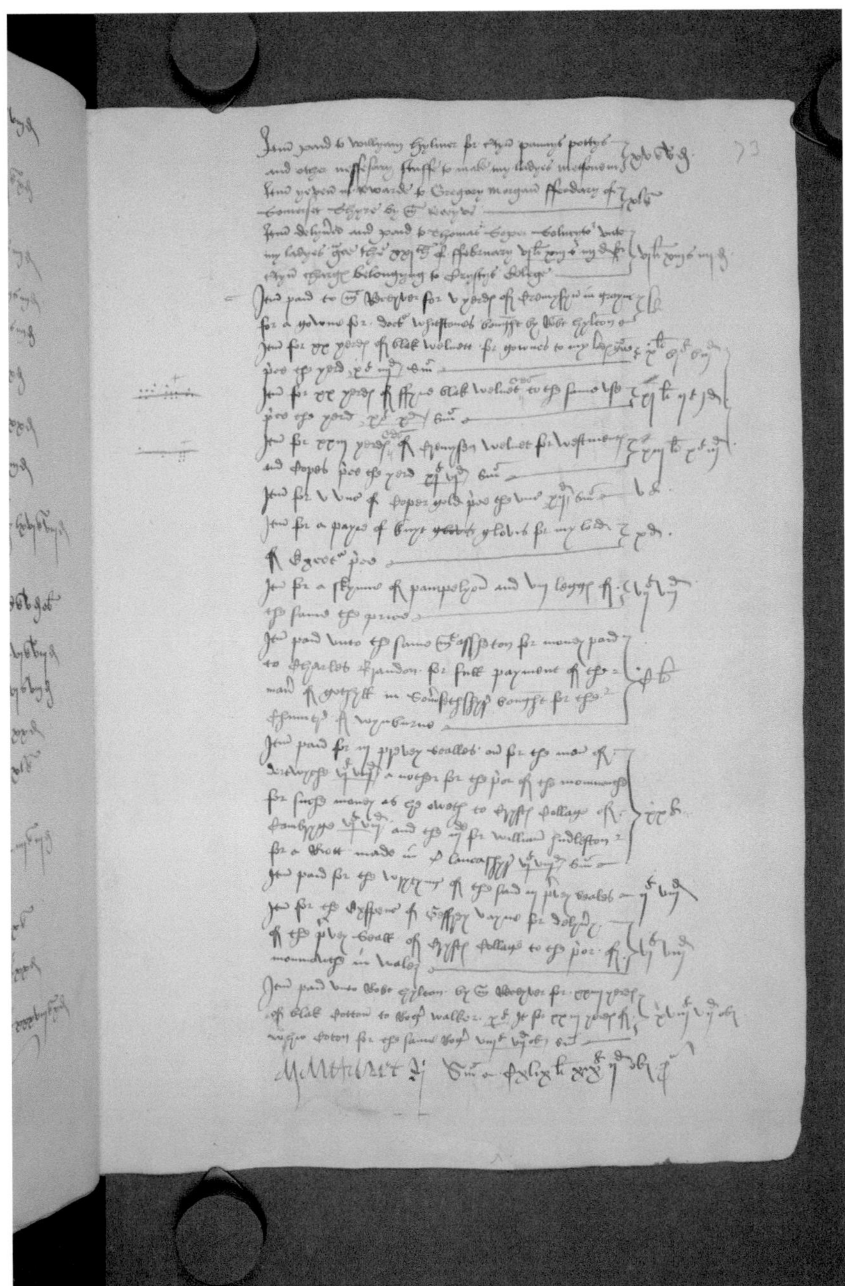

Plate 16 D91.19 (SJLM/1/1/3/3), p. 73

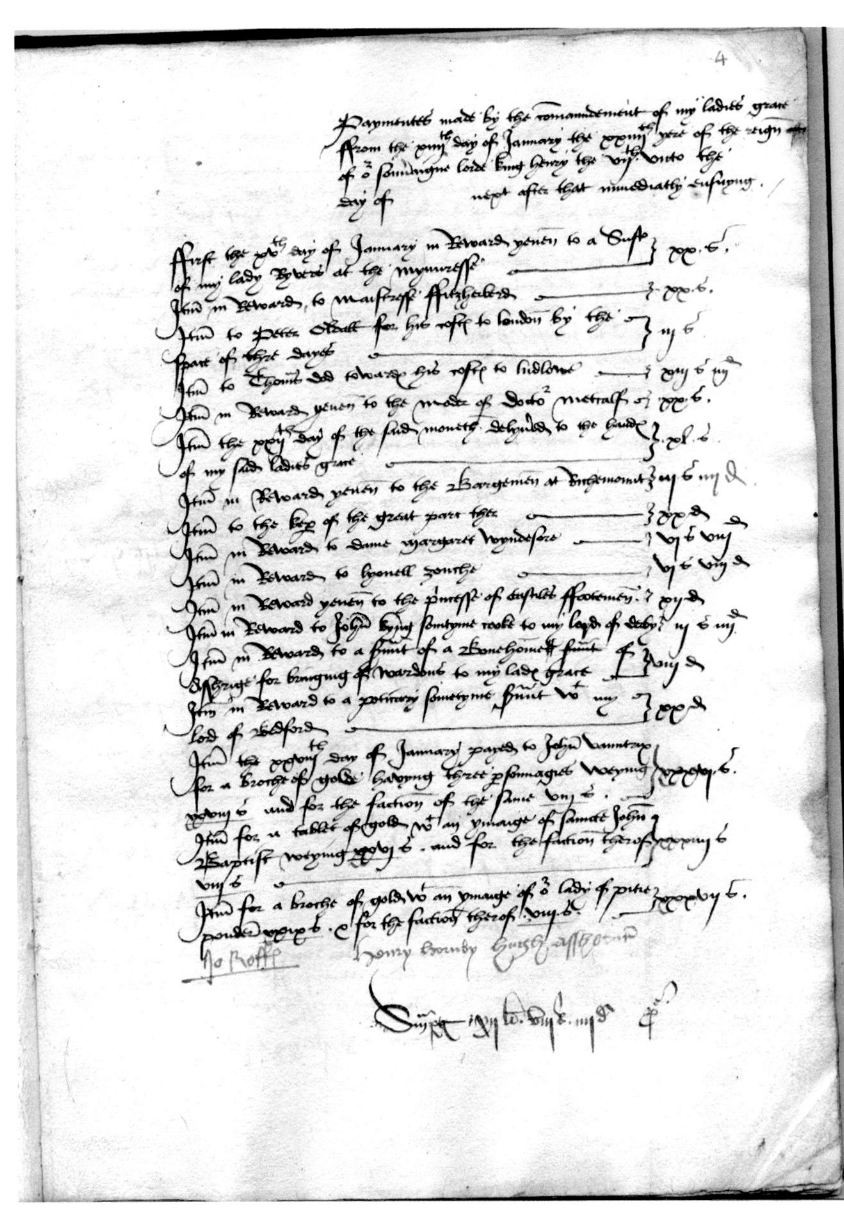

Plate 17 D102.1 (SJLM/1/1/5/1), f. 4r

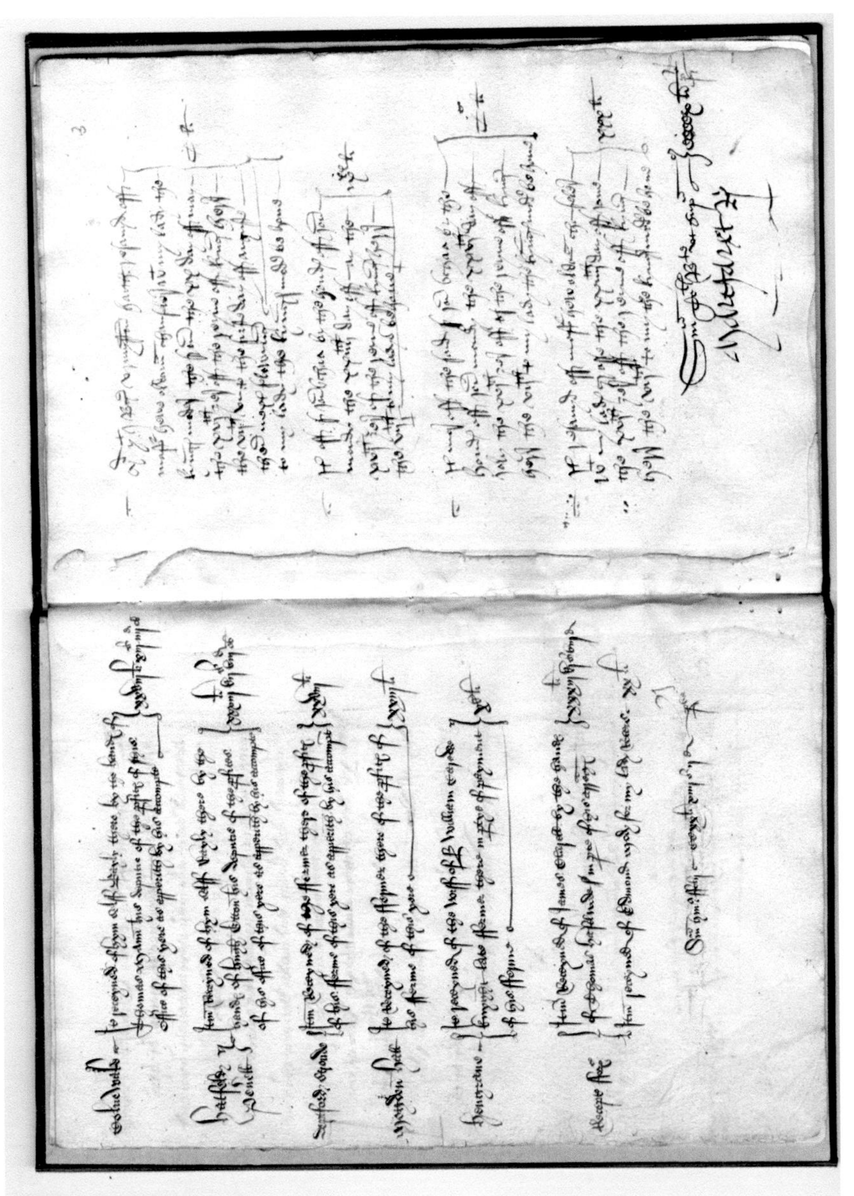

Plate 18 D102.2 (SJLM/1/1/4/1), pp. 2–3

INTRODUCTION

This edition of selected household accounts of Lady Margaret Beaufort, mother of Henry VII, had its inception in my interest in the monastery of St Saviour and St Birgitta, known as Syon Abbey, the only English house which followed the order of St Birgitta of Sweden. Founded by Henry V in 1415, shortly after he had founded a new Carthusian house at Sheen, these two elite monasteries faced each other on opposite banks of the Thames, Sheen on the south bank within the royal manor of that name (renamed Richmond in 1501). As a scholar and editor of medieval and early modern religious and devotional texts, both in manuscript and print, I was intrigued by suggestions that Lady Margaret Beaufort was responsible for the publication of texts originating at Syon or promoted within Syon. My interest coincided with the publication in 1992 of the seminal book on Lady Margaret, *The King's Mother: Lady Margaret Beaufort, Countess of Richmond and Derby*, and led to my visiting the Lady Margaret archives at St John's College, Cambridge, one of Lady Margaret's two college foundations.[1] From there, the intrinsic value and interest of the accounts led to my proposal to the British Academy of an edition, which I embarked on in the autumn term of 2009.

I was guided in my choice of accounts to edit and in all my early knowledge of the College Archives, and indeed of Lady Margaret herself, by the then Archivist, Malcolm Underwood, co-author of *The King's Mother*. This Introduction aims to place these edited accounts in context. Divided into five sections, it first introduces Lady Margaret herself and the archival context of her accounts, and then offers a brief comparison with the edited accounts of other contemporaneous households before an introduction to the accounts edited here and a briefer synopsis of those in the St John's archives which remain unedited. Section 2 introduces the personnel responsible for the edited accounts and discusses what can be learnt from the accounts of the management, structure and daily running of Lady Margaret's household. Section 3 moves to an analysis of the edited accounts, that is, the accountants, the format of the accounts and their compilation, the audit, and the respective roles of accountant and auditor, in as far as these things can be gleaned from the documents themselves. Section 4 provides detailed descriptions of the

[1] My study of these archives confirmed Lady Margaret's close contact with Syon and led to a series of articles and a book (see Select Bibliography at the end of this edition).

individual edited accounts, both as material objects and as records of Lady Margaret's life, while Section 5 provides the empirical evidence for the discussion in Section 3 and takes the form of a palaeographical analysis of the document hands.

1 Lady Margaret Beaufort and her Household Accounts

Lady Margaret Beaufort (1443–1509) was the mother of Henry Tudor (1457–1509) by her first husband, Edmund Tudor, who died before his son was born. In January 1458 Lady Margaret was married to her second husband, Henry Stafford, son of the duke of Buckingham, who died in 1471. In another speedy re-marriage, by June 1472 her third husband was Thomas, second baron Stanley, steward of Edward IV's household and virtual overlord of Lancashire.[2] 1485 saw the battle of Bosworth Field in which Thomas and his brother, William, overlord of extensive lands in north-east Wales, supported Henry Tudor, albeit at the last moment. Under Henry VII the two brothers became respectively lord constable and chamberlain. In February 1495 William Stanley was executed as a traitor.

This extremely potted history has been given to establish the context of the household accounts edited here. It may be that the execution of Stanley made it desirable for Lady Margaret to establish a distance between herself and her husband, and it is tempting to see that as the catalyst for Lady Margaret's vow of chastity and her establishment of a household entirely apart from her husband's principal houses at Lathom and Knowsley [Lancs.]. Collyweston, on the Northamptonshire/Lincolnshire border, had originally been the property of Ralph, lord Cromwell (1393–1456), whose estate at Tattershall had been granted to Lady Margaret by her son in the 'Great Grant' of 22 March 1487.[3] The earliest account edited here (D91.17) covers a period from the summer of 1498, when she was occupied in a royal progress with the king through East Anglia, until early 1499. The preparation of Collyweston as her official home is recorded in this account of her then cofferer, James Clarell, and it is the locus of the accounts of his successor,

[2] Her wardship and marriage had previously (in 1450) been granted to William de la Pole, earl of Suffolk, for his son John. For full details of the life of Lady Margaret: M. K. Jones and Malcolm G. Underwood, *The King's Mother: Lady Margaret Beaufort, Countess of Richmond and Derby* (Cambridge: Cambridge University Press, 1982) (her marriages pp. 35–65, her separation from Stanley 153–6).

[3] For the Great Grant, by which Lady Margaret received from her son substantial estates free of any interest to Thomas Stanley: Jones and Underwood, *The King's Mother*, pp. 99–103 and Appendix 2, B and C (pp. 264–6).

Miles Worsley, from February 1502 until January 1505.[4] The following two years are audited from Croydon, the palace of the archbishops of Canterbury, and from 14 January 1507 from Hatfield, the palace of the bishops of Ely, the office held by her stepson James Stanley.[5]

The extant accounts of the period of Lady Margaret's life from 1498 until her death 29 June 1509, two months after her son, are kept at her second Cambridge foundation, St John's College. Her first foundation, Christ's College, was endowed and founded during her last years,[6] whereas the considerable negotiations needed for the foundation of St John's were barely underway when Lady Margaret started to fail, perhaps late in 1508 at a time of increased vigilance and anxiety over the health of her son. John Fisher, bishop of Rochester and her close confidant, may well have attempted to speed up a process in which he was himself practically and emotionally involved, but the situation was not satisfactory at Lady Margaret's death, and the persistence of Fisher, with the assistance of two of her other executors, Henry Hornby and Hugh Ashton,[7] in securing lands and property for St John's rather than allowing them to go into the new king's coffers led in time to an animosity which may have contributed to some extent to Fisher's execution in 1535.[8] However that may be, the fact that St John's holds these accounts and has held them from its foundation may be attributable to their being kept at the college for scrutiny in negotiations with the king, in order to establish Lady Margaret's clear intentions with regard to the foundation of the college.[9]

[4] No cofferer's accounts survive for the intervening period.

[5] On the houses used by Lady Margaret: Malcolm G, Underwood 'Politics and Piety in the Household of Lady Margaret Beaufort', *Journal of Ecclesiastical History*, 38 (1987), 39–52 at 40–2; on the houses and household: Jones and Underwood, *The King's Mother*, chapter 5 ('Household Life').

[6] See the accounts for 1505–9 passim (D91.21, D91.19, D102.1).

[7] Richard Rex, 'Fisher , John [St John Fisher] (*c.* 1469–1535)'; Malcolm G. Underwood, 'Hornby [Horneby], Henry (*c.* 1457–1518)'; Claire Cross, 'Ashton, Hugh (*d.* 1522)' (*ODNB*).

[8] For Fisher: Malcolm G. Underwood, 'John Fisher and the Promotion of Learning', in *Humanism, Reform and the Reformation: The Career of Bishop John Fisher*, ed. B. Bradshaw and E. Duffy (Cambridge: Cambridge University Press, 1989), pp. 25–46.

[9] For the foundation of Christ's and St John's colleges: Jones and Underwood, *The King's Mother*, pp. 202–31; Malcolm G. Underwood, 'The Lady Margaret and her Cambridge Connections', *The Sixteenth Century Journal*, 13 (1982), 67–82 at 75–80; for Christ's: A. H. Lloyd, *The Early History of Christ's College, Cambridge: derived from contemporary documents* (Cambridge: Cambridge University Press, 1934); for St John's: Thomas Baker, *History of the College of St John the Evangelist, Cambridge*, ed. J. E. B. Mayor, 2 vols (Cambridge: Cambridge University Press, 1869); Richard Rex, 'The Sixteenth Century', in *St John's College, Cambridge: A History*, ed. Peter Linehan (Woodbridge: Brewer, 2011), pp. 5–92 passim.

1.1 The Accounts of Lady Margaret Beaufort

The documents relating to Lady Margaret Beaufort which are held in St John's College, Cambridge are a remarkable collection, perhaps not matched in the period except by those elsewhere which relate to her son, the king himself (discussed below at 1.4). Until recently they were almost unknown outside Cambridge itself. The town clerk and historian of Cambridge, Charles Henry Cooper, had used them copiously in 1839 in making a detailed study of Cambridge documents relating to Lady Margaret and her two colleges. This remained in manuscript at his death and was then edited and published by his close academic friend, the St John's fellow and Kennedy Professor of Latin, John E. B. Mayor.[10] Members of the College had used them and often written about them in the College magazine, the *Eagle*, which had been co-founded by Mayor in 1859. In particular, R. F. Scott, mathematician and later barrister, who served as Master of St John's 1908–33, had discussed, in the *Eagle* and elsewhere, archival material relating to Lady Margaret. However, this rich resource remained largely of College interest until the publication in 1992 of *The King's Mother: Lady Margaret Beaufort, Countess of Richmond and Derby*, written with extensive use of the archival documents by two historians, Michael Jones and the then archivist of St John's, Malcolm Underwood.

These archival documents consist of household accounts; accounts of the clerk of works, James Morice; deeds and other records, various in matter and scope; inventories; and executors' accounts.[11] Few of these have been edited, and none of the household accounts, which are here edited for the first time and discussed in the following sections of this Introduction.[12] The largest group consists of five books of chamber accounts, kept by successive cofferers, James Clarell, Miles Worsley and Robert Fremingham; these run from 1498

[10] Thompson Cooper, rev. by John D. Pickles, 'Cooper, Charles Henry (1808–66)' (*ODNB*); C. H. Cooper, ed. by J. E. B. Mayor, *Memoir of Margaret, Countess of Richmond and Derby* (Cambridge: Cambridge University Press, 1874); 'Mayor, John Eyton Bickersteth': John Venn and J. A. Venn, *Alumni Cantabrigienses*, 2 vols in 10 (Cambridge: Cambridge University Press, 1922–54). Mayor was also responsible for the editing and publication of the extensive history of St John's by the non-juring (and so ejected) fellow, Thomas Baker: *History of the College of St John the Evangelist, Cambridge*. For Baker: Frans Korsten, 'Baker, Thomas (1656–1740)' (*ODNB*).

[11] For the fullest published list of that part of the St John's archive which relates to Lady Margaret and which was used by Jones and Underwood: *The King's Mother*, Select Bibliography, pp. 297–8. See too the St John's College Archives (SJCA) at <https://www.sjcarchives.org.uk/institutional/index.php/the-records-of-lady-margaret-beaufort>. Neither is a complete record: *The King's Mother* lists those documents used in writing the book, while there are more documents yet to be added to the website.

[12] They are listed in *Household Accounts from Medieval England*, ed. C. M. Woolgar, RSEH n.s. 18, 2 vols (Oxford: Oxford University Press, 1992–3), II: 693 sub 'Beaufort, Margaret, Countess of Richmond'.

until 1509, with accounts missing for the years 1499–1501.[13] The chamberlain's accounts survive only for the year 1501–2, when the office was held by Roger Ormeston.[14] There are no diet accounts, but the annual cash, corn and stock account survives for the year 1506–7, kept by the treasurer, William Bedell, and this appears to serve as a template for other years.[15] Finally, the whole period 1499–1509 is covered in Lady Margaret's own book of receipts and expenses, kept by her secretary and dean of chapel, Henry Hornby.[16]

1.2 The Edited Accounts

The accounts edited here occur in four forms:

1.2.1 First, for just one year (1506–7), there is the computus (**D91.16**, now SJLM/1/1/1/1) of the treasurer of the household, William Bedell. In Latin and in roll form, it details the foodstuffs and provisions used by the household at both Croydon and Hatfield throughout that year; the dorse is a stock account. It refers frequently to a 'liber abbreviamentorum' (e.g. sheets 20, 3d, 4d, etc.) or to the 'abbreviamenta' (e.g. sheets 4d, 5d, 10d, 11d, etc.) themselves, i.e. (the book of) 'breves', abbreviated/summary accounts (*OED* **breve** *n.* 1c); there are also frequent references to a book of provisioning the household, 'liber provisionis (hospicii)' (sheets 4, 9, 10, etc., 1d, 4d, 5d, etc., cf. *DMLBS* **provisio** 4), i.e. making bulk purchases of provisions.[17] Other records mentioned are (once) a quire of names (presumably names of those who qualify for livery) kept by James Morice, clerk of the counting-house ('in quodam quaterno de nominibus per Jacobum Morres clericum countrie hospicii predicti', sheet 31d); once (in a corrected passage) to a book with itemised accounts (*DMLBS* **parcella** 3b) ('in libro de parcellis' 19d); and once to another small book kept by the treasurer ('in quodam parvo libro de nominibus & summis penes Willelmum Bedell thesaurarium hospicii predicti remanenti') (sheet 21).

1.2.2 There is a single book of receipts and payments (**D102.10**, now SJLM/1/1/6/1), recorded principally by Lady Margaret's secretary/dean of chapel (later chancellor), Henry Hornby. It covers 1 January 1499 to 3 October 1509, i.e. the full ten years of her running her own household entirely inde-

[13] D91.17, D91.20, D91.21, D91.19, D102.1 (now SJLM/1/1/2/1, /1/1/3/1, /1/1/3/2, /1/1/3/3, /1/1/5/1). See above, pp. xi–xii, for the procedure in referencing documents edited here.
[14] D102.2 and D102.6 (now SJLM/1/1/4/1 and /1/1/4/2).
[15] D91.16 (now SJLM/1/1/1/1).
[16] D102.10 (SJLM/1/1/6/1).
[17] D91.16 ('þe accompt of þe same tresorere', D91.20/194) is distinct from this 'boke of the houshold' (D91.20/64).

pendent of her husband, Thomas Stanley; the book is kept up beyond her death on 29 June 1509 with material culled from earlier records in order to bring the accounts to a complete conclusion, and the executors infill some of the empty or near-empty pages with their own details.[18] It appears that this was Lady Margaret's own 'boke of receytes'.[19] Compare, for example, the payment recorded at D91.19/60 ('wherof he [Miles Worsley] hath delyvered unto the coffers of the seid prynces of suche money as he receyved of my lord of London as yt appereth in the boke of receytes of the seid prynces ... l i.')[20] with the entry for the same period in the book of receipts and payments at D102.10/131 ('Item receyved the same day [13 December 1507] by Myles Worsley of my lord of London in partie of payment of C li. of money lent unto hym ... l li. «allocatur»').[21]

1.2.3 In addition, there survive the account books of the successive cofferers (the term 'treasurer of the chamber' is used from 14 January 1506), James Clarell, Miles Worsley and Robert Fremingham. By the second half of the fifteenth century the chamber had become the place to receive and spend money, large sums and small.[22] The chamber accounts commence in the peripatetic summer of 1498 (24 June) when Collyweston was being prepared as Lady Margaret's permanent home, but these first accounts of James Clarell (**D91.17**, now SJLM/1/1/2/1) continue only until the first audit (12 January 1499), after which no accounts survive until Miles Worsley's begin 2 February 1502 and continue in three books (**D91.20**, **D91.21**, **D91.19**, now SJLM/1/1/3/1, /1/1/3/2, /1/1/3/3) until 13 January 1509. Robert Fremingham then takes over as acting treasurer of the chamber with a book (**D102.1**, now SJLM/1/1/5/1) which ends on the day of Lady Margaret's death.

1.2.4 Finally, the accounts of the chamberlain, Sir Roger Ormeston, survive in two (originally one) small volumes (**D102.2**, **D102.6**, now SJLM/1/1/4/1, /1/1/4/2), covering only the period from May 1501 to February 1502 (with a month's gap from approximately 18 December to 9 January).

The 'lib[er] de parcellis' noted above may be one of several mentioned in other contexts: these were books with detailed itemised entries. One 'boke of

[18] The dissolution of a household was not immediate after death. It continued to function as a body, and Lady Margaret allowed for its continuance for six months after her death: D4.7, p. 50.

[19] Cf. 'þe boke off þe receytes off þe seid pryncez' (D91.21/90).

[20] Cf. 'and so he [Miles Worsley] oweth Dlxxv li. viii d. qua. wherof delyvered unto þe pryncez as yt may appere in hur boke of receytes ... l li.' (D91.19/50).

[21] Note too the references to Lady Margaret in the first person in 'myn almes mony' (p. 10) and 'into oure own coffers' (p. 22), and the correction of second to first person in '<your> my cofers' (p. 11).

[22] A. R. Myers, 'The Household of Queen Elizabeth Woodville 1466–7', *Bulletin of the John Rylands Library*, 50 (1968), 1–68 at 2.

parcelles' (*OED* **parcel** *n.* 5a, b) contained details of the exhibitions supported by Lady Margaret, was signed by her and was in her keeping (D91.20/64; D91.21/152); this is presumably the same as one said to have been made by Worsley and in her keeping (D91.20/194). (Worsley also kept a book, 'the boke of the saide Myles', or 'þe booke of accompt of þe seid Miles', which is distinct from his cofferer's accounts since it is mentioned within those (D91.20/134, 194).) Another 'booke of parcelles' contained details of Lady Margaret's legal transactions, including those associated with Christ's; it had been prepared by her solicitor Thomas Soper and was kept by her receiver general, Hugh Ashton (D91.21/67, 148; D91.19/55). Ashton is also recorded as keeping the executors' accounts for the former chamberlain Roger Ormeston (D91.21/80, 163). There may also have been another book kept by Ashton, a narrative record or 'remanbrance' (D91.21/148, cf. *OED* **remembrance** *n.* II.6a). There appears also to have been a book specific to the Christmas entertainments devised by John Harrison: 'a booke therof ['the dysgysenges & playes in Crystemasse'] made in the countynghowse' (D91.19/112).

1.3 The Unedited Accounts

Extant but not edited here are the accounts of James Morice, clerk of the counting house ('clericum countrie hospicii predicti' D91.16/31d) and Lady Margaret's clerk of works.[23] These accounts survive for almost the whole period 1500–7: D102.9 (6 January 1500 – 6 January 1501, Collyweston), D91.14 (16 September 1502 – 13 January 1504, Collyweston), D91.13 (13 January 1504 – 13 January 1505, Collyweston), D91.22 (13 January 1505 – 13 January 1507).[24] However, they appear to be only partial for the earlier years and missing for the last years, and they may even be incomplete in the years covered. For example, there is very little on the building works for Christ's College: only D91.22 contains a little information (pp. 128–37) on money received by Morice for payment to John Syclyng, master of Christ's.[25]

[23] Cf. 'the boke of the accompte of the same James', 'the boke of accompte of the saide James' (D91.20/64, 194).

[24] These are: SJLM/1/2/1, 1/2/2/1, /1/2/2/2, /1/2/3. All but the last are payments for works at Collyweston; the last covers works at Collyweston, Fotheringhay, Croydon, Haling, Christ's College, Hatfield and Coldharbour.

[25] For details of expenses for the chapel of Christ's College see the account of the fellow, John Scott, in D106.1 (SJLM/8/2/3/5), discussed in Anya Heilpern, '"Souvent me souvient": Remembering Lady Margaret Beaufort's painted glass in Cambridge', in *Medieval Art, Architecture and Archaeology in Cambridge: College, Church and City*, ed. Gabriel Byng and Helen Lunnon, British Archaeological Association Conference Transactions, 43 (Abingdon and New York: Routledge, 2022), pp. 227–72 at 250–1. For further records relating to Christ's: D105.89 (SJLM/8/2/3/3), a letter from Hornby to Fisher; D57.172 (SJLM/8/2/3/4), Fisher's injunctions as Visitor to Christ's.

The bulk of the information (pp. 128–31) consists of payments amounting to a sum total of £572 11s. 7¼d., with an extra £432 13s. 1d. paid out later (p. 132). However, these books, disassembled and partial as they are, are the remains of the computus referred to in the household accounts, some of which can be matched. For example, two entries in D91.21 (Worsley's accounts for 1505–7) are cancelled with the annotation 'quia in computo Jacobi Morez' (pp. 28, 35). Both are for June 1505, the first (19 June) recording 100s. paid to Syklyng and the second (22 June) £66 13s. 4d.; these can be compared with the same amounts for the same dates in Morice's account D91.22 (p. 128).

Of great interest are the inventories of Lady Margaret's goods (D57.43; D91.1–6, 10–12, 15; D91.24.1; D102.4, 12–19),[26] some of which were made during her lifetime, e.g. of goods delivered to Robert Hilton, her yeoman of the wardrobe, 21 August 1500 (D91.6), or of the goods and clothes of Henry Hornby, her dean of chapel, December 1504 (D102.14), or of hangings and coverings, made at Hatfield by Robert Hilton 28 October 1505 (D91.24.1), or of the wardrobe of beds, made at Hatfield in March 1509 (D91.12). Robert Hilton's last inventory is extant (D91.4), started at Hatfield 14 January 1509 and continuing until 16 August, two months after her death. It notes the distribution of her clothing, some during her lifetime, the rest afterwards, and a valuation was undertaken 6 September by the notary Oliver Scales (D91.2). A valuation of her bequests is preserved in D91.17. Wardrobe stuff was transported in July 1509, after her death, from Hatfield to London (D56.148, now SJLM/7/5/10), and another inventory (D102.19) was made at Hatfield 8 August 1509 by Richard Gough, clerk of the kitchen, Peter Baldwin, the keeper of her place at Coldharbour, and Richard Lister.[27]

Of the rest listed above, D102.13 and D91.15 ('the book of the Revestrie') replicate material on the chapel, the first marked by cancellations and annotations in the hand of John Fisher (before and after her death), the second a fair copy. D91.1 is a list of household plate and D91.3 is a list of bequests of other plate; D91.5 records the robes and spices and plate kept in coffers and closets; D102.4 and D102.15 are inventories of the wardrobe of beds; D102.16 lists hangings; D102.17 are bequests, D102.18 is an inventory of goods in Lady Margaret's chest and chamber, and D91.10 and D102.12 list her jewels in the keeping of Lady Margaret's gentlewoman, Edith Fowler; D91.11 lists various odds and ends at the house of the chanter of St Paul's; D57.43 is an inventory of plate and jewels given to Christ's College after Lady Margaret's death.[28]

[26] SJLM/8/2/3/1; SJLM/2/1/3, /2/3/3/2, /3/2/5, /2/2/2, /2/3/3/1, /2/1/2, 2/3/3/4, /2/4/1, /2/3/1/3, /2/3/2/1; SJLM/2/3/1/5; SJLM/2/3/1/2, /2/3/3/3, /2/3/2/2, /2/1/1, /2/3/1/1, /2/3/5, /3/2/3, /2/3/1/4, /2/2/1.

[27] The latter includes the Hatfield inventory at D91.12, but with valuations.

[28] R. F. Scott, 'On a List (preserved in the Treasury of St John's College) of the Plate, Books and Vestments Bequeathed by the Lady Margaret to Christ's College', *Proceedings of the Cambridge Antiquarian Society*, 9 (1896), 349–67.

Executors' accounts exist from 1509 to 1519 (D91.24.2, now SJLM/1/3/1), which were edited by Charles Cooper, together with the 1505 Hatfield inventory mentioned above (D91.24.1).[29] Other documents dealing with the executors include D91.7, a draft of their accounts 1511–13; D91.8, lists of payments made; D91.9, receipts and expenses of Nicholas Metcalfe, 1510; D56.172, expenses of the executors early in 1513; and D57.34, Henry Hornby's account of money received by the executors 1509–16.[30]

1.4 Accounts of Other Households

The range and variety of extant archival material relating to Lady Margaret Beaufor is remarkable. The fact that all the material of her prime, approximately the last ten years of her life (1498–1509), is concentrated in a single depository, St John's College Archives, is also unusual. A brief review of a selection of other medieval household accounts may serve to put Lady Margaret's into context.

For the Staffords, closely related to Lady Margaret through her second marriage to Henry Stafford (*c.* 1425–71), son of the first duke of Buckingham, numerous records survive in a variety of current locations, the most extensive for Humphrey (1402–60), earl and then first duke of Buckingham, and for his wife Anne Neville as dowager duchess (she died in 1480), and for Edward (1478–1521), third duke, who with his brother was a ward of Lady Margaret after Bosworth. They have been comprehensively studied by Carole Rawcliffe.[31] As magnates whose wealth at death was at least £5,000 p.a., the dukes of Buckingham might seem to compare with Lady Margaret, although her Stafford marriage was only to a younger son and her great wealth at death (£15,000 in moveable goods and around £3,000 p.a. in landed wealth) was largely a result of her son's victory at Bosworth.[32]

Those of the Stafford accounts which relate to Henry Stafford provided Jones and Underwood with valuable information on Lady Margaret's earlier life and consist of household accounts, estate accounts, and deeds and other

[29] Cooper, *Memoir of Margaret*, Appendix, II.1 'A vew' (pp. 178–9), i.e. D91.24.1; II.2–6 'Anno secundo' (pp. 179–214), i.e. D91.24.2, discussed briefly below (2.2).

[30] SJLM/1/3/3 (D91.7 and D91.8), SJLM/1/3/2, SJLM/7/5/11, SJLM/1/3/6.

[31] Carole Rawcliffe, *The Staffords: Earls of Stafford and Dukes of Buckingham* (Cambridge: Cambridge University Press, 1978); *Household Accounts from Medieval England*, ed. Woolgar, II: 713–15. See too C. M. Woolgar, *The Great Household in Late Medieval England* (New Haven and London: Yale University Press, 1999), passim.

[32] For wealth at death: Carole Rawcliffe, 'Stafford, Humphrey, first duke of Buckingham (1402–1460)'; C. S. L. Davies, 'Stafford, Edward, third duke of Buckingham (1478–1521)'; Michael K. Jones and Malcolm G. Underwood, 'Beaufort, Margaret [*known as* Lady Margaret Beaufort], countess of Richmond and Derby' (1443–1509)' (all *ODNB*).

records, all extant in Westminster Abbey.[33] The household accounts are those of Henry Stafford and his wife at their manors of Woking [Sur.] and Bourne [Lincs.] from 1466 until 1471, and take the form of journals of purchase and provisions and diet accounts.[34] They thus cover the last five years of their life together before her husband's death in 1471, whereas the other documents stretch as late as 1508–9.[35] (The St John's accounts similarly cover the end of an epoch, the last years of Lady Margaret's own life at her house in Collyweston [Lincs.] and her two borrowed houses, Croydon and Hatfield.)

Both Woking and Bourne had been the property of Lady Margaret's grandmother, Margaret Holland, duchess of Clarence.[36] Bourne was one of the family estates which established the Beaufort position in Lincolnshire, and Lady Margaret had used it regularly.[37] However, it was only in 1466 (the start-date of the household accounts of Henry Stafford and Lady Margaret) that the couple acquired Woking by royal grant after the execution of Lady Margaret's Beaufort cousin, Henry, duke of Somerset. The location of Woking led to a more active political life for Stafford, and, at least by proxy, for Lady Margaret herself. The years just before Stafford's death (1469–71) saw the Yorkist defeat by Warwick the Kingmaker at Edgecote, in which William Herbert, earl of Pembroke, was killed. Margaret's son, Henry, was Herbert's ward and at Edgecote with him, and uncertainty about his fate and future encouraged Margaret to lobby for recognition of her son during the exile of Edward IV and readeption of Henry VI. Warwick was killed at the battle of Barnet on 14 April 1471, and 4 May saw final defeat for the Lancastrians at the battle of Tewkesbury. On 4 October Margaret's husband died of the wounds incurred at Barnet.[38]

Partly contemporaneous with the Stafford accounts discussed above are those of John Howard, a lifelong Yorkist who rose under Edward IV and was created duke of Norfolk by Richard III in 1483, dying at his side at Bosworth in 1485.[39] These are (unedited) diet accounts for 1445–50 and (minimally edited) books of expenses covering 1462–71 and 1481–3.[40] Extending to the

[33] Jones and Underwood, *The King's Mother*, Select Bibliography, pp. 301–2; cf. *Household Accounts from Medieval England*, ed. Woolgar, II: 714 sub 'Stafford, Henry'.

[34] WAM 12181–90.

[35] WAM 19606 (1508–9) is the account roll of the refectorer of the abbey, where Lady Margaret died and was buried.

[36] For life in both households: Jones and Underwood, *The King's Mother*, pp. 137–43.

[37] For Lady Margaret's Lincolnshire property: ibid., pp. 127–33.

[38] Exciting times are rarely reflected in household accounts, but for an analysis of the period in relation to Lady Margaret and the Stafford household accounts: ibid., pp. 47–58.

[39] Anne Crawford, 'Howard, John, first duke of Norfolk (*d.* 1485)' (*ODNB*).

[40] The latter featured in the nineteenth-century Roxburghe Club volumes, *Manners and Household Expenses of England in the XIIIth and XVth Centuries*, ed. Beriah Botfield (1841) and *Household Books of John Duke of Norfolk and Thomas Earl of Surrey; temp. 1481–90*, ed. J. Payne Collier

end of the fifteenth century are the accounts of an ecclesiastical (rather than secular) magnate, William Worsley (*c.* 1435–99), dean of St Paul's 1479–97.[41] Worsley may have been related to Lady Margaret's cofferer, Miles Worsley, who was appointed in the year of the dean's death and may well have been part of the extended Worsley/Booth family connections from which William Worsley benefited considerably.[42] The accounts of Worsley's receiver, Roger Radcliff, survive from 1479 until 1498 and, together with other similar records, provide a clear picture of his revenue from estates and benefices, estimated at over £300 and perhaps over £400 p.a., approximately half of which (on average £181 p.a.) was consumed by his household either at the deanery at St Paul's or at his inherited house in Hackney: 'This placed him among the very wealthiest of English clergy below the episcopal level'.[43]

Lady Margaret's household accounts cover the cusp of the sixteenth century, the years of Henry VII's gradual settlement into the royal role which had been so hard won and which was contested until the later 1490s.[44] The accounts of another woman survive from a much earlier period but are in many ways comparable to those of Lady Margaret.[45] Elizabeth de Burgh (1295–1360) had similar interests and preoccupations to Lady Margaret and, like her, founded a Cambridge college, Clare College. Her mother, Joan of Acre, was a daughter of Edward I, and Lady Margaret herself descended

(1844). For a list of the accounts: *Household Accounts from Medieval England*, ed. Woolgar, II: 703–4 sub 'Howard, John'. There is no modern edition, although parts of the Roxburghe Club volumes, with other material, have been (re)printed with an introduction by Anne Crawford: *The Household Books of John Howard, Duke of Norfolk, 1462–1471, 1481–1483* (Stroud: Alan Sutton, 1992).

[41] *The Estate and Household Accounts of William Worsley Dean of St Paul's Cathedral 1479–1497*, ed. Hannes Kleineke and Stephanie R. Hovland, Richard III and Yorkist History Trust, London Record Society Publications, 11 (Donington: Shaun Tyas, 2004). For a list of the accounts: *Household Accounts from Medieval England*, ed. Woolgar, II: 721 sub 'Worsley, William'.

[42] *Estate and Household Accounts*, ed. Kleineke and Hovland, pp. 3–17; Michael J. Bennett, 'Worsley, William (*c.* 1435–1499)' (*ODNB*); Susan Powell, 'Lady Margaret Beaufort as Patron of Scholars and Scholarship', in *Patrons and Professionals in the Middle Ages*, ed. Paul Binski and Elizabeth A. New (Donington: Shaun Tyas, 2012), pp. 100–21 at 111–12.

[43] *Estate and Household Accounts*, ed. Kleineke and Hovland, pp. 31, 36. His involvement in the Perkin Warbeck conspiracy led to his attainder, from which he was pardoned at some cost, including the loss of his Hackney and Tottenham estates to Reginald Bray and the goldsmiths John Shaa and Bartholomew Rede: ibid., pp. 5, 15.

[44] There had been internal rebellions until 1497 (the Yorkist risings and Yorkshire and Cornish rebellions); the pretender Lambert Simnel had been defeated in 1487 and another pretender, Perkin Warbeck, was finally removed at the start of Lady Margaret's first extant account (1498–9).

[45] *Elizabeth de Burgh, Lady of Clare (1295–1360): Household and Other Records*, ed. and transl. Jennifer Ward, Suffolk Records Society, 57 (Woodbridge: Boydell, 2014). Over one hundred relevant documents survive: *Household Accounts*, ed. Woolgar, II: 696 sub 'Burgh, Elizabeth de, Lady of Clare'.

from Edward I through Edwards II and III, although her great-grandfather, John of Gaunt, son of Edward III, had fathered her grandfather, John Beaufort, earl of Somerset, by Katherine Swynford while he was still married to his second wife, Constance of Castile.[46] Both Elizabeth de Burgh and Lady Margaret held considerable estates but had suffered privations and early widowhood; both were successful and entrepreneurial *femmes soles* who ran their households, estates, manors and regions through their officers and council, Elizabeth's based on Clare [Sfk] and Lady Margaret's on Stamford [Lincs].[47] Both supported young men as scholars and involved themselves in the University of Cambridge to the extent of founding colleges.[48] More similarities might be listed, but the overwhelming difference, of course, is that Lady Margaret negotiated against adverse odds to bring her son to the throne of England and through that success came to perform on a national, not local, stage.

And so, finally, the most valuable accounts to view in tandem with Lady Margaret's are the chamber accounts of her son, Henry VII.[49] These comprise three books of receipts covering 1487–95 and 1502–5 (TNA, E101/413/2/1, E101/413/2/2, E101/413/2/3), one book of Elizabeth of York's expenses 1502–3 (TNA, E36/210),[50] and seven books of payments (in chronological order, TNA, E101/414/6; E101/414/16; E101/415/3; E36/210; London, BL, Add. MSS 59899 and 21480; TNA, E36/214).[51] They provide a fascinating perspective of life at Henry VII's court, one which is comparable in many ways to life in Lady Margaret's household,[52] and with several items of which

[46] Constance died in 1394 and John of Gaunt married Katherine in 1396. For the unstable progress of their descendants' legitimisation: Jones and Underwood, *The King's Mother*, pp. 19–26.

[47] Ward estimates around one hundred household members towards the end of Elizabeth de Burgh's life: *Elizabeth de Burgh*, p. xx within a discussion of the household records, pp. xix-xxiv. For Lady Margaret's household see 2.2 below.

[48] Elizabeth de Burgh first supported University Hall and then was encourged to support the foundation of the college named after her family estate at Clare.

[49] *The Chamber Books of Henry VII and Henry VIII, 1485–1521*, ed. M. M. Condon, S. P. Harper, L. Liddy, and S. Cunningham and J. Ross: <https://www.tudorchamberbooks.org/>; Sean Cunningham and James Ross, *Kingship and Political Society in England, 1485–1529: The Projection and Reception of Royal Authority under Henry VII and Henry VIII* (Oxford: Oxford University Press, forthcoming).

[50] Previously edited by Nicholas Harris Nicolas: *Privy Purse Expenses of Elizabeth of York* (London: William Pickering, 1830).

[51] In addition, London, BL, Add. MS 7099 contains antiquarian extracts from a lost book of Henry VII (October 1492–1509). For the documents: <https://www.tudorchamberbooks.org/editorial-method/>. The web edition as a whole covers 1495–1521, ending with the withdrawal from office of the long-serving treasurer of the chamber, John Heron, whose career had begun as deputy to Sir Thomas Lovell in 1485.

[52] For discussions of the documents themselves and what they reveal of life at the court of Henry VII: Margaret Condon, Samantha Harper and James Ross, 'The Chamber Books of Henry VII

Lady Margaret's accounts may be compared, for example, in the progress of their joint plans for burial at Westminster Abbey, or the use of the same City goldsmiths for their New Year's gifts. While the king inevitably dealt with issues of national significance and Lady Margaret largely with issues of regional and personal significance, the phrase used by the editors of the chamber books resonates with the present editor of Lady Margaret's cofferers' accounts: 'the incredible variety of entries in the Chamber Books, from small payments for strawberries to massive subsidies to foreign allies, as well as the financial instruments known as bonds and recognisances'. In Lady Margaret's case these accounts similarly move from small payments for apples, pears and rose water to large payments towards the refoundation of Christ's College, Cambridge, as well as loans and debts made to and incurred by her household and others well beyond.

2 Lady Margaret Beaufort and her Officers and Household

2.1 The Personnel

2.1.1 The computus (D91.16) of the treasurer of the household, William Bedell

William Bedell was the treasurer of the household throughout the period of Lady Margaret's single status (1498/9–1509).[53] It is likely that he began his career in the service of the Staffords; from 1487 until the duke came of age in 1498 he served Lady Margaret as receiver of the estates of the young third duke of Buckingham, Edward Stafford, whose wardship, with that of his brother Henry, she had been granted soon after Bosworth.[54] Between 1493 and 1498 he was also receiver-general for all her estates, and in 1498 he became treasurer of her household, a post he is also recorded as having held in 1493. This was an important role with responsibility for all the monies entering and leaving the counting house. Bedell's wife Cecily was propertied in her own right and held land at Cheshunt, the manor of which Lady Margaret had received in the 'Great Grant' of 1487. In the latter half of 1508, Lady Margaret spent six weeks in Cheshunt, ten miles south-east of Hatfield, at Cecily's manor house, Tongs (see D91.19/101).

and Henry VIII, 1485–1521: An Analysis of the Books and a Synopsis of Henry VII and his Life at Court' at <https://www.tudorchamberbooks.org/chamber-books-analysis-and-synopsis–2/>.

[53] Laura M. Wood, 'Bedell, William (d. 1518)' (*ODNB*), in which see further for his career after Lady Margaret's death. Note: Bedell was not an executor of Lady Margaret, *pace ODNB*. See too Jones & Underwood, *The King's Mother*, p. 269 and passim.

[54] Rawcliffe, *The Staffords*, pp. 56, 200–1. Bedell's will (TNA PROB 11/19/116) refers several times to his 'lord', the duke of Buckingham.

Bedell's status may be assessed by the fact that on his death in 1518 he was buried, as his will requested, 'at the lower ende in my ladies chapell at Westminster called Scala Celi', in a tomb no longer extant.[55] (Of the other of her household officers whose accounts are edited here, burial was presumably in their parish church, with the exception of Henry Hornby, who seems to have been buried in what is now Little St Mary's, Cambridge, at that time the chapel of Peterhouse, where he was master.[56])

2.1.2 The book of receipts and payments (D102.10) of Lady Margaret's secretary/dean of chapel (later chancellor), Henry Hornby

Henry Hornby (*c.* 1457–1518) may have been the son of an employee of Lady Margaret and Thomas Stanley at their Maxey estate in Lincolnshire.[57] He appears to have been born in Baston [Lincs.], where he is said to have founded a grammar school.[58] There is a strong likelihood that Lady Margaret supported his education at Cambridge, from which he eventually emerged D.Th. in 1495.[59] He was her secretary already in the 1490s and became dean of her chapel from its consecration at Collyweston in 1498/9;[60] from the turn of the year 1504/5 he also served as her chancellor.[61] As Lady Margaret's nominee he had become master of Peterhouse in 1501 and may eventually have been buried there.[62] He was also master of Tattershall college for most of the 1500s

[55] TNA PROB 11/19/116. For Scala Celi: Nigel Morgan, 'The Scala Coeli Indulgence and the Royal Chapels', in *The Reign of Henry VII*, ed. Benjamin Thompson (Stamford: Paul Watkins, 1995), pp. 82–103.

[56] Susan Powell, 'Cambridge Commemorations of Lady Margaret Beaufort's Household', in *Commemoration in Medieval Cambridge,* ed. John S. Lee and Christian Steer (Woodbridge: Boydell, 2018), pp. 123–51 at 133–6. See too for biographical details of Ashton and Fisher, whose monuments are/were in Cambridge, and others of her household who were buried there.

[57] A George Hornby looked after the horses at Deeping [Lincs.] in 1483: Jones & Underwood, *The King's Mother*, pp. 168, 276. For Hornby: Malcolm G. Underwood, 'Hornby [Horneby], Henry (*c.* 1457–1518)' (*ODNB*); Underwood, 'The Lady Margaret and her Cambridge Connections', 72–3; Powell, 'Lady Margaret Beaufort as Patron', 111–12.

[58] Jones & Underwood, *The King's Mother*, p. 276, although the entry refers to Boston, whereas Hornby's allegiance appears to have been to Baston, to which he left in his will altar cloths and vestments for the use of the Guild of the Blessed Mary, as well as money to repair the bridge: TNA PROB 11/19/69 (where, like Bedell, he requires prayers for the soul of Lady Margaret).

[59] He is recorded 19 March 1506 as 'in \sacra/ theologia doctoris et predicte excellentissime matris cancellarii' in a slip of paper at the end of the book of receipts and payments which he kept for Lady Margaret (D102.10/182).

[60] Lady Margaret received the licence for the chapel in September 1498: D91.17/42.

[61] In these edited accounts his usual title is 'dean', and he is only referred to by name as chancellor (a role he took over from Oldham in late 1504) in 1509 (see Hornby in the PEOPLE index); at D91.19/82 references to masters chancellor, dean and receiver would suggest three separate persons, but the number of beds is revised to two.

[62] His will refers to his burial 'in ecclesia vbi deus ex sua speciali gratia me obire voluerit'. See the discussion of his burial place in Powell, 'Cambridge Commemorations', pp. 133–6.

and 1510s, and dean of Wimborne, where Lady Margaret's parents were buried, from 1509 (the year of her death). His importance to the household cannot be overestimated, and with John Fisher, bishop of Rochester and her spiritual and secular confidant, he was the most long-serving and diligent of her executors.

2.1.3 The chamber accounts

2.1.3.1 The chamber accounts (D91.17) of James Clarell (24 June 1498–12 January 1499)

Little is known about James Clarell, other than that he was Lady Margaret's cofferer before and also after her separation from Thomas Stanley.[63] He is recorded as such in 1494, and the note of his arrears 24 June 1498 (D91.17/1) shows that he was also cofferer for the previous set of accounts, but whether he continued in that role beyond 12 January 1499 is unknown since the following three years of accounts are missing. However, it is unlikely that he continued in that precise capacity, not least since Lady Margaret brought a suit of debt against him *c.* 1501, which he paid off in part in that year (D102.2/2).[64] Thereafter a man of the same name is recorded as sending fifteen yards of tawny medley from London in June 1504, a transaction cited again in a list of debts at the end of the year (with the debt recorded correctly as 45s. 7½d.), and again in 1506, 1507 and 1508 (when accounting errors have reduced the debt to 45s. 5½d. and it was still unpaid).[65]

2.1.3.2 The chamber accounts (D91.20, D91.21, D91.19) of Miles Worsley (2 February 1502 until 13 January 1509)

Similarly, little is known of Miles Worsley, cofferer throughout 1502–8 (called treasurer of the chamber from 14 January 1506).[66] The Worsleys appear to have been northern in origin, and from 1479 until his death in 1499 William Worsley, who was mentioned above (1.4), was dean of St Paul's, and was originally attainted in 1494 along with William Stanley, Thomas Stanley's brother. A James Worsley was groom of the robes to Henry VIII,[67] and it seems likely that Miles (appointed in the year of William Worsley's death) was a member

[63] Jones and Underwood, *The King's Mother*, p. 271 (p. 107 for his debt to Lady Margaret *c.* 1501, p. 154 for the assumption that he was dismissed after the 1498–9 accounts).

[64] Jones and Underwood, *The King's Mother*, pp. 107, 271 (but for 'SJC.D102.2, p 8' read 'p. 2').

[65] D91.20/158, 194; D91.21/79, 162–3; D91.19/61, 123. For more litigation associated with Clarell: TNA C 1/294/85; C 1/291/55; C 1/205/71; C 1/338/12; C 4/9/170.

[66] D91.21/83; his title at 14 January 1505 is missing due to a damaged page but appears still to be 'clerk of the coffers' (D91.21/1). For the little that is known: Jones and Underwood, *The King's Mother*, p. 187 (and index); Powell, 'Lady Margaret Beaufort as Patron', p. 111.

[67] For his wardrobe book 1516–21: *The Great Wardrobe Accounts of Henry VII and Henry VIII*, ed. Maria Hayward (Woodbridge: Brewer, 2012), p. xxi and index.

of the same family. No will appears to survive, but he is cited in various documents in relation to landed estates and litigation thereof during Henry VIII's reign (1515–16).[68]

2.1.3.3 The chamber accounts (D102.1) of Robert Fremingham (20 January – 29 June 1509)

What is known about Robert Fremingham is that, with Richard Bothe, bailiff of Lady Margaret's estates at Wykes and Frampton [Lincs.], he was involved in litigation with Worsley and his wife Margaret in 1507.[69] His name first appears in the accounts on 18 February 1505 (D91.21/10),[70] but his elevation to treasurer of the chamber in the 1509 accounts (D102.1) was only in an acting capacity, perhaps occasioned by Worsley's duties elsewhere after Lady Margaret's death 29 June, or other reasons.[71] (For the suggestion that he worked in the wardrobe of robes, see 5.4.1 below.) The fact that he is named among the gentlemen of Lady Margaret's household in the lists of mourning apparel for the funeral of Henry VII (see further below) may suggest his status in the household.[72]

2.1.4 The accounts (D102.2, D102.6) of the chamberlain, Sir Roger Ormeston (20 May 1501 until 11 February 1502)

More is known of Ormeston (d. 1504),[73] who was a northerner like Hornby and perhaps Worsley, and was the cousin of Hugh Oldham, another northerner and a protégé of the Lancashire-born William Booth, archbishop of York 1452–64.[74] Ormeston is recorded as constable of Corfe castle in 1492,

[68] TNA E 150/680/2; E 150/680/3; C 142/30/49–2; C 142/30/96; CP40/980.

[69] TNA CP40/980; see too Jones and Underwood, *The King's Mother*, p. 274, and TNA C 1/309/39 for litigation after Fremingham's death relating to his late wife Joan Swanne.

[70] He is not mentioned in Henry Hornby's book (D102.10) until p. 151 (4 February 1508), but if the hand at D91.20/28 (18 June 1502) is actually the 'curly' hand and the 'curly' hand is that of Fremingham (see 5.4.1 below), his first appearance in Lady Margaret's household was earlier still.

[71] Fremingham refers to himself as 'occupantis officium thesaurarii camere', D102.1/2r. An erasure before 'occupantis' may indicate that he started to write 'thesaurii camerarii' and was corrected, or corrected himself, to 'occupying the office of treasurer of the chamber'.

[72] His surname is there given as 'Fernyngham', which suggests that his family may originally have come from Farningham [Kent].

[73] He himself spells his surname 'Urmyston' (D102.2/3 (Plate 18), 5, 7, etc.), and Ur- is also the recorded spelling of his wife and kinsmen, cf. Urmston [Lancs.]. However, Orm- is found in other hands, e.g. D102.2/1 and D102.10/18, and the spelling 'Ormeston' is so consistently used in Jones and Underwood, *The King's Mother*, that it is adopted here.

[74] Jones and Underwood, *The King's Mother*, p. 279–80 (sub Oldham and Ormeston); for the northern networks in Lady Margaret's household: Powell, 'Lady Margaret Beaufort as Patron', pp. 107–13. For a suit in the Court of Chancery in which a Robert Worsley of Eccles [Lancs.] and

when Oldham was deputy receiver for Lady Margaret's West Country estates. He acquired a knighthood and became chamberlain of Lady Margaret's household in 1501, the same year as Oldham became chancellor; Oldham was appointed bishop of Exeter in November 1504, again the same year that Ormeston became steward of the University of Cambridge (but was dead by 6 April).[75] The last record in Lady Margaret's accounts of his being alive (or at least the date of the last submitted payment) is 4 March 1504 (D91.20/191); his will was written 28 March and proved 29 June,[76] so that he was dead not much more than two years after the completion of D102.2/6. At the start and end of the 1504/5 financial year, references are made to his executors (D91.20/144, 194). He was to be replaced as chamberlain by Lady Margaret's kinsman, Sir John St John II of Bletsoe.

2.2 The Household[77]

Later in the present edition, a comprehensive index of PEOPLE provides an index by name and occupation, from which evidence of Lady Margaret's household can be gleaned. However, given that these details of personnel cover ten years, the role of the person is only occasionally stated, their rise or otherwise in the household is rarely marked, and only occasionally are distinctions made between servants of Lady Margaret and of the king or queen, the accounts edited here provide only a partial view of the household, and the numbers employed in it cannot easily be estimated.[78]

A contemporary account, however, suggests as many as 440. In his New Year's gift to Henry VIII's eldest daughter, Mary, probably presented in 1556, at the beginning of the year after her accession to the throne, Henry Parker (a name which will feature more below) recalled a lavish NewYear's feast when he was a fifteen-year-old sewer to Mary's great-grandmother, Lady Margaret Beaufort, and was followed to her table by twenty-five attendants,

William and John Ormeston of Leigh [Lancs.] were defendants: TNA C 1/368/39.

[75] 28 May according to Jones and Underwood (*The King's Mother*, p. 280), but the document cited is dated 6 April and deals with the stewardship vacancy 'per mortem nuper Aurati equitis Rogeri Ormston': C. H. Cooper, 'On the Earlier High Stewards of the University of Cambridge', in *Antiquarian Communications: Being Papers Presented at the Meetings of the Cambridge Antiquarian Society*, I (Cambridge: Cambridge University Press, 1859), pp. 273–8 at 274.

[76] TNA PROB 11/14/211.

[77] For analyses of Lady Margaret's income and household: Jones and Underwood, *The King's Mother*, chapters 4, 'The countess and her property', and 5, 'Household life' (pp. 93–136, 137–70).

[78] Over 150 names in the PEOPLE index appear to have been members of the household for long or shorter periods between 1498 and 1509 (but there are no accounts extant from January 1499 until May 1501).

of whom his father was one.[79] The memory led him to expatiate on Lady Margaret's largesse, liberality and humanity: 'although that she had in her checker roule contynually two and twenty score of ladies, gentylmen, yeomen, and offycers, yet it ys a wonder to tell, ther was neither man nor woman, if thei were of any reputatyon, but she coulde call them by ther names'.[80] Such a number on her household payroll is large, and Jones and Underwood dispute it, suggesting that so many could only have been reached at particularly grand occasions. However, they confirm that 'the broader impression is borne out by the documentary evidence', citing £1,542 spent on the household in the year 1506–7, apart from other expenditure, including £115 on New Year's gifts. By then, they note:

> Her establishment was now the greatest in the realm after the king's. Forty years ago she had helped manage a small household of thirty. Now she presided over a hierarchy of officers and departments.[81]

The household of thirty male servants and two female was that she maintained with her husband Henry Stafford in Bourne [Lincs.] until his death in 1471.[82] However, the discussion that follows here will begin in 1498 at the time of her refurbishment of Collyweston as her main home, and it will use what evidence exists in the present edited accounts to suggest, not so much numbers, as rather the extent of her actual household and those who were in her purlieu, to whom she disbursed obligations and from whom she received service.

In the accounts edited here, the earliest evidence for her household is provided by the details of the riding household she employed on her progress with the king through East Anglia in the summer of 1498.[83] D91.17/46–7 lists wages for the period ending at Michaelmas term and cites thirty-seven men, of whom the chamberlain Roger Ormeston, the clerk of the spicery William

[79] For Jones and Underwood, *The King's Mother*, p. 158, the occasion was a celebration of William Smith's elevation to the see of Lincoln (1496); certainly Smith was present and it was held before 1499 when Lady Margaret's half-brother John, viscount Welles, died, as he is also said to have been present.

[80] The gift was a vellum presentation copy of Parker's own account of a past time before the religious and political upheavals of recent years. The manuscript, London, British Library, Add. MS 12060, has been edited by James P. Carley and Richard Rex as 'The Account of the Miracles of the Sacrament', in *Triumphs of English: Henry Parker, Lord Morley, Translator to the Tudor Court*, ed. Marie Axton and James P. Carley (London: British Library, 2000), Appendix 7 (pp. 253–69). For the quotation see p. 263 (Add. MS 12060, f. 22r).

[81] Jones and Underwood, *The King's Mother*, p. 159, citing SJCA D91.21 (now SJLM/1/1/3/2, edited here).

[82] Ibid., p. 138. At his death she maintained a reduced household of sixteen: ibid., p. 144.

[83] Susan Powell, 'Lady Margaret Beaufort: a Progress through Essex and East Anglia, 1498', in *The Elite Household in England, 1100–1550*, ed. C. M. Woolgar (Donington: Shaun Tyas, 2018), pp. 295–316.

Hilmer, the cofferer James Clarell, and the future yeoman of the wardrobe Robert Hilton held, or were to hold, important roles in her household.[84] The first to be named is the physician Thomas Denman, master of Peterhouse, whose wage is said to be for half a year (£10), while no term is given for the others in the entry: Ormeston 23s. 4d., Hilmer 40s., and Latimer, Stukeley and the launderer 20s. each. Two others (John Brownyng and Richard Dawson) were paid 10s. and 5s. respectively as quarter-year wages. Clarell was paid 16s. 8d. a quarter plus horse livery expenses. Eighteen individuals were paid 10s. a quarter and 6s. 8d. for horse livery; the grooms received 5s. a quarter. Apart from the named officers, only the status of the ten grooms is given,[85] and we may assume that the others were gentlemen of the household (or perhaps co-opted from outside the household for the progress itself). Of this male riding household at the start of Lady Margaret's independent life, over a quarter were still in her service at the end of her life.[86] Denman and Ormeston were both dead, Clarell and others had moved elsewhere, but four of her original riding household had advanced sufficiently to be chosen as part of her retinue of twenty-seven men at her son's funeral over a decade later – Nicholas Aughton, George Fraunces, William Hilmer and Robert Hilton (see further below).

The thirty-seven of 1498 do not include the members of her counting house and her provisioning departments, presumably because they were not part of the riding household. However, nor are counting-house officers mentioned in what might seem to be a comparable household, that of Elizabeth of York, listed in an undated document preserved again in St John's College, Cambridge (D102.11, now SJLM/9/2/1). The post-holders are the chamberlain, vice-chamberlain, confessor, carvers, cup-bearer, secretary, sewers, gentlemen ushers, sewers for the chamber, squires attendants, sergeant-at-arms, yeoman ushers, yeomen, grooms and pages of the chamber, chaplains, physician, clerk of the closet, and apothecary. Next are listed the departments of the household: the bakehouse, pantry, cellar, buttery, ewery, kitchen, accatry, larder, and almonry,[87] while the rest of the document lists stable staff

[84] The household wages for the period June 1498 to January 1499 came to £43 11s. 8d. (D91.17/67).

[85] Hilton is named among them; he was taken along 'for his workmanship as a skynner' (D91.17/47).

[86] The estimate is based on their remaining in the accounts as late as D91.19 (1507–9): Aughton, Coke (aka Ludlow), Edlyn, Fraunces, Hilmer, Hilton, Pole, Shirley, Walter, Worsley. Of these, Coke and Hilmer featured in Lady Margaret's will, and Aughton, Edlyn, Fraunces and Hilton featured in the posthumous list of 'Rewardes' (see further below and Appendix).

[87] In the treasurer's roll for 1506–7 (D91.16), several members of Lady Margaret's provisioning departments are cited by name and job title: butchers, recent and present (Davy, Unwyn), the clerk of the spicery (Hilmer), yeomen of the bakehouse (Casse, Cox), the brewhouse (Canwyke), the cellar (Vaux), the chandlery (Kylner), the dry larder (Hill), the pantry (Davenport, Fyssh), the pastry house (Daye), and a groom of the scullery (Hynkersall). Of these, Canwyke,

(at least twenty-two posts) and ends with a short list of Katherine of Aragon's servants. As it stands, relatively few names are attached to the posts (only forty-one out of a minimum of forty-six offices, apart from the stable staff), and the list may have been compiled as a template or desideratum rather than as a complete record of post-holders.[88] Again, it does not include any women (although over forty women can be identified who served her at one time or another throughout her reign), and it can be augmented considerably from Elizabeth of York's privy purse expenses.[89]

No strict correlation between Elizabeth of York and her mother-in-law may anyway be likely: unlike the queen, Lady Margaret lived as *femme sole*, and she exercised considerably more authority (as noted slyly by court visitors), not just the personal authority recorded of her as the autocratic mother of the king and his principal adviser, but also, for example, regional authority through her own council, which met at her purpose-built council house at Collyweston, where a convenient prison-house had also been constructed.[90] Lady Margaret Beaufort was also a very wealthy woman in her own right. After Bosworth her son endowed her with considerable property, largely through the 'Great Grant' of 1487. This provided her with a total income of £1,960, and the death of her husband Thomas Stanley in 1504 increased her landed income to £3,000.[91]

As a small indication of the potential compass of the king's household, the lists of those who were accorded mourning attire at his funeral, two months before Lady Margaret's own death, are useful.[92] Those of the king's household are named, by office or by Christian name and surname, to the number of over four hundred in forty-two different categories. Even at the end of her life Lady Margaret's household was of course smaller, if a comparison is made with the 188 proposed mourners at her own funeral (see further below).[93] However, these lists of mourning attire for her son's funeral are helpful in providing details of the most senior members of Lady Margaret's household and those closest to her at the end of her life. Her female servants

---

Davenport, Daye, Hill, Kylner, and Vaux were rewarded after Lady Margaret's death (see Appendix), and Hilmer was named in her will.

[88] 'A boke made aswell for the nombre of all thofficers and servauntes of the Quenes chambre as for other ministres as officers and servauntes suing for grace in howsholde and stable as folowyth'.

[89] *Privy Purse Expenses*, ed. Nicolas, which was used, with other sources, in Alison Weir, *Elizabeth of York: A Tudor Queen and her World* (New York: Ballantine, 2013), Appendix II ('Elizabeth of York's Ladies and Gentlewomen').

[90] Jones and Underwood, *The King's Mother*, pp. 85–6.

[91] Ibid., pp. 100, 115.

[92] *Letters and Papers, Foreign and Domestic, Henry VIII*, ed. J. S. Brewer, I (London: HMSO, 1920), no. 20 (pp. 11–21), based on TNA LC 2/1 (Lord Chamberlain's Department, Record of Special Events, Accounts of Funerals and Mournings).

[93] SJCA D4.7 (now SJLM/3/1/4), pp. 31–8.

may be considered first. Allowances of mantlets, kerchiefs, and cloth were made to many ladies for attendance at Henry VII's funeral, amongst whom are named Lady Margaret herself and an entourage of thirteen, specified as Jane Guildford and Elizabeth Willoughby (ladies, with two unnamed gentlewomen attendants), Anne Clifford, Edith Fowler, Alice Parker, Elizabeth Radcliffe, Alice Stanhope, Elizabeth Webbe, and Margaret Yan (gentlewomen), and Perrot Doryn and Jane Walter (chamberers).[94] All are recorded in the accounts edited here, Edith Fowler and Alice Parker, her kinswoman and the wife of Henry Parker quoted above, most frequently.[95] Those men in Lady Margaret's household who were granted allowances of cloth were her counsellors (masters chancellor, chamberlain, steward, and Morgan),[96] her chaplains (masters confessor, almoner, and Peksall),[97] her gentlemen (master Parker, George Hevenyngham, George Frauncesse, Robert Fernyngham, Roger Ratclyff, and John Lee), her yeomen (Robert Merbury, William Hylmer, Nicholas Aughton, Richard Aderston, John Merycoke, Robert Newssewyke, Robert Hylton, John Madyson, and William Love), and her grooms (Hugh Carr, Henry Abney, Hugh Worsley, John Hasylby, and Robert Clyff).[98] These thirty-eight named women and men might be seen as comprising the inner circle of Lady Margaret's household, her chamber staff.[99]

Information on Lady Margaret's own funeral exists in SJCA D4.7 (now SJLM/3/1/4) and D91.24.2 (now SJLM/1/3/1), as well as in her will (on which D4.7 is based).[100] The estimate of funeral expenses in the document SJCA D4.7, which was prepared at Hatfield 17 January 1509, provides mourning cloth for many more than the thirty-eight members of her household who had been supplied for the king's funeral, and the number 188 given above comprised (with no names attached) four ladies, twelve gentlewomen and

[94] *Letters and Papers*, ed. Brewer, I: 11, 13. The surname Doryn (Jones and Underwood, *The King's Mother*, p. 272 sub Doryn, Perrot) is not recorded in these edited accounts, but see SJCA D56.29 (SJLM/7/3/1) for the signature 'Perrott Dorryn', SJCA D3.78 (SJLM/7/3/2) for 'Perote Deron' and SJCA D91.4 (SJLM/2/2/2), p. 14 for 'Perot Doryn'. For Margaret Yan: S. Powell, *The Birgittines of Syon Abbey: Preaching and Print* (Turnhout: Brepols, 2017), pp. 219–22.

[95] For Edith Fowler, the only woman to be buried in Christ's College chapel: Powell, 'Cambridge Commemorations', pp. 128–31. For Alice Parker (a St John by birth) see below.

[96] That is, Henry Hornby, Sir John St John II, Sir William Knyvet; Philip Morgan was her physician. There is no entry for 'controller' in the document.

[97] That is, Edmund Wilsford, Robert Bekinsall, and master Peksall. William Fell was in Rome in 1507 (D91.19/19, 54) and Bekinsall is referred to as her almoner April 1508 (D91.19/82).

[98] *Letters and Papers*, ed. Brewer, I: 13. Names are as spelt in the document.

[99] There are no staff from the counting house (if we exclude Fremingham, perhaps attached to the wardrobe of robes (see 5.4.1 below), not even William Bedell, her treasurer, or James Morice, her clerk of works.

[100] *Collegium Divi Johannis Evangelistae 1511–1911* (Cambridge: Cambridge University Press, 1911), Appendix: 'The Will of the Foundress' (pp. 101–26).

eight knights; eight chief chaplains; ten chaplains, twelve gentlemen and eight choristers from the chapel; six chief officers and councillors; ten gentlemen of the household and 110 yeomen and grooms.[101] The black cloth had been estimated (D4.7, p. 36) at around £100 (not all the calculations are accurate); in the event, in the account of expenses paid out by Henry Hornby (D91.24.2, pp. 58–9), it came to a total of £384 16s. 0½d.[102]

The estimated overall cost for the funeral had been £1,033 2s. 8d. (D4.7, p. 38), whereas the final cost was £1,021 6s. 7½d. (D91.24.2, p. 59). However, the items in each document vary to some extent, and only a full comparison would establish precise differences in cost. For example, the estimate document did not include final expenses paid for the lying in state, that is, for leading the body (66s. 8d.), painting the appropriate coats of arms (£96 5s. 11d.) and paying the heralds of arms (£15 10s.), and making an elaborate canopy ('maiestie') to hang over the hearse (53s. 4d.). On the other hand, the estimate document included various costs anticipated by her death elsewhere, such as the rituals to be performed at and around her place of death and en route to London and thence to Westminster Abbey (D4.7, pp. 31–2). Of course, Lady Margaret's dying at Westminster had removed these costs altogether. Similarly there must have been expenses associated with the mass of her month's mind, celebrated at the abbey on 29 July 1509, but no account survives of the costs or details, although the event is commemorated in the sermon ('a mornynge remembraunce') preached by her close confidant and friend, John Fisher, bishop of Rochester, and, in true Lady Margaret style, published by him through Wynkyn de Worde (*STC* 10891).[103]

After the funeral there was some unhappiness in the household over the delay in rewarding Lady Margaret's servants,[104] and a second useful document may relate to this unhappiness. Headed 'Rewardes' (D56.131, now SJLM/7/5/8), it lists payments made to her household staff after her death

[101] SJCA D4.7, pp. 31–8. In addition cloth was to be provided for fifty gentlemen servants (or gentlemen's servants) specifically said not to be on the checker roll, and 140 torchbearers.

[102] Edited by Cooper, *Memoir of Margaret*, pp. 188–90 (12). The only explicit records in Lady Margaret's household book citing payments to Ashton for 'funerall expenses' are two entries for £55 9s. and £50 (D102.10/133). (The same page records the distributions in alms of four lots of £33 6s. 8d. each, as stipulated in D4.7 and in her will.)

[103] Edited by J. E. B. Mayor, *The English Works of John Fisher now first Collected by John E. B. Mayor*, EETS ES 27 (London: Trubner 1846), pp. 289–310; now superceded by *John Fisher's Court Sermons: Preaching for Lady Margaret 1508–1509*, ed. Cecilia A. Hatt (Oxford: Oxford University Press, 2021), pp. 345–80 (with commentary). See Veronica O'Mara, 'Unearthing the History of an Early Printed Sermon: John Fisher and St John's College, Cambridge', in *Middle English Manuscripts and their Legacies: A Volume in Honour of Ian Doyle*, ed. Corinne Saunders and Richard Lawrie with Laurie Atkinson (Leiden and Boston: Brill, 2022), pp. 212–33. See below for Lady Margaret's own printing ventures.

[104] Jones and Underwood, *The King's Mother*, pp. 245–6.

(see Appendix) and may be (although the sums differ slightly) the document referred to in D102.10/132: 'Item delyvered the viii[th] day of Septembre to pay the rewardes of my ladys servauntes by advise and determinacioun of my lord of Wynchestre ... CC li.'. If so, it merely executes a codicil to Lady Margaret's own will: 'Also the said princesse willed that hir householde seruauntes which had long contynyed and done to hir good seruice shulde be rewarded with part of hir goodes by the discrecion of the Reuerend fader in God Richard Bishhope of Wynchestere vponn informacionn yeven vnto hym of theire good seruice and merites.'[105] There are ninety-one names, with payments totalling £200 16s. 8d. Most of the names are known members of the household (e.g. Hugh Ashton, Lady Margaret's receiver general; Laurence Canwyke, yeoman of the storehouse; John Merycok, yeoman of the chamber), but not all: for example, Christopher Myddelton (56/3) was a London notary, Jaques Yerwell is recorded at Lady Margaret's college of Fotheringhay (56/4), and John Parker is likely to have been clerk of the king's buttery (56/5). Several yeoman of the various household offices are mentioned, and just one bailiff, her Hatfield bailiff, Nicholas Warcoppe.[106]

The extent of Lady Margaret's household was clearly not defined solely by those who feature most in the accounts edited here, but they are invaluable in demonstrating the vectors of her influence and the numbers who were drawn within her penumbra. For example, there are frequent references to members of her chapel, and this is an area where comparison can be made with the king, a comparison which was made in her own day but which can be corroborated by extensive scholarly research.[107] In his New Year's gift cited above, Henry Parker informed Queen Mary that her great-grandmother 'kept her chapple egall with the king her sonne'.[108] In the accounts edited here,

[105] 'The Will of the Foundress', p. 125 (148). It is also recorded in D91.24.2 as given to the household servants 'at theyr departyng by the dyscrecyone of thexecutours that tyme' (p. 60). The earlier document (D4.7) had anticipated continued payment of wages to the household for six months after Lady Margaret's death (p. 50). D102.10/133 records £20 given to the Hatfield household.

[106] The recipients of the 'Rewardes' are marked by [R] and the recipients of Lady Margaret's will by [W] in the PEOPLE index in this edition. The reimbursement appears to have been largely for those not otherwise rewarded in Lady Margaret's will (only the Stukeleys are in both).

[107] The research is that of Fiona Kisby: 'The Early-Tudor Royal Household Chapel, 1485–1547' (unpub. doctoral thesis, University of London, 1996), esp. chapter 4 (pp. 161–306) and Appendix 5 (pp. 540–4). For a synopsis of these sections: Fiona Kisby, 'A Mirror for Monarchy: Music and Musicians in the Household Chapel of Lady Margaret Beaufort, Mother of Henry VII', *Early Music History* 16 (1997) 203–34. Also valuable in relation to Westminster Abbey: Roger Bowers, 'The musicians and liturgy of the Lady chapels of the monastery church, c.1235–1540', in *Westminster Abbey: The Lady Chapel of Henry VII*, ed. Tim Tatton-Brown and Richard Mortimer (Woodbridge: Boydell, 2003), pp. 33–57.

[108] London, British Library, MS 12060, f. 22r (Carley and Rex, 'The Account of the Miracles of the Sacrament', p. 264).

around thirty personnel are noted as connected to the chapel at some stage in the last ten years of Lady Margaret's life, and the document mentioned already above (SJCA D4.7, now SJLM/3/1/4) records twelve priests, twelve laymen and ten choristers of her chapel at the end of her life (p. 33). It was served by her dean Henry Hornby and the subdean William Clerk, with other chaplains, gentlemen (singing men) and children (choristers), apart from Leonard le Fevour, usually called 'Leonard of the vestry', who was groom of the vestry and responsible for various tasks to do with the chapel books and Lady Margaret's own books. This compares well with the forty-two members of the Chapel Royal listed in the funeral ordinances for Henry VII – a dean and sub-dean, six priests, eighteen gentlemen, eleven chapel children, a sergeant, yeoman and groom of the vestry, and perhaps two 'pistelers'.[109]

Loyalty to Lady Margaret was high within the household, as evidenced by the statements of John Fisher and Henry Parker (Lord Morley by the time he wrote his reminiscences of Lady Margaret for her great-granddaughter).[110] It is evidenced in the wills of her closest servants: William Bedell, her treasurer, and Henry Hornby, her secretary, asked for prayers for her soul, and Bedell left a cup of gold and two great chains of gold (approx. 89 oz.) for charitable works 'for the soule of my most singuler good lady Margarete countes of Richemount by whom I had all that I haue'.[111] Richard Lynne, her vice chamberlain, referred to her with warmth in calling one of his executors, Hugh Ashton, 'countroller to the right excellent pryncesse moder to our souereigne lord kyng Henry the vijth'.[112] At his death in 1504 her chamberlain, Roger Ormeston, left 'vnto my ladis grace' a standing cup with a gilt cover, acknowledging gratitude to her son as he bequeathed to his wife and her heirs 'all suche landys as I had by reason of the kyngis gifte to me'.[113]

Wills also provide some indication of relationships, as kin or as colleagues, within the household. Richard Lynne chose colleagues, the almoner Robert Bekinsall as well as the controller Hugh Ashton as executors of his will;[114] beside his sons, James Morice cited 'my lord Morley my supervisor', that is, Henry Parker, as supervisor of the executors; Ormeston chose a man who

[109] *Letters and Papers*, ed. Brewer, I: 15, 18. For a full discussion of the Royal Chapel: Kisby, 'The Early-Tudor Royal Household Chapel'. At the time various chaplains read the gospel and epistle, so that the terms 'gospeller' and 'epistler' 'did not describe an office in the formal sense' (ibid., p. 88).

[110] For an overview: R. M. Warnicke, 'The Lady Margaret Beaufort, Countess of Richmond (d. 1509) as seen by John Fisher and by Lord Morley', *Moreana*, 19 (1982), 47–55.

[111] Bedell TNA PROB 11/19/116 (probate 12 July 1518); Hornby TNA PROB 11/19/69 (probate 16 March 1518).

[112] Lynne: TNA PROB 11/16/179 (probate 28 March 1509).

[113] Ormeston: TNA PROB 11/14/211 (probate 29 June 1504).

[114] For Bekinsall: Underwood, 'The Lady Margaret and her Cambridge Connections', 74–5; for Ashton, pp. 73–4.

was both kin and former colleague, 'my cousyn maistur Hugh Oldam'. The duplication of surnames in the PEOPLE index provided later in this edition indicates the extent of family involvement in Lady Margaret's household: Henry and Hugh Ashton; John and William Bedell; Nicholas and Walter Compton; William and Robert Fell; Richard and William Lynne; James and Morgan Morice; Elizabeth, John, Roger, Thomas, and William Urmeston. John Bedell was deputy to William and certainly a family member; Morgan Morice was a servant of John Fisher and James Morice's nephew; John and William Urmeston served in Lady Margaret's household, and Thomas ('my Brother parsonne' in Roger's will) was receiver and vicar of Kendal [Westm.]. Sometimes family connections are not apparent from surnames: as noted above, Roger Ormeston was the cousin of Hugh Oldham, chancellor until 1503/4; Hugh Ashton, receiver, was the uncle of Thomas Mawdesley, a chaplain in the household; Henry Hornby, secretary, was the uncle of Robert Pulvertoft, bailiff of Tattershall.[115]

Some of Lady Margaret's own kin found positions in her household, and many are mentioned in these accounts. Although she had no siblings and no children other than Henry VII, Lady Margaret had numerous siblings of the half-blood, who married and produced offspring who figure in these accounts.[116] The first husband of Margaret Beauchamp, Lady Margaret's mother, had been Oliver St John, and the accounts are full of the St Johns, and Sir John St John II (son of Sir John St John I of Bletsoe, Oliver's son) was Lady Margaret's chamberlain after Ormeston.[117] Her gentlewoman Alice Parker was his daughter and the wife of Henry Parker, gentleman of the household, mentioned several times above; Lady Margaret supported them both and appears to have been fond of them and their children, as her accounts often mention nurses and midwives for Alice and gifts for the children.[118] The Frogenhalls and Zouches, often mentioned in the accounts, were descended from Mary St John (sister of Sir John St John I), who had married Sir Richard Frogenhall, and her sister Elizabeth, who had married William, lord Zouche. Among others, Lady Margaret paid exhibitions for

[115] Ashton: TNA PROB 11/21/58; Hornby: TNA PROB 11/19/69.

[116] See the PEOPLE index, and see the (sometimes faulty) genealogical tables in Jones and Underwood, *The King's Mother*, unpaginated (before p. 1). For the St John family tree the following is fuller and more accurate: Linda Ehrsam Voigts and Ann Payne, 'Medicine for a Great Household (ca. 1500): Berkeley Castle Muniments Select Book 89', in *Studies in medieval and renaissance history*, third series, 12 (AMS Press: New York), pp. 87–270 (Genealogy Chart II).

[117] Apart from those listed under St John, see too in the PEOPLE index: Elizabeth Bigod, Anne Clifford, Elizabeth Fitzgerald, Eleanor Grey, Gruffydd ap Rhys, Mary Conyers, Eleanor Verney.

[118] For example, D91.21/ 32, 37, 75, 89 (so too D91.20 and D91.19 passim); 20/92 ('a knytt cote for maister Parkers son'; 19/75 ('a bonett bought for lytell maistres Parker'), 111 ('for yonge maistres Parker iiii popettes ').

John and Joan St John of Lydiard Tregoze, Henry and Alice Parker, John and Anne Markham (see further below), and Alexander and Margaret Frogenhall (see, for example, D91.21/77).

Margaret Beauchamp's third husband (after Lady Margaret's father, John Beaufort, duke of Somerset) was Lionel, lord Welles. His son John, Lady Margaret's half-brother, died in 1499, leaving as his widow Cecily, a daughter of Edward IV who had been married into the family after Bosworth. Cecily was another favourite of Lady Margaret, and Parker noted that she was especially honoured at the New Year's feast he recalled in his memoir for Queen Mary: 'by her person under her clothe of estate [was] the lady Cecyle, king Edwardes doughter, your aunte'.[119] At the time of her death in August 1507 (D91.19/59) Cecily was with Lady Margaret at Hatfield as a lady sojourner (see further below).

Lady Margaret's interest extended to the families of her husbands. The Tudors were supported in different ways by Henry VII, the son of Lady Margaret's first husband, Edmund Tudor, and she herself retained servants of the family of her second husband, Henry Stafford, son of the first duke of Buckingham.[120] Stafford's sister Joan, long after his death, married Sir William Knyvett, Lady Margaret's steward. After Bosworth Lady Margaret had housed as wards Edward Stafford, third duke of Buckingham and his brother Henry (both of whom are mentioned in the accounts), perhaps with their sisters Elizabeth and Anne.[121] Lady Margaret's last husband, Thomas Stanley, features in her accounts in his own right until his death in 1504, as do his servants, of whom many are mentioned.[122] His son James was, through Lady Margaret's offices, bishop of Ely, but in return she commandeered the bishop's palace at Hatfield for the last years of her life.[123] Stanley's heir had been another son, George le Strange, who pre-deceased him in odd circumstances (allegedly poisoned at a banquet); his widow Joan and his daughter Eleanor are mentioned in the accounts, the latter dying in Lady Margaret's household in December 1503, the same month as her father (see 4.3.2 below). The heir to the Derby title was therefore Thomas Stanley II, who stayed at Collyweston with his grandfather in August 1502 and is also recorded as

[119] London, British Library, MS 12060, f. 21v (Carley and Rex, 'The Account of the Miracles of the Sacrament', p. 263).

[120] Reginald Bray, who later became Henry VII's receiver general, had held that position before in the household of Henry Stafford and Lady Margaret; William Bedell had been Lady Margaret's receiver for the Stafford estates before he became her treasurer.

[121] For Elizabeth, who became head of the household of Lady Margaret's granddaughter Mary, Queen of the Scots, see the PEOPLE index sub Radcliffe.

[122] See the PEOPLE index sub Henry Barlow, Henry and Richard Conway, Henry Cotton, Roger Dalton, Davy Harvey, John Hill, George Rygmaydon, Henry Starkey.

[123] For his own hard bargain (after her death) in relation to the founding of St John's College: Jones and Underwood, *The King's Mother*, pp. 242–3

staying overnight after his grandfather's death two years later to the month (D91.20/36–7, 168).

Lady Margaret's household might therefore be swelled by visitors from time to time, but its numbers included semi-permanent residents, some of them paying guests, 'sojourners'. Already in 1501 James Morice's accounts for building works at Collyweston (D102.9, now SJLM/1/2/1) record refurbishment of rooms for 'Lady Scroppe', 'Frognall', 'Lady Bray', 'My lord', 'Lady Jane', and one for 'Lady Revers and lady Powis', as well as 'The Quene chamber' and 'Harry Clegges and Whytytngtonis chamber'.[124] Frogenhall was a kinsman, as mentioned above. Lady Bray was the wife of Sir Reginald Bray, who had held the position of receiver general in the household of Henry Stafford and Lady Margaret, had supported Henry VII in exile abroad, and had then become his own receiver general. She is the only one of Lady Margaret's womenfolk to be mentioned in the 1498 progress through East Anglia (D91.17/17/37, 38, 45, 59, 63). 'My lord' was Thomas Stanley and 'the Quene' Elizabeth of York. 'Lady Jane' was Jane Guildford (née Vaux), who was brought up with her brother in Lady Margaret's household and became in time one of her ladies (she is named as such at the funeral of Henry VII). These were all members of the household, but Lady Scrope, Lady Rivers and Lady Powis were not. They come into a category of 'distressed gentlewomen', and Lady Margaret seems to have been especially thoughtful of such women.

Mary Rivers's mother, Elizabeth Beaufort, was a first cousin of Lady Margaret; her first husband, Anthony Rivers, had been executed in 1483, after which she had married George Neville ('the bastard') who, however, lived in exile abroad from at least 1492. This sufficiently explains Lady Margaret's provision of a room (or share of a room) for her.[125]

Lady Scrope and Lady Powis were also in need of support and were housed by Lady Margaret as paying guests, as noted at the end of Lady Margaret's book of receipts and payments: 'Receytes of the ladies sojornynge with my lady the xiiii yere of the reigne of our soveran lord kinge Henry the vii' (D102.10/138, also 142–3).[126] These receipts seem to be a post-mortem

[124] D102.9/11, 27, 37, 41, 45, 47, 92, 100. Clegg and Whittington were footmen (see the PEOPLE index).

[125] Lady Margaret gave £100 towards the marriage in 1501 of Mary Rivers's daughter, Anne Neville, to John Markham, supported the couple, and paid for Anne's midwife and burial in 1505: D102.10/46; D91.21/45, 47, 75. She also supported Mary Rivers's cousin, Margaret Lewis (see the PEOPLE index), a nun at the Minories, whose sister Alice was prioress: Jens Röhrkasten, *The Mendicant Houses of Medieval London, 1221–1539* (Münster, London: LIT Verlag, 2004), pp. 130, 254.

[126] The receipts give full details of duration of stay and numbers of servants, with the costs of each category of sojourner. For these lady sojourners see the PEOPLE index sub SOJOURNERS; see too Jones and Underwood, *The King's Mother*, pp. 161–4.

gathering of payments (perhaps in the form of actual receipts) for the period 1499–1506.[127] Elizabeth Scrope was a Neville by birth, whose first husband, Thomas, sixth lord Scrope of Upsall and Masham, had died in 1493 and her second, Sir Henry Wentworth, in 1500.[128] Lady Powis was the widow of John Grey, first baron Grey of Powis, who had died in 1497. As the daughter of William Herbert, who had had responsibility for the upbringing of Henry VII in his castle at Raglan, she had been a child companion of Lady Margaret's son, and she was clearly someone Lady Margaret was fond of: she was still living in her household at her death in 1506 (see 4.3.2 below).

What appears to be significant in Lady Margaret's accommodating these women is that they were widows, ladies of standing who were in need of shelter and who could also pay for their upkeep.[129] Other lady sojourners who are mentioned are Lady Clifford in 1499, Lady Cheney with 'lady Wayneford' (i.e. Scrope) in 1501, and Lady Cecily in 1504 and 1506. Anne Clifford was a St John, the sister of Lady Margaret's chamberlain, Sir John St John II; she had married Henry Clifford, tenth baron Clifford, the extremely difficult 'shepherd lord', but seems to have left him in 1499 and found shelter along with her two daughters at Collyweston.[130] Margaret Cheney may have been a god-daughter of Lady Margaret; her husband Sir John, baron Cheney, had died in 1499 and she herself died in 1503. Cecily Welles has been mentioned above as a daughter of Edward IV (and so sister of Elizabeth of York, Lady Margaret's daughter-in-law). She had been married to Lady Margaret's half-brother, John Welles, in 1487,[131] and, as noted above, was a favourite of Lady Margaret, who supported her against the king after she married for a third time in 1502.[132] Indeed, the receipt for 1504 records payment by 'my lady Cicill and hir husbonde' for a half-year at 21s. 8d. a week for herself and only 6s. 8d. for her esquire husband (Thomas Kyme). By 1506 only Cecily was in residence, and in some debt, part of which she repaid in the form of three

[127] Both ladies are recorded for 1500, lady Scrope (as 'lady Wayneford') in 1501, and Lady Powis also for 1501, 1504 and 1506.

[128] For Lady Margaret's support in a legal wrangle with Wentworth's son and heir: Jones and Underwood, *The King's Mother*, p. 163.

[129] In this category may also be considered Margaret Pole, who was not accommodated at Collyweston but did receive financial support from Lady Margaret when she was lodging with her children at Syon Abbey after the death in 1505 of her husband, Sir Richard Pole, the son of Lady Margaret's half-sister Edith St John: Susan Powell, 'Margaret Pole and Syon Abbey', *Historical Research*, 78 (2005), 563–7, rev. in *The Birgittines of Syon Abbey*, pp. 215–18, 223–7.

[130] Jones and Underwood, *The King's Mother*, pp. 163–4. Henry Summerson notes: 'by 1499 a separation was being mooted [but] the couple remained together until Anne died in 1508': 'Clifford, Henry, tenth baron Clifford (1454–1523)' (*ODNB*).

[131] Her first marriage to Ralph Scrope, brother of Thomas Scrope, husband of Elizabeth Scrope mentioned above, was dissolved in 1486.

[132] For details: Jones and Underwood, *The King's Mother*, pp. 133–5.

costly gowns (see D91.16/7 and D102.10/143). She was to die at Hatfield in August 1507, a year to the month after Lady Powis had died in Lady Margaret's household.

Perhaps to be considered in a similar 'sojourner' category in Lady Margaret's household, but supported by Lady Margaret rather than paying for their board and lodgings, are her wards and her almsfolk. Like all aristocrats, she had many wards (twelve are named in these edited accounts). The most prominent had been Edward Stafford, third duke of Buckingham, and Henry, earl of Wiltshire, his younger brother, whose father, the second duke, had been executed in the Buckingham rising against Richard III in 1483.[133] (She is also said to have housed the daughters of Edward IV and the earls of Warwick and Westmorland.[134]) As for her almsfolk, their social class was quite different. Charitable giving was an essential duty of the aristocrat, and Lady Margaret's almsgiving was controlled by her almoner (at the time of her son's death Robert Bekinsall), who supervised her Maundy Thursday almsgiving (see 4.3.2 below) as well as her day-to-day acts of spontaneous charity. But more than this, she kept an almshouse at each of her main residences, as well as joining with her son in establishing one at Westminster Abbey to house thirteen poor men (the thirteenth a priest).[135]

Although both men and women were almsfolk at Hatfield, as attested by Fisher (see below), the almsfolk mentioned by name in these edited accounts are women (apart from one male child), and the keeper at Collyweston in 1504 was a woman, 'moder Maryon' (D91.20/182).[136] Refurbishment of the almshouse at Collyweston is recorded in the 1505 building account of James Morice (D91.22/13, now SJLM/1/2/3), and Lady Margaret also had almshouses at Croydon and Hatfield.[137] Her almsfolk were twelve in number, as recorded in both her will and Fisher's month's mind sermon: 'Poore folkes to the nombre of twelve she dayly and nyghtly kepte in her house'.[138] (He goes

[133] The mother of the second duke had been a Beaufort, Lady Margaret's cousin (and another Margaret Beaufort); Lady Margaret's second husband, Henry Stafford, had been the duke's uncle.

[134] William Campbell, *Materials for a History of the Reign of Henry VII*, 2 vols (London: Longman, 1873–7), I: 311.

[135] For the building of the Westminster almshouses: Jones and Underwood, *The King's Mother*, p. 233 (note also 'my ladys warkes at Westmynster' D102.10/47). For full details of the hall, chapel, etc.: H. M. Colvin, D. R. Ransome, John Summerson, *The History of the King's Works*, III:I (London: HMSO, 1975), pp. 204–10.

[136] See the PEOPLE index sub Alson, Davy (a child), Dawson, Elyn, Kettell, Marion.

[137] For Croydon and Hatfield: Jones and Underwood, *The King's Mother*, pp. 154–6. For payment of a half-year rent for the almshouse to the Hatfield bailiff in 1509 see D102.1/9r.

[138] For her will: 'Also the said princesse willed that the nowmber of .xij. poore menn and womenn that hir grace kepte and founde at Hatfeld in hir lif tyme shuld be kept and maynteyned at hir costes during all the lyues of the said poore menn and womenn': 'The Will of the Foundress', p. 125 (140). A memo of Roger Notte (SJCA D56.146, now SJLM/7/1/9) refers to the costs at

on to specify Lady Margaret's service to her almsfolk in terms of the seven works of corporal mercy derived from Matthew xxv: 41–6, that is, performing charitable tasks throughout their lives and then attending their deaths and funerals.)

The almschildren, like her chapel children, will have been found paths in life after they left her household, although the future of only one child is recorded here, Nicholas Davy, who was apprenticed in London (D91.21/117). Certainly the chapel children were furthered in life after their voices broke. Some might move on to further chapel service, such as the chapel child John Mason, who became a chaplain at the college at Tattershall of which Lady Margaret was patron, or the chapel man William Farthing who went to the Chapel Royal. To ensure excellent singing of the Latin services, they had been taught Latin grammar, and Lady Margaret's accounts record grammar books and desks.[139] Lady Margaret supported the more academic at school and university: Thomas Bury and William Watwod at Eton, Thomas Freston at Winchester, Richard Moyne at the London charterhouse, Thomas Peper at Oxford. It may have been through her chapel that Lady Margaret first entered the world of authorship and publication. Her ambition in church ritual was remarkable, and in 1493, even before the establishment of her Collyweston chapel, she appears to have initiated through papal licence the celebration of the new feast of the Holy Name with a liturgy written for her by her secretary, Henry Hornby, and printed (presumably at her request) by Richard Pynson (*STC* 15851).[140] She herself had an academic interest in scholarship, which she developed not only vicariously but also through her own translations and her arrangements with two printers, Wynkyn de Worde and Richard Pynson, to print those translations and the works of others.[141] It was in this way that de Worde printed Fisher's sermons on the penitential psalms in 1508 and his funeral sermon for Henry VII in 1509 (*STC* 10902, 10900),[142] and it was a

Hatfield of seven women and three men (3 November 1510, eighteen months after Lady Margaret's death). For Fisher's comment: Mayor, *The English Works of John Fisher*, p. 297, ll. 16–17; Hatt, *John Fisher's Court Sermons*, p. 362, ll. 191–2.

[139] D91.20/102; D91.21/19; see too D102.9/17, 51 (SJLM/1/2/1) for desks and presses.

[140] Powell, *The Birgittines of Syon Abbey*, pp. 168–71 (pp. 162–4 for her impressive liturgical books). For Hornby's composition and setting to music of anthems in 1498 see D91.17/61; for the services for the feasts of the Transfiguration and the Name of Jesus in 1504 see D91.20/160, 166, 171.

[141] For her role in the printing of several books in the 1490s and 1500s: S. Powell, 'Lady Margaret Beaufort and her Books', *The Library*, Sixth Series, Vol. 20 (1998), 197–240, rev. as Chapter 6 of Powell, *The Birgittines of Syon Abbey*, pp. 153–214: for the Feast of the Holy Name, pp. 168–71, for her own translations, pp. 179–87, and see too Brenda Hosington, 'Lady Margaret Beaufort's Translations as Mirrors of Practical Piety', in *English Women, Religion, and Textual Production, 1500–1625*, ed. Micheline White (Farnham: Ashgate, 2011), pp. 185–203.

[142] Edited, together with Henry VII's funeral sermon, by Mayor, *The English Works of John Fisher*, and Hatt, *John Fisher's Court Sermons*.

path which, it was suggested above, John Fisher followed in having de Worde print his own sermon on Lady Margaret herself.

This sermon may be considered the last printing venture initiated by Lady Margaret Beaufort, one of many influenced by her own example to others. Fisher's eloquence in this 'mornynge remembraunce' (*STC* 10891) preached at Lady Margaret's month's mind on 29 July 1509 is considerable. Highly rhetorical, it might be dismissed in the twenty-first century as flattery, even though Fisher asserts that his intention is not 'vaynly to extol or to magnyfye aboue her merytes', and even though his sermon only a few months previously at Henry VII's funeral service had been frank about the dead king's extortions.[143] In assessing Lady Margaret's sphere of influence above, I have tried to touch on her extended 'familia' as well as her immediate household, that is, those who were not, perhaps, on the 'checker roule', but whom she supported and influenced as an active Martha rather than a passive Mary.[144] Fisher himself identified the members of this extended family in his encomium on Lady Margaret's 'hospytalyte and charytable delynge to her neyghbours': 'her owne houshold', 'straungers', 'suters' (those approaching her for justice), 'the poore creatures', and in describing her deathbed he expatiated further on all those who had cause to weep, not just those within the household, that is, her ladies and kinswomen, her gentlewomen, her chamberers, her chaplains and priests, and 'her other true and faythfull seruauntes', but also her almsfolk 'to whome she was always pyteus and mercyfull', the students of Oxford and Cambridge 'to whome she was as a moder', the scholars of England 'to whome she was a veray patronesse', all good people, both secular ('to whome she was as a louynge syster') and religious ('whom she so often was wont to vysyte and comforte'), all good priests and clerks 'to whome she was a true defenderesse', all noble men and women 'for whom she was a myrroure and exampler of honoure', and all the common people 'for whom she was in theyr causes a comon mediatryce'.[145] Only a study of the accounts edited here may allow the individual to assess, in a very different and secular context, how far Lady Margaret may have deserved Fisher's praise.[146]

[143] Mayor, *The English Works of John Fisher*, p. 293, l. 25; Hatt, *John Fisher's Court Sermons*, p. 360, l. 109. For the sermon on Henry VII: Mayor, pp. 268–88; Hatt, pp. 309–43.

[144] This is the theme of Fisher's sermon, preached on the feast day of St Martha and structured around the verses Luke x: 38–9 in the gospel story of Martha, Mary, and the raising of their brother Lazarus.

[145] Mayor, *The English Works of John Fisher*, p. 300, l. 27 – 301, l. 17; Hatt, *John Fisher's Court Sermons*, pp. 361–2, ll. 161–286.

[146] See below (4) for an overview of each account edited here, which identifies some of the charitable acts praised by Fisher.

3 The Compilation of the Accounts

3.1 The Accountants

Charge and discharge accounting, together with an audit system, developed at the royal exchequer at the start of the twelfth century.[147] It was a seemingly simple record of the charge (income) and discharge (expense) of the exchequer: what was received, what was spent, what was owed. In the case of the charge and discharge accounts edited here each individual officer is clearly indicated as responsible for his own document.[148] The treasurer's roll begins: 'Computus Willelmi Bedell thesauraurii hospicii' (D91.16/1, 1d);[149] the chamberlain's accounts begin: 'Thaccompte of sir Roger Ormeston knyght' (D102.2/1); and the cofferer/treasurer of the chamber accounts begin, respectively: 'The accomptes of James Clarell cofferere' (D91.17/1), 'Thaccompte of Miles Worsley cofferare' (D91.20/4),[150] 'Thaccompt of Myles Worsley clerk' (D91.21/1),[151] 'Thaccounpte of Miles Worsley tresourer of the chambre' (D91.19/1),[152] and 'Computus Roberti Fremyngham <...> occupantis officium thesaurii camerarii' (D102.1/2r).[153] Only the book of receipts and payments (D102.10), which appears to be acephalous, has no formal introduction of the material and its author.

The body of the text in all these documents is written entirely or mainly in the hand of the accountant responsible for the document (and, in the case of D102.10, in the hand of Henry Hornby, Lady Margaret's secretary and dean of chapel, later chancellor). This may seem strange, since these were busy men, and clerks might be expected to do such work. However, there were clearly advantages to the officer taking full responsibility for his document, unless circumstances made it impossible. In his account of 'The Household of Queen Elizabeth Woodville 1466–7', A. R. Myers was able to demonstrate that Thomas Holbeche, clerk of the receipt and chief assistant to the treasurer

[147] For accounting in a monastic context: Alisdair Dobie, *Accounting at Durham Cathedral Priory: Management and Control of a Major Ecclesiastical Corporation*, 1083- 1539 (Houndmills: Palgrave, 2015); *The States of the Manors of Westminster Abbey c.1300–1422*, ed. Barbara Harvey and C.M. Woolgar, 2 vols, British Academy, Records of Social and Economic History, n.s. 57–8 (Oxford: Oxford University Press for the British Academy, 2019), Introduction (pp. 1–31).

[148] For the evidence for these men as their own scribes and a demonstration of the features of the different hands, named and unnamed, see below (5.4) and the Description to each edited text.

[149] The title on sheet 1d is seen when the roll is scrolled up.

[150] 'Thaccompte of Myles Worsley coferare ...', 'Thacompt of Miles Worsley clerk [of þe coffers] ...' (D91.20/71, 141).

[151] 'Thaccompte of Mylys Worsley tresourer of the chamber ...' (D91.21/83).

[152] 'Thaccompt of Miles Worsley tresaurere of the chambr ...' (D91.19/65).

[153] As well as 'account' and 'computus', the term 'indenture' is used at D91.21/161 (see the footnote to 'his new indenture').

(and receiver-general) John Forster, wrote up documents such as obligations and rolls of knights' fees and, most interestingly, compiled the actual account book.[154] However, Lady Margaret Beaufort ran a tight ship. Her officers were known to her personally, some over many years. It was pragmatic, hard-working and sensible men whom she favoured and with whom she worked closely. She was not the sort of woman to allow delegation to inferiors. Of Oldham, her chancellor until 1504, John Hooker in 1578 said that he was 'a man having more zeal than knowledge'; of Ashton, another northerner, Claire Cross has remarked on his expertise in administration and estate management, despite the absence of a formal university education.[155] Of the accounts edited here, only Hornby (whose account is written as her secretary, rather than as an accountant), was university-trained, and for that training he was indebted to Lady Margaret. Practical men were what Lady Margaret sought as her servants, and it seems in keeping with her character that the men who ran her household, who were legally responsible for their accounts to her, should be held to account even to the extent of writing them up themselves. (See below for William Bedell's presentation of his computus D91.16 to Lady Margaret in the presence of her council.)

In this regard, Carole Rawcliffe's comments on accountants and their accounts may usefully be quoted:

> By the late thirteenth century most estate and household accounts were based on the long-established principle of individual liability. In accordance with this carefully balanced system of charge and discharge each official was responsible for the arrears of previous years as well as for the immediate issues of his manor or receivership. Any legitimate expenses were then deducted from the total charge, while overdue rents, unauthorised payments and cash in hand were all technically regarded as debts to be settled at the next audit.[156]

3.2 The Format of the Accounts

The majority of the accounts edited here are accounts of the costs and expenses of the financial year,[157] most (D91.17, D91.20, D91.21, D91.19, D102.1) compiled by the cofferer (later known as the treasurer of the chamber), but one (D102.2, D102.6) by the chamberlain (for a shorter

[154] Myers, 'The Household of Queen Elizabeth Woodville', 7, 47 ('et soluta Thome Holbache clerico recepte regine scribendo istum librum', with a list of documents he wrote).

[155] Hooker cited by Nicholas Orme, 'Oldham, Hugh (*c.* 1450–1519)' (*ODNB*); Claire Cross, 'Ashton, Hugh (d. 1522)' (*ODNB*).

[156] Rawcliffe, *The Staffords*, p. 50.

[157] In these accounts the financial year normally begins on or after 13 January, at that time the feast day of St Hilary (officially the date for resuming legal business after the New Year, e.g. in the Court of Arches), but see further below (3.5).

period). The treasurer's roll (D91.16) and the book of receipts and expenses (D102.10) are different, compiled respectively by William Bedell and Henry Hornby; their format will be discussed separately below.

A close analysis of D91.21 (for the years 1505–6, 1506–7) may serve to explain the format of these documents. Each year of the account begins with the location in the margin ('Croydon', p. 1; 'Hatfeld' p. 83), followed by the formal introduction to the account, naming the accountant (Miles Worsley, 'clerk [of the coffers])' p. 1, 'tresourer of the chamber' p. 83) and the term of the account (14 January 1505–14 January 1506, p. 1; 14 January 1506-[1]4 January 1507, p. 83). First come Worsley's arrears ('arrerages', pp. 1, 83) as listed at the end of the previous year's accounts (D91.20/194, D91.21/78), followed by details of moneys received from the coffer during the year ('Furst receyved ...', p. 2; 'Recepta denariorum extra cofferas domine principisse', p. 84), followed by other receipts (pp. 4, 86–7) in the course of the year, with a grand total (pp. 5, 89).[158] Thereafter begin the main details of the accounts, the costs and expenses (pp. 7–67, 91–160, cf. 'Cost*es* and exspenc*e* w*i*th other dyv*er*se payment*es* and reward*es*' p. 7, 'Costys and exspencys with other dyverse payementes and rewardes' p. 91) paid out by Worsley in the course of the year, with a formal introduction giving the term of the account and the accountant ('paid by the handes of Myles Worsley as hereafter hit doth appere', p. 7, cf. p. 91). The total for an entry is entered to the right of each entry after a bracket, and the final total ('Summa') of a series of entries, or a page, or a financial year, is usually set apart to the right of the page.[159]

Within the main body of the text (the costs and expenses throughout the period of the account) the entries are broadly in chronological order, but (with the exception of D91.17) not noted on a daily basis. Items are sometimes introduced by a marginal heading (e.g. 'Tharrerages', p. 1) or names are given in the margin (e.g. 'Conysby' p. 92, sometimes bracketing several items, e.g. 'Robert Hylton', pp. 13–14). At times the date is given but more often not. The entries record all payments dealt with by the cofferer, some noted as paid out in accordance with a 'byll assigned' (p. 7), or 'by his byll therof made', or 'by his bylles assigned' (pp. 7, 55, 116). The random appearance of the bills (or random transcription) means that large items of money and small are recorded together, for example, the entries spanning pp. 76–7 which include a cup of gold worth over £100 for the king's New Year gift, five tin bottles at 3s. 4d., and the purchases of Diseworth and Roydon for Christ's College at £710

[158] For the second year of the accounts, there are details (p. 90) of payment made by Worsley to the coffers 'inmedyatly after þe determinacioun off his last acompt' and a part-payment of a debt.

[159] In the edited texts footnotes record right brackets, if they enclose more than one item, and the total is shown on the next line; otherwise three dots (with a single space before and after) lead to the total for an entry and are also used after the final page total ('Summa').

and £880 respectively. Many items relate to sums repaid to members of the household for dispensing rewards on Lady Margaret's behalf, e.g. 'Item paid unto maister Morgan for a reward yeven to a man', 'Item delyvered to maistres Stannop for a reward yeven to maistres Massy', and 'Money paid to maister chaunceller for a reward yeven to the kynges servand for a hawke' (p. 122). Larger sums of money are also entrusted to trusted members of the household, such as Robert Merbury (£102 to deliver to master Syclyng for Christ's College, p. 122) and Edith Fowler (66s. 8d. to buy pearls in London, p. 123). Sums are also advanced direct to Lady Margaret, such as (when she is at Hatfield) 66s. 8d. 'to Hughe Carre to delyver to my ladys grace the same day', or (when she is at Cambridge) 100s. 'by the handes of maistres Foler', or 'delyvered …to hyre almes purse' (pp. 124, 127, 128). Normally each page is signed by Lady Margaret ('Margaret R'), sometimes twice at different points in the page.[160]

At the year end there is a grand total of the sums paid from the coffer by Worsley, from which is deducted the earlier grand total of his receipts to reveal his debt to the coffer (pp. 72, 152). The breakdown of the grand total, as it relates to individuals or items or services rendered, then occurs over several pages, introduced by 'Wherof in' (pp. 71–7, 153–60), and the sum of the allowances is given (pp. 77, 161), followed by the cofferer's debt and further allowances due to him, from which his debt is calculated anew ('And so all thynges deducted & alowed he oweth…', p. 78, 'And as yet resteth dew·unto þe seid princes', p. 161). The year ends with the position with regard to debts and loans (pp. 79–80, 162–5). Thereafter are listed those debtors for whom the cofferer cannot be held liable, with a summary of their debts (pp. 79–80, 162–4), sometimes stretching over several years.[161] The sum of the debts outstanding at the end of the year is noted, and the cofferer's own debts are given: 'And resteth thys uppon the saide accomptant of his owne arrerages' (p. 80, cf. p. 165).

3.3 The Stages of Compilation of the Accounts

It is clear that the chamber accounts were written up from other sources throughout the financial year. The entries seem to have been copied in batches,[162] presumably from drafts and from bills, which are very often

[160] D102.1 (1509) is not signed by Lady Margaret but by Henry Hornby, John Fisher and Hugh Ashton.

[161] For example, D91.21/164 summarises 'all the money dew and not payd of siche as was prestyd [lent/advanced] the last yere and in ii other yeres befor past'.

[162] For example, D91.20/120 shows variation in the colour of the ink (the first two entries darker than the next three), followed by a marginal 'Summa', after which there is one more entry, another written smaller, and then the rest of the page copied all at once in a paler ink. At

mentioned (e.g. 'by a byll assigned/assygned/assyned' 20/83, 21/94, 19/92, etc.). Many entries are undated, and others are not in chronological order, perhaps because they were piled up and copied as they came to the accountant's hand, like the entries at 20/165–8, which, if dated, deal in random order with 5, 7 and 16 August, then the feast of the Assumption (15 August), then 16 August followed by the Assumption again, after which dated items are for 18 August, 23 August (followed by 22 August and then back to 23 August and even earlier to 14 August), then a return to 25 August, followed by 20 August and 10 July.

These summaries of the material (the costs and expenses) were completed largely in one hand in each document; only the accounts for which Worsley was responsible (D91.20, D91.21, D91.19) are at times in more than one hand.[163] However, the summarising material at the beginning and end of each year (part-year in the case of D91.17, D102.1 and D102.2, D102.6) was prepared after this, most plausibly at the time of the audit. To demonstrate this: the Recepta denariorum (e.g. D91.20/5–7, 73–4, 142–4), which occurs at the start of any one year, lists receipts for that whole year, which could only be recorded at the end of that year. As further evidence: an entry at the start of the 1504 financial year (D91.20/144) refers to Roger Ormeston's executors, whereas the body of the text includes entries on payments made by him (the date of the last submitted payment is 4 March 1504, D91.20/191). Ormeston's executors are also mentioned at the end of the financial year (D91.20/194). Clearly Ormeston was still alive 4 March 1504,[164] whereas the start of that financial year (14 January, D91.20/140) refers to his executors. In the case of the last account (D102.1), the opening rubric precisely dates the term of the account, a quarter year and sixty-seven days (f. 2r), whereas the costs and expenses, written by the accountant Robert Fremingham, leave the end date blank (f. 4r), because they were written earlier.

If the summaries at both the beginning and end of the year were written at the time of the audit, it may seem impossible that the body of the accounts (the costs and expenses) should have been written throughout the year. Surely a document begins at the beginning and goes through to the end? And yet, how might there be time to copy up all the items of costs and expenses at the end of the year, with the audit pending? The answer may lie in the make-up of the individual account books. It seems that these were made up in advance,

D91.19/48 the last entry before the cancelled mid-page 'Summa' is in darker ink from the entries above; after the 'Summa' the rest of the page seems to have been completed in one stint in a paler ink. At D91.19/109 a change of hand in December 1508 seems to involve catching up with accounts dating back to May.

[163] See below (5.4) and the Descriptions to the edited texts for the evidence that the main hand was always that of the accountant responsible for the document.

[164] He was dead by 6 April (see 2.1.4 above).

presumably into quires loosely stitched together. For example, the costs and expenses for D91.20 begin (p. 11) with payment to Leonard of the vestry for the book in which the accountant is writing, and other years were expected to be added, since the year ends within a quire at p. 200 with two blank quires left.[165] Space may have been left at the start of a quire for the initial summary, e.g. D91.20 (year 1502–3), where pp. 1–3 and p. 10 are blank (with the preliminary matter on pp. 4–9 and the 'Costes and exspense' starting on p. 11); or where the 1503–4 year ends at the end of a quire (p. 68) and the first two pages of the next quire (pp. 69–70) are blank;[166] or an extra quire might have been inserted later for the initial summary, which may have been the case at the start of the 1504–5 year when the initial material (pp. 141–4) is on a bifolium, i.e. a single quire of one folio sheet folded and inserted before the costs and expenses of that year.[167]

As for the summaries at the end of any one year, those could of course only be recorded at the end of the year. To take D91.20 as an example, the final summary for 1502–3 starts on the verso (p. 64) of the last costs of the year and ends the quire; that for 1503–4 carries on straight after the costs of that year and ends the quire; that for 1504–5 starts on the same page as the end of the costs for that year. There is some evidence that the full copying of the accounts had not been completed at the time of the audit, in that several entries are often added to the end of the costs and expenses, perhaps having come to light during the audit; in these cases Lady Margaret does not sign the extra entries, presumably because they were added under the auditor's direction (and sometimes by the audit team). For example, at the end of the 1506–7 financial year, she does not sign any pages after D91.21/145, i.e. 8 January 1507, whereas the entries continue in the hand of the accountant Miles Worsley through pp. 146–9 (the first entry p. 146 is also 8 January), with the final sums (pp. 146–7, 150) in the summary hand, as is the end-of-year summary (pp. 151–65). None of this material is signed by Lady Margaret, but it has all been overseen by the auditor.

The conclusion is that the rubrics and summaries at the beginning and end of each financial year in the chamberers' accounts were compiled at the same time, at the time of the audit; the hands in which they were written are referred to here by the blanket term 'the summary hand', and they may be

[165] The reason for the (medieval) binding of the chamber accounts D91.20, D91.21 and D91.19 into those divisions of years (1502–5, 1505–7, 1507–9) is not clear, and might be random; they might, on the other hand, relate to different auditors.

[166] Both the first and fourth quires have also had pages removed. Blank pages and removed pages may suggest too much space left for the initial summary. Cf. D91.17 where pp. 6–18 are blank, after the initial summary but before the 'Costes and exspences'.

[167] For details of the quiring of each document see the Description to each edited text. It has not been possible to study the watermarks of each document.

assumed to be the hands of the auditor(s) and/or clerk(s). The intervening material, the costs and expenses, may have been copied up through the year in batches and scrutinised and signed by Lady Margaret at the end of each page and each batch. Sum totals are usually provided for the page, but sometimes within the page, which may provide further evidence of a pause in the copying up of the accounts, e.g. D91.21, pp. 102 and 106, where the entries above the mid-page 'Summa' have been signed by Lady Margaret, who also signs the end-of-page 'Summa' when the page has been completed. Only the latter is approved by the auditor (and the mid-page 'Summa' is cancelled p. 102).[168] The sequence of events would appear to be the block writing-up of bills and drafts and their subsequent signing by Lady Margaret (perhaps also several pages at a time). There is no indication that the accounts were written up daily, or even weekly, and Lady Margaret is clearly signing the entries rather than the checked sum totals.[169]

3.4 Checking the Accounts

As seems to be common in accounting documents, there is less arithmetical accuracy than one might expect, although a system of dots is sometimes used as an aid in calculation, generally in a margin or at the foot of a page (e.g. 20/7; 21/105; 19/73, Plate 16, etc.).[170] The calculations of (presumably) the audit team in the summaries at the beginning and end of the year appear to be diligent and careful: there are no errors, for example, in the 'Summe' written small on D91.21, pp. 153–60, 164, at the end of the 1506–7 year.[171] Elsewhere some calculations are out by very little,[172] some by a large amount, perhaps to be expected in lengthy sums but not in short entries such as 20/55, where seven yards of cloth at 11s. 6d. a yard come to £4 0s. 6d. (not £4 0s. 2d.), or 21/17, where 4 lb. of thread costing respectively 15d., 13d., 12d. and 11d.

[168] The mid-point 'Summa' on p. 102 incorporates the 'Summa' of p. 101, whereas that on p. 106 deals only with p. 106.

[169] She signs centrally at the bottom of a set of entries, usually at the foot of the page (but sometimes mid-page, e.g. D91.21/102); 'probatur' is however written close to the 'Summa'. (In the texts edited here it has been convenient to attach ^{M} (to signify the signature 'Margaret R') to the front of the 'Summa' and ^{P} (for 'probatur') to the end.)

[170] For an explanation of this system of dot calculations: C. T. Martin, *The Record Interpreter* (London: Stevens & Sons, 2nd ed. 1910), pp. xii-xiii; for an informative discussion of its use in a monastic context: Dobie, *Accounting at Durham Cathedral Priory*, pp. 147–8.

[171] However, the individual entries still have some errors, e.g. p. 154, where five gifts of 40s., one of 20s. (altered from 40s.) and another of 26s. 8d. are at first added correctly (£12 6s. 8d.) but the 'xii' then apparently altered to 'xi'. Evidently the checker assumed that the reduction of 20s. had not already been recorded in the total. The end-of-page 'Summa' is then 20s. short.

[172] For example, in the last entry at D91.21/129, where each individual item is priced and a total of 38s. 3d. recorded, the 3d. is cancelled, despite 38s. 3d. being correct. This may indicate a practice of rounding up or down.

per lb. should reach a total of 4s. 3d. (not 3s. 3d.), and the final total of the page is wrong.[173] In another example (21/16) four attempts at calculating the final 'Summa' (two of them in the Worsley hand, and the other two both approved) are all incorrect (although the final sum is only 1s. over). Cancellations of sums, and their replacement by new calculations, are common (but not always correct),[174] although calculating errors can sometimes be explained by changes to the document.[175] For example, the addition of 8d. to one of the items at 21/13 ('Item paid to John Skynner') necessitates a change to the total, which is incorrect at the first attempt, whereas an even simpler addition at 21/142 is wrong ('Item paid to Henry Wenstanley').

All the documents bear evidence of a system of checking (both internal and external), often resulting in alterations to both individual and sum totals. Annotations, invariably in Latin, record allowances, payments, and non-payments of debts, etc., as at 20/93, 21/79, 19/21, etc. Interim checks and ad hoc calculations may be noted at the foot of a page (e.g. 20/12, 21/7) or in the margin (e.g. 21/18, 57; 19/50, Plate 15);[176] page and mid-page totals approved by the auditor are marked 'probatur' (^{P} in the edited text), sometimes with a mark of notation which perhaps identifies the individual auditor or indicates a second checker.[177] By no means all totals marked 'probatur' remain uncorrected, e.g. D91.19/44 where the total in the main hand is marked 'probatur' but cancelled and the correct total given (with no 'probatur'), or the last entry of 21/64, where the total 'xiiii li. xiiii s. viii d.' has been cancelled, together with the 'probatur' alongside, and the correct sum ('xiiii li. viii s. iiii d.') added, with a second 'probatur'.[178]

[173] Frequent checks of the calculations have been made by the editor but are only recorded when notably incorrect or of some significance. However, as an indication of the reliability of the accounts, one whole chamber account (D91.20) has been checked completely against totals marked 'probatur'; footnotes record discrepancies only. In addition, the footnotes to the edited texts provide details of any erroneous calculations of cloth in D102.2/9–32; the long Hilton entries of D91.19/102–3, 106 are all correctly calculated or corrected.

[174] For example, the correction at 20/156 of twenty-one yards of cloth at 2s. 6d. a yard from 56s. to 53s. (it should be 52s. 6d.).

[175] Cancellations are mostly of individual sums, but sometimes of entries (often with a note to explain why) and even whole pages, e.g. D102.10/24–5, 35. Entries and their totals may sometimes be cancelled after the final total of a page has been calculated, with the result that their inclusion in the final total needs re-calculating when the page is checked (see, e.g., footnotes to 20/96, 98).

[176] The fact that these notes are written small, cancelled, and neither signed nor marked 'probatur' confirms that they are checks.

[177] For example, D91.20 shows two different writings of 'probatur' and two different checking marks, broadly relating to different financial years (see below (5.3) and the footnotes to the Description of the edited text).

[178] The re-calculated sum was first written small, in a hand seemingly not that of the 'Summa', to the left at the foot of the page and was then cancelled (presumably after it had been written out fair above).

3.5 The Audit

The audit seems to have been completed by the second week in January, and the financial year begins on the octave of the Epiphany, that is, on or after 13 January, the feast day of St Hilary and the start of the Hilary term.[179] An entry in D91.16 (sheet 16, Plate 1) records its presentation to Lady Margaret - the entry is dated 22 January 1507. The auditing team consisted of auditors and clerks. As Christopher Woolgar explains, in relation to the early medieval auditing of Westminster Abbey:

> There were two groups of personnel especially associated with the accounts. Firstly, there was a cadre of professional auditors and estate administrators of some distinction, whose main interests lay in working with these documents, checking the detail of the financial position and making calculations to understand the functioning of the estate ...They were supported by a second group, clerks whose principal tasks were collating information, drafting routine documents and then copying them out fair ...[180]

The situation may be broadly comparable to Lady Margaret's accounts much later in the medieval period, in that we may assume an auditor was responsible for overall comparison of records, checking, and annotating, while his clerk(s) copied out from drafts the preliminary and final summary material (although the division between auditor and clerk is not clear in the accounts edited here). Auditors named in the documents are Thomas Hobson and master Croke, and his clerk Bartholomew. Hobson was an important professional auditor, recorded as one of Henry VII's auditors, along with Robert Watnoo, Thomas Tamworth and John Saxey, and as auditor for Oliver King, bishop of Bath and Wells (TNA SC 1/51/177). He is referred to by name in all the documents (except D102.1 and D102.2/D102.6) ,[181] whereas Croke is mentioned only in accounts for 1504 through to 1506 ('master Crokes clerkes' 20/145, 'maister Croke auditor' 20/166; 'Bertylmew maister Crokes clerk' 21/8, 'master Croke' 21/91, 'maister Crokes clerkes' 21/92).[182] It seems likely that Hobson was 'master auditor' throughout the accounts; perhaps Croke acted under him or was brought in at particularly busy times.

[179] Bedell's computus runs from 13 January; the chamber accounts D91.20, D91.21, D91.19 all cite 14 January (but D91.20/4 runs from 2 February, the Purification of the Virgin, to 14 January); D91.17 runs from 24 June, the Nativity of St John the Baptist, until 13 January; D102.1 cites 20 January as the start date.

[180] *The States of the Manors of Westminster Abbey*, ed. Harvey and Woolgar, p. 28.

[181] The references to 'maister auditour' (D91.20/7, 11; D91.19/109) must be assumed to be to Hobson, who is mentioned by name in the previous and following entries which refer to an auditor.

[182] In an earlier generation a Richard Croke had been an exchequer attorney of Henry VI's queen, Margaret.

3.6 Accountant and Auditor

The respective roles of accountant (i.e. officer responsible for the document) and auditor would appear to be clear-cut: the accountant presents his account for audit, after which the auditor is responsible for checking the details across all the relevant accounts. This is not always verifiable in the absence of some documents and uncertainty about the relative hands involved in corrections, checks, annotations and the like.[183] However, it is usually possible to ascertain that page (and mid-page) totals are normally in the accountant's hand, and corrections are often in the same hand, e.g. D91.21/57 where three mid-page 'Summe' are all in the main hand, or D91.21/108 where two 'Summe' are in that hand. As for corrections to sums, if not in the main hand, they may be in one or two other hands, e.g. D91.21/63, where only the first of three mid-page 'Summe' is in the main hand (and the final 'Summa partis' is perhaps in none of these hands), or the next page where alterations in the cost of russet cotton are all in the main hand, which has altered the total from 2s. 6d. to 3s. 6d. so messily that a different hand cancels it and writes it more clearly above.

The Latin annotations which are found throughout D91.20, D91.21 and D91.19 are mostly written with a thick nib and black ink, that is, the same thick nib and black ink as the formal summary material, which is written in the Bastard Anglicana script throughout D91.20, D91.21 and D91.19, but here writing in a fast cursive hand with much abbreviation of the Latin.[184] Although this hand (the 'sprawling' hand) is so distinctive as to be instantly recognisable, it cannot be said beyond doubt that it is responsible for all the annotations, some of which are very short indeed. However, a clear example of this hand working closely together with the accountant is found at D91.21/162, where Worsley writes a marginal note on an entry in his own hand, the content of which is confirmed by a Latin annotation in the 'sprawling' hand, which may be assumed to be an auditor's hand. Another example of their joint practice is found at D91.19/44, where the page total (£38 6s. 8d.) in the main (Worsley) hand has been cancelled and a new total (£35) added in a different hand; the Worsley total includes an entry for 66s. 8d., whereas the corrected total removes the sum of the entry and is likely to be the same hand that has cancelled that entry and noted 'postea in pede'. Such notes as 'postea (allocatur) in pede' or '(quia) (postea) in pede' are common, as well as 'quia allocatur in computo thesaurarii' (D91.20/93), 'quia in computo Jacobi Morez' (D91.21/28), 'quia solvitur' (D91.19/63), etc. Sometimes the note is more extensive, e.g. D91.20/91, where the Latin note explains just what is wrong with the first entry on the page; D91.21/29, where the Latin note

[183] Some of the evidence that exists will be discussed under the individual documents below and is noted in the footnotes to the edited texts, but for a fuller discussion of the hands see below (5).
[184] These are marked by double angle brackets in the edited texts.

explains the cancellation of the entry ('quia postea in diversis parcellis deliberatis per magistram Lynche'); D91.19/50 (Plate 15), where the accountant's debt is noted as 'oneratur in computo sequenti' and an English note directs one to 'serche in the vth lef folowyng for ferther allowaunce' (in both cases these cross-references can be checked).[185] Sometimes the note is accompanied by an annotating note or checkmark such as + (perhaps a mark by a checking clerk to alert to a need for scrutiny), as at D91.20/91 just cited.[186] Sometimes the entry is vigorously and decisively cancelled to allow no error.[187]

The 'sprawling' hand mentioned above is so called because it often works in a hurry and produces a chaotic and undisciplined text. It is found in all the documents edited here (except the earliest, D91.17), and is responsible for the annotations discussed above. Apart from the annotations, it intervenes most frequently in the summary material at the end of a year, writing up material, adding material, and again annotating material. It works closely with Henry Hornby in Lady Margaret's book of receipts and payments. (For all this see further below, and for a description of the hand see 5.2 below).

The question of who was responsible for these interventions (whose was the body attached to the 'sprawling' hand) is not proveable, although it has been assumed so far that all interventions not in the hand of the accountant responsible for the document (Bedell, Clarell, Worsley, Fremingham, Ormeston) are the result of the auditing process and so written by a member of the auditing team. The authoritative wording of 21/152 (in the 'sprawling' hand) might suggest so: 'as it appereth more playnly in a booke of parcelles therof made and appon this accompt examyned'. Even the occasional occurrence of this hand within the body of 'Costs and expenses', rather than in the summary material, occurs at audit time, e.g. at D91.20/60, entries four and five in the 'sprawling' hand occur within early January material being copied up just before the audit; they are not insignificant entries but deal with payments made to Lady Margaret's solicitor, Thomas Soper (his fee for the year and his costs for suits undertaken for Lady Margaret). Again, at D91.21/67, the first entry occurs at audit time (the second entry on the page is dated 14 January) and deals with the purchase for £740 of the manor of Diseworth to endow Christ's College. However, before we turn to the individual documents for scrutiny, it may be useful to consider whether an internal member of the counting house might have been responsible, that is, whether the 'sprawling' hand might be internal to the household rather than external.

[185] See the footnotes to D91.19/50. Where cross-references can be checked within the same document or against other documents, the result is footnoted in the edited texts.

[186] Only ^{3} is reproduced (in the edited text for D91.16), but other symbols are normally noted in the Description and/or footnotes to each edited text.

[187] See, e.g., the footnotes to D91.19/93–5, 98, 101. See the penultimate entry D102.10/35 for a sum not just crossed through but also pricked.

In an illuminating and influential note of some fifty years ago, James R. Hooker problematised then current opinions on the bureaucratisation of Henry VII's administration.[188] While the king's systems cannot entirely have been replicated by Lady Margaret, whose household was smaller, and who had had many more years in which to develop her own systems than her son had had, it is worth considering some of Hooker's comments here. His focus is on the three main officers involved in the administration of the household: the treasurer (who had charge of comestibles and stock), the controller (who was charged with particular areas of the treasurer's remit, such as spices), and the cofferer (who received and paid out money as the treasurer dictated and submitted accounts annually to the controller for audit). The treasurer is relevant to the accounts of Lady Margaret edited here, since we possess his computus for one year, 1506. The cofferer is also relevant, since we have his accounts for several years. However, in Henry's household the treasurer handled no money; instead it was handled by the cofferer, who was responsible to the controller, so that the three together were responsible for managing the expenses of the household. The accounts of Lady Margaret's cofferer, however, do not record the daily expenses for table and stables (which may be assumed to be lost): instead all payments from the coffer, small and great, including regular payments (of fees, exhibitions, etc.) are recorded, but not regular household expenses.[189]

In Henry's household the cofferer and controller kept their own separate books of the daily expenses, so that the cofferer's final account for the year could be checked against the controller's. (In the first years of Henry's reign, a third check was provided by the treasurer's final account.) This provides a context for the checking and annotation of the cofferer's accounts mentioned above and suggests that there was a separate book against which the cofferer's accounts could be checked. To some extent this is the case, as will be shown below, when discussion moves to the individual documents edited here, but the checking is not (or not only) done against a book kept by the controller, but against a book kept by Lady Margaret (D102.10, written largely by her secretary, Henry Hornby), and against the computus of James Morice, and probably against another or other lost books (see further below).[190] That the

[188] R. Hooker, 'Some Cautionary Notes on Henry VII's Household and Chamber "System"', *Speculum* 33 (1958), 69–75; discussed in Steven Gunn, *Henry VII's New Men and the Making of Tudor England* (Oxford: Oxford University Press, 2016), pp. 67–70.

[189] The treasurer's account D91.16/14–15 records the cost of the horses throughout the year, and the total costs of livery, diet expenses and wages for the servants. The earliest chamber account, D91.17/46–7, records the wages and servant/horse payments for the riding household of 1498, as discussed above (2.2).

[190] The pivotal role of Lady Margaret in managing her money may perhaps be compared with that of her son. In a discussion of the extension of chamber finance in his household, Margaret

controller had a role in the counting house seems indisputable, and there are occasional references to that role, such as a record of £66 15s. delivered by master controller and master auditor 20 September 1502 (D91.20/7). But it seems impossible that the controller could have been the 'sprawling' hand, since the role appears not to have been invested in any one single person over the years of the 'sprawling' hand's interventions (that is, all the documents from 1501 on).[191]

One thing that Hooker notes is the problem of making definitive statements about Henry VII's administrative systems 'so long as the men who supposedly performed these offices remain nebulous figures' (p. 70), a statement which becomes more pertinent when he later questions whether named holders of offices held such offices in any permanent sense, or even performed the duties of those offices themselves.[192] This has some relevance to Lady Margaret's officers, in that (as Hooker shows for Henry VII) there is overlap and uncertainty in relation to some named officers. If the office of controller was important in the king's household, its importance in Lady Margaret's cannot be ascertained, since no documents survive which are specifically attached to that post, and the office seems to have been sporadic. It is a post which William Bedell held in 1499, which William Merbury is known to have held in 1502, which John Fothede held in 1505 and 1506, and which Ashton held in 1509, but the continuity or otherwise of these post-holders is not known.[193] Given that the office of controller is, however, omitted from the mourning wear recipients at Henry VII's funeral,[194] and is left blank in the legacies of Lady Margaret's will,[195] it may be the case that the position was not a single and specific one in Lady Margaret's household but perhaps adopted by an officer as and when necessary. For example, Bedell must have been treasurer as well as controller in 1499, Ashton remained receiver general

---

Condon notes: 'The concentration of cash and administration in the King's own hands removed a whole dimension from the political scene. It gave the king financial, and, in consequence, political independence.': M. M. Condon, 'Ruling Elites in the Reign of Henry VII', in *Patronage, Pedigree and Power in Late Medieval England*, ed. Charles Ross (Gloucester: Alan Sutton; Totowa NJ: Rowman and Littlefield, 1979), pp. 109–42 at 127.

[191] The earliest examples are at D102.10/18; D102.6/2.

[192] Margaret Condon says, of Henry VII's reign, that whereas 'the cofferership grew immeasurably in stature', 'major household offices ...were left vacant for long periods at a time': Condon, 'Ruling Elites in the Reign of Henry VII', p. 127.

[193] See the PEOPLE index sub Bedell, Merbury, Fothede, Ashton, and (for references to 'master controller' which give no name) sub CONTROLLERS.

[194] *Letters and Papers,* ed. Brewer, I: 11, based on TNA LC 2/1, f. 122r.

[195] Although 'oure Comptroller' is left blank among the legacies of her will (in the probate copy SJCA D4.7, now SJLM/3/1/5), Ashton is named as 'Comptrollour of our householde' in the list of her executors, cf. *Collegium Divi Johannis Evangelistae*, p. 123 (136) with p. 109 (40). For the different versions of Lady Margaret's will at St John's College, Cambridge: Jones and Underwood, *The King's Mother*, Appendix 4 (pp. 288–90).

as well as adopting (it seems) the office of controller in 1509, and it may be that Lady Margaret's steward, Sir William Knyvett, served as controller to some extent, but again no account related to him is extant and he is rarely mentioned by name or role in the documents edited here.

No name is given in the accounts of anyone who might be thought to fulfil the crucial senior role of the 'sprawling' hand. The hand is not that of a clerk, unless a senior and experienced clerk, since it intervenes so freely, and in such an undisciplined way, scribbling, correcting and annotating. The summary material, particularly at the end of a financial year, is highly important, in that the book must be balanced, and it is mostly at the end of a year that the 'sprawling' hand may assert itself beyond the confines of the formulaic account. Cursive material within the rubrics is sometimes chaotically inserted, e.g. D91.20/194 (last entries on extension); calculations may be corrected, e.g. D91.19/63; memoranda may be added, e.g. D91.20/194 (back of extension); extra entries may be added, e.g. D91.21/90.

The hand is not that of the chamberlain, Roger Ormeston, not only because he died in 1504, but because his hand is documented in his extant account, D102.2 and D102/6 (discussed below), nor could it (on the basis of both likelihood and his signature in the Foundation Charter of St John's College, D4.17, now SJGR/1/1) be that of his successor, Sir John St John II, who anyway seems not to have played a very active part in the accounts. After Ormeston's death references to the vice-chamberlain, Richard Lynne, proliferate, whereas St John is not called chamberlain by name at any point in the edited accounts ('master chamberlain' is used, but without specification).[196] A possible candidate, and one who must have been very familiar with the accounts and was certainly there at the time of the audit,[197] is the receiver general, Hugh Ashton, but the only extended document in his hand (D56.12, SJLM/7/1/1) does not bear this out, nor the evidence of the same (Ashton) hand in the post-mortem pages of D102.10 (see Plate 7 and footnotes to pp. 126–8, 131–3).[198] The decisive argument in favour of a member of the auditing team is perhaps that the hand is most prominent in the audit summaries, although one has to admit that, however talented an auditor he was (and he was very talented), his scribbles and scrawls and crossings out and abbreviated and truncated Latin annotations do not superficially inspire confidence.[199]

[196] He is named as chamberlain in Lady Margaret's will.

[197] Two of the payments to the auditing team are made by the receiver: 10s. to Bartholomew, Mr Croke's clerk, 'at the audet tyme' (D91.21/8) and to Hobson's clerks (19/69).

[198] This is confirmed also by comments in the 'sprawling' hand which would be impossible if the hand were Ashton's, for example: 'Item the vi[th] daie of February paied for a dever for my ladyis grace councell as the receyvour knowith' (D91.20/191).

[199] The hand is not that of Thomas Hobson, the main auditor, since at least two memoranda

4 The Edited Accounts

The previous section has served as a preliminary to the following discussion of the individual documents, which survive largely as codices, with one roll (D91.16).[200]

4.1 Computus provisionis (roll) of the treasurer of the household, William Bedell (D91.16, now SJLM/1/1/1/1)

Only this single Latin *computus provisionis* survives, that of the treasurer, William Bedell, for the year 13 January 1506 - 13 January 1507, when Lady Margaret's household was first at Croydon, the palace of the archbishop of Canterbury, and then at Hatfield, the palace of the bishop of Ely (her step-son, James Stanley).[201] The treasurer was normally responsible for preparing a composite statement of expenditure in the four main household offices, kitchen, pantry, cellar, and chamber, as well as outside the household; Bedell presented the computus to Lady Margaret at Hatfield 22 January 1507, where she announced in the presence of her council that he should be awarded a fee of £10 for his labour (sheet 16, Plate 1).

Compiled just a few years before Lady Margaret's death, D91.16 shows the economy of the household at the height of her power, when it was one of the grandest in the kingdom after that of her son himself.[202] In the form of a Chancery-fashion roll, it provides a general account of the provisioning for the complete household in the year 1506–7: cash receipts and expenses are detailed and balanced on the front, with the cash value of the stuff remaining in the different offices of the household, while the dorse holds a stock account (*de stauro*) which accounts for the commodities by volume, i.e. the amount used and the amount left.

The front begins with details from the previous computus (for 1505–6, now lost): arrears owed (£173 9s. 6½d.) and value of unused stuff (£418 1s. 9¼d.). Money received from Lady Margaret's coffer at various times during

---

written in the 'sprawling' hand (D91.20/194 (Appendix to the edited text); D102.10/23) refer to Hobson, but it might be the hand of one of his clerks, or the other auditor, Croke, or his clerk Bartholomew.

[200] A full Description is provided at the start of each edited document. For personnel see above (2.1); for the hands at work in the documents see below (5).

[201] The account of Miles Worsley dated 14 January 1505 was written at Croydon, and that dated 13 January 1506 at Hatfield (D91.21/1, 83).

[202] A total of £1,542 was spent on the upkeep of the household during that year: Jones and Underwood, *The King's Mother*, p. 159.

the year amounts to £2,008 12s. 7½d.[203] These amounts are calculated: £2,600 3s. 11¼ d. Receipts are then listed with marginal sub-headings: stuff sold outside the household (total £11 6s. 5d.); rents received from pastures and meadows reserved for household use (£35 3s. 5d.); gifts in kind from several persons (£23 12s. 6½d.). Thereafter sales are noted: woollen cloth sold outside the wardrobe; hides, skins, suet, wool, intestines, wheat, bread, candles (but nothing received from the last four for reasons which are stated). Receipts from outside the household are Cecily Welles's board and lodging and the rent of pasture land.[204] Then the whole amount of receipts with the previous arrears is totalled (sheet 7): £2,779 11s. 0¼d., followed by the allowances for stuff left over and gifts in kind, which together total £237 10s 11¼d. With these two sums left hanging, and both verified ('probatur'), the account moves on to the expenses: the purchase of corn, ale and beer, wine, cattle, sheep; the costs of pasture land for grazing; the purchase of livestock, salted fish, spices, rushes, salt, oil, candles and wax; the costs of rewards, firewood, payments outside the household, 'necessary payments' (a catch-all), items bought for the chapel children and for the kitchen boys, horse livery, servants' diet (£13 10s. 3½d.), livery cloth (£134 1s. 7d.), fresh birds and fish (£288 11s. 2½d.), servants' wages (£278 19s. 4d.). The summary (sheet 16, Plate 1) is followed (sheet 17) by named individuals and their debts (some noted as (un)paid), leading to a computation (sheet 21) which absolves Bedell of any due debt. A heading (sheet 22) introducing the cash value of stock remaining 13 January 1507 leads through the granary, bakehouse, pastry house, pantry, buttery, cellar, and then deals with cattle, sheep, poultry, the wet and dry larders, the chandlery, fuel, hay, oats, the scullery and spicery, and closes (sheet 26) with the total value of stuff remaining in the household (£233 6s. 1½d.).

The dorse lists the stock left over from the previous year's computus by volume and the amount used in the current year of cereal, beverages, livestock, fish, salt, oil, honey, candles, dried, crystallised and preserved fruit, spices, nuts, sweetmeats, oils, paper, soap, pulse, hay, wood and wool, all sub-divided into categories. To explain the first item (sheets 1d–2d), wheat (Frumentum): the amount left over from the previous year (1505) and the amount provided for the household during the current year (1506), with extra amounts relating to the heaped measures of grain ('lez hepes'), are added together. Next, the amount delivered to the Croydon and Hatfield millers, the amount used for the poultry, and the amount sold on the open market are

[203] The latter was recorded (sheets 2, 16) in an indentured bill, half kept by Lady Margaret, half by Bedell. For an example of a computus that has been cut indenture-style (i.e. in an indented line) see 21/1 (Plate 13).

[204] For Cecily Welles see further below and 2.2 above. For her sojourn with her husband at Hatfield see D102.10/143; for her burial there August 1507 see D91.19/30, 35.

calculated, together with three bushels sold to John Fish (this is also written small in the left margin below the subheading, Frumentum). Simple division renders the amount of flour now remaining. Three individuals and the Hatfield granary are noted ('unde in manu') as holding certain amounts of flour, which happily confirms the amount remaining.

The next item, wheatmeal (Farina frumenti), proceeds in the same way (sheets 2d–3d): so much was left over from the previous computus; so much was received from the millers for use, for example, in the pastry-house; two bushels were missing in the previous computus; and so the sum of wheatmeal is calculated. The amounts used in the pastry house during the year for various forms of bread and rolls are then calculated. There was no allocation for waste nor was anything sold outside the household, but three bushels were delivered to Lady Margaret in Cambridge in August 1506 (sheet 2d).[205] There should now be two quarters and five bushels remaining, but ('unde super') Walter Cox, valet of the pastry house, owes two bushels which he has been forgiven (the auditor holds a bill signed by Lady Margaret to confirm this). Therefore two quarters and three bushels are left. And so it continues.

The system is the same throughout; let us take as a final example the last item (sheet 31d), woollen cloth (Pannum laneum): 30¾ verges were noted as left over in the 1505 computus; 640½ verges were received for livery for the household in 1506 plus an extra 10½ (the result of inconsistencies in the measuring process), making the amount received during the year 681¾ verges. As for the amount used, James Morice, clerk of the counting house, has a 'quire of names' which contains details of members of the household who received cloth for livery to the amount of 612⅝ verges;[206] Lady Margaret herself has signed a bill (noted at the end of the previous computus) agreeing the delivery to various persons of 26⅛ verges; 25¼ verges have been sold to various servants for 104s. 8d. In all 664 verges are accounted for. Deduction of the amount distributed and sold from the original amount held for the year results in 17¾ verges remaining.

James Morice's 'quire of names' ('ut patet in quodam quaterno de nominibus per Jacobum Morres clericum countrie hospicii predicti', sheet 31d) may serve to introduce a note on how evidence for the various amounts owed or paid was submitted. James Morice had a book with the names of those who had·been given cloth for their liveries (and presumably of how much cloth), and the cloth was delivered to various persons by a bill with

[205] Lady Margaret travelled from Hatfield to Cambridge in August (sheet 13), and several deliveries of different foodstuffs were made to her there (sheets 2d, 3d, 7d, 9d, 13d). See too D91.21/123–136 passim.

[206] The royal households were unusual in providing livery as cloth, rather than as ready-made garments.

Lady Margaret's sign manual.[207] Other bills are mentioned: an indentured bill,[208] a bill signed with Lady Margaret's sign manual which remained with the auditor,[209] and various signed bills.[210] Tallies are a common means of contract for payment with workmen such as the millers of Croydon and the officers of the pastry and poultry houses,[211] or between the baker and the officer of the pantry (sheet 3d), and the butcher and the officer of the larder (sheet 7d), and so on.

The single hand in which the roll is written moves freely between a formal script for marginal and in-text rubrics, e.g. 'Summa allocacionis', 'Et debet', 'Postea oneratur de', 'Et debet dicta summa conjuncta', etc. (sheet 16, Plate 1), and a small, low, slanting cursive hand for the body of the text. It is clear that the material was copied up fair from an earlier draft or drafts onto a prepared template. Entries are carefully positioned on the page, e.g. the entries begin halfway down sheets 3 and 22; there is a large gap between the first and second entries on sheet 4; the material on the short sheet 7 is positioned in the centre of the sheet. The two entries on sheet 15 are positioned in the middle of the otherwise blank sheet so that the elaborate 'Summa' and its rubrics can occupy all sheet 16 (Plate 1). The effect of the template is more marked on the dorse, the commodity listed in the margin and brackets enclosing a space which was perhaps determined by the previous year's computus.[212] Either there is too much space (e.g. 1d, 6d, 29d–31d), often because there is little or nothing to report, e.g. sheet 9d (Plate 3), where entries for 'Carcasia bovettorum' and 'Carcasia vaccarum' have been drawn up and bracketed for 6 cm. but have only a scribbled 'nichil'. Less commonly, there is too little space, and some entries needed extra space to note the further distribution of the commodity under consideration. (Indentation of 'Super' and its dependents constricts the space further, e.g. sheets 13d, 17d.) Amongst other examples, 'Confeccions' (26d) is squeezed into a very small space, and the templated 'Summa' of the first entry ('Suger valans') at 21d (Plate 4) has been cancelled because the accountant has had to write over and around it in order to continue his notes on further expenditure of the sugar. Perhaps perforce, the completion of the dorse seems to have been a hurried and even cursory job

[207] 'Et deliberantur diversis personis per mandatum domine per billam de nominibus signo manuali sub signo de panno remanenti in fine ultimi computi' (sheet 31d).

[208] 'ut patet per billam indentatam inter predictam principissam et ipsum computantem confectam' (D91.16/2).

[209] 'ut patet per billam signo manuali <s> signatam penes auditorem remanentem' (sheet 3d).

[210] 'ut patent diverse bille signate' (sheet 20d). Signed bills are the invariable form of submitting an expenses claim (sheets 21d, 23d, 24d, 25d, etc.). (For an extant signed bill see D102.10/182.)

[211] 'ut patet per xii tallias super hunc computum ostensas convinctas probatas et dampnatas etc.' (sheet 2d).

[212] 'Porci' is templated on both sheets 11d and 12d.

(this becomes apparent from sheet 5d), and there are frequent errors and corrections to both text and calculations, seemingly in the same hand (and perhaps with the intention of balancing the accounts as much as anything else). Sheet 19d ('Weke') provides a good example of this: 'Et remanent' is written formally in thick black ink, as is the number 'lxxix', but the annotations relating to this number have been filled in much more hurriedly in a fast hand (with corrections in the same hand). The lack of care (or time), or faults in the drafts, thus appear to extend to the calculations, e.g. 'Saunders' (sheet 22d), when the accountant mistakenly repeats the amount remaining from the last computus (4½ lb.) as the amount provided during the time of the present computus; at some point this has been cancelled (in the same hand) and replaced by a new sum (10½ lb.) which is also the total (i.e. even if correct, it ignores the amount remaining from the last computus). Even minor corrections can be wrong, e.g. sheet 23 ('Pultre'), where the omitted number of pheasants is added but either the total (20d.) or the number is wrong ('In \ ii/ fesanis de exenniis precio pecie ii d.'), or sheet 19d, where the amount of wick left is correctly noted as 79 but then corrected to 67 ('lx<xix>\vii/ lib.').

The main language of the roll is Latin, but many of the terms (particularly towards the end of the front and on the dorse) are English or French (naturalised by this date but still sometimes used with 'le(z)'). It is sometimes difficult to assess whether a word is Latin or English/French, especially since Latin inflections are anyway contracted. For example, in the phrase 'In xxxiiii lib. di. amigdale' (sheet 26), *amigdale* may be French or Latin or even English (*OED* **amygdal** *n.*). Again (sheet 24), *tortis* has been taken to be Latin in the phrase 'pro tortis' (cf. *DMLBS* **torta** 4), although its use with English adjectives ('In tortis hole & broken') might suggest it was thought of as an English word (*OED* **tortis** *n.* 1).[213] On the dorse (sheet 17d), 'de viii tortis fractis ponderantibus lxi lib.' is a wholly Latin phrase, but at 16d this type of candle is described with others in a fully macaronic phrase, 'in tortis ceriis sices prikettes & ab luminibus factis'. As here, languages are often used side-by-side, e.g. sheet 25 (Plate 2), where 'confectio' (Lat.) and 'confettes' (English, of French origin) appear (from the contractions used) to occur within three entries ('In iiii lib. di. i qr. ...ii d. ob'). It seems likely that the clerks responsible for the provision of the household thought in English but wrote with stylised Latin formulae and standard French terms. English becomes much more common as the roll proceeds; at sheet 21 the subheading (up to this point always in Latin) is written in English ('Dyverse servauntes of house') and then cancelled and re-written in Latin, but the marginal subheadings that follow on the front of the roll are almost all in English.

[213] It is also French (OF **tortis**). Cf. too 'pro staff torches' (sheet 24).

4.2 The book of receipts and payments, kept principally by the secretary/dean of chapel, later chancellor, Henry Hornby (D102.10, now SJLM/1/1/6/1)

This book (ninety-one folios, 240 x 170 mm., written mostly in English) records sums of money received by the treasury as due payments to a receiving house, or delivered out of the treasury, normally to the treasurer, William Bedell, or the cofferer/treasurer of the chamber, Miles Worsley (in 1509 Robert Fremingham), for running the household, e.g. 'for my ladys almes' p. 46, 'for the houshold' p. 47.[214] It begins at the start of Lady Margaret's establishment at Collyweston and runs from 1 January 1499 beyond her death (29 June 1509) until 3 October of that year (the last entries written on formerly blank pages). Up to the end of the 1501 financial year sums are received into the treasury from Nicholas Compton as receiver general, after which Hugh Ashton replaces him;[215] sums of money are also received from Hugh Oldham, both as receiver of Lady Margaret's west country estates (e.g. pp. 4, 23) and as chancellor: the last reference to him by name as 'master chancellor' is for 5 August 1504 (p. 32). By the end of the year he had been elevated to the see of Exeter (where he had served as archdeacon for many years), and Hornby had perhaps taken over his role.[216] Others responsible for delivering sums of money to the treasury include the chamberlain (e.g. pp. 28, 32, 33, etc.), who was at first Roger Ormeston and then Sir John St John II, and the vice-chamberlain, Richard Lynne (pp. 144, 178), as well, of course, as stewards, bailiffs, feodaries and others.

D102.10 is Lady Margaret's own book;[217] payments delivered to Lady Margaret by Worsley can be traced in D102.10, e.g. D91.19/50 'delyvered unto þe pryncez as yt may appere in hur boke of receytes ...l li.', and again, more specifically, 'delyvered unto the coffers of the seid prynces of suche money as he receyved of my lord of London as yt appereth in the boke of receytes of the seid prynces ...l i.' (p. 60), are recorded at D102.10/131. Another example: a note in one of the chamber account books about a bag of money which was short of the full amount ('as yt appereth in my ladys boke of receytes and paymentes of þis yere in þe tytle of Mony delyvered unto þe tresourer of household ... <xxx> <xxiiii li. ii s. iiii d.> xxiiii li. ii s. iiii

[214] Fremingham both delivers and receives money during his occupancy of the role of treasurer of the chamber (in place of Worsley) in 1509.

[215] Compton is last mentioned (always by full name, never as receiver (general)) at p. 40 (16 January 1502).

[216] Jones and Underwood, *The King's Mother*, p. 278 (but Hornby is not so named until 1509 in these accounts).

[217] There are occasional first-person references: 'myn almes mony' (where the marginal rubric reads, 'Remayninge in my ladys handes'), 'my landes', 'my chauntre' (pp. 10, 23, 148), and (if these might be thought to involve faulty omission of 'ladys') the cancellation of 'your' and replacement by 'my' in 'my cofers' (p. 11).

d.', D91.19/3) duly appears in D102.10 under 'Money delyvered unto Myles Worsley tresowrer of chambre from the viii day of January anno xxiii[cio] H. vii[mi] unto [*blank*]': 'Fyrst delyvered unto the seid Miles the day of January anno xxiii[cio] as money due by hym uppon the determinacione of his accompte ended the viii[th] day of January anno predicto with xxiiii li. ii s. iiii d. wantyng oute of a bag ...' (p. 159).[218]

Such notes often refer one to allocations in the computi of individual years (e.g. pp. 4, 5, 15, etc.), and to the computus for each year kept by the receiver (e.g. p. 16), and so several references can be traced to the chamber accounts. For example, the sums of money recorded as delivered into the coffers during 1502 (D102.10/55–8) are replicated in Miles Worsley's computus as sums received by him in the course of the year (D91.20/5–8). D102.10/33 notes that Miles Worsley's computus records a receipt from the chancellor (at this date Hugh Oldham) of 60s. 'for certen prentytt bokes bought for my ladys grace'; the relevant computus at this date is the chamber account D91.20, which records (p. 129) the payment of the 60s. to Oldham. Similarly, on 7 February 1502 Worsley was given £18 11s. 4½d. in relation to the arrears of his last account (D102.10/26); this sum is recorded as received by Worsley in his chamber account: 'In primis of my debt of my last accountes' (D91.20/5). Worsley's arrears can be checked through several accounts, e.g. the sum of £86 3s. 7¾d. delivered to the coffers 13 January 1507 leaves Worsley with £44 9s. 8¾d., which is (as the entry says) 'charged in his new indenture for thys next yere' (D102.10/113, Plate 6), and the entry is duly recorded with the remaining debt in Worsley's accounts D91.21/152 and D91.19/1–2. And, elsewhere, a clear parallel can be traced between all the 'mony delyvered unto Myles Worsley' (D102.10/123–5) and 'Recepta denariorum extra cofferas domine principisse' (D91.21/84–5). A final example: the undated details of sums of money received by Worsley (D102.10/103–04) can be traced to either Worsley's account for 1505 (D91.21/4, 58, 77) or the list of loans/advances at the end of 1504 (D91.20/194).[219] The total of the receipts on p. 104 of D102.10 (£28 1s. 0¾d.) is noted in the 'Summa partis' at the end of the page and annotated as subsumed within the sum of £368 12s. 9½d. in Worsley's computus ('quod oneratur in computo dicti Milonis infra summam CCClxviii li. xii s. ix d. ob.'); in D91.20/194 that sum appears: 'And so there ys awyng ... CCClxviii li. xii s. ix d. ob.' The annotation to that statement ('ergo oneratur in computo sequenti') then refers one to D91.21/1 , where the sum is recorded as Worsley's arrears at the end of 1505.[220]

[218] The bag is charged in Worsley's debts for 1507 (D91.19/63).

[219] See footnotes to pp. 103–4.

[220] The entry is damaged but is clear enough for one to be sure of this.

This careful practice of recording, checking, annotating, and cross-referencing is only traceable in the chamber accounts, since only D91.16 of the treasurer's accounts, D102.2 and D102.6 of the chamberlain's accounts, and no others, have survived. Were more accounts extant, doubtless an examination of D102.10 with the various computi of various officials would provide all the parallels to demonstrate the tight system used in Lady Margaret's household and recorded assiduously (if not always neatly) in this, her own household book. As implied, D102.10 is a workaday book, intended as a record rather than a public document. The rubrics are not in a formal hand (except for p. 149), nor is the material signed at any point (in comparison with the chamber accounts) or calculations approved. Rubrics in English or Latin introduce either receipts (by Bedell or Worsley) or payments from (usually) 13 January throughout the specified year. Several rubrics are incomplete, e.g. 'Receytes of mony at divers tymes from the xx day of Aprill the xvith yere of our soveran lord kyng Herry the viith unto the [*sic*]', p. 21).[221] Extra entries are often added at the end of the year, followed by a summary of receipts/payments of the year, often followed by blank pages. For example, the sums delivered to Bedell from 21 November 1500 (p. 38) end incomplete p. 40 and are followed by two blank pages. After Lady Margaret's death 29 June 1509 blank pages 126–9 (see Plate 7) and 131–3 were filled with post-mortem receipts in the hands of three executors, Fisher, Hornby and Ashton, the same executors who had signed each page of her final chamber account, D102.1 (see Plate 17). Paper slips (some still in situ, e.g. pp. 1, 182) were sewn in to secure bills and similar relevant material.

The sums of money were normally paid out from the treasury and received into it by the treasurer, William Bedell,[222] who kept his own account, referred to at the end of the year 1506/7: 'the whiche somme ys charged in þe tresourerys acompt' D102.10/114. By luck, the treasurer's computus for this same year survives, the only one to do so, and the sum is found there (D91.16/3). On a few occasions money was handed over by the cofferer himself, Miles Worsley, or by the controller of the household (pp. 101–03), or by the chancellor and the controller (p. 108). The fact that this is recorded suggests that it was unusual (cf. 'delyvered ...in the absence of the tresorere by the <absence> handes of Miles', p. 12) and that the treasurer was normally solely responsible for delivering money from the treasury. In this, Lady Margaret's system may differ from that of her son, for whom, as noted above, the treasurer and the controller were responsible for signing off sums to the cofferer.

[221] At p. 26, but more frequently from p.46, the English rubrics are shortened to a mere 'Anno' note.

[222] His clerk appears to have been a relative, John Bedell, whose name occurs frequently.

The book was largely compiled for Lady Margaret by her secretary and dean of chapel, Henry Hornby. The 'sprawling' hand encountered in most other documents (and assumed to be a member of the auditing team) appears to be responsible for many of the rubrics and some entries (which become more frequent as the years advance); these entries often occur at the end of a section (p. 67, Plate 5), sometimes followed by blank pages, as noted above, after which the rubric/memorandum and first entry or two of the new section are also in the 'sprawling' hand.[223] For example, the 'sprawling' hand finishes p. 78 (written in the Hornby hand) by adding a further entry, (probably) cancelling a previous entry, and calculating the 'Summa partis' and complex 'Summa totalis'. In another example, Hornby's stint (which began p. 111) ends after three entries on p. 113 (Plate 6), when the 'sprawling' hand takes over for p. 114; pp. 115–16 are blank, the 'sprawling' hand supplies the rubric for p. 117, after which Hornby returns. In the final pages of the book (pp. 176–82), where receipts over the years from lands held in wardship by Lady Margaret are recorded, Hornby (pp. 176–8, 181–2) and the 'sprawling' hand (pp. 179–80) work in tandem.

An occasional addition in the 'sprawling' hand modifies or elaborates the original entry, e.g. the first entry on p. 102, where 'over ...Cambrigge' and the corrected sum are in this second hand.[224] The hand often notes what has happened to the moneys in many entries, e.g. 'allocatur' (p. 113, Plate 6), 'oneratur', and fuller notes, e.g. 'allocatur in computo recepte de anno xv', 'allocatur in computo de anno xvi^{o}', 'allocatur in computo precedenti' (p. 16), sometimes marking them by checkmarks (see Description to the edited text). It is the 'sprawling' hand which is responsible for the lengthy rubrics, macaronic in language, and often with the end date incomplete: 'Receytes off mony to my ladys coffers from the xvth daye off Januare anno xx^{mo} regis Henrici vii^{mi} unto the [*sic*]', 'Memorandum off mony delyvered unto the tresoure off household from þe xiiith daye off Januere anno xx^{mo} regis Henrici vii^{mi} unto the [*sic*]', 'Item delyvered to þe seid Milez þe [*blank*] daye off [*blank*] anno [*blank*] by þe handes off master controller for landes purchesed off sir Herry Erbet knyght ...DCCxl li. «oneratur»' (pp. 85, 91, 102).

In the course of the document, we glean something of other accounting documents and practices. A large sum of £162 3s. for tin, sold by the chancellor (at this date Hugh Oldham) and received into the treasury from him, was given 'ad manus proprias domine' (p. 29), straight into Lady Margaret's own hands. Expenses for the upkeep of the household when Lady Margaret was in London in April 1505 are for £205 16s. 4d. 'as appereth by billettes in the

[223] See, for example, footnotes to the edited text, pp. 86–104.

[224] The Hornby hand provides notes in the left margin (e.g. 'quia rediit \ideo/ cancellatur', p. 123), not (like the 'sprawling' hand) in the right hand margin above or below the 'Summa'.

bagges' (p. 182). Bags of money and other receptacles feature prominently in the post-mortem notes on the formerly blank or near-empty pages in the book. On 2 July 1509, just three days after Lady Margaret's death, £1,240 7s. 5½d. was found 'in my ladys litill standerd' (p. 133) and used for various payments, such as her funeral expenses (£55 9s.) and alms to the bedridden in thirty London parishes (£33 6s. 8d.). 'A litill bagge of lynen cloth' full of coins was taken from the coffer and given to Ashton, along with other specified types of coin (p. 133). Money was also found in coffers kept by Edith Fowler and was put into 'oon bagge sealed with <se> the seale of sir John Seynt John', and a blue pincase contained £46 13s. 8d. (p. 126, Plate 7). Sums of money received from John Fotehede (master of Michaelhouse and former controller of the household) on 12 July 1509 were received and paid out (p. 132) by the executors (here Fisher, St John and Hornby), and what was left (in one bag of £333 6s. 8d. and another of £80) was 'put in the cofer with jewellis' on 3 October, 1509, together with two other bags of money (pp. 126, 132). The total sum of receipts into the coffers from money retrieved, or received from officers of the household and others, or obtained by small sales (such as two silver-gilt pots decorated with portcullises, sold to the dean of Lincoln for £30 5s. 8d., or a chest sold to mistress Massey for 10s., p. 127) was calculated at £3,926 13s. 10d. (p. 131).

4.3 The chamber accounts (D91.17, D91.20, D91.21, D91.19, D102.1)

4.3.1 The chamber accounts of James Clarell (D91.17)

D91.17 may be considered separately from the following three chamber accounts (D102.1 will also be considered separately at the end of this section). It is the first (certainly, first extant) book to deal with Lady Margaret's Collyweston household,[225] and runs only from 24 June 1498 until 12 January 1499. It therefore differs from the next three account books in covering not much more than six months, rather than a year at a time.[226] This is because it begins 24 June (the Nativity of St John the Baptist) with Lady Margaret's arrival in London at the start of a four-month period during which she and her son went on progress through East Anglia, travelled together to Collyweston, and then spent six weeks at Woodstock.

Initial and final material is written in a summary hand using formal script, whereas the main body of accounts is in one hand, seemingly that of Clarell himself. The structure is the same as the later chamber accounts, although the

[225] References to Clarell's 'last accompte' (1) and 'my laste boke' (27) provide evidence of this volume as the continuation of previous account(s).

[226] D102.1 also covers a short period, since Lady Margaret died less than half-way through the year.

costs and expenses are laid out differently, as will be seen. D91.17 begins with the debt of James Clarell carried forward from the previous (lost) account, together with the receipts during the period of the account (pp. 1–5, followed by 6–18 blank). It is then itemised by the day (unlike the later account books), with the place and date given in the margin (but no date after p. 26), and the day of the week centred in the body of the text (not replicated in the edited text). The sum total is given at the end of each week as the last item on a page. After the usual preliminaries of arrears and settlements, the volume begins 24 June 1498 at Westminster and details payments made there until 28 July (pp. 19–28).[227] Thereafter, starting at the Tower of London (29 July), the major part of the volume provides daily details of the expenses ('Item payd', rarely 'Item delyverid') of the riding household in an itinerary taken by Lady Margaret 31 July – 22 October 1498 (pp. 29–51).[228] A brief return to Collyweston (7 September, with the king), perhaps to check the state of the refurbishment being undertaken there, lasted only a few days (pp. 37–8), after which Lady Margaret travelled south, spending the rest of September and most of October with the king, largely at Woodstock (pp. 38–50).[229] Her return to Collyweston 22 October established her there for the rest of the year and the duration of the account, which provides a page for each week's entries at Collyweston until 12 January 1499 (pp. 51–65). Within the account may be noted her preparations for the chapel at Collyweston, such as the delivery of an organ and of a licence to use the chapel (pp. 38, 42), and the funding (out of her own coffers at this stage) of her readers at Cambridge and Oxford (Dr John Smyth, pp. 37, 55, and Dr Edmund Wilsford, pp. 42, 46).[230] At the end the sum of all the allowances and payments for the period is given, together with Clarell's debt, and a summary of the payments by type and person, including a payment (p. 67) of £148 14s. 9d. to Henry Hornby (the bill in Hornby's hand is sewn to p. 66 (Plate 9), and there is a bill in the hand of the merchant Nicholas Nynes for £240 received from Hugh Oldham sewn to p. 67).

[227] There is a foray to Sheen, Windsor and Easthampstead, recorded 24 – 30 June (D91.17/19, Plate 8).

[228] The details of Powell, 'Lady Margaret Beaufort: a Progress' now supercede those of Jones and Underwood, *The King's Mother*, Appendix 1 (pp. 260–1) and are more accurate than Terry Breverton, *Henry VII: The Maligned Tudor King* (Stroud: Amberley, 2016), pp. 304–11.

[229] An entry on Wednesday 10 October refers to the costs of 'the kynges beynge at Colyweston' (D91/17/48). A payment of £21 10s. Monday 29 October is to James Morice, her clerk of works, for works and repairs to Collyweston; another is dated Saturday 17 November (£28 10s.), and for further payments see pp. 54, 58, 61, 64, 65.

[230] Also mentioned (p. 42) is John Fawne, then her scholar at Oxford, but to be her first official preacher funded through Westminster (see further below).

4.3.2 The chamber accounts of Miles Worsley (D91.20, D91.21, D91.19)

Clarell calls himself 'cofferere to the most excellent princesse Margaret' (D91.17/1), but the next accounts to survive are those of a different cofferer, Miles Worsley, whose accounts may be considered together. There are three volumes extant (chronologically, **D91.20, D91.21 and D91.19**), covering the years 1502–8. (There are no extant accounts between the close of Clarell's account, 12 January 1499, and the start of Worsley's D91.20 account, 2 February 1502, apart from the chamberlain's accounts, D102.2 and D102.6, 20 May 1501–11 February 1502.) From at least 14 January 1506 the term 'cofferer' is replaced by 'treasurer of the chamber' (D91.21/83).[231] The three years of D91.20 (2 February 1502–14 January 1505) are all localised to Collyweston; the two years of D91.21 (14 January 1505–14 January 1507) are written first (1505) at Croydon and then (1506) at Hatfield;[232] Lady Margaret largely remained at Hatfield during the following two years, 1507 and 1508 (D91.19, 14 January 1507–14 January 1509).

These are large documents, written on paper of approximately the same size as D91.17 (the length of page is usually approximately 305 mm. and the width approximately 215 mm.),[233] apart from D91.19 which is larger (345 × 240 mm.). Each survives within its original vellum wrapper, the back edge of which folds over to contain the whole document, while the upper and lower edges front and back fold in and down.[234] The accounts seem at some stage to have been kept together on a shelf ('Pressus 11', D91.21, D91.19, possibly in Fisher's hand). Only D91.21 displays traces of having been treated as an indenture, in that the early pages are cut zig-zag fashion to ensure their authenticity (Plate 13).[235]

During these years much happened in the royal household which is only dimly recorded in these chamber accounts. The death of Henry VII's son Edmund in 1500 is not recorded because no chamber account exists (but see D102.10/9), but the accounts survive for the periods which saw the

[231] The introductory rubric for the previous year (D91.21/1) is damaged but is legible as 'clerk'; the year previous to that uses 'clerk of þe coffers' (D91.20/141). Both previous years use the same term as Clarell: 'cof(f)erare' (D91.20/1, 71).

[232] The single extant computus of William Bedell (D91.16) overlaps with D91.21; it covers expenditure at both Croydon and Hatfield.

[233] D91.21 is only 285 mm. long.

[234] There may be some reason why these specific years were bound together (such as that they were all audited by the same auditor), but no reason is apparent.

[235] They are sometimes referred to as indentures, e.g. 'xliiii li. ix s. viii d. ob. qua. remanynyng in his handes and ys charged in his new indenture ayenst paymentes to be made this next yere' (D91.21/152), cf. D91/19/2 (the next year's account book): 'First receyved the xvith day of January apon the fote of his accounpte anno xxii^{do} ... xliiii li. ix s. viii d. ob. qua.'.

deaths of Arthur and Elizabeth of York in 1502 and 1503,[236] the death of Lady Margaret's husband Thomas Stanley in 1504 (D91.20/168),[237] and the death of Lady Margaret's fool Skip in 1508 (D91.19/75). Those who died in Lady Margaret's own residences were Eleanor Stanley, Lady Margaret's step-granddaughter, at Collyweston, in December 1503,[238] Anne Grey, Lady Powis, at Collyweston in August 1506,[239] and Cecily Welles, widow of Lady Margaret's half-brother, at Hatfield in August 1507.[240] (Most devastating of all to Lady Margaret was the death of her son, which took place in the year of her last chamber account D102.1 (see below).)

There were also happier times, both small, such as the christening of Mary Conyers's child (D91.20, 163, 197) or one of James Morice's children (D91.21/9), and great. In 1501 she had refurbished Coldharbour for the arrival from Spain of Katherine of Aragon to marry her grandson Arthur (the preparations for which are recorded in some detail in Roger Ormeston's 1501–2 account discussed below), and in 1503 she prepared Collyweston for the stay of Princess Margaret en route to Scotland for her marriage to James IV, for which she may have borrowed plate from the king himself: 'Item to the same for caryage of all the plate from Colyweston to London which was provided for my ladies grace agaynest the kynges comyng' (D91.20/111). The accounts record rewards to Nicholas Aughton for riding out to meet the king's entourage as it approached Collyweston, having left London 8 July 1503, and for riding part of the way with Princess Margaret's entourage when it left (20/113). The wedding of her young kinswoman, Elizabeth Zouche, to the heir of the earl of Kildare was celebrated at Collyweston at the same time, but it may be noted only in the general business surrounding the king's visit, such as the movement of beds and 'rewardes to syngyng men at the kynges beying at Colyweston' (D91.20/102–10 passim).

In 1506 Philip I, duke of Castile, and Queen Joanna (Katherine of Aragon's sister) had to be unexpectedly entertained at court when grounded

[236] The last reference to Arthur is for garters for him and his brother Henry, recorded 16 April 1502 when he had already been dead fourteen days (D19.20/21); the last reference to the queen is a payment to her midwife (she died 11 February after childbirth) (D19.20/191).

[237] He died 29 July and his servant was rewarded 2 August for bringing the news from Lancashire to Collyweston (D91.20/164), after which the religious houses of Stamford were all paid for funeral obsequies and cloth was bought and 700 yards of 'say' (fine serge or silk) dyed black (p. 166).

[238] The burial, washing of the chamber, expenses, etc. are recorded 20/125, 139, 146. Oddly, her father died (supposedly of poison) at a banquet the same month.

[239] D91.21/121, 124, 159. Lady Powis was a daughter of William Herbert, with whom the young Henry Tudor had been brought up at Raglan Castle [Mon.].

[240] D91.19/30, 35. Lady Margaret had always been fond of Cecily and had championed her third marriage to Thomas Kyme in 1502. She and Lady Powis both had their own rooms at Collyweston. See above (2.2).

by storms as they were en route from the Netherlands to Spain. Lady Margaret entertained them at Croydon and commissioned an account of their enforced stay;[241] payments are recorded at both the court and Croydon to Philip's minstrels (D91.21/99, 103, 108, 110). (Philip died the same year, and a proxy marriage took place in December 1508 between his son Charles and Henry VII's daughter Mary, who became 'princess of Castile'.)[242]

During all these years the most frequent records are purchases of textiles, silks, metals and furs, either to be made up into apparel for Lady Margaret herself and her household, or ready-made (in the case of smaller items like bonnets and hose). Textiles were also bought to furnish her houses, her litter, her chair of estate, and the like (particularly in the refurbishment of Coldharbour recorded in D102.2 and D102.6).[243] The most regular records of events are religious ones: Lenten preaching, Maundy Thursday and Easter rituals, and celebrations at St Nicholas's Eve and Christmas/New Year.[244] Visits to the court and elsewhere are noted by payments to service staff at her departure, as at Woodstock in October 1498 (D91.17, 49–50) and at Richmond in June 1505 and January 1507 (D91.21/27; D91.19/11); visits to monastic institutions also required reimbursement for hospitality rendered, as at the abbey at Westminster in May 1507 and March 1508 (D91.19/18, 76), or to Richard, butler of the charterhouse at Sheen (D91.20/85), or for 'bred & ale at Syon' (D91.19/12), where she regularly travelled by barge when at Richmond.[245] Conversely, when the king visited her, his servants were rewarded, as in July 1503 at Collyweston, when, as noted above, he accompanied Princess Margaret part of the way to Scotland for her marriage (20/109–11). Every church and shrine visited by Lady Margaret is recorded by offerings made, often at Syon, or at Westminster to Our Lady of Pew, perhaps nearer

[241] Lady Margaret gave a reward to 'oon þ*at* brought a booke to my lad*ys* g*ra*ce of the comyng of the kyng*e* of Castell' (D91.21/103). For the book (SJCA D105.162, now SJLM/9/2/2) : 'The Meeting of Henry VII and the King of Castile', *The Eagle*, 15 (March 1889), 1–4.

[242] She is so called in D102.1 and in Lady Margaret's will. The marriage was delayed and in 1514 she married Louis XII of France.

[243] Susan Powell, 'Textiles and Dress in the Household Papers of Lady Margaret Beaufort (1443–1509), Mother of King Henry VII', in *Medieval Clothing and Textiles 11*, ed. Robin Netherton and Gale R. Owen-Crocker (Woodbridge: Boydell, 2015), pp. 139–57; Maria Hayward, *Dress at the Court of King Henry VII* (Leeds: Maney, 2007), 83–6 (p. 85 for a summary of Lady Margaret's expenditure 1498–1509).

[244] Her preachers on the Sundays of Lent were eminent (see SCHOLARS AND PREACHERS in the PEOPLE index). For Easter celebrations 1502–8 see D91.20/16, 90, 152; D91.21/15, 107–8; D91.19/14–16 and 83–9 passim. On St Nicholas Eve (5 December) in 1504 Lady Margaret rewarded both her own boy bishop and the Collyweston parish church boy bishop (D91.20/183); for Christmas and New Year, with its disguisings and gift-giving, see the entries at the end of each year of the accounts.

[245] Lists of rewards occur frequently at her departure from (usually) Richmond, e.g. D91.20/86, 109; D102.1/4v.

Collyweston to Our Lady of Holywell,[246] but also further afield at Sudbury, Bury St Edmunds, Walsingham or King's Lynn when on progress in 1498.

The Maundy Thursday celebrations are worth remarking on here. As noted above (2.2), Lady Margaret had built almshouses at Collyweston and Westminster, and she ran almshouses at Croydon and Hatfield, but her princely charity was not confined to her almsfolk. Each Lent records Lady Margaret's purchase of bonnets, hose and shoes for poor folk (for example, in 1507, six dozen white bonnets 'for my ladyes maunde' and six dozen women's hose, D91.19/12), and her gift of 13d. each, all to an increasing number of poor folk, the number dependent on her age. There were fifty-nine in 1502, sixty in 1503, sixty-one in 1504, sixty-two in 1505, sixty-three in 1506, sixty-four in 1507, sixty-five in 1508, and then in 1509 the number rises to sixty-seven, having been altered from sixty-six.[247] The details are of interest because, if Lady Margaret was born in 1443, as Jones and Underwood have convincingly argued,[248] she was sixty-five on Maundy Thursday 1509 (5 April) and not sixty-six (still less sixty-seven) until 31 May. Perhaps the alteration to sixty-seven was an error, although, even if so, all the earlier numbers are anyway a year over, unless she calculated her age (as does the present monarch) in terms of the year, rather than the exact date, i.e. 1509 was the year in which she entered into her sixty-sixth year on earth.

During all the years of these accounts Lady Margaret was working towards her foundation of Christ's College, Cambridge.[249] The first record in the chamber accounts is D91.20/190, where a reward of 20s. is given on 13 January 1505 to John Syclyng, then master of God's House before its refoundation as Christ's.[250] In the spring of 1505 (D91.21/16, 25) he visited Collyweston with four fellows (perhaps more accurately, the four fellows). In the later accounts, D91.21 (1505–7) and D91.19 (1507–9), Lady Margaret

[246] For Syon: S. Powell, 'Syon Abbey and the Mother of King Henry VII: The Relationship of Lady Margaret Beaufort with the English Birgittines', *Birgittiana*, 19 (2005), 211–24, partly incorporated into Powell, *The Birgittines of Syon Abbey*, Chapter 6 ('Lady Margaret Beaufort: Books, Printers, and Syon Abbey') at pp. 184–5. For Our Lady of Pew: Matthew Payne, 'The first chantry chapel of Lady Margaret Beaufort at Westminster Abbey', in *Performance, Ceremony and Display in Late Medieval England*, ed. Julia Boffey (Donington: Shaun Tyas, 2020), pp. 273–83. For Holywell, which (from the context of occurrences) may be the Huntingdonshire chapel in Holywell-cum-Needingworth rather than the London priory of Augustinian canonesses, see the PLACES index. It is not the Welsh shrine of St Winifred: Powell, *The Birgittines of Syon Abbey*, pp. 174–5.

[247] D91.20/16, 88, 151; D91.21/15, 107; D91.19/26, 97l; D102.1/15v.

[248] *The King's Mother*, p. 34. Much has been made, on the basis of this date, of the youth of Lady Margaret at the time she gave birth; the previously accepted year of her birth was1441.

[249] Jones and Underwood, *The King's Mother*, pp. 215–31.

[250] The earliest reference (in a section of Lady Margaret's book of receipts and payments which lists money delivered to the clerk of works, James Morice, from 2 March 1505) records £66 13s. 4d. 'for þe beldyng off Cristez Collage in Cambryge' (D102.10/107).

acquired property to fund the college and, later, books and chapel goods to furnish it,[251] and payments are frequent, usually to Syclyng.[252] By February 1508 the statutes were being copied and a memo being sent to Rome (D91.19/72).[253] Another outlay was her project for stabilising the fens around her properties in Lincolnshire, regularly damaged by floodwater; she established a commission to tackle the problem, which was achieved by means of a ram and sluice (D91.20/32, 62, 162, 165; D91.21/80; D91.19/61, 124; see too D102.10/2; D102.2/7, D102.6/5).[254] A third longterm project was the result of the decision by herself and her son to be buried in the abbey at Westminster, rather than at Windsor which had been their earlier intention.[255] For this she conveyed lands to the abbey, from which the monks were also to fund the stipends for her two University readers and her preacher in divinity.[256] (As Jones and Underwood note, the establishment of the Westminster chantry is 'inseparable from that of the lectureships and preachership which Margaret founded'.[257]) One entry in particular, in her account for 1506, may be mentioned here, since it refers to a document (London, British Library, Lansdowne MS 441) which summarises all the clauses of her settlement with the abbey.[258]

[251] Scott, 'On a List of the Plate, Books and Vestments'.
[252] For an extant bill of receipt by Syclyng of payments for Christ's: D102.10/182.
[253] See too the 1509 account (D102.1) passim, where the last reference to Christ's is for work to the tune of £325 2s. 3d. (f. 18r). For the statutes: *Early Statutes of Christ's College, Cambridge*, ed. H. Rackham (Cambridge: Fabb and Tyler, 1927).
[254] M. K. Jones, 'Lady Margaret Beaufort, the Royal Council, and an Early Fenland Drainage Scheme', *Lincolnshire Historical and Archaeological Society*, 21 (1986), 11–18. See too the chamberlain's account, D102.2 and D102.6, below.
[255] Earlier still Lady Margaret had favoured Wimborne, where her parents were buried. For the cartulary of a chantry at Wimborne: TNA E 135/3/21. For the evolution of Lady Margaret's plans for burial: Jones and Underwood, *The King's Mother*, pp. 206–8, 233–4; Payne, 'The First Chantry Chapel'. For the king's provisions for his burial: Margaret Condon, 'God Save the King: Piety, Propaganda, and the Perpetual Memorial', in *Westminster Abbey*, ed. Tatton-Brown and Mortimer, pp. 59–97. For Lady Margaret's tomb: R. F. Scott, 'On the Contracts for the Tomb of Lady Margaret Beaufort', *Archaeologia*, 66 (1912–15), 365–76.
[256] For the fullest details: Jones and Underwood, *The King's Mother*, pp. 196–7, 206–12; Underwood, 'The Lady Margaret and her Cambridge Connections', 69–72; for an earlier account see Cooper, *Memoir of Margaret*, pp. 89–93. For specific details of the two Westminster readerships (established 8 September 1503) at Oxford and Cambridge (first held respectively by John Roper and John Fisher), and the preachership at Cambridge (established 30 October 1504 and first held by John Fawne), see Jones and Underwood, *The King's Mother*, p. 206, and Richard Rex, 'Lady Margaret and her Professorship 1502–1559', in *Lady Margaret Beaufort and her Professors of Divinity at Cambridge 1502 to 1649*, ed. P. Collinson, R. Rex, and G. Stanton (Cambridge: Cambridge University Press, 2003), pp. 19–56.
[257] Jones and Underwood, *The King's Mother*, p. 206.
[258] For the details of the indenture (which also cites her previous endowments): Cooper, *Memoir of Margaret*, pp. 105–7 (which wrongly cites '*MS. Lansd.* 444'). See the description, with a full abstract, in *A Catalogue of the Lansdowne MSS in the British Museum* (London: 1812–19), II: 122–3 (MS 441). For the indenture in relation to Lady Margaret's chantry at Westminster: Payne,

In that year she granted land in Great Chesterford (Essex) and executed an indenture between herself and the abbey to fund two additional chantry monks, aided by a lay brother, for a perpetual celebration on the anniversary of her death. The writing and enrolling of the writ for the land, and the vellum, binding, limning, silk laces, velvet lining, clasps, crosses, decoration, buckram bags and seal cases for the indentures, made 'boke fassion', are recorded at D91.21/149.

The final material at the end of each year provides useful evidence of a careful bureaucracy, in that references are made to several books to be checked for confirmation of transactions and figures. For example, in the end-of-year summary for 1503 (January 1504), it is noted that Worsley's delivery of £402 19s. 2½d. to James Morice, Lady Margaret's clerk of works, can be confirmed 'bothe by the boke of accompte of the saide James as by the boke of the saide Myles' (20/134).[259] The same summary records that £331 10s. 2½d. delivered to Bedell, the treasurer, can be confirmed 'in his [Bedell's] accompte and also in a boke of parcelles of the said Miles' (20/134).[260] This sum, made up of five payments, can be found in Lady Margaret's book of receipts and payments (D102.10, discussed above) under the heading 'Memorandum off mony delyvered unto the forseid tresourere' (D102.10/61); presumably it could also be found in Bedell's own account and Worsley's book of parcels, were these extant. In the same summary a scribbled note in the 'sprawling' hand records that Worsley's end-of-year residue has been paid into the coffers on 16 January 1504, as detailed 'in the boke off the seid princes and also in a payre off indentures made betw[e]ne the princes and Miles' (D91.20/134, cf. p. 142). While the indentures do not survive, the sum is found in Lady Margaret's book (D102.10/75). Also mentioned, at the end of the next financial year (January 1505), is a 'warant of þe seid countiez' which allows Miles £20 (20/194). Another form of record is written on the back of the paper extension to this page (see Appendix to the edited text of D91.20) and serves as a memorandum to discuss with Hornby the matter of the expenses paid to the priest Harry Norton in relation to the estate of Thomas Welby of Moulton, administered by the clerk of the king's hanaper, George Kirkham.[261]

'The First Chantry Chapel'; for several indentures associated with Henry VII's chantry there: Condon, 'God Save the King'.

[259] Cf. 'in computo Jacobi Morres' 21/28, 35.

[260] Cf. 'certen goodez bought at London & sent to Colyweston for þe use of þe seid houshold as in þe accompt of þe same tresorere it appereth', 20/194. For Worsley's book of parcels, i.e. individual entries, cf. 'another boke of parcelles signed with the hande of the forseid counties and in hur kepyng remaynyng' (20/64) and 'a booke of parcelles þerof made by þe seid Myles & remanyng in þe custody of þe seid countiez' (20/194).

[261] See Jones and Underwood, *The King's Mother*, p. 129.

As for other personnel, Hugh Ashton, Lady Margaret's receiver general, kept his own computus ('in computo Hugonis Assheton clerici recepte', 20/147) and also kept the record made by the executors of Roger Ormeston, Lady Margaret's chamberlain, who had died in 1504: 'þe booke made by thexecutourz of þe same sir Roger & remaynyng in þe kepyng of maister Ashton' (20/144, cf. 20/194). And, interestingly, there is also some reliance on memory: 'And also [it can be confirmed] by the knowlege of the saide James [Morice]', cf. 'the boke of the accompte of the same James by his owne <h> knolegh' (20/64); 'paied ...as the receyvour [Hugh Ashton] knowith' (20/191); 'þe booke of accompt of þe seid Miles and also by þe knowlech of þe seid James' (20/194).

4.3.3 The chamber accounts of Robert Fremingham (D102.1)

This is the final of these chamber accounts, of the same dimensions as D91.21 but only twenty-two folios rather than eighty-six. It needs to be considered separately from the previous years because it covers only the last months of Lady Margaret's life (20 January 1509 - 29 June 1509), is not linked to a specific place (such as Collyweston, Croydon or Hatfield), and was the responsibility of an acting treasurer of chamber. As the initial rubric makes clear by citing the dates 20 January 1509 to 29 June 1509 (f. 2r), the preliminary material was written up after Lady Margaret's death on 29 June. It seems likely that the 'Paymentes' were also written up, at least in part, after her death, since an entry for 26 July was partly copied out amongst earlier entries and then cancelled (f. 15r),[262] and the entries are anyway disordered chronologically at this point, which suggests perhaps that they had been imperfectly organised for copying. The treasurer of chamber is here Robert Fremingham, acting in that capacity (f. 2r) perhaps because Miles Worsley was involved elsewhere after Lady Margaret's death.[263]

Lady Margaret had suffered ill health for a number of years, as the references throughout her accounts to physicians, potions, rose water, cramp rings and suchlike testify. Medicinal preparations are recorded in 1509 both before and after her son's death (ff. 4v, 15r), the total for the six months' medicines being 29s. 6d. (f. 17r), and there is a reference in late April or early

[262] The previous dated entry is for 8 June (f. 14v) and the next for 14 April (f. 15r). The cancelled entry does not recur.

[263] Worsley was certainly in post in 1509, as an entry records his being paid at Easter for hiring a room in Hatfield for 'his stuf' for eighteen weeks 'at the tyme of the auditt' (f. 9r). Whether this was the annual audit or an inventory is unclear (such a statement does not occur anywhere else). The most likely inventory is perhaps that carried out by Robert Hilton 14 January – 16 August 1509 (D91.4, now SJLM/2/2/2), but it does not mention any involvement by Worsley, only by Bedell and Morice (p. 22).

May, after the trauma of her son's death, to the 'time of hir sekenesse' (f. 15r).[264] Since at least the spring of 1507 she had been pre-occupied by his ill health, and had spent Christmas and Easter (and perhaps longer) away from Hatfield, but his eventual death late in the evening of 21 April is recorded only in her move from Coldharbour to Richmond, the bringing of her fool Reginald and two of her gentlewomen from Hatfield to Richmond, the provisioning of black cloth, and finally a reward to Robert Merbury for coming to Richmond to give her an account of her son's funeral procession from there to St Paul's Cathedral, and thence to Westminster Abbey (ff. 9v–12r passim).[265] Just after the funeral the account notes her removal to the Tower for the coronation of the new king, and then to Richmond and Greenwich, from where she sent John Fisher's funeral sermon to be printed by Wynkyn de Worde (ff. 11v–13v passim). The end-of-year summary records payment for the house in Cheapside from which on 24 June she and her grandchild Mary watched the coronation procession of her grandson Henry and his queen, the former wife of his dead brother Arthur (f. 17r).[266]

The final summary in D102.1 of the six months' expenses includes customary entries for offerings and alms, as well as other charitable duties: 'Rewardes yeven att the cristyng of dyvers childer' (f. 17r), 'Money payed for the mariage of maistres Yan' (f. 17v), and a total of 66s. 8d. to Margaret Pole (ff. 9v, 12v, 15v). Gold, silver and textiles, with their working by her embroiderer, came to nearly £200, with a further £68 10s. 3d. for stuff bought by her yeoman of the wardrobe, Robert Hilton; 35s. 6d. went on books direct from Wynkyn de Worde,[267] and £4 11s. 0d. for bullions to decorate the books she was giving to Christ's College (f. 17v).[268] The largest single sum for payments from January to June 1509 was £325 2s. 3d. (f. 18r) for the 'reparacion' (as the building work was normally called, in recognition of its being a refoundation) of Christ's College. Only in this last account is reference made (27/28 March) to St John's Hospital, to be refounded eventually as St John's College, her second foundation in Cambridge: 'Item to Thomas Bellingeham maister comptrollours servant for riding to Cambrige by the space of iiii dayes for certayn wrytinges concernyng Sainct Johns house' and 'Item to master

[264] Henry Parker attributed her death to the eating of a cygnet: London, British Library, Add. MS 12060, f. 23r-v (Carley and Rex, 'The Account of the Miracles of the Sacrament', p. 264).

[265] The sermon was preached at St Paul's on 9 May (neither the new king nor Lady Margaret attended: Hatt, *John Fisher's Court Sermons*, p. 311). For an account of her actions in 1509 and those of others after her death: Jones and Underwood, *The King's Mother*, pp. 234–50.

[266] Fisher commented in his sermon for her month's mind that even at the coronation she feared unhappy times ahead: Fisher, *The English Works*, p. 305, l. 33 - p. 306, l. 9; Hatt, *John Fisher's Court Sermons*, p. 366, lines 386–90.

[267] For details of the books: f. 5v; at her death de Worde was in debt for an advance of £20 (f. 18v).

[268] For the books: N. McLean, 'Books given to the Library of Christ's College Cambridge by the Lady Margaret', *The Library*, n.s. 8 (1907), 218–23.

Assheton comptrollour of my ladyes houshold for riding to London at iii dyuerse tymes and ther abiding in all by the space of viii dayes aboute the alteracion of Sainctt Johns house in Cambrige into a colleige of secular studentes and also to unyte the priory of Bromholme in Norffolk dissolued unto the same house' (f. 8r).[269]

No page of D102.1 is signed by Lady Margaret, but that is unsurprising if her accounts were normally written up and signed at the end of the financial year (or even in batches throughout the year) and she was otherwise preoccupied. Instead they are signed by her close colleague in all her projects, John Fisher, together with her secretary and chamberlain, Henry Hornby, and her receiver general and controller, Hugh Ashton (see Plate 17).

4.4 The accounts of the chamberlain, Sir Roger Ormeston (D102.2, D102.6)

These two volumes were once one book, an account of the receipts and payments of Lady Margaret's chamberlain, Sir Roger Ormeston, from 20 May 1501 to 11 February 1502, which directly precedes the earliest chamber account, D91.20, which begins 2 February 1502.[270] As noted above (2.1.4), he died some time between 28 March and 6 April 1504 and was replaced as chamberlain by Lady Margaret's kinsman, Sir John St John II of Bletsoe.

D102.2 and D102.6 appear, like the other account books, to have been written up by the officer responsible for the account, in this case Ormeston himself,[271] with the rubrics and summary material at beginning and end written in a summary hand (compare pp. 2 and 3, Plate 18). The account largely deals with the preparations for the reception in London of Katherine of Aragon, the bride of Lady Margaret's grandson Arthur. As chamberlain, Ormeston was in charge of the occasion, and the books record his receipts and payments for such items as cloth of gold and accoutrements for Lady Margaret's horses and litter, as well as for the refurbishment of Coldharbour itself for entertainment of the royal party. The two most involved in the refurbishment were William Bolton, the talented Austin canon of St Bartholomew

[269] Further indirect references (ff. 6r, 18r) are to her purchase of the manor of Bassingbourn, which in the event was not to be conveyed to St John's until 1512. For Bromholm and Bassingbourn: Jones and Underwood, *The King's Mother*, p. 234. For the long-drawn-out foundation of St John's after Lady Margaret's death: ibid., pp. 241–9; Rex, 'The Sixteenth Century', esp. pp. 5–17; R.F.S. (R. F. Scott), 'Notes from the College Records', *The Eagle*, 16 (December 1890), 341–57; M. G. Underwood, 'Records of the Foundress', *The Eagle*, 68 (Easter 1979), 7–23 at 14–19.

[270] The rubric (D102.2/1) gives the end-date as 18 December, but the last dated item in the book is 11 February 1502 (D102.6/9).

[271] 'I Roger Urmyston', pp. 3, 5; 'by me Roger Urmyston', p. 7, etc.

the Great, Smithfield,[272] and Peter Baldwin ('Peter of Coldharbour'), the general manager of the property,[273] who were paid a total of £32 9s. 9d. and £8 4s. respectively 'for reparacionus off Coldherbare', including Peter's 'makyng off the garden' (D102.2/10, D102.6/6).

After some vicissitudes Katherine had landed at Plymouth on 2 October 1501, after which she progressed slowly to London. Her reception into London on 12 November was lavish,[274] as were the receptions for her entourage the next day, hosted by Lady Margaret at Coldharbour and by her husband at Derby House.[275] Lady Margaret and her gentlewomen attended the marriage itself in St Paul's on 14 November (D102.6/5). Katherine and Arthur were at Windsor until 21 December when they left for Ludlow, which was to be Arthur's own seat of government; his death there on 2 April returned Katherine to London until, after several very difficult years, she married Henry, Arthur's younger brother, on 11 June 1509.

A secondary thread running through D102.2 and D102.6 deals with the payments for the sluice at Boston, which was briefly mentioned above in relation to the chamber accounts. Ormeston's account is therefore useful in providing evidence for the project prior to the earliest extant chamber account (D91.20), when Ormeston appears to have been responsible for payments: 'Memorandum payd by Roger Ormeston knight for divers necessaries and implementtes to þe slewes att Boston of my lady þe kinges moder money' (D102.6/9). Lady Margaret owned two important manorial estates in Lincolnshire, Deeping and Maxey, and her own palace at Collyweston was just over the border in Northamptonshire. The silting of the lower part of the River Witham, combined with the tidal flow, caused considerable flooding of her land and that of other local landowners, and it threatened the revenues

[272] For Bolton as master of the king's works, notably the Henry VII Chapel: Colvin, Ransome, Summerson, *The King's Works*, III:I, pp. 210–22 at pp. 213–14. On the man: Judith Etherton, 'William Bolton (d. 1532)' (*ODNB*). This early date for Bolton's involvement with Lady Margaret appears to be previously unknown; he was promoted to prior in 1505 (he is here called 'the master of Seint Bartilmewes', e.g. D102.6/6). James Morice and Richard Gough were also involved in the refurbishment, which included glazing by Robert Stones at a cost of 44s. 3d. (D102.2/8, 10–12, 14, D102/6/6). For Coldharbour: C.L. Kingsford, 'On some London Houses of the Early Tudor Period', *Archaeologia*, 71 (1921), 17–54 at 21–8.

[273] Baldwin doubled as a scribe and bookbinder, e.g. copying out inventories (D91.17/24) or 'lynyng and dressyng of a booke' (D91.20/25). Matthew Payne has suggested privately (as a suggestion of Margaret Condon) that there is some reason to think he might have been the nephew of Quentin Poulet, the king's librarian.

[274] See *The Receyt of the Ladie Katerine*, ed. Gordon Kipling, EETS OS 296 (1990). For Katherine and her Spanish courtiers: Theresa Earenfight, 'A Precarious Household: Catherine of Aragon in England, 1501–1504', in *Royal and Elite Households in Medieval and Early Modern Europe: More than Just a Castle*, ed. Theresa Earenfight (Leiden/Boston: Brill, 2018), 338–70.

[275] *The Receyt of the Ladie Katerine*, ed. Kipling, Book III, Chapter 5 (pp. 47–8, ll. 313–59).

Lady Margaret received from her Boston tenants.[276] A royal commission was set up to investigate the problem, and in 1499 Lady Margaret provided a loan 'towardes the werkes in the said Boston for defense of watier' (D102.10/2). The commission recommended a sluice at Boston bridge, for which Lady Margaret financed a brass ram (to drive in the piles of the bridge and sluice), which was sent from London to Boston in 1501/2 (D102.6/5). In June 1502 her receiver general, Hugh Ashton, together with her secretary/dean, Henry Hornby, and controller, William Merbury, rode to the area of Lincolnshire known as Holland 'and serten places in the fenne to see the convayaunce of the water' (D91.20/28), after which the master carpenter of the sluice was paid for his work (p. 32). Lady Margaret's works protected her lands, the manors she had inherited from her mother around Deeping and Maxey, on the edge of the fens, and the honour of Richmond lands around Boston (part of the 'Great Grant' of 1487). They were innovative for the time, although they did not last (as no fen drainage scheme lasted until comparatively recently), and they were remembered at least into the early seventeenth century, when the cartographer Joost de Hondt noted: 'Many conclusions have been tried for the draining of the Fens, and have not been undertaken only by mean men, but also by the greatest of the Countrie; ... one of the principal was the Lady Margaret, Countess of Richmond'.[277]

5 The Hands

As already discussed, most of the documents edited here have fixed preliminary material to each year (description of the document, arrears, receipts, etc.) and fixed final material (sum total, debt of the accountant, summary of payments, other debts, balancing the account of the year). This summary material is largely written in a formal script (Bastard Anglicana), called here the 'summary hand' (which was not a single hand throughout these documents). Within these bookends of the year the accountant (i.e. the originator of the document) writes out the individual payments throughout the year in a free cursive hand.[278]

[276] For a detailed study: Jones, 'Lady Margaret Beaufort, the Royal Council'.

[277] G. Mercator and J. Hondius, *Atlas, or a geographicke description ...*, 2 vols (Amsterdam: Hondius-Janssonius, 1638). I, p. 66, quoted in Jones, 'Lady Margaret Beaufort, the Royal Council', p. 11.

[278] Sometimes added material in the summaries is written, not in a formal script, but in a cursive Anglicana/Secretary script, such as is used for the main body of the accounts.

Both types of hand in the documents considered here display characteristics of the court hands identified by Jenkinson in *The Later Court Hands*.[279] Doubtless Jenkinson would have seen the hands which wrote some of these documents as (in a formal script) 'apparently derived from bad models of Bastard, very freely written', or (in a cursive script) 'typical rough Free Hands of the late fifteenth century' or even at times 'the worst type of script in which parts of individual letters, especially m, n and other short letters, almost disappear from extreme rapidity of writing'.[280] Common features which he identifies in English spelling are found in the documents edited here: 'the use of ȝ and þ'; 'superior letters ...y^{e} for the and ȝ^{ou} for you', many of which 'appear to be quite meaningless'; the abbreviation 'pd' for 'paid';[281] elision with 'the' in 'thandes'; initial <ff> 'where certainly no capital is intended' (as is the normal function of <ff> initially).[282]

The description of the hands which follows is not intended as a palaeographic exercise but as an attempt to identify the accountants who created these documents (in the cursive hands) and to say a little about the auditors who worked with them (in the summary hand). However, in the case of the latter at least, it must be borne in mind that training was similar for all these men, so that letter forms cannot always certainly identify individuals. As will be seen, English spelling and abbreviation habits tend to be more helpful, and in this the cursive hands are much more distinctive than the summary hand, since they were not trained in the same way as the auditors; Hornby, for example, was university-trained, and the others were not necessarily originally trained in a counting house.[283] Another consideration is the working circumstances which might affect the individual hand, sometimes working fresh, sometimes at the end of a long day, sometimes with little to note in the document, sometimes with a great deal to copy out from draft. With these considerable caveats, there follows here an analysis of the named and some unnamed hands in the edited documents, an analysis which has informed the earlier discussions in this Introduction.

[279] C. Jenkinson, *The Later Court Hands in England from the Fifteenth to the Seventeenth Century* (Cambridge: Cambridge University Press, 1927). See particularly Alphabets 1–3 and Plates XXIV-XXVII, XXIX.

[280] Ibid., p. 154 (of private household accounts 1432–3) and p. 156 (of a merchant's account book 1487).

[281] This is found when a long list of payments made to Robert Hilton is copied out at D91.21/31–2.

[282] Ibid., pp. 154–9 passim.

[283] Henry Hornby's invocation to 'Jesus' (D102.10/9) and Roger Ormeston's invocations to Christ and the Virgin (D102.2, first unfoliated page and then pp. 5, 7, 21) are normally found in a learned/monastic scribal context.

5.1 The Summary Hand of the Audit

The summary hand is not a single hand; the term therefore has a different meaning from the individual cursive hands of the accountants, cited in the edited documents as 'the MW hand', 'the HH hand', etc. As noted above, all the documents edited here have preliminary and final (i.e. summary) material which introduces and concludes the financial year within the document (17/66, Plate 9; 20/4, Plate 10).[284] There are set formulae for the introduction of various accountancy practices within the document, and these are normally written with a thick nib and strong black ink in the formal script known as Bastard Anglicana, large for the most important rubrics (e.g. 'Thaccompte ...dais' D91.20/4 (Plate 10), 'And so he owith ...ii d. ob.' 20/64, etc., sometimes with a decorated initial, e.g. 'Summa ...vii d. ob.' 20/64, etc.), and smaller, normally written with a finer nib, for lesser rubrics (e.g. 'Friste ...appere' 20/4, 'wherof ...remaynyng' 20/64). The lists of loans and summaries of payments according to items/people which are found at the end of each financial year are normally written in a neat small script, perhaps in a different hand, e.g. D91.20/65–8, 135–40, 195–200. In D91.20, which is used as an exemplum here, an especially neat, closely written script is used for the loans listed at the end of each year on extensions to pp. 64, 134 (Plates 11–12) and 194. The receipts on pp. 142–4 and the last pages of the document (pp. 191–200) are written in a tall, careful hand (which favours the spelling 'paied').Within the formulae the relevant material for the year is infilled in a cursive Anglicana/ Secretary script, e.g. 'The whiche somme' (20/134) to the end of the page (Plate 12).

As already discussed, the summary material is the responsibility of the auditor and his clerk(s); one individual is perhaps responsible for the main rubrics and another for the lists and summaries.[285] Features of the spelling of the summary hand are the elision of 'the' with a following vowel, e.g. 'Thaccompt(e)' or similar at 20/4, 71; 21/1, 83; 19/1, 65; a double <ff> in all positions in a word, not just medial (e.g. 'ffest" 17/1, 'ffrome' 20/71, 21/1, 19/1; 'whereoff' 20/134, 21/152, 161; 'off' 19/51, 52, 54–5, 1/18r); the occasional use of thorn (e.g. 'þe' 17/20, 20/141–4, 21/77, 19/3. 19/65, 1/17r).[286] However, a set formal script does not allow for much individualism of hand, and the rubrics are standard formulae with only minor variation. The present editor has studied the individual letter-forms of the initial and final summary

[284] For details see the Description to each edited text. In D102.10 the summary material is rudimentary and largely informal; D91.16 and D91.17 appear each to be written in only one hand, which switches between formal and cursive script.

[285] They sometimes exhibit misunderstanding of their copytexts, e.g. 'or for' for 'cofor' D91.17/67; 'Petur Ayason' for 'Pepur and Mason' 21/154.

[286] The use of thorn may be particularly associated with the 'sprawling' hand discussed below.

material in each document, particularly the formation of <I> (e.g. 'Item', 'January') and the writing of <m> (e.g. 'Miles', 'Margarete'), as well as the individual spelling and wording of the summary hand in its formal script.[287] Although differences and similarities exist, they do not helpfully correlate in such a way as to enable one to make definitive statements about the different hands used for the summary material; indeed, variants of letter-formation may even be found within the same brief stint, such as the writing of <m> at D91.17/1. Although it seems certain that more than one hand was responsible for the summary material over the ten years of these edited accounts, only one member of the auditing team writes in a hand that is entirely distinctive, and that distinctiveness is discernible, not in the formal script of the summary material, but in a cursive script within the summary material, and also in the main body of the accounts.[288] This is a hand which has been mentioned several times already in the earlier sections of this Introduction, the 'sprawling' hand.

5.2 The 'Sprawling' Hand

This hand is particularly distinctive, in that, when writing extempore, it is sprawling and undisciplined,[289] although if it is the same hand that also writes in the formal Bastard Anglicana script (e.g. D91.19/50, Plate 15), it is more disciplined and restrained. It is an easily recognisable hand in its cursive form. It uses a thorn fairly frequently (marked by its lack of an ascender, like <p>) and sometimes uses a yogh finally in place of <s> (the yogh is transcribed in these edited texts as <z>, e.g. 'Crystez' D91.21/67, 'Mylez' D102.10/125); it uses <ff> in 'ffor' D91.20/64, 'ffyrst', 'ffewell' D102.10/18, etc. and 'off' D91.20/194, D91.21/67, etc. Its double-lobed Anglicana <a> has a particularly sloppy upper lobe, very noticeable when it occurs as the second letter in a word, e.g. 'payde'. Latin comes more naturally to this hand than English and is always used for the annotations. The 'sprawling' hand often slips into Latin when writing dates, e.g. 'Item receyved of the seid master Hugh by the handes of Roger Ormysten xiiii^{mo} die July anno xv', 'Primo the xxith day of Aprill' (D102.10/20–1), and at D102.10/29 the writing of the phrase 'John

[287] The hands at beginning and end of the documents appear to be the same, as would be expected since both the initial and final material were written at the time of the audit.

[288] This is not to say that this hand does not write any of the formal material, simply that the hand is not easily detectable in formal script.

[289] Even without an image (Plate 5), the transcription of the last two entries on D102.10/67 would give an idea of the lack of discipline in the hand when writing fast. It may even be the same hand which occasionally writes with an odd slanting duct (see Description to D102.10 and footnotes to the edited text passim).

Hoo <q> late reve off Cheshunt' reveals that the Latin 'quondam' (former) came first to mind but had to be cancelled for the English 'late'.

For 'master' (which is the usual spelling found in uncontracted forms) this hand uses a single <m> with a flourish from the final stroke under the letter and over the top; it often elides the definite article and noun, e.g. 'thabbot' (D102.10/4, 25, 132), 'thandes' (D102.10/33, 67, 101, etc.);[290] it sometimes has an excrescent –t, e.g. 'Hught' (D102.10/19, 20, 33, 131); and it has occasional but not consistent northern spellings, e.g. 'awinge' (owing), 'aght' (owed), 'mawyng' (mowing) D102.10/21, 69, 114; 'aweth' D91.20/194 (Appendix to the edited text), 'awinge' D102.10/21, 'awght' D102.10/64, 'mawyng' D102.10/114, etc. It always writes 'Herry' (D91.20/194 (Appendix to the edited text), D91.21/67, etc.). This hand makes several mistakes of transcription from at least p. 58 of D102.10, e.g. 'dayly' and 'devered' for 'bayly' and 'delyvered' (p. 58), and makes many false starts, e.g. 'mirhe' for 'Miles' (p. 61), 'dete' for 'Decembere' (p. 67), and 'syd' for 'seid' (p. 75), all cancelled and corrected, and (uncorrected) 'herensues' for 'revenues' (p. 131). This indicates speed when copying, and perhaps unfamiliarity with the material, but anyway the spelling of English in this hand is sometimes eccentric, even by Early Modern English standards, e.g. 'syche', 'sewetes', 'tacon' D91.20/60; 'clemyth' D91.20/194 (Appendix to the edited text); 'Whyt' (for 'wyth') D91.21/161, etc.; 'monyht' (for 'monyth', month) D102.10/34, 61, 83, etc.

The 'sprawling' hand is therefore an impatient, or busy, hand when writing in a cursive hand. Its cursive forms (which, as noted already, are readily recognisable) occur in copying, as when it adds occasional payment entries (e.g. D91.20/60, fourth and fifth entries, or D91.21/67, first entry), or annotating entries to indicate payments resolved or cancelled and why,[291] or adding and enlarging on summary material at the end of a year, e.g. D91.20/60, 134 (Plates 11–12), 194; D91.21/67, 85, 90, 150, 152, 161 (and perhaps more); D91.19/3, 50 (Plate 15), 114; D102.1/16r-v (and perhaps more).[292]

5.3 The Auditors and Accountants

Although the individual hands of the auditors cannot be definitively assessed, different writing habits might appear to provide some indication of how many were responsible for calculations. Some confidence might be placed in the writing of 's.' ('solidi') in calculations. In the chamber accounts of Miles

[290] At D102.10/61 this hand starts to write 'tha' (for 'thandes') but corrects it to 'the handes off'. It even writes 'Thobson' (D102.10/62) for 'T. Hobson', perhaps from a draft.

[291] Annotations (indicated in the edited texts by double angle brackets) are generally written with a thick nib and strong black ink (as used for the large Bastard Anglicana script in the summaries).

[292] See the Descriptions and footnotes to the edited texts.

Worsley, the main (MW) hand uses a simple delta; the first calculation for the ‘Summa’ at D91.21/87 and the first cancelled ‘Somme totall’ on p. 89 are written with a single-lobed <s> with a high curly ascender (which creates a more elaborate delta-shaped <s> than Worsley’s), while the other calculations (the correction p. 87 and the second cancelled total and the corrected total p. 89 use a single-lobed <s> with a tiny curly ascender).[293] Since these occur in summary material at the end of the year 1505–6, these final calculations may be assumed to be those of the auditor and/or his clerks, and this appears to be confirmed by the fact that in other contexts the ‘sprawling’ hand (which may be that of the auditor) uses the single-lobed <s>, e.g. D91.21/150 (‘Somme’) and 151.[294]

Such examples may be multiplied in different forms throughout the accounts and have generally influenced any opinions expressed on hands in the footnotes to the edited texts, as at D91.20/167, where the accountant (as usual) writes the totals of individual entries and the sum total of the page, but the corrections to two entries and to the sum total are in a different hand, and what appears to be a third hand corrects the corrections of one entry and the sum total. Presumably the auditor and his clerk were at work here. A caveat is, however, necessary: as noted above, the summary material is mainly written in a formal script, either a large display script (particularly noticeable in the decorated initial ‘S’ of ‘Summa’) or a smaller formal script, both based on a type of script known as Bastard Anglicana. This script allows for different representations of <s>, and indeed there are cases where what is clearly a summary hand (‘the ‘sprawling’ hand) uses both a single-lobed <s> and in more formal contexts an elaborate delta <s>.[295] Nevertheless, the MW hand uses only one type of <s> and so can be differentiated from other hands in his documents.

The writing of 1,000s and 100s might also be thought to indicate different hands. These large sums normally occur in the summary material at the beginning and end of the accounts, e.g. D91.19/2, where there is a ‘Summa partis’, two jotted calculations to left and right at the foot of the page, and a dot calculation. The first jotted calculation represents 2,000 as ‘ij^{ml}’, the

[293] There are many examples, e.g. D91.19/22, where the writing of ‘s.’ (‘solidi’) differentiates the MW hand of the ‘Summa’ (there are two on the page) from the single-lobed superscript curly <s> of ‘s.’ in the ‘Summa partis’. See too 19/56 where the elaborate delta <s> in the second total (£26 5s. 5½d.) is corrected to £29 10s. 6½d. by the hand which uses the small single-lobed ‘s’.

[294] For several annotations recording the status of loans in the same end-of-year summary material, where again two hands are at work noting debts, allowances and payments, see the footnotes to D91.21/79.

[295] Thus in D91.21/79 (see previous footnote) the ‘two hands ...at work’ may simply be the same ‘sprawling’ hand writing at different times and in different contexts. So too in the footnote prior to the last where at 19/56 the two implied hands may simply be one employing a different <s>.

second as 'm^{l} m^{l}'; both are then cancelled, and the formal 'Summa partis' confirms the second cancelled calculation and uses 'ij^{ml}'. However, all appear to use the single-lobed <s> in 's.' ('solidi') and to be in the same hand. In fact, a perusal of the documents shows that 'm^{l}m^{l}' and similar combinations are the norm in formal script (Bastard Anglicana), while the Roman numeral with superscript '^{ml}' is sometimes used informally (it is arguably less liable to error than the other use). For example, at D91.19/3, a jotted sum total uses 'iij^{ml}', whereas the sum total written fair to the right uses 'm^{l}m^{l}m^{l}'; likewise at D91.19/50 (Plate 15) a jotted sum total (which has been cancelled) uses 'ij^{ml}', whereas the grand total in the body of the text has 'm^{l}m^{l}'.[296] The case is similar in the writing of 100s, where the formula 'DC' and equivalent is used in formal script but 'vj^{C}' and equivalent may be found informally. For example, in D102.2/6 the hand of the 'Somme totall' uses 'DCCCC' for 900 but the jotting at the foot of the page uses 'ix^{C}' for the same number. In D91.20/6 the cancelled 'Summa' uses 'D' for 500, but the correction below prefers 'v^{C}'.[297] (Given the uncertainties about the significance of the representation of these numbers, 1,000s are throughout this edition transcribed 'MM' (2,000) and 100s 'DCCCC' (900).)

Even if the respective writing of <s> in 's.' ('solidi') and of 1,000s and 100s provides no useful evidence of the number of auditors working on the accounts, some evidence may be found in the indications of approval of the accounts and the individual checkmarks used in these approvals. For example, in the chamber accounts a trefoil normally accompanies the 'probatur' of approval by the auditor, but at least two other marks are also found,[298] and in D91.16 a distinctive long-tailed <z> (ʒ in the edited text) suggests a different auditor again. Some evidence may also be gleaned from the writing of 'probatur': in D91.20 for the year 1502–3 'probatur' is written 'p*ro*b*atur*', i.e. with the letters <p> and <b> written out and the rest contracted, but from the year 1503–4 (from p. 78) only <p> is written in full (and the rest contracted), suggesting that a different auditor/clerk took over at this point.[299]

As noted above, in the case of the MW hand, it has been possible to distinguish auditor (who switches scripts) from accountant (who does not switch scripts). This is less clear in the other hands. The most distinctive feature of what is here called the 'curly' hand is a single-stroke secretary <s> with a loosely curving ascender, but the scribe employs an elaborate delta version of this too (see Plate 16, where the first three entries are in the 'curly'

[296] Compare D102.10/149 (where the 'sprawling' hand writes the sum total formally as 'm^{l}m^{l}DCiiii^{xx}v') with p. 153, where the same hand informally uses 'iiij^{ml}'.

[297] See too D91.21/151 and 152 for mixed use in the 'sprawling' hand ('m^{l}vij^{C}xlii', 'DCC').

[298] See the Descriptions to the edited texts.

[299] The trefoil also appears to change from three dots with a tail to three black dots.

hand and the rest in the MW hand).[300] Similarly, Henry Hornby's loose, curling single-lobed <s> bears similarities with the more tightly curled <s> of the 'sprawling' hand.[301] However, the 'sprawling' hand is so distinctive in any sustained bout of writing that it is generally recognisable.

For example, in D102.10, Henry Hornby's book of receipts and payments, the 'sprawling' hand works closely with Hornby; again it is largely responsible for the summary material, i.e. the introductory and concluding material for each year and the entries around it. In this document the summary material is always informal and cursive.[302] However, it is possible that the 'sprawling' hand, so recognisable in its sprawling cursive hand, may be less recognisable in the formal Bastard Anglicana scripts of the summary material. Reference was made above (5.2) to a formal script perhaps used by the 'sprawling' hand: 'if it is the same hand that also writes in the formal Bastard Anglicana script (e.g. D102.1/18v), it is more disciplined and restrained'. Indeed, it might be the case that the summary material at both the beginning and end of D102.1 might be in the summary hand (it is the only chamber account that has an opening rubric in Latin, the preferred language of the 'sprawling' hand). One might further speculate, for example, that much of the summary material for the end of the years 1505–6 and 1506–7 (D91.21/70–80, 150–65), and perhaps for other ends (or even beginnings) of year, might be written in the 'sprawling' hand, but the fact disguised by the variety of scripts.[303] Interesting as this speculation is, it would probably be unwise to put the onus of too much copying, particularly routine draft copying of lists and summaries (as mentioned above), on the 'sprawling' hand, a hand whose duties are clearly senior and authoritative and who would be unlikely to take on the role of a copying clerk in normal circumstances. The term 'summary hand' is therefore used for all the summary material, and no attempt is made to identify the individual hands, apart from the 'sprawling' hand.

5.4 The Cursive Hands of the Accountants

There are five named hands in the documents, viz. William Bedell (D91.16), James Clarell (D91.17), Miles Worsley (D91.20, D91.21, D91.19), Robert Fremingham (D102.1), and Roger Ormeston (D102.2, D102.6). All of these

[300] For the 'curly' hand see below. It occurs sporadically throughout the chamber accounts (see Description to the edited texts).

[301] In the writing of 100s Hornby uses the superscript '^{C}', e.g. 'ii^{C}' (not 'CC'), 'vi^{C}' (not 'DC'), e.g. D102.10/11, 50. (Only Hornby's document, D102.10, employs such large numbers in the non-summary material.)

[302] Only the rubrics on pp. 151, 155, 159 are written in an approximation of the Bastard Anglicana script.

[303] Note the use of thorn even in the formal script throughout these pages.

announce themselves at the start of their documents, and sometimes within the documents, and it appears that they write in their own hands. Another hand which can be identified is that of Henry Hornby, who, as Lady Margaret's secretary, is largely responsible for D102.10, her own book of receipts and payments.[304] These hands all display a script which is a mixture of Anglicana and Secretary letter shapes (with a preponderance of one or the other), but the duct (i.e. the angle and direction of the pen and the pressure brought to bear on the pen) and the individual hand (the characteristics of the formation of letters, etc.) are usually sufficiently different to identify each hand when it occurs elsewhere. In English texts the preferred spellings and sometimes letters (e.g. 'th', written either as <þ> or <y> or <th>) provide helpful additional criteria by which to identify a hand.

5.4.1 The 'curly' hand

Most of the documents display evidence of other hands in the main body of the text, sometimes for just one or a few entries, sometimes recurring, sometimes for a longer stretch. The briefer entries cannot be more closely identified,[305] but one hand which is responsible for increasingly longer stints of work is called here the 'curly' hand. As an occasional scribe in the chamber accounts and Lady Margaret's household book, the 'curly' hand is tight and controlled, with a distinctive curly <I> in 'Itm' (first three items of 19/73, Plate 16). It uses the contractions 'm' for 'master' and 'Robrt' for 'Robert', and represents final –er as 'o' with a contraction to indicate 'ur', e.g. 'Peto*ur*' for 'Peter' (19/6, 7, 17, etc.). It occasionally uses distinctive spelling combinations, e.g. 'ue' as in 'nue' (19/95) and 'nct' in 'saincte' (19/93–5). It also favours the (by this date) semi-archaic weak plural ending in –n, now confined largely to the south of England, e.g. 'shone' for 'shoes' (20/124–5, 148), 'hosyn' for 'hose' 20/125, 148. This hand may perhaps be identified with that of Robert Fremingham, the accountant responsible for the whole of Lady Margaret's last chamber account, D102.1 (below), who, it has been suggested above, 2.1.3.3), may have derived from Farningham in Kent. The curly <I> is similar (but not invariable), as is a delicate up-stroke on a final secretary –e (this is common in secretary script, such as in Bedell's document, D91.16). Most distinctive in D102.1 is the <s> of 's.' ('solidi'), a secretary <s> with a delicate upward curve (Plate 17). Although this is different from the delta <s> most used by the 'curly' hand in the chamber documents,[306] those documents do

[304] For the ascriptions see below and the Descriptions to the edited texts.
[305] They are noted in footnotes to the edited texts.
[306] The <s> of the 'curly' hand entry totals in D91.20 and D91.21 normally emulates the MW <s> (or may indeed be written by the MW hand, who certainly writes the page totals). In D91.19

have occasional examples of the <s> of D102/1 in the 'curly' hand, e.g. D91.20/82–3, 85, 171, D91.21/25, 91. Compare, for example, the first two entries at D91.19/73 with the third, all in the 'curly' hand (Plate 16).[307] It may be that the two letter forms relate to some extent to a more or less formal style, since, for example, D91.19/96 displays the simpler <s> in the entries and the more elaborate <s> in the totals at the end of each entry.[308]

5.4.2 The hand of D91.16 (SJLM/1/1/1/1) (Plates 1–4)

Apart, perhaps, from the rubric at the top of sheet 1d ('Croydon et Hatfeld. Computus Willelmi Bedell'), this Latin roll appears to be written in one hand, which uses a Bastard Anglicana court hand for rubrics, marginal headings and formulaic material (e.g. 'Et debet', 'Et remanent', etc.) and a cursive hand (Anglicana with Secretary influence) for the main body of the text. The cursive hand writes smoothly and fluently in a small hand using a fine nib, with an occasional awkward feature derived from his familiarity with court hand, e.g. an occasional square-cornered <o>. The scribe's <d> noticeably slants to the left with a pointed lobe, while descenders flourish to the right, e.g. <h>. The hand appears to be that of the treasurer and originator of the document, William Bedell ('Infrascriptus Willelmus reddit computum de', sheet 1d), i.e. the undersigned William renders account. This is confirmed by a rental in Bedell's hand when he was receiver general for the Buckingham estates managed by Lady Margaret during the nonage of her ward, the third duke.[309]

Occasional alterations appear to be in the same hand, e.g. sheet 9 (end of sheet calculations), as do interim calculations, which are usually to the right at the foot of a sheet but sometimes to the right after a section, e.g. sheet 2 (before 'Stuffura'). Such calculations are preceded (less commonly, followed) by a long-tailed <z> (ȝ in the edited text), which appears to act as a checking

---

a more elaborate delta <s> is used, and the page totals are often in this hand when it is responsible for the entries.

[307] Compare, for example, the 's.' ('solidi') of the page totals of 19/28 (delta) and 29 (simple), or the mixed 's.' of the entry totals at 19/98, 105. Note also the single example in the twelfth entry of D91.20/126 and the first entry of D91.21/26.

[308] It appears to be the same hand as SJCA D91.4 (SJLM/2/2/2), Robert Hilton's 1509 Hatfield inventory of the wardrobe of robes, with which Bedell and Morice were also involved (p. 22). The document refers several times to Fremingham and the purchases of cloth made by him and recorded in his account book (pp. 1, 5–6, 9–12, 14–15). James Clarell, the first recorded cofferer, may also have been involved in the purchase of cloth for Lady Margaret (see 2.1.3.1 above), and both Clarell and Fremingham had responsibility for writing the chamber accounts at different times (in D91.17 and D102.1).

[309] WAM 32364 (in particular, the <d> is distinctive). For Bedell's role in the Buckingham estates: Rawcliffe, *The Staffords*, pp. 56, 200, 201. It is conceivable, but not ascertainable, that both documents are in the hand of his deputy, John Bedell (not mentioned in Rawcliffe).

mark, e.g. sheets 9 and 12 (where the symbol may have been added later to the right of the calculation), sheet 12d and after (where it occurs before marginal annotations), and from sheet 20d on (alongside 'Et remanent'). It would seem likely that another hand than the main one was responsible for these checks, but (as noted above) there is no visible difference; even an apparent difference between the main hand's vertical double-lobed <s> on the line and corrections in a horizontal superscript double-lobed <s> in 's.' for 'solidi', e.g. sheet 8 (calculation for 'Allocacio stuffure'), may be a random variation.[310] 'Probatur' (^{P} in the edited text) is rare (twice on sheet 8 and once on sheet 11), and it may be that the long-tailed <z> is the check mark of the auditor or his clerk, or even of an internal checker, although its form is exactly that of <z> as used by the main hand, e.g. 'bz' (bushels) sheet 3d. Another symbol, perhaps to be read as 'nA' ('nota(tur)'?) but probably just a decorative feature, is frequently used from p. 22 to introduce a bracket after a marginal subheading and is not reproduced in the edited text. On the dorse, which is templated, seemingly in the same hand, annotations about the remaining stock become common, again seemingly in the same hand and, even if added later (sometimes apparent from a different shade of ink),[311] written in the same hand usually straight after the total of remaining stock, e.g. sheets 15d and 19d (the fate of the four remaining cades of sprats, or of the figs). The speed and neatness suggests throughout that the details have been copied from a draft rather than added extempore.

5.4.3 The hand of D102.10 (SJLM/1/1/6/1) (Plates 5–7)

Unlike the other accounts, no specific name is attached to D102.10, although the main hand can be identified from other extant documents. D102.10 is Lady Margaret's own book, kept for her by her secretary, Henry Hornby, dean of chapel and later chancellor of the household. It is several times referred to as 'my ladys boke of receytes and paymentes' (D91.19/3) and similar, and it was kept up throughout the period of her final ten years (it runs from 1 January 1499 beyond her death, 29 June 1509, until 3 October of that year). It is a workaday book, without Lady Margaret's signature or any clear intervention by an auditor, although, as noted above, the 'sprawling' hand, which is assumed to be that of an auditor, occurs often, especially at the start and end of a year's details of receipts into, or deliveries from, the treasury.

Although Hornby does not specifically acknowledge it as his own hand, nor is the book specifically acknowledged in the text as Lady Margaret's, this

[310] For example, the correction at the end of 'Empcio multonum' (sheet 9) is definitely in the same hand as the entry, but uses the horizontal <s> for 's.'.

[311] See the footnotes to sheets 18d–19d.

may be because it appears to begin imperfect with a badly-damaged first page. As just noted, it is occasionally referred to in other documents as her own book, and these cross-references can be verified in D102.10 (see 4.2 above). As for Hornby as its main scribe, his hand is attested by the note 'Per me H. Hornby' (p. 77) alongside two cancelled items in the same hand (the phrase 'the HH hand' will nevertheless be used, in line with the nomenclature of other hands). More evidence is provided by a note in his hand sewn to p. 66 of D91.17 (Plate 9), and if the loosely curved <I/J> of that note may contrast with the distinctive flat horizontal top stroke of <I/J> in D102.10 (esp. in the frequent examples of 'Item'), an insertion into and below the sixth clause of SJCA D6.4 (not yet re-catalogued), one of the four versions of an agreement to convert St John's Hospital into St John's College, is clearly in the same hand, beginning with 'In' and 'Idem' respectively, displaying the same <I> as D102.10 (see Plate 6).[312]

Hornby writes an easy, loose, cultured hand, much influenced by the Secretary script, e.g. <a> and <g>,[313] and with no use of the thorn or yogh. There appear to be no distinctive features of spelling, beyond the normal variation of the period; the abbreviation of 'master' is 'm*aster*' with a broad stroke sweeping to the left below the <m> and curving over the top to end in a <t>. The hand differs markedly from the 'sprawling' hand, which first appears lower down p. 18 to record extra receipts at the time of the audit of January 1501 and then reappears in similar contexts, i.e. at the end and beginning of sections of dated receipts/deliveries, throughout the document, e.g. pp. 19–21 (receipts April 1501), 33–4 (receipts at the audit January 1504), 61–2 (extra deliveries to the treasury 1503), etc. In line with its lack of neatness, it may be capable of writing differently at different times (see especially the footnote to p. 135 in the edited text).[314] The 'curly' hand, i.e. Fremingham, appears occasionally (see footnotes to the edited text).

Of interest in D102.10 is the fact that some pages between pp. 126–33 (some of which, but not all, were left blank when the pages were first written up) have been used by Lady Margaret's executors to record transactions after her death. Apart from Hornby's own hand, the two other main hands can be identified as those of Hugh Ashton (in particular the duct of this square stocky hand and his distinctive writing of 'I'/'J'),[315] and John Fisher (a spiky

[312] The addition directly after the clause, dated 12 March 1508 (24th regnal year), must have been required of her secretary by Lady Margaret, who signs it after Hornby.

[313] As, incidentally, does Lady Margaret in her signature.

[314] The writing of 's.' ('solidi') in several different-looking entries confirms that they are likely all to be in the 'sprawling' hand.

[315] Comparison with the bill of deposit D56.12 (SJLM/7/1/1) confirms the hand.

italic hand, very distinctive).[316] (See Plate 7, and see footnotes to the edited text for full details of their interventions.)

5.4.4 The hand of D91.17 (SJLM/1/1/2/1) (Plates 8–9)

The rubrics and initial and final material of D91.17 (pp. 1–5, 66–67) are written in a Bastard Anglicana script, while the main body of the text is in an Anglicana/Secretary cursive hand. Both the formal and cursive scripts have yogh (edited here as <z>) for genitive singular or (all cases) plural -s when no abbreviation is used (e.g. 'arreragez' p. 4, 'rewardez', 'costez', 'chargez', pecez' p. 19, Plate 8); both use a distinctive tall 2-lobed Anglicana <a>, noticeable especially when single or in second-letter position (e.g. 'paymentes' p. 66, Plate 9; 'payde', p. 27); both use initial ff- (e.g. 'ffest' p. 1, 'ffeachynge' p. 42). It is therefore possible that the document is entirely in one hand, which switches from formal to informal script. James Clarell identifies himself as the cofferer of the document (p. 1) and frequently refers to himself in the third person.[317] We may assume therefore that he was responsible for writing the document, the first chamber account extant, which largely deals with Lady Margaret's riding household in the summer of 1498.[318] There are occasional marginal notes in another (tall thin) hand, e.g. 'Conysby' (once), 'Shoyng' (often),[319] similar to the hand of a marginal 'Null' in a much later document, D102.1/2r (where it may be in the same hand as the informal summary material on the same page). Corrections to the sums are rare, but at the foot of p. 48 is a sum total in Clarell's hand which has then been cancelled and replaced by a new sum total (both are marked 'probatur') in a different hand, presumably that of an auditor; this other hand is also responsible for the Latin annotation.[320] The long-tailed <z> of D91.16 is also found as a checking mark in D91.17, but only with 'probatur' and only from pp. 54–60. Lady Margaret signs below the sum totals.

[316] See, for example, D57.17 (SJLM/7/8/1) in which Fisher writes to William Bolton, prior of St Bartholomew's, Smithfield, asking him to pay £4 to Roger Notte, and D57.18 (SJLM/7/8/2) in which Fisher writes to Sir Thomas Mawdesley, asking him to deliver to Mr Parker £9, the residue of the £19 due to Parker at the christening of his children. For a comparable italic hand see Thomas More's Latin hand: Anthony G. Petti, *English literary hands from Chaucer to Dryden* (London: Arnold, 1977), Plate 18 (p. 66).

[317] See the Description to the edited text.

[318] Intervening chamber accounts are missing between D91.17 and D91.20, i.e. between January 1499 and February 1502.

[319] For page references, see the Description of the edited text.

[320] The correcting hand represents 's.' in 'solidi' as a single tight lobe with an ascender curling tightly to the left (as also the correction at D91.17/58); Clarell uses a broken lobe with an ascender drifting to the right. The tight-lobed <s> occurs throughout all the accounts, although in formal script a double-lobed <s> with an ascender moving from the middle to the right is also found.

5.4.5 The hand of D91.20, D91.21, D91.19 (SJLM/1/1/3/1, SJLM/1/1/3/2, SJLM/1/1/3/3) (Plates 10–16)

The main body of the accounts is in a current hand, seemingly that of Miles Worsley according to the entries in D91.20/5 ('In primis of my debt of my last accountes') and D91.21/22 ('Item in exspenc*e* at Coldherbor*e* and for my botte hyre at suche tyme I receyved money'), where the entry is annotated 'Myles Worsley' in the same hand (Plate 14). Although this ascription is in D91.21, all the chamber accounts except the final one, D102.1, are written mainly in the MW hand. This (mostly Secretary) hand uses Secretary <a> and <g> and an elaborate <R> and distinctive <B>. In fast writing the hand slopes slightly to the right, and the digraph <th> is often written as a single curving letter. The spelling has distinctive characteristics, e.g. the digraph <ai> ('maister', e.g. 20/61, 21/8, 19/5; 'maistres/z'/'maystrez', e.g. 20/54, 21/22, 19/9; 'spaice', e.g. 20/62, 21/21, 19/74; 'waiges'/'wayges', e.g. 20/90, 21/33, 19/78), and the yogh, which is used both for /z/ (e.g. 'daiez', 20/92, 21/33, 19/76, etc.) and /j/ (e.g. 'Lydeȝard' 19/36).[321] Contractions include '(un)t' with a short flourish (for '(un)to'), 'm' with a flourish under to the left and over to the right (for 'maister'), 'wth' (for 'with'), and 'It' with a flourish (for 'Item'). The initial and final <ff> is common (but only medial and final <ff> is transcribed in the edited text), e.g. 'off', or 'ffol(l)er', the surname of Edith Fowler, one of Lady Margaret's six gentlewomen, always found in the MW hand (and no other) with this spelling. There are occasional northern dialect features, e.g. <aw> (for <ou>, <ow>, e.g. 'sawdyor' 20/97, 'awne' 21/109), <ss> in 'wassyng' (e.g. 20/182; 21/12, 62, 94; 19/86, etc.), <qu> (for <w(h)>, and the <y> form of <þ>, which was itself an old-fashioned form at this date, <th> being usual.[322] In particular <qu> for <wh> is a northern feature which the accountant tries to suppress: at D91.21/27 'quytyng' is altered to 'whytynge', at p. 45 'quyte' to 'whyte', and at p. 51 the MW hand starts to use <q>, which he then cancels, writing 'white' instead.[323] Not a northern feature (it is one associated with London from the sixteenth through to the nineteenth centuries) is <w> for <v> and vice versa, e.g. 'Vestmynster' 21/112, 'wesselles' 21/113, 'wellom' 21/111, 19/83, 'wewe' 19/47, etc. Occasionally there is an excrescent –th, e.g. 'Davyth' 21/97 ('Davy' 21/103, 106). Other significant

[321] Since these forms (apart from 'maister', often anyway abbreviated) are not regularly found, they may indicate a native dialect surfacing occasionally (although they might relate to the copytexts, i.e. drafts, bills, etc.).

[322] The 'y'-type thorn (not reproduced here) is particularly found in relative clauses with 'þat', e.g. 'a woman of Dodyngton þ*at* kepes Nicholas Aughton chylde', 'a frer*e* of Stampforth þat prechud' (20/112, 150), but also (rarely) in 'þe' and 'þis'. The summary hand also uses <þ>, but not in the <y> form, e.g. 21/67, 71, 80, 150, 152, 154 (x 2), 156, 159–61.

[323] For Worsley's presumed northern connections (and that of other members of the household): Powell, 'Lady Margaret Beaufort as Patron', p. 111.

features of this hand include the spellings ‘servand(e)’, ‘wardrop(p)’ and, ‘afoure’ (rare, e.g. 21/114).

D91.20 is the earliest of the documents. As noted above, the ‘curly’ hand appears from time to time from p. 28, the letter forms very similar to the Worsley hand, but consistently using a cramped and curly <I> in ‘Itm’, while the Worsley hand uses a loose curving <I> with usually just a flourish after the -t- of ‘Item’. It prefers ‘master’ and ‘mastres’ (not the <ai> of the Worsley hand) and ‘Fowler’ to ‘Foller’, both with ff-; ‘master’ is abbreviated to <m> with a curling tail from the right below the body of the letter and back up over the top to the right with a <t> through it. As noted above, the ‘curly’ hand is also found in D91.21 and D91.19, and is particularly frequent in D91.19, and it seems to be identifiable with the hand of D102.1 (discussed below). Other hands may also be involved, but variation in letter forms and duct may simply be the result of Worsley starting new stints, although a difference in material and spelling sometimes suggests a new hand, as noted above (5), when a list of payments to Robert Hilton, clerk of the wardrobe, on D91.21/31–2 appears noticeably different from the previous pages, including the abbreviation ‘pd’ for ‘paid’ rather than the usual full spelling.

Marginal headings to D91.20 are often provided in the Worsley hand and cite the person or occasion to which the item refers, but marginal notes and comments may date from any period of the document in a variety of hands; they may then be the result of later checking or editing of the document, e.g. D91.20/90–1, 96–7. Lady Margaret signs most pages ‘Margaret R’ below the last entry (^{M} in the edited text). Alongside (and sometimes mid-page) is a ‘Summa’, i.e. a sum total of the page (or part of page, or pages), written in the MW hand and usually corrected in the same hand. This is marked ‘probatur’ (^{P} in the edited text), sometimes with a symbol which may indicate different auditors, e.g. a trefoil or a cross.[324] Sometimes a correction is in a hand different from the MW hand and can be assumed to be that of the auditor (where discernible, these are noted in the footnotes to the edited text).[325] In all three documents there are Latin marginal annotations, often written in a thick nib and black ink (as used in the large Bastard Anglicana rubrics) and often marked with a + (which also marks some entries without comments, e.g. 20/109), which record details relating to the sum of an entry, e.g. first entry 20/91, penultimate entry 21/28, ninth entry 19/6.

[324] See the Descriptions to the edited texts, and note the different representations of ‘probatur’ in D91.20, discussed above (5.3).

[325] They are mainly discernible by the different use of the <s> in ‘s.’ (‘solidi’), as mentioned above.

5.4.6 The hand of D102.1 (SJLM/1/1/5/1) (Plate 17)

This last account of Lady Margaret provides some interesting evidence about both the 'curly' and 'sprawling' hands. The 'sprawling' hand, as discussed above, seems to be responsible for the usual interventions in the summaries (certainly f. 16r-v), but the uneven large Bastard Anglicana script of the opening Latin rubric, as well as the tall thin hand of the smaller formal script (both to be seen on f. 2r),[326] also display the same letter forms as the cursive script of the 'sprawling' hand. This is perhaps particularly evident at f. 18v, where the annotation of the cancelled last entry of the whole document seems to be written in the same hand as the entry, and indeed the whole page of the document (which itself compares with all the summary material). It is possible that the 'sprawling' hand is switching (cursorily) between styles in completing the whole of the summary material himself. And, as again noted above, this raises questions about the summary hand in other documents, and what part the 'sprawling' hand may have played in the more formal parts of the summaries.

The main hand of the document, as argued above, appears to be the 'curly' hand of the earlier documents. In terms of spelling, rare features of the 'curly' hand noted above are more common in D102.1, that is, 'nue' (also 'Andrue') and 'saincte' at ff. 6r-v, 10r-v and ff. 4r, 15r, respectively. However, distinctive features of D102.1 are a marked use of –esse, e.g. 'maistres(se)' f. 4r (but cf. 'maisteresse' D91.20/126), 'Frauncesse' f. 12v, 'quincesse' f. 13r.[327] Other distinctive spellings are 'ai'/'ei'/'ie' in 'mariaige', 'portaige', 'knowleige' and 'wief' (ff. 5r-v, 8r, 9r-v). Otherwise the spelling in D102.1 is very variable: 'mastir', 'master/mastres', 'maister/maistres', and once 'maisteresse', as noted above, and there are relatively few contractions. It may be the case that the greater idiosyncracies of D102.1 relate to a greater freedom in Fremingham's responsibility for the whole account and his inclination to use his own preferred forms more than those of his copy-text (although the possible influence of a scribe's copy-text must always be borne in mind).[328]

This 'greater freedom' arises from the fact that Fremingham was entirely responsible for this last account of Lady Margaret's life, when he was standing in as treasurer of the chamber (presumably for Miles Worsley, who was

[326] For the large formal script see also ff. 2v–3r, 16v, 18r-v, and for the smaller formal script ff. 17r–18v. (Where appropriate, large and smaller formal scripts interact on the same page, with the sprawling 'cursive' script most evident in interventions, such as the calculations on f. 16v.)

[327] While this might suggest a different hand from the 'curly' hand, the spelling in D102.1 is very variable: 'mastir', 'master/mastres', 'maister/maistres', and once 'maisteresse', as noted above; there are relatively few contractions.

[328] As, for example, in the single northern form, 'awner' (i.e. owner), found only at f. 9v; Fremingham otherwise displays no specific regional characteristics.

perhaps involved in other matters after her death).[329] The 'curly' hand appears first in an entry for 18 June 1503 (D91.20/28) but not in Lady Margaret's household book (D102.10) until p. 112 (23 August 1506). It then occurs increasingly over the years, particularly in 1508 (D91.19/89–109), as one might expect if Fremingham were becoming a more senior member of the counting house.[330]

5.4.7 The hand of D102.2 and D102.6 (SJLM/1/1/4/1, SJLM/1/1/4/2) (Plate 18)

This document (now in two parts, D102.2 and D102.6) is dated 1501 and is therefore earlier than all the other documents edited here, apart from D91.17. It appears, like the other account books, to have been written by the officer responsible for the accounts, in this case Ormeston himself,[331] with the rubrics and summary material at beginning and end written in the summary hand.[332] Ormeston's is a very distinctive hand in appearance and spelling choices; it is also a sometimes fast, illegible and/or inaccurate hand, with particular confusion over the forms of e/o/(a), and an odd choice of vowel in 'Jon', 'Joly', 'Somma' (where –u- would be expected).[333] In script it is Anglicana with Secretary elements, and in duct it is tall and spiky. There is a noticeable flourish on many words (here represented as –e). The old-fashioned yogh <ʒ> is used both finally, where its phonological value is /z/ and it is edited here as <z> (e.g. 'harnesez', 'porcolyez' p. 3), but also initially, where it means /j/ (e.g. 'ʒere', p. 5), and medially (e.g. 'bowʒht', 'browʒht', pp. 5, 25), where it must by this date be merely an alternative form of <g> without phonological value.[334] The old-fashioned thorn <þ>, written as <y>, is also used, e.g. in the phrase 'Memorandum þat' (D102.2/3 (Plate 18), 5, 7, 21),[335] although its equivalent, the digraph <th>, is found too. An excrescent h- is found occasionally, e.g. 'helne' (ell), 'heyge' (edge) (pp. 28, 29), and 'off' is preferred (like the summary hand). The northern vowel combination of –ai- occurs in 'haith' (pp. 3, 5), and 'mast*er*' and 'mast*er*is' are the preferred contracted forms. Spelling is

[329] Worsley's own death, or ill health, is a possibility. He was not at Henry VII's funeral, nor is he mentioned in her will nor in the later 'Rewardes' (see Appendix).

[330] For details see the Descriptions to the edited texts.

[331] 'I Roger Urmyston', pp. 3, 5; 'by me Roger Urmyston', p. 7, etc.

[332] The summary hand uses more elaborate forms of 's.' ('solidi') than the RO hand, which uses a looser single-lobed <s> with a high loose curve to the right.

[333] The illegibility improves a little with the change of nib at D102.2/17; for the inaccuracies see the footnotes passim, especially those for pp. 9–32 where the cloth calculations have all been checked for this edition. Some words are especially hard to elucidate, and 'Alderbornedyne' at p. 30 has eluded the present editor.

[334] In the edited texts, <z> is used finally but <ʒ> initially and medially.

[335] This northern feature has also been noted in the MW hand (5.4.5 above).

very idiosyncratic, e.g. 'my ladys grasse',[336] 'Herr' with a flourish for Henry/Harry, 'Watour' for Walter,[337] or the sentence: 'Item paid the same day for xliiii loodes off sownd browʒght to Goldherbare. Price the loyd iiii d.' (p. 25).[338] Ormeston's age and/or infirmity may account for some of the characteristics and problems of his hand. As noted above (2.1.4), the date of his last submitted payment was 4 March 1504 (D91.20/191), shortly before he died and just two years after the completion of D102.2 and D102.6. At the start and end of the 1504–5 financial year references are made to his executors (D91.20/144, 194). He was to be replaced as chamberlain by Lady Margaret's kinsman, Sir John St John II of Bletsoe.

5.5 The Signature Hand

Finally, given that all we have in these documents of Lady Margaret's own hand is her signature, the reader may be directed to a letter (TNA SC 1/51/189) in her own hand, a cultured secretary hand, dated by The National Archives [1497?] and so just prior to the earliest of the documents edited here. In this letter to Thomas Butler, earl of Ormond, she uses the signature 'M Rychemound', whereas in all the accounts after her independent settlement at Collyweston her signature is 'Margaret R'. As Jones and Underwood have noted, this was a change from the normal aristocratic sign manual (initial plus title) to one 'distinctly regal, mirroring the king's "HR", employed since 1492, and the queen's "Elizabeth R"'. Jones and Underwood remain uncommitted as to whether the distinctly regal Lady Margaret intended 'R' for 'Richmond' or for 'Regina'.[339]

[336] Cf. 'gresse' (grease), 'peysse' (piece), and even 'thysse' (this), etc. (pp. 35, 22, 11, etc.). The spellings 'grasse' and 'gresse' (and perhaps others) may reflect northern pronunciations at this date.

[337] D102.2/7, cf. 'Water Reve' D102.6/5. Recorded by sixteenth-century orthoepists as the pronunciation of the time.

[338] See too the footnotes to D102.2/14, 31.

[339] Historical novelists (such as Philippa Gregory, *The Red Queen*) have been less reticent.

D91.16 (SJLM/1/1/1/1) Latin roll (*computus provisionis*): household expenses and stock account of William Bedell treasurer of the household, 13 January 1506 – 13 January 1507, Croydon and Hatfield.

Discussion See Introduction 4 and Plates 1–4.

Description Paper, in the form of a Chancery fashion roll, written on both sides (edges frayed, right side torn in three places sheets 1–2, repaired and restitched 1977). Sheet size approx. 390 x 285 mm.[1] (approx. 45 mm. of first sheet turned inwards, away from dorse, and down with '1d' (MGU) and (later) 'SJLM/1/1/1/1' upside down top right, i.e. the first page of the dorse). 32 sheets slip-stitched (1977) head to tail, paginated per sheet top left 1–32, dorse 1d–32d (27–32, 32d blank). Left margin variable, approx. 45–75 mm. (contains headings); right margin variable; upper and lower margins not applicable. Roll cased in a rectangular grey conservation-grade boxboard box with tie ('SJLM/1/1/1/1' on white pasted slip),[2] replacing the waterproof buckram cylinder of 1977 . One main hand (Anglicana/Secretary), probably that of William Bedell; rubrics in a formal Bastard Anglicana script.[3] Sum totals within the text and at the foot of the page, as well as corrections and confirmation of corrections, appear to be in the same hand and are marked by a long-tailed <z> (^{3} in the edited text). The usual mark of an auditor's confirmation ('probatur') occurs only three times, twice on sheet 8 and once on sheet 11 (^{P} in the edited text). Lady Margaret's signature does not occur.

Summary

FRONT: Rubric (Croydon and Hatfield, Bedell, 13 January 1506 – 13 January 1507, i.e. years **21–22**), arrears of previous year (1505) and value of remaining stuff, 1; receipts: cash receipts and stuff sold outside household, 2; receipts from pastures and meadows managed for the use of the household, 3; gifts in kind from several persons, woollen cloth sold outside the wardrobe, 4; hides, skins, suet, 5; wool, intestines, wheat, bread, white candles, 6; receipts from outside the household, 7–8; sum total of receipts and arrears, and allowances for the stuff left over and the gifts in kind, 8; expenses: the purchase of corn, ale and beer, wine, cattle, sheep, 9; pasture rented, the purchase of livestock, salted fish, 10; spices, rushes, 11; salt, oil, candles and wax, rewards to several persons, firewood, 12–13; payments outside the household, 13; 'necessary payments' (a catch-all), items bought for the chapel children and for the

[1] Sheet length normally varies little: the original length was 400 mm., as demonstrated by the unstitched first and last sheets; however, 7/7d is only 180 mm. long.

[2] This dates from the 2014–15 repair and conservation.

[3] The rubric on the dorse (1d) may be in a different hand.

kitchen boys, horse livery, diet for servants, livery cloth, 14; fresh purchases, wages, 15; sum total of allowances to treasurer, his debt and further allowances, 16; debts owed to treasurer, balance of his account (nothing owed), 17–21; cash value of stock remaining 13 January 1506: granary, bakehouse, pastry house, pantry, 22; buttery, cellar, cattle, sheep, poultry, wet and dry larders, 23–4; chandlery, fuel, hay, 24; oats, scullery, spicery, 25–6; sum total of stuff remaining, 26

DORSE: Rubric (Croydon and Hatfield, Bedell, 13 January 1506 – 13 January 1507), 1d. [Commodities by volume: each item deals with the amount left over at the end of the previous year, the amount consumed during the year, and the balance, together with any allowances.] wheat, 1d–2d; wheatmeal, 2d–3d; bread (manchets), 3d;bread (chets and trencher bread), ale, 4d; beer, Gascon wine, 5d; sweet wine, 6d; oxen, 7d–8d; heifers, cows, 8d; carcases of oxen, heifers and cows, sheep, 9d–10d; carcases of sheep, calves 10d–11d; lambs, pigs, 11d; wool, pigs, 12d; ling, cod, salt cod, stockfish, 13d; sturgeon, salted salmon, salted eels, salted conger, white herring, 14d; red herring, sprats, 15d; oil, 15d–16d; honey, white candles, 16d; wax, 16d–17d; rosin, large wax candles, 17d; supperlights, sizes and prickets, wax candles (two types), 18d; wick, 18d–19d; figs, large raisins, 19d; candied fruit, preserves, coarse and whole sugar, powdered sugar, sugar from Crete, 20d; sugar from Valencia, currants, pepper, grains, cloves, 21d; mace, nutmeg, sanders, 22d; large cinnamon, 22d–23d; small cinnamon, ginger, capers, pickled olives, 23d; dates, sweetmeats (four types), 24d; green ginger, lemons and candied fruit, pickled lemons, quinces in syrup, oranges in syrup, 25d; English saffron, 25d–26d; confections, prunes, almonds, turnsole, rice, 26d; blanchpowder, 26d–27d; liquorice powder, galangal, agnus castus seed, honey, salad oil, 27d; frankincense, fine and coarse strainers, paper (three types), 28d; white and black soap, oats, 29d; beans and peas, hay, 30d; firewood, 30d–31d; bark, woollen cloth, 31d [32d blank]

Edited Text

[*sheet 1*] *Croydon et Hatf\eleld Episcopi.* Computus Willelmi Bedell thesauraurii hospicii excellentissime principisse Margarete comitisse Richmondie et Derbeie ac matris domini regis nunc Henrici septimi ibidem a xiii° die Januarii anno xxi° regni regis Henrici \vii°/ predicti usque xiii^{um} diem mensis Januarii extunc proximo sequenti anno dicti domini regis <x> xxii^{do} inclusive scilicet per unum annum integrum.

Arreragia. De arreragiis ultimi computi finientis predicto xiii° die Januarii anno xxi° regni regis Henrici vii predicti ut pro tantis denariis pendentibus super diversas personas prout in pede eiusdem computi plenius patet … Clxxiii li. ix s. vi d. ob.

Precium stuffure de remanentia in fine ultimi computi. De precio diverse stuffure remanentis non expendite in fine dicti ultimi \computi/ finientis predicto xiii° die

Januarii anno xxi° regni regis Henrici vii° supradicti prout in pede eiusdem computi particulare patet … CCCCxviii li. xxi [d. qua.][4]

[*sheet 2*] *Denarii recepti extra cofuram domine principisse per indenturam.* De denariis receptis de predicta principissa ad diversas vices infra tempus huius computi ut patet per billam indentatam inter predictam principissam et ipsum computantem confectam datam xvi die Januarii anno xxi° regni regis nunc Henrici vii predicti huic computo annexatam … MMviii li. xii s. vii d. ob.

[3]MMDC li. iii s. xi d. qua.[5]

Stuffura vendita extra hospicium.[6]

De precio vi qr. ii bus. frumenti venditorum extra hospicium infra tempus huius computi precio bus. ix d. sic venditorum Willelmo Warre et aliis prout in dorso huius computi patet[7] … xxxvii s. vi d.

De precio xxx bus. salis de Bay venditorum extra hospicium predictum infra tempus huius computi sic venditorum Thome Hyll ingrosso etc. … ix s. xi d.

De precio unius congre <salis> salse vendite infra tempus huius computi sic vendite domine Johanne Haw prout in dorso huius computi patet … xii d.

De precio <vi> <\xxvi/> \vi/ multonum debilium venditorum extra hospicium infra tempus huius computi sic venditorum ingrosso Roberto Hopkyn ut in dorso patet … v s.

De precio xx multonum <s> venditorum extra hospicium Thome Snow de Croydon pecia pro xii d. ut in dorso huius computi patet … xx s.

De precio lxv carectarum corticis nuper remanentium apud Colyweston sic venditarum Johanni Thomson de Depyng barker ingrosso per recognicionem dicti computantis super hunc computum … vii li. xiii s.

[3]xi li. vi s. v d.[8]

[*sheet 3*] *Diverse pasture et prata domine reservate ad usum hospicii eiusdem.* De denariis receptis de diversis ministris computabilibus prefate principisse et pro redditibus et firmis diversarum pasturarum et pratorum reservatorum tam pro agistamento boum et multonum provisis pro hospicio predicto quam pro expensis equorum eiusdem principisse etc. videlicet \<viii li. ix s.> x li. v s. viii d./ de ballivo de Ware ut pro firma xviii acrarum prati in Closelaunde liiii s. x acrarum prati in Chaldwell xxx s. \iii acraris prati in Burymede ix s./ precio feni decimalis ibidem empti viii s. et pro falcacione

[4]The rest of the calculation is lost through damage to the right edge; the total below shows that the missing material is 'd. qua.'.

[5]The total of 'Arreragia', 'Precium stuffure' and 'Denarii recepti', written small in the same hand below the right-bracketed sum of 'Denarii recepti'.

[6]Each marginal heading covers the items until the next marginal heading; brackets are not used until sheet 22 ('Garnare').

[7]Warre is not mentioned on the dorse, nor Haw, Hopkyn or Snow (but for Snow, see sheet 21). The reference must be to 'lez hepes' of corn (sheet 1d).

[8]The total of the 'Stuffura', written small in the same hand to the right at the foot of the sheet.

fenifacture et cariagio herbagii provenientis de pasturis predictis lxviii s. necnon pro firma retroherbagii xvii acrarum prati in Chaldwell et Burymede x s. ac pro firma herbagii parci ibidem xxvi s. viii d. [9]Preposito de Chesthunt \xliii s. iiii d./ pro precio xiiii carectarum feni de ipso habitarum xxxvii s. iiii d. et pro cariagio et mo[d]iacione dicti feni etc. vi s. Ballivo de Burne \x li./ pro firma unius magni clausi de novo inclusi infra mariscam domine ibidem. Ballivo de West Depyng \liii s. viii d./ pro firma xxviii acrarum di. prati xxxvii s. et pro falcacione fenifacture et cariagio herbagii provenientis de prato predicto xvi s. viii d. et pro falcacione fenifacture et cariagio herbagii provenientis de dicto prato lii s. et ballivo de Colyweston \xl s./ pro firma cuiusdem pasture ibidem vocate le Serte. In toto ut in computis predictorum minist[r]orum pro uno anno integro finienti ad festum sancti Michaelis archangeli anno xxii^{do} regni regis Henrici vii plenius patet … xxxv li. xiii s. v d.

[*sheet 4*] *Exennia data prefate principisse per diversas personas.* De denariis per ipsum computantem receptis ut in precio diversorum exenniorum prefate principisse infra tempus huius computi datorum videlicet vi boum iiii li. x multonum xvi s. viii d. vi capriolorum <iiii> \ii/ s. xlvii signett*es* iiii li. xiiii s. ix signett*es* de stauro domine xviii s. vi cranes viii s. iiii^{xx}vii fesanorum lviii s. xix pavonum xix s. iiii^{xx}v perdicum xiiii s. ii d. <Cxix> \lix/ quayles ix s. x d. xiiii bytt*ou*rs ix s. iiii d. iiii^{xx}xiii teles xiiii s. v d. xvi shovelers x s. viii d. xlix herons xxxii s. viii d. iiii^{xx}xi caponum xxx s. iiii d. quinque gallinarum x d. xii pull*es* xii d. xii malard*es* ii s. Clvii cuniculorum xix s. xi d. ob. xxiiii lez rabett*es* ii s. i pecie rumbi recepte v s. i salmonis recepti ii s. iii dentricum iii s. quinque lez tenches xx d. ii lez gonard*es* viii d. x roches viii d. i barell vini dulcis vocati osey x s. xlvi quync*es* ii s. et iii carectarum feni dati per episcopum Roffensem \v s./. In toto ut in libro provisionis de tempore huius computi in titulo Regarda pro huius exenniis plenius apparet ultra diversos cervos et damas dicte principesse datos hic non specificatos etc. … xxiii li. <xiiii> \xii s./ vi d. ob.

[3]<xxxx> lix li. v s. xi d. ob.[10]

Pan[n]um laneum venditum extra garderobam domine. De precio xxv virg. i quart*er* panni lanei venditarum extra garderobam domine diversis serviencibus hospicii eiusdem domine infra tempus huius computi ad diversa precia ut in dorso huius computi plenius patet[11] … Ciiii s. viii d.

[3]Ciiii s. viii d.[12]

[*sheet 5*] *Vendicio corriorum boum bovettorum vaccarum et vitulorum.*

De precio Cxxxiii corriorum boum provenientium de bobus ad usum hospicii predicti infra tempus huius computi necatis sic venditis <sic venditis> diversis \personis/ pecia

[9] 'Preposito ...vi s.' is preceded by ///, 'Ballivo de Burne ...ibidem' by //, 'Ballivo de West Depyng' by // (as a means of separating them).

[10] The total of the 'Diverse pasture' and 'Exennia' (sheets 3–4), written small in the same hand below the right-bracketed sum totals.

[11] See sheet 30d.

[12] The total of the 'Pannum laneum' written small in the same hand to the right at the foot of the sheet, followed by a large gap.

pro iii s. iiii d. sed minus in toto iii s. iiii d. prout in dorso huius computi plenius patet[13] ... xxii[14] li. <vi s. viii d.>

De precio iiii corriorum boum provenientium de tot bobus infra tempus huius computi mortuis ex morina venditis Roberto None pecia pro ii s. ut in dorso huius computi patet ... vi s.

De aliquibus proficiis provenientibus de vendicione corriorum vitulorum infra tempus huius computi provisorum et ad usum hospicii predicti per dictum tempus necatorum. Nichil hic in onere eo quod conceduntur clericis dicti hospicii nomine et feodo sed ut satis constat super hunc computum ... nichil

De precio DCCCCxxv pellium multonum infra tempus huius computi ad usum hospicii predicti necatorum sic venditorum diversis personis ad diversa precia \<vi li. xviii s. xi d. ob.> vii li. iiii s. vii d./ unde CCxxi pellium vocatarum wolefell precio pecie vii d. ob. CCCCiiii pellium vocatarum wynterfell precio pecie iiii d. \vi li. xiiii s. viii d./ CCC pellium facientium xxv dd. vocatarum shyrlyng*es* precio p<re>ecie iii d. \lxxv s./ in toto prout in dorso huius computi plenius liquet[15] ... xvii li. xiiii s. iii d.

Notandum pro pellibus morinatis huius anni quia nullus valor ut dicitur. Tamen memorandum.[16]

Vendicio pellium multonum agnellorum et capriolorum. De precio lxxiiii pellium vocatarum moryns modici valoris remanentium non venditarum annis xx^mo^ et xxi^mo^ Henrici vii^mi^ sic venditarum Johanni Cokk*es* ingrosso per recognicionem dicti computantis super hunc computum ... iii s. iiii d.

De aliquibus proficiis provenientibus de pellibus agnellorum infra tempus huius computi provisorum et [ad] usum hospicii predicti infra tempus supradictum necatorum. Nichil hic in onere eo quod pertinent clericis dicti hospicii racione officii suorum per relacionem factam super computum ... nichil

De aliquibus proficiis provenientibus de pellibus capriolorum infra tempus huius computi provisorum et necatorum etc. ut supra. Nichil hic in onere eo quod pertinent predictis clericis hospicii etc. ... nichil

Vendicio cepi. De precio D<xvii>xxxi pet. [*blank*] cepi provenientium de bobus et multonibus infra tempus huius computi ad usum hospicii predicti necatis sic venditis diversis personis ad diversa precia prout in dorso huius computi plenius apparet[17] ... xviii li. xviii s. i d. ob.

[13] For this and the following entry see sheet 8d.

[14] MS 'xxjj'.

[15] See sheet 10d.

[16] Written small in the same hand above the marginal 'Vendicio ...capriolorum'.

[17] See sheet 12d.

[*sheet 6*] *Vendicio lane.* De precio xxxv pet. [*blank*] lane provenientium de CClx velleribus multonum infra tempus huius computi tonsuratorum quelibet pet. continens xiiii lib. precio pet. ii s. iiii d. sic liberate Willelmo Wyllyn de Chesthunt ut in dorso huius computi patet[18] ... iiii li. xx d.

^{3}lxiii li. iii s. iiii d. ob.[19]

Interiora animalium. De aliquibus proficiis provenientibus de interioris animalium videlicet de bobus et multonibus infra tempus huius computi necatis. Nichil hic in onere eo quod <pertin> pro tempore estivali pertinent carnifici racione officii sui et pro tempore yemali reservantur ad usum hospicii predicti per relacionem factam super hunc computum ... nichil

Furfur. De aliquibus proficiis provenientibus de precio furfuris provenientis de frumento infra tempus huius computi ad usum hospicii predicti furnito nichil hic in onere eo quod pertinent pistore racione officii sui ut gestatum est super hunc computum ... nichil

Chippynges panum. De aliquibus proficiis provenientibus de lez chippyng*es* panis humani videlicet maunchett*es* chett*es* et trencher bred nichil hic in onere eo quod medietas <p> eorundem pertinent officiariis panetrie et alia medietas reservatur pro pulletria ad usum hospicii predicti provisionis per relacionem factam super hunc computum ... nichil

Candele albe. De precio [*blank*] dd. candelarum albarum factarum de cepo domine prouenienti de bobus et multonibus infra tempus huius computi ad usum hospicii predicti necatis ultra Dxxxi pet. cepi ut supra venditas diversis personis superius oneratas quia nulle vendite fuerant[20] ... nichil

[*sheet 7*] [21]*Recepta forinseca.* De denariis receptis \de/ domina Cecilia in partem solucionis pro dieta sua et tabula serviencium suorum per recognicionem dicti computantis super hunc computum ... xx li.

De denariis receptis de firma unius pasture de Burne fenne \vi li. xiii s. iiii d./ et unius pasture vocate Shyllyngthorpe \vi li. xiii s. iiii d./ ac alterius pasture vocate le Serte \xl s./ reservatarum ad usum hospicii predicti sic dimissarum diversis personis pro uno anno integro finienti ad festum anunciacionis beate Marie virginis anno xxi^{mo} Henrici vii^{i} per recognicionem dicti computantis etc. ... xv li. vi s. viii d.

De denariis receptis de firma predicte pasture de Burne fenne pro medietate anni finienti ad festum sancti Michaelis archangeli anno /[*sheet 8*] xxii^{do} regni regis Henrici vii^{mi} per recognicionem dicti computantis etc. ... C s.

[18] See sheet 12d.

[19] The total of sheet 5 and this first entry on sheet 6, written small in the same hand below the right-bracketed sum totals.

[20] See sheet 5.

[21] The entry begins halfway down a short page.

[3]xl li. vi s. viii d.[22]

Summa totalis. Recepta cum arreragiis[23] … [P]MMDCClxxix li. xi s. qua.

De quibus

Allocacio stuffure de remanentia. Idem computat in precio diverse stuffure remanentis in fine ultimi computi finientis xiii^{mo} die Januarii anno xxi^{mo} regni regis Henrici vii^{mi} videlicet frumenti vinum cervisie boum multonum pissium salsorum salis et aliorum superius super dictum computantem onerate et infra tempus huius computi preter remanentia expendite ultra Clxiii li. <lib.> vi s. viii d. deductos de precio focalis bosci et carbonis silvestris remanentium apud Colyweston eo quod pendet inferius super Willelmum Justyce supervisorem dicti focalis et ultra xxx li. de precio certi mearemii nuper remanentis apud Colyweston predictum et modo deliberati versus reparacionem collegii domine apud Cantibrigiam et inferius in pede huius computi allocati ac ultra x li. xvi s. viii d. de precio certi corticis hoc anno venditi etc.
… <CCxxiiii li. xv s. i d. qua.> \CCxiii li. xviii s. v d. qua./[3]

Allocacio exenniorum. Et in precio diversorum exenniorum superius super dictum computantem oneratorum et ad usum hospicii predicti infra tempus huius <compi> computi preter remanentia expenditorum …xxiii li. xii s. vi d. ob.

[P 3]CCxxxvii li. x s. xi d. ob. qua.[24]

[*sheet 9*] *Empcio frumenti.* Et in precio CCCxlvi qr. vi bus. frumenti per ipsum computantem ad usum hospicii predicti infra tempus huius computi provisi ad diversa precia ut in libro provisionis dicti hospicii per tempus predictum plenius patet … iiii^{xx}ix li. v s. qua.

Empcio cervisie et birre. Et in precio CCxv [*blank*] dol. xli lag. cervisie ad usum hospicii predicti infra tempus huius computi provisorum ad diversa precia unde xiii dol. i pipe xxx lag. precio cuiuslibet dol. xxxii s. et lag. ii d. \xxi li. xvii s./ iiii^{xx}vi dol. iii lez hogg*es* et xxxii lag. di. precio dol. xxiiii s. et lag. i d. ob. \Ciiii li. vi s. ob./ et Cxiiii dol. i pip xxvi lag. di. precio cuiuslibet dol. xx s. et lag. i d. qua. \Cxiiii li. xii s. ii d. ob. qua./ et pro precio iiii dd. viii lag. <emp> cervisie emptorum de diversis uxoribus in villa \vii s. i d./ ac pro precio iiii[25] lez kylderkynnes birre emptorum etc. \vi s. viii d./ necnon pro expensis valetti promtuarii diversis vicibus equitandi ad providendum cervisiam predictam \ xii s./. in toto ut in libro provisionis hospicii predicti patet … CCxlii li. xii d. ob.

Empcio vini. Et in precio xvii dol. \i hogg/ vini Gascon \iiii^{xx} li. xvi s. viii d./ videlicet rubii clarette \vi dol. iii hog*e*/ et albi \viii dol. <\hog i dol.> i hog*e*/ per ipsum computantem ad usum hospicii predicti infra tempus huius computi provisorum ad diversa precia et pro precio unius le butte malmessey \lxvi s. viii d./ i butte romney \xlvi s. viii d./ xli lag. di. et i quarte muscadell \lvi s./ xvi lag. di. et i q*u*arte osey \xvi s. ix d./ ac

[22] The total of sheet 7 (plus the *nichil* entries of sheet 6), written small in the same hand below the right-bracketed sum totals..

[23] 'Summa ...arreragiis' in the formal script (Bastard Anglicana), 'Summa' lavishly decorated with penwork.

[24] The total of both 'Allocacio', written small in the same hand to the right at the foot of the sheet.

[25] MS 'iijj'.

eciam pro denariis solutis \viii li. <xviii s.> xix s. xi d. ob./ pro portagio lacagio et cariagio \xi d. ob./ vini predicti in toto ut in predicto libro provisionis hospicii de tempore predicto patet … iiii^{xx}xix li. ii s. viii d. ob.

Empcio boum. Et in precio Clxxiii boum per eundem computantem provisorum infra tempus huius computi ad usum hospicii predicti ad diversa precia cum vi s. i d. solutis pro di. carcasii et cum vi li. v s. i d. solutis pro \diversis/ expensis factis in provisione dictorum boum et stigacione eorundem ut in dicto libro provisionis hospicii plenius liquet … Cxlvi li. <lib.> xix s.

Empcio multonum.

Notandum quia Cxxii multonum \xii li./ parcella dictorum Miiii^{xx}xiii multonum \[...]/ *onerati fuerant in dorso computi anno proximo precedenti et nulli denarii pro eiisdem soluti dicto anno sed parcella dicte summe Cxiii li. xi s. vi d. Ideo memorandum.*[26] Et in precio Miiii^{xx}xiii multonum per dictum computantem provisorum ad usum dicti hospicii infra tempus predictum ad diversa precia ut in libro provisionis dicti hospicii plenius patet … cum xxxv s. ii d. solutis pro expensis in provisione et stigacione dictorum \multonum/ … <Cxiii li. xi s. vi d.> Cxv li. vi s. viii d.

^{3}DCiiii^{xx}xii li. xiiii s. v d. qua.[27]

[*sheet 10*] *Diverse pasture conducte et reservate pro bobus et multonibus. Notandum pro vi li. xiii s. iiii d. solutis per firma pasturarum de Shillyngthorpe pro anno xxi^{o} Henrici vii quia extra tempus huius computi.*[28] Et in denariis allocatis pro firma diversarum pasturarum conductarum de diversis personis pro sustentacione boum et multonum provisorum ad usum hospicii predicti etc. cum Ci s. viii d. pro firma unius pasture vocate Marbures \lx s./ unius clausi vocati Haucros feld \vi s. viii d./ ii parvorum clausorum iuxta gardinum manerii de Croydon \ v s./ et unius clausi conducti de vicario de Croydon \ x s./ ac pro firma unius clausi cum le slaught*er*howse apud Hatfeld \xx s./. vi li. xiii s. iiii d. pro firma pasture de Shyllyngthorpe pro uno anno integro finienti ad festum sancti Michaelis archangeli anno xxi^{mo} Henrici vii prius non allocata lx s. solutis magistro Hugoni Asshton clerico pro pastura xl <s> boum et vi jume[n]tarum depasturatorum infra novum clausum de Burne pro uno anno integro etc. lxx s. pro firma unius pasture apud Barnette \xl s./ et alterius pasture \xxx s./ apud Hatfeld vocate <C> \le/ Conynger xiiii s.[29] <iii d.> \ix d./ solutis pro clausura predictarum pasturarum et cum iii s. vi d. solutis diversis personis conductis ad supervidendum dictas pasturas \ac onus xiii li. xvi s. viii d. pro diversis pasturis domine reservatis ad usum dicti hospicii superius oneratis/. In toto ut in predicto libro provisionis plenius patet … <xix li. iii \v/ s. xi d.> <Item xiii li. xvi s. viii d.^{3}> \xxxiii li. ii s. vii d./[30]

Empcio aprorum porcorum vitulorum agnellorum et capriolorum. Et in precio x aprorum iiii^{xx}xviii porcorum CCCxxxii vitulorum \di./ \CCCxxvii/ agnellorum et xxxvii

[26] Written small in the same hand below the marginal heading 'Empcio multonum'.

[27] The total of sheet 9, written small in the same hand to the right at the foot of the sheet.

[28] 'Notandum ...computi' written small in the same hand below the marginal heading 'Diverse pasture ...multonibus'.

[29] MS 'xijij'.

[30] The first calculation was made before the added sum ('Item'), after which both were canc. and the final sum add. above.

capriolorum provisorum ad usum hospicii predicti infra tempus huius computi ad diversa precia ut in libro provisionis dicti hospicii plenius aparet ... iiii^{xx}ii li. vii s. v d.

Empcio pissium salsorum. Et in denariis per prefatum computantem solutis pro precio diverse stuffure quadragesimalis ad usum dicti hospicii provise infra tempus huius computi ad diversa precia videlicet pro precio MDCCli lyng*es* <salsorum> xxx li. vi s. x d. MDCCCCxv pissium salsorum vocatorum haberdeyne et codd*es* xxi li. x s. MDCiiii^{xx} fungiarum xiiii li. xiii lez congres salsorum xiii s. iiii d. xiiii barell*es* salmonium salsorum xix li. x s. ii d. ii lez barell*es* rumbi vocati sturgyo*u*n lvii s. viii d. di. barell et i fyrkyn anguillarum salsarum xxxv s. lx lez lampreyes salsorum xxiiii s. xx barell*es* allecis albi xi li. ix d. xiiii cad*es* Dviii allecis rubii iiii li. xiii d. iii cad*es* lez sprott*es* iiii s. viii d. ii lez barell*es* mellis xl s. et pro portagio et cariagio stuffure predicte cum expensis in provisione eiusdem stuffure vii li. vii s. iii d. In toto ut in libro provisionis predicti hospicii per tempus predictum partiter patet ... Cxvi li. x s. ix d.

^{3}CCxxxii li. v d.[31]

[*sheet 11*] *Empcio specierum et aliorum*. Et in denariis solutis pro speciebus variorum generum per ipsum computantem ad usum hospicii predicti infra tempus huius computi provisis videlicet pro precio iiii^{or} tappenett*es* ficorum de orto vi s. ii d. lez sortez ficorum marchaunt xxiiii s. viii d. <l> Diiii lib. rasonorum magnorum xxiiii s. viii d. DCClxix lib. le sug*er* course et hole x li. ix d. ob. xlviii lib. le sug*er* powder viii s. xii lib. iii qr. ii oz. le sug*er* valans v s. x d. qua. di. lib. sug*er* <val> candey iiii d. Clxxv lib. rasonorum corans xxv s. xlviii lib. pip*er*is liiii s. xxviii lib. c*or*reynes xix s. x d. xiii lib. cloves lviii s. xiii lib. mases iiii li. vii s. xiii lib. nuttemugg*es* xxx s. iiii d. vi lib. saunders vii s. xv lib. quinque oz. synamome petyt xlv s. vii d. xviii lib. <zinsis> zinsiperi xxvi s. xii lib. cap*er*s ii s. ix d. di. lag. et iii pynt*es* lez olyves in pykell xiiii d. Cl lib. dactulorum xxxv s. vii lib. lez comfettes carewes iii s. vi d. xlvii lib. di. lez comfett*es* plat*es* <ii s. viii d.> \xviii s. ii d./ ii lib. lez comfett*es* byskett*es* xx d. ii lib. lez long comfett*es* ii s. viii d. vii lib. lez confecc*io*ns v s. x d. xii lib. grene gyng*er* xii s. xliiii lib. iii q*u*art*er* di. lez lymons et succad*es* xxii s. v d. ob. iiii^{xx}x lib. lez lymons in pykell xiiii d. quinque lib.et quinque lez buc*es* croci <iiii lib. iiii> iiii li. iiii d. Ciiii^{xx}i lib. di. prewnes xxxs. Clxviii lib. amigdalarum xxxvi s. vi d. ii lib. le turnesale iii s. iiii d. ii lib. lez oreng*es* in syrope xii d. C^{mi}l aliorum oreng*es* xiiii d. C^{ma} pomorum vocatorum pyppyns xii d. quinque lib. di. le blaunch powder ii s. ix d. iiii lib. lycoryse xvi d. vii lib. lez agnes sede xxi d. ii lag. iii pynt*es* le salet oyle ii s. i lag. vini acri albi viii d. iiii lib. thuris v s. iiii d. lxvi virg. les streyno*urs* viii s. i quaterni et ii foliorum papiri regalis vi d. i reme papiri de Gene ii s. vi d. ii <p> lez remes papiri Francie iiii s. iiii d. et pro expensis in provisione et cariagio stuffure predicte cum denariis solutis pro diversis vasis et aliis neccessariis emptis pro dictis speciebus imponendis lxiiii s. iii d. ob. In toto ut in predicto \libro/ provisionis hospicii partiter patet necnon pro denariis solutis pro colleccione et direccione croci domine hoc anno crescentis apud Coleweston etc. xvii s. ... ^{P} ^{3}lii[32] li. <v s.> \ii s./ vii d. ob. qua.[33]

[31] The total of sheet 10 written small in the same hand to the right at the foot of the sheet.

[32] MS 'ljj'.

[33] The total of 'Empcio specierum' (incorrect).

Empcio cirporum. Et in denariis solutis pro precio cirporum \lxxvii s. viii d. ob./ infra tempus huius computi ad usum hospicii predicti provisorum cum cariagio eorundem vt in dicto libro provisionis hospicii predicti plenius patet … Cv s. ob.

[3]lvii li. vii s. viii d. qua.[34]

[sheet 12] *Empcio salis.* Et in denariis solutis pro precio xi qr. salis albi \lv s. iiii d./ et iii <wa> wayes di. iii qr. \ii bus./ salis de Bay \liii s. viii d./ [*blank*] per eundem computantem provisorum ad usum hospicii predicti infra tempus huius computi et pro cariagio \<xxxix s. viii d.>/ \portagio xxxviii s. xi d./ dicti salis ut in predicto libro provisionis hospicii patet … vii li. vii s. xi d.[3]

Empcio olei. Et in denariis solutis pro precio ii barell*es* olei vocati rape oyle emptorum ad usum dicti hospicii infra tempus predictum cum x d. solutis pro precio i le barell empti etc. ut in dicto libro hospicii <predicti> patet … xxv s. x d. ob.[3]

Empcio candelarum albarum et smigmatis nigre cum le wyke. Et in denariis solutis pro precio CCCxlvii dd. \di./ candelarum albarum precio cuiuslibet dd. xii d. xvii li. vii s. vi d. et pro precio quinque dd. di. candelarum albarum vocatarum wacchyng candell*es* precio cuiuslibet dd. xviii d. viii s. iii d. ac pro precio ii qr. xii lib. le <candell> weke emptorum v s. viii d. necnon pro precio ii lez barell*es* smigmatis nigre xxviii s. iiii d. emptorum ad usum hospicii predicti infra tempus huius computi ut in libro provisionis eiusdem hospicii per dictum tempus plenius patet … xix li. ix s. ixd.[3]

Empcio cere cum aliis neccessariis. Et in denariis per ipsum computantem solutis pro precio xiiii lib. le torche weke et tap*er* weke emptarum ad usum dicti hospicii infra tempus predictum ut in dicto libro \provisionis/ hospicii patet … xxi d.[3]

Regarda pro exenniis et aliis. Et in denariis solutis pro regardis datis diversis personis tam pro exenniis quam ab regardis per mandatum dicte principisse solutis infra tempus huius computi ut in libro provisionis eiusdem hospicii particulariter patet … <xix li. xix s. iiii d.> [3] <Item liii s.> \xxii li. xii s. iiii d./[35]

[3]l li. xvii s. vii d. ob.[36]

Custus focalis. Et in denariis per eundem computantem solutis pro focale empto et proviso ad usum hospicii predicti infra tempus huius computi videlicet pro precio MD talwod et CCClviii carectarum le hardwod xvii li. xv s. x d. XVIMDCCC di. fagott*es* xiiii li. vii s. vi d. Clxiiii carectarum et x qr. carbonis silvestris quodlibet carecta continens xxiiii qr. xlviii li. xv s. x d. denariis solutis pro cariagio CCxxviii carectarum \dicti/ focalis a bosco vocato le [*sheet 13*] Whytehorse usque Croydon unde Ciiii^{xx}xviii carectarum \cxv s. vi d./ quodlibet carecta ad vii d. et xxx carectarum \xv s./ quodlibet carecta ad vi d. vi li. x s. vi d. stipendio diversorum laborariorum conductorum ad prostrandum et dirigendum lez talwod hardwod byllet et fagott*es* predictos cum denariis solutis pro cubacione eiusdem focalis etc. ix li. xvii s. ii d. ob. ac pro diversis expensis factis in provisione predicti focalis cum denariis solutis pro tabula Philippi colyer

[34] The total of sheet 11, written small in the same hand to the right at the foot of the sheet.

[35] The first calculation was made before the added sum ('Item'), after which both were canc. and the final sum add. above.

[36] The total of sheet 12, written small in the same hand to the right at the foot of the sheet.

xxvii s. x d. In toto ut in predicto libro provisionis hospicii supradicti pro tempore predicto plenius aparet ... iiii^{xx}xviii li. xiiii s. viii d. ob.[3]

Soluciones forinsece. Et in diversis solucionibus forinsecis per ipsum computantem factis et solutis infra tempus huius computi cum viii li. xix s. iii d. ob. pro expensis prefate principisse et serviencium suorum in itenere suo equitantium a Croydon usque Syon videlicet secundo die Marcii infra tempus huius computi et de ibidem usque Croydon predictam in toto per ii dies Cii s. ii d. pro expensis dicte principisse et serviencium suorum in itenere suo equitantium a Croydon predicta usque Rychemond et de ibidem domorsum etc. videlicet predicto mense Marcii etc. iiii li. xii s. vi d. pro consimilibus expensis eiusdem principisse et serviencium suorum in itenere suo equitantium a Croydon supradicta usque London et ibidem \spectantium/ et deinde usque Croydon videlicet mense Aprilis infra tempus predictum xxiiii s. iiii d. pro expensis diversorum serviencium dicte principisse equitantium a Rychmond cum domina principissa et domina Maria filia domini regis usque Croydon videlicet mense Maii infra tempus supradictum x li. iiii d. pro expensis predicte principisse et serviencium suorum in itenere suo equitantium a Croydon predicta usque Westmonasterium et ibidem spectantium per ii dies cum <exi> expensis eiusdem principisse et serviencium suorum de ibidem usque Syon et deinde usque Croydon videlicet predicto mense Maii etc. xv li. xv s. vii d.; pro consimilibus expensis eiusdem principisse et tocius familie sue \tempore/ remocionis \sue/ a Croydon predicta usque Hatfeld videlicet mense Junii infra tempus computi xix li. x s. vi d. solutis pro cariagio diverse stuffure dicte principisse et serviencium suorum a Croydon predicta usque Hatfeld supradictam dicto mense Junii etc. necnon cum lxxiii li. xvii s. viii d. ob. pro expensis predicte principisse et serviencium suorum in itenere suo equitantium a Hatfeld predicta usque Cantibrigiam et ibidem \spectantium/ ac deinde domorsum usque Hatfeld videlicet mense Augusti infra tempus computi in toto per ix dies ut in predicto libro provisionis hospicii plenius liquet ... Cxlvi li. xix s. vi d.[3]

[3]CCxlv li. xiiii s. ii d. ob.[37]

[*sheet 14*] *Soluciones neccessarie.* Et in diversis solucionibus necessariis per ipsum computantem factis et solutis ad usum dicti hospicii infra tempus predictum cum Cxiii s. vi d. solutis pro precio MMMCCCCxxx ciphorum silvestrium lv s. pro escambio vasorum electrorum xix s. iii d. <solutis pro precio xix s. iii d.> solutis pro iiii^{or} lez materas et iiii lez bolsters emptis pro eisdem xlvii s. pro iii \magnis/ peciis de le say xiii s. iiii d. solutis pro duobus qr. lez mustard sede et cum xviii s. iiii d. solutis pro cariagio i paris organorum et alie stuffure a Colyweston usque Hatfeld predictam in toto ut in libro provisionis hospicii predicti pro tempore supradicto partiter patet ... xxxviii li. xvii s. iii d. qua.[3]

Empcio diversorum ornamentorum et aliorum neccessariorum pro pueris capelle. Et in denariis per dictum computantem solutis pro diversis ornamentis et aliis neccessariis emptis et provisis ad usum puerorum predicte capelle dicte principisse infra tempus huius computi cum l s. ii d. solutis pro diversis neccessariis emptis pro eadem capella ut in dicto libro provisionis patet ... vi li. xvi s. ii d. ob.[3]

[37] The total of sheet 13 written small in the same hand to the right at the foot of the sheet.

Empcio ornamentorum et aliorum neccessariorum pro garcions coquine. Et in denariis solutis pro diversis ornamentis emptis pro garcions coquine infra tempus predictum ut in eodem libro \provisionis/ hospicii partiter patet … xxviii s. viii d.[3]

Liberatura equorum. Et in denariis per ipsum computantem solutis pro liberatura palafridorum et aliorum hakkenett*es* dicte principisse infra tempus huius computi cum xiii li. ix s. ii d. solutis pro tabula custodis dictorum equorum usque xiii^{m} diem Januarii in clauso huius computi x s. solutis pro pane equino xv li. xiiii s. v d. solutis pro iiii^{xx}xvi qr. avene vii li. ix s. viii d. solutis pro xl carectis feni cum cariagio eiusdem xl s. ix d. pro ferris \equorum/ lxxvii s. xi d. solutis pro expensis predictorum equorum cum dietis custodis eiusdem venientis a West Depyng usque Croydon et alibi diversis vicibus in toto cum xxi li. xvi s. ix d. pro firma diversorum pratorum domine reservatorum etc. … <xlvi li. viii s. i d.> <Item xxii li. xvi s. ix d.>\lxviii li. iiii s. x d./[38]

Diete et tabula diversorum serviencium domine. Et in denariis solutis pro dietis et tabula diversorum serviencium predicte principisse ad diversas vices infra tempus huius computi ut in predicto libro provisionis hospicii etc. plenius patet … xiii li. x s. iii d. ob.[3]

Empcio panni lanei pro liberatura serviencium hospicii domine. Et in denariis per ipsum computantem solutis pro precio DCxl virg. di. [*blank*] panni lanei emptarum pro liberatura serviencium dicte principisse ad diversa precia ut in libro provisionis pro dicto hospicio huius anni patet cum xxxix s. pro liberature diversorum non allocatis anno proximo precedenti … Cxxxiiii li. xix d.[3]

[3]CClxii li. xviii s. x d. qua.[39]

[*sheet 15*] [40]*Accata recentia.* Et in denariis solutis accatore pro accatis recentibus per ipsum emptis et provisis ad usum hospicii predicti infra tempus huius computi videlicet tam pro signis lez cranys ffesaunt*es* aucis porcellis caponibus gallinis pullis et aliis volatilibus quam pro dentricibus lengiis anguillis et pissibus marinis ac lacticinio prout in libro provisionis hospicii predicti plenius patet … CCiiii^{xx}viii li. xi s. ii d. ob.[3]

Vadia serviencium hospicii. Et in denariis allocatis pro vadiis serviencium hospicii predicte principisse pro uno anno integro finienti ad festum natalis domini anno xxii^{do} regni regis nunc Henrici vii ut in libro hospicii predicti partiter apparet … CClxxviii li. xix s. iiii d.

Dlxvii li. x s. vi d. ob.[41]

[*sheet 16*][42]

Summa allocacionis … MMCCCxlvi li. xiiii s. ix d. Et debet … CCCCxxxii li. xvi s. iii d. qua. Postea oneratur de … <CCxvii li. iiii s. v d. ob.> \CCxxxiii li. vi s. i d. ob./ de

[38] The first calculation was made before the added sum ('Item'), after which both were canc. and the final sum add. above.

[39] The total of sheet 14 written small in the same hand to the right at the foot of the sheet.

[40] The entries on sheet 15 are centred to allow a full page for sheet 16 calculations.

[41] The total of sheet 15, written small in the same hand to the right at the foot of the sheet.

[42] Parts of the rubrics on sheet 16 ('Summa allocacionis', 'Postea …de', 'Et …coniuncta', 'Tamen', 'Et …ultra', 'De quibus', 'Et debet', 'De quibus', 'Et debet', 'Et …ei', 'Et ...ultra', 'Unde') are written in a larger and more formal script. See Plate 1. Cf. too sheet 17, 'Super'.

precio certe stuffure remanentis non expendite \in fine huius computi/ sed reservate versus expensa hospicii predicti pro anno futuro ut inferius in pede huius computi patet. Et debet dicta summa conjuncta … <DCl li. viii d. ob. qua.> \DClxvi li. ii s. iiii d. ob. qua./ Tamen respectuantur ei … <CCxlii li. iiii s. v d. ob.> \CCxxxiii li. vi s. i d. ob./ pro precio diverse stuffure <in fine> in fine[43] huius computi \remanentis/ non expendite sed reservate pro expensis predicti hospicii pro anno futuro etc. Et debet ultra … CCCCxxxii li. xvi s. iii d. qua. De quibus allocantur ei … xxx li. pro precio certi mearemii nuper remanentis apud Colyweston superius in titulo De Remanentia.[44] Oneratur eo quod deliberantur versus reparacionem collegii domine apud Cantibrigiam prout testatum est super hunc computum. Et debet … CCCCii li. xvi s. iii d. qua. De quibus allocantur ei … x li. xvi s. viii d. de precio certi corticis de remanentia ultimi computi superius dupliciter onerato videlicet in titulo De Remanentia[45] ad x li. … xvi s. viii d. et in titulo De Vendicione stauri extra hospicium[46] ad vii li. xiii s. ea de causa hic in allocacione posito etc. Et debet … CCCiiii^{xx}xi li. xix s. vii d. qua. De quibus allocantur ei … x li. pro feodo dicti computantis pro hoc anno <prius non allocato hic in allocacione posito> per mandatum predicte principisse ore tenus coram concilio suo super declaracionem huius computi apud Hatfeld xxii^{do} die Januarii anno xxii^{do} regis predicti etc. Et ei … iii^{xx}i li. xv s. iiii d. qua. pro tantis denariis hic exoneratis eo quod onerantur in quadam indentura inter prefatam principissam et <da> … dictum computantem confecta data xxii^{do} die Januarii anno xxii^{do} regni regis Henrici vii^{mi} predicti <ut p> ut in eadem patet. Et debet ultra … CCC li. iiii s. iii d.

Unde

[*sheet 17*] *Super*[47]

Ricardum Page pro parte xviii li. vi s. viii d. de precio xx boum eidem venditorum etc. superius onerato inter Arreragia[48] … lxvi s. viii d.

Willelmum Jay de London pro viii dd. et ii pellibus multonum eidem venditis anno [*blank*] superius oneratis inter Arreragia … xxxii s. viii d.

Michaelem Williamson de Okeham de precio corticis eidem venditi anno xvi^{o} regni regis Henrici septimi adhuc non soluto ultra lx s. solutos ad manum Johannis Bedell etc. superius onerato inter Arreragia … xx s.

Executores Ricardi Fleccher pro precio bosci eidem venditi per rectorem de Cliff adhuc non soluto superius onerati inter Arreragia … xxiii s. iiii d.

Eosdem executores Ricardi Fleccher pro precio diverse stuffure eidem Ricardo vendite extra hospicium anno ii^{do} precedenti adhuc non soluto videlicet pro precio unius barrell allecis albi \xii s./ vii carectarum veteris feni \xviii s. viii d./ et M fagott*es* \xi s. viii d./ superius onerato inter Arreragia … xlii s. iiii d.

[43] The first 'in fine' (canc.) ends a line; the second begins the next line.

[44] See sheet 8 ('Allocacio stuffure de remanentia').

[45] *Ibid.*

[46] See sheet 2 ('Stuffura vendita extra hospicium').

[47] 'Super' is actually in the margin of sheet 19 but bracketed to include sheets 17–21.

[48] 'Inter Arreragia' (sheets 17–20 passim) refers back to the composite sum on sheet 1 ('Arreragia').

Willelmum Burbage pro precio i barell salmonium salsorum eidem venditi anno xix^{o} regni regis Henrici vii^{i} adhuc non soluto superius onerato inter Arreragia … xxi s. iiii d.

Willelmum Marbury pro precio unius cade allecis rubii eidem venditi extra hospicium anno xix^{o} regni Henrici viii^{i} adhuc non soluto superius onerato inter Arreragia … iiii s.

Willelmum Worsop pro precio ii boum eidem venditorum extra hospicium anno ii^{do} precedenti adhuc non soluto superius onerato inter Arreragia … xxxii s.

Johannem Sharow pastorem de Burne pro precio unius corrii morinati per ipsum habiti anno ii^{do} precedenti adhuc non soluto superius onerato inter Arreragia … ii s. viii d.

Johannem Thorp serviencem abbatis de Pipwell pro precio Cxxxi corriorum boum per ipsum habitorum extra hospicium infra tempus <huius> computi anno ii^{do} precedenti ultra xvi li. solutos anno proximo precedenti adhuc non soluto superius onerato inter Arreragia … Cxvi s. viii d.

Eundem Johannem Thorp pro precio lxvii corriorum boum eidem venditorum anno proximo precedenti adhuc non soluto superius onerato inter Arreragia … xi li. iii s. iiii d.

[*sheet 18*] Executores Rogeri Urmeston militis pro precio unius dol. vini Gascon eidem venditi extra hospicium anno xx^{mo} regni regis Henrici vii^{mi} adhuc non soluto superius onerato inter Arreragia … iiii li. vi s. viii d.

David Cecyll pro precio unius pipp vini Gascon eidem venditi extra hospicium dicto anno xx^{o} Henrici vii^{i} adhuc non soluto superius super dictum computantum onerato inter Arreragia … xlvi s. viii d.

Eundem David Cecyll pro precio iii hogg*es* vini eidem venditorum extra hospicium anno xxi^{mo} regis Henrici vii^{mi} predicti etc. … lxii s. vi d.

Robertum <Slak> Lake et Robertum Slye de Luthyngton pro precio lxxv pet. lane eiisdem venditarum extra hospicium anno xx^{mo} regni regis Henrici vii^{i} adhuc a retro existenti non soluto superius onerato inter Arreragia ultra vi li. solutos hoc anno … vi li. x s.

Dictos Robertum Lake et Robertum Slye pro precio [*blank*] pet. lane eiisdem venditarum extra hospicium anno xxi^{mo} regis Henrici vii^{mi} precio cuiuslibet pet. [*blank*] adhuc non soluto etc. … C s. Notandum quia nondum ad certum ut plenius patet in dorso computi de dicto anno xxi^{o} Henrici vii.[49]

Willelmum Kylnere pro precio CCCCiiii^{xx}x pet. et ix lib. cepi eidem venditarum extra hospicium anno <xxi>^{mo} \xix^{o}/ Henrici vii adhuc non soluto superius onerato inter Arreragia \ultra viii li. vi s. solutos eodem anno/ ultra lxx s. iii d. solutos <dicto> anno xxi^{o} et ultra xl s. solutos hoc anno … vi li. xii s. ix d.

Johannem Langton pro precio CCCCxxxviii pellium multonum vocatorum shyrlyng*es* et CClxi pellium vocatarum wynt*er*fell eidem venditarum anno xx^{o} Henrici vii^{i} adhuc

[49] ‘Notandum …vii’ written small in the same hand to the right of the sum.

a retro existenti non soluto superius onerato inter Arreragia ultra C s. solutos anno xxi^{mo} dicti regis et ultra xxx s. solutos hoc anno … iiii li. vi s. iiii d.

Dictum Johannem Langton pro precio CCCxxviii pellium multonum \x li. xviii s. viii d./ vocatorum wulfell precio pecie viii d. xx pellium vocatarum wulfell provenientium de morina \x s./ precio pecie vi d. et pro precio lxxvi pellium vocatarum shirlyngys \xix s./ precio pecie iii d. eidem Johanni venditorum anno xxi^{mo} Henrici vii^{mi} adhuc non soluto etc. … xii li. vii s. viii d.

Willelmum Lynne pro precio Ciiii^{xx}vii pellium multonum vocatorum wulfell sibi venditorum extra hospicium anno xx^{mo} Henrici vii etc. … vi li. iiii s.

Magistrum collegii de Fodryngay pro precio viii qr. frumenti \lxiiii s./ unius qr. farine frumenti \viii s./ et vi signett*es* \xiiii s./ eidem venditorum extra hospicium anno xxi^{o} Henrici vii adhuc non soluto etc. superius super dictum computantem onerato inter Arreragia ultra lxxii s. solutos hoc anno … xiiii s. Perdonantur ut dicitur.[50]

[*sheet 19*] Magistrum Gryndell pro precio certe stuffure per ipsum habite extra hospicium anno xxi^{o} regis Henrici vii^{i} predicti videlicet i qr. iii bus. <frumenti> farine \viii s. iii d./ unius hogg cervisie \vi s./ iiii lyngys \xx d./ et vi fungiarum \ix d./ adhuc non soluto superius onerato inter Arreragia … xvi s. viii d.

Magistrum Martyn nuper de Croydon pro precio unius hog. cervisie per ipsum habiti extra hospicium dicto anno xxi^{mo} Henrici vii^{mi} adhuc non soluto superius onerato inter Arreragia … vi s.

Magistrum Moreton nuper de le Whytehorse pro precio unius hogg cervisie per ipsum habiti extra hospicium anno xxi^{o} predicto adhuc non soluto superius onerato inter Arreragia … vi s.

Johannem Tanne pro precio iii pipp vini Gascon per ipsum habitorum extra hospicium dicto anno xxi^{mo} Henrici vii^{i} etc. ut supra … [*blank*]

Thomam Cheney militem pro precio unius pipp vini Gascon per ipsum habiti extra hospicium dicto anno xxi^{mo} Henrici vii^{i} etc. … xli s. viii d.

Davidum Philipp militem pro precio unius hogg*e* vini Gascon per ipsum habiti extra hospicium dicto anno xxi^{mo} Henrici vii^{i} etc. adhuc non soluto superius onerato inter Arreragia … xx s. x d. Solvitur.[51]

Edwardum Vause pro precio xx lez sesternes vini Gascon per ipsum venditorum extra hospicium dicto anno xxi^{mo} Henrici vii^{i} adhuc non soluto etc. ut supra … xxvi s. viii d.

Willelmum Houghton de Chesthunt barker pro precio lxvii corriorum boum sibi venditorum extra hospicium <as> eodem anno xxi^{mo} Henrici vii^{i} adhuc non soluto superius onerato inter Arreragia ultra x li. xvi s. viii d. Solvitur.[52] … vi s. viii d.

Robertum Sharow de Burne pro precio unius corrii boum morinatorum per ipsum habiti extra hospicium anno xxi^{o} predicto etc. … xviii d.

[50] 'Perdonantur ut dicitur' written small in the same hand to the right of the sum.

[51] 's' (i.e 'solvitur') add., probably in the same hand.

[52] 's' (i.e 'solvitur') add., probably in the same hand.

Willelmum Holden de Sothewark[53] pro precio lii multonum sibi venditorum extra hospicium anno xxii^{mo} Henrici vii pecie[54] adhuc a retro existenti non soluto superius onerato inter Arreragia … lii s.

Willelmum Bysshope de Sothewar\k/[55] pro precio CCxl pellium vocatarum wynterfell \iiii li./ precio pecie iiii d. CCxlviii pellium vocatarum shyrlyng*es* \lxii s./ precio pecie iii d. et iii pellium morinatarum \vi d./ precio pecie ii d. [*sheet 20*] eidem venditarum extra hospicium anno xxi^{mo} regni regis Henrici vii^{mi} predicti adhuc non soluto superius onerato inter Arreragia ultra vi li. xv s. iiii d. solutos hoc anno … vii s. ii d.

Willelmum Banast*er* de Oxstede iuxta Croydon pro precio CCiiii^{xx} pet. dicti cepi sibi venditarum extra hospicium anno xxi^{mo} Henrici vii^{mi} precio cuiuslibet pet. x d. adhuc a retro existenti non soluto superius onerato inter Arreragia ultra vii li. x s. solutos hoc anno … iiii li. xi s. viii d.

Robertum Tales de Stampford pro precio CCCCvi lib. cere sibi venditarum extra hospicium anno xxi^{mo} regni Henrici vii adhuc non soluto superius onerato inter Arreragia ultra iiii li. xvii s. vii \ob./ solutos hoc anno … iiii li. Nota pro Ciiii^{xx}xii lib. cere parcella dictarum CCCCvi lib. quia deliberata \fuerat/ ad usum hospicii per relacionem W. Kylner adhuc non deductis pro defectu certitudinis etc. tamen dicta cera oneratur in dorso huius computi.[56]

^{3}Ciiii li. xvii s. v d.[57]

Willelmum Justyse supervisorem boscorum et focalis domine pro precio certi focalis bosci et carbonis silvestris remanentium apud Colyweston adhuc non venditorum superius super dictum computantem onerato … Clxiii li. vi s. viii d. ex mandato Thome Hobson[58]

^{3}Clxiii li. vi s. viii d.[59]

Johannem Cokk*es* pro precio CCxii pellium vocatarum wulfell precio pecie vii d. ob. \ vi li. xviii s. xi d. ob./ CCCxlvi pellium vocatarum wynt*er*fell precio pecie iiii d. \Cxv s. iiii d./ CCC pellium vocatarum shyrlyng*es* precio \pecie/ iii d. \lxxv s./ et lxxiiii pellium debilium vocatarum morens \iii s. iiii d./ sibi venditarum infra tempus huius computi superius onerato adhuc non soluto … xvi li. xii s. vii d. ob.

Clericos hospicii pro precio ix pellium vocatarum wulfell precio pecie vii d. ob. \v s. vii d. ob./ et lxviii pellium vocatarum wynterfell precio \pecie/ iiii d. \xix s./ deficientium in <def> necligencia eorundem et non deliberatarum extra hospicium ut in libro abbreviamentorum huius anni patet superius super dictum computantem onerato … xxiiii s. xi d. ob.

[53] Alt. from 'Sothewarth'.

[54] The isolated 'pec*ie*' may be part of an original 'precio pecie' with price, as in the next entry, cf. the second entry under 'Multones' (sheet 22) which also omits 'precio' but has the price.

[55] Alt. from 'Sothewarth'.

[56] 'Nota ...computi' written small in the same hand to the right of and below the sum. For 'in dorso huius computi', see sheet 16d.

[57] The total of sheets 17–20 (up to and incl. the Robert Tales entry and written below it).

[58] 'ex ...Hobson' add. in the same hand after the sum.

[59] The total of this entry written small in the same hand below the right-bracketed sum.

Robertum None pro precio iii corriorum boum sibi venditorum extra hospicium infra tempus huius computi adhuc non soluto etc. ... x s.

Dictum Robertum pro ii corriis boum vocatis morens sibi venditis infra tempus huius computi precium ii s. adhuc non soluto ... iiii s.

[*sheet 21*] Willelmum Thomson de Sancto Albano pro precio unius le way cepi eidem venditi infra tempus huius computi etc. ... x s.

Thomam Snow de Croydon pro precio xx multonum debilium eidem venditorum extra hospicium infra tempus huius computi precio pecie <ii> s. \xii d./ ultra xv s. solutos etc. ... v s.

Johannem Fyssh pro precio iii bus. frumenti sibi venditorum extra hospicium infra tempus huius computi precio bus. ix d. adhuc non soluto ... ii s. iii d.

Johannem Thomson de Depyng pro precio certi corticis eidem venditi infra tempus huius computi ingrosso etc. ultra iiii li. solutos hoc anno ... lxxiii s.

Willelmum Wyllyn de Chesthunt pro precio xxxv pet. lane provenientis de multonibus infra tempus huius computi tonsuratis et eidem Willelmo deliberatis ad usum domine precium cuiuslibet pet. ii s. iiii d. ... iiii li. xx d.

<Dyv*erse* *ser*va*un*t*es* of house> Diversos serviences hospicii pro precio certi panni lanei per ipsos habiti extra garderobam prefate principisse infra tempus huius computi adhuc non soluto ut patet in quodam parvo libro de nominibus et summis penes Willelmum Bedell thesaurarium hospicii predicti remanenti superius super dictum computantem onerato ultra viii s. solutos per manum Jacobi Morres etc. ... iiii li. xvi s. viii d.

[3]xxxii li. ii d.[60]

[3]Summa pendens ... CCC li. iiii s. iii d.[61]

<*debet iiii*^{xx}*xi li. xii s.* \<*xv s.*>/ *iiii d. ob. qua.*>[62] dictum computantem[63] ... <iiii^{xx}xi li. xv s. iiii d. qua.> nichil. Et eque. Et quietus est.[64]

[*sheet 22*] [3]Stauro tam vivo quam mortuo[65] hospicii prefate principisse remanenti non expendito xiij^{o} die Januarii anno regni regis nunc Henrici vii xxij^{do} ut inferius sequitur.

Garnare.[66] In precio ix qr. <frument> di. iij pec. frumenti remanentium in manu Henrici Knotte precio qr. vi s. viii d. ... lxiii s. xi d. ob.

[60] The total of the entries on sheets 20 (beginning with 'Johannem Cokk*es*') and 21, written small below the right-bracketed sum totals.
[61] 'Summa ...iii d.' written small to the right lower down the sheet.
[62] Written small (and canc.) to the left of 'dictum computantem'.
[63] Written in the formal script.
[64] 'Et quietus est' written below 'Et eque'.
[65] The only heading clearly taking the dative/ablative case, as shown by 'viuo' written in full ('Staur*o* tam viuo q*u*am mort*uo*'). This heading is preceded by 'nA', perhaps 'nota', perhaps merely decorative; the following headings (except 'Bakhouse') are followed by 'nA' up to and including *Pultre* (sheet 23). See further below.
[66] From this point the headings in the margin are bracketed to link all related items.

In precio i qr. di. remanentium in manu Walteri Cokk*es* precio qr. vi s. viii d. … quia disperatur[67]

In precio ii qr. vi bus. iii pec. frumenti remanentium in manu Georgii Aughton … quia disperatur

In precio xxxii qr. frumenti remanentium in granario apud Hatfeld unde i qr. <pre-cio.> iiii bus. precio qr. v s. et xxx qr. iiii bus. precio qr. iiii s. viii d. … vii li. ix s. x d.

Bakhouse. In precio i bus. farine \frumenti/ pro lez maunchett*es* remanentis in pistrino <precio> … xii d.

In ii qr. farine frumenti pro lez chet*es* inde fiendis remanentium in dicto pistrino precio qr. iiii s. viii d. … ix s. iiii d.

In <ffari> precio i bus. farine vocate fome floure remanentis … viii d.

In <fa> precio i bus. trencher meyle remanentis … iiii <bus.> d.

Past<e>re. In iiii bus. farine frumenticie remanentibus in pasteria precio bus. vii d. … ii s. iiii d.

Pantre. In precio CCCxxviii chet*es* <etc.> remanentium in panetria precio trium i d. … ix s. i d.

[*sheet 23*] *Buttre*. In precio i <pip s> hogg \x lag./ cervisie pro domina remanentium precio ix s. viii d. et ii dol. xx lag. cervisie remanentium pro hospicio precio dol. xx s. … xlix s. viii d.

Seller. In precio ii dol. i pip vini rubii remanentium precio dol. [*blank*] … xiii li. vi s. viii d.

In precio i dol. ii hogg vini clarett*e* <de> remanentium precio dol. vi li. … ix li.

In precio iii hogg*es* vini clarett de vetere vino proviso remanentium … Nichil quia nullus valor.[68]

In i butt xxxii lag. malvesy remanentium precio <C s.> … C s.

In lxiii pichers romney remanentibus precio [*blank*] … xxx s.

In precio x pich*er* mustedell remanentium <precio> [*blank*] … xiii s. iiii d.

Bestes.

In \precio/ xl boum remanentium apud Colyweston precio pecie xvi s. … xxxii li.

In precio xix boum remanentium apud Hatfeld precio pecie xviii s. … xvii li. ii s.

In precio iiii boum \ii/ remanentium apud Beauo*ur* castell \i/ in custodia ballivi de Burne et \i/ in custodia Ricardi Davy precio pecie xxs. … iiii li.

Nota.[69] In i bove deficienti … [*blank*]

Multones. In <mutons> precio xiii multonum remanentium apud Hatfeld precio pecie ii s. … xxvi s.

[67] 'quia disperatur' here and below written small to the right after the entry (there are no totals).
[68] 'nichil ...valor' written small to the right after the entry in the same hand (there is no total).
[69] Written small in the left margin.

In \precio lxv/ multonum debilium remanentium apud Hatfeld predictum pecie ad x d. … liiii s. ii d.

In precio lxvii multonum deficientium … [*blank*]

Pultre. In precio i signi apud Croydon … ii s.

In precio vii signorum de exen[ni]is precio pecie ii s. iiii d. … xvi s. iiii d.

In precio vi caponum remanentium precio pecie iiii d. … ii s.

In xvi perdicum precio pecie ii d. … ii s. viii d.

In \ii/ fesanis de exenniis precio pecie ii d. … xx d.

In vii pavonibus de exenniis remanentibus … vii s.

In i bitt*our* remanenti precio … x d.

In iiii gruibus remanentibus precio pecie xx d. … vi s. viii d.

In precio viii qr. avene precio qr. xvi d. … x s. viii d.

Wete larder. In precio i carcasii ii pec*es* di. boum <l> remanentium … xvi s. viii d.

In iiii^{or} carcasiis multonum remanentibus precio … vi s. viii d.

In iii carcasiis vitulorum remanentibus precio … vii s.

In i carcasio agnelli remanenti precio … xvi d.

Drye larder. In precio MCv^{xx}vii ling*es* remanentium precio <pec> C^{ma} xliii s. iiii d. … xxv li. xix s.[70]

In precio DCClxii haberden*es* remanentium precio … ix li.

In precio MCClxxiii fungiarum remanentium … xii li. xii s. ii d.

[*sheet 24*] In precio iii q*uarter* vnius barell stirgeon remanentium precio barell xxx s. … xxii s. vi d.

In precio x barell*es* salmonium salsorum remanentium … xiii li. vi s. viii d.

In precio xiii congres salsarum remanentium precio pecie xii d. … xiii s.

In precio i <bus.> qr. v bus. salis de Bay remanentium … v s.

In precio x bus. salis albi remanentium precio bus. viii d. … vi s. viii d.

In precio i barell i firkyn mellis remanentium … xxxiii s. iiii d.

In precio iii <py> dentricum remanentium … iii s.

In precio i tenche remanentis … xii d.

In oleo remanenti iiii lag. … iiii s.

In precio viii cad*es* di. allecis rubii remanentium … xxxiiii s.

In precio xi barell*es* allecis albi remanentium … Cvi s. iiii d.

[70] The number of ling is oddly expressed and should read 'MCiiii^{xx}xvii' to agree with the sum.

[71]*Chaundre*. In precio xi dd. v lib. candelarum albarum<de> remanentium precio dd. xii d. … xi s. v d.

In tortis hole et broken xxiii pond \ponderantibus/ CCCviii lib. \iiii d./ … Cii s. viii d.

In precio xxvii staff torches ponderantium in cera lvii lib. precio lib. v d. … xxiii s. ix d.

In xii new staf*es* mearemii emptis pro staff torches precio … iii s.

In xlvi lib. cere operatis in quarrears precio lib. v d. ob. … xxi s. i d.

In Cxii lib. <cak*es*> rosyn remanentibus precio … iii s. iiii d.

In precio iiii^{xx}xiiii lib. cere non operatarum remanentis precio lib. v d. ob. … xliii s. i d.

In viii <lib.> \pet./ weke pro tortis <prec> quodlibet pet. continens viii lib. precio <lib.> \pet./ vi d. … iiii s.

In iii lib. tapweke precio lib. i d. … iii d.

Focale. In <ss> xx carectis fagott*es* remanentibus apud Hatfeld precio carecte x d. … xvi s. viii d.

In precio xx carectarum tallewod et herdwod remanentium ibidem precio carecte <idem> x d. ut supra … xvi s. viii d.

In precio xxii carectarum carbonum silvestrium remanentium apud Hatfeld … xii li. x s. viii d.

Fenum. In precio x carectarum feni remanentium apud Hatfeld … xl s.

In precio xxxvii carectarum feni remanentium apud <Hatfeld> Depyng … lxxiiii s.

In precio lvi carectarum feni remanentium apud Ware … viii li. viii s.

In precio xiiii carectarum feni remanentium apud <Barnett> Chesthunt … xlii s.

In precio xii carectarum feni remanentium apud Barnett … xxxvi s.

[*sheet 25*] [72]*Avena*. In precio lxi qr. avene remanentium apud Depyng Colyweston Maxsey Ware et Hatfeld precio qr. xx d. … Ci s. viii d.

Scolery. In i hogg \iiii lag./ vinacr*e* remanentibus … x s.

In precio i hogg iiii lag. vertjuse remanentium … vi s. viii d.

In precio iii hogg aleacre remanentium … x s.

In precio ii qr. senvy sed remanentium … xiii s. iiii d.

Memorandum pro xvii virg. iii quarter panni lanei <rem> adhuc non aperciatis remanentibus in garderoba. Ideo memorandum erga proximum.[73]

Spicere. In CCiiii^{xx}iii lib. i qr. sug*er* hole precio lib. iii d. qua. … lxxvi s. vii d. ob. qua.

[71] 'B' in left margin before 'Chaundre'.

[72] 'A' in left margin before 'Avena' and also before 'Scolery' (below). See Plate 2.

[73] Written small in the same hand in the left margin below the entries for 'Scolery', followed by a gap before 'Spicere'.

In precio xiiii lib. di. sug*er* powd*er* precio lib. ii d. … ii s. v d.

In vi lib. iii qr. sug*er* valans precio lib. v d. … ii s. ix d. ob.

In xiiii lib. rasen correnis precio lib. i d. ob. qua. … ii s. ob.

In ix lib. di. iii oz. di. piperis precio lib. xiiii d. … x s. viii d.

In xvii lib. graynes precio lib. viii d. ob. … xii s. ob.

In i lib. ii buc*es* clowes remanentium precio lib. iiii s. … iiii s. vi d.

In i lib. i qr. iii buc*es* di. mac*es* precio lib. vii s. … xi s. qua.

In ii lib. i buce i qr. le buc*e* nutmugg*es* precio lib. ii s. iiii d. … iiii s. x d. qua.

In iii buc*es* saunders precio le buce i d. … iii d.

In ii lib. et di. buc*e* cinamon large precio lib. iii s. iiii d. … vi s. ix d. qua.

In vi lib. iii qr. cinamon petyt precio lib. ii s. vi d. … xvi s. x d. ob.

In v lib. iii qr. et di. buc*e* zinziberi precio lib. xvi d. … vii s. viii d. ob.

In iiii lib. di. cap*er*es precio lib. ii d. ob. … xi d. qua.

In iii pynt*es* olyff in le pykell … vi d.

In xvii lib. di. dactus precio lib. ii d. … ii s. xi d.

In iiii lib. di. i qr. ii buc*e* confectionum caraweyes precio lib. vi d. … ii s. v d.

In vii lib. di. confett*es* plat*es* precio lib. iiii d. ob. … ii s. ix d. ob. qua.

In i qr. co*n*fett*es* biskett*es* precio lib. x d. … ii d. ob.

In vii lib. iii qr. ii buc*e* grene gyng*er* precio lib. xii d. … vii s. x d. ob.

In x lib. iii qr. et iii buc*e* lemond*es* et succad*es* precio lib. vi d. … v s. vii d.

In precio quadraginta lemond*es* in pekyll … vi d.

In di. lib. quynces in cirop … ii d.

In croco … nichil hic tamen memorandum pro croco remanenti in custodia magistre Fouler[74]

In i qr. ii buc*e* confecc*i*ons precio … iii d.

In xxxii lib. prunes precio lib. ii d. … v s. iiii d.

[*sheet 26*] In xxxiiii lib. di. amigdale precio lib. iii d. … viii s. vii d. ob.

In iii lib. ryse precio lib. i d. ob. … iiii d. ob.

In ii lib. blaunche powd*ur* precio lib. vi d. … xii d.

In iii lib. pouder lucrise precio lib. iiii d. … xii d.

In iiii lib. agnes sedes precio lib. iii d. … xii d.

[74] See sheet 26d below.

In i potell i \q*u*art*e* di./ sallett oyle <de> precium … xii d.

In xxxviii virg. streyn*er*es fyne et course precio virg. ii d. … vi s. iiii d.

In i reme viii quaternis et xiii foliis papiri Francie … iii s. iiii d.

In lxiii lib. i qr. i buce smigmatis albe remanentis precio lib. ii d. … x s. vi d.

Summa totalis stuffure predicte remanentis[75] … CCxxxiii li. vi s. i d. ob.

[75] Preceded by ‘nA’ and written large in the formal script.

DORSE

[*sheet 1d*]

Croydon et Hatfeld.[76]

Computus Willelmi Bedell thesaurarii hospicii excellentissime principisse Margarete comitisse Richmondie et Derbeie ac matris domini regis nunc Henrici vii[mi] \ibidem/ pro uno anno[77] integro finienti xiii[mo] die Januarii anno regni regis Henrici vii predicti xx[ii][do 78]

[79]*Frumentum.* [80]Infrascriptus Willelmus reddit computum de[81] ... xxvi qr. di. ii pec. di. frumenti de remanentia ultimi computi anni proximi precedentis. Et de ... CCCxlvi qr. vi bus. frumenti de provisione dicti computantis infra tempus huius computi ut in libro provisionis hospicii predicti patet. Et de ... x qr. vi bus. di. provenientibus de lez hepes predicti frumenti infra tempus huius computi provisi videlicet de quolibet qr. i pec. etc. Et de ... ii qr. di. bus. provenientibus de incremento mensure de frumento hoc anno provisi ut supra ultra predictos x qr. vi bus. di. frumenti provenientes de lez hepes dicti frumenti superius oneratos.

Summa ... CCCiiii[xx]vi qr. i bus. di. et di. pec.[82]

[*sheet 2d*] De quibus liberantur molendinariis de Croydon \Cxxxiii qr./ et Hatfeld \ Clxxi qr./ ad molendandum pro expensis hospicii predicti infra tempus huius computi ut patet per xii tallias super hunc computum ostensas convinctas probatas et dampnatas etc. ... CCCv qr. frumenti. Et liberantur dictis molendinariis de Croydon et Hatfeld ad molendandum pro officio de le pastre ut patet [per] unam talliam etc. ut supra ... xxiiii qr. frumenti. Et liberantur pro sustentacione pulletrie provise ad usum hospicii domine apud Croydon et Hatfeld infra tempus huius computi ut patet per i talliam etc. ... v qr. frumenti. Et venduntur in foro apud [*blank*] cum iii bus. venditis Johanni Fissh ... vi qr. ii bus. frumenti pro ... xxix s. ii d.

Summa ... CCCxl qr. ii bus.

ʒxxix s. ii d. inde super Johannem Fissh pro iii bus. frumenti ... ii s. iii d. Nota.[83]

Et remanent ... xlv qr. vii bus. di. et di. pec.

[76] Written at the top of the sheet so as to be seen when rolled up.

[77] 'anno' rep.

[78] The rest of the rubric is torn away; [ii] is conjectured on the basis of the rubric on sheet 1.

[79] On the dorse the lavish left margins with headings in formal script leave little room for the entries (often with cancellations, additions, notes, etc.).

[80] Preceded by 'nA' (cf. sheets 22–3 above); so too 'Summa' (1d, 2d, 5d, etc.), 'Et remanent (ultra)' (3d–4d, etc.), and before the brackets in some items, e.g. 'Cervisia' (4d), 'Birra' (5d), etc.

[81] 'Infrascriptus ...de' and 'Summa' (1d) in the formal script; so too 'Et remane(n)t (ultra)', 'Et (de)', 'Unde' (sheets 2d–9d).

[82] At the foot of the sheet, written in the formal script.

[83] 'ʒxxix s. ...Nota' written small in the left margin below 'Frumentum' and alongside the Fish entry.

Unde in[84]

manu Ricardi Knott … ix qr. di. iii pec.

Walteri Cokk*es* … i qr. di.

Georgii Aughton … ii qr. di.

garnario apud Hatfeld … xxxii qr.

Farina frumenti. Et de … iiii qr. iii bus. di. farine frumenticie de remanentia ultimi computi. Et de … \CCCv qr./[85] farine frumenti receptis de molendinariis de Croydon et Hatfeld infra tempus huius computi ut patet per [*blank*] tallias inde confectas etc. ut supra. Et de … xxiiii qr. frumenti receptis de dictis molendinariis de Croydon et Hatfeld pro officio de le pastre ut patet per i talliam inde confectam etc. Et de … ii bus. de farina deficientibus in ultimo computo anni proximi precedentis prout patet in dorso eiusdem.

[86]Summa … CCCxxxiii qr. v bus. di.

De quibus furnuntur in lez manchett*es* chet*es* et trencher bred infra tempus huius computi ut patet per [*blank*] tallias inde confectam etc. … CCCiiii qr. ii bus. Et liberantur officiariis de le pastr*e* pro artocriis et ab inde fiendis pro hospicio predicto etc. ut patet per talliam etc. … xxvi qr. iii bus. di. Et allocatur molendinariis pro vasto facto in molacione frumenti pro hoc anno etc. … nichil. Et venduntur extra hospicium infra tempus predictum … nichil. Et deliberantur pro expensis domine apud Cantabrigiam mense Augusti infra tempus computi … iii bus. farine

Summa … CCCxxxi qr. di. bus.

Et remanent … ii qr. v bus.

Unde

Super

Walterum Cokk*es* valettum pistrine pro farina deficienti in officio suo anno xxi° regni Henrici vii^{i} … ii bus. Perdonatur per dominam super hunc computum ut patet per billam signo manuali <s> signatam penes auditorem remanentem.[87]

[*sheet 3d*] … Et remanent ultra … ii qr. iii bus.

Farina frumenti deliberata pro le pastry. Et de … vi bus. de remanentia ultimi computi. Et de … xxvi qr. iii bus. di. farine frumenticie receptis infra tempus huius computi ut patet per talliam etc. Et de … i qr. i bus. farine deficientibus in officio pasterie in annis xx \v … bus./ et xxi° \iiii bus./ Henrici vii^{i} prout patet in dorso <c> ultimi computi. Summa … xxviii qr. ii bus. di.

[84] Indented and bracketed to include the next four lines ('manu' on the next line should be included in 'unde in'); the bracket is introduced with 'ata' (probably merely decorative).

[85] Preceded by a badly blotted amount deleted and rewritten.

[86] Preceded by an arrangement of dots for calculation.

[87] 'Perdonantur …remanentem' add. to the right of the sum in the same hand.

De quibus expenduntur pro artocriis et aliis ad usum hospicii predicti infra tempus huius computi … xxvi qr. iii bus. di.[88] Summa … xxvi qr. iii bus. di.

Et remanent … i qr. vii bus.

Unde

Perdonantur per dominam super hunc computum per billam signatam penes auditorem remanentem.[89]

Super[90]

Thomam Case vallettum pasterie pro farina deficienti in officio suo in annis xx \v bus./ et xxi \iiii bus./ regni regis Henrici vii^{i} … i qr. i bus.

Robertum Daye valettum pasterie pro farina deficienti in officio suo hoc anno … ii bus.

Et remanent ultra … iiii bus.

*Maunchet*es. De maunchett*es* de remanentia ultimi computi … nichil. Sed reddit de … <XD[...]> \XMDx/ manchett*es* receptis de pistore ad diversas vices infra tempus huius computi \<cum CCxl deliberatis pro expensis domine apud Cantabrigiam>/ ut patet per [*blank*] tallias inter dictos pistorem et officiarium panetrie confectam super hunc computum convinctam probatam et dampnatam etc. Et de … CCCCiii m*aunchettes* deficientibus in ultimo computo anni proximi precedentis prout in dorso eiusdem patet. <Et de>

Summa … IXMDCCCCxiii

De quibus expenduntur infra hospicium predictum per tempus huius computi ut in libro abbreviamentorum dicti hospicii per dictum tempus plenius patet … IXMDCxxxiii m*aunchetes*. Et deliberantur expensis domine apud Cantibrigiam mense Augusti infra tempus huius computi … CCxl m*aunchetes*

Summa … IXMDCCClxxiii

Et remanent … Mxl

Unde

Perdonantur per dominam ut supra[91]

Super[92]

Johannem Fissh valettum panetrie pro maunchett*es* deficientibus in officio suo per librum abbreviamentorum … CCCCiii m*aunchettes*

<Eundem Johannem Fissh> \Riginald Davenport/ et Riginald Davenport vallettum dicte panetrie pro lez m*aunchettes* deficientibus in officio suo hoc anno per librum abbreviamentorum … DCiiivii

Et remanet ultra … nichil

[88] The total is in lighter ink.

[89] Written small in the same hand to the left of 'Super'.

[90] Indented and bracketed to include the next two entries.

[91] Written small in the same hand to the left of 'Super'.

[92] Indented and bracketed to include the next two entries.

[*sheet 4d*] *Chetys et trencher brede*. Et de ... CCCx chet*es* et trencher bred de remanentia ultimi computi. Et de ... LXVMCCCxxi ... chet*es* et trencher bred receptis de pistore ad diversas vices infra[93] tempus huius computi ut patet per [*blank*] tallias inter dictos pistorem et officiarium panetrie confectam super hunc computum convintam probatam et dampnatam etc. Et de ... DCCiiii^{xx}xii chet*es* deficientibus in <p> dorso predicti ultimi computi anni xx^{i} precedentis. Et de ... MMMM chet*es* deficientibus non deliberatis per pistorem iuxta racionem frumenti expenditi infra tempus huius computi in defectu dicti pistoris.

Summa ... LXVIMCCCCxxiii. Item ... MMMM[94]

De quibus expenduntur infra hospicium predictum per tempus huius computi ut in libro abbreviamentorum dicti hospicii per idem tempus patet ... LXIIIIMCCCCiiii^{xx}x [95] di. ... chet*es* et trencher bred. Et allocatur pro pane undicendo quolibet die dominica videlicet pro qualibet septina i chette ... lii chet*es*. Et allocatur pro liberature officiario ... nichil quia supra infra summam LXIIIIMCCCCiiii^{xx}x di. ut parcella eiusdem ut patet in libro abbreviamentorum. <Et de ... MMMM chet*es* deficientibus non deliberatis per pistorem iuxta racionem frumenti expenditi infra tempus huius computi in defectu dicti pistoris>

Summa ... LXIIIIMDxlii di. <Item ... MMMM>[96]

Et remanent ... MDCCCiiii^{xx} ch*etes* di. ... Item

MMMM[97]

Unde

Perdonantur ut supra[98]

Super[99]

Johannem Fissh valettum panetrie pro chet*es* etc. deficientibus in officio suo pro anno xxi^{o} Henrici vii ut patet in dorso ultimi computi ... DCCiiii^{xx}xii

<Eundem> Johannem Fissh et Riginald Davenport valletos dicte panetrie pro chet*es* deficientibus in dicto officio <huius anni> hoc anno per librum abbreviamentorum ... DCClx di.

Walter Cokk*es* pro lez chet*es* deficientibus in defectu <...> MMMM

Et remanent ultra ... CCCxxviii

Cervisia. Et de ... iiii dol. i pip cervisie de remanentia ultimi computi. Et de ... CCxv dol. xli lag. <rec> cervisie receptis de provisione dicti computantis infra tempus huius computi ad diversa precia ut in libro ... provisionis eiusdem hospicii per dictum

[93] 'infra' rep. next line.

[94] 'Item ...MMMM' add. in the same hand in lighter ink.

[95] A blot (of cancellation?) occurs after 'LX'.

[96] Add. and canc. in the same hand.

[97] Add. small below the total.

[98] Written small in the same hand to the left of 'Super'.

[99] Indented and bracketed to include the next three entries.

tempus patet etc. Et de ... xiiii dol. i pip viii lag. deficientibus ut patet in dorso ultimi computi.

Summa ... CCxxxiiii dol. i hogg iii lag.

De quibus expenduntur ad usum hospicii predicti infra tempus huius computi <in> ... Ciiii^xx^xvi dol. i q*u*art. Et in cervisia allocata pro lez dragg*es* bus. pro quolibet dol. viii lag. per relacionem factam super diversa computa precedentia etc. ... nichil quia allocatur inter abbreviamenta etc.

Et in cervisia allocata pro laccagio de cervisia habita ad usum hospicii predicti apud Croydon et Hatfeld ut in libro provisionis hospicii plenius liquet ... i dol. xxviii lag. Et in cervisia debili distributa pauperibus patrie ad diversas vices infra tempus huius computi ut in libro abbreviamentorum dicti hospicii patet ... <vi dol. xxxii lag.> \ nichil/. Et in cervisia debili vocata broken ale liberata [*blank*] Hynkersall grome de le scolery pro aleager et ale salsia in inde fiendis per testimonium Johannis Rose unius clericorum dicti hospicii ... i dol. iii hog. Et liberantur ad usum pauperum elimosinarie domine apud Croydon et Hatfeld ut in libro abbreviamentorum dicti hospicii patet ... vi dol. xxxii lag.

Summa ... CCiiii dol. iii hogg lx lag. i q*u*art*e*

Et remanent ... xxix dol. xxxiiii[100] lag. iii q*u*art*e*

Unde

Perdonantur ut supra[101]

Super[102]

Laurencium Canwyke valettum promptuarii pro cervisia deficienti in officio suo anno xx^o^ \x dol. xxxxii lag./ et xxi^o^ \iii dol. i hog. xxiii lag./ regni regis Henrici vii prout patet in dorso ultimi computi ... xiiii dol. i pip x lag.

Eundem Laurencium pro cervisia deficienti in officio suo hoc anno per librum abbreviamentorum ... xii dol. xl lag. iii q*u*art*e*

Et remanent ultra ... ii dol. i h*og* xxx lag.

[*sheet 5d*] *Birra*. De remanentia ultimi computi ... nichil. Sed reddit de ... i ... kynderkyn beare recepto de provisione dicti[103] computantis infra ... tempus predictum ut in libro provisionis eiusdem hospicii per idem tempus patet.

Summa ... i kynd*erkyn*

< De quibus> \Quorum/ Expenduntur ad usum hospicii predicti infra tempus huius computi ut in libro abbreviamentorum dicti hospicii per tempus predictum patet <etc.> i kyn.

Summa ... nichil

Et remanet ... nichil

[100] MS 'xxxiijj'.

[101] Written small in the same hand to the left of 'Super'.

[102] Indented and bracketed to include the next two entries.

[103] 'dicti' rep. next l.

Vinum Gascon. Et de ...vi dol. i hogg <ix> \viii/ sex. di. <d> vini Gascon[104] remanentibus ultimi computi unde in manu magistri Hugonis Oldom nunc episcopi Exoniensis et Nicholai Mattok iii hogg etc. Et de ...xvii dol. i hogg vini Gascon receptis de provisione dicti computantis infra tempus huius computi ut in libro provisionis dicti hospicii per tempus predictum patet etc. Et de ...i dol. i sest*er*ne de <df> deficientibus ut patet in dorso ultimi computi. Summa ... xxv dol. ix sest*er* di.

De quibus expenduntur ad usum hospicii predicti infra tempus huius computi ut in libro abbreviamentorum dicti hospicii pro tempore predicto patet … xvi dol. iii hogg ii sest*er* iii p*ip* \ii q*u*art*e* di. pynt/. Et in vino deficienti de mensura videlicet per pollicem etc. … nichil. Et allocatur pro lez lyez videlicet pro quolibet pip quinque sest*er*nes quilibet le sesterne continens iiii^or lag. scilicet pro predictis [*blank*] dol. [*blank*] expenditis infra tempus huius computi … nichil hic quia allocantur inter abbreviamenta etc. Et in vino deliberato pro capella domine ad diversas vices infra tempus huius computi per discrecionem officiarii etc. … i hogg. Et in vino deliberato pro vino acri inde fiendo ut in libro abbreviamentorum dicti hospicii patet … i dol. Et in vino dato Edwardo Vause valetto sellarii ex assensu officiarii domine \apud Croydon/ ut in libro abbreviamentorum dicti hospicii continetur … ii hogg brokyn wyne.

Summa … xvii dol. ii <sest*er*> hogg*es* ii sest*er* iii p*ip* ii q*u*art*e* di. pynt

Et remanent … vii dol. ii h*og* vi sest*er* ii p*ip* ii q*u*art*e* di. pynt

Unde

Perdonantur ut supra[105]

Super[106]

Edwardum Vause valettum sellarii pro vino deficienti in officio suo anno xxi° regni regis Henrici vii prout patet in dorso ultimi computi … i dol. i sest*er*ne

Eundem Edwardum pro vino <de> deficienti in predicto officio hoc anno prout patet in dorso computi eiusdem anni … ii hogg v sest*er* ii p*ip* ii q*u*art*e* i di. pynt

Hugonem episcopum Exoniensem et Nicholaum Mattok <apud Colyweston> pro vino per ipsos habito … iii hogg. Notandum quia non perdonatur[107]

[*blank*] pro vino debili remanenti apud Colyweston … i hogg vini debilis

Et remanent ultra … quinque dol. vini \ii dol. di./ rubii et \ii dol. di./ claret*te*

[*sheet 6d*] *Vinum dulce.* Et de … i butt et iii q*u*art*er* i butt malvesey de remanentia ultimi computi. Et de … di. but romney de remanentia ultimi computi. Et de … [*blank*]

Et remanent … i dol. unde in malvesy i butt xxxii p*ip*. In romeney lxiii p*ip* et in mustadell x p*ip*

[rest of sheet 6d blank]

[104] Followed by a blot.

[105] Written small in the same hand to the left of 'Super'.

[106] Indented and bracketed to include the next four entries.

[107] 'Notandum ...perdonatur' written in the same hand to the right of 'iii hogg'.

[*sheet 7d*] *Boves*. Et de ... xxiii bobus de remanentia ultimi computi cum ii \de vetere/ deficientibus etc. Et de ... Clxxiii bobus <d> receptis de provisione dicti computantis infra tempus huius computi ut in libro provisionis dicti hospicii patet. Et de ... vi bobus receptis de exenniis diversorum personarum infra tempus huius computi ut in libro provisionis hospicii predicti in titulo Regarda pro exenniis etc. plenius patet.

Summa ... CCiiii

De quibus mactantur ad usum hospicii predicti infra tempus huius computi ut patet per [*blank*] tallias inter carnificem et officiarium lardarii confectam super hunc computum convinctam probatam et dampnatam etc. ... Cxxix boum. Et venduntur extra hospicium infra tempus predictum ... nichil. Et in morina mortuis infra tempus huius computi per testimonium[108] thesaurarii domine super computum ... iii \apud Croydon Ware et Colyweston/. Et mactantur ad usum hospicii predicti domine apud Cantebrigiam mense Augusti infra tempus huius computi ... iiii boves. Et fore furatis per latrones infra tempus huius computi \apud Croydon/ per recognicionem predicti thesaurarii super computum ... ii

Summa <alloc> ... Cxxxviii

Unde [...] l corriorum venditorum

[*sheet 8d*] Super

John Chambelett de Blechyngley pecia pro iii s. iiii d. ultra iii s. iiii d. perdonatos eidem per discreccionem officiarii domine ... viii li. iii s. iiii d.

[3]*viii li. iii s. iiii d.*[109]

lxxix corria vendita Roberto None de Hertford pecia pro iii s. iiii d. ... xiii li. iii s. iiii d.

[3]*xiii li. iii s. iiii d. Inde super dictum Robertum xiii s. iiii d.*

iiii corria vendita apud Cantebrigiam pecia pro iii s. iiii d. ... xiii s. iiii d.

[3]*xiii s. iiii d.*

et iii corria morinata vendita <de> predicto Roberto None pecia pro ii s. ..vi s.

[3]*vi s. super eundem Robertum None pro ii corriis iiii s.*

<Deficiunt ii boum de vetere remanentia>[110] Et remanent ... lxvi

Unde

Super[111]

<Nota pro ii bobus deficientibus de veteribus remanentibus> Stet.[112]

[108] 'testimonium' rep.

[109] This and the other italicised sums are noted in the left margin alongside the relevant item.

[110] Written small in the same hand to the left of 'Et remanent' and canc.

[111] Bracketed to include the next three entries,.

[112] Written small in the same hand above 'Super', alongside 'Ricardum ...'; canc. and restored ('Stet').

<Nota pro> Memorandum quod ii bos remanent apud Coliweston anno proximo precedenti.[113]

Ricardum David nuper carnificem hospicii domine pro [*blank*] bobus deficientibus in defectu eiusdem <[...] de veteribus deficientibus>[114] ... ii de veteribus

Ballivum de Burne \i boum/ <et apud> \set/ \ ii boum/ castro de Beau*our* ... iii

Henricum Unwyn carneficem dicti hospicii hoc anno deficienti in officio suo ... i qui nuper remanet apud Coliweston

Bovette vocate steres. Et remanent ultra
... lix boves apud Colyweston \xl/ et Hatfeld \xix/

De remanentia ultimi computi ... nichil. Sive de provisione etc. ... nichil

Summa ... null[115]

Et remanet ... nichil

Vacce. De remanentia ultimi computi ... nichil. Sive de provisione etc. ... nichil

Summa ... null

... Et remanet ... nichil

[*sheet 9d*][116] *Carcasia boum.* Et de ... ii carcasiis i pece boum de remanentia ultimi computi. Et de ... Cxxix carcas boum receptis de tot bobus infra tempus huius computi ad usum hospicii predicti necatis ut patet superius etc. Et de ... iiii^or^ carcasiis receptis de tot bobus necatis ad usum hospicii domine apud Cantibrigiam. Et de ... i q*uar*t*er* i pec*e* carnium boum emptis in foro per dictum computantem ut patet in libro provisionis.

Summa ... Cxxxv carcasia i q*uar*t*er* ii pecez

De quibus expenduntur ad usum hospicii predicti infra tempus huius computi ut in libro abbreviamentorum dicti hospicii pro tempore predicto patet ... Cxxx carcasia <i q*uar*t*er*> ix pec*es* <[.....]> Et expenduntur apud Cantebrigiam ad usum <d> hospicii domine ibidem mense Augusti ... iiii carcasia.

Summa ... Cxxxiiii carcasia ix pec*es*

Excedit in abbreviamentis ... vii pec*es*.[117] Et remanent ... xii pec*es* di.

Carcasia bovettorum ... nichil[118]

Carcasia vaccarum ... nichil

[113] Written small in the same hand below 'Super'; 'Nota pro' is perhaps a false start.
[114] The legible part of a heavily cancelled passage.
[115] From this point 'null' is used as well as 'nichil'; it is left unexpanded here because of the problems of properly recognising the referent.
[116] See Plate 3.
[117] Written small in the same hand to the left of 'Et remanent'.
[118] 'nichil' here and below written small.

Multones. Et de ... Cxlix multonibus de remanentia ultimi computi. Et de ... Miiii^{xx}xiii multonibus per dictum computantem provisis infra tempus huius computi ut in libro provisionis dicti hospicii plenius patet. Et de ... x multonibus receptis de exenniis diversis infra tempus huius computi ut[119] in libro provisionis hospicii predicti in titulo Regarda pro exenniis plenius liquet etc. Summa ... MCClii

[*sheet 10d*] De quibus necantur ad usum hospicii predicti infra tempus huius computi ut in libro abbreviamentorum dicti hospicii patet ... DCCCCxxv. Et venduntur extra hospicium diversis personis infra tempus huius computi etc. ... xxvi multones debiles pro ... xxv s. Et in multonibus ex morina mortuis infra tempus computi ... xxxiiii. Et allocatur pro multonibus allocatis in ultimo computo dicti computantis et oneratis in libro provisionis \hospicii predicti/ huius anni ... Cxxii Summa ... MCvii

[120]unde iiii^{xx}xiiii pelles que faciunt vii dd. x pelles provenientes de pellibus multonum necatorum inter xiii diem Januarii et diem cinerum infra tempus computi etc. pecia pro iiii d. ... xxxi s. iiii d. sic vendite Johanni Cokk*es* CCxii pelles vocate wollefell que faciunt xvii dd. viii pelles <dd. ad vii s. vi d.> venduntur dicto Johanni Cokk*es* pecia pro vii d. ob. et dd. <pro> \ad/ vii s. vi d. ... vi li. xviii s. xi d. ob. CCC pelles vocate shirly*nges* que faciunt xxv dd. sic vendite dicto Johanni pecia pro iii d. ... lxxv s. CClii pelles que faciunt xxi dd. necate inter festum sancti Martini et xiii^{m} diem Januarii in clauso huius computi vocate wynt*er*fell vendite <d> predicto Johanni pecia pro iiii d.[121] ... iiii li. iiii s. et lviii pelles vocate wynt*er*fell <ac> pecia ad iiii d. ac ix pelles vocate wollefell pecia ad vii d. ob. de pellibus multonum venditis per clericos hospicii et non specificatis per talliam ... xxiiii s. xi d. ob. Necnon lxxiiii pelles morinate de remanentiis de annis xx^{o} et xxi^{o} Henrici vii^{o} vendite prefato Johanni Cokk*es* pro iii s. iiii d.

Et remanent ... <lxvii> \Cxlv/ multones

Unde

Super[122]

Henricum Unwyn carnificem hospicii predicti pro multonibus deficientibus hoc anno ... lxvii notandum[123]

Et remanent ultra ... lxxviii <unde> qui remanent apud Hatfeld in custodia Johannis a Greve unde \lxv/ <lxiii> debiles multones

Carcasia multonum. Et de ... vi carcasiis multonum de remanentia ultimi computi. Et de ... DCCCCxxv multonibus receptis de tot multonibus infra tempus huius computi ad usum hospicii predicti necatis ut patet superius etc. Summa ... DCCCCxxxi

De quibus expenduntur ad usum hospicii predicti infra tempus huius computi ut in libro abbreviamentorum dicti hospicii patet ... DCCCCxxxiiii Summa ... patet

Excedit in abbreviamentis ... iii carcasia multonum[124] Et remanent ... iiii carcas

[119] 'ut' rep. next l.

[120] 'unde ... pro iii s. iiii d.' written in the same hand straight after 'Summa ...MCvii'.

[121] MS 'iijj'.

[122] Indented and bracketed to include the next entry and 'Et remanent ...multones'.

[123] 'lxvii notandum' written as one comment.

[124] Written small in the same hand to the left of 'Et remanent'.

Vituli. Et de … v carcasiis vitulorum de remanentia ultimi computi. Et de … CCCxxxii \di./ carcasiis vitulorum ad usum hospicii predicti infra … tempus huius <hisus> computi provisionis ut in libro provisionis dicti hospicii patet. Et de … i carcaso di. de deficientibus prout patet in dorso ultimi computi. Summa … CCCxxxix

[*sheet 11d*] De quibus expenduntur ad usum hospicii predicti infra tempus huius computi ut in libro abbreviamentorum dicti hospicii patet … CCCxli i q*uart*er

Summa … patet

Excedit in abbreviamentis … v carcasia i q*uarter*[125] Et remanent … iii carcasia

Agnelli. De remanentia ultimi computi … null. Sed reddit de … CCCxxvii agnellis receptis de provisione infra tempus huius computi ut in libro provisionis hospicii ut in libro provisionis hospicii supradicti plenius liquet. Et de … xvi carcasiis iii q*uart*er de agnellis deficientibus ultimo computo prout in dorso eiusdem patet.

Summa … CCCxliii carcasia iii q*uart*er

De quibus expenduntur ad usum hospicii predicti infra tempus huius computi ut in libro abbreviamentorum dicti hospicii patet … CCCxiii Summa … patet

Et remanent … xxx carcas

Unde

Perdonantur per dominam super hunc computum ut supra[126]

Super[127]

Thomam Hill pro agnellis deficientibus anno xxi° regni regis Henrici vii^{i} prout patet in dorso computi eiusdem anni … xvi carcasia iii q*uart*er

Eundem Thomam Hill pro agnellis deficientibus hoc anno … xiii carcasia i q*uart*er

Et remanet ultra … i carcas

Porci. De remanentia ultimi computi … nichil. Sed reddit de … iiii^{xx}xviii porcis de provisione dicti computantis infra tempus huius computi ad usum hospicii predicti etc.

[128]Supra … … iiii^{xx}xviii[129]

Tamen expenduntur ad usum hospicii predicti infra tempus predictum … iiii^{xx}xviii carcasia i q*uarter.*

Excedit in abbreviamentis … i q*uarter*[130] Et remanet … nichil

[*sheet 12d*] *Lana.* Et de … null de remanentia ultimi computi. Sed reddit de … xxxv pet. lane in CCiiii velleribus etc. quelibet pet. continens xiiii lib. pet. ad ii s. iiii d. sic liberantur Willelmo Wyllyn de Chesthunt pro … iiii li. xx d.

[125] Written small in the same hand to the left of 'Et remanent'.
[126] Written small in the same hand to the left of 'Super'.
[127] Indented and bracketed to include the next two entries.
[128] The rest of sheet 11d is indented and written as continuous text.
[129] See sheet 10 ('Empcio aprorum porcorum').
[130] Written small in the same hand to the left of 'Et remanent'.

[3]<[...]> *iiii li. xx d.*[131] Summa ... xxxv pet. que liberantur Willelmo Wyllyn etc. ut supra[132]

<De quib>

Memorandum quod quilibet waye continet xiiii pet. et quelibet pet. continet xiiii lib.[133]

Cepum proveniens de bobus et multonibus.[134] Et de ... <x>xvi pet. cepi de remanentia ultimi computi. Et de ... xxxvi wayes xi<i> pet. cepi provenientis de bobus et multonibus infra tempus huius computi ad usum hospicii predicti necatis ut patet per [*blank*] tallias super hunc computum convinctam probatam et dampnatam etc.

Summa ... <xxxix wayes <i>i pet.> xxvii wayes xiii pet.

De quibus liberantur pro luminibus albis inde fiendis ad usum hospicii predicti inferius specificatis ... nichil. Et venduntur Thome Dyer de Croydon ut de cepo provenienti de bobus et multonibus necatis ad usum hospicii predicti <inter> apud Croydon inter xiii^{m} diem Januarii et primum diem Junii extunc proximo sequenti infra tempus huius computi accidentis precio le waye x s. et pet. ad viii d. ob. ... <x>viii way di. pro iiii li. v s.

[3]*iiii li. v s.*[135]

Et venduntur apud Cantabrigiam provenientes de iiii^{or} bobus ibidem necatis ad usum hospicii domine pet. pro viii d. ... xxiii pet. ... xv s. iiii d.

[3]*xv s. iiii d.*

Et venduntur Willelmo Thomson de Seynt Albons de cepo provenienti de bobus et multonibus necatis etc. inter \dictum/ primum diem Junii et xiii^{m} diem Januarii in clauso huius computi precio le way x s. et pet. viii d. ob. ut supra ... xxvi wayes xi pet. ... xiii li. vii s. ix d. ob.

[3]*xiii li. vii s. ix d. ob. Inde super W. Thomson x s. pro i le waye cepi.*

Et venduntur Willemo Kyln*er* ... i way cepi pro ... x s.

[3]*x s.*

Summa ... xxvii wayes xiii lib. que continent in <libris> pet. ... Dxxxi

Et remanet ... nichil

Porci.

Nichil hic quia antea.[136]

De remanentia ultimi computi ... null. Sed reddit de ... [*blank*] porcis infra tempus huius computi ad usum hospicii predicti provisis ut in libro provisis ut in libro provisionis dicti hospicii per tempus predictum patet etc. Summa ... null hic quia antea

[131] ‘[3]...xx d.’ written small in the left margin above ‘Lana’.
[132] See sheets 6 and 21 above. All written in the same hand.
[133] Written small in the same hand above the marginal heading ‘Cepum ...multonibus’.
[134] Written small in the same hand alongside ‘Et de ...’.
[135] This and the other italicised sums are noted in the left margin alongside the relevant item..
[136] Written small in the left margin after ‘Porci’. See the last entry on sheet 11d and footnote.

[*sheet 13d*] *Lynges*. Et de … DCCC \<...> iiii^{xx}xix/ lyng*es* de remanentia ultimi computi. Et de … MDCCli lyng*es* receptis de provisione dicti computantis infra tempus huius computi <et> ad usum dicti hospicii etc. cum [*blank*] lez <pro> taleffisshes. Et de … … xxxvii ling*es* de defectu in ultimo computo prout patet in dorso eiusdem.

Summa … MMDCiiii^{xx}vii <[...]>

Item xxxvii[137]

De quibus expenduntur ad usum hospicii predicti infra tempus huius computi[138] in libro abbreviamentorum dicti hospicii patet … MCCv lyng*es* di. Et liberantur pro expensis domine apud Cantibrigiam mense Augusti etc. … iiii   Summa … MCCix

Et remanent … MCCCClxxvii<i>

Item … xxxvii.

Unde

Perdonantur ut supra[139]

Super[140]

Thomam Hill valettum lardarii sicci hospicii predicti pro ling*es* deficientibus in officio suo anno xxi° H. vii^{i} … xxxvii

Eundem Thomam Hyll pro lyng*es* deficientibus in dicto officio hoc anno <ut patet per dictum> librum abbreviamentorum … li

Et remanent ultra … MCCCCxxvii lyng*es*

*Codd*es *et haberdeyne*. <Et de> De codd*es* et hab*er*deyns de remanentia ultimi computi … null. Sed reddit de ...Ciiii^{xx}iii codd*es* et hab*er*deyns deficientibus in <ii> annis xx° et xxi° regni regis Henrici vii^{i} prout patet in dorso ultimi computi. Et de … MDCCCCxv receptis de provisione dicti computantis infra tempus huius computi etc.

Summa … MMiiii^{xx}xviii

De quibus expenduntur ad usum hospicii predicti infra tempus huius computi etc. ut in libro abbreviamentorum dicti hospicii patet … DCCCCiiii^{xx}iiii   Summa … patet.

Et remanent … MCxiiii.

Unde

Perdonantur ut supra[141]

Super[142]

Thomam Hyll <z> valettum lardarii dicti hospicii pro dictis pissibus salsis deficientibus in officio suo in <ii bus.> anno xx° \Cxvii/ et xxi° \lxvi/ regni regis Henrici vii^{i} … Ciiii^{xx}iii

[137] Add. in the same hand after 'Summa'.

[138] Followed by a blot.

[139] Written small in the same hand to the left of 'Super'. See sheet 11d.

[140] Indented and bracketed to include the next two entries.

[141] Written small in the same hand to the left of 'Super'.

[142] Indented and bracketed to include the next two entries.

Eundem Thomam pro pissibus deficientibus in officio predicto per librum abbreviamentorum hoc anno ... xxix

Et remanent ultra ... DCCCCii

Fungie. Et de ... Dxlvi fungiis de remanentia ultimi computi. Et de ... MDCiiii$^{x[x]}$ fungiis receptis de provisione dicti computantis infra ... tempus huius computi etc. ut <p> in libro provisionis dicti hospicii patet. Et de ... iiii^{xx}ix fungiis deficientibus in annis xx^{o} et xxi^{o} Henrici vii^{i} ut patet in dorso ultimi computi anni proximi precedentis.

Summa ... MMCCCCxv

De quibus expenduntur ad usum hospicii predicti infra tempus huius computi ut in libro abbreviamentorum dicti hospicii patet ... DCClxviii

Summa ... patet

Et remanent ... MDCxlvii.

Unde

Perdonantur ut supra[143]

Super[144]

Thomam Hill valettum lardarii hospicii predicti pro fungiis deficientibus in officio in annis xx \lxv/ et xxi \xxiiii/ regni regis Henrici vii^{i} prout patet <per> in dorso ultimi computi ... iiii^{xx}ix

Eundem Thomam pro fungiis deficientibus in officio suo hoc anno ... xlv

Et remanent ultra ... MDxiii

[*sheet 14d*] *Sturgyon*. Et de ... i barell i q*uarter* barell sturgyons de remanentia ultimi computi. Et de ... ii barell*es* receptis de provisione dicti computantis infra tempus huius computi ut in libro provisionis dicti hospicii patet.

Summa ... iii barell*es* et i q*uarter*

<De quibus> \stet/ <\Et ... > expenduntur ad usum hospicii predicti infra tempus huius computi etc. ... ii barell*es* di. Summa ... [*blank*]

Et remanent ... iii q*uarter* unius barell

Salmones salsi. Et de ... vii barell*es* salmonium salsorum de remanentia ultimi computi. Et de ... xiiii barell*es* salmonium salsorum receptis de provisione dicti computantis infra tempus predictum etc. Summa ... xxi

De quibus expenduntur ad usum hospicii predicti infra tempus huius computi etc. ut supra ... xi b*arelles* Summa ... patet

Et remanent ... x barell*es*

143 Written in the same hand to the left of 'Super'.

144 Indented and bracketed to include the next two entries.

Anguille salse. De remanentia ultimi computi … nichil. Et de … i <xiiii> barell i firkyn anguillarum salsarum receptis de provisione dicti computantis etc. ut supra.

Summa … i barell i firkyn que expenduntur ad usum hospicii predicti etc.

Et remanet … nichil.

Congre salse.[145]

Et de … i congre de remanentia ultimi computi. Et de … xiii de provisione dicti computantis etc. Summa … xiiii.

Et remanent … xiii congr*e*.

^{3}*xii d.*[146] De quibus venditur extra hospicium infra tempus predictum etc. … i congre pro … xii d. Summa … patet.

Allec album. De remanentia ultimi computi … null. Sed reddit de … xx [*blank*] barell*es* \di./ receptis de provisione dicti computantis infra tempus huius computi etc.

Summa … xx^{ti} di. barell*es*

De quibus expenduntur ad usum hospicii predicti infra tempus huius computi … ix barell*es* di.

Summa … patet.

Et remanent … xi barell*es*

[*sheet 15d*] *Allec rubium.* De remanentia ultimi computi … null. Sed reddit de … xiiii cad*es* Dviii cad*es* allecis rubii receptis de provisione dicti computantis infra tempus predictum etc.[147]

Summa … xiiii cad*es* Dviii

De quibus expenduntur ad usum hospicii predicti infra tempus huius computi etc. … vi cad*es* CClxviii allecis Summa … patet.

Et remanent … viii cad*es* di.

*Sprott*es. De remanentia ultimi computi … null. Sed reddit de … iiii^{or} cadys sprott*es* <de> receptis de provisione dicti computantis infra tempus huius computi etc. ut supra.

Summa … iiii que expenduntur ad usum hospicii predicti infra tempus huius computi.

Et remanent … null

Sal.

Memorandum quod i way salis continet [*blank*].[148] Et de … iii qr. salis de Baye <et ii bus. salis albi> de remanentia ultimi computi <...>. Et de … ii bus. salis albi de remanentia ultimi computi etc. Et de <iii way di.> \xi qr./ salis albi receptis de provisione dicti

[145] Within the entry for 'Anguille salse' but bracketed with separate marginal subheading.
[146] Written small in the left margin alongside the entry.
[147] 'cades(2) ...etc.' written in darker ink.
[148] Written small in the same hand alongside 'Et de …iii way …'.

computantis infra tempus huius computi ut in libro provisionis dicti hospicii patet. Et de … iii way di. iii qr. ii bus. salis de Bay receptis de provisione dicti computantis infra tempus huius computi etc. ut supra.

Summa … iii wayez di. vi qr. ii bus. salis de Baye et xi qr. ii bus. salis albi

De quibus expenduntur ad usum hospicii predicti infra tempus predictum de sale de le Bay … iii wayez di. vii bus. Et expenduntur ad usum dicti hospicii infra tempus predictum de sale albo … x qr.. Et venduntur Thome Hill de Croydon … xxx bus. salis de Baye pro … ix s. xi d.

[3]*ix s. xi d.*[149] Summa … iii wayes di. xiiii qr. v bus.

Et remanent … ii qr. vii bus. unde in sale de Bay i qr. v bus. et in sale albo x bus.

Oleum. De remanentia ultimi computi … null. Sed reddit de … ii barell*es* continentibus [*blank*] lag. olei <recept'>[150] de rape per predictum computantem provisis infra tempus huius computi etc. Et de … nichil [*blank*] olei vocati lampe oyle per dictum computantem proviso etc. ut supra. Summa … ii barell*es*

[*sheet 16d*] De quibus expenduntur ad usum hospicii predicti infra tempus huius computi etc. videlicet de oleo de le rape … ii barell*es*. Et expenduntur in oleo vocato lampe oyle infra tempus predictum … nichil. Summa <patet> … ii barell*es*.

Et remanent … iiii lag.

Mel.[151]

De remanentia ultimi computi … nichil. Sed reddit de … [*blank*] de provisione dicti computantis infra tempus predictum. Summa … [*blank*]

De quibus expenduntur ad usum dicti hospicii infra tempus predictum … [*blank*]

Et remanent … i barell i fyrkyn.

Candele albe.

Nota quod quodlibet dd. continet xiii lib.[152]

Et de … xxvii dd. i lib. candelarum albarum de remanentia ultimi computi. Et de … CCCxlvii dd. candelarum albarum receptis de provisione dicti … computantis infra tempus huius computi ut in libro provisionis hospicii predicti patet. Et de … null[153] candelarum albarum receptarum de <prefa> stauro prefate <d> principisse etc. Et de … xv dd. di. candelarum vocatarum wacchyng candell*es* de provisione computantis etc. ut supra. Et de … iiii^{xx}vi dd. vi lib. di. de candelis deficientibus in annis <xx^{o}> xix^{o} et xxi^{o} regni regis Henrici vii^{i}.

Summa … CCC<C>lxxvi dd. di. que faciunt VIMCiiii^{xx}ix lib. di.

[149] Written small in the same hand alongside 'ix s. xi d.'.

[150] 'olei' rep. next line.

[151] Within the entry for 'Oleum', but bracketed with a separate marginal subheading.

[152] Written small in the left margin alongside 'Et de ...xxvii dd.'.

[153] Inserted into a gap in the template for the number of candles.

De quibus expenduntur ad usum hospicii predicti infra tempus huius computi ut in libro abbreviamentorum hospicii predicti patet … MMMDCCiiii^{xx}xviii lib. \di./ candelarum albarum. Et allocatur pro lez quarryers et <le> wacchyng candell*es* expenditis infra hospicium predictum infra tempus huius computi … xxv lib. que faciunt ii dd. i lib.

Summa … MMMDCCCxxiii lib. di.

Et remanent … MMlxxvi lib.

Unde

Perdonantur ut supra[154]

Super[155]

Willelmum Kiln*er*e valettum chaunder*e* hospicii domine pro candelis deficientibus in officio suo annis xx^{o} \xxxviii dd. vi lib. di./ et xxi^{o} \lviii dd./ regni regis Henrici vii^{i} … iiii^{xx}xvi dd. vi lib. di.

Eundem Willelmum pro candelis deficientibus in dicto officio hoc anno … iiii^{xx}ix dd. ii lib. di. que faciunt Mlxx lib. di.

In libris Cxxxii.[156] Et remanent ultra … xi dd. v lib.

Cera. Et de … Dxlvii lib. cere operatis et non operatis de remanentia ultimi computi. Et de … null … cere per dictum computantem infra tempus huius computi proviso ut in libro dicti hospicii patet. Et de … Ciiii^{xx}xii lib. receptis de Roberto Tales de Staunford ut parcella CCCCvi lib. cere eidem venditarum extra hospicium anno proximo precedenti per recognicionem Willelmi Kyln*er*e valetti chaunder*e* etc. Et de...CCClxxvii lib. iii qr. de cera deficientibus in dicto officio chaunder*e* in annis xix^{o} et xx^{o} H. vii^{i}.

Summa … <C>MCxvi lib. iii qr.

De quibus expenduntur ad usum hospicii predicti infra tempus huius computi ut in tortis ceriis sic*es* prikett*es* et ab luminibus factis ad usum dicti hospicii ut in libro abbreviamentorum eiusdem hospicii patet … Dx lib. i qr. cere. Et allocatur pro quinque dd. di. quarryes continentibus xviii lib. cereis continentibus ix lib. di. syses iii lib. et prykett*es* v lib. remanentibus in fine ultimi computi prius non allocatis in toto … xxxv lib. di. Et allocatur pro lez quarryes ceriis sisez et prykett*es* remanentibus hoc anno … nichil.

Summa … Dxlv lib. iii qr.

Et remanent … Dlxxi lib.

Unde

[154] Written small in the same hand to the left of 'Super'.

[155] Indented and bracketed to include the next two entries.

[156] Written small to the left of 'Et ...lib.'.

[*sheet 17d*] Perdonantur ut supra[157]

Super[158]

Willelmum Kiln*er*e valettum chaunder*e* pro cera deficienti in dicto officio in annis decimo nono \CClxxiiii lib./ et vicesimo \Ciii lib. iii qr./ regni regis Henrici vii^{i} … CCClxxvii lib. iii qr. Nota quia non deficit abbreviamentiis ut supponitur.[159]

Eundem Willelmum pro cera deficienti in dicto officio tam pro hoc anno quam anno proximo precedenti … liii lib. i qr.

Et remanent ultra … Cxl lib. xlvi lib. operate non operate iiii^{xx}xiiii lib.[160]

Rosyn. Et de … CCiiii^{xx}xiii lib. rosyn de remanentia ultimi computi. Et de … null <libris> rosyn per dictum computantem proviso infra tempus huius computi etc.

Summa … CCiiii^{xx}xiii

De quibus expenduntur ad usum hospicii predicti infra tempus huius computi etc. ut supra … Ciiii^{xx}<xiii>i lib. Summa … patet.

Et remanent … Cxii[161] lib.

Torti. Et de … xxiiii tortis hole ponderantibus CCxxxiiii lib. de remanentia ultimi computi. Et de … viii tortis fractis ponderantibus lxi lib. de remanentia dicti ultimi computi. Et de … xiiii staff torches hole ponderantibus xxxii lib. de remanentia ultimi computi. Et de … xix staff torchys fractis ponderantibus xl lib. de remanentia dicti ultimi computi. Et de … [*blank*] tortis.

Et remanent … [162]

In torches hole …

In tortis fractis …

xxiii ponderantibus CC<C>C\viii lib./<iiii^{xx}iiii lib.>[163]

In staffe tortis ponderantibus … lvii lib.

In staf*es* for torches … xii p*r*ice iiis.[164]

[*sheet 18d*] [165]*Supp*er*light*es. Et de … quinque dd. viii lib. ponderantibus in toto xviii lib. de remanentia ultimi computi. Et de … [*blank*]

Et remanet … null.

[157] Written small in the same hand to the left of 'Super'.
[158] Indented and bracketed to include the next two entries.
[159] See sheet 16d.
[160] 'xlvi … iiii^{xx}xiiii lib.' written small in the cramped space to the right of 'Cxl lib.'.
[161] MS 'xjj'.
[162] The following entries on the page are actually above and to the right of the templated 'Et remanent'.
[163] The total of the two entries above, bracketed to the right of the entries.
[164] 'price iii s.' add. in lighter ink.
[165] 'Supperlightes ...de' add. above and to the right of the templated 'Et remanet'.

*Syses et Prikett*es. Et de … iii lib. syses de remanentia ultimi computi. Et de … v lib. prikett*es* de remanentia dicti ultimi computi. Et de … [*blank*]

Et remanet … nichil.

Cerii et mortes. Et de … ix lib. ceriorum de remanentia ultimi computi. De morteys de remanentia … null.

Sed reddit de … [*blank*].

Et remanet … null.

Weke. Et de … lvi lib. torche weke de remanentia ultimi computi. Et de … xx lib. tap*er* weke de remanentia ultimi computi. Et de … xiiii lib. le weeke de provisione dicti computantis infra tempus huius visus. Summa … iiii^{xx}x [lib.][166]

[*sheet 19d*] De quibus expenduntur ad usum hospicii predicti infra tempus computi … xxi lib. Summa … patet.

Et remanent … lx<xix>\vii/ lib. unde in torche <way> \weke/ viii pet. … quelibet pet. continens … viii lib. … lxiiii lib. Tap*er* weke … iii lib. <et le weke pro staff*es* torche s … xii lib.>

Fici. De remanentia ultimi computi … null. Sed reddit de … iiii toppenott*es* ficorum de orto et iiii^{or} sort*is* ficorum de marchaunte per ipsum computantem provisis ad usum hospicii predicti infra tempus huius computi etc.

Summa … iiii^{or} sort*es* ficorum de marchaunte et iiii^{or} toppenott*es* ficorum de orto que expenduntur ad usum hospicii predicti infra tempus predictum.

Et remanet … nichil.

Rasoni magni. Et de … C lib. rasonorum magnorum de remanentia ultimi computi <per usum>. Et de … Diiii lib. rasonorum per dictum computantem provisis infra tempus huius computi ut in libro provisionis dicti hospicii patet.

Summa … DCiiii lib.

De quibus expenduntur ad usum hospicii predicti infra tempus huius computi ut in libro <abbreviamentorum dicti> \de parcellis <per clericos>/ hospicii pro tempore predicto <patet> \scripto penes Willelmum Elm*ere* clericum spicerie remanentibus/ … Cxlvi lib. Et allocatur pro vasto facto et perdito in custodia dictorum rasonorum per tempus huius computi per discreccionem officiarii etc. … [*blank*].

Et allocatur pro pondere de lez frayles etc. per discreccionem officiarii etc. … [*blank*].

Summa … [*blank*].

Et remanet … [*blank*].

[166] MS 'd'.

[*sheet 20d*] *Succad*es. De remanentia ultimi computi … nichil. Sive de provisione infra tempus huius computi … nichil. Summa … null.

Et remanet … nichil.

Marmelade. De remanentia ultimi computi … null. Sive de provisione infra tempus huius computi … nichil. Summa … null.

Et remanet … nichil.

Suger course et hole. Et de … Clxxvii lib. iii qr. suger course et hole de remanentia ultimi computi. Et de … DCClxix lib. [*blank*] per predictum computantem provisis ad usum hospicii predicti infra tempus huius computi etc. ut in libro provisionis <dci>[167] dicti hospicii patet.

Summa … DCCCCxlvi lib. iii qr.

De quibus expenduntur ad usum hospicii predicti infra tempus huius computi etc. … DClv lib. di. Et expenduntur ad usum dicti hospicii ut patent diverse bille signate … viii lib. Summa … DClv lib. di.

Item viii li.[168]

³Et remanent … CCiiii^{xx}iii lib. i qr.

Suger powder. Et de … lxxix lib. di. suger powder de remanentia ultimi computi. Et de … xlviii lib. [*blank*] de provisione dicti computantis infra tempus huius computi etc.

Summa … Cxxvii lib. di.

De quibus expenduntur ad usum hospicii predicti infra tempus huius computi etc. … Cxiii lib. Summa … Cxiii lib.

³Et remanent … xiiii lib. di.

Suger candy. De remanentia ultimi computi … nichil. Sed reddit de … di. lib. de provisione dicti computantis infra tempus huius computi etc.

Summa … di. lib. quod expenditur ad usum hospicii predicti etc.

Et remanet … nichil.

[*sheet 21d*][169] *Suger valans*. De remanentia ultimi computi … nichil. <Et de … > Sed reddit de … xii lib. iii qr. ii oz. per dictum computantem provisis ad usum hospicii predicti infra tempus huius computi etc. ut in libro provisionis dicti hospicii patet.

Summa … xii lib. iii qr. ii oz.

De quibus expenduntur ad usum hospicii predicti infra tempus huius computi etc. … iiii lib. \di./ <iii q> iii oz.

[167] Heavily blotted.
[168] Add. below in the same hand.
[169] See Plate 4.

Et allocatur pro le sug*er* valans habito de Willelmo Elmere clerico spicerie domine de proprio stauro suo et ad usum hospicii \dicte/ domine infra tempus computi anni proximi precedentis <Summa> expendito prout in dorso computi dicti anni patet … iii oz.. Et expenduntur ad usum hospicii predicti ut patet per billam signatam … i lib. i qr. Summa … vi lib. ii oz.

[3]Et remanent … vi lib. iii qr.

Rason corans. De remanentia ultimi computi … nichil. <Et de> Sed reddit de … Clxxv lib. de provisione dicti computantis infra tempus huius computi etc.

Summa … Clxxv lib.

De quibus expenduntur ad usum hospicii predicti infra tempus huius computi etc. … Cliiii lib. Et allocatur pro lez reson corans habitis de Willelmo Elmere clerico spicerie domine de proprio stauro suo et ad usum hospiciii dicte domine infra tempus computi anni proximi precedentis expenditis prout in dorso computi dicti anni patet … vii lib.

Summa … Clxi lib.

Et remanent … xiiii lib.

*Pep*ur. Et de … xxvi lib. di. oz. <de> pep*ur* de remanentia ultimi computi etc. Et de … xlviii lib. pep*ur* de provisione dicti computantis infra tempus huius computi etc.

Summa … <lxiiii lib. i> lxxiiii lib. di. oz.

De quibus expenduntur infra hospicium predictum infra tempus huius computi etc. … lxiiii lib. i qr. et i oz.. Summa … lxiiii lib. i qr. et i oz.

[3]Et remanent … ix lib. di. iii oz. di.

Greynes. De remanentia ultimi computi … nichil. <Et de> \Sed reddit de/ … xxviii lib. greynes de provisione dicti computantis etc.[170] [3]Summa … xxviii lib.

De quibus expenduntur ad usum hospicii predicti infra tempus huius computi etc. … vii lib. Et allocatur pro lez greynes habitis de Willelmo Elmere clerico <hospi> spicerie domine de proprio stauro suo et ad usum hospicii dicte domine infra tempus computi anni proximi precedentis expenditis ut in dorso computi dicti anni patet … iiii lib.

Summa … xi lib.

[3]Et remanent … xvii lib.

Clovys. Et de … i lib. \di./ iii oz. di. clowys de remanentia ultimi computi. Et de … xiii lib. de provisione infra tempus huius computi. Summa … xiiii lib. di. iii oz. di.

De quibus expenduntur ad usum hospicii predicti infra tempus huius computi … xiii lib. di. i oz. di.

[170] 'greynes ...etc.' continues straight on from the previous text but with a gap which suggests that it was add. later.

[*sheet 22d*] ... Et remanent ... i lib. ii oz.

Masys. Et de ... i lib. di. i oz. i q*uar*t*er* le oz. de remanentia ultimi computi. Et de ... xiii lib. provisis infra tempus huius computi. Summa ... xiiii lib. di. i oz. et i q*uar*t*er* le unc*e*

De quibus expenduntur infra tempus huius computi ad usum hospicii predicti etc. ... xiii lib. iii q*uar*t*er* le unc*e*. Summa ... xiii lib. iii quart*er* le unc*e*

[3]Et remanent ... i lib. <di.> \i q*uar*t*er* iii oz./ et di. oz.

*Nutmug*es. Et de ... ii lib. iii qr. ii oz. et i q*uar*t*er* le unce de remanentia ultimi computi. Et de ... xiii lib. provisis infra tempus huius computi ad usum eiusdem hospicii etc.

Summa ... xv li. iii qr. ii oz. et i q*uar*t*er* le unc*e*

De quibus expenduntur ad usum hospicii predicti infra tempus huius computi etc. ... xiii lib. i qr. et i oz. Summa ... xiii lib. i qr. et i oz..

[3]Et remanent ... ii lib. di. <i qr.> i oz. et i \q*uar*t*er* le unc*e*/

Saunders. Et de ... iiii lib. di. de remanentia ultimi computi. Et de ... <iiii lib. di.> \x lib. di./ provisis infra tempus huius computi etc. Summa ... x lib. di.

De quibus expenduntur ad usum hospicii predicti infra tempus predictum ... x lib. i qr. et i oz..

[3]Et remanent ... iii oz.

Synamome large. De remanentia ultimi computi ... null. <Et de> \Sed reddit de/ ... xv lib. quinque oz. provisis infra tempus huius computi etc.

Summa ... xv lib. quinque oz.

[*sheet 23d*] De quibus expenduntur ad usum dicti hospicii infra tempus predictum etc. ... x lib. iii oz. di.

Et allocatur pro le synamom large habito de Willelmo Elmere clerico spicerie domine de proprio stauro suo et ad usum hospicii dicte domine infra tempus computi anni proximi precedentis expendito prout in dorso computi eiusdem anni patet ... i lib. quinque oz.. Et expenduntur \etc./ ut patet per billam signatam ... i lib. i qr.

Summa ... xi lib. di. et di. oz.

Item ... i lib. i qr.[171]

[3]Et remanent ... ii lib. <iii qr.> \di./ et di oz.

Synamome petit. De remanentia ultimi computi ... nichil. <Et> \Sed reddit/ de ... xx lib. i qr. synamome petit de provisione infra tempus huius computi.

Summa ... xx lib. i qr..

De quibus expenduntur ad usum hospicii predicti infra tempus huius computi ... xiii lib. i qr.

[171] Add. below in the same hand.

Et allocatur pro le synamom petytte habito de Willelmo Elmere clerico spicerie domine de stauro suo proprio et ad usum hospicii dicte domine infra tempus computi anni proximi precedentis expendito prout in dorso computi dicti anni patet … i qr.

Summa … xiii lib. di.

[3]Et remanent … vi lib. iii qr..

Gynger. Et de … vi lib. di. et di. oz. de remanentia ultimi computi. Et de … xviii lib. zinziberi provisis infra tempus huius computi etc. Summa … xxiiii lib. di. et di. oz.

De quibus expenduntur ad usum hospicii predicti infra tempus huius computi … xviii lib. i. qr. et i oz..

Et expenduntur ad usum dicti hospicii ut per diversas billas signatas etc. … i qr. iii oz.

Summa … xviii lib. i qr. et i oz.

Item … i qr. iii oz.[172]

[3]Et remanent … v<i> lib. <iii oz. > \iii qr./ di. \oz./.

Capers. Et de … iii lib. <de p> cap*er*es de remanentia ultimi computi. Et de … <xv> \xii/ lib. provisis infra tempus huius computi etc. Summa … xv lib.

De quibus expenduntur ad usum hospicii predicti infra tempus huius computi … x li. di. cum iii lib. allocatis per billam signatam. Summa … x lib. di.

[3]Et remanent … iiii lib. di.

Olyves in pykell. Et de … i pynt olyves de remanentia ultimi computi. Et de … i potell iii pynt*es* provisis infra tempus huius computi etc. Summa … i gallon.

De quibus expenduntur ad usum hospicii predicti infra tempus huius computi … i potell i pynte. Summa … i potell i pynte.

[3]Et remanent … iii pynt*es*

[*sheet 24d*] *Dat*es. De remanentia ultimi computi … null. Sed reddit de … Cl lib. [*blank*] provisis infra tempus huius computi etc. Summa … Cl lib.

De quibus expenduntur ad usum hospicii predicti infra tempus huius computi … Cxxiii lib. di. Et allocatur pro lez dat*es* habitis de Willelmo Elmere clerico spicerie domine de stauro suo proprio et ad usum hospicii dicte domine infra tempus computi anni proximi precedentis expenditis prout in dorso computi eiusdem anni patet … ix lib. Summa … Cxxxii lib. di.

[3]Et remanent … xvii lib. di.

*Comfet*tes *Carewes*. Et de … ii lib. i qr. confectionum carewes de remanentia ultimi computi. Et de … vii lib. provisis infra tempus huius computi etc.

Summa … ix lib. i qr.

[172] Add. below in the same hand.

De quibus expenduntur ad usum hospicii predicti infra tempus huius computi … <di. lib.> iiii lib. i qr. ii oz. cum di. lib. allocato per billam signatam etc.

Summa … iiii lib. i qr. ii oz.

[3]Et remanent … iiii lib. di. i qr. ii oz..

*Comfett*es *plat*es. De remanentia ultimi computi … nichil. <Et> \Sed reddit/ de … xlvii lib. di. provisis infra tempus huius computi etc. Summa … xlvii lib. di.

De quibus expenduntur ad usum hospicii supradicti infra tempus huius computi … <xvi lib. di.> \xxxvi lib. di./.

Et allocatur pro lez comfett*es* plat*es* habitis de Willelmo Elmere clerico <hospicii> spicerie domine de proprio stauro suo et ad usum hospicii dicte domine infra tempus computi anni proximi precedentis expenditis prout in dorso computi dicti anni patet … iii lib. di. Summa … xl lib.[3]

[3]Et remanent … vii lib. di.

*Long comfett*es. De remanentia ultimi computi … null. Et[173] \reddit/ de … ii lib. [*blank*] provisis infra tempus huius computi etc.

Summa … ii lib. que expenduntur ad usum hospicii predicti etc.

[3]Et remanet … nichil.

*Comfett*es *byskett*es. Et de … iii qr. i lib. de remanentia ultimi computi etc. Et de … ii lib. provisis infra tempus huius computi. Summa … ii lib. iii qr..

De quibus expenduntur ad usum hospicii predicti infra tempus huius computi … ii lib. di. cum di. lib. allocato per billam signatam. Summa … ii lib. di.

[3]Et remanet … i qr.

[*sheet 25d*] *Grene gyng*er. Et de … xiii lib. i qr. grene gyng*er* de remanentia ultimi computi etc. Et de … xii lib. <de> provisis infra tempus huius computi etc.

Summa … xxv lib. i qr.

De quibus expenduntur ad usum hospicii predicti infra tempus huius computi etc. … xvii lib. i qr. ii oz. cum i lib. iii qr. allocatis per billam signatam.

Summa … xvii lib. i qr. ii oz.

[3]Et remanent … vii lib. iii qr. ii oz.

*Lymond*es *et Succad*es. De remanentia ultimi computi … null. Sed reddit de … xliiii lib. iii qr. di. provisis infra tempus huius computi etc.

Summa … <xx> xliiii lib. iii qr. di.

De quibus expenduntur ad usum hospicii predicti infra tempus huius computi etc. … xxvii lib. di. iii oz.

[173] Written over alteration.

Et allocatur pro lez lymons et succad*es* habitis de Willelmo Elmere clerico spicerie domine de stauro suo proprio et ad usum hospicii dicte domine infra tempus computi anni proximi precedentis expenditis ut in dorso computi eiusdem anni patet … vi lib. i qr.
Summa … xxxiii lib. iii qr. iii \oz./

[3]Et remanent … x lib. iii qr. iii oz.

*Lymond*es *in Pykell.* Et de … xii lymond*es* de remanentia ultimi computi. Et de … iiii^{xx}<vi>\x/ lymond*es* de provisione dicti computantis etc.

Summa … Cii

De quibus expenduntur ad usum hospicii predicti infra tempus huius computi etc. … lxii.
Summa … lxii.

[3]Et remanent … xl.

Quynces in syrope. Et de … di. lib. de remanentia ultimi computi. De provisione … … nichil.
Summa … di. lib. quod remanet.

[3]Et sic remanet … di. lib.

Nota pro i lib. i qr. etc. habitis de W.E. non allocatis[174]

Orrenges in syrop. De remanentia ultimi computi … null. Sed reddit de … ii lib. provisis infra tempus huius computi.

Summa … ii lib. que expenduntur infra tempus huius computi.

Et remanet ...nichil.

Saffron inglyssh. De remanentia ultimi computi ...nichil. <Et> \Sed reddit/ de ... quinque lib. quinque oz. provisis infra tempus huius computi etc.

Summa ...quinque lib. quinque oz.

De quibus expenduntur ad usum hospicii predicti infra tempus huius computi ...i lib. Et allocatur pro le[175] /[*sheet 26d*] saffron habito ad usum hospicii domine de Willelmo Elmere clerico spicerie dicte domine de stauro suo proprio et infra tempus computi anni proximi precedentis expendito prout in dorso computi eiusdem hospicii pro dicto anno proximo precedenti patet ...quinque oz. Et liberantur magistre Fowler etc. ...iiii lib.
Summa … v lib. v oz.

[3]Et remanet … nichil tamen memorandum pro iiii lib. remanentibus in custodia magistre Fowler[176]

Confeccions. De remanentia … nichil. Sed reddit de … vii lib. provisis etc. De quibus <libera> expenduntur etc. … vi lib. \di./ <i qr.> ii oz.

[3]Et remanent … i qr. ii oz.

Prunes. De remanentia ultimi computi … nichil. Sed reddit de … Ciiii^{xx}i lib. di. provisis infra tempus huius computi etc.
Summa … Ciiii^{xx}i lib. di.

[174] Written small in left margin above ‘Orrenges in syrop’. W.E. is William Elmer/Hilmer, clerk of the spicery (see sheet 26d below).

[175] ‘le’ rep. on next sheet.

[176] See sheet 25 above.

De quibus expenduntur ad usum hospicii predicti infra tempus huius computi etc. ... Cxxxiiii lib. di.

Et allocatur pro lez prewnes habitis de Willelmo Elmere clerico <hospicii> spicerie domine de stauro suo proprio et ad usum hospicii dicte domine infra tempus computi anni proximi precedentis expenditis ut in dorso computi eiusdem anni patet ... xiiii[177] <di.> Summa ... Cxlviii lib. di.[3]

[3]Et remanent ... xxxiii[178] lib. <di.>

Almondys. Et de ... lxxviii lib. di. almond*es* de remanentia ultimi computi. Et de ... Clxviii lib. [*blank*] provisis infra tempus huius computi <ad> etc.

Summa ... CCxlvi lib. di.

De quibus expenduntur ad usum hospicii predicti infra tempus huius computi ... CCxii lib. Summa ... CCxii lib.

[3]Et remanent ... xxxiiii lib. di.

Turnesale. De remanentia ultimi computi ... null. Sed reddit de ... ii lib. [*blank*] provisis infra tempus huius computi etc.

Summa ... ii lib. que expenduntur ad usum hospicii predicti etc.

[3]Et remanet ... nichil.

Ryse. Et de ... xxxii lib. di. de remanentia ultimi computi. De provisione ... nichil.

Summa ... xxxii lib. di.

De quibus expenduntur ad usum hospicii predicti infra tempus huius computi ... xxix lib. di. Summa ... xxix lib. di.

[3]Et remanent ... iii lib.

Blaunch powder. De remanentia ultimi computi ... nichil. Sed reddit de ... quinque lib. di. provisis infra tempus huius computi.

[*sheet 27d*]

Summa ... quinque lib. di.

De quibus expenduntur ad usum hospicii predicti infra tempus huius computi etc. ... ii lib.

Et allocatur pro le blaunche powder habito de Willelmo Elmere clerico <hosp> spicerie domine ad usum hospicii predicte domine et infra tempus computi anni proximi precedentis expendito ut in dorso computi dicti anni patet ... i lib. di.

Summa ... iii lib. di.[3]

[3]Et remanent ... ii lib.

Powder of licoryse. De remanentia ultimi computi ... nichil. Sed reddit de ... iiii lib. provisis infra tempus huius computi etc. Summa ... iiii lib.

[177] MS 'xiijj'.
[178] MS 'xxxijj'.

De quibus expenditur ad usum hospicii predicti infra tempus huius computi etc. … i lib. Summa … i lib.

[3]Et remanent … iii lib.

Galyngale. De remanentia ultimi computi … nichil. Sive de provisione … nichil.

Summa … null.

[3]Et remanet … nichil.

Agnes Sede. De remanentia ultimi computi … nichil. Sed reddit de … vii lib. provisis infra tempus huius computi etc. Summa … vii lib.

De quibus expenduntur ad usum hospicii predicti infra tempus huius computi etc. … iii lib.

[3]Et remanent … iiii lib.

Hony. Nichil hic quia antea.[179]

Salet oyle. Et de … i lag. iii pynt*es* olei vocati salett oyle de remanentia ultimi computi. Et de … i lag. provisa infra tempus huius computi etc. Summa … ii lag. iii pynt*es*

De quibus expenduntur infra tempus huius computi ad usum hospicii predicti etc. … i lag. i potell \di. p[ynte]/[180] Summa … i lag. i potell di. pynte

[3]Et remanent … i potell <iii pynt*es*> \i quarte di. p*ynte*/

[*sheet 28d*] *Frankensense*. De remanentia ultimi computi … null. Sed reddit de … iiii lib. [*blank*] provisis infra tempus huius computi etc. Summa … iiii lib.

De quibus expenduntur ad usum domine infra capellam suam per tempus huius computi etc. … ii lib.

Et allocatur pro le fra[n]kensense habito de Willelmo Elmere clerico spicerie domine <ad> de stauro suo proprio et infra capellam eiusdem domine infra tempus computi anni <ann> proximi precedentis expendito prout in dorso computi dicti anni proximi precedentis patet … ii lib. Summa … iiii lib.

[3]Et remanet … nichil.

Strenors fyne and course. Et de … l virg. iii qr. de remanentia ultimi computi. Et de … lxvi virg. \di./ fyne et course provisis infra tempus huius computi etc.

Summa … Cxvii virg. i qr.

De quibus expenduntur ad usum hospicii predicti infra tempus huius computi etc. … lxxix virg. cum ii virg. allocatis per billam signatam etc. Summa … lxxix virg.

[3]Et remanent … xxxviii virg. i \qr./.

[179] Written small in a large templated space. See 16d ('Mel').

[180] 'ynte' lost at edge of sheet.

Papire regale. De remanentia ultimi computi … nichil. Sed reddit de … i quayre et ii foliis papiri regalis infra tempus huius computi provisis etc.

Summa … i quaternum et ii folia que expenduntur etc. ut supra

³Et remanet … nichil.

Papire de Gene. De remanentia ultimi computi … null. Sed reddit de … i reme papiri proviso infra tempus huius computi etc.

Summa … i reme quod expenditur infra tempus huius computi etc.

³Et remanet … nichil.

Papire Francie. Et de … iii remes ix quaternis et xxi foliis papiri Francie de remanentia ultimi computi. Et de … ii remes provisis infra tempus huius computi etc.

Summa … quinque remes ix quayres xxi folia

De quibus expenduntur ad usum hospicii predicti infra tempus predictum etc. … iiii remes i q*u*ayre et viii folia. Summa … iiii remes i q*u*ayre viii folia.

³Et remanent … i reyme viii q*u*ayre xiii folia

[*sheet 29d*] *Smygmatis albe*. Et de … iiii^{xx}xix lib. iii qr. iii oz. smigmatis albe de remanentia ultimi computi. De provisione … nichil.

<De quibus expenduntur infra tempus huius computi etc. … xxxvi lib. di. ii oz.

Summa … xxxvi lib. di. ii oz.

Et remanent … lxiii lib. i qr. i oz.>

Summa … iiii^{xx}xix lib. iii qr. iii oz.

De quibus expenduntur infra tempus predictum ad usum hospicii predicti etc. … xxxvi lib. di. \ii/ oz.

Et remanent … lxiii lib. i qr. et i oz.

Smygmatis nigre. [*blank*][181]

Avene. Et de … xiiii qr. avene \de/ remanentia ultimi computi apud Croydon. Et de … ii qr. avene de remanentia ultimi computi apud West Depyng etc. Et de … Cxvi qr. [*blank*] avene de provisione dicti computantis infra tempus huius computi ad usum hospicii predicti etc.

Et remanent … lxix qr.

Unde[182]

apud Hatfeld pro pulletria … viii qr.

apud Depyng …

Colyweston Maxsey …

[181] See sheet 12 ('Empcio candelarum albarum et smigmatis nigre cum le wyke').

[182] The following five entries are bracketed to the right of 'Unde'.

Ware et Hatfeld …

pro equis domine …

lxvi qr.[183]

[*sheet 30d*] *Fabe et Pise*. De remanentia … nichil. Sive de provisione … nichil.[184]

Et remanet … null.

Fenum.

Et remanent[185]

apud Ware … lvi carecte

<West Depyng>

Chesthunt … xiiii carecte

Colyweston … nichil

West Depyng … xxxvii carecte

Maksey … nichil

Hatfeld … x lod*es*

Barnet … xii carecte

Focale etc. videlicet talwod [*sheet 31d*] *fagott*es *et carbonum.*

Et remanent[186]

in herdwod … xx lod*es*

in bavyn … xx lod*es*

in carbono silvestri … xxii <ca> lod*es*

Cortex.

³*vii li. xiii s. Inde super ipsum Johannem lxxiii s.*[187]

Et de … lxv carectis corticis de remanentia ultimi computi. De provisione … nichil

Summa … lxv carecte que venduntur Johanni Thomson de Depyng pro … vii lib. xiii s.

Pannum laneum.

[183] The total of the four entries above, bracketed to the right of the entries.

[184] 'de ...nichil' written small at the top of a largely blank bracketed space; there are several gaps between text on this sheet.

[185] The following eight entries are bracketed to the right of 'Et remanent', with the amounts bracketed further right; the whole is written over halfway down the otherwise blank bracketed space.

[186] The following three entries are bracketed to the right of 'Et remanent'; the whole is written near the foot of an otherwise blank bracketed space.

[187] Written small below 'Cortex' in the same hand as the main text.

[188]*Emptum pro liberatura <ho> serviencium hospicii etc.*

[3]*Ciiii s. viii d.*

Memorandum quod N. Saunders recepit de parte dicte summe … vii s.

Et de … xxx virg. iii quart*er* de remanentia ultimi computi. Et de … DCxl virg. di. receptis de provisione infra tempus huius computi <ad> pro liberatura domine ut in libro provisionis hospicii plenius liquet. Et de … x virg. di. panni provenientibus de incremento mensure in deliberacione dicti panni etc.

Summa … DCiiii^{xx}i virg. iii q*u*art*er*.

De quibus deliberantur diversis serviencibus hospicii pro liberatura eorundem ut patet in quodam quaterno de nominibus per Jacobum Morres clericum countrie hospicii predicti confecto super hunc computum ostenso probato et examinato etc. … DCxii virg. di. et di. q*u*art*er*. Et deliberantur diversis personis per mandatum domine per billam de nominibus signo manuali sub signo de panno remanenti in fine ultimi computi … xxvi virg. di. q*u*art*er* panni lanei. Et venduntur diversis serviencibus dicti hospicii cum iii^{bus} virg. de remanentia ultimi computi … xxv virg. i q*u*art*er* pro … Ciiii s. viii d.

Summa … DClxiiii virg.

Et remanent … xvii virg. iii q*u*art*er* panni lanei.

[sheet 32d blank]

[188] The following three marginal notes are written small, perhaps in the same hand (the second and third later), each below the other and below the marginal heading ‘Pannum laneum’.

D102.10 (SJLM/1/1/6/1) Book of receipts and payments kept principally by Henry Hornby, secretary and dean of chapel, later chancellor, 1 January 1499 – 3 October 1509.

Discussion See Introduction 4 and Plates 5–7.

Description Paper (badly damaged at imperfect(?) start, with edges of pp. 1–4 frayed and remounted), written on both sides, with many blank pages (pp. 8, 14, 30, 41–2, 49, 54, 63–4, 68, 72–4, 80–2, 85–6, 88–90, 94–100, 105–6, 110, 115–16, 121–2, 134, 145, 150, 154, 163–4, 166–8, 170–5), some written on later (pp. 126–9, 132–3). Page size approx. 240 x 170 mm., paginated recto 1–181 top right in pencil (MGU). 91 ff. in five quires: 1^{20} (wants 2 cut out), 2^{20}, 3^{20}, 4^{16}, 5^{16}.[1] Left margins approx. 30–40 mm. (with annotations), right margins variable, upper margins 10 mm. (sometimes contain headings, e.g. 'Recepta pro anno xviii', p. 31), lower margins variable depending on number of entries. Most pages show signs of stitching and/or pin or spike holes, e.g. pp. 3–34, 35–64, 65–71, 85, 91, 101, 117–30, 131–54, etc.). Paper slips are attached to several pages (see Summary below and text passim), and two paper slips (see p. 101 below) are now in an envelope marked 'from parchment cover, discovered while under repair' (MGU). Sewn at different points down the outer edges of pp. 85/86, 91/92, 101/102, 151/152, 155/156, 159/160 are strips of paper folded in half (now approx. 30 x 40 mm.) which act as markers of regnal years and of other information.[2] The quires are stitched into the original parchment wrapper with two modern leather and string strengtheners on the spine; the irregularly-cut parchment is tucked in and sewn to the approx. size 250 x 170 mm. '102.10' in pencil (MGU) inside front cover on upper fold-over has been cancelled and 'SJLM /1/6/1' added; scribbled bills and calculations are on both sides of the back cover.[3] The whole is contained in a modern box of brown/grey waterproof buckram ('D102.10' altered to 'D102/10' on a white pasted slip bottom right front cover of slip-case, now erased to 'SJLM /1/1/6/1').[4] Mostly in one hand, seemingly that of

[1] I.e. pp. 1–38, 39–78, 79–118, 119–50, 151–182.

[2] Some are cut off, e.g. pp. 85/86; only a few letters can be read on the remains of some, e.g. pp. 91/92 recto 'p*ro*', verso 'u*er*ed'; others are fuller, e.g. p. 151/152 recto 'Receytes of money pro anno x[xiij^{mo} regis Henrici vii^{mi} (?)], verso 'Receytes of money pro anno x[xiij(?)] H. vii'; p. 155/156 recto 'Money delyv*er*ed unto the tresourer of howshold', verso 'Mony delyv*er*ed unto the the*sauerer*e of household'. Some of the stitching holes noted above may relate to lost markers.

[3] Inside back cover bottom right: 'Summa obligacionium valencium x Decembris anno ii^{do} regis H. viii per estimacionem ...MClxiii li. xv s. iiii d.'; sideways on right side indecipherable. Outside of back cover top right 'DCxxxiiii li. xiii(?) s.'; upside down top right two lines of writing in a very small hand (illegible even under ultra-violet light).

[4] This dates from the 1976–78 repair and conservation of the accounts and inventories.

Henry Hornby ('the HH hand'),[5] who is also responsible for corrections and page totals. 'Jesus' written in the upper margin in the HH hand p. 9. There is also another distinctive and idiosyncratic hand (the 'sprawling' hand), which is responsible for summary material and entries around the beginning and end of sections.[6] A thin, slanting hand (which in language has some of the characteristics of the 'sprawling' hand) is footnoted at pp. 111, 117, 123–4, 135, 148, 155–6, 165. The 'curly' hand (perhaps Robert Fremingham) occurs on pp. 112, 118–19, 124, 151–2, 165.[7] Latin annotations occur in the 'sprawling' hand, which notes the reasons for cancellations of entries, etc.[8] These annotations often direct one to other accounts ('computi'), beginning with the 14th regnal year (p. 3); cross-references are attempted in the footnotes when the extant records allow comparison. Originally blank pages pp. 126–8 (see too pp. 129, 131), 132–3 have been used for post-mortem accounts.[9]

Summary
1499–1509 (including post-mortem notes) (years 14–24)
Note: The summary that follows notes the first and last date recorded within a rubric or a category, but it should be noted that some entries are undated or are added out of chronological order. The year given is that referred to in the rubrics, which seem to follow the calendar year (i.e. the period of the yearly accounts) rather than the strict regnal year. (The full potential range of years is given for pp. 176–82.)

Miscellaneous receipts and payments (regnal years 13, 15, 17 cited), pp. 1–2 (paper slip sewn to p. 1); receipts 1 January - 10 October 1499 (**year 14**), pp. 3–7 (paper slip sewn to p. 4) [8 blank]; money delivered, mainly to Miles Worsley, 13 January - 10 October 1499 (**year 14**), pp. 9–13 [14 blank]; receipts 13 January 1500 - 1 January 1501 (**year 15**), pp. 15–18; receipts 13 January - 19 April 1501 (**year 16**), pp. 19–20; receipts 20 April 1501 – 31 January 1502

[5] See the note to the fifth entry on p. 77 below. Early in the document the HH hand writes of himself in the third person, e.g. 'the dean of my said ladies chapell', p. 3; indeed the accounts are at first occasionally written as if by Lady Margaret herself, e.g. 'myn almes mony' p. 10, 'into oure own coffers' (p. 22), 'my cofers' (alt. from 'your') p. 11.

[6] See further in footnotes to the edited text. Except for the rubrics pp. 151, 155, 159, the introductory and concluding material for each year is here cursory and cursive, unlike the mainly formal script of the summary hand in the chamber accounts D91.17, D91.20, D91.21, D91.19, D102.1, and the chamberlain's account D102.2/D102.6.

[7] See footnotes for other (unknown) hands.

[8] Annotations to the text (in the 'sprawling' hand unless otherwise noted) are indicated by double angle brackets. + is sometimes used as a checking mark, e.g. at the total fourth entry from end p. 10; alongside annotation fifth entry from end and alongside total p. 26; alongside annotation fourth entry from end and alongside total p. 31, etc. Another annotating mark is similar to a secretary <a>, e.g. second to fourth and ninth to eleventh entries p. 11; first, second, fourth, seventh and last entries p. 12; first, seventh and eighth entries p. 13, etc.

[9] Pp. 129, 131 were not blank but have been added to post-mortem.

(**year 16**), pp. 21–5; receipts 7 February 1502 - 21 January 1503 (**year 17**), pp. 26–9 [30 blank]; receipts of Hugh Ashton and Hugh Oldham 13 February 1503 - 17 January 1504 (**year 18**), pp. 31–4; money delivered, mainly to Bedell 14 January - 29 December 1500 (**year 15**), pp. 35–7; money delivered to Bedell 21 November 1500 - 21 January 1502 (**year 16**), pp. 38–40 [41–2 blank]; money delivered to Worsley 14 January 1500 – 18 April 1501 (**year 15**), pp. 43–5; money delivered to Worsley 14 January 1501 - 22 January 1502 (**year 16**), pp. 46–8 [49 blank]; money delivered to Bedell 7 February 1502 – 17 January 1503 (**year 17**), pp. 50–2; tin delivered to John Dantre 21 August [1502], p. 53 [54 blank]; money delivered to Worsley 7 February 1502 – 19 January 1503 (**year 17**), pp. 55–8; money delivered to Bedell 13 January 1503 – 13 February 1504 (**year 18**), pp. 59–62 [63–4 blank]; money delivered to Worsley 19 January 1503 – 10 January 1504 (**year 18**), pp. 65–7 [68 blank]; money delivered to Bedell 14 January – 11 December 1504 (**year 19**), pp. 69–71 [72–74 blank]; money delivered to Worsley 14 January 1504 – 7 January 1505 (**year 19**), pp. 75–79 [80–82 blank]; receipts 17 January 1504 – 15 January 1505 (**year 19**), pp. 83–84; receipts 15 January 1505 – 13 February 1506 (**year 20**), pp. 85–87 (marker once sewn to p. 85/86) [88–90 blank]; money delivered to Bedell 13 January 1505 – 12 January 1506 (**year 20**), pp. 91–93 (marker sewn to p. 91/92) [94–100 blank]; money delivered to Worsley 13 January – 13 December 1505 plus some undated (**year 20**), pp. 101–103 (paper slips in a loose envelope are perhaps from pp. 101–2)[10]; undated receipts, pp. 103–4 [105–16 blank]; money delivered to James Morice 2 March – 19 June 1505 (**year 20**), pp. 107–109 [110 blank]; receipts from 15 January 1506 – 18 January 1507 (**year 21**), pp. 111–114 [115–16 blank]; money delivered to Bedell 13 January 1506 – 15 January 1507 (**year 21**), pp. 117–120 [121–22 blank]; money delivered to Worsley 13 January 1506 – 10 January 1507 (**year 21**), pp. 123–25; receipts 3 October 1509 (post mortem), pp. 126–29 (lower half); money delivered to Morice 3 November and 11 December 1506 (**year 22**), p. 129 (upper half); receipts 13 January – 13 December 1507 (**year 22**), pp. 130–31; receipts, mostly July 1509 (post mortem), pp. 131(foot of page) - 133 [134 blank]; money delivered to Bedell 13 January 1507 – 7 January 1508 (**year 22**), pp. 135–7; receipts of lady sojourners 1499 and 1500 (**years 14, 15**), p. 138; occasional receipts 1498–1501 (**years 14, 15, 17**), pp. 139–40; receipts of lady Powis 1506 (**year 21**), p. 141; receipts of lady sojourners 1500–4 (**years 16, 17, 19**), p. 142; receipts of sojourners Cecily Welles and Thomas Kyme 1503–6 (**years 19, 21**), p. 143; receipts for the juncture of Alice Parker 1500–1 (**year 16**), p. 144 [145 blank]; money delivered to Worsley 13 January – 31 December 1507 (**years 22–23**), pp. 146–9 [150 blank]; receipts 8 January 1508 – 16 January 1509, pp. 151–3

[10] The slips record groats, which are the subject matter of pp. 101–2 and are recorded below on p. 101; pp. 101–2 have pin marks (groats are also mentioned p. 77, but this has no pin marks).

(marker sewn to p. 151/152) [154 blank]; money delivered to Bedell for the year 8 January 1508 – 2 January 1509 (**years 23–24**), pp. 155–7 (marker sewn to p. 155/156); obligations, p. 158; money delivered to Worsley 8 January 1508 – 10 January 1509 (**years 23–24**), pp. 159–61 (marker sewn to p. 159/160); receipts of Robert Fremingham 20 January – 26 May 1509 (**year 24**), p. 162 [163–4 blank]; money delivered to Bedell 20 January – 31 July 1509 (**year 24 & year 1 HVIII**), p. 165 [166–8 blank]; money delivered to Fremingham 20 January – 28 June 1509 (**year 24 & year 1 HVIII**) p. 169 [170–5 blank]; receipts from John St John's lands 1500–4/5 (**years 20, 15–17, 19**), pp. 176–7; receipts from Jane Rykyl's lands 1499/1500–1501/02 (**years 15–17**), p. 178; money delivered to the coffers from these and other lands 1505–6 (**years 20–21**), pp. 179–80; (canc.) money delivered to James Morice to buy cattle 9 August 1502 (**year 17**), p. 181; receipts from Margaret Gonsell's lands 19 May 1503 (**year 18**), money delivered to John Fothede for household expenses 19 April 1505 (**year 20**), p. 182 (paper bill of John Syclyng 19 March 1506 sewn to p. 182).

Edited Text

[*p. 1*][11] [paper slip 88mm. x 24 mm. stitched to top of page]

xxxiii oz. iii qr. di.

[12]Memorandum weyte of a standinge cope sent to my lord for his New Yer*es* yeft the xxviii day of Decembre wich was bought of s*ir* John Shaa \is this/ [...]

Item bought of m*aster* Hugh Oldom a standing cuppe with a cover gilte and graven wych was yeven to my lord of Bath for his New Yer*es* yeft weying xxxi unc*e* iii quarteriis. Price the unce iii s. [...]

Memorandum the xvii day of Aprill \anno regni regis Henrici vii/ delyv*er*ed unto m*aster* Rose s*er*vante to my lady Scrop for the bichofe of my lady Scrop [...]

Memorandum <d> Rec*eyved* the xxiiii day of Decembr*e* the xvii[th] yere of the reigne of king Henrie the vii of doctor Thomas Hutton executo*ur* to John Hutton late decessed by the hand*es* of Ric*hard* Lynne i*n* full co*n*tentacio*u*n for the mano*ur* of Ov*er*hall w*ith* [.....] the town off Boxworth i*n* the count*ie* of Cambrige [.....] wych mano*ur* w*ith* the purtena*n*ce the said John i*n* his live tyme bought of us CClxvi li. [...]

[13]a ... of l mark*es*

2 ... of C li. xvii s. xiiii d. ob.

CClxvi li. [.....]

[11] The outer edge of p.1/2 is damaged and torn. Sums are not readable even under ultra-violet lamp.

[12] The HH hand starts here.

[13] These notes at the foot of the page are written in a different ink and hand (John Fisher?).

[*p. 2*] Memorandum the ix day off Decembre the xiii yer*e* of the reigne off o*ur* soverain lord kinge Henry the vii that the secretary receyved of Gregory Skypwith for Burgoy*n*is land*es* i*n* p*ar*tie of payment due for the yer*e* ended i*n* the fest of Saint Michaell last passed … xiii li. vi s. viii d.

Item receyved of Willyam Michell the xx^{ti} day of July for horses by <s> him sold at div*er*se tymes … xi li. xvi s. ii d.

Item of Wyllyam Daniell receyved the xx^{ti}ii day of Octobre for c*er*tain horses bought of my lady i*n* p*ar*tie of payment of vii li. … iii li. xiii s. iiii d.

Memorandum that the xxv day of Octobre the xvth yer*e* of the reigne of o*ur* soverain lord kinge Henry the vii my lady lent furth of hir cofers to s*ir* John Husy and other men of Boston as appereth by an obligacion beringe date afor*e*said <for> toward*es* the werk*es* i*n* the said Boston for defense of watier … xl li.

Item r*eceyved* of William Daniell i*n* p*ar*tie of payment for horses boght of my lady the viii day of August … xli s. iiii d.

[*p. 3*] Receyt*es* at div*er*se tymes from the first day of January the xiiii yer*e* of the reigne off oure soverain lord kinge Henry the vii by my lady

First at Colyweston by the hand*es* of m*aster* Hugh Oldom the vi day of January next folowinge in gold … Clxviii li. v s. vii d. qua.

wheroff yeven to my lord Welles … xx li.

Item yeven to the said m*aster* Hugh … v s. vii d. qua.

Item rec*eyved* the same tyme and place of the said m*aster* Hugh i*n* anothere*e* bagge in gold and silv*er* … lx li.

Item of James Clarell by the hand*es* of the dean of my said ladies chapell at Colyweston the xiiith day of the said moneth … Cxlviii li. xiiii s. ix d.

Item of the said m*aster* Hugh the xxviii of January at Grenwych of the lordshipp of Manerber*e* in Wales … xl li.

Item the first day of February at Grenwych of the said m*aster* Hugh of the lordshipp of M*ar*ton in Westmorland … xx li.

Summa recepte CCCCxxxvii li. iiii d. et qua.[14]

Nota. Item the ix day of February receyved of Langton for the joynto*ur* of Alice Parkar of the lord Morles land*es* … l marce

Nota. Item the vi day off <o> January of Gregory Skipwith of Burgoy*n*s landes … xx li.

[14] The correct total of the receipts on p. 3 up to this point, written small in the left margin, probably in the HH hand.

[*p. 4*] Item rece*yved* the xvi day of February of thabbot of Syscito*ur* for fee ferm of the town of Siscito*ur* due for oon hole yer*e* ended at the fest of saint Michael last passed … xxx li.

Item rece*yved* of m*aster* Hugh Oldom of the duchye of Excestre the xx^{ti}v day of the said moneth … l li. xiiii s. x d.

Item rece*yved* the said day of Nicholas Compton by the hand*es* of Miles Worsley … Clxii li.

<Item rece*yved* of Nicholas Compton the fourth day of March … iiii^{xx} li.>

Item rece*yved* of James Clarell by the hand*es* of the sayd Miles the iiiith day of March … iiii^{xx} li.

Item rece*yved* of sir \Willyam/ Walles of the lordship of Kendale for arrerag*es* of the same the xiii day of March … xvi li. xiii s. iiii d.

Item \the same day/ of the said s*ir* Willyam for rent*es* of the same lordshypp due at the fest of saint M*ar*tyn last past … xx li. «allocatur in computo de anno xv^{mo}»[15]

Item the xvth day of March rece*yved* of Nicholas Compton by the hand*es* of the \said/ Miles … Clx li.

Item rece*yved* the xi day of Aprill of Wyllyam Denton for Rychmounte fee … xxvi li. xiii s. iiii d. «allocatur in computo de anno xv^{mo}»

Summa huius lateris 5C46 li. 18 d.[16]

Summa utriusque lateris 9C83 li. 22 d.[17]

Item rece*yved* the [*blank*] day of May of Nicholas Compton … C li.

Item rece*yved* the v day of Juyn of the said Nicholas … Cii li.

Item rece*yved* the same day of s*ir* Raufe Longford … iiii li.

[paper slip 80 x 135 mm. stitched onto p. 4, still in the HH hand]

Memorandum receyved of Hugh Warde of Boston x li. for the wych m*aster* Hugh Oldom at Excestre hath payed by my ladies co*m*maundment at the desir*e* of the said Hugh Warde to the purser*e* of his shipp … x li.

Item delyv*er*ed at Excestre to the said purser*e* by the said m*aster* Hugh for wynes bought of the said Hugh Ward … xx li.

[*p. 5*] Item rece*yved* of the said Miles wych he had of Hugh Ward of Boston for mony that <w> my lady payed for the said Hugh at Excestre … x li.

Item rece*yved* by the hand*es* of the said Miles of Nicholas Compton the xxviii day of Juyn … lxxvi li.

[15] The cofferer's account for the 15th regnal year (1500) is not extant (see Latin annotations pp. 4–5), nor for the 16th (see Latin annotations pp. 5, 17–19).
[16] The correct total of the receipts (without the canc. item) on p. 4 up to this point, written small in the left margin, probably in the HH hand.
[17] The total of the receipts noted on pp. 3 and 4, probably written in the HH hand.

Item rec*eyved* by the hand*es* of the said Myles of Nycholas Compton the xii day of Octobr*e* … lxvi li. xiii s. iii d.

Item rec*eyved* by the hand*es* of the said Miles of the same Nicholas Compton the xxvii day of October … CCCCxx li.

Item rec*eyved* by the xxx day of Octobre by the hand*es* of the said Miles of Nicholas Compton … l i.

Item rec*eyved* the last day of Octobre by the hand*es* of the said Miles of John Stakhouse balife of Cotyngham … liii li.

Item rec*eyved* of Nicholas Compton by the hand*es* of <Miles> the said Miles the xvii day of Novembre … lxiii li.

Item rec*eyved* of sir William Wall the xxviii day of Nove*m*bre by the hand*es* of Miles … Cxx li.

Item rec*eyved* of Ric*hard* Galee by the hand*es* of Miles \the ii^{d} day of Decembre/ … v li. vi s. viii d. «allocatur in computo de anno xvi^{mo}»

Item rec*eyved* of sir Raufe Langford by the hand*es* of his s*er*vant Oliv*er* Haye the xiiii day of Decembre … xviii li. «allocatur in computo recepte de anno xv^{mo}»

Summa totalis recepte pro anno xv^{mo} … Mlxxxviii li.[18]

[*p. 6*] Item r*eceyved* of Gregory Skypwith by the hand*es* of my lady Bray the xix day of Decembre … xl li.

Item receyved of the baliffe of Tateshale by the hand*es* of Miles the xxix day of Decembre … xx li. «allocatur in computo recepte»

Item r*eceyved* by the hand*es* of the said Miles of Gregory Skypwith the viith day of January i*n* p*ar*tie of payment of the revenuse of a hole yer*e* ended at the fest of saint Michell last passed for the man*er* of the Overhall and Boxwith i*n* the count*ie* of Cambrige p*ar*cell of my lad*ys* purchesed land*es* … x li.

[*p. 7*] Memorandum that the so*m*mes folowinge wer*e* taken forth of my ladies cofers

First that was receyved of Wyllyam Michell for c*er*tain horses sold by hym i*n* tyme passed … xi li. xvi s. ii d.

Item to make payment unto s*ir* Edward Brampton for land purchessed of hym in Chestonte … Cxx li.

Item the vii day of Septembre for p*ro*visio*u*n at Stirbyche fayr*e* … Clx li.

Item the xxi day of Septembre … xx li.

Item the xxvii day of Septembre … xx li.

Item the first day of Octobre … xxvi li. xiii s. iiii d.

Item the iiii day of Octobre … xi li.

[18] The correct total of the receipts on p. 5, plus those since the last total on p. 4 (but without those on the sheet sewn on to p. 4).

Item the v day of Octobre … lxiiii li.

Item the viii day of Octobre … xxxv li.

Item the x day of Octobre … l li.

Item the same day … l li.

[*p. 8 blank*]

[*p. 9*] Delyveraunce at div*er*se tymes by my lady of the foresayd so*m*mes receyved

First to Miles Worsley by the hand*es* of the dean of my ladis chapell the xiiith day of January the xiiii[19] yer*e* of o*ur* soverain lord kinge Henry the vii … xxxvii li. xiiii s. iiii d.

Item the xix day of the said moneth to the said Miles by the hand*es* of the said dean … lii li.

Item the xxiii day of the same moneth to the same Miles and by the <su>said dean … lix li. v d.

Nota. Item the ix day off February that was receyved of Tho*ma*s Longland for maisteres Alic*e* P*ar*ker*e* for Michaelmasse rent last past … xxxiii li. vi s. viii d.

Delyvered to Miles for the same.[20] Item the <last> \xxiiii/ day of February to the cristenynge of my lord Edmound … C li.

Item the same tyme yeven to the norshrye … iii li. vi s. viii d.

Item to the midwife … xl s.

Item delyv*er*ed to the said Miles the last day of February … xli li. xviii s. viii d.

Item delyv*er*ed to the said Miles the secu*n*d day of March … xx li.

Item delyv*er*ed to the same the iiiith day of March … xxxiii li.

Item to the said Miles the viiith day of March … xxxii li. xvi d.

Item dely[21]

CCCCxiiii li. viii s. i d.[22]

[*p. 10*] Item delyv*er*ed to the said Miles the xix day of March … xx li.

Item delyv*er*ed to the same the xx^{ti} day of March … xx li.

Item to the same the xxiii day of March … xlvi li.

Item to the same the xxviii day of March … xxv li.

[19] MS 'xiijj'.

[20] Bracketed to include the next three items.

[21] Entry incomplete.

[22] The correct total of the items on p. 9, written small to the right at the foot of the page in the HH hand.

Item to the same the ix day of Aprill … xiiii li. vi s.

Item to the same the xi day of Aprill the som … xxvi li. xiii s. iiii d.

Item to the same the xxiiii day of Aprill … xxxv li.

Item to the same the xxvii day of Aprill … xxv li.

Item to the same the xxviii day of Aprill … xxx li.

Item to the same the iiii day of May … lxv li. xiii s. viii d.

Item to the same the x day of May … xl li.

Item to the same the xvii day of May … xx li.

Item to the same the xx [*blank*] day of May … C li.

Item to the same the v day of Juyn … xxiiii li.

Item delyv*er*ed to the same the xxii day of Juyn … xxxv li.

*Remayninge i*n *my lad*ys *hand*es.[23] Item kepte for myn almes mony … x li.

Item delyv*er*ed <th> to the same Miles the xxviii day of Juyn … lxxvi li.

Item delyv*er*ed to the same Miles the xiii day of July … xx li.

Item delyv*er*ed to the same Miles the xxiiii day of July … xlii li. xiii s. iiii d.

DClx<x>iiii li. vi s. viii d.[24]

[*p. 11*] Item delyv*er*ed to the said Miles the iii day of Auguste … lx li.

Item delyv*er*ed to the countroll*our* the ix day of August … xxvi li. <xiii s. iiii d.>

Item delyv*er*ed to the same the xix day of the same moneth … xxiiii li. <xiii s. x d.> xviii d.

Item delyv*er*ed to the same the xx^th^ day of the same moneth … xxvii li.

Item delyv*er*ed the xxviii day of August to Miles Worsley … xx li.

Item delyv*er*ed the vii day of Septembre to the said Miles … <xx li.> xl li.

<Item delyv*er*ed the same day to the countroll*our* for thexpenses of houshold … xx li.>

Item delyv*er*ed to the said Miles the xvi day of Octobre for <yo*ur*> my cofers … xxxiii li. vi s. viii d.

Item the same day delyv*er*ed to the said Miles for the tresorer*e* … xxxiii li. vi s. viii d.

Item delyv*er*ed the last day of Octobre to the said Miles for the tresorer … liii li.

Item delyv*er*ed the xiiii day of Novembr*e* to the tresorer*e* by the hand*es* of Will*i*am Adderton … xl li.

[23] Written in the left margin in the HH hand.

[24] The total of the page, written small to the left at the foot of the page in the HH hand; the correct total is £675 6s. 4d.

Item delyv*er*ed to Miles the xxv day of Novembre … xxx li.

<CClxix li. xiii s. iiii d.> Clxxxiii li. vi s. viii d.[25]

[*p. 12*] Item delyv*er*ed the last day of Nove*m*bre to John Bedell i*n* the absence of the tresorer*e* by the <absence> hand*es* of Miles … xl li.

Item <to de> delyv*er*ed the secu*n*de day of Dece*m*bre for the expenses of houshold to Miles i*n* the absence of the tresorer*e* … xxxvi li.

Item delyv*er*ed to the said Miles the viith day of Decembr*e* … xl li.

Item delyv*er*ed to the said Miles the x day of Decembre for the houshold … xliiii li.

Item delyv*er*ed to the said Miles the xvi day of Decembre … xviii li.

Item delyv*er*ed to the said Miles the xix day of Decembre … xl li.

Item delyv*er*ed to the tresorer*e* the xxiii day of Decembre … xl li.

Item the same day to Miles … xx li.

Item delyv*er*ed to the said Miles the xxix day of Decembre … xx li.

Clxxv li. xvii s. i d.[26]

Item delyv*er*ed to the said Miles the vii day of Januarye … lxxvii li. xvii s. i d.

Item delyv*er*ed unto Miles the vi day of Septembre … xi li. xvi s. ii d.

Item delyv*er*ed unto the tresorer*e* for p*ro*vision at Stirbiche fayr*e* the vii day of Septembre … Clx li.

[*p. 13*] Item delyv*er*ed to the said tresorer*e* for payment made to s*ir* Edward Brampton … Cxx li.

Item the xxi day of Septembre delyv*er*ed to the said Miles … xx li.

Item the xxvii day of Septembre delyv*er*ed to Miles … xx li.

Item the first day of Octobre delyv*er*ed to the tresorer*e* … xxvi li. xiii s. iiii d.

Item the iiiith day of Octobr*e* to Miles … xi li.

Item the v day of Octobre to Miles … lxiiii li.

Item the viii day of Octobre to the tresorer*e* … xxxv li.

Item to the same the x day of Octobre … l li.

Item the same day to Miles … li li.

[25] The total of the page, written to the right at the foot of the page; both calculations are seriously out and the total should be £386 14s. 10d. The first can be explained as the total of the last eight items on the page; the corrected total is £6 short of the last five items on the page. Both totals are in the HH hand.

[26] Another strange calculation, written in the left margin alongside the last line of this entry in the HH hand; the total so far on the page is £200 more than this (£375 17s. 1d.).

[*p. 14 blank*]

[*p. 15*] Receyt*es* at div*erse* tymes from the xiiith day of January the xvth yer*e* of the reyngne of *our* soverain lord kinge Henry the vii by my lady

First receyved the day above rehersed of Robert Brewster deputie to Edward Vavyser*e* of the revenuys of Billinge by the hand*es* of Miles Worsley … vi li. xiii s. iiii d.

Item receyved of the fee ferme of Waltham abbey by the hand*es* of the said Miles the day above exp*re*ssed … xi li.

Item receyved of m*aster* Hugh the xxi day of January … CCCv li. ob. di. qua.

Item rec*eyved* of Nicholas Compton by the hand*es* of Miles the first day of February … Clxi li.

Item rec*eyved* of the said Nicholas by the hand*es* of Miles the iiiith day of February … lxxxviii li.

Item rec*eyved* of the said Nicholas by the hand*es* of Miles the viiith day of February … lx li.

Item rec*eyved* the xiii day of February of Willyam Denton for Richemond fee … xvi li. «allocatur in computo recepte de anno xv^{o}»

Item rec*eyved* the xix day of February of Nicholas Compton by the hand*es* of Miles Briknet for the lordshipp of Cotyngham … lxi li.

[*p. 16*] Item rec*eyved* the xiiiith day of March of s*ir* Wyllyam Wall by the hand*es* of Miles Worsley … Cxl li. «allocatur in computo recepte de anno xv»

Item rec*eyved* of the xvth day of March of John Oliffe deputie to the balife of Tateshale of arrerag*e* … vii li. «allocatur in computo recepte»

Item r*eceyved* the xxi day of Aprill of m*aster* Hugh Oldom … iiii^{xx}xiii li. xvii s. x d.

Estur rent. Item r*eceyved* the xxiiii day of Aprill of Nicholas Compton … viii^{xx} li.

Item r*eceyved* the first day of May of m*aster* Hugh Oldom as appereth by div*erse* billes … DCCxv li. vi s. vii d. ob. qua.

Item r*eceyved* the same day of Gregory Skypwith … x li. xix s. ix d. ob. «allocatur in computo de anno xvi»

Estur rent. Item r*eceyved* of the balife of Burn … x li. xi s. v d.

Estur rent ut creditor. Item r*eceyved* of s*ir* William Karew knyght for the ferme of Hengrave the xxiiii day of May … xv li. «allocatur in computo precedenti»

Item r*eceyved* the ii^{d} day of Juyn of John Olyfe s*er*vante to Ric*hard* Parker balife of Tateshall for arerag*es* due at the fest of saint Michaell last past … x li. «in computo de anno xvi^{o}»

*Es*tur *rent*. Item r*eceyved* the xx^{ti} day of Juyn of Nicholas Compton by the hand*es* of Water*e* Compton for Estur rent … lxxx li. «in computo de anno xvi^{o}»

Estur rent. Item r*eceyved* the iiii day of July of Nicholas Compton by the hand*es* of Waltier Compton for Estur rent ... Clxxxii li. vi s. viii d. «in computo de anno xvi°»

[*p. 17*] *Estur rent ut creditor.* Item r*eceyved* the v day of July of s*ir* William Wall for Estur rent ... xx li. «allocatur in computo de anno xvi°»

Item r*eceyved* the xiiii day of Juyll of Thomas Philipps of Rikills lande i*n* Kent ... v li.

Item r*eceyved* the xviii day of Septembr*e* of Nicholas Compton by the hand*es* of Will*i*am Bedell ... lxxxxviii li. «allocatur in computo de anno xvi°»

Item r*eceyved* of s*ir* Willyam Walle of the lordesheppe of Kendall for the t*er*me neded at Whytsontyde the xii day of Octobre ... lxxxx li. «allocatur in computo de anno xvi^{mo}»[27]

Michaelmasse rent. Item r*eceyved* of Nicholas Compton for Michaelmes rent the xxvii day of Octobre ... lxix li. «allocatur in computo de anno xvi^{mo}»

Item r*eceyved* of the bayly of Gayton sooke the xxx^{ti} day of Octobre ... xx li. «in computo de anno xvi°»

Item the same day of Ric*hard* Galee of the office of feodam ... xxiii li. «allocatur in computo de anno xvi^{mo}»

Item the same day of Nicholas Compton ... lx li. «allocatur in computo de anno xvi^{mo}»

Item r*eceyved* the ix day of Decembre of s*ir* Raufe Langforth by the hand*es* of John Haghe for Dalbury and Dalburies Lees ... xviii li. vi s. viii d. «allocatur in computo de anno xvi°»

Item r*eceyved* the xiiii day of Decembre of the baliff*es* deputie of Tateshall by the hand*es* of Miles Worsley ... xx li. «allocatur in computo xvi°»

[*p. 18*] Item r*eceyved* the xxii day of Decembre of m*aster* Hugh Oldom by the hand*es* of Miles Worsley ... CCxlviii li. xix s. vi d. «allocatur in computo de anno xvi»

Item r*eceyved* the xx^{ti}ix day of Decembr*e* of m*aster* Hugh Oldom by the hand*es* of Myles Worsley ... lx li. «allocatur in computo de anno xvi»

Item r*eceyved* the vii day of January of Nicholas Compton by the hand*es* of Myles Worsley ... CCCxii li. «allocatur in eodem computo»

Item r*eceyved* the xii day of January of s*ir* William Walles by the hand*es* of the said Miles ... lx li. viii s. «allocatur in computo de anno xvi°»

[28]Item receyved of Herry Nicholson the xth day of Januar*y* anno xvi by the hand*es* of Myles Worsley ... xiii li. «allocatur in computo predicto»

[29] *Myles Worsley Cl li. xi s. v d.*

[27] The cofferer's account for the 16th regnal year (1501) is not extant (see Latin annotations pp. 5, 17–19).

[28] The 'sprawling' hand is responsible for the rest of the page, incl. the annotations.

[29] The three marginal entries are written below each other alongside the entry below, with a canc.

Thesaurarius xxii li.

John Style xxvii li. viii s. vii d.

Item rec*eyved* of m*aster* Hugh Oldom the fyrst day of Januar*y* anno xvi^{mo} per manus Roger Ormyston w*ith* xxii li. payd to N. Matick for iiii butt*es* of malvesey and a ton of Gascon wyne ov*er* and besyde xxvii li. viii s. vii d. payd for certen stuff bought for þe slewse of Boston the whiche John Style most repay … Clxxii li. xi s. v d.[30] «allocatur in computo predicto»

Thesaurarius in computo super Cl li. quid sic habuit allocatum in computo suo de anno xvi^{mo}. Item receyved of the m*aster* Hugh by the hand*es* of m*aster* Empson for wode of hym bought for my lad*ys* fewell … xl li. «allocatur in computo de anno xvi^{mo}»

[*p. 19*] [31]Receyt*es* at div*er*se tymes from the xiiith day of January the xvi yer*e* of o*ur* sov*er*ain lord kinge Henry the vii

First the viii day of February of Ric*hard* Galy by the hand*es* of Myles Worsley… x li. xv s. x d. «allocatur in computo de anno xvi^{mo}»

Item \r*eceyved*/ the vi day of February of Tho*m*as Amias … xx li. «allocatur in eodem computo»

Item \r*eceyved*/ of Water*e* Compton depute to Nicholas Compton by the hand*es* of the said Miles the viii day of March … Clxvi li. «allocatur in eodem computo»

[32]<Item rec*eyved* the iii^{de} day of Aprill of Thomas Philippes of the reveneus of Kendall deu at M*ar*tilmasse last past by the hand*es* of the said Miles … Clxiiii li. ii d. «caveat quid postea»

Item rec*eyved* of Robert Polv*er*toft balife of Tateshall by the hand*es* of the said Miles … xii li.>

[33]Item rec*eyved* of Nicholas Compton the xviiith day of Aprille anno xvi^{mo} H. vii by the hand*es* of Myles … Clx li. «allocatur in eodem computo»

<*Milles W.*> *Miles W.* Item receyved of the seid m*aster* Hught as mony by hym payd for C elne of lynen cloth. P*r*ice le elne iiii d. ob. … xxxvii s. vi d. «allocatur in eodem computo»

Miles Worsly. Item receyved of the seid m*aster* Hugh as mony by hym payd to Paull Gygles for cariage of a b[o]x and corporas casez to Rome … xl s.

[*p. 20*] *Miles Worsley*. Item receyved of the seid m*aster* Hugh by the hand*es* of Roger Ormysten xiiii^{mo} die July anno xv for to provyde stuff for my lad*ys* grace … Cxl li. «allocatur in computo predicto»

dot calculation above; each is preceded by a long-tailed <r> ('respice'?) (so too pp. 19 (last two entries), p. 20 (but not the last entry, which has a canc. marginal note), and note to p. 129 below..

[30] The total of the first two marginal receipts.

[31] The HH hand returns here.

[32] This and the next entry are canc. because (as the note says) they occur again below (p. 21).

[33] The 'sprawling' hand returns here and continues (incl. the annotations) up to and including the rubric and first two entries p. 21. A canc. note is alongside this entry in the margin.

Miles Worsley. Item receyd of the said m*aster* Hught the same day by the hand*es* of R. Ormyston … xxvi li. xvi s. viii d. «allocatur in eodem computo»

M. Worsley. Item receyved of the seid m*aster* Hugh by the hand*es* of the same Roger Ormyston … CCxix li. xix s. vi d. «allocatur in eodem computo»

Miles W. Item receyved of the m*aster* Hugh by the hand*es* of Will*i*am Bayly s*er*vant to the quene x li. viii s. viii d. <and> to purve stuff for my lad*ys* grace. And by the hand*es* of Petrer*e* of the Coldherber*e* for to purve lyke stuff xxii s. iii d. ob. … xi li. x s. xi d. ob. \allocatur in eodem computo/

Item receyved the xix day of Ap*r*il anno xvi^{mo} <by> of Roger*e* Ormysten as mony by hym receyved of Edmound Page <Bally> bayly of Darford in Kent by the hand*es* of Miles Worsley … x li. «allocatur ut supra»

[*p. 21*] Receyt*es* of mony at div*ers* tymes from the xx day of Aprill the xvith yere of our sove*r*an lord kyng Herry the viith unto the [*blank*]

Primo the xxith day of Aprill the forseid xvith yere of Thomas Phylippes of the reveneus of Kendall for Martylmes last past by the hand*es* of Myles Worsley … Clxiiii li. ii d. «allocatur in computo»

Item rec*eyved* of Rob*er*t Pulvertoft bayly of Tatyshall the <ixth> \xxii/ day of Ap*r*ill anno xvi … xii li. «allocatur in computo»

[34]Item rec*eyved* of Nicholas Compton by the hand*es* of the said Miles the xxvi day of Aprill … xl li. «allocatur in computo»

Item rec*eyved* of s*ir* John Gren for money awinge by Gregory Skipwith i*n* p*ar*tie of payment of a mor*e* som the first day of May … xxxiii li. vi s. viii d.

Item rec*eyved* of the execut*ours* of s*ir* William Carew knyght for his ferme of the halfe yer*e* rent of Ingrave payable at Est*er* last past the ii^{de} day of Juyn … xv li. «allocatur in computo»

[*p. 22*] [35]Item rec*eyved* the xviith day of Juyn of Nicholas Compton by the hand*es* of William Bedell into our*e* own coffers … Cxxxii li. «allocatur in computo»

Item rec*eyved* the ii^{de} day of July of the baylife of Tateshall by the hand*es* of Miles Worsley … vi li. «allocatur in computo»

Item rec*eyved* the xi day of August of s*ir* Raufe Langford for the ferme of Dalbery and Dalbery leys … vii li. «allocatur in computo»

Item rec*eyved* the xi day of August of m*aster* chauncceler*e* of the revenus of Exit*ur* land*es* by the hand*es* of Miles Worsley … xxxvi li.

Item rec*eyved* the xix day of August of Thomas Par*e* in p*ar*tie of payment for his gres\o/mes i*n* Kendall by the hand*es* of Thomas Hobsom audit*our* … xx li. «allocatur in computo»

[34] The HH hand returns here.

[35] This entry is perhaps written in a different hand.

Item rec*eyved* the same day of Nicholas Compton of the reveneus of Som*er*sett*es* land*es* by the hand*es* of the said Miles … lxvi li. xiiii s. iiii d. «allocatur in computo»

Item rec*eyved* of Nicholas Compton the thred day of Nove*m*br*e* by the hand*es* of the said Miles … CCCxx li. «allocatur in computo»

Item r*eceyved* the vi day of Nove*m*br*e* of Tho*m*as Philipps of the revenews of Kendall … Cxli li. «allocatur in computo»

Item rec*eyved* of Olyv*er* Hay for Dalbery and Dalbury leys \the vii day of the same/… xvii li. «allocatur in computo»

[*p. 23*] Item r*eceyved* the viii day of Nove*m*br*e* of Edward Vavese*re* … xx^{ti}vii li. «allocatur in computo»

Item rec*eyved* the same day of Nicholas Compton by the hand*es* of the said Miles … xx li. «allocatur in computo»

Frongnall. Item rec*eyved* the xix day of the said moneth of s*ir* Hugh Ashton of the land*es* of Frongnall*es* in Kent … x li. ii s. ii d. «memorandum of ix li. rec*eyved* by Thomas \Hobson/ of the same <of> the whiche so*m*me the said Thomas ys charged w*ith*all for*e* makyng of my lad*ys* breve»

Item rec*eyved* of Nicholas Compton for the fee ferme of Waltham abbey the iii^{de} day of Decembre «anno xvii^{mo} in partem solucionis de arreragiis dicte feodi firme pro anno xvi^{mo}» … xxx^{ti} li. «allocatur in computo»

Item rec*eyved* the xxiii \day/ of Novembr*e* of John Kinge … viii li. «allocatur in computo»

Item rec*eyved* the ii^{de} day of Decembr*e* of the bayly of Dertwych … xi li. «allocatur in computo»

Item rec*eyved* the viii day of Decembr*e* of William Denton for Babram … xxvi li. iii s. iiii d. «allocatur in computo»

Item rec*eyved* the ix day of Decembr*e* of m*aster* Hugh Oldom of my la*n*d*es* in the west countree «cu*m* CClxxiii li. xii s. vi d. receptis de Nicholao Compton pro feofamento» … DCCiii li. vi s. <viii d.> iiii d. «allocatur in computo»

Item rec*eyved* the xxi day of Decembr*e* of Nicholas Compton of such money as by hy*m* was putt to kepinge of the abbot of Peturburgh … vii^{xx}xvii li. xvii s. vi d. «allocatur in computo»

[*p. 24*] [36] <Item rec*eyved* the xx^{ti}ix day of Decembr*e* of the baylyfe of Enderby by the hand*es* of Myles Worsley … vi li. xv s. viii d. «allocatur in computo»

Item rec*eyved* the ii^{de} day of January of the bailife of Colston Basset … x li. ix s. viii d. «allocatur in computo»

Item rec*eyved* the same day of <the> Robert Polv*er*toft bailife of Tateshall … xxv s. vii d. ob. «allocatur in computo»

[36] Pp. 24–5 are canc.

Item rec*eyved* the same day of the baylife of Bassingburn … xiiii li. xvi s. iii d. qua.

Item rec*eyved* of Richard Galie the iii^de day of January … xi li. «allocatur in computo»

Item rec*eyved* the same day of Edward Heven … vii[37] li. xii s. i d. «allocatur in computo»

Item rec*eyved* the iiii^th day of January of the baylife of Oveston … v li. «allocatur in computo»

Item rec*eyved* the same day of the late wife of Ric*hard* Par*ker*e late baylife of Tateshall i*n* par*te* of payment of his arrerag*es* … vi li. «allocatur in computo»

Item rec*eyved* the ix^th day of January of the baylife of War*e* … xl li. «allocatur in computo»

Item rec*eyved* the xvi^th day of January of Nicholas Compton by the hand*es* of Miles Worsley … CClxxv li. xix s. iiii d.[38] «allocatur in computo»

Item rec*eyved* the same day of Nicholas Compton by the hand*es* of John Bedell … xl li. «allocatur in computo»

[39]*Nota.* Memorandum to receyve of s*ir* Hugh Asshton iiii li. that he receyved <of> of Margeret Parker*e* late wyff unto <John> Richard P*ar*ker*e* late bayly of Tatishald.

[*p. 25*] Item rec*eyved* of Thomas Philip the last day of January … xx li. «allocatur in computo infra aliam summam de Kendall»[40]

Item rec*eyved* of John Wren for fee ferme of thabbot of Cristall the same day … iiii li. vii s. ob.

Item rec*eyved* the same day of the said John for the reveneus of Scotton and Brerton … xvii li. x s.

Item rec*eyved* the same day of Oliv*er* Hudilston and John Thornby baliff*es* of Wasshingborogh for the reveneus of the same … xii li.>

[*rest of page blank*]

[*p. 26*] Anno xvii

Recepta. Money receyved the vii day of February the xvii yer*e* of kinge Henry the vii of Miles Worsley of his debet of his last accounte ended at Candelmas last past … xviii li. xi s. iiii d. ob.[41]

Item rec*eyved* the xviii day of February of s*ir* Hugh Asshton of the arrerag*es* of the last accompte … lxxvi li. vii s. viii d.

[37] MS 'vjj'.
[38] MS 'xv' alt. to 'xxv'? 'iii' alt. to 'iijj'?
[39] This entry is written small at the foot of the page in the 'sprawling' hand.
[40] See p. 25 below.
[41] See D91.20/5.

Item rec*eyved* the vii day of March of John Dalkyns by the hand*es* of William Mayn of the arrerag*es* of Holdernes deu at Michaelmesse anno xi° H*en*rici vii i*n* p*ar*tie of payment of lxx li. … xx li.

Item rec*eyved* the xvth day of March of s*ir* Hugh <arrerag*es*> Asshton of arrag*es* … xiiii li.

Item rec*eyved* the xvii day of s*ir* Hugh Ashton by the hand*es* of John Wren of the arrag*es* of Cotyngham … viii li.

Nota quia habet billam de xxxii li.[42] Item of the same the said day for a quarter*e* ended at M*ar*tynmasse … <xxii li.> xxxii li.

Item rec*eyved* of m*aster* chaunceler*e* by the hand*es* of Miles the xxvii day of March … CClxxxx li. xvi s. iiii d.

Item rec*eyved* of Ric*hard* Galee of his arrerag*es* the ii^{de} day of Aprill by the hand*es* of the same Miles … xxx li.

Item rec*eyved* the xx^{ti}v day of Aprill of s*ir* Hugh Asshton by the hand*es* of Miles … xi li. v s. iiii d.

Item rec*eyved* the iii^{de} day of Aprill of the bailiffe of Tateshall … v li.

Summa partis … CCCCiiii^{xx}xvi li. viii d. ob.[43]

[*p. 27*] Item rec*eyved* the vii day of May of s*ir* Hugh Ashton … xlix li.

Item rec*eyved* the same day of Thomas Philipps of the receite of Kendale … Clxxii li.

Item rec*eyved* the xth day of Juyn of s*ir* Hugh Asshton by the hand*es* of Miles … Ciiii^{xx}v li. ii s. ii d.

Item rec*eyved* the xxviii day of Juyn of Thomas Philipps for the gressom of Tho*m*as Parr*e* … xx li.

Item rec*eyved* the ii^{de} day of July of m*aster* Hugh Oldom … CClxxxviii li. xiii s. iiii d.

Item rec*eyved* the same day of s*ir* Hugh Asshton … xx li. vi s. viii d.

Item rec*eyved* the xxiiii day of July of s*ir* Hugh Asshton … lxxi li. vi s. viii d.

Item rec*eyved* the xxvii day of July of s*ir* Hugh Asshton … xv li. vii d. ob.[44]

Item rec*eyved* the xxx day of July of the[45] same s*ir* Hugh … x li.

Item rec*eyved* the iiiith day of August of the same s*ir* Hugh … xv li.

Item rec*eyved* the xxiiii day of August of the arrerag*es* of Holdernesse by the hand*es* of Willia*m* Mayn … xvii li.

Item rec*eyved* of Thomas Philipps for Kendall the xx^{ti}iiii day of Septe*m*br*e* … <[…]>Cxxxvi li.

[42] Written in the margin in the 'sprawling' hand with + above 'Nota' and above the canc. total.
[43] The total (correct before the alterations), written at the foot of the page, still in the HH hand.
[44] 'ob' add. later.
[45] 'the' rep.

Item rec*eyved* the xii day of Octobr*e* of s*ir* Hugh Asshton … xiii li.

[*p. 28*] Item rec*eyved* the xx day of Octobr*e* of Ric*hard* Galee of his office of feodary … xxix li. xiii s. iiii d.

Item rec*eyved* the xx^{ti}v day of Octobr*e* of s*ir* Hugh Asshton … xl li. ix s.

Item rec*eyved* the xxviii day of Octobr*e* of Ric*hard* Both for Dodington … xix li.

Item rec*eyved* of Willia*m* Mayn the last day of Octobr*e* of the arrerag*es* of Holdernesse … xii li. xiii s. iiii d.

Item of Ric*hard* Galee the first day of Nove*m*bre … xxix li. x s.

Item rec*eyved* of s*ir* Hugh Asshton the first day of Nove*m*br*e* … CCxiii li. xiii s. ix d. ob. qua.

Item rec*eyved* the viii day of Nove*m*bre of the bayliffe of Tateshall … xx li. xiii s. iiii d.

Item rec*eyved* the xx day of Decembr*e* of s*ir* Hugh Asshton … CCCxlix li. xi s. vii d. ob.

*Wherof payed to m*as*t*er *Conyngsby the vi day of January vi^{xx} li.*[46] Item rec*eyved* the xxiii day of Decembr*e* of m*aster* chambirlain for money rec*eyved* of m*aster* Conyngsby … CCl li.

Item rec*eyved* the same day of m*aster* chauncelere of his receyte … CCCCCxl li.

Item rec*eyved* the last day of Decembr*e* of s*ir* Hugh Asshton … Cxxii li. xi s. iiii d.

Item rec*eyved* the same day of the said s*ir* Hugh … xl s.

Item rec*eyved* the viii day of January of s*ir* Hugh Asshton … CCCCxxxvii li. xiiii s. ob.

Item receved of m*aster* chauncelere the same \day/ for money delyv*e*red to m*aster* chambirlain the xx^{ti}ix day of August … xx li.

[*p. 29*] Item rec*eyved* the same day of m*aster* chauncelere … xxvi li. xvi s. x d.

Item rec*eyved* the xi day of January of m*aster* chauncelere for money by hym payed for tynne … Cxlvii li. xvii s. vi d.[47]

Ad manus proprias domine. Item rec*eyved* the same day of m*aster* chauncelere for tynne by hym sold … Clxii li. iii s.

Item rec*eyved* the same day \of m*aster* chauncelere/ by the hand*es* of Willia*m* Hilmere to p*r*ovide spices for my ladis houshold … xiii li. vi s. viii d.

[48] Item rec*eyved* of m*aster* Hugh Assheton by the hand*es* of Thomas Soper of tharrerages of John Hoo <q> late reve off Cheshunt … xxvi li. viii d.

[46] Add. in left margin, still in the HH hand.

[47] See p. 53 below.

[48] This and the next entry are in the 'sprawling' hand.

Item rec*eyved* off John Butteller late bayly of Sheldon and Wolford Magna the whiche war*e* in my lad*ys* hand*es* by the nonnage of my lord off Bukyngham by the hand*es* off Thomas Soper … vii li.

Item rec*eyved* of s*ir* Thomas Laurence k*night* by Tho*m*as Philipps … vi li. xiii s. iiii d.

Item rec*eyved* the same day of Thomas Franke by the said Tho*m*as Philipps … iiii li. iiii s.

Item rec*eyved* the xixth day of January of Will*i*am Denton … xvii li. iii s. iiii d.

Item rec*eyved* the same day of Ric*hard* Galey … iii li. viii s. i d. ob.

Item rec*eyved* the xx^{ti}i day of January of s*ir* Hugh Asshton … xlv li. iiii s. ix d.

[*p. 30 blank*]

[*p. 31*] Recepta pro anno xviii

Receyt*es* made by s*ir* Hugh Assheton «and m*aster* Hugh Oldom»[49]

Furst receyved of the said s*ir* Hugh the xiiith day of February anno xviii^{o} … Clxxii li. iiii s. viii d.

Item rec*eyved* of s*ir* Hugh Asshton the xviiith day of February at Richmount… xxi li. iiii s. iiii d.

Item rec*eyved* of the same the xiiiith day of March at Richmounte … xlvi li. xi s. v d.

Item rec*eyved* of m*aster* chauncel*er*e the first day of Aprill … CCxx li.

Item rec*eyved* the xth day of Aprill of s*ir* Hugh Asshton … xli li. xi s. vi d.

Nota pro computo videmus.[50] Item rec*eyved* the same day of s*ir* Roger*e* Urmeston for the joynct*our* of maistres Alice P*ar*kere … xxxiii li. vi s. viii d.[51]

Item rec*eyved* the xx^{ti} day of Aprill of s*ir* Hugh Asshton … xviii li. xix s.

Item rec*eyved* the xvth day of May of the <v> m*aster* Thomas Urmeston vicar*e* of Kendall … Clxxxxiiii li. xi d.

Nota quantum stet de C marcis.[52] Item rec*eyved* the viii day of February for the dutie of John Dalkyn of Holdernes by the hand*es* of Willia*m* Mayn … x li.

[*p. 32*] Item rec*eyved* the xxx^{ti} day of May of s*ir* Hugh Ashton … <v> lvi li. xiiii s. ix d.

Item rec*eyved* of the same the ii^{de} day of Juyn … xv li. vi s. viii d.

Item rec*eyved* the viii day of Juyn of John Turney for the warde of Jane Godston i*n* p*ar*tie of payment of a mor*e* s*er*vice … xl li.

[49] Add. in the HH hand.
[50] Written in the margin in the 'sprawling' hand with + above 'Nota' and above the canc. total.
[51] For another instalment see p. 144 below.
[52] Written in the margin in the 'sprawling' hand (see p. 26 above).

Nota quantum debet ultra.[53] Item rec*eyved* the xii day of Juyn of m*aster* chambirlain for money rec*eyved* of s*ir* John Grene … xx li.

Nota quantum debet ultra. Item rec*eyved* the said day <for> of the same m*aster* chambirlain for money rec*eyved* of m*aster* Conyngsby … Cxi li.

Item rec*eyved* the xxi day of Juyn of s*ir* Hugh Asshton … lxxxix li. xii s. viii d.

Item rec*eyved* the xxii day of Juyn of the same s*ir* Hugh … xvi li.

Item rec*eyved* the iiii^th^ day July of m*aster* chauncerler*e* … CCxl li.

Item rec*eyved* the xii day of July of s*ir* Hugh Asshton … lxix li. v s. iiii d.

Conyngsby. Item rec*eyved* the xth day of Juyn of Thomas Smyth of Okham i*n* par*t*ie of payment of such money <of> as m*aster* Conyngsby then owth unto my lady … ix li.

Item rec*eyved* the vth day of August of m*aster* Hugh Oldom my lad*ys* chauncelere … xl li.

Item rec*eyved* the xix^th^ day of August of s*ir* Hugh Asshton … xliii li. xi s. iiii d.

[*p. 33*] Item rec*eyved* the vii^th^ day of Septembr*e* of s*ir* Hugh Asshton … xlvi li. vi s. viii d.

Item rec*eyved* the ii^de^ day of Nove*m*br*e* of Ric*hard* Gale … xx li.

Item rec*eyved* the same day of the vicar*e* of Kendall … Cxliii li. x s. i d.

Item rec*eyved* the xiii^th^ day \of Decembre/ of s*ir* Hugh Asshton by the hand*es* of Miles … CCCCxxi li. vii d. ob.

Item rec*eyved* the xiiii^th^ day \of Dece*m*br*e*/ of the same by the hand*es* of the said Miles … Clxxxiiii li. xi s. iiii d.

Item rec*eyved* the xx^ti^vii of Decembr*e* of m*aster* chauncellere … DCClxx li. xxi d. ob. di. qua.

[54]Item rec*eyved* of the seid m*aster* Hugh Assheton xxi^mo^ die Decembris anno xix^no^ <wheroff> as that was payd to m*aster* chamberlyn … Cxxi li. xiii s. iiii d.

Item receved off m*aster* chauncellere the last day off Decembr*e* anno xix^no^ for the man*ere* off Cote pro termino mensis Decembris anno \per manus Milonis/ … x li. vii s. vii d. qua. di.

Oneratur in computo dicti Milonis Worsley et allocatur ibidem.[55] Item rec*eyved* off m*aster* chauncellere [*blank*] eiusdem mensis Decembris for certen prentytt bok*es* bought for my lad*ys* grace … lx s.

Item receyved of m*aster* Hught Assheton the xth day off Januar*y* by the hand*es* off Miles Worsley by thand*es* of m*aster* chamb*er*lyn for certen stuff by hym baught … xxiii li. iii s. vii d. ob.

[53] This and the note below are written in the margin in the 'sprawling' hand

[54] The 'sprawling' hand returns here and continues to the end of p. 34.

[55] See D91.20/129.

[*p. 34*] Item receyved the xvith daye off Januar*y* anno xix^{no} regis predicti off m*aster* Hugh Assheton … DCCxxx li. xviii s.

Item receyved off the same m*aster* Hugh the xviith day off the same monyht … xxxix li. xv s. vi d. ob.

[*rest of page blank*]

[*p. 35*] [56]<Delyv*er*aunce at div*er*se tymes by my lady from the xiiiith day of January the xvth yer*e* of *our* soverain lord kinge Henry the vii the so*m*mes folowinge.

First to Wyllyam Bedell tresorer*e* of my lad*ys* household the day above rehersed … xl li.

Item to the same the xxix day of January … xl li.

Item to the same the xiith day of February by the hand*es* of John Bedell … xlvi li. ii s. vi d.

Item to the same the xx^{ti}viii day of March by the hand*es* of John Bedell … xxi li. ix s.

Item to the same the ii day of March by the hand*es* of John Bedell … xx li.

Item delyv*er*ed to the said Wyllyam Bedell the xx^{ti} day of March … xl li.

Item the xxx^{ti} day of March … lxix li.

Item to the same the xv day of Aprile … l \li./ xiii s. iiii d.

Item to the same the xviii day of Aprile … xxxvii li.

Item the xxvii day of Aprill to the same … <xx li.>[57] xl li.

Item delyv*er*ed to the same the first day of May be the hand*es* of John Bedell … xl li.>

[*p. 36*] Item delyv*er*ed unto the same the xxiiii day of May … xv li.

Item delyv*er*ed to the same the secu*n*de day of Juyn … xxxiii li.

Item delyv*er*ed to the same the xiii day of Juyn … lxiiii li. xiii s. iiii d.

Item delyv*er*ed to the same the xvi day of Juyn … xxx^{ti}iiii li. vi s. viii d.

Item to the same the xxv day of Juyn … xxix li.

Item to the same by the hand*es* of John Bedell the first day of July … lxiii li.

Item delyv*er*ed to the same the v day of July by the hand*es* of John Bedell … xl li.

Item to the same the xiiiith day of July by the hand*es* of John Bedell … xx li.

Item to the same the xxviii day of July … <xli d.> xli li.

Item to the same the v day of August … Cvii li. x s. x d.

[56] The HH hand returns here. The whole page is canc.

[57] Pricked as well as canc.

Item delyv*er*ed to the same the xxii day of August … lxxxxiii li. xiii s. iiii d.

Item to the same <at> i*n* another bagge the forsaid day … iiii^{xx}xiii li. xvii s. x d.

[*p. 37*] Item delyv*er*ed to the tresorer*e* the xvi day of Octobre … xlvii li.

Item delyv*er*ed to John Bedell the xxvii day of Octobr*e* … xxxiiii li.

Item delyv*er*ed to John Bedell the xiiith day of <February> Novembre … xl li.[58]

< Item delyv*er*ed to the same John Bedell the xxi day of Novembre … xxii li. ii s. iiii d.

Item the iii day of Decembre delyv*er*ed to William Bedell … xliii li.

Item delyv*er*ed to John Bedell the xii day of Decembre … xx li.

Item delyv*er*ed the xviii day of Dece*m*bre to William Bedell tresorer*e* … C li.

Item delyv*er*ed the xxix day of Decembr*e* to William Bedell … xx li.>

[*rest of page blank*]

[*p. 38*] Delyv*er*aunce at c*er*tain tymes by my lady co*m*maundment to William Bedell tresorer*e* of hir houshold from the xx^{ti}i day of Novembre the xvi yer*e* of kinge Henry the vii for thexpenses of hir houshold the somes folowing

First the xxi day of Nove*m*bre delyv*er*ed to the same … xxii li. ii s. iiii d.

Item delyv*er*ed to the same the iii^{de} day of Decembr*e* … xliii li.

Item to the same the xii day of Decembr*e* … xx li.

Item to the same the xviiith day of Decembr*e* … C li.

Item to the same the xx^{ti}ix day of Decembr*e* … xx li.

Item to the same the xviiith day of January … xxv li.

Item delyv*er*ed the first day of February to the same by the hand*es* of John Bedell … iiii^{xx}iii li.

Item delyv*er*ed the xxiii day of February to the same by the hand*es* of John Bedell … xlv li.

Item delyv*er*ed the xix day of March to the same … iiii^{xx}xii li. viii s.

Item delyv*er*ed to the same the xxx^{ti} day of March … Cviii li.

Item delyv*er*ed to the same the x day of Aprill … xxxix li. iiii s.

[*p. 39*] Item delyv*er*ed the xii day of Aprill to the same for so moch money allowed for wode boght of the kinge[59] i*n* Westhay upon his <l> acounte i*n* anno xvi … l li.

[58] A line is drawn under this entry and the rest of the page is canc.

[59] Alt. from 'kings'(?).

Item delyv*er*ed the same day to the same for iiii bott*es* of malvesey and a tonne of Gaskeyn wyne p*ro*vided at London by Roger*e* Urmeston … xxii li.

Item delyv*er*ed the xxiiii day of Aprill to the same … lxvi li. vii s. iiii d.

Item delyv*er*ed to the same the xxvii day of Aprill … [*blank*]

Item delyv*er*ed the vi day of May to the same … xxxii li.

Item delyv*er*ed the xxiiii day of May to John Bedell … xlviii li. xix s. vi d.

Item dylyv*er*yd to the seid Willia*m* Bedyll treserar the xith dai of June … xxxiiii li.

Item delyv*er*ed to the same the xxv day of Juyn … lxxi li. v s. viii d.

Item delyv*er*ed the xv day of July to John Bedell … xxxiii li. vi s. viii d.

Item delyv*er*ed the xxiii day of July to the same John … lxx li.

Item delyv*er*ed the xii day of August to William Bedell … xxxvi li.

[*p. 40*] Item delyv*er*ed to the said tresorer*e* the x\i/xth day of August … iiii^{xx}xiii li.

Item delyv*er*ed to the same the xxvii day of August for p*ro*vision at Stirbissh fair*e* … Cxxxiii li. vi s. viii d.

Item delyv*er*ed to m*aster* tresorer the xviii day of Decembr*e* … C li.

Item delyv*er*ed the xvith day of January to m*aster* tresorer by <John Bedell> \Nicholas Compton/ … xl li.

Item delyv*er*ed to the same the xxi day of January … xxv li. vi s. viii d.

<Item delyv*er*ed the iiii day of July>

[*rest of p. 40 and pp. 41–42 blank*]

[*p. 43*] *Vacat.*[60]

[61]<Delyv*er*aunce at <ty> div*er*se tymes from the xiiiith day of January the xvth yer*e* of the reigne of oure soverain lord kinge Henry the viith the so*m*mes folowinge

Vacat.[62]

First to Miles Worsley the xvth day of March … x li.

Item the xxvi day of March … xiii li. vi s. viii d.

Item the xxx^{ti} day of March … xlix li. iii s. iiii d.

Item delyv*er*ed to the said Miles the first day of May … DCCxv li. vi s. vii d. ob. qua.

Item to the same the day abovesaid … x li. xix s. ix d. ob.

Item to the same the day abofesaid … x li. xi s. v d.

[60] 'Vacat' here and below written in a neat small hand.
[61] Pp. 43–5 lightly canc.
[62] Bracketed to include all the entries on the page.

Item to the same the iiii day of May … xxv li. iii s. iiii d.

Item to the same the xiii day of Juyn … xl li.

Item to the same the xx^{ti} day of Juyn … x li.

Item to the same the iii day of Auguste … xi li. xiii s. iiii d.

Item to the same the said day … xi li.

Item to the same the xxii day of Auguste … v li.

Item to the same the xx^{ti}v day of Auguste … vi li. xiii s. iiii d.

[*p. 44*] Item delyv*er*ed to Myles Worsley the xxviith day of August anno xvi^{o} regis H. vii at Notley … xlviii li. xiii s. iiii d.

Item delyv*er*ed to the same the xxiii day of Septembr*e* at Wodstok … xl li.

Item to the same at Lidington the x day of Octobre … xxi li.

Item to the same the xxvii day of Octobre … x li.

Item delyv*er*ed to the same the secu*n*de day of Nove*m*bre … xx li.

Item delyv*er*ed to the same the iii day of Novembre <for a rewarde yeven to> … vi li. xiii s. iiii d.

Item delyv*er*ed to the same the vii day of Novembre … xx li.

Item delyv*er*ed to the said Miles upon Saint Michael even to *con*tent the king*es* grace for the wardshipp of Rikell*es* … CC m*arce*

Item delyv*er*ed to the same the x day of Novembre … xvii li.

Item delyv*er*ed to Miles the ix day of Decembre … xviii li. vi s. viii d.

Item delyv*er*ed to the said Miles the xxx day of Decembr*e* … xl li.

Item delyv*er*ed to the same Miles the ii^{de} day of January … xv li.

Item delyv*er*ed to the same the said day wich was rec*eyved* of Stile … <x\l/ li.> xl li.

[*p. 45*] Pro anno xv^{mo}

Item delyv*er*ed the xiii day of January to the said Miles … xviii li.

Item delyv*er*ed to the same the xviiith day of Aprill … C li.[63]

Item>

[*rest of page blank*]

[63] This entry is out of place chronologically.

[*p. 46*] Anno xvi^{o} Henrici vii

Delyv*er*aunce at div*er*se tymes from the xiiiith day of January the xvi yer*e* of *our* soverain lord kinge Henry the vii to Miles Worsley

First delyv*er*ed to the same Miles Worsley the xvi day of January next e*n*suynge … xix li.

Item delyv*er*ed to the same Miles the xxii day of January … xxvi li.

Item delyv*er*ed to the same the xi day of February … xx li.

Item the viii day of March delyv*er*ed to the same … lvi li.

Item delyv*er*ed to the same the iii^{de} day of Aprill … xxi li. xvii s. vi d.

Item delyv*er*ed to the same the xviith day of Aprill … lxv li. vi s. x d.

Item delyv*er*ed to the same the xth day of Novembr*e* for money receyved of Rikels land*es* … x li. xvi s. viii d.

Item delyv*er*ed the xxii day of Aprill to the same for money rec*eyved* of He*n*ry Nicholson … xiii li.

Item delyv*er*ed to the same the xxviiith day of Aprill for my lad*ys* almes … xiii li. vii s.

Item delyv*er*ed to the same the said day of April … xl li.

Item delyv*er*ed the secu*n*de day of Juyn to the same Miles … xxiii li.

Item delyv*er*ed to the same Miles the xviii day of Aprill for the <w> mariage of Marcham son … C li.

[*p. 47*] Item delyv*er*ed to Myles Worsley the xvi^{t} day of Juyn … viii li. ii s. iiii d.

Item delyv*er*ed to the said Myles the xixth day of Juyn … xxxiii li.

Item delyv*er*ed to the said Miles the xxv day of Juyn … xviii li.

Item delyv*er*ed to the said Miles the xxix day of Juyn … xx li.

Item delyv*er*ed to the said Miles the xix day of July … xl li.

Item delyv*er*ed to the said Miles the xii day of August … xvii li.

Item delyv*er*ed to the said Miles the xixth day of August … lxxii li.

Item delyv*er*ed to the same Miles the viii day of August for my lad*ys* wark*es* at Westm*ynster* … xx li.

Item delyv*er*ed to the same Miles the xth day of August … xxvii li.

Item delyv*er*ed to the same Miles the xviiith day of Octobr*e* … xlv li. xiii s. <v>iiii d.

Item delyv*er*ed the viii day of Nove*m*br*e* to the said Miles … Cxxi li.

Item delyv*er*ed the xx^{ti}i day of the said moneth to the same Miles for the houshold … <xlxxx li. ii s. ii d.> \lxx li. ii s. ii d./

Item delyv*er*ed the same day to the said Miles to pay for a garnyshe of silv*er* vesell … viii^{xx} li. and xx s.

[*p. 48*] Item delyv*er*ed to the same Miles the iiii day of Decembr*e* … lxix li.

Item delyv*er*ed to the said Miles the viii day of Decembr*e* … xxvii li.

Item delyv*er*ed the same day to the said Miles … xxxv li.

Item delyv*er*ed the same day to the said Miles … xxvi li. xiii s. iiii d.

Item delyv*er*ed to the same the xx^{ti}viii day of Decembr*e* … Clxx li. ix s.

Item delyv*er*ed the last day of Decembr*e* to the same Miles for the quenes New Yer*es*[64] yeft … xlii li. vi s. viii d.

Item delyv*er*ed to the same the iii^{de} day of January … xiii li. xii s. i d.

Item delyv*er*ed to the same Miles the xx^{ti}ii day of January … Cxl<i>xix li.

[65]Item delyv*er*ed by the hand*es* of my lady Jane … C s.

Item

[*rest of page and p. 49 blank*]

[*p. 50*] Anno xvii

Money delyv*er*ed to the tresorer*e* for the expenses of hir houshold from the vii day of February anno xvii regni regis Henrici vii^{mi}

First i*n* full *con*tentacion of his surplisage of his accompte ended at the fest of Purificacio*un* of *our* Lady last past … xxxi li. ix s. vii d. ob.

Item delyv*er*ed the \viii/ <same> day \of the said moneth/ to the said tresorer*e* for the expenses of this New Yer*e* … lv li. vii s. x d. ob.

Item delyv*er*ed the xi day of March to John Bedell … C li. xi s. iiii d. ob.

Item delyv*er*ed the xxvi day of March to the said tresorer*e* … xxxiiii li. xii s. viii d.

Item delyv*er*ed the xvi day of Aprill to m*aster* tresorer*e* … xxiiii li.

Item delyv*er*ed the xxvii day of Aprill to m*aster* tresorer*e* … lxxi li.

Item delyv*er*ed the xvii day of <ap> May … lxxii li.

Item delyv*er*ed the xxiiii day of May to the said tresorer*e* by the hand*es* of John Bedell … xlv li. v s. iiii d.

Item delyv*er*ed the xi day of Juyn to the said m*aster* tresorer*e* … iiii^{xx} li.

DCxxxvii li. iiii s. ii d.[66]

[64] MS 'yrer*es*'.
[65] The entry is written in the 'sprawling' hand, with 'Item' below in the HH hand..
[66] The correct total for p. 50, written small to the right at the foot of the page, still in the HH hand.

[*p. 51*] Item delyv*er*ed the last day of Juyn to m*aster* tresorer*e* by the hand*es* of John Bedell ... xxxix li. xiiii s. viii d.

Item delyv*er*ed the iiii day of July to the said tresorer*e* ... xxxiiii li. xvi s. viii d.

Item the xvith day of July dylyv*er*yd unto the seid tresorar ... lxx li. vi s. iiii d.

Item delyv*er*ed the xxx^{ti} day of July to John Bedell ... xxv li. vii d.

Item delyv*er*ed the vi day of August to John Bedell ... lxxii li.

Item delyv*er*ed the xxvi day of August to John Bedell ... lxvi li.

Item delyv*er*ed the x day of Sept*em*br*e* to John Bedell ... lxii li. xiii s. iiii d.

Item delyv*er*ed the xvith day of Sept*em*br*e* to John Bedell ... xliiii li.

Item delyv*er*ed the xx^{ti}v day of Sept*em*br*e* to John Bedell ... iiii^{xx}viii li. iiii s. ii d.

<Item rec*eyved* the xiith day of Octobr*e* of s*ir* Hugh Ashton ... xiii li.> *Vacat*.

Item delyv*er*ed the xxi day of Octobr*e* to m*aster* tresorer*e* ... xxix li. xiii s. iiii d.

Item delyv*er*ed the xx^{ti}vi day of Octobr*e* to m*aster* tresorer*e* ... iiii^{xx}xv li. vi s. vi d.

Item delyv*er*ed the xii day of Nove*m*bre to m*aster* tresorer*e* ... xx li.

Totalis ... DCvii li. xv s. ix d.[67]

<CCClxx li. xi s. vi d.> <CCCl li. xi s. vii d.>[68]

[*p. 52*] Item deliv*er*ed the ii^{de} day of Decembr*e* to John Bedell ... xxix li. x s.

Item delyv*er*ed the xiiii day of Dece*m*br*e* to m*aster* tresorer*e* ... xxviii li. xi s. vi d.

Item delyv*er*ed to m*aster* tresorer*e* the <xvi> xx^{ti} day of Decembr*e* ... Cxviii li. <v> vi s. ix d. ob. qua.

Item delyv*er*ed to m*aster* tresorer*e* by the hand*es* of Willia*m* Hilmer*e* for money delyv*er*ed to hym by m*aster* chauncelere for p*ro*vision of spices ... xiii li. vi s. viii d.

Item delyv*er*ed to m*aster* tresorer*e* by the hand*es* of John Bedell the xvii day of January ... Cxii li. iiii s. ii d.

[*rest of page blank*]

[*p. 53*] Memorandum delyv*er*ed by the hand*es* of m*aster* chaunceler*e* to John Dantre of South Hamton xxi day of August i*n* tynne wich su*m*me is charged byfor*e* amonge the receyt*es*[69] ... <Clxii li. iii s.> Cxlvii li. xvii s. vi d.

[*rest of p. 53 and p. 54 blank*]

[67] Written in the 'sprawling' hand to the left below the entries (the hand uses the form 'vj^{C}' for 600). The total for the page (minus the canc. £13) should be £647 15s. 7d.

[68] Both canc. calculations are written to the right at the foot of the page in the HH hand.

[69] See the second entry p. 29.

[*p. 55*] Anno xvii

Delyveraunce to Miles. Money delyv*er*ed to Myles Worsley the vii[th] day of February <the> anno xvii regni regis Henrici vii[mi].

First to the said Miles the same day of his arrerag*es* of his last accounte … xviii li. xi s. iiii d. ob.[70]

Item delyv*er*ed the same day to the said Miles of money receyved of my lady Powes … xxi li. xx d.

Item delyv*er*ed the same day to the said Miles … xii li.

Item delyv*er*ed the xxi day of February to the same Miles … viii li.

Item delyv*er*ed the ii[de] day of March to the same Miles … x li.

Item delyv*er*ed the iiii[th] day of March to the same Miles i*n* money receyved of my lady Waynefford … viii li. vi s. viii d.

Item delyv*er*ed the vii day of March to the said Miles … xx li.

Item delyv*er*ed the xvii day of March to the said Miles … xiiii li.

Item delyv*er*ed the xxi day of March to John Saint John for my lady Bygod for hir dower*e* of the land*es* of the king*es* gift by the hand*es* of the said Miles … xx li.

Item delyv*er*ed to the said Miles the xxvii day of March … xxxiiii li. x s. ii d.

Summa partis … Clxvi li. ix s. x d.[71]

[*p. 56*] Anno xvii.

Item delyv*er*ed the ii[de] day of Aprill to the said Miles … xxx li.

Item delyv*er*ed the xiiii[th] day of Aprill to the same Miles … xxiiii li. v s. viii d.

Item delyv*er*ed the xxii day of the same moneth to the said Miles … xx li. ii s. x d. ob.

Item delyv*er*ed the xxiii day of Aprill to the same Miles … v li.

Item delyv*er*ed to the same Miles the xi day of <apri> May … xxxviii li.

Item delyv*er*ed the xvii day of May to the said Miles … xxx li. xiii s. iiii d.

Item delyv*er*ed to the same Miles the xxix day of May … xxviii li.

Item delyv*er*ed the x[th] day of Juyn to the same Miles … xxxi li. viii s. vi d.

Item delyv*er*ed the xii[th] day of Juyn to the said Miles … xxix li. ii s. iiii d.

Item delyv*er*ed the xx[ti]vi day of Juyn to the said Miles … xx li.

Item delyv*er*ed to Miles the ii[de] day of July … xxx li. <v> iii s. vi d.

Item delyv*er*ed to the same Myles the iii[de] day of July … xii li.

Item delyv*er*ed the xxvi day of July to the same Miles … lxxi li. vi s. viii d.

[70] See D91.20/5–7 for all these receipts.

[71] The correct total for p. 55, written at the foot of the page in the same (HH) hand.

Item delyv*er*ed the same day to the said Miles for money lent to the bisshop of Carlisle elect to Duresme … C li.

<Summa partis … CCCClx li. ii s. x d. ob.>[72]

[*p. 57*] Item delyv*er*ed the vth day of August to the said Miles … xv li.

Item delyv*er*ed the xvth day of August to the said Miles … xvii li. xv s. viii d.

Item delyv*er*ed the xxii day of August to the said Miles … xxix li.

Item delyv*er*ed the vi day of Septembr*e* to the said Miles … xlix li. iii s. ix d. ob.

Item delyv*er*ed the vii day of Septe*m*br*e* to the said Miles … xxix li.

Item delyv*er*ed to Miles the xx^{ti} day of Septembr*e* anno xviii^{mo} regis Henrici vii^{mi} … lxvi li. xv s.

Item delyv*er*ed the xx^{ti}iiii day \of Septe*m*br*e*/ to the said Miles … xx li.

Item delyv*er*ed the xvth day of Octobr*e* to Miles … xli li. ii s. vi d.

Item delyv*er*ed the xvth day of Octobr*e* to the same Miles … xxi li. x s.

Item delyv*er*ed the xx^{ti}vii day of Octobr*e* to the said Miles … xx li.

Item delyv*er*ed the vith day of Nove*m*br*e* to the said Miles … xvii li.

Item delyv*er*ed the xii day of Nove*m*br*e* to the said Miles … xx li. xiii s. iiii d.

Item delyv*er*ed the xix day of Nove*m*br*e* to the same Miles … xix li.

Item delyv*er*ed the ii^{de} day of Decembr*e* to the said Myles … Cxvii s. viii d.

<Totalis … DCCCxxxiii li. vii s. ii d. ob.>[73]

<DCvi li. xiiii s. v d. ob.>[74]

[*p. 58*] Item delyv*er*ed the xth day of Decembr*e* to the said Miles … xv li. xvii s. x d.

Item delyv*er*ed the xx^{ti} day of Decembr*e* to the said Miles … xii li.

Item delyv*er*ed the same day to the said Myles … xx li. xii s. viii d.

Item delyv*er*ed to the said Miles the xxiiii day of Decembr*e* … iiii^{xx}iii li.

Item delyv*er*ed the same day to the said Miles … x li. xi s. viii d.

Item delyv*er*ed the xxvii day of Decembr*e* to the said Miles … li li. vi s. viii d.

Item delyv*er*ed the last day of Decembr*e* to the said Miles … xlviii li. v s.

[72] The total for p. 56, written at the foot of the page in the same (HH) hand; the canc. sum is £10 short.

[73] The total of the 'Summa partis' (p. 56) and p. 57 (£371 17s. 11½d.), written small to the right below the entries in the HH hand; the correct total would be £842 10d.

[74] Written small to the left at the foot of the page, perhaps in the same HH hand.

[75]Item de[ly]v*er*ed the viiith day off Januar*y* anno xviii^{mo} by the hand*es* of John Butteller*e* late [b]ayly[76] of Sheldon and Wolford Magna by the hand*es* of Thomas Soper … vii li.

Item <Rec> de[ly]v*er*ed by the hand*es* off the seid Thomas Soper as mony receyved of John How late reve off Cheshunt … xxvi s. <vii d.> viii d.

Item delyv*er*ed the xixth day of January to the said Miles … xx li. xi s. v d. ob.

[*p. 59*] *Anno xviii. Delyv*er*aunce to the tresorer*e. Money delyv*er*ed to Willia*m* Bedell tresorer*e* of my lad*ys* houshold from the xiiith day of January anno xviii^{mo}.

Hic desunt 2^{e} summe que tamen stant in indenturis. B.[77]

First delyv*er*ed to the same the xith day of Aprill … C li.

Item delyv*er*ed to the same the first day of May … iiii^{xx}viii li. vii s. vi d.

Item delyv*er*ed to John Bedell the xi day of May … xliiii li. v s. iiii d.

Item delyv*er*ed the xx^{ti}ii day of May to the same John Bedell … lxxxiii li. viii <d.> s.

Item the ixth day <anno> of Jun*e* to the same Wyllyam … Cxxvii li. xix s. x d.

Item delyv*er*ed the first day of July to m*aster* tresorer*e* … Ciiii^{xx}xiii li. xii s. x d.

Item delyv*er*ed the xxv day of July to John Bedell … lxxix li. xii s. viii d.

Item delyv*er*ed the ixth day of August to John Bedell … <x li.> xl li.

Item delyv*er*ed the xxviiith day of August to John Bedell … xlvii li. vi s. viii d.

Item delyv*er*ed the viith day of Septembr*e* to the said John … lxxxii li.

Item delyv*er*ed to the said John the vii day of Septe*m*br*e* … xlvi li. vi s. viii d.

Item delyv*er*ed the xviiith day of Septe*m*bre to the same John … C li.

[*p. 60*] [78]Item delyv*er*ed unto the forsaid Willia*m* Bedell the furst daye of Octobr*e* … xlviii li.

Item delyv*er*ed the xxiiii day of Octobr*e* to John Bedell … xlviii li.

Item delyv*er*ed the viith day of Nove*m*bre to m*aster* tresorer*e* … xl li.

Item delyv*er*ed the xvith day of Nove*m*br*e* to m*aster* tresorer*e* … xl li.

Item delyv*er*ed the first day of Dece*m*bre to m*aster* tresorer*e* \for money rece*yved* of my lady Cecill/ … lii li.

Item delyv*er*ed the xvii day of Decembr*e* to m*aster* tresurer*e* … vi^{xx} li.

[75] This and the next entry are in the 'sprawling' hand.

[76] MS 'dayly'.

[77] The missing two sums may relate to pp. 59 and 60. A line from 'B' leads to where they should appear on the page (before 'First')..

[78] This entry and the last on the page are written in a different hand, the same as that at pp. 91, 117, 147, 161 (see footnotes).

Item delyv*er*ed the xx^{ti}iii day of Decembr*e* to m*aste*r tresurer*e* … iiii^{xx}<li.>i li. xviii s. iii d. ob.

Item delyv*er*ed the xiith day of Januar*y* to the forsaid m*aste*r tresorer*e* … lix li.

[*p. 61*]

[79]*A*. Item delyvered <of> the xiiiith day off Januar*y* anno xviii^{mo} fo[r] the arrerages off the last acompt … l li. xii d. qua.

Item delyv*er*ed the viiith day off Feveryere next folowyng … xlv li. iiii s. ix d.

Item delyv*er*ed the xiiith off <j> the same monyht … Ciii li. xvi s. v d.

Summa … [*blank*]

Memorandum off mony delyvered unto the forseid tresourer*e* by <tha> the hand*es* off Myles Worsley wheroff the <a> seid <mirhe> Miles hath alowance in hys acompt <off> \among/ foryn payment*es*.

Fyrst <a> on tyme Ciiii^{xx}xi li. xviii s. iii d. Anothere tyme xxxiii li. xiiii s. ix d. ob. Anothere tyme lxiiii li. xvii s. And anothere tyme xx li. And anothere tyme viii li. iii s. iiii d. … Cxviii li. xiii s. <viii d.> iiii d. ob.[80]

Item delyv*er*ed to the tresorer*e* <ffor*e*> in the p*r*ice off iiii^{xx}iiii yard*es* off blake cloth … xii li. xvi s. x d.

Summa … CCCxxxi li. x s. ii d. ob.[81]

[*p. 62*] Memorandum off money receyved by the seid tresourer*e* off certen p*er*sones <f> off syche mony as they awght unto my ladys grace for certen stuff unto them sold as yt appereth in \the/ fote hys last acompt at large videlicet de anno xviii^{mo} regis predicti.

Fyrst receyved off John Atwode off Eslyngham in Kent by the hand*es* of Thobson for the rest whete off hym bought ayenst the mariage off the prince \Arthur*e*/ … C s.

Item receyved [*blank*]

[*the rest of p. 62 and pp. 63–64 blank*]

[*p. 65*] [82] xviii.

To Miles.

Anno xviii.

Money delyv*er*ed to Miles Worsley from the xixth day of January in anno xviii^{mo} Henrici vii.

[79] Pp. 61–2 are written in the 'sprawling' hand. The marginal 'A' is bracketed to include the first three items on the page, all of which relate to 'arrerages', i.e. arrears, cf. notes to pp. 69, 92, 146.
[80] The total is correct.
[81] The sum total is correct (written in the 'sprawling'hand).
[82] The HH hand returns here.

First delyv*er*ed to the said Miles the same day … xv li. xviii s.

Item delyv*er*ed the xx^{ti}i day of January to the same Miles … xxvi li. xiiii s.

Item delyv*er*d to the said Myles the xiiith daye of February next folowyng … CClx li. vi s. ix d.

Item delyv*er*ed unto the said Myles the forsaid <d> xiii daye of February … iiii^{xx}xix li.

Item delyv*er*ed to the same Miles the first day of Aprill … iiii^{xx} li. viii s.

Item delyv*er*ed to the same the xiith day of Ap*r*ill … xxi li. iiii s. iiii d.

Item delyv*er*ed the same day to the said Miles … xxv li. viii s. ix d.

Item delyv*er*ed the xx^{ti}ii day of Aprill to the same Miles … xlvi li. xi s. v d.

Item delyv*er*ed the xx^{ti}vii day of Aprill to the same Miles … xviii li. xix s.

Item delyv*er*ed the iii^{de} day of May to the same … xvii li. iii s. iiii d.

Item delyv*er*ed the xi day of May to the said Miles … xix li.

Item delyv*er*ed the xx^{ti}ii day of May to the same … xxiii li.

[*p. 66*] Item delyv*er*ed the xxii day of May to the same Miles … xii li.

Item delyv*er*ed the same day to the said Miles … Clxxxxiiii li. xi d.

Item delyv*er*ed to the same Miles the xiii day of July … CCxliii li. xvii d.

Item delyv*er*ed the xi day of July to the said Miles … Cxxviii li. viii s. vi d.

Item delyv*er*ed the xvi day of July to the said Miles … lxix li. v s. iiii d.

Item delyv*er*ed the xxvii day of July to the said Miles iii^{xx}iiii li. xii s. vi d. … lxiiii li. xii s. vi d.

Item delyv*er*ed to the said Miles the xxixth day of July … xx li.

Item delyv*er*ed the xxviii day of August to the said Miles … xliii li. xi s. iiii d.

Item delyv*er*ed the viiith day of <August> Septe*m*br*e* to the same Miles … xxxi li. xiii s. iiii d.

Item delyv*er*ed the same day to the said Miles … xvi li. xvii s. xi d.

Item delyv*er*ed to the said Miles the viiith day of Octobr*e* … lxii li. vi s. ix d.

Item delyv*er*ed the xvith day of Octobr*e* to the same Miles in denariis riallis … xx li.

Item delyv*er*ed the xx^{ti}iii day of Octobr*e* to the same Miles … xv li. xvi s. <v>iii d.

[*p. 67*] Item delyv*er*ed the iiiith day of Nove*m*br*e* to the same Miles … xx li.

Item deliv*er*ed the xvith day of Nove*m*br*e* to the said Miles … xviii li.

Item <to> delyv*er*ed the xx^{ti}vii day of Nove*m*br*e* to Myles by the ha*n*d*es* of Nicholas Sander … xiii li. x s. i d.

Item delyv*er*ed the xiiiith day of Dece*m*br*e* to the same Miles … Ciiii^{xx}iiii li. xi s. iiii d.

Item delyv*er*ed the xixth day of Decembr*e* to the said Miles … <xliiii li. vi s. viii> xli li. vi s. viii d.

Item delyv*er*ed to the said Miles the xxx^{ti} day of Dece*m*bre … DCxx li.

[83]Item delyv*er*ed to Myles off the the[so]rye off m*aster* Hugh Assheton by thand*es* off m*aster* chamb*er*lyn the xth day off <Janier*e*> Janiver*e* anno <xviii^{mo}> xix^{no} … xxiii li. iii s. vii d. ob.

Item delyv*er*ed < … > [*blank*] off <dete> Decembr*e* anno xix^{no} regis H. vii^{mi} by thand*es* off m*aster* Hugh Oldom for bok*es* by hym bought … lx s.

[*p. 68 blank*]

[*p. 69*] Anno xix^{no}

Memorandum off mony delyvered to Will*i*am Bedell tresour[er]e off household from the xiiiith daye Januare anno xix^{no} regis Henrici vii^{mi}

B.[84] Fyrst delyvered unto the seid tresourer*e* the xviith day off Januar anno predicto … lxi li.

A. Item deliv*er*ed unto the same as for suche clere money þ*at* he aght in thende of his last accompte ended the xiii day of Janyvere last passed … lix li. xv s. v d. ob.

[85]Item delyv*er*ed unto the same the iii^{de} day of February for payment made to the m*aster* of Fodringay for woode of the king*es* bought of the said m*aster* … xx li.

Item delyv*er*ed to the same the xvith day of February by the hand*es* of James… xxxviii li. xii s. iii d.

Item delyv*er*ed the vth day of March to m*aster* tresorer*e* by the hand*es* of James Morice … xx li.

Summa partis … Ciiii^{xx}xix li. vii s. ix d. ob.[86]

[*p. 70*] Anno xix^{no} regni regis Henrici vii^{mi}

Item delyv*er*ed to m*aster* treserer*e* the ix day of March by the hand*es* of James Morice … xxxi li. vi s. viii d.

Item delyv*er*ed the xx^{ti}iii day of March to m*aster* tresurer*e* … Cxix li. v s.

Item delyv*er*ed the xith day of Aprill to m*aster* tresurer*e* by John Bedell … l li.

[83] This and the next entry are in the 'sprawling' hand, which also writes the Memorandum and first two entries on p. 69. See Plate 5.

[84] 'B', with 'A' below, may indicate that the entries need to be reversed chronologically. On the other hand, 'A' appears to relate to 'arrerages', i.e. arrears, cf. notes to pp. 61, 92, 146.

[85] The HH hand returns here.

[86] The total is written at the foot of the page, perhaps not in the HH hand; all the *Summe partis* from now on are correct (not all perhaps in the HH hand).

Item delyv*er*ed the xxiii day of Aprill to m*aster* tresurer*e* by the hand*es* of Nicholas Saunder … lxxii li.

Item delyv*er*ed the xx^{ti}v day of Aprill to m*aster* tresurer*e* by the hand*es* of the said Nicholas … xxx li.

Item delyv*er*ed the xx^{ti}viii day of Aprill to m*aster* tresurer*e* by the hand*es* of the said Nicholas … C li.

Item delyv*er*ed the xx^{ti}i day of May to m*aster* tresurer*e* … lxxx li.

Item delyv*er*ed the xx^{ti}v day of May to the same m*aster* tresurer*e* … iiii^{xx} li. xii li. xiii d.

Item delyv*er*ed the iii^{de} day of Juyn to m*aster* tresorer*e* … lviii li. xi s.

Item delyv*er*ed the xx^{ti}ii day of Juyn to the m*aster* tresaurer*e* by the hand*es* of John Bedell … iiii^{xx} <li.> x li. v s. v d.

Item delyv*er*ed the xx^{ti}iiii day of Juyn to the same by the hand*es* of the said John … lx li.

Summa partis … DCCiiii^{xx}iii li. ix s. ii d.

[*p. 71*] Item delyv*er*ed the xx^{ti}viii day of Juyn to m*aster* tresaurer*e* by the hand*es* of John Bedell … CCxix li. v s. viii d.

Item delyverd the xvii day of August to m*aster* tresarer … <C li.> Cvi li. xiii s. iii d.

Item delyv*er*ed the xxx^{ti}i day of August to m*aster* tresorer*e* … Cxiiii li. xiiii s. iiii d.

Item delyv*er*ed the viith day of Septembr*e* to m*aster* tresaurer*e* by John Bedell … Ciii li. viii s. iiii d.

Item delyv*er*ed the ix day of Septembr*e* to m*aster* tresaurer*e* … lxviii li. viii s. iiii d.

Item delyv*er*ed the xx^{ti}vi day of Sept*em*br*e* to m*aster* tresaurer*e* … CCxliiii li. xiiii s. ii d.

Item delyv*er*ed the iiiith day of Nove*m*br*e* to the said m*aster* tresaurer*e* … xxxix li. xii s. xi d.

Item delyv*er*ed the same day unto the said m*aster* tresaurer*e* … iiii^{xx}x li.

Item delyv*er*ed the xx^{ti}v day of Nove*m*br*e* to the same by John Bedell … xl li.

Item delyv*er*ed the viith day of Dece*m*br*e* to the same by John Bedell … iiii^{xx}vii li.

Item delyv*er*ed the xith day of Dece*m*br*e* to to the same by John Bedell … CCxxiiii li. iii s. ii d.

Summa partis … M<C>\CCC/xxxviii li. xiiii d.

Total delyv*er*ed to m*aster* tresorer*e* … MMCCCxx li. xviiii s. i d. ob.[87]

[*pp. 72–74 blank*]

[87] The correct total of the *Summe partis* pp. 69–71 (see p. 78), written to the left at the foot of the page in a different hand.

[*p. 75*] [88]Memorandum off mony delyv*er*ed unto Miles Worsley from the <xvith> \xiiiith/ day off Januar*y* anno xix^{no} regis H. vii^{mi} unto [*blank*]

Fyrst delyv*er*ed unto the seid Miles as mony by hym dew uppon the det*er*mi[n]acio*u*n off his last acompt endyd the xiiith daye off the <seid> Januar*y* anno xix^{no} regis predicti as yt appereth in [*blank*] ... xxix li. xvi s. ii d. qua.

Item delyv*er*ed unto the <syd> seid Miles as mony by \hym/ receyved off Thomas Cordall for*e* wode by hym sold at Colyweston ... xi li. x s. vi d.

[89]<Item delyv*er*ed unto Miles the iii^{de} day of February to yeve unto m*aster* of Fodringay for p*ar*tie payme*n*t for wode of the king*es* bought of the said m*aster* ... xx li.>[90]

Item delyv*er*ed to the said Miles the xvith day of February ... xx li.

Summa partis ... lxi li. vi s. viii d. qua.

[*p. 76*] Anno xix^{no}

Item delyv*er*ed the xxv^{ti} day of February to the same Myles ... xx^{ti}v li. vi d. viii d.

Item delyv*er*ed the vth day of March to the said Miles ... xvi li.

Item delyv*er*ed the xx^{ti}ii day of March to the said Miles by the hand*es* of James Morice ... xxii li. xiii s. iiii d.

Item delyv*er*ed the xiith day of March to the said Miles ... xliii li. v s. v d.

Item delyv*er*ed the iii^{de} day of Aprill to the same Miles ... l li.

Item delyv*er*ed the xx^{ti}viii day of Aprill to the same Miles ... xliii li.

Item delyv*er*ed the same day to the said Miles ... xxiii li. viii s. iiii d.

Item delyv*er*ed to the same Miles the xvith day of May ... xxiii li. xiii s. iiii d.

Item delyv*er*ed the[91] last day of May to the said Miles ... xxxvii li. vii s. ii d.

Item delyv*er*ed the same day to the said Miles ... lxxiii li. xvi s. vii d.

Item delyv*er*ed the xx^{ti}vii day of Juyn to the said Miles ... lv li.

Item delyv*er*ed the iii^{de} day of July to the same Miles ... xxxi li.

Item delyv*er*ed the ixth day of July to the said Miles ... xxiiii li.

Summa partis ... CCCClxviii li. x s. x d.

[*p. 77*] Anno xix^{no}

Item delyv*er*ed the xth day of July to the said Miles ... lxviii li. iii s. iiii d.

Item delyv*er*ed to the same the said xth day ... CCxxxv li. xii s.

[88] The memorandum and the first two entries are written in the 'sprawling' hand.

[89] The HH hand returns here.

[90] Canc. because entered on p. 69 above.

[91] MS 'thei'.

Item delyv*er*ed to the same the xx^{ti}ix day of July … x li. xvi s. v d.

<Item delyv*er*ed to the same the vth day of Auguste … iiii^{xx} li. v s.

Item delyv*er*ed to the same the vth day of Auguste … lxxix li. v s.>

Per me H. Hornby.[92]

Item delyv*er*ed to the same Miles the vth day of Auguste … lxxv li. xv s.

Item delyv*er*ed the last day of August to the said Miles … xviii li. xi s. iii d. ob.

Item delyv*er*ed the ixth day of Septembr*e* to the said Miles … xvii li. xv s. viii d.

Item delyv*er*ed the xx^{ti}vi day of Septe*m*br*e* to the said Miles … xlvi li. xxi d. ob. di. qua.

Item delyv*er*ed the xviiith day of Septe*m*br*e* i*n* clipped grot*es* to the said Miles to be co*n*veyed to London by s*ir* Hugh Asshton … Cxviii li. xviii s. ix d.

Item delyv*er*ed the same day <of t> to the said Miles … xix li. vi s. viii d.

Item delyv*er*ed the ii^{de} day of Octobr*e* to the same Miles … iiii^{xx}ii li. vi s. viii d.

Item delyv*er*ed the xixth day of Octobr*e* to the said Miles … x li.

Summa partis … DCCiii li. vii s. vii d. di. qua.

[*p. 78*] Item delyv*er*ed the iiiith day of Nove*m*br*e* to the said Miles … xxxv li. viii s. iii d.

Item delyv*er*ed the xx^{ti}v day of Nove*m*br*e* to the said Miles … xx li.

Item delyv*er*ed the xith day of Dece*m*br*e* to the said Miles … Cxviii li. viii s. i d.

Item delyv*er*ed the same day to the said Miles i*n* denariis riall*es* and xxx d. … xx li. x s.

<Item rece*yved* the xx^{ti}i day of January of s*ir* Hugh Asshton by the hand*es* of the said Miles … CCCCiiii^{xx}ii li. iii s. xi d.>

Item delyv*er*ed unto the said Miles the xx day of Dece*m*br*e* … <lxv> l li. xvii s. x d.

[93]Item delyv*er*ed to þe Miles vii^{mo} die Januarii anno xx^{mo} … xix li. xvii s. ix d. ob.

Summa partis … <CCxlv li.. iiii s. iii d.> CClxv li. ii s. ob.

Total delyvered to Miles … MCCCClxxviii li. ix s. iiii d. qua. di.[94]

[92] Written in the left margin alongside the two canc. items for 5 August (the next item for 5 August is presumably correct). The note in the same hand as the entries provides evidence that the main hand is that of Hornby.

[93] This entry is in the 'sprawling' hand, which appears to be responsible for the rest of p. 78, p. 79, and certainly for the rubric and the first entry on p. 83.

[94] The correct total of the *Summe partis* (pp. 75–78) should be £1,498 7s. 1¾d. (see last sum on this page).

Summa totalis delyvered … [95]<MCCCClxxviii li. ix s. iiii d. qua. di.>
<MMMDCCiiii^{xx}xix li. vii s. v d. ob. qua. di.>
MMMDCCCxix li. v s. iii d. di. qua.
[96]to m*aster* tresoror*e*
MMCCCxx li. xviii s. i d. ob.
[97]Miles
<MCCCClxxviii li. ix s. iiii d. qua. di.>
MCCCCiiii^{xx}xviii li. vii s. i d. ob. qua. di.

[*p. 79*] <MCCCCiiii^{xx}xviii li. vii s. i d. ob. qua. di.> <DCCCxix li. v s. iii d. di. qua.>[98]

[*pp. 80–82 blank*]

[*p. 83*] *Anno* <*xix*> *xx^{mo}*. Receytes off mony from the xviith day off Januar*y* the xix yere off kyng Herry the viith <unto þe xv daye off þe same monyht the yere off the reigne off the seid kyng>

Fyrst receyved off m*aster* Hugh Assheton the xx^{ti}iii[99] day off the seid monyht … xiii li. vi s. viii d. «allocatur»

[100]Item rec*eyved* of m*aster*Asshton the xx^{ti}v day of February by the[101] hand*es* of Miles Worsley … iiii^{xx}iii li. vi s. viii d.

Item rec*eyved* the viith day of March of m*aster* Tho*m*as Urmeston receyvor of Kendall … lxxx li.

Item rec*eyved* the iii^{de} day of Aprill of my lorde of Duresme for money lent unto hym by the hand*es* of Miles Worsley … C li. «in computo Milonis Worsley»[102]

Item rec*eyved* of sir Hugh Asshton the xiith day of March … xliii li. v s. v d. «allocatur»

Item rec*eyved* the vth day of Aprill of dame Katherine Ameas «per pelt off C m[…]»… xiii li. vi s. viii d.

[95] All three sums (the last perhaps in a different hand) occur below each other, bracketed to the right after 'Summa … delyvered'. The final calculation is the correct sum of both Bedell's and Worsley's receipts (Bedell's are totalled p. 71, Worsley's p. 78). Below to the left is a dot calculation.
[96] Bracketed to the right after the two canc. sums above, and bracketed to the calculation, which is correct (see p. 71).
[97] Bracketed to the right after the two canc. sums above (below 'to master tresorere') and bracketed to the calculations; the corrected total is now correct at £1,498 7 s. 1¾d..
[98] Written in the same (i.e. 'sprawling') hand at the foot of the otherwise blank page; the two sums are correct for, firstly, Worsley's receipts, and, secondly, the sum total on p. 78 (as divided between Worsley and Bedell), minus the 3,000, which has not been jotted down.
[99] MS 'xxijj^{ti}'.
[100] The HH hand returns here.
[101] 'the' rep.
[102] See D91.20/134.

Item rec*eyved* the xi day of Aprill of Ric*hard* Galee … v li. «allocatur»

Item the same day of Charles <Ryym> Yarborogh … v li. «allocatur»

Item of Ric*hard* Both the xiiith day of Ap*r*ill … xxxiii li. «allocatur»

Item rec*eyved* the xx^{ti}viii day of Ap*r*ill of s*ir* Hugh Asshton i*n* *par*te of payme*n*t for the ferme of Manereber*e* … lx i. «allocatur»

[*p. 84*] Item rec*eyved* the xixth day of May of the vicar*e* of Kendall by the hand*es* of the said Miles … lxxx li. «allocatur»

Item rec*eyved* the last day of May of s*ir* Hugh Asshton of the land*es* i*n* the west *par*ties … CCCiiii^{xx}ii li. iii s. ii d. «allocatur»

Item rec*eyved* the xiiiith day of Juyn of s*ir* Hugh Asshton … lxxviii li. «allocatur»

Item rec*eyved* the xth day of July of s*ir* Hugh Asshton … CCxxxv li. xii s. «allocatur»

Item rec*eyved* of the same the xx^{ti}ix day of July … x li. xvi s. v d. «allocatur»

Item rec*eyved* the xv day of August of s*ir* Hugh Asshton … xviii li. xi s. iii d. ob. «allocatur»

Item rec*eyved* the xix day of August of the same … Cxiiii li. xiiii s. iiii d. «allocatur»

Item rec*eyved* the xiith day of Septe*m*br*e* of the said s*ir* Hugh … xix li. vi s. viii d. «allocatur»

Item rec*eyved* the viith day of Dece*m*br*e* of s*ir* Hugh Asshton … MCxxviii li. xviii s. vii d. «allocatur»

Item r*eceyved* the xx^{ti}i day of Dece*m*br*e* of s*ir* Hugh Asshton by the said Miles … CCCiiii^{xx}ii li. iii s. xi d. «allocatur»

[103]Item receyved off m*aster* Hugh Assheton the xvth day off Januar*e* anno xx^{mo} by the hand*es* off the seid Miles … Dvi li. v s. vi d. «allocatur»

[*p. 85*] Receyt*es* off mony to my lad*ys* coffers from the xvth daye off Januar*e* anno xx^{mo} regis Henrici vii^{mi} unto the [*blank*]

First rec*eyved* the xxi day of January of s*ir* Hugh Asshton by the hand*es* of Miles Worsley … Cxii li. ix s. xi d. «allocatur»

< Item rec*eyved* \the xiii day of Febru*ary*/ of sir John Twhayt*es* at Parise by <his> his brother \Tho*m*as/ Twhayt*es* for money lent unto the said s*ir* J. Tw\h/ayt*es* by my lady … xiii li. vi s. viii d.> «quia postea»[104]

Item rec*eyved* the xx^{ti}i day of February of s*ir* Hugh Asshton … vi li. xiii s. viii d. «allocatur»

Item rec*eyved* of s*ir* Hugh Asshton the xx^{ti}iii day of February … Clxxix li. viii s. viii d. ob. «allocatur»

[103] This and the rubric on p. 85 are in the 'sprawling' hand.

[104] The entry is canc. 'because [it occurs] later', i.e. p. 87.

Kendall. Item rec*eyved* the viith day of March of s*ir* Hugh Asshton … CCxi li. x s. vii d. «allocatur»

Item rec*eyved* the ixth day of March of s*ir* Hugh Asshton … xli li. vii d. «allocatur»

Item rec*eyved* the xx^{ti}iii day of March of s*ir* Hugh Asshton … xliiii li. «allocatur»

Item rec*eyved* the xx^{ti}ix day of Ap*r*ill of s*ir* Hugh Asshton … CCCCvi li. ix s. «allocatur»

Item rec*eyved* of the same the vi day of May … Cv li. xiii s. ix d. «allocatur»

Item rec*eyved* the xxi day of May of the said s*ir* Hugh … xlv li. viii s. ob. «allocatur»

Item rec*eyved* of the same the xx^{ti} day of Juyn … Cxxviii li. xii s. v d. «allocatur»

[*p. 86*] *Kendall.* Item rec*eyved* the xvith day of Septe*m*br*e* of s*ir* Hugh Asshton of the revenews of Kendall … Clxv li. vi s. viii d. «allocatur»

Item rec*eyved* the same day of the said s*ir* Hugh … CCCli li. xvi s. viii[105] d. ob. «allocatur»

Item rec*eyved* the same day of <of> the said s*ir* Hugh … xxx li. xvi s. viii d. «allocatur»

Item rec*eyved* of the said s*ir* Hugh Asshton the xviiith day of Nove*m*br*e* … DCCCCl li. x s. «allocatur»

Item rec*eyved* of the same the xiiith day of Dece*m*br*e* … Miiii^{xx}xix li. v s. v d. «allocatur»

Item rec*eyved* the said day of the same s*ir* Hugh … lxi li. xi s. v d. «allocatur»

[106]Item \rec*eyved* as/ mony delyv*er*ed to Will*iam* Bedell tresourer*e* off household as for certen medewes and pastures þ*a*t war*e* occupied to the use off my lad*ys* household … xlvi li. ii d. «allocatur»

[*p. 87*] So*m*me totall off all mony receyved off Hugh Assheton clerke w*i*thin the tyme aforseid … MMMMCii li. iii s. vii d. ob.[107]

theroff[108]

to my lad*ys* coffers … MMMMlvi li. iii s. v d. ob.

to Will*iam* Bedell … xlvi li. ii d.

Item rec*eyved* <off> þe xiiith day off Feveryere þe xx^{ti} yere off s*ir* John Twhayt*es* at Pares by his brother*e* Th. Twhaytes for mony lent unto þe s*ir* John … xiii li. vi s. viii d.

[*pp. 88–90 blank*]

[105] MS 'vijj'.

[106] The entries from here until the second entry on p. 91 are in the 'sprawling' hand.

[107] The sum total is divided below between the coffers (£4,056 3s. 5½d.) and the treasury (£46 2d.).

[108] Written to the right below the sum total (above), 'theroff' introduces the sums delivered to the coffers and to Bedell.

[*p. 91*] Memorandum off mony delyv*er*ed unto the tresour*e* off household from þe xiiith daye off Januer*e* anno xx^{mo} regis Henrici vii^{mi} unto the [*blank*]

Fyrstt delyv*er*ed to Will*i*am Bedell tresorer*e* of houshold the xxv day of Januarii … l li. xviii s. x d.

[109]Item delyv*er*ed the xiiii day of February to the said tresaure by the hand*es* [of] Nicholas Sander*e* … xlii li. ix s. iii d.

Item delyv*er*ed the ii^{de} day of March to m*aster* tresaurer*e* by the said Sander … lxxx^{ti} li. vi s. iiii d.

Item delyv*er*ed the xixth day of <m> March to m*aster* tresaurer*e* by Sander*e* … lxxxx li.

Item delyv*er*ed the vth day of March to m*aster* tresaurer*e* by Sander*e* … xliiii li.

Item delyv*er*ed the xviiith day of Aprill to m*aster* tresaurer*e* by Sander*e* … lxxxxvi li. ii s. viii d.

Item delyv*er*ed the xiiith day of Juyn to m*aster* tresaurer*e* by Sander*e* … Cxli li. xiiii s. viii d.

Item delyv*er*ed the xxii day of Juyn to m*aster* tresaurer*e* … <lxix> lxvii li. ix s.

[110]Item delyv*er*ed to m*aster* tresourer the xxvith day of July … CCvi li. xiii s. v d.

Item delyv*er*ed to m*aster* tresaurer the xvith day of August … lxxi li.

Item delyv*er*ed the xxith [111] day of August to m*aster* tresaurer*e* … Cxxxvii li. v s. ii d.

[*p. 92*] Item delyv*er*ed the iiiith day of Sept*em*br*e* to m*aster* tresaurer*e* by Nicholas Sander*e* … lxxvi li. viii s. x d.

Item delyv*er*ed the xx^{ti} day of Sept*em*br*e* to m*aster* tresaurer*e* by the hand*es* of Nicholas Saunder*e* … lxxiiii li.

Item delyv*er*ed the xx^{ti}vii day of Sept*em*br*e* to m*aster* tresaurer*e* by Nicholas Sander*e* … xlii li. vi s. viii d.

Item delyv*er*ed the same day to the said m*aster* tresaurer*e* by the same Nycholas… xxx li. xvi s. viii d.

Item delyv*er*ed the xi day of Octobr*e* to the tresaurer*e* <and \to/ the> by the said Nicholas … xxxii li.

Item delyv*er*ed to the same by the said Sander the xviiith day of Octobr*e* … xxxvi li.

Item delyv*er*ed the xx^{ti}ii day of Octobr*e* to m*aster* tresaurer*e* by the said Saunder*e* … xlvi li.

Item delyv*er*ed the xiiith day of Dece*m*br*e* to m*aster* tresaurer*e* by the said Sander … CCxix li. xix s.

[109] The HH hand returns here.

[110] This entry is written in a different hand, the same as that at pp. 60, 117, 147, 161 (see footnotes).

[111] MS 'xxjth<jj>'.

Item delyv*er*ed the xx^{ti}i day of <march> Dece*m*br*e* to the same m*aster* tresaurer*e* … C li.

[112]*A*. Item delyv*er*ed unto þe seid tresourer*e* for þe areragez off his last acompt … Cvi li. vii s. viii d. ob.

[*p. 93*] Item delyv*er*ed unto þe seid tresourer*e* þe xx^{ti}ii daye off þe seid month… xlvi li. ii s. iiii d.

Item delyv*er*ed unto þe same tresour*e* þe <xiii>\viiith/ daye off Januar*e* anno xxi^{mo} … lxix li. vii s. xi d.

Item delyv*er*ed unto þe same ther*e* þe xii day off the same monyht … CCli li. xii d.

So*m*me totall off þe hole mony delyv*er*ed to the seid tresour*e* … MMClxi li. ix s. v d. ob.

wheroff ys off tharerages off þe seid tresourerys last accompt … Cvi li. vii s. viii[113] d. ob.

and so redy mony delyv*er*ed out off my ladys coffers … MMlv li. xxiii d.

[*pp. 94–100 blank*]

[*p. 101*]

[two torn and irregular paper slips approx. 35–40 x 150 mm., now kept in an envelope (see Description above), may have belonged here:

In grott*es* … Clxi li. vi d. in two bagg*es*

In grott*es* … iiii^{xx}vii li. iii s. viii d.]

Memorandum off mony delyv*er*ed unto Myles Worsley from the xiiith day off Januar*y* anno xx^{mo} regis Henrici vii^{mi} unto the [*blank*]

Furst <receyved by> \delyv*er*ed to/ the said Myles of his arrerag*es* of the last account … xxxix li. xi s. i d. qua.[114] «oneratur»

Item in recepta est. <Item delyv*er*ed to the said Myles the xxvii day January in cleppyd grott*es* send to London to the receyver … Cvi li. vii s. ii d. «ex recognicione Johannis Fothed»>

Item delyv*er*ed the same day to the said Myles by thand*es* of John Fothed comptroll*er* … xxxiii li.

[115]Item delyv*er*ed the xiiii day of February to the said Miles for payment of money lent to the scluse at Boston … xlv li. ix s. iiii d. «oneratur»

[112] The entries from here on (up to and incl. the memorandum and first three entries on p. 101) are in the 'sprawling' hand. The marginal 'A' appears to relate to 'arrerages', i.e. arrears, cf. notes to pp. 61, 69, 146.

[113] MS 'viij', but the sum delivered to the coffers (below) is assessed as if this were 'vi'.

[114] See D91.20/194 and p. 103 below and footnote..

[115] The HH hand returns here.

Item delyv*er*ed the xx^{ti}ii day of February to the said Miles … xxiiii li. ii s. vi d. «oneratur»

Item delyv*er*ed the last day of February to the said Miles … xxxii li. xvii s. «oneratur»

Item delyv*er*ed the iii^{de} day of March to the said Miles … x li. xiiii s. ii d. ob. «oneratur»

Item delyv*er*ed the same day to the said Miles … xx li. xix s. x d. «oneratur»

Item delyv*er*ed the xix day of March to Miles … iiii li. ii s. iiii d. «oneratur»

Item delyv*er*ed to Miles the xixth day of Aprill … lxvi li. «oneratur»

[*p. 102*] Anno xx^{mo}

Item delyv*er*ed the xixth day of Aprill to Miles Worsley i*n* clipped grot*es* to be chaunged at London «ov*er* and besyd*es* lxxi li. xiii s. iiii d. delyv*er* to James for Cambrigge» … <Cxiii li. xviii s. v d.> xlii li. v s. i d.[116] «oneratur»

Item delyv*er*ed the xvi day of Juyn to Miles by the hand*es* of Saunder … xx li. «oneratur»

Item delyv*er*ed the xx^{ti}i day of Juyn to Miles by the hand*es* of Saunder … CCClxxvii li. vii s. viii d. ob. «oneratur»

Item delyv*er*ed the xxii day of Juyn to the said Miles … Cxviii li. xiii s. iiii d. «oneratur»

Item delyv*er*ed to the same Miles the xx^{ti}vii day of July … xxxv li. xvii s. vii d. «oneratur»

Item delyv*er*ed the xvith day of Septe*m*br*e* to the said Miles … lxvii li. xvi s. ii d. «oneratur»

Item delyv*er*ed the same day to the said Miles … xx li. «oneratur»

Item delyv*er*ed the xx^{ti}ix day Octobr*e* to the said Miles … xxviii li. x s. «oneratur»

Item delyv*er*ed the xiiith day of Dece*m*br*e* to the said Miles … DCxix li. xii s. xi d. «oneratur»

[117]Item delyv*er*ed to þe seid Milez þe [*blank*] daye off [*blank*] anno [*blank*] by þe hand*es* off m*aster* controller for land*es* purchesed off s*ir* Herry Erbet knyght … DCCxl li. «oneratur»

[*p. 103*] Item delyv*er*ed to þe seid Milez þe [*blank*] day off [*blank*] anno predicto by þe hand*es* off the seid m*aster* controller*e* for land*es* purchesed off the lord Fytzwater*e* videlicet for þe full payment off <DCCCiii^{xx} li.> DCCCiiii^{xx} [118] … CCCClxxvi li. «oneratur»

So*m*me off all the hole mony delyv*er*ed unto Myles Worsley w*ith*in þe \tyme/ aforseyd … MMDCCCiiii li. xix s. i d. qua.

[116] The corrected sum as well as the annotation are in the 'sprawling' hand.

[117] The entries from here until the end of p. 104 are in the 'sprawling' hand.

[118] See D91.21/58, 77.

wheroff was off his awn proper arrerage of his last acompt … xxix li. xi s. i d. qua.[119]

and cu*m*me out off my lad*ys* cofferes … MMDCCCxv li. viii s.

Item he hath receyved off Thomas Soper my lad*ys* solist*er* for the p*ar*te off Gregore Skypwithys dett … xx li.[120] «oneratur»

Item receyved off the same Thomas Soper*e* for the parte off the ladys Skreneys det … iiii li. «oneratur»

[*p. 104*] Item he hath receyved off Olyv*er* Holand in þe p*ar*te off payment off xv li. xiiii s. i d. … viii li. xvi s. vi d. ob. qua.[121]

Item receyved off Will*iam* Elmer*e* as mony þe last yere to hym lent … xiii li. vi s. viii d.

Item receyved off maistris Wyndysore as mony to hur*e* þe < … > last yere prestyd… xvii s. x d.

Item receyved off Nicholas Awghton as for mony to hym lent … xlvi s. viii d.

Item receyved off Richard Atherton for mony to hym prestyd þe last yere … liii s. iiii d.

Summa partis … xxviii li. xii d. ob. qua. «quod oneratur in computo dicti Milonis infra summam CCClxviii li. xii s. ix d. ob.»[122]

[*pp. 105–6 blank*]

[*p. 107*] [123]Money delyv*er*ed to James Morise for the work*es* from the ii^{de} day of March anno regni regis Henrici vii^{mi} xx^{mo}.

First delyv*er*ed to the said James the iii^{de} day of March … viii li. x s. «oneratur»

Item delyv*er*ed to the said James the iiiith day of July … Ciiii[124] li. xx d. «oneratur»

[125]Item the xx day of July recevid be the said James \as it doth apere by[126] indenture of the said sommes/ … iiii^{xx}vii li. viii s. iii d. «oneratur»

Item delyv*er*ed the xvith day of Septe*m*br*e* to the said James … xxx li. x s. «oneratur»

Item delyv*er*ed the xii day of Nove*m*br*e* to the said James … xxxii li. v d. ob. «oneratur»

Nota. Item delyv*er*ed the xiiith day of Dece*m*br*e* to James Morise … lxxiiii li. x s. «oneratur»

[119] See p. 101 above and footnote.
[120] For this and the next entry see D91.21/4.
[121] For this and the other entries on p. 104 see D91.20/194.
[122] See D91.20/194 (twice noted) and footnotes.
[123] The HH hand returns here.
[124] MS 'Cijij'.
[125] This entry (and the addition) are written in a different hand.
[126] 'appeire of' add.

Item delyv*er*ed to the same <s> the said day for rep*ar*acions at Coldherborogh … vii li. xviii s. v d. «oneratur»

[127]Item delyv*er*ed to þe seid James þe xxvii day off <Ja> June by the hand*es* off Miles Worsley for þe beldyng off Cristez Collage in Cambryge … lxvi li. xiii s. iiii d. «oneratur»

Item delyv*er*ed at another*e* tyme þe xixth day off June anno regis by þe hand*es* off þe seid Miles toword þe seid rep*ar*aciones … C s. «oneratur»

[*p. 108*] Item delyv*er*ed another tyme [*blank*] day off [*blank*] anno xxi^{mo} regis predicti by the hand*es* of m*aster* chanceller and m*aster* controller*e* toward þe forseid reparaciones off Cristes Collage in Cambrigge to <by> þe hand*es* off m*aster* Sykelyng … Cxxxvii li. vi s. viii d.

[*p. 109*]

So*m*me totall off all þe hole mony delyv*er*ed unto þe forseid Jamez Mores w*ith*in þe tyme aforseid … Dliii li. xviii s. ix d. ob.

Item he ys charged w*ith* tharerages off his last acompt … xxxii li. xix s. xi d.

Totalis liberacionum … Ciiii^{xx}vii li. xviii s. viii d. ob.[128] «computus coram Thomas Hobson auditore»

extra[129]

[*p. 110 blank*]

[*p. 111*] Receyt*es* off mony from þe xvth day off Januar*e* the xx^{ti}i yere off kyng Herry the viith unto [*blank*]

[130]Fyrst rec*eyved* the xx^{ti} day of January of Miles Worsley i*n* p*ar*te of his arrerage of his last accompte … Cxii li. xv s. iiii d.

Item rec*eyved* the <x> \viith/ day of February of s*ir* Hugh Asshton by the hand*es* of Miles Worsley … CClx li. ix s. v d. ob. «allocatur»

Item rec*eyved* the xiith day of <January> \February/ of s*ir* Hugh Asshton … iiii^{xx}vii li. xiii s. viii d. «allocatur»

[131]Item rec*eyved* off s*ir* Hugh Ashton the laste dey off M*arch* by the hand*es* off Miles Worsley off the receyt*es* off Kendall … Clxxvii li. xiiii s. iiii d. «allocatur»

Item rec*eyved* of the same day off the seyd s*ir* Hugh by the hand*es* off the sayd Myles off the gen*er*all rec*eyvour* … CCl li. xiii s. iiii d. «allocatur»

[127] The entries from here up to and including the rubric on p. 111 are in the 'sprawling' hand.
[128] The total cash delivered to Morice plus his arrears (£1 over).
[129] Written below the annotation ('extra', i.e. outside the treasury).
[130] The HH hand returns here.
[131] The need to use the space economically may explain the thin, slanting hand for this and the next entry, which in language has the characteristics of the 'sprawling' hand, cf. notes to pp. 117, 123–4, 135, 148, 155–6, 165.

Item rec*eyved* the xixth day of May of the said recey[v]o*ur* by Myles Worsley... CCClvii li. viii d. «allocatur»

Item rec*eyved* the same day of the said receyvo*ur* for the receyte of Kendale ... C s. «allocatur»

Item rec*eyved* the xx^{ti} day of Juyn of the said s*ir* Hugh ... xx li. «allocatur»

[*p. 112*] Item rec*eyved* the xx^{ti}i day of Juyn of s*ir* Hugh Asshton ... xvii li. vi s. viii d. «allocatur»

Item rec*eyved* the xx^{ti}viii day of Juyn of the said s*ir* Hugh ... xx li. «allocatur»

Item rec*eyved* the xviii day of July of s*ir* Henry Willoghby by the said Miles p*ar*te of payment of CC li. for money to hy*m* lent ... l li. «allocatur in computo Milonis Worsley»[132]

Item rec*eyved* the xxx^{ti} day of Juyn of John Turney for the warde of Jane Godston... xx li. «allocatur»

[133]Item receyved the xx^{ti}iii day of August of s*ir* Hugh Asshton by the hand*es* of Myles Worsley ... iiii^{xx}xiiii li. xix s. iii d. «allocatur»

Item receyved the ixth day of September of the recepto*ur* of Kendal ... Ciiii^{xx}v li. iiii s. ix d. ob. qua. «allocatur»

Item received the same day of the same s*ir* Hugh Asshton by the hand*es* of the said Myles ... CCCiiii^{xx}viii li. vi d. «allocatur»

Item receyved of the said s*ir* Hugh the xx^{ti}iii day of Septembre by the hand of the said Myles ... iiii^{xx}i li. xvii s. iiii d. «allocatur»

Item rec*eyved* the xiiiith day of Octobr*e* of the said s*ir* H[u]gh[134] ... xviii li. «allocatur»

Item rec*eyved* the ii^{de} day of Nove*m*br*e* of the same ... DCCCx li. xviii s. v d. «allocatur»

[*p. 113*] Item rec*eyved* the xiii day of Nove*m*br*e* of s*ir* Hugh Asshton ... iiii^{xx}xii li. x s. x d. «allocatur»

Item rec*eyved* the xx^{ti}vi day of Nove*m*br*e* of the same ... Cxxxii li. xiii s. iiii d. «allocatur»

Item rec*eyved* of the same s*ir* Hugh the xixth day of Dece*m*br*e* ... Mlx li. xv s. iiii d. «allocatur»

[135]Item rec*eyved* viii^{vo} <da> die Januarii anno xxii^{do} ... Ciiii^{xx}xvii li. iii s. viii d. ob. qua. «allocatur»

Item rec*eyved* in <y> þe p*r*ice off certen plate by the hand*es* off Ric*hard* Both for certen felons good*es* ... xiiii li. xiiii s. ix d. ob. «allocatur»

[132] See D91.20/134.

[133] This and the next two entries are written in the 'curly' hand.

[134] MS 'high'.

[135] The entries from here up to and incl. the rubric on p. 117 are in the 'sprawling' hand. See Plate 6.

Item rec*eyved* off Myles Worsley in þe full payment off his arrerages off his acompt endyd þe xiiith daye off Januar*e* anno xxii^{do} regis H. vii w*ith* xliiii li. ix s. viii d. ob. qua. remaynyng in hys hand*es* <as> and ys charged in his new indentur*e* for thys next yere … iiii^{xx}vi li. iii s. vii d. ob. qua.[136]

Item rec*eyved* off Will*iam* Bedell tresourer*e* off household in þe pa[r]te off payment off his arrerages de anno xxi^{mo} regis H. vii … iiii^{xx} li. xix s. xi d. \oneratur in computo/

Totalis recepte de magistro H. Assheton … <MMMMCCiiii^{xx}xii li. xvi s. v d. ob.>[137]

[*p. 114*] Item receyved off s*ir* Herry Willughby knyght by the hand*es* of Myles Worsley in þe p*ar*te off payment off CC li. to hym lent … l li. «oneratur in computo dicti Milonis inter arreragia»[138]

Item receyved off James Mores clerke off the warkes þe xviiiith day off < … > Januar*e* anno xxii^{do} H. vii … <iiii li. vii s. vii d. qua.> Ciiii s. vii d. qua.

Item receyved in þe p*r*ice off certen pastures and medowes w*ith* þe makyng and mawyng off hey for*e* þe sustentacion \as wele/ of oxson and <shepe> shepe as off palffrayes and horses off þe seid princes <and he ys charged> the whiche so*m*me ys charged in þe tresourerys acompt … xxxv li. xiii s. v d.

[*pp. 115–16 blank*]

[*p. 117*] Mony delyv*er*ed unto þe tresourer off household from þe xiiith day off Januar*e* anno xxi^{mo} regis H. viith unto þe [*blank*]

[139]Fyrst delyv*er*ed the xx^{ti}iii day off January to the said tresaurer*e* by the hand*es* of Nicholas Sander*e* … Cxii li. v s. iiii d. «oneratur»

Item delyv*er*ed the xi day of February to the said tresaurer*e* by Nicholas Saunder… C li. «oneratur»

Item delyv*er*ed the iiiith day of March to the tresaurer*e* … Ci li. «oneratur»

[140]Item delyv*er*yd unto the same the xxiiiith day of M*ar*che … iiii^{xx}ii li. «oneratur»

<Item delyv*er*yd the>

Item delyv*er*yd the iiiith day of Aprill to the tresaurer by the hand*es* off Nicholas Sawnder … iiii^{xx}xxiii li. iiii s. xi d. ob. «oneratur»

[141]Item delyv*er*d the xxiith day of Aprille to the tresourer by Nich*olas* Saunder… lxxi li. «oneratur»

[136] See D91.21/152.

[137] Written at the foot of the page, still in the 'sprawling' hand.

[138] See 21/79, 90, 153, 162.

[139] The HH hand returns here.

[140] This and the next two entries are written in a slanting hand, cf. notes to pp. 111, 123–4, 135, 148, 155–6, 165.

[141] This entry is written in a different hand, the same as that at pp. 60, 91, 147, 161 (see footnotes).

[142]Item delyv*er*ed the xth day of May to the tresaurer by Nicholas Saunder ... lxxii li. «oneratur»

Item delyv*er*ed the xixth day of May to the tresaurer by Nicholas Sander*e* ... lxxvi li. «oneratur»

[*p. 118*] Item delyv*er*ed the xxx^{ti} day of May to m*aster* tresaurer by Nicholas Saunder ... xx li. «oneratur»

Item delyv*er*ed the vii day of Juyn to the tresaurer by Nicholas Sander*e* ... lxv li. ii s. vi d. «oneratur»

Item <rec*eyved*> delyv*er*ed the xx^{ti} day of Juyn to the tresaurer*e* ... xxx li. vi s. viii d. «oneratur»

Item delyv*er*ed the iii^{d} day of July to the said tresaurer*e* by Nicholas Sander*e* ... xxx li. vi s. viii d. «oneratur»

Item delyv*er*ed the xi day of July to the tresaurer by Nicholas Saunder ... xxx li. vi s. viii d. «oneratur»

Item delyv*er*ed the xx^{ti}v day of July to the tresaurer by Sa*n*der ... l li. «oneratur»

Item delyv*er*ed the xxx^{ti} day of <Juyly>[143] July to the tresaurer by Saunder ... li li. vi s. viii d. «oneratur»

Item delyv*er*ed the viith day of August to the tresaurer by Sander ... iiii^{xx} li. «oneratur»

Item delyv*er*ed the xx^{ti}i day of August to the tresaurer by Saunder ... Cviii li. xiiii d. «oneratur»

[144]Item deliv*er*ed the xx^{ti}v day of August to the tresourer by Saunder ... lvi li. v s. <xi> x d. «oneratur»

Item deliv*er*ed the xii day of September to the said tresourer*e* by Saunders ... iiii^{xx}x li. «oneratur»

[*p. 119*] Item deliv*er*ed unto the tresourer*e* the xii day of September by Saunder ... lxxviii li. <v s. i d.> «oneratur»

Item deliv*er*ed the iiiith day of Octobre unto the tresourer by Nicholas Saunders ... xx li. «oneratur»

Item deliv*er*ed unto the said Saunders the ixth day of Octobre ... xxxiii li. v s. vi d. «oneratur»

[145]Item delyv*er*ed the xiith day of Octob*re* to the tresaurer*e* by the said Nicholas ... Cxxiii li. xiii s. iiii d. «oneratur»

142 The HH hand returns here.
143 A failed attempt to alter 'Juyn' to 'July'.
144 This and the next entry, as well as the first three entries on p. 119, appear to be in the 'curly' hand.
145 The HH hand returns here.

Item delyv*er*ed the iii^{de} day of <Nove*m*ber to the tresaurer*e* by> the said Nicholas … <lii li. xii s. v d.> «oneratur» «cancellatur hic quia oneratur super Jacobum Mores»

Item delyv*er*ed the xxviii day of Nove*m*br*e* to the tresauro*ur* by the said Nicholas … Cxii li. xvii s. vi d. «oneratur»

Item delyv*er*ed the xith day of Dece*m*br*e* to the tresauror by the said Nicholas … Cxiii li. «oneratur» «cancellatur hic quia oneratur super Jacobum Mores»

Item delyv*er*ed the xixth day of Dece*m*br*e* to the tresaurer by the said Nicholas … xvi li. «oneratur»

Item delyv*er*ed the xx^{ti}ii day of Dece*m*br*e* to the tresaurer by the said Nicholas … iiii^{xx}ii li. x s. «oneratur»

[*p. 120*] [146]Item delyv*er*ed the xth daye off Januar*e* anno xxii^{do} regis H. vii in rede mony receyved at ii tymes by þe hand*es* off Richard Shyrley bayle off Ware xxv li. xiii s. iii d. and in þe price x q*u*art off whete receyved off Reynold Adeson xliii s. iiii d. in all … xxvii li. xvi s. vii d.

Item delyv*er*ed unto þe seid tresourer*e* þe arrerages off his last acompt videlicet de p*ar*te iiii^{xx}x li. xix s. xi d. as yt appereth in þe fote off his seid last acompt … <iiii^{xx} li.> iiii^{xx} li. xix s. xi d.[147]

[148]Item delyv*er*ed the xvth day of January to the tresaurer by Nicholas Sander … xxxix li. vi s. viii d.

Item delyv*er*ed <t> unto þe seid tresourer*e* by þe hand*es* off div*er*s p*er*sones in þe part of payment of thayre arreragez dew uppon þis det*er*minacion …[149]

[*pp. 121–2 blank*]

[*p. 123*] [150]Mony delyv*er*ed unto Myles Worsley from þe forseid xiiith day off Januar*e* anno xxi^{mo} unto þe [*blank*]

[151]Fyrst delyv*er*ed the xxi day of January to the said Miles \of his arrerag*es*/ … lxvi li. vii d. <ob.> qua. «oneratur inter arreragia»

Item delyv*er*ed the xxx^{ti} day of January to the same Miles … lxvii li. iiii s. «oneratur in computo»

Item delyv*er*ed the xiith day of February to the said Miles … iiii^{xx}vii li. xiii s. viii d. «oneratur in computo»

Item delyv*er*ed to the said Miles the xx^{ti}vi day of February … xxxii li. «oneratur in computo»

[146] Apart from the third entry on p. 120 (in the HH hand), p. 120 is in the 'sprawling' hand,.
[147] See the last entry on p. 113 above.
[148] The entry is in the HH hand.
[149] There is no sum and the rest of the page is blank.
[150] For the sums below see D91.21/84–5.
[151] The HH hand returns here.

Item delyv*er*ed the vth day of Marche to the said Miles … xlv li. «oneratur in computo»

Quia rediit \ideo/ cancellatur[152] <Item delyv*er*ed the xiith day of Marche to the said Miles> … <Cvi li. xiii s. viii d.> <iiiixxvi li. xiii s. vii d.>

Item delyv*er*ed the xiiiith day of March to the said Miles … Ciiiixx li. «oneratur in computo»

Item delyv*er*ed to the same Miles the xiiith day of March … vi li. <vi> ii s. <viii d.> «oneratur in computo»

[153]Item delyv*er*yd unto the same Miles the xviiith day off M*ar*ch … xxi li. iii s. i d. «oneratur in computo»

Item delyv*er*yd unto the same Miles the fyrst day off Aprill … xx li. vi s. viii d. «oneratur in computo»

[*p. 124*] Anno xxi.

Item delyv*er*ed unto Myles Worsley the vith daye off Aprill … xli li. «oneratur in computo»

[154]Item delyv*er*ed the viith day of May unto the same Miles … xxvii li. xiii s. iiii d. «oneratur in computo»

Item delyv*er*ed the xixth day of May to the said Miles … v li. «oneratur in computo»

Item delyv*er*ed the xxxti day of May to the said Miles … vii li. ii s. vi d. «oneratur in computo»

Item delyv*er*ed the first day of Juyn to the said Miles for C*r*ist*es* College … CCv li. vii s. xi d. «oneratur in computo»

Item delyv*er*ed the xxti day of Juyn to the said Miles … xx li. «oneratur in computo»

Item deliv*er*ed the same day to the said Miles … xxxii li. «oneratur in computo»

Item delyv*er*ed the iiideday of J\u/ly to the same Miles … vii li. «oneratur in computo»

Item delyv*er*ed the xi day of July to the same Miles … xx li. «oneratur in computo»

Item delyv*er*ed the same day unto the said Miles … Cxvii s. «oneratur in computo»

Item delyv*er*ed the xixth day of July to the said Miles … xxi li. vii s. viii d.[155] «oneratur in computo»

Item delyv*er*ed the first day of August to the said Miles for the bildinge of Crist*es* College i*n* Ca*m*brige … Cii li. «oneratur in computo»

[152] The HH hand notes in the margin that the entry is canc. because the money has been returned (it's not in the list at D91.21/84).
[153] The last two entries on p. 123 and the first on p. 124 are written in a slanting hand, cf. notes to pp. 111, 117, 135, 148, 155–6, 165.
[154] The HH hand returns here.
[155] MS 'vijj d.'.

[156]Item deliv*er*ed the xx^{ti}v day of August to the said Myles … xxxviii li. xiii s. iiii d. «oneratur in computo»

[*p. 125*] [157]Item deliv*er*ed the xxi day of Septemb*er* to the seyd Myles … lxvi li. «oneratur in computo»

Item deliv*er*ed the xx^{ti}iii day of Septembre to the said Myles … iiii^{xx}i li. xvii s. iiii d. «oneratur in computo»

Item delyv*er*ed the xiiiith day of Octobr*e* to the said Miles … xviii li. «oneratur in computo»

Item delyv*er*ed the xvth day of Octobre … xx li. «oneratur in computo»

Item delyv*er*ed the iii^{d} day of Nove*m*bre to the same … xlviii li. «oneratur in computo»

Item delyv*er*ed the viith day of Nove*m*br*e* to the said Miles … Cviii li. «oneratur in computo»

Item delyv*er*ed the xiiith of Nove*m*br*e* to the said Miles … C li. «oneratur in computo»

Item delyv*er*ed the xx^{ti}viii day of Nove*m*br*e* to the said Miles … xxxix li. vii s. iiii d. «oneratur in computo»

Item delyv*er*ed the xixth day of Dece*m*br*e* to to the said Miles … xxxiiii li. ii s. «oneratur in computo»

[158]Item delyv*er*d þe iii day off Juyn … xxviii li. iiii d. «oneratur in computo»

Item delyv*er*ed unto þe seid Mylez þe xth dayе off Januar*e* anno xxii^{do} H. vii … Cxxix li. iiii s. vi d. «oneratur in computo»

Item delyv*er*ed unto þe seid Miles as mony receyved by hym off s*ir* Herry Willughby knyght in þe p*ar*te off payme*n*t off CC li. to hym lent <oneratur l [.....] l li. delyv*er* to Myles Worsley> … l li. «oneratur in computo <inter> inter arreragia»[159]

[*p. 126*][160] The iii^{de} day of Octobre the first yer*e* of kinge Henry the viii. Memorandum that of the money receyved of m*aster* Fotehede as appereth i*n* the thred lefe folowinge ther remaineth the day of afor*e* writen as appereth i*n* lower ende of the said iii^{de} lefe the p*ar*cellis ensuinge.

[156] This entry is written in the 'curly' hand.

[157] This and the next entry are written in a different hand (which may not be the same as that of the previous note)..

[158] The rest of the items on p. 125 are in the 'sprawling' hand.

[159] See D91.21/153, 162; D91.19/60.

[160] Pp. 126–128 (on previously blank pages) are an intrusion of material relating to receipts after Lady Margaret's death (so too pp. 132–3 below). There are three hands: the HH hand, responsible for the material up to and including the second rubric ('Money ...day'); a square awkward hand (that of Hugh Ashton), responsible for the rest of the page and the first entry on p. 127, as well as the word 'Item' at the start of the next entry; and the distinctive hand of John Fisher for the rest of pp. 127–8. Various marks of annotation are used for each item; ° and ⁺ are used below to indicate a dot and a cross. See Plate 7.

1.° First i*n* on bagge … CCCxxxiii li. vi s. viii d.

2.° Item i*n* another bagge … lxxx li. wich two bagg*es* wer*e* put i*n* the cofer w*ith* jewellis.

[161]Item i*n* the same cofer wer*e* also put the said day the su*m*mes folowinge.

3.° First i*n* on bagge … iii^{xx}xi li. xi s. iiii d. and xxiii s. xi d. rec*eyved* by m*aster* Pexall.

4.° Item i*n* another bagge … iii^{xx} li. xxviii s.

Dxlvii li. ix s. xi d.[162]

Money rec*eyved* <hy> \of/ other p*er*sones the said day.

xxvii li. *xx s.*[163] 5.° First of John Mundy goldsmyth of London in parte of payement for pla<y>te sold unto hym … CCCCC mark*es* \CCCxxxiii li. vi s. viii d./[164]

Nichil hic quia oneratur in alio libro.[165] 6.°Item of money found in the coffers in the custody of maistr*es* Edyth Fowler as apperith in oon bagge sealed w*ith* <se> the seale of s*ir* John Seynt John … vii li. xvi s.

7.° Item <c> in a blew pyncase in gold … xlvi li. xiii s. viii d.

Mettcalf.[166] Item receved the same tyme of sir Thomas Maudysley as well for plate as for oth*er* stuff of my lad*ys* by hym sold … CCCi li. x s. vi d.

[*p. 127*]

⁺8.° Item receyved of the dean of Lincoln for ii pott*es* of silv*er* gylt <j> chased w*ith* portcolions uppon the coppe conteynyng a Clxiii unc*es*. P*r*ice the unce iii s. x d. … xxx li. v s. viii d.

9. 10. Item receyvid of sir Thomas Mawdislee in ii bagg*es* ass apperith in a bill of the same … Cli li. xvii s. xiiii d. ob. Ciiii^{xx}xiiii li. xiiii s. ix d. ob.[167]

11. Item in another bagg … xiiii li. xiiii d.

Mettcalf. Item of Morgan Mores … lxxv li. vii s. i d. ob.

⁺12.° Item <an obligacio> of John Mu*n*dey for the resydew of golld plate and jewells over and byside his oblig[a]cions … liii li. xvi s.

⁺° Item of the same … xxii s. ii d.

Mettcalf. Item by \m*aster*/ Penda*n*t froo my lady of Surraye for certayne furrus and ii hyngyng*es* oon of Parys another of Nabugdonosor … xliiii li.

[161] Preceded by an annotation mark like a secretary 'a'.
[162] The correct total of items 1–4, jotted in the left margin, perhaps in Fisher's hand.
[163] In the left margin alongside the entry, perhaps in Fisher's hand.
[164] i.e. 500 marks in £sd.
[165] Written neatly in the left margin (perhaps in the 'sprawling' hand).
[166] This and the following instances of marginal 'Mettcalf' may be in the same hand as the previous marginal note.
[167] Presumably the two sums relate to the two bags. 9. and 10. are written below each other, as are the two sums (rather clumsily).

Metcallf. Item of Morgane Moress for vii yerd*es* of cloth of golld att xvi s. the yeard ... v li. xii s.

Mettcallf. Item of the same for a cloth of astate payned with[168] cloth of tisshew and velwett embrourderd with roses ... xxiiii li.

Mettcalf. Item receyvid of <m*aster*> oon obligacion of m*aster* Marneys for certane stuff by hym boght ... vii li. x s.

<*Mettcallf.*> Item off James Morres \in p*ar*te of payment/ for the rivnews and prof-itt*es* off land*es* putt in mortmayne ... iiii^{xx} li.

Mettcalf. Item for a chest solld to m*astr*es Massye ... x s.

[*p. 128*]

13. Item receyvid of s*ir* Henry Marneys obligacio*u*n ... lix li.

14. Item of John Mu*n*dees obligacio*u*n ... CCCCi li. «deficit»[169]

in the which is allowance of [*blank*]

15. Item of the same Mundee ... CCCCi li.

[*p. 129*] 1937 li. 4 s. vii d.[170]

[171]Mony delyv*er*ed unto James Mores from þe forseid xiiith daye unto [*blank*]

[172]*Mores*. Fyrst delyv*er*ed unto þe seid James by þe hand*es* off Nicholas Sander iii^{cio} die Novembris anno <xxi^{mo}> xxii^{do} H. vii^{mi} ... lii li. xix s. viii d. «computus»

Mores. Item delyv*er*ed unto þe same James by þe hand*es* off the seid Nicholas xi° die Decembris dicti anno xxii^{do} ... Cxiii li. «computus»:

[173]Su*m* of monay receyvid into the coffers byside Mu*n*dees.

Item m*aster* M[174] Marners. Item James Moress ... MCCiii^{xx}i li. xv s. iii d. ob.

wherof abate m*aster* Mettcalf*es* expens*e* et remanet ... DCCviii li. xv s. i d.

[*p. 130*] [175]Receytt*es* of mony from the xiiith day of Januar*e* anno xxii^{do} regis Henrici vii unto the [*blank*]

[168] 'with' rep.
[169] Add. in the same hand.
[170] Neither a correct calculation of the preceding items, nor of the money delivered to Morice (lower down the page); written in the top margin (hand uncertain).
[171] This rubric and the next two entries (written in the 'sprawling' hand) were on the page originally, before the post-mortem interventions at the top and bottom of the page.
[172] This and the next marginal heading are preceded by a long-tailed 'r' ('respice'?) forming the vertical of a decorative cross (for other examples, see note to p. 18 above).
[173] Fisher has added this material at the foot of the page.
[174] An initial, or an error?
[175] The 'sprawling' hand is responsible for the rubric.

[176]First the third day of March of s*ir* Hugh Asshton my lad*ys* receyvo*ur* … lxxi li. xviii s. viii d. «allocatur»

Item rec*eyved* the last day of March of the same s*ir* Hugh … Dlx li. xix s. «allocatur in ii summis»

Item *receyved*/ of my lad*ys* chauncelo*ur* for a chalesse sold unto hy*m* weyng*e* xi unc*e* di. at iii s. iiii d. by unc*e* … xxxviii s. iiii d.

Item the xxx day of May of s*ir* Hugh Assheton by the hand*es* of Mylys Worsley … CCCClxxvi li. xvi s. v d. ob. «allocatur»

Item rec*eyved* the xx^{ti}v day of Juyn of Edward Forsett < by the hand*es*> for land*es* sold i*n* Billesby … xl li.

< Item rec*eyved* the ix day of Sept*em*br*e* of s*ir* Hugh Asshton of the revenewes of Kendall … CCxl li.>

Item rec*eyved* the same day of the said s*ir* Hugh … CCCviii li. xv s. iii d. «allocatur»

Item rec*eyved* the ix day of Sept*em*br*e* of s*ir* Hugh Asshton of the revenews of Kendall … Clxxi li. xiii s. vii d. ob. qua. «allocatur»

Item of the said s*ir* Hugh the xviiith day of Sept*em*br*e* … iiii^{xx}xiiii li. vi s. iiii d. qua. «allocatur»

[*p. 131*] Item rec*eyved* the viii day of Nov*em*br*e* of the said s*ir* Hugh Asshton … DCCCCxxxix li. xi s. «allocatur»

Item rec*eyved* of s*ir* Hugh Asshton the iiiith day of Dec*em*br*e* by […][177] allowed … xxxii li. xix s. v d. «allocatur»

Item rec*eyved* of s*ir* Hugh Asshton the xiiith day of Dec*em*br*e* … DCCCx li. «allocatur»

Item rec*eyved* the same day by Myles Worsley of my lord of London i*n* p*ar*tie of paym*en*t of C li. of money lent unto hy*m* … l li. «allocatur»

[178]Item receyved of s*ir* Hugh Assheton by þe hand*es* of Myles of Worsley as mony delyv*er*ed unto Thomas Sop*er* my lad*ys* solist*er* by þe seid s*ir* Hught \\Assheton/ … viii li. xix s. viii d. «allocatur»

Item <delyv*er*ed by by> receyved by the hand*es* of the tresourer of houshold … xxiiii s.

So*m*me of all þe hole receyte unto þe coffers w*ith* l li. receyved <of> of my lord of London and xxiiii s. by þe[179] tresaurer*e* of household for [rev]enues[180] receyved of þe bayly of Makesey … MMMDCCCCxxvi li. xiii s. x d.

[181]M*aster* Ashton … DCCxx li. v s. ix d. ob.

[176] The HH hand returns here.

[177] A spike inserted halway-down through pp. 131–154 has left a hole in the pages here.

[178] This entry and the rest on p. 131 are in the 'sprawling' hand.

[179] 'the' rep.

[180] MS 'herensues'.

[181] Written by Fisher, using the space at the foot of the page.

[*p. 132*] [182]Memorandum receyved the xiith day of July of m*aster* John Fotehed m*aster* of Michaellhouse i*n* Ca*m*brige the first yer*e* of the reigne of kinge He*n*ry the viii by my lorde of Rochestre s*ir* John Saint John and Henry Hornby the so*m*mes of money folowinge.

Paymentes made of money receyved of mas*t*er *Fotehed.* First of money delyv*er*ed to thabbot of Peturborogh to be kepte for my lad*ys* use … DCxxxiii li. vi s. viii d.

*M*as*t*er *Asshton.* Item of money delyv*er*ed unto the said m*aster* Fotehed to be kepte for my lad*ys* use … DClxvi li. xiii s. iiii d. [183]wherof taken the xviith day of July to delyv*er* m*aster* Hugh Asshton … Cviii li. xv s. «oneratur »

Nicholas Saunder. Item delyv*er*ed the vi day of August to Nicholas Sander for the houshold … xl li. «oneratur »

Saunder. Item delyv*er*ed the ixth day of August to Nicholas Sander … lx li. «oneratur»

*Mais*t*er Morgan.* Item delyv*er*ed the xvth day of August to m*aster* Morgan … xxvi li. xiii s. iiii d.[184]

Saunder. Item delyv*er*ed the said day to Nicholas Sander … iiii^{xx}xvii li. xviii s. iiii d. «oneratur »

For Cristes college. Item delyv*er*ed the same day by the ha*n*d*es* of James Morice for the bilding*es* of Crist*es* college … C li.

*For rewarde*s. Item delyv*er*ed the viiith day of Sept*em*br*e* to pay the reward*es* of my lad*ys* s*er*vaunt*es* by advise and det*er*minaciou*n* of my lord of Wynchestre … CC li.[185]

Saunder. Item delyv*er*ed the xvi day of Sept*em*bre to Nicholas Sander … iii^{xxx}vi li. xiii s. iiii d. \oneratur/

For Cristes college. Item delyv*er*ed the same day to m*aster* Tomson m*aster* of Crist*es* college for bildinge of the same college … iiii^{xx}vi li. xiii s. iiii d.

<*For* p*ro*b*ate of my lad*ys *testame*n*t.* Item delyv*er*ed to *con*tent <for my> p*ar*te of payment for the fine of my lord of Ca*n*terbury for p*ro*bate of my lad*ys* testame*n*t … lx li.> [186]Iterum recipitur <D> Thomas Maudesley oneratur.

Saunder. Item delyv*er*ed the xith day of Sept*em*br*e* to Nicholas Saunders by m*aster* Pecsall as appereth by a bill of the said Nicholas … lx li. «oneratur »

The remane*n*t is in ii bagg*es* wherof the on *conteyneth* CCCxxxiii li. vi s. viii d. and the other lxxx li. wich was put i*n* the cofer w*ith* jewellis[187]wherin also was \<i*n* a iii^{de} bagge[188]/> putt iii^{xx}xi li. xi s. iiii d. and i*n* a fourth bagge was putt iii^{xx} li. and xxiii s. xi d. rec*eyved* by m*aster* Pecsall r*eceyved* <of sir T. Maudesly> ageyn and xxviii s.

[182] Pp. 132–3 (on previously blank pages and in the HH hand) are an intrusion of material relating to receipts after Lady Margaret's death.

[183] Add. in the same (HH) hand with a line linking it to the marginal name.

[184] See also p. 133 below. For other of Morgan's expenses in relation to the sale of Lady Margaret's goods, and for a book of the sales written by him: D56.97 (SJLM/7/1/3).

[185] See Appendix 1.

[186] Add. in the same (HH) hand.

[187] The …jewellis' at the foot of p. 132 is continued ('wherin …xxviii s.') at the foot of p. 133.

[188] Alt. from 'pak'?

[*p. 133*]

Memorandum ther*e* was founde the ii^{de} day of <Junly> July the first yer*e* of kinge Henry the viiith i*n* my lad*ys* litill sta*n*derd … MCC\xl li./ vii s. v d. ob.

Oneratur in alio libro.[189]

Assheton. Wherof was delyv*er*ed the same day unto m*aster* Asshton my lad*ys* comptroll*our* for payment*es* of hir fun*er*all expe*n*ses … lv li. ix s. «oneratur »

Item delyv*er*ed the vi day of July to doctor Willesford to be yeven i*n* almes to bedrede p*er*sones w*ith*in xxx^{ti} p*ar*isshes i*n* London … xxxiii li. vi s. viii d.

Oneratur super magistrum Assheton.[190]

Item delyv*er*ed the same day to doctor Ha*n*son for like i*n*tent i*n* other xxx^{ti} p*ar*[i]sshes … xxxiii li. vi s. viii d.

Item delyv*er*ed the same day to doctor Tomson for the same i*n*tent w*ith*in other xxx^{ti} p*ar*isshes … xxxiii li. vi s. viii d.

Item delyv*er*ed the said day to m*aster* John Grindel for the same purpose i*n* other xxx^{ti} p*ar*isshes … xxxiii li. vi s. viii d.

M*aster* Asshton.[191]

Item delyv*er*ed the vii day of July to my lad*ys* said comptroll*our* for the said fun*er*all expe*n*ses … D li. «oneratur »

Item delyv*er*ed the same tyme to the said comptroll*our* … xlviii li. vi s. viii d. «oneratur»

Item delyv*er*ed the xith day of July to m*aster* Asshton … CC<lxxi li. x s.> \lxxii li. iii s. iiii d./ «oneratur »

Item delyv*er*ed the xiith day of July to m*aster* Morgan for div*er*se payment*es* … x li.

Sanders. Item delyv*er*ed the xviith day of July to James Morice for the household at Hatfeld … xx li. «oneratur super Sanders »

Item taken forth of the coffer to delyv*er* unto m*aster* Hugh<t> Asshton the said xviith day of July first i*n* a litill bagge of lynen cloth *con*teignynge i*n* crisadous*e* and other gold … xxviii li. xv d.

Item i*n* grossis minut*es* xiiii unc*e* … xliiii s. iiii d.

Item i*n* clipped money xxvii unc*e* … iiii li. v s. vi d.

Item i*n* gode money … xx s. viii d. ob.

Item i*n* gold … C li.

[189] Add. in the left margin, perhaps in the 'sprawling' hand writing neatly.
[190] Add. in the left margin, perhaps in the 'sprawling' hand; bracketed to include the next four items.
[191] Bracketed to include the next three items.

Cxxxv li. xi s. ix d. ob.[192] «oneratur »

Summa totalis … MM<D><C>l li. x s. ix d. ob.

[*p. 134 blank*]

[*p. 135*] [193]Mony delyv*er*ed unto Will*i*am Bedell esquier tresourer*e* of household ffrom þe xiiith day of Januar*e* anno xxii^{do} regis H. vii unto þe [*blank*]

First delyv*er*ed unto the same tresaurer*e* the xx^{ti}iii day of January … iii^{xx}xviii li. ix s. iiii d.

Item delyv*er*ed the xx^{ti}ii of January to the same upon his arrerag*es* of his last accompte \as money resting i*n* his hand*es*/ … iiii^{xx}i li. xv s. <v> iiii d. <ob.>

Item delyv*er*ed to Willi[a]m Bedell \the xxxth day off Januar*e*/ by the hand*es* off Nicholas Saunder … iiii li. ii s. v d. ob. qua.

Nota caret xxiiii li. ii s. iiii d. et ex confessione Milonis Worsley. Item delyv*er*ed unto the same tresourer the viii day of Februarii … <Cxi li. vi s.> iiii^{xx}vii li. iii s. iiii d.

Item delyverd unto the same treserer*e* the xviiith day of Februarii … xl li.

Item delyverd unto the same treserer*e* the xxv day of Februarii … <xl> l li.

Item delyverd unto the same treserer*e* the vith day of Marche … xxxvii li. xi s.

[194]Item delyv*er*ed the xxvii day of March unto the tresaurer by Nicholas Sander*e* … v^{xx}iiii li.

Item delyv*er*ed the xth day of May to m*aster* tresaurer by Nicholas Sander … l li.

[*p. 136*] Item delyv*er*ed the xx^{ti}iii day of May to m*aster* tresauro*ur* by the said Nicholas … xxviii li. ii s. viii d.

Item delyv*er*ed the same day to m*aster* tresauro*ur* by the said Nicholas … vi li.

Item delyv*er*ed the xiith day of Juyn to m*aster* tresaurer by Nicholas Sander … Cxix li. xviii s.

Item delyv*er*ed the viii day of July to m*aster* tresaurer by Nicholas Saunder … liiii li.

Item delyv*er*ed the xxi day of July to the said tresauro*ur* by Nicholas Sander… lxxix li. vi s. viii d.

Item delyv*er*ed the vi day of August to m*aster* tresaurer*e* by Nicholas Sa*n*der*e* … iiii^{xx}iii li. viii d.

[192] This (correct) total is written to the right of the five entries above, loosely bracketed to the items. For the post-mortem item add. at the foot of the page see the last item on p. 132.

[193] The original text returns here in a variety of hands. The first two and last two entries are in the HH hand, but the rubric and the fourth entry are in the 'sprawling' hand, the third entry (incl. the addition above line) is in a slanting hand (cf. notes to pp. 111, 117, 123–4, 148, 155–6, 165), and the fifth to seventh entries are in a different hand.

[194] The HH hand returns here.

Item delyv*er*d the xi[th] day of August to m*aster* tresorer by Nycholas Saunder … lii li. xii s. iiii d.

Item delyv*er*ed the xxii day of August to m*aster* tresaurer by Nicholas Sander … Clx li.

Item delyv*er*ed the xxix day of August to m*aster* tresaurer … xxviii li. iiii s. ii d.

Item delyv*er*ed the xth day of Septe*m*bre to the tresauro*ur* … CClx li. xvi s. iii d.

Item delyvered the xv[th] day of Octobere the xxiii[th] of o*ur* suffrayn lord kyng Henri the vii[th] to the[195] said Wil*i*am Bedell tresorer «by thand*es* of James Morese» … xxxi li. v s.

Item delyv*er*ed the viii[th] day of Nove*m*br*e* to the said tresauro*ur* by Sander … xxxii li. v s. v d.

Item delyv*er*ed the ix[th] day of Nove*m*br*e* to the tresauro*ur* by Sander … Cxxi li.

Item delyv*er*ed the first day of Nove*m*br*e* to the tresauro*ur* by James Morice … lxvii li. v s. vii d.[196]

[*p. 137*] Item delyv*er*ed the xiii[th] day of Decembr*e* to the tresauro*ur* by Nycholas Sander … iiii[xx]xiii li.

[197]Item delyv*er*ed þe vii daye of Januar*e* anno xxiii[co] regis predicti by þe hand*es* of m*aster* Hugh Assheton … Cii li. iii s. ii d.

MDCCCCxxviii li. xiii s. v d. ob. qua.[198]

So*m*me of all the mony delyv*er*ed unto <mast*er*> þe seid <Miles> tresourer*e* … MDCCCCxxviii li. xiiii s. v d. ob. qua.

[*p. 138*] [199]Receyt*es* of the ladies sojornynge w*ith* my lady the xiiii yer*e* of the reigne of o*ur* soveran lord kinge Henry the vii.

<Fist> First of my lady Clifford the v day of Decembrer for hir sowrnyng*e* w*ith* my lady from the xviii[th] day of Aprill unto the iiii[th] day of Decembr*e* anno xv regis H. vii for hirsilfe hyr*e* two doughters and iii s*er*vant*es* by the space of xx[ti]ii wok*es* ev*er*y weke for hirselfe vi s. viii d. and for ev*er*y of hir childern and s*er*va*u*nt*es* a weke xx d. Summa i*n* the weke viii s. iiii d. … <xxiiii li.> xxiiii li.[200]

Receyt*es* of the ladies sojornynge w*ith* my lady the xv[th] yer*e* of the reigne of o*ur* soverain lord kinge Henry the vii[th] «the xxviii day of February»[201]

[195] 'the' rep.

[196] Add. later (out of sequence) in a lighter ink but the same HH hand.

[197] This entry and the rest of the page are in the 'sprawling' hand.

[198] The sum total (as below), written small in the left margin in the 'sprawling' hand.

[199] The HH hand returns here.

[200] The total is correct for 32 weeks (not 22 as above); other calculations below are correct. A line is drawn under the entry and the next heading is indented (as is the normal practice pp. 138–43, 177–8).

[201] Add. in the right margin in the same (HH) hand.

First of my lady Powes by the hand*es* of James Moryce from Allhaloutide i*n* the xiiii yer*e* of H. vii unto the last day of the <said> moneth of Octobr*e* then next folou<l>ynge by the space of a hole yer*e* for hir silfe ev*ery* weke vi s. viii d. wich is i*n* the yer*e* xvii li. vi s. viii d. and for hir woman ev*ery* weke xx d. that is i*n* the yer*e* iiii li. vi s. viii d. and for hir twoo s*er*vant*es* ev*ery* weke ii s. viii d. that is i*n* the yer*e* vi li. xviii s. viii d. wich so*m*me totale amounteth to xxviii li. xii s. wheroff abated for hir attendaunce at Grenwich upon my ladys grace for hir and hir iii s*er*vant*es* by the space of xiii wek*es* vii li. iii s. and so is clerly receyved … xxi li. ix s.

Item for my lady Scrope from the xx^ti^v day of Octobre unto the xv day of February for hir silfe and four*e* s*er*vant*es* for hir silfe ev*ery* weke x s. and ech of hir s*er*vant*es* xx d. The so*m*me totale … xiii li. vi s. viii d.

[*p. 139*] Receyt*es* of div*er*se casualties the xiiii^th^ yer*e* of H. the vii.

*By the hand*es *of* mas*t*er *Hugh Oldom.* First receyved of Trevilian for the ward of Cokworthy payable at the fest of the nati*vi*te of Saint John Baptest last past yn the begynnynge of August also last past the xiiii yer*e* of the reigne of o*ur* soverain lord kinge Henry the vii … l li.

Item r*eceyved* of Tho*m*as Po\r/mard[202] for a fyne of his outhlaury the xxviii of Octobr*e* … iii li. vi s. viii d.

[*p. 140*] Receyt*es* of div*er*se casualties the xv^th^ yer*e* of H. the vii^th^.

First r*eceyved* of Ric*hard* Gallee the xiii^th^ day of March for the good*es* of a felon seased by Robert Eland … iii li. «in computo de anno xvi^o^»

Receit*es* of casualties from the xxix day of May anno xvii.

First <the> rec*eyved* the xxix day of May of Ric*hard* Galee by the hand*es* of Miles Worsley for two knight*es* fees payed by s*ir* Nicholas Heron knight wherof my lady p*ar*doned hym xl s. and so he payed … viii li.

Item rec*eyved* of Thomas Cordall the iii^de^ day of July for wodde sold outh of the mair*e*sall by the hand*es* of Miles Worsley … xii li.

Item rec*eyved* the xxvii day of Septembr*e* of Thomas Cordall for woode sold ought of the mair*e*sale … iiii li.

Item rec*eyved* of the p*ar*son of Cliffe the xi day of Octobr*e* for wodde sold outht \of/ the quenes sale … xiiii li. x s.

Item rec*eyved* the xxviii of Octobr*e* of Tho*m*as Cordall for bark of wode sold by hy*m* … iiii li. vi s. viii d.

Item rec*eyved* the ii^de^ day of August of the same Tho*m*as for woode sold by hym i*n* the sale of Eston woode … xiiii li.

[203]Item rec*eyved* off the seid <miles> Thomas for the sondre wode sale by thand*es* off Miles su*m* tyme Cx s. vi d. and anothere tyme vi li. in all … xi li. x s. vi d.

[202] 'Po\r/inard' (?).

[203] The entry is written in the 'sprawling' hand.

[*p. 141*] Receyt*es* for my lady Powes anno xxi.

First rec*eyved* the iiii[th] day of July of the baron of Dudley by the hand*es* of Robert Fremyngh*am* i*n* p*ar*te of payme*n*t of a mor*e* fine due unto the lady Powes … xx li.

Item rec*eyved* at Croydon the xviii day Juyn i*n* cheynes of gold and other juyles praysed by my lorde of Ca*n*turburies pryser i*n* p*ar*te of payme*n*t … [*blank*]

[*p. 142*] Receit*es* of the lady sojornaunt*es* w*ith* my ladies grace the xvi[th] yer*e* of Henry the vii[th].

First of my lady Powes the xv day of Novembre for hir silfe oon gentilwoman and ii men s*er*vant*es* … xxii li. ii s. iiii d.

Money receyved of the ladies sojornaunt*es* w*ith* my ladies grace the xvii[th] yer*e* of kinge Henry the vii[th].

First the first day of February of my lady Powes for hir silfe and hir woman ev*er*y weke viii s. iiii d. unto this present day … xxi li. xx d.[204]

Item rec*eyved* the iiii[th] day of March of my lady Wayneford for the tyme of xx[ti]v wek*es* ended the last day of February for hir silfe and ii s*er*vant*es* ev*er*y weke <u>vi s. viii d.</u>… viii li. vi s. viii d.

Item rec*eyved* the xx[ti]v day of Octobr*e* of my lady Cheyney for hir sojornynge w*ith* my lady … lxxvi s. viii d.

Anno xix[no]. Item rec*eyved* of my lady Powes the xx[ti]viii of Septe*m*br*e* i*n* p*ar*te of payment for hir sojornynge … xx li.

Item rec*eyved* the xxviii day of Ap*r*ill i*n* the xix[th] yer*e* of Henry the vii[th] of my lady Powes for hir and hir s*er*vant*es* i*n* full *con*tentac*io*n unto the first day of February last past … xxiii li. viii s. iiii d.

[*p. 143*] Anno xix[no].

Received of my lady Cicill and hir husbonde for their*e* sogiornynge that is to say for hir silfe ev*er*y weke xxi s. viii d. for hir*e* husband vi s. viii d. for two gentilwomen iiii s. ii gentilmen iiii s. ii yomen xl d. ii gromes ii s. viii d. wych i*n* a yer*e* amounteth to the su*m*me of a Cx li. xv d. wherof receyved the first day of Dece*m*br*e* anno xix[no] for their*e* said sorgiornynge for oon halfe yer*e* … lii li.

Anno xxi[mo].

Receyved the iii[de] day of August of my lady Cecill by the hand*es* of Henry Salford and of Miles Worsley i*n* p*ar*te of payment of Cxiiii li. xvi s. iiii d. due the xx[ti]iii day of Juyn last past … xx li.

Item rec*eyved* the iii[d] day of Nove*m*br*e* of my lady Cecill for hir burde wag*es* … xx li.

Anno xxi. Item rec*eyved* the iii[de] day of Juyn for my lady Cecill by the hand*es* of Henry Salford and Miles Worsley i*n* money … xxviii li. iiii d.

[204] See D91.20/5.

Item rec*eyved* the same tyme of the said lady Cecill i*n* iii gownes of cloth of golde and silke to the val*our* of … xxvi li. xiii s. iiii d.

And so remaigneth due by my said lady Cecill unto my lady for old arrerages … lxxiiii li. xvi s. viii d.

[*p. 144*] <Memorandum receyved the xxii day of Decembre the xvi yer*e* of kinge Henry the vii for the ioinct*our* of maisteres Alice Parker*e*.

First of m*aster* vichambirlain the day above said … xxxiii li. vi s. viii d.

Item r*eceyved* the xixth day of Aprill \the xvi yer*e*/ of Tho*m*as Langlond receyvo*ur* to s*ir* William P*ar*ker*e* by the hand*es* of the vichambirlain … xx li. iiii s.

Item rec*eyved* the xth day of Decembr*e* by the hand*es* of my lady Morley for the said ioinct*our* … xxxiii li. vi s. viii d.>

[*p. 145 blank*]

[*p. 146*] [205]Mony delyv*er*ed unto Myles Wursley tresourer of the chamb*er* from þe seid xiiith day off Januar*e* anno xxii^{do} regis predicti unto þe [*blank*]

First the xviiith day of January delyv*er*ed to the said Miles for the bilding*es* of Crist*es* college as money payed by m*aster* John Siclinge ov*er* and above his receypt*es* … xx li. \b/[206]

Item delyv*er*ed the xx^{ti} day of January to the said Myles … xvii li. xi s. vii d.

Item delyv*er*ed the xvi day of January to the said Miles upon his arrerag*es* of his accompte … xliiii li. ix s. viii d. ob. qua. \a/

Item delyv*er*ed the xith day of Ap*r*ill unto the said Miles … DCxxxiiii li. xvi s.

Item delyv*er*ed the iiiith day of May [t]o[207] the said Miles for the work*es* of Crist*es* college … Cxi li.

[208]Item delyv*er*ed the xxx day off May to the seyd Milis … xxii li. iii s. x d.

Item delyv*er*t the viii day of Junii to the seyd Mylys … C li.

Item delyv*er*ed the iiiith day of July to the said Miles … xxxvii li. xii s. iii d.

Item delyv*er*ed the xiith day of July to the said Miles … xl li.

[*p. 147*] Item delyv*er*ed the xxi day of July to the said Miles … iiii^{xx}v li. iiii s. ix d. ob. qua.

[205] The rubric is in the 'sprawling' hand.

[206] This 'b' after the total, with 'a' in the same position in the next entry but one, may indicate that the entries need to be reversed chronologically. On the other hand, 'a' appears to relate to 'arrerages', i.e. arrears, cf. notes to pp. 61, 69, 92.

[207] MS 'fo'.

[208] This and the next entry are in a different hand.

Item delyv*er*ed the xxvii day of July to Myles for payment unto the kinge for Creyke and Manerber*e* ... CCCl li.

Item delyv*er*ed the vi day of August to the same ... xv li. xv s. x d.

Receptum est iterum. <Item delyv*er*ed the viiith day of August to the same Myles to paye the kinge for Wokinge> ... xxvi li. xiii s. iiii d.> xxvi li. xiii s. iiii d.

Item delyv*er*ed the xxiii day of August to the same Miles to send unto the maist*er* of Crist*es* college by maist*er* Scotte <for> in full payment unto m*aster* Crosley for his mese by the said college ... x li.

Item delyv*er*ed the xx^{ti}v day of August to the same Miles for money lent to the beriall of my lady Cecill and sent by s*ir* Tho*m*as Maudesley hir confesso*ur* ... xx li.

Item delyv*er*ed the xiith day of Septe*m*br*e* to the said Myles ... xiii li.

Item delyv*er*ed the same day to the said Myles ... xliii li. xv s.

Item delyv*er*ed unto the said Miles the xviiith day of Septe*m*br*e* ... xxvi li.

[209]Item delyv*er*ed to Myles by the hand*es* of James Moric*e* the xixth day of Sept*embre* ... C li.

[*p. 148*] Item delyv*er*ed to the sayde Miles the iiiith day off Octobr*e* by thand*e* off James Mores ... lvi li. xiii s. iiii d.

Item delyv*er*ed the xx^{ti}vi day of Octobr*e* to the same Miles for the bildinge at C*r*ist*es* college by Nicholas Sander ... xx li.

Item delyv*er*ed the first day of Nove*m*bre to the said Miles ... xl li.

Item delyv*er*ed unto the say[de] Miles the xvith day off the sayd moneth ... xxviii li.

Item delyv*er*ed the iiiith day of Nove*m*bre to the same Miles ... xxxii li. xix s. v d.

Item delyv*er*ed the said day to the said Miles <for> i*n* p*ar*tie of payment of land*es* purchesed of <s*ir*> Charles Brandon for my chauntre i*n* Wynborn ... C li.

Item delyv*er*ed the xiiith day of Decembr*e* to the said Myles ... xxxii li. xiii s. iiii d.

Item delyv*er*ed the xx^{ti} day of Dece*m*bre to the said Miles \for Heymu*nde*/ ... C li.

Item delyv*er*ed the last day of Decembr*e* to the said Miles ... l li.

Item delyv*er*ed to the said Miles the last day of Dece*m*bre for mony payed i*n* the begynnynge of February last past to s*ir* Edward Haward for <m*aster* P*ar*ker*e*> redemynge of m*aster* P*ar*kers land*es* ... D mark*es*

Item delyv*er*ed the same day unto the said Miles for the king*es* New Yer*es* gift*es* ... Cx li. x s.

Item the same tyme for other New Yer*es* gift*es* ... iiii li. xi s. iii d. ob.

[209] This entry is written in a different hand, the same as that at pp. 60, 91, 117, 161 (see footnotes). The first and fourth entries on p. 148 are written with a slanting hand, cf. notes to pp. 111, 117, 123–4, 135, 155–6, 165.

[*p. 149*] [210]Item delyv*er*ed unto þe seid Miles by þe hand*es* of s*ir* Hugh Assheton receyvo*ur* as mony by hym payed to s*ir* Thomas Soper my lad*ys* solist*er* … viii li. xx s. viii d.

Summa totall of þe hole mony delyv*er*ed unto þe seid Myles w*ith*in þe tyme aforseid … MMDCiiii^{xx}v li. xvi s. i d.

[*p. 150 blank*]

[*p. 151*]

[211]Receytes of money from the viii day of January the xxiii yere of the reigne of kyng Henry the vii unto [*blank*]

[212]First receyved the xxvii day of January of s*ir* Hugh Asshton my lad*ys* receyvo*ur* … xiii li. vi s. viii d. «allocatur»

Item rec*eyved* the iiiith day of February of Robert Fremyngham by the hand*es* of Miles Worsley for div*er*se jwell*es* that he had of my lad*ys* g*r*ace which wer*e* my lady Powes xxvii li. xvi s. iiii d. and also i*n* full payment of all money due unto my said lad*ys* g*r*ace by the said lady Powes v li. xi s. viii d. … xxx^{ti}iii li. viii s.

Item rec*eyved* the first day of March of my lad*ys* said receyvo*ur* of the revenouse of Kendale … Clxxiii li. xiii s. ii d. «allocatur»

Item rec*eyved* the said day of my lad*ys* said receyvo*ur* of other receyt*es* … CCCCxxi li. vi s. v d. «allocatur»

Item rec*eyved* the ii^{d} day of March by Myles Worsley of my lord of Rochestr*e* for stuffe bought that was my lad*ys* Cecile … vi li.

Item rec*eyved* the xx^{ti}ii day of Juyn of m*aster* Asshton by Nicholas Sander … Diiii^{xx}v li. xvi s. iiii d. «allocatur»

[213]Item receyved the xiiiith [214] day of Septembr*e* of the rec*eytes* of Kendall by the hand*es* of Myles Worsley … CCv li. x s. «allocatur»

Item rec*eyved* the same day of s*ir* Hugh Assheton by the hand*es* of the said Myles Worsely … CCCCxvii li. ii s. iiii d. «allocatur»

Item receyved the ii^{de} day of Novembr*e* of s*ir* Hugh Asshton by the hand*es* of Myles Worsely … DCCCCxxvi li. vii s. i d. ob. «allocatur»

[*p. 152*] Item rec*eyved* the xxth day of Novembr*e* of s*ir* Hugh Assheton gen*er*all receyvo*ur* by the hand*es* of Myles Worsely … Clvii li. «allocatur»

[210] This page is in the 'sprawling' hand.
[211] The rubric appears to be written by the 'sprawling' hand in a formal script.
[212] The HH hand returns here.
[213] The 'curly' hand is responsible for the rest of the page and the first entry on p. 152.
[214] MS 'xiijjth'.

[215]Item rec*eyved* the xxiii[th] day of Dece*mbre* of m*aster* Assheton by the hand*es* of Miles … DCxi li. v d.

[216]Item receyved þe x[th] day of Januar*e* by þe hand*es* of Miles Worsley for þe kyng*es* New Yeres gyft … C li. «allocatur»

Item receyved þe secund day as mony payed <t> unto Thomas Soper*e* my lad*ys* solistere by þe hand*es* of þe seid Myles … xiii li. xii s. viii d. «allocatur»

Item rec*eyved* of s*ir* Hugh Asheton clerk o*ur* gene*r*all receyvo*ur* the xvi[th] day of Januar*e* anno xxiiii[to] regis Henrici vii[mi] … DCiiii[xx] li. xviii s. vi d. ob. «allocatur»

[*p. 153*]

Summa totall of all þe hole receyte … MMMMCCClxiii li. ii s. vii d.

wer[o]f by[217]

m*aster* Hugh Assheton … MMMMCCCxxiii li. xiiii s. vii d.

Miles Worsley for div*ers* juell*es* … xxxiii li. viii s.

my lord of Rochester for stuff … vi li.[218]

[*p. 154 blank*]

[*p. 155*] [219]Money delyv*er*ed unto William Bedell esquyer tresourer of howshold from the viii[t] day of January anno xxiii[cio] unto [*blank*]

Fyrst delyv*er*ed unto the seid tresourer the xii[th] day of January anno xxiii[cio] as money due by him uppon the determ*inacion* of his accompte … Ciiii[xx]vii li. xii d.

Item delyv*er*ed the xx[ti]vi daye of Januar*e* anno xii[i][cio] regis Henrici vii … C li.

[220]Item delyv*er*ed the ix[th] day of February to the tresauro*ur* by James Morice i*n* the absence of Nicholas Sander … xxviii li.

Item delyv*er*ed the xv[th] day of February to the tresauro*ur* by Nicholas Sander … lxiiii li.

Item delyv*er*ed the xx[ti]iii day of February to the tresauro*ur* by Sander … Cv li. viii s.

Item delyv*er*ed the xxiii day of March to the tresauro*ur* … Clii li. x s. ii d. ob.

[221]Item delyv*er*ed the laste day off Aprill to the tresaurer*e* … <C li.>

[215] This entry is in the HH hand.

[216] The rest of p. 152 and p. 153 are in the 'sprawling' hand.

[217] Written to the right of 'Summa ...receytes'; -o- is written over an original –e-.

[218] The three lines 'master ...vii d.', 'Miles ...viii s.', 'my ...li.' are bracketed to the right of the previous material.

[219] The rubric and the first entry may be in a different hand from the 'sprawling' hand of the third entry.

[220] The HH hand returns here.

[221] This entry is written in a slanting hand, cf. notes to pp. 111, 117, 123–4, 135, 148, 156, 165.

Item delyv*er*ed the iii^{de} day of May to the tresaurou*r* by Nicholas Sander … CCxl li.

Item delyv*er*ed the xth day of Juyn to the tresaurou*r* by Nicholas Sa*n*der*e* … iiii^{xx}xvi li.

[*p. 156*] Item delyv*er*ed the xx^{ti}ii day of Juyn to the tresaurou*r* by Sander … C li.

Item delyv*er*ed the xx^{ti}ix day of Juyn to the tresaurou*r* by Nicholas … xiii li.

Item delyv*er*ed the xixth day of July to the tresaurou*r* by Nicholas … xxx^{ti}vi li. xviii s. iiii d.

Item delyv*er*ed the xx^{ti}vi day of July to the tresaurou*r* by Sander … lx li. xi s. iii d.

Item delyv*er*ed the viiith day of August to the tresaurou*r* by Saunder … Clx li.

Item delyv*er*ed the last day of August to the tresaurou*r* by Nicholas Sander … Cxxxv li.

[222]Item delyv*er*ed the xiiiith day off Octob*re* to the tresauror*e* by Nicholas Sander … xxx li.

Item delyv*er*ed the xxvi day of Octob*re* to the tresowrer by Nicholas Sand*er* … xxxv li.

Item delyv*er*ed the xxxi day of Octob*re* to the tresowrer by Nicholas Sander*e* … iiii^{xx}xvii li. xiii s. i d.

Item delyv*er*ed the xx day of Nove*m*br*e* to the tresorer by Nicholas Sander*e* … Clvii li.

Item delyv*er*ed the xx ^{ti}vii day of Nove*m*br*e* to the tresaurou*r* by Nicholas Sander … Cxviii li.

Item delyv*er*ed the xvith day of Dece*m*br*e* to the tresaurou*r* by Sander … lx li.

Item delyv*er*ed the ii^{de} day of January to the tresaurou*r* by Sander … xliii li. vi s.[223] viii d.

[*p. 157*] [224]Summa off all the hole payment*es* aforseid … MMCxix li. viii s. vi d. ob.

[*p. 158*] [225]Obligacions

[226]In þis an obligac*ion* of s*ir* Will*ia*m Urmeston clerke \domine Margarete/ … xxv li. xvii s. iiii d.

Item another of dame Elizabeth Scrop dicte domine … CC li. to save har meles and discharge ayenst Ric*hard* Weyntworth

[222] This entry is written in a slanting hand (see the previous footnote).
[223] Alt. from or to 'viij'?
[224] This page is in the 'sprawling' hand.
[225] This page is in a different hand.
[226] Each entry except the second, fifth, seventh, tenth, twelfth, and twenty first, is preceded by a sign consisting of two dots with a squiggle above them (these marks are canc. in the twentieth and last four entries).

Item anoþ*er* of George Hevenyngham dicte domine ... x li.

Item anoþ*er* of Ric*hard* Yon dicte domine ... xx li.

Item anoþ*er* of Ric*hard* Pr*e*ston dicte domine super arbitrium ... C li.

Item anoþ*er* John ap H*owe*l and Gruf ap Rees dicte domine to kepe and p*e*rfor*m*e c*e*rten covenau*ntes* ... C li.

Item anoþ*er* of Hue Warde dicte domine super arbitrium ... CC li.

Item an endent*ur* of dame Jane Bewford and John Russell gent*leman* ... [*blank*]

Item an oblig*acion* of s*ir* Robe*r*t Curson dicte domine ... xxiiii li.

Item anoþ*er* of John Lloyd Will*iam* Walt*er* Rog*er* Bygge dicte domine \in CC marcis/ super [... ..]

Item another of John Lomley dicte domine to obs*er*ve and kepe c*er*ten covenau*ntes*... quinque marc*es*

Item anoþ*er* of Joh*n* Crakenthorp et aliorum dicte domine ... xx li.

Item anoþ*er* of Edward Blount armigeri dicte domine ... x li.

Item another of Roger Belle dicte domine ... iii li. v s. vi d.[227]

Item anoþ*er* of Rog*er* Lyngam tenere episcopo Coventrie and Lichfeldie and Regnaldo Bray militi ... C li. to content and paie c*er*ten arrerag*es*

Item anoþ*er* of Thom*as* Hawke de Stone dicte domine ... xx li.

Item anoþ*er* of Edmu*n*d Page dicte domine ... xl^{ti} marke

Item anoþ*er* of Thom*as* Cretou*r* of Wrastlyngworth et aliorum teneri Joh*ann*i comite Somerset in xxxv li.

Item anoþ*er* of s*ir* Harry Wyllughby et aliorum dicte domine ... C li.

Item anoþ*er* of Nicholas Elemeden dicte domine ... iiii li.

Item anoþ*er* of James Stanley clerk et aliorum dicte domine ... CC li.

Item anoþ*er* of s*ir* John Shaa dicte domine ... v^{xx} marc*es*

Item anoþ*er* of Will*ia*m Browne and Jo*hn* Mondy dicte domine ... CCCCC li.

Item anoþ*er* of Humfri Connysby and Chr*isto*fr*e* Pykering dicte domine ... C li.

Item anoþ*er* of George Nevill lord Burgevenny ... iii^{xx} li.

[*p. 159*] [228]Money delyv*er*ed unto Myles Worsley tresowrer of chambr*e* from the viii day of January anno xxiii^{cio} H. vii^{mi} unto [*blank*]

*This sum*me *is canceled her for bycause it is charged emong*es *the arr*er*agez of his accompt anno xxiii^{to} Hen*ri*ci vii^{mi}*. <Fyrst delyv*er*ed unto the seid Miles the day of

[227] A bond of Roger Bell for exactly half this amount is extant, but for a much earlier date, 1503 (D57.160; SJLM/1/1/6/2).

[228] The rubric (in a formal script) and the first two entries may be in the 'sprawling' hand.

January anno xxiii^{cio} as money due by hym uppon the determi*nacio*ne of his accompte ended the viiith day of January anno predicto w*ith* xxiiii li. ii s. iiii d. wantyng oute of a bag … Ciii li. xvi s. v d. ob. qua.>[229]

Item delyv*er*ed unto the seid Milys the xxvth daye of January anno xxiii^{cio} by the hand*es* of James <Mondy> Mores as money due by the seid Jamys uppon his accompt ended the seid viii day of January anno supradicti … xl s. qua.

[230]*This was b\r/oght yn ageyn.* <Item delyv*er*ed the last day of January to the said Miles <for> wich was delyv*er*ed to Tho*m*as Babyngton <s> to content for the recov*er*y of all the land*es* beinge of the joynture of my lady Shirley … xxvi li. xiii s. iiii d.>

Item delyv*er*ed the first day of March unto the said Miles … Cxlii li. xvi s. ii d. ob.

Item delyv*er*ed the iii^{de} day of March to the said Miles at my lad*ys* removinge from Hatfeld to the Base … CCCxiii li. vi s. v d.

[*p. 160*] Item delyv*er*ed the xx^{ti}v day of March to the said Miles by James Morice for the bilding*es* of C*r*ist*es* College i*n* Cambrige … lxxix li.

Item delyv*er*ed the xx^{ti}ii day of Juyn to Miles by Nicholas Sander to *con*tent for the charg*es* i*n* the exchekere for the secu*n*de recury of the land*es* i*n* Disworth agaynste the lord Barkley and for <fr> discharge of disme restinge upon the church of Malton and for purchesse of Che[c]heleys[231] land*es* i*n* Malton and Barington … xix li.

Item delyv*er*ed the same day to the said Miles by the said Nicholas for rep*ar*acions at Ca*m*brige … xx li.

Item delyvered the xx^{ti}ix day of Juyn to Miles by Nicholas … iiii^{xx}iiii li. iii s. iiii d.

Item delyv*er*ed the xixth day of Ju\l/y<n> to Miles by Nicholas for money lent to m*aster* Conyngsby to be repayed at Ca*n*delmasse next e*n*suynge as appereth by his obligacion remaynynge i*n* the kepinge of my lad*ys* grace … C li.

[232]Item delyv*er*ed the xiii day of Septe*m*br*e* to Mylys Wursley by thand*es* of Nicholas Sandur*e* … xxiii li. vi s. viii d.

Item delyv*er*ed to the seyd Mylys the seyd day … CClxiii li. xx d.

Item delyv*er*ed the xxiiith day of Dece*m*br to the said Miles … Clxi li. ii s.

[*p. 161*] [233]Item <r*eceyved*> \ delyv*er*ed unto/ the said Miles the ixth day of January … xiii li. vii s. i d.

Item the x day of January for money paid for the kyng*es* New Yer gyft*es* by the said Myles … C li.

[229] See D91.19/3, 63.
[230] The HH hand returns here.
[231] MS 'Chethesleys'.
[232] This and the next entry are written in a different hand.
[233] These three entries are written in a different hand, the same as that at pp. 60, 91, 117, 147 (see footnotes).

Item <*receyved*> for money delyv*er*ed to Thomas Sop*er* my lad*ys* solicit*ur* … xiii li. xii s. viii d.

[234]Summa totalis … <MCCCCxxxviii li. xii s. vi d. ob.> MCCCxxxiii li. xvi s. ob. qua. i. «unde predictus <idem> Milo oneratur in computo suo de anno xxiiii[to] sicut continetur ibidem»[235]

[*p. 162*] [236]Receytes of money from the xx[ti] day of January the xx[ti]iiii yer*e* of kinge Henry the vii[th].

First of m*aster* Hugh Asshton the <xx> xiiii[th] day of February by Rob*er*t Fremyngham … CCxlix li. vi s. vi d. ob.

Nota pro residuo.[237] Item rec*eyved* the xx[ti]ii day of January of Miles Worsley \by the said Rob*ert*/ for his debet upon his accompte … lxii li. ix s. iii d.[238]

Item the v[th] day of Ap*r*ill of m*aster* Asshton by the said Rob*er*t … xx li.

Item rec*eyved* the xxvi[th] day of May <of> the first yere of the reigne of kinge He*n*ry the viii[th] of m*aster* Asshton by the hand*es* of Rob*er*t Fremyngham … CCClix li. vi s. x d.

[*pp. 163–64 blank*]

[*p. 165*] [239]Money delyv*er*ed unto Will*i*am Bedell esquyer tresurrer of howshold from the xx[th] day of January the xxiiii[to] yere of the reign of kyng Henr*y* the vii[th].

First delyv*er*ed the xxi[th] day of the same moneth unto the said Will*i*am as money <unto> \by/ hym dwe apon the detirmynacion of his accompt endyd the viii[th] day of the said January … Ciiii[xx]xviii li. xvii s. vii d.

Item <rec*eyved* the> to the same the iii[th] day of February by Nicholas Saundr … iiii[xx]xiii li.

[240]Item delyv*er*ed the first day of March unto the said tresauro*ur* by Saunder… Cvi li. xviii s.

Item delyv*er*ed the xi[th] day of March to the tresauro*ur* by Saunder … iiii[xx]xii li. vii d.

Item delyv*er*ed the xxviii day of March unto the seyd tresauro*ur* by Nicholas Sander … Cxl li. ii s. viii d.

Item delyv*er*ed the ix[th] day of Ap*r*ill to the tresauro*ur* by Sander … li li. xiii s. iiii d.

Item delyv*er*ed the xxviii[th] day of Ap*r*ill to the tres*ur*ar by Sander … Cvi li.

[234] The page is completed in the 'sprawling' hand.
[235] See D91.19/66.
[236] The HH hand returns.
[237] The marginal note is in a different hand.
[238] See p. 169.
[239] The rubric and the first two items appear to be written in the 'curly' hand.
[240] The HH hand returns for the rest of the page, except the penultimate entry, which is written in a slanting hand, cf. footnotes to pp. 111, 117, 123–4, 135, 148, 155–6.

Item delyv*er*ed to the tresaurou*r* by Saunder the last day of July … lxv li. x s.

[*pp. 166–168 blank*]

[*p. 169*] [241]Money delyv*er*ed from the xx^{ti} day of January the xx^{ti}iiii yer*e* of kinge Henry the vii unto Robert Fremyngham.

First delyv*er*ed to the said Robert the xx^{ti}ii day of January of money receyved of Miles Worsley … lx^{ti}ii li. ix s. iii d.

Item delyv*er*ed unto the same the xvith day of February … CCxlix li. vi s. vi d. vi d. ob.

Item delyv*er*ed unto the said Rob*er*t the vith day of Ap*r*ill … xx li.

Item the ixth day of Ap*r*ill … CClxxxxv li.

Item delyv*er*ed unto the same Rob*er*t the xx^{ti}viii day of Juyn the first yer*e* of kinge Henry the viiith … Clx li.

[*pp. 170–75 blank*]

[*p. 176*] Receite*s* of John Saint Johnis lande*s* a festo sancti Michaelis in anno regni regis Henrici vii xx^{mo}.

First the xx^{ti}vii day of Octobr*e* of s*ir* James Plogh and Tho*m*as Masleyn for the halfe yer*e* rent of Legdarde Tregose ended at the fest of Michaelmesse afor*e* said … v li. viii s. iii d.

Item rec*eyved* the viith day of Nove*m*br*e* of the said s*ir* James … xiiii li. xv s.

[*p. 177*] Receyte*s* of the lande*s* of John Saint John the xvth yer*e* of H*enry* the vii.

*xvth yer*e. First the v\i/i day of January by the hande*s* of Miles of Gregory Skypwith in p*ar*tie of payment of a hole yer*e* ended at the fest of saint Michell last passed … lvii li. xvii s. i d.

xvith. Item r*eceyved* the xxii day of Decembre the xvi yer*e* of kinge Henry the vii of William Bedell by the hande*s* of Myles Worsley of the lordship of Garsington i*n* Oxonfordshyr*e* … xv li.

Item rec*eyved* the v day of January of Margaret Skipwith wydeu late wife of Gregory Skipwith decessed … xxvi li.

Item rec*eyved* the vi day of August of Will*i*am Bedell by the hande*s* of Miles Worsley of the lordshipp of Garsington … x li.

Item rec*eyved* the iii day of Decembr*e* of William Bedell of the lordshipp of Garsington … xx li.

Item rec*eyved* the[242] vith day of Decembr*e* of my lad*ys* chambirlain of the lordshipp of Hatf[el]d[243] Pev*er*ell … xviii li. xiii s. ii d.

[241] The HH hand completes the rest of the document (apart from pp. 179–80).
[242] the *rep*.
[243] MS ‘Hatford’.

Item the same day of the same for the lordshipp of Depford ... xvi li. vi s. x d.

Anno xvii.

First rec*eyved* of m*aster* chambirlain the xx^{ti}v day of Decembr*e* ... xxiiii li.

Anno xix^{no}.

Item rec*eyved* the xx^{ti}iiii \day/ of Octobr*e* of Tho*m*as Maslinge fermour of Legeard Tregose for the behove of m*aster* Saint John for the halve yer*e* rent ended at Michaelmes ... xv li. xvi s. ii d.

Item rec*eyved* the xix day of May of s*ir* James Plowgh for the halfe yer*e* rent ended at the fest of o*ur* Lady the anu*n*ciacion last passed ... xv li. iiii s. vii d.

[*p. 178*] Receyt*es* of Rikyls land*es* the xvth yer*e* of H*enry* the vii.

First <of> the vii day of January by the hand*es* \of/ Miles Worsley of Gregory Skypwith of the revenuse of the man*er* of Mugdenhall i*n* the counte of Esex the fest of saint Michell last past ... xl [li.][244]

Also receyved of the said landes the xvith yer*e* of kinge Henry the vii.[245]

First the x day of Novembr*e* of hir land*es* i*n* <be> London by the hand*es* of the vichambirlain ... x li. xvi [s.]

Item rec*eyved* of the same of the revenews of the said land*es* at Richmounte the ii^{de}day of Nove*m*br*e* ... xl li.

Anno xvii.

First rec*eyved* the xx^{ti}v day of Decembr*e* of m*aster* chambirlain ... xxiiii li.

Item rec*eyved* the x day of January of m*aster* chambirlain ... iiii li.

[*p. 179*] [246]Anno xx^{mo}

Item delyv*er*ed to my ladys coffers þe xvi day off Januar*e* anno xx^{mo} regis Henrici vii^{mi} by the hand*es* off m*aster* Hugh Assheton off the revenewes off Rykyll*es* and Thrognall*es* land*es* for the seid xx^{ti} yere ... xxxix li. xi s. v d.

Item delyv*er*ed to þe seid coffers þe forseid daye and yere off the revenewes off m*aster* Seint Johns land*es* for the seid xx^{ti} yere ... xxxvi li. xvii s. v d.

[*p. 180*] Anno xxi^{mo}

Memorandum off mony delyv*er*ed unto my lad*ys* coffers by the hand*es* [off] m*aster* Hugh Assheton off parte off the yssues off Frognall*es* land*es* and Rykyll*es* land*es* þe xiiiith day off Januar*e* anno xxi^{mo} Henrici vii^{mi} by the hand*es* off Miles Worsley... lx li. xiii s. [...]

[244] Text lost here and below because of damaged inner edge of pp. 178–182.

[245] Add. later.

[246] Pp. 179–80 are in the 'sprawling' hand.

Item delyv*er*ed unto þe said coffers die et anno <predicto> predictis by the hand*es* off þe seid Miles Worsley off the part off the yssues off maist*er* Seint Johns land*es* ov*er* and besyde xiiii li. xv s. delyv*er* befor*e* unto þe seid coffers by the hand*es* off the seid Miles as appereth in þe iii lefus before[247] ... Cii li. ix s. vi d. ob.

[*p. 181*] [248]<Anno xvii.

Memorandum delyv*er*ed to James Morice the ix day of August to bye catall to put i*n* my lad*ys* fermys of Burn and Depinge ... xliiii li.>

[*p. 182*] Receites for Margaret Gonsell anno xviii^{o}.[249]

First of Will*iam* Grymston the xix day of May of the p*ro*fitt*es* of the land*es* of the said Margaret due at the fest of saint M*ar*tin i*n* wynter last past i*n* parite of payme*n*t... x li. [...] s.

Memorandum delyv*er*ed the xixth day of Aprill anno xx^{mo} regni regis Henri[ci] to m*as*-t*er* le comptroller*e* of my lad*ys* howsehold f[or] the expe*n*ses of hir howshold the tyme of beying*e* of hir grace at London to be by hym delyv*er*ed at tymes co*n*venient to Nicholas Sander*e* or to James Moryce for expe*n*ses or p*ro*vision to be made for my lad*ys* said howsehold ... CCv li. xv<i>i s. iiii d.

[250]as appereth by billett*es* i*n* the bagg*es*

[251]To m*aster* Colet ... DCC li.[252]

To my lord Fytzwater*e* ... DCCCxix[253]

[paper slip 215 x 115 mm. sewn to the outer edge of p. 182:

Testatur per istam billam factam xix^{o} die mensis Marcii anno regni regis Henrici septimi xxi^{o} quod ego Johannes Syclynge magister sive custos collegii Christi in universitate Cantabrigiensi recepi de excellentissima matre regia per manus magistri Metecalffe sexto die mensis predicti xxvi li. xiii s. iiii d. Et predicto xix^{o} die Marcii recepi de predicta matre regia per manus Henrici <Hornebe> Hornby in \sacra/ theologia doctoris et predicte excellentissime matris cancellarii Clxxx li. pro edificacione collegii predicti. Per me Johannem Syclynge.][254]

[255]MMMMMCCiiii^{xx}xii li. xvi s. v d. ob.

MMMMCCCxxviii li. ix s. x d. ob.

[247] See p. 176 above.
[248] The HH hand returns here.
[249] MS 'xvijj^{o}'.
[250] Add. in the same (HH) hand.
[251] This and the next entry are scribbled in a different hand to the left lower down the page.
[252] See p. 77 above and D91.21/77.
[253] See p. 102 above and D91.21/58, 77.
[254] See D91.21/97, 99
[255] These two sums of money are jotted in a different hand lower down the page.

D91.17 (SJLM/1/1/2/1) Account of James Clarell cofferer: 24 June 1498 – 13 January 1499

Discussion See Introduction 4 and Plates 8–9.

Description Paper, with minor repair to frayed edges and faded from p. 29 (quire 2), written on both sides, approx. 305 x 215 mm. 38ff. in three quires: 1^{14} 2^{14} 3^{10},[1] preceded and followed by a modern flyleaf. Paginated recto 1–75 (excluding flyleaves) top right in pencil (MGU); pp. 6–18, 68–76 and flyleaves blank. Left margins approx. 50–5 mm. (with some subheadings); right margins variable; upper margins 15–20 mm.; lower margins variable. Bills sewn into pp. 66 and 67 are in the hands of Henry Hornby (with his seal) and Nicholas Nynes. Bound into a brown/grey buckram cover in a slipcase of the same material. A slip inside the volume records in a 19th c. hand: 'N° 23 in Hist. MSS. Report/ Accompt of James Clarell .../With signature "Margaret R" at end of each week'. One main hand (Anglicana with Secretary influence), which appears to be that of Clarell himself.[2] The summaries, i.e. initial and final material (pp. 1–5, 66–67), use a formal script (Bastard Anglicana, with a large decorated initial 'S', pp. 4, 66). Occasional marginal notes in another (tall thin) hand, e.g. 'Conysby' (p. 26), 'Shoyng' (pp. 21, 33, 34, 39, 40).[3] Corrections to the sums are rare.[4] Sum totals are marked 'probatur' (^{P} in the edited text), which on pp. 54–60 is preceded by a long-tailed <z> (^{ʒ} in the edited text), probably the auditor's system of checks and spot-checks; Lady Margaret signs below the sum totals (^{M} in the edited text).

Summary

1498–9 (years 13–14) statement of account (Clarell, 24 June 1498 – 12 January [act. 13] 1499), arrears of last account, p. 1; receipts, pp. 1–3; sum total of receipts with arrears, pp. 4–5 [6–18 blank]; costs and expenses, pp. 19–65; sum total and allowance, p. 65; sum of allowances and payments, debt of James Clarell, pp. 66–7 [paper bill in Henry Hornby's hand sewn to p. 66, paper bill in Nicholas Nyne's hand sewn to p. 67] [68–75 blank]

[1] I.e. pp. 1–28, 29–56, 57–76.

[2] 'as it apperyth by my laste boke' p. 27, 'purveyde by me', 'Item for my costez at London for myne accompte' p. 28, 'payde ... by me' p. 31, 'payde to me for my iii horssez ... my servauntez dyetes' p. 34 (two entries), 'payde to me for rydynge' p. 40, 'my servaunte' p. 44, 'to me', 'payde to me' p. 46, 'payde to me' p. 52, 'gaffe me' p. 59, 'bought by me' p. 62, 'payde to me', 'my servaunte' p. 65. Note too: 'Item payde for my ladys offerrynge when *youre grace* departed from oure Ladye of Wauleshyngham' (p. 35, my italics).

[3] The hand is similar to that which writes 'Null' in the margin at D102.1/2r.

[4] But see footnotes to pp. 48 (with an annotation marked here by double angle brackets) and 58.

Edited Text

[*p. 1*] The accompt*es* of James Clarell cofferer*e* to the most excellent princesse Margaret countesse of Richmond and Derbe and moder unto our*e* sovereign lord kyng Henry the viith that nowe is that is to sey from the fest of the Nativite of Seynt John Baptist in the xiiith yere of our*e* seid sovereign lord unto the xiith day of Januar*y* in the xiiiith yere of the seid kyng that is to sey by halff a yere and xx^{ti} daiez.

*Arre*r*agez of the last accompte.* The<is> seid \James/ Clarell oweth of the arre*r*agez of his last accompte as appiereth in the fote of the same ... xlvii li. v s. vii d. qua. iii p*artes* qua.

Summa ... xlvii li. v s. vii d qua. iii p*artes* qua.

*Receyt*es *of money of John Heron.* Also he hath receyved of John Heron on of the kyngez s*er*vant*es* at ii tymes that is to sey the fi[r]ste day of July in the xiiith yere of the reign of the seid kyng in p*ar*tie of payment of a more so*m*me for the lordship of Breknok xl li. and the xth day of Octob*er* in the xiiiith yere of our*e* seid sov*er*eign lord as for money by s*ir* Thomas Lovell knyght lent to my ladiez grace C li. ... Cxl li.

Summa ... Cxl li.

[*p. 2*] *Receyt*es *of money of Nicholas Compton.* Also he hath receyved of Nicholas Compton on of my ladiez receyvo*ur*z at dyverse tymez that is to sey in the moneth <of> Juny[5] in the xiiith yere of our*e* seid sov*er*eign lord iiii^{xx}x li. the xth day of July in the same yere Clx li. the moneth of Septembr*e* in the xiiith yere of the seid kyng by the hand*es* of the baillye of Dertwich xix li. the iiiith day of Decembr*e* in the same yere by the hand*es* of the baillie of Dalburley and Dalburleys xvii li. another tyme the same day and yere by the hand*es* of the seid Nicholas CCCCxxxii li. xi s. v d. another tyme the same day and yere by the hand*es* of John Walssh fermer*e* of Dere and Pennale xl li. anothere tyme the same day and yere by the hand*es* of James Mawdesley xl li. another tyme the same day and yere by the hand*es* of John Stakhouse xlvi li. and another tyme the same day and yere by the hand*es* of Richard Shirley xxxv li. In all ... DCCClxxix li. xi s. v d.

... So*m*me ... DCCClxxix li. xi s. vd.

[*p. 3*] *Receyte of money <f> of* sir *John Shawe.* Also he hath receyved of s*ir* John Shawe knyght the xvith day of July in the xiiith yere of the reign of our*e* seid sovereign lord as in money by hym lent to my ladiez grace ... Dxl li.

Summa ... Dxl li.

Receytes of money the busshop of Rochestre. Also receyved of my lord of Rochestere the first day of January in the xiiith yere of the reign of oure seid sov*er*eign lord as in the repayment of money that he borowed of my seid ladiez grace ... lxvi li. xiii s. iiii d.

Summa ... lxvi li xiii s. iiii d.

*Receyt*es *of money of the seid countesse.* Also the seid accomptant hath receyed by the hand*es* of the seid countesse that is to say the xvith day of \Auguste/ in the xiiith yere of the reign of our*e* seid sov*er*eign lord < ... > by the hand*es* of m*aster* Hornby xxxix li.

[5] June? July?.

xvs and the xviii day of Septemb*er* in the <x> xiiiith yere of the reign of our*e* seid sov*er*eign lord CC li. in all ... CCxxxix li. xv s.

Summa ... CCxxxix li. xv s

ther is more of the other side [6]

[*p. 4*] [7]*Somme of the hole receipt with the arrer*ag*ez* ... MDCCCCxiii li. v s. iiii d. qua. iii pars qua.

[*p. 5*]

wherof receyved of the

arre*r*agez of the last accompte ... xlvii li. v s. vii d. qua. iii pars qua.

John Heron ... Cxl li.

Nicholas Compton ... DCCClxxix li. xi s. v d.

s*ir* John Shawe ... Dxl li.

busshop of Rochester*e* ... lxvi li. xiii s. iiii d.

seid countesse ... CCxxxix li. xv s.

[*pp. 6–18 blank*]

[*p. 19*] *Westmyster*. [C]ostes[8] and exspences rewardez w*ith* other div*er*se paymentes of the excelent princes Margerett countes off Richemonde and Derbye and moder unto our sov*er*ayne lorde kynge Henrye the viith don and recey[v]de by the hondes off James Clarell as hereafter apperyth.

Schene. xxiiii^{o} de Junii anno xiii^{o}. Sondaye. Mydsomer daye.[9] Item payde to Thomas Wheteley a skoller of my ladys at Cambryge for his co*m*mensement there ... xl s.

Wyndsore. xxv^{o} die. Mondaye. Item payde to s*ir* John Schaa for diverse costez leyde out by hym for Mouse my ladys servante ... xx s.

Estamstede. xxvi^{o}die. Tewysdaye. Item payde to Will*ia*m Danyell yoman of my ladys charyett for div*er*se costez and chargez layd out by hym by a bill signed ... vii s. x d.

xxvii^{o} die. Wedynsdaye. Item payde for a peyre of writtyng*e* tabullys for my lady*e* ... xii d.

[6] Written small centrally at the foot of the page in the same hand.

[7] The text is very elaborately set out across the whole of pp. 4–5. 'Somme ... arreragez' is bracketed to the right with the total after the bracket; the total is bracketed to the right to 'wherof receyved of the', which itself is bracketed to the right with names/details and amounts listed below each other after the bracket.

[8] 'c' lightly written in preparation for expected decoration. See Plate 8.

[9] The Latin subheading is written in the left margin throughout, and the English day written centrally above the entry.

Wyndsore. xxviii^o die. Thursedaye. Item payde for ii pecez of redd saye to Chr*isto*ffer Richardson*e* … xxxvi s.

xxix^o die. Frydaye. Item payde to <Chr*isto*ff> Richarde Stukley for a pownde of golde of Venys for my ladys worke … xix s.

Schene. ultimo die Junii. Saturdaye. Item payde for my ladys offerrynge at master Seynt Johns mariage … xx d.

[M]Summa totalis … vi li. v s. vi d.[P]

[*p. 20*] *Westmyst*er. *primo die Jullii.* Sondaye. Item payde to Richarde Carr for hevynge a coffer unto þe Toure from master Heron hensse at Westmyst*er* … iiii d.

ii^o die. Mondaye. Item payde in a rewarde to John Mundye to bye hym a gowen … xx s.

iii^o die. Tewysdaye. Item payde to Will*i*am Sandez for the costes and espencez of master P*ar*ker and of yonge Burgon beynge at Oxfforde at skole by a bill signed … iii li. xxi d.

iiii^o die. Wedynsdaye. Item payde for standardez gardevyans and for mendynge of coffers by a bill signed w*ith* my ladys honde … iii li. xvii s. x d.

v^o die. Thursdaye. Item payde to Bestyan Mussheka[10] broder for makynge of flourys and other thyngez by a bill signed … vii li.

vi^i die. Frydaye. Item payde to John Lyberde for cheynez \a/ hope and other thyngez w*ith* þe makynge by a bill signed … xxviii li.

vii^o die. Saturdaye. Item payde to Roger Ormeston for þe makynge of div*er*se thyngez <p*er*teynge> p*er*teynynge to my ladys chare of crymsyn welvett by a bill signed … iiii li. vi s. vi d.

Item payde to the same Roger for Brugez satten and bokeram by anoder bill signed … xxiiii s. viii d.

Item payde to þe same Roger for bredd ale and wyne for master Seynt Johns weddynge by anoder bill signed … xiii s. iiii d.

[M]Summa totalis … xlix li. iiii s. v d.[P]

[*p. 21*] *Westmyst*er. *viii^o die Julii*. Sondaye. Item payde in a rewarde to Hobbson my ladys audito*ur* … xx s.

Item payde in a rewarde to his clerke … v s.

ix^o die. Mondaye. Item payde to Portkullys for his costez goynge into Fraunce uppon my ladys messag*es* … liij s. iiii d.

x^o die. Tewysdaye. Item delyv*er*d unto my ladys grace unto hir almez pursse … ix li.

[10] Perhaps 'Musteka' as p. 38 (both of which forms show correction).

xi° die. Wedynsdaye. Item payde to Olyv*er* Seynt John for his costez rydynge w*ith* my ladys grace from Schene to Wyndsore to Estmastede and so to Schene ayen by his byll signed … viii s. v d.

Item payde to master Denman for rydynge to Wyndsore from Schene w*ith* my ladys grace and there a daye stondynge aft*er* and so to Estamstede and þere a daye stondy-nge and to Wyndsore ayen and there a daye stondynge and so to Schene and there a daye stondynge for iii horssez on at v d. a daye and þe other ii at iii d. a pece þat is to sey by iiii days rydynge \iiii s. iiii d./ iiii days stondynge aft*er* iiii d. on horsse and iii d · the other \ii s. viii d./ two his s*er*vantez dyet*es* by viii dayes \ii s. viii d./ … x s. iiii d.

Item payde to master amner for rydynge w*ith* his ii horssez by þe same iiii days \ii s. viii d./ and for iiii days stondynge \ii s./ his s*er*vantez dyet*es* by viii days \ii s. viii d./ schoynge /vi d./ … vii s. x d.

Item payde to master secretorye for his ii horssez rydynge the same tyme by iiii days rydynge \ii s. viii d./ and iiii days stondynge \ii s./ his s*er*vantez dyet*es* by viii days \ii s. viii d./ schoynge \vii d./ … vii s. xi d.

Shoyng. Item payde to master Fell for his ii horssez þe same tyme rydynge \ii s. viii d./ and for iiii days stondynge \ii s./ his s*er*vantez dyet*es* by viii days \ii s. viii d./ schoynge \v d./ … vii s. ix d.

Item payde to Will*i*am Pole and Edwarde Heven for theyr iii horssez rydynge the same tyme by iiii days \iiii s./ and for iiii days stondynge \iii s./ theyre s*er*vantez dyet*es* by viii days \ii s. viii d./ schoynge \viii d./ … x s. iiii d.

Item payde to the seyde Edwarde Heven for rydynge by ii days from Estamsted unto Westmyst*er* upon my ladys message … xvi d.

Item payde to John Fysshe and Richarde Cheke theyre rydynge schoynge w*ith* other costez by a bill signed … xiiii s. iiii d.

[*p. 22*] *Westmyster*. Item payde to Richarde Kylte and Roger Kardon for theyre iii horssez rydynge the same tyme by iiii days \iiii s./ and for iiii days stondynge \iii s./ theire s*er*vantez dyet*es* by viii days \ii s. viii d./ schoynge \v d./ … x s. i d.

Item payde to Henrye Coke and Roberde Smyth for rydynge the same tyme w*ith* iii horssez \iiii s./ and iiii days stondynge \iii s./ theire s*er*vantez dyet*es* by viii days \ii s. viii d./ schoynge \ v d./ … x s. i d.

Item payde to Osmunde Notte and Raffe Schurley for theyre iii horssez rydynge by iiii days \iiii s./ and for iiii days stondynge \iii s./ there s*er*vantez dyet*es* by viii days \ii s. viii d./ schoynge \iiii d./ … x s.

Item payde to George Frauncez for ix days rydynge before to make loggyngez for my ladys \g*r*ace/ with ii horssez at xvi d. the day … xii s.

Item payde to Will*i*am Adthirton rydynge w*ith* hym to make redye my ladys loggenge at viii d. þe day … vi s.

Item payde to Thomas Philippez for rydynge before to take loggyngez for my ladys s*er*vantez and horssez at xii d. the daye … ix s.

Item payde to *Christ*offer Bygom for goynge w*ith* my ladys stuffe [to] Roberde Hilton by vi days at div*er*se tymez … vi s.

Item payde to R[i]charde Carre and Will*ia*m Adthyrton for goynge from <Schene> Westmyst*er* to Schene and from Schene to Westmyst*er* by ii tymez <at> by iiii days … iiii s.

Item payde to the seyde Will*i*am for a stole for my ladys grace … vi d.

Item payde to the ii fotemen for runnynge w*ith* my ladys grace by iiii days \ii s. viii d./ and for ii peyre of schone for theyme \xii d./ … iii s. viii d.

Item payde to Edwarde Heven for my ladys offerrynge at the rode w*ith*in the charterhousse at Schene … xii d.

Item payde for my ladys bote hyre the same tyme … viii d.

Item payde to Will*i*am Pole for rydynge by iii days uppon my ladys message unto Skyppw*ith* … ii s.

Item payde to Nicholas of Aughton for a rewarde geven to my ladys bedman at Wyndsore … xii d.

Item payde to *Christ*offer Richardson for lopys and for makynge of hangell*es* to my ladys bedde … iii s. viii d.

Item payde for a peyre of slypp*er*s and schone for master John Seynt John \xvi d./ and for hys loggenge and his broders at div*er*se tymez \xviii d./ and for wassheynge of his schurtez \iiii d./ … iii s. ii d.

Item payde for this boke … x d.

Item payde for crule to mende my ladys hanggyngez at Colyweston at ii s. the pounde and iii li. att xii d. þe li. … vii s.

[*p. 23*] *Westmyst*er. *xii*^{o} *die.* Thursedaye. Item payde to mastres Fyherberde for sope and other thyngez by a byll signed w*ith* my ladys honde … xi s. v d.

xiii^{o} *die.* Frydaye. Item payde unto Roger Ormeston for þe makynge of kkottshyns of golde and portkullys w*ith* other thyngez for my ladys chare by a bill signed … xliiii s.

xiiii^{o} *die.* Saturdaye. Item payde to mastrez Fynche for div*er*se sylke hadde of hir as well by mastrez Cursson as by mastrez Lacye as it apperyth by ii billys signed w*ith* my ladys honde … iiii li. x s. iiii d.

[M]Summa totalis … xxix li. iii s. v d.[P]

[*p. 24*] *Westmyst*er. *xv*^{o}. Sondaye. Item payde by my ladys co*m*maundement unto mastres Fyherberde … v li.

Item payde in a rewarde to on Betras Abseley … v s.

xvi^{o}. Mondaye. Item payde in a rewarde to mastrez Wyndsore my ladys god doughter … xx s.

Item payde to mastres Massey for mendynge of a cloke … iiii s. iiii d.

Item payde for a lok for the same clokk … xii d.

Item payde to Will*ia*m Danyell and his felowys for drynkynge by the wey by vi days … ii s.

Item payde for lycoure for the chare /ii d./ and for a whipp \i d./ … iii d.

Item payde to the ferror*e* for xxv horsse schoyn \ii s. x d./ CCCC naylez \xxvi d./ and for his rydynge from Okynge to Ware \viii d./ … iiii s. x d.

Item payde to master Horneby in a rewarde that he gaffe to *Christ*offer Bygom when he was syke … vi s. viii d.

Item payde also to hym in a rewarde gewon to John Stantons son … vi s. viii d.

Item payde to Raffe Schurley for the borde wagez of my ladys stabull men and for p*ro*vendur dep*ar*tynge w*ith* my lad*ys* horssez from Cheston to Okynge and for the costez of the same as it apperyth by a bill signed … liiii s. vi d.

xvii. Tewsdaye. Item payde in a rewarde to a Skott at Wyndsore … iii s. iiii d.

Item delyv*er*id unto my ladys grace at the autur*e* at Schene … iii s. iiii d.

Item payde for bote hyre of my ladys gentylwomen from Westm*yster* unto Schene … xii d.

Item payde in a rewarde to a Skottysshe woman at Schene … xiii s. iiii d.

Item payde unto \dame/ Agnes <dompne> Colles at þe Menery … <x> vi s. viii d.

Item payde <in a> for my ladys offerrynge at Seynt Brygitez … xx d.

Item payde for my seyde ladys offerrynge at o*ur* Ladye of Pew … xx d.

Item payde to mastrez Curson for div*er*se leyde out by hyr by a bill signed … iiii s. i d.

Item for martes for my ladys gentylwomen … xii d.

Item payde to Petur of Coldeherber for writtynge of my ladys bokys <at> of hir stuffe … xx s.

Item for the hyre of a barge from Schene to Syon and ayen to Schene for my ladys grace … ii s.

[*p. 25*] *Westmyst*er. *xviii° die.* Wedynsdaye. Item payde in a rewarde to on Alys Essex … xx d.

Item payde in a rewarde to the balyffe of Dertfforde for bryngynge of a image of the trynete unto my ladys grace … xii d.

Item delyv*er*id unto m*aster* Horneby to be gowen in almes to the house of Syon and at the charterhousse … iii li.

Item payde in almes to the ii ancreces at Seynt Albons … xvi s. viii d.

Item payde to mastres Massey for a sarkett schone and hossen for Godstons doughter … xiiii d.

Item payde to Henrye Coke for erbez smale fysshes and other thyngez by a bill signed … iii s. vii d. ob.

Item payde to mastrez Massey for a stantarde … xxvi s. viii d.

Item payde for my ladys offerryngez at Poulys to the rode and to oure Ladye of Grace … vi s. viii d.

Item payde in a rewarde to on Roberde Castell … iii s. iiii d.

Item payde in a rewarde to a harmyt*e* þat brought perys … xii d.

Item payde to Will*i*am potyknarye for sugur and other thyngez for medcyns by a bill signed … xvi s. ii d.

Item payde in a rewarde to Jakson of Wyndsore for makynge of broches for my ladys grace … iii s. iiii d.

Item payde in a rewarde or almes to a Douche woman þat sued to the kynge for hir husbonde beynge in p*re*son … xx d.

Item payde for brochys þat were sent unto my lorde of Yorke and unto my ladye <m*er*gene> Margerett … viii d.

Item payde in almez to div*er*se pore men and women by þe hondez of m*aster* Hornebye … xx d.

Item payde in a rewarde to a pore woman of Eyton … iii s. iii d.

Item payde for my ladys offerrynge at Wyndsore iii pec*es* of thyrtye penis … vii s. vi d.

Item payde to master Whytamore <for> in p*ar*te of payement for his costez at Wyndsore for my ladys work*es* … iii li.

Item payde in a rewarde to a woman þat brought cherys … xii d.

Item payde in a rewarde to s*ir* John Thomson of Wyndsore … iii s. iiii d.

Item payde in a rewarde to a s*er*vante of master Maddes … xii d.

Item payde in a rewarde to mastrez Jane Gower … xx s.

Item payde in a rewarde to a pore woman in almez … iiii d.

Item payde in almez to the burrynge of \on/ Blake Petur … xx d.

Item payde in a rewarde to Madde Crystyan … xx d.

Item payde in a rewarde to a pore man that <for> sued to my ladys grace comynge of <out> Brukyshyre … ii s.

Item payde to master Horneby for his bote hyre to Schene and ayen upon my ladys message … ii s.

[*p. 26*] *Westmyst*er. *xix^{o} die.* Thursedaye. Item payde in a rewarde to a pore woman called Elyzabeth Johnson … vi s. viii d.

Item payde in a rewarde to master John Fawne a skoller of my ladys at Cambryge … xxvi s. viii d.

Item payde to *Christ*offer Bygom for hokes crochett*es* and other necessary bought by hym by a bill signed … iii s. vi d.

Item payde to Richarde Karre goynge w*ith* my ladys <stuffs> stuffe at dyv*er*se [tymes] by iiii days … ii s.

Item payde to Roberde Edlyn goynge w*ith* the stuffe by viii days … iiii s.

Item payde to Richarde Stukley for weyffynge stollys and other thyngez by a bill signed … viii s.

Frydaye. *xx*^{o} *die.*

*Money delyv*erid *for my ladys housesolde.*[11]

Item delyv*er*ed unto Richarde Gough clerke of my ladys kechyne for oxen bought at Coventre feyre … lxvi li. xiii s. iiii d.

Item delyv*er*id unto the same Richarde for oder p*ro*vysyons … l li.

Item delyv*er*id unto Will*i*am Bedell for more p*ro*vysyons … xlvi li.

Item delyv*er*id unto the same Will*i*am anoder tyme … l li.

Saturdaye. *xxi*^{o} *die.*

Item payde to my lorde tresorer for a greate bedde of cloth of golde for my ladys grace … l li.

Item delyv*er*id unto John Pykton of London mercer to <p*er*> p*ur*vey tapestrez and lynen cloth for my ladys grace … l li.

Conysby. Item delyv*er*id unto master Conysbye for p*ur*chassynge of certayne inlonde in p*ar*te of payment by a bill of his honde … Cxl li.

[M]Summa totalis …CCCCiiii^{xx}i vii d. ob.[P]

[*p. 27*] Sondaye. Item payde to Will*i*am Dyse a westment maker*e* for makynge of westmenstez for my ladys grace by a byll signed … xv s.

Item payde to Laurence Canwyke for div*er*se thyngez spent for master*e* P*ar*ker by a bill signed … iii s. iiii d.

Mondaye. Item payde to John Love for furrys and powderyngez by a bill signed … iii li. xviii d.

*Memorandum that the said xxviii li. iiii s. be answ*ered *to my ladys grace.* Item delyv*er*de unto John Mundye servante unto sir John Schaa knyght in romayn money the whiche is not covante … xxviii li. iiii s.

Item payde unto R[i]charde Schurley for the borde wagez of my ladys horsse kep*ers* and for p*ro*vendur as it apperyth by ii billys signed … ix li. v s. vi d. ob.

Item payde unto Palmer sadeler for makynge of my ladys new sadell*es* w*ith* bokell*es* pendauntez and all man*er* off oder stuffe as it apperythe by a bill signed wherof he was payde x li. as it apperyth by my laste boke the whiche bill <anou> amounteth to þe s*u*me of xxix li. xvi s. ix d. so now payde … xxix li. xvi s. ix d.

[11] Bracketed to include the next four items.

Item payde to the same Palm*er* for div*er*se thyngez for my ladys chare of cloth of golde by anoder bill signed … xxxviii s. v d.

Item payde to the same Palm*er* for div*er*se stuffe hadde and taken by R[i]charde Schurley by anoder byll signed … iiii li. vii s. viii d.

Tewysdaye. Item payde to Roger Kardon for sylkez wollen cloth w*ith* manye other div*er*se thyngez bought by hym by a bill signed … lxxii li. xvii s. x d.

Wedynsdaye. Item payde in a rewarde to my ladye Man*er*s at hir dep*ar*tynge from my ladys grace … vj li. xiii s. iiii d.

Item payde in a rewarde to my ladye Sandez … liii s. iiii d.

Item payde in a rewarde to mastres Jane Gower*e* … x li.

Item payde in a rewarde to Fayreffaxe … vi s. viii d.

Item payde in a rewarde to the preste of oure Ladye of Pew … xx s.

Item payde in a rewarde to Olyv*er* Seynt John … xl s.

Item payde in a rewarde to a prest þat brought my ladys grace boxes w*ith* pouders … xx s.

Item payde in a rewarde to doctur Brenkley … xl s.

Item payde in a rewarde to fryer Candysshe … vi s. viii d.

Item payde in a rewarde to William potyknar*es* wyffe for bryngynge of drynkes and rosse levys … vi s. viii d.

Item payde in a rewarde to dame Agnez Collys … vi s. viii d.

[*p. 28*] Thursedaye. Item payde in a rewarde to m*aster* Roberde surjoyne for the helynge of m*aster* Parkers legge … x s.

Item payde to <the> Rowlande my ladys cordenar for schone and slypp*er*s for my ladys grace … xxi d.

Frydaye. Item payde in a rewarde to m*aster* John Seynt John to put in his pursse … vi s. viii d.

Item payde for the loggyngez of his s*er*vante w*ith* his costez havynge his horsse to Ware and ayene him selffe … ii s.

Item payde for a horsse for master P*ar*ker goynge to my lorde princ*e* … xx s.

Item payde for a stantarde for the stabull stuffe … xvi s.

Item payde for ii lokk*es* and ii keys to the chare of crymsyn welvett … xvi d.

Item payde to Wodwarde the golde wyer drawer for golde wyer by a bill signed … vi li. iiii s.

Saturdaye. Item payde for a pece of cloth of golde of damaske vyolett *con*teynynge xvi yardez iii <qa> quarter*e* and di. at l s. the yarde … xlii li. iii s. ix d.

Item payde to Guyberde Guylpyne for the chargez of my lad*ys* horssez and kep*ers* lyenge at Okynge by a bill signed … xlv s. ii d. ob.

Item payde for lynen cloth cloth of golde tuke for my ladys grace p*ur*veyde by me by a bill signed … xxiii li. xiiii s. ix d. ob.

Item for my costez at London for myne a*c*compte w*ith* bote hyre at div*er*se tymez and at London <*sur*> aboute my ladys matter … ix s.

Item payde for loggyngez as well at Schene Westmyst*er* and at the Toure by viii wekez for all my ladys for xii bedds … xlviii s.

Item payde to Petur of Coldeherberde for mendynge of my ladys bok*es* w*ith* other thyngez by a bill signed … xxvi s. ob

Item payde to the kyngez sadeler for makynge of the kyngez sadell and for thynges lo*n*ggynge to the same by a bill signed … xxxvii s. iiii d.

[M]Summa totalis …CCxli[12] li. x s. iii d.[P]

[*p. 29*] *At the Towre*. Sondaye. Item payde to Balye the quenys s*er*vante for haulffe a pownde of white thredde for my ladys grace … iiii s.

Item payde to hym for a pownde of thredde of anoder sorte … ii s.

Mondaye. Item payde for ii ell*es* of hollonde cloth for the fole … xiii d.

Tewysdaye. Item payde in a rewarde to John Pyktons s*er*vante that bought div*er*se stuffe for my ladys grace and brought p*ar*te thereof to the Toure … vi s. viii d.

Item payde in a rewarde to the gentylmen of the kyngez chapell … xx s.

Stratfforde abbey.[13]

Item payde for the dyet*es* of Richarde Schurley w*ith* a xi p*er*sons at London by ii melys … iiii s. viii d.

Item payde for horsse mete for xix greate horssez and vii hakneys … xii s. iiii d.

Haverynge of the boure. Wedynsdaye. Item payde for <fo> the dyetez of Richarde Schurley with xi p*er*sons by ii melys at Stratfforde abbey … iiii s. iiii d.

Item for horsse mete for xix greate horssez and vii hakneys … viii s.

Item payde in a rewarde to my ladye Kateryns chylde at Haverynge of the Boure … xl s.

*M*aster *Tyrell*es. Thursedaye. Item payde for <horssemete> the dyet*es* of Richarde Schurley w*ith* xxi p*er*sons by ii melys at Haverynge[14] … iiii s. viiii d.

Item for horsse mete for <xx> xix grete horssez and vii hakneys … viii s. vi d.

Mastres Bardvyles. Frydaye. Item payde for <horssemete> the dyet*es* of Richarde Schurley with a xi p*er*sons at sir Thomas Tyrell*es* by ii melys … iiii s. viii d.[15]

Item payde for horsse mete for <xvii> xix grete horssez and vii hakneys … viii s. x d.

[12] -i over blot.

[13] Written alongside the next two items.

[14] 'at Haverynge' add. by the main hand in the same ink as the entries below.

[15] The same charge as for twenty-one people two entries above.

My lorde of Ormunndes. Saturdaye. Item payde for the dyet*es* of Richarde Schurley w*ith* a xi p*er*sons by ii melys w*ith* the drynkyngez at m*astres* Bardevylez … iii s.

Item payde for xix greate horssez and vii hakneys … viii s. x d.

[M]Summa totalis …vii li. xix d.[P]

[*p. 30*] *My lorde of Ormunndez*. Sondaye. Item payde for my ladys offerrynge to oure Ladye of Oultynge … xx d.

Hennyngham. Mondaye. Item payde for the dyet*es* of Richarde Schurley w*ith* a xi p*er*sons by ii days at my lorde of Ormu*n*ndez … vii s. vi d.

Item payde for horsse mete for xix grete horssez and vii hakneys by ii days … xviii s. viii d.

Tewysdaye. Item payde to Ormeston that he payde unto John Lybarde for certayne thyngez made for my ladys grace … xxxviii s.

Wedynsdaye. Item payde in a rewarde to a Ducheman that gaffe my ladys grace a clokk … xx s.

Thursedaye. Item payde in a rewarde to a chanon that <gaf> kept a clok the whiche my <ladys> lorde of Oxfforde gaffe unto my ladys grace … vi s. viii d.

Frydaye. Item payde in a rewarde to a s*er*vante of the byschope of Murrey in Skotlonde … vi s. viii d.

Item delyv*er*id unto a preste for to by pap*er* for to write … iii s. iiii d.

Item [*blank*]

Saturdaye. Item payde to Will*i*am Danyell for chare clowtys for horsse mete and mannys mete w*ith* other necessar*es* for my ladys chare and for halyinge it to Colyweston and for the costez fettchynge my ladys litt*er* to Henyngham as it apperyth by ii billys signed … xx s. v d.

[M]Summa totalis …vi li. ii s. xi d.[P]

[*p. 31*] *Hennyngham*. Sondaye. Item payde in a rewarde to a messenger that kam from my lorde p*r*ince … ii s.

Mondaye.[16] Item payde in a rewarde to the yoman of the seller w*ith* my lorde Oxfforde … x s.

Item payde for the dyet*es* of R[i]charde Schurley with x p*er*sons by vii days … xi s. viii d.

Item payde for horsse mete for xvii greate horssez and v hakneys by the space of vii days … xxxvi s. vii d.

Item payde for loggyngez at Hennyngham for vi beddez for my ladys s*er*vantez by a weke … iii s.

Burry. Tewysdaye. Item payde for my ladys offerrynge at oure Ladye Sudburye … ii s.

[16] Preceded by an annotation mark.

Item payde for the dyet*es* of Richarde Schurley w*ith* ix p*er*sons at Lanam and for theire drynkkynge … ii s. viii d.

Item payde for horsse mete for xiii greate horssez and ix hakneys the same tyme … viii s.

Wedynsdaye o*ur* Ladys daye þe Asumpc*i*one. Item payde for my ladys offerrynge there … v s.

Item payde for my ladys offerryngez at hir fyrst co*m*mynge … v s.

Item payde for my ladys offerynge >tha> when hir grace went in to the churche in the evenynge to Seynt Edmonde schryne … xx d.

Item payde the same tyme for hir offerrynge to our Ladye of Undercrofte there … xii d.

Thursedaye. Item payde in almez to the ancre at Bury … iii s. iiii d.

Oure Ladye of Wullepitt. Frydaye. [17]Item payde for my ladys offerynge at o*ur* Ladye of Wullpitt ii pec*es* of thyrtye pens … v s.

Item payde in white money by me xx d. iii s. iiii d. and by Ormeston \xx d./ … viii s. iiii d.

Item payde for[18] xv pownde of waxe for iii tapers to sett byfore oure Ladye there at viii d. þe pownde … x s.

Item for the makynge of the same iii tapers … xii d.

Item for ii pownde and a haulffe for anoder lytyll taper … xx d.

Item for the makynge thereof … iii d.

Item for bredde ale and wyne for the kyngez s*er*vantez and my ladys there in the cowrte that they drank … ii s. ii d.

Item payde for waxe to bryne byfore my ladys grace at hir masse … xvi d.

[*p. 32*] *Thettforde*. Saturdaye. Item payde for my ladys offerrynge at Seynt Edmondes schryne the same daye that hir grace dep*ar*ted from Bury … ii s.

Item for my ladys offerrynge at the relykkez there … xx d.

Item payde for the dyet*es* of R[i]charde Schurley with ix p*er*sons by v days at Bury … xii s. vi d.

Item for horsse mete for <c> xiii grete horssez and ix hakneys there … xxvi s. x d.

Item payde for a brusshe for my ladys sadell*es* … iiii d.

Item payde for lx horsse schone from Okynge to Burye … vii s. viii d.

Item payde for DCC naylez at iiii d. the hundred … ii s. iiii d.

[M]Summa totalis …viii li. xv s.[P]

[17] Very faint to foot of page (read under ultra-violet light).

[18] 'for' rep.

[*p. 33*] *Buknam castell.* Sondaye. Item payde for the dyet*es* of Richarde Schurley w*ith* ix p*er*sons by ii melys at Thettforde … iii s. viii d.

Item for horsse mete for xiii grete horssez and ix hakneys … viii s. iiii d.

Norwhiche. Mondaye. Item payde for the dyet*es* of Richarde with ix p*er*sons by ii melys at Buknam … iiii s.

Item for horsse mete for xiii grete horssez and ix hakneys … vii s. viii d.

Item payde for my ladys offerryngez a pece of v s. and a xl in pens … viii s. iiii d.

Item payde to a fole that mett my ladyez grace at Bukna*m* w*ith* a tabur*e* … iiii d.

Tewysdaye. Item payde that my ladys grace sent for a tokens to <mx?> my ladye Bemownde … vi s. viiii d.

At sir *William Boleyns.* Wedynsdaye. Item payde for the dyet*es* of Richarde Schurley w*ith* ix p*er*sons by ii days at Norwhiche … viii s. vi d.

Item for horsse mete for xiii grete horssez and ix hakneys … xvii s. x d.

Waulesshyngham. Thursedaye. Item payde for the [*blank*] of Richarde Schurley w*ith* ix p*er*sons at s*ir* Will*i*am Bolleyns … ii s. viii d.

Item for horsse mete for xiii grete horssez and ix hakneys … viii s.

Item payde for my ladys offerrynge at the hye aulter when my ladys grace kam in fyrst … xx d.

Item for my ladys offerrynge to oure Ladye the same tyme … xx d.

Frydaye. Item payde in a rewarde to the kyngez ha<r>begur*e* … xx d.

Item payde in a rewarde to Reynolde my lord*es* servant … vi s. viii d.

Item payde for a bruche of golde that was sent to my lorde … v s.

Item for other brochez that my ladys grace gaffe away of sylv*er* and gylt … xvi d.

Item payde to master Denman for rydynge w*ith* my ladys grace from London to Wauleshyngham w*ith* iii horssez by xiiii days rydynge and v days stondynge his owen horsse at v d. a day rydynge and the other at iiii d. a pece and stondynge iiii d. and the other ii at iii d. a daye his s*er*vantez dyet*es* by the seyde xix days at iiii d. a daye. Summa <schoynge> \xx d./ Summa … xxvii s. iiii d.

Shoyng. Item payde to master amner for rydynge w*ith* ii horssez by the seyd xiiii days at iiii d. þe horsse and for v days stondynge at iii d. þe horsse his s*er*vantez dyet*es* by þe seyde xix days at iiii d. his schoynge and remeveynge \xix d./ … xix s. ix d.

Item payde to m*aster* secretorye for his rydynge w*ith* ii horssez by xiiii days and v days stondynge his s*er*vantez dyet*es* by xix days schoynge \xviii d./ … xix s. viii d.

[*p. 34*] *Wauleshyngham.* Item payde to doctur Fell for rydynge the same tyme w*ith* ii horssez by xiiii days \ix s. iiii d./ and v days stondyng \ii s. vi d./ his s*er*vantez dyet*es* by xix day*es* \vi s. iiii d./ schoynge[19] and remeveynge \xvi d./ … xix s. vi d.

[19] MS 'sochynge'.

Item payde to [*blank*] Verney for his iii horssez by þe seyde xiiii days \xiiii s./ and for v days stondynge \iii s. ix d./ his s*er*vantez dyet*es* by xix days \vi s. iii d./ schoynge \xv d./ … xxv s. iii d.

Item payde to Roger Ormeston for rydynge the same tyme w*ith* his ii horssez by xiiii days \ix s. iiii d./ and for v days stondynge after \ii s. vi d./ his s*er*vantez dyet*es* by xix days \vj s. iiii d./ schoynge and remeveynge \xii d./ … xix s. ii d.

Item payde to me for my iii horssez the same tyme by xiiii days rydynge \xiiii s./ and for v days stondynge \iii s. ix d./ my s*er*vantez dyet*es* by xix days \vi s. iii d./ schoynge and remeveynge \xiii d./ … xv s. i d.

<Item payde to me for the dyet*es* of me and my ii s*er*vantez att London to tarrynge behynde to paye paymentez and other thyngez for my ladys grace by iii days \iii s./ and my horsse mete \iii s./ … vi s.>

Item payde to Richarde Kylte and John Walter for rydynge with theyre iii horssez by xiii days \xiiii s./ and for v days stondynge after \iii s. ii d./ theire s*er*vantez dyet*es* by xix days \v s. iiii d./ schoynge \vii d./ … xxiii s. i d.

Shoyng. Item payde to Richarde Cheke and Mylez Worseley for rydynge the same tyme w*ith* iii horssez by xiiii days \xiiii s./ and for v days stondynge \iii s. ix d./ theire s*er*vantez dyet*es* by xix days \vi s. iii d./ schoynge \viii d./ … xxiiii s. ii d.

Item payde to John Leche and Raffe Schurley for rydynge w*ith* their iii horssez by xiiii days \xiiii s./ and for v days stondynge \iii s. ix d./ theire s*er*vantez diet*es* by xix days \vi s. iiii d./ schoynge \x d./ … xxiiii s. iiii d.

Item payde to Will*i*am Pole and Roberde Smyth by xiiii days rydynge \xiiii s./ and for v days stondynge \iii s. ix d./ theire s*er*vantez dyet*es* by xix days \vi s. iiii d./ schoynge \viii d./ … xiiii s. ii d.

Item payde to John Fysshe and Laurence Canwik for rydynge w*ith* theire iii horssez by xiiii days \xiiii s./ and for v days stondynge after \iii s. ix d./ theire s*er*vantez dyet*es* by xix days \vi s. iiii d./ schoynge \viii d./ … xxiiii s. ii d.

Item payde to Henry Coke and Osmu*n*de Nott for theyre iii horss*es* the same tyme by xiiii days \xiiii s./ and for v days stondynge \iii s. ix d./ theire s*er*vantez dyet*es* by xix days \vi s. iiii d./ schoynge and remeveynge \viii d./ … xxiiii s. ii d.

Item payde to Roger Kardon and Chr*ist*offer Richardson for theyre iii horssez by xiiii days \xiiii s./ and for v days stondynge \iii s. ix d./ s*er*vantez dyet*es* by xix days \vi s. iiii d./ schoynge \xii d./ … xxiiii s. vi d.

Item payde to George Frauncez for rydynge before to take and make redy my ladys loggyngez w*ith* his ii horssez by xix days at xvi d. a day … xxv s. iiii d.

Item payde to Will*i*am Adthirton for rydynge the same tyme w*ith* on horsse by xix days att viii d. … xii s. viii d.

Item payde to Thomas Philippez for rydynge before to take upp loggyngez for my ladys horssez and s*er*vantez by xx^{ti} days at xii d. … xx s.

[*p. 35*] *Wauleshyngham*. Item payde to Roberde Edlyn Will*i*am Thomason Roberd Hilton and Mowse for goynge w*ith* my ladys stuffe by xiii days from London to Wauleshyngham at vi d. the man … xxvi s.

Item payde to Nicholas of Aughton and Richarde Carr fotemen for runnynge w*ith* my ladys grace by the seyde xiii days at iiii d. the man … viii s. viii d.

Item payde for vi peyre of schone for theym þe seyde journey … iii s.

Item payde to the ii litt*er* men for theire drynkynge by the wey by xiii days at ii d. the man … iiii s. iiii d.

Item payde to Roberde Edlyn for rydynge upon my ladys message from Heny*n*ngham to mastres Bardwylez by a day … viii d.

Item payde to John Fysshe for rydynge to Wauldon upon my ladys message by a daye for Ric*harde* Stukley … viii d.

Item payde to Richarde Cheke for a litull botell for my ladys grace … vi d.

Item payde for hym for rydynge upon my ladys message from Hennyngham to Ipwhiche by iii days … ii s.

Item payde to hym for rydynge upon my ladys message from Thettforde to Bury by ii days … xvi d.

Item payde to hym for a potell \and a pynt/ of rumney at Norwyche … x d.

Item payde to the clerke of my ladys signett for his haulfe yeres wagez endynge at Lammasse last passed … xxxiii s. iiii d.

Item payde to hym for his loggengez from the xxix daye of Marche unto the xxiii daye of Septembr*e* that is to sey by xxiii wekez at iii d. a wek … v s. ix d.

Saturdaye. Item payde for my ladys offerrynge when youre grace dep*ar*ted from oure Ladye of Wauleshyngham … v s.

Item payde in a rewarde to my ladye of Suthffolk … iii li. vi s. viii d.

Lyn. Item payde in a rewarde to the prest of Wauleshyngham … vi s. viii d.

Item payde to hym to maynten my ladys lyght there … iii s. iiii d.

Item payde in almez to my ladys foles fader … viii d.

Item payde in a rewarde to a woman that brought þe fole … viii d.

Item payde for the dyet*es* of Richarde Schurley w*ith* ix p*er*sons by ii days at Wauleshyngham … vii s. ix d.

Item payde for horsse mete for xiii greate horssez and viii hakneys by the seyde ii days … xviii s. x d.

Item payde for mendynge of the lokk*es* of the coffer þat the sadell*es* be caried in … iiii d.

Item payde for new ryban for the litt*er* … x d.

Item payde for mendynge of þe forseyde coffer … iii d.

Item payde for a quarter of guylt*e* naylez for the litt*er* … xiiii d.

Item payde for horsse shone from Hennyngham to Wauleshyngham … xviii d.

Item payde for CCC horsse nayles … xii d.

[M]Summa totalis …xxxiiii li. vi s. iiii d.[P]

[*p. 36*] *Lyn*. Sondaye. Item payde to the holy woman at Lyn … xx d.

Item in a rewarde to hir that kepeth hir … iiii d.

Mondaye. Item payde in a rewarde in almez to the ancur*e* at Lyn … iii s. iiii d.

Item payde for my ladys offerrynge at oure Ladye at the Mounte … xx d.

Item for hir offerrynge to ii seyntez und*ur* oure seyde Ladye … ii s.

Item payde in a rewarde to a fryer <as> Lyn … vi s. viii d.

At my lady Benyffeldez. Tewysdaye. … Item payde for loggengez at Lyn for div*er*se of my ladys s*er*vantez by iii nyghtez for viii <med> beddez … ii s. ii d.

Item for the dyet*es* of Richarde Schurley w*ith* ix p*er*sons by iii days … xi s. x d.

Item for horsse mete for xiii greate horssez and viii hakneys … xxvi s. ii d.

Item for a gyrth \iiii d./ a peyre of pastoron \iiii d./ … viii d.

Item for CCC naylez \xii d./ and for xvi horsse schone \xxiii d./ … ii s. xi d.

Brandon ferrey. Wedynsdaye. … Item payde for the dyet*es* of Richarde Schurley w*ith* ix p*er*sons by ii melys at my lady Beneffeldes … iiii s. ii d.

Item for horsse mete for xiii grete horssez and viii hakneys … viii s. vii d.

<Item for>

*At m*aster *Cottons place*. Thursedaye. Item payde for the dyet*es* of Richarde Schurley with ix p*er*sons by ii melys at Brandon ferrey … iii s. ix d.

Item for horsse mete for xiii greate horssez and viii hakneys … ix s.

Ely. Frydaye. … Item payde for my ladys offerrynge to Seynt Audre \xx d./ and to iiii schrynez above \iiii s./ and to Seynte Audres hedd and reliques \xx d./ … vii s. iiii d.

Cambrige.[20] Saturdaye. … Item payde for the dyet*es* of Richarde Schurley w*ith* ix p*er*sons by iii days at m*aster* Cottons housse … vii s. v d.

Item[21] payde for ii oun*cez* of Seynt Audrez lacez for my lad*ys* grace … iii s.

Item payde for horsse mete for xiii grete horssex and ix hakneys … xvii s. vi d.

Item for the batynge of the horssez at Ely … xii d.

[M]Summa totalis … vi li. xiiii d.[P]

[20] Preceded by 'R'.

[21] Preceded by 'A'.

[*p. 37*] *Cambrige*. Sondaye. Item payde to Henry Coke for fuell in the kechyn and for fuell in my ladys chamb*er* and for my ladye Braye at Brandon ferrey … xviii d.

Item for wyne vynagur and vergus to seth my ladys fysshe … iiii d. ob.

Mondaye. Item payd in a rewarde to the wife of the housse where my ladys grace was logged … xx s.

Item delyv*er*de to my ladye to hir owen hond*es* to hir pursse … x s.

Huntyngdon. Item payde for a cheyne of golde to John <Lybarde> \payde/. Price … iiii li. x s.

Item payde to doctur Smyth reder in my ladys lectur in Cambrige for his terme ended at Lammasse last passed … l s.

Item payde to master Palm*er* for the wrytynge of the workez of master Chubbis for ii termez ended at mydsom*er* last … xl s.

Item to s*ir* Thomas Colman of Gregory Hostell the quenez skoller and my \ladys/ for his haulffe yerez exibyc*io*n ended at Mychelmasse <las> next co*m*mynge … xiii s. iiii d.

Item payde for a rewarde sent to mastres Sand by Bulst[ro]de[22] … xiii s. iiii d.

Item payde for the dyet*es* of Richarde Schurley w*ith* ix p*er*sons by ii days at Cambrige … vii s. x d.

Item payde for horsse mete for xiii grete horssez and viii hakneys … xviii s. viii d.

Tewysdaye. Item payde John Walter for his jo*ur*neynge into Lankyschire to my lorde and to other placez by a bill signed … xxi s. iii d.

Peturborough. Wedynsdaye. … Item payde for the dyetez of Richarde Schurley w*ith* ix p*er*sons at Huntyngdon by ii days … viii s. x d.

Item payde for horsse mete for xiii grete horssez and viii hakneys … xviii s. viii d.

Thursedaye. Item payde … nichil

Colyweston. Frydaye. Item payde for the dyet*es* of R[i]charde Schurley w*ith* iiii p*er*sons by ii days at Peturborowe … ii s. iiii d.

Item for horsse mete for iii litt*er* horssez and ii hakneys … iiii s. ii d.

[M]Summa totalis …xvj li. v s. iii d. ob.[P]

[*p. 38*] *Colyweston*. Sondaye. Item payde to Bestyan <muskel> Musteka broderer for broderynge of portkullys and <west> branchez of rosez by a bill signed … x li. v s.

Item payde in a rewarde to hym for his costez to Colyweston … vi s. viii d.

Mondaye. Item payde in a rewarde to a s*er*vante of my lorde marques for bryngynge a message unto my ladys grace … vi s. viii d.

Tewysdaye. Item payde in a rewarde to a s*er*vante of my lorde Wellis for bryngynge of a horsse unto my ladis grace … xx s.

[22] MS 'Bulstorde'.

Wedynsdaye. Item payde in a rewarde to Whitynge gentylman ussher of the kyngez chamb*er* … x s.

Item payde in a rewarde to <a> div*er*se s*er*vantez of my ladye of Northffolke for bryngynge of a p*re*sent to Colyweston … xx s.

Harowdon. Thursedaye. … Item payde in a rewarde to master John Seynt John in his pursse … vi s. viii d.

Item payde for a quarters wagez for his s*er*vante … vi s. viii d.

Item payde in a rewarde to a s*er*vante of my lordys þ*at* brought letturs unto my ladys grace unto Colyweston … iii s. iiii d.

Item payde to my lady Braye for a rewarde to Pers Barb*ur* … vi s. viii d.

Item payde to hir for a rewarde gewen to Nycholas Clyff … vi s. viii d.

Item payde to hir for a rewarde gewen to Fauldrynge … vi s. viii d.

Item payde <f> to hir for that scho hadde leyde oute for my ladys grace for other thyngez … xx s.

Item payde to on that caried a peyre of organs from Seynt Albons to Colyweston and for other necessary for theyme and for his dyet*es* as it apperyth by a bill signed … iii li. v s. vi d.

Item payde in a rewarde to Petur of Coldherberd for his diligence <d> to delyv*er* bok*es* at Colyweston … xiii s. iiii d.

Northampton. Frydaye. Item payde for the dyet*es* of Richard Schurley w*ith* xi p*er*sons at Harowden by ii melys … iiii s. viii d.

Item for horsse mete for xiiii doubull horssez and x hakneys … ix s. xi d.

Item payde for my ladys offerrynge at oure Ladye of Grace … v s.

Item payde in a rewarde to a pore man that brought my lady grapez … xii d.

Ochecott. Saturdaye. … Item payde for the dyet*es* of Richard Schurley with xi p*er*sons at Northampton by ii days … vii s. vi d.

Item payde for horsse mete for xiiii grete horssez and ix hakneys the same tyme at Northampton by ii days … xvii s.

[M]Summa totalis …xxii li. viii s.. xi d.[P]

[*p. 39*] *Ochecott*. Sondaye. Item payde in a rewarde to John Kynge my ladys s*er*vante … vi s. viii d.

Mondaye. Item payde to Thomas Philippez for rydynge about Cromers maners and other tymez by a bill signed … vi s. viii d.

Tewysdaye. Item payde … nichil

Banburye. Wedynsdaye. Item payde for the dyetes of Richarde Schurley with xi persons at Ochecote by iiii days … ix s. iiii d.

Item for horsse mete for xiiii grete horssez and viii hakneys the same tyme by iiii days … xxxi s.

Wodstok. Thursedaye. … Item payde for the dyet*es* of Richarde Schurley w*ith* a xi p*er*sons at Banbury by ii melys … iii s. xi d.

Item for horsse mete for xiiii grete horssez and viii hakneys … viii s. iii d.

Item payde in a rewarde to mastres Grewell at Banburye … vi s. viii d.

Frydaye. Item payde for the dyet*es* of Roberde Schurley at Wodstok by ii melys dep*ar*tynge into Lyncolneschire to Lyndsey … iii s. v d.

Item for horsse mete for xiiii grete and ix hakneys þe same tyme … ix s. vi d.

Item for xxix horsse shone \iii s. x d./ DCC nayle \ii s. viii d./ … vi s. iiii d.

Item for xvi lib. of here for the sadell*es* … xv d.

Item for a gravell for the litt*er* horsse … vi d.

Shoyng. Saturdaye. Item payde to master Talbott for rydynge w*ith* his iii[23] horses from Peturborow to Wodestok by vii days rydynge his owen horsse at v d. and þe other at iiii d. and for iiii days stondynge his owen horsse at iiii d. and the other at iii d. his s*er*vantez dyet*es* xi days at iiii d. schoynge \viii d./ … xv s. iii d.

Item payde to m*aster* Denman for rydynge w*ith* his doubull horsse and ii hakneys from Wauleshyngham to Wodstoke by xiiii days at v d. his doubull horsse and iiii d. þe hakney and for viii days stondyngez his doubull horsse at iiii d. þe hakney at iii d. his s*er*vantez dyet*es* by the seyde xxii days at iiii d. schoynge \viii d./ … xxix s. x d.

Item payde to master amner rydynge by xiiii days w*ith* ii horssez at iiii d. þe horsse and for viii days stondynge at iii d. þe horsse his s*er*vantez dyet*es* by xxii days at iiii d. schoynge \vi d./ … xxi s. ii d.

MSumma totalis …xxii li. viii s. xi d.P

[*p. 40*] Item payde to master secretorye for rydynge w*ith* his ii horssez by xiiii days at iiii d. a horsse and for viii days stondyng at iii d. þe horsse and his s*er*vantez dyet*es* by xxii days at iiii d. schoynge \vi d./ … xxi s. ii d.

Item payde to doctur Fell for rydynge w*ith* his ii horssez the same tyme by xiiii days and for viii days stondynge his s*er*vant*es* dyet*es* by xxii days at iiii d. schoynge \vi d./ … xxi s. iiii d.

Item payde to Olyv*er* Seynt John for his horsse mete by xxvii[24] days rydynge from London to Wauleshyngham and so to Wodstok and for iii wek*es* stondynge for on horsse and his s*er*vantez dyet*es* by xxvii days schoynge \vi d./ … xxx s.[25] ii d.

Item payde to Varney for rydynge w*ith* his iii horssez by þe seyde xiiii days \xiiii s./ and for viii days stondynge \vi s./ his s*er*vantez dyet*es* by xxii days \vii s. iiii d./ schoynge \ viii d./ … xxviii s.

[23] 'hor' add. but not canc.
[24] MS 'xxvjj'.
[25] Alt. from 'xix s.'.

Item payde to Roger Ormeston for rydynge w*ith* his ii horssez by xiiii days \ix s. iiii d./ and for viii days stondyngez \iiii s./ his s*er*vantez dyet*es* by xxii days \vii s. iiii d./ schoynge \xii d./ … xxi s. viii d.

Item payde to me for rydynge w*ith* iii horssez by xiiii days \xiiii s./ and for viii days stondynge \vi s./ my s*er*vantez dyet*es* by xxii days \vii s. iiii d./ schoynge \x d./ … xxviii s. ii d.

Item payde to Richarde Kylt and John Walter for rydynge w*ith* there iii horssez by xiiii days (\xiiii s./ and for viii days stondynge \vi s./ theire s*er*vantez dyet*es* by xxii days \vii s. iiii d./ \vi d./ … xxvii s. x d.

Schoynge.[26]

Item payde John Leche and Raffe Schurley for rydynge w*ith* iii horssez by xiiii days and for viii days stondynge theire s*er*vantez dyet*es* by xxii days schoynge \x d./ … xxviii s. ii d.

Item payde to John Fysshe and Laurence Canwyk for iii horssez by xiiii days rydynge and viii days stondynge there s*er*vantez dyet*es* by xxii days schoynge \viii d./ … xxviii s.

Item payde to Richarde Cheke and Mylez Worseley for rydynge w*ith* iii hors*es* by xiiii days and for viii days stondynge theire s*er*vantez dyet*es* by xxii days schoynge \viii d./ … xxviii s.

Item payde to Will*ia*m Pole and Roberde Smyth for rydynge w*ith* iii horssez by xiiii days and for viii days stondynge theire s*er*vantez dyet*es* by xxii days schoynge \viii d./ … xxviii s.

Item payde to Henry Coke and Osmunde Nott for rydynge w*ith* iii horssez by xiiii days and for viii days stondynge theire s*er*vantez dyet*es* by xxii days schoynge \viii d./ … xxviii s.

Item payde to Roger Kardon and Chr*ist*offer Richardson for rydynge w*ith* theire iii horssez by xiiii days and viii days stondyng theire s*er*vantez dyet*es* by xxii days schoynge \x d./ wheroff a bate for Chr*ist*offer for viii days rydynge and iiii stondynge … xxiiii s. vi d.

[*p. 41*] Item payde to George Frauncez for rydynge before to make redy my ladys loggengez from Wauleshyngham to Wodstok w*ith* ii horssez by xxii days at xvi d. þe day … xxix s. iiii d.

Item payde to Will*ia*m Adtherton a grome rydynge w*ith* hym by þe seyde xxii days w*ith* on horsse at viii d. … xiiii s. viii d.

Item to Thomas Philippez for rydynge to make redy loggynge for my ladys s*er*vantez and horssez by xxii days at xii d. … xxii s.

Item payde to Roberd Edlyn Will*ia*m Thomson Mousse and Nicholas Cotton by xiii days goynge w*ith* my ladys stuffe and to Roberde Hilton also at vi d. þe man a daye … xxxii s. vi d.

[26] Written in margin alongside 'vi d.' above.

Item payde to John Love for goynge w*ith* my ladys stuffe from Colyweston to Wodstoke by v days at vi d. … ii s. vi d.

Item payde to Edwarde Heven for rydynge from Ochecote to Wodstok by ii days and a daye stondynge … xi d.

Item payde to John Leche for rydynge from Colyweston to Hyntyngdon at div*er*se tymez and to Cambrige for wyne for the kynge by vi days … vi s.

Item payde to the ii fotemen <ryd> runnynge w*ith* my ladys grace by xiii days at iiii d. þe man … viii s. viii d.

Item payde to the ii litt*er* men for theire drynkyngez by the wey by xiii days at ii d. the man … iiii s. iiii d.

[M]Summa totalis …xxix li. iii s. v d.[P]

[*p. 42*] *Wodstoke*. Sondaye. Item payde in a rewarde to <my> the gardener of Wodstoke that gaffe my ladys grace a hounde … iii s. iiii d.

Item payde in a rewarde to a woman that brought my ladys grace a p*re*sent of fysshe … xx d.

Mondaye. Item payde for a D guylt nayle to mend my ladys litt*er* … ii s. vi d.

Item payde for the costez of the saddeler \ii d./ feachynge the[27] same nayle at Oxfforde and for his horsse mete at Wodstok by iii days \ix d./ … xi d.

Item payde in a rewarde to the same saddeler for his waytynge upon my ladys stuffe all the last jo*ur*ney … x s.

Item payde in a rewarde to a clerke of the p*re*vey seale for a p*re*vey seale for a warde of my ladys in Devonshyre … iii s. iiii d.

Tewysdaye. Item payde in a rewarde to my ladye Harryngton that was borowed of s*ir* Richarde Pudsey … xl s.

Item payde in a rewarde to Mewtys the kyngez Frensshe secretorye … xl s.

Wedynsdaye. Item payde in a rewarde to Richemonde the harowde for his costez goynge into Fraunce upon my ladys message … v li.

Thursedaye. Item payde in a rewarde to the chaunceler of Lyncolnes s*er*vante for bryngynge of a licence for the devyne service to be hadde at Colyweston in my ladys chapell … iii s. iiii d.

Item payde for the exibyc*io*n of John Fawne my ladys skoller at Oxfforde as it apperyth by a bill signed … xix s. ix d. qua.

Frydaye. Item payde in a rewarde to doctur Wylforde my ladys reder in devenyte at Oxfforde … vi s. viii d.

Saturdaye. Item payde to the kyngez amner for the costez for the forseyde John Fawne for his exibyc*io*n … xx s.

[M]Summa totalis …xii li. xi s. vii d. i qua.[P]

[27] 'the' rep.

[*p. 43*] Sondaye. My[c]helmasse[28] daye. Item payde for the dyet*es* of iii horsse kep*ers* by v melys at Wodstoke co*m*mynge from lyverey from Stratton Awdeley <by> for to goo w*ith* my ladys grace to Langeley … ii s. vi d.

Item payde for horsse mete for v grete horssez and a hakney by ii days etc. … vi s. viii d.

Mondaye. Item payde to Henrye Coke for smale fysshes butt*ur* and egges for my ladys grace by a bill signed … iiii s. xi d.

Tewysdaye. Item payde in a rewarde to a s*er*vante of the p*r*ior of Lantony for bryngynge of chessez unto my ladys grace … iii s. iiii d.

We<n>dynsdaye. Item payde for the dyet*es* of iii p*er*sons w*ith* theire drynkyns at Langeley by ii <melys> days … xx d.

Item payde for horsse mete for v grete horsses and a hakney by the seyde ii days … vi s. iii d.

Thurssdaye. Item payde for the dyet*es* of iii p*er*sons at Wodstok co*m*mynge from Langley for ii melys … xiii d.

Item payde for horsse mete for v grete horsses and a hakney the same tyme … ii s. vi d.

Item payde for pynnes for the litt*er* \i d./ and for schoynge \ii d./ … iii d.

Frydaye. Item payde to master Denman rydynge w*ith* my ladys grace from Wodstok to Langley by a day and a daye lyenge there and for anoder daye to Wodstok ayen and there a daye stondynge w*ith* his grete horsse and ii hakneys at v d. þe grete horsse and iii d. the other ii a pece that is to sey ii days rydynge \ii s. ii d./ and for ii days stondynge \xx d./ his s*er*vantez dyet*es* by iiii days \xvi d./ schoynge \iii d./ … v s. vi d.

Item payde to master amner for rydynge the same tyme w*ith* ii horssez by ii days \xvi d./ and for ii days stondynge \xii d./ his s*er*vantez dyet*es* by iiii days \xvi d./ … iii s. viii d.

Item payde to master secretorye for rydynge the same tyme with his ii horssez by ii days \xvi d./ and for ii days stondynge \xii d./ his s*er*vantez dyet*es* by iiii days \xvi d./ … iii s. viii d.

Item payde to doctur Fell for his rydynge w*ith* ii horssez by ii days \xvi d./ and for ii days stondynge \xii d./ his s*er*vantez dyet*es* by iiii days \xvi d./ … iii s. viii d.

[*p. 44*] Item payde to Richarde Kylt and John Leche for theire iii horssez rydynge unto Langley and ayen unto Wodstoke by ii days rydynge \ii s./ and for ii days stondynge \xviii d./ theire s*er*vantez dyet*es* by iiii days \xvi d./ … iiii s. x d.

Item payde <for> to Richarde Cheke and Mylez Worseley for rydynge the same tyme by ii days w*ith* iii horssez \ii s./ and for ii days stondynge \xviii d./ theire s*er*vantez dyet*es* þe seyde iiii days \xvi d./ … iiii s. x d.

[28] MS 'Mythelmasse'. The Sunday (30 September) was the day after Michaelmas.

Item payde unto Laurence Canwyke and Henrye Coke for theire iii horssez the same tyme \ii s./ and for ii days stondynge \xviii d./ theire *ser*vantez dyet*es* by iiii days \xvi d./ … iiii s. x d.

Item payde unto Will*ia*m Pole and Roberde Smyth for theire iii horssez by ii days rydynge \ii s./ and for ii days stondynge \xviii d./ and for theire *ser*vantez dyet*es* by þe seyde iiii days \xvi d./ … iiii s. x d.

Item payde to Roger Kardon and to Raffe Schurley for rydynge w*ith* iii horssez by ii days \ii s./ and for ii days stondynge \xviii d./ theire *ser*vantez dyet*es* by iiii days \xvi d./ … iiii s. x d.

Item payde for the costez of my *ser*vant*e* w*ith* on horsse by ii days rydynge \viii d./ and for ii days stondynge \vi d./ … xiiii d.

Item payde to George Frauncez rydynge before to make redy <[…]> my ladys loggynges fyrst at Cornebury and then my ladys grace kam not there by ii days and so to Langley by ii days before w*ith* ii horssez at xvi d. a daye \v s. iiii d./ and a daye rydynge ayen to Wodstok \viii d./ and there a daye stondynge \vi d./ his *ser*vantez dyet*es* þe seyde ii days \viii d./ … vii s. ii d.

Item payde to Will*ia*m Adthirton grome rydynge the same tyme by[29] v days as well to Cornebury to Langley and to Wodstok ayen at viii d. a daye … iii s. iiii d.

Item payde to John Fysshe rydynge the same tyme before to make loggyngez as well for my ladys *ser*vantez as hir horssez by iii days to <Langley> \Cornebury/ and iii days to Langley at xii d. a daye … vi s.

Item payde to Roberd Edlyn Mouse Nicholas Cotton Will*ia*m Thomson Roberd Hylton by ii days goynge w*ith* my ladys stuffe at vi d. by þe day þe man … v s.

Item payde to Nycholas of Aughton and Richarde Karr*e* fotemen for ii days runnynge at iiii d. a day … xvi d.

Item payde for ii peire of schone for theyme … xii d.

[*p. 45*] Saturdaye. Item payde to my ladye Braye for a rewarde gewen to Mountney my ladys *ser*vante … xii s. iiii d.

Item payde in a rewarde to a *ser*vante of my lorde <m*ar*ques> m*ar*ques that brought word of the delyv*er*ance of my ladye his wiffe … x s.

Item payde in a rewarde to a *ser*vante of the proctur*es* of the charterhousse in London … iii s. iiii d.

Item payde in a rewarde to John Gryse … vi s. viii d.

Item payde in a rewarde to Thomas Flewde a synger … xx s.

Item payde in a rewarde to Pers Champyon … xx s.

Item payde in a rewarde to the abbas of Godstow … xx s.

Item payde in a rewarde to my ladye Jane Bougham housbonde … vi s. viii d.

[29] 'by' rep.

Item payde in a rewarde to Jaques Haute … vi s. viii d.

Item payde in a rewarde to mastres Grewell … vi s. viii d.

Item payde in a rewarde the ancrer … xx d.

[M]Summa totalis …x li. ix s. x d.[P]

[*p. 46*] Sondaye. Item payde in a rewarde to Richarde Carr goynge to London … iii s. iiii d.

Item payde to doctur Edmonde Wilsforde my ladys red*er* in divinite in Oxfforde for his haulffe yeres w[a]ges endynge at Mychelmasse last passed … x li. xiii s. iiii d.

Mondaye. Item payde unto div*er*se of my ladys s*er*vantez for theire wages endynge at Mychelmas last passed that is to sey to master Denman for his haulffe yeres wages \x li./ to Roger Ormeston \xxiii s. iiii d./ to Will*ia*m Hylm*er* \xl s./ to Hew Latym*er* \xx s./ to Richarde Stewkley \xx s./ the laundur \xx s./ … xvi li. xiii s. iiii d.

Item payde to John Brownnynge for his quarters wages … x s.

Item payde unto Richarde Dawson for his quarters wages … v s.

Item payde to other div*er*se of my ladys s*er*vantez for theire quarters wages and for theire horsse lyverey that is to sey to me for my quarters wages \xvi s. viii d./ and for my iii horsse lyverey \viii s. iiii d./ … xxv s.

Item also payde to me for iii quarters wages after x m*a*rke the whiche my ladys grace gaffe me at Chr*ist*emasse last passed the whiche aminteth above the olde wagez afore reherced for <rehe> þe seyde iii quarters … l s.

Item payde to George Frauncez for his quarters wagez \x s./ and for his horsse lyverey \vi s. viii d./ … xvi s. viii d.

Item payde to John Leche for his quarters wages \x s./ and for his horsse lyverey the seyde space \vi s. viii d./ … xvi s. viii d.

Item payde unto Richarde Schurley for his quarters wagez \x s./ and for his horsse lyverey \vi s. viii d./ … xvi s. viii d.

Item payde to Will*ia*m Pole for his quarters wagez \x s./ and for his horsse lyverey \vi s. viii d./ … xvi s. viii d.

Item payde to Laurence Canwyck for his quarters wagez \x s./ and for his horsse lyverey \vi s. viii d./ … xvi s. viii d.

Item payde to Will*ia*m Whytyngton for his <q> wagez \(x s./ and for his horsse lyvery \vi s. viii d./ … xvi s. viii d.

Item payde to Henrye Clegg for his <haulffe yer> quarters yerez wagez \x s./ and for his horsse lyverey \vi s. viii d./ … xvi s. viii d.

Item payde to John Walt*er* for his <haulffe ye>re quarter wagez \x s./ and for his horsse lyverey \vi s. viiii d./ … xvi s. viii d.

[*p. 47*] Item payde Henry Coke for his <haulffe yeres> wagez \x s./ and for his horsse lyverey for a quarter … xvi s. viii d.

Item payde to Osmunde Nott for his quarters wagez \x s./ and for his horsse lyverey \vi s. viiii d./ … xvi s. viii d.

Item payde to Roberde Smyth for his quarters wagez \x s./ and for his horsse lyverey \vi s. viii d./ … xvi s. viii d.

Item payde unto Chr*ist*offer R[i]chardson for his quarters wagez \x s./ and for his horsse lyverey \vi s. viii d./ … xvi s. viii d.

Item payde to Raffe Schurley for his quarters wagez \x s./ and for his horsse lyverey \vi s. viii d./ … xvi s. viii d.

Item payde to Thomas Philippes for his quarters wagez \x s./ and for his horsse lyverey \vi s. viii d./ … xvi s. viii d.

Item payde to Roger Kardon for his quarters wagez \x s./ and for his horsse lyverey \vi s. viii d./ … xvi s. viii d.

Item payde unto Portkullys for his quarters wagez \x s./ and for his horsse lyverey \vi s. viii d./ … xvi s. viii d.

Item payde to Richarde Cheke for his quarters wagez \x s./ and for his horsse lyverey \vi s. viii d./ … xvi s. viii d.

Item payde to Mylez Worseley for his quarters wagez \x s./ and for his horsse lyverey \vi s. viii d./ … xvi s. viii d.

Item payde to the gromes for theire quarters wagez that is to sey to Chr*ist*offer Bygom \v s./ Will*i*am Adthirton \v s./ Robertt Edlyn \v s./ Will*i*am Thomson \v s./ Richarde Mouse \v s./ Nicholas Cotton \v s./ Nicholas of Aughton \v s./ Richarde Carr \v s./ John Love \v s./ and for his workmanship as a skynner Robert Hilton \v s./ … lv s.[30]

<Tewysdaye. Item delyv*er*id money for the houssolde fyrst to Richarde Gough <Clr> clerke of the kechyn … xxvi li. xiii s. iiii d.>

Item delyv*er*id unto m*aster* controller at on tyme in London … xiiii li. vi s. viii d.

Item delyv*er*id for xii tonne of wyne to <Sche> Stephen Bulle at v li. the tonne … lx li.

Item payde to Mark Cristen my ladys servant for malmeseye … iiii li. vi s. viii d.

Item delyv*er*id unto John Kynge my ladys s*er*vante … xl s.

Item delyv*er*id unto Hugh Latym*er* my ladys s*er*vante … xx li.

Item delyv*er*id to viii weyne men in a prest for cariage … liii s. iiii d.

Item delyv*er*id unto John Kynge anoder tyme at London … xxv s. viii d.

Item payde unto John Leche for a remanent of malmesey and for lodynge and hevynge þe seid wyne by his bill … xlii s. xi d.>

[30] The rest of the page is crossed through and not entirely legible.

[*p. 48*] Wedynsdaye. Item payde unto the cofferer of the kynges housse for þat he leyde out <m> money for the charges at the kynges beynge at Colyweston w*ith*out div*er*se p*ro*vysyo*u*n of my ladys owen store ... lxxii li. iii s. i d.

Thursedaye. Item payde to my ladys owen hondez for juell*es* that is to sey <of> rynges <beddes> bedes of golde and other thynges bought of a Frensshe man ... x li. xiii s. iiii d.

Frydaye. Item payde in a rewarde to John Collop my ladys arras mender ... iii s. iiii d.

Saturdaye. Item payde in a rewarde to the p*r*ior of the charterhouse of Hentons s*er*vante for bryngynge of a wylde bore to my ladys grace ... vi s. viii d.

<PSumma totalis ... CClxx li. xi s. viii d. «Ista summa est indiritta»>

PCxxix li. <x>viii s. i d.[31]

[*p. 49*] Sondaye. Item payde to Hugh Latymer for his borde wages and for rydynge for thredde hokk*es* and for borde wagez for a arrow maker w*ith* other thyngez by a bill signed ... iii li. v s. viii d.

Item payde to Olyv*er* Seynt John for his horsse lyverey and for his s*er*vantez dyet*es* by a bill signed ... xxix s. iii d.

Mondaye. Item payde for the exibycon of Richarde Burgon that lerneth at Oxfforde by a byll signed ... xxix s. iii d.

Item payde to William Sandes for the costez of Jone Osborne w*ith* hir borde wages as it apperyth by a bill ... xlvi s. ii d.

Item delyvered unto m*aster* controller for my ladys housolde ... xx li.

Tewysdaye. Item payde to Laurence Canwyke for the costes havynge yonge master Park*er* to Ludlow and hymselffe ayen and for rydynges into other*e* placez on[32] my ladys messagez by his bill signed ... xxviii s. viii d.

Wedynsdaye. Item payde for CCC and a haulffe of powderynges for my ladys bonett pric*e* þe hundreth xiiii d. ... iiii s. i d.

Item payde for a quarter of white cloth for þe same bonett ... ii s.

Thursedaye. Item payde for the dyet*es* of iii horsse kepers kepynge my ladys horsses at Stratton Awdley by iii wekez at xii d.a weke ... ix s.

Item payde for the borde wagez of a sadeler there by a weke ... xii d.

Item payde for hey and litt*er* for vi horssez for xxi[ti] days at ii d. daye and nyght ... xxi s.

Item payde for hey and litt*er* for the sadelers horsse by vii days ... xiiii d.

Item payde for p*ro*vendur for the seyde horssez by iii wek*es* ... x s.

[31] The original sum ('CClxx li. xi s. viii d.') included the entries canc. p. 47 and, although originally marked 'probatur', is now itself canc.The corrected sum is written before 'Summa totalis' in the same hand as the Latin annotation (and also marked 'probatur'. Neither sum is exactly correct.
[32] Written over alteration.

Item payde to Richarde Schurley for his costez w*ith* iii p*er*sons for horsse mete and mannys mete for havynge my ladys horsse from Wodstok to Depynge and comynge ayen to Wodstok as it apperyth by his bill*es* … xxxiii s. vii d.

Item payde in a rewarde to mastres Jane … xx s.

Item payde in a rewarde to mastres Varney at hir dep*ar*tynge from þe court to Colyweston … xx s.

Item payde in a rewarde to mastres Lacye … x s.

Item payde in a rewarde to mastres Elnore Jonez … xv s.

Item payde in a rewarde to mastres Lee … vi s. viii d.

Item payde in a rewarde to mastres Brent … vi s. viii d.

Item in a rewarde to El[i]zabeth Frauncez … vi s. viii d.

[*p. 50*] Frydaye. Item payde in a rewarde to Wyndsore the harowde … x s.

Item payde in a rewarde to the offycers of the kyngez housse at my ladys dep*ar*tynge to Colyweston … xxvi li. xiii s. iiii d.

Item payde in a rewarde to the kyngez chamb*er* … x li.

Item payde in a rewarde to the quenes chamb*er* … vi li. xiii s. iiii d.

Item payde in a rewarde to the porters … xx s.

Item payde in a rewarde to cart takers … vi s. viii d.

xlv li. iiii s.[33]

Item payde for loggynges for div*er*se of my ladys s*er*vantez at Wodstok for xii beddes by iiii wekez … xxiiii s.

Item payde in a rewarde to m*aster* John Jakson a skoller of my ladys in Oxfforde … vi s. viii d.

Item payde in a rewarde to Roberde Bewley of Brystow … iii s. iiii d.

Item payde for the dyet*es* of Will*iam* Mychell with a xi p*er*sonez at Wodstok by ii melys dep*ar*tynge to Banburye … ii s. vi d.

Item payde for horsse mete for xxi grete horssez and viii hakneys by a daye and nyght … ix s.

Banburye. Item payde for master John Seynt Johns ii horssez theire mete … ix d.

Saturdaye. Item payde in a rewarde to the quenes fotemen … v s.

Item payde in a rewarde to Clement grome of the kynges chamb*er* … v s.

Item payde in a rewarde to a woman þat kam from Cambryge … ii s. iiii d.

Item payde for horsse mete for xxi grete horssez and viii hakneys by a nyght … xi s. vi d.

[33] The (incorrect) total of the six items above, bracketed to the right of the items.

Item payde for fuel and candell*es* … vi d.

Item payde in a rewarde to a woman that brought my ladys grace flowres to hir litt*er* … viii d.

Northampton. Item payde for my ladys offerrynge at the rode … ii s. vi d.

[34]Item payde for hir offerrynge at oure Ladye of Grace … v s.

[M]Summa totalis …iiii^{xx}viii li. ii s. i d.[P]

[*p. 51*] *Northampton.* Sondaye. Item payde in a rewarde to a woman that brought my ladys grace a rolle of preyers … ii s.

Item payde <in a R> for the dyet*es* of Will*i*am Danyell yoman of the charyett and for the grome of the same co*m*mynge from Colyweston to Northampton … x d.

Item for his dyet*es* and his felowys in North[a]mpton … vi d.

Item payde for horsse mete for xxvi grete horssez and ix hakneys by a nyght … xv s. xi d.

Item payde to the ferrer for l^{ti} schone there … iiii s. xi d.

Item payde for DCCC nayle … ii s. viii d.

Item payde for a brusshe … iiii d.

Keterynge. Mondaye. Item payde in a rewarde to a *ser*vante of my <ladys> lady Vauses for bryngynge of flaggons of wyne … xx d.

Item payde for horsse mete for xxvii^{ti} horssez and viii hakneys by a nyght … xv s. xi d.

Item payde for schon for þe horsses \x d./ and for CC nayle \viii d./ … xviii d.

Colyweston. Tewysdaye. Item payde to Richarde Schurley for xviii pownde of waxe and for serynge of the cloth for þe litt*er* at vi d. þe lib. … ix s.

Wedynsdaye. Item payde to master Talbott for jo*ur*neynge w*ith* his doubull horsse and ii hakneys by iiii days rydynge and a daye stondynge after his doubull v d. a daye \xx d./ his hakneys at iiii d. a pece \ii s. viii d./ and for stondynge iiii d. for doubull horsse and his hakneys iii d. \vi d./ þe horsse schoynge \x d./ … vi s. <ii d.>

Item payde to m*aster* Denman for his <h> rydynge the same tyme for his doubull by iiii days \xx/ and a daye stondynge \iiii d./ and for his ii hakneys by iiii days rydynge \ii s. viii d./ and for a daye stondynge after \vi d./ schoynge \viii d./ … v s. x d.

Item payde to doctur*e* Fell for his jo*ur*neynge w*ith* ii horssez <at> by iiii days \ii s. viii d./ and for on daye stondynge \vi d./ … iii s. ii d.

Item payde to master secretorye for rydynge w*ith* his ii horssez by iiii days \ii s. viii d./ and for a daye stondynge \vi d./ … iii s. ii d.

Item payde <for> to master <Ame> amner*e* for rydynge w*ith* his ii horsses the same tyme by iiii days \ii s. viii d./ and for a daye stondynge \vi d./ … iii s. ii d.

[34]This entry add. in darker ink in the same hand.

[*p. 52*] Item payde <for> to Roger Ormeston for rydynge the same tyme w*ith* his iii horsses for iiii days \iiii s./ and for a daye stondynge after \ix d./ … iiii s. ix d.

Item payde to me for my iii horsses rydynge the same tyme by iiii days \iiii s./ and for a daye stondynge \ix d./ … iiii s. ix d.

Item payde to Raffe Varney for his jo*ur*neynge w*ith* iii horsses by iiii days \iiii s./ and for a daye stondynge after \ix d./ … iiii s. ix d.

Item payde to Henry Bygott for his costez comynge from his housse to Wodstok by iii days w*ith* iii horsses at viii d. a daye man and horsse … vi s.

Item payde to hym for a daye lyenge at Wodstok w*ith* his seyde iii horssez after iii d. the horsse \ix d./ his s*er*vantez dyet*es* by a daye \iiii d./ and for rydynge by iiii days <from> \to/ <Cl> Colyweston from Wodstok w*ith* my ladys gr*ace* w*ith* his iii horssez \iiii s./ and for a daye stondynge after \ix d./ … v s. x d.

Item payde unto Clement for his co*m*mynge from London to Wodstoke by ii days w*ith* ii horssez … <xvi d.> ii s. viii d.

Item payde unto hym for <for> rydynge w*ith* his ii horssez by [*blank*] from Wodstok unto Colyweston by iiii days \ii s. viii d./ and for a daye stondynge after \vi d./ … iii s. ii d.

Item payde unto Strangquysshe for his rydynge w*ith* ii horssez fro Wodstok to Colyweston by iiii days \ii s. viii d./ and for a daye stondynge after \vi d./ … iii s. ii d.

Item payde to hym for the costez of John Seynt John for horsse mete and mannys mete as it apperyth by a byll … v s. iiii d.

Item payde to master John my ladys coke for his co*m*mynge fro Seynt Albons to Wodstoke w*ith* ii horssez by ii days \ii s. viii d./ and for rydynge before by a daye from Wodestok to Banburye \xvi d./ and for iii days to Colyweston w*ith* my ladys grace w*ith* ii horssez \ii s./ and for a daye stondynge after \vi d./ schoynge \vi d./ … vii s.

Item payde to Richarde Kylt and John Leche for iiii days rydynge from Wodstoke to Colyweston w*ith* iii horssez \iiii s./ and for a daye after \ix d./ … iiii s. ix d.

Item payde unto Edwarde Heven and Raffe Schurley for rydynge the same tyme by iiii days w*ith* iii horssez \iiii s./ and for a daye stondynge \ix d./ … iiii s. ix d.

Item payde to Will*iam* Whittyngton and Thomas Chattoke for iiii days rydynge the same tyme \iiii s./ and for a daye stondynge \ix d./ … iiii s. ix d.

Item payde unto Mountney for rydynge the same tyme w*ith* his iii horssez by iiii days \ii s. viii d./ and for a daye stondynge \vi d./ … iii s. ii d.

Item payde to John Fysshe and Laurence Canwyke for iii days rydynge w*ith* iii horssez \iiii s./ and for a daye stondynge after \ix d./ … iiii s. ix d.

Item payde to Will*iam* Pole and Roberde Smyth for rydynge the same tyme by iiii days w*ith* iii horssez \iiii s./ and for i daye stondynge \ix d./ … iiii s. ix d.

Item payde unto Richarde Cheke and Myles Worseley for[35] rydynge by iiii days w*ith* iii horssez \iiii s./ and a daye stondynge \ix d./ … iiii s. ix d.

[35] 'for' rep. next l.

Item payde to Henrye Coke and Roger Kardon for iiii days rydynge w*ith* iii horssez \ iiii s./ and for a daye stondynge \ix d./ … iiii s. ix d.

Item payde to John Kynge for iiii days rydynge \xvi d./ and a daye stondynge \iii d./ … xix d.

[*p. 53*] Item payde to George Fraunceż for rydynge w*ith* his ii horssez before by <iiii> v days to make redy my ladys loggynges \vi s. viii d./ and for a daye stondynge after <vi d./ his servantez dyet*es* by a daye iiii d. … vii s. vi d.

Item payde to Will*i*am Adthirton for rydynge w*ith* hym w*ith* on horsse by v days … iii s. iiii d.

Item payde to him for his rydynge upon my ladys message from Colyweston to Cambryge by ii days … xvi d.

Item payde to hym for rumney for my ladys grace … <xvi d.> xi d.

Item payde to hym for a lampe … iii d.

Item payde to Randall Wodd and Henrye Clegg for rydynge before to make redye my ladys s*er*vantez and horssez loggyngez by v days ii horssez … x s.

Item payde unto <the> Roberde Edlyn \ii s./ Mouse \ii s./ Will*i*am Thomson \ii s./ Nicholas Cotton \ii s./ John Bygg \ii s./ by iiii days goynge w*ith* the stuffe … x s.

Item payde to Richarde Karre \xvi d./ and Nicholas of Aughton \xvi d./ for goynge w*ith* my ladys grace by iiii days … ii s. viii d.

Item payde for ii peyre of schone for theyme … xii d.

Item payde to the ii litt*er* men for theire drynkyns att Langley from Wodstok and to Colyweston by vi days … ii s.

Item payde to Roberde Hilton John Love goynge w*ith* the stuffe the next wey from Wodstok to Colyweston by iiii days … ii s.

Item for wauchynge the stuffe … vi d.

Thursdaye. Item payde to Richarde Chek for rydynge to the kinge to Nottley abbey by iii days … ii s.

Frydaye. Item payde to Nicholas of Aughton for a rewarde that he gaffe to a woman that brought appullys to my ladys gr*ace* … xii d.

Saturdaye. Item payde <in a Rewar> to Nicholas of Aughton for rydynge to Burry upon my ladys message by iiii days … ii s. viii d.

[M]Summa …ix li. ix s. ii d.[P]

[*p. 54*] Sondaye. Item payde in a rewarde to a s*er*vante of my lady Nevell*es* … vi s. viii d.

Mondaye. Item payde <ffirst> to James [M]orice[36] clerk of the work*es* of Colyweston for the work*es* and <reparcon> rep*ara*ci*o*ns of the same … xxi li. x s.

[36] MS 'Norice'.

Tewysdaye. Item payde[37] unto master controller at Banburye … x li.

Wedynsdaye. Item payde to Roger Kardon for chamlett wollen cloth lynynge w*ith* other necessary by a bill signed … xli. xviii s. ix d. qua.

Thursedaye. Item payde to <Hugh Calkott>[38] the balyffe of Colyweston for wodde for my ladys housse … xiiii li.

Frydaye. Item payde for my ladys offerynge upon All Hallowen day … v s.

Saturdaye. Item payde in a rewarde to master Chubbys … x s.

[M P3]Summa …lvi li. x s. v d. qua.

[*p. 55*] Sondaye. Item payde to master Bekensale for his exibycon at Cambryge … xxvi s. viii d.

Mondaye. Item payde to Nicholas of Aughton for his costez rydynge to my lorde of Dyrham by my ladys co*m*maundement … xiii s. iiii d.

Tewysdaye. Item payde in a rewarde to Olyv*er* Seynt John … xl s.

Wedynsdaye. Item payde to Richarde Cheke for his jo*ur*neynge to the kinge by ix days … vi s.

Thursedaye. Item payde in a rewarde to Frye the kyngez s*er*vante … xxvi s. viii d.

Frydaye. Item payde in a rewarde to a woman that brought my ladys grace a fawne … iii s. iiii d.

Saturdaye. Item payde in a rewarde to a pore man of Waulessyngham … xii d.

Item payde to doctur Smyth my ladys reder in Cambryge for his quarters wagez endynge at All Hallowen tyde last … l s.

Item payde to Will*i*am Hylmer for div*er*se necessar*es* for my ladys gr[a]ce by a bill signed … xii s.

[M]Summa …viii li. <xviii> s. xix s. [3P 39]

[*p. 56*] Sondaye. Item payde in a rewarde to doctur Chubbys at his dep*ar*tynge … xx s.

Mondaye. Item payde to master Seynt John to bye hym a bowe … ii s. <viii d.> iiii d.

Tewysdaye. Item payde in a rewarde to Dawtre the quenez s*er*vante … iii s. iiii d.

Wedynsdaye. Item payde to s*ir* Hew Assheton for the kepynge of a yonge woman that wul be a nonne … xix s. vi d.

Thurseday. Item payde to Jokye for his costez to Cambryge … vii d.

Frydaye. Item payde in a rewarde to the deane of Lyncolne s*er*vante for bryngynge of iiii fessauntez to my ladys grace … ii s.

[37] 'delyv*er*id' add.

[38] 'to' rep.

[39] The cancellation and addition are in the same ink as 'probatur'.

Item payde in a rewarde to a wiff that brought my ladys grace capons … ii s.

Saturdaye. Item payde to Jamez [M]orice clerke of the work*es* for the rep*ara*c*io*ns at Colyweston … xxviii li. x s.

[M]Summa …xxx li. xix s. ix d.[3P]

[*p. 57*] Sondaye. Item payde in a rewarde to on John Hyll … iii s. iiii d.

Mondaye. Item payde in a rewarde to Norrey the harrowde … vi s. viii d.

Tewysdaye. Item payde in a rewarde to a s*er*vante of doctur Chubbys … xii d.

Wedynsdaye. Item payde in a rewarde to a s*er*vante of þe quenez called John Hollonde … vi s. viii d.

Thursdaye. Item payde in a rewarde to the vyker of Maxsey … xxxiii s. iiii d.

Frydaye. Item payde to Thomas Phylippez for my ladys grace … viii s. iiii d.

Saturdaye. Item payde to a boke prynter for bok*es* for my ladys grace … xvi s.

Item payde to Roger Berell for a dyall … vii s.

Item payde in a rewarde to a s*er*vante of Thomas Amyas for bryngynge of iii chyldren from Tetersale … v s.

Item delyv*er*id unto Richarde Gough clerke of þe kechyn … x l li.

[M]Summa …xliiii li. xi s. viii d.[3P]

[*p. 58*] Sondaye. Item payde in a rewarde to Will*i*am Mychell … x s.

Mondaye. Item payde in a rewarde to a p*r*este that kam from mastres Seynt John … x s.

Tewysdaye. Item payde in a rewarde to master Lathe … vi s. viii d.

Wedynsdaye. Item payde in a rewarde to Dawson … x s.

Thursdaye. Item payde to James <Norice> Morice clerke of the work*es* for the buyldyngez at Colyweston … xxx li.

Frydaye. Item payde in a rewarde to master Lathe … vi s. viii d.

Saturdaye. Item payde in a rewarde to Chr*ist*offer Richardson by my ladys co*m*maundement … xxxiii s. iiii d.

[M]Summa totalis …xxxiii li. <vi s. viii d.> xvi s. viii d.[3P][40]

[*p. 59*] Sondaye. Item payde to my lady Braye for a rewarde gewen unto Coney my lordes s*er*vante … v s.

Item payde unto my seyde lady for a rewarde gewen unto the gromez of the quenez stabull … vi s. viii d.

[40] Corrected in a different hand.

Mondaye. Item payde in a rewarde to George Bekensale … vi s. viii d.

Tewysdaye. Item payde in a rewarde to a s*er*vante of Roger Wales … xx d.

Wedynsdaye. Item in a rewarde to the clerkez on Seynt Nicholas nyght … v s.

Thurssedaye. Item payde to a joyner for ii bordez and ii peyre of trestell*es* … xiii d.

Fryday <o*ur* lady>. Item payde to James Morice clerke of the work*es* at Colyweston for the work*es* of the same … xxxiii li. vi s. viii d.

Saturdaye o*ur* Ladys daye. The Concepcon. Item payde for my ladys offerynge the same daye … v s.

Item payde in a rewarde that my ladys grace gaffe me … iii li. vi s. viii d.

Item payde in a rewarde for my ladye Man*er*s … xx s.

[M]Summa totalis …xxxix li. xvii s. iiii d.[3P]

[*p. 60*] Sondaye. Item payde to Chr*ist*offer Bygom for his horsse mete w*ith* other charges leyde oute by hym by a bill signed … xi s. viii d.

Mondaye. Item payde to Hugh Latymer for wull to make matres for beddez w*ith* other necessar*es* by a bill signed … xx s. iiii d.

Tewysdaye. Item payde in a rewarde to doctur Smyth … x s.

Wedynsdaye. Item payde in a rewarde to doctur*e* Hanson … xx s.

Thursedaye. Item payde in a rewarde to Rowley master s*ir* Edwardes s*er*vante for his syngynge in the chapell … vi s. viii d.

Frydaye. Item payde in a rewarde to on that brought a lettur unto my ladys grace … vi s. viii d.

Saturdaye. Item delyv*er*id to Will*iam* Mychell in a prest … iiii li.

[M]Summa totalis …vii li. xv s. iiii d.[3P]

[*p. 61*] *Colyweston*. Sondaye. Item payde to Water Coke yoman of the bakhouse … v s.

Item payde to Henry Curtas grome of the same by my ladys co*m*mandement … iii s. iiii d.

Item payde to m*aster* Hughe s*er*vante for ridynge upon my ladys message … ii s. vi d.

<Tewysdaye> Mondaye. Item payde to Thomas Whetley skoller of Cambrige for his haulffe yeres exibycon endynge at Chr*ist*emasse next co*m*mynge … xxvi s. viii d.

Tewysdaye. Item payde to John Fawne towarde his exibycon at Cambrige … vi s. viii d.

Wedynsdaye. Item payde in a rewarde to a s*er*vante of the capteyne of Garsey for bryngynge of goweges by master Brays comaundement … xx s.

Thursedaye. Item payde in a rewarde to George Newton that pleyth at oragam … iii s. iiii d.

Frydaye. Item payde to a man that kam from Burry in a rewarde … iii s. iiii d.

Saturdaye. Item payde to James <l> Moryce for the work*es* at Colyweston … xxx li.

Item payde in a rewarde to on that brought a chylde from Lenton abbey … ii s.

Item payde to the deane for wrytynge and settynge of antymys … xvi s. vi d.

[M]Summa totalis …xxxxiiii li. vi s. x d.[P]

[*p. 62*] Sondaye. Item payde on a rewarde to John Bigg … iii s. iiii d.

Mondaye. Item payde in a rewarde to on William Corhonde a synger … v s.

Item payde in a rewarde to s*ir* Nicholas Vausez for bryngynge of p*re*sent to my ladys grace … vi s. viii d.

Item payde for sylkez golde wyer wollen cloth and other necessar*es* bought by me by a bill signed … iiii^{XX}xix li. xiii s. x d.

Item delyv*er*id unto my ladys grace for hir alm*us* pursse … xl li.

Tewysdaye. *Ch*risten*n*mass daye. Item payde for my lad*ys* offerynge at iii masses in hir clossett … iii s.

Item for my lad*ys* offerrynge at the hye masse … v s.

Wedynsdaye. Item payde for my ladys offerynge on Seynt Stephens daye … xii d.

Thursedaye. Item payde for my lad*ys* offerynge on Seynt Johns daye … xii d.

Frydaye. Item payde for my ladys offerynge on Child*ur*mass daye … xii d.

Saturdaye. Item payde for my ladys offerynge on Seynt Thomas day … xii d.

[M]Summa totalis …Cxi li. x d.[P][41]

[*p. 63*] Sondaye. Item payde in a rewarde to the p*r*ior of mysru[l]e[42] … iii s. iiii d.

Mondaye. Item payde for a press in the revestry for my ladys stuff there … x s.

Item payde on a rewarde to a childe of Fordynghay … iii s. iiii d.

Item payde for my ladys offerynge in the clossett … xii d.

Tewysdaye. Newyer*es* daye. Item payde for my ladys offerrynge yn hir clossett … xii d.

Item payde for my lad*ys* offerrynge at the hiy masse … v s.

Item payde to master Braye to his New Yer*es* gyft … vi li. xiii s. iiii d.

Item payde to my lady Braye to hir New Yer*es* gyft … vi li. xiii s. iiii d.

Item payde in a rewarde to master Talbott … v li.

Item payde delyv*er*id unto my ladys owen hond*es* for rewardez … iii li. vi s. viii d.

[41] Sum in darker ink and another hand.
[42] MS 'mysrure'.

Item payde in a rewarde to the abbott of mysrule … xx s.

Item payde in a rewarde to the p*r*ior of the same rule … xx s.

Item payde in a rewarde to Cony my lord*es* s*er*vante … v s.

Item payde in a rewarde to Stanley my lord*es* s*er*vante … v s.

Item payde in a rewarde to Frye the kyngez s*er*vante for bryngynge of the kyngez New Yer*es* gyft to my lad*ys* grace … v li.

Item payde in a reward to <the> Lacye the quenes s*er*vante for bryngynge hir New Yer*es* gyft … iii li. vi s. viii d.

Item payde in a rewarde to the byshopp of Excest*ers* s*er*vante for bryngynge of a New Yer*es* gyft … x li.

Item payde in a rewarde to Will*i*am Hylm*er* … xx s.

Item payde in a rewarde to Will*i*am Mychell*es* wife … vi s. viii d.

Item delyv*er*id unto my ladye Braye for my ladys gr[a]ce … x s.

Item payde in a rewarde to þe priorez of M*ar*gate … xx s.

Item payde in a rewarde to a prest of the Newerke of Leycestur*e* … iii s. iiii d.

Item payde in a rewarde <too> \to/ Byggley a synger comynge from Peturborough … iii s. iiii d.

Item payde in a rewarde to John Seynt John … iii s. iiii d.

[*p. 64*] Wedynsdaye. Item payde in a rewarde to a preste that kam from Welynge <upo> besyde Grantham … iii s. iiii d.

Item payde to the player at <Ord> organs to by hym lynynge for his gowen … iii s. iiii d.

Thursedaye. Item payde to Brownynge for his quarters wages … x s.

Item delyv*er*id unto James Morice for the work*es* at Colyweston … x li.

Item payde to Roberde Ferro*ur* for rydynge costez by a byll signed … v s. i d.

Frydaye. Item payde in a rewarde to my lord*es* mynstrell*es* … xiii s. iiii d.

Saturdaye. Item payde in a rewarde to master s*ir* Edwardez taborett*es* … vi s. viii d.

Item payde for a peyre of crewet*es* … xii d.

Item payde for ii paxes … xx d.

Item payde in a rewarde to a harowde of armez … vi s. viii d.

[M]Summa totalis … li li. xiii s. xi d.[P]

[*p. 65*] Sondaye. Twelveth daye. Item payde for my ladys offerrynge In the clossett … xii d.

Item payde for hir offerrynge at the hye masse … v s.

Mondaye. Item payde in a rewarde to a sargaunte of armes … xx s.

Tewysdaye. Item payde in a rewarde to Richarde Lyn … xx s.

Wedynsdaye. Item payde to master deanez s*er*vante for rydynge upon my ladys messagez by a bill signed … vi s. x d.

Thursedaye. Item payde to Skypw*ith* for his yer*es* fee w*ith* <his> other costez by a bill signed … iiii li. xvii s. viii d.

Frydaye. Item payde in a rewarde to a drover … iii s. iiii d.

Saturdaye. <Item>

<Summa totalis …vii li. xiii s. x d.>[M 43]

Item payde to James Morice clerke of the work*es* at Colyweston for the surplysage of his acounpte[44] … v li. xi d.

Item payde to Richarde Cheke rydynge w*ith* master[45] to Burne by iii days … ii s.

Item payde to me for my quarters wagez … xxxiii s. iiii d.

Item for my horsse lyverey by viii wekez at ii d. a daye and nyght the horsse for iii horssez … xxxv s.

Item for the dyet*es* of my s*er*vante by viii wek*es* at xii d. … viii s.

[M]Summa totalis …xvi li. xiiii s. i d.[P]

Totalis allocata huc … MDCxxvii li. vii s. viii d. ob.[46]

[*p. 66*] Item paied to m*aster* Henry Horneby the xiii[th] day of Januar*y* in the xiiii[th] yere of kyng Henry the vii[th] as appiereth by a bill her*e*to this leyff sued
… Cxlviii li. xiiii s. ix d.

Summa …patet

So*m*me of all allowance and payment*es* aforeseid … MDCClxxvi li. ii s. v d. ob.

And the seid accomptant oweth … Cxxxvii li. ii s. x d. ob. qua. iii[c] pars qua.

[paper slip 110 x 185 mm. sewn to p. 66, written and signed by Henry Hornby, sealed and stamped with his rebus, a horn and a double 'h'][47]

This bill made at Coliweston the xiii day of January the xiiii[th] yere of the reigne of king Henry the vii[th] witnesseth that I m*aster* Henry Horneby have receyved of m*aster* James Clarell Cxlviii li. xiiii s. ix d. to the use and behove of my lady the king*es* moder. In witenesse wherof I the said m*aster* Horneby have set to this bill my seale and signe manuel the day year and place above.

… Henry Horneby

[43] Canc. because extra items add.; the revised summa is at the foot of the page. Lady Margaret signs both.
[44] Four minims for 'm'.
[45] No name add.
[46] Written small to the left at the foot of the page in the formal hand.
[47] See Plate 9.

[*p. 67*] [48] *Wherof is paied to my ladiez* [*c*]*ofor*[49]

Offeryngez at dyverse tymez … vi li. xi s.

Almes purse … xx li.

Almes … iiii li. xi s.

Reward*es* to div*er*se p*er*sonez at dyv*er*se tymes \with xlv li. iiii s. gyffen to the kyng*es* s*er*vant*es* and the quenez/ … Cxli li. iiii s. viii d.

Exhibicon of my ladiez scolers … xxiii li. xvii s. v d.

Household wagez … xliii li. xi s. viii d.

Cloth of gold silk*es* furrez wollen cloth and other necessarez bought for my ladiez grace … xvii s. v d. ob. qua.

Goldsmyth warke and juellys … xliii li. iii s. iiii d.

Gold wyer*e* and brawdery warke … xxiii li. ix s.

Dyv*er*se stuff bought … Cii li. xi s.

M*aster* Whitamore for my ladiez wark at Wyndesore … lx s.

Repairyng of my ladiez chare … x li. xiii s.

Sadillez w*ith* necc*essar*ies to them belongyng … xxv li. xxi d.

M*aster* Skipwith for his yerez fee w*ith* cost*es* in lawe … iiii li. xvii s. viii d.

Cofferer*e* of the kyngez house for the kyng*es* cost*es* whilst the <w> kyng*es* g*r*ace was at Colyweston … lxxii li. iii s. i d.

Clerk of my ladiez warkez at Colyweston … Clviii li. viii s. vii d.

Wode for my ladiez houshold <at> \bought by the baillye of/ Colyweston … xiiii li.

Rewardez on Neweyrez day to dyv*er*se p*er*sonez … xxxvii li. xvi s. viii d.

Sir*e* John Shawe in Romayne grotez … xxviii li. iiii s.

M*aster* Conyngesby for a purchase of land … Cxl li.

Will*i*am Gough clerk of my ladiez kechyn … Clvi li. xiii s. iiii d.

Will*i*am Bedell countroller*e* of my ladiez houshold … Cxxvi li.

Cost*es* and expensys for my seid ladiez ridyng and other*e* wyse as in the diett*es* of hir*e* s*er*vant*es* shoyng of horsez and other div*er*se thyngez as appiereth wokely in the boke of accompte signed w*ith* my seid ladiez hand w*ith*in the tyme of this accompte … Ciiii^xx^ii li. xiii s. ob. qua.

M*aster* Henry Horneby as appiereth by his bill to the next leyff her*e* in this boke afore sued … Cxlviii li. xiiii s. ix d.

[48] This is a continuation of p. 66 ('Somme of all allowance … iii^c^ pars qua'); 'Wherof … for' is written in the left margin, bracketed left (to p. 66 'Somme … qua') and right to include all the entries on p. 67.

[49] MS 'or for'.

[paper slip folded 20 mm. vertically at left and stitched to top left of page, final size 195 x 190 mm., sewn to p. 67,written and signed by Nicholas Nynes]

Be it knowen to all men that I Nicholas Nynes of London have receved the day of makyng of this present byll of maist*er* Hugh Oldom clerk to delyv*ere* to Humfrey Conyngesby s*er*ieant of the lawe to thuse of my lady the kyng*es* moder too hundr*e* and forty pound st*erling*. In witnesse wherof I the seid Nicholas wrotte this byll with myne oune honde the viiith day of Decemb*er* in the xiiiith yere of kyng Henr*y* the viith

By me Nicholas Nynes

[On back:] Receyvet off my lad*ys* g*r*ace ... MM li. de quibus solvitur[50] infra

[*pp. 68–75 blank*]

[50] MS 'sol utt'.

D91.20 (SJLM/1/1/3/1) Account of Miles Worsley cofferer: Collyweston, 2 February 1502 – 14 January 1505[1]

Discussion See Introduction 4 and Plates 10–12.

Description Paper, in a good state, with only very minor repair, written on both sides; page size approx. 300 x 215 mm. 124 ff. in thirteen quires of irregular numbers of leaves: 1^{10}(wants 8 cut out), 2^{12}, 3^{14}(wants 12 cut out), 4^{8} (wants 2 cut out), 5^{10}, 6^{12}, 7^{10}(wants 6, 9 cut out), 8^{2}, 9^{10}(wants 1 cut out), 10^{12}, 11^{12}(wants 3 and 4 torn out), 12^{12}, 13^{10}(wants 8 torn out).[2] Paginated top right (recto only) 1–247 (but 125, [126], 126[(b)], [126c], 127); pp. 1–3, 8, 10, 69–70, 72, 76, 130, 132–3, 193, 201–248 blank. The lengthy sum totals on pp. 64, 134 and 194 extend onto an extra sheet of paper stitched to the foot of the pages (225 x 200 mm. folded upward, written on the front only p. 64; 290 x 210 mm. folded upward, written on the front only, p. 134; 425 x 270 mm. folded inward, upward from the bottom to the stitching line, and then upward to the page, written on front and back with back writing visible when page open, p. 194). Pages 141–44 are a bifolium, slightly smaller in length and width than the other pages (approx. 285 x 200 mm.). Left margins approx. 55 mm. (with some subheadings); right margins variable; upper margins 10–15mm.; lower margins variable. Sewn with white thread 135 mm. down the outer edge of pp. 71/72 is a blank strip of paper approx. 20 mm. x 45 mm. which acts as a marker to the new financial year (1503–4). Another marker tab (65 mm. x 25 mm.) is sewn 135 mm. down the outer edge of pp. 141/142, 'anno xx^{mo}' written on both sides.[3] The quires are stitched into the original membrane wrapper with two modern leather and string strengtheners on the spine;[4] the irregular-ly-cut unscraped parchment is approx. 600 x 700 mm. at its largest points when opened out (the upper and lower edges front and back fold in and down, and the back edge of the wrapper folds over to contain the whole document). A contemporary hand has recorded in ink on the front cover: 'Computus milonis Worsley Expensionum Stuffure in anno Regis henrici vii^{mi}' (diplomatic transcription), with the years 'xviii^{o}', 'xix^{o}', 'x[x^{o}]'. The

[1] This is the only account in which the editor has fully checked the page and mid-page totals; footnotes record all the incorrect totals, but not those that are correct. Individual entries have been spot-checked.

[2] That is, pp. 1–18, 19–42, 43–68, 69–82, 83–102, 103–26, 126(b)–40, 141–44, 145–62, 163–86, 187–206, 207–30, 231–48. F. 12 of quire 3, f. 6 of quire 7 and f. 3–4 of quire 11 may have been used for the extensions to pp. 64, 134 and 194 respectively. See p. 11 for Leonard of the vestry's payment for the preparation of at least the first part of the book.

[3] Page 141 actually starts the 19th year (it may have been misplaced in conservation). These marker tabs are folded over and stitched to both sides of the page, i.e. they are of double thickness.

[4] The book itself was prepared by Leonard of the vestry (see p. 11).

whole is contained in a modern box of brown/grey waterproof buckram ('D91.20' in pencil on a white pasted slip, bottom right front cover of slipcase, now erased to 'SJLM/1/1/3/1').[5] The summaries, i.e. initial and final material for each year of the accounts (pp. 4–9, 64–71, 75, 134–44, 194–200), use a formal script (Bastard Anglicana, with a large decorated initial'S' pp. 9, 64, 75, 134, 144, 194) for the rubrics, infilled with either a smaller formal or a cursive script.[6] The main body of the accounts, the marginal headings, and the page totals aremostly in a current hand (Anglicana, with Secretary influence), the same as that in D91.21 and D91.19, seemingly identifiable as the hand of Miles Worsley himself ('the MW hand').[7] Another hand (the 'curly' hand) occurs on pp. 28, 74, 82–3, 85, 120–9, 145–9, 157–8, 171.There are clear interventions in the distinctive 'sprawling' hand: at pp. 60, 134, 194 (both the text and the memorandum on the back of the paper extension: see Appendix at the end of this edited text).[8] Latin annotations and other interventions (some with +, e.g. 'Nota' 20/107, 138) occur occasionally in a hand (probably the 'sprawling' hand) which notes (often with a thick nib and very black ink) the reasons for cancellations of entries, etc.[9] Page and (rarer) mid-page totals are written, and often corrected,in the MW hand;[10] most are marked 'probatur'([P] in the edited text), and signed by Lady Margaret ('Margaret R', [M] in the edited text).'Probatur' is often accompanied by a trefoil, which is not noted in the edited text; from p. 153 the trefoil is replaced by a squiggle and line and from the beginning of the year 1503–4 'probatur' is written differently, suggesting a change of auditor.[11]

Summary

1502–3 (years 17–18) [1–3 blank], rubric (Collyweston, Worsley, 2 February 1502 – 14 January 1503), arrears of last account, p. 4; receipts, pp. 5–7 [8 blank]; sum total of receipts with arrears, p. 9 [10 blank]; costs and expenses, pp. 11–63; sum total of allowance and payments, debt of MW, further pay-

[5] On p. 1 'D91.20' is canc, and replaced by 'SJLM/1/1/3/1'.

[6] The blanket term, the 'summary' hand, is used for what may be one or more of the hands used in D91.20, D91.21, D91.19, D102.1,and D102.2/6.

[7] E.g. 'my last accountes', pp. 5, 88.

[8] See the footnotes for precise details of material written in the 'curly' and 'sprawling' hands.

[9] See footnotes to p. 126c. Annotations are indicated by double angle brackets; marginal and above-line interventions are noted in the footnotes.

[10] They may be assumed to be in the MW hand, unless noted otherwise; when not in the main hand, the hand must be that of the auditor/clerk,but only the term 'different (hand)' is used here. The MW hand uses a delta-shaped 's.' ('solidi') which differs from the 's.' of the 'probatur' hand(s).

[11] Until p. 63 the abbreviation is 'p*r*ob*atur*'; from p. 78 it is 'p*robatur*' (but note 'p*robatur*' p. 123, both contractions p. 129, and p*r*oba*tur* p. 160).

ments by MW, debt of MW, loans/advances, sum held by MW, p. 64; summary of expenses by item/person, pp. 65–8 [69–70 blank];

1503–4 (years 18–19) rubric (Collyweston, Worsley, [14 January] 1503 – 14 January 1504), arrears of last account, p. 71 [72 blank]; receipts, sum of receipts, pp. 73–4; sum total of receipts with arrears, p. 75 [76 blank]; costs and expenses, pp. 77–129 [130 blank]; single extra payment, p. 131 [132–3 blank]; sum total of expenses and payments, debt of MW, further payments by MW, debt of MW, single extra payment (incomplete), debt of MW, loans/advances, sum held by MW delivered to coffers 16 Jan. 1504, p. 134; summary of expenses by item/person, pp. 135–40;

1504–5 (years 19–20) statement of account (Collyweston, Worsley, 14 January 1504 – 14 January 1505), arrears of last account, p. 141; receipts, pp. 142–4; sum of receipts, sum total of receipts with arrears p. 144; costs and expenses, pp. 145–90; total payment and debt of MW, p. 190; allowance to MW, p. 191; receipts of Roger Ormeston from 20 January 1504, pp. 191–2 [193 blank]; sum total of expenses and payments, debt of MW, payments by MW to offset debt, further payments to MW, loans/advances, money still in hands of executors of RO, sum held by MW, p. 194; summary of payments by item/person, pp. 195–200 [201–48 blank].

Edited Text
[*pp. 1–3 blank*]

[*p. 4*] [12]*Colyweston*. Thaccompte of Miles Worsley cofferare of the most excelent princes Margaret counties of Richmound and Derby and moder unto oure sov*er*aigne lord the kynge that nowe ys kynge Henry the seveneth frome the fest of Puryficaciou*n* of oure Lady the xviith yere of the reigne of the seid sov*er*aigne lorde unto the xiiiith day of January then next folowyng that ys to sey by the space of iii quarters of a yere and lxxiii dais.

*Tharr*er*ages*. Friste the seid accomptaunte ys charged with tharrerag*es* of his last accompt as in the fote of the same more playnly doyth appere … xxvii li. xviii s. ob.[13]

Summa … xxvii li. xviii s. ob.

[*p. 5*] [14]Receyved by Miles Worsley of my ladies g*r*ace from the last day of February anno regni regis Henrici viith thiez p*ar*cell*es* folouyng*e* videlicet

<In primis of my debt of my last account*es* … xviii li. xi s. iiii d. ob.>[15]

[12] The summary hand begins the document. See Plate 10.
[13] The previous account is not extant.
[14] The MW hand starts here.
[15] See p. 4 and see also D102.10/55–8 for all these receipts.

Item the same day of my lady Powes for hir sudiorne for hurself and hyr woman from the xiiiith day of Decembr*e* unt*o*[16] this day … xxi li. xx d.

Item receyved of my lad*ys* g*r*ace <bi> the viith day of Februar*y* … xii li.

Item receyved the xxi day of February for money delyv*er*ed to <Iany> Jamys Moric*e* by m*aister* Hugh Assheton at London … viii li.

Item receyved the ii^{de} day of Februar*y* by delyv*er*ance of m*aister* dean … x li.

Item receyved of my lady Waynsforth the iiiith day of M*ar*che for hir sudiorne w*i*th my lad*ys* g*r*ace by the spaic*e* of xxv wek*es* ended the last day of Februar*y* ev*er*y weke for hirself and ii s*er*vand*es* vi s. viii d. … viii li. vi s. viii d.

Item receyved the <xxvii> \xxi/ day of M*ar*che of John Dalkyn by the hand*es* of William Mayn*e* of the arrerag*es* of Haldernes which was dew at Michaelmas anno xi° regis Henrici vii^{timi} in p*ar*te of payment of lxx li. … xx li.

Item receyved of my lad*ys* g*r*ace the xvii day of M*ar*che … xiiii li.

Item receyved the xxi day of M*ar*che of money receyved of John Wren for the payment of my lady Bygott …xx li.

Item receyved the xxvii day of M*ar*che by a byll of allowanc*e* of m*aister* chauncellers m*aister* Hughe Oldoms … xxxiiii li. x s. ii d.

Item receyved the ii^{de} day of Aprell … xxx li.

Item receyved the xiiiith day of Aprell … xxiiii li. v s. viii d.

Item receyved the xxi day of Aprell … xx li. ii s. x d. ob.

Item receyved the xxiii day of Aprell … C s.

Summa … <CCxlv li. xviii s. v d.> CCxxvii li. vii s. ob.^{P}[17]

[*p. 6*] <Item rec*eyved* of John Bedell the xxx day of Aprell for m*aister* Hevenyngham in p*ar*te of payment of lx s. as aperith in the foot of my last accompt*es* … xl s.> «cancellatur hic quia oneratur superius inter[18] arreragia infra dictum annum …xxvii li. xviii s. ob.»[19]

Item rec*eyved* the xith day of Maii of my lad*ys* g*r*ace … xxxviii li.

Item receyved the xviith day of May … xxx li. xiii s. iiii d.

Item receyved the xviith day of May of s*ir* Nicholas Byrron knyght for two knyght*es* fee … viii li.

Item receyved the same day furth of my lad*ys* coffers … xx li.

Item rec*eyved* <of> the xth day of Juyn of s*ir* Hugh Assheton … xxxi li. viii s. vi d.

Item rec*eyved* the xiith day of Juyn of s*ir* Hugh Assheton … xxix li. ii s. iiii d.

[16] 'the' add.

[17] The revised total is in a different hand.

[18] MS 'intter'.

[19] Written small to the right of the canc. entry.See p. 4.

Item rec*eyved* the vth day of Juyn … xx li.

Item rec*eyved* the iiiith day of July … xii li.

Item rec*eyved* the same day as by a byll rec*eyved* of m*aister* chaunceller …xxx li. iii s. vi d.

Item receyved the xxv day of July … lxxi li. vi s. viii d.

Item rec*eyved* the same day for money lant to my lord Carlyle ellecte to be bysshop of Durham … C li.

Item rec*eyved* the vith day of August … xv li.

Item rec*eyved* the xv day of August … xvii li. xv s. viii d.

Item receyvde the xxith day of August … xxix li.

Item rec*eyved* the vith day of Septembr*e* … xlix li. iii s. ix d. ob.

Item rec*eyved* the viith day of Septembr*e* … xxix li.

<Summa … Dxxx li. xv s. ix d. ob.> Summa … Dxxx<ii> li. xiii s. ix d. ob.[P][20]

[*p.* 7] Item rec*eyved* the xxth day of Septembr*e*<of>by delyv*er*anc*e* of m*aister* controller and m*aister* audito*ur* … lxvi li. xv s.

Item r*eceyved* the xxiiiith of Septembr*e* <\of/ [.....]/> … xx li.

Item r*eceyved* the xv day of Octobr*e* … xli li. ii s. vi d.

Item r*eceyved* the same <daii> day … xxi li. x s.

Summa … Cxlix li. vii s. vi d.[21]

Item receyved the xxvith day of Octobr*e* … xx li.

Item receyved the vith day of Novembr*e* … xvii li.

Item receyved the xiith day of Novembr*e* … xx li. xiii s. iiii d.

Item receyved the xixth day of Novembr*e* … xix li.

Item receyved the ii^{de} day of Decembr*e* … Cxvii s. viii d.

Item receyved the xth day of Decembr*e* … xv li. xvii s. x d.

Item <…> receyved the xxth day of Decembr*e* … xii li.

Item receyved the same day as by a byll of allowanc*e* for s*ir* Hugh Assheton for stuff bought for my lad*ys* g*r*ace at London … xx li. xii s. viii d.

Item r*eceyved* in money the same day … xi li.

Item receyved the xxiiith day of Decembr*e* by a byll of allowanc*e* for m*aister* chamberlayn … iiii^{xx}iii li. <ix s. iiii d.>

[20] Both calculations appear to be in the MW hand, but the canc. sum uses ‘D’ and the correction uses ‘v^{C}’ (both rendered ‘D’ here).

[21] The total of the four entries on the page, written to the left of the entries in the MW hand and canc.

b.[22] Item receyved the xxviith day of Decembr*e* … li li. vi s. viii d.

a. Item rec*eyved* the xxiiith day of Decembr*e* by a bill of alouanc*e* of m*aister* chauncellers m*aister* Hugh Oldom … x li. xi s. viii d.

Item r*eceyved* the last day of Decembr*e* in gold <…d> w*i*th xl s. delyv*er*ed to my lad*ys* g*r*ace by s*ir* Hughe Assheton … xlviii li. v s.

Item receyved the xith day of Januar*y* of money receyved by Soper*e* … viii li. vi s. viii d.

Item r*eceyved* the xixth day of Januar*y* of money receyvdd of Willyam Denton xvii li. iii s. iiii d. Item of Ric*hard* Galley lxviii s. i d. ob. … xx li. xi s. v d. ob.

<*Summa … CCClxiiii li. ii s. xi d. ob.*^{P}>[23]

Summa partis … <D\C/xiii li. xv s. v d. ob.> D<C>xiii li. x s. v d. ob.[24]

[*p. 8 blank*]

[*p. 9*]

[25]So*m*me totall of all the receytt*es* with the arre*r*ag*e* afore wryten … <MCCCi li. ix s. iiii d.> MCCiiii^{xx}ix li. ix s. iiii d.

[*p. 10 blank*]

[*p. 11*] [26]Cost*es* and exspens*e* w*i*th other dyv*er*se payment*es* and reward*es* of the most excellent prynce*s* Ma[r]garete countes of Richmound and Darbye and moder unto our*e* sov*er*aigne lord kyng*e* Harry the viith from the furst day of Februar*e* in the xviith yer*e* of our*e* said sov*er*aigne lord paid by the hand*es* of Miles Worsley as herafter foloweth.

Furst delyv*er*ed unto a Grek the same day in reward … x s.

Candylmas day. Item delyv*er*ed unto Georg*e* Fraunc*es* apon Candylmasse day for my lad*ys* offryng v threttypens of gold. Summa … xii s. vi d.

Vicar of Makseye. item paid the iii^{de} day of February unt*o* s*ir* Wyllyam Greves vicar*e* of Makessey for the tythe of ii closses called the P*ar*ke and the New <Cr> Closse for oon yer*e* … xxiiii s.

[22]The marginal notes ‘b’ and ‘a’ (see next item) indicate that they need to be transposed chronologically.
[23]The total of the items since the last ‘Summa’, written to the left of the entries (not in the MW hand) and canc.
[24]The first total is of the items since the mid-page total; the second total includes that mid-page total. Both are in the same hand (not the MW hand). There is a dot calculation in the bottom right corner of the page, with ‘xxiij d. ob.’ to the right of it.
[25]The summary hand returns here with a decorated initial ‘S’.
[26]The MW hand returns here.

Item paid to Lenard of the vestry for a booke for the names of suche p*er*sons as be retayned w*i*th my ladiez grace vi d. and for this book xvi d. … xxii d.

Edward Heyvon. Item paid t*o* Edward Heyvon and Rob*er*t Pulv*er*toft for their*e* cost*es* ridyng w*i*th m*aister* countroller t*o* the sessyons kept at <…> Lyncolne as aperith by their*e* byll assigned … xxxi s.[27] iiii d.

Auditur and his clerk. Item paid the vith day of Februar*y* unto <the> my ladies g*r*ace for a reward yeven unt*o* m*aister* audit*ur* … lxvi s. viii d.

Item the same day in reward unt*o* his clerk … x s.

Item t*o* John Brydde for reward yeven unt*o* a man that brought word of the comyng t*o* Stampforth of ii Skottysshe knyght*es* from London … iii s. iiii d.

R. Bothe. Item paid unt*o* Richard Bothe the xth day of February ridyng in my lad*ys* messag*es* t*o* my lord Hastyng*es* by iii daiez comyng and goyng at xii d. a day … iii s.

*Chyld*er *of the chappell.* Item paid unt*o* m*aister* countroller for a reward yeven unt*o* the chylder of the chappell syngyng of dyv*er*se ballett*es* afour*e* my lad*ys* g*r*ace …iii s. iiii d.

*M*aister *countroller.* Item paid unto Willyam Merbury countroller for his exspens*e* w*i*th iii horsis from Colyweston unt*o* Spaldyng <and> Boston and Lyncolne t*o* the sessyons and their*e* beyng w*i*th goyng and comyng by the spaic*e* of viii daiez ov*er* and besyd*es* his exspens*e* at Spaldyng at the p*r*iors charge by ii daiez hey and lytt*er* for his hors*es* and su*m* other charg*es* at Wyllyam Cutlers cost*es* … v s. iiii d.

^{M}<Summa … viii li. xi s. iiii d.^{P}> «nichil hic quia in dorso istius folii»[28]

viii li. xi s. iiii d.[29]

[*p. 12*] *Goldsmyth of Stampforth.* Item paid the xiith day of Februar*y* unt*o* m*aister* Gryndell for money by hym paid unt*o* the goldsmyth of Stampforth for the makyng of an ever of sylv*er* weying*e* xxix unc*e* iii q*uarter* di.[30] at viii d. the unc*e*. Summa … xix s. iiii d.

Item t*o* the same for the gyldyng*e* of the pyx for the sac*r*ament … vi s.

Item for a reward yeven t*o* a prest of m*aister* Feldyng*es* … vi s. viii d.

Item for a portuas of ii <vlmes> volmes bought of the hardwar*e* man. P*r*ice …v s. iiii d.

Item the same day yeven in reward unt*o* a s*er*vand of m*aister* Hobsons comyng*e* in messag*es* t*o* my lad*ys* g*r*ace … v s.

[27] See p. 12. Alt. from 'l.' to 's.'.

[28] 'nichil …folii' add. after the total indicates that the total is to be ignored because included in the total p. 12.

[29] Written small to the right at the foot of the page.

[30] MS 'd', perhaps for 'half', perhaps for 'pennyweight'. In either case the total sum accounts only for 29 oz.

Item paid unt*o* a monke of Vaude in reward which brought my lady wryting wherby she and hir howsold s*er*vand*es* be brethren and sustren of the order thrughe the reme …vi s. viii d.

Item the xiii[th] day of Februar*y* paid unt*o* Georg*e* Hevyngham for a payr*e* of clarycord*es* whiche he bought at London for maistres P*ar*ker … vi s. viii d.

Item the xvi[th] day of Februar*y* paid unt*o* m*aister* Morgan for a reward yeven unt*o* doctur Wotton a frere of Stampforth … iii s. iiii d.

Item delyv*er*ed the same day unt*o* Rog*er* Radclyff for a reward yeven unto Hughe Warde of Boston … vi s. viii d.

Item delyv*er*ed unt*o* maistres Massy for money paid unto Georg*e* of the chapell for the stryngyng*e* of a pair of clarycord*es* for maistres P*ar*ker … xii d.

Item paid unto John Brydde <for> which he betoke unt*o* my ladies g*r*ace for hir offryng … v s.

[M]Summa … xii li. iii s.[P][31]

lxxi s. viii d.[32]

[*p. 13*] Item delyv*er*ed to Willyam Fertheng*es* wyff in reward … xii d.

Item delyv*er*ed to maistres Foler for a reward yeven unt*o* a s*er*vand of my lady Wauce the xxiiii day of Februar*y* … xx d.

Item paid t*o* Rob*er*t Hylton the xxv day of Februar*y* for vi yerd*es* of blew for a cotte for Skyppe. P*r*ic*e* the yerd xiiii d. … vii s. vii d.

Item t*o* the same for a yerd of blew for the gardyng of an horse howse … xiiii d.

Item t*o* the same for a pair*e* of shoez for Skypp … viii d. Item for a hatt for hym …. viii d. … xvi d.

Item t*o* the same for a fire panne … i d.

Item delyv*er*ed unt*o* m*aister* countroller the xxvi day of Februar*y* for a reward yeven unt*o* m*aister* Gabryell of Clare hall in Cambryg*e* which prechett afour*e* my lad*ys* g*r*ace the iii[de] Sonday of Lent … x s.

Item delyv*er*ed unt*o* my lad*ys* g*r*ace for a reward yeven unt*o* maistres Spens*er* … xx s.

Item paid t*o* Hugh Latym*er* for the cost*es* of hyr*e* s*er*vand*es* and hir <for> horsis beyng*e* their*e* a nyght … ii s. vi d.

Item paid the iii[de] day of M*ar*che to m*aister* dean for a reward yeven unt*o* m*aister* chaunceller s*er*vand bryngyng*e* wrytyng*es* from London unt*o* my lad*ys* g*r*ace … v s.

Item for a reward yeven unt*o* m*aister* Free … xx s.

Item in reward unto Churche exchet*ur* of the countie of Lyncoln … xx s.

Item to a chapplen of the bysshop of Morrey … v s.

[31] The total of pp. 11 and 12.

[32] The total of p. 12, written small to the left at the foot of the page.

Symprynham. Item to the p*r*ior <of> \and/ the nonnes of <sj> Sympryngham ... vi s. viii d.

Item paid the iiiith day of M*ar*che to John Fysshe Nicholas Cotton John More Water Cokk*es* Edward Vauce and Hughe Bowker*e* for their*e* cost*es* ridyng into the fenne for a day and a nyght ... x s.

Item paid the same day unt*o* oon Paskall of Peturborogh for dyenge of xliii pec*es* of roc*es* for a bedd ... v s.

[M]Summa ... Cxvii s. [P][33]

[*p. 14*] Item paid the vith day of M*ar*che unto Lenard grome of the vestry for xii smale bok*es* of clene paup*er* for my ladies g*r*ace. P*r*ice ... ii s.

Item paid to the same for the stuf spent aboute the byndyng*e* of a maseboke and a p*ro*sessionall besyd*es* the byndyng*e* ... ii s.

Item to the same for a pax ... iiii d.

Item for the stuff spent aboute the byndyng*e* of a p*r*imer besid*es* the labur of byndyng*e* ... viii d.

Item paid to the same for syngyng bred ... xviii d.

Item the same day yeven in reward unt*o* ii freres of Yerlande ... iii s. iiii d.

Item t*o* Thomas Boyfeld of Stelton for ridyng*e* apon my lad*ys* message t*o* Huntyngton ...xx d.

Item for a reward yeven unt*o* p*ar*son Bybe the xxvi day of Februar*y* ... vi s. viii d.

Item delyv*er*ed for a reward yeven unt*o* a monke of Ely which preched afour*e* my lad*ys* g*r*ace the iiiith Sonday of Lent ... x s.

Item yeven in reward unt*o* Willyam Mayn the viith day of M*ar*che ... xx s

...[M]Summa ... <xxviii s. ii d.> xlviii s. ii d. [P][34]

Item yeven in reward unto ii s*er*viaund*es* of my lady Cessell*es* for bryngyng*e* of a fellon*e* t*o* Colyweston ... vi s. viii d.

*My lady Rev*e*rse.* Item delyv*er*ed the xth day of M*ar*che unt*o* my lady Rev*er*se by my lad*ys* comaundement for suche money as m*aister* chamberleyn receyved of hyr*e* ...viii li. x s.

[*p. 15*] *Shoez bought for poure folk*es. Item paid the xvi day of M*ar*che to Jakson of Stampforth for iiii dd. and xi payr*e* of shoez. P*r*ice the dossen iii s. iiii d. and for the xi pair*e* at iiii d. a payr*e*. Summa ... xix s.

Item paid the same day to Adam Forster*e* for xxii plyet of lynan clothe at iiii d. ob. the plyet. Summa ... viii s. iii d.

[33] The total of p. 13.

[34] The first total omits the last 20s.; the second is correct; both appear to be in the MW hand.

Item paid for xxxii plyett of lynam clothe at iiii d. ob. the plyett and iiii d. ov*er* in all. Summa … xii s. iiii d.

Item payd for xxiiii <l> plyet of harden clothe at iii d. the plyet. Summa … vi s.

Item for xvi plyett of harden clothe at iii d. qua. the plyett. Summa … iiii s. iiii d.

Item payd for xxi pleytt of herden clothe at iii d. ob. the plyett. Summa … xii d. ob.

Item payed for ii elles of Flemyshe clothe at vi d. qua. the elle. Summa … xii d. ob.

Item for a panne … xii d.

Item for a payr*e* of bellows … iii d. ob.

Item for a pounde of blew thredd … xi d.

Item for ii payr*e* of knytt howse for Elesabeth Jane. P*rice* … iii d. ob.

Item for vi yerd*es* of tawny for Richard Laborer and moder Elyn at xx d. the yerd … x s.

Item for a bonett for moder Elyn. P*rice* … vii d.

*Howse bought for power folk*es.

Item paid for xviii payr*e* of howse at iii d. the payre … iiii s. vi d.

Item for xlii payr*e* of howse at iii d. ob. a payr*e* … xii s. iii d.

Item paid for a payr*e* of sheres for Richard broderer … xvi d.

Item for caryeg*e* of the same stuff from Stampforth … iiii d.

Item paid for iiii baues of iiii chylder of the chappell at <viii d.> \vi d. ob./ the pes … ii s. ii d.

Item paid for other iiii bawes for other iiii chelder of the chappell. P*rice* the baw viii d. … ii s. viii d.

[M]Summa … xiii li. x s. i d.[P] [35]

[*p. 16*] Item delyv*er*ed unt*o* maystres Foler for a reward yeven unt*o* m*aister* Denton …xx s.

Item delyv*er*ed to Rob*er*t grome of the chambr*e* t*o* be take unt*o* my lad*ys* g*r*ace …xiii s. iiii d.

*My lad*ys *almes gowne and bonett*es *bought for the maundy.*[36]

Item paid to Jamys Moric*e* the xvi[th] of M*ar*che for iiii dd. of almes bonett*es* bought by hym at London. P*rice* the dd. vi s. Summa … xxiiii s.

Item to the same for anoder dosen. P*rice* … vii s.

Item for a reward yeven unt*o* Jane Gower … vi s.viii d.

[35] The total includes the two items after the total on p. 14.

[36] Bracketed to include the next five items.

Item for iii yerd*es* of derke tawny for my lad*ys* maundy gowne. P*ric*e the yerd iiii s. … xii s.

Item paid for ii elnes of bombas and a corde to trusse the said stuff w*i*th … viii d.

Item delyv*er*ed unto Wyllyam Wadforth for his cost*es* ridyng*e* at dyv*er*se tymes from Colyweston to Lenyssey and int*o* the contrey therabowt*es* apon my lad*ys* messag*es* … xx s.

*Nota. Money yeven unto pore folk*es *at the maundye*. Item delyv*er*ed to my lad*ys* g*r*ace at the maundy for lix pore folk*es* ev*er*y pec*e* xiii d. Summa … lxiii s. xi d.

*My lad*ys *offrynge apon Goode Fryday and Est*ur *day.*[37]

Item delyv*er*ed for my lad*ys* offryng*e* apon Goode Fryday … xxx s.

Item delyv*er*ed for my lad*ys* offryng*e* apon Est*ur* day … vii s. vi d.

Item payd unto Adam Forster for a reward yeven t*o* Wyle the kyng*es* messeng*er* the xiiii[th] day of M*ar*che … vi s. viii d.

Item paid to m*aister* Gryndell for money delyv*er*ed to the p*ar*son of Seynt Mergett*es* besyd*es* Eyton … vi s. viii d.

Item paid to the same <fo> whiche was yeven to a man of Bukden that went in pylgramege for my lad*ys* g*r*ace … xii d.

Item paid to Gryffeth m*aister* deans s*er*vand for a reward yeven t*o* thexchet*ur* s*er*vand of Lyncoln … xx d.

Item payd t*o* m*aister* chamberleyn for a reward yeven unt*o* Willyam Hamerton and George <a> Hamerton … x s.

*To the cook*es *at Est*ur *and to the sauc*ery.[38]

Item delyv*er*ed to the same which was yeven unt*o* the cook*es* for their*e* w*i*th att Est*ur* … xxvi s. viii d.

Item to the sauc*er*y and squyllerry … v s.

[M]Summa pagine … xiii li. ii s. ix d.[P]

[*p. 17*] Item paid to Ric*hard* Carre for money by hym delyv*er*ed t*o* my lad*ys* g*r*ace at Bukden playing at the blanke … x d.

Item to the same for his bot hir*e* from London to Richemounde w*i*th a bonnet for the counties of Spayne … xiiii d.

Item to the same for his cost*es* ridyng*e* aft*ur* the said countes t*o* Gylford and from thens t*o* London t*o* make delyv*er*anc*e* of the said bonett … xvi d.

Item to the same for his horse hir*e* the same journey … xii d.

[37] Bracketed to include the next two items.

[38] Bracketed to include the next two items.

Item payd the xxviith day of M*ar*che t*o* m*aister* chaunceller as aperith by his byll assigned for a token to the lady of Scotland a bo[n]et[39] ryall … x s.

Item for xi yerd*es* of tawny damaske. P*ric*e the yerd vi s. vi d. Summa … lxxi s. vi d.

Item t*o* the same for xxiiii^{ti} yerd*es* of tawny chamlet. P*ric*e the yerd ii s. x d. … lxviii s.

Item t*o* Pawle<s> Gygles for c*er*ten bulles p*ur*cheset for my lad*ys* g*r*ace … x li.

Item for a prynted porthuse in ii volymes … v s. iiii d.

Lynnen clothe bought for the maundy. Item for CC elnez of lynnen clothe for pour*e* folk*es*. P*ric*e the elne v d. … iiii li. iii s. iiii d.

Item <d> t*o* the same for money by hym delyv*er*ed t*o* Willyam Hylm*er* for sylk*es* and other stuff bought by hym for my lad*ys* g*r*ace … iiii li. ii s.

Item to the same for money delyv*er*ed t*o* Watson at his dep*ar*tyng*e* by the byddyng*e* of m*aister* Bray … viii li.

Item t*o* the same for a large coffer w*i*th loke and key send t*o* Coldherborow. P*ric*e … x s.

Item paid the xxviii day of M*ar*che to Willyam Hylm*er* for a gret pec*e* of fig*es* yeven to the gentylwemen and chaumberers weying iiii^{xx} and iiii lib. at a ob. a lib. Summa …iii s. vi d.

Item to the same for crewle bought for gert*er*is for your*e* g*r*ace xii yerd*es* … xii d.

Item to the same for dyv*er*se sed*es* t*o* sau … iiii d.

^{M}Summa … xxxiiii li. xix s. iiii d.^{P}

[*p. 18*] *Primo die mensis Aprellis.* Item paid to Rob*er*t Smyth for his cost*es* for hymself and his horsis in ridyng*e* on my lad*ys* messag*es* to delyv*er* hir letters in Rutland by the spaic*e* of iii dayes ev*er*y day xii d. by a byll … iii s.

Item paid to Willyam Hylm*er* for money payd by hym to Rob*er*t Beeke cariar of Kendall for dyv*er*se stuffe caryed of my lad*ys* as harnes lynnen clothe and wollen clothe from Coldherboroghe to Colyweston to the wheȝt of CCC and x lib. at ob. lib. … xiiii s. v d.

Item payd to Rich*ard* Laghton of Stampforthe for iii unc*e* of frenge delyv*er*ed to Ric*hard* Stewkeley. P*ric*e iii s. for vi unc*e* of sylk of dyv*er*se colowres at ix d. the unc*e*. Summa iiii s. vi d. Item for a unc*e* and a half of clen gold and sylv*er*. P*ric*e ix d. Summa …viii s. iii d.

*M*aister *Fessher.* Item yeven in reward unt*o* m*aister* Fessher sargant … xx s.

*M*aister *Bekynsall.* M*aister* Bekynsall for a q*uar*t*er* of a yere ended at Est*er*…xxvi s. viii d.

Conysby s*ergant.* item in reward yeven unt*o* m*aister* Conysby the ii^{de} day of Aprell … xl s.

[39] A conjectural emendation for 'aboet ryall'.

Item delyv*er*ed unt*o* Rog*er* Radclyff for a reward yeven to m*aister* Whitamore … vi s. viii d.

Item the vth day of Aprell yeven in reward unt*o* a s*er*vand of Willyam Dentons …iii s. iiii d.

Item payd to Nicholas of Aughton for ii daies ridyng from Bugden to maist*er* Fysshere the juge <by the spaic*e* of> ev*er*y day viii d. Summa … xvi d.

Item payd to the same for iiii dayez t*o* Brymygam and to Colyweston … ii s. viii d.

Item t*o* the same for vii daiez from Colyweston to Lodlow … iiii s. viii d.

Item for vii dayez from Colyweston to Grenewyche … iiii s. viii d.

^M Summa istius septimane … vi li. xv s. viii d.^P

[*p. 19*] Item payd the xth day of Aprell t*o*<adi> Adam Forster for money by hym payd t*o* a s*er*vand of m*aister* Bryknell man of law for thyngrossyng*e* of thon p*ar*te of a payr*e* of indenturs conc*er*nyng*e* the mariage betwix s*ir* Rauf Shyrley and my lady his wyff …vii s. viii d.

Item to the same for anoder peyr*e* conc*er*nyng*e* the same marieg*e* w*i*th the draught*es* … iii s. iiii d.

Item paid to the same Adam for his cost*es* ridyng*e* and delyv*er* c*er*tain letters that is to say oon l*ett*re t*o* the chaunto*ur* of Lincoln another to m*aister* John Chambers and the iii^de letur*e* t*o* Rob*er*t Cellam in Notinghamshir*e* by the spaic*e* of ii daiez … ii s.

Item to the same for ridyng t*o* s*ir* John Marcham and agayn by the spaic*e* of ii daiez …ii s.

Item to the same for ridyng to oon Botheby in Nothynghamshir*e* by ii daiez w*i*th my lad*ys* le*tt*re … ii s.

Item payd t*o* Richard Bothe for ridyng apon my lad*ys* messag*es* un t*o* my old lady Hastyng*es* and bryngyng unswar*e* ayen by the spaic*e* of iii daiez … ii s.

Item payd the xii^th day of Aprell to Wyllyam Aderton for the cost*es* ii p*er*sons and vi horsis from Colyweston to Bykelleswade to the feyr*e*<and> by <vii> v dayez … xii s. viii d.

Item payd t*o* the same for his coste*s* t*o* Okam and their*e* abydyng t*o* se the mustur*e* of such p*er*sons as wer*e* apoynted t*o* do the kyng*es* s*er*vys by ii daiez … xvi d.

Item to the same for his cost*es* ridyng*e* from Colyweston t*o* Grenewyche t*o* the kyng by iiii daiez … ii s. viii d.

Item paid the same day t*o* John Hyggeson in reward oon of the gromes of the stabell …iiii s.

^M Summa … xxxix s. viii d.^P

[*p. 20*] Item paid the xiii^th day of Aprell t*o* John Skynn*er* for black trede … iii d.

Item t*o* the same for whit[40] thredd … x d.

[40] 'Tr' add. but not canc.

Item the same day for a reward yeven unto doctur Jubbis ... xx s.

Idem.[41] *M*aister *Palm*er *of the unyvers*i*te of Cambryg*e. Item delyv*er*ed unt*o* Roger*e* Radclyff for m*aister* Palmer of the univ*er*site in Cambryge for his stypend from Michaelmas to Estur last passid ... xl s.

Item paid to Rog*er* Radclyff which he delyv*er*ed unt*o* the Frenche chyld when he toke his ryghtis at Est*ur* ... xii d.

Item the xv day of Aprell yeven in reward unt*o* m*aister* Whitstones ... lxvi s. viii d.

Item the same day in reward unto Thomas Hyll and Wyllyam Hegge jardyners for drayinge of the pound*es* ... xx d.

Item for a reward yeven unt*o* John More ... vi s. viii d.

Nota.[42] Item payd to m*aister* chamberleyn for money by hym payd t*o* Mergery Welson for c*er*tayne evydance conc*er*nyng Jane Godstonys ... xl s.

Item to the same for a reward yeven t*o* John Wyllyams wyff for laboryng for the said evydenc*e* ... iii s. iiii d.

*M*aister *chamberlayn*. Item to the same for a reward yeven to the kyng*es* attourney for suyng of m*aister* Seynt Jones plee and for puttyng of hit in the Excekker*e* ... x s.

Item paid to the same for money payd to Wodward the goldwyr*e* drawer*e* a pownde of gold of <damark> damaske. P*r*ic*e* ... lvi s.

Item for ii pec*es* of bukram. P*r*ic*e* the pes ii s. <vi d.> viii d. ... v s. iiii d.

Item t*o* maistres Fynche for ii unc*e* of sylk. P*r*ic*e* the unc*e* xi d. Summa ... xxii d.

Item to maistres Bucke fo[r] xxv yerd*es* of tawny medly. P*r*ic*e* the yerd iii s. vi d. ... iiii li. vii s. vi d.

Item for a reward yeven unt*o* Olyv*er* Seynt John ... x s.

Item for iii dd. of napkynse. P*r*ic*e* the dd. viii s. ... xxiiii s.

Item for vi elnez of yelow sarsynet. P*r*ic*e* the elne iii s. iiii d. ... xx s.

Item for vi yerd*es* of whit tewke. P*r*ic*e* the yerd xiii d. ob. ... vi s. viii d.

Item payd the xvi day of Aprell by m*aister* tresorers comaundement for the bryngyng of a prysoner from Colyweston to Hornecastell ... v s.

[M]Summa ... xx li. vi s. ix d.[P]

[*p. 21*] Item payd the xvith day of Aprell to maistres Wynesour*e* for ii unc*e* of damask golde which was spent upon ii garters oon for my lord prince another for my lorde of Yorke. P*r*ic*e* the unc*e* v s. ... x s.

Item payd to the same for flatte golde occupied abowte the same garters a q*u*art*er* dwt. P*r*ic*e* ... ii s. vi d.

Item the same day yeven in reward t*o* Thomas Symson grome of the wardrop of the robis ... i s. viii d.

[41] Doubtful. Faint and in a different hand.

[42] Written in a different hand.

Item paid the xviith day of Aprell to John Walter as aper[i]th by his byll for a payr*e* of sheris p*rice* viii d. for a bell roppe ix d. for a pec*e* of lyne for the vayle iii d. for ii pec*es* lyne for the canopes iii d. ob. for CCCC small tentyr hok*es* iiii d. for lib. of threden reban for vestment*es* ii s. viii d. for a lib. of tukkyngyrdell xiiii d. for a pounde of fyne redd threde and grene ii s. for a pound of Cotnall threde x d. for a pound of crulys and half a q*u*art ii s. iii d. …xi s. ii d. ob.

Item paid to the same for iii q*u*art*er* of warpyng*e*<tr> threde and for a q*u*art*er* of blew threde xii d. for a lib. of wollen yerne blew grene and yelow vi d. for bromys i d. for a glasse for the lampe ii d. for a pec*e* of olde sylk rybonde for a coope of red bawdkyn weying a unc*e* x d. Item for his cost*es* to Stampfor for the same stuff ii d. … ii s. ix d.

[43]<Item payd to Wyllyam Frodsham of Byrmyngham for lx byll*es* for my lad*ys* g*r*ace. Pric*e* of ev*er*y pece \nichil/ ix d. Summa … xlvi s. vii d.

Item for caryage of the same from Byrmyngham t*o* Colyweston \at ii tymes/ … iii s. iiii d.>

Item payd by m*aister* tresorer t*o* Wyllyam Fredsham of Brymgham for xl byll*es* bought by Nicholas Aughton. Pric*e* ev*er*y pec*e* ix d. … xxx s.

Item in reward for the bryngyng of the same xl byll*es* … iii s. iiii d.

Item paid to the same Wyllyam for other xx byll*es* delyv*er*ed the xith day of Aprell. Pric*e* the pec*e* w*i*th the carieg*e* x d. Summa … xvi s. viii d.

[M]Summa … iiii li. iii s. i d. ob.<[P]>[P]

[*p. 22*] Item for a reward yeven to s*ir* John Carter prest of the closse of Lycheffeld the xviith day of Aprell … v s.

*Ric*hard *Carre*. Item payd to Richard Carr*e* for his cost*es* ridyng*e* from Colyweston to Ludlow and <th> their*e* abydyng*e* w*i*th goyng*e* and comyng*e* by the spaic*e* of vii daiez for his self and the hyr*e* of his horse ev*er*y day xii d. … vii s.

*Th*omas *Pellett*. Item payd to s*ir* Everaude Feldyng knyght by Wyllyam Aderton for the diett of Thomas Pellett from the xviith day of Januar*y* unto the xx day of Aprell by the spaic*e* of ix wek*es* at x d. a weke. Summa … vii s. vi d.

Item to the same for a reward yeven to his prest … iii s. iiii d.

Item in reward to Coney my lord*es* s*er*vand … vi s. viii d.

Item delyv*er*ed to Willyam Aderton for money by hym delyv*er*ed to Thomas Pellett*es* tewter at Cambrige to by hym howse shoez and other ness*esaryez* … x s.

Item paid to the same Wyllyam for ridyng w*i*th the same Thomas to Cambryg*e* for ii p*er*sons and iii horsis by the spaic*e* of iii daiez … v s. ii d.

Item paid to maistres Massy the xxii day of Aprell for stuff and other ness*esaryez* bought for the ii yong gentylwomen as by a byll assigned ov*er* and besyd*es* vi s. viii d. delyv*er*ed to the said maistres Massy by my lad*ys* g*r*ace … xi s. vii d.

[43] This and the next item are canc. and recorded more accurately in the following three entries.

Item paid to m*aister* tresorer for a reward yen to the nonnes of Stampforth … <vi s. viii d.> xx d.

Browynyng. Item paid to John Stoke for to delyv*er* unto John Browynyng of Burne for a q*uarter* of a yer*e* ended at the fest of our*e* Lady last passid … x s.

Item in reward yeven unt*o* John Debalbus the xxvii day of Aprell … xx s.

Item in reward yeven to John Harison the same day … xx s.

Item for a reward yeven to John Foske syngyng man … vi s. viii d.

Item paid the xxx day of Aprell for the cost*es* of my lady Cessell s*er*vand*es* and hir horse meyte beyng in the towne … vi s. xi d.

^{M}Summa … vi li. xviii d.^{P}

[*p. 23*] Item payd the last day of Aprell t*o* Rob*er*t Hylton for iiii yerd*es* of blak cotton for the lynyng*e* of my ladiez maundy gowne at v d. the yerd. Summa … xx d.

Item paid to Anne Rede for a reward yeven unt*o* a s*er*vand of my lady Vauc*e* … xx d.

Item the iii^{de} day of Maii in reward yeven to Ossemounde … vi s.viii d.

Item paid to Roger Radclyff for my lad*ys* offryng at the mariage of Rede and maistres Frevell … xii d.

Item paid the iiiith day of May to Rob*er*t Smythe for his cost*es* ridyng t*o* the kyng*e* by the spaic*e* of v daiez … v s.

Item delyv*er*ed to George Fraunc*es* for my lad*ys* offryng apon Holy Thursday … v s.

Item the vith day of May yeven in reward unto John Collop … x s.

Item paid to Edward Heyvon for money yeven unt*o* the May kyng at Colyweston … xx d.

Item to the same <h> Edward for my lad*ys* offryng at Holywell iii s. iiii d. Item to a bourdez iii s. iiii d. … vi s. viii d.

Item paid to Gryffeth m*aister* deans s*er*vand for a reward yeven unto a s*er*vand of Ric*hard* Gillez convaying of my lad*ys* le*tt*re … xx d.

Item to Wyllyam Pole for my lad*ys* offryng apon the Dedycacion Day … v s.

Item the xiii day of May for my lad*ys* offryng at the pardon … xlvi s. viii d.

Item delyv*er*ed to Wyllyam Hylm*er* for my lad*ys* offryng at the said p*ar*don the xix day of Maii … vi s. viii d.

Item delyv*er*ed unto Georg*e* Fraunc*es* for my lad*ys* offryng*e* apon Witsonday … v s.

Item paid to Willyam Aderton for his cost*es* ridyng to London from Colyweston and ayen by the spaic*e* of ix daiez at viii d. a day … vi s.

^{M}Summa … Cx s. iiii d.^{P}

[*p. 24*] *My lord*es *mynstrels*. Item delyv*er*ed for a reward yeven to iiii menstrels of my lord*es* the xxii day of May … vi s. viii d.

Item for a reward yeven unto m*aister* countroller at his goyng to London … xx s.

Item payd unto Wyllyam Pole for a booke to wryte the wardropp stuff in. P*rice* … vi d.

Item paid to Maydwell shomaker in Stampforth for a payr*e* shoez and a pair*e* sleppers and for the fotyng of a payr*e* of buskyns for my lad*ys* grace … xviii d.

Item delyv*er*ed for my lad*ys* offryng apon Trenyte Sonday … v s.

Frawyk. Item delyv*er*ed to m*aister* dean for a reward yeven to m*aister* Frowyk the kyng*es* s*er*uaunt … lxvi s. viii d.

Item for a reward yeven unto m*aister* Fysher … xl s.

Item to m*aister* Conysby in reward at the same tyme … xl s.

Bekynsall. Item delyv*er*ed the xxiiii day of May to m*aister* Bekynsall toward*es* his charg*es* of his comensement of bachiler of devinitie … iiii li.

Fawne. Item delyv*er*ed to m*aister* Fawne for his stipend for an half yer*e* to be ended at midsom*er* … xxvi s. viii d.

Item paid to Richard Stewkeley for money by hym payd to a man that cariet tent bemes yeven by Whittyngton from Donstabyll unto Colyweston … ii s. iiii d.

Item paid to m*aister* Gryndell for money by hym payd the last day of Marche for a payr*e* of shoez for Wyllyam Laborer … iiii d.

Item to the same for money yeven to John Debalbus in p*er*fourmyng of his reward … iii s. iiii d.

[M]Summa … xiiii li. xiii s.[P]

[*p. 25*] Item delyv*er*ed for my lad*ys* offryng apon Corpus Chr*ist*i day … v s.

*M*aister *chamberlayn*. Item paid the xxviii day of May to m*aister* chamberleyn for ii yerd*es* of scarlett. P*rice* the yerd ix d. … xviii s.

Item to the same for a pec*e* of red bokeram. P*ric*e the pec*e* vi s. viii d. Item for anothe[r] pec*e* of bokeram. P*rice* the pece v s. iiii d. … xxii s. viii d.

Item to maistres Fenche for ii unc*e* of twyne cremessyn sylk. P*rice* the unc*e* xi d. … xxii d.

Item payd to the kyng*es* attournay for causyng of m*aister* Seynt Johnez plee to be enterd … xiii s. iiii d.

Item yeven to my lord p*r*ive sell t*o* send t*o* m*aister* Watson by m*aister* Brayez comaundement … xl s.

Item payd to Augustyne Spynell for new count*er*fet arres a[s] by his byll …viii li. xvi s. v d.

Item payd t*o* Petur*e* of Coldherborogh for lynyng and dressyng of a booke by my lad*ys* co*m*maundement … liiii s.

Item paid t*o* Blagge of the exchekker*e* for c*er*ten enteres and fees t*o* hym and other of the said plaic*e* for fenyssyng of m*aister* Seyn Johnes mat*er*ez … lviii s. iiii d.

Item paid to the same m*aister* chamberlayn for a reward yeven to maistres Caro … vi s. viii d.

*Rob*e*rt Hylton.*Item paid to Rob*er*t Hylton the last day of May for v yerd*es* of medly for litell Burton the chyld of the chappell. P*rice* the yerd ix d. … iii s. ix d.

Item for xxiiii yerd*es* of blak cotton. P*rice* the yerd iiii d. Summa … viii s.

Item payd to the same for caryeng of c*er*ten stuff bought by hym at Lecest*er* fayr*e* …xii d.

Item to the same for anlett*es* by hym bought agaynest Wytsontyd … iiii d.

Item to the same for ii kyppe and a half of whit lambe. P*rice* the kypp xv d. …iii s. i d. ob.

MSumma … xx li. xii s. v d. ob.P

[*p. 26*] *Mense Juyn.* Item paid[44] to m*aister* Gryndell for money yeven to <a> \ii/ por*e* men[45] in Stampforth … xiii d.

Item yeven in reward unto a s*er*vant of the baileff*es* of Burne for the bryngyng of ii hawkes unto my lad*ys* g*r*ace … iii s. iiii d.

Item for a reward yeven unto <the> a s*er*vand of the bysshop of Carli[l]e … iii s. iiii d.

Item paid unto John Leche for money yeven by my ladies comaundement unto maistres Morgan … xiii s. iiii d.

Item paid unto Nicholas Saunders for a pec*e* of medly cont*eynyng* …xxiiii yerd*es* di. P*rice* the yerd ii s. x d. … lxix s. v d.

Item t*o* the same for a pec*e* of medly cont*eynyng* xx yerd*es*. P*rice* the yerd …ii s. viii d. Summa … liii s. iiii d.

Item for a pec*e* of medly cont*eynyng* vi yerd*es*. P*rice* the yerd … iii s. ii d. … xix s.

Item for a pec*e* of blak cotton cont*eynyng* xlviii yerd*es*. P*rice* the yerd v d. … xx s.

Item for vi yerd*es* of canvas t*o* trusse in the same clothe. P*rice* the yerd … iii d. qua. … xix d. ob.

Item for ii lib. of blew thredd. P*rice* … ii s. ii d.

Item for a lib. of whit thred … viii d.

Item paid for iiii kypp of blak lambe. P*rice* the kypp vi s. viii d. Summa …xxvi s. viii d.

Item for a dd. of bonett*es* for the chylder of <of> the chappell … xi s. viiii d.

Item for CCC neld*es* … x d.

Item for xiii thymbyll*es* … vi d.

[44] 'the' add.
[45] Alt. from 'man'.

Item for the cariag*e* of the same stuff … xvi d.

^{M}Summa … xi li. viii s. iii d. ob.^{P}

[*p. 27*] Item in a reward [to] a man þ*a*t came from s*ir* Thomas Dalaland to be gardyn*er* … xx d.

Item the viith day of Juyn in reward yeven unto John Harris s*er*vand unto m*aister* Curson for a booke yeven of the feodareship of Lyncolnshir*e* … x s.

Item delyv*er*ed to Ric*hard* Kylt to bye bonett*es* at London … xl s. viii d.

Item paid to John Brydd for ix glasses for styllyng waters. The p*rice* … xiiii d.

Item to the same for a doss*en* of sylk poynt*es* for the lytt*er* … iiii d.

Item to the same for his cost*es* ridyng to Okam to take the must*er* ther*e* by ii daiez … xvi d.

Item paid to Edward Heyvon the xth day of Juyn for xxix payr*e* of bregynders w*i*th sallett*es* splent*es* gussett*es* standard*es* and fold*es*. P*rice* the payr*e* xvi s. viii d. …xxiiii li. iii s. iiii d.

Item payd to the same for a barrell of blak sope … xii s.

Item payd to the porters for beryng of the said harnesshe and <Sp> sope from the ship unt*o* the hall garthe vi d. and from thens t*o* the boott vi d. … xii d.

Item yeven in reward t*o* the same Edward for his gud delygenc*e* bying of the same stuff w*i*th other by hym bought for the howsehold … xx s.

Doctor Roper. Item payd unto m*aister* tresorer for money by hym delyv*er*ed t*o* doctor Roper of Oxforth for redyng of devynetie theire for his stipend for a holl yer*e* to be ended at mydsom*er* next t*o* come … xiii li. vi s. viii d.

^{M}Summa … xli li. <xvi s. vi d.>[46] xviii s. ii d.^{P}

[*p. 28*] *Nichil* <Item delyv*er*ed unto m*aister* dean for a reward yeven unto Foske syngyng man … x s.> «nichil»[47]

Item payd the xiiith day of Juyn to the goldsmyth of Stampforth for makyng and gyldyng of a spone for my lad*ys* clossett … iii s. iiii d.

Item paid unto p*ar*son Bybe for ii premers bought by hym for my lad*ys* g*r*ace … viii d.

Item payd the xiiiith day of Juyn t*o* Rob*er*t Edlyn for money payd for s*ir* Crystofers horse meyte oon of the quenys chapleyns beyng at Colyweston … xvi d.

Brownyng. Item paid the xviiith day of Juyn unto John Brownyng for oon q*u*art*er* of a yer*e* to be ended at mydsom*er* next … xx s.

46 Corrected in the same hand.

47 The item is canc. (and 'nichil' inserted both after the total and in the margin), but it was a different amount given to Foske earlier (p. 22).

[48]Item paid unto Richard Galee the xviii day of Juyn iiii li. which was sent by him unto London to be deliverd in rewarde unto oon that broght a breve from the popes holynes unto my ladies grace of c*er*tain indulgence and p*ar*don … iiii li.

Assheton. Item payd the same day unto < m*aister*> s*ir* Hughe Assheton for the cost*es* of m*aister* dean m*aister* countroller and hymself ridyng to Holand and s*er*ten plac*es* in the fenne t*o* see the convayaunc*e* of the wat*er* … x s. x d.

Item payd to Henry almoigner for iii payr*e* of shoez for Skippe and for makyng clene of his cotys at dyv*er*se tymez … xxii d.

vthday of Juyn. Item payd to Thomas Bekke of Kendall for xi yerd*es* and a half of blew damaske. P*r*ic*e* the yerd iii s. viii d. … xxxviii s. vi d.

^{M}Summa … vii li. vi s. vi d.^{P}

[*p. 29*] Item payd the xxvith day of Juyn t*o* Ric*hard* Kylt for the cost*es* of Richard Moyne oon of the chyldren of the chappell for the cost*es* of hymself and his horse from Colyweston to <t> London and their*e* abydyng iiii daiez and so to the chart*er*-howse. Summa in all … ix s. iiii d.

Item to the same for a reward yeven to m*aister* Fyssher … xl s.

Item paid the last day of Juyn for the cost*es* of Wyllyam Aderton and ii persons w*ith* hym ridyng to London and ayen to Colyweston by the spaic*e* of vi dayez and a half for my lad*ys* lytter … xix s. viii d.

Item payd to Wyllyam Hylm*er* for a reward yeven unto doctor Jubb*es* … vi s. viii d.

Item delyv*er*ed t*o* maistres Wensour*e* for a payr*e* of shoes for the Frenche chyld …xii d.

July. Item paid the furst day of July to Wyldebor*e* caryar for the caryage of viii saddels w*ith* <w bytt*es*> brydell*es* and bytt*es* from London to Colyweston … ii s. viii d.

Item for the caryag*e* of a fardell of clothe weying cwt di. … xvi d.

Item payd to Wyllyam Aderton for vi ell*es* of canvas for t*o* trusse the horse harness*es* in … ii s. i d.

Item t*o* the same for v yerd*es* and iii q*u*art*er* of vyolett. P*r*ic*e* … xii s. vi d.

Item for ii dosen thymbyll*es* … x d.

Item for CC neld*es* … viii d.

Item for a red lasshe skynne … iiii d.

Item for ii brosshes for the lytt*er* … viii d.

^{M}Summa … iiii li. xvii s. ix d.^{P}

[*p. 30*] Item payd the iiiith day of July to m*aister* Hughe Oldom chaunceller for iii yerd*es*<of> and a half of violett in grayne for maist[r]es Anne F[r]evell. P*r*ic*e* le yerd x s. iiii d. … xxxvi s. ii d.

[48] This entry is written in the 'curly' hand.

Item t*o* the same for money delyv*er*ed t*o* m*aister* Bray in full payment for the lordship-p*es* of Padington and Drayton … xx li.

Item to the sexten of Pawlis for iiii palmez … xiii s. iiii d.

Item to the same for c*er*ten stuff bought for Ric*hard* Moyne my lad*ys* scoler at the cherte*r*howse … xiiii s.

Item to the same for a rynge of fyne gold w*ith* a large saffer … C s.

Item paid to Rob*er*t Edlyn for a reward yeven unto maistres Morgan for chekyns … xii d.

Item to John Urmeston for a reward yeven to a s*er*vand of the bysshop*es* of Derram …v s.

Item delyv*er*ed t*o* my lad*ys* g*r*ace for hir almes purse the iiii[th] day of July … lx s.

Item in reward to Lenard of the vestry … vi s. viii d.

Item paid t*o* m*aister* chamberlayn the xiiii[th] day of July for my lad*ys* offryng t*o* Seynt Johens hed besyd*es* Burne … xii d.

Item for my lad*ys* offryng at Sympryngham … xx d.

Item for my lad*ys* offryng t*o* the rode in Boston … xx d.

Item in reward to the ancrysse at Boston … xx d.

Item for my lad*ys* offryng at the whit frer*es* … xx d.

Item for my lad*ys* offryng at the gray frer*es* … xx d.

<Item to a in Boston chyseh>

Item for offrynge*s* to a saynt in Boston chyryche … iiii d.

Item for my lad*ys* offryng on Seynt Thomas Day at Boston … v s.

[M]Summa … <xxx li.> xxxii li. x s. x d.[P]

[*p. 31*] Item paid to m*aister* chamberlayn for a reward yeven to fesshers þ*at* dreu the polie in Tatsall hethe … iii s. iiii d.

Item for my lad*ys* offryng at Tat*er*sall … xx d.

Item for my lad*ys* offryng at Cryshed … xx d.

Item for my lad*ys* offryng on Trenyte Sonday … v s.

Item for my lad*ys* offryng at Lyncoln … v s.

Item for my lad*ys* offryng t*o* the shryne at Lyncoln iii s. iiii d. and to a saynt at aft*ur* supp*er* iiii d. … iii s. viii d.

Item in reward to the nonnez at Lync*o*ln … vi s. viii d.

Item in reward to the frer*es* at <gl> Grantham … xii d.

Item for a reward yeven to a s*er*vand of my lord of Northumberland … vi s. viii d.

Item in reward to Ric*hard* Sherley towarde*s* his coste*s* awaytyng apon my lad*ys* g*r*ace t*o* Boston … x s.

Item paid to m*aister* Morgan for money by hym delyv*ere*d for my lad*ys* offryng at Seynt Mergette*s* besyde*s* Tatsall send by a prest … xx d.

Item the xvi day of July in reward to a s*er*vand of s*ir* Edward Sawage for bryngyng of an hert from Hatfeld chasse … xiii s. iiii d.

Item for a reward yeven t*o* thenbassyt*ur* of Skotland … iiii li.

Item paid to John browderer for iii emag*es* of gold werk … vi s. viii d.

Item paid to Hughe Latym*er* for the cost*es* of thenbassytors horsis and his s*er*vand*es* … iii s. viii d.

[M]Summa … vii li. x s.[P]

[*p. 32*] Item payd to Edward Heyvon for a reward yeven t*o* the maryners for shotyng*e* of gonnys … x s.

Item t*o* the same for money delyv*ere*d t*o* the gelde of Corpus Chr*ist*e … xliiii s.

Item to the gelde of our*e* Lady … xiii s. iiii d.

Item to the Trinite gelde … vi s. viii d.

Item t*o* the m*aister* carpent*er* of the cluse at Boston in reward … vi s. viii d.

Item to the gray frer*es* in reward … vi s. viii d.

Item paid the xxth day of July t*o* a s*er*vand of m*aister* Cutlerd for copieng and wrytyng uppe of[49] indentures of the offic*e* of Bovett … xx d.

Item payd to m*aister* chaunceller for a reward yeven t*o* a woman of Wemondan and hir dought*ur* … ii s.

Item yeven in reward unt*o* Mathew jugler s*er*vand t*o* my lord Oxforth … vi s. viii d.

Item payd t*o* maistres Frevell for a reward yeven t*o* a s*er*vand of the deans of Ly[n] colne … iii s. iiii d.

Item paid to Roger Radclyff for my ladys offryng at Kyme to the heghe auter in the abbey xx d. Item to anoder saynt in the same <p> chyrche iiii d. … ii s.

Item payd the xxi day of July for a reward yeven by Wyllyam Hylm*er* to the nonnes of Sympryngham … xx s.

Item t*o* the same Wyllyam for a panyer t*o* trusse in appulls … iiii d.

Item payd to the same Willyam Hylm*er* as aperith by a bill assigned for the hir*e* of werkmen for his garden and herb*es* t*o* the same and for spyc*es* and other nessesaryez bought for my lad*ys* g*r*ace … xxii s. vi d.

[M]Summa … vii li. v s. x d.[P]

49 'of' rep. next l.

[*p. 33*] Item payd to Willyam Hylm*er* the xxi day of July for ix unc*e* of sylk. P*ri*c*e* the unc*e* xi d. Summa … viii s. iii d.

Item t*o* the same for iiii unc*e* of sylk iii s. viii d. Item for ix unc*e* of vestment reben at xi d. the unc*e*. Summa … viii s. iii d. Item for a frenge weiyng viii unc*es* di. at xiii d. the unc*e*. Summa … ix s. ii d. ob. … xxi s. i d. ob.

Item in reward unto John browderer for his cost*es* to Lynne … xx d.

Item paid to m*aister* Gryndell for money by hym payd t*o* the goldsmyth of Stampforth for sowderyng of the cover of the coppe of <gl> gold which my lad*ys* g*r*ace dayly drynkythe in … xx d.

Item payd to the same for the mendyng of a grett gylt pott … iii s. iiii d.

*M*aister *chamberleyn*. Item paid the xxiiiith day of July to m*aister* chamberlayn for a reward yeven to m*aister* Frawyk and m*aister* Conysby for theyr*e* councell in my lad*ys* mat*er*es … xiii s. iiii d.

Item for a reward yeven to Bretnell at the same tyme … iii s. iiii d.

Item paid to the same for iii pec*es* of grene say. P*ri*c*e* the pece xxxiiii s. Item for ii pec*es* of red say at xxxiiii s. the pece. Summa … viii li. x s.

Item paid to the same for iiii pec*es* of bokeram wherof oon pec*e* blak another blew and ii grene. P*ri*c*e* the pec*e* iiii s. viii d. … xviii s. viii d.

Item for iii elnez di. of canvas. P*ri*c*e* the elne iiii d. … xiiii d.

Item to a broker for his labur*e* iiii d. and for the cariag*e* of the same stuff from Colherborow t*o* the Fawcon in Gracious Strete iii d. … vii d.

Item paid to the same for vii yerd*es* of clothe of gold of grene. P*ri*c*e* the yerd xxviii s. … ix li. xvii s.

Item to maistres Fench for xiiii uncz i q*u*art*er*. P*ri*c*e* … xvi s. vii d.

Item paid to Petur*e* Palmers s*er*vand for dwt C of gylt neyll*es* … xviii d.

[M]Summa … xxii li. xviii s. ii d. ob.[P]

[*p. 34*] Item payd the xxviith day of July to Adam Forster for his cost*es* ridyng to the bishoppe of Karlill by the spaic*e* of v days ev*er*y day xii d. … v s.

Item t*o* the same for ridyng to Sympryngham Boston to Tatsall and to Kyme by the spaic*e* of iii daiez … iii s.

Item for his cost*es* ridyng*e* from Colyweston to Wodstok to the kyng*e* by iiii daiez … iiii s.

*M*aister *Bekynsall*. Item paid to m*aister* dean for money by hym paid to m*aister* Bekynsall t*o*ward*es* his exibuc*ion* betwix this and Est*er* next comyng … xl s.

Item to the same for a reward yeven to Robert Ferfax the kyng*es* s*er*vand … vi s. viii d.

Item delyv*er*ed to George Fraunc*es* for a reward yeven unto Perith Champion the kyng*es* s*er*vant … xx s.

Item payd for his horse meyt*e* at the Bayles … xxiii d.

Item to m*aister* dean for a reward yeven to an armett for makyng*e* of an hegh way betwix Boston and Tatsall … vi s. viii d.

Item t*o* maistres Reyde in reward … xiii s. iiii d.

[M]Summa … C s. vii d.[P]

Item in reward to Rob*er*t Pulv*er*toft at Tatsall … vi s. viii d.

[*p. 35*] Item delyv*er*ed to my ladies g*r*ace for my lady marques the xxvii day of July …vi s. viii d.

Item payd the xxviiith day of July to the hardwar*e* man for ii lytell glassis of yvery. P*r*ice … iii s. iiii d.

Item for ii papers of ymagry. P*rice* … vi d.

Item for xviii rynge*s* for tokyns … xii d.

Item for iii ymag*es*[50] in parchement <ye> oon of the pety of our*e* Lord another of Seynt Anne and the thred of Seynt Ursula. P*rice* … iiii s.

Item paid the xxviiith day of July to Rob*er*t Hylton for ii yerd*es* di. of tawny yeven to Rob*er*t Fermor my lad*ys* sheppard at ii s. iiii d. ev*er*y yerd … v s. x d.

Item paid for a yerd q*uarter* and naill of t[a]wny kersay for John fottman ii s. ii d. … ii s. x d.

Item for a yerd and q*uarter* of the same for Harry fotman … ii s. viii d. ob.

Item for makyng*e* and lynyng*e* of the same … xx d.

Item to the same for ii payr*e* of shoez for the fotmen … xii d.

Item paid the xxviii day of July to Rob*er*t Smythe for his cost*es* and horse hir*e* ridyng*e* to Lodlow from Colyweston at ii tymes apon my lad*ys* messag*es* by the spaic*e* of xviii daiez … xviii s.

Item yeven in reward to John Kyngysland for his cost*es* ridyng to Tatsall and awaytyng*e* apon my lad*ys* counsell and at Colyweston by m*aister* chamberlayns comaundement …v s.

Item delyv*er*ed to m*aister* Whaytt*es* in reward the iiide day of August … vi s. viii d.

Item to the same to delyv*er* unto Peris Mychon my lad*ys* vokett in Parr*es* … iiii li.

[M]<Summa … vii li. v s. x d. ob.><vi li. x d.> Summa vii li. v s. x d. ob.[P] [51]

[*p. 36*] Item paid to the hardwar*e* man for xiii crusifux of moder of perle. P*rice* the pec*e* ii d. Summa … ii s.

[50] MS 'yamag*es*'.

[51] The total is canc. and another add. to the right (also canc.); the original total is then rewritten and approved, all in the main hand. It is correct and includes the final item after the total on p. 34.

Item for xi tokyns of sylv*er*. P*r*ice the pec*e* ix d. Summa … viii s. iii d.

Item for viii other tokyns at viii d. a pec*e*. Summa … v s. iiii d.

Item for iiii baskett*es* … iiii d.

Item for an emage of Mary Mawdeleyn in clothe … v s.

Item paid t*o* Wyllyam Aderton for ridyng to Grantham by the spaic*e* of ii dayez at viii d. a day … xvi d.

Item to the same for ridyng to Wodstok to the kyng the spaic*e* of iiii daiez … ii s. viii d.

Item t*o* the same for ridyng to Slefford for Bovett for iii p*er*sons by ii daiez … ii s. ii d.

Item paid the vth day of August to m*aister* dean for money by hym payd to a man of Boston for carieg*e* of c*er*tain stayned clothes belangeing to o*ur* Ladies guylde at Boston … xx d.

Item t*o* the same þ*a*t was yeven unto an Irishe prest whiche was in preson … xii d.

Item delyv*er*ed to Rob*er*t grome of the chambr*e* which was yeven unto s*ir* Thomas Stanley to play w*i*th my lord … vi s. viii d.

*W. Hylm*er.

Debetur … ii s.

<b> per byllam.[52]

Item payd to Willyam Hylm*er* for the cost*es* of Wyllyam Watwod chyld of the chappell from Colyweston to Eton as aperith by a byll assigned … xi s. iiii d.

Item t*o* the same for xx unc*e* of slevyd sylk of dyv*er*se colors. P*r*ic*e* the unc*e* x d. …xvi s. viii d.

Item to the same for iii unc*e* of webbe sylk at xi d. the unc*e* … ii s. ix d.

M<Summa … iiii li. v s. vi d.> Summa … lxvii s. ii d.P [53]

[*p. 37*] Item paid to Harry Bygod wich was yeven to a chyld þ*a*t played afour*e* my lad*ys* g*r*ace at Boston … xii d.

Item payd to s*ir* Hughe Assheton for xxx elnez of Normandy canvas at v d. the elne and for cariage from London to Colyweston iiii d. … xii s. x d.

Item yeven in reward unto m*aister* Foler toward*es* the cost*es* of Calcott*es*<…> ridyng w*i*th hym into Norfolk for tytell*es* of lande … xx s.

Item paid the vii[th] day of August to John Urmeston for his cost*es* ridyng from Colyweston unt*o* Newerk by the spaic*e* of iiii daiez … iiii s.

*M*aister *Fessher*.

[52] Each marginal phrase is written at different times, both in the main hand.

[53] Both the canc. total and the approved one are in the main hand.

xi day of August.[54]

Item delyv*er*ed unto m*aister* Willyam Pykerell for m*aister* Fyssher reder of my lad*ys* lectures in divinitie in Cambryg*e* for an half yer*e* ended at mydsom*ur* last passyd … C s.

Item to m*aister* s*ir* Thomas Stanley to play w*i*th my lord at tabuls … iii s. iiii d.

Item payd to m*aister* Morgan for a reward yeven unt*o* a s*er*vand of < m*aister*> \doct*ur*/ Harryngtons … xii d.

Item yeven in reward unto a s*er*vand of Thomas Robertson … iii s. iiii d.

Item delyv*er*ed for my lad*ys* offryng apon thAnunciacion day of *our* Lady … v s.

Item in reward to [*blank*] þ*at* preyched afour*e* my lad*ys* g*r*ace the same day … v s.

Item payd to Georg*e* Fraunc*es* for a rewarde yeven to m*aister* Davy Phyllypp*es* þ*at* shewed his hors*es* … xx d.

Item payd to p*ar*son Bybe for my lad*ys* offryng at Peturborow to *our* Lady and Seynt Oswald*es* arme … iii s. iiii d.

[M]Summa … viii li. xviii d.[P]

[*p. 38*] Item paid the xviiith day of <J> August to Nich*olas* Aughton for his cost*es* from Colyweston to <Tat*er*> Wyndesore and from thens to Tat*er*sale by the spaic*e* of viii daiez … v s. iiii d.

Item to the same for v daiez into Cheyssher*e* apon my lad*ys* messag*es* … iii s. iiii d.

Item to the same for ii daiez after Wyllyam Hylm*er* to Heygham Ferres … xvi d.

Item for a day aft*er* m*aister* countroller … viii d.

Item for his horse meyte from Tat*er*sall to Lyncoln and from thens to Colyweston by the spaic*e* of iiii daiez … xvi d.

Item to the same for ii daiez to the pryer of Seynt Andrewes in North[ampton] … xvi d.

Item to the same for ii daiez to m*aister* Seynt Johns … xvi d.

Item for a reward yeven to Steven Tabret … iii s.iiii d.

*M*aister *Derley.*[55]

Item payd to m*aister* Derley of the univ*er*site of Cambryg*e* for a matresse bought for Thomas Pellett p*r*ic*e* ii s. viii d. a payr*e* of shett*es* ii s. iiii d. a bolster xvi d. a cov*er*let ii s. viii d. … ix s.

Item to the same for hause and shoez and for other nessessariez for the same Thomas t*o* be bought … v s.

Item in reward to a prest that came from Wendesore which kepith Kyng Harry their*e* …vi s. viii d.

[54] Each marginal phrase is written at different times, both in the main hand.

[55] Bracketed to include the next two items.

Item in reward to Hughe Ward … vi s. viii d.

[M56]Summa … xlv s. iiii d.[P]

[*p. 39*] Item in reward to John Collop by m*aister* dean … xx d.

Item delyv*er*ed t*o* my lad*ys* g*r*ace for Davy Hervy … xx d.

*M*aister *Jamys Denton*. Item delyv*er*ed to Edward Vauce for the stypend of m*aister* Jamys Denton beyng at Orlyance for oon holle yer*e* ended at Est*ur* last passyd … xl s.

Item to my lad*ys* g*r*ace for hir almez purse … xl s.

*Kyng*es *mynstrels*. Item t*o* the kyng*es* mynstrels in reward … xx s.

Item payd to Lenard of the vestry for the heylyng of ii chylder \of/ a pour*e* womans at Stampforth … vi s. viii d.

Item the xxiiith day of August t*o* an hermyte of Brokwod in almys … iii s. iiii d.

Nota. Item payd to William Aderton the xxiiiith day of August for the cost*es* of v horsis by hym bought at York*es* wold by the spaic*e* of vii daiez … vii s. viii d.

Item in reward yeven to a s*er*vande of m*aister* Newport*es* for bryngyng of a greyt horse yeven by his m*aister* unto my ladiez g*r*ace … xiii s. iiii d.

Item payd to m*aister* countroller for his exspenc*e* w*i*th iiii horsis from <l> Colywen unt*o* Lyncoln to the assyse their*e* tarying and ayenby viii daiez ev*er*y day xvi d. and fro the meyte and drynke of his horse keper ii s. viii d. … xiii s. iiii d.

*Cost*es *of Erley*. Item delyv*er*ed by[57] Nicholas Saunders t*o* Thomas Prechett*es* for the cost*es* of Erley won of the chylder of the chappell to London … vi s. viii d.

Item for a reward yeven to Sothewyk syngyng man by the same Saunders … iii s. iiii d.

Item payd to Nicholas Aughton for his cost*es* ridyng from Colyweston to Raglond and ayen by ix daiez …vi s.

Item paid the xxviiith day of August to m*aister* Felle for money yeven unto the frer*es* obs*er*vant*es* of the New Castell … x s.

Item t*o* the same for the nonnes of Catley … iii s. iiii d.

[M]Summa … viii li. xvii s.[P]

[*p. 40*] Item paid t*o* m*aister* Felle for money yeven unto the gylde of Ihesu at Grantham … xii d.

Item t*o* the same for money yeven unto the proktur*e* of Saynt Johnez hospitall in Rome … xx d.

Item to the same for my ladiez offryng at Eld*er*nall … iiii d.

Item payd to Rob*er*t Edlyn for money delyv*er*ed unt*o* m*aister* chamberlayn for the cost*es* of presoners which wer*e*<…> takyn at war … vi s. viii d.

Item payd t*o* Wyllyam Hylm*er* for oon dossen of brothryng brochis. P*r*ic*e* … xii d.

[56] Some text canc. after Lady Margaret's signature.
[57] Written over 'to'(?).

Item for fustik and for starche iiii d. … xvi d.

Septembre. Item the iiiith day of Septembre in reward yeven to Water Lambe of Wensor syngyng man for dyv*er*se song*es* yeven unto my lad*ys* g*r*ace … vi s. viii d.

Item paid unto Gye Erby of Stelton for bryngyng of Thomas Pellett unto Colyweston … xii d.

Item paid <p> unto Wensent for a rynge w*ith* a saffur*e* … liii s. iiii d.

Item payd unto John Brydde for ridyng from Colyweston to Barkeley castell t*o* the kyng by the spaic*e* of vi dayez at viii d. a day … iiii s.

Item paid the vth day of Septembr*e* to the parech prest of Colyweston for styllyng of dyv*er*se wat*er*es for my lad*ys* g*r*ace in reward … x s.

Jane Gower. Item delyv*er*ed unto Thomas Symson to betake unto Jane Gouer t*o*ward*es* hir fyndyng at London … xx s.

Item paid to maistres Foler for a reward yeven unto my lord*es* s*er*vand*es* toward*es* their*e* cost*es* eyteng of a buke at Stampforth … vi s. viii d.

^{M}Summa … Cxii s. viii d.^{P}

[*p. 41*] Item the vith day of Septembr*e* in reward unto a s*er*vande of my lady Hastyng*es* for bryngyng*e* of rose wat*er*ez unto my lad*ys* g*r*ace … iii s. iiii d.

Item paid to Elizabeth Webbe for <fo> money yeven to a sust*er* of the nonnez of Sympryngham … viii d.

Item paid for my ladiez offryng to our*e* Lady of Hallywell the ixth day of Septembr*e* …xx d.

Item in raward the xith day of Septembr*e* to Water Cokk*es* of the bakhowse toward*es* the losse of an horse …ix s. iiii d.

Item delyv*er*ed to <gerorg> Georg*e* Fraunc*es* for my ladies offryng apon the Ascencion day of our*e* Lady[58] … v s.

Item paid t*o* m*aister* Grendell for a r[e]ward yeven unto the frer*e* for his labur in the garden … iii s. iiii d.

Item t*o* the same for a howse clothe for Ric*hard* Laborer … xviii d.

Item for makyng of the same and for lynyng for a doblet for hym … x d.

Item paid to Rob*er*t Hylton for a payr*e* of shoez for Skypp … vi d.

Item to the same for a bonet for a chyld founde of almys by my lad*ys* g*r*ace vi d. Item for a pair*e* of howse ii d. Item for a payr*e* of shoez iii d. … xi d.

^{M}Summa … xxvii s. i d.^{P}

Item delyv*er*ed to John Collop in reward … v s.

Item t*o* Willyam Webbe of Clyff for goyng to Throp Wat*er*feld to se for such stuff as wer*e* nessesarie for my lad*ys* werk*es* at Colyweston … viii d.

[58] i.e the Assumption, 15 August.

Item to Wyllyam Merbury at the same tyme … viii d.

[*p. 42*] Item the xiiith day of Septembr*e* yeven t*o* Weston and Hasulrygg the kyng*es* s*er*vand*es* in reward … xl s.

Item paid to Rob*er*t Merbury for his cost*es* ridyng to Huntyngton and ayen by the spaic*e* of ii daiez in message to m*aister* chaunceler … xvi d.

Item in reward for the bryngyng of an hawke yeven by the kyng unto my ladiez g*r*ace … x s.

[59]Item paid to Jamys Moric*e* for money by hym paid to John Kyng*e* of Bykkelyswade for the bryngyng of <*cer*se se> *cer*ten tenaund*es* of Medcroft afour*e* my lad*ys* councell ayenest the bayly ther*e* …iii s. iiii d.

Item to the same for a reward yeven to a s*er*vand of the lady Taylebosse for bryngyng of a glasse of rose wat*er* unto my lad*ys* g*r*ace … xii d.

Item in reward to Nicholas Gray won of the clerk*es* of the kyng*es* work*es* toward*es* his losses in <bryng> brynyng of his howse and god*es* at Richmound … xl s.

[60]Item in reward to Gye Everby of Stelton for the bryngyng of x pertrych t*o* my lad*ys* g*r*ace … ii s.

Item the xxth day of Septembr*e* in reward to Frawyk sargant of lawe … xl s.

Kynges mynstrels. Item for a reward yeven unt*o* the kyng*es* mynstrles … xx s.

Item paid to Edward Wauce for a C of neld*es* bought by hym at London for my lad*ys* g*r*ace … iiii d.

Item paid the xxiii day of Septembr*e* unto m*aister* chamberlayn for money payd t*o* Rauffe Laythum for ii <claspyssy> claspes sylv*er* and gylt weying ii unc*e* … xiii s. iiii d.

Item to the same for a claspe for my lad*ys* booke sylv*er* and gylt weying a unc*e* d. … x s.

<Item to maistres Fench for ii pounde of gylt gold. P*r*ic*e* the pounde xvi d. … xxxii d.>

[*p. 43*] Item payd the xxiiiith day of Septembr*e* unto Willyam Pole and Thomas Prechet and a s*er*vand for their*e* cost*es* by ii daiez to Grantham … v s. iiii d.

Item to the same Willyam for a bell bought for my lad*ys*<dwe> dove … ii d.

Item paid to s*ir* Hughe Assheton for a reward yeven unto Olyv*er* Seynt John … xiii s. iiii d.

Item to the same for iiii yerd*es* of tawny to the said Olyv*er* for a gowne. P*r*ic*e* the yerd iiii s. x d. Summa … xix s. iiii d.

Item for iiii yerd*es* of blak fryse. P*r*ic*e* the yerd xiiii d. … iiii s. viii d.

Item t*o* the same for vi unc*e* of golde of Venys. P*r*ic*e* of a unce ii s. iiii d. … xiiii s.

[59] Preceded by 'n' ('nota'?).
[60] Preceded by 'n' ('nota'?).

Item for wollen thred and crewle … viii s.

Item paid to m*aister* countroller for a reward yeven to the kep*er* of the bysshopp of Lyncolns place for usyng of hangyng*es* carpett*es* and other stuff at tyme of my lad*ys* councell settyng ther*e* … xx d.

Item the xxvith day of Septembr*e* to m*aister* dean for a reward yeven t*o* Thomas Watson syngyng man of Westm*ynster* … vi s. viii d.

Item to Conysby s*er*gant in reward the xxix day of Septembr*e* … xx s.

Item for a reward yeven unt*o* maistres Feherber … x s.

Item to m*aister* dean for a reward yeven unt*o* a prest of Lechefeld the xiii day of Septembr*e* … iii s. iiii d.

[M]<Summa … xvi li. vi s. ii d.><vi d.>

Summa … xiiii li. xiiii s. ii d.[P] [61]

[*p. 44*] Item in reward unto Rog*er* Heyton s*er*vand to m*aister* chaunceller comyng in missag*e* to my lad*ys* g*r*ace … iii s. iiii d.

Primo die Octobris. Item delyv*er*ed unto my ladiez g*r*ace for reward*es* yeven to my lady Verney and maistres Brent … lxvi s. viii d.

Item delyv*er*ed unto Willyam Pole for a reward yeven unto on bayly of Eston for makyng of raten bane … v s.

Item paid to Willyam Pole for a reward yeven unto Willyam Pole the quenys s*er*vande … iii s. iiii d.

Item in reward to Edward ap Rees by m*aister* chambrelain … vi s. viii d.

Item paid the vith day of Octobr*e* unto Jamys Moric*e* for dyv*er*se stuff bought for my lad*ys* g*r*ace at Scewresbryg fayr*e* as aperith by a byl assigned … xii li. xix s. vi d.

Item payd the vith day of Octobr*e* for the cost*es* of xii horsis of my lady Verneys and for the diett of hyr kep*ers* by the space of iiii daiez … xv s. viii d.

Item payd to H<…>ugh Latym*er* for a bayle for a canepe … iiii d.

Item to Wyllyam Egge and Thomas Hyll in reward … iii s. iiii d.

Item in reward to Georg*e* Kyrkam s*er*vand for bryngyng of an hawke from Peturboro … xii d.

Item to Byllesby for the costis of m*aister* Bretnell*es* horsis and his kep*er* … iii s.

[M]Summa … xviii li. vii s. x d.[P]

[*p. 45*] Item in reward yeven to oon Peche the quenes s*er*vant the xiith day of Octobr*e* … vi s. viii d.

[61] This is the first total since that on p. 41; the corrected total, written small below the original total (both in the main hand), is correct.

Item payd to Rob*er*t Merbury for a reward yeven unto a skottysshe fole at my lad*ys* goyng*e* to Eldernall … ii s.

Item the xvii^th^ day of Octobr*e* in reward unto maistres Layce … xiii s. iiii d.

Item in reward unto m*aister* Mordant … C s.

Item paid the xviii^th^ day of Octobr*e* to John fotman for ridyng to Bytam a day … xii d.

Item for a day ridyng to Vawde for Gremsby … xii d.

Item for ii daiez ridyng to Estun and Depyng for oon Pope … ii s.

Item for <goyng> ridyng for palfreis for to <set> go for my lady marques … iiii d.

Item paid to Nich*olas* Aughton for ridyng t*o* Crolande by ii daiez … xvi d.

Item t*o* the same for vi daiez ridyng int*o* Yorkshir*e* … iiii s.

Item for his bot hir*e* ov*er* Humber*e* … vi d.

Item for ridyng t*o* Harbaro … viii d.

John Brownyng. Item payd to John Brownyng for a q*uarter* of a yer*e* ended at Mychaelmas last … x s.

Item paid to Wyllyam Weldbor*e* for the cariage of Thomas Watsons stuff from Westm*ynster* unto Colyweston … xv s.

Item payd to Ric*hard* Aderton for a payr*e* of buskyns and a payr*e* of pensons bought by hym for my ladiez g*r*ace … ii s.

Item yeven in reward to the same Ric*hard* for laboryng of my lad*ys* mat*er*ez at London … iii s. iiii d.

[M]Summa … viii li. iii s. ii d.[P]

[*p. 46*] Item paid unt*o* s*ir* Hughe Assheton for a reward yeven unto John Collop at his goyng to London … iii s. iiii d.

Item payd to m*aister* Morgan for money by hym payd unto m*aister* Fessher my lad*ys* reder in Cambryge for a q*uarter* of an yer*e* ended at Mychaelmas <lass> last passid … l s.

Item paid unto m*aister* countroller the xxviii^th^ day of Octobr*e* for a reward yeven unto ii s*er*vand*es* of s*ir* Harry Wellybes comyng w*i*th ii goshawk*es* … x s.

Item the same day in reward to a prest of Brettan … vi s. viii d.

Item payd to <ma> Morgans wyff for the cost*es* of maistres <lacey> Lacy horsis …iii s.

Item in reward unto John Clowyle of the Yle of Purbek … x s.

<Item in reward unto Thomas Rob*er*tson s*er*vant for bryngyng of letturs unto my lad*ys* g*r*ace … vi d.>

Item delyv*er*ed unto George Fraunc*es* for my lad*ys* offryng apon Halhallow day … v s.

Item to the same for my lad*ys* offryng apon Alsowle day … v s.

Item delyv*er*ed to m*aister* countroller for a reward yeven unto a Walshe man oon of the kyng*es* mynstrels … v s.

Item delyv*er*ed to m*aister* dean for a reward yeven unto John Stakhowse <*ser*> for bryngyng of *cer*ten horsis unto my lad*ys* g*r*ace … xxvi s. viii d.

Item to the same for a reward yeven unto Wyllyam Mayn … xl s.

Item payd to m*aister* tresorer for a reward yeven unto oon Cot*es* of Grantham … iii s. iiii d.

[M]Summa … viii li. <ix s. iiii d.> \viii s./[P][62]

[*p. 47*] *Primo die* <*Decembris*> *Novembr*is. Item payd the furst day of <Decembr> \ Novembr*e*/ unto Wyllyam Hylm*er* for rau sylke to make alkermes. For d. lib. … v s. vi d.

Item for new g*r*ane for the same alkermes i q*uarter* … xvi d.

Item for swette appuls a panyer to cary theym in and for the cariage fro London to Colyweston for the same alkermes … viii d.

Item for a payr*e* of shoez bought by the same … v d.

Item for blak reben i yerd iii q*uarter* … vii d.

Item for a payr*e* of sokk*es* and anoder of bulwerk*es* knytt for your*e* g*r*ace … xiiii d.

Item payd to the same for dressyng settyng and sawyng of dyv*er*se herb*es* in the styl hows garden by xii daiez … ii s.

Item paid the same day to Rob*er*t Hylton for iii yerd*es* of medly for a gowne for a pore woman at the maundy. Ev*er*y yerd p*r*ice ii s. ii d. … vi s. vi d.

Item to the same for ii yerd*es* and a halfe of rede cloth for the same woman. P*r*ice the yerde xviii d. Summa … vii s. ix d.

Item paid to Rob*er*t Hylton for x yerd*es* of white for \iii/ horse howses. P*r*ic the yerd v d. … <…>iiii s. ii d.

Item paid for a payr*e* of shoez for Skyppe … vi d.

Item payd to Thomas Prechett in full payment ov*er* vi s. viii d. delyv*er*ed to hym for the cost*es* of Ernelay oon of the chyldrer of my lad*ys* chappell from Colyweston unt*o* Wenchest*er* and from thens t*o* his fader … ii s. viii d.

Item paid to m*aister* Grendell for a reward yeven unto John Kynok*es* my lad*ys* s*er*vand … xii d.

Item to the same for money payd to the goldsmyth of Stampforth for sowdryng of ii bassyns and a candylstyk … iii s. iiii d.

[M]Summa … xxxvii s. vii d.[P]

[62] The corrected total (also in the main hand) is correct.

[*p. 48*] Item payd the ii^{de}day of <Decembr*e*> Novembr*e* for iiii parr*es* ring*es* to the hardewar*e* man bought by Rog*er* Radclyff … ii s. viii d.

Item in reward unto the quenys mydwyff the iiiith day of Novembr*e* … x s.

Item in reward unto maistres Molynex … vi s. viii d.

Item payd to Jamys Moric*e* the viith day of Novembr*e* for an horse bought for my lad*ys* g*r*ace … xxvii s.

Item payd to Lenard of vestry by a byll assigned … xxi d.

Item payd to m*aister* dean for a reward yevenn unto oon Cot*es* of Grantham … ii s.

Item t*o* the same for a reward yeven unto Thomas Rob*er*tson s*er*vand <Cony> comyng from London … xvi d.

Item paid the xiith day of Novembr*e* to Willyam Grevell for ii daiez ridyng*e* for m*aister* Mordaunt for his horse hir*e* and his cost*es* … ii s.

Item paid the xvth day of Novembr*e* to <…> Edward Heyvon for xi yerd*es* \di./ of tawny. P*r*ic*e* the yerd v s. … lvii s. vi d.

Item t*o* the same for iiii < yerd*es*> mynk*es*. P*r*ic*e* a pece ii s. viii d. … x s. viii d.

Item paid to the same for a payr*e* of bag rynge*s* of sylv*er* and gold weying vi unc*e* and iii q*uarter*. P*r*ic*e* the unce vi s. … xl s.

Item paid for a yerd and a nayll velued t*o* cov*er* the same bagg*e* <Rig> ryng*es*. P*r*ic*e* the yerd ix s. viii d. …x s. iii d.

Item for perlyng of the same bagg*e* and makyng botons and lasys t*o* the same … v s. iiii d.

Item p*ai*d to a bag maker for makyng of the same bagg*e* … xvi d.

Item paid for iiii mynk*es*. P*r*ic*e* a pec*e* ii s. vi d. … x s.

^{M}Summa … <ix li. viii s. vi d.> ix li. viii s. vi d.^{P}

[*p. 49*] Item payd t*o* the same <Jamys> Edward for a pec*e* of blew sarsynet *conteynyng* xvi ell*es*. P*r*ic*e* the ell iii s. iiii d. … liii s. iiii d.

Item to the same for oon pec*e* sypor*is* … ii s. viii d.

Item paid to the same for xlii ell*es* of canvas. P*r*ic*e* the ell iii d. ob. … xii s. iii d.

Item payd to Ric*hard* Carr*e* the viiith day of Novembr*e* for ridyng to Estamstyd t*o* the kyng by the spaic*e* of viii daiez comyng and goyng … viii s.

Item t*o* the same for ridyng for s*ir* John Seynt John by <ii daiez> a day …<xvi d.> viii d.

Item payd to Willyam Aderton the xiith day of Novembr*e* for v bytt*es* for the palffereys … v s.

Item paid unto John Bedell for an horse bought for my lad*ys* g*r*ace … xxx s. vi d.

Item payd to Wyllyam Mochell for his cost*es* w*i*th other w*i*th hym and iii hors*es* from Colyweston to Lenton fayr*e* for hors*es* … iiii s. viii d.

Item in reward t*o* the kep*er* of Harryngworth p*ar*ke … iii s. iiii d.

Item paid the xixth day of Novembr t*o* m*aister* dean for money delyv*er*ed to m*aister* Palm*er* of the unyv*er*site in Cambryg*e* for his stypend from Est*ur* unto Michaelmas last passid … xl s.

Item paid for a reward yeven unto Morice Seynt John … xl s.

^{M}Summa … x li. <xii d.> \v d./^{P}

[*p. 50*] Item the xxth day of Novembr*e* to John Bygg in reward … xiii s. iiii d.

Item payd unto John Fyssher of Stampforth pewterer for iii bassyns … ii s.

Item in reward to Edward Heven s*er*vand for bryngyng of verdurs unto my lady … ii s.

Item payd unto Jamys Clarrell for a fyveshillyngez in gold delyv*er*ed to John Debalbus for the gyldyng of ii lytell saltez … v s.

Item payd to the goldsmyth of Stampforth for mendyng of oon of my lad*ys* candylstykk*es* of hir chappell the xxith day of Novembr … <ii s.> xii d.

Item in reward unto ii s*er*vand*es* of m*aister* Bulkeleys for convaying of an goshauke from Blewmar*is* unto Colyweston … xxvi s. viii d.

Item paid the xxiith day of Novembr unto Wyllyam Laborer oon of the gromes of the stabyll for convaying of iiii hors*es* from Colyweston unto Calic*e* as aperith by his byll therof made … lvi s. iiii d.

Item delyv*er*ed unto m*aister* dean the same day for a reward yeven unto a s*er*vand of Willyam Aderton for convaying of ii letturs from London unto my lad*ys* g*r*ace …iii s. iiii d.

Item payd to m*aister* Gryndell the same day for money payd by hym unto the goldsmyth of Stampforth for makyng of ii candelstykk*es* sylv*er* weying xxviii unc*e* for ev*er*y unc*e* facyon vi d. Summa … xiiii s.

^{M}Summa … vi li. iii s. viii d.^{P}

[*p. 51*] Item payd to Richard Carr*e* the xxvith day of Novembr for ridyng w*i*th the baily of Burne for to inqwyre for Bowett*es* land*es* by the spaic*e* of ii daiez … xvi d.

Item t*o* the same for ridyng to Grantham for Thomas Phillipp*es* by a day … viii s.

Item for makyng of a payr*e* of buskynce for my lad*ys* g*r*ace and a payr*e* of shoez … x d.

Item to the same for ridyng into Lyncolnshir*e* for oon John Turner by the spaic*e* of v daiez … iii s. iiii d.

Item delyv*er*ed unto m*aister* John Seynt John toward*es* his cost*es* ridyng unto my lady marques … xiii s. iiii d.

Item to the same for to delyv*er* unto my said lady marques … xx s.

Item in reward unto my lady marques woman at Colyweston … vi s. viii d.

Item in reward unto s*ir* Wyllyam Notman of Burne for bryngyng of wardons … xx d.

Item paid unto Wyllyam Hylm*er* for v candylstyk*es* of latten for my lad*ys* g*r*ace … ii s.

Item delyv*er*ed unto my lady Rev*er*se the xxviiith day of Novembr*e* for a reward yeven unt*o* maistres P*ar*kers mydwyff … v s.

Item paid to John Brydd the xxx^{te} day of Novembr*e* by a byll assigned for ridyng to Bytham Spaldyng and Ele at dyv*er*se tymez by the spac*e* of xxvi daiez at viii^{d} the day. Summa … xvii s. iiii d.

^{M}Summa … lxxii s. ii d.^{P}

[*p. 52*] Item delyv*er*ed unto my lad*ys* g*r*ace the xxx day of Decembr*e* for money yeven unto maistres Flee and maistres Webbe to bye ether of them a gowne … xxx s.

Item for money yeven to the p*ar*son Bybe in rewarde by my lad*ys* g*r*ace … xx s.

Item the iiiith day of Decembr*e* unt*o* Ric*hard* Bothe for a reward yeven unto Jane Gower … x s.

Item delyv*er*ed to m*aister* Gryndell for a reward yeven unto the p*r*ior of Thorney þ*at* preched a<for> four*e* my lad*ys* g*r*ace … vi s. viii d.

Item on Seynt Nicholas even unt*o* Seynt Nicholas and his clerk*es* … v s.

Item to the clerk of the towne … ii s.

Item paid the ixth day of Decembr*e* unt*o* Richard Carre for ridyng unto s*ir* John Seynt John at delyv*er*aunce of maistres P*ar*ker by the spaic*e* of ii daiez … xvi d.

Item t*o* the same for a day unt*o* Peturboro for a myter apon seynt Nich*olas* even and for the bryngyng of the same myter unto Peturborow ayen … xvi d.

Item paid to m*aister* Grendell for money payd for the makyng of iiii claspys for bok*es* sylv*er* and gylt weying ii unce at v s. the unc*e*. Summa … x s.

Item payd to the same for money payd t*o* John Trygg of Peturborow for a paynted table which standythe in my lord*es* closett … xl s.

^{M}Summa … vi li. vi s. iiii d.^{P}

[*p. 53*] Item payd the xiith day of Decembr*e* unto m*aister* Gryndell for a payr of shoez by hym bought for Richard Laborer vi d. and for makyng of his dublett vii d. … xiii d.

Item paid to the same for money payd t*o* a laborer for carying of dong*e* int*o* the garden for iiii daiez at iii d. the day … xii d.

Item delyv*er*ed unt*o* m*aister* stuarde for a reward yeven unto my lord marques the xiiiith day of Decembre at his beyng at Colyweston … C s.

Item payd for his horse meyte and for the diett*es* of his kepers <and> paid to Hughe Latym*er* vii s. x d. Item to Bradley viii s. Summa … xv s. x d.

Item delyv*er*ed unto Worssop toward*es* his cost*es* for the caryage of an wyld bore from Colyweston to the kyng … vi s. viii d.

Item paid the xxth day of Decembr*e* unto s*ir* Hughe Assheton for money by hym delyv*er*ed unto Edmond Nycholas the hardware man for stuff bought for my lad*ys* g*r*ace …xvi li. xx d.

Item to the same for money payd unto maistres Benett for half a lib. of gylt gold. P*r*ice …ix s.

Item to the same for iii bonett*es* of black velvet. P*r*ic*e* the pec*e* xii s. … xxxvi s.

Item t*o* the same for a bonet of lettysse … vi s.

Item for a lib. of gylt golde. P*r*ic*e* … xvi s.

Item for ii baskett*es* to carry in the said stuff … viii d.

Item for a tymbr*e* of fyne gray … xiii s. iiii d.

Item for another tymbr*e* of curss gray … x s.

[M]Summa … xxvi li. xvii s. iii d.[P]

[*p. 54*] Item delyv*er*ed t*o* my ladiez g*r*ace the xxth day of Decembr*e* for hyr*e* almes pursse … x li.

Item payd to Rob*er*t Hylton for a payr*e* of buskync*e* for my lad*ys* g*r*ace … xii d.

Item paid to the same for ix yerd*es* of fryce for Skypp. P*r*ic*e* the yerd iiii d. ob. … iii s. iiii d. ob.

Item payd to the same for iiii pec*es* of blak cotton ev*er*y pec*e* cont*eynyng* xxiiii yerd*es*. P*r*ice <[...]> ev*er*y pece viii s. … xxxii s.

Item payd to the same for anlytt*es* … iii d.

Item payd to m*aister* chamberlayn the xxiiith day of Decembr for v yerd*es* of morrey clothe. P*r*ic*e* the yerd iii s. iiii d. … xvi s. iii d.

Item for an elne of canvas t*o* trusse hit in … iiii d.

Item for ii lib. of gylt golde bought of maistres Fynche. P*r*ic*e* … xxxii s.

Item to m*aister* Shaw by the same for money sende unto maister Thwaytt*es* by my lad*ys* comaundement … xvi li.

Item for iii yerd*es* and a q*uarter* of morrey clothe. P*r*ic*e* the yerd iiii s. viii d. … xv s. ii d.

Item to maistres Fench for iiii pounde of gylt golde. P*r*ic*e* the lib. xvi s. … iii li. iiii s.

Item for a boxe to trusse in the said golde … iiii d.

Item for ii dossen nappkynce. P*r*ic*e* … x s.

Item for ii pec*es* of canvas. P*r*ic*e* … xxxv s.

Item payd for oon pece of blew bokeram … iii s. viii d.

Item for other ii peces of blew bokeram … vi s. viii d.

[M]Summa … xlii li. xiii s. ii d. ob.[P]

[*p. 55*] Item payd to the same m*aister* chamberlayn for CC curten rynges. P*rice* … xviii d.

Item for oon hundreth of gret hok*es*. P*rice* … xii d.

Item for iii M of crochett*es*. P*rice* … ix s.

Item payd for iii dosen of fyne gylt paup*er* … iii s. vi d.

Item for ii dosenn of fyne sylv*er* paup*er* … iii s.

Item for iiii dd. of red paup*er* … ii s. viii d.

Item for iii dd. of grene paup*er* … ii s.

Item payd for oon pounde of gold foyle … xii d.

Item for a yerd of canvas t*o* trusse the same … iii d.

Item for ii mynke skynnes. P*rice* … iiii s. viii d.

Item payd for oon furre of calabur*e*. P*rice* … xviii s.

Item for ii pec*es* of curse lawne. P*rice* … xviii s.

Item payd for xviii yerd*es* and oon q*uarter* of tawny satten. P*rice* the yerd v s. iiii d. … iiii li. xvii s. iiii d.

Item payd for xxviii yerd*es* of tawny damaske. P*rice* the yerd v s. iiii d. …vii li. ix s. iiii d.

Item payd for vii yerd*es* of tawny velvet of golde colowr*e*. P*rice* the yerd xi s. vi d. … iiii li. ii d.[63]

Item payd to maistres Fenche for iii pounde of gylt golde. P*rice* the pounde xvi s. … xlviii s.

Item paid for a payr*e* of howse for Ric*hard* Mowen my lad*ys* skoller ii s. ii d. Item for a shert xiiii d. Item for a fustian doblet ii s . viii d. … vi s.

Item payd for a payr*e* of howse for Wyllyam Wodward iiii d. for a payr*e* shoez vii d. Item for a shert \xiiii d./ … ii s. i d.

Item paid to the same m*aister* chamberlayn for money payd t*o* a brotherer*e* for c*er*tan stuff for my lad*ys* g*r*ace … xvi li. vi s. viii d.

[M]Summa … xxxviii li. xv s. ii d.[P] [64]

[*p. 56*] Item payd to the same m*aister* chamberleyn for money payd for vi lib. of golde foyle … vi s.

Item payd for ii dd. of bell*es*. P*rice* … ii s.

[63] The pence should be 6d.

[64] The total is 1s. over.

Item payd for oon pec*e* of curse lawne … viii s.

Item for x yerd*es* of s*ar*cynet of gold color*e*. P*ric*e the yerd iii s. viii d. …xxxvi s. viii d.

Item payd for oon eln*e* of canvas to trusse the said stuff in … iiii d.

*Jane Gower*e. Item to the same for money delyv*er*ed unto Jane Gower*e* … x s.

Item paid the xxiii[th] day of Decembr unto m*aister* chamberlayn for money delyv*er*ed unto Wyllyam Grevell at London to bye iiii dosen of gold papur*e* and iii dd. of sylv*er* papur*e*. Pryce … vi s. viii d.

Item for ii payr*e* of shoez x d. and for an elne of canvas iiii d. and for ii dd. gold foyle ii dd. of tyn foyle and for ii dd. of bellez xvi d. … ii s. vi d.

Item payd to m*aister* chaunceller for ii Spaynessh skynnez oryng*e* coler. P*ric*e … v s. iiii d.

Item for a hundreth yerd*es* of lyre … ii s. iiii d.

Item to the same for vi pec*es* of lennen clothe delyv*er*ed to m*aister* chamberlayn. P*ric*e the pece xxxiii s. iiii d. … x li.

Item payd for carryage of the same from Exeter unto London … iiii s.

Item payd to Worshoppe of Colyweston for his cost*es* and labur*e* w*i*th ii horsis from Colyweston unto the kyng caryeng of a wylde bore send by my lad*ys* g*r*ace for his labur*e* by vii daiez and the hir*e* of his ii hors \in full payment ov*er* vi s. viii d./ … <xvii s.> x s. iiii d.

[M]Summa … xiiii li. xiiii s. ii d.[P]

[*p. 57*] Item paid the xxx[ti] day of Decembr*e* to maistres Massy for a reward yeven unto maistres Anne Buknowr*e* the quenys gentylwoman … vi s. viii d.

Item payd the last day of Decembr*e* to Rychard grome yssher of the hall for the heyleng of a chylde oon of my lad*ys* ward*es* and for Skypp and Made Besse … xxvi s. viii d.

Crystemas Day. Item <i> delyv*er*ed to George Fraunc*es* for my lad*ys* offryng apon Crystemas Day … v s.

Item delyv*er*ed to my lad*ys* g*r*ace by m*aister* Hughe Assheton … xl s.

Item delyv*er*ed unto maistres Merbury for money yeven Kyrbes wyff for the kepyng*e* of <mag> Mergett oon of my lad*ys* ward*es* … iiii s.

Item paid the iii[de] day of Januar*y* unto Richard Boothe a rewarde which my lad*ys* g*r*ace had of him for a s*er*vant of the kinges … vi s. viii d.

Item paid the same day unto the <golde>smyth of Stamford for makyng of ii ewers of silv*er* weyng x lib. 5 unc*e* iii quart*er* aft*er* iiii d. the unc*e* … xv s. iii d.

*New Yer*es *day*. Item delyv*er*ed to m*aister* Bygot for the quenes Neuyerr*es* gyft in angill*es* … xl li.

Item to the same for m*aister* Brayez … vi li. xiii s. iiii d.

Item to the same for my lady Braye … liii s. iiii d.

Item to the same for to delyv*er* unto the bysshop of Ely s*er*vande ... xl s.

Item to m*aister* Free for bryngyng of the kyng*es* Newyer*es* gyft*es* ... C s.

Item for bryngyng of quenys Newyr*es* gyft*es* ... lxvi s. viii d.

Item t*o* William Hylm*er* ... xx s.

Item t*o* Leghe s*er*vant ... xx s.

Item to Scasbryg*e* ... vi s. viii d.

Item to Robert Leghe ... vi s. viii d.

[M]Summa ... lxvii li. x s. xi d.[P]

[*p. 58*] Item to Coney my lord*es* s*er*vand ... vi s. viii d.

Item to yonge Coney ... iii s. iiii d.

Item for my lad*ys* offreng the same day ... v s.

Item to Raynold Stanley ... vi s. viii d.

For maister *chamberleyns Newyer*es *gyft*. Item delyv*er*ed the last day of <No> Decembr*e* to Willyam Pole for my lad*ys* g*r*ace ... xl s.

<Item to my lad*ys* g*r*ace by s*ir* Hughe Assheton ... xl s.>

Item payd to Harry Coke the same day for a brasse panne bought by hym for my lad*ys* clossett. P*r*ic*e* ... x d.

Item paid to Ric*hard* Carr*e* the last day of Decembr*e* for ridyng from Colyweston to London to se the convayanc*e* of a bor*e* send to the kyng by my lad*ys* g*r*ace ... vi s.

Item in reward to a s*er*vand of m*aister* Wak*es* by m*aister* chamberlayn comaundement ...xx d.

Item paid to Richard Stewkeley by a byll assigned for hempsed for brydd*es* and for lyres for tent*es* w*i*th other ness*esaryez* bought for the same and for ledd enke and papur. The summa ... viii s. viii d.

Item payd unto s*ir* Wyllyam for shoez and howse w*i*th other ness*esaryez* bought for William Gybon ward unto my lad*ys* g*r*ace as aperith by a byll ... ii s. i d.

*Doctor Rop*er. Item payd to m*aister* tresorer for money payd to doct*ur* Roper*e* for redyng of my lad*ys* lectur*es* in Oxforth for the t*er*me ended at Mychaelmas last ... lxvi s. viii d.

*Par*s*on of Coldherboro*. Item payd to the same for money payd by hym unto m*aister* Roston for the tythe of Coldherborogh for two yer*es* ended at Mychaelmas last passid ...Cvi s. viii d.

[M]Summa ...xii li. xiiii s. iii d.[P]

[*p. 59*] *Brownyng*. Item payd to the [s]u[f]frycans[65] prest to betake unto John Browynyng*e* of Burne for the t*er*me ended at Crystemas last ... x s.

[65] MS 'ffusfrycans'.

Item payd the xth day of Januar*y* to John Kemys for his exspenc*e* ridyng from Colyweston <in> to my lad*ys* lordshipp*es* in north Wales and south Wales by the spaice of xvi daiez at xii d. the day and for reward*es* yeven unto dyv*er*se p*er*sons þ*at* was his gydys w*i*thin the said countrey v s. ... xxi s.

Item delyv*er*ed to <pr> George Fraunc*es* for my lad*ys* offryng apon the Xiith Day ... v s.

Conysbe. Item in reward unto m*aister* Conysby s*er*gant ... lxvi s. viii d.

Item for his horse meyte and the diett*es* of his s*er*vant*es* ... xiiii s.

<Item payd unto Sop*er* my lad*ys*<l> solystit*er* ov*er* and besyd*es* vii li. receyved of John Botteler and xxvi s. viii d. receyved of Ric*hard* Corwell> ... xxii s. viii d.

Item payd unto Rob*er*t Pulv*er*toft for a cote of fence made of platt*es* ... vii s. vi d.

Item payd to m*aister* Lynne for a reward yeven to a messeng*er* comyng from s*ir* Thomas Dassy to the kyng ... iii s. iiii d.

Item payd to John Bedell for money payd by hym for the caryag*e* of a tonne of ale from Colyweston to the kyng ... xxiii s. iiii d.

Item to the same for money payd for the caryag*e* of a fardell of lynyn cloth for pore folk*es* ... v s. ix d.

Item delyv*er*ed unto m*aister* dean for a reward yeven to a prest þ*at* came from Lychfeld toward*es* the caryag*e* of his stuff from thens to Colyweston ... xiii s. iiii d.

Item delyv*er*ed to maistres Foler for a reward yeven to m*aister* Elmes ... xl s.

Item delyv*er*ed to Richard Gowgh in reward ... xiii s. iiii d.

[M]Summa ... <xii li. v s. xi d.> xi li. iii s. iii d.[P][66]

[*p. 60*] Item payd to m*aister* dean the xth day of January for a reward yeven to maistres Rede ... x s.

Item to the same for a reward yeven \to John Penter/ of the chappell ... x s.

Item payd the xith day of January unto John Harryson as aperith by a byll assigned for dyv*er*se stuff bought for dysgyssyng*es* in Crystemas ... Cxiiii s. viii d. ob.

[67]Item payed to Thomas Soper*e* my lad*ys* solyster*e* for hys fee for an[68] hole yere endyd at Cristymes anno xviii^{mo} regni Henrici vii^{mi} ... lxvi s. viii d.

Item payed to the same Thomas Soper for syche[69] cost*es* and expenc*e* as he hath payed for syche sewet*es* as he hath tacon in my lad*ys* name as appereth by a byll signed w*ith* my ladys hand and delyvered ... vi li. <vi s. viii d.> ii s. viii d.

[66] The canc. total is correct (both are in the main hand).

[67] This entry and the next are written in the 'sprawling' hand.

[68] Followed by an ink blot.

[69] MS 'syches'. Perhaps it was mistaken (or intended) as 'syrches' (OED **search***n*. 2b), but note 'syche' ('such') in the same sentence (and see Appendix for 'syche' in the memorandum, p. 194).

Item delyv*er*ed unto my lad*ys gr*ace apon New Yer*es* even for Newyer*es* gyft*es* … iiii li.

Item payd unto m*aister* chamberlayn for so myche money delyv*er*ed by hym ov*er* his account for Rikles land*es* by s*ir* Hughe Assheton hand*es* … vi s. viii d.

Item delyv*er*ed unto Steven <S> Taberet in reward … iii s. iiii d.

Item paid the xii[th] day of Januar*y* unto the hardware man for iii couffers … xvii s.

Item to the same for iii comb*es* of yvery … v s.

Item for ii ymag*es* of clothe oon of our*e* Lady and anoder of Mary Mawdelen … viii s.

Item for ii glyst*er* pypes. P*rice* … vi s.

Item for oon clothe of neld*es* … xx d.

Item for ii payr*e* of yevery beyd*es* … ii s. viii d.

[M]Summa … xxii li. xiiii s. iiii d. ob.[P]

[*p. 61*] Item payd to the same for a dossen gloves … iii s. iiii d.

Item paid for iiii payre of candyl snoffers[70] … viii d.

Item delyv*er*ed for money delyv*er*ed unto Thomas Pellett*es* tewter*e* at Cambryge vi s. viii d.

Item for a cote and othe[r] nessessariez for hym t*o* be bought other vi s. viii d. …xiii s. iiii d.

Item paid to Thomas grome of the stabyll for the cost*es* of bryngyng of the same Thomas Pellet to Cambryg*e* … iii s. x d.

Item to m*aister* dean for a reward yeven unto an armet besyde Boston … iii s. iiii d.

Item for a reward yeven unto Hyde the <q> quenys s*er*vande … <vii> vi s. viii d.

Item in reward unto John Browne grome of the bedd*es* delyv*er*ed the same tyme … vi s. viii d.

Item the xiiii[th] day of Januar*y* to an aget mynstrell belongyng*e* to s*ir* Thomas Cheny …xx d.

Item delyvered unto m*aister* dean for a reward yeven unto John Harryson for his dysport*es* in Crystemas … xx s.

Item in reward unto Lowthe faukener*e* … xiii s. iiii d.

*The kyng*es *players*. Item the xv day of Januar*y* in reward unto the kyng*es* players … xl s.

[70] MS ‘sknoffers’.

Item payd the same day unto Richard Bothe for yeving his attendance upon maister p*re*sident at Leicest*er* in thexaminacion of the variaunce betwene the bysshop of Lincolne and my lorde Hasting*e* conce*r*ning affray co*m*mitted by their*e* s*er*vand*es* the abydyng and going and comyng the spaic*e* of thre dayez ... iiii s.

Item to the same yeving his attendance at Grantham upon the counsaill the space of vii dayes hymself a s*er*vant and two horses ... ix s. iiii d.

Item in reward unto m*aister* Petur the kyng*es* secretary s*er*vant delyv*er*ed to m*aister* dean ... vi s. viii d.

Item in reward to a s*er*vant of oon Richard Parker*e* of the eyle of Ely delyv*er*ed to m*aister* dean ... ii s.

MSumma ... vi li. xiiii s. x d.P

[*p. 62*] Item delyv*er*ed the xvii[th] day of Januar*y* unto maistres Fowler for a reward yeven unto m*aister* Morgance dought*ur* at hir maryag*e* ... x s.

Item delyv*er*ed unto m*aister* dean the same day for a reward yeven unto m*aister* Brytnell man of law ... xl s.

Item the same day in reward to m*aister* Cutlerd ... xl s.

Item delyv*er*ed unto m*aister* dean for a reward yeven unto the p*r*ior of Urmesby in Lensey ... x s.

Item t*o* the hardwar*e* man for iii dd. brochis and a dosen tavelynce delyv*er*ed unto maistres Massy ... iii s.

Item paid to Jamys Morice the same day for his cost*es* at Spaldyng to ov*er*se the workmen ther*e* that clensid the rev*er* by the spaic*e* of vi daiez he and his s*er*vande at xx d. a day. Item to Willyam Aderton by the same spaic*e* at vi d. the day ... xvi s.

Item paid to the same for the exspenc*e* of m*aister* Hughe Assheton and hymself by the spaice of iii daiez for to ov*er*se the sewer of Wilond ... vii s. ii d.

Item paid to the same Jamys for the hyr*e* of an horse for Ric*hard* Fyndon for to carre the same Ric*hard* to the kyng*es* g*r*ace at Langley by the spaice of vi daiez and from thens to Colyweston ev*er*y day his hyr*e* iiii d. and for his meyte iii d. Summa ... iiii s.

Item for the diett of the same Ric*hard* from Colyweston to Langley by iii daiez at iiii d. the day. Summa ... xii d.

Item in reward yeven unto m*aister* Cutlerd clerk for wryting of a pair*e* of indenturs for my lad*ys* g*r*ace ...iii s. iiii d.

Item paid to m*aister* Cutlerd for serchyng of a coawarante ... vi s. viii d.

[*p. 63*] Item paid to Thomas Robertson of Boston for vi lib. of whit gold of Venys. P*r*ic*e* the lib. iii li. ix s. Flemyche and in sterling*e* money the lib. xlv s. Summa totalis in Flemyche money xviii li. iiii s. vi d. the which maketh in st*er*lyng money after xxvii s. for the lib. xiii li. x s. sterlyng ... xiii li. x s.

Item paid to the same for cours gylt gold vi lib. at ix s. the lib. Flemyche money. Summa liiii s. the which mak*es* in st*er*lyng money of Englond aft*er* xxvii s. Flemyche for the pounde. A lib. standes in vi s. viii d. st*erlyng* … xl s.

Item paid t*o* the same for ii pec*es* of red and grene sarssenyt contaynyng thay bothe lii s. Flemych stik*es*. P*r*ice the stik ii s. ii d. Flemych. Summa <cl> Cxii s. viii d. Flemych which mak*es* sterlyng iiii li. iii s. vi d. sterlyng. The yerd standith in ii s. ii d. ob. sterlyng …iiii li. iii s. vi d.

Item paid to the same for ii pec*es* of fyne verdur contaynyng lv Flemych styk*es*. P*r*ic*e* the styk iii s. viii d. Flemyche. Summa x li. xx d. the wich makythe sterlyng vii li. vi s. viii d. A stik standith in ii s. viii d. st*erlyng* … vii li. <di> vi s. viii d.

Summa … xxxiiii li. ii s. iiii d.[P] [71]

[*p. 64*] [72]Summa of all the allowance and paiment*es* afor wrytten … DCCiiii li. xvi s. viii d. ob.

And so he owith … Diiii^{xx}xiiii li. xi s. vii d. ob.

wherof

the seid Mylys hath delyuerd to James Mores clerk of the work*es* at div*er*se tymes as yt apperith in the boke of the accompte of the same James by his owne <h> knolegh … CCCl li. x s. i d. ob. Also he delyuerd to Will*i*am Bedell tresourer of houshold by the hand*es* of John Bedell as yt apperith in the boke of the houshold … l li. And also he hath paid for thexibic*i*on of maister Seynt John and his wyff xxxiii li. vi s. iiii d. for thexhibicion of maister P*ar*ker and his wyff ix li. ix s. vd. ob. Thexhibic*i*on of Richard Frognall and Alexander his broder vii li. v s. vii d. thexhi[bi]c*i*on of Jane Rykylys and Ellissabeth Godesto*u*n xxxv s. vii d. ob. thexhibic*i*on of m*aister* M*ar*kehame lxxiiii s. v d. ob. and thexhibic*i*on of the French childe xl s. x d. In the hole … lvii li. xii s. iii d. ob.[73] As yt p*ar*ticlarye doyth appere in another boke of p*ar*cell*es* signed with the hande of the forseid counties and in hur kepyng remaynyng.

And so the [seid] Milys owithe … Cxxxvi li. ix s. ii d. ob.

wherof

[paper extension sewn to the bottom of p. 64, written small and neat]

*In prest*es *delyverd by my ladyes comaundment that ys to sey*[74]

Richard Conwey so*m*me tyme on of the clerk*es* of my la[d]ys chapell as in money to hym delyverd by my ladys co*m*maundment … iiii li.

Maister Arthur at London … <l> xx s. «debetur»

Rychard Carre for so much money by hyme delyverd to my ladys grace … vi s. viii d. «debetur»

My lorde of Durisme … C li.

[71] The total of pp. 62 and 63 (but 1s. over).

[72] The summary hand returns here.

[73] The total of the exhibitions.

[74] Bracketed to include all the next items on the paper extension.

John Innez of Stanneford … x li.

Maister Bekynsale … xl s.

George Hevenynghame … vii li. xvii s. vi d.

And so remayneth in the hand*es* of[75] the seid Miles … xi li. v s. ob.

[*p. 65*] Almes yeven to div*er*se p*er*sones ad div*er*se tymes … viii li. iiii s.

Money delyverd at div*ers* tymes to my ladys almes purse … xix li.

Certen pecez of wollen cloth bought for pore folk*es* … xxiiii li. iiii s.

li li. viii s.[76]

Money paid to the goldesmyth at Stanneford as well for certan*e* plate by hyme bought as for mendyng of div*ers* plate at[77] certen*e* tymes with[78] paid for a rynge of gold … xxiii li. xi d.

Exhibyc*io*n of my ladis scolers with the kepyng of my ladis lecturez at Oxenford and Cambrigge … xl li. iiii s.

Money sent to maister Twaytt*es* my ladys scoler at [*blank*] … xvi li.

Money delyverd at div*ers* tymes within this accompte for my ladys offerynge … xi li. xx d.

Exhibic*io*n of Richard Moyn at the charterhouse … xxiiii s. ix d.

Exhibic*io*n of Skyppe ad div*er*se tymez … xvii s. iiii d. ob.

Certen stuff bought for the childern of the chapell … xxvii s. iiii d.

Money delyverd to Brownyng of Burne my ladys almes man for a hole yer*es* fee … xl s.

Money delyverd to Peers Mychyn my ladis woket at Pares … iiii li.

Money paid to the vicare of Makesey for the tyth of ii closses there … xxiiii s.

[*p. 66*] Money delyverd to Richard Kelke to bye sonett*es* for men and childern … xl s. viii d.

Costez don at the lawe for the recov*er*ey and makyng sewer of maister Seynt John land*es* … iii li. xx d.

Money paid to maister Mordaunt for his fee … C s.

Horse bought of John Stakehouse … iiii li. iiii s. ii d.

Cost*es* of the cariage of iiii horses to Calyce … lvi s. iiii d.

Money paid for a staundyng tabull in my lord*es* c\l/osset … xl s.

[75] 'of' rep. next line.

[76] The total of the first three items on p. 65, bracketed to the right of the items.

[77] Written over 'off'?

[78] There is no gap for the missing sum.

Money delyverd to my lady Revers by my ladys co*m*maundment … viii li.

Newe counterfett arez bought for my ladis grace … xvi li. iii s. i d.

Div*er*s furres bought for my ladies grace … iiii li. xvi s. viii d. ob.

Div*er*s necessary stuff bought by my ladys co*m*maundment as well for hir grace as other … vii li. iii s. xi d. ob.

Cloth of gold bought for my ladys grace … ix li. xvii s.

Money delyverd to James Morice to bye certen stuff for my lad*ys* grace at Sturbrigge faire … xii li. xix s. vi d.

Money yeven to Jane Gowre at div*er*s tymes … xxx s.

Cost*es* don*e* for certen*e* ornament*es* of my ladys chapell … lxvii s. ii d.

Div*er*se sylk*es* bought as velvett damaske saten chamlytez sarsenett and other … xxxix li. x s. i d.

Gold and gold wyre bought for my ladys grace at soundre tymes … xlii li. xx d.

[*p. 67*] Money delyverd to Edward Nycholas hardwar man to bye certen*e* stuff for my ladys grace in Flanders … xvi li. x d.

Bonett*es* and frountelette*s* bought for gyntilwemen … xlii s.

Certen wollen cloth bought by my ladis co*m*maundment … xxii li. xviii s. iiii d.

Certen lynyn cloth bought for my ladis grace … xv li. iii s. i d. ob.

Certen peces of grene say bought … viii li. x s.

Money delyverd to Thomas Rob*er*tson for certen stuff by hyme bought for my ladys grace … xiii li. x s.

Money delyverd to John Harryson for stuff bought for the dysgysyng in Cristumase … Cxiiii s. viii d.

iii coffers and other certen stuff bought of the hardwarman … xliii s. viii d.

Money dylyverd to Edward Hevyn for to bye <stuff> xxix paire of brygonders … xxiiii li. ix s. x d.

Certen forest byll*es* bought … lxxii s. viii d.

Money delyverd to Poule Gyles for certen bull*es* and wrytyng*es* that come from Rome … xiiii li.

Money delyverd to maister Bray for the full paymennt of the maner of Padyngton and other … xx li.

Money paid to doctor Rounston for the tyeth of Coldherborowe of ii yerez endid at Michelmase anno xviii[[m]o] regis Henrici vii[mi] … Cvi s. viii d.

Money paid to Thomas Soper my ladys solicet*our* for his fee lxvi s. viii d. and for cost*es* of sewte of the lawe vi li. ii s. viii d. … ix li. ix s. iiii d.

[*p. 68*] Cost*es* do*n*n vppon lytell Gybon my ladys ward … ii s. i d.

Money delyverd for the quenes New Yerez gift*es* xl li. maister Braye x marc*e* my lady Braye liii s. iiii d. and to my ladys hand*es* for to gyve in Newyere gyft*es* iiii li. in all … liii li. vi s. viii d.

Money delyverd to Oliver Seynt John at div*er*se tymes … xliiii s.

Reward gyffon to Watson with xl s. payd for certen [*blank*] to m*aister* Braye … x li.

Reward gyffen for the kepyng of a goshauke … xxvi s. viii d.

Money delyverd to maistrez Flye and maistrez Webbe by my ladys co*m*maundment … xxx s.

Rewarde yeven to div*er*se p*er*sones at soundre tymes within the tyme of this accompte … Cxxxiiii li. xii s. iiii d.

Foren expenc*e* of my ladys s*er*vant*es* in rydyng vppon hur messagez to div*er*s places at soundre tymes and other expens*e* of hur counsell … xx li. xv s. ix d. ob.

totalis … DCCiiii li. xvii s. viii d. ob.[79]

[*pp. 69–70 blank*]

[*p. 71*] [80]*Colyveston*. Thaccompte of Myles Worsley coferare of the most excellent prynces Margaret countes of Rychmound and derby and moder unto oure sov*er*ane lord the kynge that nowe ys kynge Henry the viith frome the \<fest off the Puryficac*i*on off our*e* Lady>/ <xiiiithday of January> \stet/ the xviiith yere of the seid sov*er*ayn lord unto the xiiiith day of January then next folowyng that ys to sey by the space of <iii q*u*arters off a yere> an hole yere.

Tharreragez. Fryste the seid accomptand ys charged with tharreragez of his last accompte as in the same more playnly yt doth appere … Cxxxvi li. ix s. ii d. ob.

Summa … Cxxxvi li. ix s. iid. ob.[81]

[*p. 72 blank*]

[*p. 73*] [82]Receyved of my ladiez g*r*ace from the xiiii day of January anno regni Henrici vii xviii^{o}

Furst receyved the xix day of Januar*y* … xv li. xviii s.

Item r*eceyved* the xxi day of January … xxvi li. xiiii s.

Item r*eceyved* the xiii day of February … CClx li. vi s. ix d. ob.

Item r*eceyved* the same day … iiii^{xx}xix li.

[79] Written small to the left at the foot of the page in the same hand (it is £1 over the correct total of pp. 65–8).
[80] The summary hand begins the new year.
[81] See p. 64.
[82] The MW hand returns here.

Item r*eceyved* the furst day of Ap*r*ell … iiii^{xx}x li. viii s.

Item r*eceyved* the xii day of Ap*r*ell … xxi li. iiii s. iiii d.

Item r*eceyved* the same day … xxv li. viii s. ix d.

Item r*eceyved* the xxii day of Ap*r*ell … xlvi li. xi s. v d.

Item the xxvii day of Ap*r*ell … xviii li. xix s.

Item r*eceyved* the iii^{de} day of May … xvii li. iii s. iiii d.

Item r*eceyved* the xith day of May … xix li.

Item r*eceyved* the xxii day of May … Ciiii^{xx}xiiii li. xi d.

Item r*eceyved* xxiiii day of May … xxiii li.

Item r*eceyved* the xxv day of May … xii li.

Summa … DCCClxix li. xiiii s. vi d. ob.[83]

Item r*eceyved* the xiii day of Juyn … CCxliii li. <v d.> xvii d.

Item r*eceyved* the xith day of July … Cxxviii li. viii s. vi d.

Item r*eceyved* the <x> xvi day of July … lxix li. v s. iiii d.

Item r*eceyved* the xxviii day of July … lxiiii li. xii s. vi d.

Item r*eceyved* the xxix day of July … xx li.

Item r*eceyved* the xxviii day of August … xliii li. xi s. iiii d.

Item the viii day of Septembre … xxxi li. xiii s. iiii d.

Item the same day … xvi li. xvii s. xi d.

Item the viii day of Octobr*e* … lxii li. vi s. ix d.

Item the xvi day of Octobr*e* … xx li.

Item the xxiii day of Octobr*e* … xx li.

Item the same day … xv li. xvi s. iii d.

Summa … DCCxxxv li. <xiii s.[84] *v d.> \xiii s. iii d./*[85]

Summa pagine recepte … MDCv li. vii[86] s. xi d. ob.

[*p. 74*] Item iiiith of Novembr*e* … xx li.

Item rece*yved* the xvith day of Novembr*e* … xviii li.

[87]Item rece*yved* the xxviith day of Novembr*e* … xiii li. x s. i d.

[83] The total so far, written small in left margin.
[84] MS 'xiij'.
[85] The total since the last noted total, written small in left margin (the canc. sum is 1d. over and the corrected sum, in a different hand, is 1d. under).
[86] MS 'vjj'. The total of the whole page of receipts (1d. over).
[87] The rest of the page may be written in the 'curly' hand.

Item rec*eyved* the first day of Decembr*e* … xvi li.

Item r*eceyved* the xiiiith day of Decembr*e* … Ciiii^{xx}iiii li. xi s. iiii d.

Item rec*eyved* the xix day of Decembr … xli li. vi s. viii d.

Item rec*eyved* the xxx day of Decembr … DCxx li.

<DCCCiiii^{xx}xiii li. viii s. i d.>[88]

Item rec*eyved* the xiii day of January of m*aister* chamberlayn by byll*es* of allowance … xxiii li. iii s. vii d. ob.

Item receved of m*ais*t*er* chaunceller the last day of Decembr … lx s.

Summa partis … DCCCCxxxix li. xi s. viii d. ob.

So*m*me off the hole receyt*es* … MMDxliiii li. xix s. viii d.[89]

[*p. 75*] [90]Some of all the receytez with tharra*r*ag*es* … MMDCiiii^{xx}i li. viii s. x d. ob.

wherof

payed as foloweth

[*p. 76 blank*]

[*p. 77*] [91]Cost*es* and exspenc*e* w*i*th other dyv*er*se payment*es* and reward*es* of the most excellent prync*es* Margarete countesse of Rychemound and Darby and moder unto our*e* sov*er*aigne lord kyng Harry the viith from the xiiiith day of January in the xviiith yer*e* of our*e* said sov*er*aigne lord payd by the hand*es* of Myles Worsley.

Furst payd to m*aister* dean for a reward yeven unto Wyllyam Whyttyngton xx^{ti} day of January … vi s. viii d.

Item paid to Wyllyam Merse of Depyng for ii yerd*es* di. of tawny medly at iii s. the yerd … vii s. vi d.

Item payd unto the same for xiiii yerd*es* di. of tawny medly at ii s. vi d. the yerd … xxxvi s. iii d.

Item paid to the same for xliiii yerd*es* of blak lynyng. P*r*ic*e* the yerd v d. … xviii s. iiii d.

Item for ii lib. of blew thredd. P*r*ic*e* … ii s. ii d.

Item for carryag*e* of the same stuff from Coventr*e* unto Colyweston … xx d.

[88] The total is alongside the 30 December entry and is £20 short because it was calculated before the first entry was added (see note above).

[89] Both totals are written in the 'sprawling' hand lower down the page from the entries; the 'Summa partis' is correct, but the total of all the receipts is 2d. over.

[90] The summary hand returns here. The total is correct in terms of the totals above.

[91] The MW hand returns here.

Item paid unto Saunder skynner for workyng apon my ladys stuff and his servand by the spaice of ix daiez and nyghtes agaynest Crystemasse for every day and nyght viii d. … vi s.

Item paid unto maister tressorer for a reward yeven to a servande of maister Perpoyntes comyng in message unto my ladys grace in Crystemasse … ii s.

Item payd unto maister dean for a reward yeven to a servande of George Kyrkam for bryngyng of letturs from London unto my ladys grace … xii d.

Item paid the xxi day of January unto maister Gryndell for money payd unto the goldsmyth of Stampforth for mendyng of the fote of a gylt pott … xii d.

Item to the same for makyng of a new saucere of sylver … ii s. iiii d.

[*p. 78*] Item payd the xxiiii day of January to maistres Foler for a reward yeven to the prior of Seynt Cattrens of Lyncoln … vi s. viii d.

Item paid to the same for a payre of shoez for Merget Golsell … iiii d.

Candylmasse day. Item for my ladys offryng apon Candylmasse day … thretty pens of golde …xii s. vi d.

Item the iii^{de} day of February to a frere of Grenewyche that prechet afoure my ladys grace … iii s. iiii d.

Item the iiiith day of February to maister dean for a reward yeven unto Orton my ladys servande … vi s. viii d.

Item paid to maister dean for a reward yeven unto Richard Aderton comyng from London in message to my ladys grace … x s.

Item payd the vii day of February to a armorer for dressyng of xxix payre of sallettes with splentes gussettes standardes and scurtes of mayle … xiiii s. viii d.

Item the same day to my ladies grace for money delyvered to my lady marques … xiii s. iiii d.

Item payd to Nicholas Aughton by a byll assigned for xi daiez ridyng to Richmounde and ayen … vii s. iiii d.

Item to the same for ridyng to Foteringay to maister Denton for his dyner and horse meyte … iiii d.

Item to Willyam Hylmer by a byll assigned for sylkes and golde bought by hym at London … lxii s. iii d.

Item to John Kyng of Bykelleswade in reward for bryngyng worde unto my ladys grace of the parsonage of Wrastlingworth the xth day of February … iii s. iiii d.

Item delyvered to maistres Foler for the maryage of maister Frognoll … vi s. iiii d. … ^{M}Summa … <xii li xii s.> xi li. xii s.^{P}[92]

[92] The total of pp. 78 and 79.

[*p. 79*] Item paid the xii^th^ day of February unto m*aister* tresorer for a reward yeven unto a s*er*vande of m*aister* Peyrepoynt*es* comyng in message unto my lad*ys* g*r*ace ... ii s.[93]

Item payd the xiii^th^ day of February unto Richard Carr*e* by a byll assigned for ridyng to Fenne Stretford for iii daiez ii s. Item for ridyng ii daiez by m*aister* countrollers comaundement xvi d. Item for the cost*es* of the brother wyff husbound xvi d. ... iv s. viii d.

Item paid unto m*aister* Gryndell for money paid to the goldsmyth of Stampforth for makyng of angellett*es* of sylv*er* for my lad*ys* g*r*ace ... xii d.

Item to the same for makyng of a vice of the cover of a cupp of gold ... xii d.

Item to the same for a reward yeven unto the procto*ur*s of Cambryge ... vi s. viii d.

Item paid the xiiii^th^ day of February for a reward yeven to John Duffeld ... vi s. viii d.

Item the xvi day of Februar*y* delyv*er*ed to Codde at Am*er*sam to betake unto my ladies g*r*ace ... vi s. viii d.

Item paid to Nich*olas* Aughton for his cost*es* ridyng t*o* London by v daiez goyng and comyng ... iii s. iiii d.

*M*aister *Fawne*. Item payd to m*aister* Morgan for money by hym payd to m*aister* Fawne my lad*ys* scoller in Cambryg*e* for a half yere endet at Crestemasse ... xxvi s. viii d.

Item delyv*er*ed to s*ir* Hughe Assheton the xix day of February delyv*er* to a nonne in Camse abbey ... x s.

Item delyv*er*ed the same day t*o* William Hornywold m*aister* deanes s*er*vand to bye ii tapers ether of theym of v lib. weght to be offerd afour*e* Seynt Margett*es* in Lensey ... vi s. viii d.

^M^Summa pagine ... lxxv s. iiii d.^P^

[*p. 80*] Item paid to George Fraunc*es* for a reward yeven toward*es* the mendyng of a brygg betwix Northampton and Stone in Stretforth ... xii d.

Item paid the xxvi day of Februar*y* to m*aister* chamberlayn for v mantelett*es* of Pares ... xxv s.

Item for ii kerchiff*es* of pares. P*r*ice ... viii s.

Item for makyng of a barbbe ... xii d.

Item for vi yerd*es* of pares. P*r*ic*e* the yerd xx d. ... x s.

Item paid unto m*aister* dean for money delyv*er*ed to the Walshemen the kyng*es* s*er*vaund*es* apon Seynt Davies Day ... vi s. viii d.

Item to the same for money yeven unto Ric*hard* Aderton m*aister* chambre*laynes*[94] s*er*vand ... <v> iiii d.

[93] Perhaps entered in error (cf. p. 77).

[94] MS 'm*aister* Chambr^e^' over erasure.

Item paid to the same for a reward yeven unto the kyng*es* confessor toward*es* the byldinge of a howse of obs*er*vant*es* in Fraunce ... xl s.

Item paid the ii[d] day of Marche to Rob*er*t Hylton for money by hym paid to a skynner of Stampforth for makyng up of armyn womes ... v s.

Item paid to the same for v yerd*es*<of> and a half of dark tawny for cot*es* for the two lett*er*men. P*rice* of ev*er*y yerd ii s. x d. Summa ... xv s. vii d.

Item paid for makyng of the same cot*es* ... xii d.

Item paid for the yerd q*uarter* and a half q*uarter* of tawny kersey for John fotman. P*rice* of an yerd ii s. ii d. ... ii s. xi d. ob.

Item paid for a yerd q*uarter* of the same tawny for Herry fotman aft*er* the same p*r*ice ...ii s. viii d. ob.

Item paid for makyng and lynyng of the same howse ... xx d.

Item paid for two payr*e* of shoez for the same fottmen. P*rice* the payr*e* vi d. ... xii d.

[*p. 81*] Item paid t*o* the same for money paid to my lady Scrop for basse past wyer and pynnes ... xxiii d.

Item paid for a chaffyng dysshe ... ii s.

Item for a fyer shovyll \and a pair*e* of belowes/ ... xii d. ob.

Item paid for viii elnez of canvas for a palett case. P*rice* the elne iii d. ob. ... ii s. iiii d.

Item paid for helpe for the makyng of my lad*ys* sloppe vi d. Item forryng of the same xvi d. ... xxii d.

Item paid t*o* the same Rob*er*t for his cost*es* at London by the space of iiii daiez beying their*e* by my ladiez co*m*maundement ... xvi d.

Item to the same for carryag*e* of my ladies stuff from London at ii tymes ... xvi d.

Item paid to George Fraunc*es* for a reward yeven to a s*er*vand of thabbott*es* of Glawcet*er* for bryngyng of a bake lamprey t*o* my ladiez g*race* ... iii s. iiii d.

Item delyv*er*ed to m*aister* dean for money yeven unto maistres Denton of hir fee ... lxvi s. viii d.

Item paid to Willyam Aderton the vi[th] day of M*ar*che for v horsis bought by hym in the north countre which wer*e* send into France ... vii li. xvi s. ii d.

Item in reward to Crystofer Fezaunt ... vi s. viii d.

Item paid to John fotman by a byll for caryag*e* of a couffer from Richmound to London and for sawlyng of a payr*e* of shoez for my ladiez grace ... ii s.

Item the same day delyv*er*ed to m*aister* chamberlayn for my ladiez offryng to Seynt Brygyt ... ii s.

Item paid to the wat*er*men for a reward convaying of my ladiez g*r*ace betwix Richmond and Syon ... iii s. iiii d.

[M]Summa ... xviii li. xiii s. x d. ob.[P]

[*p. 82*] Item paid the vi[th] day of M*ar*che to William Hylm*er* for xviii unc*e* of sylk bought of maistres Fench. P*r*ic*e* the unc*e* xi d. … xvi s. vi d.

Item paid t*o* the same for blak reben of the brod sorte ii unc*e* iii q*uarter*. P*r*ic*e* …ii s. ix d.

Item paid to the same William for a wyker hamp*er* and a lok for the same. P*r*ic*e* … xiiii d.

Item for a gret wassyng bolle. P*r*ic*e* … xx d.

Item for a gret wat*er* jugge of leder*e* … ii s. viii d.

Item for a wat*er* chaffur of brasse weyng xiiii lib. at iii d. ob. the pound … iiii s. i d.

Item paid for a fyr*e* panne of yrne … viii d.

Item for a lytell brasse panne w*i*th a steyle … viii d.

Item for blak crule for your*e* g*r*ace … viii d.

Item paid for iiii whitt bonett*es* … xvii d.

Item paid for a botte for carryag*e* of ii yonde stolis and a fourme for my ladiez g*r*ace …iiii d.

[95]*M*aister *chamb*er*lain*.[96]

Item paid the xi[th] day of M*ar*che at Richemond unto maister chamberlain for two pounds of gilt golde at xvi s. the lib. … xxxii s.

Item iiii stone bottelles … xii d.

Item oon pece of tany chamlet. P*r*ic*e* … xxxvi s. viii d.

Item a C of whit bugge … xxvi s. viii d.

Item two tymber lott*es* … xvi s. viii d.

Item for thre yerd*es* of blak satten … xx s.

Item paid unto maister chamberlain for a reward yeven unto Hugh Dennes … vi s. viii d.

Item to the same for a reward yeven unt*o* Munde … iii s. iiii d.

Item yeven in reward unto maister Twat*es* s*er*vant for conveing of a foreinge woman unto my ladies grace … xiii s. iiii d.

[*p. 83*] Item the xiiii[th] day of Marche yeven in rewarde unto my lady Kat*er*in Courtney sustur to the quenes g*r*ace decessed … xx s.

Item the same day in reward to doctor Atkinson chaplain unto my lady Brey … xx s.

Item the same day yeven in rewarde unto Arture Som*er*sete … xl s.

[95] The 'curly' hand is responsible for these entries relating to the chamberlain and the first three entries on p. 83.
[96] Bracketed to include the next eight items.

Maistres Frognoll. Item the same day for a rewarde yeven unto maistres Frognoll at London … lxvi s. viii d.

*M*aister *almoigner.*[97]

Item payd to m*aister* almoigner for a reward yeven unto maistresse Alienor Johannes … x s.

Item t*o* the same for a pounde of wax bought by hym for my ladiez g*r*ace … vii d.

Item payd unto John Fysshe for his cost*es* from Colyweston unto Richmound w*ith* c*er*ten stuff of my ladiez g*r*ace by iiii daiez … iiii s.

Item in reward unto Mylez [B]oesse[98] my lady Scropp*es* s*er*vande for bryngyng of mavessy to my ladiez g*r*ace <to> at Richmound … xx d.

Item delyv*er*ed unto Nicholas Aughton and John Fisshe for bryngyng of maistres Frognoll*es* from London into Kent for hir cost*es* and theyr*es* … x s.

Item paid to George Fraunc*es* for money yeven to my ladiez g*r*ace for hir offryng to Seynt Bregett at Syon the Saturday the furst wek in Lent … xii d.

Item to the same for money yeven to the wat*er*men convayng of hir g*r*ace from Richmond to Syon and ayen to Richmond … iii s. iiii d.

Item payd the xvith day of M*ar*che to Wylliam Hylm*er* for medicens and other ness*esaryez* for my ladiez g*r*ace as aperith by a byll assigned … v s. ii d.

[M]Summa … xviii li. xvi d.[P99]

[*p. 84*] Item the xvith day of M*ar*che unto s*ir* Samson Norton s*er*vant in <t> rewarde and for the cost*es* of a Frenche woman from Calice to Richmound … xx s.

Item the same day in rewarde to <hew> Hughe Denys wyff by Ric*hard* Bothe …vi s. viii d.

Item to maistres Flee for money betakyn unto my ladiez g*r*ace … vi s. viii d.

Item paid to maistres Wenysowr*e* for iiii M pynnesse bought by hir for my ladiez g*r*ace … ii s. vi d.

Item paid unto m*aister* dean for a reward yeven unto Garter the kyng of herold*es* … vi s. viii d.

*M*aister *Jamys Denton.* Item paid the xvith day of M*ar*che t*o* m*aister* Jamys Denton my ladiez skoller in Orlyance toward*es* his exibuc*ion* for the yer*e* to be ended at our*e* Lady Day in Lent … xl s.

Item paid unto m*aister* dean for a reward yeven unto maistres Fitzherberd … vi s. viii d.

Item the xxii day of M*ar*che delyv*er*ed to my ladiez g*r*ace for money delyv*er*ed to the ankur*e* at the chart*er*house … xx d.

[97] Bracketed to include the next two items.
[98] MS 'Roesse'.
[99] The total is 10s. under.

Item in reward to Campynet beyng seke at London … x s.

*Cost*es *of Ric*hard *Carr*e. Item paid to Ric*hard* Carre for his cost*es* and horse hyr*e* rydyng to serch the way betwix Richmond and Synt Albonys the spaic*e* of a day … xii d.

Item to the same for ridyng t*o* Ware t*o* cont*er*maunde my ladiez horsis ii daiez … ii s.

Item the xxiii day of M*ar*che paid to Georg*e* Fraunc*es* for a reward yeven t*o* Peris Barburs wyff … vi s. viii d.

Item delyv*er*ed t*o* my ladiez g*r*ace for a reward yeven to maistres Sowche w*i*th the quene of Skott*es* … vi s. viii d.

Item for a reward yeven unto Gret Elyzabeth … iii s. iiii d.

Item in reward to m*aister* Laice fesicion … x s.

Item in reward to m*aister* Lynche … xx s.

[M]Summa … viii li. x s. vi d.[P]

[*p. 85*] Item paid the xxii day of M*ar*che to m*aister* Morgan for a reward yeven to Botton my ladiez s*er*vand for bryngyng of a brasse of greyhound*es* to my ladiez g*r*ace at Richmound … vi s. viii d.

Item paid to the <sam> same for two pair*e* of po<r>thowse bought for my ladiez g*r*ace … x s.

Item paid to m*aister* chamberlayn for money delyv*er*ed by hym to my ladiez g*r*ace at Colyweston … xxx s.

Item t*o* the same for a reward yeven to my ladiez oste at Kettryng … iii s. iiii d.

Item to the same for money paid t*o* oon of Ketreng þ*at* went to Colyweston for my ladiez count*er*peynt for hir lytell bedd … viii d.

Item to the same for a reward yeven to a man þ*at* was robbett at Am*er*sam … ii s. iiii d.

Item in reward t*o* the bargeman þ*at* browght my ladiez g*r*ace ov*er* the wat*er* at Richmound … xx d.

Item paid to maistres Flee for a reward yeven to a man þ*at* brought a glasse of rose wat*er* t*o* my ladiez g*r*ace from my lady Ryv*er*se sust*er* at Myn*er*ez … xii d.

Item paid unto maistres Wenysowr*e* for a reward yeven to a s*er*vand of my lady of Syon bryngyng of butt*ur* t*o* my ladiez g*r*ace … xii d.

Item to the same for iiii[C] neld*es* … xiiii d.

[100]Item yeven in reward unto da[n]e[101] John Eline … iii s. iiii d.

Item to dane Silvestre … iii s. iiii d.

[100] The last three entries on the page were added in the 'curly' hand using a darker ink.
[101] MS 'dame'.

Item to Richard butleir*e* of the charturhouse … iii s. iiii d.

<Summa … […] vii s. x d.> Summa … iii li. viii s. x d.[P]

[*p. 86*] Item delyv*er*ed t*o* Grewell for my ladiez offryng apon our*e* Lady Day … v s.

Item the same day delyv*er*ed to my ladiez g*r*ace for a reward yeven unto Hugh Denyse …xx s.

Item in reward to Weston … x s.

Item in reward unto Jamys Braybroke … vi s. viii d.

Item to Peris Barbur in reward … vi s. viii d.

Item to Fraunc*es* in reward … vi s. viii d.

Item to Thomas Wolv*er*ston in reward … iii s. iiii d.

Item to m*aister* dean for a reward yeven t*o* m*aister*<at> Arthur … xx s.

Item to Nicholas Gray in reward … xiii s. iiii d.

Item to the scole maist*er* of the chart*er*howse for Ric*hard* Moyne … iii s. iiii d.

lx s.[102]

Item to the proct*our* of the chart*er*howse t*o* p*ro*vide for Ric*hard* Moyne a gowne and a pair*e* of howse … xiii s. iiii d.

Item to Hasulrygg in reward … x s.

Item to the pantr*e* … xx s.

Item t*o* the buttre in reward … xx s.

Item to the seller in reward … xx s.

Item t*o* the kychen in reward … xxvi s. viii d.

Item to Thomas Coke and his felow … x s.

Item t*o* the squyllery and colehowse … v s.

Item t*o* the porters … vi s. viii d.

Item t*o* the wodyard … vi s. viii d.

Item t*o* the spyc*er*y … v s.

Item to Shyrley m*aister* clerk of the kychen … xx s.

Item to Elyzabeth Leghe … vi s. viii d.

Item in reward to a <Suss> sust*er* of my lady Rev*er*se at Myn*er*esse … iii s. iiii d.

Item in reward to my lady Verney … xiii s. iiii d.

ix li. xvi s. viii[103] d.[104]

[102] The total of the previous seven items, bracketed to the right of the items.
[103] MS 'vijj d.'
[104] The total of the previous fifteen items (10s. over), bracketed to the right of the items.

Item for my lad*ys* offryng at our*e* Lady of Pewe ii s. vi d. Item to the rode of northe dore in Pawles ii s. vi d. t*o* our*e* Lady of G*r*ace … ii s. vi d. Summa … vii s. vi d.

[*p. 87*] *M*aister *chauncellere*.[105]

Item paid unto m*aister* chaunceller for money payd to Polles Gygles for a bull of non residence for my ladiez chapell prest*es* … xiiii li.

Item paid to the same for my ladiez offryng at Saint Albones … x s.

Item payd to Willyam Aderton for a reward yeven to the <ques> quenes fotmen … ii s.

Item paid to maistres Webbe for a reward yeven to Edith Burton for bryngyng of walnott*es* in c*er*yppe to my ladies g*r*ace at Richmound … iii s. iiii d.

Item paid to John Urmeston for his cost*es* and bot hyr*e* to Richmound apon my ladiez messag*es* … viii d.

Item paid to Crystefer Bygynsse for two brusshes for the wardrop … vi d.

Item to my ladiez g*r*ace for offryng at Northampton to our*e* Lady of G*r*ace … ii s. vi d. Item by m*aister* confessor for money betakyn to my ladiez g*r*ace the same tyme xvi d. … iii s. x d.

Item for my ladiez offryng t*o* the rode of Walle in Northampton … ii s. vi d.

Item paid to John fotman for a reward yeven to the lytermen … iii s. iiii d.

Item t*o* the same for a reward yeven to a wyffe of Weldom þ*a*t brought a dysshe of appuls … iiii d.

[M]Summa … xxx li. v s. vii d.[P 106]

[*p. 88*] Item t*o* John Urmeston for a reward to Weston … vi s. viii d.

Item delyv*er*ed t*o* my ladies g*r*ace by Richard Carre as aperith in the fote of my last accountes[107] … vi s. viii d.

Item payd the vii[th] day of Ap*r*ell to George Fraunc*es* for iii dd. beydes bought at Syon for my lad*ys* g*r*ace … iii s. ii d.

Item the xii day of Ap*r*ell to my lad*ys* g*r*ace for hir almes pursse … x li.

*Money delyv*ered *at the mawndy to pore folk*es. Item the xiii[th] day of Ap*r*ell yeven to lx pore folk*es* at the maundy ev*er*y pece xiii d. Summa … lxv s.

Item delyv*er*ed to George Fraunc*es* for my ladiez offryng apon Palme Sonday … v s.

Brownyng. Item paid to m*aister* dean for mone delyv*er*ed unto John Brownyng for his anuitie for the t*er*me endet at our*e* Lady Day in Lent … x s.

[105] Bracketed to include the next two items.
[106] The total of pp. 86–7 is correct in terms of the intermediate marginal calculations, although it does not reflect the alteration from 'vij' to 'vijj' on p. 86.
[107] See p. 68 above.

Item in reward to the baly of Tatsall s*er*vande for the convaying of a l*ett*re <for> from my lady Cecill to my lad*ys* g*r*ace … xx d.

Item in reward to a s*er*vande of doct*ur* Haryngton comyng in messag*es* unto my ladiez g*r*ace … iii s. iiii d.

Item paid to Rob*er*t Edlyn for a dosen of arroez for the chylder of chappell … v d.

Item in reward yeven to Holt m*aister* chamberlayn s*er*vant … xx d.

Item paid to the same Rob*er*t for a reward yeven to Hugh Denys s*er*vant for bryngyng of two bottels of wyne to my ladiez g*r*ace … xii d.

Item yeven <in> by maistrez Curson to Hugh Carre and to Rob*er*t Bonett … viii d.

Item for an erthen pott bought by Rob*er*t Edlyn … iii d.

Item paid to a lander for wasshyng of my ladiez clothes at Richmounde … iii s.

[*p. 89*] Item paid to Rob*ert* Edlyn for money paid for the dying and dressing of Perrett gown … xvi d.

Item paid to s*ir* John
 Blotte for money to be delyv*er*ed to John brotherers wyff at Stone in Stretforth … xiii s. iiii d.

*M*aister *Assheton.*[108]

Item paid the xth day of Ap*r*ell to s*ir* Hughe Assheton for money yeven t*o* William Barkers wyff for a bedde for Olyve*r* Seynt John … x s.

Item paid to the same for a reward yeven t*o* Jane Goer at London … xx s.

Item for iiii elnez of lynnen clothe for the same Jane. P*r*ice the elne viii d. … ii s. viii d.

*M*aister *chamberlayn.*[109]

Item paid to m*aister* chamberlayn for a reward yeven to Campynet of my lad*ys* chappell beyng seke at London … iii s. iiii d.

Item paid to the same for lvi yerd*es* of grene s*ar*cynet. P*r*ice the yerd ii s. viii d. … vii li. ix s. iiii d.

Item paid to the same for vi yerd*es* of blak fostyan to make fotmen doblett*es*. P*r*ice the yerd vii d. … iii s. vi d.

Item paid to Palm*er* sadler for a cheyre tr[e]de … vi s. viii d.

Item paid for a C neld*es* … iiii d.

Item paid for iii pec*es* of red bokeram. P*r*ice … xx s.

Item paid to the same m*aister* chamberlayn for money delyv*er*ed to Ric*hard* Carre for t*o* bye iii pec*es* of red bokeram … xx s.

Item paid for a lib. of golde of damask t*o* Wodward*es* wyff … lx s.

Item for my lad*ys* offryng at Senalbonis t*o* the shryne … xx d.

[108] Bracketed to include the next three items.
[109] Bracketed to include the rest of the items on p. 89.

Item for my lad*ys* offryng at Donstabyll … iii s. iiii d.

Item for a reward yeven to the waytt*es* of Northampton … iii s. iiii d.

[M]Summa … xxxi li. vii s. iiii d.[P 110]

[*p. 90*] *My ladiez offryng on Gode Fryday and Est*ur *Day.*[111]

Item for my ladiez offryng apon Goode Fryday in v s. of golde … xxx s.

Item for my lad*ys* offryng apon Est*ur* Day in the mornyng xx d. and at <…> masse v s. … vi s. viii d.

Item for a reward yeven to m*aister* Parker the xiii day of Aprell … iii s. iiii d.

Item paid to m*aister* Morgan for a glyst*er* pype bought by hym … ii s.

Item paid the xiii[th] day of Aprell to m*aister* Grendell for money paid for the cost*es* of the prior of Thorney comyng to preyche at Colyweston apon Mydlent Sonday … ii s. iii d.

*M*aister *Par*kers *chyld.* Item the xv day of Aprell delyv*er*ed to maistres Merbury for money paid t*o* Fremans wyff for kepyng of m*aister* Parkers chylde … x s.

Nonnez of Catley. Item delyv*er*ed to the prior of Sympryngham for a reward to the nonnez of Cattley … vi s. viii d.

*A horse bought of J. Moric*e.[112]

Item the xxix day of Aprell to Jamys Morice for an horse by hym bought for my lad*ys* grace at Stampforth fair*e*. Price … xxxviii s. iiii d.

Item for shoyng of the same horse … viii d.

Item paid to Hugh Latym*er* for a manys waig*es* and help to drye clothes in the wardrop of my lad*ys* beyng at London … xii d.

*To the cook*es *for theire with at Est*er.[113]

Item in reward to the cok*es* for theyr*e* with at Est*er* … xxvi s. viii d.

Item t*o* the sawc*er*y and squyllery … v s.

Item paid t*o* John Browne m*aister* coke for safferon delyv*er*ed to Palm*er* sadler at London which was occupied for harnesse ayenst the mariag*e* … xi s.

[M]Summa … vii li. iii s. vii d.[P]

[*p. 91*]

*Thomas Rob*ert*son.*[114]

[110] The total of pp. 88–9.
[111] Bracketed to include the next two items.
[112] Bracketed to include the next two items.
[113] Bracketed to include the next three items.
[114] Bracketed to include the next four items.

«*Nota attingere iuxta retro ii s. viii d. le <b> yerde ad xvii li. vi s. <vii> viii d.*»[115]

Item paid to Thomas Robertson of Boston for ii pec*es* of tapystre cont*aynyng* vi^{xx} and x Flemysshe ellis at iii s. viii d. Flemyssh and in sterlyng money ii s. viii d. Summa … xvii li. vi d.

Item paid to the same oon pece of curser warke contaynyng lxv F[lemyssh] elnet at iii s. iiii d. Flemyssh. Summa in sterlyng money … vii li. xiii s. xi d.

Item paid to the same for iiii pec*es* of cremesyn satten of Brug*es* at ii s. iiii d. Flemyssh the furst pec*e* *contaynyng* lxv ellnes. ii^{de} lviii i q*uarter*. iii^{de} lxviii and q*uarter*. iiiith xlviii. and summa CC Flemyssh elnez. Summa stuffure … xx li.

Item paid for cariag*e* of the same from London to Boston ii s. vi d. Item from Boston t*o* Colyweston iiii s. iiii d. Summa … vi s. x d.

Item paid to Lenard of the vestry for syngyng bredd and other ness*esaryez* for the chapell as aperith by his byll … ii s. ix d.

Item in reward t*o* ii s*er*vand*es* of m*aister* Peyrepoynt*es* bryngyng of ii men t*o* my ladis gr*a*ce … iii s. iiii d.

For ale send to the kyng.[116]

Item paid the xxiii day of Ap*r*ell to Jak of Lydyngton for a tonne of ale sent to the kyng*es* gr*a*ce to London … xxxii s.

Item for hopying of iiii hogyshed*es* for the same ale … xiiii d.

Item for caryag*e* of the same ale to Coldherborow … xxiii s. iiii d.

*M*aister *Fawnee.*[117] Item paid the xxiiii day of Ap*r*ell to m*aister* Fawne my ladies scoller in Cambryge in full payment for a q*uarter* of a yer*e* endet at Est*er* last … xiii s. iiii d.

Item yeven in reward t*o* the hardware man … iii s. iiii d.

Item to Harr*y* Cotton my lord*es* s*er*vande in reward … vi s. viii d.

^{M}Summa … xlix li. vii s. ii d.^{P}

[*p. 92*] Item the xxvith day of Ap*r*ell yeven in almes to an hermyte of <yelande> Irnam … xx d.

Item the same day in reward to a s*er*vande of m*aister* Cutlerd for the convaying of my ladies l*ett*ers to s*ir* John Blott … xii d.

*Rob*ert *Hylton.*[118]

[115] Written in the left margin alongside the above entry, this is the first of a number of marginal annotations (often accompanied by +) in the 'sprawling' hand. As the note says (referring to the first entry), 130 ells at 2s. 8d. sterling is indeed £17 6s. 8d., not £17 6d.
[116] Bracketed to include the next three items.
[117] Bracketed to include the single item.
[118] Bracketed to include the rest of the items on p. 92.

Item paid the same day to Rob*er*t Hylton for vi^{xx} elnes of canvas. P*r*ic*e* the elne iii d. qua. … xxxii s. vi d.

Item t*o* the same for viii elnes of canvas. P*r*ice the elne ii d. ob. … xx d.

Item paid to the same for v dd. cappys … xxix s. ii d.

Item for iii other cappis. P*r*ic*e* … xvii d.

Item for a knytt cote for m*aister* Parkers son … vi d.

Item for a bonet for the same … ii d. ob.

Item for <his> cost*es* of the said R*o*ber*t* to London for p*ro*vicion of the said stuff … viii d.

Item for cariag*e* of the same from London to Rychemount … viii d.

Item for <i>iii elnez of lynyn clothe. P*r*ic*e* the <enle> elne xvi d. … iiii s.

Item paid for caryag*e* of a coffer fro s*ir* John Shawez t*o* Coldherborow and to Richmount … xii d.

Item paid for the cost*es* of the same Rob*er*t Hylton at London by the spaic*e* of ii daiez for delyv*er*eng*e* of my lad*ys* lev*er*y their*e* … viii d.

Item for iii elnez of lynen clothe. P*r*ic*e* elne xii d. … iii s.

Item for x elnez of canvas t*o* make a pak. P*r*ic*e* the elne iii d. qua. … ii s. viii d. ob.

Item paid for cord t*o* make pakk*es* … xviii d.

Item paid to the porters for makyng of the same pakk*es* and for playttyng*e* and pakthredd … xviii d.

Item paid for xxxii elnez of canvas aft*er* iii d. qua. the elne. Summa … viii s. viii d.

^{M}Summa … iiii li. xii s. vi d. <ob.>^{P}

[*p. 93*] *Rob*er*t Hylton.*[119]

Item paid to the same Rob*er*t Hylton for iiii yerd*es* of blak cotton for Perett*es* gowne. P*r*ic*e* … ii s.

Item paid for the soing*e* of the same gowne … viii d.

Item paid for a payr*e* of sheris for maistres Curson for <ch> shapyng of my ladiez almez smok*es* … iiii d.

Item paid t*o* the same Rob*er*t Hylton by his byll for iiii yerd*es* of blak for a mantyll for my ladiez g*r*ace. P*r*ic*e* the yerd iiii d. … <xvi d.><xvi s.> «quia allocatur in computo thesaurarii»[120]

Item paid for v dd. of almez howse. P*r*ic*e* the dd. iii s. … xv s.

Item paid for v pounde of blew thredd. P*r*ic*e* the pounde xi d. … iiii s. vii d.

Item for half a hundreth of neld*es* … ii d.

[119] Bracketed to include all the items on p. 93.

[120] 'quia …thesaurarii' add. to explain the canc. totals.

Item for viii elnez of canvas t*o* pak in the said stuff. P*rice* the elne iii d. … ii s.

Item for malyng corde … iiii d.

Item for his cost*es* by iiii daiez at Coventr*e* t*o* p*ro*vide the said stuff … iii s.

Item paid to the same for my lad*ys* offryng*e* at o*ur* Lady of the town … v d.

Item for v dd. of almez shone. P*rice* … xix s. iiii d.

Item for viii yerd*es* of Kyntyssh kyndall t*o* mak Skypp a cote. P*rice* the yerd ix d. … vi s.

Item paid for a payr*e* of howse for Perott … viii d.

Item for a payr*e* of shone for moder Elyn … iiii d.

Item for a payr*e* of <sleppers> slep*er*s for P*e*rott*es* … vi d.

Item for a payr*e* of shoez for Margett Golson … vi d.

MSumma … <lxxii s. x d.> lvi s. x d.P [121]

[*p. 94*] Item paid the ii^de day of Maii to William Hylm*er* by his byll assigned for a pott to putt in a lectuar*y* for my lad*ys* g*r*ace … iii d.

Item paid t*o* the same for a pair*e* of shoez sengle soled for my lad*ys* g*r*ace … v d.

Item t*o* the same for a hamp*er* and a lok to the same … xvi d.

Item for a lib. of pakthred for Ric*hard* Stukely … iiii d.

Item paid t*o* Herr*y* Wynstanley for iii payr*e* of shoez for Skyppe … xviii d.

Item for ii pair*e* of howse … xii d.

Item for wasshyng*e* of his clothis … vi d.

Item paid to Maydwell of Stampforth for vii payr*e* of shoez for the yonge gentylwomen … ii s.

Item paid to maist*er* Morgan for m*aister* Wallis horse meyte oon of the kyng*es* chapplens … iii s. iii d.

Brograve. Item paid the iiii^th day of May to John Brograve in p*ar*te of payment of a mor*e* summa … xx li.

Item delyv*er*ed to John Haryson for a reward yeven to a s*er*vande of m*aister* p*re*sydent*es* comyng oute of his way fro[m][122] London to Colyweston … xx d.

Item paid for a reward yeven to a s*er*vande of arched[ek]en of Bangowr*es* for convaying of an l*ett*re from his maist*er* unto my lad*ys* g*r*ace … iii s.

*My lad*ys *offrynge on Dedycacion Day*. Item delyv*er*ed unto Georg*e* Fraunc*es* for my ladiez offryng apon the Dedycacion Day … v s.

[121] The first total includes the canc. total of 16s. (fourth entry, p. 93); the second total removes the 16s. Both are anyway 1s. over.
[122] MS 'fron'.

Item paid to m*aister* dean for a reward yeven t*o* a monke of <w><Sy> Sempryngham … xii d.

[M]Summa … xxi li. <xvii d.><vii d.> \xv d./[P]

[*p. 95*] <Item the xi[th] day of May t*o* my ladies g*r*ace for money yeven unt*o* my lady <marquese><markques> … xx s.>

Item the xi[th] day of Maii t*o* my ladies g*r*ace for a reward yeven t*o* my lady markques …xx s.

Item in reward to m*aister* Crow of the chappell … x s.

Item delyv*er*ed unto m*aister* dean for a reward yeven unto Rog*er* Heyton m*aister* chauncellers s*er*vande comyng in message from his maist*er* unto my lad*ys* g*r*ace … vi s. viii d.

Item in reward unto John Warde m*aister* Brayez s*er*vande … vi s. viii d.

Item paid to Griffith Ric*e* for money yeven in almes to a por*e* man and his wyff of Kendall … xx d.

Item paid the xx day of May to John Urmeston for iii payr*e* of spektakels bought at the hardware man … vi d.

Item paid to m*aister* Gryndell for the makyng of Ric*hard* Laborers gowne … vi d.

*M*aister *Jubb*es. Item paid the xxii[th] day of May to doctor Jubbes toward*es* the byldyng of the colage of Ih*es*u in Cambryge … xxvi li. xiii s. iiii d.

Item the xxii[th] day of May to oon Carre that came w*ith* the erle of Boughen son from Berwyck in reward … vi s. viii d.

<Item paid to Richard Carr*e* for viii yerd*es* of blake. P*r*ice the yerd iii s. … xxiv s.> «allocatur per thesaurarium»[123]

*Ric*hard *Carr*e. Item to the same for ix yerd*es* of tawny fustyan. P*r*ice the yerd vii d. … v s. iii d.

Item for a pound of wyre vi d. Item for caryage of the same from Coventr*e* to Colyweston vi d. … xii d.

[M]Summa … <xxx li. xvi s. iii d.> xxix li. xii s. iii d.[124]

[*p. 96*] *Cost*es *of Ric*hard *Carre for ridyng*. Item paid to Ric*hard* Carre the xxiiii[th] day of May for his cost*es* ridyng to London to the kyng*e* and their*e* abydyng by the spac*e* of vii daiez … viii s.

Item paid to the same for ridyng to the abbey of Thornam by the spaic*e* of v daiez … iii s. iiii d.

[123] 'allocatur …thesaurarium' add. to explain the cancellation.

[124] The canc. total in the MW hand allows for the canc. first entry on the page but not for the canc. entry of 24s. which the corrected total (in a different hand from MW) deducts.

Item paid to the same for ridyng to Coventre by the spaic*e* of iii daiez … ii s.

*Kyn*ges *mynstrels*. Item paid the xxv day of May to Henr*y* of Lasebury and other the kyng*es* mynstrels in reward … xxvi s. viii d.

Item delyv*er*ed to m*aistres* Foler for my lad*ys* offryng apon Holy Thursday …v s.

*Kyn*ges *messeng*er. Item paid the xxix day of May to m*aister* amener for a reward yeven unto <a> the kyng*es* messeng*er* …v s.

«<*attingat ad […..]*>» Item paid to Deygre Adeys <of> Alton besyd*es* Newerk for xxiii unc*e* di. of fyne golde of damaske <of the> \at iiii s. iiii d. the unce/ … Ci s. x d.

*Hor*ses *bought by John Stakhowse.*[125]

Item paid to John Stakhowse for iii horsis oon <by> bay. P*r*ice xlvi s. viii d. Oon greseld horse xxx s. Another blake xxiii s. <Summa> and for the ferry of the said iii horsis at Barton apon Umber*e* vi d. For the cost*es* of theym from Cottyngham to Colyweston iii s. … Ciii s. ii d.

Item for the cost*es* of the same John Stakhowse bryngyng of the same horsis <…> by v daiez at xvi d. the day … vi s. viii d.

Item for the ferry of his horsis … viii d.

Cx s. vi d.[126]

*R. for how*kes. Item in reward to a man of Barrodowne for bryngyng of a cast of lanners to my lad*ys* g*r*ace paid to Rog*er* Radclyff … iii s. iiii d.

^{M}Summa … xiii li. v s. viii d.^{P}

[*p. 97*] Item paid to John Bedell for a reward yeven to George of the chappell at my lad*ys* dep*ar*tyng toward*es* Richmound for makyng of an antem of Gawde[127] Flore … vi s. viii d.

*My lady*s *offryng apon Vitsonday*. Item delyv*er*ed to George Fraunc*es* for my lad*ys* offryng apon Vitsonday … v s.

Item delyv*er*ed to <Twaytt*es*> Thawytt*es* sawdyor of Calles in reward the furst day of Juyn … xxvi s. viii d.

Item in reward the ii^{de} day of Juyn t*o* a messeng*er* of the kyng*es* … iii s. iiii d.

Item to Joke oon of the gromes of the stabyll for horse bred for my lad*ys* horsis bryngyng*e* of my lady marques to Colyweston … viii d.

Item paid the iiiith day of Juyn for the hyr*e* of ii tailiors by xi dayez werkyng in the wardrop of the bedd*es* at iiii d. a day a pec*e* … vii s. viii d.

Item delyv*er*ed t*o* a s*er*vande of <R> m*aister* Rukleys for convaying of vi hobby horsis from his m*aister* to my lad*ys* g*r*ace … lxvi s. viii d.

Brograve. Item delyv*er*ed t*o* John Brograve the viith day of Juyn … xxvi li. xiii s. iiii d.

[125] Bracketed to include the next three items.
[126] The total of the three items above, written in the left margin.
[127] Alt. to or from 'gawdy'.

Item paid the xth day of Juyn to Wyllyam Hylm*er* for a payr*e* of buskynce and pynsons bought at London for my ladies g*r*ace … xvi d.

*W. Hylm*er. Item paid to the same for a lib. of gylt golde t*o* brother w*ith*. P*r*ice the lib. … xv s.

Item paid to the same for carying of ii pec*es* of red bokeram and a pec*e* of grene sarsynet weying x lib. and di. lib. pakthred from London to Stampforth … vii d.

[M]Summa … xxxiii li. vi s. vi d.[P]

[*p. 98*] *M*aister *chamberlayn.*[128]

Item paid to m*aister* chamberlayn the xiith day of Juyn by his byll assigned for iii pec*es* of blak bokeram. P*r*ice the pec*e* iii s. … ix s.

Item t*o* the same for a hundreth of canvas. P*r*ice… xxxiii s.

Item for meyteng*e* of the same at Styllyard … ii d.

Item for ii pec*es* of red bokeram. P*r*ic*e* the pec*e* vi s. … xii s.

Item for xxiii yerd*es* of grene <bokeram> sarsynet. P*r*ic*e* the yerd iii s. iii d. … lxxviii s.

«xxiii virg. ad iii s. iii d. le virg. … lxxiiii s. ix d.»[129]

Item paid to the same for money delyv*er*ed to m*aistres* Fynch for a pounde of blake reben and frenge for my lad*ys* litter xvi s. Item for i lib. of golde of Vennes xliii s. for v lib. gylt gold. P*r*ic*e* the [unce] xvi s. Summa iiii li. Item for viii unc*e* of sleved vii s. iiii d. Item for ii grene freng*e* waying xxxiiii unc*e*. P*r*ic*e* unc*e* xii d. … ix li. xvi d.

Item t*o* the same for ii lib. of blak crewle at ii s. iiii d. Item for on lib. of open sylk <xiii s. vii d.> \xiiii s. viii d./ for iii unc*e* of open sylk ii s. ix d. … xix s. ix d.

Item paid to m*aister* chamberlayn for a pec*e* of canvas contaynyng a hundreth yerd*es*. P*r*ice … xxxii s. viii d.

Item for meytyng*e* of the same … ii d.

Item paid for lxiiii «yerd*es*» of blak velvet. P*r*ic*e* the yerd ix s. … xxviii li. xvi s.

Item for viii yerd*es* of blak velvet for my lad*ys* pylleon and <c> sadell and horse harnesses. P*r*ice the yerd ix s. … lxxii s.

Nota pro C^{ma}.[130] Item for a hundreth yerd*es* of <s> sarsynet of dyv*er*se colowrez. P*r*ic*e* the yerd iii s. iiii d. … xvi li. xiii s.

Item paid for v pec*es* of lyr*e*. P*r*ic*e* the pec*e* viii d. … iii s. iiii d.

Item for a pounde of foll*er* lyr*e*. P*r*ice … vi d.

[128] Bracketed to include all the items on p. 98.

[129] Written in the margin alongside the next entry but referring to this one; the note indicates that the total is wrong for 3s. 3d. per yard (it would be correct for 3s. 4d.).

[130] Although the marginal notes here and three below appear to read 'C^{ma}', 'centum majus', i.e. 120, rather than 'C^{mi}', 'centum minus', i.e. 100, the sums are more correct for 100 (this entry is 4d. short and the entry below 10d. short).

Nota pro C^{ma}. Item for a hundreth yerd*es* of s*ar*cynett and ii yerd*es* and a q*uarter*. P*r*ice the yerd iii s. iiii d. ... xvii li.

Item for vi pec*es* of lyr*e*. P*r*ice the pec*e* viii d. ... iiii s.

[*p. 99*] Item paid for vi yerd*es* of blak bokeram for lynyng of my lad*ys* pelyon. P*r*ice the yerd iii d. ... xviii d.

Item for iii yerd*es* of canvas t*o* trusse the sylk*es* in ... x d. ob.

Item in reward to the bayly of Coldehorton for carying of sylk*es* from London to Colyweston ... iii s. iiii d.

Item for trussyng pap*er* and pakthred ... i d. ob.

Stet. <Item for iii yerd*es* di. of blak cloth for my lad*ys* g*r*ace ... xlvi s. viii d.> \stet/ «per thesaurarium»[131]

Item for vi hundreth powdreng*es*. P*r*ice the hundreth ... viii s.

Nota. Si virg. ad xii d. attingat nisi ad xii s.[132] Item t*o* maistrez Fench for xii yerd*es* of frenge waying an unc*e* di. P*r*ice the unc*e* xii d. ... xxvi s. vi d

Item for vi unc*e* of sylk at xi d. the unc*e* ... v s. vi d.

Item for xl yerd*es* of freng*es* wayng vi lib. viii unc*e*. P*r*ic*e* the lib. xvi s. ... Ciiii s.

Item for pec*es* of reband wherin was an unc*e* di. of Venys golde. P*r*ic*e* vi s. iii d. and an unc*e* di. of sylk. P*r*ice xviii d. ... vii s. ix d.

*M*aister *chamberlayn*. Item for a blak small freng*e* for the garnysshyng of my lad*ys* pelyon ... x s.

Item for a pelyon of downe ... xx d.

Item for ii pec*es* of blak bokeram at iii d. the pec*e* ... vi d.

Item for xxx yerd*es* of cord ... viii d.

Item paid to Palm*er* sadeler for makyng of a pelyon and horse harnesshe and for makyng of an cheyr*e* for my lad*ys* g*r*ace ... xxxix s.

Item for his s*er*vand*es* cost*es* bryngyng of the same stuff to Colyweston ... xx d.

Item for vii pec*es* of cord. P*r*ic*e* the pece iii d. ... xxi d.

Item for a reward yeven to Rob*ert* Pellett by m*aister* chamberlayn ... x s.

Summa ... <iiii^{xx}xvii li. ix s. xi d.><xvi li. iii s. iii d.^{P}> iiii^{xx}xviii li. ix s. xi d.[133]

[131] Canc. but restored ('stet' twice).

[132] The marginal note highlights the discrepancy but fails to notice that each yard weighs one and a half ounces. The calculation is still incorrect (it should be 18s.).

[133] The total of pp. 98–99. Despite the several calculations (all in the MW hand), the correct total would be £98 4s. 5d.

[*p. 100*] Item the xiiith day of Juyn in reward to a messeng*er* of the kyng*es* … v s.

Item the same day in reward to my lad*ys* solycet*ur* … x s.

*Trinitie Sonday my lad*ys *offryng*. Item for my ladies offryng apon Trinite Sonday … v s.

Item delyv*er*ed to m*aister* pr*es*ydent for a reward yeven to m*aister* Nevell man of law … vi s. viii d.

Item paid to Nicholas Aughton for xii daiez jorneying as aperith by his byll assigned …viii s.

Item paid to George Fraunc*es* for a reward yeven unto maistres Lacy the xiiith day of Juyn … xx s.

Item delyv*er*ed to the same George for a reward yeven unto a s*er*vande of bysshop of Morrey … iii s. iiii d.

Brownyng. Item paid the xv day of Juyn t*o* Willyam Brownyng t*o* delyv*er* unto his fader John Brownyng for his anuyte for the t*er*me at mydsom*ur* … x s.

*My lord*es *mynstrles*. Item in reward to my lord*es* mynstrles beyng w*i*th my lad*ys* g*r*ace the iiiith day of Juyn … vi s. viii d.

Item paid to m*aister* dean for a reward yeven to the chyld*er* of the chappell for syngyng of a balett befour*e* my lad*ys* g*r*ace at the woddsyde … xii d.

Item to the same for a reward yeven to a s*er*vande of m*aister* Wallis for convaying of a <lc> l*ett*re from my lad*ys* g*r*ace unto his maist*er* t*o* Pet*ur*borow … xx d.

Item t*o* the same for a reward yeven to George Fraunc*e*s s*er*vande for goyng for my lorde of Lyncolnes chaunceller … xx d.

Item the xxvi day of Juyn in reward to m*aister* Thawythis … xl s.

^{M}Summa … lxxix s.^{P}

[*p. 101*] *Wollen cloth*.[134]

*Stuf bought at Coventr*e.[135]

<Item paid for a pec*e* of blak conteynyng*e* xxx^{ti} yerd*es* at iii s. ii d. the yerd. Summa …iiii li. xv s.

Item paid for anoder pec*e* of blak cont*eynyng* xviii yerd*es* at ii s. viii d. the yerd … xlviii s.>

per thesaurarium[136]

Item paid for vi lib. of blew thredd iii lib. at xii d. the pounde and other iii lib. at ix d. the pounde … v s. iii d.

[134] Written in the top left margin in faded ink and probably a different hand from the MW hand.
[135] Bracketed to include the next eleven items.
[136] Bracketed to the right of the two items above.

Item paid for vi lib. of whit thredd v lib. at x d. the pounde and oon pounde at vii d. ... v s. ix d.[137]

Item paid for iii pec*es* of blak bokeram ii pec*es*<at> at xii s. and oon pec*e* at v s. ... xvii s.

Item paid for iii unc*e* of opyn sylk at x d. the unc*e* ... ii s. vi d.

Item paid for ii unc*e* of twyne sylk at <[...]> x d. ... xx d.

Item paid for vi cov*er*lett*es* iii at iii s. viii d. a pec*e* and other iii at v s. a pec*e* ... xxvi s.

Item paid for iii pec*es* of holmes fustyan at viii s. vi d. the pec*e* ... xxvi s.

Item paid for viii elnes of canvas to trusse the said stuff in ... ii s. viii d.

Item for trussyng cord ... vi d.

Item paid t*o* John Smyth for caryag*e* of the same from Coventr*e* to Colyweston ... xvi d.

Doctor Collett. Item paid to m*aister* Morgan for a reward yeven the xi[th] day of Juyn t*o* doctor Collett xx s. and for his cost*es* and horse meyte vi s. ix d. ... xxvi s. ix d.

Item the same day t*o* m*aister* Powell of Oryall college in Oxford that prechit afour*e* my lad*ys* g*r*ace apon Corpus Christi day ... x s.

Item delyv*er*ed for my lad*ys* offryng the same day ... v s.

<[M]Summa ... xiiii li. xvii d.[P]> vi li. xviii s. v d.[P] [138]

[*p. 102*] Item paid to John Bedell for a reward yeven to Ric*hard* Aderton m*aister* chamberlayns s*er*vande for ridyng to London ... x s.

Item paid to William Elton of Cambryge and his s*er*vant broderers for workyng apon a<t> gret bedde by the spaic*e* of vii wek*es* from the xxv day of Aprell unto the xv day of Juyn ev*er*y weke for hymself and his s*er*vande iiii s. ... xxviii s.

Item paid to m*aister* amener for a reward yeven to George Fraunc*es* s*er*vande for ridyng unto Crolande <...> apon my lad*ys* messag*es* ... xx d.

*Caryag*e *of bedd*es *from Boston and Spaldyng.*[139] Item paid the xxiii day of Juyn for the hyr*e* of ii cart*es* from Waldram Hall to Colyweston w*i*th beddyng sent from Spaldyng and from Thomas Rob*er*tson of Boston ... ii s. viii d.

Item in reward to ii s*er*vand*es* of the p*r*ior of Spaldyng and Thomas Rob*er*tson for convaying*e* of the same stuff t*o* Waldram Hall by wat*er* ... vi s. viii d.

Suffrycan. Item paid for the hir*e* of a cart from Huntyngton t*o* Colyweston w*i*th beddyng sende by the suffrycan ... xii d.

Item the xxvi[th] day of Juyn in reward to Paskall brotherer for workyng apon my lad*ys* work*es* ... xiii s. iiii d.

[137] The total is 1s. over.

[138] The canc. and approved total (all in the MW hand) includes the two canc. items that begin the page.

[139] Bracketed to include the next two items.

Item paid to Lenard of vestry for v bok*es* dressyng new … iiii s.

Item for ii gram*er* bok*es* for m*aister* Coup*er* … viii d.

Item in reward to m*aister* Myddelton of London notarie the xxvii day of Juyn … xx s.

Item t*o* his clerk in reward … vi s. viii d.

Item in reward t*o* Rauff Carr*e* of Edynbor*e* … vi s. viii d.

[M]Summa … Ci s. iiii d.[P]

[*p. 103*] *Brydd.*[140]

Item paid the xxviii[th] day of Juyn to John Brydde for rydyng to m*aister* Marcam by ii daiez … ii s.

Item paid to the same for a payr*e* of sleppers and shoez bought by hym for my lad*ys* g*r*ace … xi d.

Item paid to the same for a reward yeven by hym in <R> Northampton for wardons yeven t*o* my lad*ys* g*r*ace … viii d.

Item to the same for ridyng \in/ to Cambrygeshyr*e* to the shreff and other dyv*er*se gentylmen by vi daiez … iiii s.

Item t*o* the same for ridyng t*o* Cambryge t*o* the asyse and for to pay money to Rauf Chamberlayn and for rydyng to Malton by vii daiez … iiii s. viii d.

Item paid to the same for x elnez of canvas. P*r*i*ce* the elne <u>iii d. ob.</u> … ii s. xi d.

Item for iii pounde of cotton … <xv> xviii d.

Item for a C neld*es* … iiii d.

Item in reward for oreng*es* … iiii d.

Item t*o* the same for rydyng t*o* my lord Lyncoln … iiii s. <vii d.> viii d.

Item t*o* the same for ridyng t*o* Croland by the spac*e* of ii daiez … xvi d.

Summa xxiii s. iiii d.[141]

Item in reward t*o* Thomas Hyll the last day of Juyn for drawyng of the pound*es* … iii s. iiii d.

Item in reward to Nicholas Baxter and John Fraunc*es* for their*e* labur at the same tyme … xx d.

*M*aister *dean.*[142]

[140] The marginal note is one-third of the way down p. 103 and is unbracketed, but it includes all the entries relating to Brydd.
[141] The total of the previous eleven entries on p. 10, written in the margin just below 'Brydd' (see the previous note).
[142] Bracketed to include the rest of the entries on the page.

Item paid the iii[d] day of July to m*aister* dean for money paid to George Aughton for ridyng*e* w*i*th ii horsis by the spaic*e* of ii daiez for <d> convaying of [a] chyld of my lad*ys* chappell t*o* Higham Ferr*es* … ii s.

Item t*o* the same for a reward yeven to John Walter … vi s. viii d.

Item in reward by the same t*o* a sust*er* of John <Jurer> Joyners of Stampforth … iii s. iiii d.

[M]Summa … xl s. <iiii d.> v d.[P]

[*p. 104*] Item paid the vi[th] day of July to m*aister* Quytstones p*re*sydent of my lad*ys* councell for money paid to a prynter in London for pryntyng of my ladies bok*es* … xl s.

Item paid to William Kylke s*er*vande to maistres Talbott for a half yer*es* waig*es* … xiii s. iiii d.

Item t*o* the same in reward for his cost*es* beyng at Colyweston … xx d.

*M*aister *chaunceller*. Item paid to m*aister* chaunceller for xxxiiii elnez of holland cloth bought for my lad*ys* g*r*ace … xviii s. vi d.

Item paid to m*aister* Elmez for money by hym paid for the cost*es* of m*aister* Walles s*er*vaunt*es* and m*aister* Waghan s*er*vaunt*es* and their*e* horsis in Stampforth from Sonday at nyght the xxv day of Juyn unto Tewisday at morow … xii s. x d.

Item paid to Ric*hard* Bothe for a reward yeven to a s*er*vant of my lady Hungerforth for bryngyng of rose wat*er*ez to my lad*ys* g*r*ace … iii s. iiii d.

Item paid to Georg*e* Fraunc*es* for xii bowlez … xvi d.

Item yeven in reward to m*aister* Cottrell of Fodryngay syngyng man the vii[th] day of July … iii s. iiii d.

Item paid to Lenard Patryk syngyng man … v s.

Item paid to m*aister* chamberlayn for a reward yeven to the quene of Skott*es* fotmen …v s.

Item paid the xii[th] day of July to Nicholas of the wardrop for the hyr*e* of viii men workyng*e* in the wardrop of bedd*es* by the spaic*e* of a day … ii s. viii d.

Item paid to the same oon man workyng by the spaic*e* of xviii daiez at iii d. the day … iiii s. vi d.

[M]Summa … Cxi s. vi d.[P]

[*p. 105*] Item paid the xii[th] day of July unto s*ir* Hughe Assheton for a reward yeven to my lady Ryv*er*se sust*er* a nonne of the Myn*er*esse … x s.

Item paid to the same for ii frontlett*es* bought by hym for my lad*ys* g*r*ace … xvi s. iiii d.

Item paid to the same for vi chambr*e* bolles of pewt*er* … iii s. iiii d.

R. Carr. Item paid to Ric*hard* Carre for his cost*es* ridyng to London and other plaic*es* apon my lad*ys* messag*es* by the spaice of xxviii daiez at viii d. the day as aperith by his byll assigned … xviii s. viii d.

Item paid to the same for the hyre of a horse the same spac*e* as by the same byll aperith … iii s.

Item in reward t*o* John Haryson the xiith day of July to toward*es* his jorney to Skotland …xx s.

W. Aderton. Item paid the xviiith day of July to Willyam by a byll assigned for v yerd*es* and a half of grene clothe. P*ric*e the yerd xiiii d. and viii d. the half yerd. Summa … vi s. viii d.

Item paid to the same for ii daiez ridyng from Colyweston to Northampton to the kyng …ii s.

Item paid to the same for the cost*es* of vi hoby horsis yeven to my lad*ys* g*r*ace by oon nyght … xiiii d.

*Rewar*des *to syngyng men at the kyng*es *beying at Colyweston*. Item yeven in reward to s*ir* Thomas Stephyns prest which came from Cambryg*e* … vi s. viii d.

Item in reward to John Smyth of West*mynster* syngyng man for iii wek*es* beying in my lad*ys* chappell … xx s.

Item in reward t*o* Conwey the same tyme … v s.

Item in reward t*o* Pykryng of Tatsull … v s.

^{M}Summa … Cxvii s. <x d.> viii d.^{P}

[*p. 106*] Item paid the xviiith day of July to m*aister* Gryndell for money paid for the horse meyte of Chr*ist*ofer Mydelton … xvi d.

Item to the same for money paid to Davy Wyll*i*ams goldsmyth for the facion and gyldyng of a cope of assey weying vi unc*e* iii q*uarter* for ev*er*y unc*e* … xi s. iii d.

Item to the same for the makyng of a holy water stokke weying xi unc*e* and for the facion of ev*er*y unc*e* viii d. … vii s. iiii d.

Item paid to the same for the mendyng and sawdryng of a bason which was broken in the ewrye … xvi d.

*Rewar*des *yeven to a syngyng man*. Item the xiith day paid in reward yeven by the same t*o* s*ir* Thomas Fox syngyng man … xx s.

*Gardyn*er. Item the xx^{ti} day of July to John Gardyner syngyng man … vi s. viii d.

Gowghe. Item the same day to Ric*hard* Goughe … xx s.

Nota. Item to Ric*hard* Bothes s*er*vand for ridyng to Sutterton besyde Boston for the vycar of the same … xvi s.

Item in reward t*o* oon Cot*es* of Grantham for his comyng*e* to my lad*ys* g*r*ace … xx d.

Item paid to m*aister* dean for <a> money delyv*er*ed to Thomas Watson for convaying oon of the chyld*er* of the chappell t*o* Oxforth and agayn … x s.

*M*aister *chamber*l*ayn*. Item delyv*er*ed to my lad*ys* g*r*ace \by/ the same for a reward yeven to m*aister* chamberlayn … x li.

*R. Carr*e. Item paid to Ric*hard* Carre for his cost*es* ridyng t*o* London to m*aister* Bray by v daiez and to Lawnd abbey t*o* the kyng for i day … iiii s.

Item paid t*o* Ric*hard* Aderton for his cost*es* ridyng from London t*o* Colyweston w*i*th iii horsis bryngyng of c*er*ten plate for my lad*ys* howse at the kyng*es* beyng their*e* … v s. x d.

Item in reward to the suffrycan s*er*vand*es* for carryag*e* of bedstuff f[rom][143] Colyweston to Burne which was occupied at the kyng*es* beyng their*e* … xii d.

[M]Summa … xv li. vi s. v d.[P]

[*p. 107*] *W. Hylm*er.

xxiii day of July.

Item paid to Wyllyam Hylm*er* for dyv*er*se stuff bought for my lad*ys* g*r*ace as aperith by his byll assigned … iiii s. vii d.

*M*aister *Twaytt*es. Item delyv*er*ed to maister <Whay> Twhaytt*es* for his cost*es* into Fraunce apon my lad*ys* messag*es*<o> the xxviii day of July … xx li.

Brograve. Item paid the xxix day of July to John Brograve in p*ar*tie of payment of a mor*e*. Summa … xx li.

iii hobies. Item the same day in reward to Willyam Blabe for bryngyng of hawk*es* unto my lad*ys* g*r*ace … xx d.

Item paid t*o* Willyam Pole the same day for a reward yeven to m*aister* Bretnels clerk … iii s. iiii d.

Item paid unto m*aister* Gryndell for a reward yeven unto s*ir* Crystofer Crosley goyng*e* apon my ladies messag*es* to the bysshop of Lyncoln … xx s.

S*ir H. Norton.*

Nota. Item paid unto s*ir* Harr*y* Norton in p*ar*tie of payment for mone dew unto the excecutors of m*aister* Welbyes … iiii li.

[M]Summa … xlv li. ix s. vii d.[P]

[*p. 108*] Item paid unto m*aister* chamberlayn as by a byll assigned for thiez p*ar*cell*es* for ii pec*es* of rossett damaske. P*r*ic*e* the yerd v s. viii d. for lxiiii yerd*es* … xviii li. ii s. viii d.

Item for ii pec*es* of tawny damaske *conteynyng* l yerd*es* and one q*uarter*. P*r*ic*e* the yerd v s. viii d. … xiiii li. iii s. iiii d.

Item t*o* the same for one pec*e* of blake damaske *conteynyng* xxxiiii yerd*es* at v s. vi d. the yerd … ix li. vii s.

[143] MS 'for'.

Item t*o* the same for ii pec*es* of crewell of the mydelyst assyse. Pric*e* the pec*e* iii s. … vi s.

Item t*o* the same for iii M hok*es*. Pric*e* the M iii s. … ix s.

Item for xl grett hok*es*. Pric*e* … iiii d.

Item for vi pec*es* of small cord at iii d. the pec*e* … xviii d.

Item for iiii pound of lyre. Pric*e* the pounde iiii d. … xvi d.

Item for vi payr*e* of caibuls w*i*th the men. Pric*e* the payr*e* ix d. … iiii s. vi d.

Item for xlii pounde and a q*uarter* of fyne downe at vi d. the pounde … xxi s. i d. ob.

Item for on pec*e* of blak saten *conteynyng* xxxii yerd*es*. Pric*e* the vi s. viii d. … x li. xiii s. iiii d.

Item for ii pair*e* of gardyvyanc*e* to carre my lad*ys* plate in from London … xxviii s.

Item for viii elnez of canvas to trusse in the said plate. Pric*e* the elen iii d. ob. … ii s. iiii d.

Item to ii porters for beryng*e* of the said stuff from Coldherbor*e* unto m*aister* Shaez …v d.

Item paid to a carryor for carryeng of my lad*ys* stuff by m*aister* Shaez comandement …xiii s.

Item paid t*o* a vestement maker*e* for workyng of c*er*teyn stuff for my lad*ys* g*r*ace … xiii s. iiii d.

Item for x pec*es* of <fus> fustian. Pric*e* the pec*e* xvi s. … viii li.

[*p. 109*] Item paid unto the same for iii pounde of crule … vi s.

Item for x unc*e* of sleved blak and gold colour*e*. Pric*e* the unc*e* xi d. … ix s. ii d.

Item paid for oon M of gylt nayle … iii s. iiii d.

Item to the same for D of gylt nayles … ii s. iiii d.

Item t*o* the same for a reward yeven to Rob*er*t Wynfeld … vi s. viii d.

Item for a reward yeven t*o* the erle of Kyldar*e* s*er*vande for bryngyng of iii hobiez unt*o* my ladiez g*r*ace … xiii s. iiii d.

Item in reward to Henr*y* Odoll … xx s.

Item in reward to the quenys mynstrles … xiii s. iiii d.

Item in reward to Nich*olas* Clyff … vi s. viii d.

Item for a reward yeven to Hasulrygg … vi s. viii d.

Item paid to the same for money paid t*o* m*aister* Shaye for makyng of c*er*ten stuff for my lad*ys* g*r*ace … xxv li. x s.

Item t*o* the same for a reward yeven to s*ir* Charles … C s.

Item in reward to Rob*er*t Wynfeld … vi s. viii d.

Item in reward to Henr*y* Odoll … xx s.

Item in reward to Knollez … vi s. viii d.

Item in reward to Quytyng … vi s. viii d.

Item in reward to Rob*er*t Jones … xx s.

Item in reward to Greneway … x s.

Item in reward to Hughe Denysse … vi s. viii d.

Item to Perith Barbur … x s.

Item t*o* the kyng*es* howsehold in rewarde … xx li.

Item t*o* the kyng*es* chamb*er*l*ayn* and t*o* the garde … x li.

Item t*o* Sherley m*aister* clerk of the kyng*es* kychen … xx s.

Item t*o* Nich*olas* Clyff in reward … vi s. viii d.

Item to the kyng*es* porters … xiii s. iiii d.

Item t*o* the quenys chamb*er*l*ayn* in reward … iii li. vi s. viii d.

Item t*o* the quenys mynstrlez in reward … xiii s. iiii d.

[*p. 110*] Item paid t*o* the same m*aister* chamb*er*l*ayn* for a reward yeven t*o* the kyng*es* phessycions … xx s.

Item t*o* the kyng*es* fotmen in reward … xx s.

Item in reward to the kyng*es* bedd*es* … xx s.

Item in reward unto Mathew Baker*e* … xx s.

Item in reward to Mewth … xx s.

Item in reward to the kyng*es* bagpype … iii s. iiii d.

Item t*o* Mathew Baker comyng in messag*es* t*o* my lad*ys* g*r*ace from the kyng … x s.

Item t*o* yong Staunton in rewarde … vi s. viii d.

[M]Summa … Cxlv<i>i li. xi s. iiii d. ob.[P] [144]

[145]Item paid the xxviiith day of July t*o* Wyllyam Wyllyamson baily of Maksey for the cost*es* and charg*es* of dyv*er*se p*er*sons of my lord of Wenchest*er*s beyng at Maksey w*i*th his horsis the tyme of the kyng*es* beyng at Colyweston … xxvii s. vii d.

[M]Summa … xxvii s. vii d.

[*p. 111*] Item in reward unto the warden of the frer*es* of Carnerven in Wales … vi s. viii d.

[144] The total of pp. 108–9 and p. 110 up to this point (1s. over).

[145] This entry is in the same hand (the MW hand), written lower down the page after a gap.

*Stuff of m*aister *Cutlerd send to Boston and of m*aister *Red*es. Item paid the iiii^th^ day of August to John Rober[t]*es* for carrying of bedstuff to Boston to m*aister* Cutlerd and Rede w*i*th ii cart*es* ... xii s.

*M*aister *presdyent*. Item paid unto m*aister* dean for money delyv*ere*d t*o* m*aister* presydent for his cost*es* goying apon my ladies messag*es* to London ... lxvi s. viii d.

Lenard. Item paid t*o* Lenard of the vestry for byndyng of Legenda Auria xx d. Item for a stok lok vii d. ... ii s. iii d.

Walter. Item paid unto John Walter for iiii yerd*es* di. of blew bokeram for a vestement. P*ric*e the yerd vi d. ... ii s. iii d.

Spaldyng. Item paid t*o* Warssop of Colyweston for carying of bedd*es* to Waldram Hall of the p*ri*or of Spaldyng ... xvi d.

Moder Elyn. Item paid to Freman of Colyweston for a bedde for moder Elyn by the spaic*e* of liii wek*es* at a i d. the wek ... iiii s. vi d.[146]

Kyrbyes wyff. Item paid to Kyrkbyes wyff for kepyng of a chyld of the chapell by iii wek*es* beyng seke and for wachyng w*ith* Elyzabeth Frognell ... ii s. iiii d.

*M*aister *chaunceller*.[147]

Item paid the vth day of August to m*aister* chaunceller for iii yerd*es* of tawny medly. P*ric*e the yerd v s. iiii d. ... xvi s.

Item to the same for a pece of blak bokeram ... vi s.

Item to the same for caryag*e* of all the plate from Colyweston to London which was p*ro*vided for my ladies g*r*ace agaynest the kyng*es* comyng ... viii s.

Item t*o* the same for a gardyvyan which came to Colyweston w*i*th stuff at Crystemas anno xv^mo^ [148] ... vi s. viii d.

^M^Summa ... vi li. xiiii s. viii d.^P^

[*p. 112*] *R. Hylton*.[149]

Item paid the vth day of August to Rob*er*t Hylton for ii pec*es* of blak cotton ... xv s. viii d.

Item to the same for ii bassyns of puter ... xiiii d.

Item for a payr*e* of shoez for Skypp ... vi d.

Item paid for viii yerd*es* of popyngay colo*ur* kersay for a cote for the same Skyp. P*ric*e the yerd xii d. ... viii s.

*The kyng*es *att*o*urney*. Item in reward to the kyng*es* attorney the vth day of August at Lydyngton ... lxvi s. viii d.

Item for a pair*e* of howse bought by Rob*er*t Hylton for m*aistres* Parott ... ix d.

[146] The total is 1d. over.
[147] Bracketed to include the next four items.
[148] Christmas in the 15th year would be December 1500.
[149] Bracketed to include the next four items.

Item paid to Henry Wynstanley for a rewarde yeven to a woman of Dodyngton þ*a*t kepes Nicholas Aughton chylde … xii d.

Item yeven in reward unto Mowse at Colyweston … vi s. viii d.

Item paid to George Fraunc*es* for rydyng to Fodryngay and to Lydyngton to <ei> eyther place ii tymez and for ii daiez to Leycet*ur* and ayen to Colyweston … v s. iiii d.

Item the xiith day of August to m*aister* dean for a reward yeven to \sir/ Crystofer*e* Crosseley oon of my lad*ys* chapplenc*e* … xx s.

Summa vi li. v s. ix d.[150]

*R. Plom*er.[151]

Item paid the same day to Ric*hard* Plomer for ridyng from Lyddyngton to Bryncasterton w*i*th c*er*tain rentall*es* t*o* the kyng*es* solycit*ur* … viii d.

Item to the same for rydyng to Colyweston from Lyddyngton and abydyng their*e* iii daiez … xii d.

Item t*o* the same for makyng of oon forme for my ladiez clossett … ii d.

Item to the same for makyng of a lok t*o* a coffer of my lad*ys* g*r*ace … iii d.

[*p. 113*] Item paid to the balyes wyff of Lyddyngton for the cost*es* of ii doct*ours* w*i*th their*e* horse meyte and their*e* s*er*vand*es* for a nyght … ii s. v d.

Item paid to ii men remevyng*e* of bedd*es* at Lyddyngton at my ladies comyng … x d.

Hardware man.[152]

Item paid to the hardware man the xiiith day of August for ii lytell coffers of yvery … ii s.

Item to the same for a M neld*es* … ii s. vi d.

Item to the same for xviii smale ymag*es* in parchement … vi d.

Item to the same for a fyne ymage yeven to my lady Cessell … iii s. iiii d.

Item delyv*er*ed to George Fraunc*es* for my lad*ys* offryng apon <…> thAnunciacion day of our*e* Lady … v s.

Heymonde Glasse. Item paid the xv day of August to the hardwar*e* man for lxiiii stikk*es* and a half of dyapur at vi d. Flemyssh and in sterlyng … xxii s. x d.

Item paid to m*aister* dean for money delyv*er*ed unto maistres Foler which was yeven in reward unto oon of the quene of Skott*es* gentylwomen … iii s. iiii d.

Item paid to s*ir* Hughe Assheton for his cost*es* ridyng from Lyddyngton to Levsted abbey as aperith by his byll assigned … viii s.

N. Aughton. Item paid to Nycholas Awghton the xxii day of August for ii daiez ridyng*e* for s*ir* John Seynt John doughtur … xvi d.

[150] The correct total to this point, written small in the margin by the MW hand.
[151] Bracketed to include the rest of the entries on the page.
[152] Bracketed to include the next four items.

Item to the same for a day ridyng to mete the kyng*es* g*r*ace or he came at Colyweston … viii d.

Item for a day rydyng after the quene of Scott*es* … viii d.

Item to the same for ridyng to Bukden for the lycense of maistres Souche … xvi d.

[M]Summa … ix li. ii s. vii d.[P]

[*p. 114*] Item paid to the hardware man for ii yerd*es* and oon q*uarter* of blew reban. P*r*ic*e* the yerd ii d. … iiii d. ob.

Item yeven t*o* m*aister* dean for the cost*es* of George Fraunc*es* s*er*vande comyng from his m*aister* from the courte … xii d.

Item delyv*er*ed to my ladies g*r*ace for a reward yeven to Flee yemon of the kyng*es* wardrop … xx s.

Item in reward unto a Flemyng oon Nicholas Stuard … iii s. iiii d.

Item in reward unto the kep*er* of Rokyngham p*ar*ke … iii s. iiii d.

Item yeven in rewarde unto Henry Barlow my lord*es* s*er*vande bryng[yng] of merlyons to my lad*ys* g*r*ace … v s.

Item paid for the cost*es* of ii frer*es* of Grenewich by ii daiez … xii d.

Item paid to Nicholas Aughton for ridyng to the p*r*ior of Lecet*ur* a day … viii d.

Item t*o* the same for ridyng to the kyng t*o* Cotyngham iii daiez … ii s.

Item in rewarde unto the chappell toward*es* the cost*es* of etyng of a buk yeven to theym by my ladiez g*r*ace … vi s. viii d.

Item paid for my ladies offryng apon our*e* Lady Day the Nativitie … v s.

Item paid to Ric*hard* Carr*e* for ridyng at c*er*ten tymes as aperith by his byll assigned by xxviii daiez … xviii s. viii d.

Item t*o* the same for C curtayn rync*es* … vi d.

Item paid to Griffith Richard*es* for ridyng w*i*th ii horsis w*i*th maist*er* p*re*sydent and other of my lad*ys* councell to Lyncoln to thassise by the spaic*e* of viii daiez … xiii s. iiii d.

[M]Summa … iiii li. x d. ob.[P]

[*p. 115*] Item payd the last day of August to Thomas <kingy> Yngellysby grom of the stabell for the cost*es* of hym<h>self and iii horsis from Colyweston to London for m*aister* Markam and m*aister* Frognoll … vii s. iii d.

Item paid to John Fenton of Lyddyngton for gooyng in message of my ladies g*r*ace to the baily of Elmeton … xii d.

Item paid unto s*ir* William Beawpre for cost*es* of the exibucion of William Gybbon oon of my lad*ys* ward*es* … ii s. iiii d.

Item paid unto m*aister* dean for a reward yeven to Masson oon of the chylder of the chappell … ii s. iiii d.

Item paid unto Richard Bothe for a reward yeven to the survaiers s*er*vande whiche rode in message to doctor Batemanson … v s.

Item paid unto Ric*hard* Bothe for ridyng from Lyddyngton to <Cloz> Crolande w*i*th c*er*ten money to the prior … xx d.

Item payd to Thomas Rede of London brauderer*e* for iii vestment*es* w*i*th the <app…> aparell oon whit another redde and the iii^{de} blew … lxi s. viii d.

Item delyv*er*ed to m*aister* chamberlayn for a reward yeven to the kyng*es* plaiers comynge from Skotlonde to Colyweston … xiii s. iiii d.

Item paid to maistres Flee for money yeven in almes to a prest of the North Country goyng oon pylgramege to Canturbury … xx d.

Item the vii day of Septembr to m*aister* Bekynsall for a rewarde yeven unto a frere of Lychefeld … xii d.

Item delyv*er*ed to my lad*ys* g*r*ace for a reward yeven unto maistres Odell … xx s.

^{M}Summa … Cxviii s. iii d.^{P}

[*p. 116*] *Kep*er *of Horyngworth parke*. Item the xvith day of Septembr*e* to the kep*er* of Horryngworth p*ar*ke in reward … x s.

Item delyv*er*ed to George Fraunces for a reward yeven unto s*ir* John Thomson prest … iii s. iiii d.

Jamys Morice.[153]

Item paid to Jamys Morice for money paid to Thomas Forster for workyng in the wardrop of the bedd*es* by the spaic*e* of ix wek*es* endid the xx day of July … x s.

Item paid to Paskall brotherer the same tyme for his workyng … vii s. viii d.

Item t*o* the same for a reward yeven t*o* a s*er*vande of my lady Norfolk*es* … v s.

Item t*o* the same for a rewarde to Roger Dalton my lord*es* s*er*vande at his goyng from Lyddyngton t*o* my lorde … iii s. iiii d.

Item for a reward yeven to Robert Dey of London which is amytted oon of the m*aister* cok*es* … iii s. iiii d.

Item t*o* the same for a reward yeven t*o* Wat*er* Cokke*s* and his feloez beyng at the mylne … xii d.

*Olyv*er *Hollande*.[154]

Item paid the xxith day of Septembr*e* to Olyv*er* Holande for ridynge from Lyddyngton to Lanam in message to my lorde of Oxforth by iiii daiez … iiii s.

[153] Bracketed to include the next six items.

[154] Bracketed to include the next four items.

Item paid to the same for ridyng to Epsewich for m*aister* Folers mat*er* by vi daiez … vi s.

Item to the same for ridyng t*o* Esby de la Sowche in message <j> to my lorde Hungerforth by ii daiez … ii s.

Item t*o* the same for the convayng*e* of an lett*ur* by m*aister* deanys comaundement from Cambryg*e* to Chest*er*forth … iiii d.

W. Pole.[155] Item paid to William Pole for a reward yeven to Burtons moder on of the cheld*er* of the chapell … iiii s. iiii d.

[M]Summa … lix s. iiii d.[P]

[*p. 117*] Item in reward to Bonyfface my lord*es* s*er*vand for c*er*ten medycens yeven to m*aister* Markam for a desease in his legge … iii s. iiii d.

Item paid to Thomas Flemyng grome porter for his cost*es* and horse hyr*e* ridyng from Lydyngton to Kyllyngworth w*i*th m*aister* Elmez by m*aister* chamberlayns comaundement by the spaic*e* of vi daiez … vi s.

R. Aderton. Item paid the xxiiii day of Septembr*e* to Ric*hard* Aderton for ridyng*e* apon my ladiez messag*es* t*o* the kyng and to Crolande and other plac*es* by the spaic*e* of xxv daiez for his cost*es* and in rewarde … xxvi s. viii d.

*Pre*s*ydent.* <Item in reward to m*aister* pre*sydent toward*es* his cost*es* goyng to London the xxvii day of Sept*em*br … <xl s.> «nichil»

Item delyv*er*ed to my ladiez g*r*ace the xxviii[th] day of Septembr*e* for a rewarde yeven t*o* a s*er*vande of the bysshop of Wenchest*er* for the convaying of c*er*tan hangyng*es* and other stuff agaynest*es* the kyng*es* comyng to Colyweston and for the carryage of theym agayn …<lxvi s. viii d.> liii s. iiii d.

\ *x s.*/ *doc*tur *Harryngton.*

xx s./ *docto*ur *Batmanson.*

xx s./ *do[c]*tur *Robynson.*[156]

Item delyv*er*ed to m*aister* dean for a reward yeven to the doct*ur*us at their*e* beyng at Colyweston … l s.

Lande of Benyfeld. Item in reward unto the kep*er* of the lande of Benyfeld at my lad*ys* beyng their*e* … xx s.

Item paid unto his wyff for iii dd. bredd iii s. v dd. ale vii s. vi d. ii gese x d. ii pigg*es* x d. peions bake vi past*es* xii d. beff and motton xii d. chese iiii d. … xv s. ii d.[157]

Item in reward to doctor Batemanson the same tyme … xx s.

Item in reward to Nicholas Collis lerned man … vi s. viii d.

Item in rewarde unto Paston my lord of Oxforth s*er*vande … vi s. viii d.

[155] Bracketed to include the single item.

[156] These three lines, each below the other in the left margin, are bracketed to the next item.

[157] The total is 8d. over.

Item paid unto John Urmeston for his cost*es* ridyng to Kyllyngworth to my lord of Wenchest*er* by the spaic*e* of iii daiez <fo> w*i*th ii horsis … v s.

[M]Summa … <xiii li. vi s. ii d.> <x li. xiii s. iiii d.> x li. xii s. x d.[P]

[*p. 118*] *Jamys Morice.*[158]<Item paid the last day of Septembr*e* to Jamys Morice for a pece of blak clothe cont*eynyng* xxiiii yerd*es* di. P*ri*ce the yerde iii s. iiii d. … lxxiii s. vi d.>[159] …«nichil per thesaurarium]»

Item for a pec*e* of witte cotton cont*eynyng* xxxix yerd*es* … xvi s. x d.

Item for a pece of russett cotton cont*eynyng* xxi yerd*es* … ix s. x d.

Item paid for ii yerd*es* and iii q*uarter* of kersey of gyng*er* color. P*ri*c*e* the yerd xv d. … iii s. vi d.

<Item for v pec*es* of russett fustian ev*er*y pec*e*>

Item for iiii lib. of whitt thredde at vii d. the lib. … ii s. iiii d.

Item for a pece of hollonde clothe cont*eynyng* xxvii elis at xiiii d. the elne. Summa of all … xxxi s. vi d.

Item for ii wachyng candylstik*es*. P*ri*c*e* … xvi d.

Item for a coffer of waynskott. P*ri*c*e* … iiii s.

Item for CCCC skynnez of blak lambe at xvii s. vi d. the C … lxx s.

Item paid for iii yerd*es* iii q*uarter* of derk tawny. P*ri*c*e* the yerd ii s. ii d. …viii s. i d. ob.

Item paid for xii pec*es* of lynnen clothe cont*eynyng* xv^{xx} elnes. P*ri*c*e* the ele v d. … vi li. v s.

Item paid for vi elnez of canvas to trusse in the said cloth w*i*th a pec*e* of corde … ii s. i d.

Item for <xii> \xvi/ elnez of lynnen clothe at xii d. the elne … xvi s.

Item delyv*er*ed to Thomas Codde for my ladies offryng*e* apon the Dedicacion Day at Lyddengton … ii s. vi d.

Item paid the xiith day of Octobr*e* to Rob*er*t Hopwode m*aister* tresorers s*er*vande for ridyng apon my ladies messag*es* to the bysshop of Wenchest*er* to Langley … iii s. iiii d.

Item paid unto m*aister* dean for a reward yeven unto m*aister* Brudnell toward*es* his charg*es* at the fest of the s*er*gant*es* … C s.

Item in reward to m*aister* Cutlerd the same tyme … lxvi s. viii d.

Item in reward to Nicholas Trygg*e* of Stamford for his cost*es* comyng from Gretford to Lydyngton … xx d.

Item yeven in rewarde unto John Stevenson of Crolande … iii s. iiii d.

[158] Bracketed to include the next fourteen items.

[159] The correct total would be £4 1s. 8d.

[*p. 119*] Item the xiith day of Octobr in rewarde to Robert Cluer maister of the queristers in Stokelar for bryngyng of a syngyng chyld unto my lady … iii s. iiii d.

Item paid to John Bredd for a reward yeven t*o* my lorde of Oxforth s*er*vande <n> Mathew Jogeler … vi s. viii d.

Item paid to m*aister* dean for a reward yeven to a s*er*vande of m*aister* Stanleyes of Staffordshir*e* for bryngyng of a lett*ur* to my lad*ys* g*r*ace from Suttons Chasse … xx d.

Item in rewarde to a s*er*vande of Rob*er*t Buttons for bryngyng of quync*es* to my lad*ys* g*r*ace … xii d.

Item the xiiith day of Octobr*e* in rewarde to William Bek m*aister* p*re*sydent s*er*vande …v s.

Item paid unto Nicholas Saunders for a reward yeven to doctor Batmanson …liii s. iiii d.

Item in reward the xvith day of Octobr*e* to John Collop arres maker … vi s. viii d.

Item paid the xx day of Octobr*e* to Gryffyth Richard*es* for a reward yeven to m*aister* Medelton s*er*vande for bryngyng of dyv*er*se letters from London … v s.

Item to the same for reward yeven to a man for convaying of my lad*ys* letters to Ric*hard* Lynne conc*er*nyng*e* Ric*hard* Stukeley mat*er* … viii d.

Item t*o* the same for a reward yeven to oon Overton … xii d.

*M*aister *Fawne*. Item paid the xx^{ti} day of Octobr*e* to m*aister* Fawne for a half yer*e* ended <the> at Michaelmas … xxvi s. viii d.

Item paid to m*aister* dean for a reward yeven to ii p*er*sons for convaying of ii chyldren from Tutbury to Lyddyngton to be in the chappell w*i*th my lad*ys* g*r*ace … iii s. iiii d.

Item yeven in reward to a s*er*vant of Mylez Busshe for bryngyng of quynsus unt*o* my lad*ys* g*r*ace the xxith day of Octobr*e* … xx d.

^{M}Summa … <xxxii li. xvii s. vi d. ob.^{P}> xxix li. iiii s. ob.^{P} [160]

[*p. 120*] Item paid the xxiith day of Octobr*e* to m*aister* John Hechyn of Ihesu Colage in Cambrige for the exibucion of Thomas Pellett … v s.

Item t*o* the same for arreyment nessessary to be bought for the same Thomas Pellett … vi s. viii d.

Item paid the xxiiith day of Octobr*e* to Edith Foler for a reward yeven unto Mergett Stukeley … xxvi s. viii d.

Item to the same for a reward yeven to Flyntt*es* wyff … iii s. iiii d.

Item t*o* the same for a reward yeven t*o* a mydwyff of Lyddyngton … xx d.

Summa totalis DCCvii li. viii d.[161]

[160] The total of pp. 118–19 (the correction, still in the MW hand, is 10s. over).

[161] The sum total to this point, written small in the left margin.

Item delyv*er*ed to m*aister* dean for a reward yeven to m*aister*<Bart...> Burton ... xx s.

Item delyv*er*ed for my ladies offryng apon Alhallo Day ... v s.

[162]Item paid unto John Elston for his cost*es* and horse hir*e* bringyng of a buke unt*o* Croyland t*o* my ladies counsaill the iii^{de} of Novembr*e* ... xvi d.

Item paid unto maister dean for a rewarde unto Richard Aderton at Lidington ... iii s. iiii d.

Item a rewarde yeven unto Willia*m* Hilm*er* s*er*vant for conveyng Thomas Pellet unto Chambrig*e* ... xvi d.

Item paid to a shomaker of Lidington for two pair of shoes unto my ladies grace ... xii d.

Item to Roger Radclyf for money deliv*er* unto the p*ar*sone of Saint Margaret*es* at Ketesby ... iii s. iiii d.

Item in reward unto Ric*hard*<Goney> Coney my lord*es* s*er*vant at Lidington ... x s.

[*p. 121*] Item paid to maister tresarer for a rewarde yeven unto vi Spaynerd*es* that daunsed the morice ... vi s. viii d.

Item in rewarde unto Ric*hard* Aderton the xth day of November ... vi s. viii d.

Item in rewarde unto a s*er*vant of my lord of Oxonford*es* for bringyng fesaunt*es* ... vi s. viii d.

Item paid unto Richard Boothe for riding unto my ladye Hasting*es* by comaundement of my ladies grace by the spaic*e* of <...> iii dayes ... iiii s.

[163]Item paid to Adam Forster for a unc*e* of saten sylk ... xvii d.

Item paid to Ric*hard* Carre for ridyng from Liddyngton to the kyng at Astlay and foloyng his g*r*ace to Kyllyngworth by vi daiez ... iiii s.

Item t*o* the same ridyng for s*ir* John Seynt John by two daies ... xvi d.

Item t*o* the same for ridyng to Tatsall to m*aister* dean by iii daies ... ii s.

Item t*o* the same for ridyng to Burne to the baily a day ... viii d.

Item t*o* the same for ridyng to Windsore to the bisshop of Wynchestr*e* and so to London to maist*er* chamberlayn ... vi s.

Item to the same for riding to s*ir* John Maskam by iii daies ... ii s.

[164]Item paid to Olyv*er* Holand for the cost*es* of mastir Jubbys beyng at Ledyngton ... xx d.

[162]The ‘curly’ hand takes over here and is also responsible for the first four entries on p. 121.
[163]The MW hand returns here.
[164]The ‘curly’ hand returns here and continues, closely written, until the end of p. 126c and then from p. 127 up to and including the penultimate entry on p. 129.

Item paid to the said Olyv*er* for rydyng to Cambrygge for mastir chamberlayns mater … iiii s.

Item to the same for his cost*es* into Notynghamshire … iii s. iiii d.

^{M}Summa … vi li. xix s. i d.^{P}

[*p. 122*] Item paid the xxth day of <l> Novembr*e* to Nicholas Aughton for rydyng to the kyng by the space of viii days … v s. iiii d.

Item paid the same tyme to Henr*y* Fysher oon of my ladyes chappell for the co*n*veyng of two chyldren of the chappell from Tyddbery to Colyweston … xxiii s. ob.

Item paid the same tyme to mastres Fowler for money by hir paid to mast[ir][165] Morgans wyff for chekons and i pygge and othir vetell for the ladyes brekfast*es* … ii s. x d.

Item paid the same tyme to Lenard of the vestry for byndyng of lxxvi bokys of master John Gersons pryntyng at i d. ob. the boke … ix s. iiii d.

Myles. Item paid the same tyme to mastir Gryndell for i carte for to cary hom Coke and his wiff out of <the> Colyweston to Worthorp … viii d.

Item paid unto the same for money by hym paid unto mastirs Morgan and the bayllyf for the charges of the docto*urs* of the Arches at Colyweston … xix s. viii d.

Item paid to the same for a rewarde gevyn unto mastir Chr*ist*ofer Cros[l]y[166] … xx s.

Item paid in reward to John Tanne for brynging of a gossehauke by my ladyes comaundment … iii s. iiii d.

Item payd in reward to Henr*y* Lodlowe for foder delyv*er*ed to mastres Masse at dyv*ers* tymes for my ladyes g*r*ace … xx s.

Item paid the xxiiiith day of Novembr*e* unto the pryo*ur* of Sympryngham for the bord of Angues Swoche from the first day of May unto Alhaloutyd last past … xx s.

Item paid to the said prio*ur* for to dystrybute in almes for my ladyes g*r*ace … vi s. viii d.

Item paid the same tyme to Nicholas Saundre for i pece of canvas b[o]ught at Lenton fayor co*nteynyng* xxiii yerd*es*. P*r*i*ce* the yerde ii d. ob. and iiii d. over all … v s. i d. ob.

Item t*o* the same for a pece of canvas co*nteynyng* xlviii yerd*es*. P*r*i*ce* the yerde ii d. ob. qua. … xi s.

Item t*o* the same for i pece of blacke cotton co*nteynyng* xxi yerd*es*. P*r*i*ce* … vi s.

Item t*o* the same for i pece of russet co*nteynyng* xviii yerd*es*. P*r*i*ce* the yerde v d. … vii s. vi d.

[*p. 123*] Item paid to Nicholas Saunder for i pece of russet clothe co*nteynyng* xxii yerd*es*. P*r*i*ce* the yerde v d. … ix s. ii d.

[165] MS 'mastres' ('r' alt. to 'i'?).

[166] MS 'Crosby'.

Item paid to the same for i pece of white cotton co*n*te*ynyng* xli yerd*es*. P*r*ic*e* the yerde v d. ... xvi s. viii d.

Item to the same for i pec*e* of white carsey co*nteynyng* xvi yerd*es*. P*r*ic*e* the yerde vi d. ...viii s.

Item t*o* the same for trussyng corde to truse in the said clothe ... iiii d.

Item yevyn in rewarde to s*ir* John \Blot/ veker of Newporte Paynell for his co*m*myng to my ladyes g*r*ace by hir co*m*maundment ... iii s. iiii d.

Item paid the xxvi[th] day of Novembr*e* to docto*ur* Felle my ladyes aumno*ur* for money by hym leid out for my ladyes almes from the <i> vii[th] day of May last past unto the xviii[th] day of Novembr*e* ... xviii s. i d.

Item paid the xxvi[th] day of Novembr*e* to Henr*y* Wynstanley for viii days rydyng into Lancashire and home again ... viii s.

Item paid the same tyme in rewarde to a Frenche pryste by m*astir* deane ... ii s.

Item paid the same tyme to my lady Revers for iii lib. of damask gold. P*r*ic*e* ev*er*y pu*n*d l s. ... vii li. x s.

Item paid the same tyme in reward to a s*er*vant of my ladye prynces ... iii s. iiii d.

Item yevyn the same tyme in reward to Raeff Carre for brynging of letters from Scotlond to my ladyes g*r*ace ... xiii s. iiii d.

Item delyv*er*ed to my ladyes g*r*ace in hir lyttor goyng to oure Lady of Halywell ... iii s. iiii d.

Item paid the xxix[th] day of Novembr*e* by the co*m*maundment of my ladyes g*r*ace to Henr*y* Ludlowe for rep*ar*acyons doune <a> upon his howse in Colyweston the which now Hugh Ratclyff dwellyth in ... iiii li.

Item paid the same tyme to mastir Gryndell for a tap*er* wayng vii lib. at viii d. the pund ... iiii s. viii d.

Item to the same for a powder box of sylv*er* and for the fasshyn of the same ... viii s.

Item yevyn in rewarde the same tyme to Jamys the kyng*es* purcyvant by [my] ladyes co*m*maundment ... iii s. iiii d.

Item paid the last day of Novembr*e* t*o* Richard <Pul> Plu*m*mer for my ladyes overyng on Seynt Andrewys day ... v s.

[M]Summa ... xxiiii li. <xvii s. i d.> <xiii s. iiii d.> \xvii s. i d./[P 167]

[*p. 124*] Item paid the first day of Decembr*e* in rewarde to a man for kepyng of Skyppe at <le> Ledyngton by mastir Morgan ... xx d.

Item paid to the said master Morgan for the cost*es* of mastir Fyssher at Ledyngton ... xvi d.

Item to the same for a payer of dubbyll soled shone for my ladyes g*r*ace ... viii d.

[167] The final, approved total of pp. 122–3 is in paler ink than the other calculations (which are in the MW hand).

Item paid the ii^{de} day of Decembr*e* to mastres Fowler for a taper for our*e* Lady of Halywell … v s.

Item paid the iiith day of Decembr*e* to Richard Carre for rydyng to Robert Nevell in <s> Notynghamshyr*e* and home a<yene>gein by iiii days … ii s. viii d.

Item yevyn in reward the iiiith day of Decembr*e* to mastres Rede by my ladyes co*m*maundment … vi s. viii d.

Item the same tyme yevyn in reward to a s*er*vant of my lorde of Cyldare for brynging of a <halke> gossehalke … xiii s. iiii d.

Item yevyn the same tyme in rewarde to the master of the hospytall in Stampford for makyng of a s*er*mon byfoir*e* my ladyes g*r*ace … v s.

*Seynt Nicholas clerk*es.[168]

Item yevyn the vth day of Decembr*e* in rewarde to the bysshop w*ith*in my ladyes <zelayere> place on Seynt Nicholas Evyn by my ladyes co*m*maundment … v s.

Item paid the same tyme to the bysshop of the towne of Colyweston in lyke wyse … xx d.

Item paid the viiith day of Decembr*e* for the offeryng of my ladyes g*r*ace at the Concepcion of oure Lady … v s.

Item yevyn the same tyme in reward to a fryo*ur* by mastir confessor by the co*m*maundment of my ladyes g*r*ace … viii d.

Item paid the ixth day of Decembr*e* in rewarde to the gardyner by [my] ladyes co*m*maundment … xx d.

Item paid the same tyme to mastir Gryndell for sowderyng and mendyng of iii sylv*er* pott*es* of the sellor and oon of the buttre … v s. iiii d.

Item paid the same tyme to Robert Hylton for vi yerd*es* of black cotton for a <run> jackit <of> for docto*ur* Jubbys … ii s. vi d.

Item to the same for vi yerd*es* of white <lyngne> lynyng for the same … xviii d.

Item paid to the said Robert for ii payor of shone for Skyp … xii[169] d.

Item to the same Robert for v yerd*es* of white cotton for to make the said Skyppe a petycote … xvii d. ob.

Item paid the same tyme to Madwell of Stampford for shone bought at dyv*er*s tymes for the ii yong gentylwomen … ii s.

[*p. 125*] Item paid to the same Robert for ii shepe skynnys for the skynn*er* … v d.

Item to the same for v yerd*es* of russet cotton for a jacket for Henr*y* the kyng*es* godson …ii s. i d.

Item for v yerd*es* of whit*e* for lynyng for the said jacket … xvii d. ob.

[168] Bracketed to include the next two items.
[169] MS 'xjj'.

Item for ii yerd*es* of tawne fustyan fo[r] a dublat for the said Henr*y* … xii d.

Item for a yerde and a halfe of white for lynyng of the same doblet … v d.

Item for canvas to the same … i d. ob.

Item for a yerde of wachet for a payer of hosyn to the same Henr*y* … ix d.

Item for makyng and lynyng of the same hose … vi d.

Item for a russet bonet for the same Henr*y* … x d.

Item for a payer of shone for the same Henr*y* … v d.

Item for a dosyn of point*es* for the same … i d.

Item paid to the said Robert for iii yerd*es* of blacke lynyng for a gowne of mastres Perot … xii d.

Item for a payer of shone for the same mastres Perot … vi d.

Item paid to the same for the lynyng of the plyt*es* of iii gownys of mastres Webbe … xii d.

Item for armletes for the same gownes … iii d.

Item to the same for iii yerd*es* of black [c]otton[170] for lynyng of a kyrtyll of the same mastres Webbys … xii d.

Item t*o* the same for vi yerd*es* of black lynyng for a gowne for Thomas Pelet … ii s.

Item to the same for iiii yerd*es* of white cotton for lynyng for a cote for the said Thomas … xiiii d.

The bereall of Elynor Stanley. Item paid the same tyme for the cost*es* and charg*es* of the bereall of mastres Elynor Stanley. To the pryst*es* clerk*es* and chylderyn vi s. for iiii men to bere hir to chyrche viii d. for ii men that made the grave viii d. for ix ryngers to ryng all the bereall xviii d. for the weryng of the bell*es* xii d. to power folk iiii s. vi d. for the waste of iiii tapers vi d. in lyk*e* wyse for the torchys vi d. for brekyng of the growne in the chauncell vi s. viii d. to Utherbyis wyffe for wa<t>chyng wasshyng and makyng clene of the chamber vii s. iiii d. to Thomas Bakers wyffe xvi d. to another woman xvi d. to Love for his labor and wache ii s. …xxxiiii s.

[M]Summa … Cxiii s. i d. ob.[P] [171]

[*p. 126*] *Land*es *bought in Chesterfford*. Item paid the xiiiith day of Decembr*e* unto s*ir* Hugh Assheton for money by hym paid to master chamberleyn for land*es* bought of <sir Thomas Terell> Gardener*e* in Chesterff[or]d [172] … Cxx li.

Item paid to the same for money paid to mastres Benet for ii pecys of grene tartren … xxxviii s.

Item to the same for money paid to John <Brow> Browgrave … xxx li.

[170] MS 'Sotton'.

[171] The total of pp. 124–25, preceded by a blot (it is 6s. 8d. over).

[172] MS 'Chesterffeld' (see p. 159 below).

Item to the same for a garnysshed bonet for mastres Flee … xxiiii s.

Item paid to Margaret Frognal in p*ar*te of payment of hir joi[n]to*ur*[173] … lxvi s. viii d.

Item paid the same tyme to John Heron for byldyng made at Wokyng … xxvi li. xiii s. iiii d.

Item paid for a gret portuse for my ladyes g*r*ace … xiiii s.

Item paid for another of ii voloms … iii s. iiii d.

Item paid for rep*ar*acyons done at Coldharborogh … xii s.

Item the xviii day of Decembr*e* in reward unto John the French chyld … x s.

Item the same day in reward to a s*er*vande of my lady Norfolk*es* … iii s. iiii d.

Item a rewarde yeven to m*aster* Brudnell*es* s*er*vant for gooing of my ladies message to London … xiii s. iiii d.

Maistrez Denton. Item paid unto m*aster* dean the xviii[th] day of <Octobre> December for maisteresse Dento*ns* fee due at the feest of Saint Mychaell tharchangell last passed …iii li. <x> vi s. viii d.

Item paid the xx[th] day of Decembr*e* to John Brownyng for oon halfe yere for his annewyte enddyd at Crystemas next co*m*myng … xx s.

Item paid the same tyme to John Byrde for <mo> money paid to Thomas Richar[d] son for his cost*es* w*ith* iii horsis to London for master Parker and Thrognall and for carying up of Henr*y* the kyng*es* godson to London … vii s. ix d.

Item paid the same tyme to Henr*y* Bygod for <j> oon federbedde w*ith* the bolster. P*r*ice xx s. For another federbed w*ith* the <bost> bolster viii s. For ii corse matres ii s. For ii payer of fastenys viii s. iiii d. For iii payer of blanket*es* iiii s. For oon payer of shet*es* of iii bred*es* viii s. iiii d. For iiii payer of shet*es* of ii bred*es* at xx s. For ii payer of shet*es* of ii bred*es* xii s. For vi payer of corse shet*es* viii s. For the best counterpoynte xvi s. viii d. For iiii coverlett*es* iiii s. For a long pelour*e* of baudkyn vi s. viii d. … Cxviii s.[174]

[*p. 126b*] Item delyv*er*ed to John Byrde for my ladyes offeryng apon the Twelfeday … v s.

Item paid the vi[th] day of January to Willyam Quttyller s*er*gant[175] in rewarde … xl s.

Item the same tyme delyv*er*ed to mastres Fowler for a rewarde yevyn to my lady markes s*er*vant … vi s. viii d.

Item delyv*er*ed the same tyme to John Peyton for money delyv*er*ed to my ladyes g*r*ace …vi s. viii d.

Lord and abbot off mysrewle.[176]

[173] MS 'joimto*ur*'.

[174] There is no page total here (it should be £196 10s. 5d.); the total for the next page (p. 126b) does not include this page (which is in fact included, without comment, in the page total for p. 127).

[175] Alt. from 's*er*vant'?

[176] Written in the left margin with a thick nib and black ink in the 'sprawling' hand; bracketed to

Item the same tyme paid to John Haryson for makyng of dysgysing*es* and his sport*es* in Crystemas ... lvi s. vi d.

Item in rewarde to the same ... xiii s. iiii d.

Item in rewarde to Thomas Prechet abbot of mysserowell ... vi s. viii d.

Item paid to mastir Cuttyler <serv> clerk*es* for wrytyng of the copyes of the g*r*aunt of Colyweston in Est*er* *ter*me and for wrytyng of a payor of indentures of covena*un*t*es* for maryage of mastres Webbe ... iii s. viii d.

Item to the same for wrytyng of the copye of evydences bytwext my ladyes g*r*ace and my lady Cycell ... viii d.

Item to the same for wrytyng of iii shet*es* of paup*er* for my ladyes g*r*ace for makyng of ewydenc*es* ... ii s.

Item payd the xith day of January to Ric*hard* Flecher for the cost*es* of John browderer from Lynne to Colyweston ... ii s. vi d.

Item paid to the same for the norsyng of a powir chylde by the space of iii wekes ... <viii d.> ii s.

Item paid to the same for <iuge> inqueryng <o> for the moder of the chylde ... xiiii d.

Item paid the xiith day of January to Willya*m* Wyldebore for carying of a coffer of evydenc*es* and a clothe sak sent by m*astir* chamberlen from London ... vii s. iiii d. ob.

Item also paid to mastir Gryndell for a rewarde yevyn to a Frenche prest co*n*fessor to mastres Perot ... xx d.

Item to the same Gryndell for a rewarde yevyn to mastir Chr*isto*fer Crosley ... vi s. viii d.

[M]Summa ... viii li. ii s. vi d.[P 177]

[*p. 126c*] Item paid the xiiith day of January to m*astir* chamberlen for a rewarde yevyn unt*o* m*astir* Conysby for my ladyes maters at the Kyng*es* Hede in London ... vi s. viii d.

Item in rewarde to mast*ir* Brewtenell the same tyme ... vi s. viii d.

Nota bene.[178] Item the same tyme for a rewarde yevyn to the kynges attorney for the examynyng of my ladyes maters in the Cheker ... xiii s. iiii d.

*le unc*e *iiii s. viii d.*[179] Item to the golde wyer drawer for i lib. of <flatte> rollude golde of damaske \le unce iiii s. viii d./ ... lvi s.

include the next three items.

[177] ½d. short.

[178] This 'Nota' and the other marginal notes (except the last two) and above-line insertions (several marked with +) are written with a thick nib and black ink (probably in the 'sprawling' hand).

[179] Written in the left margin alongside the item. The total requires 1 lb. of gold to be 12 oz.

le unce <i pece> v s. viii d. Item paid to the same golde wyer drawir for vi unc*es* of flate golde of damaske \le unce v s. vii d./[180] … xxxiiii s.

Item paid to s*ir* John Hussey and to Rob[e]rt Hussy for certeyn land*es* lying in Byllysby … Ciii^{xx} li.

Item paid unto s*ir* Thomas [T]errell[181] for certeyn londes lying in [Ma]lton[182] … Clxii li.

Item paid to Gardener for makyng of <my> wrytyng to Wodstok … v s.

Item paid to Nicholas Turpyn for parte of c*er*teyn lond*es* lying in Byllysby …liii li. vi s. viii d.

Item for ii gamys of <of> chestmen for my ladyes g*r*ace … xvi d.

Item for ii unc*es* of sylke … xx d.

Item paid to the same for ii preve <selles> sealles for Stannop … vi s. viii d.

Item paid for i pece of blacke velvet co*nteynyng* xxi yerd*es* i q*uarter*. P*rice* the yerde viii s. x d. … ix li. viii s. v d.

Notatur quia attengitur in se ad ix li. vii s. viii d. ob. plus quam prius per ix d.[183]

Item paid t*o* the same for money paid for weyng of a gret co[ffe]r[184] w*ith* evydenc*es* and for carying of the same to the carte and for corde to the same <covir> coffer … vii d.

Item paid to Conysby clerk in rewarde … <vi s. viii d.> xxvi s. viii d.

Notatur et li. oneratur domina.[185]

Item paid the same tyme to a stayn*er* that came from Scotlond … vi s. viii d.

*M*astir *chamberlayn for m*astir *Thaytt*es. Item paid the same tyme to master chamber*-*len for money delyv*er*ed unto master Twhayt*es* for my ladyes <g> maters in Fraunce … xiii li. vi s. viii d.

[M]Summa … CCCCxxvi li. vii s.[P]

[*p. 127*] *R. Stukeley*. Item paid unto Richard Stewkeley the xxvii day of Decembr*e* by his byll assigned for a pece of gerthe webbe for the gret bemes … viii d.

Item to the same for a pece of <lyrce> lyre … vi d.

Item to the same for crewsis bought for my ladies g*r*ace at Lyddyngton iiii d. and for hempsed viii d. … xii d.

[180] The marginal cost of 5s. 8d. is correct, although the entry above line appears to read 'v s. vij d.' (in the same thick nib and black ink as the marginal note).
[181] MS 'derrell'.
[182] MS 'wolton'.
[183] The marginal note points out that the total given is 9d. more than the correct total, £9 7s. 8d.
[184] MS 'covir'.
[185] Doubtful transcription, but the note and correction to the total may refer to 20s. given Coningsby p. 128.

Item in reward unto Jamys the kyng*es* pursyvant delyv*er*ed unto George Fraunc*es* … v s.

Item delyv*er*ed unto m*aster* Morgan for a reward yeven unto Thomas Ferthyng*es* wyff … ii s.

Item delyv*er*ed unto maistres <wyf> Wynesowr*e* in reward … x s.

Item delyv*er*ed to George Fraunc*es* for a reward yeven unto the prync*es* fotman … iii s. iiii d.

Item paid unto s*ir* Hughe Assheton for a garnesshed bonet for maistres Webbe agaynest hir mariage … xxiii s. iiii d.

Item paid to the same for cariage of a hundreth of prynted bok*es* w*i*th other of my lad*ys* stuf from London … xviii d.

Item t*o* the same for a reward yeven to <the> a goldsmyth that came from London … xx d.

Item paid unto Heugh Latym*er* for wolle for a mattresse for Skypp … xii d.

Item delyv*er*ed unto George Fraunc*es* for my ladiez offryng apon Crystemas Day in money x s. and in gold v s. … xv s.

Item to the same to delyv*er* unto m*aster* Atkynson chapplen unto my lady<es> Bray … liii s. iiii d.

Item paid unto Jamys Morice for money paid by hym for dyv*er*se matt*es* for ii gallerys … xvii s.

Item the last day of Decembr*e* to my ladies g*r*ace by the hand*es* of m*aster* chaunceller … vii s. vii d. qua. di.

Item delyv*er*ed unto my ladies g*r*ace the xix day of Decembr*e* for hir almes purse … x li.

[M]Summa … CCxiii li. xiii s. iiii d. qua. di.[P] [186]

[*p. 128*] Item delyv*er*ed unto my ladies g*r*ace the last day of Decembr*e* to yeve for Newyer*es* yeft*es* … x li.

Newyers Day. Item delyv*er*ed unto m*aster* Free for bryngyng of the kyng*es*<newy> Nevyergyft*es* … C s.

Item delyv*er*ed unto my ladies g*r*ace for William Hylm*er* … xx s.

Item for m*aster* chamberlayne … xl s.

Item for m*aster* Morgan … xl s.

Item to Leghe s*er*gant … xx s.

Item to Steven Taberet … iii s. iiii d.

Item to Henry Cony for bryngyng of my lord*es* Newyersgyft … xx s.

[186] The total includes the unwritten total of p. 126.

Item delyv*er*ed to William Pole for my ladies offryng the same day … v s.

Item the ii^{de} day of January unto the exchet*ur* of Lyncolnshyr*e* in reward … xx s.

Item in reward unto Conysby s*er*gant … xx s.

Item paid unto m*aster* Bretnell s*er*vande in full payment for his cost*es* to London apon my ladies materez ov*er* <u>xiii s. iiii d.</u> which he receyved afour*e* … ix s. ii d.

Item delyv*er*ed unto m*aster* dean for a reward yeven to m*aster* Fessher my lad*ys* reder in Cambryg*e* … x s.

Stet. Item to the same for a reward yeven to <s*ir* Hugh Assheton> \to my lad*ys* solycetur*e*/ … xl s.

Item to the same for a reward yeven unto Roger Heyton m*aster* chauncellers s*er*vant … xx d.

Item paid the vth day of Januar*y* unto m*aster* Brewtnell*es* clerk for his labur <vr> wrytyng of dyv*er*se endentures for my lad*ys* g*r*ace … xi s. viii d.

^{M}Summa … xxxii li. x d.^{P}

[*p. 129*] Item paid unto m*aster* chamberlayn for a reward yeven unto m*aster* Fessher oon of the jug*es* of the Comen Place … iiii li.

Item paid unto John Bredde for money payd unto s*ir* Herry Boynton and Isabell his wyff in full payment of all dutees and bargayns seales and p*ro*mysses made betwyxx my lad*ys* g*r*ace and the said s*ir* Herry and Isabell … iii li. vi s. viii d.

<Summa partis … vii li. vi s. viii d.>

Item paid to s*ir* Hugh Assheton brother for his cost*es* into Walis … vi s. viii d.

Item paid unto s*ir* Hughe Assheton for money delyv*er*ed unto John Brograve … xx li.

Item paid to John Bredd for his cost*es* and Willyam Wodforth William Fitzwill*ia*m ridyng to Sleforth and to Byllesby in Lyndsay for <taty> takyng of possession in c*er*ten land*es* theyr*e* and from thens to Grantham by the spaic*e* of viii daiez at <u>xii d.</u> a day … xxiiii s.[187]

[188]Item paid to m*aister* chaunceller for c*er*ten prynted bok*es* by hym bought at London …lx s.

Summa … <xxviii li. x s. \xvii s./ viii d.>^{P} xxxi li. xvii s. iiii d.^{P}[189]

[*p. 130 blank*]

[*p. 131*] [190]Item payed <for> \to/ maister Saynt John and my mastres his [wyfe] for theyre exhibic*io*n

[187] Lady Margaret's signature occurs below this entry and then not again until p. 145.

[188] This final entry (after a gap) is in the MW hand.

[189] The sums are in different hands (neither the MW hand); the canc. sum is marked 'p*r*o*batur*' and the corrected (and correct) sum is marked 'p*r*o*batur*'.

[190] An unfinished entry (in the summary hand of p. 134ff.) on an otherwise blank page.

[*pp. 132–3 blank*]

[*p. 134*] [191]Some t[ot]all[192] of all expensis and paymentes byfore wryten … MCCCCxli li. xvii s. viii d. ob. qua.

And so he oweth … MCCxxxix li. xi s. i d. ob. qua. wherof he hath deliv*er*ed unto James Mores clerk of the werk*es* at divers tymes … CCCCii li. xix s. ii d. ob. as hit dothe p*ar*ticularly appere bothe by the boke of accompte of the saide James as by the boke of the saide Myles. And also by the knowlege of the saide James. Also delivered unto Will*iam* Bedyll tresourer of houshold at div*er*s tymes as hit doth appere in his accompte and also in a boke of p*ar*celle*s* of the said Miles w*ith* xii li. xvi s. x d. for iiii^{xx}iiii yerde*s* of blak deliv*er*ed for lyverey … CCCxxxi li. x s. ii d. ob. And also he hathe payed for thexybyc*i*on of maystyr Seynt John and his wyff xxvi li. xii s. x d. for thexhibic*i*on of maistyr P*ar*ker and his wyff xv li. xii s. vi d. qua. for thexhibic*i*on of mayst*er* Frognoll and his wyff x li. xiii s. iiii d. in all as yt doth appere in the forsaid boke of p*ar*celle*s* … lxii[193] li. xv s. vi d. qua. And so he owethe …CCCCxlii li. vi s. ii d. ob. whereoff the seid Miles hath payd to James Mores for*e* the sup*er*plus off his acompt … xxxix s. ii d. qua.

[paper extension sewn to the bottom of p. 134, written small and neat]

And so he aweth … CCCCxl li. vii s. qua.

*In prest*es *delivered by my lady*s *co*m*maundme*nt *that ys to saye*

to[194]

My lord of Duresme … C li.[195]

*r*eceyved *and delyv*ered *to my lady*s *couffers*[196]

Richard Conway of the chappell … iiii li.

John Joynes … x li.

George Hennyngham over iiii li. payed by John Bedyll … lxxvii s. vi d.

Recepta de Johanne Bedell xiiii^{o} die Januarii l s.

Maistyr Bekynsall … xl s.

Will*iam* Pole … xi li.

[191] The 'sprawling' hand is responsible for this page (apart from the list of names on the extension, which is probably in a different hand, although the 'sprawling' hand returns at the end of the list). See Plates 11–12.

[192] MS 'talall' (alt. to 'tatall').

[193] Alt. from 'lxiij'.

[194] To be read as following on from 'And so …qua.', the marginal 'in …saye' is bracketed to 'to' which is itself bracketed to include all the next items on the paper extension as far as 'And so remayneth'.

[195] See D102.10/83.

[196] Noted in the MW hand in the left margin; the other marginal notes on the page may also be in this hand (but more cramped).

Syr John Melton knyght … xvi li. xiii s. iiii d.

Maistres Curson … lx s. «rec*eyved* ii^{de} day of Septembr*e*»

Nota. Mayster Burwell … iiii li. «\fine allocatur/» «recepta»[197]

Pryour of Crowlande … xl li.

Water Cokk*es* … xliii s. iiii d.

Richard Carre … x s.

Recepta de Ricardo Carre[198] *xiiith die me*[*n*]*sis*[199] *Marcii.*

Will*i*am Farthyng … xiii li. vi s. viii d.

Syr Henry Willoughby knyght … CC li.[200]

CCCCx li. x s. x d.[201]

And so remayneth in the handys of the sayde Myles …<xxxxvi li. xv s. iiii d. ob.> xxix li. xvi s. ii d. qua.[202]

[203]The whiche som*m*e off <xxx> xxix li. xvi s. ii d. qua. the seid James[204] hath delyvered unto \the/ coffers off seid princes <as> the xvith daye off Januar*y* anno xix^{no} regis predicti as yt appereth in the boke off the seid princes and also in a payre off indentures made betw[e]ne the princes and Miles at large.

Sic debentur ultra per personas predictas … CCCCx li. x s. x d.

[*p. 135*]

[205]*Wherof in*[206]

Almes yeven to div*er*ce p*er*sons at soundre tymes … vii li. xiii s. vi d.

Money delyverd at soundre tymes to my ladys almes purse … xxii li. xvii s. vii d. qua.

Money delyverd to doctor Jubbys toward*es* the byldyng of Jh*esu*s College in Cambrigge … xxvi li. xiii s. iiii d.

lvii li. iiii s. v d. qua.[207]

Money delyverd [at soundre] tymes for my ladys offeryng … ix li. ii s. vi d.

[197] See p. 172 below.
[198] MS 'Crarre'.
[199] MS 'messis'.
[200] See D102.10/112.
[201] The correct total of debts from loans, written in the left margin and again at the foot of the page.
[202] The total of debts recovered deducted from MW's debt.
[203] The 'sprawling' hand finishes the page.
[204] Presumably an error for Miles (perhaps explicable given the reference to James Morice higher up the page).
[205] The following pages (until p. 141) are probably written in the hand of the extension on p. 134.
[206] Bracketed to include all the items on p. 135.
[207] The total of the first three items on the page, bracketed to the right of the items.

Certen peces of wolen cloth and div*er*ce pecez of frese bought for pore folk*es* ... xiii li. xviii s. x d. ob.

Exhibic*i*on of certen of my ladys scollers at Oxenford and Cambrigg ... <vi li. xi s. vi d.> vii li. xviii s. ii d.

Exhibic*i*on of Skipp my ladys fole ... xxi s. vii d.

Certen plate bought with the mendyng of other plate at soundre tymes ... xxvii li. x s. iii d.

Ale bought and send to the kyng*es* grace with cariag*e* of the same ... lvi s. vi d.

Dyverce pecez of certen lynyn cloth and canvas bought at dyv*er*ce[208] tymes ... xx li. xiiii s. ix d.

Summa partis ... Cxli li. xx d. ob. qua.

[*p. 136*] Gold and goldwyre and workynge sylk and rebyn at soundre and div*er*ce tymes bought ... xlvii li. v s. iiii d. ob.

Certen sylkes bought as saten damaske chamlett*es* sarsenett*es* and other sylk*es* of soundre colers ... Cx li. ii s. iiii d.

Div*er*ce pecez of velve bought ... xli li. xvi s. v d.

Diverce pecez of fustion and bokeram bought ... x li. Iii s. iii d.

Div*er*ce stuff necessary bought for my lad*ys* grace ... lviii s. xi d.

Certen other necessary stuff bought at soundre tymes ... viii li. xvii s. i d. ob.

Money paid to Thomas Rob*er*tson and other for certen cov*er*yng*es* and hangez of tapstre werk ... xxvi li. xxiii d.

Div*er*ce furres bought for my ladys grace at soundre tymes ... vi li. xiiii s. ii d.

Certen fether bedd*es* and other stuff bought of Henry Bygot ... Cxviii s.

Div*er*ce horses bought of soundre p*er*sones ... xxxviii li. xix s. viii d.

Too garnysshed bonett*es* bought for maistris Flye \xxiiii s./ and maistres Webbe \xxiiii s./ ... xlviii s.

Cost*es* and expens*es* of many and div*er*ce of my ladys s*er*vaunt*es* ryding apon hure messeng*es* to soundre and div*er*s placez ... xx li. <xi s. vii d. ob.> viii s. xi d. ob.

Summa partis ... CCCxxi li. xiiii s. ob.

[*p. 137*] Cost*es* and expenc*es* of my lord of Wynchester s*er*vaunt*es* at Makesey when the kynge was at Colyveston ... xxvii s. vii d.

Certen foryn cost*es* and expenc*es* necessary ... iiii li. xii s. v d.

Cost*es* of the carrag*e* of div*er*ce stuff to div*er*ce placez at soundre and div*er*ce tymes ...lxi s. i d. ob.

[208] 'dyu*er*ce' is spelt with three minims for <u>.

Reward yeven to John Haryson and other in Cristimas … lxxvi s. viii d.

Div*er*ce reward*es* yeven to soundre p*er*sons at many and div*er*ce tymez …iiii^{xx}xviii li. v s. viii d.

Reward yeven to maistres Frognall \and/ for hure juncture … xi li. xiii s. iiii d.

Reward*es* yeven to s*ir* Charles Som*er*set C s. and div*er*s other of the kyng*es* s*er*vaunt*es* at his beyng at Colyveston xlvi li. vi s. viii d. … xlvi li. vi s. viii d .

Reward yeven to s*ir* Roger Urmeston my ladys chamb*er*lyn … x li.

Reward*es* yeven to the kyng*es* attorney lxvi s. viii d. m*aister* Cuteler lxvi s. viii d. and m*aister* Brudell C s. … xi li. xiii s. iiii d.

Reward yeven to div*er*ce lerned men by m*aister* chamb*er*lyn … xxvi s. viii d.

Reward yeven to doctor Atkynson my lady Bray chaplyn … liii s. iiii d.

Reward*es* yeven to m*aister* Cony*n*gsby \C s./ and to m*aister* Fyssher \iiii li./ the jugge … ix li.

<Ciiii^{xx}v li. xv s. viii d.> Ciiii^{xx}xiiii li. xv s. viii d.[209]

Summa partis … CCiii li. xvi s. ix d. ob.

[*p. 138*] Money delyverd to m*aister* Twayt*es* for my ladys maters in Fraunce …xxxiii li. vi s. viii d.

Nota. Money paid to s*ir* Henry Norton for m*aister* Welby dette … iiii li.

Cost*es* of the cariag*e* of certen stuff that my lord of Wynchester lent ayenst the co*m*myng to Colyveston frome London and theder agayn … liii s. iiii d.

Money paid to maister Hugh Oldome my ladys chauncler \lx s./ m*aister* president \xl s./ and certen other \xxvi s. viii d./ for prynted bok*es* by them bought … vi li. vi s. viii d.

Money delyverd to maistris Denton for hure fee anno xix^{no} … vi li. xiii s. iiii d.

Money delyverd to Palmer sadeler for div*er*s horse harnes for my ladys grace bought … lxxvi s. i d.

Money paid for a bede bought for Olyver Seynt John … x s.

Cost*es* and expensez of m*aister* Parker childe … xiii s. ob.

Certen thing*es* bought for the chapell … vii s. v d.

Money delyverd to maistres \Jane/[210] Gower … xxii s. viii d.

Money paid to maistres Talbot \s*er*vant/ \xiii s. iiii d./ <and m*aistr*is Fawne \xxvi s. viii d./> … <xl s.> xiii s. iiii d.

[209] The correct total of the nine items above relating to rewards, bracketed to the right of the items.

[210] Written with a thick nib, probably in the 'sprawling' hand (unlike the corrections to the entry below).

Money paid to John Brownyng for his anuite for a yere at Cristmasse anno xix^{no} … xl s.

Summa partis … lxii li. ii s. vi d. ob.

[*p. 139*] Money delyverd to Paule Gygles for a bull of non residence for my ladys chapell … xiiii li.

Cost*es* and charg*es* of the burying of maistrez Elynor Stanley … xxxiiii s.

Cost*es* of maister p*re*sident at London by my ladys commaundment … lxvi s. viii d.

Money paid to the priour of Sempringham for the borde of Agnes Souche … xx s.

Money delyverd to Henry Ludlowe for certen rep*ar*aci*o*ns done vppon his house that Hugh Ratclyff dewelled in … iiii li.

Rep*ar*aci*o*ns done at Coldherburgh … xii s.

Money paid to John Heron in the parte of paymennt of CC marc*e* dew to the kynge for certen rep*ar*aci*o*ns don at Wokyng … xxvi li. xiii s. iiii d.

Money paid to Gardyner for lande bought of hyme at Chesterf[or]d[211] Cxx li. to s*ir* Husie and his broder for land*es* of them bought lying in Billysby Ciiii^{x} li. to Nycholas Turpyn for his land*es* lying in Malton Clxii li. and to Brograve for land*es* of hym bought lying in Malton Cxvi li. xiii s. iiii d. … DCxxxii li.

Summa partis … DCiiii^{xx}iii li. vi s.

[*p. 140*] Money delyv*er*ed to my ladyes g*r*ace for Neweyeres gyft*es* … x li.

Money delyv*er*ed to divers p*er*sones by my ladyes co*m*maundme*n*t for ther Newye[re]s gyft*es* … viii li. viii s. iiii d.

xviii li. viii s. iiii d.[212]

Money delyv*er*ed to maist*er* Frye bryngyng the king*es* Newyeres gyft … C s.

Money delyv*er*ed to s*ir* Henry Boynton … lxvi s. viii d.

Money payed for iii vestment*es*<vestment*es*> … lxi s. viii d.

Summa partis … xxix li. xvi s. viii d.

[*p. 141*] [213]*Colyweston.* Thacompt of Miles Worsley clerk of þe coffers of þe most excellent pryncesse M*ar*garete countez of Richemond and Derby and mother of our sov*er*aygne lord þe kyng þ*at* nowe is kyng Henry þe viith from þe xiiiith day of Januar*e* in þe xixth yer*e* of þe seyd sov*er*aigne lord unto þe same xiiiith day of Januar*e* next ensuyng in þe xxth yer*e* of þe seyd sov*er*aigne lord þat is to say by a hole yer*e*.

211 MS 'Chesterfeld' (cf. p. 126 above).
212 The total of the first two items on the page, bracketed to the right of the items.
213 The summary hand begins the new year.

Tharrerages. Furst the seid accomptant is charged wyth þe arreragez of his last accompt as it doth more playnly apper*e* in þe fote of þe same … CCCCx li. x s. x d.[214]

Summa … CCCCx li. x s. x d.

[*p. 142*] [215]*Recepta denariorum*. Furst receyved of tharrerag*es* of his last accompt endet þe xiiith day of Januar*y* in þe xixth yer*e* … xxix li. xvi s. ii d. qua.[216]

Item receyved þe same tyme <bj> by þe hand*es* of Thomas Cordall for wode by hym sold … xi li. x s. vi d.

Item receyved þe xvith day of Februar*y* … xx li.

Item receyved þe xxv^{ti} day of Februar*y* of s*ir* Hugh Ashton by bill*es* of allowance for money by hym paied for my ladiez \g*race*/ … xxv li. vi s. viii d.

Item receyved <of> þe vth day of M*ar*che … xvi li.

Item receyved þe xiith day of M*ar*che by þe hand*es* of s*ir* Hugh Ashton clerk … xliii li. v s. v d.

Item receyved <of> þe xxiith day of M*ar*che by þe hand*es* of James Morys … xxii li. xiii s. iiii d.

Item rec*eyved* þe iii^{de} day of Aprill … l li.

Item rec*eyved* þe xxviii^{ti} day of Aprill … xliii li.

Item rec*eyved* þe same day … xxiii li. viii s. iiii d.

Item rec*eyved* þe xvith day of May … xxiii li. xiii s. iiii d.

Item receyved þe last day of May of s*ir* Hugh Ashton … xxxvii[217] li. vii s. ix d.

Item receyved the same day … lxxiii li. xvi s. vii d.

Item receyved the xxvii^{ti} day of June … lv li.

[*p. 143*] Item receyved þe iii^{de} day of July … xxxi li.

Item receyved þe ixth day of July … xxiiii li.

Item receyved þe xth day of July … lxviii li. iii s. iiii d.

Item receyved þe same day by þe hand*es* of s*ir* Hugh Asheton … CCxxxv li. xii s.

Item rec*eyved* þe xxixth day of July by þe hand*es* of þe same … x li. xvi s. v d.

Item receyved þe vth day of August … lxxv li. xv s.

Item receyved þe last day of August anno xx^{o} … xviii li. xi s. iiii d. ob.

Item rec*eyved* þe ixth day of Septembr*e* … xvii li. xv s. viii d.

[214] See p. 134 above.
[215] The receipts (pp. 142–4) are no longer in the MW hand, but in the summary hand (here a tall, stiff hand as pp. 191–200).
[216] See p. 134 above.
[217] Alt. from ‘xxxviij’.

Item rec*eyved* þe xxvi day of Septembr*e* … xlvi li. xxi d. ob. di. qua.

Item rec*eyved* þe xviiith day of Septembr*e* in clipped grotez delyv*er*ed to s*ir* Hugh Ashton <rec*eyved* for þam> … Cxviii li. xviii s. ix d.

Item rec*eyved* þe same day of Septembr*e* … xix li. vi s. viii d.

Item rec*eyved* þe ii^{de} day of Octobr*e* … iiii^{xx}ii li. vi s. viii d.

Item rec*eyved* þe xixth day of Octobr*e* … x li.

Item rec*eyved* þe iiiith day of Novembr*e* … xxxv li. viii s. iii d.

Item rec*eyved* þe xxvth day of Novembr*e* … xx li.

Item rec*eyved* þe xith day of Decembr*e* … Cxviii li. viii s. ii d.

Item rec*eyved* þe same day … xx li. x s.

Item rec*eyved* þe xxi^{ti} day of Decembr*e* … l li. xvii s. x d.

Item rec*eyved* þe viith day of Januar*y* … xix li. xvii s. ix d. ob.

[*p. 144*] Item receyved of s*ir* Roger Urmyston knyght as for certen s[t]uff by hym bought and for oþer payment*es* in like wise by hym made as it may apper at large in þe booke made by thexecuto*urz* of þe same s*ir* Roger and remaynyng in þe kepyng of m*aister* Ashton …lxvi li. viii s. ii d.

So*m*me totall of all þe receipt*es* of this yer*e* … MDlxiiii li. xv s. iii d. ob. qua.[218]

Some totall of all þe receiptez wyth þe arrerag*es* befor wrytten … MDCCCClxxv li. vi s. i d. qua. di.[219]

wherof[220]

[*p. 145*] [221]Cost*es* and expenc*e* w*ith* other dyv*er*se payment*es* and rewardes of the most excellent prynces Margaret countesse of Richemound and Derby and modr unto our sov*er*ayne lorde kyng Henr*y* the viith from the xiiiith day of January in the xixth yere of the reign of our*e* said sov*er*ayne lord paid by the hand*es* of Myles Worsley as here after more playnly doith apere.

Fyrst the xvth day of January paid to Nicholas Aughton for rydyng to the abbot of Leceyto*ur* … xvi d.

Item to the same for rydyng to Cotton in Huntyngtonshyre by ii dayes … xvi d.

Item to the same for rydyng to the kyng at Hampton Corte and from thens to London by viii dayes … v s. iiii d.

[218] The total is 8¼d. under.

[219] In terms of the accountant's calculations the total is correct with the addition of the arrears at the end of p. 134.

[220] Written to the right at the foot of the page, 'wherof' introduces the costs and expenses of the year, which begin p. 145.

[221] Pages 145–8 are in the 'curly' hand.

Item the same tyme in rewarde to Thomas White oon of the gromys of the stabyll ... vi s. viii d.

Item paid the same tyme to master Gryndell for a rewarde yevyn to a[222] baker of Ely ...vi s. viii d.

Item paid the same tyme to Willyam Adrton for his cost*es* to Grantham by ii dayes and a nyght sendyng to my lorde of Northhumbirlond ... ii s.

Item yeven the xxiiith day of January in reward to Thomas Andrew ... vi s. viii d.

Item the same tyme yevyn in rewarde to George of the chappell at his dep*ar*tyng ... vi s. viii d.

Item paid the same tyme to mastres Stannop for a reward yeven to mastres Parkers mydwyff ... v s.

Item the same tyme yevyn in rewarde to mastres Parkrs norse ... iii s. iiii d.

Item paid the xxiiiith day of January in rewarde yevyn to dame Johne Frankyn a nonne ... iii s. iiii d.

Item paid the same tyme to *sir* Hugh Assheton for a rewarde yevyn to master Crok*es* clerk*es* ... xiii s. iiii d.

Item paid the same tyme to Robert Powdrell for i lib. iiii unc*es* of golde of damaske at iiii s. ii d. the unc*e* ... lxvi s. viii d.[223]

Item paid the same tyme to master Gryndell for a rewarde yevyn to John Collop toward*es* his cost*es* to London ... vi s. viii d.

R. Dey. Item paid the same tyme to Rob*er*t Daye cok in rewarde for a q*uarter* of a yer*e* endyng at Crystemas last past ... vi s. viii d.

^{M}Summa ... vii li. xx d.^{P}

[*p. 146*] Item paid the xxixth day of January to master deane for a rewarde yevyn to Ric*hard* Gought ... xl s.

Item paid for the offeryng of my ladyes g*r*ace on Candylmas day ... xii s. vi d.

E. Stanley. Item paid the same tyme to master Morgan for a rewarde yevyn to Bradleys wyffe for wasshyng of the clothes of mastres Elynor Stanleys and makyng clene of the chamb*er* ... i s. viii d.

Item paid the same tyme to master deane for a rewarde yevyn to a s*er*vant of master John Edmond*es* for bryngyng of letters from the kyng to my ladyes g*r*ace ... xx d.

Item <paid in Re> yevyn in reward to Peper oon of the chyldryn of the chappell ... iii s. iiii d.

Item paid the xxixxth day of January to Olyv*er* Holland for rydyng to my lord of Oxford by the space of vi dayes ... vi s.

[222] 'oon' add.

[223] The total is correct for only 1 lb. of gold of damask. (It is clear from p. 148 that there are 16 oz. to the lb.)

Item paid the xxiiith day of February to John Nicholas skynn*er* for DCl pynk*es* for a gowne of blacke velvet w*ith* a smalle ege of let*es*. P*rice* the C xvi d. … viii s. viii d.

Item to the same for \di./ a pound of smale white thred vi d. for <A p> halfe a pounde of corser threde iiii d. … x d.

Item to the same for his expenc*e* at Colyweston by the space of two dayes the tyme of my ladyes g*r*ace beyng at Ledyngton … xvi d.

[M]Summa … iiii li. xii d.[P]

Memorandum to a fee[224]*send from doctur Standysh.* Item delyv*e*red unto Rob*er*t s*er*vant to master deane for a rewarde yevyn to doct*our* Standyshe … iii s. viii d.

Item delyv*e*red the xiith day of February unto John Carter master deanys s*er*vant for the borde of mastres Angnc*e* Sowche … xx s.

Item delyv*e*red to the same for money yevyn toward hir apparell … xx s.

Item delyv*e*red to the same John for a rewarde yevyn to a monck of Sympryngham … xx d.

Item delyv*e*red to master Morgan for money yevyn to master Jobbys whicht was delyv*e*red to master Denton for Jhesu Colege in Camebryge … xii s.

[*p. 147*] Item paid the same tyme to mastres Massey for money by hir payd for dyv*ers* t[h]yng*es* co*nser*nyng to mastres Thrognall and Jane Gostone as apperyth by a byll asyned … ix s. v d.

Item paid to Willyam Hylmer for dyv*er*se spyec*es* and metsons menestred to my ladyes g*r*ace as apperyth by a byll … iii s. vii d.

Item delyv*e*red to my ladyes g*r*ace the whicht was yevyn to my lady Cycell … xx s.

Item delyv*e*red to Ric*hard* Aderton for a rewarde yevyn to <doc> master Fyssher my ladyes reder in Cambrygge … x s.

Item delyv*e*red to George F*r*aunc*es* for a rewarde yevyn to Henr*y* Starkey my lordes s*er*vant … v s.

The fyrst Sonday in Lent. Item delyv*e*red to master deane the xxiiiith day of February for a rewarde yevyn to oon of the <ffy> fryo*ur* Austyns of Stampford the whicht pre-chyd byfor*e* my ladyes g*r*ace the fyrst Sonday in Lente … v s.

Soper. <Item paid the xxvth day of February to s*ir* Hugh Assheton for money paid to Soper my ladyes celyster for fynes and recov*er*es of dyv*ers* landes … xx li.> «cancellatur hic quia allocatur in computo Hugonis Assheton clerici recepte infra xxxiiii li. xii d.»

*M*astres *Thrognall.* Item t*o* the same for money paid to mastres Thrognall for <l> hir jounynto*ur* for a hole yere endyd at Michelmas last past … lxvi s. viii d.

Jane Gore. Item paid to the same for money delyv*er*ed to Jane Gore … xl s.

[224] MS 'ffre'.

Item paid the iiith day of Marche to Olyv*er* Lowthe in reward toward his cost*es* beyng at London … iii s. iiii d.

*Docto*ur *Ednam the ii Sonday*. Item in reward to docto*ur* Ednam for prechyng byfore my ladyes g*r*ace the ii Sonday in Lent … xx s.

Item paid for the cost*es* of his iiii horse and a s*er*vant stondyng at Ric*hard* Flechers … iiii s. viii d.

Item in rewarde to mastres Talbot by s*ir* Hugh Assheton … x s.

Item in rewarde to a s*er*vant of the eschetors of Lyncolnshyre by master deane the vith day of Marche … iii s. iiii d.

[*p. 148*] Item in rewarde to a s*er*vant of my lady Cycell for brynging of a gowne from London of my ladyes g*r*ace … xii d.

Item to the same in rewarde yevyn by master deane … xx d.

Item in rewarde to master Brewtnell s*er*g*au*nt of lawe by master deane … xl s.

*Thomas Lumb*er. Item paid to Thomas Genowe Lumb*e*rd for vi unc*e* of golde of damaske. P*r*ic*e* the unc*e* iiii s. iiii d. … xxvi s.

Item in rewarde to the same … v s.

Item paid to Ric*hard* Carre the xith day of Marche for rydyng to my lorde into Langkynshyre by xiith dayes … viii s.

Item to the same for rydyng to Peterborogh for a myto*ur* on Seynt Nicholas Evyn … viii d.

Item to the same for rydyng for the abbot of Petorborogh for crystenyng of master Parkers chylde … viii d.

Item to the same for rydyng to my lorde w*ith* my ladyes Newyers yefte by a xi <d> dayes … vii s. iiii d.

Summa … <xx>xvii li. ix s. viii d. [P225]

Item paid the xvth day of Marche to James Mores for a reward yevyn to a woman of Brystowe … iii s. iiii d.

Item to the same for a rewarde yevyn to Alyse Lynne … x s.

Item paid to Rob*e*rt Hylton for a payer of hosyn for mastres Parot … viii d.

Item <the> to the same for a payer of hosyn for modr Elyn … v d.

Item to the same for a payer of shone for the said Elyn … iiii d.

Item to the said Robert for vii yerdes of cotton for to lyne the angcrys mantyll … ii s. iiii d.

[225] The cancellation refers to the £20 canc. under Soper (p. 147). The total since the last total on p. 146 is 1s. over.

[*p. 149*] [226]*Maister Conysby*. Item paid the xiiiith day of M*ar*che to Richard Fleccher for the cost*es* of m*aister* Conysby s*er*vaund*es* and xiii horsis by a day and ii nyght*es* … ix s. viii d.

Item paid to John Brydd the xviiith day of M*ar*che for his cost*es* ridyng for Bowett*es* wyff and hir chyld w*i*th iii horsis by iii daies … vi s.

Item paid to the same for ridyng to the same place to se c*er*ten wodd by v daiez … v s.

Item delyv*er*ed unto m*aister* dean for a reward yeven to Thomas Rob*er*tson of Boston … x s.

Item delyv*er*ed to the same for a reward yeven to m*aister* Parker … vi s. viii d.

Item to the same for a reward yeven to a s*er*vand of the p*r*ior of Croland … iii s. iiii d.

Item paid to William Grevell the xix day of M*ar*che for his cost*es* ridyng to Boston for Thomas Rob*er*tson by iii daies … iii s.

Stakhowse. Item paid to John Stakhowse for a gresseld horse bought by hym for my lad*ys* g*r*ace … iiii li. x s.

Item paid to the same for the kepyng and bryngyng of the said horse to Colyweston …x s.

[227]Item paid the same tyme to Chr*ist*ofer Richardson for rydyng w*i*th master Fyssher to Grantham by ii dayes … ii s.

^{M}Summa … viii li. ii s. ix d.^{P}

[*p. 150*] Item paid the xx^{ti} day of Marche for a reward yeven to John Hyll my lord*es* s*er*vande … xii d.

Item paid to Richard <Carre> Aderton the xxiii day of Marche by his byll assigned for ridyng to London and tarrying their*e* the spaic*e* of xiii daiez at viii d. the day … viii s. viii d.

Item paid the same tyme unto Richard Carre by his byll assigned for ridyng to London and abydyng their*e* the spaic*e* of ix daies … vi s.

Item in rewarde to a frer*e* of Stampforth þ*a*t prechud afour*e* my lad*ys* g*r*ace … v s.

Item delyv*er*ed to m*aister* dean for a reward yeven to Rog*er* Heyton m*aister* chauncellers s*er*vande … v s.

Item delyv*er*ed to George Fraunc*es* for my lad*ys* offryng apon the Anunciacion Day of our*e* Lady … v s.

Item paid unto maistres Foler for a reward yeven unto maistres P*ar*kers <nurse> nurse …xx d.

Item in reward to the p*r*ior of Thorney that prechid afour*e* my lad*ys* g*r*ace on our*e* Lady Day … vi s. viii d.

[226] The MW hand returns here.
[227] This entry is written in the 'curly' hand.

Brownyng. Item paid to m*aister* dean for money delyv*er*ed to John Brownyng for the t*er*me endit at our*e* Lady Day in Lent … x s.

Sir Thomas Stanley.[228]

Item paid to John Bradley for cost*es* of x horsis and his kep*er* … viii s. vii d.

Item paid to Richard Fleccher for two horsis … xvii d.

Item paid to m*aister* dean for a reward yeven to a s*er*vande of maistres Denton … iii s. iiii d.

R*obert* Hylton. Item paid to Rob*er*t Hylton for ii pec*es* of blak cotton contaynyng xxiiii yerd*es*. P*ric*e the pec*e* vii s. … xiiii s.

Item for two other pec*es* of blak cotton. P*rice* … xiii s. iiii d.

Item ii pec*es* of whit cotton conteyning xxiii yerd*es*. P*rice* the pec*e* vi s. iiii d. … xii s. viii d.

Item for oon pece of blak bokeram cont*eyning* xv yerd*es* … iiii s. x d.

Item for another pece of blak bokeram cont*eyning* xv yerd*es* … v s. viii d.

[*p. 151*] Item paid to Rob*er*t Hylton for a <fyr*e* panne> \pair*e* tong*es*/ … vi d.

Item to the same for ii payr*e* of bellowes … v d.

Item t*o* the same for v dd. and ii pair*e* of almes howse. P*rice* the dossen iii s. vi d. … xvii s. ix d.

Item paid for a brusshe for the wardrop … vi d.

Item to the same for his cost*es* by ii tymes to p*ro*vide the said stuff w*i*th other for maist*er* P*ar*ker and maist*er* Markam … viii d.[229]

Item in reward to a s*er*vande of my lord of Duresme comyng in messag*es* to my lad*ys* g*r*ace the xxvi day of Marche … xx s.

Item delyv*er*ed to m*aister* dean for a reward yeven to a s*er*vande of William Polis comyng from London to Colyweston the furst day of Ap*r*ell … iii s. iiii d.

Item delyv*er*ed to my lad*ys* gr*a*ce the iii^{de} day of Ap*r*ell for the crystenyng of maistres Mounteney chylde … xl s.

Item delyv*er*ed to my lad*ys* gr*a*ce the same day for her almes purse … C s.

*Money delyv*er*ed to pore folk*es *at the maundy*. Item the iiiith day of Ap*r*ell yeven to lxi pore folk*es* at the maundy ev*er*y pece xiii d. … lxvi s. <v>i d.[230]

*My lad*ys *offryng apon Gode Fryday*. Item delyv*er*ed to George Fraunc*es* for my ladies offryng apon Goode Fryday in v s. of gold … xxx d.

[228] Bracketed to include the next two items.

[229] Alt. from 'vij d.'

[230] The number of almsfolk (cf. 61 pairs of shoes, p. 153) refers to Lady Margaret's age. If born in May 1443, she would still be 60 in April 1504 (but might think of this as her 61st year).

Item paid unto m*aister* dean for a reward yeven unto ii s*er*vaund*es* of of thabbott*es* of Vestm*ester* … xi s. viii d.

Item t*o* the same for a reward yeven unto maister receyvers clerk … iii s. iiii d.

Item paid unto maistres Wyndesowr*e* for money delyv*er*ed unto my lady Cecill t*o* offer <v> for my lad*ys* gr*a*ce to our*e* Lady at Halywell … xx d.

Item in reward t*o* Thomas late s*er*vande unto m*aister* Pyee ridyng apon my lad*ys* messag*es* … v s.

^{M}Summa … xx li. xiii s. ix d.^{P}

[*p. 152*] Item delyv*er*ed to John fotman the vth day of Ap*r*ell to delyv*er* to my lad*ys* gr*a*ce for a reward yeven to Ric*hard* Stewkeley … vi s. viii d.

*Es*t*er Day my lad*ys *offryng*. Item for my lad*ys* offryng apon Est*er* Day in the mornyng xx d. and at masse v s. … vi s. viii d.

*For the with at Es*t*er to co*k*es*. Item in reward to the cokes for theyr*e* withe at Ester … xxvi s. viii d.

Item to the sawc*er*y and skollery in reward … v s.

Item in reward unto William Mylner a French prest which came to conffesse maistres Perrott and John Shottley … iii s. iiii d.

*Es*t*er terme. R. Dey*. Item paid unto Rob*er*t Dey coke ov*er* xl s. paid to hym for his waig*es* by the yer*e* in rewarde … vi s. viii d.

Item paid the xth day of Ap*r*ell unto Nicholas Saunders for money paid at Stampforth for the cost*es* of my lord of Northumberlayn horsis and his s*er*vand*es* beyng their*e* iii daiez …xlvii s. ix d.

Item paid to the same for his cost*es* at Stampforth oon nyght t*o* content \for/ the said horse meyte … vi d.

Item paid the xiith day of Ap*r*ell to John Gerott for ridyng to London and their*e* abydyng <by> for my lad*ys* messag*es* by vii daiez … vii s.

Almes shoez. Item paid to Rob*er*t Hylton for money paid t*o* Jakson of Stampforth for lxi pair*e* of shoez for pore folk*es* yeven by my lad*ys* gr*a*ce at the mawndy … xx s.

*M*aister *Fawne*. Item paid the xi day of Ap*r*ell to m*aister* Fawne of the unyv*er*site of Cambryge for his stipend for an half yer*e* ended at the fest of the Anu[n]ciacion of our*e* Lady … xxvi s. viii d.

Item paid to the same toward*es* his entre to be bachyler of deuinitie … lx s.

Item paid to the same for money paid unto m*aister* Holt for dette of Rauff Fawne … xl s.

R. Aderton. Item paid the xiii day of Ap*r*ell unto Ric*hard* Aderton for xii daiez ridyng to London and tarying their*e* … viii s.

Item paid to the same for ii daiez ridyng to ov*er*take Henry Clegg … xvi d.

^{M}Summa … xiii li. vi s. iii d.^{P}

[*p. 153*] Item the xvith day of Ap*r*ell paid unto John Brydde for his cost*es* and John Rose the survayars s*er*vande from Colyweston to Byllysby Chesterforth Royston Knesworth Waddon and Malton to syrvay c*er*tan land*es* their*e* as aperith by their*e* byll assigned …xvii s. xi d.

Item paid the xvi day of Ap*r*ell to George Fraunc*es* for my lad*ys* offryng at <Kettryng> \Bulwyck/ … xvi d.

Item delyv*er*ed to the same Georg*e* for my lad*ys* offryng at Northampton … iii s. iiii d.

Item delyv*er*ed to m*aister* Morgan for my lad*ys* offryng at Northampton iii s. iiii d. and to John fotman xx d. … v s.

Item delyv*er*ed to my lad*ys* gr*a*ce for a reward yeven unto m*aister* Lolle of Northampton … xx s.

Item t*o* my lad*ys* gr*a*ce for a reward yeven to maist\r/ez Odall the same tyme … x s.

Item delyv*er*ed to m*aister* Mounteney for a rewarde yeven to the nonnes of Ravell … iii s. iiii d.

Item paid unto Rob*er*t Asse of Bulwyk for vii bowlez w*i*th i d. for the bryngyng … viii d.

Item paid unto William Hylmer by his byll assigned for money delyv*er*ed to Rob*er*t Bonet towardes his cost*es* to London … ii s.

Item to the same for vi urenall*es* … vii d.

*Oly*v*er Holande.*

Item paid to Olyv*er* Holande for lx elnez of canvas bought by hym at London for my lad*ys* gr*a*ce … xx s.

Item paid to the same for vi pec*es* of bocrome ev*er*y pec*e* price v s. Summa … xxx s.

Item t*o* the same for oon pownde of westment thredde … xiii s. iiii d.

Item for carying of the same stuff … iii s. vi d.

Item for his cost*es* by x daiez from Colwyston to London and ther*e* abydyng … x s.

lxvi s. x d.[231]

Walmesforth brygge. Item delyv*er*ed to John <Holande> \Halley/ the <xxviii day of Aprell> \xi day of May/ toward*es*the rep*ar*acion of Walmesforth brygg … vi li. xiii s. iiii d.

J. Collop. Item delyv*er*ed unto m*aister* amener for a reward yeven to John Collop toward*es* *his* cost*es* to London … vi s. viii d.

[M]Summa … xiiii li. xii d.[P]

[231] The total of only the first four items above, although the bracket to the right includes all five items.

[*p. 154*] Item the xxviii day of Aprell to John Nelson <ti> in rewarde towardes the losse of an horse which diett by the way to London … xxvi s. viii d.

Item paid the same day unto m*aister* conffessor for his exspence by the way ridyng w*i*th my lad*ys* g*r*ace to Northampton by iiii daiez … vi s. i d.

Item paid to m*aister* countroller in lyke wyse for ridyng the same iourney w*i*th my lad*ys* g*r*ace … iiii s. iiii d.

*Doct*ur *Jubb*es *for Ihesu Collage*. Item delyv*er*ed to my lad*ys* g*r*ace for doctor Jubbis toward*es* the byldyng*es* of Ih*es*u Colage in Cambrige … vi li. xiii s. iiii d.

Item paid unto George Fraunc*es* for a reward yeven to Thomas Hyll and John Leghe jardyners … iii s. iiii d.

Item delyv*er*ed unto my lad*ys* g*r*ace for a rewarde yeven to John Gardyner the xxviii day of Ap*r*ell … iii s. iiii d.

Item paid the same day to maistres Massy for a reward yeven unto a pore woman of Coventre … xx d.

Item paid unto Nicholas Aughton for a payr*e* of sleppers bought by hym at London for my lad*ys* g*r*ace … viii d.

Item paid to the same for canvas to trusse iiii yerd*es* of tawny medly bought by the same Nicholas at London for maistres P*ar*ker and hir chyld … iiii d.

Item for my lad*ys* offeryng at Crolande delyv*er*ed t*o* maistes Wenesowre to our*e* Lady … xx d.

Item to Seynt Gudlake shryne … xx d.

Item at Lynne to our*e* Lady at the frerys … xii d.

Item to Seint Saviowr*es* … xii d.

Item to our*e* Lady of the Mownt … xx d.

vii s.[232]

Item to the freris at Lynne in reward … v s.

Item to the ancur*e* at the same plais … iii s. iiii d.

Item at Walsyngham to the mylk of our*e* Lady … iii s. iiii d.

Item t*o* our*e* Lady … xii d.

Item to Seynt Laurence … iiii d.

Item t*o* our*e* Lady … xx d.

Item for a tapur of wax … xx d.

Item t*o* the prest of our*e* Lady chappell … iii s. iiii d.

Item t*o* the ermette … iii s. iiii d.

[232] The total of the five items above, bracketed to the right of the items.

Item for my lad*ys* offeryng t*o* our*e* Lady in the mornynge in gold … v s.

[M]Summa … x li. xiii s. ix d.[P]

[*p. 155*] Item delyv*er*ed at Lynne to Edward Goldyng to delyv*er* to dame Mergaret London a nonne of Camse abbey … vi s. viii d.

Item the xiii day of May in reward to ii freris of Ware toward*es* the byldyng of their*e* chyrch … xx s.

Item delyv*er*ed unto George Fraunc*es* for my lad*ys* offryng apon the Dedicacion Day …v s.

Item paid unto John fotman by his byll assigned for money yeven in reward by the way to Walsyngham to dyv*er*se persons … ii s. iiii d.

Item paid the viii day of May unto m*aister* countroller for a reward yeven t*o* a man of Boston bryngyng unswar*e* of a mat*er* conc*er*nyng my lord Conyas … ii s.

Item paid t*o* Olyv*er* Holande and Richard Aderton for convaying*e* of a p*re*soner to London and for their*e* cost*es* homward by vii daiez at xii d. the day … xiiii s.

Item for keping*e* of the same p*ri*soner the spaic*e* of iiii daiez … iiii s.

Item for the cost*es* of the horse at London and home agayne by iii daiez \w*i*th his hir*e*/ … ii s.

Item paid the xviii[th] day of May unto Richard Aderton for his cost*es* from Wesbych to London and ther*e* tarying by the spaic*e* of ix daiez and in reward toward*es* the helyng*e* of his arme which was hurt the same <iou> iorney … x s.

Item paid unto Henry Wenstanley for ii payr*e* of hose and for iii pair*e* of shoez to <Ski> Skypp … ii s. vi d.

Item for wasshing and mendyng of his clothes … viii d.

Item for the hyr*e* of a horse for hym from Lydington to Colyweston and theder agayn …iiii d.

Item delyv*er*ed for my lad*ys* offryng apon the Assencion Day … v s.

Item in reward to a frere of Stampforth that prechet afour*e* my lad*ys* g*r*ace the same day … v s.

*M*aister *controller for Seynt Mary chyrch in Cambr*ige. Item delyv*er*ed to m*aister* countroller the xvi day of May to delyv*er* t*o* the univ*er*site of Cambrige toward*es* the byldyng of Seynt Mary chirch … x li.

Item for my lad*ys* offryng apon Witsonday … v s.

[M]Summa … xiiii li. iiii s. vi d.[P]

[*p. 156*] Item paid the last day of May to a s*er*vand of the baylies of Burne for kepyng of a cast of laners for my lad*ys* g*r*ace in reward … iii s. iiii d.

Item in reward to a frer*e* of Lynne þ*a*t made a s*er*mond afour*e* my ladies g*r*ace …vi s. viii d.

Item paid Renold Davempord for appuls and wyne which he paid four*e* at the ancryse of Stampforth at my lad*ys* beyng their*e* … xii d.

Item paid to m*aister* Hughe Assheton for xiiii pec*es* of holland clothe cont*eynyng* CCClxx elnez at vi d. the elne … ix li. v s.

Item paid to the same for money delyv*er*ed unto m*aister* \chaunceller for m*aister*/ Thawytez for my lad*ys* mat*er*ez at Parr*es* delyv*er*ed by Rauf Lathom … xiii li. vi s. viii d.

Item paid to the same for cost*es* of William Long and ii of m*aister* chauncellers s*er*vand*es* takyng*e* lev*ery* and possession in <fer> forest*es*[233] land*es* at Cory Ryv*er* to my lad*ys* usse … viii s. iiii d.

Item paid to the same for xxi yerd*es* of sersenett. P*r*ice the yerd ii s. vi d. … <lvi s.> liii s.[234]

Item for iii unc*e* of selk bough[t] by Nicholas Aughton paid to the same s*yr* Hughe … ii s. viii d.

Item for vi yerd*es* of russet damaske. P*r*ic*e* the yerd iiii s. vi d. … xxvii s.

Item for xxiii yerd*es* of ʒalow damaske at iiii s. vi d. … Ciii s. vi d.

Item for xi yerd*es* of blew damaske and i q*u*art*er* and di. at iiii s. vi d. the yerd … li s. ii d. qua.[235]

Item paid to the same for money delyv*er*ed to Rob*er*t Jenson my lady Cecell s*er*ua*u*nt for a bonet and a payr*e* of buskync*e* for my lad*ys* g*r*ace … xvi s. viii d.

Item t*o* the same s*yr* Hughe for a p*re*sentacion for s*yr* John Carter on of my lad*ys* chappell … xxiiii s. i d.

Item paid to the clerk*es* of the kyng*es* signet for a lett*ur* to make m*aister* Bredenell cust*os* rotulo*rum* in Keston … vi s. viii d.

[M]Summa … xxxvii li. xv<iii> s. ix d. qua.[P]

[*p. 157*] Item paid to maistres Wynesowr*e* the iii[de] day of Juyn by hir byll assigned for my lad*ys* offryng*e* at Castill Aker t*o* the heghe awter … iii s. iiii d.

Item t*o* the arme of Seynt Phyllyp … xii d.

Item to Seynt Thomas of Westacre … xii d.

Item in reward to the keper of the chyme at Lynne … xii d.

Item t*o* the chyrche of Seynt Petur at Wysbyche … xii d.

Item t*o* our*e* Lady of the see at Wysbyche … xx d.

Item t*o* the <Rel> relykes at Crolande … xii d.

[233] 'Forestes' (?).

[234] The correct total is 52s. 6d. The first total is in the MW hand, the second in a different hand marked with +.

[235] The total is for 11¼ yards, although the entry records 11⅜ yards.

Item t*o* the heghe awter at Peturborogh … iii s. iiii d.

Item t*o* the relykes at Peturborogh … xx d.

Item in reward to Molynes son … xii d.

Item to maistres Frognolles kyneswoman … xx d.

Item to maist*er* Morgan for the ancur*e* at Lynne … xx d.

xix s. iiii d.[236]

Item for CC neld*es* … viii d.

[237]Item paid the vi[th] day of June to John B[e]dell[238] for a matres oon payer of shet*es* and a cov*er*let w*ith* the caryage bought for Peper vi s. viii d. for vii yerd*es* of lenyne clothe for a surplys ii s. ob. for v yerd*es* of blancket of ii yerd*es* brode iiii s. for a bonet xii d. for makyng of his gowne x<ii> d. for a hose clothe of blak xviii d. … xvi s. ob.[239]

Item paid the same tyme to Nicholas Saunder for money paid to Ric*hard* Flechers wyfe and Hugh Latym*er* for the dyet of my lady markes s*er*vant*es* w*ith* hir horse mete … xxi s. ii d.

Item the same in rewarde yevyn by master deane to the nonnys of Kelsey for the rep*ar*acyou*n* of their place … xl s.

Item yevyn in rewarde to a s*er*vant of mast*er* Fouke Odellys … iii s. iiii d.

[240]Item paid the same tyme to Edward Hevyn for the expenc*es* of hymself and his ii s*er*vant*es* rydyng from <Colyweston> Bostone unto Byllysby and Garnethorp and from thens to Colyweston by vi dayes at iii s. the day xviii s. … xviii s.

Item paid to the said Edward for a man for rydyng from Bostone to Lyncoln and from Lyncoln to Bostone by ii days ii s. viii d. and to another man for rydyng from Bostone to[241] Sowgh Holand and Kestehevyn by ii days ii s. viii d. … v s. iiii d.

Summa … vi li. iii s. x d. ob. [P]

[*p. 158*] Item paid the vi[th] day of June to Edward Hevyn for a man rydyng from Bostone unto Barton of <the> Umbre <to spyke> for to delyv*er* a lett*er* to master Kelle by iii dayes iiii s. … iiii s.

Item paid to the same in almys yevyn for <of the C> byldyng of the chyrche of the fryo*ur* mynors in Bostone … xl s.

[242]Item paid to Jamys Clarell the same day for xv yerd*es* of tawny medly at v s. the yerd … lxxvii s. vi d.

[236] The total of the items so far on the page, bracketed to the right of the items.
[237] This entry as far as (and including) the second entry p. 158 are in the 'curly' hand.
[238] MS 'Bodell'.
[239] The total is correct, taking into account the correction.
[240] This and the next item are bracketed (separately) to the left, but with no name in the margin.
[241] 'vnto' add.
[242] The MW hand returns.

Robert Hylton.[243]

Item paid to Rob*ert* Hylton by his byll assigned for a pair*e* of slippers for maistres Perrott … vii d.

Item t*o* the same for ii payr*e* of shoez for the fotmen … xii d.

Item to the same for a yerd q*uarter* di. of tawny for a payr*e* of <how> hose to John fotman at ii s. ii d. … ii s. xi d. ob.

Item for makyng and lynyng of the same … x d.

Item for a yerd q*uarter* di. of the same for Henry fotman … ii s. viii d. ob.

Item for makyng and lynyng of the same … x d.

Item to the same for money paid to a caryer of Fodryngay for bryngyng of stuff from London send by m*aister* Clarell … xii d.

Item for a payr*e* of hose for maistres Perrott … viii d.

Item for ii yerd*es* di. of cardynall <g> whytt for the lynyng of a damaske gowne of my lad*ys* g*r*ace. P*r*i*ce* the yerd iii d. and for half a yerd of bokeram to p*er*fourme the same gowne … x d. ob.

<vii s.> xi s. v d. ob.[244]

[245]Item to the same Rob*ert* by another byll assigned for iiii yerd*es* of violett for maistrez Zouch of Sympryngham. P*rice* the yerd iii s. viii d. Summa … <xv s. viii d.> xiiii s. viii d.

Item for xviii yerd*es* of whytte kersey for the same. P*rice* the yerd xi d. … xvi s. vi d.

Item for vii yerd*es* of whitt kersey for the same at ix d. the yerd … v s. <v d.> iii d.

Item paid to Nicholas Aughton for ridyng afoure to make serche of the way betwyx Colyweston and Walsyngham by iiii daiez goyng and comyng … iiii s.

Item delyv*er*ed for my lad*ys* offryng apon T*r*inite Sonday to Georg*e* Fraunc*es* … v s.

[M]Summa … viii li. <xix s. vi d. ob.> xviii s. iiii d. ob.[P 246]

[*p. 159*] <Item paid the vi[th] day of Juyn to maistres Massy for>

Item paid the vi[th] day of Juyn to John Brograve in full payment of Cxxxiii li. <viii s.> vi s. viii d. for land*es* lying in Malton … xvi li. xiii s. iiii d.

Item delyv*er*ed to Ric*hard* Aderton to delyv*er* to Thomas Pellett tuter at Cambryche for such stuff as is nessessary to be bought for hym … x s.

Item in reward to Roger Orton … vi s. viii d.

Item for my lad*ys* offryng apon Corpus Chr*ist*i Day … v s.

[243] Bracketed to include the next twelve items.
[244] The total (correct as corrected) of the nine items above, bracketed to the right of the items.
[245] This and the next-but-one entry are preceded by black dots (pres. check-marks).
[246] The corrected total (not MW) is correct and takes into account the corrected items.

Item in reward to m*aister* Conynsby ... iiii li.

Item to iii of his clerk*es* ... xx s.

Item to m*aister* dean for a reward yeven to Thomas Bury oon of the chylder of the chappell ... xx d.

Item t*o* the same by John his s*er*vande for a reward yeven to the kep*er* of the juell*es* at Crolande ... xii d.

Item to the same which was yeven in almes at Rudam ... xii d.

Item in reward to a s*er*vande of the abbott*es* of Westm*ynster* the vi^th^ day of Juyn ... xx s.

Item payd the same day unto John Rose the survayers s*er*vande for ridyng to Byllesby and other plac*es* to s*ur*vay c*er*ten land*es* by my lad*ys* comaundement ... vii s. viii d.

Item paid the xii^th^ day of Juyne to Worsop of Colyweston for the hyr*e* of iii horsis for iii pr[e]seners[247] from Colyweston to Northampton ... ii s.

Item paid to Thomas Flemyng and William P*ar*ker for their*e* cost*es* convaying of the same p*er*sons by the spaic*e* of ii daiez ... iiii s.

Item for the diett of the said presoners ... xviii d.

Item in reward to John Collop the same day ... vi s. viii d.

Item paid to the same John yerne bought for my lad*ys* g*r*ace ... xx d.

Item paid to Nicholas Aughton for his cost*es* ridyng to London from Colyweston by vi daiez ... iiii s.

^M^Summa ... xxv li. vi s. ii d.^P^

[*p. 160*] *Brownyng*. Item paid the xvi^th^ day of Juyne to John Brownyng for a q*uar*t*er* of a yer*e* to be endet at mydsom*er* next ... x s.

*M*aister *Coup*er. Item in rewarde to m*aister* Coup*er* for settyng of dyv*er*se song*es* for my lad*ys* chappell ... vi s. viii d.

Item delyv*er*ed to the said m*aister* Coup*er* towardes the pryntyng of the stories of the fest*es* of our Lorde oon of the Transfiguracion and the other De Nomine <Jeshu> Jh*es*u ... C s.

Item in reward to m*aister* Clarrell ... xx s.

*Hardwar*e *man.*[248]

Item paid to the hardware man for iiii elnez of reben. P*r*ice the elne iiii d. ... xvi d.

Item t*o* the same for a payr*e* of yvery beyd*es* of iiii unc*e* at vi d. the unc*e* ... ii s.

Item t*o* the same for a gyrdell w*i*th tassels ... xx d.

[247] MS 'proseners'.

[248] Bracketed to include the next three items.

R. Aderton.[249] Item paid to Ric*hard* Aderton by his byll assigned for ridyng to Bury Nettelsted and to Emeswell by the spaic*e* of v daiez ... iii s. iiii d.

R.Kylt. Item in reward to Ric*hard* Kylt <...> by m*aister* survayer ... vi s. viii d.

Maistres Youch.[250]

Item paid to Worsop of Colyweston for carying of dyv*er*se stuff to Sympryngham to maistres Youch w*i*th ii horsis for too tymes beyng their*e* ... iii s. iiii d.

Item paid to Olyv*er* Holland for a sylv*er* spone bought for the said maistres Youch ... v s. iiii d.

*Exchet*ur *of Lyncoln*. Item in reward to the exchetur*e* of Lyncolnshyr*e* by m*aister* survayer ... xl s.

An armet of Cambrige. Item to an armett of Seynt Anne chappell in Cambryge toward*es* the byldyng of the same chappell in almes ... xx s.

Maistres Youch. Item paid to maistres Marbury for money yeven to maistrez Youch ...xiii s. iiii d.

Item paid to Rog*er* Radclyff for a reward yeven to a s*er*vand of m*aister* Parr*es* a safferon setter ... iii s. iiii d.

*R*obert *Dey. Mydsom*er *t*er*me*.[251] Item paid the xxvii day of Juyne to Rob*er*t Dey coke ov*er* xl s. yeven to hym for his waig*es* by the yer*e* in reward ... vi s. viii d.

[M]Summa ...xii li. iii s. viii d.[P]

[*p. 161*] Item the xxiii day of Juyne to maistres Foler for a reward yeven to maistres Seynt John mydwyff ... v s.

Item to the same for a reward yeven to hir nurse ... iii s. iiii d.

Item paid to the same for money yeven to William Parker ridyng to Tatsall to m*aister* dean by ii daiez ... ii s.

Item paid unto maist*er* Margam for a reward yeven to doctor Crystofer a physsicion in Cambrig*e* ... vi s. viii d.

Item delyv*er*ed the xxiiii day of Juyne to my lad*ys* g*r*ace for money yeven to my lady marquesse ... iii li. vi s. viii d.

Item paid to Hughe Latym*er* for exspenc*e* of my lord marquesse horsis and the diett*e* of the kep*ers* ... xii s. iii d.

Item paid to William Aderton for a yerd q*uarter* of purpyll welwet xviii s. viii d. Item for yerd q*uarter* of tawny welvet xiiii s. iiii d. ... xxxiii s.

Item in reward to the same Wylliam ... v s.

Item paid to Ric*hard* Aderton for ridyng to sir John Melton and to Spaldyng by ii daiez ... xvi d.

[249] Bracketed to include the single item.
[250] Bracketed to include the next two items.
[251] Two marginal notes in two different hands.

Frere Austens in Stampforth. Item delyv*er*ed to m*aister* Edmound Deland oon of the frere austens in Stampforth toward*es* the rep*ar*acions of theire plaice … lxvi s. viii d.

Item in reward to a s*er*vande of thabbott*es* of Peturbor*e* for bryngyng of a cast hawk*es* to my lad*ys* g*r*ace … iii s. <v>iiii d.

Item paid to m*aister* Bygod for the exspenc*e* of Willyam Farfax <doj> doghtur*e* comyng from hir father unto my lad*ys* g*r*ace … iii s. v d.

Item paid in reward yeven to a s*er*vande of my lady Fegarett*es* comyng to my lad*ys* g*r*ace … iii s. iiii d.

Item paid to m*aister* dean for money delyv*er*ed unto m*aister* confessor for a q*u*art*er* of a yer*e* endet at mydsom*er* last passid … lxvi s. viii d.

Item to the same toward*es* his exspenc*e* to London … xl s.

Item in reward to m*aister* Catysby a s*er*vande of my lord of Lyncolnes … vi s. viii d.

[M]Summa … xvi li. v s. iiii d.[P]

[p. 162] Item paid to maister dean for a man to convay a horse that John Masson of the chappell brought to Colyweston from Wynchestre … xx d.

Item delyv*er*ed to m*aister* <Twaytt*es*> Thawytt*es* to delyv*er* to m*aister* Morice Seynt John toward*es* his cost*es* and charg*es* in propayring of hymself as a man of armys in the kyng*es* s*er*vice … vi li. xiii s. iiii d.

Item delyv*er*ed to the same to bye c*er*ten juell*es* for my lad*ys* g*r*ace in Fraunce … xx li.

Item to the same in rewarde for his cost*es* beyng at Colyweston … xx s.

Item in rewarde to John Shottley the viii day of July toward*es* his exspenc*e* into Fraunce … xx s.

Item paid to William Wyldebore the same day for carying of lynnen clothe and other stuff of my ladies g*r*ace *conteynyng* in weght <u>cwt di.</u> at <u>xiiii d.</u> the cwt … xxi d.

Item to the same for carying of a couffer w*i*th c*er*ten stuff of my lad*ys* g*r*ace by maist*er* survayers p*ro*vicion … v s. iiii d.

Item payd to maistrez Foler for mone delyv*er*ed to maistrez Mounteney to bye c*er*ten sylk*es* at London … xx s.

Item paid to the same for a reward yeven to George Fraunc*es* for p*ro*viding of rosis for my lad*ys* g*r*ace … vi s. viii d.

Item in reward to John Smyth servande for bryngyng of a laveret from Stow P*ar*k … iii s. iiii d.

Nota. Item paid unto s*ir* Henry Norton the x day of July for money oying by my lad*ys* g*r*ace to m*aister* Welby for his exspenc*e* to Kendall and other plaic*e* apon my lad*ys* mat*er*ez … iiii li.

*Walmesforth brygg*es. Item delyv*er*ed to John Halley of Wittryng towardes the rep*ar*acion of Walmysforth brygg*es* the xii day of July … <xll> xl s.

[M]Summa … xxxvi li. xii s. i d.[P]

[*p. 163*] Item payd the xii[th] day of July to s*ir* Hughe Assheton for the gyldyng of a lytell buk and a claspe to the same for my ladiez g*r*ace … iiii s. viii d.

Item paid to the same for money yeven to a nonne of the Myn*er*ez suster unto my lady Rev*er*se … x s.

Item paid to the same for iiii[xx] and x yerd*es* of clothe of golde bought for my lad*ys* g*r*ace … iiii[xx]x li. xii d.

Item paid to the same for a bonett bought for my lad*ys* g*r*ace by maistrez Massy … xiii s. iiii d.

Item paid to the same for Newyer*es* gyft*es* yeven to the kyng*es* g*r*ace and my lord of Ely at Crystemas anno xix[mo] … Cxxiii li. xviii s. ix d.

Item paid to the same for money delyv*er*ed to Petur*e* of Coldherborow toward*es* the rep*ar*acion of the same … lx s.

Item in reward to the quene of Skott*es* feman the xiiii[th] day of July … iii s. iiii d.

Item delyv*er*ed the xvi day of July to m*aister* countroller for the crystenyng of my lady Conyas chylde … lxvi s. viii d.

Item delyv*er*ed for a reward yeven to m*aister* Jamys Denton my [ladys][252] scoller at Orlyaunce … xl s.

Item in reward to Hasulryg grome of the bedd*es* w*i*th the kyng … vi s. viii d.

Item the xix day of July in reward to the p*r*ior of Duresme s*er*vand for bryngyng of a pelow of downe of Cutbert foules to my lad*ys* g*r*ace … vi s. viii d.

Item paid the xxi day of July to Bradley for cost*es* of xiii horsis of s*ir* Thomas Stanleys …v s. vi d.

Item paid for ix horsis standyng at m*aister* Morgance of the same s*ir* Thomas … iiii s. viii d.

Item paid the xxviii day of July to Hughe Latym*er* s*er*vande for cost*es* of Masson horse standyng their*e* ix dayez and ix nyght*es* … ii s.

Item paid to m*aister* Morgan for a reward yeven to the vicar of Seynt Stevens at Stampforth for styllyng of waturs … iii s. iiii d.

[M]Summa … CCxxv li. vi s. vii d.[P]

[*p. 164*] Item payd the xxix day of July unto s*ir* Hughe Assheton for vi unc*e* and d. q*u*artron of sylke ryband for vestment*es*. The unce at xii d. … vi s. ii d.[253]

Item paid unto the same for iiii pec*es* of bokeram of dyv*er*se colowres. P*r*ice the pece iiii s. x d. … xix s. iiii d.

Item paid to the same for a elne of canvas to trusse the said stuff in … iiii d.

Item paid to the same for money paid unto my lady Bray for sylk*es* bought by hyr unto my lad*ys* g*r*ace … vii s. vi d.

[252] Om. MS.

[253] The total has been rounded up from 6s. 1½ d.

Item payd to the same s*ir* Hughe for money by hym payd in opteynyng*e* of a generall p*ar*don of the kyng*es* g*r*ace for such somes of money as wer*e* sett owte uppon my lad*ys* g*r*ace in the Eschequer at Vestm*ester* as aperyth by a byll therof … ix li. iii s. i d.

Item in reward to John Lowthe for bryngyng of a goshawke unto my lad*ys* g*r*ace the xxix day of July … vi s. viii d.

Item delyv*er*ed to s*ir* Hughe Assheton the last day of July in reward yeven to Hughe Denyes … xx s.

Item delyv*er*ed to maistres Foler for a reward yeven to maistrez P*ar*kers norse … xii d.

Item delyv*er*ed to George Fraunc*es* for a reward yeven to Osmounde Notte … vi s. viii d.

Item delyv*er*ed to William Pole for a reward yeven to my lord*es* s*er*vande … iii s. iiii d.

Item delyv*er*ed to mais*t*er Bekynsall apon a reknyng for ridyng into Lancashir*e* the furst day of August … xx s.

Item <in> to George Rygmaydon my lord*es* s*er*vande toward*es* his cost*es* from Lancashyr*e* to Colyweston the iii^{de} day of August … iii s. iiii d.

Item delyv*er*ed to Ric*hard* Aderton to delyv*er* to the gray freris of Stampforth for dyrge and masse for my lorde vi s. viii d. Item t*o* the whitte freris vi s. viii d. item to the blak frerys vi s. viii d. Item t*o* the frere austens vi s. viii d. Item to the nonnes v s. Item to the channons of Newstyd v s. Item to ii prest*es* of the almes howse xvi d. Item to xii beyde men xii d. Item t*o* the blak monk*es* iii s. iiii d. … xlii s. iiii d.

^{M}Summa … <x li.> \xv li./ xix s. ix d.^{P}

[*p. 165*] Item paid to s*ir* Davy Phillipp*es* for a reward yeven to a s*er*vande of my lord of Northumberland for bryngyng of a goshawke and iii merlyons the v day of August … xx s.

Item the vii day of August t*o* Lowthe fokener*e* for his cost*es* laboryng for hawkys for my lad*ys* g*r*ace … x s.

Item paid to m*aister* dean for a reward yeven to a s*er*vande of s*ir* John Hussy at my lad*ys* goyng to Halywell on <ply> pylgramege … xx d.

Item t*o* the same for a reward yeven to a s*er*vande of maist*er* Brownes of Walcott for bryngyng of satten fro London to my lad*ys* g*r*ace … xx d.

Item paid to Richard Lynne for the cost*es* of the co*m*myssyon of sewers as a<be>perith by his byll … xvi s. viii d.

Item paid to the same for a reward yeven to Tempest for bryngyng of a cast of lavars …iii s. iiii d.

Item to the same for his cost*es* ridyng into the Yle of Ely for Stukley mater*e* … iii s. iiii d.

Item paid to Holt by the same for v daies ridyng to London and ayen … v s.

Item yeven to the same Ric*hard* Lynne in reward for his cost*es* to London … xxvi s. viii d.

R. Aderton. Item paid to Ric*hard* Aderton for ridyng to London and ayen by v daiez as aperith by his byll assigned and for v dayez ridyng into Lyncoln<ss>shyr*e* a day to Burne and ii daiez ridyng to Spaldyng and Crolande in all … viii s. viii d.

Item delyv*er*ed to George Fraunc*es* for my lad*ys* offryng apon our*e* Lady Day the Assumpcion[254] … v s.

Item paid to maister*e* dean for to bye suche thyng*es* as shalbe necessary to John Masson for his fyndyng at Tatsall <viii>vi s. viii d. and xx d. to have in his purse at his goyng …viii <l.> \s./ iiii d.

[M]Summa … Cx<v> s. iiii d.[P]

[*p. 166*] Item paid the xvith day of August to Heymounde Nicholasson hardware man for a pece of brodde dyapur*e* cont*eynyng* in lenketh xxxviii yerd*es* at xv d. ob. the yerd. Summa … xlix s. i d.

Item for a pece of dyapur*e* cont*eynyng* xxxvi yerd*es*. P*r*ice the yerd xi d. ob. … xxxiiii s. vi d.

Item a pece of smale dyapur*e* cont*eynyng* xxxv yerd*es*. P*r*ice the yerd iiii d. qua. … xii s. iiii d. ob. qua.

Item for ii coffers iiii s. vi d. Item for another couffer iiii s. vi d. i dossen of fyne glovis iii s. iiii d. For ii glassis of yvery vi s. ii elnez of ryban viii d. i payr*e* of spektakles w*i*th case iii d. For a skene of sylk ii d. For iii howk*es* hodd*es* and ii payr*e* of bell*es* by Hevengham xii d. Summa … xx s. v d.

Item paid to s*ir* Hughe Assheton for his cost*es* ridyng to the kynge apon my lad*ys* mat*er*ez the xvi day of August … xix s. iii d. ob.

Item paid to m*aister* dean for a reward yeven to a gray frere þ*at* <pe> prechyd afour*e* my lad*ys* g*r*ace apon our*e* Lady Day the Assumpcion … vi s. viii d.

Item paid to the same for money paid to a prynter of London for pryntyng of xii massis of No*mine* Jh*es*u … vii s.

Item in reward to m*aister* Croke auditor … x s.

Item paid for the dyeng of DCC yerd*es* of say into blak. P*r*ice of iii yerd*es* ii d. … xvi s. viii d.[255]

Item paid to m*aister* dean for money yeven to the p*r*ior of Thorney the xvi day of August … vi s. viii d.

Item paid to Jamys Morice for a payr*e* of awndeyrnes x s. iiii d. ob. and for a wachyng candylstik ii d. … xi s. iiii d. ob.[256]

Item paid to the same for caryag*e* of a fardell of lynnen clothe sende by Olyv*er* Holland w*i*th a hamper*e* w*i*th y[e]rne stuff from London … vi s. viii d.

[M]Summa … x li. viii s. ob. qua.[P]

[254] MS 'a assumpcion'.

[255] The calculation is for 300 (CCC) yards, but the number appears to be 'DCC', i.e. 700.

[256] The total is correct for a 12d. candlestick.

[*p. 167*] Item paid to Ric*hard* Aderton for a reward yeven to a caryar of Stampforth for convaynge of my lad*ys* lettur*es* to London … iiii d.

Item paid to the same for ridyng to London apon my lad*ys* message by vi daiez … iiii s.

Item paid the xviii day of August to Jamys Morice for a reward yeven to a s*er*vande of the vicar of Kendall … iii s. iiii d.

*Bought at Coventr*e *by R. Hylton.*

Item paid the xxiii day of August to Rob*er*t Hylton by his byll assigned for a pece of tawny medly cont*eynyng* xxvi yerd*es* at iiii s. the yerd … v li. iiii s.

Item paid to the same for anoder pece of tawny medly cont*eynyng* xxiiii yerd*es* at ii s. x d. the yerd … lxviii s.

Item paid to the same for a pece of violett cont*eynyng* xxv yerd*es*. P*r*ice the yerd ii s. iiii d. … <lxv s.> lviii s. iiii d.[257]

Item paid to the same for a pece of russett fryce for pore folk*es* cont*eynyng* xl yerd*es*. P*r*ice the pece … xv s.

Item to the same for iii kypp of blak lambe. P*r*ice the kypp v s. vi d. … <\xvi s. vi d./> <xi s.> \<stet>/ xvi s. vi d.[258]

Item paid for ii yerd*es* di. of tawny kersey. P*r*ice the yerd ii s. … v s.

Item paid for ii lib. of blew thredde. Oon lib. at xii d. another at <[…]> x d. … xxii d.

Item for xii elnez of canvas. P*r*ice … iii s. iii d.

Item for ii rollez of corde. P*r*ice … iiii d.

Item for vi payr*e* of wemen <hows> hose … iii s.

Item for cariag*e* of the same stuff from Coventr*e* to Colyweston for ii pakk*es* … iii s.

Item paid to the same Rob*er*t for his cost*es* by iiii daiez p*ro*vidyng of the same stuff … iiii s.

Item payd to the same Rob*er*t as aperith by another byll assigned for a yerd q*u*art*er* of whitt kersey for hose to Thomas Bury at ix d. the yerd … xii d.

Item for lynyng and makyng of the same … vii d.

Item for a payr*e* of shoez to Rawffe þ*a*t lyeth seke at Ric*hard* Flecchers … vi d.

Item paid for a payr*e* of shoez for Skyppe … vi d.

[M]Summa … xiiii li. <xix s. \vii s./ ii d.> \xii s. vi d./[P 259]

[257] The new (correct) total is in a different hand.

[258] The original sum (in the MW hand) was changed by a different hand and then changed back again (with 'stet') by another hand (see the next footnote).

[259] The original sum (in the MW hand) was partly canc. and alt. in a different hand and then re-calculated above the line in another hand.

[*p. 168*] Item yeven in reward the xxii day of August to doctor Gabryell Selvester for comyng in message from my lord of Oxforth to my lad*ys* g*r*ace … vi s. viii d.

Item paid to John Walter for <xxi> xxxi yerd*es* of sere clothe for vestment*es* and copis xvii d. and for wasshyng of the same clothe and his cost*es* at Stampforth iii d. … xx d.

Item paid the xxiii day of August for horse meyte of xlvii horsis of my lord of Derbyes at Colyweston by a day and ii nyght*es* … xxxv s. iiii d.

Item delyv*er*ed the same day for dyeng of dyv*er*se sayez into blake and for the caryag*e* of the same to Stampforth and ayen. … xv s.

Item the xiiii day of August to m*aister* Morgan for a reward yeven to m*aister* Fraunc*es* physicion … vi s. viii d.

Item payd to William Grevell for his cost*es* and for the hyre of his horse to Burne w*i*th a suete of westment*es* … xii d.

Item delyv*er*ed to maistres Foler*e* for a reward yeven to the quene of Skott*es* lander*e* the xxv day of August … iii s. iiii d.

Item paid <t> to Willyam Hylmer*e* for urynall*es* and other glasses and for dyv*er*se herb*es* for my lad*ys* g*r*ace as aperith by his byll assigned … xvii s. xi d.

Item paid to m*aister* dean for money yeven to Olyv*er* Holande s*er*vande comyng from London w*i*th dyv*er*se lettur*es* to my lad*ys* g*r*ace and for goyng ayen to m*aister* confessor to London … v s.

Item delyv*er*ed to John Carter m*aister* deans s*er*vande for money yeven to John Walter*e* for his cost*es* to London … x s.

Item paid to Nicholas Aughton the xx day of August for a yerd of blak for ii payr*e* of howse for my lad*ys* g*r*ace … ii s. viii d.

item for a payr*e* of buskynce xii d. Item for <a> \ii/ payr*e* of shoez viii d. bought by the same Nicholas <al> at London the x day of July … xx s.

[M]Summa … Cvi s. xi d.[P]

[*p. 169*] Item paid the xxvii day of August to Nicholas Aughton for his cost*es* ridyng from Thornall to Canterbury to the kyng by the spaice of x daiez at viii d. … vi s. viii d.

Item paid the same day unto m*aister* Morgan for a reward yeven to a s*er*vande of my lady Hungerforth bryngyng of rose wat*er*ez to my lad*ys* g*r*ace … vi s. viii d.

Item paid to Rob*er*t Hylton for <a> ii yerd*es* of grene clothe to receyve mone apon at ii s. iiii d. the yerd … v s. x d.

Item paid to Rob*er*t Hylton by his byll assigned the xx[ti] day of August for makyng of a payr*e* of buskynce of oriege ledder for my lad*ys* g*r*ace … vi d.

Item paid for makyng of a payr*e* of shoez of the same ledder … iii d.

Item for ii payr*e* of sleppers. P*r*ice the payre vii d. … xiiii d.

Item for ii payr*e* of shoez. Pryc*e* … x d.

Item for a payr*e* of shoez for Ric*hard* Laborer … vi d.

Item for a payr*e* of shoes for Skypp … vi d.

Item for makyng and lynyng of a payr*e* of howse for John fotman x d. Item for makyng and lynyng of a payr*e* of howse for Henr*y* fotman x d. … xx d.

Item paid for makyng and lynyng a payr*e* of howse for Ric*hard* Laborer … x d.

Item paid to John Collop to by **ȝerne** at Stamforthe of dyv*er*se colores[260] … ii s.

^{M}Summa … xxvii s. v d.^{P}

[*p. 170*] Item in reward the last day of August to a s*er*vande of my lorde of Kyldar*es* bryngyng of iii merlyons to my lad*ys* g*r*ace … iii s. iiii d.

Item paid to m*aister* dean for a reward yeven to [P]ellett[261] somtyme oon of the chylder of the chappell … xx d.

Item paid to Olyv*er* Lowthe the furst day of Septembr*e* by a byll assigned for his cost*es* from Thornall to my lord prynce w*i*th hawk*es* fro my lad*ys* g*r*ace … xii s. iii d.

R. Dey. Item paid to Rob*er*t Daye for the t*er*me ended at Mychaelmas … vi s. viii d.

Item in reward to my lord prynce menstrels the iii^{de} day of Septembr*e* … vi s. viii d.

Item in reward to Newby m*aister* stuard*es* s*er*vande comyng in message to my lad*ys* g*r*ace at Thornall …v s.

Nichil. <Item delyv*er*ed to m*aister* Morgan for a reward yeven to m*aister* Davy Phillipp*es* wyff toward*es* their*e* cost*es* at my lad*ys* beyng their*e* … vi li.> nichil[262]

Item in reward to the keper of the p*ar*ke and of his conyez … vi s. viii d.

Item in reward to other of m*aister* Davy s*er*vand*es* … vi s. viii d.

Item in reward to maist*er* Seynt Johnez nurse … xii d.

Item the vth day of Septembr*e* in reward to oon Castell of the kyng*es* Exchekere … xl s.

Item paid to John fottman for my lad*ys* offryng at Wencent … xii d.

Item the same day to Jamys Atkynson sadeller for ix daiez workyng apon my lad*ys* lytter and for cov*er*yng of horse harnesshe w*i*th blak … x s.

Item paid to oon William Davy for helpyng hym t*o* worke by v daiez at iii d. the day …xv d.

^{M}Summa … <ix li. ii s. ii d.> Cii s. ii d.^{P}

[*p. 171*] Item delyv*er*ed the vii day of Septembr*e* to John Collop for yerne bought at Stampforth of dyv*er*se colores … ii s. vi d.

[260] \r/ over alteration.

[261] MS 'mellett'.

[262] Both 'nichil's are written in the MW hand.

Item delyv*er*ed to maistrez Foler for money yeven to a pore woman that came to have ben in my lad*ys* almes howse … iiii d.

Item delyv*er*ed to the same for money yeven to the woman þ*a*t kepith the pore folk*es* … xii d.

Item paid unto Ric*hard* Aderton for neld*es* bought for the sadeler ii d. for vernysshe ii d. for whet led ii d. for threde i d. … vii d.

*Walmesforth brygg*e. Item paid to John Halley of Wetteryng in full payment of ix li. yeven by my lad*ys* g*r*ace toward*es* the rep*ar*acion of Walmesforth brygge … vi s. viii d.

Item delyv*er*ed for my lad*ys* offryng apon our*e* Lady Day the Nativite … v s.

Item delyv*er*ed to my lad*ys* g*r*ace for a reward yeven to Crathornes wyff … xx s.

Item delyv*er*ed the ix day of Septembr*e* to m*aister* dean for a reward yeven to doctor Smythe þ*a*t prechet afour*e* my lad*ys* g*r*ace apon our*e* Lady Day the Nativite … x s.

Item <d>delyv*er*ed to m*aister* dean for a rewarde yeven to s*ir* Geffrey Trafforth xx s. and to Davy Hervy xx s. my lord s*er*vand*es* … xl s.

Item paid unto William Aderton for a M blake nayle for my lad*ys* lytter … ii s.

[263]Item paid the xvith day of Septembr*e* to Nicholas Saunder for ii lib. of threde of all colors xx d. for xii unc*es* i q*uarter* of frenge xi s. iiii d. for i lib. of brode rybon for vesteme[n]t*es* xiii s. iiii d. for C of large curtyn rynge*s* vi d. for CC of smale ryng*es* xi d. for i pece of launde viii s. for ii pec*es* of cotton viii s. for ii hampers xviii d. for ii lock*es* to the hampers x d. … xlvi s. i d.

Item paid the same tyme to John Walter for botonnys of threde of all colers … xii d.

Item delyv*er*ed to Lenard Delese for viii premars ii s. for v bok*es* of In Nomine Jhesu xii d. for oon bok*e* wryton w*i*th raggyd hand vi d. for oon boke in prynt iiii d. for oon bok*e* of Miserere i d. … iii s. xi d.

[M]Summa … vi li. xix s. i d.[P]

[*p. 172*] Item paid to m*aister* tresorer the xvii day of Septembr*e* for lynnen clothe bought of Rob*er*t Dobbis of London CCliiii ell*es*. P*r*ice the elle iii d. … lxiii s. vi d.

Item paid t*o* the same for vi pec*es* bought by hym of the same Rob*er*t cont*eynyng* Ciiii^{xx}xviii ellis di. at ii d. ob. ev*er*y ell … xli s. iiii d.

Item paid for a cart to cary the same clothe to Coldeherbor*e* … iiii d.

Item paid to John Hogeson for medcyns to my lad*ys* geldyng … xvi d.

*Pepur*e *payd to doctour*e *Rop*er. Item paid to doctur*e* Roper*e* for exibucion of Pepur*e* beyng in Oxforth as aperith by a byll therof made xiii s. iiii d. ob. qua. Item delyv*er*ed to the same apon a rekenyng to bye suche stuff as shal be thought nessesary for hym xx s. …xxxiii s. iiii d. ob. qua.

[263]The last three entries on the page are in the 'curly' hand.

Nichil. <Item paid to John Collop for threde bought at Stampforth of dyv*er*se colowr*es* t*o* mende arr*es* clothes … ii s. vi d.><in alio>[264]

Item paid unto m*aister* Burvell for stuff by hym bought at London for my lad*ys* g*r*ace the xiii day of August anno xix° regis Henrici septimi … iiii li.

Item in rewarde unto doctur Roper þ*at* prechitt afour*e* my lad*ys* g*r*ace the xv day of Septembr*e* … vi s. viii d.

Item in reward to John Hodgeson oon of the gromes of the stabyll toward*es* his charg*es* of byeng of his fuell … v s.

Item paid unto Richard Aderton for riding[265] from Colyweston to Clopton to oon Dudleys wyff by a day viii d. Item for ridyng t*o* Burne to my lord suffrycan a day viii d. … xvi d.

Item in reward to a servande of <h> thabott*es* of Peturborow for bryngyng of iii pertrych and a baskett w*i*th safferon levis to my lad*ys* g*r*ace … viii d.

Brownyng. Item paid to John Brownyng of Burne for his anuitie for a q*u*art*er* endet at Mychaelmas last passyd … x s.

MSumma … xii li. iii s. vi d. ob. qua.P

[*p. 173*] Item the xxvi day of Septembr*e* in reward unto Sop*er* my lad*ys* solicito*ur* … xx s.

Item for ii sawters bought by m*aister* comptroller for ii cheldren that s*ir* William Bewpre hathe in gov*er*na*u*nce … xii d.

Item paid to m*aister* Grendyll for money by hym paid for sawdryng of a gylt potte xx d. Item for sawdryng of a candylstyk þ*at* was broken in the chappell \viii d./ … ii s. iiii d.

Item in reward to m*aister* Jerowme Baptist … xl s.

Item paid the xxviii day of Septembr*e* unto maister amener for a reward yeven to a s*er*vande of thabott*es* of Peturboro for bryngyng of saff[r]on levis unto my lad*ys* g*r*ace … viii d.

Item paid to maister chaunceller the last day of Septembr*e* for money by hym payd for the byndeng prent*is* of a dought*er* of John Walters in London by my lad*ys* comaundement … liii s. iiii d.

Item paid to John Holt for his exspenc*e* ridyng unto maist*er* Emson to his <s> place at Eston by ii daiez xvi d. Item for ii daiez ridyng to Crolande xvi d. Item for a day ridyng to Sleforthe t*o* s*ir* John Hussey viii d. … iii s. iiii d.

Item paid unto the same for ii daiez ridyng unto Ramessey … xvi d.

Nota et locatur cum episcopo Exonensi. Item delyv*er*ed to my lad*ys* g*r*ace the ii^de^ day of Octobr*e* by the hand*es* of m*aister* dean … lxvi li. xiii s. iiii d.

[264] Canc. and noted ‘nichil’ in the margin because it was the first entry on p. 171 (‘in alio’).
[265] MS ‘ridimg’.

Item paid for m*aister* Conyesby horse meyte standyng at Richart Flecchers … xiii s. iiii d.

Item delyv*ere*d unto m*aister* dean for a reward yeven unto Justice the quene of Skott*es* s*er*vande … v s.

[M]Summa … lxxiii li. xiii s. viii d.[P]

[*p. 174*] Item paid the xvi[th] day of Octobr*e* unto Jamys Morice for vi pec*es* of whitte frice bought by hym at Stewrisbryge fayr*e* cont*eynyng* CCxlii yerd*es* … lxviii s.

Item paid to the same for vi pec*es* of whitte blankett*es* and vii yerd*es*. Summa totalis lxvi brode yerd*es*[266] … xli s. x d. ob.

Item payd for x coverlett*es*. P*r*ice of ev*er*y cov*er*lett ii s. viii d. … xxvi s. viii d.

Item paid for xi matteres at ii s. vi d. the pec*e* … xxvii s. vi d.

Item for iii counterpoynt*es* of werders and oon of <Jym> imagry. P*r*ice of ev*er*y of thaym viii s. … xxxii s.

Item paid for xi casis of tykk for bolsters. P*r*ice … ix s. viii d.

Item paid for xv pec*es* of whitte corde and other trussyng corde … ii s. xi d. ob.

Item for oon payr*e* of beloes … iii d.

Item paid for iii fyr*e* panys … iii s.

Item paid for oon pec*e* of locram clothe co*nteynyng* iiii[xx]xvi < yerd*es*> ell*es*. P*r*ice … xxxiii s. iiii d.

Item paid for oon pec*e* of whitte kersey cont*eynyng* xviii yerd*es* … xiii s. iiii d.

Item paid for oon pece of blak kersey cont*eynyng* xviii yerd*es* … xxxv s. iiii d.

Item paid for ii kyppe of blak lambe … x s. iiii d.

Item for oon kyppe of whitte lambe … ii s. viii d.

Item for vii candylstik*es* … ii s. iiii d.

Item paid for a couffer to putt in the said stuff … iiii s. viii d.

Item for iii pec*es* of russett fryce cont*eynyng* vi[xx] yerd*es* … xl s.

Item paid for a furre of shanke … xi s.

Item paid for ii furris of pot*es* … xii s.

Item paid for ii brusshes for the wardrop … xii d.

Item for a carde for furr*es* … iii d.

Item for xii yerd*es* of stamen … xxiiii s.

Item paid to the same for v pec*es* of blake cotton bought at Stampforth co*nteynyng* Cxv yerd*es* … xxxv s.

[266] 'yerd*es*' add. in lighter ink by the same hand.

Item to the same for ii pec*es* of whitte cotton cont*eynyng* xlvi yerd*es* … xiii s. iiii d.

Item paid to the same for iii matteres … viii s.

Item for v treenn boll*es* xiii treen platters and dysshes viii copp*es* … xvi d.

Summa partis … xxiii li. iiii s. x d.[267]

[*p. 175*] Item paid to the said Jamys for a brasyn panne weying xxviii lib. cont*eynyng* xvi galons at ix s. iiii d. Item for a yrne treveit waiying xxv lib. ii s. vi d. Item for a brasyn ladyll. P*ri*ce vi d. xiiii treen boll*es* and copp*es* xvi d. for i dd. trenchers and i dd. of tren sponys iii d. Summa … xiii s. xi d.

Item paid to the same for wyer bought by Rob*ert* Hylton … vi d.

Item paid to William Hylm*er* for a lib. starche … i d. ob.

Item to the same for sokk*es* and bulwerk*es* and for fyne papur*e* half a reme … ii s. viii d.

Item paid unto Nicholas Aughton for ridyng to Chechester and from thens to Porchester and so to Colyweston the space of xii daiez … viii s.

Item to the same for ridyng to Wenchester and agayn to Colyweston by xii daiez … viii s.

Item paid unto m*aister* Morgan for a reward yeven to a nonne of Sympryngham to by hir coolis … iii s. iiii d.

<*Nichil*>[268] Item paid unto Edward Vauce for his cost*es* ridyng into the north countre for the p*ar*sonage of Lythe by x daiez x s. Item for his botte hyr*e* ov*er* Hombere viii d. For a gyde ii daiez ov*er* Blakamor*e* xii d. Summa … xi s. viii d.

Item in reward to a s*er*vande of s*ir* Rauffe Bygod comyng to seall the said voosen … vi s. viii d.

Item paid unto m*aister* dean towardes the exibucion of John Mason at Tatsall … vi s. viii d.

Item in reward to a man that brought quync*es* and wardons from Wakerley … viii d.

Item paid unto m*aister* dean for a reward yeven unto m*aister* Brudenell s*er*jeaunt of lawe … xl s.

Item in reward unto his clerk … vi s. viii d.

Jane Gower. Item paid to John Browne m*aister* coke for money delyv*er*ed to Jane Gooer by the survaiers comaundement the vii day of Octobr*e* … xxvi s. viii d.

Item delyv*er*ed unto s*ir* Crystoffer Crosley my lad*ys* chappleyn to delyv*er* unto Thomas Bury tuter at Eton … x s.

[M]Summa … xxx li. v s. iiii d. ob.[P] [269]

[267] Written small (not in the MW hand) to the right at the foot of the page (5s. over). Not approved nor signed by Lady Margaret, it is included in the total for p. 175, where the excess of 5s. is corrected.
[268] Faint in the left margin.
[269] The total for pp. 174–5, followed by what looks like 'C hus'.

[*p. 176*] Item paid unto Raynold Davemport for ridyng to Lyncoln apon my lad*ys* messag*es* buy the space of iii daiez ... iii s.

Item in reward unto John Collopp the xth day of Octobre ... vi s. viii d.

Item paid to Petur of Coldherboro the xii day of Octobr*e* ov*er* lxvi s. viii d. delyv*er*ed to hym by the receyvo*ur*<S> Hughe Assheton for the cost*es* of the bryngyng of a nonne from Shepay to Colyweston ... xi s. ix d.

Item delyv*er*ed to the said Petur for convaying of the nonnes woman from Colyweston to Shepay abbey ayen ... xiii s. iiii d.

Item in reward unto the said Petur for his labur and cost*es* ... xiii s. iiii d.

Item yeven in reward the xiiith day of Octobr to a s*er*vande of thabbott of Ramesey ... vi s. viii d.

Item paid the xiiii day of Octobr*e* unto Nicholas Aughton for vi daiez ridyng to London and ayen ... iiii s.

Item paid to m*aister* Gryndell the same day for makyng of v beydis of golde and for burnysshyng of other v beyd*es* ... iiii s. viii d.

Item paid the same day to William Parkar for iii daiez ridyng for Wak*es* moder and for the kep*er* of Molton parke ... iii s.

Item paid to Richard Aderton for ridyng to Caldwell abbey besyd*es* Bedforth apon my lad*ys* messag*es* by ii daiez ... xvi d.

Item to the same Richard for ridyng to Cambrig*e* to oon Hamden ii daiez ... xvi d.

Item paid to the same Richard for a yerd and iii q*uarter* of redde for half a horse clothe for a horse yeven to my lord Bukyngham ... xviii d.

Item paid to the same for a day ridyng unto Peturboro ... viii d.

Item paid the xix day of Octobr*e* for horse meyte of viii horsis of my lord Henry of <Bukkyngham> \Stafforth/ ... vi s. vi d.

Item for v horsis of my lord \John/ marqueyes the same tyme ... iiii s. iiii d.

Item for diett*es* of their*e* s*er*vand*es* ... ii s. ix d.

^{M}Summa ... iiii li. <v s.> \iiii s./ iiii d.^{P}[270]

[*p. 177*] *J. Morice*[271]

Item payd unto Jamys Morice the xxix day of Octobr*e* for ii pec*es* of blake cotton cont*eynyng* v^{xx}xviii yerd*es* ... xlviii s.

Item paid to the same of oon pece of fryse cont*eynyng* xxxix yerd*es* bought at Coventre ... xv s.

Item paid to the same for the cost*es* of Rob*er*t Hylton to Styrbryge fayr*e* to provide stuff for my lad*ys* g*r*ace ... iiii s.

[270] The first total (in the MW hand) is corrected in a different hand but is still 6d. short.

[271] Bracketed to include the next three items.

*Oly*ver *Holand.*[272]

Item paid to Olyv*er* Holande the same day for xi pec*es* of Parys at … vi li. xi s. iiii d.

Item to the same for dyeng of a bedd w*i*th curtyns into blakke … xxiii s.

Item for ii burd*es* of paste iiii d. Item for cariag*e* of the bedd and the freng*e* xii d. … xvi d.

Item paid to the same for a ell of canvas to trusse in the Parris and the said bedd … iii d.

Item for vi^{xx}xiiii ell*es* of canvas at iiii d. the ell … xliiii s. viii d.

Item for ii pec*es* of hollande clothe cont*eynyng* lxiiii ell*es* at v d. the elle …xxvi s. viii d.

Item to maistres Cotton for suche stuff as she dyd send to my lad*ys* g*r*ace … ii s.

Item for waying of the said lynnen clothe and for cariage of the same to Wildebore … iiii d.

Item for ii ell*es* of canvas to trusse hit in … ix d.

Item for the cost*es* of the said Olyv*er* Holande w*i*th his s*er*vande and two horsis by the space of xvi daiez at ii s. the day … xxxii s.

Item paid to John Holt for ridyng to Ramessey by the spaice of ii daiez xvi d. Item for ridyng to Huntyngton ii daiez xvi d. Item for ridyng to Lytell Paunton the space of oon day viii d. … iii s. iiii d.

Item paid unto Thomas m*aister* countrollers s*er*vande for going in message to my lord Clyfford … iii s. iiii d.

Item paid to m*aister* Morgan for a reward yeven to oon Ogyll*es* wyff of Prescott in Lancashir*e* … x s.

Item in reward to a man that brought my lad*ys* furris from London … xii d.

Item in reward to s*ir* Rauff Werney chamberlayn to the quene of Skott*es* at his beyng at Colyweston … xl s.

[M]Summa … xix li. vii s.[P]

[*p. 178*] Item delyv*er*ed to m*aister* dean for a reward yeven unto m*aister* Coup*er* towardes his cost*es* and charg*es* ridyng to London Wynesowr*e* and into the west partiez to make <s> serche for chyldren for my lad*ys* chappell w*i*th the cost*es* of ii chyldren which he brought with hym the said tyme … lxvi s. viii d.

Item delyv*er*ed to maistrez Massy for a reward yeven to maistrez Lacy the xxix day of Octobr*e* … vi s. viii d.

Item in reward unto a s*er*vand of Myles Busshe for bryngyng of quync*es* to my lad*ys* g*r*ace … xx d.

[272] Bracketed to include the next ten items.

Item delyv*er*ed to Ric*hard* Aderton for his cost*es* ridyng to m*aister* Fereffax place … viii d.

Item delyv*er*ed the last day of Octobr*e* to my lad*ys* g*r*ace for hir almes purse … vi li. xiii s. iiii d.

[M]Summa … x li. ix s.[P273]

Item the furst day of Novembr*e* delyv*er*ed unto Rog*er* Radclyff for my lad*ys* offryng apon Alhallow day … v s.

Item delyv*er*ed the same day unto a s*er*vande of m*aister* Hochyns toward*es* the exibucion of Thomas <plett> Pellet at Cambryche … xiii s. iiii d.

Item the iii^{de} day of Novembr*e* to Edward Heyvon to delyv*er* unto the gray freris of Boston in almys … vi s. viii d.

Item delyv*er*ed to maistrez Foler for a reward yeven unto my lord of Rochesters moder …vi s. viii d.

Item the vth day of Novembr unto maistrez Curson for x lib. of wex for ii tapurs to be sett afour*e* the rode and our*e* Lady at Boston. For ev*er*y lib. vi d. ob. and for the makyng iiii d. … v s .ix d.

[*p. 179*] Item delyv*er*ed the viiith day of Novembr*e* unto John fotman for a reward yeven to oon Bonyface of Northampton … vi s. viii d.

Item paid to Rob*er*t Hylton for money paid unto Rob*er*t Passelaw for vii daiez and a half workyng w*i*th my lad*ys*<skiner> skynner by the day vi d. … iii s. ix d.

Item paid to Rob*er*t Hethe for v daiez and a half takeng the day iiii d. … xxii d.

Item paid unto Thomas Buttelare for v dayez workyng taykyng the day vi d. … ii s. vi d.

Item paid the xiii day of Novembr unto maister John Seynt John for a payr*e* of course shet*es* xvi d. iiii tabulclothes ii s. vi d. for v towell*es* ii s. iii d. ob. for ii paynted clothis viii d. for a potte and a possnet xxii d. … viii s. vi d. ob.

Item delyv*er*ed unto m*aister* stuard for a reward yeven <for> to a man þ*at* came from Huntyngton with a lett*ur* to my lad*ys* g*r*ace fro my lord Rochester … xx d.

Item paid unto my lord Rochester for money paid at dyv*er*se tymes by hym for my lad*ys* g*r*ace … xx s.

Item delyv*er*ed to maistres Randull for a reward yeven to m*aister* Morgans doughtur the ii^{de} day of Novembr … vi s. viii d.

Item delyv*er*ed to George Fraunc*es* for a reward yeven to Ric*har*d Flecchers wyff at my lad*ys* goyng to se maistrez Stan*n*op … xx d.

Item paid unto Olyv*er* Hollande the xv day of Novembr for a <sparvese> sparver t*o* a bedd for the ancryse iiii s. <j> for iiii staned clothis for hir chambr*e* iiii s. viii d. … viii s. viii d.

273 Followed by a gap on the page.

Item in reward to maistrez Parkers nurse … xx d.

Item paid unto m*aister* dean for money yeven to the ancryse at the nonnez of Stampforth toward*es* hir fyndyng … x s.

Item in reward to Fraunc*es* oon of the kyng*es* physsicions the xiii day of Novembr*e* … v s.

[M]Summa … Cxvi s. ob.[P]

[*p. 180*] *xxvi*º *die Novemb*ris[274]

Item paid unto John foteman for money delyv*er*ed for my ladies offryng apon Mychaelmas Day at the nonnes of Stampforth … xx d.

Item paid unto John Brydde for a booke of Vitam Patris bought by hym at London for my ladies g*r*ace … v s.

Item paid unto Richard Aderton for his cost*es* ridyng apon my ladies message unto Seynt Ned*es* … xvi d.

Item paid unto maist*er* amener the xxiii day of Novembr*e* for a reward yeven to the p*r*ioris of the nonnes of Stampforth … vi s. viii d.

Item paid unto maistres Morgan for ii stone of wolle bught by hyr to make carpett*es* …v s. viii d.

Item paid unto William Hylm*er* by his byll assigned the xxv day of Novembr*e* for a payr*e* of knytte hose for my lad*ys* g*r*ace … xx d.

Item to the same for a doss*en* of grett beyd*es* for my lad*ys* almes folke … xii d.

Item t*o* the same for a dossen of box beyd*es* … xviii d.

Item for [*blank*] paid to the same for vi unc*e* di. of raw sylke fyne at viii d. the unc*e* … iiii s. iiii d.

Item paid to the same for fyne grayne half a lib. at … ii s. viii d.

Item for ii grett stones of chalke … ii d.

Item paid unto the same for a barrell of succade waying in clere succade lxviii lib. at v d. the lib. Summa xxviii s. iiii d. and for the carying of the said barrell from London to Colyweston weying lxxvi lib. at a ob. the lib. Summa iii s. <iii d.> \ii d./ … xxxi s. vii d.[275]

Item paid unto John Bedell the xxvi day of Novembr*e* for money delyv*er*ed to my lad*ys* g*r*ace for the crystenyng of m*aistres* Stanopp*es* chylde … liii s. iiii d.

[M]Summa … Cxvi s. vii d.[P]

[*p. 181*] Item paid the xxvi[th] day of Novembr*e* unto Rob*er*t Hylton for a payr*e* of slyppers for my lad*ys* g*r*ace … vii d.

[274] Bracketed to include the next three items.

[275] The second 'Summa' has been reduced by a penny, but the total does not take account of this and is a penny over.

Item for a payr*e* of shoez for maistres Perrott … vi d.

Item for vi payr*e* of <howse> \shoez/ for vi beyde men at vi d. a payr*e* … iii s.

Item for vii beyde women vii payr*e* shoez at iiii d. … ii s. iiii d.

Item for a payr*e* of shoez for pore Rauff … vi d.

Item for ii almouse children ii pair*e* shoez … v d.

Item paid for viii yerd*es* lynyng for thankorise gowne at iii d. the yerd … ii s.

Item paid for makyng and lynyng of ii payr*e* of howse for Thomas Bury … xvi d.

Item paid for the hyr*e* of a tayleo*ur* makyng of almesse folke stuff and the chyldren of the chappell by the spaic*e* of x daiez at iii d. the day … ii s. vi d.

…xiii s. <iii> ii d.[276]

Item for a payr*e* of shoez for Skyppe … vi d.

Item paid unto the same Rob*er*t for a pece of blak bought at Coventre cont*eynyng* xxxv yerd*es* at iiii s. … vii li.

Item for another pece of blake cont*eynyng* xix yerd*es* at iii s. iiii the yerd … lxiii s. iiii d.

Item to the same for a pece cont*eynyng* xxix yerd*es* at iii s. iiii d. the yerd …iiii li. xvi s. viii d.

Item for a pece of tawny fustian cont*eynyng* xv yerd*es* … ix s.

Item for xxiiii yerd*es* of whit cotton at v d. the yerd … x s.

Item for v pounde of blew threde oon of xiiii d. another xii d. the thred xi d. and two at x d. the pounde … iiii s. <vii d.> <x d.> ix d.

Item for the cost*es* Rob*er*t Hylton at Coventr*e* by iiii daiez at xii d. the day and for cariag*e* of the same stuff from Coventr*e* unt*o* Colyweston iii s. x d. … vii s. x d.

[M]Summa … xvii li. v s. iii d.[P]

[*p. 182*] Item paid the xxvi day of Novembr*e* unto John Brownyng of Burne for a q*u*art*er* to be endet at Crystemasse next for his anuytie … x s.

Item paid for a grete cowle to beyre clothes in to the water and ii paylez for the pore folk*es* … xv d.

Item paid for a kettell bought for the same pore folk*es* … xx d.

Item for a panne ix d. and xiii dysshes ii grette platturs and ii sawcerez. P*r*ic*e* xiiii d. Item for pott*es* bought by Marion þ*at* kepith the almes folk*es* ii d. Item for sawlyng of Nicholas shoez oon of the almez chyldren ii d. Item for a bolle to wasshe in their*e* clothis viii d. Item in exspenc*e* at Stampforth for p*ro*vicion of the said stuff ii d. Summa … iii s. i d.

[276] The total of the first nine items on p. 181, bracketed to the right of the items.

Item payd unto Thomas Mounteney for a pece of blak satten count*eynyng* xxv yerd*es*. Pr*ice* the yerd vii s. x d. bought by hym at London for my lad*ys* g*r*ace … ix li. xv s. x d.

Item paid to the same for a yerd of blak kersey bought for my lad*ys* g*r*ace. Pr*ice* … iii s. iiii d.

Item the xxvi day of Novembr*e* unto Ric*hard* Makblythe proctur*e* of Seynt Crystofers and Seynt Jorge gyelde in Yorke in full payment for a p*ar*don lett*ur* to my lad*ys* g*r*ace … xx s.

Item delyv*er*ed to m*aister* dean for money yeven in almes to a pore man goyng w*ith* croches in Stampforth … xii d.

Item delyv*er*ed to the proctur*e* of Cambryge the ii^{de} day of Decembr*e* toward*es* the byldyng of seynt Mary cherche in Cambryge ov*er* x li. delyv*er*ed unto m*aister* countroller for the same use … x li.

Item delyv*er*ed unto m*aister* dean for a reward yeven to doctor Smythe for prechyng afor*e* my lad*ys* g*r*ace the iiiith day of Decembr*e* … <x s.> vi s. viii d.

Item in reward to Ric*hard* Gowghe at his beyng at Colyweston … xxvi s. viii d.

Item delyv*er*ed to the same for money yeven to Petur*e* of Coldeherbor*e* for his \lev*er*y/ gowne … xii s. iiii d.

Item to the frat*er*nitie of our*e* Lady and Seynt Thomas of Canturbury gylde in the chyrche of Seynt Magnus in London … xx s.

Item delyv*er*ed to the same for a goblett … liii s. iiii d.

^{M}Summa … xxvii li. xv s. ii d.^{P}

[*p. 183*] Item in rewarde the iiiith day of Decembr*e* unto Feyreffax of the kyng*es* chappell … x s.

Item paid the vith day of Decembr*e* unto Nicholas Saunders for ii unc*es* of purlyng golde bought for my lad*ys* g*r*ace at London by m*aister* tresorer … ix s. iiii d.

Item t*o* the same for i unc*e* of saten sylke … ii s. iiii d.

Item for makyng of a ryng … ii s.

Item the vth day of Decembr*e* yeven unto the bysshop w*i*thin my lad*ys* place apon Seynt Nicholas Even … v s.

Item in lyke wyse to the bysshop of the towne of Colyweston … xx d.

Item in reward to a s*er*vande of thabbott*es* of Peturborogh for bryngyng of a mytur*e* apon Seynt Nicholas Even … xii d.

Item delyv*er*ed for my lad*ys* offryng apon Seynt Andrew day … v s.

Item delyv*er*ed to George Fraunc*es* for my lad*ys* offryng apon our*e* Lady Day … v s.

Item the viith day of Decembr*e* yeven unto the priores of the nonnys of Stampforth at the p*ro*fession of the ancryse their*e* … xx s.

Item paid unto William Wyldebore for CCC di. and i q*uarter* weght caryeng of the said ancryse stuff from London unto Colyweston … iiii s. iiii d. ob.

Item in reward unto s*ir* William Norman toward*es* his cost*es* from Wynesowr*e* to Colyweston and ayen to Wenysowr*e* … xxvi s. viii d.

Item yeven to the same s*ir* William by m*aister* dean … iii s. iiii d.

Item paid unto m*aister* dean for a reward yeven to Justice the quene of Skott*es* se*r*vande … v s.

Item to the same for a reward yeven to a man þ*at* came from Kettryng w*i*th a box of letturs from m*aister* p*re*sydent to my lad*ys* g*r*ace … xii d.

[M]Summa … C s. xx d. ob.[P]

[*p. 184*] Item the ix[th] day of Decembr*e* delyv*er*ed unto my lad*ys* g*r*ace for money yeven unto the ancryse at the nonnys of Stampforth … x s.

Item for a reward unto Hughe Denysse delyv*er*ed the same tyme … x s.

Item paid unto John Bradley for the burde of a woman that Hughe Latym*er* hade a chylde by the space of xv daiez ii s. Item for fechyng of hir chylde from Clyff iiii d. Item to a man that convayed hir to Stampforth ii d. … ii s. vi d.

Item paid unto s*ir* Hughe Assheton receyver for money by hym paid at London for carryage of ii grete chyst*es* on grette fardell and a small fardell from the Ile of Sheppey to London … v s.

Item paid unto the same for the diett of the ancryse syst*er* and hir man by ii melis at London … viii d.

Item for theyr*e* bedde by iiii nyght*es* … iiii d.

Item for kepyng of the said stuff in a howse at Byllyng*es*gate … iiii d.

Item for caryage of the said stuff from Byllyngate to Coldehe\r/boro … ii d.

Item paid unto the same for money yeven unto a nonne of the Myn*o*res syst*er* unto my lady Rev*er*se … x s.

Item for ii furres of mynyvere. P*r*ice of theym … xl s.

Item paid to the same for ii furres of gray … xl s.

Item paid for a tymber of gray. P*r*ice … xii s.

Item paid unto the same for money by hym paid for my lad*ys* Neweyere yeft*es* for i grosse of sylv*er* and gylt weying xxviii unc*e* i q*uarter* di. at v s. the unce … vii li. xxii d. ob.

Item for oon gylt goblett weying viii unce di. at *v s.* the unce … xlii s. vi d.

Item for another gylt goblett weying viii unce and i q*uarter* at v s. … xli s. iii d.

Item for another gylt goblett weying viii unce i q*uarter* at v s. the unce … xli s. iii d.

Item for i gylt pax waying <viii unc*es* \<[…]>/ di. at v s.> viii unc*es* di. at v s. the unce …xlii s. vi d.

[M]Summa … xxii li. iiii d. ob.[P]

[*p. 185*] Item paid unto the same for iii gylt spones weying iii unc*es* di. q*uart*e*r* at v s. … xv s. vii d. ob.

Item for x sylv*er* spones waying xv unc*es* at iii s. viii d. the unc*es* … lv s.

Item for iii pec*es* and a half of crest clothe. P*r*ice the pece xxxii s. …<vii li. iiii s.> Cxii s.[277]

Item paid to the same for money by hym paid to Petur*e* of Coldherbor*e* for the cost*es* of a nonne from the Ile of Sheppey to Colyweston … lxvi s. viii d.

Item paid to the same for rep*ar*acions done at Coldeherbor*e* as in tylyng tymberwerk mendyng of go<i>ttures makyng of i chemney mendyng of flores and of the led*es* as it apereth more planly by a byll made by the said Petur of the parcell*es* and remaneth w*i*th hym … xi li. ix s. ii d.

Item paid unto Richard Aderton the x day of Decembr*e* for rydyng to Burne for the suffrycan … viii d.

Item paid unto the same for horse meyte of my lad*ys* palfferes at Stampforth at the profe[ss]ion[278] of the ancryse … xv d.

Item paid unto William Parker for his cost*es* ridyng to Leycest*er* for a wedow and their*e* abydyng by the space of v daiez … v s.

Item paid unto Olyver Lowthe for rydyng unto Wysbech the space of ii daiez w*i*th ii horsis as aperith by his byll assigned … iii s.

*Jamys Moric*e. [279]

Item paid unto Jamys Morice for xiii yerd*es* of blake by hym bought at London at ix s. the yerd … Cxvii s.

Item paid unto the same for a dosen rossett bonett*es* … viii s.

Item paid for oon dosen of whit bonett*es* … ix s.

[280]Item for x unce of furine golde of Venesse at iii s. iiii d. …<xliii s. iiii d.> xxxiii s. iiii d.[281]

Item for ii <vn> unce of smaller golde. Price … viii s.

Item for iiii unce di. of gylt golde at xiiii d. the unc*e* … v s. iii d.

[277] The (correct) correction is in a different hand.
[278] MS 'p*r*ofection'.
[279] Bracketed to include all seven items to the end of the page.
[280] Preceded by a black dot (check-mark).
[281] The (correct) correction is in a different hand.

Item for iii furres <[...]> of pot*es* of grey ... xv s.

[M]Summa ... <xxxvi li. v s. xi d. ob.> xxxiiii li. iii s. xi d. ob.[P][282]

[*p. 186*] Item paid unto the same Jamys for a furre of womb*es* of gray. Price ... xiii s.

Item t*o* the same for ii payr*e* of knytt sokk*es* ... ii s. viii d.

Item for ii payr*e* of knytte bulwerk*es* ... ii s. viii d.

Item for iii elnez of canvas and corde ... xiii d.

Item paid t*o* the same for the cost*es* of the ancryse syster from Shepey to Stampforth w*i*th hir s*er*vand ... xxii s.

Item paid for the caryage of the same from London to Colyweston ... ii s.

[M]Summa ... xliii s. v d.[P]

Item paid unto maistrez Wendesore the xiiii day of Decembr*e* for money yeven unto a skoller of Cambrigh whiche was lately made prest ... xx s.

Item paid unto Lenard of the vestry for byndyng of c*er*ten book*es* for the chappell ... v s. vii d.

Item yeven in reward to the same Lenard ... iii s. iiii d.

Item the xvii day of Decembr*e* unto my lad*ys* g*r*ace by maistres Foler for a reward yeven unto maistres Wendesowre ... xx s.

Item delyv*er*ed the same day to m*aister* dean for a reward yeven unto a s*er*vande of my lord <duesme> \Duresme/ ... v s.

Item the xviii[th] day of Decembr*e* delyv*er*ed to m*aister* dean for a reward yeven to s*ir* Richard Verun prest in London towordes his cost*es* comyng t*o* my lad*ys* g*r*ace ... xiii s. iiii d.

Item in reward to a yonge man þ*at* came w*i*th <hym> the same prest ... xx d.

Item for money yeven to the anker*e* in the Valle at London ... iii s. iiii d.

Item to the ankeryes w*i*thowte Bysshopp*es*gate ... xx d.

Item to the ankeries at Westm*ynster* ... xx d.

Item to maist*er* dean for a reward yeven to maist*er* Belle a prest of Fodryngay xxi day Decembr ... iii s. iiii d.

[M]Summa ... iii li. xviii s. xi d.[P]

[*p. 187*] Item paid unto Richard Aderton the xxi day of Decembr*e* for ridyng unto Burne and to s*ir* Thomas Delaland*es* and other dyv*er*se plac*es* w*i*th my lad*ys* lettur*es* to make serch for dyv*er*se felons and robbers by the spaice of ii daies ... xvi d.

[282] The calculation in the MW hand is replaced by one which takes account of the two corrections above and is in the same hand as those corrections. There is a dot calculation to the left at the foot of the page.

Item paid the same day for a reward yeven by maister Morgan unto a gray frere of Stampforth … iii s. iiii d.

Item delyv*er*ed to m*aister* dean at the nones of Stampforth to delyv*er* unto my lad*ys* g*r*ace … x s.

Item paid unto Nicholas Freman for lodgyng and kepyng of Skyppe the space of lix wek*es* at ii d. the weke. Summa … ix s. x d.

Item paid unto m*ais*t*er* Gryndell for money by hym paid for myndyng of a holy wat*er* stik for my lad*ys* clossett … iiii d.

Maystres Wynesowre. Item paid unto maistres <wenysoure> Wendysore as by hir byll assigned for a reward yeven to the carpent*er*ez xx d. Item to the layers of wodde xx d. Item to Lenard for <byngyng> \byndyng/ of book*es* xx d. to the same Lenard in reward xii d. Item for offryng at my lord*es* moneth mynde xx d. Item to the ankeryes woman xii d. Item to George Fraunc*es* s*er*vand xii d. Item to maist*er* Odell s*er*vande xx d. Item to Ric*hard* Stukeley for ankeres stuff ii s. viii d. Item to the same Richard in reward iii s. iiii d. Item to the olde ankeris ii s. Item to maistrez Stannopes nurse xx d. Item to the almes women viii d. Item for pynnys vi d. Summa … xxii s. ii d.

Item t*o* the procture of Jhesu gylde at Grantham … xii d.

Item paid unto Thomas Velles clerk of Eston for the comyns beddyng wassing and other nessessaries of a pore chylde by the space of xiii wek*es* ended apon the Concepcion Day of oure Lady every wek viii d. … viii s. viii d.

[M]Summa … lvi s. viii d.[P]

[*p. 188*] Item the xxvi day of Decembr*e* delyv*er*ed to my lad*ys* g*r*ace for hir almes purse … x li.

Item delyv*er*ed to maistres Foler for a reward yeven to Henr*y* Wynstanley … v s.

Item t*o* the same for a reward yeven unto John Walter*e* … vi s. viii d.

Item paid to maistres Massy by a byll assygned for money by hir paid for moder Elynes bedde … lii s. vi d.

Item for kepyng of a pore woman in sekenes … iiii d.

Item paid for a lace for maistres Frognoll … iii d.

Item paid for a kombe for hyr ii d. for mylk i d. for two book*es* viii d. for a gyrdell ii d. for ii lac*es* of sylk vi d. for whit sope i d. for a payre of knyves iiii d. for vi dosen poyn-t*es* vi d. for mylk iii d. in reward for quync*es* viii d. … iii s. v d.

My ladys offryng apon Crystemas Day and xii daiez.[283] Item delyv*er*[ed] to maistres Foler for my lad*ys* offryng on Crystemasse Day in gold v s. and in money for the xii daiez x s. Summa … xv s.

Debetur per billam Ricardi Goughe.[284]

[283] Bracketed to include the single item.

[284] Bracketed to include the next two items.

Item paid the xxx day of <j> Decembr*e* unto John Kleton goldsmyth for a goblett w*i*th a cov*er* gylt waying xiiii unc*e* q*uarter* di. and ferthyng gold weyght at v s. the unc*e*. Summa … lxxi s. x d. ob.[285]

Item paid unto the same for anoder gylt goblett w*i*th a cov*er* gylt waying xv unc*e* di. q*uarter*. Summa … lxxv s. vii d. ob.

Item in reward to maister Fawne that prechet afore my lad*ys* g*r*ace the last day of Decembr*e*… vi s. viii d.

Newyer gyftes.[286] Item delyv*er*ed unto my lad*ys* g*r*ace the same day to yeve in Newyer gyft*es* … xiii li. vi s. viii d.

Item for maist*er* Morgan Newer gyft … xl s.

Item to William Hylm*er* … xx s.

Item for Steven Taberet … iii s. iiii d.

Item <for m*aister* controller Newyer gyft … x li.>

Item delyv*er*[ed] to Henr*y* Salforth for my lady Bray Newer gyft … liii s. iiii d.

Summa … <xlviii li. xi s. xi d. ob.> \viii d./> \viii d./ xxxviii li. xi s. viii d.[P 287]

[*p. 189*] Item for my lad*ys* offryng apon Newer*es* Day … v s.

Item delyv*er*ed to maister A[r]thur*e* for the bryngyng of the kyng*es* Newer gyft*es* unto my lad*ys* g*r*ace … C s.

Item to a s*er*vande of the bysshop of Ely for the bryngyng of a Newyer gyft unto my lad*ys* g*r*ace … xl s.

Item paid the ii^{de} day of Januar*e* unto s*ir* Richard Royston maister of the collage of Seynt Laurence Pulteney in London for the tythe of Coldherbor*e* by ii yer*es* last past …Cvi s. viii d.

Item delyv*er*ed to Maryon oon of the almes women apon a reknyng to bye stuff nessessary for theym … iii s.

Item for a reward yeven unto his clerk*es* … xiii s. iiii d.

Item in reward to maister Brudnell … iiii li. vi s. viii d.

Item in reward to Ric*hard* Stukeley for my lad*ys* offryng apon the xiith day … v s.

Item in reward to the suffrycan … lxvi s. viii d.

Item the vith day of Januar*e* to oon <Johene> Jone Alwen by Alysander Frogoll … iii s. iiii d.

Item paid unto John Bradley for the cost*es* of maister <Col> Conyesby horsis … xx s. iiii d.

Item in reward to my lad*ys* solicit*ur* … xx s.

[285] The total is correct but the farthing weight (see Glossary) has been lost.

[286] Bracketed to include the rest of the items on the page.

[287] The (correct) correction is in a different hand from the first total in the MW hand.

Item for his horse meyte standyng at Ric*hard* Fleccher … xii s.

Item delyv*er*ed unto m*aister* dean for a reward yeven unto m*aister* Denton my lad*ys* scoller … xl s.

^{M}Summa … xxxi li. ii s.^{P}[288]

[*p. 190*] *Robert Dey*. Item paid the xth day of Januar*e* to <Ric*hard* Ade\r/ton> Rob*er*t Dey for a q*uarter* waig*es* ended at Crystemasse … vi s. viii d.

Item paid unto Ric*hard* Cotmote grome isshar*e* of the haull for his cost*es* to London …v s.

Item the xii day of Januar*e* unto George Fraunc*es* for a reward yeven to Ric*hard* Clement and Nicholas Hyde the kyng*es* s*er*vand*es* … vi s. viii d.

Item in reward to John Haryson for his dysgysynge in Crystemasse … xx s.

Item paid to the same for a cote and a hud lynyng and makyng x s. viii d. Item þ*at* was yeven to chylder þ*at* dauncet the XII Nyght iiii d. … xi s.

Item paid for a masse booke for my lad*ys* g*r*ace … v s.

Item the xiii day of Januar*e* in reward to m*aister*<Sicyly> Syklyng maister of Godd*es* Howse in Cambryge … xx s.

^{M}Summa … lxxiiii s. iiii d.^{P}[289]

Item delyvered to my ladys grace apon Newyer*es* Day … x li.

Totalis solucio … <DCCCClvii \li./ vi s. v d. ob.><\xi s. xi d. ob./> DCCCCxxxvii li. xi s. xi d.

Debetur … Dxx li. <iii s. viii d.> xviiii s. i d. ob.

[*p. 191*] [290]Item paied to John Mundy of London goldsmyth for ii pott*es* of silv*er* gilted for the kyng*es* New Yeres gift*es* at Cristenmas anno xx^{mo} H. vii weyng CCCiiii^{xx}xvi unce. P*r*ice the unce v s. the whiche amounteth in gode money <unto iiii^{xx}ix li. \iiii^{xx}xix li./> And for the same pott*es* was delyv*er*ed unto the seid John Moundy in clipped grott*es* \and so my lady leses w*ith* thexchaunge of x li. in grot*es*/ that James Mores had xxxvi li. xiii s. i d. And so the seid Myles moste have allowaunce of Cxxvii li. iii s. xi d. for he is charged w*ith* the seid clipped grott*es* in his receyte as gode and laufull money.

Paied by the seid s*ir* Roger Urmeston by the comaundement of my ladyis grace sence the xx^{ti} daie of January the xixth yere of kyng Henry the viith as ensueth.

Firste delyv*er*ed to the hand*es* of my ladyis grace for a reward to the quenez medwyff … x s.

[288] From here on the 'Summa' calculations appear to be in the summary hand.There is a dot calculation to the left at the foot of the page, preceded by 'totalis', and another to the right above the page total.

[289] The 'Summa' and the rest of the page are in the summary hand, with the final calculations ('Totalis …i d. ob.') written small to the left at the foot of the page.

[290] This and the next page are written in a neat cursive summary hand.

Item the vith daie of February paied for a dev*er* for my ladyis grace councell as the receyvo*ur* knowith ... xvii s. iiii d.

Item paied to Will*i*am Botery the xx^{ti} da[i]e of Februar*e* for xxvii ell*es* and di. of cameryke cloth at iiii s. viii d. the elne ... vi li. viii s. iiii d.

Maistrez Denton. Item the xxvith day of February paied to Richard Haryson in Flet Strete for a reward from my ladyis grace to be conveyed to m*aistres* Denton ... C s.

Item paied the iiiith daie of March for v doss*en* white bonett*es*. P*r*ice the pece vi d. ... xxx s.

Item paied for iii yerd*es* and i q*uarter* blakk. P*r*ice the yerde vi s. ... xix s. vi d.

Item paied for iii yerd*es* and i q*uarter* tawny medley for my lady. P*r*ice the yerde iiii s. ... xiii s.

Item paied for ii M pynnes at vi d. the M ... xii d.

Item paied for a doss*en* of white bonett*es*. P*r*ice the pece vi d. ... vi s.

Item paied to John Middelton for xxiiii^{ti} yerd*es* of blakk damask. P*r*ice the yerde vii s. ... viii li. viii s.

Summa ... xxiiii li. xiii s. ii d.

Summa pagine ... <Cxlix li. vi s. iiii d.> Cli li. xvii s. i d.[291]

[*p. 192*] Item paied <to John> for ii ell*es* canvas ... viii d.

Item paied for cariage of vi doss*en* bonett*es* weyng li lib. Price the pounde ob. ... ii s.[292]

Item paied for vi <ell*es*> yerd*es* of lynsey wolseay for my lady. Price the yerde viii d. ... iiii s.

Item in reward to m*aister* Lacy the xvi daie of M*ar*ch for my lady ... iii s. iiii d.

Summa ... x s.

Money laied owte for Frognall.[293]

Friste delyv*er*ed to hym at Colyweston the same mornyng that he co*m*me forth to pay for certeyn stuff that he hadd bouth ... ii s.

Item delyv*er*ed to the same Frognall at London the xx^{ti} daie of January for his bord wages and other necessares ... xx s.

Item paied for his horse mete the space of iii daies ev*ery* daie v d. ... xv d.

Item delyv*er*ed to Frognall the vith daie of Februar*e* at the Kyng*es* Hed ... xx s.

[291] The total of £24 13s. 2d. (previous line) plus MW's allowance (top of p. 191) of £127 3s. 11d, written small centrally at the foot of the page in the same hand as the material at the foot of p. 190.

[292] The total is 1½d. short.

[293] Bracketed to include the next five items.

Item delyv*er*ed to Frognall the xvith daie of Marche … xiii s. iiii d.

Summa … lvi s. vii d.[294]

Money layd oute for Parker.[295]

Firste to the pryncipall of Barnard*es* Ynne for Parker*es* co*m*myns by the space of ii wek*es* complet … ii s. viii d.

Item paied for his pencion the space of ii t*er*mes … xx d.

Item paied to the principall for money that he lent to P*ar*ker … xx d.

Summa … vi s.[296]

Summa pagine … lxxii s. vii d.

Totalis huius folii …<Clix li.> Clv li. ix s. viii d.[297]

[*p. 193*] Totalis allocacio … Miiii^{xx}iii li. xix d.[298]

[*p. 194*] [299]Summa totalis of all þe expenses and paym*entes* afor wrytten … Miiii^{xx}iii li. xix d.

And so he oweth … DCCCiiii^{xx}xii li. iiii s. vi d. ob. qua. di.

wherof

he hath delyv*er*ed unto þe coffr*e* of the seid countiez by þe hand*es* of þe bisshop of Duresme for money to hym lent befor… C li. And also he hath delyv*er*ed to þe tresorer*e* of houshold by þe hand*es* of s*ir* Roger*e* Urmyston knyght as in certen goodez bought at London and sent to Colyweston for þe use of þe seid houshold as in þe accompt of þe same tresorer*e* it appereth … vii li. viii s. And also delyv*er*ed to James Mores clerk of werk*es* at div*er*se tymes as it doth p*ar*tic*ul*arly apper*e* aswell by þe booke of accompt of þe seid Miles and also by þe knowlech of þe seid James … CCCi li. xvi s. ob. And also he hath paied for þe exhibic*i*on of m*aister* Seynt John and his wif xi li. v s. thexhibic*i*on of m*aister* Henr*y* P*ar*ker*e* and his wyiff xvi li. vii s. iiii d. thex[hi]bic*i*on of m*aister* Keham lxxi s. vii d. and thexhibic*i*on of m*aister* Thrognall and his wiff xviii li. xii s. viii d. ob. in all as it doth p*ar*tic*ul*arly apper*e* in a booke of p*ar*cell*es* þ*er*of made by þe seid Myles and remanyng in þe custody of þe seid countiez \<xl> xlix li. xvi s. vii d. ob./ And þ*ere* is allowed hym… xx li. by a warant of þe seid countiez dated þe xvth day of Januar*e* anno xx° regis H. vii^{mi}. And also he hath delyv*er*ed to James Morys apon þe det*er*mi*na*c*i*on of this accompt … C s. And so he oweth yet …

[294] The total of money laid out for Frognall.

[295] Bracketed to include the next three items.

[296] The total of money laid out for Parker.

[297] Noted centrally at the foot of the page, this is the (correct) total of the sheet ('folium') pp. 191–2.

[298] Written small to the left on an otherwise blank page, and again formally on p. 194.

[299] The summary hand of p. 194 (apart from the list of names on the extension) is clearly the 'sprawling' hand, which (as at p. 134) returns at the end of the list.

CCCCviii li. iii s. x d. ob. qua. wherof ys alowed … xxxix li. xi s. i d. qua. for syche as ys dew by hym and now

[paper extension sewn to the bottom of p. 194, written small and neat; for the back of the extension see the Appendix at the end of this edited text]

charged in hys indentur*e*. And so there ys awyng … CCClxviii li. xii s. ix d. ob.

«ergo oneratur in computo sequenti»[300]

Firste to Richard Convay of the chapell … iiii li.

Item to John Joyner … x li.

Item to John Henyngham … xxvii s. vi d.

Item to m*aister* Beconsawe … xl s.

Item to Will*iam* Pole … xi li.

Item to s*ir* John Melton \knyght/ … xvi li. xiii s. iiii d.

Item to the prio*ur* of Croland … xl li.

Item to Walter Cokk*es* … xliii s. iiii d.

Item to Will*iam* Farthyng … xiii li. vi s. viii d.

Item to s*ir*<Will*iam*> Henry Willyby knyght … CC li.

R*eceyved of Olyv*er *Holland by his byll of allowaunce viii li. xvi s. vi d. ob. qua. etsolvitur vi li. xvii s. vi d. qua. xxiiii*^{o} *die Septembris.*[301] Item to Olyver Holand at ii tymes … xv li. xiiii s. i d.

Item to Willmez Hilm*er* … xiii li. vi s. viii d. «solvitur »

Solvitur. Item to maistres Wyndesore … xvii s. x d. «solvitur»

Item to James Clarrell by the hand*es* of Henry Salford iiii li. xv s. and by Olyver Holland xlvi s. viii d. wherof the seid James bought xv yerd*es* of tawny medley lxxvii s. vi d. and for money delyv*er*ed to Frognall xviii s. vi d. ob. and so he outhe clere … xlv s. vii d. ob.

R*eceyved of N. Awgton.* Item to Nicholas Aughton … xlvi s. viii d. «solvitur per byllam xxvi s. and xx s. viii d.»

R*eceyved of Ri*chard *Aderton the xxiiii day of Januar*e. Item to Richard Aderton … liii s. iiii d. «recepta»

Item to John Walter … iii s. iiii d.

Item in money prested unto m*aister*<Twsatt*es*> Thwat*es* my ladys scoller at Parres for my ladyis mat*er*ez theire by the hand*es* of s*ir* Roger Urmeston knyght the iiiith daie of M*ar*che anno xix° H. vii by the hand*es* of Rauff Lathum ov*er* and beside xx mark*es* paied to m*aister* Hugh Assheton the laste daie of Decembr*e* anno xix° for as muche money as he did delyv*er* unto m*aister* Hugh Oldom at Excet*ur* and the same m*aister*

[300] Add. below the total (see D91.21/1 and D102.10/104).

[301] This and the marginal notes below record in the MW hand the repayment (or not) of the loans; similar notes have been added after the sums of other loans below.

Hugh Oldom seith that he delyv*er*ed as xx mark to the forseid Rauffe Lathum and to the seid m*aister* Twhaytt*es* and therfore hit is to inquire [i]f[302] m*aister* Twhaytt*es* had xl marke or but xx[ti] mark …xiii li. vi s. viii d.

*Som*m*e totalle off alle þe prest*es. *CCClxviii li. xii s. ix d. ob.*[303]

[304]Item in mony remaynyng in the hand*es* off thexecuto*urs* off s*ir* Roger*e* Urmyston knyght as yt appereth in the fote of acompt by them made restyng in þe kepyng off m*aister* Hugh Assheton … xvii li. vii s. ix d.

And so resteth in þe hand*es* of þe seid Miles … <xxxix li. xi s. i d. qua.> \oneratur in indentura/[305]

CCClxviii li xii s. ix d. ob.[306]

[*p. 195*] [307]Alm*es* yeven to diverse p*er*sones at sondry tymes … xix li. x s. ii d.

Money delyv*er*ed at sondrie tymes to my ladies almes purse … xxx li. xi s. ii d.

l li. xvi d.[308]

Money delyv*er*ed to docto*ur* Jubbes for bildyngg Jh*es*us college in Cambr*ige* …<xiii> vi li. xiii s. iiii d.

Money delyv*er*ed for bildyng of Seynt Mary church. P*r*ice … x li.

Money delyv*er*ed for rep*ar*aci*o*nz of Walmesforth bridge … ix li.

Money delyv*er*ed to Jane Goer late my ladies s*er*vant … lxvi s. viii d.

Money yeven for þe bildyng of the Austyne frers in Stanneford … lxvi s. viii d.

Cost*es* and expens*es* of þe nonne þ*at* cam fro Shiphey to Stanneford … lxvi s. viii d.

xxxv li. xiii s. iiii d.[309]

Money delyv*er*ed at sondry tymes for my ladiez offeryng*es* … viii li. vii s. iii d.

Certen pecez of wolen cloth and div*er*s peces of frees and cottons bought at div*ers* p*r*ices … lix li. ix s. vii d.

Div*er*se and certen peces of lynen cloth of div*er*se prices bought at sondry tymes … xvii li. xvii s.

Summa partis … Clxxi li. viii s. vi d.

[302] MS 'of'.

[303] Written in the left margin alongside 'Item' below, this records the total of the loans (£368 12s. 9½d.).

[304] The 'sprawling' hand returns here.

[305] Written small above the line. See p. 194 (before the list of loans).

[306] Written small to the right at the foot of the page (probably in the MW hand), this is the amount owed p. 194 (before the list of loans).

[307] The summary hand continues (not the 'sprawling' hand).

[308] The total of the first two items on p. 195, bracketed to the right of the items.

[309] The total of the six items above, bracketed to the right of the items

[*p. 196*] Div*er*s silk*es* as velvet damaske saten sarsnet <saten sarsnet and> oþ*er* bought … xxxii li. xi s. vi d. qua.

xxvii ellys of cameryk clothe. P*r*ice þe elne iiii s. viii d. … vi li. viii s. iiii d.[310]

Certen canvas bokerame fustian bought at sondr*e* tymes … xiiii li. x s. xi d.

Certen cloth of gold bought for my lady … <xiiii li. x s. xi d.> \iiii^{xx}x li. xii d./

Certen rawe silk*es* bought for my ladiez g*r*ace … Ciii s. x d.

Gold wire and gold of damaske … lxxiii s. ii d. ob.

Certen peces of diap*er* bought … iiii li. xv s. xi d. ob. qua.

Exhibic*i*on of Skipp … xiiii s. ii d.

Cost*es* of cariage of certen stuff … xx s. ob.

Thexibic*i*on of m*aister* Fawne … vi li. vi s. viii d.

Thexhibic*i*on of Pellett … xxiii s. iiii d.

Thexhibic*i*on of Pepir*e* … xvi s. ob.

Thexhibic*i*on of James Denton my ladyes scoler*e* at Orlyaunce … iiii li.

Thexhibic*i*on of John Mason of Tateshall … xv s.

xiii li. xii d. ob.[311]

Money delyv*er*ed yerly to John Brownyng of Burne … xl s.

Money delyv*er*ed to a man of London to take John Walt*er*s doughter to pryntes … liii s. iiii d.

Summa partis … Clxxvi li. xiii s. iiii d. ob.

[*p. 197*] Money delyv*er*ed to m*aister* controller*e* for þe cristnyng of my lady Conyers child … <liii s. iiii d.> \lxxvi s. viii d./

Money yeven to m*aistres* Stanehop at þe cristynyng of h*er* child … liii s. iiii d.

Money yeven <to> at þe cristonyng of m*aistres* Moynteneys child … xl s.

Money delyv*er*ed to m*aister* Thwayt*es* for my ladies mat*er*es at Paris ov*er* and besid*es*<lxvi s. viii d.> \xx marc/ made in p*r*est in þe foote of this booke[312] … xiii li. vi s. viii d.

Certen necc*essa*riez of stuff bought for my ladies g*r*ace for her owne were as certen <stuff> \clothe/ and oþ*er* necessariez … xxvi li. xiii s. iiii d.

Certen oþ*er* necc*essa*ri stuff bought for[313] many causes … xvi li. vii s. vi d.

[310] The correct total is £6 6s.

[311] The total of the five items above, bracketed to the right of the items

[312] See p. 194 on the extension to the page.

[313] 'my' add.

Cost*es* of my ladiez s*er*vant*es* ridyng apon her*e* messagez to sondry placez … xxi li. xix s. ii d.

Foryn and necc*essar*iez expens*e* as for cost*es* of div*er*se and many straung*er*s and of þ*er*e horsez abydyng at Stanneford … xvi li. xvi s. viii d.

Reward*es* yeven to sondre p*er*sones at div*er*s tymes … iiii^{xx}viii li. xiiii s. v d.

Reward*es* yeven to m*aister* Conyngesby w*ith* xxxiii s. iiii d. for his clerk*es* … x li. xiii s. iiii d.

Reward to m*aister* Brikenell at div*er*se tymes … viii li. xiii s. iiii d.

Reward to þe exchetou*r* of Lincolnshire … xl s.

Cx li. xiiii d.[314]

Summa partis … CCxiii li. iiii s. vi d.[315]

[*p. 198*] Reward*es* yeven to m*aister* <Thre> Arthur*e* \C s./ bryng*yng* of þe kyng*es* Newyer*es* yeft*es* and to my lord of Elys \xl s./ s*er*vant*es* … vii li.

Reward yeven to m*aister* Cowp*er* … lxvi s. viii d.

Reward*es* yeven to my lady m*ar*k*es* … lxvi s. viii d.

Reward yeven to m*aister* confessou*r* … Cvi s. viii d.

Reward to m*aister* Morys Seynt John … vi li. xiii s. iiii d.

Reward yeven to John Castell of <Thesq> þe Eschequyer*e* … xl s.

Reward yeven and send to <q> mastreis Denton w*ith* þe qwen of Scott*es* … C s.

Reward yeven to þe suffregan … lxvi s. viii d.

xxi x li.[316]

Money paied to Brograve for þe full paiement of his land*es* bought by my lady … xvi li. xiii s. iiii d.

Money paied for þe tith of my ladies place called Coldeherburgh for ii yerez … Cvi s. viii d.

Div*er*se book*es* bought by m*aister* Cowp*er* and oþ*er* for þe chapell and oþ*er* … vi li. vii s. vi d.

Certen furres bought for my ladiez g*r*ace … ix li. ix s. v d.

Money delyv*er*ed for þe bord of mastres Anne Souche w*ith* her apparell … lviii s. viii d.

Money delyv*er*ed for xi peces of Pares bought for my ladiez g*r*ace … vi li. xii s. viii d.

Summa partis … iiii^{xx}iii li. viii s. iii d.

[314] The total of the four items above (1d. over), bracketed to the right of the items.
[315] Correct in terms of the bracketed total (see the previous note).
[316] The total of the seven items above, bracketed to the right of the items

[*p. 199*] Oon barell of succad bought for my lady … xxxi s. vii d.

Certen plate and oþ*er* jewell*es* bought for my ladies g*r*ace … xxvii li. xix s. vi d.

Certen rep*ar*aci*on*s don at Coldherburgh … xiiii li. xv s. x d.

Delyv*er*ed to my lady in money … lxvi li. xiii s. iiii d.

Dieng of certen saies for my ladies chamb*er* … xxiiii s.

Div*er*se urinall*es* and glass*es* w*ith* oþ*er* necc*ess*a*r*iez bought for my ladies g*r*ace … xvii s. xi d.

Money delyv*er*ed for my ladies p*ar*don w*ith* certen charg*es* and costes in þe Escheqwyer*e* … ix li. iiii s. i d.

Neweyerys yeft*es* yeven to þe kyng and my lord of Ely at Cristmas anno xix° regis Henrici vii^{mi} … Cxxiii li. xviii s. x d.

Money paied for like Newyerys gift*es* yeven to þe kynng and to my seid lord at Cristemas anno xx° which was made of clippid grotez … Cxxvii li. iii s. xi d.

Money delyv*er*ed to my ladies g*r*ace for certen oþ*er* Newyeres gift*es* yeven to many oþ*er* sondrie p*er*sones … xlvi li. x s. <ii d.> ix d.

Money paied to s*ir* Roger Urmyston knyght for thexhibici*on* of m*aister* Thrognall at London … lxvii s. i d.

Money paied in like wise by þe same s*ir* Roger*e* Urmyston for þe exhibici*on* of m*aister* P*ar*ker*e* … vi s.

Money delyv*er*ed for certen stuff bought for m*aister* Seynt John … viii s. vi d. ob.

Summa partis …. CCCCxxiiii li. <ix d. ob.> xvi d. ob.[317]

[*p. 200*] *Nota pro iiii li. et iiii li. in anno precedenti et li. oneratis per Kirkham.* Money delyv*er*ed to s*ir* Henr*y* Norton for money due by my lady to m*aister* Welby ov*er* and besid*es* iiii li. allowed in þe last accompt … iiii li.[318]

Money delyv*er*ed to m*aistres* Thrognall*es* moder for her junctur*e* … lxvi s. viii d.

Oon horse bought of John Stakhouse w*ith* cost*es* of þe cariage of þe same … C s.

Cost*es* of þe mendyng of my ladies horse litt*er* and oþ*er* necc*essar*iez … xiiii[319] s. x d.

Money paied for þe p*re*sentaci*on* of a benyfice for s*ir* John Cart*er* … xxiiii s. i d.

Summa partis … xiiii li. <iiii s. vii d.> \v s./[320]

Summa totalis … Miiii^{xx}iii li. xix d.

[*pp. 201–48 blank*]

[317] The (correct) correction to the summary hand calculation appears to be in the MW hand.
[318] See the Appendix below for the details of this entry.
[319] MS 'xiijj s.'; the shilling add. here is also add. to the 'Summa partis' below (see next footnote).
[320] 'v s.' is correctly add. above line (see the previous footnote) and 'iiii s.' correctly canc., but 'vii d.' should not be canc. with it (the correct total is £14 5s. 7d.).

[APPENDIX: the back of the extension p. 194, written in the 'sprawling' hand]

Memorandum to co*m*myn w*ith* <my> m*aster* deane for <[…]> viii li. payd to s*ir* Herry Norton for syche mony as he clemyth <w*ith*> to have off m*aster*<Conys><Conysby> Welby and þ*at* þe m*aster* Welby dema*n*neth the <at s> same so*m*me off my lady for hys cost*es* rydyng*e* in Kendall and to þ*at* Thomas Hobson sheweth þ*at* <at> þe seid m*aster* Welby aweth to have nothyng for hys seid cost*es* for <a> þe same sayeth þ*at* he payd for all hys cost*es* goyng and comyng and þ*er*for*e* yt ys wele don to speke w*ith* Kyrkeh*a*m þ*at* hath the mynstraciou*n* off the good*es* off the seid m*aster* Welbys þ*at* he pay the seid viii li. ayen unto my lady grace.

D91.21 (SJLM/1/1/3/2) Account of Miles Worsley cofferer/treasurer of the chamber: Croydon and Hatfield, 14 January 1505 – 14 January 1507

Discussion See Introduction 4 and Plates 13–14.

Description Paper (occasional wormholes, esp. pp. 85–110, the bottom outer corners frayed and remounted); page size approx. 285 x 210 mm. 86 ff. in eight quires of irregular numbers of leaves: 1^{10}, 2^{10}, 3^{10}, 4^{14}, 5^{10}, 6^{12}, 7^{12}(wants 11, 12), 8^{10}.[1] Paginated top right (recto only) 1–171; pp. [i-ii], 68–69, 81–82, 88, 166–72 blank. A strip has been cut off square from 15 mm. from the inner edge of the top of pp. 81/82 to a depth of 35 mm. A piece of paper approx. 280 x 210 mm., torn across at the lower edge, has been written on, turned sideways, folded and stitched between pp. 62/63. Left margins approx. 50 mm. (with some subheadings); right margins variable; upper margins 10–15mm.; lower margins variable. The quires are stitched into the original membrane wrapper with two modern leather and string strengtheners on the spine; the irregularly-cut unscraped parchment is approx. 530 mm. x 590 mm. at its largest points when opened out (the back edge of the wrapper folds over to contain the whole document, and the upper and lower edges front and back fold in and down). A contemporary hand has recorded in ink on the front cover: 'Pressus 11', and contemporary notes read 'xiii li. xvii s. ix d.' (on the back fold-over, facing up when the book is closed) and 'xxv day of June' '[.....]ay ffoller of [.....] to hur delyv*er*ed [...] iii [...] et deb ii [...]' (on the back of the casing). The front vertical edge of the wrapper is cut down zig-zag top right to bottom centre (including the first two sheets) to indicate cancellation after completion and approval of the audit; the cut defaces the first folio of writing (pp. 1–2), and the second folio recto (p. 3) is variably legible. The whole is contained in a modern box of brown/grey waterproof buckram ('D91.21' in pencil on a white pasted slip, top left front cover of slipcase, now erased to 'SJLM/1/1/3/2'). The summaries, i.e. initial and final material for each year of the accounts (pp. 1–5, 70–80, 83–91, 161–5), use a formal script (Bastard Anglicana, with a large decorated initial 'S' pp. 5, 68, 89, 152) for the rubrics, infilled with either a smaller formal or a cursive script.[2] The main body of the accounts and the marginal headings are mostly in a current hand (Anglicana with some Secretary influence), the same as that in D91.20 and D91.19, seemingly identifiable as the hand of Miles Worsley himself

[1] That is, pp. 1–20, 21–40, 41–60, 61–88, 89–108, 109–32, 133–52, 153–72.

[2] The blanket term, the 'summary' hand, is used for what may be one or more of the hands used in D91.20, D91.21, D91.19, D102.1, and D102.2/6.

('the MW hand', 'the main hand').[3] Another hand (the 'curly' hand) occurs pp. 25–6, 91; the 'sprawling hand' is responsible for entries on pp. 67, 85, 90, 150 ('Somme'), 152, 161 (and perhaps even all the end-of-year summary for 1505–6, pp. 70–80 and 1506–7, pp. 150–65).[4] Lady Margaret signs 'Margaret R' at the bottom of each page of entries (^{M} in the edited text, placed to the left of the page total).[5] Page and (rarer) mid-page totals are normally written, and often corrected (if not by the auditor), in the MW hand;[6] they are marked 'probatur' (^{P} in the edited text), normally with a trefoil symbol, as in D91.20,[7] or (pp. 91–132) an elongated delta with two horizontal lines across it, as well as the trefoil.[8] Latin annotations and other interventions (some with +, e.g. *Nota* p. 116, fourth entry p. 150) occur occasionally in a hand (probably the 'sprawling' hand) which notes (often with a thick nib and very black ink) the reasons for cancellations of entries, etc.[9]

Summary

1505–6 (years 20–21) rubric (Croydon, Worsley, 14 January 1505 – 14 January 1506), arrears of last account p. 1, receipts, pp. 2–4; sum total of receipts and arrears, p. 5 [6 blank]; costs and expenses, pp. 7–67 [68–9 blank]; sum total of costs and expenses, debt of MW, extra payment by MW, debt of MW, p. 70; summary of expenses by item/person, pp. 71–7; sum total of MW's allowances, p. 77; debt of MW, p. 78; loans/advances, pp. 79–80; sum total of loans/advances, debt of MW delivered to coffer, p. 80 [81–2 blank];

1506–7 (years 21–22) rubric (Hatfield, Worsley, 14 January 1506 – 14 January 1507), arrears of last account, p. 83; receipts, pp. 84–5; extra charge on MW, p. 86; further receipts, p. 87 [88 blank]; sum total of receipts and arrears, p. 89; money delivered to coffer by MW, p. 90; costs and expenses, pp. 91–160; sum total of costs and expenses, debt of MW, payment to coffer by MW, debt of MW, p. 161; loans/advances, pp. 162–4; outstanding loans/advances, sum total of loans/advances, debt of MW cleared, p. 165.

[3] E.g. marginal note p. 162, cf. 'my', 'I', p. 22. For marginal notes in several hands, see, for example, pp. 91–5.

[4] See footnotes for changes of hand and other hands.

[5] She does not sign any pages after p. 145, i.e. 8 January 1507.

[6] They may be assumed to be in the MW hand unless noted otherwise; when not in the main hand, the hand must be that of the auditor/clerk, but only the term 'different (hand)' is used here.. The MW hand uses a delta-shaped 's.' ('solidi') which differs from the 's.' of the 'probatur' hand(s).

[7] There is a trefoil but no 'probatur' at the mid-page 'Summa' pp. 102, 106.

[8] These must be the check-marks of the auditor and/or his clerk(s); they are not shown in the edited text.

[9] Annotations are indicated by double angle brackets; marginal and above-line interventions are noted in the footnotes. + also occurs alone as an annotating mark, e.g. eight times on p. 109.

Edited Text

[*p. 1*] *Croydon.* [10]Thaccompt of Myles Worsley clerk [.....] of the most excellent pryncesse M*ar*garete [.....] Rychemond and Derby and moder*e* unto [.....] the kynge that nowe ys kyng Henry th[.....] frome the xiiiith daye of Januar*y* in [.....] the yere of the said souv*er*ayne lorde un[.....] xiiii daye of Januar*y* next ensuyn[.....] xxith yere of the seyde sov*er*ayn lo[.....] to saye by the space of an hole [.....]

*Tharrerag*es. Furst the said accomptant ys charged wit[.....] the arrerag*es* of his last accompte as it doth [.....] more playnly appere in the fote of the sam[.....]

Summa ... CCClxv[...][11]

[*p. 2*] Furst receyved of <tharrerag*es*> \as money remanynyng in his hand*es*/ of his last accompte ended the xiiith daye of Januar*y* in the xxth yere ... xxxix li. xi s. i d. qua.[12]

Item receyved the same daye in redy money ... xxxiii li.

Item receyved the xiiiith daye of February ... xlv li. ix s. iiii d.

Item receyved the xxiith daye of February ... xxiiii li. ii s. vi d.

Item receyved the last daye of February ... xxxii li. xvii s.

Item receyved the iii^{de} daye of Marche ... x li. xiiii s. ii d. ob.

Item receyved the same daye ... xx li. xix s. x d.

[...]m receyved the xixth daye of Marche ... iiii li. ii s. iiii d.

[.....] receyved the xixth daye of Apryll ... lxvi li.

[.....] receyved the same daye in clypped grotys [.....] and besyd*es* lxxi li. xiii s. iiii d. delyv*er*ed [.....]es Mores for to delyv*er* to maystyr [.....] for the rep*ar*aci*o*nes of Crystez College [.....]ge ... xlii li. v s. i d.

[.....]ed the xvith day of Juyn by the [.....] Nicholas Saunders ... xx li.

Summa partis ... CCCxxx\ix/<viii> li. xvi d. ob. qua.

[*p. 3*] Item receyved the xxith daye of June ... CCClxxvii li. vii s. viii d. ob.

Item receyved the xxiith daye of June ... Cxviii li. xii[13] s. i d.

Item receyved the xxvii daye of July ... xxxv li. xvii s. vii d.

Item receyved the xvi daye of Septemb*er* ... lxvii li. xvi s. ii d.

Item receyved the same daye ... xx li.

Item receyved the xxii daye of Octob*er* ... xxx[...]

Item receyved the xxix daye of Octob*er* ... [...]

[10] The summary hand begins the document. Lacunae are the result of indenture-style cutting of the first pages (see Plate 13).

[11] For the sum see D91.20/194.

[12] See D102.10/101, 103.

[13] MS 'x ii' (perhaps with an intermediate letter canc.).

Item receyved the xiiith daye of Decemb*er* … […]

Item receyved the [*blank*] daye of [*blank*] […]y the hand*es* of mastyr comptroller for money pa[…] unto syr Henry Colett knyght for the purchase […] Dyesworth with the membr*e* … [.....]

Item receyved the xviiith daye of Decemb*er* by the hand*es* of the sayd mastyr comptroller for the purches of Roydon for to p*er*fo*ur*me DCCC<[…]>\[…]/i li. … […]l[…] x[…]i li.

So*m*me totall off þe indentur*e* … MMDCCCliiii li. xix s. di. qua.

Summa partis … MMDxv li. xvii s. viii d. ob.

[*p. 4*] *[…]ren recept*es. Item receyved of syr John Grene knyght at ii tymes by thand*es* of Thomas Soper my ladyes solicit*our* in parte of suche money as Gregorye Skyppewith owyth my ladye … xx li.

Item receyved of the lady Skrene late wyff unto Herper late my ladys receyvo*ur* of the duke of Bokynghams land*es* at ii tymes by the handes of the said Thomas Soper in parte of payme*n*t of suche money as the said Herper owght my ladye … iiii li.

Summa … xxiiii li.

[*p. 5*] Some totall of all the receptes with tharrerag*es* byfore wrytten … MMMCCxlvii li. xi s. x d. ob. qua.

[*p. 6 blank*]

[*p. 7*] [14]Cost*es* and exspenc*e* w*i*th other dyv*er*se payment*es* and reward*es* of the most excellent prynces Margarett countesse of Richmound and Derby and moder unto our*e* sov*er*aigne lorde kyng Henry the viith from the xiiiith day of January in the xx^{ti} yere of the reign*e* of our*e* said sov*er*aigne lord paid by the hand*es* of Myles Worsley as hereafter hit doth appere.

Furst paid unto Rob*er*t Hylton by his byll assigned for ii yerd*es* and iii q*u*art*er* of derk tawny for a nyghtgowne for my ladies g*r*ace. P*r*ice the yerd ii s. … v s. vi d.

Item paid unto the same for makyng of vi payrs of <ho… > hose for my lad*ys* bedmen at iiii d. the payr*e* … ii s.

Item for lynyng of oon of the said payr*e* hose … iiii d.

Item paid for vii payr*e* of hose for my lad*ys* bedwomen at v d. the payr*e*. Summa … ii s. xi d.

Item paid for so<w>lyng*e* of a payre of shoes for moder Margarett oon of the almes women … ii d.

Item for ii payr*e* of shoes for ii pore almes chyldren at iii d. the payre … vi d.

[14] The MW hand starts here.

Item paid to the same for money paid to George Skynner for workyng*e* by iiii daiez and a half \at iiii d. the day/ … xviii d.

Item paid unto John Holt by his byll assigned for his cost*es* rydyng \to/ Grymosby of S[c]oterthorp[15] … viii d.

Item paid unto the same for vi daies rydyng to the co*ur*te and home to Colyweston \at viii d. the day/ … iiii s.

Item paid unto William Hylm*er* by his byll assigned for vi nest*es* of longe coffyns for lettur*es*. \Pryce the nest ii d./ … xii d.

Item for fyne pakthrede for carpett*es* v lib. \P*r*ice the i lib. ii d./ … xx d.

Item for wachyng lyghet*es* and whit lyght*es* <med> made w*i*th cotton and send from Cambryge \P*r*ice the dd. xviii d./ … xv s.

Item paid for the hyre of a horse and a man and their*e* diett*es* from Cambryge unto Colyweston w*i*th the said candyll*es* by iii daiez and a half at xvi d. the day … iiii s. viii

Item for caryage of vi carpett*es* fro London to Colyweston … xii d.

[M]Summa … xl s. xi d.[P]

viii d.[16]

[*p. 8*] Item paid unto Richard Adderton by his byll assigned for ridyng to London and ayen by ix daiez \at viii d. þe day/ … vi s.

Item to the same for a pounde of sylv*er* of Vennys … xxx s.

Item delyv*er*ed to maister Parker at his goyng unto his father the xvi day of January … xx s.

Item delyv*er*ed unto William Pole for a reward yeven unto maistres Odell at hir beying at Colyweston … xx s.

Item in reward to George Hamerton the kyng*es* *ser*vande … v s.

Item paid the xxi day of January unto Heymond Nycolson hardware man for vi doss*en* napkyne of dyaper. P*r*ice the dd. vii s. … xlii s.

Item paid unto the same for ii pec*es* of diapur cont*eynyng* lxxvi yerd*es* at xv d. the yerd … iiii li. xv s.

Item for ii pec*es* of dyapur tuell cont*eynyng* lxviii yerd*es* … xlii s.

Item for a pece of diapur*e* cont*eynyng* lxviii yerd*es* at xx d. the yerd. Summa … Cxiii s. iiii d.

Item for a pece of dyapur*e* cont*eynyng* xxxviii yerd*es* of tabell brede at x d. the yerd … xxxi s. viii d.

Item for a dosen payr*e* of French glovis. \P*r*ice the payre iii d./. Pric*e* … iii s.

Item for iii payr*e* of every beyd*es* at \<xv> ii s. viii d. the payr*e*/ … viii s.

[15] MS 'Stoterthorp'.
[16] Written small to the left at the foot of the page in the MW hand.

Item in reward unto Bertylmew maist*er* Crok*es* clerk by the receyver at the audet tyme … xx s.

Item paid unto John Brydde for a reward yeven unto a s*er*vande of the dean of my lord Oxforths chappell for bryngyng of a mare send from his maist*er* unto my lad*ys* grace the xxi day of Januar*y*… xiii s. iiii d.

Item paid unto maistres Bygott the xxiii day of January for a gowne of blak damaske … xlvi s. viii d.

Item paid unto John Stakhowse by the hand*es* of the receyver syr Hughe Assheton for a bey horse for my lad*ys* letter. The pryce … liii s. iiii d.

Item in reward to Henry Orlow of Norwyche syngyng man for his cost*es* to Colyweston … vi s. viii d.

[M]Summa … xxvii li. xvi s.[P]

[*p. 9*] Item paid unto m*aister* tresorer the xxvi day of January for a reward yeven unto the kyng*es* players … xxvi s. viii d.

<Item delyv*er*ed to m*aister* Gryndell in cleppyd grott*es* to be send oute to the receyver syr Hughe Assheton to London for the myndyng of c*er*ten plate for my lad*ys* g*r*ace … Cvi li. vii s. ii d.>

Item delyv*er*ed to my lad*ys* g*r*ace the same day for the crystenyng of Jamys Morice chyld … xx s.

Item paid unto syr Crystofer clerk of the clossett for a booke bought for my lad*ys* g*r*ace \called/ <cald> Vergill … vi s. viii d.

Item the <v> xxviii day of January delyv*er*ed unto maistres Foler for a reward yeven unto Marmyon at his goyng to the courte … xx s.

Item paid the same day to m*aister* Gryndell for a reward yeven to a s*er*vand of thabbot of Pet*er*boro … xii d.

Masson at Tatsall. Item paid unto m*aister* dean the xxix day of January toward*es* the exibucion of John Masson at Tatsall … xx s.

Item paid unto the same for a reward yeven unto the p*ar*son of Seynt Mergarett*es* … iii s. iiii d.

*Oly*ver *Holand.*[17]

Candylmas day. Item delyv*er*ed to Olyv*er* Holland for my ladiez offryng apon Candylmas day v <tr> thretty penc*e* in gold … xii s. vi d.

Item paid unto the same Olyv*er* for stuff bought by hym at London in the moneth of January. Furst for xii yerd*es* of welvet at xi s. viii d. the yerd … vii li.

Item paid unto the same for vii yerd*es* and a half of brodde reban for my lad*ys* g*r*ace. P*r*ice … v s. viii d.

Item for his bot hyr*e* to Grenewich at ii tymez vii d. and to Westm*ynster* i d. … viii d.

[17] Bracketed to include the next seven items.

Item for canvas and corde to trusse the said stuff … viii d.

Item for caryage of the same to Stampforth … xii d.

Item paid unto the same Olyv*er* for his cost*es* the space of xiii daiez \at xii d. the day/ … xiii s.

[M] Summa … <Cxix li. xviii s. iiii d.> xiii li. xi s. ii d.[P] [18]

[*p. 10*] Item payd unto m*aister* dean for a reward yeven unto doctur*e* Smythe vichaunceller of Cambrige that prechyd afour*e* my ladies g*r*ace the furst Sonday in Lent … vi s. viii d.

Item paid the xv day of February to William Radclyff for iii skynnes of <chevaler> cheverell. P*r*ice xii d. and for iii other skynnes of red lether. The[19] p*r*ice ix d. Summa … xxi d.

N. Saunders.[20]

Item paid the same day to Nicholas Saunders for <s> two pec*es* of lynnen clothe conteynyng lxviii elnes d. P*r*ice the ellne ix d. Summa … li s. iiii d.

Item paid unto the same for a pec*e* of <… > cont*eynyng* xxxiiii elles di. at vii d. the ell … xx s. i d. ob.

Item for iii ellys of canvas to trusse the said clothe in … ix d.

Item to the same for two book*es*. \Pryce the boke ii s. viii d./ of Scala Perfeccionis … v s. iiii d.

Item to the same for a reward yeven to maist*er* Cowp*er* and Ric*hard* Rowley for pryckyng … xx s.

[21]Item paid the xviii day of February to Rob*er*t Fremyngham for a reward yeven to Waywyn execut*ur* to doctur Mawdysley … vi s. viii d.

Item delyv*er*ed the same day to m*aister* countroller by the hand*es* of Nicholas Saunders at my lad*ys* goyng to the ancryse of Stampforth … xvi s. viii d.

Item delyv*er*ed unto m*aister* dean for a reward yeven unto the noones of Sympryngham … xx s.

Item to Bonyface Stanley in reward comyng from Northampton by my lad*ys* comaundement … xiii s. iiii d.

Item delyv*er*ed unto m*aister* dean for a reward yeven to a s*er*vand of m*aister* Conysby the xxi day of February … xx d.

[M]Summa … viii li. iiii s. iii d. ob.[P]

[18] Both calculations are in the MW hand; the total has been altered because the second item on the page was canc.

[19] MS 'redletherthe'.

[20] Bracketed to include the next five items.

[21] This and the following item are bracketed to the left but with no name in the margin.

[*p. 11*] Maister *Assheton.*[22]

Item paid the xxiiith day of February to syr Hughe Assheton receyver by a byll assigned for half a pounde of grene reban w*i*th golde. The p*r*ice … viii s.

Item for iii unc*es* of blew sylk. P*r*ice … iii s. ii d. ob.

Item to the same for di. pounde of red threde … xii d.

Item to the same for money paid unto syr John Hussey for his fee … C s.

Item paid to the same for money paid unto John Castell of the kyng*es* <exchyker> exchaker*e* bothe for respit of omage for m*aister* John Seynt John and suche feoffers as be feffed to the p*er*fourmance of my lad*ys* last wyll … Cii s.

Item paid unto John Holt the same day by his byll assigned for ridyng to Cakston after Nicholas Aughton by two daiez \at viii d. the day/ … xvi d.

Item to the same for ridyng to Wyldebore and to Stelton to my lord of Rochest*er* … viii d.

Item for ridyng to Peturboro for m*aister* subdeans p*re*sentacion by a day … viii d.

Item paid the same day unto Rob*er*t Pulv*er*tofte for his cost*es* ridyng to se c*er*ten land*es* for my lad*ys* use by the spaice of iiii daiez \at xii d. the day/ … iiii s.

Item in reward to a frere þ*at* prechit afour*e* my lad*ys* grace the ii^{de} Sonday in Lent … iii s. iiii d.

Item paid the xxvii day of February unto m*aister* Morgan for a reward yeven to a scoller of Cambryge … v s.

Item paid to the same for money yeven to a nonne of Sympryngham … xx d.

Item paid unto John Tanne of Lynne for vi carpett*es* bought at Southampton. P*r*ice the pece xii s. vi d. Summa … lxxv s.

Item for pakkyng of the same carpett*es* … vi d.

^{M}Summa … xv li. vi s. iiii d. ob.^{P}

[*p. 12*] Item paid unto Richard Aderton for his cost*es* ridyng unto syr John Melton in Yorkshir*e* by the spaice of vi daiez at viii d. by the day … iiii s.

Item to the same for the cost*es* of my lad*ys* palferes at Stampforth at my lad*ys* goyng t*o* the pardon of the nonnes the furst day of M*a*rche … xii d.

Item in reward unto a gray frere of Stampforth that prechid afour*e* my lad*ys* grace the iii^{de} Sonday of Lent … vi s. viii d.

Item in reward to the p*ar*son Bybe the iii^{de} day of Marche … xx d.

Item paid unto <m*aister* dean> \maistres Foller/ for a reward yeven unto Bell of <Cambryche> \Foderingay/ … vi s. viii d.

Item to the same for sylk bought for my lad*ys* use[23] … iii s.

[22] Bracketed to include the next five items.

[23] MS 'vuse'.

J. Brownyng. Item paid the iiiith day of Marche to John Brownyng*e* of Burne by Ric*hard* Stok for his anuytie for a q*uarter* of a yere to be ended at our*e* Lady Day … x s.

Item the vith day of Marche in reward unto Bonyface Stanley for his labur*e* and cost*es* comyng from Northampton to Colyweston … xx s.

Item the viith day of Marche in reward to a armett of Brokwod … x s.

Item paid unto Maydwell of Stampforth for a payer of slyppers and a payre of heghe pynsons for the ancryce at the nonnes delyv*er*ed by maistres Marbury … x d.

For oure Lady lyght at Walsyngham. Item paid unto maister Gryndell for money delyv*er*ed by hym for the repayryng of a lyght afoure our*e* Lady at Walsyngham paid the v day of March … iii s. iiii d.

Item paid unto m*aister* Morgan for a reward yeven unto a s*er*vande of maist*er* Sekelyng that brought appuls and oreng*es* unto my lad*ys* g*r*ace … ii s.

[M]Summa … iiii li. vii s. vi d.[P]

[*p. 13*] Item paid the viiith day of [Ma]rche[24] unto syr William Beaupray for the exspenc*e* of William Gibon my lad*ys* warde from Est*er* unto Crystemas as aperith by his byll assigned … ii s. vi d.

Item delyv*er*ed unto George Fraunc*es* the ixth day of M*ar*che to delyv*er* unto my lad*ys* g*r*ace for a reward yeven unto maister Carter … vi s. viii d.

Item paid to John Skynner the x day of M*ar*che by his byll assigned for half a C of <armynt> pynk*es*. P*r*ice viiid. Item for CCC doz. of fyne pynk*es* occupyed in a gowne of blak damaske iiii s. \viii d./ Item in a bonett of armyns CC powdryng*es*. P*r*ic*e* ii s. Item for ii pound of threde. P*r*ic*e* xviii d. … viii s. <ii d.> <viii d.> x d.

*Rob*er*t Hylton.*[25] Item paid unto Rob*er*t Hylton the xiith day of M*ar*che for xxv yerd*es* of medly. P*r*ic*e* the yerd ii s. ii d. Summa … liiii s. ii d.

Item paid unto the same for vi pec*es* of blak cotton iii pec*es* at vii s. the pece. Summa … xxi s. And the other iii pec*es* at vi s. viii d. the pece xxs. … <l>xli s.

Item for iiii pec*es* of whitt cotton. P*r*ic*e* the pec*e* vi s. iiii d. … xxv s. iiii d.

Item for xix yerd*es* of medly <… > clothe for kyrtell*es* for pore wemen at ix d. the yerd … xiiii s. iii d.

Item for iiii ellez and iii q*uarter* of blak worsted. P*r*ice the elle iiii s. … xix s.

Item for ii pec*es* of bokeram. P*r*ic*e* a grette … xi s.

Item for vi dd. of <how> [hosy]n. P*r*ic*e* the dd. iiii s. … xxiiii s.

Item for vi payr*e* of fyne hosyn. P*r*ic*e* the payr*e* vii d. … iii s. vi d.

Item paid for caryag*e* of the same stuff from Stampforth to Colyweston … iiii d.

Item for the cost*es* of the said Rob*er*t bying of the said stuff by ii daiez … viii d.

[24] MS '[…]rche'.

[25] Bracketed to include all the next items up to and including the sixth item on p. 14.

Item for xviii yerd*es* of whit kersey. P*rice* the yerd ix d. … xiii s. vi d.

^{M}Summa … xi li. iiii s. <vii d.> ix d.^{P}[26]

[*p. 14*] Item paid the xiith day of M*ar*che unto Rob*ert* Hylton by his byll assygned for ii payr*e* of shoez for my lad*ys* almouse chyldren at ii d. ob. the payr*e* … v d.

Item for sawlyng of iiii payr*e* of shoez for iiii of the almes wemen at ii d. the payr*e* … viii d.

Item for a payr*e* of shoez for Skyppe … vi d.

Item for a payr*e* of <hov> hose to hym … v d.

Item for makyng and lynyng of a payr*e* of hose for Henry the kyng*es* godson … viii d.

Item for a payr*e* of shoez for the same Henry … <v> iiii d.

Item delyv*er*ed unto maister Morgan the xii day of M*ar*che in reward … xx s.

Item paid unto Jak*es* Yarwell of Fodryngay for his cost*es* ridyng to Stretton in Strete by the space of a day … viii d.

Item to the same for ridyng by the comaundement of my lad*ys* councell to certen townes within Lyncolnshire by the spaice of v daiez at viii d. … iii s. iiii d.

Item to the same for his awne labur*e* by the said space at iiii d. the day … ii s.

Item to the same for his horse labur*e* the said space of vi daie[s][27] at iiii d. the day … ii s.

Item paid unto Thomas [W]elles[28] clerk of Eston for the bourde and lernyng*e* of a pour*e* chylde by the spaice of xiii wek*es* endet \at viii d. the weke/ the x day of M*ar*che … viii s. viii d.

Item delyv*er*ed the xviiith day of M*ar*che unto m*aister* chaunceller for a reward yeven unto m*aister* Conysby … liii s. iiii d.

Item to the same for a reward yeven unto my lad*ys* solicit*ur* … xx s.

Item to the same m*aister* chaunceller for vi p*ar*don lettur*es* … iiii s. vi d.

^{M}Summa … Cxvii s. vi d.^{P}

[*p. 15*] Item paid the xxith day of M*ar*che unto Jacson of Stampforth for v dd. and ii payr*e* of shoez. P*rice* the dossen iiii s. and for ii payr*e* viii d. Summa … <xix>xx s. viii d.

Item paid to the same for vi payr*e* of shone for my lad*ys* almes men. P*rice* the payr*e* vi d. … iii s.

Item paid to the same for vii payr*e* of wemen shoez. P*rice* the payr*e* iiii d. … ii s. iiii d.

Item to the same for iii payr*e* of shoez for pore chylder … ix d.

[26] The correction is also in the MW hand.

[27] MS 'daie'.

[28] MS '[…]elles'.

Item delyv*er*ed to lxii pore folk*es* at the maundy ev*er*y pece xiii d. Summa ... lxvii s. ii d.

<*Nota* >.[29] *My ladys offrynge apon Goode Fryday.* Item for my lad*ys* offryng apon Goode Fryday in v s. of gold ... xxx s.

Item paid unto Richard Aderton for ii daiez ridyng to m*aister* Antwyssell place in Leycet*ur*shyr*e* \at viii d. the day/ ... xvi d.

Item in reward to doct*ur* Hamer þ*at* prechyd afor*e* my lad*ys* g*r*ace apon Goode Fryday ... vi s. viii d.

Item yeven to the cok*es* at Est*er* toward*es* theyr*e* with in reward ... xxvi s. viii d.

Item to the soc*er*y and skollery ... v s.

*Es*t*er day my lad*ys *offrynge*s. Item for my lad*ys* offeryng apon Est*er* day at the resurrexson ii s. vi d. and at masse v s. ... vii s. vi d.

Item for my lad*ys* offreng apon our*e* Lady Day the Anu[n]ciacion[30] ... v s.

Item paid unto William Aderton the xxiiii day of M*ar*che by the receyv*er*se comaundement for hey by hym bought at Chesthunt in the moneth of February anno xix^{o} for my lad*ys* horsis ... ix s.

^{M}Summa ... ix li. <iiii> \v s./ s. i d.^{P}[31]

[*p. 16*] Item the xxx^{ti} day of M[ar]ch[32] unto George Hamerton in reward ... v s.

Item paid unto John Collop the furst day of Aprell for threde to amende carpett*es* ... xvi d.

Item paid unto maistrez Wenesowr*e* the iii^{de} day of Aprell for money payd to Lenard for vi Frenche book*es* ... v s.

<*Nota* >. Item paid unto m*aister* chaunceller for vi pardon letturs at ix d. a pece ... <v s. iii d.> iiii s. vi d.

Item delyvered to m*aister* chaunceller for a reward yeven unto maister Sekelyng m*aister* of Godd*es* howse in Cambryg*e* toward*es* his cost*es* at Colyweston ... xx s.

Item to iiii other of his felowez of the same howse at the same tyme ... <xx s.> xxvi s. viii d.

Item delyv*er*ed the vith day of Aprell to m*aister* chaunceller for a reward yeven unto m*aister* Brettnell ... xl s.

Item payd unto John Walter for iii yerd*es* of bokeram and a half. P*r*ice ... xxi d.

Item paid unto the same for seryng of iii tabyll cloths ... xii d.

Item the vii day of Aprell unto maistrez Corson in reward < þ*at*> \for <his> recompenc*e* of hur want*es* ... xl s.

[29] Written and canc. above the marginal heading.
[30] MS 'anuciacion'.
[31] The corrections are also in the MW hand.
[32] MS 'M[...]ch'.

Nota. Item paid unto Ric*hard* Aderton by his byll assigned for xi yerd*es* and i q*u*art*er* of lynnyn clothe bought at London … xlv s.

Item paid for viii ell*es* of lynyn clothe. P*ric*e … xxvi s. viii d.

Item paid for a pownde […] di. uncz of frynge … xvi s. vi d.

Item paid for a pounde and di. uncz of rubene … xvi s. vi d.

Item paid for a half pounde of threde the whiche John Walter owght … xii d.

Item paid for half a pounde of the same thredde … xii d.

Item paid for a q*u*art*er* of threde … iiii d.

Item paid for a panyer to carry stuff in … ii d.

Item paid for corde … i d.

Item paid […] for caryage of the same stuff from London unto Huntyngton … xii d.

Item paid for a male pelyon to cary on the said stuff … iiii d.

[M]Summa … <xii li. vii s. xi d.> <xiiii s. vii d.>

<xiiii li. viii s. vd.> [P]

xii li. xiii s. x d. [P][33]

[*p. 17*] Item paid unto the same Rychard Aderton for his cost*es* rydyng from Colyweston to London and there abydyng*e* by the space of vii daiez \at viii d. the day/ … iiii s. viii d.

Item to the same for rydyng unto Cambryge by the space of iii daiez \at viii d. the day/ … ii s.

H. for the nonne of Sympryngham.[34]

Item paid unto m*aister* Morgan for money by hym paid for the dying of viii yerd*es* of lynyn clothe at viii d. a yerd for a nonne at Sympryngham … v s. iiii d.

Item to the same for money paid for the makyng of iii cowles and ii kyrtell*es* … iii s. iiii d.

Item paid unto Rob*er*t Hylton by his byll assigned for iii yerd*es* di. of fyne brode whitte at iiii s. the yerd … xiiii s.

Item for iii yerd*es* of courser whitt at iii s. iiii d. the yerd … xi s. viii d.

Item for other iii yerd*es* of whitt at iii s. ii d. … xi s. <i d.> < v d.> i d.

Item for v brode yerd*es* of whytte ev*er*[y] yerd at iii s. … xv s.

Item for oon yerd of violett cloth for a scapelary … iii s. viii d.

[33] Only the first two calculations are in the MW hand; the final approved total (1s. over) may be in the 'curly' hand.

[34] Bracketed to include the next seven items.

*Hylt*on.[35] Item payd unto the same for iii yerd*es* of blak for my lad*ys* g*r*ace at v s. the yerd … xv s.

Item for xv yerd*es* of blak for my lad*ys* lytter and horse harness*es* ev*er*y yerd at iii s. … <xl s.> xlv s.

Item paid for iiii pounde of blew threde for my lad*ys* g*r*ace wherof oon was at xv d. another at xiii d. another at xii d. and that other at xi d. Summa … iii s. iii d.[36]

Item paid for xxv yerd*es* of blak cotton at v d. the yerd … x s. v d.

Item for xxiiii yerd*es* of whitt cotton at v d. the yerd … x s.

Item paid for a doss*en* of hose for my lad*ys* almesse women … iii s.

Item paid for ii rolles of corde to trusse in the said stuff iiii d. and for carying of the said stuff iii s. … iii s. iiii d.

Item paid t*o* the same Rob*er*t for his cost*es* at Coventr*e* to p*ro*vide the said stuff … iii s.

Item paid unto the same for a new booke to wryte in the wardrop stuff … iiii d.

Item paid unto the same for xxiiii skynnes of whitte lambe to p*er*fourme my lad*ys* nyght slop. \Pryce the skyn i d. qua./ … ii s. vi d.

[M]Summa … viii li. vii s. vii d.[P 37]

[*p. 18*] Item paid unto maister Morgan for money yeven unto Orton s*er*vande … xx d.

Item delyv*er*ed unto m*aister* countroller for a reward yeven unto a s*er*vant of the bysshop of vest Chest*er* for convaying of a horse yeven unto my lad*ys* g*r*ace … xx s.

Item the x day of Aprell delyv*er*ed unto m*aister* countroller for a reward yeven unto ii skollers of the Quenys Colage in Cambryge … xiii s. iiii d.

Item the xi[th] day of Aprell unto m*aister* dean for a reward yeven unto a prest of Skottland … vi s. viii d.

<xli s. viii d.>[38]

*<Nota.> Olyv*er *Holand.* Item payd unto Olyv*er* Holland the xiiii[th] day of Aprell for xxiiii yerd*es* of blak welvett at xi s. <the> iiii d. the yerd … <xiii li. xii d.> <vii li. xviii s. viii d.> xiii li. xii s.

Item to the same for a pece of hollande clothe cont*eynyng* xxviii ell*es* at xiiii d. the elle … xxxii s. viii d.

Item for ii pec*es* of elle brode clothe at v d. the elle one pec*e* cont*eynyng* xxxiiii ell*es* the other cont*eynyng* xxxiii ell*es* iii q*u*art*er*. Summa … xxviii s. ii d. ob. qua.

[35] Bracketed to include the next ten items.

[36] The correct total of this simple sum is 4s. 3d.

[37] The correct total is £8 3s. 11d.

[38] The total of the entries so far on p. 18, written small in the left margin in the MW hand (and canc.).

Item paid to the same for bott heyr*e* from London unto Grenewych and ayen … viii d.

Item paid for ii homers for the wardrop … xii d.

Item paid to the same for his cost*es* and the caturs w*i*th iii horsis by x daiez at ii s. viii d. a day for <con> convaying of bake bremes to the kyng*e* from my lad*ys* g*r*ace … xxvi s. viii d.

Item to the same for frenge reban and crewle … xviii s. iiii d.

Item paid for a bare hyde […]. P*r*ice … xxvi s. viii d.

Item payd for a grette clothe sake. P*r*ice … xx s.

Item for a payr*e* of gardyviance. P*r*ice … xvi s.

Item paid to the same for a pec*e* of canvas of xlviii ell*es* and a half at v d. the ell … xx s. ii d.

Item for v doss*en* bonett*es* and a half at vi s. the dd. … xxxii s. vi d.

Item for carying of the said bonett*es* to Harbaro … xiiii d.

Item for sendyng to Harbaro for the said bonett*es* at ii tymes … xii d.

Item to the same for carying of my lad*ys* stuff from London and certen book*es* to Colyweston … iii s. ii d.

Item for his cost*es* to London \at xii d. the day/ by the space of viii daiez … viii s.

Item for convaying of <tuff> stuff from Fodryngay to Colyweston … viii d.

[M]Summa … xxvii li. xi s. vi d. ob. qua. <xli s. viii d.>[P]

[*p. 19*] Item the xith day of Aprell delyv*er*ed unto m*aister* countroller for <a R> money yeven unto my lady marquesse toward*es* hir horse meyte at Colyweston … xx s.

Item delyv*er*ed unto maister chamberlayn for a reward yeven to a chylde <of> that hade a berde and came forth of Skottland … v s.

Kynges mynstrels. Item to the same for a reward yeven unto the kyng*es* mynstrels … xx s.

*Chyrche exchet*ur *of Lyncoln.* Item the xiiii day of Aprell delyv*er*ed unto George Fraunc*es* for money yeven unto <Chyl> Chyrche exchet*ur* of Lyncolnshyr*e* for his fee xx s. and in reward the same tyme vi s. viii d. … xxvi s. viii d.

Item delyv*er*ed to m*aister* chaunceller for money yeven to oon Cowen somtyme baily of Hoveden … iii s. iiii d.

John Masson at Tatsall. Item delyv*er*ed to the same for money yeven unto John Masson at Tatsall for his exibucion … xvi s. viii d.

Item payd unto George Fraunc*es* for a reward yeven unto the p*r*ioris of the nonnys of Stampforth at my lad*ys* beyng theyr*e* … iii s. iiii d.

Item paid the xvi day of Aprell unto Richard Aderton for his cost*es* and Jokye of the stabyll to Sympryngham … xiiii d.

Item paid unto maister countroller the xx^{ti} day of Aprell for money delyv*er*ed unto my lad*ys* g*r*ace at Stampforth to the ancryse theyr*e* iii s. iiii d. Item to an old gyntelwoman iii s. iiii d. Item to ancryse of the nonnys at Stampforth iii s. iiii d. … x s.

Item payd to William Grevell for ridyng to Bottesford by the space of two dayez \at xii d. the day/ … ii s.

Item paid unto maistrez <w> Merbury for a reward yeven to a prest of Foddryngay þ*at* prechyd at the chyrche at Colyweston … vi s. viii d.

Item payd to the same for my lad*ys* offryng*e* to the rode at Boston*e* iiii d. and to Seynt Margaret*es* iiii d. … viii d.

Summa … Cxv s. vi d.[P]

[*p. 20*] Item paid unto maistres Wynesowr*e* by hir byll assigned for a reward yeven unto maist*er* Odell s*er*vant … iii s. iiii d.

Item in almes to ii bedred men at Eston … iiii d.

Item yeven unto the p*r*ioris at Stampforth … <x d.> xx d.

Item to the olde ancryse … xii d.

Item to my lord of Rochest*er* s*er*vand in reward … ii s.

Item in reward unto maistrez Molenars … vi s. viii d.

Item to Rob*er*t Merbury for Romney … iii d.

Item in reward t*o* Lenard … xii d.

Item yeven unto the almez folk*es* … xiiii d.

Item paid unto maistrez Massy by hyr byll assigned for ii saulters for my lad*ys* g*r*ace xvi d. and for mylk and almound*es* for Hubbek*es* and Elyzabeth Frogoll*es* \in all/ … ii s. x d.

Item to the same for money yeven to pore Rauff … v s.

Item in reward to John Collop at Warre … iii s. iiii d.

Item in rewarde yeven to Radclyff wyff of Stampforth and Davy Cecell wyff and Trygg*es* wyff beyng at Colyweston … xx s.

Item paid unto Rog*er* Radclyff for money delyv*er*ed for my lad*ys* offryng at the frerys at Ware … iii s. iiii d.

Item to the same for money yeven to a botman at the same tyme … xx d.

Item paid unto the same for a bottell of muskadyne bought at London for my lad*ys* g*r*ace … xiiii d.

Item payd unto m*aister* chamberlayn for money delyv*er*ed for my lad*ys* offryng to the rode at Huntyngton … xx d.

Item paid to the same for my lad*ys* offryng to a ymage of our*e* Lady standyng in a crosse betwyx Waltham and London … xii d.

Item payd unto Elyzabeth Raundull for cypers bought for my lad*ys* g*r*ace ... iii s. iiii d.

^{M}Summa ... lx s. x d.^{P}

[*p. 21*] Item delyv*er*ed the xxviii day of Aprell unto m*aister* Bekynsall to yeve unto the gray frer*es* of Grenewych ... xx d.

Item the same day delyv*er*ed unto my lad*ys* g*r*ace at hir goyng to my lady Northfolk ... xl s.

Item in reward yeven unto the seller at my lady Northfolk ... x s.

Item in reward yeven unto the kechyn theyr*e* ... x s.

Item to my lad*ys* g*r*ace for money yeven to the ancryse besyd*es* Bethelem ... iii s. iiii d.

Item for my lad*ys* offryng to our*e* Lady of Barkyng ... ii s. vi d.

Item for my lad*ys* offryng t*o* the rode \of/ northe dore ... ii s. vi d.

Item for my lad*ys* offryng to our*e* Lady of g*r*ace at Powlis ... ii s. vi d.

Item paid unto Rob*er*t Merbury for a prem*er* bought for my lad*ys* g*r*ace at London ... ii s. viii d.

Item paid unto m*aister* confessor for money delyv*er*ed unto a suster of my lord marques at Myn*er*es ... vi s. viii d.

J Holt.[39]

Item paid the iii^{de} day of May unto John Holt by his byll assigned for rydyng to Lecet*ur* by the spaice of two dayez \at viii d. the day/ ... xvi d.

Item to the same for ridyng t*o* Moche Petleng by the space of oon day ... viii d.

*W Hylm*er. Item paid the viiith day of May unto William Hylm*er* by his byll assigned for medecynes and other nessesariez bought for my lad*ys* g*r*ace ... xliiii s. ii d.

John fotman. Item paid unto John fotman for buskynce and shoez and reward*es* yeven for appull*es* and t*o* the presoners of Stampforth as aperith by his byll assigned ... v s. x d.

Item payd to m*aister* chaunceller for a reward yeven at Colyweston unto the generall of the quytte freris ... lxvi s. viii d.

^{M}Summa ... x li. xviii s. x d.^{P}

[*p. 22*] *Assheton.*[40] Item payd the ixth day of May unto syr Hughe Assheton for xiiith yerd*es* of fyne blak velvett. P*r*ice the yerde xiii s. iiii d. Summa ... viii li. xiii s. iiii d.

Nota. Item paid unto the same for xxv yerd*es* d. of blake sarsenet. Pryce the yerd iii s. x d. Summa ... <iiii li. xvii s. ix d.> \stet/ <iiii li. xvii s. ix d.>[41]

[39] Bracketed to include the next two items.

[40] MS 'Asshreton', bracketed to include the next four items.

[41] Both sums are the same (although the first may have been altered), both are correct, and both

Item paid to the same for x yerd*es* of course velvett. Pryce the yerd xi s. Summa … Cx s.

Item for xvii[th] yerd*es* and 1 q*u*art*er* blak satan. Price the yerd viii s. Summa … vi li. xviii s.

Item payd for a booke of Scala Perfeccyonis for my lad*ys* g*r*ace … ii s.

Item delyv*er*ed unto my lad*ys* g*r*ace the vth day of May at West*mynster* … xx li.

Assheton.[42] Item payd unto syr Hughe Assheton the vi[th] day of May for money delyv*er*ed <unto> for my lad*ys* offryng apon the Assencion day at Westm*ynster* … v s.

Assheton. Item to the same for a reward yeven unto maistrez Burne … vi s. viii d.

*M*aistrez *Stannop.* Item payd unto maystrez Stannop for a reward yeven unto the p*r*ioris s*er*vand of Depforth … xx d.

Item payd unto m*aister* chaunceller for money yeven unto the byldyng of a chyrche in Kyrton in Holland … xx d.

Myles Worsley. Item in exspenc*e* at Coldherbor*e* and for my botte hyre at suche tyme I receyved money of the receyver syr Hughe Assheton … xii d.[43]

R. Aderton. Item paid to Richard Aderton for his bot hyr to London at ii tymez and for ii dayez lying in London to p*r*ovide of welvett for my lad*ys* g*r*ace … x d.

<*R*eward *yeven to dame Mergaret Pole*>. <Item delyv*er*ed unto my lad*ys* g*r*ace the xii[th] day of May at the Syon in gold \for a reward/ yeven to dame Margaret Pole … xx s.>

[M]Summa … <xlvi li. xvi s. xi d.> \xvii s. ix d./[P44]

[*p. 23*] *J. Holt.* Item payd the xiiii[th] day of May to John Holt for his cost*es* ridyng from Richemound to Colyweston and ayen by iiii dayez \at viii d. day/ … ii s. viii d.

Item the same day delyv*er*ed unto iii monk*es* of the charterhowse at my lad*ys* beying theyre … xiii s. iiii d.

Item to the ancur*e* at the chart*er*howse … iii s. iiii d.

Item in reward yeven to oon Dalton s*er*vande unto my lord Derby for <bryig> bryngyng of <al> appuls to my lad*ys* g*r*ace … xii d.

Item to syr Edward Bothe the xii[th] day of May for half a lib*er* of wax for my lad*ys* g*r*ace … iiii d.

*M*aistrez *Foller.*[45] Item delyv*er*ed unto my lad*ys* g*r*ace the xii day of May by maistrez Wenysowr*e* and maistrez Foler*e* at Syon for reward*es* yeven ther*e* … xl s.

have been cancelled, all in the MW hand. The first is restored by the superscript 'stet', i.e. 'let it stand'. See Plate 14.

[42] Written faint alongside the first of the two Ashton entries bracketed together; the second entry alongside the second item repeats the name in the same hand but darker ink.

[43] Note 'my', 'I'.

[44] The calculation in the MW hand is corrected by another hand.

[45] Bracketed to include the next three items (of four relating to Fowler).

Item paid unto maistrez Foler for a reward yeven unto Mergett Wettnall somtyme kep*er* of my lord*es* place in London … iii s. iiii d.

Item to the same for a reward yeven unto Thomas Symson … iii s. iiii d.

Item to the same for money yeven to maistres Pero*te* … viii d.

Item payd unto John Haryson for ii yerd*es* of whytte bought for my lad*ys* g*r*ace \at iiii d. the yard/ … viii d.

Item in reward to the kep*er* of the deanys place at Wynesowr*e* at my lad*ys* beyng their*e* … v s.

Item delyv*er*ed to m*aister* dean for a reward yeven to the kyng*es* speyr*es* at Wynesowr*e* … vi li. xiii s. iiii d.

Item for the bot hyr*e* of Mylez Worsley from Richmound to London and ayen to Richmounde and for exspenc*e* by ii daiez at London to receyve money of m*aister* receyver for cleppyd grott*es* and to content for dyv*er*se plate bought of John Moundy … ii s.

<l> *My ladys offryng apon Corpus Christi day*. Item for my lad*ys* offryng apon Corpus Chr*ist*i day at Richmound … v s.

Item in reward the same day to a pore woman þ*at* bought peysecodd*es* and poundgarnard … xx d.

Item in reward unto the kyng*es* olde godson the same day … xx s.

[M]Summa … xi li. xv s. viii d.[P]

[*p. 24*] *Velvet*. Item payd the xxi day of May unto syr Hughe Assheton for xii yerd*es* of Lewk*es* welvett. P*r*ice þe yerd xvii s. … x li. iiii s.

Maistres Denton. Item payd the xxii day of May to William Morrant to delyv*er* unto maistrez Denton w*i*th the quene of Skott*es* for her fee … lxvi s. viii d.

John Mondy. Item payd to syr Hughe Assheton for money payd to John Moundy goldsmyth for dyv*er*se plate bought for my lad*ys* g*r*ace ov*er* and besyd*es* c*er*ten brokyn plate which he receyved of the said syr Hughe Assheton … xxxix li. viii s. ob.

Item the xxiii day of May to George Fraunc*es* for a reward yeven to a s*er*vande of Henry Wyett … xx d.

Item payd to William Grevell for ridyng from Richmound to my lord of Rochest*er* to Bromley by a day … viii d.

*Buryez tut*er. Item yeven <in reward> unto Thomas Buryes tuter in the collage of Eyton toward*es* his exibucion … xx s.

Item yeven in reward unto the scolemast*er* of Eyton for teycheng of the said Thomas … iii s. iiii d.

Item the xxiiii day of May in reward to dame Merget Pole … xl s.

Item the same day in reward to maistrez Wynesowr*e* at Syon … xl s.

Item payd unto Alex*ander* de Bruxell*es* for dyv*er*se rynge*s* made by hym for my lad*ys* g*r*ace and for a george. P*r*ice in all … vi li.

Organs bought. Item paid unto syr Ric*hard* Cressall p*r*ior of the new hospitall of our*e* blessyd Lady w*i*thowte Bysshopyate in London for a payr*e* of grett organce standyng in my lad*ys* chappell … C s.

Jane Gowre. Item to Jane Gowre by the hand*es* of John Browne m*aister* coke the xxv day of May … xxvi s. viii d.

[M]Summa … lxx li. xi s. ob.[P]

[*p. 25*] Item payd the furst day of Juyn unto maistrez Stannop for sypres and pynnes bought for my lad*ys* g*r*ace … vii s. Ii d.

Item in reward to Skelman kep*er* of Eltham at my lad*ys* beyng*e* theyr*e* … vi s. viii d.

Item paid for theschaunge of iiii pewter bassynce and for the mendyng of a chaffyng dyssh … ii s. viii d.

*By m*aister *dean*. Item in reward to maistrez Cromeyr*e* … vi s. viii d.

Item in reward unto maist*er* Fabbe and m*aister* Nun felloez of Godd*es* howse in Cambryge … xxvi s. viii d.

Item to Nicholas Coles oon of the <pli> procture*s* of the Arches … x s.

Item to the kep*er* of Richmound p*ar*ke in reward … iii s. iiii d.

To T. Bury. Item to Thom*as* Bury at Wynesowr*e* … xx d.

Item yeven in reward to a woman þ*at* brought cak*es* <v> to my lad*ys* g*r*ace unto my lord of Excet*eres* place … xii d.

Item in reward to m*aister* Baptyst oon of the kyng*es* fecicions … xx s.

Item delyv*er*ed unto syr Edward Bothe for ii westment*es* iii awbis w*ith* theyr*e* apurtynance … liii s. iiii d.

[46]Item in rewarde to the kep*er* of the gardyn at my lorde chamb*er*len at Hampton Corte … iii s. iiii d.

Item in rewarde for a s*er*vant of my lorde of Bokyngham for bryngyng of two buck*es* to Richemound to my lady … vi s. viii d.

Item in rewarde to my lady Cateryn by m*astres* Fowler … iiii li.

Item in rewarde to Mary rydyng by m*astres* Fowler … xl s.

Item delivered to my lad*ys* purce by m*astres* Fowler … iiii li.

Item in rewarde to master chauncellers suster by m*astres* Fowler … xx s.

Item in rewarde to William Hylmers wyffe by m*astres* Fowler … xx s.

Item in rewarde to mastres Crowmer by m*astres* Fowler … vi s. viii d.

[46]The 'curly' hand is responsible for the rest of the entries on p. 25 and also p. 26 (but the totals may be in the MW hand).

Item in rewarde to my lorde prynces norse by m*astres* Fowler … vi s. viii d.

[M]Summa … xviii li. Ii s. vi d.[P]

[*p. 26*] Item in rewarde to[47] Weston the ii^{de} day of June … xx s.

Item paid the same tyme to Ric*hard* Aderton for a wevyng stole xiiii d. for two puppets ii d. for two payer of sheets xvi s. for oon unce of gold iiii s. viii d. for a unce and iii q*u*art*er* of saton sylke ii s. iiii d. for oon unce of saton sylke xvi d. for a unce of webe sylke xi d. for a wevyng frame x d. for a payo*ur* of syssou*rs* and a payo*ur* of sherys iii d. for wyer ii d. for wyer pynnes i d. for a pounde of threde viii d. for half a unce of flat gold iii s. x d. for thre rede skynnes ix d. for a blacke hat iii s. iiii d. for iii dd. bed*es* iii s. for i lib*er* di. of dyv*er*s colerys sylks xxii s. … lxvii s. vi d.

Item paid the same tyme to the said Ric*hard* Ad[e]rton for rydyng from Rychemound to Ware by the space of two days xvi d. Item for rydyng from Rychemound to Ware for my lad*ys* horsys by iii days ii s. for rydyng to Wynso*ur* by ii days xvi d. for his cost*es* in London by iii days xii d. for rydyng from London to Chartsey by oon day viii d. Item for rydyng from Chelsey into Kent and from thens to London by iii days ii s. … viii s. iiii d.

Item paid to the said Ric*hard* Ad[e]rton for a unce of pyrlyng golde iiii s. viii d. for a dd. of nedell*es* iiii d. for ii ell*es* of canvas viii d. for money yevyn to the kyng*es* confessou*r* liii s. iiii d. Item to m*aster* Sygelyn m*aster* of Goddys howse in Cambryge xl s. … iiii li. xix s.

Item yevyn to the chefe juge to my lorde Frowyk my lady Braye and to the Cyon. Fyrst a tonne of claret of wyne. P*rice* iiii li. vi s. viii d. For oon pype of red wyne xl s. For the caryage of a pype viii d. For another tonne of claret wyne lxxiii s. iiii d. For a runlet of malmeset xii s. ii d. Paid for the runlet xiiii d. For barryng sponyng lodyng and caryage of the said wyne xv d. … xii li. x s. ii d.

[M]Summa … xxii li. v s. i d.[P]

[*p. 27*] [48]Item delyv*er*ed to my lad*ys* g*r*ace by syr Edward Bothe at Richmound the ii^{de} day of Juyn … C s.

Item in reward yeven to the pantre … xx s.

Item to the buttre … xx s.

Item to the seller … xx s.

Item to Brant of the p*r*evy seller … vi s. viii d.

Item to the sargant of the seller … xx s.

Item to the kechyn … xxvi s. viii d.

Item to two lardyners … x s.

Item to the squllery and colehowse … x s.

[47] 'to' rep.
[48] The MW hand returns here.

Item to the porters … x s.

Item to the pultre … v s.

Item to the spyc*ery* … vi s. viii d.

Item to Sherley m*aister* clerk of the kechen … xx s.

Item to the wardrop of the bedd*es* … xx s.

Item to Ric*hard* caretaker*e* … v s.

Item to Knoll*es* and <quytyng*e*> \Whytynge/ … xxvi s. viii d.

Item to Rider Rob*er*t Allen and Arnold ysshers of my lady Maries chambr*e* … xl s.

Item to Mathew jugeler by maistrez Stannop … v s. viii d.

Item to maistrez Foller for a reward yeven to maistrez Catysby … xx s.

Item to maistrez W[e]ston[49] by maistrez Foller … vi s. viii d.

Item to Gret Elyzabeth … vi s. viii d.

Item to a monke of Rochest*er* by maistres Foller … vi s. viii d.

Item to a s*er*vand of thabbott*es* of Westm*ynster* for convaying of bedd*es* from Richmound … vi s. viii d.

Item to Ric*hard* Pynson for C prynted book*es*. P*r*ic*e* … x s.

Item to the butteler at <Syon> \charterhowse/ … ii s.

Item delyv*er*ed to Rob*er*t Merbury at Bysshop Hatfeld to delyv*er* to maist*er* Dodley … lxvi s. viii d.

Item yeven to my lord John at Hatfeld … xl s.

Item payd for his horse meyte … iii s. viii d.

[M]Summa … xxvii li. ii s. iiii d.[P]

[*p. 28*] Item payd at maist*er* Conysby place for horse meyt of maist*er* Morris Seynt John … xx d.

Item to a pore woman at Richmound by John Bredd … xii d.

Item the vii[th] day of Juyn to maist*er* <c> Thawytt*es* at Barkley to bye for my lad*ys* g*r*ace at Parr*es* rynge*s* of golde waying oon unce and vi pendent*es* for gyrdels. Summa … iiii li.

Item to maist*er* chaunceller for a reward yeven to maist*er* Reyde tresorer unto my lord prynce … xx s.

Item paid to maist*er* vichamberlayn for money yeven unto the nonnes at <ffo> Soffham … iii s. iiii d.

Item for my lad*ys* offryng at Ihe*s*u Colage … xx d.

[49] -e- lost by a hole in the paper.

Item at Frere Austens for my lad*ys* offryng … xx d.

Item to maistrez Lacy by maistrez Foler in rewarde … vi s. viii d.

Item to oon þ*at* brought lemons and orag*es* at Richemound in reward by maistrez Foler … xx d.

Item to maistrez Perrott by maistrez Foler … iiii d.

Item to maistrez Stannop for a reward yeven to a potycuryez wyff of Cambryge … vi s. viii d.

Item paid unto Hughe Carr*e* for money payd for a booke byndyng at Westm*ynster* … ii d.

Item payd unto Ric*hard* Sherly for a reward yeven unto the blake frer*es* for bryngyng of straberis at Cambryge … iii s. iiii d.

Item to the botmen at Cambryge for convaying of my lad*ys* g*r*ace to the scoles … xx d.

Item in reward unto the waytt*es* at Cambryge … iii s. iiii d.

Item delyv*er*ed the xix day of Juyn to m*aister* Sekelyng m*aister* of Godd*es* howse in Cambryge toward*es* the byldyng of the same howse … <C s.> «quia in computo Jacobi Morez»[50]

Item payd to Ric*hard* Plom*er* for ii elnez of reban bought at Richmound for my lad*ys* g*r*ace … xii d.

Summa … <xi li. <\xi li./>[51] xvii s. vi d.> vi li. xvii s. vi d. [P]

[*p. 29*] [52]Item paid to m*aister* Bessaner the xx^{ti} day of Juyn for carying of a clok from Grenewich to London … viii d.

Item payd to the said m*aister* Bessaner þe said day for an elne white sarsenet. P*r*ice … iiii s. viii d.

Item paid to the said m*aister* Bessaner for money that he paid to Rob*er*t Pynson of London skynner … iiii li. vi s. viii d.

<Item paid to the same for money that he paid to maistres Lynche of London to bestowen[53] stuff for my lad*ys* g*r*ace … <xx li.> «quia postea in diversis parcellis deliberatis per magistram <ss> Lynche»[54]

Item paid to the same for a paire gardivians … x s.

Item paid to the same for carying of iii gardivians w*i*th plaite from London to Richemond … xxii d.

[50] Add. in the 'sprawling' hand.

[51] This has been add. above line to clarify the first 'xj' which is written over an alteration.

[52] Another hand appears to be responsible for this page (the writing of 'Item' and the form of 's.' differ from the MW hand). See too p. 31.

[53] MS 'be stowen'.

[54] 'quia … Lynche' add. in the 'sprawling' hand.

Item paid to the same for money that he paid to John Mundy of London goldsmyth for a george weyt … lxviii s.

Item to the same for makyng of the said george … xx s.

Item to the same for a perle to the said george … iii s. iiii d.

Item to the same for the makyng of a ryng of gold … iii s. iiii d.

Item to the same for the mendyng of a cros of sylver and gylt … x s.

Item to the same for a stewyng pot of silv*er* weis lxxvi uncz iii q*u*art*er* at iii s. x d. þe unce. Summa … xiiii li. xiiii s. i d.

Item to the said maist*er* Bessaner for his cost*es* from Foderynghay to Leycester, Thurcaston, [D]ithesworth, Kegworth for bying of lyffelod … x d.

[M]Summa … <xlv li.> \xxv li./ xii s. vii d.[P]

[*p. 30*] [55]Item delyv*er*ed to m*aister* stuard for money yeven unto Morice Seynt John at his dep*ar*tyng from Fodryngay … vi li. xiii s. iiii d.

Item to the same for money yeven unto Greffeth Donne … xl s.

<Item to Ric*hard* Pynson at Syon by m*aister* chaunceller for a C prynted book*es*> … nichil[56]

Item payd unto m*aister* tresorer for a reward yeven to the kyng*es* fotmen \at Syon/ … xx s.

Item t*o* the same for a reward yeven to William Lowman \at Barkwey/ … x s.

Item for a baskett of wekers and a hangyng lokk bought for my lad*ys* grace … xiii d.

Ancryse of Stampforth. Item delyv*er*ed unto m*aister* Grendell the xxi day of Juyn for a q*u*art[er] wayg*es* for the ancryse of Stampforth from our*e* Lady Day unto mydsom*er*… xxvi s. viii d.

Item paid the xxi day of Juyn to John Haryson for chessemen bought at Richmond … vi d.

Item payd unto Raynold <Davemp<p>ed> \Davemport/ for his cost*es* from Okyng to Richmound wi*th* a buk sende to my lady Mary … ii s.

Item payd unto Jamys Morice for a reward yeven t*o* the p*re*sydent of Stampforth at my lad*ys* dep*ar*tyng from Colyweston … x s.

Item paid unto George Fraunc*es* for money delyv*er*ed for my lad*ys* offryng at Fodryngay to the heghe aut*er* … iii s. iiii d.

Item to the same for money yeven unto the fisshers þ*a*t drew the rev*er* at Fodryngay … xx d.

[M]Summa … xii li. viii s. vii d.[P]

[55] The MW hand returns here.

[56] Add. in the MW hand (nothing here because cited earlier at p. 27).

[*p. 31*] [57]*Hylton.*[58]

Item p*ai*d to Rob*er*t Hilton the xxth day of June for vi yard*es* of blak for coot*es* to the ii litt*er*men … xii s.

Item p*ai*d for ii yard*es* of blak for a sumpter cloth … ii s.

Item yoven to werkmen for makyng of the same … xx d.

Item p*ai*d for i yerd di. of yelow for the same … ii s. vi d.

Item p*ai*d for a q*u*art*er* of blonket for pyk*es* to the same … iii d.

Item p*ai*d for i yerd q*u*art*er* and di. of tawny kersey for a peyr of hoses to John footeman … iii s. ii d. ob.

Item for a yerd and a q*u*art*er* of the same to Henr*y* foteman … ii s. xi d.

Item for makyng and lynyng of the said ii peir*e* hoses … xx d.

Item for a payr of shoes to John footeman … vi d.

Item for a payr of hose to Long Thomas cloth lynyng and makyng … iiii s.

Item for ii peyr of shoos to the same Thomas … xii d.

Item for i payr of hose to Henry footeman clothe makyng and lynyng … iii s. v d.

Item for ii peyr of shoos for the same Henry … xii d.

Item for C di. of pukys. P*ri*c*e* C <u>xvi d</u>. … ii s.

Item for i furre of poot*es* … vi s.

Item for i kyp of blak lambs to my ladies g*r*ace … vi s. viii d.

Item for vii yard*es* of blak cotton whiche made a gowne for a patron to my lady … iii s. vi d.

Item for iiii yerd*es* of fyne blak for my lad*ys* g*r*ace … xxxii s.

Item for vi lettes. P*ri*c*e* the pece iii d. … xviii d.

Item for i yard and i q*u*art*er* of sarsenet for a typpet at <u>iii s. x d.</u> a yard … iiii s. ix d.

Item for iii yard*es* of rybbon. P*ri*c*e* the yerd <u>ii d</u>. … vi d.

Item for a rowle of fyne bokram for my lady … iii s.

Item for a yerd and di. of brode rybbon for a girdill … xvi d. ob.

Item for furryng of a peyr of slevis of a gown … iiii d.

Item for iii yerd*es* of bokerham for lynyng of my ladies pilion … xv d.

Item for whyt twyne and blak thred … viii d.

[57] Perhaps the same hand as p 29 above, or yet another hand ('paid' is abbreviated 'p^{d}').
[58] Bracketed to include all items on this page.

Item p*ai*d for a cloth sake for the wardrop of the bedd*es* … xiiii s.

MSumma … Cxiii s. viii d.P [59]

[*p. 32*] Item p*ai*d for seryng candell*es* … iiii d.

Item p*ai*d for iiii cases to ii bedd*es* w*i*th the hedd*es* to the same … xvi s.

Item p*ai*d for furryng of a kyrtill of damask and a peyr of sleves … xiiii d.

Item p*ai*d for ii yard*es* of bokerham for a case for my ladies cloke at vi d. a yard … xii d.

Item p*ai*d for ii brusshes … x d.

Item p*ai*d for a booke to thuse of the wardrops … x d.

Item p*ai*d for \blak/ cotton whiche lyned my lad*ys* playth of hir mantelet … ii d.

Item p*ai*d for cotton for lynyng of a stomacher to my ladies grace … iii d.

Item p*ai*d for furryng of a kyrtill of blak velwet w*i*th grey poot*es* … viii d.

Item p*ai*d to iiii skynners by the space of iiii days … viii s.

Item p*ai*d to a taylo*ur* to help to sowe my ladies gere by the space of iiii days … xx d.

Item p*ai*d for the boordyng of the same skynn*er*s by iiii days … ii s. viii d.

Item p*ai*d to a taylo*ur* to help to sew maistres Perott*es* gowne and kyrtill … xii d.

Item p*ai*d for a payr of hose for maistres Perot at Rychemond … viii d.

Item for i pare of hose and shoos for Skypp … x d.

Item for a cote cloth for Henry my lad*ys* godson cont*eynyng* ii yerd*es* di. at ii s. a yerd … v s.

Item for makyng of the same … viii d.

Item for i pair of hose cloth makyng and lynyng … xx d.

Item for i payr of shoos for the same Henry … v d.

Item p*ai*d for a shirte for the same Henry … xi d.

Item p*ai*d for a doseyn of poynt*es* for the same Henry … i d.

MSumma … xlvi s. viii d. ob.P [60]

[*p. 33*] [61]Item delyv*er*ed to maistrez Foller the xxii day of Juyn for a reward yeven to Henr*y* Wenstanley and Thomas Forster fottmen … vi s. viii d.

Item paid to Jamys Morice for a reward yeven to maistrez Stannop norse … xx d.

[59] The total is not in the MW hand.
[60] The total is in the MW hand.
[61] The MW hand returns here.

R. Hylton by a byll assigned.[62]

Item paid to Rob*er*t Hylton by his byll assigned for his bourd waig*es* at Grenewyche … xvi d.

Item for bot hyr to London at ii tymes … ii d.

Item for his bourde wayg*es* at Coldherburogh by the space of iiii daiez … xvi d.

Item for his bord waig*es* at London by ii dayez at my lad*ys* being at Richmound … viiid.

Item for his bot hyr*e* from London to Richmound at dyv*er*se tymes w*i*th my lad*ys* stuff … ii d.

*William Hylm*er *by a byll as*signed.[63]

Item paid unto William Hylm*er* the xxii day of Juyn for iii urynall*es* at Braynforth … iiii d.

Item for his bot hyre from Richmond to Coldherboro … xii d.

Item for iii glasse bottell*es* cov*er*et w*i*th leder and for lokk*es* … vi s. viii d.

Item for a panyar to truse theym in … iiii d.

Item for a grett hamp*er* to trusse in dyv*er*se glasses þ*at* were yeven unto your*e* g*r*ace … x d.

Item payd for a padlok and key for the same glass*es* … iiii d.

Item for iii tynne bottell*es* w*i*th vic*es* … xx d.

Item for other ii oon of a pynt viii d. another of a q*u*art xii d. … xx d.

*R. Plom*er. Item paid the xxiiii day of Juyn to Ric*hard* Plom*er* for money by hym payd for the mendyng of my lad*ys* stole … ii d.

*Money payd to m*aister *chaunceller.*[64]

Item in reward to sir Edward Bothe at his goyng to Cambryge by <[…]> chaunceller … xiii s. iiii d.

Item to m*aister* chaunceller for a pardon lett*er* for William Parker*e* … ix d.

[M]Summa … xxxix s. vii d.[P]

[*p. 34*] Item paid the xxv day of Juyne unto Rob*er*t Fremyngham for money yeven unto a pore man þ*at* folloet my lad*ys* lytter at m*aister* Conysby place … xii d.

Item payd to Rob*er*t Hylton the same day for a reward yeven to Mergett Stukeley at my lad*ys* goyng from Colyweston to the kyng … iii s. iiii d.

62 Bracketed to include the next five items.

63 Bracketed to include the next eight items.

64 Bracketed to include the next two items.

*Rob*er*t Merbury*.[65] Item paid unto Rob*er*t Merbury the same day for money paid for the furryng of a payr*e* of buskynce for my lad*ys* g*r*ace … ii s. iiii d.

Item for money payd for the same buskynce … xvi d.

Item for makyng of a payr*e* of buskynce of Spaynessh lether … viii d.

Item for a payr*e* of <pyns> pynsons of the same lether … ii d.

Item for iii payr*e* of slyppers at viii d. a payr*e* … ii s.

Item for a payr*e* of shoez … vi d.

Item for a nell of canvas to trusse hit in … iiii d.

Item <payd> \in reward/ to Thomas Forster of the wardrop of bedd*es* the xxvi day of Juyne … iii s. iiii d.

Brownyng. Item payd the same day to John Brownyng of Burne for a q*u*art*er* endet at mydsom*er* last passid … x s.

*Nicholas Aughton by his byll ass*igned.[66]

Item payd the xxix day of Juyne unto Nicholas Aughton by his byll assigned for his cost*es* ridyng into the north parties to my lord of Yorke, my lord of Duresme and to my lord Clefforth by the space of xiii dayez … viii s. viii d.

Item paid unto the same for a payr*e* of shoez and slyppers for my lad*ys* g*r*ace bought in London … xiiii d.

Item for a pype of golde for a sample … vii d.

Item for a baskett to carry spyc*es* in which were send my lad*ys* g*r*ace … iii d.

Item for ridyng to the kyng at Candelmasse by <vi> x dayez … vi s. viii d.

[M]Summa … xlii s. iiii d.[P]

[*p. 35*] *Nich*olas *Aughton by his byll ass*igned.[67]

Item payd unto the said Nicholas by his said byll assigned for ridyng to the p*r*ior of the Charterhowse besyd*es* Richmound by vi dayez … iiii s.

Item to the same for ridyng unto Cambryge for the felloez of Godd*es* howse by iii dayez … ii s.

Item for the hyre of a man for to seche for oon of the same felloez … xvi d.

Item for the carryage of viii fetherbedd*es* from Westm*ynster* unto Grenewyche … xvi d.

Summa … xxvi s.[68]

[65] Bracketed to include the next seven items.

[66] Bracketed to include the next five items (but continues on p. 35).

[67] Bracketed to include the next four items.

[68] The total of the Aughton payments pp. 34–5, written in the MW hand in the left margin below 'Nicholas … assigned'.

Item the xxix day of Juyne in reward unto *Master* Sapcott*es* prest for bryngyng of rosis to my lad*ys* g*r*ace at dyv*er*se tymez … v s.

*Rob*er*t Dey*. Item payd the xxix day of Juyne to Rob*er*t Dey coke for a <p*ar*te w> half yere waig*es* endet at mydsom*er* last passid <aft> ov*er* xls. yeven to hym by the yer*e* of household wayg*es* … xiii s. iiii d.

M*aister Sekelyng* m*aister of Godd*es *howse*. Item delyv*er*ed to Jamys Morice to delyv*er* unto <the> m*aister* Syklyng maist*er* of Godd*es* howse in Cambryge toward*es* the byldyng*e* of the same delyv*er*ed the xxii day of Juyne … <lxvi li. xiii s. iiii d.> «cancellatur quia allocatur in computo Jacobi Morres»[69]

Summa … lxviii li. iiii d.[70] Item paid to the bayle of Fodryngay for the exspenc*e* of the bysshop of Morreys horsis and his s*er*vand*es* \xxiii horsis/ … vi s. x d.

Item payd unto Richard Aderton for his cost*es* ridyng*e* to make serche for Crystofer Richartson by the spaice of iii dayez … ii s.

Item payd unto the same for ridyng*e* to Lyncolne withe William Parker for hymself and iii p*er*sons by iiii dayes xiiii s. viii d. and for diett of Parker viii d. and for wachyng*e* of hym viii d. … xvi s.

Item for the hyr*e* of his horse and meyte to the same horse by the said space … ii s. viii d.

Item to the gaylo*ur* for receyvyng hym ii d. and for corde ii d. … iiii d.

Item payd unto the same Richard for iii pec*es* of blew bokeram by hym bought at London … xv s.

[M]Summa … <lxx li. iii s. ii d.> lxix s. x d.[71]

[*p. 36*] Item payd the vith day of July unto Ric*hard* Aderton by his byll assigned for ii pec*es* of blew bokeram … ix s.

Item paid to the same for i pece of grene bokeram … iiii s. vi d.

Item paid for a pounde of golde of Wennes … xxii s.

Item paid unto the [*blank*] for a frenge bought by Ric*hard* Stukeley … ii s.

Item paid for iiii lib. of threde … iii s. iiii d.

Item paid for the dyeing*e* of vi lib. yerne of dyv*er*se colores … ii s.

Item for a gallon of malvessey and a gallon of romney … ii s.

Item for a pottell of moscadyne … viii d.

Item for a ellne of canvas to trusse stuff … iiii d.

Item paid unto the same for his bot hyr from London to Syon … vi d.

[69] Written small in the 'sprawling' hand in the right margin above the canc. total.
[70] Written in the MW hand in the left margin at the start of the item (but perhaps relevant to the previous item).
[71] The new total (not marked 'probatur' and not in the MW hand) reflects the removal of the Syclyng payment above.

Item for a reward yeven to m*aister* Conysby s*er*vande that were gyd*es* for my lad*ys* g*r*ace unto Bysshop Hatfeld … xx d.

Item paid to the same Richard for a day lying in London … iiii d.

Item payd the vii[th] day of July unto maistrez Foller for a reward yeven unto a prest of the collage at <Tat> Fodryngay for styllyng of watters for my lad*ys* g*r*ace … v s.

Item delyv*er*ed unto m*aister* dean for a reward yeven to the gentylmen of the chappell toward*es* the dyteng of a buk yeven to theym by my lad*ys* g*r*ace … xx s.

Item in reward yeven to Laurence Cotton brother unto syr Rob*er*t Cotton knyght … iii s. iiii d.

Item delyv*er*ed unto maistrez Foller for a <Re> reward yeven to maistrez Seynt Johens nurse … iii s. iiii d.

[M] Summa … <iiii> iiii li.[P]

[*p. 37*] Item the vii[th] day of July delyv*er*ed unto maistrez Foller for a reward yeven to a gentylwoman that dwellis in m*aister* Sapcott*es* place þ*at* brought rosis and rose wat*er*ez … vi s. viii d.

Item yeven in reward to John Carter s*er*vand unto m*aister* chaunceller for copying of the statut*es* of Godd*es* howse in Cambryge … xx d.

Item payd unto Jamys Morice the xi[th] day of July for money paid at Colyweston for the exspenc*e* of the bysshop of Chichest*er* and syr Gryffith Rice for theyr*e* horse meyt at my lad*ys* beyng their … xvii s. vi d.

Item to the same for a reward yeven to a s*er*vant of m*aister* Benyfeld for bryngyng of a cast of lanners … v s.

Relyk Sonday offrynges. Item for my lad*ys* offryng apon Relyk Sonday … ii s. vi d.

Item delyv*er*ed unto maistrez Foler for money yeven to maistrez Cursson at hyr beyng at Fod\r/yngay … xx s.

Gray freris of Stampforth. Item to the warden of the gray frerys of Stampforth the xiii day of July … xiii s. iiii d.

*Bysshop of Chechest*er. Item paid unto the bayle of Fodryngay for the bysshop of Chechest*er* horse meyte by iiii daiez … xv s. x d.

Gray freris of Boston. Item delyv*er*ed unto Ric*hard* Bothe for money yeven unto the gray frerys of Boston the xv day of July … xiii s. iiii d.

Item in wyne and ale spent at Bayles at the asurement of Nicholas Treverne and Jane Laxam … ix d.

M*aister Grendyll.*[72] Item paid unto m*aister* Grendyll the xviii day of July for money paid unto a goldsmyth of Stampforthe for new makyng and gyldyng of a brokyn salt … iii s. iiii d.

[72] Bracketed to include the next three items.

Item paid to the same for the mendyng of a broken crucifex and a brokyn candylstyk … xii d.

Item paid unto the same for new makyng and gyldyng of oon other brokyn salt the v day of July … iiii s.

Item paid unto m*aister* Morgan for a reward yeven unto a chappleyn of my lorde of Rochest*er* at Colyweston … vi s. viii d.

^{M}Summa … Cxi s. vii d.^{P}

[*p. 38*] *Lenard.*[73]

Item payd unto Lenard of the vestery the xixth day of July for vi doss*en* parchement skynnez at ii s. a <pece> doss*en* … xii s.

Item unto the same for iii skynnes of bukk*es* lether. P*r*ice … iiii s. viii d.

Item the xx^{ti} day of July to William Luffe in reward … iii s. iiii d.

Item paid the xxiii day of July for the cost*es* of my lord of Derbyes horsis beyng in Fodryngay for lxxx horsis … liii s. viii d.

Item paid the xxvith day of July unto Richard Aderton for ridyng from Fodryngay unto London by the spaice of viii daiez <… > goyng and comyng … v s. iiii d.

Item to the same for his cost*es* ridyng for Nicholas of the wardrop wyff by a day … viii d.

Item paid to m*aister* countroller for a reward yeven to m*aister* William Malam on of the maistres of the chauncery for his <c> horse meyte … vi s. viii d.

Item to maistrez Stannop for a reward yeven unto Lenard of the vestry for byndyng of bok*es* … iii s. iiii d.

Item delyv*er*ed to my lad*ys* g*r*ace the xxvii day of July for hir almes purse … xiii li. vi s. viii d.

Item in reward to Richard Flecchers wyff … iii s. iiii d.

Item to William of the chaundry wyff in rewarde … iii s. iiii d.

Nota. Item the xxviiith day of July to the kep*er* of the p*a*rke at m*aister* chamberlayns place at my lad*ys* beyng ther*e* … v s.

Item paid the same day to syr Rob*er*t Brewer prest for money by hym paid for exibucion of Thomas Pellett at suche tyme he was w*i*th m*aister* Feldyng as <by> aperith by a byll … vi s. iiii d. ob.

^{M}Summa … xviii li. xiiii s. iiii d. ob.^{P}

[*p. 39*] *Nota.* Item paid to Annes Tuk of Dodyngton the furst day of August for the bourde of iii chylder þ*a*t be kepyd of almes by xiii wek*es* and iiii daiez at xviii d. a weke at xii d. the iiii daiez … xx<i> s. vi d.

[73] Bracketed to include the next two items.

Item paid to the same for iii payr*e* of shoez … ix d.

Item for clowtyng of theyme … iiii d.

Item for shavyng of theyr*e* hedd*es* … i d.

Item for theyr*e* scole hyr*e* the same space … xii d.

Item delyv*er*ed to m*aister* dean for money yeven unto m*aister* Brutnell the iii^{de} day of August … lxvi s. viii d.

Item to the same for money yeven unto Kyrkam the same tyme … xl s. iiii d.

Item paid to m*aister* vichamberlayn for a reward yeven unto a s*er*vand of my lord Derbyez þ*at* delyv*er*ed a horse yeven to my lad*ys* g*r*ace … x s.

Item paid unto maistres Massy by hir byll assigned for dyv*er*se stuff bought for my lad*ys* g*r*ace the iii^{de} day of August at Fodryngay … xvii s. x d.

Item paid to m*aister* Morgan for a reward yeven to the p*ar*son of Seynt Mychaell*es* for styllyng of aquavite for my lad*ys* g*r*ace … v s.

Item delyv*er*ed unto the subdean for a reward yeven unto oon Cotterell m*aister* of the chylder of Fodryngay Colage for prykkyng of m*aister* Bell*es* masse … vi s. viii d.

Nichil <Item for a reward yeven by maistres Stannop to Lenard for byndyng of book*es* for my lad*ys* g*r*ace … iii s. iiii d.> nichil[74]

Item yeven in reward to a s*er*vande of m*aister* Wittylburyes for the bryngyng of x quayles unto my <a> lady … viii d.

Item delyv*er*ed unto maistres Foller*e* at Bassyngburne to yeve in reward unto m*aister* vichamberlayns wyffe at my lad*ys* beying theyr*e* … xl s.

[M]Summa … x li. ix s. x d.[P]

[*p. 40*] *M*aister *chaunceller*.[75]

Item paid unto m*aister* chaunceller for money yeven unto m*aister* Brednell for his cost*es* rydyng from his place besyd*es* Lyddyngton to my lord Grey Welton and from thens to London and Croydon and to London and eftsones to Croydon … liii s. iiii d.

Item paid to the same for money paid unto Pynson stacionary for a messe booke inprynted[76] in velom … lx s.

Item payd unto the same for a premer for my lad*ys* g*r*ace … xii d.

Item paid unto the same for money paid the xxvi day of July unto the maister of gramer at Tatsall for the exspenc*e* of John Masson … xix s. iiii d. ob.

*George Fraunc*es. Item paid unto George Fraunc*es* for money delyv*er*ed for my ladies offryng at the freris at Warre … xx d.

[74] 'nichil' add. faint in the MW hand in the left margin and also after the cancellation because already dealt with p. 38.
[75] Bracketed to include the next four items.
[76] MS 'in prynted'.

Item delyv*er*ed for my lad*ys* offryng to oure Lady of Pew at Westm*ynster* … ii s. vi d.

Item to Seynt Edmond*es* shryne in the abbey church … ii s. vi d.

Item in reward to oon of the gromes of the vestry v*i*th the kyng at Westm*ynster* … xii d.

Item yeven in reward unto oon Vertue oon of the m*aister* masson of the kyng*es* werk*es* at Westm*ynster* … x s.

*M*aister *Frognoll*es. Item delyv*er*ed at Lambeth to Holt for exspenc*e* of m*aister* Frognoll beyng hurt at London … xl s.

Nota. Item in reward unto the kep*er* of the kyng*es* place at Westm*ynster* … <xx s.> xx d.

*M*aister *vichamberlayn*.[77]

Item paid unto m*aister* Lynne vichamberlayn for a reward yeven unto the prokturs s*er*vand of Cambryge … xx d.

Item to the abbot of Westm*ynster* <s*er*vande> stuard in reward … vi s. viii d.

Item to the kep*er* of his chamber in reward … vi s. viii d.

Item to the buttelers … vi s. viii d.

Item to a pore man of Marton Colage … xii d.

Item to a s*er*vande of syr William Parkers in reward for a booke brought to m*aister* Lynnes at Bassyngburne … iii s. iiii d.

[M]Summa … <xi li. xvii s. iiii d. ob.> x li. xix s. ob.[P 78]

[*p. 41*] Item paid unto m*aister* Lynne the vichamberlayn for a reward yeven unto syr Parr*es* prest of Cambryge … iii s. iiii d.

Item paid to Ric*hard* Aderton for a reward yeven unto m*aistres* Seynt Johnez nurse at Fodryngay … xx d.

Item paid unto John Mondy goldsmyth for makyng of a chall*es* of golde weying xxxviii unce iii q*u*art[er]. P*r*ice the unce <u>iii s. vi d.</u> Summa … viii li. xiiii s. iiii d. ob.

Item in reward unto a s*er*vande of my lady Mary at Croydon the <xv> <x> xviii day of August … iii s. iiii d.

Item for my lad*ys* offryng to our*e* Lady at Crome apon our*e* Lad*ys* Even … xx d.

Item for my lad*ys* offryng apon our*e* Lady Day … v s.

*M*aister *Ride oon of the kyng*es *justice*. Item payd the <x> xix day of August for the exspenc*e* of m*aister* Ryde justice of the kyng*es* benche for vi horsis beying at the George in Croydon <u>xii d.</u> and for his s*er*vand*es* diett*es* <u>iiii d.</u> … xvi d.

[77] Bracketed to include the next six items.

[78] Corrected in the same ink as 'probatur' (probably in the 'sprawling' hand).

Hylton.[79] Item payd the <x> xix[th] day of August unto Rob*er*t Hylton for vi yerd*es* of tawny clothe for kyng John … iiii s. i d.

Item paid for vi yerd*es* of lynyng to the same … ii s.

Item paid for a payr*e* of shoez to the same … vi d.

Item paid for v yerd*es* for a cote to Henry the kyng*es* godson … iii s. ix d.

Item payd for a payr*e* of hoose to the same Henry … xviii d.

Item payd for a payr*e* of shoez to the same … vi d.

Item payd for a bonett to the same … xiiii d.

Item <pa>[80] payd for a elne of canvas for his doblett … ii d. ob.

Item payd for di. elne of canvas for lynyng of the same doblet … ii d. ob.

Item for a yerd of whitt cotton to the same … vii d.

Item for the makyng of the same doblett … vi d.

[M]Summa … x li. v s. xi d.[P]

[*p. 42*] Item paid the xix[th] day of August to Rob*er*t Hylton for his cost*es* by oon day at Colyweston in fochyng of the stuff of the wardrop … iiii d.

Item for a cart to carye the same stuff … xii d.

Item payd for his cost*es* for waytyng apon the stuff to Huntyngton by iii daiez … iii s.

Item for ii payr*e* of hoose to the ii fotmen w*i*th clothe makyng and lynyng … vii s. vi d.

Item for ii payr*e* of shoez to the same … xii d.

Item payd for a payr*e* of startupp*es* to Skyppe … xii d.

Item payd for two yerd*es* iii q*uarter* of blak for a cote for Willia*m* Laborer. P*r*ice the yerd <u>ii s</u>. … v s. vi d.

Item payd for makyng the same cote … vi d.

Item paid for v payr*e* of shoez for the almesmen. P*r*ice the payr*e* <u>vi d</u>. … ii s. vi d.

Item payd for vii payr*e* of shoez for the almeswomen. P*r*ice the payre <u>iiii d</u>. … ii s. iiii d.

Item payd for iiii payr*e* of hoose for the almeswomen … xvi d.

Item paid for helpyng to sowe xi gownes and xi payr*e* of hoose for the chyldren of the chappell … iii s.

Item paid unto m*aister* Grendell for the mendyng of a flagon at Stampforth … xx d.

[79] Written very lightly in the margin and bracketed to include all the next items relating to Hilton up to and including the twelfth item on p. 42.
[80] Obscured by an ink blot.

Item paid unto Rob*er*t Hylton for dressyng and dying of two gownes of m*aistres* Pott*es* … xvi d.

Item paid to maistres Merbury the xxi day of August for mylk bought for yonge maistres Parker*e* by the way from Fodryngay … v d.

MSumma … xxxii s. v d.P

[*p. 43*] Item paid unto the same maistres Merbury for a hayndeyrne … iiii d.

Item for a <Co> bonett … iii d.

Item for a panell and storropp*es* and gerth for the woman þ*a*t <Ch> carryet the chyld … ii s. ii d.

Item for the hyr*e* of a man and a horse to awayte apon theym … iiii s. vi d.

Item for baytyng*es* and other nessessaries by the way payd by the said maistres Merbury … ii s.

Item delyv*er*ed for a reward yeven unto maistrez Rede toward*es* hyr cost*es* from Fodryngay to Croydon and ayen to Boston … xx s.

Item paid unto R*ichard* Aderton for money yeven toward*es* the makyng of the stepull at Richmond … xii d.

Item paid unto Engulbred bookeseller for two messe book*es* inprynted[81] in vellem. P*r*ice … Cvi s. viii d.

In reward to the kyng*es* plaiers at Croydon the xxii day of August … vi s. viii d.

MSumma … vii li. iii s. vii d.[82]

Item paid unto Olyv*er* Lowthe the xxvi day of August for the charg*es* of the kepyng of a cast of hawkes yeven by m*aister* Benyfeld unto my lad*ys* g*r*ace … v s. viii d. ob.

Item in reward unto a s*er*vande of my lady Man*er*es for bryngyng a glasse of damask wat*er* … xx d.

Item paid unto m*aister* vichamberlayn for the cost*es* of my lady Dawbeneys s*er*vand*es* and hir horsis … iiii s. i d.

Summa … xi s. v d. ob.P [83]

Summa partis … vii li. xv s. ob.P

[*p. 44*] Item payd unto Nicholas Aughton the xxvi day of August for his cost*es* ridyng from Fodryngay unto Lyncoln aft*er* m*aister* Conysby with the kyng*es* lett*ur* by iiii daiez … ii s. viii d.

Item paid to the same for his cost*es* rydyng from Croydon to the kyng into the New Forest and ayen by vi daiez comyng and goyng … iiii s.

[81] MS 'in prynted'.
[82] The total thus far on the page, signed and approved.
[83] The total in the MW hand of the three items since the last 'Summa', followed by the total for the page in a different hand.

Item paid to the same for money yeven to a caryer for convaying of an hert yeven by the kyng to my lad*ys* g*r*ace from the New Forest to Sowthehampton … xvi d.

Item paid to the same for the hyr*e* of a man and ii horsis w*i*th his diett to convay the said hert from Sowthehampton to Croydon … x s. viii d.

Item the xxviii day of August in reward to the kep*er* of my lord of Rochest*er* parke at Bromley at my lad*ys* beyng theyr*e* … vi s. viii d.

Item to my lord Rochest*er* s*er*vant*es* delyv*er*ed to his receyver the same tyme … xx s.

*M*aister *amener*. Item payd unto m*aister* amener the iii^{de} day of Septemb*er* by a byll assigned for money yeven in almes to pore folk*es* at sondry tymes … lxvii s. vii d.

<Item delyv*er*ed to m*aister* Sop*er* solicit*ur* <unto> for my lad*ys* g*r*ace by the hand*es* of Nicholas Saunders the xxiii day of Juyne at ii tymes for wrytyng*es* had furth of the chauncery … xx li.> «cancellatur hic quia allocatur postea inter parcellas dicti Thome»[84]

*M*aister *Bell of F.* Item paid unto Nicholas Saunders for mone paid by m*aister* chauncelle[r][85] unto m*aister* Bell of Fodryngay for a quart*er* waig*es* endet at Mychelmasse next comyng … xxv s.

^{M}Summa … <xxvi li. xix s. iiii d. ob.>

vi li. vii s. xi d.^{P}[86]

[*p. 45*] Item payd the xx^{ti} day of Septemb*er* unto m*aister* Gryndell for money delyv*er*ed by my lad*ys* g*r*ace for the beryall of maistrez Markam … viii s.

Item delyv*er*ed unto maistrez Foller the xxiiii day of Septemb*er* for money yeven unto maistrez Massy for the almes <ffoll> folke … vi s. viii d.

Item paid the same day unto Jamys Morice for money yeven unto the ancryes of Stampforth … xx s.

Item to the same for money yeven unto the ancryes at the nonnes … ii s.

Item paid unto the same for money payd for the cost*es* of Lady Norton at Croydon … vi s.

T. Symson.[87]

Item payd to Thomas Symson for vii yerd*es* i q*uarter* of blak. P*r*ice the yerd iii s. x d. … xxvii s. ix d. ob.

Item for iii yerd*es* of stamyn. P*r*ice the yerd ii s. ii d. … vi s. vi d.

Item for a yerd q*uarter* of blak kersey. P*r*ice the yerd xxii d. … ii s. vi d.

Item for viii tavelyns of blak shank*es*. P*r*ice <ii d. ob.> … ii s.

[84] Add. in the 'sprawling' hand; canc. because noted at p. 67 below.

[85] -r lost by a wormhole in the paper.

[86] The first total is in the MW hand but does not allow for the canc. entry for £20; the second (correct) total is preceded by an ink blot (to delete 'xx'?).

[87] Bracketed to include the next six items.

Item for xxiiii yerd*es* <of> and a half of blak cotton. P*r*ice the yerd <u>v d. ob.</u> … xi s. ii d. ob. qua.

Item for ii yerd*es* of <quyte> whyte cotton. P*r*ice the yerd <u>vi d.</u> Summa … xii d.

Item for a payr*e* of ho<o>se to kyng John … vii d.

Item for a payr*e* of hose and a payr*e* shoez for maistrez Perrot … xvi d.

Item for a payr*e* of shoez for oon of the almes wemen … iiii d.

Item for caryage of the same stuff from London to Croydon … ii d.

Item payd for the cost*es* of the same at London … viii d.

Item payd unto Nicholas Saunders for money payd unto Bonyface Stanley for the helyng of maistrez Frognoll … vi s. viii d.

[M]Summa … Ciii s. v d. qua.[P]

[*p. 46*] Item the xxix day of Septemb*er* delyv*er*ed to maistres Foler for a reward yeven unto Ric*hard* Stukeley … v s.

*Rob*er*t Dey*. Item payd the last day of Septemb*er* to Rob*er*t Day coke for a q*uart*er endet at Michaelmas … vi s. viii d.

Item payd unto Henry Wynstanley for the cost*es* of Skyp and pore Rauff from Fodryngay to Croydon by his byll assigned … xii d.

Item for a payr*e* of shoes to Rauff … vi d.

Item for a payr*e* of hoose and a payre of shoes to Skyp … xii d.

Item payd unto m*aister* chaunceller for money yeven unto m*aister* vichamberlayn the iiiith day of Septemb*er* … xl s.

Item payd unto the same for money delyv*er*ed for my lad*ys* offryng unto Seynt Bregett at Syon … xii d.

Item paid unto maistres Foller for a reward yeven unto Thomas Williams wyff of Stampforth … v s.

Item to the same for a reward yeven unto Fllyntt*es* wyff of Colyweston … xx d.

Item to the same for money delyv*er*ed unto my lad*ys* g*r*ace the xxvii day of August … xiii s. iiii d.

Item payd unto George Fraunc*es* for money delyv*er*ed for my lad*ys* offryng at Bromley … xii d.

Item paid unto Raynold Davenport for ii dayes rydyng to London <u>xvi d.</u> and for ii daies ridyng to Richmound to my lady Mary <u>xvi d.</u> … ii s. viii d.

Item paid unto John Kemyas for a reban bought at Richmound for my lad*ys* g*r*ace … iiii d.

[M]Summa … lxxix s. ii d.[P]

[*p. 47*] Item paid unto m*aister* Grendell for money payd for the mendyng of my lad*ys* lytell clokke the ix day of Septembre ... x s.

Item for my lad*ys* offryng apon our*e* Lady Day ... v s.

N. Aughton. Item payd unto Nicholas Aughton for ridyng to the kyng unto Campforth from Croydon \at viii d. the day/ by ix daiez ... vi s.

Item payd unto m*aister* Morgan for a pound of gyng*er* ii s. viii d. for setwall xvi d. ... iiii s.

B. Stanley. Item payd unto Bonyface Stanley in p*ar*tie of payment for the heylyng of m*aister* Frognoll ... xx s.

Item paid unto maistrez Stannop for a reward yeven unto maist*res* Markham nurse ... iii s. iiii d.

Item paid for the exspenc*e* of the popes collectur*e* horsis and his s*er*vand*es* at Croydon ... ii s.

Item payd unto maistres Foller for a reward yeven to the mydwyff þ*a*t was w*i*th maistres Markam ... x s.

Item to the same for a reward yeven unto m*aister* Whitamor*e* ... vi s. viii d.

Item to the same for Mergett Walshe in reward ... iii s. iiii d.

Item to maistres Merbury for suche thyng*es* as shall belong to maistres P*ar*ker beyng at bourd waig*es* ... iii s. iiii d.

Item paid unto m*aister* countroller for the exspenc*e* of his <... > horsis at London at shuche tyme he payd money unto m*aister* Collett ... ii s. x d. ob.

Item payd unto syr Edward Bothe for suche money as he payd unto Thurstane brotherar of London for vi yerd*es* of whit satten. P*r*ice the yerd ii s. viii d. For vestment*es* in the same xx flowr*es*. P*r*ice the pec*e* vi d. Item for vi yerd*es* of bukkeram. P*r*ice the yerd iiii d. A frenge. P*r*ice ii s. The makyng. iii s. iiii d. Summa ... xxxiii s. iiii d.

[M]Summa ... Cix s. <iiii d.> \<... > x d./ ob.[P]

[*p. 48*] Item in reward yeven unto m*aistres* Werney comyng from Skotland to Halyng the xvi day of Septemb*er* ... vi s. viii d.

Item paid unto Nicholas Aughton for v daies rydyng unto the kyng to Craneburne and for the hyr*e* of a gyde from <wyic> Wynchest*er* to Fournyng Brygg*es* ... iiii s.

[M]Summa ... x s. viii d.[P][88]

The ankuryse of the nonnes of Stampforth. Item paid unto the ancryse at the nonnys of Stampforth the xiiii day of Octob*er* for a half yer*es* to be ended at Crystemas next to come ... lxvi s. viii d.

The ancryse of Stampforth. Item the same tyme delyv*er*ed unto the ancryse of Stampforth in reward ... iii s. iiii d.

[88] The total of the first two items.

Item paid unto m*aister* chaunceller for money yeven unto the lady Gray the xxiii day of Octobr*e* … xx s.

Item the xxvi day of Octobr*e* in reward to Sherly s*er*vande m*aister* clark of the kychen w*i*th the kyng þ*at* brought a lett*er* of suche p*er*sons as shuld come w*i*th the kyng to Haylyng … xii d.

Item paid unto Jamys Morice for money delyv*er*ed to my lad*ys* g*r*ace the same day … xix s. v d.

Item delyv*er*ed unto George Fraunc*es* for a reward yeven unto Weston s*er*vand … iii s. iiii d.

Item the xxix day of Octobr*e* delyv*er*ed unto my ladies g*r*ace to <you>[89] yeve in reward*es* at the kyng*es* beyng at Haylyng … lxxiii s. iiii d.

Item yeven in reward unto the <wache> garde þ*at* kept wache ii nyght*es* … xx s.

Item to Nicholas Clyff of the pantre … vi s. viii d.

[M]Summa … x li. xiii s. ix d.[P][90]

Summa partis … xi li. <v s.> \iiii s./ v d.[P]

[*p. 49*] Item to Brante and Vater*e* of the seller … xiii s. iiii d.

Item to Meryman of the kechyn … vi s. viii d.

Item to the kyng*es* fotmen … vi s. viii d.

*M*aister *Seynt John and his wyff*es *bourdes and his* ser*vand*es. Item paid unto m*aister* John Seynt John for the bourde of <his> hymself \xx d./ his wyff \xx d./ and ii s*er*vand*es* \ii s./ by the space of iiii wek*es* endyng the iiii day of Octobr*e* … <xv s. vi d.> xxi s. iiii d.

Item payd for ii pyrlyng whelis bought at Croydon … iii s. iiii d.

*Money paid unto Jamys Morice for reward*es *yeven at Blechyng Ley*. Item paid unto Jamys Moric*e* for a reward yeven to the kep*er* of the place at Blechyng Leghe … iii s. iiii d.

Item t*o* the same for a reward yeven to the workmen … iii s. iiii d.

Item to the kep*er* of the park … xii d.

Item to the keper of the garden … viii d.

Item to Rob*er*t Olyv*er* for a frame bedd for my lad*ys* g*r*ace paid by the hand*es* of Jamys Morice … xxxiii s. iiii d.

Item paid unto Raynold Davenport for ridyng to Knoll i day and ii dayes ridyng to <Richch> Richmound and to the bysshop of London … iii s.

[89] Perhaps an initial writing of 'youe', i.e. a variant form of 'yeue', to give (<u> normalised here in 'yeve').

[90] The total of the remaining items on the page in the MW hand, followed by the total for the page in a different hand.

*Money paid unto John Holt by by his byll assigned for ridyng to dyverse plac*es. Item paid unto John Holt for ridyng to Westm*ynster* to m*aster* presydent a day viii d. Item a day ridyng to my lord of Caunterburyez viii d. for ridyng to the court by <by> v daies iii s. iiii d. and for ridyng to Pensers by ii daiez xvi d. and for the hyre of a hors by <a> iiii viii d. … vi s. viii d.

*Paid unto Nich*olas *Saunders*. Item paid unto Olyv*er* Lowthe for goyng unto Calyce for hawk*es* … xx s.

Item in reward to a s*er*vand of m*aster* Dudleys by maistres Foller … iii s. iiii d.

Item in reward to doct*ur* Atkynson by maistres Foller … vi s. viii d.

Conysby. Item delyv*er*ed to Reynold Davenport for a day ridyng to Richmound the xxi day of Octobr*e* … xii d.

[M]Summa … <ix li. xiii s. vi d.> <\iiii d./> \Summa … x li. iiii d./[P]

[*p. 50*] Item the last day of Octobr*e* delyv*er*ed to maistres Foler for a reward yeven unto William Love … iii s. iiii d.

Item t*o* the same for a reward yeven unto Weston the kyng*es* s*er*vande … xx s.

*Rob*ert *Merbury*. Item paid unto Rob*er*t Merbury for ridyng unto the kyng*es* councell at Redyng \at xiii d. the day/ by viii dayez … viii s.

<*Money delyv*ere*d by m*aister *tresorer to my lady*s *solicit*ur *on a rekenyng*. Item delyv*er*ed t*o* my lad*ys* solicit*ur* apon a rekenyng by m*aister* tresorer … iiii li.> «cancellatur hic quia allocatur postea inter parcellas»[91]

Item paid the last day of Octobr*e* unto Rob*er*t Olyv*er* of Wynesour*e* for a bedde makyng for my lad*ys* grace … xxxiii s. iiii d.

Bourder.[92] Item in reward to on Mathew <a serva> a s*er*vand of the kyng*es* \at Haylynge/ … iii s. iiii d.

*M*aister *J. Seynt John bourde his wyff*es *and his s*er*vand*es. Item paid unto m*aister* John Seynt John for his bourde at xx d. the weke for his wyffes xx d. and for ii of his s*er*vand*es* at ii s. the weke by the space of iiii wek*es* endyd the furst day of Novembr*e* … <xvi s. vi d.> xxi s. iiii d.

*My lady*s *offryng apon Halhallo day*.[93]

Item for my lad*ys* offryng apon Alhallo day … v s.

Item for my lad*ys* offryng at our*e* Lady of Crome paid unto m*aister* confessor … <v s.> v d.

*Satten yeven unto my lord chamberlayns son bought by Rob*ert *Hylton.*

Nota.

[91] Add. in the 'sprawling' hand; canc. because noted at p. 4 above (it is not found at p. 67 with the collected payments to Soper).

[92] Written very small in a different hand from the MW hand responsible for the other marginalia.

[93] Bracketed to include the next two items.

Item payd unto Rob*er*t Hylton the ii^{de} day of Novembr for vii yerd*es* of russet satten which was yeven to my lord chamberlayn son. \Pryce the yard vi s./ … xlii s.

Item paid for iii unce of tawny sylk. P*r*ice the unc*e* x d. … ii s. vi d.

Item for a bonet for my lad*ys* g*r*ace bought by the same … xv s. viii d.

Item paid for xii ell*es* of lynnen clothe. Pryse the ell xiiii d. … xiiii s.

Item for xii skynnes of blak bogie … xii s.

Item paid for a cart to carry c*er*ten clothes and cotton from London to Croydon … xiiii d.

Hylton.[94]

Item paid for a pece of tawny kersey cont*eynyng* xviii yerd*es* \at xxiii d. ob. þe yard/ … xxxv s.

^{M}Summa … <xvi li. xvi s. i d.> <xiiii li. xviiii s. i d. > x li. xviii s. i d.^{P}[95]

[*p. 51*] Item paid the ii^{de} day of Novembr*e* unto Rob*er*t Hylton for money by hym paid for the sheyryng of a pece of tawny medly cont*eynyng* xviii yerd*es* … ii s.

Item paid unto the same for v yerd*es* of tawny medly at vi s. iiii d. the yerd. Summa … xxxi s. viii d.

Item for iiii yerd*es* of tawny medley at iiii s. viii d. … xviii s. viii d.

Item for iii yerd*es* and i q*u*art*er* of medely. The yerd iiii s. viii d. … xv s.ii d.

Item for viii cyppe of blak bogie. P*r*ice of ev*er* cipp xii s. vi d. … C s.

Item paid for the cost*es* of the same Rob*er*t at London to p*ro*vide for the same stuff \ at xii d. the day/ by iiii daiez … iiii s.

Item paid to the same Rob*er*t for iiii northren dosyn of brode medly at xvii s. the dosyn … lxviii s.

Item t*o* a porter for carryng of hit from the fayr*e* to Coldherboro … ii d.

Item paid for a pec*e* of <q> white cotton cont*eynyng* xxxii good*es* at vii d. the gode … xviii s. viii d.

Item paid for a pece of whit cotton cont*eynyng* xxvii good*es* at vii d. the goode … xv s. ix d.

Item to a porter*e* for*e* bryngyng of the same unto Coldherboro … ii d.

Item paid for iii pec*es* of northern blak cotton … xx s.

Item paid for a pece of whit kersey cont*eynyng* xviii yerd*es* … xiii s. iiii d.

Item paid to a porter for bryngyng of the same unto Coldherboro … i d.

[94] Bracketed to include the next item and all the items on p. 151. 'R. Hylton' is also in the left margin one-third down p. 51, bracketed to include all the entries.
[95] Perhaps only the first canc. sum is in the MW hand.

Item paid for a payr*e* of <h> shoez for moder Maryon and for a payr*e* shoez for moder Dawson and for the mendyng of ther old shoez … xvi d.

[M]Summa … xv li. <ix d.> \ix s./[P]

[*p. 52*] Item paid unto m*aister* Morgan for a reward yeven to John Wylsons wyff to remeve hir stuff furthe of Croydon the iiiith day of Novembr*e* … v s.

Item paid the viith day of Novembr*e* unto Richard Aderton for ridyng from Haylyng unto Eltham by a day … viii d.

Item t*o* the same for ridyng from Haylyng to Andover to the kyng by vi daiez \at viii d. the daye/ … iiii s.

Item to the same for ridyng to Richemound at iii tymes … ii s.

John Holt.[96]

Item paid unto John Holt for ridyng unto Cambryge the spaice of v daiez \at viii d. the day/ … iii s. iiii d.

Item to the same for ridyng to London oon day … viii d.

Item to Richmound by oon day … viii d.

Item in reward t*o* a s*er*vand of m*aister* Browne for bryngyng of iii fezaunt*es* … xii d.

N. Aughton. Item paid unto Nicholas Aughton the xiiii day of Novembr*e* for his cost*es* rydyng uppon my lad*ys* messag*es* from Croydon to Bewdeley by x dayes at viii d. the daye … vi s. viii d.

Item paid to m*aister* chaunceller for money paid unto a currer whiche brought my lad*ys* bull*es* for*e* Goddes howse from Rome for his labur*e* … lxvi s. viii d.

Item delyv*er*ed to Gerawde of Burne at his dep*ar*tyng to the kyng*es* s*er*vyce in reward xl s. and to bye hym a payr*e* of brygynders xx s. Summa … lx s.

Item delyv*er*ed to David Dyk*es* the same tyme in reward … xl s.

[M]Summa … ix li. x s. viii d.[P]

[*p. 53*] *M*aister *Genynson of Cambryg*e. Item delyv*er*ed to maistres Foller for money yeven to oon Genynson of Gregoryes ostill in Cambryg*e* the xiiii day of Novembre … liii s. iiii d.

Item delyv*er*ed to the same for a reward yeven to a s*er*vande of my lady Orton … xii d.

Item paid unto Raynold Davenport the xviii day of Novembr*e* for ridyng unto Richmound at ii tymes and for ridyng to London a day apon my lad*ys* messag*es* … iii s.

Item paid to Nicholas Saunders for his cost*es* ridyng w*i*th two horsis from Haylyng*e* to Richmounde to London and to Endvyld Chasse by the space of iii dayes at xx d. the day … v s.

[96] Bracketed to include the next three items.

Item paid unto my lady Rev*er*se for a bonet bought for maistres Parker the xx day of Novembr*e* … xxiii s. iiii d.

*Nich*olas *Aughton*. Item paid unto Nicholas Aughton for ridyng unto Croland apon my lad*ys* message … vi s.

Item paid unto John Holt for ridyng to my lady Norton by oon day … viii d.

Item to the same for ridyng*e* unto my lady Urmeston by the spaice of iii daies … ii s.

Item paid unto Olyv*er* Holland for thred bought by John Collop to mende arres clothes … v s. iiii d.

Item paid unto Rob*er*t Merbury for ridyng to London by iii daies … iii s.

Item to the same ridyng to Richemound w*i*th m*aister* receyver by the space of ii dayes … ii s.

[M]Summa … Cv s. iiii d.[P]

[*p.* *54*] *Primo die Decembris*. Item paid the furst day of Decembr*e* unto Thomas Meydwell for a payr*e* of <c> shoes for my lad*ys* g*r*ace … iiii d.

Item paid unto John Holt for ridyng to Richmound and theyr*e* abydyng*e* by ii dayes … xvi d.

Item to the same for ridyng to my lord of Wynchester by a day … viii d.

Item to the same for ridyng another tyme unto Richemound by a day … viii d.

Hylton.[97]

Item paid unto Rob*er*t Hylton for ix pec*es* of blak chamlett. P*r*ice the pece xx s. … ix li.

Item to the same for his cost*es* by a day at London … xii d.

Item payd to the same for mynke tayles … vi d.

Item to the same for v payr*e* of shoez for my lad*ys* almesmen at vi d. the payr*e* … ii s. vi d.

Item for vii payr*e* of shoes for my lad*ys* almeswemen … ii s. iiii d.

Item paid for iii payr*e* of shoes for my lady almes chyldern at ii d. ob. the payr*e* … vii d.

Item paid to the same for a pece of tawny kersey cont*eynyng* xviii yerd*es* \at xxii d. qua. the yard/ … xxxiii s. iiii d.

Item paid for a hatt for my lad*ys* g*r*ace … iiii s.

Item paid for xviii yerd*es* di. of blak welvet. P*r*ice the yerd xi s. iid. Summa … x li. vi s. vii d.

Item paid for xx yerd*es* of blew sarcynett. P*r*ice the yerd iii s. ii d. … lxiii s. iiii d.

Item payd for ii tymbr*e* of lettus. P*r*ice the tymbr*e* viii s. … xvi s.

[97] In the left margin halfway down p. 54, bracketed to include all the next items on the page.

Item paid for the cost*es* of the same Rob*ert* at London by ii dayez goyng abowte the same stuff ... ii s.

Item paid unto the same for makyng and lynyng of ii payr*e* of hoose for ii fotmen at x d. the payr*e* ... xx d.

Item paid unto Thomas Symson the furst day of Decembr*e* for a payr*e* of hose cloth for Henr*y* Baptist ... x d.

[M]Summa ... xxv li. xvii s. viii d. ob.[P]

[*p. 55*] Item paid to Thomas Symson the furst day of Decembr*e* for makyng and lynyng of a payr*e* of hose for Henr*y* Baptist ... vii d.

Item for a payr*e* of shoes to the same ... iiii d.

Item paid for a payr*e* of shoez and a payr*e* of hose for Margaret oon of the almeswomen bought by the same Thomas Symson ... x d.

Item for clowtyng of a payr*e* of the almeswomen shoez ... ii d. ob.

Item for anlett*es* ... i d.

Item paid unto John Madyson the same day for ridyng to the charterhowse a day ... xii d.

Item to the same for ridyng to London and Westm*ynster* at two tymes ... ii s.

Item paid unto Raynolde Davenport for ridyng to Rygate to m*aister* Coup*er* by a day ... xii d.

Jane Gere. Item paid unto Jane Ger by hyr*e* suster*e* the furst day of Decembr*e* toward*es* hir fyndyng ... xxvi s. viii d.

Item for a dossen and a half of[98] parchement skynnes delyv*er*ed to m*aister* chaunceller ... iii s. ix d.

Item for half a pounde of wermylyon ... iiii d.

Item paid unto Richard Stukeley by his byll assigned for gylde naylis neld*es* hok*es* ffor the clok and hempsede the xvi day of Decembr*e* ... vi s. vii d.

Item paid unto William Grevell for his cost*es* ridyng to London and to Waltham Crosse for a fecicyon for m*aister* tresorer ... ii s.

Item paid unto m*aister* amener for money yeven in almes to pore folk*es* <fto> from the xviith day of August unto the xiii day of Decembr*e* as aperith by his byll therof made ... xxxv s. iiii d. ob.

Item paid unto m*aister* receyver syr Hughe Assheton for his cost*es* ridyng to the kyng to Kylingburne and to Richemound by ii tymez ... v s.

[M]Summa ... iiii li. v s. ix d.[P]

[98] 'of' rep.

[*p. 56*] Item paid unto m*aister* receyver syr Hughe Assheton for his cost*es* and m*aister* deans to London and theyr*e* abydyng by iii daiez for my lad*ys* matters … vi s. viii d.

Item paid unto m*aister* chaunceller for money payd unto the currer which brought my lad*ys* bull*es* from Rome for Cryst*es* Collage in Cambryg*e* … xx s.

Item to the same for a reward yeven to on þ*at* brought my lad*ys* grace a <cr> chese from the popes collecto*ur* … xx d.

Item paid to the same for ii boxes for my lad*ys* wrytyng*es* … xiiii d.

Item paid unto the same for wrytyng of my lad*ys* book*es* for hir precher in Cambryge … iiii s.

Item paid unto John Carter for wrytyng*e* of my lad*ys* bok*es* of statut*es* of Cryst*es* Collage … vi s. viii d.

Brudnell. Item paid unto m*aister* chauncele*re* for a reward yeven unto m*aister* Brudnell s*er*gant of lawe … xl s.

Item to the same for a reward yeven unto m*aister* Conysby s*er*vande for dyv*er*se wrytyng*es* … xx s.

Item paid for theyr*e* horse meyte at the George in Croydon … vi s. viii d.

Item for the diett of theyr*e* horse keper*e* … vi d.

Item on Seynt Nicholas even unto Seynt Nycholas and his clerk*es* … v s.

Item t*o* Seynt Nicholas clerk*es* of the towne in Croydon … xx d.

Item delyv*er*ed unto George Fraunc*es* for my lad*ys* offryng apon Lady Day … v s.

Item paid for bo[u]rde[99] waig*es* of m*aister* John Seynt John and his wyff by v wek*es* … xxvi s. viii d.

*M*aister *Sekelyng*es. Item paid unto m*aister* Sykellyng*es* for his cost*es* from Cambryge to Croydon and for his cost*es* in Croydon yeven in reward … xlvi s. viii d.

[M]Summa … ix li. xii s. iiii d.[P]

[*p. 57*] *Almes money*. Item delyv*er*ed unto my lad*ys* g*r*ace the xiiith day of Decembr*e* for hir almes purse … x li.

*W. Hylm*er. Item paid unto William Hylm*er* by his byll assigned for medsens made for my lad*ys* g*r*ace by iiii yer*es* as aperith by his said byll … xvi li. xvi s. iii d. qua.

Item paid unto maistrez Foller for money paid unto maistrez Lenche for ii bonett*es* of welvet. P*r*ice the on xiiii s. iiii d. and the other xv s. Summa … xxix s. iiii d.

Item to the same for a pece of single sypers … iii s.

Item in reward unto John Bygge at his beyng*e* at Croydon … xx s.

Item paid unto maistres Foller for a basket to carry my lad*ys* bonett*es* in … iiii d.

[99] -u- lost by a wormhole in the paper.

Item paid unto Jamys Morice for ii hoggsedd*es* of wyne yeven to m*aister* presydent doct*ur* Quytstons ... xl s.

Item paid unto the same for a reward yeven to a s*er*vande of m*aister* Brudnell*es* ridyng in to Derbeshyr*e* apon my lad*ys* messag*es* ... x s.

<*Summa xxxi li. xviii s. xi d. qua.*>

<*Summa totalis DCClxiii*[100] *li. xi s. iiii d. ob. qua.*>[101]

Summa ... xxxi li. xviiii s. xi d. qua.[102]

Item paid unto David Dyk*es* for a horse bought for hym of m*aister* Morgan at his goyng*e* to the kyng in p*ar*te of payment of xx s. ... x s.

Item delyv*er*ed unto m*aister* vichamberlayn at Grenewich for reward*es* to be yeven their*e* ... lvi s. viii d.

Item paid unto John Beane armorer for makyng clene of xxvii payr*e* of bregonders w*i*th sallett*es* splent*es* and mayle belongyng to the same ... xxvi s. viii d.

Item paid unto m*aister* amener for money yeven unto the freris at Grenewich at my lad*ys* beying theyr*e* ... xx s.

Item delyv*er*ed to maistres Stan*n*op for a reward yeven unto the p*ar*son Bybe ... vi s. viii d.

[M]Summa pagine ... xxxvii li. xviiii s. xi d. qua.[P]

[*p. 58*] Item the xxith day of Decembr*e* paid unto my lord Fewater by the hand*es* of m*aister* countroller and Nicholas Saunders for lond*es* bought in Hartforthshyr*e* callyd the man*er* of Roydon besyd*es* Warre ... DCCCiiii^{xx} li.

Item paid for iii book*es* of clene papur*e* bought at London by Nicholas Saunders ... iii s. viii d.

Item delyv*er*ed to Rob*er*t Fremyngham for a reward yeven unto a currer þat came from Rome the xviiith day of Decembr*e* ... vi s. viii d.

Item delyv*er*ed to m*aister* chaunceller the xxii day of Decembr*e* for a reward yeven to Rog*er* Hollande of the west countre ... xl s.

Item paid unto John Brydde for money paid by hym for the horse meyte of xiii horsis of my lorde of Rochester horsis standyng at Depyng at ii tymez for v qr. iii bus. ott*es* delyv*er*ed the xii day of Juyn ... xvi s. iii d.

Item for gresse horsis the same tyme ... xiiii d.

Item paid unto Thomas Todde for his cost*es* rydyng w*i*th my lady Jane from m*aister* Mortons place unto my lady Nortons at Fullam by a day ... xii d.

Item paid unto maistres Foller for a reward yeven unto a s*er*vande of my lady Scropes bryngyng a p*re*sent ... xx d.

[100] MS 'DCClxijj'.

[101] Both calculations are written small in the left margin in the MW hand.

[102] Written small in the right margin, also in the MW hand.

Item paid unto Thomas Todde for rydyng unto Bromley to my lord of Rochester*e* by a day … xii d.

Item paid unto John Urmeston for ridyng w*i*th my lady Jane to my lady Nortons to Fullam w*i*th his s*er*vande and two horsis … xx d.

Item paid unto Nicholas Aughton for rydyng to Westm*ynster* t*o* the dean of Seynt Stevens and to m*aister* Conysby by iii dayes w*i*th his abydyng theyr*e* … ii s.

[M]Summa … <CCCCvii li. xv s. i d.> DCCCiiii^{xx}iii li. xv s. i d.[P] [103]

[*p. 59*] *My lad*ys *offrynge on Crystemasse day.*[104]

Item delyv*er*ed for my lad*ys* offryng apon Cryste*n*masse day to Georg*e* Fraunc*es* … v s.

Item for my lad*ys* offryng in grott*es* … x s.

Item paid unto m*aister* Bekynsall for a reward yeven by hym at Fodryngay unto the maister of the chylder theyr*e* for wrytyng of my lad*ys* statut*es* of Cryst*es* Collage in Cambryge … iii s. iiii d.

Item paid unto the same for a reward yeven at Fodryngay unto a <ss> s*er*vand of my lord of Rochesturs … iii s. iiii d.

Item paid unto m*aister* Grendell for money paid unto Rob*er*t van Delff ston slepper*e* of London for the percyng*e* of my lad*ys* beyd*es* that the pope sent unto my lad*ys* gr*a*ce for lxxi beydes aft*er* iiii d. the beyde … xxiii s.[105]

Item paid unto Bonyface Stanley for his horse hyr*e* and cost*es* comyng unto m*aister* Markam from London at dyv*er*se tymes to see unto his hande þ*a*t was hurt … iiii s.

Item in reward unto a prest þ*a*t came from Cambryge a syngyng man … v s.

*Newer*es *day*. Item delyv*er*ed unto my lad*ys* gr*a*ce the last day of <Janu> Decembr*e* t*o* gyff t*o* Nuer gyft*es* xiii li. vi s. viii d. and by m*aister* chaunceller on New Yer*es* day to delyv*er* unto my lad*ys* gr*a*ce vi li. xiii s. iiii d. … xx li.

Item delyv*er*ed unto my lad*ys* gr*a*ce for my lady Bray New Yer*es* gyft … liii s. iiii d.

Item delyv*er*ed to m*aister* vichamberlayn for a reward yeven unto a s*er*vande of the abbott*es* of Westm*ynster* for bryngyng of a Newer*es* gyft to my lad*ys* gr*a*ce … vi s. viii d.

Item t*o* the same for a reward yeven unto the kyng*es* messanger þ*a*t brought letturs t*o* my lad*ys* gr*a*ce … vi s. viii d.

Item delyv*er*ed to m*aister* Crowmeyr*e* for my lad*ys* offryng apon New Yer*es* day … v s.

Item delyv*er*ed to m*aister* vichamberlayn to yeve unto m*aister* A[r]thur[106] for bryngyng of the kyng*es* New Yer*es* gyft t*o* my lad*ys* gr*a*ce … iii s. iiii d.

[103] The first (canc.) total is in the MW hand, the second in a different hand.

[104] Bracketed to include the next two items.

[105] The sum would be correct for 69 beads.

[106] MS 'Athur'.

Item delyv*er*ed to the same þ*a*t was yeven unto a s*er*vande of my lord of Chechesturs for bryngynge of a New Yer*es* gyft ... vi s. viii d.

^{M}Summa ... xxxi li. xii s. iiii d.^{P}

[*p. 60*] Item paid the iii^{de} day of January unto maistres Massy for a reward yeven unto a s*er*vand of my lady Norfolk*es* that brought spektakels to my ladies gr*a*ce ... iii s. iiii d.

Item delyv*er*ed unto m*aister* chaunceller for a reward yeven unto Petur*e* of Coldherbor*e* at his beyng at Croydon ... xx s.

John Holt by his byll assigned.[107]

Item paid unto John Holt for his cost*es* ridyng to the fader of the Syon the space of oon day ... viii d.

Item t*o* the same for his cost*es* lying at the courte at the kyng*es* beyng at London ... ii s.

Item for his cost*es* ridyng unto the archedyacon of Richmound by the space of two dayes ... xvi d.

Item for ridyng to my lady Norfolk*es* and to my lady Fitzwat*er* by oon day ... viii d.

Item for ridyng t*o* the bysshop of Norwyche and unto the said lady Fitzwater by ii daies ... xvi d.

Item for ridyng t*o* my lady Dawbeney by oon day ... viii d.

Item for ridyng t*o* Richmond to my lord of Wynchester w*ith* other of the kyng*es* councell by the space of oon day ... viii d.

Item paid unto Justice the iiiith day of January for his cost*es* comyng from Cambryge to Croydon by ii daies ... xx d.

Item paid unto syr Edward Bothe for money yeven to the freris at Ware at my lad*ys* comyng uppe to Croydon ... xii d.

Item to the clerk*es* of <ffodryigg> Fodryngay ... iiii d.

Item for a box to put in my lad*ys* offreng and for takett*es* for my lad*ys* clossett ... xi d.

^{M}Summa ... xxxiiii s. vii d.^{P}

[*p. 61*] Item paid unto syr Edward Bothe the iiiith day of January for money delyv*er*ed t*o* m*aister* chaunceller which was sent to maistrez Wynesowre to Syon ... vi s. viii d.

Item paid unto maistrez Lynche the vth day of January for vi elnez of canvas \at iii d. the ell/ ... xviii d.

Item paid unto the same for money paid to a goldsmyth for a q*u*art*er* of a unce of golde and <a> half a fardyng at xxxvi s. viii d. the unce ... ix s. v d.

Item paid for makyng of the same ... iii s. viii d.

[107] Bracketed to include the next seven items.

Item paid for CC elnez of canvas vi^{xx} to the C … lxiiii s.

Item paid for trussyng corde … viii d.

Item paid to a porter for beyryng of the canvas to Peturs at Coldherboro … ii d.

Item paid for gold of Wenuth a q*uarter*e of a lib. … xvii s. iiii d.

Item for gold of Vennes a q*u*art*er* of a lib. … xvi s.

Item for sylk ii lib. … xxxii s.

Item for golde of Vennes ii lib. … lxxii s.

Item for golde of Vennes i lib. … lii s.

Item paid for iiii elis of canvas to trus the carpett*es* … xvi d.

Item paid for a pece of dowbell sypers … x s.

Item paid for two thowsand pynnes delyv*er*ed t*o* William Hylm*er* … xiiii d.

xiiii li. xv d.[108]

Item paid unto m*aister* vichamberlayn for a reward yeven unto my lord of Chechest*er* s*er*vande … vi s. viii d.

Item to the same for a reward yeven unto Steven Taberet on New Yer*es* day… vi s. viii d.

Item paid unto John Harryson for money paid unto xi workemen for workyng of the garment*es* of dysgysyng*es* by vi daies and iii nyght*es* ev*er*y person by the day vi d. and ev*er*y nyght ii d. for ii q*u*art coles xii d. and for wod to wache by xiiii d. Summa … xxxvii s. vi d.[109]

[M]Summa … xvi li. xviii s. ix d.[P]

[*p. 62*] Item the vth day of January delyv*er*ed to m*aister* chaunceller for a reward yeven unto m*aister* Conysby … lxvi s. viii d.

Item in reward to his s*er*vande … vi s. viii d.

Item paid for his horse meyte of vii horsis by v daiez … viii s. viii d.

Item paid unto John Madyson for ridyng to Grenewich to serche the way for my lad*ys* gr*a*ce … xii d.

Item to the same for ridyng w*i*th m*aister* Markam iii daiez to make serche for thevis þ*at* robyd his s*er*vand … iii s.

Item to Rob*er*t Merbury for iii dayez at the same tyme … iii s.

Item for my lad*ys* offryng apon the Twelff day … v s.

Item in reward unto Henry the kyng*es* godson the same day … xx s.

[108] The total in the right margin of the fourteen items from the second entry on the page up to this point.
[109] The total should be 40s. 8d.

Item in reward to a monke of Fethersam abbey in Kent by m*aister* confessor … xiii s. iiii d.

Item in reward to m*aister* Sop*er* my lad*ys* solicit*ur* … xl s.

Item to m*aister* conffessor for a reward yeven to doct*ur* Roper … x s.

Item in reward to a man for bryngyng of rose water*e* oon of the coven of Assherige … iii s. iiii d.

Item in reward t*o* a s*er*vande of my lord chamberlayns the vi[th] day of January … iii s. iiii d.

Item paid unto Richard Sherley the same day by his byll assigned for his cost*es* ridyng to take […]s[…]ate for my lad*ys* gr*a*ce in his lond*es* at Chest*er*forth and Roydon <at> and for his cost*es* ridyng abowte the same at dyv*er*se tymes as aperith by his said byll … xxxiii s.

Summa … x li. xvii s.

[paper slip approx. 280 x 210 mm. stitched into pp. 62/63, torn across at the lower edge[110]]

anno xxi[mo] regis H. vii[mi]

vi dd. napkins of diap*er* at vi s. the dd. … xlii s.

ii pec*es* of diap*er* cont*eynyng* xxvi yerd*es* at xv d. the y*er*d … iiii li. xv s.

ii pec*es* of diap*er* tuell cont*eynyng* lxviii y*er*d*es* … xlii s.

i pece of diap*er* cont*eynyng* lxviii y*er*d*es* at \<xv> xx d./ the y*er*d … Cxiii s. iiii d.

[*p. 63*] Item the vi[th] day of January unto a s*er*vande of m*aister* Odells þ*a*t brought chese to my lad*ys* gr*a*ce … iii s. iiii d.

Item delyv*er*ed to m*aister* countroller for a reward yeven to m*aister* Brudnell clerk for ridyng at dyv*er*se tymes for my lad*ys* matters … xx s.

Item paid unto m*aister* dean for viii unce of sylke by him bought for my lad*ys* gr*a*ce … viii s.

Summa … xxxi s. iiii d.[P 111]

Item the viii[th] day of January in reward to the kyng*es* mynstrels at Croydon … x s.

Item paid unto Raynold Davemport for ii dayez ridyng on day t*o* my lord of Rochest*er* anoder day to London at <u>xii d.</u> the day … ii s.

Summa … xii s.[P]

Item paid the x day of January to John Harryson for stuff bought for the dysgysyng*es* in Cryste*n*mas as aperith by his byll … iiii li. viii s. xi d.

Item delyv*er*ed to m*aister* Morgan for a reward yen to the nonnes of [*blank*] in Yorkshyre … vi s. viii d.

[110] Not written in the MW hand.

[111] Of the 'Summe' on the page, only this is clearly written in the MW hand.

Item paid to the same for money yeven to Pachee … xx d.

Item to the same for ii premers for ii pore chylder … viii d.

Item paid unto maistres Foler for a reward yeven to Morgan Morice þat came from my lord of Rochester … ii s.

Summa … iiii li. xix s. xi d.[P]

[M]Summa partis … vii li. iii s. iii d.[P]

Totalis solucio predicta … <MCCxxxix li. xviii s. vii d. ob. qua.><MCCxl li. xii s. v d. ob. qua.>[112]

[*p. 64*] *Hylton.*[113]

Nota.[114] Item paid unto Rob*er*t Hylton the xiii day of January for vi yerd*es* of tawny satten. P*r*ice the yerd vii s. viii d. … <l s.> xlvi s.

Item for iiii yerd*es* and a q*u*art*er* of colo*ure*d sa[t]ten.[115] P*r*ice the yerd vii s. iiii d. … xxxi<i> s. <vi d.> ii d.

Item to the same for ii pec*es* of dymysey \at xxx s. the pec*e*/ … lx s.

Item paid for vi yerd*es* of other dymysey \at xii d./ … vi s.

Item for ii pec*es* of bokeram \at iiii s. viii d. the pec*e*/ … ix s. iiii d.

Item for xxviii yerd*es* of blak fustian \at v d. ob. the yard/. P*r*ice … xii s. x d.

Item paid for a payre of shoez for maistres <Jen> Jan … viii d.

Item paid for ii payr*e* of shoez for ii fotmen … xii d.

Item paid for the makyng and lynyng of ii payr*e* of <how> hoose for the said fotmen … xx d.

Item paid unto the same Rob*er*t for ii dayes beyng at London for the said stuff … ii s.

Item paid unto the same for lx yard*es* of fryse at v d. the yerd … xxv s.

Item for l yerd*es* of blak cotton at v d. ob. the yerd … xxii s. xi d.

Item paid for iii yerd*es* of \brode/ russet cotton at <vi d.> \xiiii d./ … <iii[116] s. vi d.> \iii s. vi d./ <xviii d.>[117]

Item paid for di. pane of fox … v s.

Item t*o* the same for his cost*es* by […] dayes … iii s.

Item for dressyng and skowryng of lx yerd*es* of blak which henge in my lad*ys* chambr*e* at Colyweston … ii s. iiii d.

[112] Written small to the left in the hand of the 'totalis solucio' of D91.20/190.
[113] Bracketed to include all the items on the page.
[114] The first six entries and the thirteenth are preceded by a canc. +; a canc. + also marks the first and second entries above the totals.
[115] MS 'sacten'.
[116] MS 'ijj'.
[117] The canc. corrections are in the MW hand, but not the final sum.

Item paid for iiii ell*es* of canvas for trussyng of the said stuff … xvi d.

Item for maylyng cord for the same … iiii d.

Item for caryage of the same stuff … iiii d.

Item paid for v yerd*es* i q*u*art*er* of <crenys> cremysyn clothe at x s. iiii d. the yerd … liii s. xi d.

[M]Summa … <xiiii li. xiiii s. viii d.[P]>

xiiii li. viii s. iiii d.[P]

<xiiii li. xiiii s. viii d.>[118]

[*p. 65*] Item paid unto Rob*er*t Hylton the xiii[th] day of January for a fetherbedd and a bolster*e* … xix s. viii d.

Item paid for a frynge of blew sylk of iiii unc*e* di. P*r*ice the unce xii d. … iiii s. vi d.

Item to the same for his cost*es* by oon day … xii d.

Item paid for a nownse of throwne crymesyn sylk … xii d.

Item paid for a di. unce of grene sylk … vi d.

Item for a tymbr*e* of letuse. P*r*ice … viii s.

Item for another tymbr*e* sythen … viii s.

Item for xvi skynnes of blak bochie … v s. iiii d.

Item paid to the same Rob*er*t for his cost*es* by a day in bying of the same stuff … xii d.

Summa … xlix s.

Item paid unto Olyv*er* Holland the xiii[th] day of January by his byll assigned <for> by Nicholas Saunders for ii matres. P*r*ice … vi s. viii d.

Item for ii bolsters ii s. viii d. Item for iiii litell matres. P*r*ice viii s. for iiii bolsters iii s. viii d. for iii cov*er*lett*es* \viii s./ … for the caryage of the same from London t*o* Croydon viii d. Item for his cost*es* by vii daiez vii s. … xxx s.

Item paid unto the same for a pece of canvas cont*eynyng* lv ellis at vi d. the ell … xxxvii s. vi d.

Item for a pece of Normandy clothe cont*eynyng* xxxii <… > ellis di. at x d. the ell … xxvii s. i d.

Item paid t*o* the same for money paid t*o* Samsons wyff of Colyweston for Rauff*es* bourde … xxii d.

Item for trussyng corde … xviii d.

Item t*o* the same for his cost*es* sekyng*e* of Crystofer Richartson by iii daies … iii s.

[118] Written small to the left at the foot of the page, perhaps in the 'curly' hand. The two attempts at the sum total above are in one hand, not the MW hand.

Item for ridyng for Nicholas Treverne wyff at Clopton by a day … viii d.

[M]Summa … Cviii s. iii d.[P]

Summa partis … vii li. xvii s. iii d.[P] [119]

[*p. 66*] Item paid unto Olyv*er* Hollan the xii[th] day of January by his byll assigned by the hand*es* of Nicholas Saunders for iii cov*er*lett*es*. P*r*ice \the cov*er*lett v s./ … xv s.

Item for a hangyng lok iii d. and for smale trussyng corde x d. Item for Rauffes lodgyng at Royston \ii d./ … xv d.

Item paid to the same for money paid for caryng*e* ov*er* the gentylwomen from Westm*ynster* to Lambeth … vi d.

Item paid unto the same Olyv*er* by another byll by the hand*es* of Nicholas Saunders for C ell*es* of bokeram clothe. P*r*ice \in grete/ … xxxiiii s.

Item for the chaunge of viii unce of sylk … xvi d.

Item for ii brosses … vii d.

Item for a basket to carry colis for <[l]> straungers … ii d.

Summa … <xxxi s. x d.> lii s. x d.[P]

[120]Item payed to m*aister* tresourer for money by hym payed to m*aister* John Longlond of Magdalen Colege in Oxonford for thexhibic*i*on of Pepyr unt*o* the fest of Saint M*ar*tyn last past … xvii s. iiii d.

Item payed to m*aister* chaunceler for a [re]ward[121] geven to m*aister* Jakson goyng to Rome to pray for my lad*ys* g*r*ace … v s.

Item paid to m*aister* Clarrell by the hand*es* of Nicholas Saunders <b> for iiii daies tarrying at London in messag*es* to the kyng*es* g*r*ace for his self and ii s*er*vand*es* w*i*th iii horses … viii s. viii d.

Item t*o* the same in almes delyv*er*ed by hym to Ric*hard* Plomer*e* beyng in presson … xii d.

Summa … xxxii s.[P] [122]

Summa partis … iiii li. iiii s. x d.[P]

[*p. 67*] [123]Item payd to syr Herry Colet knyght for þe maner off Dysworth w*ith* þe members off hym bought for to gyff unto Cristez Collage in Cambryge by the hand*es* off m*astyr* controller*e* … DCCxl li.

Item paid the xiiii[th] day of January unto John Mondy goldsmyth for oon challis gylt pond*eryng* xxiiii unc*e* at v d. the unc*e* … vi li.

[119] Not in the MW hand (unlike the 'Summe' on the rest of p. 65).

[120] This and the next entry may be in a different hand (or perhaps just a new stint in the MW hand).

[121] MS '[…]ward'.

[122] This and the next 'Summa' are not in the MW hand.

[123] This entry is in the 'sprawling' hand.

Item to the same for oon gylt salt covert <pod> pond*eryng* viii unc*e* i q*u*art*er* at v s. the unc*e* … xli s. iii d.

Item to the same for oon salt gylt covert pond*eryng* x unc*e* di. q*u*art*er* at v s. the unc*e* … l s. vii d. ob.

Item paid for a cuppe of golde w*i*th a cover for the kyng*es* New Yer*es* gyfft … C li. vi s. viii d.

Item paid to the same for a rynge of golde w*i*th x s. for the makyng … xxx s.

Item payd unto Thomas Sop*er* my lad*ys* solicit*ur* for s*er*ten suett*es* by hym don by my lad*ys* comaundement w*i*th xx li. paid in the chauncery for to have lycence to mortis the chyrche of Malton and w*i*th vi li. vi s. x d. for recov*er*y of c*er*ten land*es* of m*aistres* Woldull junter and w*i*th <… > xiii li. v s. ix d. for cost*es* of other suett*es* as well for Cryst*es* Collage as other in all as hit aperith in a booke of p*ar*cell*es* remaynyng w*i*th syr Hughe Assheton … xxxix li. xii s. vii d.

Item for the cost*es* of the said Thomas comyng to Richmound and Croydon dyv*er*se tymes … xx s.

[M]Summa partis … DCCCiiii[xx]xiii li. xiii d. ob.[P]

[*pp. 68–9 blank*]

[*p. 70*] [124]Some totall of all the expens*e* and payment*es* aforsaid … MMDxxv li. xi s. qua.

And so he oweth … DCCxxii li. x d. ob.[125]

wherof

delyv*er*ed unto the coffers of the forsaid prynces the xxiii daye of Febr*uary* the xx[th] yere of the kynge Henry the vii[th] by the hand*es* of John Thwayt*es* as for money lent unto hys broder Thomas Thwayt*es* … xiii li. vi s. viii d.

And so he oweth … DCCviii li. xiiii s. ii d. ob. Nota for ferther allouanc*e* in the iiii[th] lefe folowynge.[126]

[*p. 71*] *Wherof in*[127]

Almes yeven to divers p*er*sones at sondre tymes … xiiii li. xv s. v d.

Money delyv*er*ed at sondre tymes to my ladyes almouse purse … xxvii li. xix s. vii d. ob.

xlii li. xv s. ob.[128]

[124] The summary hand returns here, perhaps, but not certainly, as the 'sprawling' hand.

[125] Having received £3,247 11s. 10¾d. (p. 4) and paid out £2,525 11s. ¼d. (above), the amount owing is correct, as are the other calculations on the page.

[126] See p. 77.

[127] Bracketed to include pp. 71–77, which are written in the neat summary hand of the extensions at D91.20/64, 94, 134.

[128] The sum of the first two entries on p. 71, bracketed to the right of these entries.

Money delyv*er*ed at sondre tymes for my ladys offerynge … vii li. xi s. i d.

Expens*e* for the p*ro*fessyou*n* of the nune at Sympry*n*gham … lxiiii s. i d.

Money delyv*er*ed as wele to the ankeres \lxviii s. viii d./ at the nunnes in Stampford as to the other ankeres \l s./ beynge at Seynte Kateryns*e* ther*e* … Cxviii s. viii d.

Certayn stuff necc*essari* bought for my ladyes almous men wemen and chyldren … vi li. xvi s. ix d.

Money delyv*er*ed at dyvers tymes unto olde Herry the kyng*es* godson and for the exhibycyou*n* of yonge Henry … lx s. x d. ob.

Exhibycou*n* of divers scolers beynge at sondre places and scolez … viii li. xv s. i d.

Money yevon unto mastyr Syklynge <of> and other scholers in Cambryge of Crystes College … viii li.

Exhibycou*n* of mastres Parott … iii s. v d.

Exhibycou*n* of Skyppe … iiii s. ix d.

Money delyv*er*ed to Jane Gower … liii s. iiii d.

Summa huc … iiii^{xx}ix li. iii s. i d.[129]

[130]Reward*es* yeven to divers p*er*sones at sondr*e* tymes … iiii^{xx}<[…]>vi li. vii s. viii d.

Rewardes yeven to the gen*er*all of þe whyte frerys … lxvi s. viii d.

Rewardes geven to mayst*er* Conyngesby at div*er*s tymes … x li. xiii s. iiii d.

Rewardes yevon to m*astyr* Bryknell at sondr*e* tymes … vii li. xiii s. iiii d.

[*p. 72*] Rewarde to George Kyrkhame … xl s.

Rewardes yevon to mastyr Moryce \x marc*e*/ Seynt John and to Gryffeth Donne … viii li. xiii s. iiii d.

Reward*es* geven to mastyr and to my m*astre*s hys wyff … iiii li.

Rewardes geven to the kynges speres … vi li. xiii s. iiii d.

Rewardes geven mastres Curson … lx s.

Money delyv*er*ed whan my lady was at Rychemond with the kynge … xxv li.

Rewarde yeven to the ladye Kateryne … xl s.

Rewarde geven to mastres Redynge … xl s.

Reward*es* \to m*astyr* P*ar*ker/ geven when he went to hys fader … xx s.

Money delyv*er*ed to my lady pryncesse … iiii li.

Divers reward*es* gevyn to divers persones at Rychm*ond* with xl s. to the lorde John and v marc*e* to m*astyr* Dudley \in all/ … xxii li. ii s. iii d.

[129] Written small to the right in the same hand.

[130] Bracketed to the right to include this item and all others up to and including the seventh entry on p. 73, with the marginal total on p. 72 (reproduced here after the seventh entry on p. 73).

Rewarde geven to Roger Holond ... xl s.

Rewarde geven to David and Jerard Osbo*ur*ne at theyr dep*ar*tynge to the kyng*es* servyce ... C s.

[*p. 73*] Reward geven to Rob*er*t Daye cok ... xx<l> s.

Rewarde geven to the kyng*es* s*er*vante when the kynge was at Halynge ... vi li. vi s. viii d.

Reward*es* geven to divers p*er*sones when my lady was at G[r]enewyche with the kynge ... lvi s. viii d.

Rewardes yeven to Thomas Soper my ladyes solycyto*ur* ... xl s.

Reward*es* geven to m*astyr* Arthur bryngynge the kyng*es* New Yerys gyfft ... C s.

Certayne wyne bought and gevyn to my ladye Braye and the chef iugge of the co*m*men place ... xii li. x s. iii d.

ii hoggeshedd*es* of wyne yeve*n* to mastyr Whetston by my ladyes co*m*maundement ... xl s.

CCxx<x>vii li. iii s. vi d.[131]

Divers sylkes bought for my ladys grace as velvett damaske satten chamlett sarsenet and other sylkys necessarye ... <\xx/> <iiii> <v li. xiii s. xi d.> lxvi li. xiii s. xi d.

Certayne other stuff neccc*essari*e bought for my lad*ys* grace ... xv li. v d. ob.

Sypers bought for my lad*ys* grace ... ix s. iiii d.

Certayne furres bought for my lad*ys* grace and by her co*m*maundment with the wages of certayne skynn*er*s at divers tymes hyred ... xiiii li. xiiii s. vii d.

Certayne goldwyre sylvyr*e* wyre goold of Venez and divers workynge sylk*es* \of sondre colo*ur*s bought with/ certayne fryng*es* and rybbans ... xxi li. iiii s. i d. ob.

Certayne worstodes fustyan and bokerame at sondr*e* tymes bought ... vi li. viii s. ii d.

[*p. 74*] Certayn wollen cloth and fresez bought for my ladyes grace and for other by her co*m*maundment ... xxix li. xv s. viii d. ob. qua.

Canvas bought at divers tymes ... vii li. xvi s. xi d.

Certayne bokys bought by my ladys co*m*maundme*n*t wherof some are masbokes p*re*nted in velime ... ix li. xiii s.

Pakethrede and of other threde of divers colo*ur*s and soortes ... xii s. iiii d.

Certayn wacchynge lyghtys and other lyght*es* bought at Cambrygge for my ladyes grace chamb*er* ... xix s. viii d.

Costys of the caryage of all the fornamed stuf at sondre tymes ... xvi s. iii d.

[131] The total of all the entries up to this point since the previous total ('Summa huc', p. 71), bracketed to the right of these entries on p. 72 (but shown here at the end of the relevant entries).

Foryn expens*e* of divers of my ladyes s*er*vant*es* rydynge uppon her messagyes to div*er*s places … xxvii li. xvii s. iiii d. ob.

Money delyv*er*ed to mastyr Bryknell for hys cost*es* <for> from Lodyngton to London and to Croydo*n* at two tymes … liii s. iiii d.

A horse bought of John Stakehouse for my ladys lytter … liii s. iiii d.

Money payed to mayster Morgan for a horse yeven to David now the kyng*es* s*er*v*ant … x s.

v yerd*es* \and i q*uarter*/ of crymysen in grayne geven unt*o* [*blank*] … liii s. xi d.

Money delyv*er*ed to syr John Husye knyght for hys fee … C s.

Money payed to mastres Denton for her fee … lxvi s. viii d.

Costys for my ladyes fotemen with other expen*se* necessarye … lxxi s. xi d.

[*p. 75*] Money payed to John Castell of the eschequyer for[132] certayn sewtes don ther for mastyr Seynt Johns land*es* … Cii s. x d.

Costes of the boredynge of mastyr Seynt John and hys wyff … lxix s. iiii d.

Money delyv*er*ed to Will*i*am Elmer for certayn spyces and medysyns made for my ladyes grace by the space of iiii yerez … xix li. xvii d. qua.

A payre of organs bought and left at Colyweston … C s.

Expens*e* of my lorde of Rochestyrs horses beynge at Colyweston and Depynge at divers tymes … l s. ix d.

Expens*e* of my lorde Dogley ys horses a[t] Fodry*n*ghay … liii s. iiii d.

Expens*e* of my ladye merques horses … xx s.

Money delyv*er*ed to mastyr Bell of Fodryngehaye … xxv s.

Certayne parchement bought and delyv*er*ed to m*astyr* chaunceler and to Leonarde … xvi s. i d.

ii bukskynnes bought and delyv*er*ed to Leonarde with the costez and byndynge of certayne bokes … viii s.

Money delyv*er*ed to Bonyface Stanley for the helynge of mastres Thrognall w*ith* other costys … xxix s. v d.

Costez of the bereynge of mastres Markehame over <u>xx s.</u> payed by my lad*ys* grace … viii s.

Money delyv*er*ed to mastres Massye for costez <for> of the kepynge of the yonge gentylwomen … xvii s. x d.

Costes of the bryngynge upp of m*astyr* Parkers chyldren from Fodrynghay to Croydon … viii s. viii d.

[132] 'for' rep. next l.

[*p. 76*] Money payed for a bonet of velvett bought for mastres Parker … xxiii s. iiii d.

vii yardes of russett satten bought and gevyn to my lorde chamb*er*layns sonne … xlii s.

Costes of my ladyes armere … xxvi s. viii d.

Costes of persynge of the bedys that wer*e* gevyn to my ladys grace by the pope … xxiii s. iiii d.

ii pecez of saye bought … lxvi s.

Mendynge of my ladys lytyll cloke … x s.

ii vestment*es* bought of divers prycez … iiii li. vi s. viii d.

Certayne glasse botelles bought … viii s. ii d.

ii chalysys gylt bought at sondre tymes … xiiii li. xiii s. iiii d. ob.

Certayn*e* plate bought at divers tymes with costys for the mendynge of plate … lxiii li. xv s. iiii d.

Certayne rynges of gold bought with a george[133] of golde … xi li. xvi s. x d.

i fetherbed with a bolster and certayn matresys and cov*er*lett*es* bought … lxxi s. iiii d.

Costez for mendynge of my ladyes horslytter … xlviii s. iiii d.

i barehyde iii clothe sakkes and ii gardevyand*es* bought … iiii li. vi s. viii d.

A coppe of golde bought for the kyng*es* New Yer*es* gyft weyinge l unc*e* di. q*u*art*er*. P*r*ice the unc*e* xxxv s. with xii li. x s. for the makynge aftyr v s. for ev*er*y unce … C li. vi s. viii d.

Money delyv*er*ed to my lady to gyf to New Yer*es* gyftys with liii s. iiii d. for my lady Bray … xxii li. xiii s. iiii d.

v tynne botell*es* bought … iii s. iiii d.

[*p. 77*] ii framed beddes bought for my lady … lxvi s. viii d.

Money payed to s*ir* Henry Collett knyght for the purchesse of the mano*ur* of Dyesworth w*ith* þe membr*e* … DCCx<l> li.

Money in lyke maner payed to the lorde Fytzwat*er* for the purches of the lordshyp of Roydon … DCCCiiii^{xx} li.

Costys of Rychard Shurley bayly of Ware for hys costes rydynge aboute to take possessio*n* ther … xxxiii s.

Money delyv*er*ed to John Haryson for the makyng of divers garment*es* for the dysgysynge with iiii li. for certayne stuff bought … vi li. vi s. v d.

Money delyv*er*ed to Thomas Soper my ladys solycyto*ur* for certayne costez of plees and seutys of acc*i*ones with xx li. payed in the chauncerye for lycence to mortes the

[133] MS 'geoorge'.

churche of Malton and vi li. vi s. x d. for the recovere of certayne landes for mastres Owdells junctur*e* ... xxxix li. xii s. vii d.

Costes of the said solycyto*ur* cu*m*mynge to Rychemond and to Croydon ... xx s.

Summa of all the said allowance w*ith* xx marc*e* delyv*er*ed to my lad*ys* coffers by mastyr Thwayt*es* ... MMDxxxviii li. xvii s. viii d. qua.

And so he awyth as ys in<t> the iii^{de} <ly> lefe byfor specyfyed[134] ... DCCviii li. xiiii s. ii d. ob.

Wherof he ys allowed <x> C li. xiiii d. ob. qua. for the exhibic*i*on of m*astyr* Seynt John and hys wyff xlii li. v s. x d. thexhibyc*i*on of m*astyr* P*ar*ker and my mastres hys wyff xxvi li. viii s. iii d. thexhibic*i*on of m*astyr* Markeham and my mastres his wyf <xvi li. ix s.> xv li. vi s. iiii d. and for thexhibic*i*on of m*astyr* Thrognall and his wyff xvi li. ix d. ob. qua.

[*p. 78*] And so all thyng*es* deducted and alowed he oweth ... DCviii li. xii s. xi d. ob. qua. «quod oneratur in computo sequenti <quod oneratur in computo sequenti>»[135]

[*p. 79*] Rychard Conway late of the chappell ... iiii li. ... «desperatur»[136] «inde allocatur xiii s. iiii d.»[137]

John Joyner late of Stampford by the surtye of Crystofer Broune by oblygacyou*n* ... x li. «totum solvitur»[138]

George Henyngham my lad*ys* s*er*vant for money by my lad*ys* grace payed unto the lady Powez for a cheyne that he lost of hyrs ... xxvii s. vi d. «desperatur»[139]

William Pole for money <s> to hym lent ... xi li.

S*ir* John Melton knyght for money to hym lent and to his wyff ... xvi li. xiii s. iiii d. «inde allocatur viii li. vi s. viii d.»[140]

The pryo*ur* of Crowland for money to hym lent ... xl li.

Water*e* Cokkes yeoman of the bakehouse for money to hym lent ... xliii s. iiii d.

Will*i*am Ferthynge late of my ladyes chappell for money to hym lent ... xiii li. vi s. viii d.

S*ir* Henry Wylloughby knyght for money to hym lent to paye the kynge for the redempcyou*n* of the mano*ur* of Coteno*ur* for mast*y*r Souche that hath maryed his doughter*e* ... CC li. «inde solvitur ad cofferam domine l li. et <and> ad manus Milonis Worsley l li.»[141]

[134] See p. 70.
[135] Add. below the total in a small hand. See p. 83 below.
[136] Add. after the total in the same hand and ink.
[137] Add. small after the total in the 'sprawling' hand.
[138] Add. small after the total in the 'sprawling' hand.
[139] Add. after the total in the same hand and ink.
[140] Add. small below the total in the sprawling' hand.
[141] Add. after the total in the 'sprawling' hand.

Olyver Holande yeman ussher of my ladyes chamber for money to hym lent … vi li. xvii s. vi d. qua.

James Clarell for money to hym delyv*er*ed by thand*es* of Henry Salfford iiii li. xv s. by the hand*es* of Olyver*e* Holand xlvi s. viii d. in all vii li. xviii d.[142] wherof the said James delyv*er*ed xv yard*es* of tawnye medley lxxvii s. vi d. and also he delyv*er*ed to Alexandr*e* Thrognall xviii s. vi d. ob. and so resteth uppon <thi> hym … xlv s. v d. ob.

John Walter for money to hym <lent> prested to by stuff for the vestre … iii s. iiii d. «desperatur»[143]

[*p. 80*] Thexecut*ou*rs of the testament of s*yr* Roger Urmyston knyght as appereth in the fote of accompte by them made restynge in the kepynge of m*astyr* Hugh Assheton … xvii li. vii s. ix d.

Summa of the money prested the last yere … CCCxxv li. iiii s. x d. ob. qua.

Rob*ert* Crathorn*e* and his felowe expendit*ou*rs of the slewes at Boston … lx li.

John Tanne of Lynne m*er*chaunt for money to hym lent by an oblygac*i*on remaynynge with Myles Worsley … xx li.

[*blank*] Rowle of the chappell for money to hym lent … lxvi s. viii d.

Rob*ert* Hilton for money to hym prested to make p*ro*vysyou*n* of stuff … ix li. xix s. iiii d.

Mastres Lynche for the p*ar*te of xx li. to her delyv*er*ed to make p*ro*vysyou*n* of stuff for my ladyes grace … lxxviii s. ix d. «totum solvitur Miloni Worsley»[144]

Thomas Soper my ladys solycyt*our* for money restynge in his hand*es* toward*es* my ladys sewtes … vii li. vii s. v d.

Totall of þe money owynge … CCCCxxix li. xvii s. qua.[145] Summa of the money p*re*sted thys yere … Ciiii li. xii s. ii d.

And resteth thys uppon the saide accomptant of his owne arrer*ages* … <Clx\x/viii li. xv s. xi d. qua.> Clxxviii li. xv s. xi d. qua.

wherof[M]

delyv*er*ed to my ladyes coffers the xxth day of Januarii … Cxii li. xv s. iiii d.[M]

[*pp. 81–82 blank*][146]

[*p. 83*] [147]*Hatfeld.* Thaccompte of Mylys Worsley tresourer of the chamb*er* with the most excellent pryncese Margaret countes of Richmound and Derby and moder to oure sov*er*ayn the kynge that nowe ys kynge Henry the viith frome the xiiiith day of

[142] The total is 2d. short (as also p. 162 below).
[143] Add. small after the total in the same hand and ink.
[144] Add. small after the total in the 'sprawling' hand.
[145] Written small, in the same hand as the main text, in the left margin alongside 'Summa … '.
[146] Top right corner p. 81 cut off square from 15 mm. to left of page to depth of 35 mm.
[147] The summary hand begins the new year.

January in the xxith yere of the seid sov*er*ayn lord unto the same xiiiith day of January next ensuynge in the xxii^{ti} yere of oure forseid sov*er*ayn lord that ys to sey by the space of an hole yere.

*Tharrerag*es. Fyrst the seid accounptant ys charged with the arrerag*es* of his last accompte as yt doyth more playnly appere in the fote of the same … DCviii li. xii s. xi d. ob. qua.[148]

Summa … DCviii li. xii s. xi d. ob. qua.

[*p. 84*] *Recepta denariorum extra cofferas domine principisse.*[149]

Firste receyved the xxx^{ti} \day/ of January … lxvii li. iiii s.

Item the xiith day of February … iiii^{xx}vii li. xiii s. viii d.

Item the xxvi day of February … xxxii li.

Item the vth day of Marche … xlv li.

Item the xiiiith day of Marche … Ciiii^{xx} li.

Item the xvith day of Marche … vi li. xiii s. iiii d.

Item the xixth day of March … xxi li. iii s. i d.

Item the first day of Aprill … xx li. vi s. viii d.

Item the vith day of Apryll … xli li.

Item the viith day of May … xxvii li. xiii s. iiii d.

Item the xixth day of May … C s.

Item the xxx^{ti} day of May … vii li. ii s. vi d.

Item the firste day of June … CCv li. vii s. xi d.

Item the iiith day of June … xxviii li. iiii d.

Item the xx^{ti} day of Juyne … xx li.

Item the same day … xxxii li.

Item the iiith day of July … vii li.

Item the xith day of July … xx li.

Item the same day … Cxvii s.

Summa partis[150] … DCCClix li. xxii s.[P]

[*p. 85*] Item the xixth day of July … xxi li. vii s. viii d.

Item the firste day of Auguste … Cii li.

[148] See p. 78 above.
[149] See D102.10/123–5.
[150] Blotted and a wormhole mended.

Item the xxvth day of Auguste … xxxviii li. xiii s. iiii d.

Item the xxi^{ti} day of Septembr*e* … lxvi li.

Item the xxiiith day of Septembr*e* … iiii^{xx}i li. xvii s. iiii d.

Item the xiiiith day of Octobr*e* … xviii li.

Item the xv day of Octobr*e* … xx li.

Item the iiith day of Novembr*e* … xlviii li.

Item the viith day of Novembr*e* … Cviii li.

Item the xiiith day of Novembr*e* … C li.

Item the <x> xxviiith day of Novembr*e* … xxxix li. vii s. iiii d.

Item the xixth day of Decembr*e* … xxxiiii li. ii s.

[151]Item rec*eyved* the viii daye off Januar*y* anno xxii^{do} … Cxxix li. iiii s. vii d.

Summa partis … <DClxxvii li. vii s. viii d.> DCCCvi li. xii s. iii d.^{P}

[*p. 86*] Item he ys charged w*ith* money that was lent unto the lady Jane Bewford by James Mores by the co*m*maundment of my ladys grace at Colyweston anno xx^{mo} H. vii^{mi} … xvi li.

[*p. 87*] [152]Receyved of Thomas Sop*er* my lad*ys* solist*er* as money by hym paid for cost*es* of my lad*ys* suett*es* and <the> charges.

Furst receyved of the same Thomas as money receyved by hym of on Ric*hard* Deseney… <xxvi s. viii d.> «nichil hic quia solvitur rere»[153]

Item receyved of the same as money by hym receyved of the said Richard for the cost*es* of his suett*es* … v s.

Item rec*eyved* of the said Thomas as money rec*eyved* of Ric*hard* Hallwell \xx d./ for the cost*es* of his suette of Thomas Tayllyo*ur* \vi s. viii d./ servientis vice camerarii for the cost*es* of his suette and off Rog*er* Appulton \v s./ for his cost*es* of his suette in all … xxxi s. viii d.

Summa … <lxiii s. iiii d.> xxxvi s. viii d.[154]

[*p. 88 blank*]

[151] This entry and that on p. 86 are written in the 'sprawling' hand.

[152] The MW hand returns here.

[153] Add. after the total in the 'sprawling' hand. Perhaps included in the entry for Soper p. 77 (the sums given fall short of the total, and the phrase 'certayne costez of plees and seutys of acc*i*ones' allows for some leeway), but see the correct sum under '*M*aister *solicit*ur' (p. 145).

[154] The two totals are written in different hands (neither is the MW hand); the same hands are responsible for the calculations on p. 89.

[*p. 89*] So*m*me totall of all the receytt*es* with tharrerag*es* byfor wryten … <MMCxlv li. ii s. v d.> <MMCClxxvi li. iii s. viii d. ob. qua.> \MMCCiiii^{xx}xii li. iii s. viii d. ob. qua./[155]

[*p. 90*] [156]Mony delyv*er*ed unto þe coffers off þe forseid pryncez by þe hand*es* off þe forseid Miles inmedyatly after*e* þe det*er*mi*n*aciou*n* off his last acompt a[s] y[t][157] appereth in þe boke off[158] þe receyt*es* off þe seid pryncez … Cxii li. xv s. <x d.> \iiii d./

Item delyv*er*ed unto þe seid coffers by þe hand*es* off syr Herry Willughby knyght in þe part off payment off CC li. ov*er* l li. payd to þe seid Miles þis <et> same yere … l li.

Summa … Clxii li. xv s. iiii d.

[*p. 91*] [159]Costys and exspencys w*ith* other dyv*er*se payement*es* and rewardes of the most excellent prynces Margaret countesse of Rychemond and Derby and moder to our*e* sov*er*eyn lord kyng Henr*y* the viith from the xiiiith day of January anno xxi° paid by the handes of Myles Worsley as hereaft*our* folowith.

*xxvi day of Jan*uar*y*. First paid to Garrard Osborne the kyng*es* s*er*vant in rewarde at his beyng at Croydon w*ith* my ladyes g*r*ace … iii s. iiii d.

Item in rewarde to Thomas Hodale for co*n*veyng of a lett*er* to the pryo*ur* and covent of the monestory of Ey … ii s.

Ancryse at the nonnes in Stampforth. Item delyv*er*ed to Grefyth ap Rychard for to delyv*er* to the ancres at the nonnys of Stampford for on q*uarter* … xxxiii s. iiii d.

Item to the same for money yevyn to the ancres of Stampford … iii s. iiii d.

Item paid the xxvith \day/ of January for the horse met of xxiiii horse of my lorde of Derbeys stondyng at George in Croydon by i day and ii nyght*es* … xiiii s. x d.

Item delyv*er*ed to master Croke for a rewarde yevyn to a man that brought i q*uart* of aqua vyte from Assheryg unto my ladyes g*r*ace … xx d.

Item paid to Bonefac*e* Stanley for his borde and a womans that kept m*aster* Markams s*er*vant by the space of a weke and for clothe to make rollys of ii s. ix d. and for aqua vyte iiii d. in all … iii s. i d.

Item paid to the same Boneface the xvith day of January by a byll of covena*u*nt*es* assyned by my ladyes g*r*ace for oon Randoll <syand> Sant <the> which the said Boneface hathe take to his prent*es* for xii yeres to lerne his syens … xli s. viii d.

Item paid to master Coper for v gramer <… > bok*es* bought for the chyldryn of the chappell … iiii s. iiii d.

^{M}Summa … <iiii li. x d.> Cvii s. vi d.^{P}

[155] The second canc. calculation (written below the first) is in the same hand as the final calculation (written small above the first) and is in a different hand from that of the first canc. calculation.
[156] This page is written in the 'sprawling' hand.
[157] MS 'at ys'.
[158] 'off' rep. next l.
[159] This page is in the 'curly' hand.

[*p. 92*] [160]*Rob*e*r*t *Dey*. Item paid the xvith day of January unto Rob*er*t Dey cooke for a q*ua*rt*er* wayg*es* ended at Cryste*n*mas last passid ov*er* xl s. paid by m*aister* tressorer in full payment of lxvi s. viii d. whiche he receyvid for his waig*es* by a yere … vi s. viii d.

Item delyv*er*ed to m*aister* chaunceller for a reward yeven to a s*er*vande of my lord Derby þ*a*t came in message unto my lad*ys* g*r*ace to Croydon … xx d.

Item the xviith day of January delyv*er*ed unto maistres Foler for a reward yeven to my lady Man*er*es at hir beyng w*i*th my lad*ys* g*r*ace at Croydon … xl s.

Item payd unto Edward Wauce for vii yerd*es* of crewle bought for my lad*ys* g*r*ace … vii d.

Item paid unto John Carter s*er*vande unto m*aister* chaunceller for money yeven to m*aister* Jakson of Cambryg*e* ov*er* v s. to hym delyv*er*ed afour*e* … xx d.

Item to m*aister* chaunceller for a reward yeven unto a s*er*vande of doct*ur* Babyngton w*i*th the quene of Skott*es* comyng in message unto my lad*ys* g*r*ace the xviii day of January to Croydon … v s. viii d.

Item payd unto Rob*er*t Edlyn for a key bought for a casse to a bottell of glasse … ii d.

Item in reward yeven to m*aister* Crok*es* cl[er]k*es*[161] … xx d.

Conysby. Item paid for the cost*es* of m*aister* Conysby horsys at Croydon for vii horsis and for the dyett of his s*er*vand*es* beyng at Warr*es* howse … v s. ix d.

Item payd the xxiiii day of January to the goldsmyth of Croydon for mendyng*e* of a chaffyng dysshe and of a lytell candylstyk f[or m]y[162] lady of sylv*er* … iiii s.

Item payd unto George Fraunc*es* for a reward yeven unto the p*ar*son of Tonnebryge < þ*at*> for yevyng my lad*ys* g*r*ace a payr*e* of knyves … v s.

Item paid unto vichamberlayn for a reward yeven to Pety John browderer to my lady Dawbeney … iii s. iiii d.

Item unto the same for a rewarde yeven unto maist*er* Hobson clerke … iii s. iiii d.

[M]Summa … iiii li. xix s. x d.[P]

[*p. 93*] Item payd unto Heymound Glasse hardware man for a gyrdell of sylke delyv*er*ed unto m*aistres* Stannop for my lad*ys* g*r*ace … xx d.

Item paid unto the same for a dosyn and two par*e* of glovis delyv*er*ed to Rob*er*t Merbury at Haylyng for my lad*ys* g*r*ace at ii s. iiii d. the dosyn and ii payr*e* at vi d. … ii s. x d.

Item paid unto the same for a payr*e* of lytell pensons … iii d.

Item for v here lassys delyv*er*ed unto maistres Stannop … xv d.

Item paid for ii elnes of brodde ryban delyv*er*ed t*o* maistres Stannop … ii s.

Item for iii elne of cremyssen sylk … xii d.

[160] The MW hand returns here.
[161] MS 'cl[…]k*es*' (wormhole in the paper).
[162] MS 'f[…] […]y' (wormhole in the paper).

Item for ii yerd*es* of whit reban delyv*er*ed unto maistres Foller. Price ... vi d.

Item paid unt*o* the same for a t*r*inyte delyv*er*ed unto George Fraunc*es* ... iiii d.

Item to the same for iiii thymbyll*es* ... i d.

Item to the same for xx neld*es* delyv*er*ed t*o* maistrez Foller ... i d.

J. Harryson. Item the xx day of January in reward unto John Haryson for his dysgyssyng*es* makynge in Cryste*n*masse ... xx s.

Gerade Osburne. Item the same day delyv*er*ed unto m*aister* chaunceller for a reward yeven unto Gerade Osburne the kyng*es* servand ... vi s. viii d.

*M*aister *Bothe.* Item unto syr Edward Bothe in reward at his goyng into Northamptonshyr*e* ... xx s.

Frere Langley. Item paid unto Warr*es* wyff of Croydon for lodgyng of frere Langley warden of the gray freris at Canturbury ... iiii d.

*Lord Barkley for the man*er *of Desworth.*[163] Item delyv*er*ed to m*aister* amener the xxix[th] day of January to delyv*er* unto my lord Barkley for his relessͤ*es* and tytell of the man*er* of Desseworth that my lad*ys* g*r*ace late purchissyd of syr Henry Collett ... <xx li.> «cancellatur hic quia postea inter alucaciones Thome Soper solisitir*is*»[164]

[M]Summa ... <xxii li. xvii s.> lvii s.[P 165]

[*p. 94*]

Item the last day of January in reward to Watson of the chappell toward his howse rent for a yere to be ended at Lamas next t*o* come ... xvi s.

*Rob*er*t Hylton by a byll assygned.* Item paid unto Rob*er*t Hylton the vi[th] day of February for <harre> the bourde of Henr*y* my lad*ys* godson by viii wek*es* at x d. the weke ... vi s. viii d.

Item paid unto the same for a frenge for a bedd of grene and blak sylke vii unc*e* at xii d. the unc*e* ... vii s.

Item payd for a stone of fyne fedthers ... ii s.

Item payd to the same Rob*er*t Hylton for his cost*es* a day ... xii d.

Item paid unto the same for the p*er*fourmyng of a furr*e* of sabull*es* ... iii s.

Item paid for ii dd. of bedstavis ... xx d.

Item paid for a chaffyng dyssh ... xx d.

Item for a matteres ... iiii s. viii d.

Item paid for his cost*es* a day ... xii d.

Item paid for mendyng and makyng of maistres Jans geyre ... iii s. iiii d.

[163] The marginal heading is in a different hand.
[164] See pp. 148, 160 below.
[165] The correction is in a different hand.

Item paid for wassyng of hyr*e* stuff … xii d.

Item paid for vi yerd*es* of blak. P*ri*ce the yerd xvi d. for my lad*ys* lytter*e* … viii s.

Item paid for makyng and lynyng of ii payr*e* of hose for ii fotmen … xx d.

Item for ii payr*e* of shoes for the same ii fotmen … xii d.

Item paid for anlett*es* *to* the use of the wardropp … iiii d.

Clothe of golde.[166]

Item payd for a pece of clothe of gold cont*eynyng* xxvi yerd*es* iii q*u*art*er* and a half q*u*art*er*. P*ri*ce the yerd xx s. … xxvi li. xvi s. vi d.

Item paid for a pece of corde … i d.

Item paid to the same Rob*er*t for his cost*es* ii dayes … ii s.

^{M}Summa … xxx li. xxiii d.^{P}

[*p.* 95] Item payd unto Ric*hard* Atherton the vith day of February by his byll assigned for his cost*es* rydyng by the space of xix dayes at viii d. the day … xii s. vIii d.

Item to the same for a gyde from Mydroff to my lord Delywar*es* place … vi s.

*Oly*ver *Lowthe.*[167]

Item payd unto Olyv*er* Lowth the same day for his cost*es* from the xxii day of Novembr*e* to the xx^{ti} day of Decembr*e* … ii s.

Item payd t*o* the same from the xxxith day of Decembr*e* unto the xxiiiith day of January for his said cost*es* … xx d.

Item payd unto m*aister* receyver the viith day of February by a byll assigned for a rynge of gold w*i*th a safer weyng*e* di. unce di. q*uarte*r. P*ri*ce … xxx s.

Item payd for a seall of sylv*er* w*i*th my lad*ys* <al> armes for the receyver of Mountesdale and Hawarden … xiii s. iiii d.

Item for ii unce of sy[l]v*er* that the new holy water stoke weys more then the olde and for makyng of the same … xiii s. ii d.

Item for the mendyng of a lytell holy wat*er* stoke and the styke … iii s. iiii d.

Item for a gylt salt w*i*th a cov*er* weying x unc*es* di. q*u*art[er] at v s. the unce … l s. vii d. ob.

Item paid unto John Holt the xth day of February for his cost*es* rydyng on my lad*ys* messag*es* by the space of viii dayes at dyv*er*se tymes as aperith by his byll assigned … v s. iiii d.

Item paid to maistres Foller the same day for a reward yeven to m*aister* Markhams nurse … ii s.

[166] Bracketed to include the next two items.

[167] Bracketed to include the next two items.

Item delyv*er*ed to the same for money yeven unt*o* maistres Carow at hir beyng w*i*th my lad*ys* grace … xx s.

[M]Summa … vii li. xiiii s. <ix d.> \vii d./ ob.[P]

[*p. 96*] Item paid the x day of February unto m*aister* Gryndell for money paid for the mendyng of a sylv*er* dysshe that came from London … xii d.

Item paid unto the wyff at the Red Lyon in Croydon for the cost*es* of my lord of Chechest*er* horsis and his s*er*vand*es* den*er* the xi day of February … xii d.

Item paid unto John Forster brotherer for his cost*es* t*o* London by ii daies at ii tymes … xii d.

*M*aister *Bell of Fodryng*. Item delyv*er*ed to the maister of Fodryngay to delyv*er* unto m*aister* Belle for a q*ua*rt*er* endet at Crystemasse last passyd … xxv s.

Offryng oon Candlylmas day. Item delyv*er*ed for my lad*ys* offryng apon Candylmasse day v threttypenc*e* in gold … xii s. vi d.

Item paid unto m*aister* Grendell for money payd unto the goldsmyth of Croydon for the mendyng of a gylt pott and a ever of sylv*er* … ii s.

Item delyv*er*ed unto m*aister* chaunceller for a reward yeven to the popys collect*ur* … xx s.

Item payd unto Maydwell of Croydon shoemaker for a payr*e* of slyppers and a payr*e* of shoez for my lad*ys* grace … xii d.

Item delyv*er*ed unto Rob*er*t Edlyn the xiith day of February to pay for two pounde of gold of Wennes bought at London for my lad*ys* grace … lx s.

Item payd unto m*aister* tressorer for money paid to m*aister* Shore shreff of London for the bourde of Ric*hard* Plomer beyng in presson … xviii s.

[M]Summa … vii li. xviii d.[P]

[*p. 97*] *Clothe of gold bought by* maister *Assheton*. Item payd the xiith day of February unto syr Hughe Assheton for money by hym payd t*o* John Prowde <fo> for iii pec*es* of clothe of golde oon pece blew cont*eynyng* xxxiiii yerd*es* iii q*ua*rt*er* oon pece red cont*eynyng* xxxii yerd*es* on q*ua*rt*er*. Item another red pec*e* cont*eynyng* xxvii yerd*es* iii q*ua*rt*er* d. q*ua*rt*er*. P*r*ice the yerd xviiii s. Summa … iiii^{xx}<x>v li. x d.

Item paid unto the same for a pounde of golde of Weness. P*r*ice … xxix s.

Item paid t*o* the same for a pounde of sylk … xiiii s. viii d.

Item paid unto Nicholas Aughton for his cost*es* ridyng apon my lad*ys* messag*es* by the space of xvi dayes at viii d. the day as aperith by his byll assigned … x s. viii d.

Item payd unto m*aister* Grendyll the xiiiith day of February for money payd for the <gyltyn> mendyng of a gylt pott … viii d.

Item in reward to Davyth Dyk*es* the kyng*es* s*er*vant … x s.

*M*aister *Conysby*. Item in reward to master Conysby the xxii day of February … xx s.

*M*aister *Brutnell*. Item in reward t*o* m*aister* Brudnell the same tyme ... xx s.

Item payd for theyr*e* horse meyte in the towne of Croydon and for his horse kep*er* diett ... iiii s. vi d.

Item paid unto m*aister* chaunceller for a reward yeven to doct*ur* Batmanson ... xx s.

Item payd unto John Carter*e* for makyng of a resyngnacion of [...][168] fre chappell in Torryngton ... xii d.

Item payd unto m*aister* Morgan for a reward yeven t*o* doct*ur* Fremyngham p*ro*vinciall of the blake freris that prechyd afour*e* my lad*ys* g*r*ace ... xiii s. iiii d.

[169]*Cambryge workes of Crystes Collage*. Item the xxiiii day of February delyv*er*ed unto maister Maytcalf to delyv*er* to m*aister* Syklyng for the work*es* of Cryst*es* Collage in Cambryge ... xxvi li. xiii s. iiii d.

[M]Summa ... C<x>xix li. vii s. ii d.[P]

[*p. 98*] Item delyv*er*ed to my lad*ys* g*r*ace the xxvii[th] day of February for hir almes purse ... x li.

Item delyv*er*ed unto maistres Foller for a reward yeven unto John Harryson ... <x>vi s. viii d.

Item paid unto the same for money yeven unto John brotherer for his goyng to London ... viii d.

Item in reward unto a s*er*vant þ*at* came from my lady Davers bryngyng worde of the decesse of m*aister* Foller ... iii s. iiii d.

Item paid unto Richart Atherton the last day of February for his cost*es* ridyng to Wynesowr*e* by two daiez at viii d. the day ... xvi d.

Item paid unto the same for ridyng to London ... viii d.

Item to the same for a pec*e* of blew bokeram ... v s. iiii d.

Item paid unto Rog*er* Radclyff by his byll assigned for ridyng to Wynesower*e* and a<gay>bydyng ther*e* by the spaice of xii daiez ... xii s.

Item t*o* the same for ridyng t*o* Richemound and abydyng there by two daies ... ii s.

Item delyv*er*ed to maistres Foller for a reward yeven to maistres Lynne the furst day of M*a*rche ... vi s. viii d.

Item to m*aister* Foderby of <of> Oxforth þ*at* prechyd afour*e* my lad*ys* g*r*ace the furst Sonday in Lent ... vi s. viii d.

Item for my lad*ys* offryng at Syon unto Seynt Breggett ... v s.

Item delyv*er*ed to my lad*ys* g*r*ace for money yeven to dame Mergaret Pole ... x s.

Item for money yeven to maistres Wynesowre ... vi s. viii d.

[168] Lost by a wormhole in the paper.
[169] Add. later in the same hand.

Item the iiiith day of M*ar*che to Hughe Carre for a rewarde yeven to maistres Merbury … vi s. viii d.

Item the vth day of M*ar*che for the exspenc*e* of syr Rob*er*t Rede at the George in Croydon … iiii s. i d.

^{M}Summa … xiii li. xvii s. < i d.> ix d.^{P}

[*p. 99*] Item delyv*er*ed the viiith day of M*ar*che unto m*aister* vichamberlayn for a reward yeven unto the kyng of Castell mynstrels beyng w*i*th my lad*ys* g*r*ace at Croydon … lxvi s. i d.

Item delyv*er*ed unto Rog*er* Radclyff to pay for theyr*e* cost*es* in the towne … vi s. vi d.

Item delyv*er*ed unto m*aister* dean for a reward yeven unto <a> frere Thomson p*r*ior of the blak freris at Langley þ*at* prechyd afour*e* my lad*ys* g*r*ace the ii^{de} Sonday in Lent … vi s. viii d.

Item delyv*er*ed unto maistrez Foller for a reward yeven to Morgan Morice my lord of Rochest*er* s*er*vande … ii s.

Item payd for the cost*es* of my lady Norton woman þ*at* brought a present to my lad*ys* g*r*ace … vi d.

*T. Pellet xiiii die M*arche. Item paid unto John Carter m*aister* chauncellers s*er*uant to delyv*er* for the exibucion of Thomas Pellett at Cambryge … vs. iiii d.

Item to the same apon a rekenyng for the same Thomas toward*es* his exibucion … vi s. viii d.

Item to the same for a reward yeven unto Marche syngyng man … xx d.

J. Plofeld. Item in reward to John Plofelde s*er*vant unto Jamys Morice for wrytyng of dyv*er*se book*es* for my lad*ys* g*r*ace … iii s. iiii d.

Item delyv*er*ed unto George Fraunc*es* t*o* delyv*er* unto my lad*ys* g*r*ace at the kyng*es* beyng at Croydon \in gold/ … xx s.

*M*aister *Sykelyng*e *of Cambryge*. Item delyv*er*ed unto m*aister* chaunceller for to delyv*er* unto m*aister* Sekelyng maist*er* of Crystes Collage in Cambryge toward*es* the work*es* of the same collage the xv day of M*ar*che … Ciiii^{xx} li.

^{M}Summa … Ciiii^{xx}v li. xix s. <vi d.> iiii d.^{P}

[*p. 100*] Item delyv*er*ed unto maistres Stannop for a reward yeven unto Jamys Moryce wyff at his dep*ar*tyng … vi s. viii d.

Item delyv*er*ed unto m*aister* confessor the xiiii day of M*ar*che in almes yeven unto the monke of Seynt Cattrens Mownte for the raunsom of c*er*ten crysten men þ*at* were takyn in hethynes … xx s.

Item paid to m*aister* receyver by his byll assigned for ridyng to London and there beyng by iii dayes and ii nyght*es* laboryng unto the bisshop of Norwych for the benyfice of Attylberue for thuse of m*aister* Sekelyng and also to m*aister* Lytchefeld for m*aister* confessor … v s.

Item payd to the same for his <… >cost*es* anoder tyme to London and there abydyng by ii dayes and ii nyght*es* for my lad*ys* mat*er*ez … iii s. iiii d.

Item payd unto Rob*er*t Hylton by his byll assigned for iiii yerd*es* of welvet. P*r*ice … xlvi s.

Item paid to the same for vii unc*e* di. of freng*e* for my lad*ys* pelyon. P*r*ice … vii s. vi d.

Item payd for a kyppe of whit lambe … iiii s.

Item paid for iii yerd*es* of medly tawny for m*aistres* Potte. P*r*ice … ix s.

Item paid to the same Rob*er*t for his cost*es* a day … xii d.

Item paid for the makyng of a payr*e* of hose for Henry my lad*ys* godson … iiii d.

Item paid for the makyng of two cot*es* for the lett*er* men … xvi d.

*For m*aister *chaunceller*. Item the xiiii day of M*ar*che delyv*er*ed to my lad*ys* g*r*ace \for a horse bought of m*aister* chaunceller and yeven to my lord p*r*ince at Croydon/ … vi li. xiii s. iiii d.

*The bourde of two pore chyld*er. Item paid to the wyff of the Swanne in Croydon for the bourde of two almes chylder by the space of ix wek*es* \at vii d./ endet the xvi day of M*ar*che … x s. vi d.

[M]Summa … xii li. viii s.[P]

[*p. 101*]

R. Hylton.[170] Item payd unto Rob*er*t Hylton the xvi^th^ day of M*ar*che by hys byll assigned for a frenge of white and blewe waying x unc*es* at xiiii d. the unce … xi s. viii d.

Item for iiii unc*e* i q*uarter* of ryban at xiiii d. the unc*e* … iiii s. xi d. ob.

Item payd for a unce of blak and blewe silk to sowe w*i*thall … xii d.

Item paid for ix unce of gylt gold w*i*th the workyng at xviii d. the unc*e*. Summa … xiii s. vi d.

Item for the workyng of x unc*e* of my lad*ys* gold … xx d.

Item for a unc*e* di. of Vennes gold at ii s. viii d. … iiii s.

Summa xxxvi s. ix d. ob.[171]

R. Hylton by a bill.[172]

Item paid t*o* the same Rob*er*t Hylton for a pece of purple velvet cont*eynyng* xix yerd*es* i q*uarter*. P*r*ice the yerd xii s. … xi li. xi s.

Item for another pece of velvet cont*eynyng* xiiii yerd*es*. P*r*ice the yerd xii s. vi d. of purple … viii li. xv s.

[170] Bracketed to include the next six items.
[171] The total of the six items, written small in the left margin within the bracket.
[172] Bracketed to include the next two items.

Summa xx li. vi s.[173]

Item paid for iii yerd*es* of blak welvet for the cov*er*yng of a sadell and the bordering of the harnes. P*r*ice the yerd xi s. vi d. … xxxiiii s. vi d.

Item for a pounde of damaske gold \conteynynge xii unce/[174] aft*er* iiii s. vi d. the unc*e*. Summa … liiii s.

Item pa[i]d[175] for a chayer … vi s.

Item payd for vi great candyll plat*es* at iii s. the pec*e* … <xii s.> xviii s.

Item paid for ii pec*e* of blak bokeram. P*r*ice the pec*e* vi s. … xii s.

Item paid for iii yerd*es* of diett tawny for my lad*ys* mawndy gowne. P*r*ice the yerd iiii s. viii d. … xiiii s.

Item paid for xxiiii yerd*es* of blak cotten. P*r*ice the yerd vi d. … xii s.

Item paid for xxiiii yerd*es* of whit cotton. P*r*ice the yerd v d. ob. … xi s.

Item payd for iiii payr*e* of wemen hoosis. P*r*ice the payr*e* vii d. ob. … ii s. vi d.

Item payd for a payr*e* of shoez for litell Henry … v d.

^{M}Summa … xxx li. vii s. ii d. ob.^{P}[176]

[*p. 102*] Item payd unto Rob*er*t Hylton in the xvith day of M*a*rche by his byll assigned for money yeven unto Palmers s*er*vande for breyngyng of[177] my lad*ys* <g> chaer to Croydon from London … iiii d.

Item payd unto the same <So> Rob*er*t for his cost*es* at London by iiii dayes … iiii s.

Item payd t*o* a man to help Richard Stukeley to make the cloth of astate by the space of iiii dayes at vi d. the day … ii s.

Item <pay> payd for a yerd di. of purpell sarsynett for lynyng of the valens of the clothe of astate. P*r*ice iii s. ii d. the yerd … iiii s. ix d.

^{M}<Summa payd to R. Hylton by his byll ass*igned* … xxx li. xviii s. iii d. ob.>

Item in reward to Thomas grome of the stabyll comyng from Ware to Croydon w*ith* a <S> lett*er* send by m*aister* chaunceller unto my lad*ys* g*r*ace … xx d.

Item delyv*er*ed to m*aister* dean for a reward yeven to P*ar*son Yonge p*ar*son of Hony Lawne in London that prechyd afoure my lad*ys* g*r*ace the iii^{de} Sonday in Lent … vi s. viii d.

Item the xvi day of M*a*rche delyv*er*ed to maistres Foller for a reward yeven t*o* \Alyse/ Stannopp*es* moder at Croydon … iii s. iiii d.

[173] The total of both items, written small in the left margin within the bracket.
[174] A caret mark after 'pounde' is canc. and placed after 'gold' instead.
[175] -i- lost by a wormhole in the paper.
[176] Not in the MW hand.
[177] 'of' rep.

Item payd unto m*aister* vichamberlayn by his byll assigned for a reward yeven unto Hughe Denysse at the kyng*es* beyng at Croydon ov*er* xx s. delyv*er*ed to hym by George Fraunc*es* … xx s.

Item to the same for a reward yeven to a goddowght*ur* of my lad*ys* g*r*ace vi s. viii d. and to hyr felow þ*at* came w*ith* hyr iii s. iiii d. … x s.

[M]Summa … <xli s. viii d.> lii s. ix d.[P] [178]

[*p. 103*] Item payd unto m*aister* vichamb*er*layn for a reward yeven to oon þ*at* brought a booke to my lad*ys* g*r*ace of the comyng of the kyng*e* of Castell … vi s. viii d.

Item paid unt*o* the same for a reward yeven to John Collop … xx d.

Item to the same for a reward yeven unto Davy Dyke*s* the kyng*es* s*er*vant … iii s. iiii d.

Item paid unto John Bredde by his byll assigned for money payd unto Palm*er* for the makyng of a new sadyll for my lord prynce … x s.

Item to the same for di. unce of Venyce gold for tuffett*es* to the same sadell … xvi d.

Item for a whyt gurthe and a dobyll payr*e* of styrrop leders … ii s.

Item for makyng of an horse harnes of stole werk borderd aboute w*ith* blak velvett … x s.

Item for ix gyld bokels and pendaunt*es* to the same sadell … vii s. vi d.

Item for vi gylt flowers to the same harnesshe … xv d.

Item for a payr*e* of steropp*es* … iii s.

Item for a coller for the horse yeven to my lord pr[i]nce … x d.

Item payd for the makyng of a chayr*e* of purpyll welvet w*ith* the stuff therto longyng … xxx s.

Item paid for iiiM and di. of gylt nayle for the same chayr*e*. P*r*ice … ix s.iiii d.

Item paid for xix gylt flowr*es* for the same chayr*e*. P*r*ice … iii s. xi d. ob.

Item payd for a new bytt and a payr*e* of gylt bossis for my lord prince … iii s. iiii d.

Item delyv*er*ed to maistres Stannop for a reward yeven unto a s*er*vande of my lord of Excetur*e* comyng in message to my lad*ys* g*r*ace … iii s. iiii d.

[M]Summa … iiii li. xvii s. vi d. ob.[P]

[*p. 104*] Item delyv*er*ed to m*aister* dean the xxi[th] day of Marche for money delyv*er*ed to m*aistres* Frognall moder for the kepyng of his brother … xiii s. iiii d.

Item delyv*er*ed to maistres Stannop for a reward yeven to a s*er*vande of the p*r*ior of the chart*er*howse in London the xxi day of M*ar*che … iii s. iiii d.

*Offryng apon our*e *Lady Day*. Item delyv*er*ed for my lad*ys* offryng apon our*e* Lady Day … v s.

[178] Only the original total is in the MW hand.

Item paid unto Nicholas Aughton for his cost*es* ridyng apon my lad*ys* messag*es* to <d> London [and] Richmound at dyv*er*se tymes as aperith by his byll assigned … iii s. vi d.

Item delyv*er*ed to maistres Foller for a reward yeven to maistres Bygott … vi s. viii d.

Item in reward to a s*er*vaunt of doct*ur* Waghan at Potteney comyng t*o* my lad*ys* g*r*ace … xx d.

Item delyv*er*ed to maistres Stannop for a reward yeven to a s*er*vant of Hughe Denysse at Croydon on our*e* Lady Even … iii s. iiii d.

Item delyv*er*ed to maistrez Foller for a reward yeven to Henry Wenstanley … v s.

Item paid for the cost*es* of m*aister* Emson horsis beyng at Warris in Croydon the xxiiii day of M*ar*che … ii s.

Item paid unto the same for the cost*es* of maist*er* presydent*es* horsis at his beyng there dyv*erse* tymes comyng to my lad*ys* g*r*ace … iii s.

Item paid for the cost*es* of my lad*ys* solicit*ur* horsis at the George in Croydon comyng w*i*th m*aister* Emson … x d.

[M]Summa … xlvii s. viii d.[P]

[*p. 105*] Item paid unto Olyv*er* Lowthe the xxv day of Marche for a hawke yeven to my lord of Bu\r/gayne … xiii s. iiii d.

R. Dey. Item paid unto Rob*er*t Dey coke ov*er* xl s. a yere payd to hym by m*aister* tressorer of his waig*es* for on q*uar*t*er* endet at our*e* Lady Day in Lent … vi s. viii d.

Item delyv*er*ed to maistrez Foller for a reward yeven to maistres Crowmeyr*e* at hir dep*ar*tyng … xx s.

*iii yerd*es *tawny p*er *R. Hilton*. Item payd unto Rob*er*t Hylton the ii^{de} day of Aprell by his byll assigned for iii yerd*es* of diet tawny for maistres Jan at iiii s. iiii d. the yerd … xiii s.

Item paid for iii yerd*es* of tawny for maistres Frognoll*es* gowne at iiii s. viii d. the yerd … xiiii s.

Item for a yerd and iii q*uar*t*er* for maistres Ursula of the same tawny … vi[i] s. v d.[179]

Item paid for iii yerd*es* of diet tawny for maistres Pott at iii s. x d. … <xvi s. vi d.> xi s. vi d.

Item paid for half a yerd of tawny medly for the body and slevis of maistres Frognoll*es* gowne … ii s. vi d.

Item paid for viii ellnes d. of wo\r/sted. P*r*ice the elle iiii s. viii d. … xxxix s. viii d.

Item for xiii yerd*es* of course northan meddeley at xviii d. the yerd … xix s. viii d.

Item for xv yerd*es* of blak cotton. P*r*ice the yerd v d. qua. … <vii s. vi d.> vi s. vi d. ob. qua.[180]

[179] -i- lost by a wormhole in the paper; it should be 7s. 2d.

[180] There is a dot calculation of 6s. 6¾d. in the left margin.

Item paid for a pounde of white threde … ix d.

Item paid unto the same Rob*er*t for his cost*es* by ii dayes at London to p*ro*vide the same stuff … ii s.

Item for iii yerd*es* of tawny medly for Pep*er* at <mad> Mawdelen Collage … x s.

[M]Summa … <ix li. ii s. x d.> viii li. vi s. ix d. ob. qua.[P 181]

[*p. 106*] *Nota.* Item payd unto Rob*er*t Hylton the ii[de]day of Aprell for vii yerd*es* of blak cotton for the lynyng of a gowne for Pep*er* at v d. the yerd … ii s. xi d.

Item paid for iiii legg*es* of bodgy for an egge for my lad*ys* gowne at iii d. the legge … xii d.

Item paid unto the same Rob*er*t Hylton for carryage of the said stuff from London to Croydon … iiii d.

E. Randull. Item in reward to Elyzabeth Randull the ii[de] day of Aprell <to> toward*es* the byeng of hir mariage geyre … C s.

*M*aistres *Morgan.* Item the same day yeven to maistres Morgan at hir depa*r*tyng … xl s.

Item delyv*er*ed to maistres Foller for money yeven to Davy Dyke*s* toward*es* the makyng of his jakett yeven to hym by the kyng … xx s.

Crystofer Genyson of Penbroke Hall. Item the same day delyv*er*ed to Crystofer Genyson of Penbroke Hall in Cambryge for an half yere to be endet at Est*er* next to come … liii s. iiii d.

Item paid unto maistres Foller for money yeven to Richard Stukeley for nelde*s* … xvi d.

[M]Summa … <x li. xviii s. xi d.>[182]

Item the iii[de] day of Aprell in reward to a messeng*er* that came from Rome … x s.

Item in reward to Gerawd Osburne the kyng*es* s*er*vant … v s.

Item for my lad*ys* offryng apon Palme Sonday … vi s. viii d.

Item yeven in reward to m*aister* Fawne þ*a*t prechet afour*e* my lad*ys* g*r*ace the same day … vi s. viii d.

[M]Summa … <xxvi> <xxviii s. iiii d.> Summa … xii li. vii s. iii d.[P 183]

[*p. 107*] *Goldsmyth.* Item payd the iii[de] day of Aprell unto Hance Wreythe of Croydon goldsmythe for the makyng of iiii sylv*er* pott*es* weying vii[xx]xiiii unce at vi d. the unce … lxxvii s.

Item paid unto the same for the settyng of two portcoll*es* in smale gylt bassynce p*er*teynyng to my lad*ys* closset … viii d.

[181] Only the original total is in the MW hand.
[182] This is noted by an annotating mark (a delta with two horizontal lines through it).
[183] Only the original total is in the MW hand.

Item paid the iiii[th] day of Aprell unto Coldherbor*e* for two cassis of tynne for seall*es* bought at London … xx d.

Item delyv*er*ed to maistres Foller for money yeven to my lady Norton at hir beyng w*i*th my lad*ys* g*r*ace at Croydon the vth day of Aprell … xx s.

Item paid unto maistres Foller for money yeven unto John Ploffeld þ*a*t was w*i*th Jamys Morice … xx d.

Item paid unto maistres Massy by hir byll assigned ov*er* x s. by hyr rec*eyved* of my lad*ys* g*r*ace for nessesaries for my lad*ys* almes folke … x s. x d. ob.

Item paid unto maistres Foller for a bonett bought for Ursula my lady Polis dought*ur* … iiii s.

Money for the mawndy. Item delyv*er*ed to <x> lxiii pore folk*es* at the mandy ev*er*y pece xiii d. Summa … lxviii s. iii d.

Gode Fryday. *My ladys offryng*. Item for my lad*ys* offryng apon Gode Fryday in fyve shellyng*es* of golde … xxx s.

Item in reward to the cokys for theyr*e* with at Estur*e* … xxvi s. viii d.

Item to the pastry sauc*er*y and skollery … v s.

Item delyv*er*ed unto m*aister* dean for a reward yeven unto Prechett oon of the chappell at his dep*ar*tyng … x s.

Item delyv*er*ed to the same for a reward yeven unto Roley of the chappell at the same tyme … x s.

[M]Summa … xiii li. v s. ix d. ob.[P]

[*p. 108*] *My ladies offryng at the resurreccion ii s. vi d. and at masse v s.* Item for my lad*ys* offryng apon Est*er* day … vii s. vi d.

Summa vii s. vi d.

Jane Gore. Item the xv day of Aprell delyv*er*ed to Andrew Ancell to delyv*er* unto Jane Gore for a q*u*art*er* endet at our*e* Lady Day in Lent … xxvi s. viii d.

Item paid the same day unto John Holt by his byll assigned for ridyng to Richmound and other plac*es* apon my lad*ys* messag*es* by iii daiez … xxvi s. viii d.

Item delyv*er*ed to m*aister* vichamberlayn for a reward yeven to oon Smerte that brought a booke to my lad*ys* g*r*ace of the comyng of the kyng of Castell and Edmound de la Pole the xviii day of Aprell … iii s. iiii d.

Item in reward to the subdean at his going to Cambryge … x s.

Item delyv*er*ed to maistres Stannop the xx day of Aprell for my lad*ys* offryng to the rode at the northe dore in Powlis … ii s. vi d.

Item for my lad*ys* offryng at our*e* Lady of G*r*ace theyr*e* … ii s. vi d.

Item to our*e* Lady of Pew at Westm*ynster* … ii s. vi d.

Item to Seynt Edmound*es* shryne <to> delyv*er*ed to maistres Stannop iiii d. and to my lad*ys* g*r*ace by maistres Foller for offryng t*o* the relyk*es* there iii s. iiii d. … iii s. viii d.

Item to the ancryse at Westm*ynster* … xx d.

Item to our*e* Lady of Barkyng … ii s. vi d.

<Item to our*e* Lady of Bethelem … iiii d.>

Item in reward to maistres Feherber at my lady Norfolk*es* the xxi day of Aprell … vi s. viii d.

Item delyv*er*ed to maistres Foller for money yeven to the p*r*ioris and covent at the Mynorys … xx s.

Item in reward to dame Mergett Lowes … x s.

Item in almes to a pore woman yeven by maistres Feherber … xx d.

[M]Summa … <Ciii s. viii d.>[P] \iiii d./ \Cix s. x d./[P][184]

[*p. 109*] *xxiii*^{o} *die Aprell*is

*Rob*er*t Hylton*. Item payd unto Rob*er*t Hylton by his byll assigned for money payd unto maistres Fynche of London for ii uncez di. of sylk. P*r*ice the unc*e* xii d. … ii s. vi d.

Item to the same for a pece of lynnen clothe in lengh iiii^{xx}xvi ell*es*. P*r*ice the pec*e* … xxxiii s.

Hoses bought for the mawndy. Item for vii dossen of wemen hoses for my lad*ys* mawndy. P*r*ice the dosen iiii s. viii d. … xxxii s. viii d.

Item payd for iiii payr*e* of fyne hose. P*r*ice the payr*e* viii d. … ii s. viii d.

*Bonett*es *bought for mawndy*. Item payd for vi dossen and i of cappes for my lad*ys* maundy and her awne almes folk*es*. P*r*ice ev*er*y dossen v s. x d. Summa … xxxv s. vi d.

Shoez bought for mawndy. Item payd for v dossen and iii payre of shoez for my lad*ys* maundy. P*r*ice the dossen [iii][185] s. iiii d. Summa … xvii s. viii d.

Item paid unto a smythe at Westm*ynster* for the mendyng of a dyall … ii s.

Item payd for a payr*e* of shoes for Henry Baptyst … v d.

Item payd unto m*aister* p*re*sydent for a clok bought for my lad*ys* g*r*ace … iii s. iiii d.

*Kyng*es *mynstrell*es. Item delyv*er*ed to Henry Glasebury and other the kyng*es* mynstrell*es* at Croydon in reward the xxvi day of Aprell … xx s.

Item payd unto Ric*hard* Aderton for rydyng to Richmound two tymes afour*e* the kyng*es* comyng to Croydon … xvi d.

Item to the same for the cost*es* of William Hussy at Croydon in Ester weke … viii d.

[184] All in the MW hand.

[185] Obscured by an ink smear; the emendation is based on 5¼ dozen at 3s. 4d. (which would be 17s. 6d.).

Item payd to the same \Ric*hard*/ <William> Aderton for rydyng to Cambryge to the kyng at two tymes by vii dayez apon my lad*ys* messag*es* the xxviii day of Aprell ... iiii s. viii d.

[M]Summa ... vii li. xvi s. v d.[P]

[*p. 110*] Item the furst day of May payd unto Myles Russell of London goldsmyth for makyng and the weght of a gold ryng for my lad*ys* g*r*ace ... v s. viii d.

Item payd unto the goldsmythe of Croydon for a gold ryng and for the makyng of the same ... v s.

Item to m*aister* Gryndell for a reward yeven unto Mondes brother ... viii d.

Item paid the vth day of May unto Thomas Maydwell for makyng of a payr*e*[186] of shoez and slyppers for my lad*ys* g*r*ace ... xii d.

Item to the same for fotyng of a payr*e* of buskynce ... iii d.

Item to the same for a payr*e* of shoez for my lad*ys* g*r*ace ... vi d.

Item for a payr*e* of corkyt shoez for maistres Pott ... viii d.

The kyng of Castell mynstrels. Item in reward to two lut*er*es of the kyng of Castell*es* þ*at* played of fore my lad*ys* g*r*ace ... xx s.

Item for the cost*es* of the same mynstrels ... v s.

Item in reward unto my lady Mary menstrels ... xiii s. iiii d.

Item delyv*er*ed to maistres Stannop for a reward yeven unto maistres Redyng w*i*th my lady Mary ... xx s.

Item delyv*er*ed to maistres Stannop for a reward yeven to[187] maistres <Denton> \ Denys/ at hir beyng w*i*th my lady Mary at Croydon ... x s.

Item delyv*er*ed unto m*aister* vichamberlayn for a reward yeven unto Crane of the kyng*es* chappell ... vi s. viii d.

Item delyv*er*ed to the same for a reward yeven to Gyles luter*e* the same tyme ... vi s. viii d.

Item payd to the same for money delyv*er*ed for my lad*ys* offryng at the maryag*e* of m*aister* Stafferton ... iiii d.

[M]Summa ... iiii li. xv s. x d.[P]

[*p. 111*] *Exibu*cion *of John Masson at Tatsall.* Item payd unto m*aister* chaunceller the xth of May for money payd to the scolemaist*er* at Tatsall for the exibucion of John Masson late chyld of my lad*ys* chappell unto the xvith day of Aprell last passyd ... xxxviii s. i d.

Item delyv*er*ed to the said scolemayst*er* apon a rekenyng ... x s.

[186] 'of a payr*e*' rep.
[187] 'unto' add.

The ancrysse at the nonnes <in S... > Stampforth. Item payd unto the ancryse of the nonnes at Stampforth for a q*uar*t*er* stypend endet at our*e* Lady Day in Lent ... xxxiii s. iiii d.

Ancryse of Stampforth. Item in almes yeven to the ancryse of Stampforth ... iii s. iiii d.

Seynt Mergettes at Catysby. Item to the p*ar*son of Seynt Mergett*es* chyrche at Catysby apon a prest for wast of my lad*ys* tapur*e* from the fest of Est*er* last passyd ... v s.

Item the x day of May in reward unt*o* the ancryse <suss> suster of Stampforth at Croydon ... iii s. iiii d.

Item payd unt*o* maistres Stannop for viii ellis on q*uar*t*er* of grene reban for my lad*ys* g*r*ace ... v s. vi d.

Item t*o* the same for ii lib. of confections and for the box ... xxii d.

Item for two gale patt*es* bought by the same ... x d.

Item for cost*es* of Rob*er*t Hylton and of the kep*er* w*i*th theyr*e* bot hyr*e* by two dayes ... xviii d.

Item t*o* the same for thembelys ... ii d.

Item payd unt*o* Rob*er*t Fremyngham for a dossen of wellom for my lad*ys* g*r*ace ... iiii s. vi d.

Item in reward to John Fysshe the xth day of May toward*es* his mariage ... xl s.

Item in reward to maistres Fetzherber the xiith day of May at Croydon ... xx s.

^{M}Summa ... viii li. vii s. v d.^{P}

[*p. 112*] *Nota.* Item delyv*er*ed to m*aister* countroller the xiiiith day of May for a reward yeven to maistres Mergett Carow at Croydon ... xx s.

Item in reward to Richart Fiyse at his dep*ar*tyng from Croydon ... xx s.

Item delyv*er*ed to maistres Foller at Westm*ynster* in pence to delyv*er* unto my lad*ys* g*r*ace vi s. viii d. and in grott*es* the same tyme xiii s. iiii d. ... xx s.

Item delyv*er*ed to maistres Stannop for my lad*ys* offryng to our*e* Lady of Pewe ... ii s. vi d.

Item to the same for offryng at Seynt Edmound*es* shryne ... iiii d

Item delyv*er*ed to m*aister* vichamberlayn for a reward yeven to the bottery at the abbey in Westm*ynster* ... vi s. viii d.

Item t*o* the seller the same tyme ... vi s. viii d.

Item t*o* the wardrop of bedd*es* ... vi s. viii d.

Item t*o* the vestry þ*at* delyv*er*ed stuff for my lad*ys* clossett ... iii s. iiii d.

Item t*o* the porters in reward ... iii s. iiii d.

My ladys offryng apon the Assencion day. Item delyv*er*ed to Georg*e* Fraunc*es* for my lad*ys* offryng apon the Assencion day at Vestm*ynster* ... v s.

Item delyv*ere*d to m*aister* vichamberlayn for my lad*ys* offryng in our*e* Lad*ys* chappell at Vestm*ynster* … xii d.

Item in reward to m*aister* Lewcie þ*at* brought half a hert from the kyng to my lady … v s.

Item in reward to Thomas Holden kep*er* of the place at Westm*ynster* … iii s. iiii d.

Item paid unto George Fraunc*es* for a elne of blak reban bought at Westm*ynster* for my lady … ii d.

[M]Summa … Ciiii s.[P]

[*p. 113*] Item delyv*ere*d to my lad*ys* g*r*ace for a reward <yeven to Stann*o*p fader at Westm*ynster*> \yeven to Elyzabeth Stafferton at Westm*ynster*/ … x s.

Item at Syon in reward to the clerk of the vestry theyr*e* for delyv*er*y of stuff for my lad*ys* clossett … iii s. iiii d.

Item the same tyme in reward unto the clerk of werk*es* for delyv*er*y of pewt*er* wessell*es* and fuell for the kechyn theyr*e* … iii s. iiii d.

Item to the howse of Syon towardes the p*ro*fescion of maistres Wenysowr*e* … x li.

Item in reward to dame Mergaret Pole the same tyme … x s.

Item in reward to two wemen norrysse to my lady Pollys two chylder*e* þ*at* wer*e* w*i*th my lad*ys* g*r*ace at Syon … vi s. viii d.

Item payd unto m*aister* vichamberlayn for money yeven to Corpus Chr*ist*i gylde at Syon … xx d.

Item to the same for money yeven to wemen that gederyt for the chyrche at Mycham … iiii d.

Item payd to Willyam Hylm*er* for money payd for the eschaunge of two pewt*er* bassynce waying two lib. more than the olde … xii d.

Item payd to the same for two <Cl> erynall*es* bought by hym at Westm*ynster* … ii d.

Item payd unto Richard Aderton by his byll assignet for ridyng to Richemount a day viii d. and to London a day and ther*e* al nyght viii d. for ridyng to the court by v dayes iii s. iiii d. … iiii s. viii d.

[M]Summa … xii li. xiiii d.[P]

[*p. 114*] Item paid the iii[de] day of Juyn to John Holt for ridyng to Grenewich to my lord of Wenchest*er* in Est*er* weke at the kyng*es* dep*ar*tyng thens … viii d.

Item paid unto the same for a casse to a great wat*er* glasse … iii d.

Item for his bot hyr*e* for the same … i d.

Item for ridyng to Richmound the day afour*e* my lady prync*es* comyng to Croydon and for ridyng the day <of> aft*er* hyr*e* dep*ar*tyng … viii d.

Item paid to the same for ridyng into Kent w*i*th the ancryse sister by the spaice of v daiez w*i*th hyr*e* cost*es* by the way … v s.

Item for the hyr*e* of a horse for m*aister* P*ar*ker to ride to London for theyr*e* exspenc*e* paid by the said Holt as aperith by his byll assigned … xvi d.

Item paid unto m*aister* Morgan for a reward yeven unto the p*ro*vinciall of the blake frerys the xxviii[188] day of May at Croydon … vi s. viii d.

Plofeld. Item the same day delyv*er*ed to John Ploffeld to bye p*ar*chement for my lad*ys* g*r*ace at London … iiii s.

Item for my lad*ys* offryng apon Witsonday … v s.

*M*aister *Thawytt*es. Item delyv*er*ed to m*aister* Thawytt*es* the furst day of Juyn apon a rekenyng t*o* bye c*er*ten stuff for my lad*ys* g*r*ace … vi li. xiii s. iiii d.

*Money delyv*er*ed to m*aister *Sekelyng for Cryst*es *Collag*e *in Cambryg*e. Item delyv*er*ed to John Bredd and Rob*er*t Merbury the furst day of Juyn to delyv*er* unto maist*er* Sekelyng toward*es* the byldyng of Cryst*es* Collage in Cambryg*e* … CCxv li. vii s. xi d.

^{M}Summa … CCxxiii li. <x>iiii s. xi d.^{P}

[*p. 115*] Item paid unto Rob*er*t Merbury the ii^{de} day of Juyn in reward toward*es* the kepyng of his horse the tyme of my lad*ys* g*r*ace beyng at Croydon … vi s. viii d.

Item to Raynold Davenport Thomas Dodde William Grevell John Madyson in lyke man*er* for kepyng of theyr*e* horsis apec*e* vi s. viii d. … xxvi s. viii d.

Item the iiiith day of Juyn in reward unto syr William Moldalle of the chappell to pay for a dyspenciacion… xxvi s. viii d.

Item for my lad*ys* offryng apon T*r*inite Sonday … v s.

Item in reward unto a s*er*vant of the warden of Manchest*ur* comyng in message from Richmounde to Croydon to my lad*ys* g*r*ace … vi s. viii d.

Plofeld. Item payd unto John Ploffeld by his byll assigned for his cost*es* from Croydon to London at dyv*er*se tymes to bye wellom for my lad*ys* g*r*ace … ii s. x d.

Item to the same in reward … iii s. iiii d.

Item payd unto John Madyson by his byll assigned for ridyng from Croydon to London[189] t*o* Westm*ynster* at two tymes … ii s.

Item delyv*er*ed to John Walter*e* t*o* by reban for copes the iiiith day of Juyn … iiii s.

Item in reward to a s*er*vande of the lady Browne that brought iiii chevens and perchis in p*r*esent to my lad*ys* g*r*ace … xii d.

^{M}Summa … <vi li. [...]i d.> iiii li. iiii s. x d.^{P}[190]

[*p. 116*] Item for my lad*ys* offryng*e* apon Corpus Chr*ist*i day … v s.

Nota Item payd unto Rob*er*t Hylton the xixth day of Juyne by his byll*es* assigned for v yerd*es* and a half of cremesyn. P*r*ice the yerd xi s. viii d. … lxiiii s. ii d.

[188] 'dd' add.
[189] 'at' add.
[190] The correction is correct.

Item paid to the same for dryssyng of a gowne of tawny medly for maistres Merget Yan … viii d.

Item paid for half a yerd of tawny for the body and slevis of the same gowne … ii s. iiii d.

Item paid for the dryssyng of a gowne for maistres Frognoll*es* and for half a yerd for the body and slevis to the same gowne in all … ii s. x d.

Item for a pece of bokeram cont*eynyng* xv yerd*es* … v s.

Item for makyng and lynyng of two payr*e* of hose for two fotmen … xx d.

Item for ii payr*e* of shoez for maistres Frognoll … viii d.

Item for a payr*e* shoez for m*aistres* Pott … vii d.

Item paid unto the same Rob*er*t for his cost*es* p*ro*vidyng the same stuff by a day … xii d.

Item for a galley copp w*i*th the cover … x d.

Item for xiii yerd*es* and i q*uarter* of grene damaske. P*r*ice the yerd vi s. viii d. … iiii li. viii s. iiii d.

Item for xxxi elnes of lynnen clothe at xx d. ell … lii s. vi d.

Item for ii payr*e* of shoez for the fotmen bought by the said Rob*er*t anoder tyme … xii d.

Item paid unto the same Rob*er*t Hylton for his cost*es* by two dayez to p*ro*vide the said stuff … xx d.

Item for iiii <tyl>lytell glassis … iii d.

[M]Summa … xi li. x s. iiii d.[P]

[*p. 117*] Item the xixth day of Juyn in reward to Bonyface Stanley vi s. viii d. and t*o* the same to delyv*er* unto a man of London which is content t*o* take unto his prentisse oon Nycholas Davy my lad*ys* almes chyld xx s. … xxvi s. viii d.

Item the xx day of Juyn unto m*aister* receyver*e* for a reward yeven unto syr George Newton somtyme of my lad*ys* chappell … v s.

Item for my lad*ys* offryng at Croydon apon the dedicacion day of the chyrch … ii s. vi d.

Item delyv*er*ed to maistres Stannop for a reward yeven to a goldsmyth of London … ii s.

Item delyv*er*ed to m*aister* Grendyll for money payd unto Hance Wreythe goldsmyth for makyng of two gylt challis w*i*th patenys ponderyng xxxii unc*e* … xxxvii s. iiii d.

Item paid unto m*aister* chaunceller for my lad*ys* offryng at Synt Thomas shryne at Canturbury at my lord of Excet*ur* beyng theyr*e* … iii s. iiii d.

Item payd unto Nicholas Saunders the xix day of Juyn for money payd for the draying of a seall for my lad*ys* g*r*ace … viii d.

Item paid unto Henry Wenstanley the xxi day of Juyn for money payd for the exibucion of Skyp as aperith by a byll assigned … ix s. i d.

Item delyv*er*ed to maistres Foller for a reward yeven to William Hylm*er* wyff at hir beyng at Croydon … v s.

Item in reward to oon Pache w*i*th the kyng at his beyng at Croydon … iii s. iiii d.

^{M}Summa … iiii li. xiiii s. xi d.^{P}

[*p. 118*] Item delyv*er*ed the xxith day of Juyn unto John Madyson for my lad*ys* offryng w*i*th syr William Moldale at his furst masse … vi s. viii d.

Item delyv*er*ed to maistres Foller for a reward yeven to maistrez Seynt John at hir dep*ar*tyng from Croydon… vi s. viii d.

Item paid unto Ric*hard* Aderton for ridyng apon my lad*ys* message*s* by two tymes to Richmound … xii d.

Item delyv*er*ed to Hughe Carre for a reward yeven to Gret Elyzabeth w*i*th my lady Mary at hir beyng at Croydon … vi s. viii d.

Item paid unto John Fodyll of Croydon shomaker*e* for iii payr*e* of shoez for iii of my lad*ys* almes folk*es* … xiiii d.

Item in reward to a s*er*vande of my lord of Norwyche for bryngyng a lett*ur* to my lad*ys* grace … iii s. iiii d.

J. Plofeld.[191]

Item in reward to John Plofeld at Croydon … vi s. viii d.

Item delyv*er*ed to the same to bye vellom at London … iiii s.

Item to my lord of Cant*er*bury preyser in reward … iii s. iiii d.

Item delyv*er*ed to my lad*ys* grace at Hampton Court … xx s.

Item the same tyme for a reward yeven to John Treglyston my lord chamberlayn*e* s*er*vand … vi s. viii d.

Item for a reward yeven to the yeman of the wardrop theyr*e* … vi s. viii d.

Item delyv*er*ed to my lad*ys* grace for a reward yeven to my lord chamberlayns son … xx s.

Item delyv*er*ed to John <v… > Urmeston for my lad*ys* offryng to our*e* Lady at Hatfeld … xx d.

Item delyv*er*ed to Ric*hard* Stukeley toward*es* his cost*es* to Colyweston for the organse and cloke to be brought to Hatfeld … v s.

Delyvered by maister *deans commawnde*. Item to John Walter*e* for his cost*es* the same tyme … vi s. viii d.

^{M}Summa … <Cvii s. vi d.> Cvi s. ii d.^{P}

[191] Bracketed to include the next two items.

[*p. 119*] *Money paid unto syr Hughe Assheton for juelles bought of Mondy goldsmyth.*[192]

Item paid unto syr <hughe>[193] Hughe Assheton for money by hym payd unto John Mondy goldsmythe for a crosse of sylv*er* and gylt weying xvii unc*ez* di. Price the unc*e* v s. … iiii li. vii s. vi d.

Item to the same for iiii rynge*s* of gold weyes[194] [*blank*] … xxvii s.

Item for the settyng of iiii rubys and the makyng of the said iiii rynge*s* … xvi s.

Item for the enamellyng of a chene and a bocull and a pendant of a gyrdell … ix s. vi d.

Reward yeven. Item in reward to a man of London that brought letturs to my lad*ys* grace that came from Rome to Hatfeld the last day of Juyn … ii s.

Jane Gore. Item to Andrew Ancell to delyv*er* unto Jane Gore for a q*uarter* ended at mydsom*ur* last passyd … xiii s. iiii d.

Money yeven to dame Margaret Pole at Syon. Item delyvered to my lad*ys* grace by maistres Foller the iii^de^ day of July for money yeven unto dame Margaret Pole at my lad*ys* beyng at Syon … x s.

Maister *Bell of Fodryngay.* Item payd unto m*aister* Bell at Hatfeld for a half yere ended at mydsom*ur* last passyd aft*er* C s. by yere … l s.

A reward to a brek layer þat cam from my lord Ely. Item the iii^de^ day of July in reward to oon Muswell a bryk layer þat came <for> from my lord of Ely to se the werk*es* at Hatfeld … vi s. viii d.

Money paid to maistres *Foller.* Item paid unto maistres Foller for money payd for makyng of Merget Jan gowne … xvi d.

*Money paid unto George Fraunc*es *for roc*es *at Croydon.* Item paid unto George Fraunc*es* for money by hym paid at Croydon to Martens wyffe for x bus. of rosis for my lad*ys* grace … v s.

Reward yeven to Plofeld. Item in reward to John Plofeld the iiii^th^ day of July for wrytyng of the statut*es* of Crystes Collage in Cambryge … v s.

^M^Summa … xi li. xiii s. viii d.^P^

[*p. 120*] *Cost*es *of Rob*ert *Fremgham to rec*eyve *money of my lord Dodlye.* Item paid unto Rob*ert* Fremyngham for his cost*es* by iiii dayes w*i*th his s*er*vant and ii horsis beying at London to receyve money of my lord Dudley for dett*es* oying to my lad*ys* grace by my lady Powes … vii s.

Item in reward to Thomas Aderton s*er*vant unto my lord of Derby the vth day of July … iii s. iiii d.

[192] Bracketed to include the next four items.

[193] Badly written and so canc.

[194] i.e. [that] weighs, cf. p. 146.

Money paid for makyng of two gylt challes with pattentes. Item payd unto Hance Wrethe of Croydon goldsmyth the xth day of July for makyng of two gylt challis w*i*th patens weying xxxii unc*e* di. … xxxvii s. xi d.

Item paid unto m*aister* chaunceller for a reward yeven to a pursyvant of the kyng*es* þ*a*t came in message to my lad*ys* g*r*ace the vi[th] day of July … iii s. iiii d.

William Hylmer.[195] Item paid xiiii[th] day of July unto William Hylm*er* for two hampers of weker … xiiii d.

Item for ii lokk*es* to the same hamp*ers* … vi d.

Item for a jonyd chayr*e* for a chyld … vi d.

Item for a pewt*er* bassyn and a porege<r> dysshe of pewt*er* … xii d.

Item for a bonett of welvet for maistres Frognoll … xiii s. iiii d.

Item for half a pece of medelyng sip*er*us … ii s. viii d.

Item for stueng*e* of iii kokk*es* … iii d.

Item for <myn]> the mendyng of a bottell of tynne … i d.

Item for a gret leder jugge of iii gallons … iii s.

Item for a wasshyng bell … viii d.

Item for a payr*e* of belloes w*i*th platt*es* … vi d.

Item for a bott from Coldherborow to Sowthewerk … ii d.

Item paid for a cart of Croydon to carry this stuff … vi d.

Item for two baskett*es* <to> that came to Hetfeld w*i*th glassis from Croydon for my lad*ys* g*r*ace … xiiii d.

[M]Summa … lxxviii s. i d.[P]

[*p. 121*] *William Hylmer*.[196] Item paid unto William Hylm*er* for his cost*es* <w*i*th> w*i*th the hyre of his two horsis for oon day to p*ro*vide the stuff afour*e* wretten … xvi d.

Item paid unto the same \for/ a unce of amber for my lad*ys* g*r*ace. The p*r*ice … xxx s.

Jok of stabyll. Item paid the xv day of July unto John Bredde by his byll asssigned for the burde of Joke of the <star> stabyll beyng seke … ix s.

Money paid to maister Morgan for rewardes.[197] Item to my lad*ys* g*r*ace by m*aister* Morgan for a reward yeven to John Walter the xi[th] day of July … xx s.

Item paid unto m*aister* Morgan for a reward yeven to a parsyvant that brought lettur*es* to my lad*ys* g*r*ace that came from Rome … xx d.

Exibucion of Skypp. Item paid unto Henry Wynstanley by his byll assyngned for money paid for Skypp*es* lodgyng and other nessessaryes bought for hym … ix s. i d.

[195] Bracketed to include the rest of the items on p. 120.
[196] Bracketed to include the next two items.
[197] Bracketed to include the next two items.

*John Holt for his cost*es *ridyng*. Item payd unto John Holt for his cost*es* ridyng apon my lad*ys* messag*es* at dyv*er*se tymes from Croydon to Richmound and London and from Hatfeld to Richmound as aperith by his byll assigned … vi s. iiii d.

*A gray horse bought for my lad*ys *grace*. Item paid unto William Barly of Ware for a gray gyldyng amblyng paid the xith day of July … xl s.

*Money paid for the cost*es *of pop*es *orrit*ur *and collettur*e *at Hatfeld with my lad*ys *grace*. Item paid at Lomons in Hatfeld for the cost*es* of the popis orrit*ur* his horsis and the diett of his horse kep*er* … vi s. x d.

A reward yeven by maistrez Foller. Item delyv*er*ed to maistres Foller for a reward yeven to Jane þ*a*t was with my lady Powes at hir goyng*e* to Colyweston … xx d.

^{M}Summa … vi li. v s. xi d.^{P}

[*p. 122*] *Rob*er*t Hylton by his byll assigned*.[198]

Item paid unto Rob*er*t Hylton for ii payer of shoez for the ii fotmen the xxvii day of July … xii d.

Item paid unto the same for lynnen clothe for the lynyng of a kyrtell to my lad*ys* g*r*ace … iiii d.

Item paid for a payr*e* of shoez korkyd for maistrez <Jan> Margaret Jan … viii d.

Item paid for a payr*e* of shoez \vi d./ for maistres Frognoll and for <a[…]lett*es*> anlett*es* … vii d.

Item for xxiiii yerd*es* of whit cotton at v d. qua. the yerd. Summa … x s. vi d.

*M*aister *Morgan money by hym paid*.

Item paid unto m*aister* Morgan for a reward yeven to a man that brought my lad*ys* g*r*ace lettur*es* that cam from Rome … viii d.

Item paid to the same for a reward yeven to the kep*er* of the p*ar*ke for takyng of conyez … xii d.

*Money delyv*er*ed to my lad*ys *g*r*ace by R. Aderton*. Item to my lad*ys* g*r*ace for a reward yeven to maistres Rede delyv*er*ed t*o* Ric*hard* Atherton … vi s. viii d.

*Money delyv*er*ed to m*aist*rez Stannop for my lad*ys *grace*.[199]

Item delyv*er*ed to maistres Stannop for a reward yeven to maistres Massy … iii s. iiii d.

Item to the same for a reward yeven to maistres P*ar*ker*e* … iii s. iiii d.

Maydwell shoemaker. Item paid the xxvith day of July to Maydwell <for> for two payr*e* of shoez for my lad*ys* g*r*ace … xii d.

Item for a payr*e* of slyppers vi d. for the makyng of payr*e* buskynce and a payr*e* shoez viii d. Summa … xiiii d.

[198] Bracketed to include the next five items.

[199] Bracketed to include the next two items.

Money paid to maister *chaunceller for a reward yeven to the kynges* ser*vand for a hawke.* Item paid unto m*aister* chaunceller the last day of July for a reward yeven to the kyng*es* s*er*vande þ*at* brought a goshwake to my lad*ys* g*r*ace … <x> x s.

[M]Summa … xl s. iii d.[P]

[*p. 123*] *Money delyv*er*ed to* maister *Sekelyng for the work*es *at Cambryg*e. Item delyv*er*ed the furst day of August to Rob*er*t Merbury to delyv*er* to m*aister* Sekelyng*e* m*aister* of Cryste*s* Collage in Cambryge for the work*e*s of the same collage in gold … Cii li.

Money paid to John Plofeld by his byll assigned.[200] Item payd unto John Plofeld for his cost*es* from Croydon[201] to London there bying a dosen of <vellon> vellom and for the bryngyng of the same to Hatfeld … ii s.

Item to the same for the rulyng of the same vellom … iiii d.

Item to the same for money by hym paid for the same vellom more then <as> he receyved … vi d.

Item paid unto the same for <fo> xvi nyght*es* lodgyng in Hatfeld … viii d.

*Money delyv*er*ed to my lad*ys *g*r*ace.* Item to Henry Abney the iii[de] day of[202] August to delyv*er* to my lad*ys* g*r*ace … xx s.

*M*aistres *Foller*. Item the vi[th] day of August delyv*er*ed to maistres Foller to bye perlys at London for my lad*ys* g*r*ace … lxvi s. viii d.

Item to the same for a reward yeven to m*aister* amener s*er*vande comyng*e* in message from London … xii d.

J. Plofeld. Item to John Plofeld the same day in reward … iii s. iiii d.

R. Pynson. Item the ix[th] day of August to Ric*hard* Pynson of London prynt*er* for half a hundreth of prynted book*es* bought at Hatfeld … xvi s. viii d.

*Henry the kyng*es *godson.* Item to Henry the kyng*es* godson in reward … xiii s. iiii d.

*M*aister solicet*ur*. Item in reward to m*aister* Sop*er* my lad*ys* solycet*ur* the same day for his labur*e* comyng to Hatfeld at dyv*er*se tymes to my lad*ys* g*r*ace … xx s.

Money paid to maister *amener*e. Item delyver*e*[d][203] the xi[th] day of August in almes yeven to two freris of Hechyn … xx d.

Item to the same for a reward yeven to Passhe … iii s. iiii d.

[M]Summa … Cix li. ix s. vi d.[P]

<Summa totalis istius xvi[mi] folii and istius lateris … DCCCCxx li. xviii s. xi d.>[P 204]

[200] Bracketed to include the next four items.
[201] MS 'Coroydon'.
[202] 'of' rep.
[203] -d obscured by a mend in the page.
[204] That is, the sum total from 'Costys and exspencys … ' p. 91 (16 ff. back). Written small to the left at the foot of the page (not in the MW hand).

[*p. 124*] Item the xiith day of August payd unto Edward Vauce for ridyng w*i*th my lad*ys* lett*ur* to a wedow at Hechyn oon Johan Mondy by ii daies … xx d.

Item paid unto m*aister* Fell amener*e* to my lad*ys* g*r*ace for suche money <to> as he delyv*er*ed to dyv*er*se p*er*sons in almes as aperith by his byll assigned … iiii li. xxii d.

Item to Hughe Carr*e* to delyv*er* to my lad*ys* g*r*ace the same day … lxvi s. viii d.

Item paid unto m*aister* Morgan for almes yeven to the ancryse of Poumfrett … xx d.

Item paid unto Ric*hard* Atherton for his cost*es* ridyng to Cambryge by iii daies … ii s.

Item for ridyng from Hatfeld to Cambryge and ther*e* abydyng iiii daies … ii s. viii d.

Item for ridyng two tymes to my lord Frawyk by the space of two dayes … xvi d.

Item paid to John Madison the xiiith day of August for money paid for the exspenc*e* of to s*er*vand*es* of m*aister* Dudles comyng to my lad*ys* g*r*ace to Hatfeld … ii s. xi d.

Item for my lad*ys* offryng on our*e* Lady Day … v s.

Item delyv*er*ed to Hughe Carre for money yeven unto syr Rog*er* Clyfford wyff at Hatfeld … xii d.

Item the xviiith day of August in reward to Stukeley m*aister* Hussy s*er*vande comyng in message t*o* my lad*ys* g*r*ace … vi s. viii d.

For my lady Powes. Item delyv*er*ed to m*aister* Carter at Croydon for money by hym paid for the buryeng of my lady Powes liiii s. i d. Item to m*aister* dean for money paid to ix prest*es* xviii clerk*es* ix chyldren xi s. x d. Item t*o* John Madyson for his cost*es* ridyng by vi daies for Umfrey hir s*er*vant vi s. viii d. in all … lxxii s. vii d.

^{M}Summa … xii li. vi s. <iii d.>^{P}

[*p. 125*] Item paid at Lomans for the cost*es* of maist*er* presyden horsis and m*aister* Dentons and for the diett of theyr*e* s*er*vant*es* the xxith day of August … ii s. i d.

Item in reward the xxiii day of August unt*o* m*aister* Denton at his beyng at Hatfeld w*i*th my lad*ys* g*r*ace … ii s. i d.

Item delyv*er*ed to maistres Foller for a reward yeven to Jak*es* <wyu> wyff þ*at* keped m*aistres* Perrot in his sekenes at Hatfeld[205] … xviii d.

J. Goer. Item delyv*er*ed to Jane Goer by hyr*e* suster at hyr beyng at Hatfeld for a q*uarter* to be endet at Mychaelmas next comyng*e* … xiii s. iiii d.

Item paid unto John Grome by his byll assigned for his cost*es* ridyng by vi daiez to the bysshop of Chest*er* … vi s.

Item delyv*er*ed to m*aister* countroller for a reward yeven Penson prynter for bryngyng of a calend*er* and other bok*es* to Hatfeld from London … vi s. viii d.

[205] The abbreviation might refer to 'maister' or 'maistres', but, despite 'his', no master Perrot is otherwise recorded in these accounts. See too p. 130 below and note the use of 'his' in the final entry of p. 140 (where 'maistrez' is written in full).

*Pep*ur. Item paid unto m*aister* tresorer for money by hym paid for the exibucion of Richard Pepur*e* from the furst day of Decembr*e* unto the fest of Seynt Bartholomew … xxx<v> s. viii d. ob.

Item paid unto John Bredd for money delyv*er*ed for my lad*ys* offryng to our*e* Lady of Whithyll xx d. Item delyv*er*ed to m*aister* vichamberlayn for my lad*ys* offryng at the same place as aperith by his byll xx d. … iii s. iiii d.

Item delyv*er*ed to m*aister* vichamberlayn for my lad*ys* offryng at our*e* Lady of G*r*ace in Cambryg*e* … xx d.

Item in the same place … iiii d.

Item in reward to the godman of the Bell in Bontyngforth … xx d.

Item for my lad*ys* offryng to our*e* Lady of Pety… xx d.

[M]Summa … iiii li. viii s. xi d. ob.[P]

[*p. 126*] Item payd unto m*aister* vichamberlayn for money yeven to the nonnes of Ikylton … vi s. viii d.

Item to the same for money yeven unto the p*re*sydent of the Quenys Collage for the breykyng of bedd*es* stydd*es* … iii s. iiii d.

Item paid unto m*aister* confessor for money yeven[206] at m*aister* Clyfforth place to c*er*ten men that came from Rotlande … iii s. iiii d.

Item payd unto m*aister* receyver for a reward yeven to on Wynslow dought*ur* þ*a*t cam to sew to be w*i*th my lad*ys* g*r*ace … iii s. iiii d.

Item in reward to John Hodson grome of the stabyll at his goyng to Waltham to lechecraft … xx d.

Item in reward to Elyzabeth Frognoll at my lad*ys* goyng to Cambryge … iii s. iiii d.

Item in reward to Perrott the same tyme … xx d.

Item delyv*er*ed to William Pole for my lad*ys* offryng on Sonday the xxx day of August … v s.

Item paid unto m*aister* confessor for money yeven unto a grey frere þ*a*t was w*i*th my lad*ys* g*r*ace at the Quenys Collage in Cambryge … vi s. viii d.

Item paid unto maistres Stannop for money yeven unto maistrez P*ar*kers nurse … xx d.

Item delyv*er*ed to Richard Bothe by m*aister* vichamberlayn comaundement to pay for the cost*es* of s*yr* John Hussy s*yr* John Cutte s*yr* Rob*er*t Sothewell s*yr* Rob*er*t Clyfforth for theyr*e* s*er*vant*es* and horsis … iiii li. x s. viii d.

Item paid unto m*aister* receyver for money yeven to m*aister* Brutnell at Cambryge … xl s.

[M]Summa … viii li. vii s. iiii d.[P]

[206] MS 'to' add. next l.

[*p. 127*] Item delyv*er*ed to Olyv*er* Holland for my lad*ys* offryng on our*e* Lady Day at Hatfeld … v s.

Item delyv*er* to my lad*ys* g*r*ace at Cambryge by the hand*es* of maistres Foler … v s.

Item paid unto Nicholas Sanders for a reward yeven unto Gerrawde Osseburne at Hatfeld … vi s. viii d.

Item paid to maistres Foller for candell*es* for maistres Frognoll*es* norse xv d. Item for sope ix d. … ii s.

Item in reward to William Love … iii s. iiii d.

*Money delyv*ered *to m*aister *Sekelyng*. Item delyv*er*ed unto m*aister* Sekelyng by the hand*es* of Jamys Morice the xii day of Septembr*e* toward*es* the work*es* of Cryst*es* Collage in Cambryge … viii li.

*M*aister *Sekelyng*. Item paid unto the same m*aister* Sekelyng for his cost*es* at Hatfeld w*i*th his comyng fro[207] Cambryg*e* and goyng ayen by v daiez \w*i*th his feloez/ … xx s. iii d.

Item paid unto m*aister* Morgan for a reward yeve to a man þ*at* came from Cambryg*e* to have ben in the spycery w*i*th my lad*ys* g*r*ace … xx d.

Item paid unto John Williams for his cost*es* goyng to my lord of Chest*er* by the space of x daiez at vi d. the day … v s.

Item paid unto Ric*hard* Aderton for the cost*es* of his s*er*vande from Cambryg*e* to <Croydon> Hatfeld apon my lad*ys* message … xx d.

Item paid unto the same for his cost*es* ridyng to the <abb> abot of Waltham and to my lord Frowyk*es* and to m*aister* Foskewes by ii daiez … xvi d.

*M*aister *Sekelyng*. Item delyv*er*ed to m*aister* Sekelyng by the hand*es* of Rob*er*t Merbury toward*es* the byldyng of Cryst*es* Collage the xxi day of Septembr*e* … lxvi li.

^{M}Summa … iiii^{xx}i li. vi s. xi d.^{P}

[*p. 128*] Item the xxith day of Septembr*e* in reward to a s*er*vand of John Stakhowse for bryngyng of worde of a warde lately falen to my lad*ys* g*r*ace oon Langdale … vi s. viii d.

Item in reward to Mondy goldsmyth beyng at Hatfeld … iii s. iiii d.

Item delyv*er*ed to maistres Foller for money sende unto dame Mergaret Pole at Syon … xx s.

Item payd unto Olyv*er* Hollande for iiii unc*es* \perle/ <pyrle> the unce at xviii s. … lxxii s.

Item paid unto the same Olyv*er* for a reward yeven to a woman that cam from London to Hatfeld to shew my lad*ys* g*r*ace certen stuff by <h> my lad*ys* comaundement … iii s. iiii d.

[207] 'fro' written over alteration.

Item paid unto the same Olyv*er* for a blak hatte bought for my lad*ys* g*r*ace … iii s. iiii d.

Item paid to the same for wormesede by hym bought … iiii d.

Item paid unto the same Olyv*er* for his cost*es* and horse hyre at London at iii tymes to p[ur]vey[208] certen stuff for my lad*ys* g*r*ace … vii s.

Item delyv*er*ed unto m*aister* Thwaytt*es* to by certen stuff at Parr*es* for my lad*ys* g*r*ace the xiith day of Septembr*e* … vi li. xiii s. iiii d.

Item delyv*er*ed my lad*ys* g*r*ace the xiith day of Septembr*e* to hyr*e* almes purse … x li.

Item paid for horse meyte of s*yr* Rob*er*t Clyfford his wyff beyng at Hatfeld w*i*th my lad*ys* g*r*ace … xii d.

Item paid unto Henry Assheton the xiith day of Septembr*e* for his cost*es* ridyng by iii daies to Byssam abbey for the p*r*ior theyr*e* … ii s.

[M]Summa … xxii li. xii s. iiii d.[P]

[*p. 129*] Item in reward unto John Chymyngton fawkener*e* for takyng of fezaunt*es* for my lad*ys* g*r*ace … v s.

*Coldeherbor*e. <Item paid unto Petur*e* of Coldherboro for money by hym paid for the repayryng of Coldherboro as aperith by his byll … xxiiii s.>

Item paid to Rob*er*t Ferror for the carryeng of iii fardell*es* from Hatfeld to Ware to be conveyed to Cryst*es* Collage in Cambryg*e* … viii d.

Item paid to m*aister* countroller m*aister* John Fothed for a pece of blew <wost> wolstyd by hym bought … xxvi s. viii d.

Item paid unto the same for a grayle wherof the secunde leff begynneth Sit Duos … xliii s.

Item paid unto the same for anoder grayle wherof the secund leff begynneth Dominum Jhesum … xliii s.

Item to the same for a large antiphaner wherof the secunde leff begynneth Debet Habere … vii li.

Item paid unto the same for another antiphaner wherof the secunde leff begynneth Te Liberantem … C s.

Item paid for another antiphaner wherof the secunde leff begynneth Aque Venture … vi li.

*Cost*es *of my lord Kent my lord Rec*e *and lord Ferr*es . Item paid for the cost*es* of my lord of Kent my lord Richart and lord Ferrys at Hatfeld by ii daiez and iii nyght*es* for horse meyte of xx horsis at Lomanes and at the Chekker*e* <u>xiiii s. ix d.</u> Item for bred

208 MS 'p*r*ovey'.

xii d. for bere oon kynd*er*kyn ii s. iiii d. wyne xiii s. viii d. sug*er* ii s. vi d. two capons xx d. appuls and payres viii d. for iii p*er*sons at den*er* vi d. for fuell for chambr*e* viii d. in candell*es* vi d. Summa xxiii s. vi d. in all … xxxviii s. <iii d.>[209]

^{M}Summa … xxvii li. <vii d.> xiii d.^{P}

[*p. 130*] Item delyv*er*ed unto maistres Foller for a reward yeven to a s*er*vande þ*a*t came from m*aister* p*re*sydent for bryngyng of a clokke unto my lad*ys* g*r*ace … xii d.

Item for a reward yeven unto my lady Norton s*er*vande for bryngyng of quync*es* to my lad*ys* g*r*ace … xii d.

Item to a s*er*vande þ*a*t came from my lady Clefford for bryngyng of a frame to make carpett*es* in … xx d.

Item to the same for bryngyng of a quysshen to my lad*ys* g*r*ace another tyme … xii d.

Item paid unto m*aister* Bowrer for money by hym paid for John Masson … ii s. iiii d.

Item paid unto maistrez Foller the iiith day of Octobr*e* for money paid unto Jak*es* wyff for the kepyng of m*aistrez* Perrott … ii s. vi d.

Sanders. Item paid unto m*aister* Coles clerk for wrytyng of the booke of p*ro*p*r*iacion of Helpston … x s.

Item delyv*er*ed to my lad*ys* g*r*ace for a reward yeven to m*aister* Hobson awdit*ur* at his beyng at Hatfeld … xl s.

Item delyv*er*ed unto m*aister* dean for money by hym paid for the <cost*es*> buryeng of John Walter*e* w*i*th vi s viii d. yeven unto his wyff … xii s. ii d. ob.

Item delyv*er*ed unto Hughe Carre to delyv*er* unto my lad*ys* g*r*ace for a reward yeven to Ric*hard* Conney … xl s.

Item to m*aister* Morgan for a reward yeven unto m*aister* Sop*er* my lad*ys* solicit*ur* the ii^{de} day of Octobr*e* … vi s. viii d.

Item delyv*er*ed to m*aister* dean for the ex[i]bucion[210] of Thomas Pellett of Cambryge … xl s.

^{M}Summa … vii li. xviii s. iiii d. ob.^{P}

[*p. 131*] Item paid unto Hughe Radclyff the xviiith day of Octobr*e* for a crosse of copper and gilte w*i*th the staff of the same and the fote of the crosse to stande apon bought for Cryst*es* Collage … lx s. viii d.

Item for ii payr*e* of candylstik*es* on more and the other lesse. P*r*ice … ix s. iiii d.

Item for a payr*e* of sensores and a ship for the same … xi s. iiii d.

Item for a chyst for the same stuff to be putt in … ix d.

Item for a stone of towe to truse the same in … viii d.

[209] The 3d. is correct.

[210] -i- lost by a wormhole in the paper.

Item for heye to trusse the same in … ii d.

Item for nayles for the same chyst … i d.

Item for lyne for the same chyste … ii d.

Item for money yeven to Palm*er* sadeler for <y[…]> \horse/ harnesse … viii d.

Item paid unto the same Hughe for his cost*es* providyng the same stuff by iii daies … iii d.

Item paid unt*o* William Radclyff for rep*ar*acions done by my lad*ys* comaundement apon the ancresse howse at the nonnes of Stamforth as aperith by a byll therof … Cvi s.

Item paid unto Wylliam Radclyff s*er*vande comyng from Stampforth to Hatfeld in reward toward*es* his cost*es* … iii s. iiii d.

Item payd unto John Pyke the xiiii[th] day of Octobr*e* for his cost*es* ridyng from Hatfeld to Excet*ur* apon my lad*ys* messag*es* by the space of xv dayes w*i*th the hyr*e* of his <hosse> horse … xv s.

[M]Summa … x li. xi s. ii d.[P]

[*p. 132*] Item paid unto George Fraunc*es* for a reward yeven to Henry the kyng*es* godson for the bryngyng of pounde garnett*es* to my lad*ys* g*r*ace … iii s. iiii d.

Item payd unto the same for a reward yeven to a s*er*vande of the abbott*es* of Seynt Abones for the bryngyng of iiii fezaunt*es* … xii d.

Item paid for the cost*es* of doct*ur* Harryngtons horse meyte beyng at the George … vi d.

Item paid unto s*yr* Edward Bothe for his cost*es* ridyng to the abbott of Westm*ynster* for hymselff and his s*er*vande by a day … <v> x d.

Item paid for the nonnes cost*es* of Chesthount at the George theyr*e* s*er*vand*es* and theyr*e* horse meyt by ii dayez and a nyght at on tyme ii s. vi d. and at another tyme for theyr*e* cost*es* in the same place x d. … iii s. iiii d.

Item payd unto m*aister* confessor s*er*vande for ridyng w*i*th the said nonnes to Chestone … viii d.

Item paid unto William Laborer for his exspenc*e* from Depyng unto Oxforth for a warde of my lad*ys* g*r*ace and from Oxforth to Hatfeld and from thens to Oxforth ayen for ix dayes … vi s.

Item for a horse hyr*e* from Barkeley unto <of> Oxforth and agayn to Barkley … xii d.

Item paid for shoyng at c*er*ten plac*es* … iiii d.

Item paid unto Rob*er*t Fremyngham for his cost*es* in ridyng to the courte by the space of iiii daiez w*i*th his horse hyr*e* and his s*er*vand … vii s. viii d.

[M]Summa … xxiiii s. viii d.[P]

[*p. 133*] Item the xxix day of Octobr*e* delyv*er* to maistrez Foller for a reward yeven unto John Gardyn*er* … xx d.

Item paid unto George Fraunc*es* for a reward yeven to my lord of Ely s*er*vande comyng in message to my lad*ys* g*r*ace to Hatfeld … iii s. iiii d.

Item paid the xxv day of Octobr*e* unto the clerk*es* wyff of Hatfeld for the lodgyng of John Plofeld by xiii wekes … iiii s. iiii d.

Item delyv*er*ed to Penson prynter in reward comyng from London to Hatfeld w*i*th book*es* to my lad*ys* g*r*ace the same day … iii s. iiii d.

Item paid unto m*aister* Bekynsall for his cost*es* ridyng from Hatfeld to London apon my lad*ys* messag*es* and their*e* abydyng by iiii daiez as aperith by his byll … vi s. ix d. ob.

Item paid unto maistrez Lynche by hir byll for a pounde of Venus silv*er* bought by hir the furst day of Aprell … xxii s.

Item paid unto the same for a pece of fyne lynnen clothe contaynyng xxviii elnes oon q*u*art*er* … lvi s. vi d.

Item paid unto the same for a pounde of gold of Damask bought the xxii day of Septembr*e* … xxvii s.

Item paid unto the same for half a lib. of sylk … viii s.

Item paid for blew worsted a pece and di. cont*eynyng* xii ellnes … xl s.

Item for <xii> iiii elnez of cremessyn wolstid … xii s.

Item for a lib. of gilt gold … xii s.

Item <ii> \x/ yerd*es* of grene welvet. P*r*ice … lxxvi s.

[M]Summa … xiii li. xii s. xi d. ob.[P]

[*p. 134*] Item paid unto maistres Lynche the furst day of Aprell as aperith by the same byll for ii pec*es* of tawny welvet the oon cont*eynyng* xxii yerd*es* a q*u*art*er* the other x yerd*es* on q*u*art*er*. P*r*ice in all … xii li. iii s. x d.

Item paid for xii yerd*es* of white welvet wantyng the half q*u*art*er* … lxxix s. ii d.

Item for iiii elnez of canvas to trusse the same in … xvi d.

Item for a pounde of golde of Damask bought the ix day of Octobr*e* … liiii s.

Item for a pounde of Vennez silv*er* … xxxviii s.

Item for iiii bonett*es* … lvi s.

Item for pirle golde a unce of damask … iiii s. vi d.

Item a pounde of vestment reban … xvi s.

Item paid unto John Williams for his cost*es* goyng to my lord of Rochest*er* two tymes … ii s.

Item delyv*er*ed for my lad*ys* offreng apon the dedicacion day at Hatfeld by the hand*es* of John Rosse … v s.

Item to maistres Foler for a reward yeven to Ric*hard* Cony iii s. iiii d. to my lord of Rochest*er* s*er*vande at two tymes iii s. iiii d. to John brotherer wyff iii s. iiii d. … x s.

Item to m*aister* p*re*sydent s*er*vande for bryngyng of pounde garnett*es* to my lad*ys* g*r*ace … viii d.

Item to Rob*er*t Fremyngham for a reward yeven to the abott of Chest*er* s*er*vande … x s.

Item paid unto Jamys Morice for xii cov*er*lett*es* … xxxii s.

Item paid unto Nicholas Saunders for a reward yeven to Lomans wyff … xx d.

Item in reward to my lady Rev*er*se s*er*vande for the makyng of two hassehok*es* for to knele on … viii d.

Item in reward to a man þ*at* brought appulls and wardons from maistrez Frowyk to my lad*ys* g*r*ace … vii d.

[M]Summa … xxvii li. xv s. vi d.[P]

[*p. 135*] Item delyv*er*ed to maistrez Stannop for a reward yeven unto Dodde at his goyng to London … vi s. viii d.

Item paid unto Watson shomaker for ii pair*e* shoez and ii pair*e* slippers for my lad*ys* g*r*ace … ii s.

Item delyv*er*ed to maistres Foller for a reward yeven to oon þ*at* came from the quene of Skott*es* … x s.

Item to the same for a reward yeven to the noones of Chesthunt at Hatfeld … xx d.

Item to the same for a reward yeven to Pendent my lord of Rochest*er* s*er*vande … xii d.

*Money delyverd \to/ Rob*ert* Merbury for Crist*es *Colege in Cambrigge*. Item paid unto John Whithed of Eston in p*ar*te of payment of x li. to hym delyv*er*ed <for> toward*es* the sclattyng*e* of Cryst*es* Collage in Cambryge … C s.

Item paid unto Rob*er*t Fremyngham for his cost*es* ridyng to the court by the space of iii dayez … v s. viii d.

Item paid to Penson s*er*vande for two prynted book*es* in vellon and vi other in pap*er* p*r*ocessioners … xxi s. iiii d.

Item for my lad*ys* offryng apon Halhallo day … v s.

Item for the proct*er* of Ihe*s*u gylde in Grantham the iii[de] day of Novembr*e* … xx d.

Item paid unto s*yr* Edward Bothe for a unc*e* of silver whiche was made in bollyons for the silv*er* and facion … v s. vi d.

Item paid unto m*aister* countroller for money by hym paid unto m*aister* Gotson notary for makyng of iiii instrument*es* and wrytyng*es* of the same of iiii book*es* of statut*es* of Cryst*es* Collage and also for the indentur*es* of the stuff sent to the same colage … viii s.

[M]Summa … viii li. viii s. vi d.[P]

[*p. 136*] Item paid unto m*aister* countroller for money paid for the byndyng of oon of the statut*es* book*es* that lyeth chened in the chappell … xii d.

Item to the same for caryage[211] of my lad*ys* clothe sak from Cambryge to Hatfeld … iiii d.

*Rob*ert *Hylton*. Item paid unto Rob*er*t Hylton the ii[de] day of Novembere for ii pec*es* of tawny fustian for kyrtell*es* for the gentylwomen at my lad*ys* fyndyng … xvii s.

Item paid for vi yerd*es* d. of satten of Sypres for a kyrtell for my lad*ys* g*r*ace. P*r*ice the yerd x d. ob. … v s. viii d.

Item for x elnez of lynnen clothe for gentylwomen smok*es* at my lad*ys* fyndyng … vi s. viii d.

Item paid for a dossen yerd*es* of tawny medly … xviii s.

Item paid for a pece of northren kersey for doblett*es* and hose for the almesmen cont*eynyng* xviii yerd*es* … xiii s.

Item for a kepp of whit lambe for thuse of the wardrop … iiii s.

Item for his cost*es* by iii dayez … iii s.

Item for iii yerd*es* of whit lynnyng for Williams Walters cote. P*r*ice … xii d.

Item for a payr*e* of hose of whit fryse for maistrez Perrot … v d.

Item paid for makyng and lynyng of two payr*e* of hose for the fotmen at my lad*ys* goyng to Cambryge … xx d.

Item paid for ii payr*e* of shoez to the same … xii d.

Item for anlett*es* for thuse of the wardrop … iiii d.

Item paid for a dossen of russett bonett*es* for the almesmen. P*r*ice … iiii s.

Item paid for xv lether lasses for pore folk*es* … iiii d.

[M]Summa … lxxvii s. v d.[P]

[*p. 137*] Item paid unto Rob*er*t Hylton for a dossen of lether gyrdell*es* … x d.

Item for two brode dossen of whitte. P*r*ice … xxiiii s.

Item for two pec*es* of whit kersey ev*er*y pec*e* xviii yerd*es* … xxviii s.

Item for a pece of northeren blak cotton. P*r*ice … vi s. viii d.

Item paid for xxviii good*es* of whitte cotton … xvi s. iiii d.

Item for a dossen of whitte capp*es* for almose wemen … viii s.

Item for a dossen of blak capp*es* for chyld*er* of chappell … xii s.

Item for ii brosshes of fyne hethe. P*r*ice … x d.

Item for a furr*e* of shank*es* … xiii s.

[211] 'when' add. but not canc.

Item for a kyppe of blak lambe … vii s.

Item for a kyppe of whit lambe … iiii s. iiii d.

Item for xxx tavelyons at ii d. the pec*e* … v s.

Item for ii broke lambe skynnes … ii d.

Item xii bogie skynnes of blak at xiiii d. a pec*e* … xiiii s.

Item for ix yerd*es* of lyght tawny medly at iiii s. iiii d. the yerd … xxxix s.

Item paid for two yerd*es* of tawny medly for maistrez Ursula. P*r*ice the yerd iii s. viii d. … vii s. iiii d.

Item for iii yerd*es* of diett tawny for my lad*ys* g*r*ace for a nyght gowne. P*r*ice the yerd iiii s. … xii s.

*Rob*e*rt Hylton.* Item paid unto Rob*er*t Hylton by another byll for a pece of whitte cotton cont*eynyng* xxvii good*es* at vii d. another pec*e* of whitte cotton cont*eynyng* xxv god*es* and a half at vii d. two pec*es* of blak cotton on cont*eynyng* xxvii god*es* and the other xxv good*es* at vii[212] d. Summa … lx s. xi d. ob.

Item paid for two pec*es* of \fryse a/ whitte <on> and a \blak cotton/ <other R[…] ssen> … xxx s.

Item for a pec*e* of cardynall whitte cont*eynyng* xxiiii yerd*es* … v s.

Item for ii porters for beyryng of the same to Coldherbor*e* … ii d. ob.

Item for a elne and q*uarter* of tawny worsted … v d.

[M]Summa … xv li. ix s. viii d.[P]

[*p. 138*] Item paid unto Rob*er*t Hylton for a yerd d. of blak satten … x s.

Item for a yerd and a half of blak damask at vii s. … x s. vi d.

Item for a C of whitte boche. P*r*ice … xxx s.

Item for a furre of shank*es*. P*r*ice … xii s.

Item viii yerd*es* of cotton russett at vii d. the yerd … iiii s. viii d.

Item for anlett*es* … iiii d.

Item for a lib. of blue threde … xii d.

Item for a pound of whitte threde … xi d.

Item for half a pounde of blak threde … viii d.

Item paid unto a colliar for carying of the same stuff … viii d.

Item for the cost*es* of the same Rob*er*t p*ro*vidyng the same … ii s.

Item for the makyng and lynyng of a payr*e* hose for blynde Thomas … viii d.

Item for the makyng and lynyng of a payr*e* hose for pore Rauff … v d.

[212] Some alteration to the number, but the total is correct for 7d.

*Crys*tes *Collage delyvered to R. Merbury*. Item dely*ve*red to Rob*er*t Merbury the viith day of Novembr*e* toward*es* the byldyng of Cryst*es* Collage in Cambryge … C li.

Item paid the xiiith day of Novembr*e* for the cost*es* of my lord of London horsis and the diett of his *ser*vand*es* being at the George in Hatfeld for xiii horsis and vi *ser*vand*es* in all … xii s. i d.

Item in reward to Ric*hard* Cony comyng in message to my lad*ys* g*r*ace from my lord of Ely … v s.

Item paid unto m*aister* receyver for x yerd*es* of russett satten by hym bought. P*r*ice of ev*er*y yerd vii s. viii d. … lxxvi s. viii d.

Item for ix yerd*es* of blak welvet. P*r*ice the yerd xi s. … iiii li. xix s.

Item for xxx yerd*es* of damask ev*er*y yerd vii s. vi d. … xi li. v s.

[M]Summa … Cxxiiii li. xi s. viii d.[P][213]

[*p. 139*] Item dely*ve*red to m*aister* chaunceller for a reward yeven unto the freris of Stampforth by the hand*es* of Roger Radclyff … vi s. viii d.

Joke of stabyll. Item paid the xvith day of Novembr*e* unto William Wylles of Waltham Crosse for the burde of Joke grome of the stabyll by the space of iiii moneth and iii daiez at xiiii d. the weke … xix s. iii d.

Item paid for the lechecraft of the same Joke … x s.

Item paid for two hok*es* of sylv*er* and gylt for my lad*ys* g*r*ace waying di. unc*e* at xviii d. and for the facion and gyltyng xviii d. Summa … iii s.

Item to Ric*hard* Cony in reward at his beyng at Hatfeld the xiiith day of Novembr*e* … v s.

Item paid unto maistrez Lynche for iii pec*es* of blew bokeram and iii pec*es* of grene bought by hyr the xxx day of Octobr*e*. P*r*ice … lii s. vi d.

Item to the same for iii pec*es* of sipers … x s. iii d.

Item to the same for a unce of red[214] sylk … xii d.

Item for a ellne and a half of canvas to trusse in the same stuff … vi d.

Item for ii unc*es* of grene sylk … ii s.

Item for half a q*u*art[er] of a <w> unce of red sylk … i d. ob.

Item to Mathew my lord of Oxforth *ser*vande in reward at his beyng at Hatfeld … xx s.

Item dely*ve*red to Edward Heyvon at his goying to Boston to dely*ve*r to the <r> gray freris theyre iii almes … xx s.

[213] The total is not in the MW hand.
[214] 'red' rep.

Item paid unto John Holt by his byll assigned for ridyng to s*yr* Rob*er*t Clyfforth a day viii d. Item to the abbot of Westm*ynster* ii daiez xvi d. Item to my lord Oxforth and to my lord Norwiche by iiii daiez ii s. viii d. … iiii s. viii d.

[M]Summa … vii li. xiiii s. xi d. ob.[P]

[*p. 140*] Item dely*ve*red unto m*aister* dean the xxvi day of Novembr*e* for a reward yeven unto iii syngyng men þ*a*t were of my lad*ys* Norfo[lk]*es*[215] chappell … xi s. viii d.

Item paid unto Henr*y* Fessher for his cost*es* to Cambryg*e* carrying of stuff for Cryst*es* Collage … iii s. iiii d.

Item paid unto Ric*hard* Aderton by his byll assigned for his cost*es* ridyng apon my lad*ys* messag*es* by vii daiez to my lord of Ely and to m*aister* p*re*sident and other plac*es* … iiii s. viii d.

Item dely*ve*red unto maistres Foller the xxvi day of Novembr*e* for money dely*ve*red to my lad*ys* g*r*ace … xl s.

Item the xxvii day of Novembr*e* to William Morrant maistrez Denton s*er*vande for a reward to be yeven to dame Alienor Werney w*i*th the quene of Skott*es* … xl s.

Item dely*ve*red to the same to dely*ve*r unto maistrez Denton of hir fee for two yer*es* ended at Mychaelmasse last passyd … vi li. xiii s. iiii d.

Item in reward to m*aister* Meddelton oon of the proctours of the Arches the first day of Decembr*e* … xx s.

Item paid unto Ric*hard* Aderton by his byll assigned for ridyng to London apon my lad*ys* message by vi daiez … iii s. viii d.

Item paid unto maistrez Frognoll*es* norse for kepyng of his chyld for a q*ua*rt*er* and iii wek*es* endet the Sonday the xx day of Decembr*e* … xi s. iii d.

… [M]Summa … xiii li. viii s. xi d.[P]

[*p. 141*] Item paid unto m*aister* Gryndell the xvi[th] day of Decembr*e* for money by hym paid unto Hance Wreythe goldsmyth of Croydon after a clere reconyng*e* of al thyng*es* þ*a*t he hathe wrought for my ladies g*r*ace in full payment … vii s. ii d.

Item paid unto Edithe Foller for money paid for dyv*er*se nessessaries bought by hyr*e* for maistrez Ursula <y> and Mergaret Lodlow as aperith by hir byll assigned … iiii s. vi d.

Item to the same for a reward yeven unto the clok maker of Westm*ynster* … iii s. iiii d.

Item in reward to a s*er*vande of my lord of Rochest*er* for bryngyng of moskadell to my lad*ys* g*r*ace … ii s.

Item paid unto m*aister* dean for his cost*es* ridyng to London and their*e* abydyng ii daies and ii nyght*es* for hymself and ii s*er*vand*es* and iii horsis … v s.

[215] MS 'Norfokl*es*'.

Item paid unto Jamys Morice for a pece of lynyn clothe cont*eynyng* xxvi ell*es* iii q*u*art*er* at xv d. ob. the ell. Item another pec*e* cont*eynyng* xiiii ell*es* di. iii q*u*art*er* at x d. the ell. Summa … lx s.

Item for v^{xx} ell*es* of canvas for thuse of the wardrop … xxx s.

Item for two unc*e* of pirle gold … ix s.

Item for iiii yerd*es* of brode blak reban … ii s. i d.

Item for a pece of lynyn clothe cont*eynyng* xxxi yerd*es* di. … xviii s. iiii d. ob.

Item paid for a boke callid Vita Cristi in Englesshe … ii s.

Item paid for oon in Frenche … xv d.

Item paid unto Richard Atherton by his byll assigned for his cost*es* ridyng to London at dyv*er*se tymes by v daiez at viii d. a d[a]y … iii s. iiii d.

[M]Summa … vii li. ix s. ob.[P]

[*p. 142*] Item to maistrez Foller to dely*ver* unto my lad*ys* g*r*ace apon Crystemasse even … xiii li. vi s. viii d.

Item dely*ver*ed to the same for money dely*ver*ed unto maistres Frognoll*es* to have in hir purse … iii s. iiii d.

Item to Merget Jan in reward … iii s. iiii d.

Item to m*aistres* Perrott … iii s. iiii d.

Item dely*ver*ed for my lad*ys* offryng apon Crystemasse day … v s.

Item for my lad*ys* offryng the xii dayez … x s.

Item to s*yr* John Carter of the chappell in reward … x s.

Item paid unto Pynson of London prynter of l book*es* the whiche my lad*ys* g*r*ace transelatyd owte of French into Englysshe … xxv s.

Item paid to Henry Wenstanley for money payd for Skypp*es* lodgyng*e* at Hatfeld by xxv wek*es* at ii d. the weke … iii s. iiii d.

Item for v payre of shoez for the same … ii s. vi d.

Item for ii payr*e* of hoose for the same … ii d.

Item dely*ver*ed to m*aister* Denton to dely*ver* to doctor*e* Batmanson in reward … x s.

Item to m*aister* Denton s*er*vande in reward … iii s. iiii d.

Item to George Fraunc*es* to dely*ver* unto my lad*ys* g*r*ace on Seynt Thomas day … vi s. viii d.

[M]Summa … xvii li. <x s. ii d.> xiii s. vi d.[P][216]

[216] Only the original total is in the MW hand.

[*p. 143*] Item paid unto Nicholas Saunders for money paid to m*aister* Bekynsall for his cost*es* at London apon my lad*ys* messag*es* … vi s.

Item to the same for vi yerd*es* of whit satan for vestment*es* … xvi s.

Item paid unto Henry Starky for lodgyng of pore Rauffe … ii s. viii d.

Item to Rauff Hopwode for wrytyng of book*es* delyv*er*ed by maistres Foller … iii s. iiii d.

Item to the brotherers wyff for a gowne of maistres Foller … x s.

Item for my lad*ys* offryng apon our*e* Lady Day afour*e* Crystemasse … v s.

Item in reward to doctor Yong þ*at* p*re*chett affore my lad*ys* g*ra*ce … x s.

Item to m*aister* dean for iii daiez ridyng to Cambryge … iiii s. ii d.

Item to m*aister* Loman for m*aister* Brewtenell horse mete the ix day of Decembr*e* … iii s. iiii d.

Item to doctor Foderby for prechyng afour*e* my lad*ys* g*ra*ce … x s.

Item to the bysshop of the <trone> towne on Seynt Nicholas Even … xx d.

Item to the fraternite of the Trinite gylde in London … xx s.

Item for reban bought by my lady Rev*er*se … iii s. v d.

Item to my lady Bray by Nicholas Aughton the xv day of Decembr*e* … liii s. iiii d.

Item to the p*ro*vinciall of the blak freris in Cambryge by m*aister* Morgan … vi s. viii d.

[M]Summa … vii li. xv s. vii d.[P]

<Summa a ultima summa usque … <CCCCxxiii li. xiiii s. ii d. ob.>[217]

[*p. 144*] Item to my lady Rev*er*se for a nownce of rebon … iii d.

Item to Lenard of the vestry by his byll assigned for makyng of dyv*er*se book*es* … v s. ii d.

Item paid for the cost*es* of m*aister* Whitstones m*aister* Harryngton and m*aister* Denton beyng at Hatfeld w*i*th my lad*ys* g*ra*ce … iiii s. xi d.

Item delyv*er*ed unto John Haryson by Nicholas Saunders toward*es* the bying of c*er*tan stuff for the plaiez in Crystemasse … liii s. iiii d.

Item to maistres Foller for my lad*ys* g*ra*ce apon New Yers day … lxvi s. viii d.

Item in reward to Peris Champion for the bryngyng of the kyng*es* New Yer gyft*es* to my lad*ys* g*ra*ce delyv*er*ed by m*aister* Lynne vichamberlayn … C s.

Item for my lad*ys* offryng apon New Yer*es* day … v s.

[217] The total of the items since the last sum total (p. 123), written small (not in the MW hand) at the foot of the page and canc.

Item to Jane Gore the ii^{de} day of January for a q*uarter* endet at Crystemasse … xiii s. iiii d.

Item to Steven Taberet in reward … v s.

Item paid to Nicholas Saunders for a reward yeven unto the kep*er* of the garden at Colyweston for a yere … xl s.

Item in reward to the abbott of Westm*ynster ser*vande delyv*ered* to m*aister* chaunceller … x s.

Item for my lad*ys* offryng apon the Twelf day … v s.

^{M}Summa … xv li. viii s. viii d.^{P}

[*p. 145*] Item delyv*ere*d to my lad*ys* g*r*ace for a reward yeven to m*aister* Coup*er* the viiith day of January … xl s.

Item for a reward yeven unto m*aister* subdean … xx s.

Item for a reward unto m*aister* Conysby at Hatfeld … xl s.

<*M*aister *solicit*ur. Item paid unto s*yr* Hughe Assheton receyver for money delyv*ere*d to Sop*er* my lad*ys* solicit*ur* at his beyng at Hatfeld the viiith day of January … xxvi s. viii d.>

Item paid for m*aister* Conysby horse meyte at the George in <Cr> Hatfeld the viiith day of January … xvi d.

Item paid to Haymound hardwareman for the hyre of his horse from Hatfeld to Cambryge w*i*th stuff for Cryst*es* Collage … iii s. ii d.

Item paid to m*aister* Bothe for dyv*er*se bok*es* bought for my lad*ys* g*r*ace of Stacion bokeseller … iii s. ii d.

Item paid unto John Haryson the viiith day of Janua[r]y toward*es* the payment*es* of c*er*tan stuff for the playez and moris dance in Crystemasse … xx s.

Item paid unto Thomas Maydwell for a payr*e* of buskynce for my lad*ys* g*r*ace … ii s. viii d.

Item to the same for a payr*e* of shoez for my lad*ys* g*r*ace … vi d.

^{M}Summa … <vii li. xv s. iiii d.^{P}> vi li. viii s. viii d.^{P} [218]

[*p. 146*] Item paid unto John Brydd the viiith day of January for iii bassens and iii ewers … xi s.

Item for a baskett corde and paper to carry theym in iii d. for iii cassis of <ten> tenne for seall*es* xii d. for a box to carry a <k> cup of gold in iiii d. for cotton corde and papur to trusse hit in ii d. … xxi d.

Item paid unto the same for his cost*es* ridyng to Oxforth for a ward of my lad*ys* g*r*ace for two horsis by the space of v da[i]es … vi s. viii d.

[218] Only the original total is in the MW hand.

Item paid unto John Harryson in full payment of vii li. xv s. vii d. for the cost*es* of the dysgysyng*es* and playes in Crystemas … lxxv s. vii d.

Item the viii[th] day of January delyv*er*ed to m*aister* receyver s*yr* Hughe Assheton to pay for a cup of gold weyez xlix unc*es* q*uarter*. P*r*ice the unce xlii s. … Ciiii li. ix s. vi d.

Item for a flower w*ith* a dyamounde weys[219] … xiii s.

Item for a flower w*ith* a ruby weyes … xii s. iiii d.

Item for the makyng of theym … xx s.

Item for a halywat*er* stok gylt weis xiii unc*es* at v s. the unce … lxv s.

Item for a halywat*er* stok all gylt weis xi unc*e* the unce v s. … lv s.

Item for two pax bred*es* bought at John Utryth weis lxix unc*es* and di. unc*e*. P*r*ice the unc*e* iiii s. … xiii li. xviii s. <xi d.>

Item for a pott for Raynesshe wyne weying x unc*e* i q*uarte*r of sylv*er* and gylt. P*r*ice the unc*e* v s. … li s. iii d.

Item delyv*er*ed to maistrez Stannop for a reward yeven to a s*er*vand of m*aister* Odall … v s.

Item to m*aister* Morgan for money yeven to my lady Rev*er*se sust*ur* at Myn*er*ez … vi s. viii d.

Summa … Cxxxiii li. xix s. ix d.[P 220]

[*p. 147*] Item paid unto m*aister* Morgan the viii[th] day of January for a reward yeven to a booke bynder of London bryngyng of tokyns from Callis to my lad*ys* grace … iii s. iiii d.

Item payd unto Nicholas Aughton by his byll assigned for his cost*es* ridyng apon my lad*ys* messag*es* at dyv*er*se tymez w*ith* vii s. paid for a cupbord … xxviii s. iiii d.

xxxi s. viii d.[221]

Item paid unto Rob*er*t Merbury for money by hym paid unto doct*ur* Thorneboro chaunceller unto the bysshop of Ely for the inpropriaciou*n* of the benyffice of Fenne Drayton and Malton … iiii li.

Item to the same[222] yeven by m*aister* Wyett to m*aister* John Godson notory of lawe … xiii s. iiii d.

Item delyv*er*ed to m*aister* vichamberlayn for reward yeven to Henry the kyng*es* godson … xiii s. iiii d.

Item to m*aister* Bell of Fodryngay for half yere endyd at Crystemasse … l s.

[219] i.e. [that] weighs, cf. p. 119.

[220] Not in the MW hand. Neither this page nor the remaining pages in the document (i.e. January 1507) are signed by Lady Margaret.

[221] In the left margin alongside the Merbury entry, but actually the total of the first two entries on the page, written in a different hand from the MW hand.

[222] 'for' add.

Item Thomas Dodde by his byll <ass> assigned for money paid to workmen for makyng of a skaffold for the lord of disport*es* in Crystemasse … iii s.

Item to m*aister* chaunceller for a reward yeven to William Ferthyng … vi s. viii d.

Item paid unto John Holt by his byll assigned for a yerd of grene clothe … ii s.

Item for ii weker bottells bought for my lad*ys* g*r*ace … viii d.

Summa pagine … xi li. viii d.[P]

[*p. 148*] *Paymentes made by Thomas Soper my ladys solister*. Item paid by Thomas Sop*er* my lad*ys* solist*er* for suet tacon ayenst div*erce* and sondre p*er*sons in dyv*er*se shyres for many p*ar*ticlar*e* cawsis as in a boke of p*ar*celle*s* made by the said solist*er* whos names causez and somes planly apere in the said boke remaynyng w*i*th the remanbrance off m*aister* Hughe Assheton receyver gen*er*all of þis yere de anno xxii[do] Henrici vii[ti] … vi li. vii s. x d.

Canford and Pole. Item payd by the said solist*er* in the chancere for the wryttyng selyng and inrollyng off the letters patent*es* for Canforth and Pole … xlix s. iiii d.

Soluciones pro Christi collegio in Cantebrygia.[223] Item paid unto the lord Berkeley for his tytell þat he clamed to have in the man*er* of Deseworth \xx li./ fine paid in the chauncere for the recov*ere* of the same \iiii li./ and paid to the lord Frowyk for the takyng of the knowledge \xx s./ and other cost*es* and charg*es* \xiii s. viii d./ … xxv li. xiii s. viii d.

Item for the interyng and inrollyng of the fyne for the man*er* of Roydon … xxiii s. x d.

Item paid for wrytyng of a charter*e* and for other wrytyng*es* made by div*er*se p*er*sons for the surenes off the man*er*s of Malton and Desworth w*i*th xxv s. ii d. for the exspenc*e* of the said solst*er* ridyng to take possession in the said man*er*es … xl s. vi d.

Item paid for the gravyng of a seall for the said collage … xl s.

Item paid for iii wrett*es* de Ad Quod Dampnum for the man*er*s of Malton Desworth and Roydon w*i*th vi li. yeven unto the escheters of Lecestr*e* Exssex*e* and Cambryge for fyndyng and makyng of inquiciou*n* and for returnyng of the same and xx s. viii d. for the wrytyng and inrollyng of the same … vii li. x s. viii d.[224]

[*p. 149*] *Soluciones pro abbacie Westmonasterii*. Item paid for another wrytte de Ad Quod Dampnum for lond*es* and tenement*es* in Chest*er*forth w*i*th xl s. yeven to the eschetur*e* of Essex and xx s. viii d. for the wrytyng and inrollyng of the same … lxiiii s.

Item payd to m*aister* Malh[am]e[225] for vellom and wryting and makyng of the indentures boke fassion betwene my lad*ys* g*r*ace and the abbot of Westm*ynster* \vi li. vi s. viii d./ byndyng lymmyng*e* and sylke lacez for the said indentures \xliii s. iiii d./ cov*er*yng \ xv s. vi d./ the said bok*es* w*i*th welvett lynyng*e* of the same \xiiii d./ claspis and crossez to the same \ii s. x d./ garnysshyng of the same boke \iiii s./ ii bagg*es* of bokerom

[223] Bracketed to include the rest of p. 148.

[224] No total at the foot of the page.

[225] -am- obscured by a mend in the page.

bought for the same boke \viii d./ and for casez for the seall*es* \viii d./ in all … ix li. xiiii s. x d.

Summa of all the holl money payd by Thomas Soper … lx li. iiii s. viii d.

Paymentes made by Robert Hylton.[226]

Item paid unto Rob*er*t Hylton for x yerd*es* of russett cotton for a cote for Skip at vi d. the yerd … v s.

Item paid for x skynnez of mynk*es* for maistrez Frognall … xii s. viii d.

Item for blak redd and grene threde for thuse of the wardrop … xii d.

Item for iiii payr*e* of wemen hose beying at my lad*ys* fyndyng at viii d. the payr*e* … ii s. viii d.

Item for iiii pec*es* of lyre for thuse of the <wr> wardrop. P*r*ice the pece iii d. … xii d.

Item for iiii tymbr*e* of lettis. P*r*ice the tymbre vii s. … xxviii s.

[*p. 150*] Item payd unto Rob*er*t Hylton for his cost*es* at London to bye the forsaid stuff by the space of iiii dayez … iiii s.

Item for the caryage of the same stuff from London to Hatfeld … viii d.

Item for vi payr*e* of hose for my lad*ys* almes wemen at v d. the payr*e* … ii s. vi d.

Item for the makyng of iiii payr*e* of hose for my lad*ys* almes wemen at iiii d. the payr*e* … xvi d.

Item paid for half a pounde of blew thred delyv*er*ed to maistrez Foller … vii d.

Item for a tymber of lettis … vii s.

Item for half a furre of Rumney shank*es* … xiii s.

Item for xii skynnes of blak lambe … iii s.

Item for anlett*es* for thuse of the <wrard> wardrop … viii d.

Item for iii yerd*es* of tawny satten. P*r*ice the yerd vii s. <vi d.> \viii d./ bought of Jamys Gentyll … xxiii s.

Item for vi yerd*es* of blak damaske. P*r*ice the yerd vii s. vi d. … xlv s. vi d.

Item for vi yerd*es* of blak satten at vii s. vi d. the yerd bought of Jamys Gentyll … xlv s. vi d.

Item for a yerd q*u*art*er* i naile of satten for fronttlett*es* for maistrez Frognoll*es* … ix s. viii d.

Item paid for vi yerd*es* of blak velvet for the lynyng of frontlett*es*. P*r*ice the yerd xi s. … lxvi s.

[226] Bracketed to include the next two items.

Madyson. Item paid unto John Madison for his cost*es* ridyng to Waynsted to the kyng by a day … xii d.

[227]Som*me* off þe payment*es* made by Rob*er*t Hylton … xiii li. xiii s. x d.[228]

[*p. 151*]

MDCCxlii li. ix s. i d. qua. <MDlix \iiii/ li. xiii s. vii d. \ix d./ qua.> <xiii li. xiiii s. ii d.>[229]

[*p. 152*] [230]Som*me* of all the hole allowance and payment*es* aforesaid in this yer*e* … MDCCxvi li. v s. i d. ob. qua. And so he oweth <yet> … Dlxxv li. xviii s. vii d. wherof is allowed hym … li li. xvii s. iiii d. for the exhibicou*n* of maste*r* P*ar*ker*e* and his wiff \xxiii li. xviii s. vi d./ and m*aster* Markehame \xxvii li. xviii s. x d./ as it appereth mor*e* playnly in a booke of p*ar*celle*s* therof made and appon this accompt examyned.[231] And so resteth yet … Dxxiiii li. xv d. <wheroff he delyv*er*ed unto þe coffers off þe p*r*inces by þe xiii daye off Januar*y* anno xxii^{do} regis Henrici vii w*i*th xliiii[232] li. ix s. viii d. ob. qua. remanynyng in his hand*es*[233] and ys charged in his new indentur*e* ayenst payment*es* to be made this next yere \iiii^{xx}vi li. iii s. vii d. ob. qua./[234] And so resteth dew … CCCCxxxvii li. xvii s. vii d. qua.>[235]

[*p. 153*] *Wherof in*[236]

Money delyv*er*ed unto my ladis coffers uppon the det*er*minaciou*n* of his last accompte … Cxii li. xv s. iiii d.

Money delyv*er*ed unto the seid coffers by s*yr* Herry Willoughby knyght in the p*ar*te of payment of CC li. … l li.

Clxii li. xv s. iiii d.[237]

Almes yevon to div*er*s p*er*sons at soundre tymes … xii li. xv s.

Money delyv*er*ed at soundre tymes to my ladis almes purse … xlvii li.

Certen stuff bought for my lad*ys* almes men women and childern … Ciii s. ix d. ob.

[227] Written in the ‘sprawling’ hand.
[228] The total of Hilton’s payments is 1d. over.
[229] Three separate calculations (the first in the ‘sprawling’ hand, the others in perhaps two different hands) written small at the foot of an otherwise blank page.
[230] The large formal script (‘Somme … yet’, ‘And so resteth’) is interspersed with the same hand in a sprawling cursive script (the ‘sprawling’ hand), followed (pp. 153–65) by a smaller formal script (perhaps also in the ‘sprawling’ hand).
[231] As noted p. 161 below.
[232] MS ‘xliijj’.
[233] See D91.19/2 (first entry).
[234] See D102.10/113.
[235] See D91.19/1. For the reason for the calculation see p. 161 below.
[236] Bracketed to include pp. 153–9.
[237] The correct total of this and the previous item, bracketed to the right of these entries.

Money delyv*er*ed to the brithren of Trinite gilde of [*blank*][238] … xx s.

Certen stuf bought and other apparell for my lad*ys* maunde … viii li. xviii s. vii d.

Money delyv*er*ed at soundre tymes to the lady Pole toward her fyndyng … lxii s.

Money delyv*er*ed at Syon for the p*ro*fession of mast*er*es Wyndesore … x li.

CCl li. xiiii s. […] d.[239]

[*p. 154*] Money delyv*er*ed unto the ancras of Stamford w*ith* Cxiii s. viii d. for certen rep*ar*acions don ther … viii li. xix s. iiii d.

… iiii^xx^xvi li. xviii s. viii d. ob.[240]

Money delyv*er*ed at soundre tymes for þe exhibicions of old Henri the kyng*es* godson and for Henri my ladis godson … xxviii s. x d.

Exhibicion of Pe[p]ur a[nd M]ason[241] and other my ladis scolers being in div*er*s places this p*re*sent yere … xi li. viii s. vii d. ob.

Money delyv*er*ed to m*astyr* Bell at divers tymes for his exhibicion … vi li. v s.

Money delyv*er*ed at soundre tymes to my lad*ys* g*r*ace for hur offering*es* … viii li. xix s.

Rewardis yevon at sondre tymes to div*er*s p*er*sones … lxxvii li. xix s. viii d.

Rewardis yevon to dame Elyno*ur* Verney xl s. m*astyr* Conyngsby xl s. m*astyr* Brudenell xl s. m*astyr* Co<l>*us* xl s. m*astyr* subdeane <xl s.> \xx s./ Thomas Sop*er* xxvi s. viii d. and rewardis yevon for kepyng of my ladys garden at Colyweston xl s. … xi<i> li. vi s. viii d.

Reward yevon to Peers Champyon bringing þe New Yeres gift … C s.

iiii^xx^xiiii li. vi s. iiii d.[242]

Cxxxi li. vii s. i d. ob.[243]

[*p. 155*] An horse bought and yevon to my lord prince … vi li. xiii s. iiii d.

Money paid for oth[er][244] horse bought to my ladis behofne … xl s.

Money payd for an hawke yevon to my lord of Burgeveny … xiii s. iiii d.

Money payd to mast*er*es Denton for hur fee for ii yeres … vi li. xiii s. iiii d.

[238] London (see p. 143).

[239] The (correct) total for the page written small at the foot of the page (the lower right corner is torn off and remounted, but the missing pence are 8½d.). The individual totals for each entry have been calculated separately, ignoring the previous sum total.

[240] The correct total of the last seven items on p. 153 and the first on p. 154, bracketed to the right of the entries.

[241] MS 'Petur Ayason'.

[242] The correct total of the three previous items ('Reward(is)'), bracketed to the right of the items.

[243] The correct total for the page, written small to the right at the foot of the page; it is correct in terms of the final sums (but note the erroneous calculation of the penultimate entry).

[244] -er obscured by a mend in the page.

Money delyverd to Jane Gower for hur fee in almes … lxvi s. viii d.

Money payd <pay> for an coppe of gold weyng xlix unc*e* i q*u*art*er*. P*r*ice le unc*e* xlii s. for þe kyng*es* New Yere gift … Ciiii li. ix s. vi d.

Money delyv*er*ed for divers other New Yeres gift*es* yevon to soundre p*er*sones … xi li. xvii s. xi d.

iii bonett*es* of velvet bought … xlvi s.

Money payd for the expenc*e* of div*er*s p*er*sones comyng to my ladis grace w*ith* other forin expenc*es* … vi li. xv s. ii d.

Money payd to Bonyface surgon for þe takyng of an chyld of my ladis to prentez and for þe mynystryng of other medicens … lxviii s. iiii d.

Cxlviii li. iii s. […][245]

[*p. 156*] Divers prentyd bokes bought for my ladis grace … lxxviii s. x d.

Money payd for threde crewle and rebyn bought for my ladys grace … xxxiiii s. iii d.

Chamlet sarsenet and bokeram bought for my ladis grace … iiii li. x s. i d.

Velvet saten and damaske of divers and soundre colers bought at divers tymes by <l> my ladys comaundment and for <vs> hur use … iiii^{xx}ii li. xv s. ii d.

Certen other stuff necessary bought for the use and behofne of my ladys grace … viii li. xiiii s. x d.

Certen other necessari stuff bought as perle vi li. xviii s. viii d. and velom xvi s. occupyed for þe writyng of div*er*s bokes for my ladis grace … vii li. xiiii s. viii d.

Certen plate juelles and rynges \xxxiiii li. xi d. ob./ bought at divers tymes w*ith* money payd at Croydon and London for the mendyng and makyng \iiii li. vii s. i d./ of certen plate … xxxviii li. viii s. ob.

Money delyv*er*ed to my lady Bray … liii s. iiii d.

Cl li. ix s. ii d. ob.[246]

[*p. 157*] Cost*es* and expenc*e* of divers and soundre p*er*sons of my ladis s*er*vant*es* ridyng at divers tymes uppon hur messages … xv li. vii s. xi d. ob.

Cost*es* for the mendyng of my ladis litter and chayre … li s. iii d. ob.

Money payd to Palmer the sadeler for the rep*ar*acou*n*s and mendyng of sadyll*es* w*ith* certen new harnes bought … xxxviii s. vi d.

Certen necessary stuff bought for my ladis fotemen … xi s. v d.

Divers nessary stuff bought for my ladis laundre and other stuf w*ith* certen necc*essary* expenc*e* … xxv s. xi d.

[245] The total for the page, written small to the right at the foot of the page (the lower right corner is torn off and remounted, but the missing pence are 7d.).

[246] The correct total for the page, written small to the right at the foot of the page.

Divers furres at soundre tymes bought for my ladis grace and for other that be at hur fy[n]dyng … vii li. xv s. i d.

Cost*es* and exhibicions of maist*er*es Parot maist*er*es Ursula Pole maist*er*es Margaret and maist*er*es Jane … Cxiii s. iiii d.

Certen necessare stuf bought for the apparell of maist*er*es Frognall … iiii li. iii s.

Money paid for cappis bought for the exhibiciou*n* of the chapell … xii s.

xx[…..]xviii[…..][247]

[*p. 158*] Workyng silkis bought at div*er*s tymes … xlv s. iii d. ob.

Workyng gold and gold wyre and silver wyre at divers tymes of sondre sort*es* and of divers p*er*sones b[ou]ght[248] … xvi li. x s.

vi^{xx} elnes of canves bought … xi li. iiii d. ob.

Certen lynnyn cloth bought … xi li. iiii d. ob.

Wolyn cloth coton and fres bought for the apparell of certen gentilmen and gentilwomen and other that be at my ladis fyndyng … x li. iii s. ob. qua.

Worstede of divers colers at soundre tymes bought … vi li. iii s. iiii d.

ii pecez of white carsey bough[t] conteynyng xxxvi yard*es* … xxxviii s.

Money payd by my ladys co*m*maundment for an dispensacion for s*yr* Will*i*am Moldale … xxvi s. viii d.

Cxi yardis and iii q*u*art[er]*es* of clo[t]h[249] of gold bought for to make copis of for Crist*es* Collage … Cxii li. vii s. vi d.

Clxiii li. iiii s. vi d. ob. qua.[250]

[*p. 159*] Certen bokes bought for the seid collage þ*a*t is to wit iii antefeners <u>xviii li.</u> ii grayles <u>iiii li. vi s.</u> an crosse of coper and gilt <u>lx s. viii d.</u> candels[…]k*es* <u>ix s. iiii d.</u> divers other necessary stuff <u>xxxvi s. iii d.</u> and also writing of certen statut*es* <u>xviii s. viii d.</u> … xxviii li. x s. xi d.

Money paid for the ap*ro*priacion of Fen Drayton and Malton unto the seid collage … Cxiii s. iiii d.

Money delyverd to m*astyr* T[hw]atis[251] to by certen stuff for my ladys g*r*ace in Fraunce … xiii li. vi s. viii d.

Certen necessare stuff bought for the wardrobe … xxxviii s.

[247] The total for the page, written small to the right at the foot of the page (the lower right corner is torn off, and the sum should be £39 18s 6d).
[248] -ou- obscured by a mend in the page.
[249] -t- obscured by a mend in the page.
[250] The correct total for the page.
[251] MS 'Twhatis'.

Cost*es* and expens*e* of s*yr* John Cutt s*yr* Robert Southwell s*yr* John Huse and s*yr* Robert Clifford knyghtez attendyng uppon my ladis grace at Cambrige in the tyme of the halowyng of Crist*es* Collage and eleccion of hur scolers þ*er* … iiii li. x s. viii d.

Cost*es* of the buryng of þe lady Powes lxxii s. vii d. and of John Walt*er* xii s. ii d. ob. … iiii li. iiii s. ix d. ob.

Money delyv*er*ed unto John Harison for certen stuff by hym bought for the disgising and mores w*ith* other disportes in Cristemas … vii li. xi s. xi d.

lxv li. xvi s. […][252]

[*p. 160*] Money payd to Herry Wynstanley for the logyng of Skipp and for other nec*essary* bought for hym … xxx s.

vi gret candel plat*es* bought … xiiii s.

Money payd at s[oun]dre[253] tymes unto Thomas Soper my ladis solister as well for div*ers* suet*es* acciou*n*s ayenst certen p*er*sones \vi li. vii s. x d./ as for the l*ett*res patent*es* for Canford and Pole \xlix s. iiii d./ and cost*es* for the recoveryng of certen landis for Crist*es* Collage \xviii li. viii s. viii d./ and \in/ lyke costis for þe makyng sewer of certen landis unto the abbey of Westm*ynster* \xii li. xviii s. x d./ … xl li. iiii s. viii d.

Money delyverd unto þe lord Berkeley for the redempcion of all suche interest and title as he claymed to have in the maner of Desworth now yevon to Cristis Collage … xx li.

Money delyverd at divers tymes unto m*astyr* Scykelyng toward*es* the beldyng of Cristis Collage Diiii^{xx}xix li. xviii d. and in lyke money delyv*er*ed to Robert Marbury for the same warke Cv li. in þe hole … DCCiiii li. xviii d.

DCClxvi li. x s. ii d.[254]

[*p. 161*] [255]So*m*me of alowaunce aforseyd w[yth][256] li li. xvii s. iiii d. for thexhibiciou*n* of mayster P*ar*ker and his wif and master Markeham as yn the v lefe \bifor/ specified[257] … MDCClxviii li. ii s. v d. ob. qua.

And so he oweth as yn the v lefe byfor specyfyd … Dxxiiii li. xv d. <Dxxiiii li. xv d.> <CCCCxxxvii li. xvii s. vii d. qua.>

Wherof delyv*er*ed unto þe seid princes as ys befor*e* specified[258] þe xiii daye off Januar*y* anno xxii^{do} regis H. vii^{t} w*ith* xliiii li. ix s. viii d. ob. qua. seid in his new indentur*e*[259] <and> etc.

[252]The total for the page written small to the right at the foot of the page (the lower right corner is torn off, and the missing pence are 4½d).

[253]MS 's… ndre'.

[254]The correct total for the page.

[255]The large formal script ('Somme', 'And so … xvii s. vii d. qua.') is interspersed with the same hand in a sprawling cursive script (the 'sprawling' hand).

[256]MS 'Whyt'.

[257]See p. 152 above.

[258]See p. 152.

[259]See D91.19/2.

iiii^{xx}vi li. iii s. vii d. ob. qua.

Reddit in computo sequenti. And as yet resteth dew unto þe seid princes as in þe v lefe byfore specified[260] … CCCCxxxvii li. xvii s. vii d. qua.… «que onerantur in computo sequenti»[261]

wheroff

<hic solvitur onus li li. xvii s. iii d. for thexh[i]bicion of m*astyr* Par*k*er and other … MDCCxvi li. iiii s. i d. ob. qua.>[262]

[*p. 162*] *uppon*[263]

Richard Conway late of \þe/ chapell over xiii s. iiii d. payd to Myles Worsley this present yere xxii^{do} … lxvi s. viii d. «unde recepti xx s. et debetur»

George Henyngham my ladis s*er*vant for mony by my ladis grace payd unto the lady Powez for an cheyne that he lost of hers … xxvii s. vi d.

William Pole for money to hym lent … xi li. «unde recepti xx s.»

[264]*Memorandum þ*at *I Myles Worsley hathe rec*eyved *this som of viii li. vi s. viii d. by the hand*es *of m*aister *Hughe Assheton.* Sir John Melton knyght for money to him lent and to his wyff over viii li. vi s. viii d. payd to Miles Worsley this p*re*sent yere xxii^{do} … viii li. vi s. viii d. «que solvuntur ad manus Milonis Wursley»

Thabbot of Crowland for money to hym lent … xl li.

Walter Cokkes yeman of the <of> bakehouse for money unto hym lent … xliii s. iiii d.

S*yr* Herry Willoughbi knyght for money unto hym lent over and besid*es* l li. paid unto my ladys coffers and l li. payd unto Miles Worsley … C li.

James Clarell for money to hym delyverd by thandis of Henri Salfford iiii li. xv s. and by thandis of Olyver Holand xlvi s. viii d. in all … vii li. xviii d. Wherof the seid James delyv*er*ed xv yerdis of tawney medley <to Alexander Trogna> lxxvii s. vi d.[265] [*p. 163*] And also he hath delyv*er*ed to Alexander Thrognall xviii s. vi d. ob. and so restith uppon him … xlv s. v d. ob.

Joh[n] Walter for money unto hym prested to by stuff for the vestrye … iii s. iiii d.

Thexecuto*urs* of the testament of s*yr* Roger Urmyston knyght as appereth in the fote of accompte by them made restyng in the kepyng of m*astyr* Hugh Assheton … xvii li. vii s. ix d.

Robert Crathorn and his felow expenditors of the slewcez at Boston … lx li.

[260] P. 152.
[261] Written small below the total. See D91.19/1.
[262] Written small over three lines to the left at the foot of the page and canc. The payment relates to the first entry at the top of the page.
[263] Bracketed to include all the following items up to and including the first item on p. 164.
[264] Written in the MW hand.
[265] See p. 79 above.

John Canne of Lynne m*er*chaunt for money to him lent by an obligaciou*n* remaynyng w*it*h Miles Worsley … xx li.

[*blank*][266] Rowle of chapell for money to hym lent … lxvi s. viii d.

My lady Jane for money unto hur by James Mores lent … xvi li.

Will*ia*m Ferthyng late of my ladis chapell for money unto hym lent … xiii li. vi s. viii d.

Olyver Holand yoman ussher of my ladys chamber for money unto hym lent … vi li. xvii s. vi d. qua.

[*p. 164*] Thomas Soper my ladys solycit*our* for money restyng in his handis toward*es* my ladis sewtes … xxxix s. v d.

CCCvii li. x s. xi d. ob. qua.[267]

So*m*me of all the money dew and not payd of siche as was prestyd the last yere and in ii other yeres befor past … CCCvii li. x s. xi d. ob. qua.

John Sint John esquier for money unto him lent … lxvi s. viii d.

Ingleberd bokebynder for money unto hym prested to by certen bokes at Pares for my ladis grace … vi li. xiii s. iiii d.

My lord of Ele for money unto hym lent … C li.

My lord of London for money unto hym lent … C li. «unde solvuntur ad manus Milonis Worsley l li.»

Nicholas Aughton for money unto him prestyd … vi s. viii d.

Cxxx li. vi s. viii d.[268]

<Cxxx li. vi s. viii d.>

[*p. 165*] So*m*me of all the money lent and \prestyd/ this present yere xxii^{do} … Cxxx li. vi s. viii d.

And so \thus/ resteth <this> uppon the seyd accomptant of his owne arrerag*es* … <iiii^{xx}vi li. iii s. vii d. qua.> «nichil quia solvuntur»

[*pp. 166–9 and [p. 170] blank*]

[266] Richard (see p. 10).

[267] The sum of pp. 162–4, written small in the left margin just above the 'Somme', in which it is written out fair.

[268] Written small, probably still in the 'sprawling' hand, in the left margin at the end of the last five (bracketed) entries, and again to the right lower down (canc.); written fair on p. 165 in a larger formal script.

D91.19 (SJLM/1/1/3/3) Account of Miles Worsley, treasurer of the chamber: Hatfield, 14 January 1507 – 14 January 1509

Discussion See Introduction 4 and Plates 15–16.

Description Paper, with fine repairs to lower edges, written on both sides, approx. 345 x 240 mm. 65 ff. in three quires: 1^{22}, 2^{20}, 3^{22}.[1] Paginated (not flyleaf [i]) recto 1–127 (but 97, [97I], 97II, [98]) top right in pencil (MGU); pp. [i/ii], 4, 49, 64, 68, 126–8 blank. Left margins approx. 55–65 mm. (with some sub-headings); right margins variable; upper margins 10–20 mm.; lower margins variable. A marker tab (25 x 80 mm.) for the new financial year is sewn 140 mm. down on the outer edge of pp. 63/64 with 'Anno xxiiii^{to} Regis henrici' (diplomatic transcription) written on the recto (cf. Description of D91.20). The quires are stitched into the original membrane wrapper with two modern leather and string strengtheners on the spine; the irregularly-cut unscraped parchment is approx. 550 x 720 mm. at its largest points when opened out (the back edge of the wrapper folds over to contain the whole document, and the upper and lower edges front and back fold in and down). A contemporary hand has recorded in ink on the front cover: 'Pressus 11' (cf. Description of D91.21). The whole is contained in a modern box of brown/grey waterproof buckram ('D91.19' (MGU) in pencil on a white pasted slip bottom right front cover of slipcase, now erased to 'SJLM/1/1/3/3); contemporary monogram and 'D91.19' in pencil (MGU) top right f. [i]r, '4' in pencil (MGU) at foot of page.[2] The summaries, i.e. initial and final material for each year of the accounts (pp. 1–4, 50–67, 114–25), use a formal script (Bastard Anglicana, with a large decorated initial 'T', p. 1 and 'S', pp. 3, 50) for the rubrics, infilled with either a smaller formal or a cursive script.[3] The main body of the accounts and the marginal headings are mostly in a current hand (Anglicana, with some Secretary influence), the same as that in D91.20 and D91.21, seemingly identifiable as the hand of Miles Worsley himself ('the MW hand', 'the main hand').[4] Another hand (the 'curly' hand) occurs on pp. 6–7, 12–14, 17, 20–2, 28–31, 72–3, 89–109.[5] The 'sprawling hand' is responsible for pp. 50 and 114 ('Somme', etc.), for the last entries on pp. 3 and 63, and for occasional interventions elsewhere (see footnotes). Lady Margaret signs 'Margaret R' at the bottom of each page of entries (^{M} in the edited text, placed to the left of

[1] That is, pp. [i]–42, 43–82, 83–128.

[2] This dates from the 1976–78 repair and conservation of the accounts and inventories.

[3] The blanket term, the 'summary' hand, is used for what may be one or more of the hands used in D91.20, D91.21, D91.19, D102.1, and D102.2 and D102.6.

[4] For example, pp. 33 'which I endentyd', 44 'my last accountes', 'delyver myself'.

[5] This hand covers a longer stint than usual at pp. 89–109 and is also responsible for the end-of-page totals. See footnotes for precise details and other hands.

the page total).[6] Page and (rarer) mid-page totals are normally written, and often corrected (if not by the auditor), in the MW hand;[7] they are marked 'probatur' (^{P} in the edited text), sometimes at first with a trefoil symbol or an elongated delta with two horizontal lines across it (e.g. pp. 5–7, 11, etc.), as in D91.20 and D91.21.[8] Latin annotations (some with +, e.g. tenth entry p. 37, fifth entry p. 78) occur occasionally in a hand (probably the 'sprawling' hand) which notes (often in very black ink with a thick nib) the reasons for cancellations of entries, etc.[9]

Summary

1507–8 (years 22–23): statement of account (Hatfield, Worsley, 14 January 1507 – 14 January 1508), arrears of last account, p. 1; receipts, sum total of receipts and arrears, pp. 2–3 [4 blank]; costs and expenses, pp. 5–48 [49 blank]; sum of allowances and payments, debt of MW, amount delivered by MW, debt of MW, p. 50; summary of expenses by item/person, payments made during the year, pp. 51–9; sum total of payments and debt of MW, p. 60; loans and advances, pp. 61–3 [64 blank];

1508–9 (years 23–24): statement of account (Hatfield, Worsley, 14 January 1508–14 January 1509), p. 65; receipts, pp. 65–6; sum total of receipts and arrears (Latin), p. 67 [68 blank]; costs and expenses, pp. 69–114; sum of allowances and payments, debt of MW, p. 114; summary of payments made during the year, pp. 115–22; sum total of payments and debt of MW, p. 122; loans and advances, pp. 123–5 [pp. 126–8 blank].

Edited Text

[*p. 1*] [10]*Hatfeld.* Thaccounpte of Miles Worsley tresourer of the chambr*e* with the most excellent prynces Margaret countes of Richmound and Derby and moder to our sov*er*ayne the kyng that nowe [is] king Henry the viith frome the xiiii day of January in the xx^{ti}ii yere of the seid sov*er*ayn lord unto the xiiii day of January next ensuyng in the xx^{xx}iii yere of our forseid sov*er*ayn lord that ys to sey by the space of [*blank*]

[6] She does not sign any pages after p. 112, i.e. 9 January 1508.

[7] They may be assumed to be in the main hand of the text (i.e. the MW hand or the curly hand) unless clearly otherwise; when not in the main hand, the hand must be that of the auditor/clerk, but only the term 'different' is used here. The MW hand uses a delta-shaped 's.' ('solidi') which differs from the 's.' of the 'probatur' hand(s).

[8] These must be the check-marks of the auditor and/or his clerk(s); they are not found after p. 39 and are not shown in the edited text.

[9] Annotations are indicated by double angle brackets; marginal and above-line interventions are noted in the footnotes. It may be this annotation hand which is responsible for cancelling entries in a double zig-zag (noted below as 'vigorously canc.').

[10] The summary hand begins the document.

Tharrerages. Fyrst the seid accounptant ys charged with tharre*rages* of his last accounpte as yt doyth more playnly appere in the fote of the same … CCCCxxxvii li. xvii s. vii d. qua.[11]

Summa … CCCCxxxvii li. xvii s. vii d. qua.

[*p.* 2] *Recepta denariorum extra cofferam domine.* First receyved the xvith day of January apon the fote of his accounpte anno xxii^{do} … xliiii li. ix s. viii d. ob. qua.[12]

Item receyved the xviiith day of January the same yere … xx li.

Item receyved the xx^{ti} day of January … xvii li. xi s. vii d.

Item receyved the xith day of Aprill the same xx^{ti} ii yere … DCxxxiiii li. xvi s.

Item receyved the iiiith day of Maye … Cxi li.

Item receyved the xxx^{ti} day of May … xxii li. iii s. x d.

Item receyved the viiith day of June … C li.

Item receyved the iiiith day of July … xxxvii li. xii s. iii d.

Item receyved the xiith day of July … xl li.

Item receyved the xx^{ti}i day of July … iiii^{xx}v li. iiii s. ix d. ob. qua.

Item receyved the xx^{ti}vii day of July … CCCC li.

Item receyved the vith day of Auguste «anno [xx]ii^{do}[13] regis predicti» … xv li. xv s. x d.

Item receyved the xx^{ti}iii day of August «anno xxiii^{cio} regis predicti» … x li.

Item receyved the xxv day of August the xx^{ti}iii yere … xx li.

Item receyved the <xiith> xiith day of Septembr*e* … xiii li.

Item receyved the same day … xliii li. xv s.

Item receyved the xviiith day of Septembr*e* … xxvi li.

Item receyved the xixth day of Septembr*e* … C li.

Item receyved the iiiith day of Octobr*e* … lvi li. xiii s. iiii d.

Item receyved the xx^{ti}vi day of Octobr*e* … xx li.

Item receyved the first day of Novembr*e* … xl li.

Item receyved the xvith day of Novembr*e* … xxviii li.

Item receyved the iiiith day of Novembr*e* … xxxii li. xix s. v d.

Item receyved the same day … C li.

Item receyved the xiiith day of <Nove> Decembr*e* … xxxii li. xiii s. iiii d.

Item receyved the xx^{ti} day of Decembr*e* … <C> C li.

[11] See D91.21, p. 152.
[12] See D91.21, p. 161.
[13] MS 'ii^{do}'.

Item receyved the last day of Decembr*e* … l li.

Summa partis … MMCCi li. xv s. i d. ob.

MM<CCxi li. xv s. i d. ob.>[14]

<MMCCii li. xv s. i d. ob.>

[*p. 3*] Item receyved the viiith daye of August anno xxii^{do} as money payed to the kyng for Wokyng … xxvi li. xiii s. iiii d.

Item <delyv*er*ed> \receyved/ to the seid Myles the last day of Decembr*e* for money payed in the begynnyng of Febr*uare* last past t*o* s*ir* E. Haward for the redemyng of m*aister* Pa*r*kers land*es* … <D marcarum> CCCxxxiii li. vi s. viii d.

Item <delyv*er*ed> \receyved/ as money payed for the kyng*es* New Yer*es* gyft … Cxv li. xv d. ob.

Item receyved of m*aister* Hugh Assheton as money payed unto Thomas Soper my lad*ys* solisito*ur* … viii li. xix s. viii d.

hucusque … CCCCiiii^{xx}iiii li. xi d. ob.[15]

[16]Item the seid Myles ys charged w*ith* mony <by> wantyng in a bagge þat dyd not contayne þe hole content by þe so*m*me of [*blank*] \as yt appereth/ in my lad*ys* boke of receyt*es* and payment*es* of þis yere in þe tytle of Mony delyv*er*ed unto þe tresourer of household … <xxx> <xxiiii li. ii s. iiii d.> xxiiii li. ii s. iiii d.[17]

So*m*me totall of all the receiptes w*ith* tharreragez byfore written … MMMCxlvii li. xvi s. qua.

MMMCxlvii li. xvi s. qua.[18]

totalis[19] …

CCCCiiii^{xx}iiii li. xi d. ob.[20]

[*p. 4 blank*]

[*p. 5*] [21]Cost*es* and exspenc*e* reward*es* w*ith* other dyv*er*se payment*es* of the most excellent prync*es* Margaret moder unto our*e* sove*r*aigne lord and countesse of Richmound and Derby paid by the hand*es* of Myles Worsley as hit dothe herafte*r* apere .

[14] Written small to the left at the foot of the page with a dot calculation in the left margin. It appears to be in the same hand as the 'Summa' written fair above it centrally and the canc. calculation written to the right at the foot of the page.

[15] Written small to the right of the page below the previous total.

[16] This entry is written in the 'sprawling' hand.

[17] See p. 63 below and D91.10/159.

[18] Written small to the left of the lower part of the total in the same hand as the calculations on p. 2.

[19] Written small to the left at the foot of the page, followed by a dot calculation.

[20] Written small to the right at the foot of the page in a different hand.

[21] The MW hand starts here.

Furst payd for the cost*es* of maister Wyette m*aister* of Cryst*es* Collage in Cambryge for his cost*es* at Hatfeld comyng to my lad*ys* g*r*ace … xiii s. x d.

Item to John Haryson in reward for his dysport*es* in Cryste*n*masse … xxvi s. viii d.

Item to Elyzabeth Stafferton … xiii s. iiii d.

Item to Thomassyn gold drayer in reward … x s.

Item to Peture[22] kep*er* of Coldherboro in reward … x s.

Item the xvi[th] day of January in reward to Pety John and Petur*e* brothere[r]s … iii s. iiii d.

Money paid unto maistrez Massy. Item paid the same day unto maystrez Massey for dyv*er*se nessessariez by <hr> \her/ bought for the iii chyldren at my lad*ys* fyndyng and for money paid for kepyng of the almes folk*es* and for weyving of napkyns \iiii s./ in all as aperith by hir byll assigned … xxx s. v d.

Item payd the xvii day of January to John Holt for his cost*es* ridyng by the space of two dayez to London apon my lad*ys* message … xvi d.

*Cryst*es *Collage. xviii day of Januar*e.[23] Item delyv*er*ed to m*aister* Rob*er*t Chappell of Peturhowse in Cambryge for the work*es* of Cryst*es* Collage <ov*er*> for suche money dew unto m*aister* Sekelyng ov*er* and above his receyt*es* … xxi li.

[M]Summa … xxvi li. v s. vii d.[P]

[*p. 6*] Item payd unto Rob*er*t Hylton the xix[th] day of January for a payr*e* of shoez for maisters Frognall … viii d.

Item for a payr*e* of pynsons for the same … iiii d.

Item for a payr*e* of shoez for m*aistrez* Perott … x d.

Item for a payr*e* of pynsons for hyr … <x> iiii d.

Item for a payr*e* of shoez for maistrez Jan … x d.

Item for ii payr*e* of [s]hoez for maistrez P*ar*ker … ii s.

*M*aist*er Parker*. Item payd unto the same Rob*er*t for iii yerd*es* of cremyssyn satten of Brygg*es*. Price the yerd iii s. for a doblett and stokk*es* for a payr*e* of hoose … ix s.

*My lord of Kent*es *tombelers*. Item to my lord of Kent*es* tomlers in reward the xix[th] day of January at Hatfeld … xx s.

Penson of London. Item delyv*er*ed unto Pynson bookeseller apon a rekenyng the xx day of <Januay> January … <x li.> «postea allocatur in pede»[24]

*William Hylm*er. Item payd unto William Hylm*er* the same day by <his> \two/ byll*es* assigned for dyv*er*se urynall*es* \iiii s. vi d./ and other glassis bought for my lad*ys* g*r*ace and for a blak welwett corsse \iiii s./ bought by the same … viii s. vi d.

[22] MS 'Perture'.

[23] Two marginal notes in the MW hand, the second below the first.

[24] See pp. 63, 122, 125 below.

Item payd unto John Carter the xxiii day of January for parchement bought by hym and delyv*er*ed to Plofelde … ii s. viii d.

[25]Item paid the xxvii^th^ day of January in rewarde to my ladyes kynneswoman at Sympryngham by John Carter notary … xx s.

*Mas*t*er Park*[e]*r*. Item the same tyme in rewarde to m*aster* Park[e]r goyng to London by my ladyes co*m*maundment … vi s. viii d.

J. Nicholas. Item paid the same tyme to John Nicholas for whyte threde viii d. for halfe a pound of fyne threde v d. for vii lether skynnes for ly[n]ing of purvillys xxi d. for v skynnes of blacke lambe xv d. for a workeman by the space of viii days iiii s. … viii s. i d.

*Peto*ur *Baldwyn*. Item in rewarde to Peto*ur* of Coldeharborght by Hugh Carre … iii s. iiii d.

Item to the said Peto*ur* for a blacke corperys … vi s.

*Tayllo*ur. Item in rewarde to a tayllo*ur* and his wyffe the which was vesyt w*ith* <ske> sykenes to voyde the towne … iiii s.

[M]Summa … iiii li. xiii s. iii d.[P]

[*p. 7*] *Mas*t*er Pexsall*. Item paid in rewarde to mastre Pexsall for his labo*ur* co*m*myng hether by master deane … iii s. iiii d.

*Peto*ur *Baldwyn*. Item paid to the said Peto*ur* of Coldeharborogh for ii dd. of rase vellym x s. for a qayer of pawper ryall viii d. for vernys ii d. … x s. x d.

Item paid to the same Peto*ur* for certeyn reparacions donne at Coldeharborgh … xlix s. ii d.

Item paid for dying of yerne for the carpett*es* … xviii d.

*Mas*t*er Wyatt*. <*Jamys Moryce*>. Item paid to <Jamys Moryce> \m*aster* Wyatt/ the xvii^th^ day of February for the byldyng of Crystys Colege by the hand*es* of m*aster* comptrollo*ur* and John Everyngham … xx li.

Money paid at Richemound. Item to s*ir* Hugh Assheton for money paid in the excheker for jogement of my lad*ys* causys … <xxx s.> xxxiii s. iiii d.

Item paid to John Mondy for a gyrdell bought for my lad*ys* g*r*ace… lii s. iiii d.

Item for makyng of the same gyrdell … xx s.

Item paid to s*ir* Hugh Assheton for xxii yerd*es* of velvet. P*r*ice the yerde xi s. iiii d. … xii li. ix s. viii d.

Item paid to the same for a pound of gold of damaske … liiii s.

Item for iiii pound*es* i unc*e* of gylte gold … liii s.

Item yevyn in rewarde to my lady Revers suster … x s.

Item delyv*er*ed to Thomas Soper my lad*ys* celyster the iii^th^ day of Marche … x li.

[25] The ‘curly’ hand starts here.

Item paid for ii reme of <p> pawper oon of pawper ryall and another smale pawper … x s.

[26]Item paid unto s*ir* Hugh Assheton for money delyv*er*ed to Thomas Ferthyng the xii[th] day of February … <vii li.> «quia in pede»[27]

Item paid unto the same for money delyv*er*ed to my lad*ys* g*r*ace to pley at the card*es* w*ith* the kynge … xl s.

Item paid unto the same for money paid unto Ric*hard* Aderton for a hamp*er* of wekers … vi d.

Item for a padlok ii d. a payr*e* of belloes iii d. for two candylstik*es* of latten viii d. for a xi lib. of blak sope ix d. for a box to put in the sope iii d. for sewyng neld*es* ii d. for his bot hir*e* to London viii d. and for his cost*es* to p*ro*vide the same stuff viii d. … iii s. vii d.

Item payd unto the same for money yeven unto maistrez Lynche for hyr*e* bot hyr*e* from London to Richmound to my lad*ys* g*r*ace … ii s.

[M]Summa … <lxvi>\ lix li./ xiii s. v d.[P]

[*p. 8*] Item payd to m*aister* Assheton receyver for money payd for xxv ell*es* of fyne holland clothe the xvii day of February … lx s. vi d.

Item paid unto the same for money yeven to the clerk*es* of the kyng*es* signett … vi s. viii d.

Item paid for iii yerd*es* of brode blak reban … xii d.

Item for my lad*ys* offryng the Saturday before the secounde Sonday in Lente delyv*er*ed by the same m*aister* Assheton … xii d.

Item for ii yerd*es* of blak reban for lassyng of my lad*ys* bagg*es* withe book*es* … iiii d.

Item for my lad*ys* offryng at the charterhowse … iii s. iiii d.

Idem. Item to the same for money paid to John Arnold goldsmyth … xx s.

Item paid for the makyng of a seall for Crystes Collage … xvi s. viii d.

Item paid to the same for money delyv*er*ed to Garter herott of armes for the makyng of a booke to weyr*e* mornyng clothes by[28] … xx s.

John Harryson. Item paid unto John Harryson for a premer for my lad*ys* g*r*ace … iiii d.

Item for syngyn bred viii d. for his cost*es* to London for clothe of gold xii d. … xx d.

Item payd unto m*aister* Assheton receyver to my lad*ys* g*r*ace for money payd to George Fraunc*es* at Richmound by his byll assigned … xxix s. v d.

Item paid unto <m*aister*> the same for money paid unto Jamys Morice by his byll … xiii s. viii d.

[26] The MW hand returns here.
[27] See p. 63 below.
[28] For the book: Powell, 'Textiles and Dress', pp. 151–3.

Item paid unto the same for a reward yeven to a s*er*vande <s> of my lad*ys* of Syon for bryngyng of vi perches to my lad*ys* g*r*ace … viii d.

Item in reward to the abbot of Glossetu*r* s*er*vande for the bryngyng of two bake lampres to my lad*ys* g*r*ace … iii s. iiii d.

Item paid to the same for money paid for the barge to convay my lad*ys* g*r*ace at two tymez from Richmond to Syon and ayen to Richmound … iiii s.

Item for a reward yeven to the Walsshe men apon Seynt Davies Day … vi s. viii d.

Item in reward to hym þ*at* kep*is* the kyng*es* lyberary … iii s. iiii d.

Item paid to the same m*aister* Assheton for moscadyll for my lad*ys* g*r*ace … xvi d.

Item to the same for money <pai> delyv*er* to maistrez Stannop the xii[th] day of February … vi s. viii d.

[M]Summa … xi li. ix s. vii d.[P]

[*p. 9*] Item payd unto John Grome for his cost*es* from Richmound to Hatfeld for Merget Stukeley … ii s. xi d.

Item payd unto maistres Lynche for xiii ellis iii q*u*art*er* of fyne lynnen clothe. P*r*ice the same … lix s. iiii d.

Item to the same for sylk*es* bought for my lad*ys* g*r*ace … ix s.

Item to m*aister* receyver s*er*vande in reward … ii s.

Item to George Fraunces s*er*vande for his c[o]st*es*[29] ridyng from Richmound to Hatfeld w*i*th maistrez Perrott … xvi d.

Item paid unto Robert Merbury for ridyng from Richmond to Norfolk to s*ir* Edward Haward for to have hym to seall a quyttance of D mark*es* for his cost*es* by the space of ix daiez … ix s.

Item payd to John Utryght goldsmyth for the makyng of a payr*e* of spectakels of gold weying half a unce a ferthyng weght. The p*r*ice of gold xix s. iiii d. the makyng iiii s. … xxiii s. iiii d.

Item to the same for a garter weying an unce and ii peny weght. P*r*ice of the gold xl s. iiii d. the makyng xiii s. iiii d. … liii s. <iiii d.> viii d.

Item payd to maister Morgan for a reward yeven unto the grome of my lad*ys* spyc*er*y … vi s. viii d.

Item to the same for a dyall of every … ii s.

Item paid unto John Holt by his byll for his cost*es* ridyng to my lord of York xiii dayez and to my lord of Oxforth iiii dayez and to my lord of Rochest*er* a day … xii s.

Item to Ric*hard* Stukeley in reward comyng to <Hatfeld> \Richmound/ … iii s. iiii d.

[29] MS 'cist*es*'.

Item to Rob*er*t Fremyngham the x day of M*ar*che for his cost*es* goyng to London for the obtaynyng of advowsen of the bysshop of Worset*ur* and ther*e* abydyng by iii dayes for hymself and his s*er*vande viii d. and for bot heyr*e* ii s. … iiii s.

Item to the same for money payd for the wrytyng of the same adwowsen … xvi d.

Item paid for a boke of Scala Perfectiones bought by Miles Worsley … ii s. viii d.

Item paid <for o> to oon person goldsmyth of London for the mendyng of a ale pot of sylv*er* more put therto by iii s. iiii d. and for the mendyng of a holy wat*er* styk and the same potte v s. … viii s. iiii d.

[M]Summa … <i>x li. <vii[30] d.> xi d.[P]

[*p. 10*] Item to John Arnold goldsmythe for the makyng of a ymage of our*e* Lady w*i*th a rubye in the fotte of the same weying xx s. and for the facion xiii s. iiii d. … xiii s. iiii d.

Rychmound. Item for the bot hyr*e* of Myles Worsley to London for the same stuff and to pay for clothe of gold … ii s.

Item delyv*er*ed to m*aister* Morgan the xith day of M*ar*che by my lad*ys* comaundement at his goyng to London … xl s.

Item payd unto m*aister* dean for a reward yeven to m*aister* Fraunc*es* fissyssion þ*at* was w*i*th my lady Norton … vi s. viii d.

Nota. Item to m*aister* Bekynsall for a reward yeven unto the ancur*e* of the chartyrhowse at Syon … xx d.

Item to the same for to delyv*er* unto the freris at Richmound … xl s.

Item to maistrez Parker and maistrez Jan at theyr*e* goyng to the pardon to Syon … iii s. iiii d.

Item to George Fraunc*es* for my lad*ys* offryng at Syon … xx d.

Item to the same George for money yeven to my lad*ys* g*r*ace at Syon for lady Wynsour*e* … vi s. viii d.

Item to my lady Mergaret Pollis norsse … iii s. iiii d.

Item payd to the kep*er* of the Marshalsee for the fees of Thom*as* Johnson and John Shaw which lay in preson ther*e* … xv s.

Item payd unto the kep*er* of Ludgate for the delyv*er*ance of John Spenc*er* presoner v s. viii d. and for the delyv*er*ance of John Chamber presoner there v s. viii d. … xi s. iiii d.

Item payd to the keper of Newgate for the delyv*er*ance of Mawde Browne wedow presoner ther … iiii s. viii d.

Item to the same for the delyv*er*ance of Elyzabeth Sawage … iiii s. viii d.

Item to the same for the fees of William Ryse p*r*esoner ther*e* … iiii s. viii d.

[30] MS 'vij jj'. £10 7d. is correct.

Item payd for a yerd and iii q*u*art*er* of right cremyssen satten for to body and sleve a gowne for maistrez P*ar*ker. The yerd xiii s. iiii d. … xxiii s. iiii d.

Item paid for a pounde of sylk of iii collers … xiii s. iiii d.

Item for two unc*e* of threde yello and tawny … iiii d.

Item for neld*es* … ii d.

Item payd for two hoggyshedd*es* of wyne redd and clarrett yeven to m*aister* Conysby. P*r*ice the pype [*blank*] … lvi s. viii d.

Item for the cost*es* bot hyre of Miles Worsley in p*ro*vidyng of the same and for <d> reideme the presoners … iiii s.

[M]Summa … xii li. xvi s. x d.[P]

[*p. 11*] Item payd unto John Utryght goldsmyth for the golde and makyng of two garters weying a unc*e* di. a i d. weght the unce xxxvii s. and for the makyng xx s. … lxxvi s. vi d.

Item for a yerd di. of <g> changeabull reban … vi d.

Item for the crystenyng of Weston chylde delyv*er*ed unto his sust*er* … lxvi s. viii d.

Item to Hughe Denysse in reward … lxvi s. viii d.

Item to my lad*ys* g*r*ace to have in pursse … iiii li.

Item to maistrez Mary Denysse in reward … xx s.

Item Wylliam Merymon of the privey kechen … vi s viii d.

Item to the kyng*es* fessecions by m*aister* Morgan … xl s.

Item to a s*er*vande of the p*r*ior of Lanthoni for bryngyng of two bake lampreys … v s.

Item to maistres Catysby in reward … xiii s. iiii d.

Item to the pantr*e* … xx s.

Item to the bottre … xx s.

Item to the seller … xxvi s. viii d.

Item to the kechyn … xxvi s. viii d.

Item to the sawc*er*y and skollery … x s.

Item to the clerk of kechyn … x s.

Item to the wodyard … vi s. viii d.

Item to the porters … vi s. viii d.

Item to the wardrop of the bedd*es* … xxvi s. viii d.

Item to the usshers of my lady Mares chambr*e* … xiii s. iiii d.

Item to Brante of the seller … v s.

Item t*o* the kep*er* of the garden … iii s. iiii d.

Item to Knolles gentylman yssher … x s.

Item t*o* William Smythe of the rob*es* … x s.

Item to the grome porter *ser*vande that bare wodde and beyryng of bedd*es* … iii s. iiii d.

Item t*o* the lander for wasshyng … ii s. viii d.

Item to Hughe Carr*e* for wolle to trusse plate in … ii d.

Item in reward to Gerrade the kyng*es* *ser*vand … vi s. viii d.

xi li. xiii d.[31]

[M]Summa … <xlii li. x ii d.> xxix li. iiii s. ii d.[P]

[*p. 12*] Item in reward to John cart taker*e* for takyng cartes … xx d.

Nota. Item payd unto the barge man for convaying of my lad*ys* g*r*ace from Richmound to Syon two tymes … iiii s.

Item for a bott to convay the stuff over the wat*er* … viii d.

Item for bred and ale at Syon … vi s. viii d.

Item to the kyng*es* fotmen in reward … iii s. iiii d.

Item paid unto Robert Merbury for two dayes ridyng from Richmound to Hatfeld to se my lady Cessell … ii s.

Item for his bot hyr*e* to London w*i*th clothe of gold … viii d.

[32]*Doct*our *Smyth*. Item paid the xxith day of Marche in rewarde to doctour Smyth for makyn of a sermon apon Passhyn Sonday by m*aster* deane … x s.

*Rob*ert *Hylton*.[33] Item paid the same tyme to Rob*er*t Hylton for iii yerd*es* of blacke clothe bought for my ladyes g*r*ace at vii s. the yerde xxi s. for iii yerd*es* medley p*r*ice the yerde v s. xv s. Item for a yerd of boltyng clothe. P*r*ice iii d. Item for ii peneworth of nedellys ii d. for a payer of hosyn for mastres Parker x d. for a payer of hosyn for mastres Jon viii d. for a payer of hosyn for mastres Perot viii d. for a payer of shone for mastres Park[e]r viii d. for a payer of shone for mastres Jon viii d. for a yerd q*uar-ter* \of/ di. \carsey/ for a payer of hosyn for master Parker at xxii d. the yerde ii s. vi d. Item for ii yerd*es* di. of carsey for the fotemens hose at ii s. the yerde v s. for makyng and ly[n]ing of the same ii payer xx d. Item for iii q*uarter* of tawney damaske for the p*er*formyng of the said fotemens dobelat*es* iiii s. viii d. Item for xiiii skynnes <of>[34] John Gesson for my lorde of Rochester of blacke bogy. P*r*ice the skynne <xx d.> xx d. xxiii s. iiii d. Item to the same John for a tymb*er* of <letys> letysse vii s. for vi dd. of whyte bonettes for my ladyes maunde. P*r*ice the dd. v s. x d. xxxv s. Item for vi dosyn

[31] The correct total of the nineteen items above, bracketed to the right of the items.

[32] The 'curly' hand returns here.

[33] Bracketed to include the rest of the items on the page, which are also bracketed to the right with a single sum total.

[34] Alt. from 'for'?

of womens hosyn. Price the dd. v s. xxx s. for his cost*es* abowte the same by ii days viii d. and for caryage of the same stuffe ii d. Item to the said Robert Hylton for his cost*es* rydyng to Hatfeld by ii tymes ii s. … vii li. xi s. xi d.

^{M}Summa … ix li. xi d.^{P}

[*p. 13*] *Robert Hylton*. Item paid the xxith day of Marche to the said Robert Hylton for nedellys for the browders ix d. Item for ii lib. of grene threde and red xii d. Item for a payer of sherys viii d. for i lib. di. of blewe threde xviii d. Item for i lib. of whyte threde xii d. … iiii s. xi d.

J. Plowfeld. Item paid the xxiiith day of Marche to John Plowfeld for a boke callyd the Shepars Calender bounded in bord*es* xvi d. Item paid for a boke callyd Horologium Sapyencie w*ith* the lyffe of Seynt Benet in the same boke xii d. For galles gomme <and> cop*er*as and vermylou*n* to make incke w*ith* xii d. … iii s. iiii d.

Offeryn. Item delyv*er*ed to Will*i*am Grevell for my ladyes offeryn at the Nunciaciou*n* of our Lady … v s.

Precher. Item the same tyme yevyn in rewarde to a blacke fryo*ur* for makyng of <of> a sermon apon the said day by master deane vi s. viii d. … vi s. viii d.

Wax. Item paid the xxviith day of Marche to master chauncello*ur* for wax to be made a taper w*ith* to set afore Seynt Margaret by the parson of Kettellsby … iii s. vi d.

J. Mason. Item paid unto s*ir* John Marshall for money occupyed for John Mason from the xviith day of Apryll unto the iiiith day of Marche … xxxvii s. ix d. ob.

Item paid for the comons of the said Mason by the said space by master chauncello*ur* … xxxiiii s. vi d.

Ancrysse. Item the same tyme in rewarde to my ladyes ancrysse at the nunnys in Stampfort by m*aster* chauncello*ur* … iii s. iiii d.

Ancrysse. Item in rewarde to the ancrysse in Stampfort towne by m*aster* chauncello*ur* … iii s. iiii d.

T. Pellet. Item paid unto master Scot of Cryst*es* College by m*aster* chauncello*ur* for ness*essary* expens*es* leid out for Thomas Pellet … xiii s. iiii d.

*M*astres *Dentons* servant. Item in rewarde the xxviith day of Marche to mastres Dentons servant for his cost*es* lying at London w*ith* money for my ladys g*r*ace … iii s. iiii d.

^{M}Summa … Cxix s. ob.^{P}

[*p. 14*] Item in rewarde to docto*ur* Fodrby for makyng of a s*er*mond apon Palme Sonday by m*aster* deane … x s.

Item in rewarde to the clocke makr for co*m*myng hether … xx d.

Item paid to <iiii> lxiiii women at my ladyes maunde at xiii d. every pece … lxix s. iiii d.

Item delyv*er*ed apon Good Fryday to George Fr*a*unc*es* for my ladyes offeryng in fyve schelyng*es* … xxx<v> s.

Item paid to Richard Wyatt for his cost*es* rydyng to the abby of Creke in Northfolke and from thens to London by the space of xii days hymselfe w*ith* iii horse ev*er*y day iiii s. … xlviii s.

Item paid in reward to s*ir* Thomas Idyll late parson of Malton … xl s.

Item paid to Will*i*am Whytmore for his q*uarter* wag*es* endyng at our*e* Lady Day in Lent … vi s. viii d.

Item paid to master receyvo*ur* for his cost*es* by iiii days[35] w*ith* iiii horse the iiii[th] day of Apryll … x s.

Item for my ladyes offeryng at the resor\r/eciou*n* by George F*r*aunc*es* ii s. vi d. Item for hir offeryng the same day v s. … vii s. vi d.

Item in rewarde to the cok*es* apon Esto*ur* Day for their wyth … xxvi s. viii d.

Item paid the vi[th] day of[36] Apryll to master receyvo*ur* by the hand*es* of Lylleg*r*ave his s*er*vaunt for money for the kyng «for Creyke abbey» … lxvi li. xiii s. iiii d.

Item paid the same tyme to m*aster* chauncello*ur* for a pece of whyte fustyan vii s. vi d. for two haffe portuys for John Mason iii s. for gravyng of my ladyes ryng iii s. iiii d. Item paid unto [*blank*] by the hand*es* of master Grove <grover> groser of London for the delyv*er*e of Thomas Chamb*er*s indentur*e* grome of <the> my ladyes spycery xl s. … liii s. x d.

Item paid for the exebesyon of <peper> Richard Peper my ladyes scoler at Oxford by the co*m*aundment of m*aster* chauncello*ur* as apperyth by a bill of the said Pepers hande … xix s. i d. ob.

Item paid to master Wyatt by the hand*es* of s*ir* Hugh Assheton for the byldyng of Crystys Colege … Cxliiii li. xiiii s. v d.

[M]Summa … CCxxxvii li. x<i> s. vii d.[P]

[*p. 15*] [37]Item payd the vi[th] day of Aprell unto John Hoo of London <goldsmyth> for the convaying of a payre of organce from London to Hatfeld w*i*th ii s. yeven hym in reward … viii s. viii d.

Item in reward to the sauc*er*y and skollery on Ester Day … v s.

*M*aister *Conysby*. Item payd at Lomans for the cost*es* of m*aister* Conysby horsis in the Ester weke … xvi d.

Item in reward to his clerk for wrytyng of c*er*ten thyng*es* for my lad*ys* [grace] the same tyme … ii s.

Item paid unto Jamys Morice for money delyv*er*ed to Olyv*er* Scallis for the cost*es* of doct*ur* Machell and m*aster* Trynam w*i*th other offic*er*ez of the bysshop of Norwyche for the inquessycion of the patronage of Artelboro … lxi s. ii d.

[35] 'at' add. at end of l.

[36] 'of' rep.

[37] The MW hand returns here.

Item paid unto the same Olyv*er* by the hand*es* of the said Jamys Morice toward*es* the chargys for the appropryacion of the personage of Helpston ... C s.

*M*aister *Bell of Fodryngay*. Item delyv*er*ed unto Jamys Morice to delyv*er* unto maist*er* Bell of Fodryngay for a q*u*art*er* endet at Ester ... xxv s.

*Crys*tes *Collage*. Item delyv*er*ed to the said Jamys Morice toward*es* the work*es* of Cryst*es* Collage in Cambryge ... iiii^{xx}ii li. xvi s. vi d.

Item in reward to the kynges courser men at my lad*ys* goyng to Seynt Albones ... vi s. viii d.

Item delyv*er*ed for my lad*ys* offryng at Seynt Albones in golde a fyve shellyng*es* furty pens and a threttypens ... x s. x d.

Item in reward to the kynges wefferer for makyng of waffers to my lad*ys* g*r*ace ... xx d.

Item delyv*er*ed to a olde monke in Seynt Albonez ... iiii s.

Item to the ancrysse at Seynt Albones ... iii s. iiii d.

Item payd unto John Brydde for a horse by hym bought for my lad*ys* g*r*ace for the lytter ... iiii li.

Item payd unto maistrez Lynche for ii pounde of golde of damaske ... Cviii s.

[M]Summa ... <Clx li. xiiii s. ii d.> Ciii li. xiiii s. ii d.[P 38]

[*p. 16*] Item the viiith day of Aprell in reward to oon þ*at* browght two yonge wodcokk*es* to my lad*ys* g*r*ace ... xx d.

Item delyv*er*ed unto m*aister* dean for a reward yeven unto Thomas Prechett oon of the chappell at his beyng at Hatfeld in the Ester weke ... vi s. viii d.

Item paid unto John <b> Pyk for his cost*es* ridyng from Hatfeld to Richmounde w*i*th a lytell coffer two daiez ii s. and another tyme w*i*th clothe for the kyng*es* shert*es* ii daiez ii s. Summa ... iiii s.

Item paid unto m*aister* receyver at Richmound for money by hym paid to Jamys Morice for rewardes yeven and other paymentes mad for my lad*ys* g*r*ace. The summa ... xlii s. viii d.

Item the xith day of Aprell delyv*er*ed to maistres Foller for a reward yeven unto Cony my lord of Derbies s*er*vand for the bryng*ing* worde of the delyv*er*aunce of my lady Derby ... vi s. viii d.

Item paid unto Nicholas of the wardrop for money delyv*er*ed to the vichamberlayn for my lad*ys* offryng at Seynt Albones iii s. iiii d. Item to Rob*er*t Merbury for my lad*ys* offryng ther*e* xx d. ... v s.

Item paid unto Rob*er*t Fremyngham for v daies ridyng from Hatfeld to London and Richmounde yeveyng attendance apon the kyng*es* councell for my lad*ys* maters ... x s.

[38] The corrected calculation is correct; both are in the MW hand.

Item the xiiii day of Aprell to maistres Foller for the bourde of Mergaret Lodlow beyng seke by vi wek*es* at vi d. the weke … iii s.

Item in reward to Thomas Sherley w*i*th the quene of Skott*es* at his goyng into Skotland the xiiii day of Aprell at Hatfeld … vi s. viii d.

Item paid unto docture Royston p*ar*son of Halhalloez for the tythe of Coldherbor*e* for two yer*es* last passyd by the hand*es* of m*aister* William Clerk subdean of my lad*ys* chappell the xiiii day of Aprell … Cvi s. viii d.

^{M}Summa … lx li. xiii s.^{P}

[*p. 17*] [39]Item delyv*er*ed the xviith day of Apr[i]ll to mastres Lynche by the hand*es* of Thomas Soper my ladyes selyster by the co*m*maundment of master chauncell*our* to bye fyne blacke satyn for my ladyes g*r*ace … x li.

Item the same tyme to the said Thomas Soper for a payer of orgons bought by Peto*ur* of Coldeharborogh and the p*ar*isshe clerk of the same p*ar*ysshe for my lad*ys* chapell … iiii li.

Item yevyn in rewarde to Hugh Warde the xviith day of Apryll by John Carter … xx s.

Item yevyn in almes to docto*ur* Darleys servant goyng to Rome by m*aster* chauncell*our* … xx d.

Item paid for the expences of mastres Lynche and hir servant w*ith* iiii horse by John Carter … iii s. i d.

Item yevyn in rewarde to the kep*er* of the letyll parcke for makyng of my ladyes g*r*ace a howse w*ith* bowys in the fylde to sope in … ii s.

Item paid for two clothys of ymagery by mastres Masse … iii s.

Item paid the xxiiiith day of Apryll to Rob*er*t Fremyngham for his cost*es* rydyng to the kyng lyng at Rychemound w*ith* ii horse by v days for maters of my ladyes … x s.

Item in rewarde to the kynges mynstrellys by m*aster* tresorer xx s. … xx s.

Item in rewarde yevyn by my ladyes commaundment to the abbot of Seynt Albons mynstrel … v s.

Item paid to Jane Gowre for hir q*uarter* wag*es* endyng at Esto*ur* by m*astres* Masse … xiii s. iiii d.

Item yevyn in rewarde to master Markhams norse by mastres Stannop … xx d.

Item <paid> \delyv*er*ed/ to mastres Lynche the xxvith day of Apryll to bye velvett*es* by master vychambrlen … x li.

Item yevyn in rewarde to master Thomas Whytamore the ii^{de} day of May by master Bekynsall … vi s. viii d.

Item delyv*er*ed to Jamys Moryce the iiiith day of May towerd the byldyng of Crystys Colege in Cambryge … Cxi li.

[39] The 'curly' hand returns here.

Item paid to Pet*our* of Coldeharborgh for a barell of muscadell co*nteynyng* v q*uarte* di. yevyn unto my lorde of Rochest*our* … vii s. iiii d.

Item paid to the said Pet*our* for makyng of a gret letter w*ith* a vynet lymyned in the first lyne of a pontyfycall … ii s. ii d.

[M]Summa … Cxl li. xi d.[P]

[*p. 18*] [40]*M*aister *Parker*. Item the xth day of May delyv*er*ed unto m*aister* Parker by George Franc*es* x s. Item at Westm*ynster* by m*aister* receyver xx s. … xxx s.

Item to the procture*s* of Corpus Chr*ist*i gylde at Seynt Paw[le]s[41] in London … iii s. iiii d.

Item for my lad*ys* offryng at the pardon at Westm*ynster* … iii s. iiii d.

Item to Roger Radclyff for money yeven unto a chyrche betwix Bernard and London … viii d.

Item in reward unto the abbot of Westm*ynster* s*er*vand*es* furst to the pantre iii s. iiii d. Item to the seller iii s. iiii d. Item to the buttre iii s. iiii d. Item to the wardrop of bedd*es* iii s. iiii d. Item to the clerk of the kechyn iii s. iiii d. Item to the porters iii s. iiii d. … xx s.

Item paid for a botte and viii roers to convay my lad*ys* g*r*ace from Westm*ynster* to Bernard*es* Castell ev*er*y roer viii d. the m*aister* xii d. the hyre of the bott iiii d. … vi s. viii d.

Item delyv*er*ed to my lad*ys* g*r*ace at the charterhowse in London … vi s. viii d.

Item to the ankur*e* in the Wall … iii s. iiii d.

Item to a prest <c> of the same place … xx d.

Item to our*e* Lady at Bethelem … ii s.

Item to William Hylm*er* s*er*vande þ*at* brought a capon to the Towre yeven to my lad*ys* g*r*ace … iiii d.

Item for hony for a medsen for my lad*ys* g*r*ace delyv*er* to Hughe Car*e* … ii d.

Item delyv*er*ed to my lady Rev*er*se at the <towse> Towre for hir syster at Myn*er*esse … xiii s. iiii d.

Item paid unto William Pole for a elne of sarsynet bought for my lad*ys* g*r*ace … iii s. viii d.

Item to John Harryson in reward … iii s. iiii d.

Item payd unto John Holt for a reward yeven unto a woman þ*at* brought chekyns and peysecodd*es* to my lad*ys* g*r*ace at the Towre … ii s.

Item payd to the same for the caryeng of my lad*ys* stuff from Westm*ynster* to the Towr*e* … viii d.

[40] The MW hand returns here.

[41] MS ‘Pawers’.

Item paid unto m*aister* Bekynsall for a reward yeven to a monke of the charterhowse in London for book*es* yeven to my lad*ys* g*r*ace … vi s. viii d.

Item in reward to a s*er*vande of dame <kateryn> Margaret Lewes of the Myn*er*esse þ*at* brought a glasse of rosewat*er* … xii d.

MSumma … Cviii s. x d.P

[*p. 19*] Item paid unto George Fraunc*es* for reward*es* yeven by my lad*ys* comaundement to the wardrop of the bedd*es* … x s.

Item to Brente of the kyng*es* seller … vi s. viii d.

Item to the lewtenand*es* botteler. Reward … iii s. iiii d.

Item to the grome porters s*er*vande … xx d.

Item delyv*er*ed to maistres Foller for reward*es* yeven at the court the x day of May … xx s.

Maistrez Lynche. Item payd unto maistrez Lynche for this stuff folloyng bought for my lad*ys* g*r*ace <as> furst for a quart of sle[v]id[42] sylk … iii s. viii d.

Item for a C neld*es* … iiii d.

Item paid for xii yerd*es* of velvett at … vii li. xiiii d.

Item for a pece of lynnen clothe … xiii s. viii d.

Item for two pec*es* of Parr*es* mantels … xx s.

Item for a pece of satten cont*eynyng* xxvii yerd*es* and half … x li. vi s.

Item for a nell of canvas … iiii d.

Item for a unc*e* of whit sylk … xii d.

< Item paid unto m*aister* dean for money delyv*er*ed unto my lad*ys* g*r*ace that was yeven unto a prest of Walis that came to se my lad*ys* g*r*ace … xiii s. iiii d.> «postea»[43]

Item delyv*er*ed the xxii day of May unto m*aister* Rob*er*t Fell to be send unto doctur*e* Fell <amer> amener unto my lad*ys* g*r*ace toward*es* his charg*es* at Rome … lxvi s. viii d.

Item for my lad*ys* offryng apon Witsonday … v s.

Item payd unto John Brydde for his cost*es* ridyng unto Tatsall and Boston for c*er*tan stuff of my lad*ys* g*r*ace for <me> hymself and his servande by iiii daiez at xx d. a day … vi s. viii d.

Item for iii cart*es* to convay the said stuff from Tatsall to Dokedyke at vi d. the cart … xviii d.

Item to iii workemen for beyryng of the stuff to the cart and the water … iiii d.

Item for a barge from Dokedyke to Cambryge w*i*th the said stuff … xii s. iiii d.

[42] MS 'slesid'.

[43] See p. 21.

Item to the same for money yeven to his s*er*vande for his cost*es* to receyve the said stuff at Cambryg*e* by iiii daiez … ii s. viii d.

Item in reward to Rob*er*t Nicholasse doughtur at Barnard þ*a*t brought cak*es* to my lad*ys* g*r*ace … xii d.

[M]Summa … <xxvii li. xi s. ii d.> Summa … xxvi li. xvii s. x d.[P][44]

[*p. 20*] Item paid unto m*aister* dean for a reward yeven unto doct*ur* Robson þ*a*t <br> prechyd afour*e* my lad*ys* g*r*ace on Witsonday … vi s. viii d.

Item paid unto m*aister* Morgan for a reward yeven to a s*er*vande of m*aister* almeners brothers that brought lettur*es* from Rome to my lad*ys* g*r*ace … ii d.

Item paid for a pener and ynkhorne for Dru<re> my lad*ys* ward the xxviii day of May … ii d.

Item the same day unto m*aister* Bekynsall for a reward yeven unto John Williams wyff of the Towre … x s.

Item to the clerke of the clossett for a pax and a sakeryng bell bought for my lad*ys* g*r*ace … viii d.

xxviii day of May. Item paid unto Thomas Maydwell for iii payr*e* of shone for my lad*ys* g*r*ace at … xviii d.

Item for the makyng of a payr*e* of buskynce … vi d.

Item for a payre of dobyll sollyd shoez … viii d.

Item for a payre of slyppers … vi d.

Item for the makyng of a payre of shone … iiii d.

Item paid unto m*aister* Mounteney for the cost*es* of the popis collect*ur* beying at Hatfeld … viii d.

Item for my lad*ys* offryng apon T*r*inite Sonday … v s.

[45]Item paid unto a nonne of the Menerys for to bye rosys and colys to make rose water for my lad*ys* g*r*ace by Rob*er*t Merbury … vi s. viii d.

Item yevyn in rewarde to master Morgan toward the cost*es* and charg*es* of the p*ro*fessyon of his wyffe at Detford in Kent by mastres Fowler … xl s.

Item yevyn in rewarde to master tresorers norse by mastres Fowler … iii s. iiii d.

Item paid to the hardward man for ii yerd*es* of vylat rebyn … xvii d.

Item in rewarde to Thomas Watson for a hole yerys rent for his howse at our*e* Lady Day last past … xi s.

Item yevyn in rewarde to master Henr*y* Bonehour*e* of Asserynge by m*aster* confess*our* … iii s. iiii d.

[44] The first (canc.) total is in the MW hand, the second in a different hand.
[45] The 'curly' hand returns here.

Item delyv*er*ed the iii^{de} day of June for my ladyes offeryng apon Corpus Chr*ist*i Day by William Hylmer … v s.

Item paid the same tyme to George Fraunc*es* for my lad*ys* offeryng to our*e* <of> Lady of Lodwyke in the p*ar*ysshe chyrche … v s.

Item paid to Rob*er*t Merbury for <l v> i unc*e* of blewe sylke redy twyned … xii d.

[M]Summa … Cv s. i d.[P]

[*p. 21*] Item paid the xxviiith day of June to master Henr*y* Wyat toward the bildyng of Crystys Colege … C li.

Item paid the xith day of June to Janne Gowre for hir q*u*art*er* wag*es* endyng at mytsomer next co*m*myng to the hand*es* of hir suster … xiii s. iiii d.

Item yevyn in rewarde to a prest that came out of Walys to se my lad*ys* g*r*ace by my lorde of Rochesto*ur* xiii s. iiii d. and by master deane xiii s. iiii d. … xxvi s. viii d.

<*Nota pro xiii s. iiii d. que solvuntur.*>[46]

Item yevyn in rewarde to the potter that maketh pott*es* at Potters Barre ii s. by George Fraunc*es* and in rewarde to the kep*er* of the gret parc for brekyng up of the parc gate iiii d. … ii s. iiii d.

Item paid the xiiiith day of June <to> in rewarde to Rob*er*t Day by m*aster* Morgan … ii s. viii d.

Item paid the same tyme in rewarde to Pynson the bokebynder by m*aster* Morgan … xx d.

Item paid the xvth day of June to the potter for pott*es* viii d. and to the same in rewarde viii d. … <xvi> xvi d.

Item paid the same tyme to s*ir* Hugh Assheton for his cost*es* two tymes beyng at London and for ryding to the corte for to obtayne the kyng*es* graunt for the abby of Creke and for ii days rydyng to London to rekyn w*ith* m*aster* Mondy the goldsmyth for soch[47] plate as was bough for Crystys Colege … xx s.

Item paid the xvith day of June in rewarde to a scoler of Oxford by m*astres* Fowler … vi s. viii d.

Item paid the same tyme to s*ir* Rauffe Varney and my lady his wyffe in rewarde by my lad*ys* hand*es* lxvi s. viii d. Item also paid for the dyett*es* of x of his servant*es* and for the mete of xviii horsys by the space of a nyght x s. viii d. … lxxvii s. iiii d.

Item yevyn in rewarde to John Willyamson for his logging at Croydon by the space of a yere by my lad*ys* co*m*maundme*n*t … vi s. viii d.

Item yevyn in rewarde the said tyme to popys collecto*ur*s chaplen for his co*m*myng to my ladys g*r*ace w*ith* letters by m*aster* deane … vi s. viii d.

Item yevyn in rewarde the xxth day of June to my lady Maryes mynstrellys … x s.

[46] See p. 19 above.
[47] MS 'sochy'.

Item in rewarde to the chylderyn of the chappell for syngyng of two songys byfore my lad*ys* g*r*ace and the bysshop of Ely by m*aster* chauncell*our* … xx d.

Item paid to John Wallys of Stampfort for money owing to hym by master Parker for a kendall cote w*ith* the ly[n]ing and the makyng of the same … xiii s. iiii d.

^{M}Summa … Cix li. x s. iiii d.^{P}

[*p. 22*] Item delyv*er*ed to John Grome for my ladyes offeryng apon Seynt <t> Awderys Day … v s.

Item paid the xxvth day of June to Ric*hard* Aderton for rydyng from Hatfeld unto my lord chambrlens playce unto the kyng by ii days xvi d. for ryding to London to master receyvo*ur* by ii days xvi d. … ii s. viii d.

Item paid to mastres Masse the same tyme for to bye flex for the power women … vi s. viii d.

[48]*M*aistres *Lynche*. Item payd unto maistres Lynche apon the xxvith day of Juyn for iii peces of sypres bought for my lad*ys* g*r*ace … x s.

Item for a half pounde of crule by the same … vi d.

Item payd for viii yerd*es* and a half and half a q*u*art*er* of satten bought by the same … liii s. vi d.

Item payd unto Wylliam Lyleg*r*ave servant unto m*aister* receyver by his byll assigned for his cost*es* ridyng and other exspenc*e* made abowte the abbey Creyk … ix li. xvii s. ii d.

Item yeven unto m*aister* Dudley for his delygent labur*e* unto the kyng*es* g*r*ace for gettyng the abbey of Creyk to Cryst*es* Colege … lxvi s. viii d.

Item paid unto John Castell of the excheker for respect of homage for land*es* þ*a*t my lad*ys* g*r*ace hathe putt in feoffament for the declaracion of hir wyll … iiii li.

Item paid unto the same for money delyv*er* to m*aister* Soper my lad*ys* solicit*ur* the xx day of May … C s.

^{M}Summa … xxvi li. ii s. ii d.^{P}

Item payd unto John Brydde for money payd for the cost*es* of my lord of Seynt Johens and m*aister* Hussy at Lomand*es* the last day of Juyn … xvi d.

Item paid for a male w*i*th a lokke and key for the clossett stuff to be caryed in delyv*er*ed to m*aister* Peksall at the Towre … iiii s. viii d.

Item delyv*er*ed unto maistrez Foller for a reward yeven for the bryngyng of rosis and straberys to my lad*ys* g*r*ace by a s*er*vande of maistrez Benstyd … iii s. iiii d.

Item the viiith day of July delyv*er*ed to my lad*ys* g*r*ace for hyr almes purse … x li.

[48] The MW hand returns here.

Item payd unto Richard Aderton for ridyng to Boston from Hatfeld by v dayez at viii d. a day ... iii s. iiii d.

MSumma ... x li. xii s. vii d.P

Summa partis ... xxxvi li. xiiii s. ix d.[49]

[*p. 23*] Item payd unto maistrez Foller for viii napkyns and two towell*es* of dyapur*e* bought of Lenard of the vestry ... x s.

Item to the same for iii payre of ambur*e* beyd*es* weying xvii unc*e* at ii s. the unc*e* ... xxxiiii s.

Item for iii ell*es* of tawny reban. P*r*ice ... iii s.

Item for iii ell*es* of grene reban ... xxii d.

Item for two ell*es* of changeabull reban ... viii d.

Item the xi[th] day of July to m*aister* Morgan for a horse bought by m*aister* Peksall clerk of my lad*ys* clossett and yeven unto my lord of Rochester*e* ... iiii li.

Item paid unto the same m*aister* Peksall for the cost*es* of his s*er*vande from Lecet*ur* bryngyng of the same horse to Hatfeld ... iii s. iiii d.

Item for the hyre of a horse the same iorney by v dayez ... xx d.

Item for the meyte of the same horse at his comyng home or he was delyv*er*ed ... iii d.

Item delyv*er*ed to Henry Salforth for my lady Cescell the same day ... vi li. xiii s. iiii d.

Item to John Mondy in reward for his horse meyte comyng from London to Hatfeld ... iii s. iiii d.

Item paid unto Rob*er*t Merbury for ii daiez ridyng from Hatfeld to Cambryg*e* and ayen to Hatfeld ... ii s.

Item payd unto Rob*er*t Fremyngham for his cost*es* ridyng to the kyng apon my lad*ys* messag*es* to Grenewiche from Hatfeld and ther*e* abydyng by iii daiez w*i*th two horsis ev*er*y day ii s. ... vi s.

Item delyv*er*ed to m*aister* chaunceller for a reward yeven unto Edward Heyvon comyng from Tatsall to Hatfeld and to London toward*es* his cost*es* ... xl s.

Item paid unto maistrez Foller for a reward yeven unto John Hyll ... iii s. iiii d.

Item to the same for a reward yeven unto maistrez Stannop*e*s norsse ... xx d.

Item delyv*er*ed to Rob*er*t Merbury for xii elles of lynnen clothe at x d. the ell ... x s.

Item delyv*er*ed to Petur of Coldherboro the vth day of July toward*es* the rep*ar*acion of the Riall in London ... x li.

MSumma ... xxvi li. xiiii s. v d.P

[49] Not in the MW hand of the 'Summa' (probably written in the 'sprawling' hand).

[*p. 24*] Item paid the xiith day of July to Thomassyn of London gold wyr*e* drawer for two pounde of rounde gold at iiii s. iii d. the unc*e*. Summa … Cii s.

Item to the same for a pounde of flatt golde ev*ery* unc*e* iiii s. x d. The summa … lviii s.

Item to my lad*ys* g*r*ace by maistres Foller the ix day of July … vi s. viii d.

Item paid unto John Carter s*er*vande to m*aister* chaunceller for a reward yeven unto m*aister* Nicholas Coup*er* s*er*vande for bryngyng of copes and vestment*es* from London to Hatfeld … xx d.

Item to William Witamor*e* s*er*vande unto m*aister* P*ar*ker for a half yer*es* waig*es* endet at mydsom*ur* last passyd … xiii s. iiii d.

Item paid unto Nicholas Aughton the xx day of July for his cost*es* ridyng apon my lad*ys* messag*es* by the space of xvii dayes unto dyv*er*se plac*es* as aperith by his byll assigned … xi s. iiii d.

Item paid unto m*aister* chaunceller for a reward yeven unto[50] m*aister* Rob*er*t Chappell toward*es* the charg*es* of his comensement … liii s. iiii d.

Item delyv*er*ed to maistres Foller for a reward yeven to Gerawde the kyng*es* s*er*vande comyng from m*aister* Lovell*es* to Hatfeld w*i*th my lad*ys* g*r*ace … iii s. iiii d.

Item to the same for a reward yeven unto Richard Laborer xx d. and to Annes Kettell won of the almeswomen xii d. … ii s. viii d.

Item to the same for money paid unto the joyner of Hatfeld for makyng of a lytell fotstole to my lad*ys* g*r*ace … vii d.

Item in reward unto a s*er*vande of m*aister* <lol> Lovell*es* for his labur*e* in helpyng to beyre stuff to my lad*ys* chambr*e* … iii s. iiii d.

Item paid unto John Harryson for xxvi ell*es* and a q*ua*rt*er* of lynnen clothe at ix d. the ell … xix s. x d. qua.

Item to the same for xxvii elles of lynnen clothe and a q*ua*rt*er*. P*r*ice the ell xx d. … xlv s. v d. \v d./[51]

[M]Summa … xvi li. <xi d.> \xviii d./ qua.[P]

[*p. 25*] *Rob*er*t Hylton*.[52]

Item payd unto Robert Hylton the xxth day of July by his bylles assigned furst for lxv elles of Normandy canvas … xx s. v d.

Item for another pece of canvas cont*eynyng* xxiii ell*es* … vi s. viii d. ob.

Item for a porter to bryng the same to the Towre … i d.

Item paid for vi yerd*es* of grene satten of Brygg*es*. P*r*ice the yerd ii s. vi d. … xv s.

[50] 'unto' rep. next l.

[51] The insertion above the line is to verify that 'v d.' is intended, since the original 'v' could be mistaken for 'x'.

[52] Bracketed to include all the items on p. 25.

Item for iii yerd*es* of blak clothe for a gowne for my lad*ys* g*r*ace at vii s. the yerd … xxi s.

Item for a yerd and a q*u*art*er* of blak welvet for the same gowne at a xi s. viii d. the yerd … xiiii s. vii d.

Item for v yerd*es* of blak bokeram for to lyne the same gowne at vi d. the yerd … ii s. vi d.

Item paid for help to make the same gowne … xvi d.

Item paid for ii payr*e* of shoez for the fotmen at my lad*ys* goyng to Westm*ynster* at vi d. the payr*e* … xii d.

Item for vi yerd*es* of tawney medly for two cot*es* for the two lyttermen. P*r*ice the yerd iii d. … xviii s.

Item paid for a pound of Coventre threde xvi d. and for a pounde of white threde x d. … ii s. ii d.

Item for fyne blak threde … iiii s.

Item for anlett*es* for thuse of the wardrop … viii d.

Item paid for vii yerd*es* of whit cotton for the lynyng of m*aister* Parkers chamlet cote at v d. the yerd … ii s. xi d.

Item for vii yerd*es* of cotton for the same cote … ii s. x d.

Item for a payr*e* of hose to the same of scarlett … vi s.

Item for a payr*e* of lether hose for the same … v s.

Item for a bonet for hym. The p*r*ice … ii s. viii d.

Item for a payr*e* of sporres for hym … x d.

Item for a payr*e* of red shoez for the same m*aister* P*ar*ker … xii d.

Item paid unto the same Rob*ert* Hylton by his byll assigned in reward for money payed more then he was allowed for the bying of almes bonett*es* and almes hose yeven at the maundy … xi s.

[M]Summa … vii li. v s. ii d. ob.[P]

[*p. 26*] *Rob*ert *Hylton.*[53]

Item paid unto the same Rob*ert* Hylton by his byll assigned for iiii yerd*es* i q*u*art*er* of Frenche tawny for a gowne for m*aister* Parker. Price the yerd v s. Summa … xxi s. iii d.

Item paid for iii yerd*es* of the same tawny for maistres P*ar*ker at v s. the yerd … xv s.

Item for iii yerd*es* of the same tawny for maistres Jan … xv s.

Item for iii yerd*es* of French tawny for maistres P*er*ot … xii s.

Item for a yerd and iii q*u*art*er* for maistres Ursula … vii s.

[53] Bracketed to include all the items on p. 26.

Item for a yerd and \a/ q*ua*rt*er* for litell m*aistres* Margett P*ar*ker … v s.

Item paid for two pec*es* of blak bokeram … x s. viii d.

Item for iiii pec*es* of grene bokeram. The pec*e* v s. … xx s.

Item for ii ell*es* of wolstid for a kyrtell for maistres P*ar*ker. The ell iiii s. <viii d.> iiii d. … viii s. viii d.

Item for ii ell*es* of wolstid for a kyrtell for maistres <Jann> Jan. P*r*ice the ell iiii s. iiii d. … viii s. viii d.

Item for ii ell*es* of wolstid for a kyrtell for maistres P*er*ott … viii s.

Item paid for viii yerd*es* of Kentisshe kendall for a cote for Skyp. P*r*ice the yerd xii d. … viii s.

Item paid for iiii pec*es* of blak cotton. P*r*ice the pece vii s. iiii d. ev*er*y pec*e* cont*eynyng* xxiiii yerd*es* for thuse of the wardrop … xxix s. iiii d.

Item paid to Maydwell for iiii payr*e* of shoez for the ii fotmen for theyr*e* jorney to Richmound and ayen … ii s.

Item to the same Rob*er*t for his cost*es* by ii daiez … xii d.

Item paid unto the same Maidwell for v dd. and iiii payr*e* of shoez for my lad*ys* maundy. The dossen iii s. viii d. … xix s. iiii d.

Item paid for ii pec*es* of whit cotton cont*eynyng* xxiii yerd*es*. P*r*ice the pece vi s. iiii d. … xii s. viii d.

Item for a payr*e* of shoez for maistres P*ar*ker … viii d.

Item for a payr*e* of shoes for maistres Jan … viii d.

MR Summa … x li. iiii s. xi d. P

[*p. 27*] Item payd unto John Harison the xxi day of July for his cost*es* and Rob*er*t Longe on of the g[r]omes of the stabyll for the convayng of a palfrey from Hatfeld to Grenewyche yeven to the kyng by my lad*ys* g*r*ace … ii s. iiii d.

Item in reward unto m*aister* Morgan toward*es* his exspenc*e* to Cambryg afore the comensement … xl s.

Item paid unto Ric*hard* Aderton for his cost*es* ridyng to Cambryge by ii dayes and for iii dayes rydyng t*o* the courte and to my lord of Bokyngham a day in all … iiii s.

*M*aister *Bell.* Item paid unto m*aister* Bell at Cambryge for a half yere to be endyd at Mychaelmasse next to come … l s.

Item delyv*er*ed unto m*aister* P*ar*ker at Royston to have in his purse … vi s. viii d.

Item delyv*er*ed to maistres Foller for to delyv*er* to my lad*ys* g*r*ace at Cambryge for reward*es* to be yeven there and at Ely … C s.

Item paid unto the vichamberleyn for money by hym delyv*er*ed for my lad*ys* offryng at Cryst*es* Collage … xii d.

Item to the same for money yeven unto a pore woman for erb*es* … iiii d.

Item payd unto m*aister* chamberlayn for money by hym delyv*er*ed for my lad*ys* offryng at the frere austens in Cambryg … xii d.

Item paid unto m*aister* vichamberlayn for money delyv*er*ed for my lad*ys* offryng at Seynt Audres shryne at Ely … iii s. iiii d.

Item to m*aister* vichamberlayn for my lad*ys* offryng in our*e* Lad*ys* chappell at Ely … xx d.

Item payd unto the same for a reward yeven unto m*aister* Fell*es* brother at Ely … vi s. viii d.

Item in reward unto m*aister* Dudleys clerk at Ely … vi s. viii d.

Item paid unto John Holt for his cost*es* ridyng to Grenewyche to the kynge by ii dayes … xvi d.

Item for calle neld*es* and pynnez and pyrlyng wyres … vii d.

Item for ridyng from Hatfeld to Cambryg iii da[y]es … ii s.

Item to a pore woman þ*a*t brought my lad*ys* g*r*ace a cake to Cryst*es* Collage … xii d.

Item to Roger Radclyff for my lad*ys* offryng at the blak frers to our*e* Lady of G*r*ace … xii d.

[M]Summa … xi li. x s. vii d.[P]

[*p. 28*] *Cryst*es *Collage*. Item delyv*er*ed unto Jamys Morice at Cambryg the xxx day of July toward*es* the work*es* of Cryst*es* Collage theyr*e* … lxx li.

Item payd unto John Madyson for a q*u*art of <ypacrys> ypacrace and a pynt of romney at Cambryge … x d.

Item the ii[de] day of August in reward to the popis collecto*ur* s*er*vand at Cambryge … xii d.

Item delyv*er*ed unto maistres Foller for a reward yeven to doct*ur* Chappell of Peturhowse in Cambryge … xx s.

Item delyv*er*ed to m*aister* chaunceller for a reward yeven to my lord of Ely comyssary at Cryst*es* Collage … xx s.

Item payd unto Ric*hard* Aderton for his cost*es* ridyng from Cambryge to London and ayen to Cambryg by iii dayes at viii d. a day … ii s.

Item in reward unto the waytt*es* of Cambryg … iii s. iiii d.

Item to m*aistres* Foller for money yeven <t*o*> m*aister* Par*ker* at Cambryge … vi s. viii d.

Item in reward to my lad*ys* goddought*ur* at Cambryg … v s.

Item paid unto m*aister* dean for money yeven in reward to the gray freris at Cambryge … iii s. iiii d.

Item delyv*er*ed to maistres Frognoll at her goyng to London … xx d.

Item unto John Haryson in reward for his cost*es* from London bryngyng of lynnen clothe and sylk*es* … iii s. iiii d.

Nota. Item payd unto s*ir* John Masson for his cost*es* from Tatsall unto Hatfeld \paid by John Carter/ … xx d.

Item delyv*er*ed the xxx^{ti} day of July to m*aister* Dudley for money payd unto the kyng for the abbey of Creyke and Man*er*bere delyv*er*ed at Ely … CCCC li.

[54]Item paid unto Nicholas Elmeden of the chappell as money unto hym lent the xiith day of August by the commaundment of my lad*ys* g*r*ace as apperyth by a nobligacion rem*aynyng* in my lad*ys* hand*es* … . <iiii li.> «quia postea in pede»[55]

[M]Summa … CCCClxx<viii li.>\iiii li./ vii s. ii d.[P]

[*p. 29*] Item paid unto the fawkener for his cost*es* into Lanckeshere to fet halkys for my ladyes g*r*ace … xi s. viii d.

Item paid to s*ir* Thomas of Cheston for caryage of a cheste \full/ of sylk*es* from London to Cheston ii s. and from Cheston to Hatfeld xiiii d. … iii s. ii d.

Item yevyn in rewarde to Henr*y* the kyng*es* godson … iii s. iiii d.

Item delyv*er*ed unto my ladyes g*r*ace for hir offeryng apon our*e* Ladys Day the Assumpciou*n* by John Grome … v s.

Item paid to Peto*ur* Baldewyn for a dosyn of rase velom … v s.

Item paid to the said Peto*ur* for a remme of smale pawper ii s. iiii d. and for a <[…]> reme of pawper of the large syse iii s. iiii d. … v s. viii d.

Item paid in rewarde to my lady Revers surgon by m*aster* chauncello*ur* … iii s. iiii d.

Item in rewarde to s*ir* John Mason by m*aster* chauncello*ur* … ii s.

Item yevyn in rewarde to the master carpenter of London bryge by my lorde of Rochesto*ur* … iii s. iiii d.

Item paid to John Holt for i day rydyng to London viii d. for i slaye viii d. for ii calle nedellys iiii d. for ii chesys xvi d. for perys and a basket xvi d. … iiii s. iiii d.

Item yevyn in rewarde to masteres Parker by m*aster* Fowler for hir expenc*e* to hir faders … x s.

Item yevyn in rewarde to docto*ur* Woddrowe for makyng of a s*er*mond apon our*e* <d> Lady Day the Assumpciou*n* by m*aster* deane … x s.

Item yevyn in rewarde to mastres Stannop norse the xxth day of August by m*aster* comptrollo*ur* … xx d.

Item paid the xxiith day of August to John Utrysshe goldesmyth for iii harnys of gold for gyrdellys w*ith* ix barys and v brochys of gold wayng iiii unc*es* di. q*uarter*. Pric*e* the unc*e* xli s. Item to the same for ii pomaunders of gold wayng ii unc*es* i q*uarter*. Pric*e* the unc*e* w*ith* the fasshyn xli s. … xii li. xiii s. vi d.

[54]The 'curly' hand returns here.

[55]See p. 125 below.

Item in rewarde to the same for his cost*es* co*m*myng hether … iii d. iiii d.

Item yevyn in rewarde to Rygecroft for bryngyng of bokys by mastres Fowler … xxvi s. viii d.

Item paid to Jamys Moryce for di. lib. of whyte sylke and halfe a lib. of blewe sylke … xxi s. iiii d.

[M]Summa … xviii li. xiii s. iiii d.[P][56]

[*p. 30*] Item paid the xxvith day of August to mastres Masse for dyv*ers* ness*essaryes* bought for the almesfolke as apperyth by hir bill … xl s.

Item paid to the hardward man for a payer of knyvys for my lady … x d.

Beryall of my lady Cycell.[57]

Item paid for the cost*es* and charg*es* of my lady Cycellys beryall that is to saye for a coffyn to close hyr in ii s. viii d. for a lib. of tapers to borne abowte hyr whan she was dede ii s. for makyng of the grave and pavyng of hyt ayene afo*ur* the moneth myne ii s. iiii d. for ii tapers wayng xx lib. \a pece/ wastyng and makyng and for ii tapers wayng xvi lib. the pece for the wastyng and makyng of all iiii tapers ii s. viii d. Item to iiii men to bere the said tapers xii d. for iiii torchys at hir beryall had of the fryers xvi d. Item for xii newe torchys for the makyng and the wastyng of the same x s. Item to the berers of the said torchys <xvi d.> iii s. for ii tapers waying i lib. vi d. Item to v bedred folk*es* the nyght of hir beryall to p*r*ay for hir xx d. Item to mastres Jane hir s*er*[v]aunt for money leyd out by hyr xx d. Item to a woman that wachyd apon hir xii d. Item to the cheffe morner<s> and hir servant*es* xxi d. Item for brekyng of the growne and for hir masse and deryge at the fryers xl s. … lxxi s. vii d.

Item paid to master Edward Bothe for his cost*es* by iiii days w*ith* ii horsys to se hir beryed viii s. … viii s.

Item paid the same tyme unto Marcellus wyffe for the borde of the said lady Cycell and hir s*er*vant*es* by the space of iii wekes and for other dyv*ers* ness*essaryes* had of the said Marcellus lxxviii s. viii d. Item for the cost*es* of hir chappelyn w*ith* ii gent*ilmen* and iii men for to convey them from London to Hatfeld xx s. … iiii li. xviii s. viii d.

Item paid to master Bothe for money yevyn to the ancrys of Seynt Albons xii d. and to two power men viii d. … xx d.

Item paid to Peto*ur* of Coldeharborogh for the rep*ar*acions of the Ryall the xxxth day of August by the hand*es* of master comptroll*our* … C s.

Item yevyn in rewarde to all my ladyes chapell to the etyng of a buk at Seynt Albons by m*aster* Carter … xx s.

Summa … xvii li. ix d.[P]

[56] There is a dot calculation after the total.

[57] Bracketed to include the next three items.

[*p. 31*] Item paid unto master Hede my lorde of Rochesto*ur*s offyshall for his cost*es* rydyng unto m*aster* Bowrers benyfyce by m*aster* comptroll*our* … xxvi s. viii d.

Item paid for a lode of hey for my lorde of Rochest*our* by m*aster* comptroll*our* … iii s.

Item yevyn in rewarde to m*aster* Fysshers keper by m*aster* comptroll*our* … iii s. iiii d.

Item paid to Pet*our* Oldehalle for i lib. di. of slevyn sylke at xiiii s. the lib. … xxi s. Item for vii unc*es* of coper sylver iiii s. viii d. Item for a yerd of blacke tarteryn ii s. iiii d. … xxviii s.

Item delyvered unto Jamys Moryce the xith day of August for the byldyng of Cryst*es* Colege in Cambryge xx li. and to the same Jamys in lyke wyse by the hand*es* of John Scot x li. … xxx li.

Item yevyn in rewarde to a s*er*vant of m*aster* Bucleys for brynging of cast of marlyns by m*aster* Bekynsall … vi s. viii d.

Item yevyn in rewarde to master tresorers norse by mastres Stannop … iii s. iiii d.

Item yevyn in rewarde to doct*our* Fayrfax for brynging of my lad*ys* g*r*ace a newe masse … vi s. viii d.

Item yevyn in rewarde to mastres Blythe my lad*ys* goddowter … vi s. viii d.

Item yevyn in rewarde to the fryers at Ware by Rob*er*t Merbury … iii s. iiii d.

Item paid to Jamys Moryce for vi yerd*es* of fustyn for mastres Jon at vii d. \the yerde/ … iii s. vi d.

Item paid to the said Jamys for ii tymber of letys for my lad*ys* g*r*ace … xvi s.

Item yevyn in rewarde to mastres Jon for hir cost*es* rydyng home into Yorkeshere to se hir fadr and hir moder by my ladyes co*m*maundment … xxvi s. viii d.

[M]Summa … xxxvi li. xiii s. x d.[P]

[*p. 32*] [58]Item delyv*er*ed unto maistres Foller for a reward yeven unto maistres Curson at Cambryge … x s.

Item delyv*er*ed to the same for a reward yeven unto maistres Rede the same tyme … vi s. viii d.

Item paid unto the clok maker s*er*vand of Westm*ynster* for the mendyng of my lad*ys* clokke the viiith day of August … v s.

Item the same day delyv*er*ed unto m*aister* chaunceller for money payd unto the kynge for Okyng … <x> xxvi li. xiii s. iiii d.

Item delyv*er*ed for my lad*ys* offryng apon our*e* Lady Day the Nativitie … v s.

Item the xth day of Septembr*e* for the cost*es* of doct*ur* Robynson horsis at Hatfeld … xvi d.

[58] The MW hand returns here.

Item paid the same day unto John Holt for ridyng to the kynge to m*aister* Empsons <s> by the[59] space of iiii daies … ii s. viii d.

Item to the same for ridyng to the kyng to Wodstok by v dayes at viii d. a day … iii s. iiii d.

Summa … xxviii li. vii s. iiii d.[60]

Item the xiith day of Septembr*e* to Forster wyff þ*at* kepis m*aister* Pa*r*kers chylde in pa*r*tie of payment for the yere … xx s.

Item paid unto Edward Heyvon by his byll assigned for his cost*es* ridyng to Helhow to receyve certen stuff of my lady <ces> Cecill*es* … xii s. xi d.

Item delyv*er*ed to m*aister* chaunceller for money by hym paid for a <dispensacion for> dispensacio*u*n for s*ir* John Mason … xl s .

Item delyv*er*ed to maistres Foller for a reward yeven to m*aister* Hevenyngham … xl s.

Item delyv*er*ed to the same þ*at* was yeven unto maist*res* Parkers norse … xx d.

Item to the same m*aistres* Foller þ*at* was yeven unto my lord of Rochest*ur* servandes to eyte a buk … vi s. viii d.

Item in reward to the kep*er*s wyff of Chesthunt … xii d.

Item in reward to the ancrysse woman of Seynt Albones … xii d.

[M]Summa … xxxiiii li. x s. vii d.[P]

[*p. 33*] Item delyv*er*ed to Hughe Carre to delyv*er* unto maistres Foller for my lad*ys* g*r*ace … xx s.

Item for my lad*ys* offryng at Seynt Albones … xx d.

Item for my lad*ys* offryng at Assherygg at two tymes … iii s. iiii d.

Item for my lad*ys* offryng at the nonrey of Seynt Margaret*es* comyng from Assherygg to Hatfeld … iii s. iiii d.

Item in reward to oon of the bretheryn of Assheryge þ*at* brought my lad*ys* g*r*ace aquavite t*o* Hatfeld … x s.

Item paid unto John Brydde for a reward yeven to a chyld þ*at* was in my lad*ys* chappell yeven at Seynt Albonez … xii d.

Nota. Nota. Item to the same þ*at* was yeven unto an aget man þ*at* came from Seynt Jamys … xii d.

Item to many chylder at Seynt Albonez at my lad*ys* comyng from Assheryg*e* … xii d.

Item in reward to the kyng*es* courser men by maist*er* tressorer at Seynt Albones … v s.

Item to my lady Cecill awdit*ur* by Nicholas Saunders in reward at Hatfeld … xx s.

[59] 'the' rep.

[60] The correct total of the eight items above, written small in the left margin.

Item paid unto John Brydd for a yerd of blak welved for my lad*ys* harnesshe ... xi s.

Item delyv*er*ed to Jamys Morice by a byll of his hande for the work*es* at Cambryge delyv*er*ed by m*aister* receyver at Cambryge the xvi day of August which I endentyd four*e* the xviii day of Septembr*e* ... xxvi li.[61]

Item delyv*er*ed to maistres Foller for a reward yeven to my lady Cecill s*er*vand comyng from London ... xx d.

Item delyv*er*ed to maistres Foller for a reward yeven to a s*er*vand of s*ir* Samson Norton for the bryngyng of quync*es* to my lad*ys* g*r*ace ... xx d.

Item paid unto William Hylm*er* for a sug*er* loff bought at Cambryge ... vi d.

[M]Summa ... xxx li. xiiii d.[P]

[*p. 34*] Item paid unto maistres Lynche the xviii day of Septembr for iii unc*e* iii q*uarter* of Venysse sylk ... v s. iiii d.

Item for my lad*ys* offryng apon Halhallo Day ... v s.

Item delyv*er*ed unto maister chaunceller for money by hym paid for the co*m*mons of s*ir* John Mason at Tatsall from the vth day of Marche in anno xxii^{do} unto the xv day of July by the space of xix wek*es* aft*er* ix^{d} the weke ... xiiii s. iii d.

Item in other exspenc*e* by the same tyme ... xix s. xi d. ob.

Item paid to the said m*aister* chaunceller for a reward yeve*n* the xxx^{ti} day of Octobr*e* to a s*er*vand of s*ir* Thomas Shefeld tresourer of Seynt Johnes for bryngyng l*ett*res from London to Hatfeld ... xx d.

Item paid unto Dodde for ridyng w*i*th my lady Cecill ii daies to London and iiii daies beying in the court ii daies beyng in London and ii dayes comyng at the same jorney as aperith by his byll assigned ... iii s. iiii d.

Nota. Item paid by the hand*es* of Jamys Moric*e* unto maister Wyett for the exibucion of Thomas Pellett and on Strache and for a tabyll clothe bought for Cryst*es* Collage as aperith by a byll therof ... xxvii s. xi d.

Item paid unto m*aister* Skott by another byll for the exibucion of the said Thomas Pellett ... xxxv s. ii d.

Item paid unto Palm*er* of London and to Jamys Gentyll for the cost*es* of a sadell makyng and harnesshe for my lord prynce ... iiii li. v s. ix d.

Item paid unto Crosley of the Kyng*es* Haule by the hand*es* of maist*er* Scotte for the purche[s] of c*er*tayn grownde and howsis adjou[r]nyng on the north side of the chappell of Cryst*es* Collage for thuse of the said collage ... x li.

Item paid to the said maist*er* Scotte for antiphen*er* for the said collage ... iiii li. xiii s. iiii d.

Item paid unto Rob*er*t Hylton by a byll assigned for the charg*es* of John Drew ... xxiiii s. v d.

[61] See p. 2 above. The MW hand, writing very fast, uses the first person pronoun ('which I endentyd').

Item to Richard Aderton and William Laborer for their cost*es* ridyng for Mergaret Stukeley to London … ii s. vi d.

[M]Summa … xxv li. xviii s. vii d. ob.[P]

[*p. 35*] Item delyv*er*ed to Jamys Morice at two tymes for Cryst*es* Collage at Sterysbryg*e* fair*e* … lxvi li. xix d.

Item for the caryage of s*er*ten stuff of my lady Cecill from Cambryge to Hatfeld … viii s. x d.

Item paid for stuff bought by Jamys Morice and Rob*er*t Hylton at Sterysbryg*e* fair*e* as aperith by a byll therof assigned \for thuse of the wardrop/ … xii li. x s. iiii d.

Item delyv*er*ed to m*aister* P*ar*ker by Nicholas Saunders at his goyng to his moder … xx s.

Item to maist*er* Collyngwod by the hand*es* of maister tressorer for his exibucion beyonde the see … xl s.

Item in reward unto a s*er*vande of m*aister* counttrollers for the bryngyng of letters from Cambryg*e* to my lad*ys* g*ra*ce … xii d.

Item the xxv day of Septembr*e* to Petur Oldam broderer by the hand*es* of maistres Foller in reward … iii s. iiii d.

Item to Jane Goer by the hand*es* [of] Andrew Ancelle for a q*u*art*er* of a yere endyd at Michaelmasse … xiii s. iiii d.

Item the xxviii day of Septembr to George Carre in reward for the bryngyng of c*er*tan lettur*es* from Hatfeld to Cambryge … xx d.

Item the same day in reward to a s*er*vand of my lord of Rochest*er* by the hand*es* of maistres Foller … xx d.

Item the same tyme to Thomas Neswik in reward by the hand*es* of maistres Foller … iii s. iiii d.

Item the ii[de] day of Octobr*e* to dame Margaret Wynsore by the hand*es* of Rob*er*t Marbury … vi s. viii d.

Item to Rob*er*t Merbury for his cost*es* ridyng to London and to the Sion by two daies … ii s.

Item the iiii[th] day of Octobr*e* to maist*er* <Bole> \Belle/ of Fodryngay to the byldyng of Seynt Goodlok chappell xx s. Item for a q*u*art*er* of his anuyte endyd at Mychaelmas xx s. … xl s.

Item for my lad*ys* offryng at sir John Masson syngyng of his furst masse … xx s.

Item to Jamys Morice by a byll for Clviii ell*es* \di./ of lynnen clothe vii li. viii s. v d. ob. qua. Item for a furre of callabor viii s. viii d. … vii li. xvii s. i d. ob. qua.

[M]Summa … iiii[xx]<xiiii[62]>xiiii li. x d. ob. qua.[P]

[62] MS 'xiijj''.

[*p. 36*] Item paid unto John Holt by the hand*es* of Jamys Morice for ridyng to Langley to the kyng and to Cambryge … v s. iiii d

Item paid unto Rob*er*t Merbury for ridyng with the kyng*es* confessor and for theyr*e* cost*es* to Cambryge … xiii s. vii d.

Item paid unto John Pyk for ridyng to Cambryg*e* ii daies … ii s.

Item payd unto Rob*er*t Hylton by the hand*es* of Jamys Morice for stuff bought for m*aister* P*ar*ker agaynest my lad*ys* goyng unto Cambryg*e* … xxxiii s. v d. ob.

Item payd unto the same Rob*er*t for stuff bought for my lad*ys* g*r*ace as reban whit thred ii pec*es* of grene bokeram as aperith by the said byll … xviii s. viii d.

Item paid unto the same Rob*er*t for hose and shoes bought for the fotmen as aperith by the said byll … ix s. viii d.

Item to s*ir* John Masson prest for a elne of wolstyd and for a bonet and for the makyng and lynyng of a payr*e* of hose … vi s. x d.

Item payd unto William Radclyff of Stampforth for money spent by hym for the rep*ar*acion of the ancrysse howse at the nonre in Stampforth … xxii s. x d.

Item to the same William for a reward yeven to the two ancryse in Stampforth … vi s. viii d.

Nota. Item unto s*ir* Jamys parrech prest of Lydeȝard Tragose <t*o*w> toward*es* the bying of a gowne delyvered by m*aister* tressorer … xiii s. iiii d.

Item to Petur*e* of Coldherboro by the hand*es* of m*aister* countroller toward*es* the rep*ar*acions of the Riall … x li.

Item t*o* Ric*hard* Aderton for his cost*es* ridyng with the kyng*es* confessor from Cambryg*e* … xiii s. i d. ob.

Item in reward to the kyng*es* bagpype by m*aister* countroller … iii s. iiii d.

Item in reward to John Vanutaysshe the <kyng*es*> goldsmythe for his labur*e* comyng to Hatfeld … iii s. iiii d.

Item in reward unto a s*er*vande of my lady Scrop*es* for the bryngyng of a bonett for m*ais*tr*es* Vaselay by m*ais*tr*es* Foller … xii d.

[M]Summa … <xviii li. iii s. i d.> xvii li. xiii s. ii d.[P]

[*p. 37*] Item delyv*er*ed the xxvi day of Octobr*e* to m*aister* Wyat by the hand*es* of Ric*hard* Aderton for Cryst*es* Collage … xx li.

Item paid unto George Carre for the cost*es* of fettyng of my lady Collys horse and for the lying of the same horse at Lomans … iii s. ii d.

Item paid for the exspenc*e* of m*aister* Brudnell horsis at Lomans … xiii d.

Item in reward <… > to John fotman by the hand*es* of maistres Foller … vi s. viii d.

Item delyv*er*ed the xvi day of Octobr*e* to maistres Stannop as in money lent to be payd ayen by the fest of All Seynt*es* next ensuyng delyv*er*ed by Jamys Morice … <xl s.> «quia in pede»[63]

Item delyv*er*ed unto my lad*ys* almesse purse by the sayd Jamys … xxx s.

Item to the wyff of Henry Mowre in reward for the kepyng of the fawkener by maistres Foller … ii s.

Item paid to John Bretane of London for iii brode yerd*es* of tawny medly for maistres P*ar*kers norsse … x s.

Item to maistres Massy for to by c*er*ten stuff for the almesse folk … ii s. iiii d.

Money delyverd to James Morece. Item paid to Bernard the kyng*es* glassyer in party of payment toward*es* the makyng of glasse wyndosse in the lybrarie in Cryst*es* Collage … +iiii li.

Nota solvitur per Morice. <Item to Lenard of the vestry as in money for the pryse of xxxv elne of lynnen clothe … xxix s. iiii d.>

Item paid unto m*aister* dean for a reward yeven to a marchant of London for the convayng of a payr*e* of organs to Hatfeld from London for my lad*ys* chappell … vi s. viii d.

Nota. Item paid unto m*aister* receyver for thiez parcell*es* bought <ly> by hym and Rob*er*t Hylton as aperith by a byll therof for a bonett for m*aistres* P*ar*ker … ii s. viii d.

Item paid for vii dos*en* of whitt bonett*es* for my lad*ys* mawndy. P*r*ice the dosyn vi s. … xlii s.

Item paid for a pese of fustian for thuse of the wardrop the which contayneth xv yerd*es*. The p*r*ice … viii s. vi d.

Item for iii yerd*es* i q*u*art*er* of kenett for m*aistres* P*ar*ker at xx d. the yerd … v s. v d.

[M]Summa … xxx<ii[64]> li. xviii d.[P]

[*p. 38*] Item paid unto the same Rob*er*t Hylton for oon fyne furr*e* of shank*es* as aperith by the said byll … xviii s.

Item to the same for courser furr*e* for thuse of the wardrop … xii s. vi d.

Item paid for l skynnes of blak bogie for the furr*e* of m*aistres* P*ar*kers gowne … xxxiii s. iiii d.

Item paid unto the same Rob*er*t for xl skynnes of courser bogie. P*r*ice of ev*er*y skynne vii d. … xxiii s. iiii d.

Item for fures bought to p*er*fourme a gowne of blak satten for my lad*ys* g*r*ace … iiii s. iiii d.

Item to Rob*er*t Hylton for his cost*es* at London p*ro*vidyng of this stuff by iii daiez at xii d. the day … iii s.

[63] See p. 63 below.
[64] MS 'jj'.

Item paid for xviii yerd*es* di. of blak welvett. P*r*ice the yerd x s. iiii d. … ix li. xi s. ii d.

Item for xxiii yerd*es* and a q*u*art*er* of blak satten. P*r*ice the yerd vii s. … viii li. ii s. ix d.

Item paid unto Lenard of the vestre by his byll assigned for a premer … xx d.

Item for a ream of paper … xvi d.

Item for caryage of the same pap*er* ii d. Item for iiii candylstik*es* iiii d. Item for the byndyng of iii Frenche book*es* \iii d./ … ix d.

Item paid unto maistres Lynche for xv unc*e* and a half of cremysen selk. P*r*ice … xx s. viii d.

Item for half a lib. of blew Venys silk*es*. P[r]ice … xii s.

Item for half a lib. of blak and tawny selk … vii s. iiii d.

Item for half a lib. of blew and tawny selk … viii s.

Item for a pounde and <un> v unc*e* of freng*e* … ii s. viii d.

Item for a lib. di. unc*e* of vestment reban … xvi s.

Item for half a lib. of lyght tawny selk. The unc*e* x d. … vii s.

Item for half a lib. of other reban … viii s.

Item paid for a pec*e* of sypers … iii s. iiii d.

Item in reward to the p*ar*son of Seynt Peturs in Cornell in London þ*at* prechyd afour*e* my lad*ys* g*r*ace apon Halhallo Day … vi s. viii d.

Item paid unto William Whitmor*e* m*aister* P*ar*kers s*er*vand for his waig*es* for a q*u*art*er* ended at Michaellmasse … vi s. viii d.

[M]Summa … xxvii li. <x s. x d.> x s. vi d.[P][65]

[*p. 39*] Item payd the ii[de] day of Novembr*e* for the cost*es* of the lady Issebell w*i*th the diett of hir servand*es* and vi horsis … viii s. viii d.

Item payd for the exspenc*e* of my lady marquesse and hir servand*es* diett and xiiii horsis … ix s.

Item in reward unto Greffithe wyff of Colyweston for the <dryng> dryeng of safferon brought to my lad*ys* g*r*ace … vi s. viii d.

Item paid unto John Hornywold for the confermacion of the covent seall for the avoyson of Reple yeven by the bysshop of Worset*ur* … xvii s.

Item in reward to the said John Hornywold for his gud delygenc*e* in the same … vi s. viii d.

Item paid unto m*aister* dean for money yeven unto s*ir* John Carter toward*es* his lechecraft at Cambryge … xx s.

[65] The first (partly canc.) total is in the MW hand, the second in a different hand (probably the 'sprawling' hand).

Item paid unto Maydwell shomaker the xv day[66] of Novembr for v payre of shoez and iii payr*e* of sleppers for my lad*ys* g*r*ace at vi d. the payre … iiii s.

Item delyv*er*ed the xvith day of Novembr*e* to Jamys Moric*e* by s*ir* Edward Artwyk for byldyng of Cryst*es* Collage … xxii li.

Item for Ihesu gylde in Grantham … xx d.

Item paid unto m*aister* receyver for money by hym payd unto George Kyrkham clerk of the kyng*es* hamp*er* for <t*o* lett> l*ett*res patent*es* of Cryst*es* Collage in Cambryge þ*at* were delyv*er*ed to the kyng*es* hand*es* by the said George at Cambrige … vii li. xix s. v d.

Item paid unto the same for money paid unto Nicholas Coup*er* stewarde of Saint Antones in London in p*ar*te of payment of suche stuff as was bought of my lady of Norfolk*es* executo*urs* … xxv li.

Item paid to the wyff of the George in Hatfeld for the cost*es* of doct*ur* Robynson horsis and his servand*es* for iiii horsis ii daies … ii s. viii d.

Item to Rob*er*t Edlyn for his cost*es* and his horse hyr*e* ridyng for Rob*er*t Lawe to Waltham Crosse … xii d.

^{M}Summa … lviii li. xvi s. ix d.^{P}

[*p. 40*] Item delyv*er*ed unto maistres Stannop the xxv day of Novembr*e* for a reward yeven to Ric*hard* Cotmote for the heylyng of William Luff … xx s.

Item paid unto Ric*hard* Aderton by his byll assigned for his cost*es* ridyng from Hatfeld unto Richemond and so to London by iii daiez paid the xxvi day of Novembr … ii s.

Item paid the same day unto m*aister* chaunceller for a reward yeven unto John Drewe my lad*ys* ward at his goying from Hatfeld into the west countre … iii s. iiii d.

Item to m*aister* chaunceller the last day of Novembr for a reward yeven unto Laurenc*e* Cuff beyng hurt in London … xiii s. iiii d.

Item to Ric*hard* Aderton <bi> for a reward yeven unto m*aister* Fellis brother comyng from London delyv*er*ed by maistres Stannop … vi s. viii d.

Item delyv*er*ed to my lad*ys* g*r*ace the iii^{de} day of Decembr for hir almes purse in penc*e* … xiii li. vi s. viii d.

Item paid unto Jamys Morice for money by hym payd for iiii pec*es* of lynnen clothe on pec*e* cont*eynyng* xxvii ell*es* wantyng the nayle ii^{de} pec*e* cont*eynyng* xxix ell*es* and half a ell iii^{de} pec*e* cont*eynyng* xxv ell*es* the iiiith pec*e* xxv ell*es* and i q*uarter*. Summa of elnez Cvi iii q*uar*t*er* at v d. ob. … xlviii s. x d.

Item paid unto the said Jamys for a reward yeven unto maister Benstid servand for fechyng of letturs þ*at* went into Skotland … viii d.

<Item paid unto Rob*er*t Hylton by his byll assigned for iii yerd*es* of tawny clothe for a gowne for maistres Lynche v s. the yerd. Summa … xv s.>

[66] 'p'? add. but not canc.

Item for a yerd iii q*uarter* of skarlett for a petycote for my lad*ys* g*r*ace at viii s. vi d. the yerd … xiiii s. x d. ob.

Item for a kyp of blak lambe for thuse of the wardrop of the rob*es* … vi s. viii d.

Item for a kyp of whytte lambe to the same use … iiii s.

[M]Summa … <xx li. […]i s. ob.> <ii s. ob.> xix li. vii s. ob.[P] [67]

[*p. 41*] Item paid unto the same Rob*er*t Hylton by the same byll for i lib. of white threde ii s. i lib. xviii d. i lib. xvi d. i lib. xiiii d. i lib. xii d. i lib. x d. and for a q*uarter* xii d. white threde as delyv*er*ed to the kepyng of maistres Foller … viii s. x d.

Item for iiii slaies delyv*er*ed to maistres Stannop … iii s. iiii d.

Item for a yerd i q*uarter* di. of skarlett for a payr*e* of hose for m*aister* Parker. P*r*ice the yerd iiii s. iiii d. … v s. xi d. ob.

Item for iii yerd*es* of blak fustian for a dobelett for the said m*aister* P*ar*ker at vii d. the yerd … xxi d.

Item for the cost*es* of the said Rob*er*t in London by two dayes p*ro*vidyng the said stuff … ii s.

Item to Apt cariar for carying the same stuff … iiii d.

Item delyv*er*ed unto Hughe Carre for a reward yeven unto maistrez Seynt Johens mydwyff þ*a*t brought cak*es* to my lad*ys* g*r*ace … xii d.

Item paid unto Rob*er*t Merbury by his byll assigned for his cost*es* ridyng to Walsyngham and to Ingham to s*ir* Edward Howard by viii daies … viii s.

Item on Seynt Nicholas Even unto Seynt Nicholas clerk*es* … v s.

Item to Seynt Nicholas clerk*es* of the towne of Hatfeld … xx d.

Item paid unto maistres Massy for <flx> flex and other nessesaries bought for my lad*ys* almes folk*es* and for litell maistres P*ar*ker as aperith by hir byll assigned … xx s.

Item payd unto Petur*e* brotherer for a pounde of gylt gold … xii s.

Item for ii pounde of carpett yerne … ii s.

Item for a M of neld*es* … iii s. iiii d.

Item for a dossen thembles iiii d. vi payr*e* of sheris vi d. for a past bourde iiii d. Summa … xiiii d.

Item delyv*er*ed to maistres Foller the \vth/ day of Dece*m*br for money yeven by my lad*ys* g*r*ace to a goldsmythe of London for certen stuff delyv*er*ed to hir g*r*ace … vii li. vii s. ii d.

For money yeven to the same goldsmythe for a pott. Item the same tyme to maistrez Foller for my lad*ys* g*r*ace … <xxxiii s. iiii d.> xxviii s. iiii d.

Item paid unto m*aister* Hevenyngham for a reward yeven unto m*aister* Letton s*er*vande at Cambryge for kepyng of a hawke … iii s. iiii d.

[67] Only the first canc. calculation is in the MW hand; the rest is probably in the 'sprawling' hand.

Item for my lad*ys* offryng apon our*e* Lad*ys* Day … v s.

[M]Summa … xiii li. xiiii d. ob.[P]

[*p. 42*] Item paid unto maistres Foller by hir byll assigned for iii pair*e* of shoes for maistres Ursula and iii pair*e* for Margaret Ludlow <ch> sethyn Seynt Th[o]mas Day afour*e* Cryste*n*masse … xviii d.

Item for vi payr*e* of hosen for theym and for ii comb*es* and <alye> a lye pott xxi d. Item for butt*ur* and egg*es* and mylk xviii d. … iii s. iii d.

Item for a pece of <f> lace for ii bokes þ*at* went to Cambryge … iii d.

Item the iiii[th] day of Decembr unto Rob*er*t Merbury to delyv*er* unto my lad*ys* solicet*ur* for land*es* purchased for Wynborne … C li.

Item to the same Rob*er*t for a reward yeven unto the exchet*ur* of Somursetshyr*e* … xl s.

Item to m*aister* chaunceller for money yeven to the exchet*ur* of Lyncolnshyr*e* for his fee for two yer*es* passid … xl s.

Item on our*e* Lady Day to a bedell of Cambryg for the bryngyng of letturs to my lad*ys* g*r*ace from my lord of Rochestur*e* … xii d.

Item to m*aister* dean for a reward yeven to a frere þ*at* <pli> prechyd afour*e* my lad*ys* g*r*ace the Sonday the xxii day of Decembr*e* … vi s. viii d.

Item for the cost*es* of maistres Smythe wedow at hir beyng at Hatfeld paid to the god man of the George for hir horse meyt and hir s*er*vandes … v s.

Item delyv*er*ed to m*aister* dean for a reward yeven unto doct*ur* Yonge þ*at* prechyd afour*e* my lad*ys* g*r*ace the Sonday the xix day of Decembr*e* … x s.

Item paid unto Rob*er*t Merbury for his cost*es* ridyng from Hatfeld to London to my lad*ys* solicit*er* by ii daies … ii s.

Item in reward to Worsop for makyng of his howse that was brent … xxiiii s.

Item paid unto m*aister* dean for his cost*es* ii daies and ii nyght*es* in horsis and in s*er*vand*es* at London for to speyke w*i*th my lord of Wenchest*er* … vi s.

Item paid to \the/ same for money paid to the p*r*ior of Seynt Albons for Hew T*ur*nar gowne \as by his byll/ … viii s.

[M]Summa … <Cii li. vii s. viii d.>[P] Cvii li. <v>vii s. viii d.[P] [68]

[*p. 43*] Item paid unto Nicholas Saunders for money by hym paid for ii lib. gallis p*r*ice x d. a lib. gu*m*me arabic vi d. a lib. cop*er*as grene iiii d. for a skynne of vellom to write in the crowne of our*e* <lord> Lady iiii d. ii pott*es* for the same ii d. Summa … ii s. ii d.[69]

[68] The corrected (correct) total is in a different hand from the MW hand.

[69] The sum allows for only 1lb. of galls.

Item xx[ti] day of Decembr*e* to Haymound Nicholasson hardware man in p*ar*tie of payment for lynnen clothe and satten of Bruges bought of hym by my lad*ys* g*r*ace … iiii[xx]viii li.

Item paid unto John Holt by his byll assigned for ridyng to the bar[o]ne of Dudley and to the bysshop of Lyncoln to Ludlow by x daies … vi s. viii d.

Item to the same for ridyng to m*aister* chamberlayn two daies … xvi d.

Item paid unto Edward Tymes for the dressyng and skowryng of c*er*ten clothes for Cryst*es* Collage the whiche was delyv*er*ed unto hym by Nicholas of the wardrop[70] … v s.

Item paid unto Edward Vaux of the seller for his cost*es* ridyng to London and ayen by iii daies as aperith <t*o*> by his byll iii s. and from London to Richmound for his bot hir*e* xvi d. Summa … iiii s. iiii d.

Item to s*ir* Rob*er*t of the chappell by his byll assigned for his cost*es* ridyng apon my lad*ys* messag*es* … xxxiii s. ii d.

Item delyv*er* for my lad*ys* offryng apon Crystemasse Day … v s.

Item delyv*er*ed to Rob*er*t Merbury for my lad*ys* offryng in the holy dayes … x s.

Item to m*aister* Bekynsall for a reward yeven unto m*aister* Roche the xxx day of Decembr*e* … vi s. viii d.

*Delyv*ered *to m*aistres *Foller*. Item paid for ix yerd*es* of blak satten bought by Rob*er*t Hylton. P*r*ice the yerd vi s. viii d. … lx s.

*Yeven to m*aister *vicechamberlayn*. Item iii yerd*es* of blak saten bought by the same vii s. ii d. … xxi s. vi d.

*Yeven to m*aister *tresorer*. Item iii yerd*es* of tawny satten. P*r*ice the yerd vi s. iiii d. … xxii s.

Item for a grey <amyas> amys bought by the same … lxvi s. viii d.

Item to the same Rob*er*t Hylton cost*es* ryding to London to p*ur*vey this stuffe by one daie di. … xx d.

[M]Summa … C li. vii s. ii d.[P]

[*p. 44*] Item to my lad*ys* g*r*ace by Hughe Carr*e* that was yeven to the lady Bowghan at hir beyng at Hatfeld … xx s.

Nwyeres Day. Item delyv*er* to the vichamberlan in reward yeven to Peris Champion for the bryngyng of the kyng*es* New Yer*es* gyft*es* to my lad*ys* g*r*ace … C s.

Item to a s*er*vand of thabbott*es* of Westm*ynster* for the bryngyng of a New Yer*es* gyft … x s.

Item to m*aister* Parker*e* in reward … xl s.

[70] MS 'wrardrop'.

Item to won of Assheregge for the bryngyng of rose water*e* delyv*er*ed to maistres Massy … iii s. iiii d.

[71]Item delyv*er*ed unto maistres Foller the last yere for Newer*es* gyfft*es* yeven by my lad*ys* <gos> g*r*ace xiii li. vi s. viii d. wherof allowed in my last account*es* lxvi s. viii d. and so remaynes unalowed x li. Item on Newer*es* Even delyv*er*ed to maistres Foller xiii li. vi s. viii d. for Neweres gyftes <to b> yeven this yer*e*. Summa in all … xxiii li. vi s. viii d.

Item the iii^{de} day of January to m*aister* chaunceller for <j> a reward yeven unto maist*er* Conysby clerk … vi s. viii d.

Item to my lady Jane by the hand*es* of Jamys Morice l s. and delyv*er* myself xvi s. viii d. Summa … <lxvi s. viii d.> «postea in pede»[72]

Item delyv*er*ed unto Thomas Pellett in reward at his beyng at Hatfeld … iii s. iiii d.

Item payd unt*o* William Whitamor*e* s*er*vande unto m*aister* P*ar*ker for a q*uar*t*er* waig*es* endyd at Crystmas … vi s. viii d.

Item t*o* the orge*n*maker that convayed the greyte organce from Hatfeld to Cryst*es* Collage in Cambryge delyv*er*ed to hym by m*aister* chaunceller … iii s. iiii d.

Item unto m*aister* Edward Bothe for money delyv*er*ed unto my lady Cecill in hir sekenes … xl s.

[M]Summa … <xxxviii li. vi s. viii d.[P]> xxxv li.[73]

[*p. 45*] *New Yeres Day offryng*. Item for my lad*ys* offryng apon Newer*es* Day … v s.

Item payd unto Fyssher of the chapell for the cost*es* of the convaying of Thomas Sherade chyld of the chappell unto his father dwellyng besyde Melton Molbrey at Stapulforde as aperith by his byll assigned … iii s. viii d.

Item payd unto George Kirkeham for money by hym paid for petye fees for the kyng*es* l*ett*res patent*es* of the lycence for purchasyng of vi li.[74] lande unto Cryst*es* Collage in Cambryge. Furst for my lord chauncell*our* fee xiii s. iiii d. the maist*er* of the Roll*es* fee iiii s. for the lace xx d. for grene wax viii d. for the examynacion iiii s. for the allowance of the warrant vi s. viii d. for the wrytyng and enrollyng xlvi s. viii d. Summa … lxxvii s.

Item paid unto <w> Thomas Maydwell for a payr*e* of sleppers for my lad*ys* g*r*ace on our*e* Lady Day vi d. Item for a payr*e* of buskyns and a payr*e* of shoes on Seynt Andrewes Day x d. Item for a payr*e* of shoes of Newer*es* Day iiii d. … xx d.

[71]The MW hand uses the first person pronoun ('my last account*es*'); see too the next entry but one ('delyver myself').
[72]See p. 125 below.
[73]The correction is probably in a different hand from the MW hand and takes account of the canc. entry above.
[74]Perhaps copied from a bill into the wrong position (it should probably come after 'Cambryge' but is not included in the total).

Item to Henry the kyng*es* godson in reward apon the Xiith Day ... xiii s. iiii d.

Item to Jane Goer for Crystemasse q*u*art*er* ... xiii s. iiii d.

Item to Steven Tabret apon New Yer*es* Day ... iii s. iiii d.

Item yeven to the preysers of my lord of Cant*er*bury preysysng my lady Cecill stuff ... <xxv s. viii d.> xxvi s. viii d.

Conysby. Item delyv*er*ed unto m*aister* chaunceller the viii day of January for a reward yeven unt*o* m*aister* Conysby ... xl s.

*Sop*er. Item the same tyme in reward unt*o* m*aister* Soper my lad*ys* solicet*ur*... xxvi s. viii d.

Item paid unto Haymond Nicholasson hardware man in full payment of lynnen clothe and satten of Brug*es* bought by hym for my lad*ys* g*r*ace ... iiii li. xviii s. iiii d.

Item paid unto m*aister* vichamberlayn for a reward yeven unto the tresorers of Seynt Johnez s*er*vand bryngyng of lettur to my lad*ys* g*r*ace þ*at* came from the Rodes ... xx d.

[M]Summa ... xv li. xv s. viii d.[P]

[*p. 46*] Item delyv*er*ed unto Petur*e* Baldwyn of Coldherboro the xith day of January for the rep*ar*acions don at Riall in London ... Cxvi s. vii d. ob.

Item paid unto Thomas Seno goldwyr*e* drayer for two pounde of rounde gold at iiii s. iii d. the unc*e* ... Cii s.[75]

Item paid unto the same for two pounde of flatt gold ev*ery* unc*e* iiii s. x d. ... Cxvi s.

Item paid unto maistres Massy for a reward yeven to my lad*ys* old lander þ*at* brought vi capons ... iii s. iiii d.

Item to maistres Foler for a reward yeven to a s*er*vand of my lady Scrop*es* ... xx d.

Item to the same þ*at* was yeven in reward unto a s*er*vand of maist*er* Bedylles ... viii d.

Item paid unto Thomas Seno of London for viii unc*e* of yelow sylk. P*r*ice the unc*e* xiiii d. ... ix s. iiii d.

Item to maistres Foller þ*at* was yeven in reward to Ric*hard* Stukely ... xx d.

Item paid unto Robert Hylton for ii pair*e* of shoes bought for <maistres> maist*er* Parker. P*r*ice ... xx d.

Item for other ii payr*e* for m*aister* P*ar*ker agaynest Criste*n*masse ... xx d.

Item paid to William Taileo*ur* for the makyng and lynyng of ii pair*e* of hose agaynest Halhallotyde ... xx d.

Item for the makyng and lynyng of other ii pair*e* agaynest Cryste*n*masse ... xx d.

Item paid for old Strengers hose ... iiii d.

[75] In this and the next entry there are 12 oz. to the lb.

Item paid for anlett*es* for the pore womens kyrtels and for the chyldren of the chappell cott*es* ... xii d.

Item paid unto the same Rob*er*t Hylton for his cost*es* at Cambryge beyng they*re* at Stewrysbryg fay*re* t*o* by stuff for my lad*ys* g*r*ace by vii daiez ... vii s.

[M]Summa ... xviii li. viii s. iii d. ob.[76]

[*p. 47*] Item paid unto Rob*er*t Hylton for CCCCC pynk*es* and a half. P*r*ice the C xvi d. Summa ... vii s. iiii d.

Item paid unto the same for CCCC powdryng*es* the hundreth xii d. Summa ... iiii s.

Item for iii skynnes of blak lambe which was occupied in my lad*ys* petycote p*er*formyng of the same ... ix d.

Item for xviii skynnes of blak lambe þ*at* was for the p*er*fourmyng of m*aister* P*ar*kers lev*ery* gowne ... vi s.

Item for the lynyng of the gentylwomens pur[fe]lls[77] þ*at* is at my lad*ys* fyndyng iiii leder skynnes. P*r*ice ev*er*[y] skynne ii d. ob. Summa ... x d.

Item paid unto Jamys Morice for money yeven unto the p*ar*son late of Malton in reward <tv> towardes his cost*es* and lost*es* goyng from the said Malton unto the chauntr*e* at M[a]xey[78] ... xl s.

Item to the same for money paid unto William Parker of Hatfeld for the carryegge of the greyte orgens from Hatfeld unto Cryst*es* Collage ... vi s. viii d.

Item paid unto Robert Borton at iii sondry tymes for the takyng downe of the organs \iii s. iiii d./ at Hatfeld and for the settyng up of the same at Cryst*es* Collaige \x s. iiii d./ and for the takyng downe of the same organs and the settyng up agayn \iiii s./. Summa ... xviii s.

Item paid unto Thomas Dalton for his cost*es* ridyng w*i*th Lellg*r*ave to Ypswyche w*i*th c*er*ten wrytyng*es* conc*er*nyng the abbey of Creyke by iii da[i]ez at xii d. the day. Summa ... iiii s.

Item paid unto Jamys Morice for his cost*es* and his s*er*vands w*i*th ii horsis ridyng to the said abbey of Creyke for to wewe the place ther*e* by iiii daies ... viii s.

Item paid unto John Harryson for dyv*er*se stuff bought for the players and moresse daunce w*i*th other dyv*er*se exspenc*e* for the abbot of mysrewle in Crystemasse as aperith by his byll ... xvi li. <x s. ii d.> xviii s. iiii d.

xvi li. x s. ii d.[79]

[M]Summa ... xxi li. <xi s.> \xii s./ <[...] s. ix d.> xi d.[80]

[76] Not marked 'probatur'.
[77] MS 'pursells'.
[78] MS 'Mxey'.
[79] Written small in the left margin in the MW hand; it has been altered later, with the result that the 'Summa' below has also been altered (in a different hand); it should be £21 13s. 11d.
[80] Not marked 'probatur'.

[*p. 48*] Item delyv*er*ed unto m*aister* Peksall for money send to m*aister* presydent for the wrytyng of a boke for my lad*ys* grace … vi s. viii d.

Item unto m*aister* presydent s*er*vande in reward … xii d.

Memorandum by the vichamberlayn *vi s. viii d. and by maistrez Foller xiii s. iiii d.* Item in reward to Gerrade the kyng*es* s*er*vande … <vi s. viii d.> xx s.

Item paid to Ric*hard* Aderton for ridyng to Waltham Crosse and ther*e* abydyng by ii daiez … xvi d.

Item paid unto Henry Wynstanley by his byll assigned for iiii payr*e* of hose for Skypp. P*r*ice … ii s.

Item to the same for iiii payr*e* of shoes … ii s.

Item for the sawlyng of the same shoes … xii d.

Item delyv*er*ed the last day of Decembr*e* unto m*aister* receyver for money paid in the moneth of February unto s*ir* Edward Howard for the savgard of m*aister* P*ar*kers land*es* … <D marc*es*> «CCCxxxiii li. vi s. viii d.»[81]

Item delyv*er*ed the same tyme to m*aister* receyver for to content for the kyng*es* New Yer*es* gyft*es* Cx li. x s. and for other New Yer*es* gyft*es* iiii li. xi s. iii d. ob. … Cxv li. xv d. ob.

Item paid for a cote clothe makyng and lynyng for Thomas Freston oon of the chylder of the chappell at his goyng to Wynchester*e* … vii s. viii d.

[M]<Summa>

Item delyv*er*ed unto Thomas Soper my lad*ys* solicitur by the hand*es* of m*aister* Assheton … viii li. xix s. viii d.

Item in reward to William Grevell at his goyng from Hatfeld … xx s.

Item paid unto John Holt for his cost*es* ridyng to London and to Richmound by iii daies … ii s.

<CCCClix li. xi s. iii d. ob.>[82]

[M]Summa partis … CCCClx li. xi s. iii d. ob. [P]

[*p. 49 blank*]

[*p. 50*]

[83]<MMDlxxii li. xv s. iiii d.> [84]Somme of all the hole allowance and paymentes aforsaide in this yere anno xxiii[cio] … MMDlxxii li. xv s. iiii d.

[81] The interpretation of 500 marks in £sd.
[82] Written small to the left of the page and written out fair below in a different hand from the MW hand.
[83] Written small to the left of 'Somme'.
[84] The 'sprawling' hand may be responsible for the formal script of the rubric as well as the cursive hand of the rest of the page (but perhaps not for 'serche … allowaunce'). See Plate 15.

[85]<Dlxxv li. viii d. qua.> And so he oweth … Dlxxv li. viii d. qua. wherof delyv*er*ed unto þe pryncez as yt may appere in hur boke of receyt*es* … l li. And so he aweth … Dxxv li. viii d. qua. «que oneratur in computo sequenti[86] \serche in the vth lef folowyng for ferther allowaunce/»[87]

[*p. 51*] *wherof in*[88]

Al<e>mes yevon unto soundre persons at divers tymes … ix li. iiii d.

Money deliv*er*ed att div*er*s tymes to my ladis grace as hur almes purse … xl li. xvi s. viii d.

Money delyvered at sondre tymes for my ladis offering … viii li. v s. vii d.

Money paid for certen stuff bought and p*ro*vided for my ladis maundy … x li. xi s. viii d.

Certen stuff bought for my ladis almes men and women … iiii li. vii s. i d.

lxxiii li. <xi s. iiii d.> xvi d.[89]

Money delyv*er*ed unto Robert Hilton for certen cottons and fresez of div*er*s colors and for other stuff for the same p*er*sones and other pore folkes and for the store of the warderope … xiiii li. xi s. vi d.

Money delyv*er*ed in the way off almes for the exhibicion of Jane Gower … liii s. iiii d.

Money delivered unto William Ratcliff of S[t]ampford for the reparacion of the ankers house there … xxii s. x d.

Exhibicion of Drewe my ladys warde … xxiiii s. v d.

xix li. xii s. i d.[90]

iiii^{xx}xii li. <xiii s. v d.> xiii s. v d.[91]

[92]Costis for the inquesic*i*on of [A]telborowe[93] … <lxi s. ii d.> lxi s.

Exhibic*i*on of scolers at my ladis finding at soundre places that is to say Thomas Pep*er* xix s. i d. ob. s*ir* John Mason vii li. xvi s. iiii d. Thomas <parett> \Pelet/ lxxviii s. ix d. m*aster* Colyngwod xl s. In the hole … xiiii li. xiiii s. ii d. ob.

Cx li. viii s. ix d. ob.[94]

[85] Written small to the left of 'And so he oweth'.
[86] See p. 65 below.
[87] See p. 60 below.
[88] Halfway down the left margin, bracketed to include all the items on the page and on the following pages up to and including p. 59 (all written in a small formal hand).
[89] The total of the five items above, bracketed to the right of the items.
[90] The total of the four items above, bracketed to the right of the items.
[91] The total of all the items so far on p. 51, bracketed to the right after the items.
[92] This item and all the next items up to and including the third item on p. 53 are bracketed to the right (for the total see p. 53).
[93] MS 'htelborowe'.
[94] The total of all the items on the page, written small to the right at the foot of the page.

[*p. 52*] Exhibic*io*n of Skyppe … xiii s.

Money delyvered unto m*aster* Bell off Fodringhay for his fee and toward*es* his exhibic*io*n … Cxv s.

xxi li. ii s. ii d. ob.[95]

[96]Costis of the approp*r*iacion of the p*ar*sonage of Helpeston unto Cristez College in Cambryge … C s.

Certen stuff bought for Cristez College as w*ith* iiii li. xiii s. iiii d. for antefeners … xvi li. xviii d.

Money payed for certen land*es* bought lying behinde the said college for to make ther orchard and gardyng … x li.

Money paied unto the kinge for the abbey of Creke to be approp*r*ied to the seid college … CCCClxvi li. xiii s. iiii d.

Money payd to m*aster* Sikelynges executo*ur*s for the sup*er*plussage of his accompte for Cristez College … xxi li.

Money yevon unto m*aster* Dudley in rewarde to soluste \þe/ kynge for the same … lxvi s. viii d.

Costis as well of William Lilg*r*ave s*er*vaunte unto my ladys receyvo*ur* and other riding div*er*s tymes unto Creke and Meniburs of the same as money payed unto the <Ex> eschetours of Norff*olk* Nort*hampton* and Leicester for the finding of divers offices … ix li. xvii s. ii d.

[*p. 53*] Costis and expens of m*aster* Richarde Clerke maister of the same college and other riding at divers tymes don uppon divers necessarez mesagez … iiii li. vi s. viii d.

Money delyverd unto the p*ar*son of Malton towardis his costis in the resingnacion his seid benifice unto the seid college … iiii li.

Money delyvered unto Jamez Morez towardes the belding of Cristez College … DCiiii^{xx}xvi li. xii s. vi d.

MCCxxxvi li. xvii s. x d.[97]

MCClxi li. xiiii d. ob.[98]

Monei paid for parte of the purches of the land that is bought for the mortez to Wimborne Mynster … <C li.> C li.

Rewardis yevon at soundre tymes to many and divers p*er*sones <lxvi li. xi s. ii d.> liiii li. xi s. ii d.

[95]The total of the last item on p. 51 and the first two on p. 52, bracketed to the right of the items.
[96]This item and all the next items up to and including the third item on p. 53 are bracketed to the right (for the total see p. 53).
[97]The total of the items since 'Costis of the appropriacion' on p. 52, bracketed to the right of the items.
[98]The total of the items since 'Costis for the inquesicion' on p. 51, bracketed to the right of the items.

Rewardis yeven unto officers and s*er*vant*es* \of the kingis/ att my ladis being at Richemount in Lent tyme … xv li. xi s. vii d.

Reward yevon to maister Morgan with[99] xl s. toward profecion of <dame> his sister dame Eleno*ur* his late wiff … iiii li.

Reward yevon to s*ir* Raff Verney and to my lady his wiff and for ther costis lying in Hatfeld … lxxviii s. iiii d.

Reward yevon to Edward Hevon … xl s.

Reward yevon unto doctour Chapell att his commensement … liii s. iiii d.

Reward yevon to divers of the kinges servantes at Ely att my ladis being þer … C s.

CCxxiii li. xxi d.[100]

<DCCCCiiii li. xiii s. vii d.> DCCCiiii^{xx}xii li. xiii s. vii d.[101]

[*p. 54*] Reward yevon to my ladis chapell … xx s.

Reward yevon to Henyngham … xl s.

Reward yevon to the escheto*ur* of Lincoln xl s. and Somersett xl s. … iiii li.

Reward yevon to Warshopp of Colyweston toward the bildyng of his house that was burned … xxiiii s.

Reward yevon unto Peers Champion bringing the kynge Newersgift … C s.

Reward yevon to maister Conyngsby xl s. and to Thomas Soper xxvi s. viii d. and to m*aster* Par*ker* xl s. and to the lady Baughan xx s. In the hole … vi li. <xvi s. viii d.> \ vi s. viii d./

ii hoggeshedis of wyne yevon unto maister Conyngsby … lvi s. viii d.

Reward yevon att the cristenyng off maister Weston child … lxvi s. viii d.

Reward yevon unto m*aster* Denys v m*a*rcs and to his wiff xx s. … iiii li. vi s. viii d.

Reward yevon unto the king*es* phisicion … xl s.

Money send unto m*aster* Fell to Rome … lxvi s. viii d.

Cxxiii li. xxd.[102]

xxxv li. vii s. iiii d.[103]

[99] MS 'whit'.

[100] The total of the eight items above, bracketed to the right of the items.

[101] The total of all the items on the page, written small to the right at the foot of the page.

[102] The total of all the items since 'Rewardis yevon at soundre tymes' p. 53.

[103] The total of all the items on the page, written small to the right at the foot of the page.

[*p. 55*] Cost*es* off divers suett*es* don by m*aster* Assheton my ladis receiv*our* in the kyngis Eschequier … xxxiii s. iiii d.

Money paied in the seid Eschequier by the same m*aster* Assheton for the respecting of homage of divers lordshippis and land*es* put in feffement to p*er*forme my ladis will nott payed for div*er*s yerez … iiii li.

Cost*es* as well of other suet*es* don by Thomas Soper my ladis solister as for the recov*er*es of certen landis bought for Wymborne and also certen money payed in the chaunsere for the selling of div*er*s writyng*es* as yt apperith in <the> a boke of p*ar*cell*es* delyv*er*ed and examaned[104] … xxvi li. xiii s. i d.

xxxii li. vi s. v d.[105]

Money paied att <ffel> Hatefeld for the costis of divers p*er*sones that come to my ladis grace … xxxi s. v d.

Costis of div*er*s of my lad*ys* servant*es* riding w*ith*in the tyme of this accompte unto soundre places uppon hur messagez w*ith* xl s. for the cost*es* of hur receyv*our* … <xxi li. xvi s. i d. ob.> xiiii li. xiii s. viii d. ob.

Costis of my lord*es* of Rochesters servantes riding to m*aster* Bowrer benyfice … xxvi s. viii d.

xvii li. xi s. ix d. ob.[106]

<lvii li. vii d. ob.> xlix li. xviii s. ii d. ob.[107]

[*p. 56*] Cost*es* off my ladis fotemen … <xl s.> xl s.

Money delyv*er*ed and paied for the finding of m*aster* Parker and of my mastres his wiff and for the wagez of his servant … vi li. xv s. iiii d.

Costis and exhibic*i*on of mastres Ursula <h> Pole m*astres* Yon<s> and off mast[re]s[108] Parrott … iiii li. iiii s. i d.

Money delyvered to m*aster* Frognall and to my mastres his wiff … xxxiiii s. iiii d.

xii li. xiii s. ix d.[109]

Certen furrez as lambe and boge bought at div*er*s tymes … xliiii s.

Certen printed bokez bought for my ladis grace … x s. ii d.

An barell of mu[s]kadele bought for my ladys grace and other swete wyne … viii s. ii d.

Certen stuff bought for my ladis grace as certen wolon cloth furrez girdell*es* rebyns and many other necessarez … xvi li. xix s. x d. ob.

[104] -m- has four minims.
[105] The total of the three items above, bracketed to the right of the items.
[106] The total of the three items above, bracketed to the right of the items.
[107] The (corrected and correct) total of all the items on the page, written small to the right at the foot of the page.
[108] MS 'masters'.
[109] The total of the three items above, bracketed to the right of the items.

iii peyer of almer bedes bought for my ladis grace … xxxiiii s.

Money paied for threde fringez thymbell*es* and nedelles at div*er*s tymez … xlviii s. ii d.

Certen other stuff bought as corpores casez brushez glases and many other thinges necessares … lxii s. ii d.

Certen velom p*ar*chement and pap*er* bought and delyv*er*ed to Hatfeld … xliiii s.

<xxvi li. v s. v<i> d. ob.> xxix li. x s. vi d. ob.[110]

xliiii li. iiii s. iii d. ob.

[*p. 57*] Money paied at div*er*s tymes to soundre p*er*sones at divers tymes for certen pecez and elnez of lynen cloth bought … xx li. vii s. ob. <qua.>

Certen other pecez of lynen cloth and diap*er* saten of Burges and certen canves bought of Haymon Nicholason the herdware man … iiii^{xx}xii li. xviii s. iiii d.

Certen elnes of cloth bought at other div*er*s tymes … xxvii s. vi d. ob.

Cxiiii li. xii s. xi d. qua.[111]

Certen pecez and yerdes of velvett at div*er*s tymes by soundre p*er*sones bought … xli li. v d.

Money paied for certen peces and yerd*es* of saten at div*er*s tymes by soundre p*er*sones bought … xxxvii li. ix d.

Money paied for sersenett and t*er*tren … vi s.

lxxviii li. vii s. ii d.[112]

Certen gilt gold lxvi s. gold of damaske viii li. viii s. vi d. rownde gold and flatt gold silver wier*e* at div*er*s tymes bought xviii li. xviii s. … xxx li. xii s. vi d.

Rawe silke Cx s. silke of Venys vi li. xiiii s. viii d. and other silke of div*er*s colers at soundre tymes bought for my ladis grace … xii li. iiii s. viii d.

… xlii li. xvii s. ii d.[113]

Certen plate bought x li. xix s. ii d. and mendyng of plate. ii garters for my lord prince lxxvii s. vi d. iii harnes girdelles of gold w*ith* ix barrez xii li. xiii s. vi d. spectakell*es* of gold xxiiii s. iiii d. and for makyng of an garter of gold liii s. viii d. … xxxi li. viii s. ii d.

CClxvii li. v s. v d. <qua.>[114]

[110] The total of the items since 'Certen furrez', bracketed to the right of the items (although the bracket does not include the first item but begins with the second). The canc. total and the corrected total are in different hands (the first is that of the total at the foot of the page).

[111] The total of the three items above (it includes the canc. farthing, which is canc. again in the total written small at the foot of the page).

[112] The total of the three items above, bracketed to the right of the items.

[113] The total of the two items above, bracketed to the right of the items.

[114] The total of all the items on the page, written small to the right at the foot of the page.

[*p. 58*] Money payed for a grey amez bought and delyv*er*ed to my ladis grace … lxvi s. viii d.

Certen stuff bought of my lady of Northfolkes execut*ours* … xxv li.

Money payed unto George Kyrkeham clerke of the hanep*er* for certen l*ett*res patens of confermac*ioun*z of Cristez College … xi li. xvi s. v d.

Lyke money payed for the writing of the vouson of Repull yevon to my ladis grace by my lord of Worsettor … xvii s.

Money in like maner paied for the delyverans of Thomas Chambers indenture … xl s.

… xliii li. i d.[115]

Money paied for the salt of gold yevon unto the kyng for his New Yeres gyft … Cxv li. xv d. ob.

Money delyv*er*ed unto my ladis grace uppon New Yerez Day by the handis of mastrez Fowler to giff in New Yeres gift*es* … xiii li. vi s. viii d.

Money alowed in this accompte for like New Yeres gift*es* deliv*er*ed the last yere and not alowed over and besid*es* v marc*e* the forseid last yere alowed … x li.

Cxxxviii li. vii s. xi d. ob.[116]

Ciiii^{xx}i li. viii s. ob.[117]

[*p. 59*] Money delyvered to John Harison lord of mysrewell for to make div*ers* disgisinges and garmentez for the morez … xvi li. xviii s. iiii d.

Money paied to the p*ar*son of Alhalowez the litill for the tyeth of Coldharbar for ii hole yerez … Cvi s. viii d.

<x<iii> li. vs.> xxii li. v s.[118]

Certen rep*ar*ac*i*ons don there by Peter of the same … xlix s. ii d.

Certen other rep*ar*ac*i*onz don at the Riall <di> in London … xxxvi li. xvi s. viii d. ob.

xxxix li. xv s. x d. ob.[119]

Money payed unto the kynge for Wokyng … xxvi li. xiii s. iiii d.

Money paied for an peyer of orgons … iiii li.

Cost*es* of the bereing of my ladi Cissell Ciiii s. v d. costis of cariage of certen hur stuff xxiii s. iiii d. and certen monei lent <pa> and paid unto divers <tymes> of hur servantez viii li. xiii s. iiii d. … xv li. xiii d.

[115] The total of the five items above, bracketed to the right of the items.

[116] The total of the three items above, bracketed to the right of the items.

[117] The total of all the items on the page, written small to the right at the foot of the page.

[118] The total of the two items above, bracketed to the right of the items.

[119] The total of the two items above, bracketed to the right of the items. Unlike the other totals, it is incorrect (10s. over).

Money delyverd unto s*ir* Edward Haward for the redempciou*n* of maister P*ar*kars landis … CCCxxxiii li. vi s. viii d.

An horse bought for my ladis litter … iiii li.

Another horse bought and gifvon unto my lorde of Rochest*ur* w*ith* certen costis of the same … iiii li. v s. iii d.

Money paied unto Palmer þe sadeler for making of an sadell and harnez for my lord prince over and besidis cloth of gold wrought in the Stok*es* for the same … iiii li. v s. ix d.

xii li. xi s. [120]

solvuntur ad [… ..][121]

[*p. 60*] Som*m*e of all the hole allowance aforsaid … MMDlxxii li. xv s. iiii d.

And so he oweth … Dlxxv li. viii d. qua.wherof he hath delyv*er*ed unto the coffers of the seid prynces of suche money as he receyved of my lord of London as yt appereth in the boke of receytes of the seid prynces … l i. And so he oweth … Dxxv li. viii d. qua.

[*p. 61*] *uppon*

Richard Conway late of \þe/ chapell over and besidis xiii s. iiii d. payed unto Miles Worseley anno xxii^{do} and xx s. payed unto the seid Miles this p*re*sent yere anno xxiii^{cio} … xlvi s. viii d.

George Henyngham my ladis servante for money by my ladis g*r*ace payed unto the lady Powez for an cheyne that he lost of hers … xxvii s. vi d.

William Pole for money unto hym lent over and besidis xx s. paied unto Miles Worsley this p*re*sent yere anno xxiii^{cio} … x li.

Thabbot of Crowland for money unto hym lent … xl li.

Walter Cokkes yemon of the bakehouse for money unto hym lent … <xliii s. iiii d.> rec*eyved t*he last day of January[122]

S*ir* Herry Willoughby knyght for money unto hym lent over and besidis l li. paied unto my ladis coffers and l li. paied unto Miles Worsley … C li.

[120] The total of the three items above, bracketed to the right of the items

[121] A partly conjectural reading. Written small to the left at the foot of the page, it is incomplete because of a mend in the paper; there are dot calculations to the right at the centre (canc.) and far right of the page.

[122] 'receyved … January' add. in the MW hand.

Jamez Clarell for money unto hym delyvered by thandis of Henry Salfford iiii li. xv s. and by thandis of Olyver Holand xlvi s. viii d. in all … vii li. xviii d.[123] Wherof the seyd Jamez hath delyvered xv yerdis of tawny <saten> medley lxxvii s.[124] and also he hath delivered unto Alexander Thrognall xviii s. vi d. ob. and so restith uppon hym … xlv s. v d. ob.

John Walter for money unto hym prested to by stuff for the vestrey … iii s. iiii d.

Thexecutours of the testament of S*ir* Roger Urmyston knyght as appereth in the fote of accompte by them made resting in the kepyng of m*aster* Hugh Assheton … xvii li. <x>vii s. ix d.

Robert Crathron and his felowe expendito[r]es[125] of the slew\c/ez at Boston … lx li.

CCxxxv li. xiiii s. ob.[126]

[*p. 62*] John Tanne of Lynne m*er*chaunte for money unto hym lent by an obligac*i*on remaynyng w*ith* Miles Worsley … xx li.

[*blank*] Rowle of the chapell for money unto hym lent … lxvi s. viii d.

My lady Jane for money unto hur by Jamez Morez lent … xvi li.

William Ferthing late of my ladis chapell for money unto hym lent … xiii li. vi s. viii d.

Olyver Holand yoman ussher of my ladis chamber for money unto hym lent … vi li. xvii[127] s. vi d. qua.

Thomas Soper my ladis solicitor for money <remayng> remaynyng in his handis uppon his last accompte anno xxiii^{cio} toward*es* my ladis sewtez … xxvi s.

John Sint John esquier for money unto hym lent … lxvi s. viii d.

Nota solvitur Miloni Worsley anno xxiiii^{to} ex suo oneracione … Cxiii s. iiii d.[128] Ingleberd bokebynder for money unto hym prested to by certen bokez att Parez for my ladis g*r*ace … vi li. xiii s. iiii d.

My lord of Ely for money unto hym lent … xx li.

Solvitur dicto Miloni hoc anno xxiiii^{to} totum ex sua recognicione. My lord of London for money unto hym lent over and besid*es* l li. paied unto Miles Worsley this p*re*sent yere anno xxiii^{cio} … l li.

Nicholas Aughton for money unto hym lent … vi s. viii d.

So*m*me of all the money dewe and not paied of suche that was prested the last yere and in iii other yerez befor past … CCClxxvi li. xvii s. v d. ob. qua.[129]

[123] 2d. short.

[124] 6d. short of its original sum at D91.20/158, 194 and D91.21/79 (77s. 6d., but it is 77s. 7d. at 21/162); the 6d. is restored at p. 123 below. For this ongoing debt see Introduction 2.1.3.1.

[125] MS 'expenditones'.

[126] The total of all the items on the page, written small to the right at the foot of the page.

[127] MS 'xvjj'.

[128] This and the next marginal note are written in the 'sprawling' hand.

[129] There are dot calculations alongside to the left and right, with another to the left at the foot of the page.

[*p. 63*] Money lent unto Thomas Ferthyng … vii li.

<Money lent unto maister Stannoppe … x li.> «quia solvitur»

Money lent unto Nicholas Elneden … iiii li.

Money lent unto Pynson the prynter uppon a prest … x li.

Money lent unto my lady Jane … lxvi s. viii d.[130]

So*m*me of all the money lent and prested this present yere anno xxiii^{cio} … <xxvi li.> \xxiiii li./ vi s. viii d.

And <\with xxiiii li. ii s. iiii d. charged uppon the seid M.> so thus restith uppon the sayd accomptaunte <of his owen p*ro*pere> arreragez> \with xxiiii li. ii s. iiii d. charged uppon the seid Miles for money wantyng oute of a bagge and <lxxix> li. \iiii^{xx}xix li./ xiiii s. ii d. ob. qua. of his owne arre*r*ages/ … <Ciii li. xvi s. v d. ob. qua.> Cxxiii li. xvi s. v d. ob. qua.[131]

debet … Cxlvii li. xiiii s. <vi d.> ob.[132]

[*p. 64 blank*]

[*p. 65*] [133]*Hatefelde*. Thaccompt of Miles Worsley tresaurer*e* of the chambr with the most excellent princesse Mergeret countesse of Richemond and Derb and mother to our*e* most sov*er*aigne lord þ*a*t nowe is kyng Henry the viith from the xiiiith day of <m*arc*> January in the xxiii^{ti} yer of our*e* said sov*er*aigne lord unto the same xiiiith day of Januar*e* then next ensueng in the xxiiii^{ti} yere of our*e* forsaid sov*er*aigne lord that is to wit by the space of on hole yer.

*Tharrerag*es. Furst the said accomptaunt is charged with the arrerag*es* of his last accompt as it doth mor*e* pleynly apper in the fote of the same … Dxxv li. viii d. qua.[134]

So*m*me … Dxxv li. viii d. qua.

*Recept*es *of money owt of my ladyes coffers*. Item receyved of his oune p*ro*pyr*e* arre*rages* lxxix li. xiiii s. ii d. ob. qua. and for money wantyng þ*a*t is charged apon him xxiiii li. ii s. iiii d. … <Ciii li. xvi s. v d. ob. qua.> «cancellatur hic quia oneratur inter arreragia»[135]

Item rec*eyved* of James Moryce the xx^{ti}v day of Januar*e* anno xxiii^{cio} of his debt for the work*es* at Cambridge … xl s. qua.

Item rec*eyved* the furst day of M*ar*che by bill*es* of allowance of m*aster* receyvo*ur* for money by him paid … Cxlii li. xvi s. ii d. ob.

[130] There is a dot calculation is to the right at the end of the entries.

[131] Apart from 'And', the rest of the entry (including all material above l.) is written small in a formal script (probably all in the 'sprawling' hand).

[132] Written small to the left at the foot of the page.

[133] The summary hand begins the new year.

[134] See p. 60 above.

[135] These sums of money are the original (unrevised) sums in the final entry of p. 63.

Item rec*eyved* the second day of M*ar*che at my ladyes removyng to Basse … CCCxiii li. vi s. v d.

[*p. 66*] Item rec*eyved* the xx^{ti}v day of M*ar*che in the said yer by the hand*es* of James Morice toward*es* the buldyng*es* of Crist*es* Collegge in Cambridge … lxxix li.

Item rec*eyved* the xx^{ti}ii day of June by thand*es* of Nicholas Saunders … xxxix li.

Item receyved the xx^{ti}ix day of June … iiii^{xx}iiii li. iii s. iiii d.

Item the xixth day of July for money lent unto mast*er* Conyngesby … C li.

Item rec*eyved* the xiiith day of Septembr*e* for money paied to Chicheley for land*es* purchased in Malton … xxiii li. vi s. viii d.

Item rec*eyved* the same tyme in redy money … CClxiii li. xx d.

Item rec*eyved* the xx^{ti}iii day of Septembr … Clxi li. ii s.

Item rec*eyved* the ixth day of January … xiii li. vii s. i d.

Item rec*eyved* the xth day of Januar*e* for money paied by m*aster* comptroller to John Mondy for the kyng*es* New Yer*es* yeft … C li.

Item rec*eyved* as in money delyv*er*ed to Thomas Sop*er* my ladies solicit*our* … xiii li. xii s. viii d.

Summa recepte … <MCCCCxxxviii li. xii s. vi d. ob.>[136]

MCCCxxxiiii li. xvi s. ob. qua.

[*p. 67*]

Summa totalis recepte cum arreragiis … <MDCCCClxiii li. xiii s. ii d. qua.> MDCCClix li. xvi s. <viii d. ob.> ix d.

de quibus

[*p. 68 blank*]

[*p. 69*] [137]Cost*es* and exspenc*e* reward*es* with other dyv*er*se payment*es* of the most excellent prync*es* Margaret moder unto our*e* sov*er*aigne lord kyng*e* Henry the viith and countesse of Richemound and Derby payd by the hand*es* of Miles Worsley as heraft*er* dothe aper*e*.

In reward to a s*er*vande of the abbot of Westm*ynster* bryngyng of a vousen of a benyfice called Seynt Nicholas Shamell*es* … iii s. iiii d.

Item paid unto m*aister* countroller for a reward yeven to m*aister* Pole for my lad*ys* besynesse delyv*er*ed by m*aister* rece*yver* … xx s.

[136] Written below the final entry on the page (and canc.), with the uncanc. calculation written smaller below it in the same hand. See D102.10/161.

[137] The MW hand returns here.

Item unto m*aister* receyver for a reward yeven unto doct*ur* Chambr*e* the xxiii day of January … xx s.

Item delyv*ere*d unto m*aister* vichamberlayn for a reward yeven unto doct*ur* Actkynson þ*at* was w*i*th my lady Bray at his beyng at Hatfeld … vi s. viii d.

Item delyv*ere*d unto m*aister* receyver for a reward yeven unto m*aister* Hobson clerk*es* … xx s.

Item to the same that was yeven unto m*aister* Nicholas Coup*er* for c*er*ten stuff bought of my lady Norfolk*es* … xx s.

Item paid unto Haymound hardware man for v ymag*es* in parchement by his byll assigned … iiii s. iiii d.

Item to the same for a dossen and v payr*e* of glovis ii s. iiii d. the dossen … iii s. iiii d.

Item in reward to the same Haymound … xiii s. iiii d.

Item payd unto Lenard of the vestry for a prymer \viii d./ in queyr*es* and for the byndyng \iiii d./ and for iiii smale bok*es* \iii d./ byndyng as aperith by his byll assigned. Summa … xv d.

[M]Summa … Cxii s. iii d.[P]

[*p. 70*] Item in reward to Pendant my lord of Rochest*ur* s*er*vand for the wrytyng of a booke yeven t*o* my lad*ys* g*r*ace … xiii s. iiii d.

Item paid unto m*aister* Morgan the xxix day of January for c*er*ten smalle bok*es* bought of Wynkyn de Ward … xvi d.

Item to the same for a jurnall xx d. and for ii other jurnalles devided in two parties every jurnall price ii s. iiii d. and for a boke of Canterbury Tales ii s. viii d. Summa … viii s. iiii d.[138]

Item delyv*ere*d to the same m*aister* Morgan for a reward yeven unto Petur*e* of Coldherbor*e* … xx s.

Item paid unto doct*ur* Royston p*ar*son of Coldherbor*e* by the hand*es* of m*aister* William Clerk subdean of my lad*ys* chappell for the tythe of Coldherbor*e* paid the xxix day of January … liii s. iiii d.

Item delyv*ere*d unto maistres Foller for a reward yeven unto the p*r*ior of the charterhowse in Coventre … vi s. viii d.

Item delyv*ere*d to the same maistres Foller for a reward yeven unto m*aister* Edward Bothe … vi s. viii d.

*Delyvered unto my lady*s *couffers agayn.* <Item delyv*ere*d unto Thomas Babyngton for the suertie of the joynto*ur* of dame Anne Sherley for a recov*er*y … xxvi li. xiii s. iiii d.>

Item in reward unto <wak> Water Cokk*es* yemon of the bakhowse w*ith* xliii s. iiii d. that was delyv*ere*d to hym in prest afour*e* and not dyscharged and in redy money now at the tyme of his ariage \xx s. in all/ … lxiii s. iiii d.

[138] The total is 8d. short.

Item delyv*er*ed unto George Fraunc*es* for my lad*ys* offryng apon Candylmasse Day in thretty pence of gold v. Summa … xii s. vi d.

Item in reward to a poticar that came from London delyv*er*ed to m*aister* Morgan … iii s. iiii d.

Item delyv*er*ed unto m*aister* P*ar*ker at his goyng to London the iii^{de} day of February … xx s.

Item in reward to frere Rob*er*t then p*r*ior of Denbeghe at Hatfeld … iii s. iiii d.

[M]Summa … <xxxvii li. v s. vi d.> x li. xii s. ii d.[P]

[*p. 71*] Item delyv*er*ed unto m*aister* dean for a reward yeven unto doct*ur* Smyth that prechyd afour*e* my lad*ys* g*r*ace oon Candylmasse Day … vi s. viii d.

Item paid unto m*aister* Peksall for mone paid unto Henry þ*at* was w*i*th my lady Rev*er*se for the makyng of a matt for hyr travyse in the clossett … xii d.

Item to the stacyonar for a sawter for my lad*ys* g*r*ace … vi d.

Item to the same for v litell bok*es* in Englysshe … vi d.

Item paid unto m*aister* chaunceller for a reward yeven unto John Pole p*r*ocat*our* unto doct*ur* Owen Pole cons*er*nyng the resignacion of Man*our*bere for his cost*es* and labor comyng from Herforth to Hatfeld and to London and ther tarying by the space of vi daies … xx s.

Item paid unto m*aister* Peter notarye for makyng of a procuracie resignacion institucion and induction and p*ro*curacie to take possession and for his lab*our*s in goyng to Neyte a place of thabott of Westm*ynster* and twysse comyng to Westm*ynster* and ones to my lord of Seynt <dat> David… vi s. viii d.

Item paid for the fee of the regestr*e* of the churche of Saint David … iii s. iiii d.

Item paid unto a scryven*er* at Westm*ynster* for wryting of the annuitie of ii obligacions … ii s. viii d.

Item paid for paper for wrytyng of div*er*se mynut*es* conc*er*nyng the said mater … i d.

Item yeven in reward to two of maist*er* president s*er*vant*es* for theyr*e* lab*our* in goyng often tymes to dyv*er*se places for the said mater … viii d.

Item paid unto the said m*aister* chaunceller for his exspens*es* at London and iii s*er*vant*es* w*i*th iiii horsis by the space of ix dayes tarying for exspedicion of the said mater by my lad*ys* comaundement … xxx s.

Summa … lxxii s. i d.

[*p. 72*] [139]Item yevyn in rewarde to mastres Benat the sylke woman by Jamys Moryce … vi s. viii d.

Item paid unto master presedent for the wrytyng of a boke of statutys for Crystys Colege v s. iiii d. for byn[d]yng of the same boke x d. for wrytyng of a mynet to Rome xx d. … vii s. x d.

[139] The ‘curly’ hand returns here.

Item paid to Richard Atherton for rydyng to my lorde of Wynchester by the space of iii days ii s. for rydyng to London to m*aster* chauncell*our* by ii days xvi d. … iii s. iiii d.

Item yeven in rewarde to my lorde of Rochest*ours* brother for bryngyng of a gossehalke … xiii s. iiii d.

Item yevyn in rewarde to J.[140] Wylkyn prynter by m*aster* Morgan … iii s. iiii d.

Item for a p*ar*done of Seynt Robert of Knavysborowe by m*aster* deane for my lad*ys* g*r*ace … xx d.

Item yeven in rewarde to a servant of the bysshop of Londons for bryngyng of a lett*our* to my lad*ys* g*r*ace … xx d.

Item yevyn in rewarde to m*aster* Bedellys mayde for bryngyng of hennys and butt*er* … viii d.

Item paid the xxiiith day of February anno xxiii^{o} to mastres Denton for hir hole yerys fee dewte to hir at the fest of Mychelmas last past by m*aster* chauncellour … lxvi s. viii d.

Item paid to Will*i*am Hylmer for certyn drogys for my ladyes g*r*ace iiii li. xiiii s. v d. ob. and for certyn metsons for my lady vi s. … C s. v d. ob.

Item in rewarde to <dame> Elyn*our* Jonys in Scotlond … vi s. viii d.

Item yeven in rewarde to masteres Dentons servant by John Plowfeld vi s. viii d. … vi s. viii d.

Item in rewarde to my ladyes wyer drawer … xx d.

Item yevyn in rewarde to my lady markes by my ladyes co*m*maundment … xl s.

Item paid to Rob*er*t Long for iii days rydyng in and out from Hatfeld to London w*ith* ii horsys to fet maystres Benet <s> sylkwoman to my ladyes g*r*ace w*ith* the expence*s* of hir and hir servant*es* by the waye \iiii s. iii d./ … iiii s. iii d.

Item yeven in rewarde to master Carter for wrytyng of certyn bok*es* for my ladyes g*r*ace … x s.

Item yevyn unto a yong man that came unto my ladyes g*r*ace from the Tower in rewarde … xx d.

Item delyv*er*ed and paid to Thomas Chamb*er* for certyn metsons to be made for my lad*ys* g*r*ace and other ness*essaryes* … xxxviii s. x d.

^{M}Summa … xv li. xv s. iiii d. ob.^{P}

[*p. 73*][141] Item paid to Willyam Hylmer for c*er*tyn pannys pottys and other nessesary stuffe to make my ladyes metsons in … xv s. v d.

Item yeven in rewarde to Gregory Morgan feodary of Somersetshyre by m*aster* receyvo*ur* … xl s.

140 Or perhaps '1', i.e. 'one'. It is likely 'Wynkyn (de Worde)' is meant.

141 The first three entries are in the 'curly' hand; the MW hand returns with the fourth entry. See Plate 16.

Item delyv*er*ed and paid to Thomas Soper solucyt*our* unto my ladyes g*r*ace the xxith of February vi li. xiii s. iiii d. for c*er*tyn charg*es* belongyng to Crystys Colege … vi li. xiii s. iiii d.

Nota. Item paid to m*aister* receyver for v yerd*es* of cremysyn in grayne for a gowne for doct*ur* Whitstones bought by Rob*er*t Hylton … l s.

Item for xx yerd*es* of blak welvett for gownes to my lad*ys* g*r*ace. P*r*ice the yerd x s. iiii d. Summa … xi li. ii s. i d.

[142]Item for xx yerd*es* of fyne blak welvet \and di./ to the same use. P*r*ice the yerd x s. x d. Summa … xi li. ii s. i d.

Item for xxiii yerd*es* \and di./ of cremysen welvet for westment*es* and copes. P*r*ice the yerd xi s. vi d. Summa … xiii li. x s. iii d.

Item for v unc*e* of coper gold. P*r*ice the unc*e* xii d. Summa … v s.

Item for a payre of knyt <glovis> glovis for my lord of Excet*ur*. P*r*ice … x d.

Item for a skynne of pampelyon and viii legg*es* of the same. The price … vii s. viii d.

Item paid unto the same m*aister* Assheton for money paid to Charles Brandon for full payment of the man*er* of Gotshyll in Som*er*setshyr*e* bought for the chauntr*e* of Wynburne … C li.

Item paid for iii prevey sealles. On for the men*er* of Dertwyche vi s. viii d. another for the p*r*ior of the Monmouthe for suche money as he oweth to Cryst*es* Collage of Cambryge vi s. viii d. and the iii^{de} for William Hudleston for a roll made in Lancashyr*e* vi s. viii d. Summa … xx s.

Item paid for the wrytyng of the said iii p*r*evey seales … ii s. viii d.

Item for the exspenc*e* of Geffrey Vayne for delyv*ery* of the p*r*evey seall of Cryst*es* Collage to the p*r*ior of Monmowthe in Walez … vi s. viii d.

Item paid unto Rob*er*t Hylton by m*aister* receyver for xxiiii yerd*es* of blak cotton to Rog*er* Walker x s. Item for xxiii yerd*es* of whit coton for the same Rog*er* viii s. vii d. ob. Summa … xviii s. vii d. ob.

[M]Summa … Cxlix li. xix s. ii d. ob.[P]

[*p. 74*] Item paid unto m*aister* receyver for money paid to Rob*er*t Hylton for a unc*e* of blew sylk to Thomysyn of London … xx d.

Item paid for the cost*es* of the same Rob*er*t at London by the spaice of two daies for this stuff and other … ii s.

Item for \two/ pair*e* of hose makyng and lynyng for the two fotmen xx d. and for two pair*e* of shoes for the same two fotmen \xii d./ … ii s. viii d.

Item paid for a yerd di. of <Sk> scarlet for a pair*e* of hose for m*aister* P*ar*ker agaynest Candylmasse. Pric*e* … vi s. vi d.

[142]This and the next entry are preceded in the left margin by dot calculations (canc.), both with + noted above them.

Item for the makyng and lynyng of the same … x d.

Item for a pair*e* of hose for the same m*aister* P*ar*ker of whit kersey. P*r*ice the yerd ii s. iiii d. Summa … ii s. vi d.

Item for makyng and lynyng of the same … x d.

Item paid for a pair*e* of bot*es* for m*aister* Parker … iii s. viii d.

Item for a pair*e* of spurr*es* for hym … xi d.

Item for Rob*er*t Hylton cost*es* ii daies for the same stuff … ii s.

Item for the cariage of[143] the same stuff w*i*th a pec*e* of welvett from London to Hatfeld … iiii d.

Item for iii yerd*es* and a q*uar*t*er* of clothe for a cote for the same m*aister* Parker. The yerd at v s. vii d. Summa … xviii s. iii d.

Item for iii paire of shoez for m*aister* P*ar*ker at x d. the payre … ii s. vi d.

Item delyv*er*ed to maistres Stannop for money paid the v day of February for v slayes cont*eynyng* MCCCxl. P*r*ice the C iii d. ob. … v s.[144]

Item to Olyv*er* Walcote to delyv*er* to a nonne of Sympryngham … xx s.

Item to maistres Foller for the cost*es* of a wedo of London that came w*i*th John Harryson to Hatfeld … v s.

Item to the same for a reward yeven to my lady Norton s*er*vande for the bryngyng of orengys … xx d.

Item to the same <þ*at*> for maistres Bennett … vi s. x d.

Item to my lady Norton s*er*vand for the bryngyng of glovis to my lad*ys* g*r*ace … xii d.

Item in reward to John Vanutrike goldsmythe … iii s. iiii d.

Item paid to Nicholas Aughton for his cost*es* ridyng to the kyng*es* g*r*ace and to Coventr*e* and to Rumsey and for the cost*es* of my lady Bougham to London as aperith by his byll assigned in all … xxiii s. iiii d.

[M]Summa … Cxii s. xi d.[P]

[*p. 75*] Item paid the furst day of M*ar*che to Henry Wynstanley for the cost*es* don for the buryeng of Skypp … ii s. x d.

Item paid for a reward to the fawkeners son for his co*m*mons at Seynt Albones … xx d.

*M*aistres *Massy*. Item paid the ii^{de} day of M*ar*che to maistres Massy by hir byll assigned for a bonett bought for lytell maistres P*ar*ker of lettuys. P*r*ice … iii s. iiii d.

Item for a rebaen and lasc*es* viii d. a co*m*me i d. for mylk ii s. for butt*ur* iiii d. iii payr*e* of shoes xi d. for flax iiii s. vii d. for spynnyng of ii lib. v d. for makyng of Strenger

[143] MS 'of' rep.

[144] Considerably rounded up.

jakett iiii d. for the makyng of pore women <shett*es*> scleff*es* xvi d. for pore folke shoes vii s. for mylk for Skypp xix d. … xix s. iii d.

Item t*o* the same þ*a*t was yeven to a man þ*a*t brought aquavite … viii d.

Item for wardens for Skypp i d. for bred and ale ii d. for candell*es* i d. … iiii d.

Item for spynnyng of kerpett yerne ix d. for dyeng of blak yerne iii d. for the mendyng of a perlyng well vi d. … xviii d.

*M*aistres *Parkers nursse*. Item to the same maistres Massy þ*a*t was yeven to maistres Parkers nurse for kepyng of the chyld … xx s.

Item delyv*er*ed the ii^{de} day of M*ar*che to Hughe Carre <at> for a reward yeve to Corwen my lord of Rochest*er* s*er*vand at my lad*ys* goyng t*o* Basse a plase of m*aister* Sayes … xx d.

*W. Hylm*er. Item the iii^{de} day of M*ar*che delyv*er*ed to William Hylm*er* in reward at his goyng from Hatfeld … lxvi s. viii d.

*Recepta. W. Hylm*er *infra vi annos*. Item delyv*er*ed to the same William the same day to be paid ayen w*i*thin vi yer*es* … <xx li.> «cancellatur hic quia inter arreragia huius anni postea»[145]

Item paid unto Thomas Maydwell for a pair*e* of sleppers delyv*er*ed to my lad*ys* g*r*ace at the Twelf Day vi d. for a pair*e* of sleppers at Candylmasse Day vi d. for a pair*e* of sleppers and a pair*e* of shoes the vth <dady> day of February xii d. oon Seynt Davies Day a pair*e* of sleppers and a pair*e* of shoes <xi> xii d. Summa … iii s.

Item in reward yeven to the brotherers at my lad*ys* departyng from Hatfeld to the Basse … ii s.

Item to maistres Foller for a reward yeven to Jane Radclyff at hir goyng w*i*th maistres Ursula to m*aister* tresorers … xx d.

[M]Summa … <xxvi li. iiii s. vii d.> vi li. iiii s. vii d.[P][146]

[*p. 76*] Item paid the iii^{de} day of M*ar*che to Nicholas Aughton for his cost*es* ridyng unto the kyng at dyv*er*se tymes … viii s. viii d.

Item to m*aister* chamberlayn for a reward yeven unto Henry Odall of the west countr*e* … xl s.

Item to m*aister* Parker in reward at his goyng to London from Basse to se the justes … x s.

Item to Richard Aderton by his byll assigned for his cost*es* ridyng to m*aister* vichamberlayn and to Depyng by the spaice of iiii daies … ii s. viii d.

Item delyv*er*ed unto maistres Stannop to delyv*er* at my lad*ys* pleasur*e* at Basse … iii s. iiii d.

Item delyv*er*ed to m*aister* chamberlayn for a s*er*vand of s*ir* Thomas Cheny that brought a fole to Basse to my lad*ys* g*r*ace … xiii s. iiii d.

[145] See p. 125.

[146] The corrected sum is in a different hand and takes account of the canc. £20.

Item delyv*er*ed to maistres Stannop for money yeven unto Henry amener at Basse for the <kyp> kepyng of the said fole … xx d.

Item to m*aister* chamberlayn for a reward yeven unto my lady Mary fotman … xx d.

Item to m*aister* dean for a boke callid a Rosarie for my lad*ys* g*r*ace … iiii d.

Item in reward at the abbey at Westm*ynster* to the seller … v s.

Item to the pantr*e* and bottre … v s.

Item to the kychen … v s.

Item to the wardrop … v s.

Item to the porters … xx d.

Item to the kep*er* of the kyng*es* palice at Westm*ynster* … xx d.

Item for my lad*ys* offryng to Seynt Edward at Westm*ynster* delyv*er*ed by m*aister* Bekynsall … iii s. iiii d.

Item paid unto Ric*hard* Aderton for his cost*es* ridyng from Basse to Bromley to my lord of Rochest*er* two daiez … xvi d.

Item to the same for money yeven unto a pore man for comyng thro his closse at my lad*ys* comyng … iiii d.

Item to maistres Stannop for a bonett of blak welvett … xii s. x d.

Item to the same for a bonett of blak welvet for m*aistres* Jan … xii s. x d.

Item to the same for a bonett of blak welvet for m*aistres* P*er*ott … xii s. x d.

Item for iii boxes for the same bonett*es* … vi d.

Item for hir bot hyr*e* from Westm*ynster* to London and ayen … vii d.

[M]Summa … v[…] li. <[…]i> \xvii s./ vii d.[P 147]

[*p. 77*] Item delyv*er*ed to maistres Stannop for a reward yeven at Coldherboro to oon of the kyng*es* messengers … xx d.

Item delyv*er*ed to m*aister* chamberlayn for a reward yeven to Wentworth gentylman yssher w*i*th the kyng*es* g*r*ace … v s.

Item in reward to my lady Boghham at Coldherboro … v s. viii d.

Item to maistres Stannop for a pounde of Venysse sylv*er* … xi s.

Item paid unto John Holt for his cost*es* ridyng to m*aister* chamberlayn plaice by ii daies … xvi d.

Item to the same from Hatfeld to m*aister* Say by a day … viii d.

Item to a s*er*vande of <of> the abbott of Glocett*ur* for the bryngyng of two bake lampres to my lad*ys* g*r*ace to Richmond … v s.

[147] The numbers are damaged and torn. The sum should be £7 9s. 7d.

Item in reward to maistres Bennett comyng to my lad*ys* g*r*ace to Coldherboro for hir bot hir*e* … xii d.

Item paid unto Madison for a yerd of reban bought at Richemound for my lad*ys* bedde … ii d.

Item for my lad*ys* offryng at our*e* Lady of Pue … xx d.

Item to the lady Wenysour*e* at Syon … vi s. viii d.

Item to my lady Margaret Pole in reward … vi s. viii d.

Item for my lad*ys* offryng to Seynt Bregett … xx d.

Item delyv*er*ed to George Fraunc*es* for a reward to oon that made lodgyng*es* in the place þ*at* m*aister* Tiler bylded at Richemound for my lad*ys* s*er*vand*es* … xx d.

Item paid for xv yerd*es* and a q*uarte*r of russett damask bought at my lad*ys* beyng at London. P*r*ice the yerd vi s. iiii d. Summa … iiii li. xvi s. vii d.

Item for xlii yerd*es* of blak sarsynett at iii s. viii d. … vi li. vi s.

Item for v yerd*es* of blak sarsynett at iii s. viii d. … xviii s. iiii d.

Item for iii yerd*es* and a half of blak welvett bought for to amend the harnesshe þ*at* longeth to my lad*ys* lytter. P*r*ice the yerd x s. iiii d. Summa … xxxvi s. <vi d.> \ii d./

Item delyv*er*ed to my lad*ys* g*r*ace by maistres Stannop at my lord of Bathes place in London … xl s.

[M]Summa … xviii li. <viii s. iii d.> vii s. xi d.[P] [148]

[*p. 78*] Item paid to maistres Stannop for hir bot hir*e* to London … i d.

Item paid unto William Love for lac*es* bought for the clothe sakke … ii d.

Item to Henr*y* Abeney for two boxes bought at my lord of Bathe place for my lad*ys* g*r*ace … i d.

Item paid unto William Quytmor*e* for his q*uarte*r waig*es* endet at our*e* Lady Day in Lent … vi s. viii d.

<*Nota* +> Item paid for xx ellnez of canvas for pallatt*es* \cassis/. P*r*ice the ellne iii d. ob. and ii d. overall … <+> v s. x d.

Item paid for two wyker bottelles … viii d.

Item delyv*er* to m*aister* P*ar*ker*e* at two tymes by m*aister* chaunceller at oon tyme xiii s. iiii d. another tyme vi s. viii d. … xx s.

Item paid for x yerd*es* and a half of wiolett kersey for the cov*er*yng of the lytter*e* at xx d. the yerd … xvii s. vi d.

Item paid for iii yerd*es* of blak clothe for the cov*er*yng of the shaft*es* of the lytter*e* and lynyng of horse collers and harnesshe. P*r*ice the yerd ii s. … vi s.

[148] The first (canc.) total is in the MW hand, the second (1s. over) in a different hand (probably the 'sprawling' hand).

Item delyv*er*ed to maistres S[t]annop the xixth day of M*ar*che to be yeven to m*aister* Chambr*e* in reward … xx s.

Item in reward to m*aister* Morgan the xxii day of M*ar*che … C s.

Item to William Love the same day by his byll assigned for ridyng from Basse to London xii d. for his dyn*er* at Coldherboro iii d. for his dyn*er* at Fulham ii d. for help to hange my lad*ys* chambr*e* at Coldherboro iiii d. for the myndyng of my lad*ys* bedd at Grenewiche ii d. for straw for pallett*es* ii d. … ii s. i d.

Item paid unto Ric*hard* Aderton by his byll assigned for ridyng from London to Hatfeld and to Basse the spaice of two daies xvi d. and <fro> for ridyng from Grenewiche to Basse and to Warre xvi d. and for ridyng from London to my lord of Rochest*er* ii tymez viii d. … iii s. iiii d.

^{M}Summa … ix li. ii s. v d.^{P}

[*p. 79*] Item in reward the xxiiii day of M*ar*che to maistres Fytzherbert … vi s. viii d.

My lord of Exetyr. Item paid unto John Untryx goldsmyth the same day by his byll for two round*es* for a bysshopp*es* glovis w*i*th two saphers in the mydd*es* weying a unc*e* i q*u*art*er*. Price the unc*e* xxxiii s. iiii d. Summa … xli s. viii d.

Item for the said two saphers … xx s.

Item for the makyng of the same … xx s.

Item in reward for a s*er*vand of my lady Surres for the bryngyng of a pressent to my lad*ys* g*r*ace … iii s. iiii d.

Item to maistres Parkar for viM pynnes bought for my lad*ys* g*r*ace … iii s.

Item to Henr*y* Abney for his bot hir*e* to London goyng for m*aister* Morgan … ii d.

Item for a baskett for my lad*ys* g*r*ace … iiii d.

Item for ii urinall*es* ii d. for ii litell boxes i d. … iii d.

Item for my lad*ys* offryng at Grenewich on our*e* Lady Day the Anunciacion … v s.

Item for my lad*ys* offryng at m*aister* Morgance furst masse at Grenewich … x s.

Item to Rob*er*t Neswyk the xxvii day of M*ar*che for a great baskett … ix d.

Item for a <g> casse of wykers for a pott of grene gynger … iii d.

Item for two hangyng lokk*es* … iiii d.

Item for bot hir*e* for John Madison for goyng to London for m*aister* Chambr*e* … iiii d.

Item in reward to Barlow m*aister* stuard*es* s*er*vand for the bryngyng of a portuouse from m*aistres* Massy … viii d.

Item in reward to a s*er*vand of Edward Heyvens for the bryngyng of bake bremes from Tatsall to Grenewich … xx s.

^{M}Summa … vi li. xii s. ix d.^{P}

[*p. 80*] Item paid for a dossen of glovis for my lad*ys* g*r*ace … ii s.

Item paid unto maistres Stannop the last day of M*ar*che for half a pounde of opyn sylk … vi s. viii d.

Item for a unc*e* di. of satten sylk*es* … xxiii d.

Item for two pec*es* of sypers … iiii s. x d.

Item for a wasshyng bolle and a pair*e* of bellewes … x d.

Item for bot hir*e* goyng to London for the said stuff … viii d.

Item the furst day of Ap*r*iell in reward to maistres Foller and maistres Massy toward*es* their*e* cost*es* from Hatfeld to Syon … iii s. iiii d.

Item to the same maistres Foller to be yeven to two ancryes at Seynt Albones … v s.

Item the same day in reward to a s*er*vaunt of my lord prince for the bryngygng of a porpasse from his g*r*ace … v s.

Item in gold yeven by my lady g*r*ace unto my lord prince the iiii[th] day of Apriell … xx li.

Item the same day to a <Cary> carpynter for cuttyng of c*er*ten stokk*es* for my lad*ys* g*r*ace … ii d.

Item the vth day of the same moneth in reward to maistres Flowrence Zouch … vi s. viii d.

Item to Wynkyn de Word the same day for c*er*tan roll*es* for saying of oure Lady sawter … viii d.

Item to John Leghe for a gardyvian for the kychen … ix s. iiii d.

Item in reward to Ric*hard* Stukeley the viii[th] day of the said moneth sent by m*aistres* Stannop … xx d.

Item for the bot hir*e* of Rob*er*t Fremyngham from Grenewich to London goyng in message to my lord of Ely for the salle of c*er*tan wodd*es* at Hatfeld … vi d.

Item delyv*er*ed the same day to my lad*ys* g*r*ace for frountlett*es* for the quene of Skott*es* and my lady Elizabeth Stafford … xl s.

[M]Summa … xxiiii li. ix s. iii d.[P]

[*p. 81*] Item in reward to maistres Stannop … vi s. viii d.

My lady Jane. Item the ix day of the said moneth as money lent to my lady Jane … <xx s.> «nichil hic quia postea inter arreragias huius anni»[149]

Item the same day in reward to William Hylm*er* … vi s. viii d.

Item to maistres Stannop for a pounde of gylt gold … xii s.

Item the thenthe day of the said moneth for a pounde of gylt gold … xii s.

[149] See p. 125.

Item the xi[th] day of the said moneth to Ric*hard* Aderton for ridyng from Grenewiche to Hatfeld and so to Cambrige by the space of iiii daies … ii s. viii d.

Item for money yeven unto ayget woman that brought apples to my lad*ys* g*r*ace … xx d.

Item to maistres Stannop the xiii day of the said moneth for a pec*e* of sypers bought for my lad*ys* g*r*ace … xx d.

Item for two ell*es* of blak reban bought by the same … xv d.

Item for iii prymers … vi d.

Item in reward to the gardyners wyff at Grenewych … xii d.

Item for the bot hir*e* of a silk woman for bryngyng of frountlett*es* to Grenewiche … ii d.

Item in reward to oon of m*aister* Sheffeld*es* s*er*vande for the kepyng of two got*es* sent from m*aister* Newport … xiiii d.

Item to William Love for a baskett … iiii d.

Item the same day for the bot hir*e* of John Utrike goldsmyth for comyng to Grenewiche … viii d.

Item the xiiii day of the said moneth in reward to my lady Bougham … vi s. viii d.

Item the same day to my lady Evarby for a gowne to be bought to maist*er* Seynt Johnes doughtur … xx s.

Item the same day in reward to a s*er*vande of *sir* Ric*e* ap Thomas for the bryngyng of certayn bacon mollyng*es* oute of Walles … xx s.

[M]Summa … <Cxv s. i d.> iiii li. xv s. i d.[P] [150]

[*p. 82*] Item delyv*er*ed to maistres Stannop the said day for the ov*er* prises of the forsaid frountlett*es* bought for the quene of Scott*es* and my lady Elizabez Stafforth … viii s. viii d.

Item in reward to a man that brought rose water from my lady Rev*er*se suster from the Myn*er*es … viii d.

Item to Rob*er*t Neswyke for goyng to London to Edward Wause to fylle a vessell of muskadell for my lad*ys* g*r*ace … viii d.

Item the xv day of the same moneth for a standyng bedde bought for my lad*ys* g*r*ace … xl s.

Item to Rob*er*t Merbury for his cost*es* and bot hir*e* goyng in message to the dean of Poll*es* from Grenewich … iiii d.

Item the same day for a pottell of muskadell … viii d.

[150] The first (canc.) total is in the MW hand, the second (which allows for the canc. 20s.) is in a different hand.

Item paid the same day to Carre of Grenewich for ii beddes for m*aister* <conffer> confessor by a moneth … iiii s.

Item to the same for ii[…] bett*es* for m*aister* chaunceller m*aister* dean and m*aister* rec*eyver* by the space of iii wek*es* … iii s.

Item paid for the hir*e* of vi bedd*es* for dyv*er*se other of my lad*ys* s*er*vand*es* by the space of v wek*es* … xvii s. vi d.

Item paid the same day for a dosen of premyrs for my lad*ys* g*r*ace … ii s.

Item delyv*er*ed to m*aister* Bekynsall my lad*ys* almener to be dystrubet for my lad*ys* almes … lxvi s. viii d.

Item paid unto maistres Stannop the xvi day of the said moneth for a border of a bonnet for maistres P*ar*ker*e* … xvi s.

Item the same day to maistres Stannop for a pounde of Venyse gold … xxviii s.

Item for a <pany> panyo*ur* … iiii d.

Item in bot hir*e* goyng for the said stuff … iiii d.

[M]Summa … ix li. viii s. x d.[P]

[*p. 83*] Item paid unto George Fraunc*es* the xix[th] day of Ap*r*iell for a reward yeven unto a laborer in the kyng*es* garden at Grenewiche … iiii d.

Item paid unto m*aister* rec*eyver* for wrytyng of a copie of the popes l*ett*res sent unto the kyng… v s.

Item to the same the said day for money sent to Thomas Bury … xx s.

Item paid unto John Ploffeld by his byll assigned for ridyng from Hatfeld to Grenewich and from thens to Hatfeld by the spaice of iiii daies … iiii s.

Item for iii queres of pauper \iiii d./ and for pennes \ii d./ and ynke … vi d.

Item for iiii skynn*es* of parchement … viii d.

Item for his bot hir*e* to m*aister* presydent*es* at Westm*ynster* and from thens to London by the space of iiii tymes … iiii d.

Item for his mete and drynk at Peturs of Coldherboro … iiii d.

Item for half a pounde of rede wax … iiii d.

Item for bot hir*e* from Vestm*yster* to Grenewiche by iiii tymes … xii d.

Item for vi skynnes of wellom … ii s.

Item the same day in reward to a woman for rose wat*er* … vi s. viii d.

Item delyv*er*ed to m*aister* P*ar*ker*e* the <v> xx[ti] day of the said moneth by m*aister* rec*eyver* … xx s.

Item delyv*er*ed on Gode Fryday to George Fraunc*es* for my lad*ys* offryng at Grenewich … xxx s.

Item the same day to maistres Parker to be yeven in almes to a pore woman … xx d.

Item the same day to Rog*er* Radclyff for a porthowse in two parties ... iii s. iiii d.

Item in reward to George Fraunces the xxii day of the said moneth ... vi s. viii d.

Item to Henr*y* the kyng*es* godson for takyng of his ryht*es* at Est*er* ... iiii d.

Item in reward to m*aister* Pecsall ... xx s.

[M]Summa ... vi li. iii s. ii d.[P]

[*p. 84*] Item delyv*er*ed unto George Fraunc*es* for my lad*ys* offryng apon Est*er* Day in the mornyng ... ii s. vi d.

Item for my lad*ys* offryng at masse the same day ... vi s. viii d.

Item to Rog*er* Radclyff s*er*vande for the conveyng by water from Coldherboro to Grenewich of two tapurs ... iiii d.

Item paid the same day for a pennard and an ynkhorne for my lad*ys* g*r*ace ... iiii d.

Item delyv*er*ed the xxv day of the said moneth to my lad*ys* g*r*ace in golde by the hand*es* of maistres Stannop ... x li.

Item the same day paid unto John Mondy goldsmyth by his byll assigned for a holy wat*er* stok sylv*er* and gylt weying xiii unce. P*r*ice the unc*e* v s. Summa ... iii li. v s.

Item for a ale cuppe sylv*er* weying xii unc*e* iii q*uarter* di. P*r*ice the unc*e* iiii s. Summa ... li s.

Item for a challes of gold weying xvi unc*e* ferthyng gold weghe. P*r*ice the unc*e* xl s. ... xxxii li. ii s. vi d.

Item for a <q> goblett of gold weying x unc*e* di. q*uarter*. P*r*ice the unc*e* xl s. ... xx li. v s.

Item for a cruse of sylv*er* gylt weyes xiiii unc*e* i q*uarter* at v s. the unce. Summa ... lxxi s. iii d.

Item for a challes sylv*er* and gylt weyng xvi unc*es* di. P*r*ice the unc*e* v s. Summa ... iiii li. ii s. vi d.

Item paid unto Davy Prat yoman of the spyc*er*y for ridyng from Hatfeld to London by a day ... xii d.

Item for his bot hir*e* comyng from London to Grenewich ... i d.

Item for his lodgyng by the space of iiii nyght*es* ... iiii d.

Item for his cost*es* ridyng from Grenewich to Hatfeld by the spaice of two daies ... ii s.

Item for his bot hir*e* ... i d.

Item for his bot hir*e* from Grenewich to London ... ii d.

Item t*o* the procters of Saint George gyld ... xx d.

[M]Summa ... lxxvi li. xii s. v d.[P]

[*p. 85*] Item delyv*er*ed to maistres Stannop for a reward yeven to Weston chylde … iii s. iiii d.

Item to m*aister* Pecsall for two casses for challes … xii d.

Item for a holy wat*er* stok w*i*th a sprynkyll … viii d.

Item the same day in reward to George Fraunc*es* … x s.

Item to Rog*er* Radclyff in reward … x s.

Item to Rob*er*t Fremyngham in reward … x s.

Item to Rob*er*t Merbury in reward … x s.

Item to Ric*hard* Aderton in reward … x s.

Item to John Madyson in reward … x s.

Item to Nicholas Aughton in reward … x s.

Item to John Leghe in reward … x s.

Item t*o* William Luff in reward … vi s. viii d.

Item to Hughe Carr*e* in reward … vi s. viii d.

Item to Henry Abney in reward … vi s. viii d.

Item to John Harryson in reward … x s.

Item to John Holt in reward … x s.

Item to John Grome in reward … x s.

Item to Thomas Porter in reward … vi s. viii d.

Item to Henr*y* Daye in reward … vi s. viii d.

Item to Thomas Dod in reward … x s.

Item in reward to the kyng*es* porters … xiii s. iiii d.

Item to the buttre in reward … xx s.

Item to the pantre … xx s.

Item to the seller in reward … xxvi s. viii d.

Item t*o* the kechyn in reward … xl s.

Item to the wodyard in reward … v s.

Item to a beyrer of wodd … iii s. iiii d.

Item to Sherley clerk of the kychen … x s.

Item to John Miklow clerk counttroller … x s.

Item t*o* the scollery in reward … v s.

Item to the sauc*er*y in reward … v s.

[M]Summa … xv li. xvi s. viii d.[P]

[*p. 86*] Item in reward to Rob*er*t Jones gentylman yssher … v s.

Item t*o* the wardrop of the bedd*es* … xxvi s. viii d.

Item to the pechyr howse … iii s. iiii d.

Item t*o* Brysse of the <preve> kychen … v s.

Item to a lander at Grenewiche for wassyng by delyv*era*unce of Hughe Carre … iiii s. viii d.

Item for a reban for my lad*ys* g*r*ace bought by maistres Stannop … iiii d.

Item in reward to William Meryman … v s.

Item in reward to John Brent … v s.

Item to lytell Laurence grome of the chambr*e* … xii d.

Item t*o* Rog*er* Radclyff <fror> for sendyng to London for keyes of the howse wher my lad*ys* g*r*ace landyd at Ratclyff … viii d.

Item in reward to the seller at m*aister* Lovell*es* … vi s. viii d.

Item to the bottre in reward … vi s. viii d.

Item to the kychen in reward … vi s. viii d.

Item to the wardrop in reward … iii s. iiii d.

Item t*o* the porter in reward … iii s. iiii d.

Item t*o* the scole maist*er* their*e* … vi s. viii d.

Item to m*aistres* Mann*er*es chyldren … iii s. iiii d.

Item for the lodgyng of Rob*er*t Fremyngham and his s*er*vant by the space of a weke beyng seke … xii d.

Item the ii^{de} day of May in reward to m*aister* Morgan … iii s. iiii d.

Item to m*aister* dean for a reward yeven unto two chyldren of m*aistres* Husses beyng at m*aister* Lovels place … iii s. iiii d.

Item to Thomas Williams for money yeven to the two ancryse of Stampforth … iii s. iiii d.

Item paid for the borde of the fawkener son at Seynt Albones the space of x wek*es* endet the ii^{de} day of May at x d. the weke viii s. iiii d. and for his scole hyre for a q*u*art*er* endyd at Est*er* xii d. and for his right*es* takyng ii d. Summa … ix s. vi d.

[M]Summa … Cxvii s. ii d.[P]

[*p. 87*] Item paid unto Robert Tayleor by Nicholasse Sanders for geyre for Henry the kyng*es* godson … xiii s.

Item for a bonett for hym … xvi d.

Item for solyng of a pair*e* of shoes for hym … iiii d.

Item for a pair*e* of new shoes for the same … viii d.

Item for money to have in his pursse … xii d.

Item paid for my lad*ys* warde callyd Henr*y* Lowe for iiii narowe yerd*es* of tawny clothe v s. for iiii yerd*es* of whit cotton for lynyng ii s. for makyng of the cote vi d. for di. yerd of <whe> whitt kersey for hosyn vi d. for makyng ii s. for a bonett ii s. for a payr*e* of shoez vi d. for the hir*e* of a horse to bryng hym to Gaddysden iiii d. … xi s.[151]

Item to Nicholas Saunders for money paid unt*o* Jane Goer … xiii s. iiii d.

Item to Ric*hard* Aderton for a reward yeven to a s*er*vand of my lord of Derbies that brought word þ*a*t my lady Derby was delyv*er*ed … vi s. viii d.

Item paid unto m*aister* dean for money delyv*er*ed to oon Maydwall for the convayng of a pair*e* of orgence … iii s. iiii d.

Item to George Fraunces for money yeven unto the freris of Warre … iii s. iiii d.

Item to m*aister* counttroller for money yeven to an armet that dwell*es* on this syde Reydyng … iii s. iiii d.

Item to William of the chaundr*e* for wax for two tappurs bought at Walsyngham … v s. ix d.

Item to George Fraunc*es* in angell*es* xiii s. iiii d. in v s. of gold two \bus. x s./ in grott*es* xvi s. viii d. … xl s.

Item for ii dossen of Walsyngham brochis … ii s.

Item for money yeven to the post at Pyknall comyng from Brandon Ferr*y* … xii d.

Item to the marshall at Walsyngham in reward … vi s. viii d.

Item to the post þ*a*t came from Babram to Brandon … xx d.

[M]Summa … Cxiiii s. v d.[P]

[*p. 88*] Item to on þ*a*t came from Brandon to my lad*ys* g*r*ace … viii d.

Item to m*aister* Chambr*e* for my lad*ys* offryng at Walsyngham … xii d.

Item for my lad*ys* offryng to the rode at Cryst*es* Collage … xx d.

Item to an armett at the Kyng*es* Collage … xx d.

Item paid unto Nicholas Saunders for a reward yeven unto John Merycoke yemon of the chambr*e* … x s.

Item to Nicholas Aughton for a prevey seall … vi s. viii d.

Item to John Carre the post by Nicholas Sanders … x s.

Item to the post at Babram by Nicholas Sanders … viii s. iiii d.

Item delyv*er*ed by the said Nicholas to Rog*er* Radclyff for my lad*ys* offryng to the heghe awter at Walsyngham … v s.

Item paid by the same to Edmounde Norrice for a serge founde afour*e* our*e* Lady at Walsyngham … iii s. iiii d.

[151] The correct total is 12s. 10d.

Item to Jamys Morice for a reward yeven unto the masons workyng apon the Kyng*es* Collage … xl s.

Item to the waytt*es* of Cambryge in reward … iii s. iiii d.

Item to m*aister* countroller for a antyphaner bought for Cryst*es* Collage … lxvi s. viii d.

Item toward*es* the byldyng of Saynt Annes chappell in Cambryge yeven by m*aister* countroller … vi s. viii d.

Item in reward to the gentylwomen and brotherers delyv*er*ed by maistres Foller … xiii s. iiii d.

Item in reward to maistres Curson … vi s. viii d.

Item in reward to the fotmen … vi s. viii d.

Item to maistres Lenche for xiiii unce of golde of Venyse. P*r*ice … xxviii s.

Item for two pec*es* of sypers … vi s.

Item in reward to maistres Lenche … x s.

Item in reward to William Hylm*er* … x s.

Item to Ric*hard* Aderton by his byll for ridyng from Grenewiche to Rochest*er* a day and a day taryng behynde my lad*ys* g*r*ace … xvi d.

[M]Summa … xii li. <viii s. viii d.> vii s.[P 152]

[*p. 89*] Item to Rob*ert* Fremyngham the iiii[th] day of May for money delyv*er*ed to m*aister* Scotte and Olyv*er* Scall*es* for the propriacion of Man*er*bere unto Cryst*es* Collage … xx li.

xxvi s. viii d. solvuntur per marcas. Item to the cok*es* for their*e* with at Ester … xxvi s. viii d.

Item to the sac*er*y and skollery … v s.

[153]Item paid to John Rose the xx[th] day of May for the borde wag*es* of John Lowe my ladyes warde for ix wek*es* endyng the said xx day at x d. the weke <u>vii s. vi d.</u> … vii s. vi d.

Item to the same to bye hym <bowys> a bowe and arowys to shote w*ith*all … viii d.

Item yeven in rewarde to mastres Parkers norse by mastres Masse … xx d.

Item yevyn in rewarde to master Morys Synt John by mastres Fowler … lxvi s. viii d.

Item yevyn in rewarde to the kyng*es* blyne mynstrell … v s.

Item yevyn in rewarde to the two ancrys of Stampford the xxiii[th] day of May by Will*ia*m Ratclyff … iii s. iiii d.

[152] Perhaps in the 'curly' hand which begins on the next page. The correct sum is £12 9s.

[153] The 'curly' hand returns here.

Item paid to mastres Parkers norse for the borde of Jane Parker by the space of <aigte> xiii wek*es* \by m*astres* Masse/ … x s.

Item paid to mastres Masse for flex … vi s. viii d.

Item paid for the mete of mastres Feharbo*urs* iii horsys and for the dyet of <Rob*er*t Merbury> hir horsekeper … xx i d.

Item delyv*er*ed the xvith day of May to Jamys Moryce toward the byldyng of Crystys Colege as apperyth by his bill … lxii li.

Item yeven in rewarde to John Vanutrysshe my ladyes goldsmyth for his cost*es* co*m*myng to Hatfeld … ii s.

Item yevyn in rewarde to mastres Moleners by mastres Stannop … xx s.

Item yevyn in rewarde to the players of the chyrche of Bokkyng … xx d.

Item yevyn in rewarde to my lorde of Elys potecary … xx d.

Item yevyn in rewarde to master Carter for translatyng of *cer*tyn bokys out of Latyn into Englysshe by m*aster* chauncell*our* … xx s.

Item yevyn in rewarde to my lady Jane Baughyn … vi s. viii d.

Item paid to Will*ia*m Kempe for caryage of my lady <I> Chaynes fole home … iii s. iiii d.

Item paid to Robert Fremyngham for his cost*es* w*ith* ii horsys rydyng from Hatfeld to Greneweche to my lorde of < Rochesto*urs*> Wynchester by ii days iiii s. and for the hyer of his bote by iiii tymes in and out from London to Greneweche xvi d. … v s. iiii d.

Item yeven in rewarde to sir Cleme[n]t of the chapell by my ladyes co*m*maundment <toward his lossys> … xl s.[154]

^{M}Summa … iiii^{xx}xiii li. xv s. vii d.^{P}

[*p. 90*] Item delyv*er* the xith day of June to George F*r*aunc*es* for my ladyes offeryng apon Whyt Sonday … v s.

Item yevyn in rewarde to the p*ro*vynceall of the blake fryers for makyn of a s*er*mond by m*aster* deane … x s.

Item yevyn in rewarde to my lorde prynces mynsterlys … iii s. iiii d.

Item yevyn in rewarde to a servant of my lorde of Burgaveyn for bryngyng of a grewhounde … iii s. iiii d.

Item delyv*er*ed the first day of June for my ladyes offeryng by Jamys Moryce … v s.

Item paid for the cost*es* of my lady Shyrleys at the syne of the George … xxi s. vii d.

Nota. Item paid for a yerd and a half \of velvet/ bough[t] by Jamys Morice … xvi s. vi d.

Item in rewarde to Clement the kyng*es* servant … vi s. viii d.

[154] There is a dot calculation to the right of the total.

Item in rewarde to a pursevant by George Fr*a*unc*es* … iii s. iiii d.

Item paid for viii whyte skynnes iii s. for i red skynne iiii d. for i tawney skynne iii d. for lether for clapsys xii d. for bord*es* x d. for threde ii d. for mendyng of surplesys iiii d. for two shorte clapsys for a grayll iii d. to Lenard le Fevo*ur* in rewarde to the said Lenard iii s. iiii d. … ix s. vi d.

Item yevyn in rewarde to mastres Fyharber by mastres Fowler … x s.

Item for my ladyes offeryng for hir pardon on Whyt Sonday … vi s. viii d.

Item delyv*er*ed to mestres Fowler to bye c*er*tyn thyng*es* for my ladyes g*r*ace … ii s.

Item paid the xx^th^ day of June to master Horman for the exebucion of[155] Thomas Bury at Eton by the hand*es* of John Holt … liii s. iiii d.

Item paid to Jane Gore for hir q*u*arter wag*es* endyng at mydsomer next co*m*myng by m*astres* Masse … xiii s. iiii d.

Item yevyn in rewarde to Margaret Stewkely toward hir cost*es* <to mast> goyng to master Odallys … iii s. iiii d.

Item delyv*er*ed for my ladyes offeryng apon Corpus Christy Day … v s.

Item delyv*er*ed the same tyme to Robert Merbury for my ladyes offeryng to the box for the newe p*ar*don … lxvi s. viii d.

Item paid to Jamys Moryce the xxi^th^ day of June toward the byldyng of Cryst*es* Colege … xx li.

Item paid for <the recovery of> a fyne for the recovery of the maner of Deseworth had ayenst s*ir* Morys Barkely … C s.

Item paid for a fyne for the recovery of the maner of Gotehyll ayenst Charlys Brandon esquyer and Margaret his wyffe … xxx s.

Item paid for the subsedy of the p*ar*sonage of Malton byfore hit was inp*ro*peryd … xl s.

Item paid to Will*iam* Kempe aforsaid[156] for the expenc*es* and charg*es* of Korse my lady Chaynes fole and for his labo*ur* to co*n*vey hym home from Hatfeld … iii s. iiii d.

[M] Summa … xli li. xvii s. <x d.> xi d.[P][157]

[*p. 91*] Item paid to Willyam Checheley and Henr*y* Checheley ten pound*es* in p*ar*te of payment <of> for soch[158] land*es* as my ladyes g*r*ace hathe bough[t] of them w*ith*in Malton and Baryngton … x li.

Item paid to Rob*er*t Fremyngham for his cost*es* w*ith* ii horsys rydyng from Wesebeche to Ely by ii days for the co*n*firmacio*un* of a voyson grauntyd by the bysshop and for the p*ro*mys of another by the pryo*ur* of the said Ely … iiii s.

[155] 'of' rep.

[156] p. 89 above.

[157] The total is £1 over.

[158] MS 'sochy'.

Item paid to John Bretyn for iii yerd*es* of tawney for a gowne for mastres Parker … xv s.

Item paid to Jamys Moryce for his cost*es* by iiii days w*ith* ii horsys rydyng to the corte to speke w*ith* c*er*tyn of the kynges councell for c*er*tyn causys of my ladyes g*r*ace and there lying by ii days to yeve attendans apon the said councell. In gret … viii s.

Nota. Item yevyn in rewarde to Nicholas Stravarme toward his charges at my ladyes beyng at the corte … vi s. viii d.

Item paid in rewarde to docto*ur* Yong for makyng of a s*er*mond apon Trenyte Sonday by m*aster* deane … x s.

Item yevyn in rewarde to a bacheler of devenyte for makyng of a s*er*mond apon Corpus Christi day … vi s. viii d.

Item paid the xxviith day of January to Edward Hevyn for the expenc*es* of George Fitzwill*i*am and Gefery Paynell w*ith* their s*er*vant*es* for rydyng to Alford Lowthe Lincoln and other plac*es* by the co*m*maundment of my ladyes g*r*ace to calle in hir reteyned s*er*vant*es* afore them for to endent w*ith* them to doe the kyng*es* g*r*ace s*er*vyce in hir <retyu> retynue by the space of ii wek*es* that is to saye first rydyng to Alford and there abydyng by v days w*ith* ix horsys xxi s. iii d. for their expenc*es* at Lowthe and there abydyng by iiii days xxxiii s. iiii d. for their expenc*es* at Lyncoln by iii days xxvi s. ii d. for their expenc*es* at Hornecastell by ii days viii s. xi d. for a man for rydyng from Tater to Mabilthorp w*ith* my ladyes letters to George Fitzwill*i*am by ii days xvi d. to John Wodford for the hyer of ii of his s*er*vant*es* rydyng abowte the country to cause dyvers of my lad*ys* s*er*vant*es* to come to Alford xx d. Item to John Atkyn of Lowthe for rydyng to dyv*ers* of my ladyes s*er*vant*es* dwellyng abowte the country ther causyng them to come to Lowthe and Lyncoln by v days iiii s. viii d. Item paid to a man for rydyng to my ladyes s*er*vant*es* dwellyng abowte Hornecastell and other plac*es* by iii days ii s. vii d. Item paid for pawper and p*ar*chement to wryte dyv*er* thyng*es* xi d. … C s. x d.

[M]Summa … xvii li. xi s. ii d.[P]

[*p. 92*] Item paid the viith day of Apryll to Richard Alcok of Bostone for rydyng into the p*ar*tyes of Lynce and into the mersshe country to yeve warnyng to my ladyes s*er*vant*es* to be at Hornecastell. For the wag*es* of hymselfe and for his horse hyer by ix days ix s. iiii d. And for the expenc*es* of Gefery Paynell and Edward Hevyn and iiii s*er*vant*es* w*ith* them at the said Hornecastyll by i day iii s. … xii s. iiii d.

Item paid in rewarde to a fryo*ur* my lady prynces confesso*ur* by mastres Fowler … xx s.

Item yevyn in rewarde to Jane Walter by m*astres* Fowler … v s.

Item yevyn in rewarde to a s*er*vant o[f] m*aster* Conysbyes for bryngyng of c*er*tyn wrytyns to my ladyes g*r*ace … xii d.

Item yeven in rewarde to a fryour for bryngyng of a payer of bed*es* from Rome the xxviith day of June by m*aster* chauncello*ur* … xl s.

Item paid to John Plowfeld by a byll asyned the said xxviith day of June for rydyng to London and Greneweche at sondery tymes and for his lying <at> there by c*er*tyn days to attende apon <the> master Scot for the p*ro*preacion of Manerbere for pawper incke parchement and velom in the hole \ w*ith* his cost*es*/ in every behalfe viii s. vi d. … viii s. vi d.

Item paid the xxviiith day of June for the borde of the fawkeners sonne at Seynt Albons by the space of viii wek*es* that is to saye from the ii^{de} day of May unto the xxixth day of the said June at x d. the weke … vi s. viii d.

Item delyv*er*ed to my ladyes g*r*ace the xxixth day of June for to yeve in almes … x li.

Item yevyn in rewarde to master comptroll*our*s s*er*vant for co*m*myng from London … xx d.

Item paid to mastres Masse for a bonet for Jane Parker vii d. for ii payer of shone vii d. for makyng and lynyng of a cote for Jane Parker xv d. for tryakyll i d. for almond*es* and sewg*er* ii d. for sewg*er* candyth ii d. for ii rybond*es* viii d. for mylke and butt*er* ii s. iiii d. for dressyng of a gowne iiii d. for the hoselyng of power folke ayenst Esto*ur* ii s. for flax and hard*es* iiii s. i d. Item to Jane Parkers norse vi s. viii d. in rewarde to a woman that brought hir hether iiii d. for power folk*es* shone iiii s. ix d. for sylke to mastres Fynche ii s. viii d. for brede and ale for moder Alson iii d. for lac*es* v d. … xxvii s. iiii d.

^{M}Summa … xvi li. ii s. vi d.^{P}

[*p. 93*] <Item delyv*er*ed the last day of June to m*aster* almoigner*e* for my lad*ys* almes … […] s.>[159]

Item yeven in reward the first day of July to singing children belonnging to the p*ar*sone of Harowe upon the hill … iii s. iiii d.

Item the same day for my lad*ys* offering at Syon … xii d.

<Item deliv*er*ed to William Laborer and Robert Feror*e* the ii^{de} day of the said moneth … xiii s. iiii d.

Item the ii^{de} day of the same to Rob*er*t Hilton in prest … vi li.>

«nichil»[160]

Item the same day to m*aster* Parker in reward … xx s.

Item <p> the same day in reward to my lady Beamount … x s.

Item for ix paire of gloves for my lad*ys* grace … ii s.

Item deliv*er*ed the iiiith day of the said monethe unto my lad*ys* grace … xx s.

Item <p> in reward the vith day of the said moneth to Wynkyn de Worde printer for bringing unto my lad*ys* grace of cirtain boke … ii s.

<Item the same day in reward to m*aster* Scotte of Crist*es* Colleige … l s. «nichil»

Item the same day in reward to my lady Boughan … vi s. viii d. «nichil»>

[159] Vigorously canc. by criss-cross lines (so too the fourth and fifth entries on the page).

[160] Bracketed to the right of the two items above, which are vigorously canc.

Item paied the same day to Nicholas Aughton by a bill signed for riding from Grenewiche to Hatfeld for litill coffres by the space of ii dayes … xvi d.

Item for riding from Grenewiche to Rochester by the space of ii dayes to <the> my lord bisshop ther*e* … xvi d.

Item for riding to my lady Scroope to Fyfeld for the p*ar*sonage of Herberowe by the space of iii dayes … ii s.

Item for riding to Cambrige for maister Scotte and Oliv*er* Scales by the space of ii dayes … xvi d.

Item for riding to Grenewiche bifore my ladies removing to Walsingham by the space of ii dayes … xvi d.

Item for lying at Ware as a post w*ith* his servant and ii horses by the space of x dayes … xiii s. iiii d.

Item for riding to Grenewiche <whan> at the reto*ur*ne of my ladies grace from Walsingham and ther*e* being the space of iiii dayes to knowe when the king*es* highnesse should remove … ii s. viii d.

Item for riding to Eltham to the king*es* grace by the space of iii dayes … ii s.

Item for riding to the kinges grace and to my lord of Wynchesto*ur* for the advowson of Conyngesby by the space of iii dayes … ii s.

Item for riding to my lord of Saincte David for the grete pardon by the space of ii dayes … xvi d.

[M]Summa … vii li. vii s.[P]

[*p. 94*] Item paied to the scribe of my said lord of Saincte David for writing of div*er*se thing*es* conc*er*nyng the said pardon … ii s.

Item for a box to put in the same pardon … ii d.

< Item paid[161] the viith day of the said moneth in preste to Rob*er*t Merbury by the comaundement of my ladies grace … xl s.>[162] «solvitur»

Item the same day deliv*er*ed unto hir grace <for> to be yevin to my lord prince for runnyng at the ring … xiii li. vi s. viii d.

Item the viiith day of <July> the said moneth in preste to Thomas Soper my ladies solycito*ur* by the co*m*maundement of hir grace … C s.

Item the same day to maister Richard Wyot for the stypend of maister Collingwood whiche shal be due for a hole yere at the feste of Saincte Mighell the archaungell next commyng … xl s.

< Item the xith day of the said moneth in prest to Rob*er*t Long oon of the gromes of the stabell … x s.> «nichil»

[161] 'the v' add. but not canc.

[162] This entry and the seventh on the page are vigorously canc. (as p. 93).

Item the xiith day of the said moneth in rewarde to a woman at Windesore for bringing of cakes unto my ladies grace … iii s. iiii d.

Item the same day for hire offering to king Henry in gold ii s. vi d. and in silver iii s. iiii d. … v s. x d.

Item for the offering of hir*e* grace the same day to Sainct George … ii s. vi d.

Item the xvith day of the said moneth to George Fraunc*es* for div*er*se reward*es* yeven by my lad*ys* co*m*maundement … x s.

Item the same day in reward to the said George … x s.

Item the same day to William Love for mending of my lad*ys* bed and convey of c*er*tain stuf over the water at Syon … viii d.

Item the same day to John Utrix by a bill assigned for mending and sodering of ii sylver pott*es* all gylt … vi s. viii d.

Item for a pair*e* of hok*es* of gold weying vi penyweight. Pric*e* the penyweight xx d. … x s.

Item for making therof … iiii s.

Item for iii pair*e* of hok*es* sylver and gylt … vi s. viii d.

Item for a pair*e* of boke claspes sylver and gylt weying a di. unc*e* … vi s.

Item for iiii pair*e* of hok*es* of gold in weight i unc*e* wanting iiii penyweight. Pric*e* … xxxi s. iii d.

Item for making of the said iiii pair*e* … viii s.

Item the same day in reward to Knowles gentilman ussher w*ith* the king*es* grace … v s.

[163]Item in rewarde to Nicholas Saunder … v s.

[M]Summa … xxvi li. viii s. ix d.[P]

[*p. 95*] Item to Bramton of the pa[ntr]ie[164] … v s.

Item to Brent Anesley and John Williams of the seller … x s.

Item to Hasilrige of the wardrobe of bed*es* … x s.

Item to the carte taker … iii s. iiii d.

Item to suche p*er*sonnes as brought bedd*es* and russhers unto my lad*ys* chamber*e* … ii s.

Item the same day to George Fraunc*es* for a reward given unto Phi*li*p and M*ar*ten the king*es* fools … xx d.

[163] This entry (still in the 'curly' hand) is squeezed into the bottom of the page; there is a dot calculation to the right of the page total.
[164] MS 'partie'.

Item to the same for the hir*e* of ii pair*e* of schet*es* for the yomen of the chamb*er* \at Richmound/ … viii s.

Item to the same for a potell of wyne which my lad*ys* grac*e* called for at Stanes … iiii d.

Item the same [day] to Hugh Carre for a launder which by the spac*e* of xvii dayes wasshed c*er*tain stuf at Richmound and Hanworth … ii s.

Item <j> to the same for an nue key of a gardevya*n* … iiii d.

[165]<Item in prest to Rob*er*t Ferror*e* the xviiith day of the said moneth … xl s.>

Item the same day to the bargeman for rowing the space of ii dayes w*ith* vi owres at vii d. an ower by the day <iii s.> \viii s./ for his wag*es* <xvi d.> \ii s./ for hir*e* of the barge xvi d. … xi s. iiii d.>

«nichil»[166]

Item the same day in rewarde to Maurice Saincte John … iii li. vi s. vi d.

Item deliv*er*ed the same day to the hand*es* of my lad*ys* grace … xx s.

Item in reward to the king*es* bargeman … xx d.

Item in reward to the feryman at Thystelworthe … viii d.

Item in reward to the king*es* fotemen … iii s. iiii d.

Item paid for the mete of my lorde chefe juggys horsys and for the expenc*es* of his s*er*vant*es* at the Cheker … iiii s. v d.

Item paid to Will*i*am Whytmore m*aster* Parkers s*er*vant for his q*uar*ters <q> wag*es* endyng at mydsomer last past … vi s. viii d.

Recepta.+ *Conynyysby. Postea.* Item delyv*er*ed the xixth day of July to master Conysby as money to hym lent to be repayd a yere at Candylmas next co*m*myng as apperyth by his obligacion remaynyng in the kepyng of my ladyes g*r*ace … <C li.> «cancellatur hic quia postea inter arreragia huius anni»[167]

Item yevyn in rewarde to Pynckeneys the Wordyes s*er*vant for bryngyng of bok*es* to Hanworth … xii d.

Item yeven in rewarde to my lady Boughyn by m*aster* chauncell*our* at Rychemound … xl s.

Item yevyn in rewarde to a s*er*vant of the rectors of Asseryge for bryngyng of chese by m*aster* deane … xii d.

[M]Summa … <Cix li. ix d.> ix li. ix d.[P]

[165] This and the next entry have vigorous cancellations.
[166] Bracketed to the right of the two items above.
[167] Add. in the 'sprawling' hand. See p. 125 below.

[*p. 96*] Item yevyn in rewarde to my lady Margaret Pole by my ladyes g*r*ace … vi s. viii d.

Item yevyn in rewarde the xxvith day of July to John Utryche my ladyes goldsmyth … <iii s. iiii d.> xx d.

Item yeven in rewarde to John Gaynysshe my lord of Burgavennes \ s*er*vant/ for bryngyng of a gossehalke … x s.

Item yevyn in rewarde to the ancrys of Seynt Albons … xx d.

Item paid to Thomas Senowe my ladyes goldewyer drauer the same tyme for v lib. and ii unc*es* of damaske gold at xii unc*es* the lib. aft*our* iiii s. iii d. the unc*e* xiii li. iii s. vi d. for i lib. of flat gold at xii unc*es* to the lib. iiii s. x d. the unc*e* lviii s. for other iiii unc*es* of flat gold at iiii s. x d. the unc*e* xix s. iiii d. for di. lib. of rounde gold at iiii s. iii d. the unc*e* xxv s. vi d. Item paid for a slathe to wark in xx d. … xviii li. viii s.

Item paid to George F*r*aunc*es* for his cost*es* by ii days rydyng from Hatfeld to Greneweche to the kyng and ayene w*ith* ii horsys … iii s. x d.

Item paid <s> to Wyncke the Worthy for bokes the xxvith day of July by m*aster* Morgan … x s.

Item paid the first day of August to Henr*y* Lodlowe for his q*u*arter wag*es* endyng at mydsom*er* last past … xx s.

Item paid the same tyme to John Willyams for goyng from Hanwod to London and from thens to Bromley and so to Stany by the spac*e* of iii days … ii s.

Item paid in rewarde to our*e* Ladyes gylde in the p*ar*ysshe of Cheston … vi s. viii d.

Item paid for ii yerd*es* of tawneny medly for a cote clothe for Lowe my ladyes warde … vi s. viii d.

Item paid to s*ir* Rob*er*t Whytelege for his cost*es* at London by the space of iiii days w*ith* his s*er*vant and ii horsys to speke w*ith* my lord bysshop of Seynt David and dyv*er*s other doct*our*s for the propreaciou*n* of the benefyce of Mano*ur*bere to Cryst*es* Colege in Cambryge viii s. … viii s.

Nota. Item paid for i gawne of rose wat*our* to Thomas Chamb*er* ii s. viii d. for a pot to put in the same viii d. … iii s. iiii d.

Item paid to Thomas Chamb*er* for xvi ellys of pekelyng ii s. iiii d. for iiii gret irne pott*es* ii s. for ii payer of sherys <iid.> iiii d. for vi stonde coffyns paynted <i>iii s. for a tabyll of coffyns viii s. for nedellys and threde i d. \for vi rowne boxys paynted iii s./ … xviii s. ix d.

Item yevyn in rewarde to Peynckeny the Worthy for bryngyng of c*er*tyn pott*es* of <y> jelafers to my ladyes g*r*ace … vi s. viii d.

Nota. Item yevyn in rewarde the iiiith day of August to c*er*tyn syngyng men of London … vi s. viii d.

[M]Summa … xxiiii li. vii d.[P]

[*p. 97*] Item yeven in rewarde to Rob*er*t Jonys the[168] xi[th] day of August vi s. viii d. Item <to> in rewarde to Broke yoman ussher iii s. iiii d. … x s.

Item in rewarde to Faughyn grome of the chambr*e* … iii s. iiii d.

Item in rewarde to Gyles lewtor … vi s. viii d.

Item in rewarde to the rybybe and other mynstrellys … x s.

Item in rewarde to \the/ kepor of the lyon … iii s. iiii d.

Item to a s*er*vant of my lorde prynces for bryngyng of a tasell in rewarde … vi s. viii d.

Item in rewarde to the kyng*es* <A> harbyngers … x s.

Nota. Item in rewarde to iiii syngers that came from London … xxxiii s. iiii d.

Item in rewarde to the fry*our*s of <Greneweche> \Richmont in Yorkshire/[169] … xl s.

Item delyv*er*ed to mastres Masse <by> to bye c*er*tyn thyngg*es* … xxvi s. viii d.

Item yeven in rewarde to the offycers of the kyng*es* seller … x s.

Item in rewarde to the kyng*es* pantry … vi s. viii d.

Item in rewarde to the kyng*es* buttry … vi s. viii d.

Item in rewarde to the clerk*es* of the kechyn … xx s.

Item in rewarde to the cokes and the pastery … xx s.

Item in rewarde to the scolery … vi s. viii d.

Item in rewarde to the porters … iii s. iiii d.

Item in rewarde to Mereman … vi s. viii d.

Item in rewarde to the pecher howse … iii s. iiii d.

Item in rewarde to the ewery … iii s. iiii d.

Item paid to Richard Atherton for rydyng to the cort by ii days xvi d. and for rydyng to London by ii days to bye sayes and other ness*essaryes* xvi d. … ii s. viii d.

Item paid to the said Richard for iii pec*es* of grene saye of iii yerd*es* depe lx s. for xii rounde chamb*er* basons of pewt*our* x s. … lxx s.

Item paid to the parson of Kettysbe for a lyght fowne afore Seynt Marget there w*ith* c*er*tyn tapers … vi s. viii d.

Item delyv*er*ed for my ladyes offeryng apon the Assumpci*oun* of our*e* Lady Day … v s.

*Bought by Rob*er*t Hylton.*[170]

Item paid to Rob*er*t Hylton for i yerd di. of kersey for my ladyes warde Burgon. P*rice* the yerd xx d. … ii s. vi d.

[168] 'the' rep.
[169] Add. in a distinctive italic hand.
[170] Bracketed to include the rest of the items on p. 97.

Item paid for lynyng and makyng of the same hose … x d.

Item paid for a payer of shoes for the said warde … x d.

Item paid for iii yerd*es* di. of medly for a gowne for the fawkeners sonne at ii s. the yerd vii s. Item for vi yerd*es* of blacke cottyn for the same gowne at v d. ii s. vi d. Item for the makyng of the same gowne vi d. Item for i yerd i q*uarter* di. of whyte carsey xvi d. ob. for makyng and lynyng of the same hosyn viii d. … xii s. ob.

[M]Summa … xvi li. xvii s. ii d. ob.[P]

[*p. 97I*] *Stuffe bought by Roberd Hylton.*[171]

Item paid for vi yerd*es* of tawney medly for letermenys cot*es* ayenst my ladyes goyng to Wasyngham at iii s. … xviii s.

Item to <S> Wyllyam Laborer for his cost*es* to bye the said clothe at London … viii d.

Item paid for ii payer of hosyn for the ii fotemen redy made vii s. iiii d. for vi payer of shone for them iii s. … x s. iiii d.

Item paid to Rob*er*t Hylton for xii yerd*es* of blacke satyn for a gowne for my ladyes g*r*ace. P*r*i*ce* the yerd vii s. vi d. … iiii li. x s.

Item for CC pinkes for the same gowne. P*r*i*ce* the C xii d. … ii s.

item for x lambe skynnes of blacke for my ladyes kyrtell slevys xx d. for furrying of the same <ii d.> iiii d. for his cost*es* ryding from Greneweche to Hatfeld to make the said gowne by ii days ii s. for his cost*es* rydyng from London to Hatfeld w*ith* my ladye Wylloughby <[…]h> and to fet my ladyes gownes by ii dayes ii s. Item for a basket for my ladyes g*r*ace vi d. Item for ii padlock*es* v d. … vi s. xi d.

Item paid for ii yerd*es* of curse medly yeven unto a power woman at Greneweche v s. for iii yerd*es* of blacke cotton for the lynyng xv d. and for the makyng of the same gowne viii d. … vi s. xi d.

Item paid for iii yerd*es* of medly for my ladyes maunde gowne at v s. l*e* yerde xv s. for v dosyn payer of shoes for the same maunde at iii s. x d. xix s. ii d. for v payer of shoys for the same maunde xx d. for vii whyte bonettes for my ladyes almes women iiii s. i d. … xxxix s. xi d.

Item paid to the same Rob*er*t for xvi yerd*es* of blacke velvet for a gowne for master Parker at x s. ii d. the yerde … viii li. ii s. viii d.

Item paid for a furre and a halfe of foynes to p*er*forme the <said gow> furre of the said gowne xxx s. Item to John God for makyng of the said gowne iiii s. … xxxiiii s.

Item for a \di./ yerd of blacke clothe for a hudde for the said master Parker ii s. viii d. for makyng and leyng in of a gowne of blacke clothe lyned w*ith* sarsenet for master Parker ii s. viii d. … v s. iiii d.

Item paid for vi yerd*es* iii q*uar*ters of tawney damaske for a jaket for master Parker at vi s. viii d. xlv s. for iiii yerd*es* \di./ of whyte cotyn for the lynyng of the same xxii d. ob.

[171] Bracketed to include all the items on p. 97I.

for makyng of the same ii s. Item for ii yerd*es* iii q*u*arters of russet damaske for a dobelet for the said master Parker at vii s. xix s. iii d. for iii yerd*es* of <ffy> fustyan for lyning of the same xv d. for canvas for the same dobelet iii d. for makyng of the same dobelat xx d. … lxxvi s. iii d. ob.

[M]Summa … xxii li. viii s. ob.[P]

[*p. 97II*] *Stuff bought by Roberd Hylton.*[172]

Item paid for a bonet for the said m*aster* Parker ii s. viii d. Item for a yerd di. of scarlet for a payer of hosyn for m*aster* Parker vii s. for lynyng and makyng of the same xii d. for ii sprewse skynnes of lether for a payer of nether hosyn ii s. for a \di./ yerd \di. q*uarter*/ <iii q*uar*ters> of kendall for the upper part*es* of the same hosyn viii d. for makyng and lynyng of the said hosyn xii d. for ii payer of kidde shoys for m*aster* Parker ii s. viii d. for ii payer of other shoys xx d. and for my[173] cost*es* to p*ro*vyde the said stuffe by the same space by iiii days xvi d. … xx s.

Item paid for xii yerd*es* \of chamlet/ for mastres Parkers gowne <at> at ii s. iiii d. ob. xxviii s. vi d. for i yerd di. and <dy> di. q*uarter* of blacke velvet afto*ur* x s. iiii d. the yerd the which is ocupyed in a egge coler and cuffys for the same gowne and the resedewe for a tepet for my ladyes g*r*ace xvi s. ix d. for a rolle of bokeram for the same gowne ii s. iiii d. for a yerd of blacke cotton for the plyt*es* of the same gowne v d. for anglett*es* for the same gowne i d. to Jamys Monkester for makyng of the same gowne iiii s. for ii ellys of blacke worsted for a kyrtell for the same m*astres* Parker viii s. viii d. for iiii yerd*es* of blacke cotton for lynyng of the same xx d. for halfe a nelle of lenyn clothe for the same kyrtell iii d. for anglett*es* i d. for a nayle of scarlet for the same kyrtell vi d. to Jamys Moncaster for makyng of the same kyrtell xx d. for a yerd di. of whyte cotyn for the lynyng of a kyrtell for m*astres* Jane Parker vii d. ob. … lxv s. vi d. ob.

Item paid for vii yerd*es* of chamlet for mastres <Jans> \Yons/ gowne xvi s. x d. Item paid for i rolle of bokerham occupyod in the same gowne ii s. iiii d. for a yerd of blacke cotton for the plytys of the same gowne v d. for iii ellys of canvas for the lynyng and the purfyll of the same gowne xii d. for anglettes i d. for makyng of the same gowne to Jamys Moncaster iii s. viii d. for ii ellys of worsted for a kyrtell for the said mastres <Jan> \Yon/ viii s. viii d. for iiii yerd*es* of black cotton for lynyng of the same kyrtell xx d. for di. elle of <leny> lenyn clothe iii d. for anglett*es* i d. for a nayle of scarlet to egge the said kyrtell vi d. Item to Jamys Moncaster for makyng of the said kyrtell xx d. … xxxvii s. ii d.

[M]Summa … vi li. ii s. viii d. ob.[P]

[*p. 98*] *Stuff bought by Robert Hylton.*[174]

Item paid for ii ellys of worsted for m*astres* Perot for a kyrtell at iiii s. iiii d. viii s. viii d. for iiii yerd*es* of blacke cotyn for lynyng at v d. the yerd xx d. for anglett*es* for the same i d. for halfe a nelle of lenyn clothe iii d. for a nayle of scarlet for a negge vi d.

[172] Bracketed to include all the items on p. 97II.

[173] 'My' prob. copied directly from Hilton's invoice.

[174] Bracketed to include the two items below.

Item to Jamys Moncaster for makyng of the same xx d. for halfe a yerd of tawneny medly for <a gowne> bodying and slevyng of a gowne of m*as*tr*es* Perott*es* ii s. … xiiii s. x d.

Item paid for iii yerd*es* of russet fustyan for a kyrtell for m*as*tr*es* Ursula at hir goyng w*ith* my lady Shyrley xxi d. for ii yerd*es* of whyte cotyn for lynyng of the same x d. … ii s. vii d.

Item yeven in rewarde to the wardon and covent of the graye ffryers of Bedford at <their> their chaptur*e* nowe beyng \the xviith day of August/ … xiii s. iiii d.

Item yeven in rewarde to master Parker by m*aster* tresorer … xxvi s. viii d.

Item in rewarde to his wyffe … x s.

Item delyv*er*ed unto the hand*es* of my ladyes g*r*ace at the kyng*es* beyng at Hatfeld xiii li. vi s. viii d. for to yeve in rewarde to the kyng*es* servant*es* … xiii li. vi s. viii d.

Item paid for the exebucions of Stanbancke my ladyes scoler at Parys … xx s.

Item paid to Thomas Chamber for his cost*es* by iii days rydyng from Hatfeld to London to p*r*ovyde <drog*es*> \drugg*es*/ and other ness*essary* metsons for my ladyes g*r*ace by m*aster* Chamber … iii s.

Item paid to Robert Merbury for rydyng from Rychemound into Wales to the Man*our* of Bere in Penbrokeshyre to receyve the arrerag*es* beyng behynde in the hand*es* of baillyffe ther*e* by xxiiith days at xii d. the day xxiii s. and in rewarde to a <garde guyde> man to helpe to guyde hym the waye ii s. i d. … xxv s. i d.

Item paid to the same Rob*er*t for vii yerd*es* iii q*uar*ters of sarcenet of oregen coler at iii s. viii d. the yerd xxviii s. v d. … xxviii s. v d.

Item for rydyng to Ware by ii days for bedd*es* ii s. for corde vi d. … ii s. vi d.

Item paid to George F*r*aunc*es* for his cost*es* by ii days rydyng from Hatfeld to Envyll w*ith* ii horsys w*ith* the hyer ii s. viii d. … ii s. viii d.

<Item delyv*er*ed the xxth day of August to Peto*ur* Oldehalle to bye certyn stuffe w*ith*all … xx s.> «intrat postea»[175]

Item paid for my ladyes offeryng at <our*e* lady of letyllmore> \Seynt Gyles in the Busshe/ besyde Cheston by George F*r*aunc*es* … iii s. iiii d.

^{M}Summa … xx<i> li. xix s. i d.^{P}

[*p. 99*] Item yevyn in rewarde the xxvth day of August to the pryo*ur* of Benham by m*aster* confesso*ur* … xx s.

Item paid to Thomas Robertson s*er*vant for the custome and the caryage of ii pec*es* of velvet i pece of blacke satyn and i pece of blacke damaske from by yen see to the maner of Tongg*es* by m*aster* chauncell*our* … xl s.

Item paid for my ladyes g*r*ace offeryn at the abby of Waltham … xx d.

[175] Add. in a very neat hand, with the entry vigorously canc. Oldhall occurs pp. 103 and 107 but not in ref. to a sum of 20s.

Item yeven to Pet*our* the fole by m*aster* chauncell*our* … viii d.

Item yeven in rewarde to Alis Bredkirke wydowe late servant to the olde lady Fithughe … vi s. viii d.

Item yeven in rewarde to my lorde prynces colyer by m*aster* chamb*erleyn* xii d. for iii q*u*arters of tryed gynger ii s. vi d. for ii lib. di. of tryakell iiii s. viii d. for a tynne potte w*ith* a cover for the same xiiii d. for a pounde i q*uarter* of powder <beyng> for my ladyes g*r*ace beyng at Rychemound xviii d. … x s. x d.

Item paid to m*aster* Seynt Johnys servant for rydyng for m*aster* chamb*er*ley[n] ayenst the kynges co*m*myng from Hatfeld to his place and ayene by iii days iii s. … iii s.

Item paid the last day of August to John Holt for ii tymes rydyng from Hatfeld to Greneweche to the kyng by iiii days ii s. viii d. and for <i>ii days rydyng w*ith* c*er*tayn plate to London and there abydyng by ii days at viii d. the day ii s. viii d. Item in rewarde to a taberett*our* at Newemarket iiii d. for a rewarde yeven to a servant of m*aster* Conysbyes for bryngyng of \c*er*tyn thyngg*es*/ <grece> to my ladyes g*r*ace iiii d. for a rewarde yeven to a heremyte xii d. for i day ryding from Chestham to Greneweche viii d. … vii s. viiid.[176]

Item paid to Rob*er*t Merbury the ii^{de} day of Septemb*er* <to Robert Merbury> for his cost*es* by ii days rydyng from Hatfeld to Bletsall to m*aster* chambrlen at xii d. the day … ii s.

Item in rewarde to s*ir* John Husseys sonnes … vi s. viii d.

Item yeven in rewarde to m*aster* Peckesall … x s.

Item paid the iiiith day of Septemb*er* to a Frenche man for \iii/ <a pec*e*> peces of counterfet arrys cont*eynyng* CCix styck*es* di. and di. q*uarter* at iii s. ii d. the stycke xxxiii li. iii s. ix d. qua. And to the same for a tapet co*nteynyng* xii stick*es* at iiii s. the sticke xlviii s. … xxxv li. xi s. ix d. qua.

Item paid the same tyme to John Democke of Andewarpe for ii blacke pec*e* of fustyn napys and i pece of tawney of the same ev*ery* pece co*nteynyng* xiiii yerd*es* at xx d. the yerd … lxx s.

Item paid to the same John Democke for i pece of blacke and i pece of tawney fustyn of napys co*nteynyng* bothe the pec*e* xxviii yerd*es*. The p*r*ic*e* in grete xliii s. iiii d. … xliii s. iiii d.

[M]Summa … xlvi li. xiiii s. iii d. qua.[P]

[*p. 100*] Item yeven in rewarde to the said John Democke … xx d.

Item paid to Rob*er*t Nesewyke for certyn <thyngg> ness*essaryes* by hym bought for my ladyes g*r*ace … vi s. viii d.

Item paid for my ladyes offeryng apon the Natyvyte of oure Lady by m*aster* Chamb*er* … v s.

Item yevyn in rewarde to a fry*our* of Cambryge for makyn a s*er*mond afore my ladyes g*r*ace apon the said Ladyes Day … x s.

[176] There is a dot calculation after the total.

Item paid in rewarde the xth day of Septemb*er* to < doct*our* Smyth> \master Baker/ for makyng of a s*er*mond afore my ladyes g*r*ace … vi s. viii d.

Item paid to John Holt for conveyng of letters to Cambryge … ii d.

Item paid to Nicholas Aughton for his cost*es* rydyng from Hatfeld to Richemound by ii dayes xvi d. for ii dayes rydyng from Hatfeld to Grenewyche xvi d. Item in lyke wyse ayene from Hatfeld to Grenewyche by ii days xvi d. for i day rydyng from Hatfeld to Waltham whan the <j> kyng*es* g*r*ace was there viii d. for i day rydyng from Tong*es* to Haveryng on the Bower to the kyng viii d. for i day rydyng from Tong*es* to a place of my lord of Seynt Johnys callyd Barwyke viii d. for iii days rydyng from Tong*es* to Eltham to the kyng ii s. for iii days from Tong*es* to Grenewyche to the kyng by iii days ii s. … x s.

Item paid in rewarde to Wynkyn the Worthy for bryngyng of bok*es* to my ladyes g*r*ace by J. Madeson … xii d.

Item paid the xith day of Septemb*er* to Nicholas Aughton for iii days rydyng from Tong*es* to Hanworth to the kyng … ii s.

Item paid the same tyme in rewarde to Wye the bysshop<ys> of Lyncoln servant by Rob*er*t Fremyngham … x s.

Item paid to Henr*y* Chychely and Will*ia*m Chychely for land*es* purchesyd of them in Malton by the hand*es* of m*aster* comptrol*our* … xxiii li. vi s. viii d.

Item yeven in rewarde to John Vanutryk my ladyes goldsmyth for his co*m*myng from London to Tongg*es* the <d> xvii day of Septemb*er* … xx d.

Item paid the same tyme to Rob*er*t Fremyngham for his cost*es* w*ith* ii horsys rydyng from Tongg*es* to my lorde of Wynchester and m*aster* Dudley w*ith* other by the space of iiii days at ii s. the day … viii s.

Item paid to Will*ia*m Hylmer of a pote w*ith* tryakyll of Jene … ii s. iiii d.

Item yeven in rewarde to the same for co*m*myng from London to Tongg*es* … iii s. iiii d.

Item yeven in rewarde to Thomas Case … iii s. iiii d.

Item yeven in rewarde to a servant of the bysshop of Lyncoln for co*m*myng to my ladyes g*r*ace to m*aster* deanys place for maters co*n*cernyng to hir g*r*ace … iii s. iiii d.

[M]Summa … xxvii li. xxi d.[P]

[*p. 101*] Item paid to Jamys Moryce for ii antefeners callyd brevys for Cryst*es* Colege … vi li. xiii s. iiii d.

Item to the same for v dd. of fyne parcheme[n]t … x s.

Item paid to the same for co*n*veying of ii letters of my ladyes from Cambryge to Nasyngton to m*aster* chauncell*our* … xvi d.

Item paid to the same for carynge of i lode of stuffe of the wardrob of robys from Cambryge to Hatfeld … v s.

<Item paid to Rob*e*rt Merbury for the <cos> cost*es* co*n*veying master Perkers chylderyn … iiii s.> «nichil hic quia postea»[177]

Item yeven in rewarde to m*aster* vichamberlens fawkener for kepyng of my ladyes tassell by m*aster* tresorer … v s.

Item yeven in rewarde to s*ir* Cleme[n]t the xixth day of Septemb*er* by m*aster* deane … vi s. viii d.

Item paid to Henr*y* Lodlowe for his q*uar*ter wag*es* endyng at Mychelmas last past … xx s.

Item paid for the berying of Will*i*am Laborer … ii s.

Item yeven in rewarde to Will*i*am Hylmer the last day of Septemb*er* by m*astres* Fowler … xx d.

Item yeven in rewarde to Perys Barbors dowter … vi s. viii d.

Item yeven in rewarde to the p*ar*ysshe clerke of Chesthaunt … viii d.

Item yeven in rewarde to mastres Bedell for the ocupying of hir howse callyd Tong*es* at my ladyes g*r*ace beyng there and hir servant*es* by vi wek*es* … xl s.

Item yeven in rewarde to mastres Wrenne for the logyng and the dyet of mastres Yon in hir howse … vi s. viii d.

Item yeven in rewarde to <t> the kep*er* of m*aster* deaynes place … iii s. iiii d.

Item yeven in rewarde to a <servant> gentylman of the kyng*es* chapell the vith day of Octob*er* … v s.

Item yeven in rewarde to a <servant of my lorde of Rochest*our*s for bryngyng of letters to my ladyes g*r*ace> <A> man of Seynt Albons for carying of leters from my ladyes g*r*ace to my lorde of Rochest*our* … xx d.

Item paid to m*astres* Jane Gore for hir quarters wag*es* endyng at Mychelmas last past … xiii s. iiii d.

Item paid to Hugh Carre for a sere clothe … xii d.

Item paid to Robert Ryse for the hyer of ii horsys by ii days carying of a chylde of the chapell to doct*our* Robynson xvi d. Item paid to the same for the hyer of ii horsys by iii days carying of m*aster* <chamberlyns chylderyn> Parkers chylderyn to m*aster* chamberlens ii s. … iii s. iiii d.

Item paid to Rob*e*rt Merbury for the dyett*es* of m*aster* Parkers chylderyn and of the said Robert and his servant from Hatfeld to Bletso by iii days w*ith* the mete of iiii horsys iii[178] s. x d. and for the hyer of his horse by the said iii days xvi d. … v s. ii d.

Item paid to the said Robert for his cost*es* by ii days w*ith* the hyer of his horse rydyng from Hatfeld to London to cary letters to the selyst*our* at xii d. the day … ii s.

[M]Summa … xiii li. xiii s. x d.[P]

[177] Add. in a very neat hand, with the entry vigorously canc. Perhaps included in the penultimate entry on this page (not elsewhere in the accounts).

[178] MS 'iiij', as if alt. to 'four', but not counted in the total.

[*p. 102*] Item yeven in rewarde to my ladyes browderers the xiiith day of Octob*er* by m*astres*[179] Fowler ... iii s. iiii d.

Item yeven in rewarde the same tyme to John Utrycks servant for bryngyng of c*er*tyn t[h]ynge*s* from London ... xii d.

Item paid to John Penred for the hyer of a horse by iii days for carying of a presoner from Hatfeld to the Marshallse aft*our* Crystemas last past xii d. and to the same for the hyer of a horse by v days to cary Coksey the fole to m*aster* Chaynes home ayene xx d. ... ii s. viii d.

Item paid to Will*i*am Hylmer the same tyme for ii pece*s* of blacke bokeram. P*r*i*ce* the pece ii s. viii d. ... v s. iiii d.

Item paid to the same for a slekyng stone ... ii d.

Item yeven in rewarde to m*aster* Morgan by m*astres* Fowler ... xl s.

Item yeven in rewarde to *master* Bedellys servant for bryngyng of a present ... iiii d.

Item paid the xvith day of Octob*er* to John Wyllyams for iiii days jorneying a fote to Cauntou*r*bury and ayene ... ii s. iiii d.

Item paid to John Holt for his cost*es* by ii days rydyng from Hatfeld to Grenewyche to the kyng ... xvi d.

Item yeven in rewarde to Jane Gowrys suster the xviiith day of Octob*er* ... v s.

Item yeven in rewarde to oon of the Bonams <at> \of/ Asryge for drawyng of a pycto*ur* of our*e* Lord apon a clothe by m*aster* Morgan ... iii s. iiii d.

Item delyv*er*ed to mastres Massey the xxiiiith day of Octob*er* to bye flex w*ith*all ... vi s. viii d.

Item paid the same tyme to Rob*er*t Hylton for lviii ellys of Normandy canvas \delyv*er*ed to m*astres* Masse/. P*r*i*ce* the elle iiii d. qua. xx s. <x d.> \vi d./ ob. For ii ellys of canvas for a bage for my ladyes stole. P*r*i*ce* viii d. Item for ii pece*s* of tawney fustyan for the use of the wardrob. P*r*i*ce* the pece ix s. xviii s. Item for ii pece*s* of blacke bokeran bought for the use of the same wardrob co*n*tenyng xv yerd*es*. P*r*i*ce* xi s. iiii d. which fustyan and bokeram is delyv*er*ed to m*astres* Fowler. Item for viii yerd*es* of kendall for a cote for m*aster* Parker at xii d. the yerd viii s. Item for viii yerd*es* of blacke cotyn for the lynyng of the same iii s. iiii d. To John God for makyng of the same viii d. Item for i yerde di. of scarlet for a payer of hosyn for the same m*aster* Parker <v s.> \vii s. vi d./. For lynyng and makyng of the same hosyn xii d. For i yerd di. of blacke for a payer of hosyn to the same m*aster* Parker. P*r*i*ce* the yerd ii s. viii d. iiii s. For lynyng and makyng of the said hosyn xii d. For a patlet of sarcenet redy made for the same m*aster* Parker vi s. For ii payer of shone for the same m*aster* Parker ii s. For i q*uarter* of tawney for to body and sleve yong m*aster* Parkers gowne xiiii d. Item <pa> for the cost*es* of the said Robert Hylton purveyng the said stuffe at London by i day viii d. ... iiii li. <vi s. vii d. ob.> \v s. x d. ob./

[M]Summa ... vii li. xvii s. <vii d.> \iiii d./ ob.[P]

[179] The scribe uses the contracted form for both masculine or feminine; 'mastres' is more likely with 'Fowler'.

[*p. 103*] Item paid to the said Robert Hylton for vi yerd*es* of satyn of Cypres for a kyrtell for my ladyes g*r*ace. P*ri*c*e* the yerd xii d. vi s. For ii yerd*es* di. of blacke cotyn for lynyng of the same at vi d. the yerde xxi d. For a holy water stocke w*ith* the sprynckyll vii d. For the cost*es* of the said Rob*er*t Hylton by i day for the p*ro*veciou*n* of the same xii d. For ii yerd*es* of blacke damaske. P*ri*c*e* the yerd vii s. iiii d. xiiii s. viii d. … xxiiii s.

Item paid to the same Rob*er*t Hylton for ii pec*es* of northyn medly for kyrtellys for my ladyes bedwomen. \P*ri*c*e*/ xlvi s. co*n*tenyng xxiiii yerd*es*. For i pece of whyte carsay cont*enyng* xviii yerd*es*. For dobelett*es* and hosyn for my ladyes bedmen. P*ri*c*e* xiiii s. x d. For a pece of blacke cotyn co*ntenyng* xxiiii yerd*es*. P*ri*c*e* <xix> \vi/ s. viii d. For iii pec*es* of blacke cotyn ev*er*y pece co*ntenyng* xxiiii yerd*es*. P*ri*c*e* xix s. viii d. For i pece of blacke lynyng playne co*ntenyng* ix yerd*es*. P*ri*c*e* vi s. viii d. Item for iii pec*es* of whyte wherof i pece is cotyn and ev*er*y pece co*ntenyng* xxiiii yerd*es* xvii s. viii d. For xxix godys of russet cotyn. P*ri*c*e* the gode vii d. ob. xviii s. i d. ob. For ii pec*es* of whyte fryce. P*ri*c*e* the pece xii s. xxiiii s. For vi pec*es* of brode whyte blanckett*es* ev*er*y pece co*ntenyng* xii yerd*es*. P*ri*c*e* lx s. For ii lib. of blewe threde. P*ri*c*e* the lib. xiiii d. ii s. iiii d. For ii lib. of blewe threde. P*ri*c*e* the <l> lib. xi d. xxii d. For ii lib. of blewe threde. P*ri*c*e* the lib. x d. xx d. For ii kyppys of lambe for the use of the wardrob the oon kyppe white and the other blacke. P*ri*c*e* viii s. ii d. For i dd. of russet bonett*es* for my ladyes bedmen. P*ri*c*e* vi s. viii d. … xi l. xiiii s. iii d. ob.

Item paid to the same Robert for vii dosyn of hosyn for my ladyes maundey. P*ri*c*e* the dd. iiii s. xxviii s. For a bonet for m*aster* Parker ii s. For a hat for the same m*aster* Parker ii s. For a corde to packe the fardell iiii d. For packyng of the same ii d. Item paid to the said Rob*er*t Hylton for hys cost*es* by iiii days <byng> bying of the said stuffe vi s. viii d. For the cost*es* of Olyver Holand by i day xii d. … xls ii d.

A pardon of Rome. Item paid the xxiiiith day of Octob*er* to the p*ar*doner of the hospytall of Seynt Thomas of Rome … xii d.

Item paid the same tyme to Peto*ur* Oldehalle for i lib. of slevyd silke wayng xvi ounc*es*. P*ri*c*e* the unc*e* x d. xiii s. iiii d. For iiii unc*es* of sylke rybon <w>. P*ri*c*e* the unc*e* x d. iii s. iiii d. Item for i lib. of blacke worsted purffull xiiii d. … xvii s. x d.

[M]Summa … xv li. xvii s. iii d. ob.[P]

[*p. 104*] *Nota*. Item paid in rewarde to hym that goith w*ith* the kyng*es* camell … xx d.

Item paid the xxvth day of Octob*er* to mastres Lynche for ii lib. of golde of Venys. P*ri*c*e* the lib. xxv s. l s. and for i q*uarter* of a lib. of blewe Venyes sylke ix s. iiii d. … lix s. iiii d.

Item paid to Robert Fremyngham the xxviiith day of Octob*er* for his cost*es* by vii days w*ith* ii horsys and his s*er*vant rydyng from Hatfeld to the kyng to Greneweche and so to hir councell lernyd at London for the mater of John Madeson and other app*er*tenyng to my lady at ii s. the day … xiiii s.

Item to the same Rob*er*t for a letter myssyve <obteny> obtayned of the kyng for the mater of the said John Madeson … xii d.[180]

[180] There is a dot calculation after the total.

Item paid for my ladyes offeryng apon All Halowe Day … v s.

Item paid the ii^{de} day of Novemb*er* to Roger Ratclyffe for a tymber of gray x s. for halfe a furre of shanckes viii s. for i skynne of mynckes ii s. iiii d. … xx s. iiii d.

Item paid the same tyme to Nicholas Aughton for iii days rydyng to the kyng from <Hatfeld> \m*aster* deanyes place/ to Greneweche at viii d. the day … ii s.

Item paid to the same for rydyng from Hatfeld to the Tower to the kyng by iii days w*ith* ii horsys … iiii s.

Item paid to the said Nicholas for money paid for the cost*es* of two fryers by oon nyght at Waltham Crosse … viii d.

Item paid to Hugh Carre for his cost*es* rydyng to Dover by iiii days goyng and co*m*myng w*ith* his bote hyer … iii s. <d> iiii d.

Item paid to Petou*r* Baldwyn for iii s[u]peraltarys[181] oon of marbyll and ii made w*ith* slate <gary> garnysshed w*ith* tymber. P*ri*ce … x s.

Item paid to Rob*er*t Fremyngham the viiith day of Novemb*er* for goyng by water from London to Greneweche to delyv*er* my lad*ys* letters unto the kyng*es* g*r*ace and to speke w*ith* my lorde of Wynchester for letters to be devysed unto the pope w*ith* the den*er* of hym and his s*er*vant … xii d.

Item yeven in rewarde to a man that brought my lad*ys* g*r*ace <pounde> pownegarnett*es* from London … vi d.

Item paid the same tyme to Edmond Tymys for the scowryng of ii pec*es* of verders w*ith* hangyng of grapys … viii s.

Item yeven in rewarde to a s*er*vant of Wynkyn the Worthyes for bryngyng of bok*es* to my lady … xii d.

Item paid to m*aster* comptrollou*r* the xiiith day of Septemb*er* for ii dd. yerd*es* of northyn medly for the almesfolke xlvi s. viii d. for another dd. of northyn medly for the same almesfolke xxii s. for the portage of the same i d. … lxviii s. ix d.

Item paid the same tyme to the said comptrollou*r* for money by hym delyv*er*ed to Thomas Soper for my ladyes causys … vi li. xiii s. iiii d.

Item paid to the said Thomas Soper for the inrollyng of a dede of feffement for mastres Stannop iiii s. … iiii s.

^{M}Summa … xvi li. xvii s. xi d.^{P}

[*p. 105*] Item paid to Rob*er*t Fremyngham for the borde of John Sedyngton my ladyes scoler by the space of x wek*es* at viii d. the weke vi s. viii d. and for his cost*es* of his beryall at Seynt Albons vi s. viii d. … xiii s. iiii d.

Item yeven in rewarde to Hugh Pole for the cost*es* and charg*es* of the <swete> sewte of his benyfyce of Manerbere lying in the dyesys of Seynt Davyes by m*aster* confessou*r* … xx s.

[181] MS 'Senperaltarys'.

Item yeven in rewarde to master Parker the xvth day of Novemb*er* by m*astres* Fowler … xx s.

Item yeven in rewarde the same tyme to my lady Elizabeth Norton … vi s. viii d.

Item to hir s*er*vant in rewarde for bryngyng of pownegarnett*es* and orygyns … xx d.

Item paid to Gasyon for nedellys and thymbellys … ii s. viii d.

Item yeven in rewarde to John Plowfeld … xx d.

Item paid to s*ir* Thomas Mawdysle for a frontelat of gold … xxiii s. iiii d.

Item yeven in rewarde to m*aster* Bedellys mayde … iiii d.

Item paid to Lenard l*e* Fevo*ur* for ii bok*es* … viii d.

Item paid to John Buckberd customer of London for certyn lenyn clothe bought by Gasyon and delyv*er*ed at Crystemas the last yere anno xxiii° H. viith … xlvi s.

Item yeven in rewarde to Humfrey Walcot for his cost*es* and expenc*es* syttyng in the p*ar*tyes of Lyncoln apon the retayners … xx s.

Item yeven in rewarde to the pryores and covent of Sympryngham by Humfrey Walcot … xx s.

Item in rewarde to my lady Sowgh nonne in the said pryores by the said Humfrey … x s.

Item yeven in rewarde to the pryores and covent of Catle <by> … vi s. viii d.

Item yeven in rewarde to Edward Asshewyn for his cost*es* and expenc*es* bryngyng of John Asshewyn his sonne to my ladyes g*r*ace from Rypley … v s.

Item paid to Nicholas Aughton for his cost*es* by ii days rydyng from Hatfeld to Bedyngton to the kyng at viii d. … xvi d.

Item paid to the same for iiii days rydyng from Hatfeld to Rypley w*ith* his <ii> s*er*vaunt and ii horsys to feche my lad*ys* fole at xvi d. the day … v s. iiii d.

Item to the same Nicholas for money delyv*er*ed unto the father of the said fole to brynge hym to Hatfeld xx d. … xx d.

Item to the said Nicholas for rydyng from Hatfeld to Grenewyche to the kyng w*ith* i horse by ii days … xvi d.

Item paid to the said Nicholas for <his> the cost*es* of the said Edward Asshewyn and his two sonnys at Madewellys … iiii d.

Item yeven in rewarde to Richard Stewkely for goyng to Cambryge by m*astres* Fowler … xx d.

Item paid to the p*ar*doner of the guylde of Jhesus in the towne at Grantham … xx d.

[182]Summa … x li. xi s. iiii d.[P]

[182]The signature is lost in a mended tear.

[*p. 106*] Item paid to Richard Atherton for his cost*es* by ii days rydyng to my lady <Scro> Scrope w*ith* ii horse … xvi d.

Item paid the xxiiiith day of Novemb*er* to mastres Massey for flax iii s. iiii d. for spynnyng of ii lib. of flax v d. for wevyng of the same v s. x d. for ii lib. of [f]laxe vi d. for di. stone of wolle <v d.> viii d. for spynnyng of ii lib. of wolle vi d. for iii payer of shoys for the chylderyn ix d. for laces viii d. for tryakyll i d. for sewg*er* <candyth> candyth ii d. for pyllyd*es* i d. for whyte bred iiii d. for ale i d. for whyte bred vi d. for butt*er* ix d. for mendyng of a payer of hosyn i d. for pynnes ii d. for makyng of Margaret Lodlowys kyrtellys xiiii d. for pyllydys for Richard Laborer and a chekon ii d. for mylke ii d. for candell*es* i d. for spynnyng of hard*es* ii d. for iii lib. of flax vii d. for warpyng of clothe iiii d. for shone for the almes folke vi s. … xxiii s. vii d.[183]

Item paid the same tyme to Rob*er*t Hylton for viii yerd*es* of blacke velvet at x s. viii d. the yerde and ii yerd*es* di. and the nayle at x s. iiii d. the yerde. Cxii[184] <x> s. ix d. ob. qua./ For vii yerd*es* of crane coleryd satyn at vi s. iiii d. the yerde xliiii s. iiii d. For vii tymbers of letys for the gentylwomen gownys which be at my ladyes fyndyng at vii s. the tymber xlix s. For a furre of shanck*es* for the gentylwomen workedays gownys xvi s. For a furre of pultys for my ladyes g*ra*ce vii s. iiii d. For vi yerd*es* of tawney medly for workeday gownys for m*aster* Parker and mastres Jan at iiii s. ii d. the yerd xxv s. For iii yerd*es* of tawney <mwsy> medly for m*astres* Perot at <ii d.> iii s. iiii d. the yerd x s. For xxx yerd*es* of whyte cotyn at vii d. the gode xvii s. vi d. For xxvi yerd*es* of blacke cotyn at viii d. the gode xvii s. <vi d.> iiii d. <for> Item to a porter for bryngyng of the same from Blackwell Haull to Coldeharborogh ii d. … xiiii li. xviii s. <viii d.> \v d. ob. qua./

Item paid to the same Rob*er*t Hylton for xlviii skynnes of blacke bodge at vii d. l*e* pece xxviii s. For xlviii skynnes of blacke bodge at v d. xx s. For xxiiii skynnes of blacke bodge at vi d. xii s. for m*aster*[185] Parker. For a yerd i q*uarter* di. of scarlet for the said m*aster* Parker at iiii s. ii d. vi s. ii d. Item for i yerd i q*uarter* di. of blacke carsey for m*aster* Parker iii s. viii d. For iii yerd*es* of Wynchester russet for ii payer of hosyn for m*aster* Parker vi s. viii d. For iii yerd*es* of whyte fustyan for m*aster* Parker xix d. ob. For a bonet for the said m*aster* Parker ii s. iiii d. … iiii li. v d. ob.

Item paid to the said Rob*er*t Hylton for vii dd. of whyte cappys for my ladyes maundy at v s. l*e* dd. which be delyvered into the kepyng of m*astres* Masse<y> xxxv s. and for the caryage of them iiii d. … xxxv s. iiii d.

[M]Summa … xxi li. xix s. ii d. ob. qua.[186]

[*p. 107*] Item yeven in rewarde to the kynge wayte … iii s. iiii d.

Item yeven in rewarde to master Varnam the xxvth day of Novemb*er* … iii s. iiii d.

Item paid the same tyme to Pet*our* Oldehaulle for ix ownc*es* of sylke rebon. P*ri*c*e* the unc*e* x d. … vii s. vi d.

[183] There is a dot calculation in the left margin.

[184] MS 'xjj'; the total is much altered but correct.

[185] MS 'mt[abbrev. for 'master']ster'.

[186] There is a tear which may have included a lost 'probatur'.

Item paid to Robert Merbury for his cost*es* by xii days rydyng into Notynghamshere to take possession of *cer*tyn land*es* for the joynter of mastres Stannop … xii s.

Item paid the xxviith day of November to Thomas Goldsmyth for the maryage \of/ mastres Merbury oon of my ladyes gentylwoman … vi li. xiii s. iiii d.

Item delyv*er*ed the same tyme to my ladyes g*r*ace for hir almes porse by mastres Fowler … xiii li. vi s. viii d.

Item paid to Nicholas Aughton the iiith day of Decemb*er* for ii days rydyng from Hatfeld to Wansted to the kyng xvi d. and in lyke wyse for ii days rydyng to Greneweche to the kyng xvi d. … ii s. viii d.

Item paid to John Holt for ii days rydyng to my lorde of Wynchester w*ith* letters to London xvi d. Item to the same for rydyng to London w*ith* master Parker by ii days xvi d. Item paid to the said Holt for rydyng to s*ir* Will*iam* Sȝaye m*aster* boteler and to the baillyffe of Ware w*ith* letters by i day viii d. … iii s. iiii d.

Item paid the iiith day of Decemb*er* to Richard Atherton for ii days rydyng to Bromely to my lorde of Rochesto*ur* … xvi d.

Item paid to Thomas Chayne of the chapell for caryage of his stuffe from London to Hatfeld … iii s. iiii d.

Item paid to Peto*ur* Baldwyn for ii payer of tabellys w*ith* the men. P*ri*ce … xx d.

Item paid to m*aster* chauncello*ur* for money sent unto my lady Shyrley inclosyd in <a> my ladyes letter for a tokyn … xx s.

Item paid to Edward Vauce for the cost*es* of the fechyng of m*aster* Varnam of Baldocke by iii days in and out … iii s.

Item the iiiith day of Decemb*er* to Rob*er*t Hylton for M di. of blacke anglett*es* for the use of the wardrob viii d. For ii lib. of whyte threde xxii d. the which is in the kepyng of m*astres* Fowler … ii s. vi d.

Item delyv*er*ed the viiith day of Decemb*er* for my ladyes offeryn apon the Co*n*sepciou*n* of [oure][187] Lady to George F*r*aunc*es* … v s.

[M]Summa … xxiii li. ix s.[P]

[*p. 108*] Item yeven in rewarde to Molson excheter of Lyncolnshere the ixth day of Decemb*er* … xx s.

Item yeven in rewarde the same tyme to master Tanne for makyng of a s*er*mond byfore my lad*ys* g*r*ace … x s.

Item paid to Nicholas Aughton in rewarde the xth day of Decemb*er* … vi s. viii d.

Item yeven in rewarde to oon of the Bonamys of Asryge for makyng of a s*er*mond the same tyme … vi s. viii d.

Item yeven in rewarde to s*ir* John <Belany> Belamy for *cer*tyn bokys of pryckesongg*es* by m*aster* Drace … xx s.

[187] Om. MS.

Item paid to Henr*y* Lodlowe the xii[th] day of December for his q*uar*ters wages endyng at Crystemas next co*m*myng … xx s.

Item paid to Richard Cotmot in rewarde the same tyme … vi s. viii d.

Item paid the same tyme to John Holt for a vestement w*ith* all thyngg*es* therto belongyng \for the chapell at Wynbo*ur*ne/ … xxvi s. viii d.

Item to the same for iii yerd*es* di. of here to ley upon the auto*ur* at the chapell of the said Wynbo*ur*ne … xiiii d.

Item paid to the said Holt for ii crewett*es*. P*r*ice viii d. … viii d.

Item paid the same tyme to Will*iam* Laborer for \his/ cost*es* w*ith* i horse rydyng from Hatfeld to Cambryge […] by iii days at viii d. the day … ii s.

Item yeven in rewarde to m*aster* Morys Seynt John s*er*vant*es* … vi s. viii d.

Item yeven in rewarde to mastres Elyn Massyngham … vi s. viii d.

Item paid to Thomas Robertson of Bostone for a pece of blacke velvet. P*r*ice xi li. xvi s. viii d. For a pece of blewe velvet. P*r*ice xi li. xviii s. iiii d. For a pece of blacke satyn. P*r*ice xi li. xviii s. vii d.[188] For a pece of blacke damaske. Pr*ice* vii li. xviii s. x d. Item paid for the cost*es* of the said sylk*es* from the marte to Calys vi s. viii d. … xliii li. xix s. i d.

Item paid to Will*iam* Hylmer for di. unc*e* of fyne amver grene. P*r*ice xx s. For i lib. of rawe sylke xiii s. iiii d. For iii q*uarter* of a lib. of fyne grayne ii s. For Ci drame of fyne gold v s. iiii d. For ii dramys of fyne perlys xii d. For vi dramys of fyne senamom iii d. For vi dramys linguin aloes iiii d. For C of quene appollys viii d. Item paid to the same for his cost*es* rydyng to London and home ayene w*ith* the p*ro*veciou*n* of the said stuffe there by iiii days iiii s. iiii d. … xlvii s. iii d.

Item yeven in rewarde to John Willyams by m*astres* Fowler … xx d.

Item yeven in rewarde to Robert Nesewyke by m*astres* Fowler … xii d.

Item yeven in rewarde to a s*er*vant of master Bokleys for bryngyng of a gosehalke by m*aster* vichamberlen … xx s. «nota non solvitur»[189]

[M]Summa … liiii li. ii s. x d.[P]

[*p. 109*] Item yeven in rewarde the xix[th] day of Decemb*er* to s*ir* John Mason … vi s. viii d.

[190]Item paid unto Thomas Maydwell for a payre of buskynce for my lad*ys* g*r*ace delyvered the xx[th] day of May … vi d.

Item for makyng of a payr*e* of shoes the same tyme … iiii d.

Item at mydsom*ur* for a pair*e* of sleppers … vi d.

Item the same tyme for a payr*e* of blak shoez … vi d.

[188] MS 'vjj'.
[189] Add. very faint in the very neat hand of pp. 98 and 101.
[190] The MW hand returns here and appears to be copying up earlier items.

Item at Barthelmewe tyde last past a payr*e* of shoes … vi d.

Item <th> on Seynt Edward*es* Day to my lad*ys* g*r*ace for a pair*e* of dowbyl-solyd shone … viii d.

Item a payr*e* of buskynce and pynsons … iii s. ii d.

Item a pair*e* of sleppers on Seynt <S> Nicholas Day for my lad*ys* g*r*ace … vi d.

Item delyv*er*ed the xxi day of Decembr*e* to maistres Stannop for a reward yeven unto a <*ser*ande> *ser*vande of maistres Odell for the bryngyng of *cer*ten chesis to my lad*ys* g*r*ace … ii s. iiii d.

Item payd unto m*aister* countroller the xxiiii day of Decembr*e* for two corsis for claspis to two premers of my lad*ys* g*r*ace … ii s. iiii d.

Item delyv*er*ed to m*aister* P*ar*ker by maistres Jan on Crystemasse even by my lad*ys* comaundement … xx s.

Item to George Fraunc*es* for my lad*ys* offrynge on Crystemasse day in golde v s. and in money x s. … xv s.

Item on Seynt Thomas Day delyv*er*ed to my lad*ys* g*r*ace to play by the hand*es* of George Fraunc*es* … vi s. viii d.

Item delyv*er*ed to maistres Foller on New Yer*es* even for my lad*ys* g*r*ace to be yeven in New Yer*es* yeft*es* … xiii li. vi s. viii d.

Item for my lad*ys* offryng apon New Yer*es* day … v s.

Item in reward to Steven Taberet … iii s. iiii d.

Item to \a/ *ser*vande of thabott*es* of Westm*ynster* for the bryngyng of New Yer*es* gyft*es* … x s.

Item to Peris Champion in reward for the <by> bryngyng of the kyng*es* Newergyft*es* to my lad*ys* g*r*ace … C s.

Item in reward to m*aister* awdit*ur* *ser*vand delyv*er*ed by maistres Foller … ii s.

Item in reward to doctor Roper þ*at* prechit afour*e* my lad*ys* g*r*ace on New Yer*es* day … x s.

[M]Summa … xxii li. xix s. iiii d.[191]

[*p. 110*] Item delyv*er*ed to maistres Massy for a reward yeven to a man of Assheryge that brought rose water to my lad*ys* g*r*ace … iii s. viii d.

Item to the same for a reward yeven unto Petur*e* of Coldherboro … v s.

Item in reward yeven to Wernam of Baldok … iii s. iiii d.

Item to m*aister* tresorer for money payd to Jamys <J> Gentyll for vii yerd*es* of fyne orege coller satten at viii s. iiii d. the yerd … lviii s. iiii d.

Item paid to maister Parker for his *ser*vand*es* waige for a half yere endyd at <Cy> Crystemasse … xiii s. iiii d.

[191] Signed but not approved.

Item paid for a bonett and a frontlett bought by John Res for maistres Heron xx s. and for a purfell of whit letice xi s. iiii d. and for the makyng of a gowne xx d. Summa … xxxiii s.

Item for my lad*ys* offryng apon the Twelft Day … v s.

Item delev*er*ed the xxvi day of M*ar*che by the hand*es* of Jamys Morice to Cryst*es* Collage … lxxix li.

Item paid unto John Brydde on the Twelft Even for purchasyng of a howse for the vicarege of Helpston by my lad*ys* comaundement w*i*th the byldyng of a parlor and chambo*ur* and makyng of two chymneyes w*i*th dores and wyndoes and other rep*ar*acions their*e* … x li.

Item paid the same day unto Gerard Godfryde and Nicholas Spernig of Cambrige stacioners for dyv*er*se bok*es* for my lad*ys* g*r*ace as aperith by byll*es* therof remay[ny] ng w*i*th my lad*ys* g*r*ace … xxviii li. iii s. iiii d.

Item to the same stacioners for money paid by my lord of Rochester for other dyv*er*se book*es* bought for my lad*ys* g*r*ace to the summa of … ix li. xix s. x d.

Item in reward to Henr*y* the kyng*es* godson for the bryngyng of c*er*ten boxes and oreng to my lad*ys* g*r*ace … xiii s. iiii d.

Item paid unto Rob*er*t Merbury for his cost*es* from Hatfeld to Richemound and their*e* abydyng by vii daies for hymself and his horse … vii s.

Item to Nicholas Trygg to delyv*er* to the ancryse of Stamforth in almes … v s.

MSumma … Cxxxiiii li. x s. ii d.P [192]

[*p. 111*] Item paid unto Roger Elys prest in suyng to the kyng*es* councell from the xiith day of Septembr*e* unto the xxi day of the same moneth for ii placard*es* \iiii s./ derected to Glyndor Dewy Keneth Owyn[193] for certen causes and for his exspenc*e* \ii s. viii d./ by the said space … vi s. viii d.

Item paid the ix day of January unto Rob*er*t Hylton for a tymber of gray for my lad*ys* g*r*ace … ix s. iiii d.

Item for a furre and a half of gray at xvi s. the furre … xxiiii s.

Item for xxi yerd*es* q*u*art*er* of tawny sarcenett at iii s. vi d. the yerd delyv*er*ed to maistres Foller … lxxiiii s. iiii d. ob.

Item for a yerd di. of grene clothe for my lad*ys* borde in hir clossed. Price the yerd iii s. Summa … iiii s. vi d.

Item for two pec*es* of sengull sypers the on pec*e* at ii s. viii d. and the other pec*e* at xx d. Summa … iiii s. iiii d.

Item for two skarlett bonett*es*. P*r*ice the bonett ix d. … xviii d.

[192] There is a dot calculation to the right at the foot of the page.

[193] MS 'Glyndordewy Kentleith owyn'. Obscure, but emended here as if the names of Welshmen, viz. Glyndor (Glyndwr, i.e. Glendower), Dewy (Dewi, i.e. David), and Owyn (Owain, viz. Owen). 'Kentleith' is less explicable, but might be an attempt at Cenydd (i.e. Kenneth).

Item for a yerd of blak sarsynett for a typett for my lad*ys* grace … iii s. viii d.

Item for iii yerd*es* of plonket rybon at viii d. the yerd … ii s.

Item for yonge maistres P*ar*ker iiii popett*es*. Price … i d. ob.

Item for a C of whit bogie for a furre for m*aister* <Soughe> \Souche/ … xxvii s. iiii d.

Item for the same a yerd i q*uarter* of Wenchest*er* russett for the same … ii s. vi d.

Item for a blak bonett bought for the same … ii s. viii d.

Item bought by the same Rob*er*t Hylton xxiiii yerd*es* of northeryn medly for thuse of the wardrop at xx d. the yerd … xl s.

Item for xxiiii yerd*es* of yellowe cotton for my lord of mysrewle. Price the yerd vi d. Summa … xii s.

Item paid to John Applis for cariage of the same stuff … viii d.

Item paid unto the same Rob*er*t Hylton for a furre of gray for the p*er*fourmyng of my lad*ys* gowne … xvi s.

Item for xx skynnes of grey bought for the egge of the same gowne. Price … iii s. vi d.

Item for a tymber of lett*es* for the p*er*fourmyng of the gentylwomens gownes at hir fyndyng … vii s.

Item paid unto Madwell for iiii pair*e* of shoes bought for m*aister* P*ar*ker at x d. the pair*e* … iii s. iiii d.

Item for makyng and lynyng of iiii pair*e* of hose for the same m*aister* P*ar*ker … iii s. iiii d.

Item payd for ii pair*e* of shoes for Henry Baptist … xvi d.

Item for the makyng and lynyng of <l> a payre of hose … viii d.

Item for ii yerd*es* iii q*uarter* of fustian bought for the same … xix d.

[M]Summa … xii li. xix s. ob.[P]

[*p. 112*] *R. Hylton.*[194]

Item paid unto the same Rob*er*t Hylton for a yerd q*uarter* of tawny fustian for a pair*e* of sleves for Stowell my lad*ys* warde … viii d. ob.

Item for makyng and lynyng of a pair*e* of howse for the same Stowell … vii d.

Item paid t*o* the same for the lynyng of iiii pair*e* of hose for the iiii almesmen … ii s.

Item delyv*er*ed to maistres Foller for a reward yeven to John fotman at his goyng from Hatfeld … xx s.

Item to the same for a reward yeven unto Thomas Casse at his beyng at Hatfeld … v s.

[194] Bracketed to include the next three items.

Item money delyv*er*ed to Petur brotherer to bye c*er*ten stuff at London for my lad*ys* g*r*ace … vii li. x s.

Item delyv*er*ed to maistres Massy at hir goyng into Leycet*ur*shir*e* … xx s.

Item paid unto John Brydde for his cost*es* ridyng to s*ir* Rauff Sherleys by the space of iii daies xx d. by the day … v s.

Item paid unto Lenard of the vestry for the byndyng of v book*es* of my lord of Rochest*er* sermond*es* xx d. Item for a game of chessemen to my lad*ys* g*r*ace viii d. … ii s. iiii d.

Item in reward unto maist*er* Fawne that <pr> preched afour*e* my lad*ys* g*r*ace in Crystemasse … vi s. viii d.

Item in reward to m*aister* Conysby at his beyng at Hatfeld … xx s.

Item in reward to his clerk … iii s. iiii d.

Item paid unto Rob*er*t Hylton for ii pounde of yerne bought by John Collop for my lad*ys* carpett*es* … ii s. iiii d.

Item paid unto John Haryson for dyv*er*se stuff bought for the dysgyseng*es* and playes in Crystemasse w*i*th xx s. yeven to the same John in reward as aperith by a booke therof made in the countynghowse. The summa … xiiii li. viii s. <xi d.> ii d. ob.

Item in reward to dyv*er*se of the chappell þ*at* plaied in Cryste*n*masse … xx s.

[M]Summa … xxx li. xvi s. <x d. ob.> \ii d./[P]

[*p. 113*] Item paid unto Ric*hard* Aderton the ix day of January for his cost*es* ridyng from Hatfeld to Carlile by the space of xxii daes at viii d. a day … xv s.

Item to the same in reward for his delygent labor … x s.

Item paid unto Thomas Sop*er* my lad*ys* solicit*ur* for the rest apon his accompt by the hand*es* of m*aister* countroller … xiii li. xii s. <vii> viii d.

Item payd to Lenard of the vestry for paper riall and parchement … iii s. iiii d.

<Item paid unto Henr*y* Lodlow for a q*uarter* waiges endett at Crystemas last … xx s. «nichil hic quia»[195]

Item unto John Mondy by the hand*es* of maist*er* countroller for a cuppe of golde for the kyng*es* Newer*es* gyft*es* … C li.

Summa … <Cxvi li. xii d. [P]> \Cxv li. xii d./

Nota. Item paid the xth day of January to Olyver Scalis for his cost*es* and exspenc*e* ridyng from Cambrige unto Hatfeld and so to Seynt Davis in Walis and for the makyng of two proxies for the resignacion of Man*er*bere as aperith by a byll assigned … lxi s. xi d.

Item unto m*aister* Par*ker* for money delyv*er*ed unto hym … vi s. viii d.

[195] See p. 108 above.

Item paid unto Rob*er*t Hylton for iii yerd*es* di. of crane collerd clothe for a cote for m*aister* P*ar*ker. Price … xvii s. vi d. \xxiiii s. ii d./[196]

Item paid unto the same Rob*er*t Hylton for a pece of blak chamlett for cotes to the two fotmen … xix s. iiii d.

Item for two pair*e* of hose for the said fotmen … viii s.

Item paid unto m*aister* Skott of Cryst*es* Collage in Cambryge for the <Es> exspenc*e* of Thomas Pellett from the xvii day of August in the xxii yere of our*e* sov*er*aigne lord kyng Henr*y* the viith unto the fest of the Nativitie of C*r*iste in the xxiiii yere of our*e* said sov*er*aigne lord as aperith by a byll therof \ov*er*/ <w*i*th> xxvi s. viii d. paid by Jamys Morice … lxviii s. viii d.

Item paid unto Nicholas Trevyrne for his cost*es* by two daies from Hatfeld to London on my lad*ys* message … xvi d.

Summa … Cxx<v>\iiii/ li. iiii s. v d.^{P}

<MCCCxlix li. v s. i d. qua.>[197]

[*p. 114*] Item delyv*er*ed to maistres Foller for a reward yeven unto Elyzabeth Stafferton at hir beyng at Hatfeld … <xiii s. iiii d.> xiii s. iiii d.

Item in reward to William Buk grome of the butre … iii s. iiii d.

Item paid unto Petur browtherer for his cost*es* to London iii daies w*i*th the hire of his horse … iii s.

Item to the same for a case for a challis by hym bought … iiii d.

Item delyv*er*ed to Jamys Morice by the hand*es* of m*aister* Skott toward*es* the byldyng of Cryst*es* Collage … for þe sup*er*plusage of hys acompt <pro> for þis yere … lxix s. v d.

Summa … iiii li. ix s. v d.

[198]Somme of all the hole allowance and paymentes aforsaid in this yere anno xxiii^{cio} regis Henrici vii^{mi} … MCClxxi li. vii s. xi d. qua. «þat is to wit»[199]

<And so he owethe … Diiii^{xx}viii li. viii s. ix d. ob. qua.>

«quia post allocaciones postscriptum»[200]

And so he oweth … Diiii^{xx}viii li. viii s. ix d. ob. qua.

«serche for further allowance in \the/ iiiith leff next ensuyng»[201]

[196] The sum ab. l. is the total of the previous two entries, add. small after the total (not in the MW hand).

[197] The total to date, written small to the right after the 'Summa' and canc.

[198] The summary hand returns here, perhaps on this page as the 'sprawling' hand.

[199] Add. small.

[200] Written small to the right between the two sums. Canc. because repeated (and also at p. 122 below).

[201] i.e. four folios further on, p. 122. Written small to the right in the 'sprawling' hand, as is the note above it.

[*p. 115*] *As in*[202]

Almes yeven to div*er*se p*er*sones at sondry tymes … vi li. ix s. i d.

Money delyv*er*ed at div*er*s tymes unto my ladyes g*r*ace as to her almose po*ur*se w*ith* x li. delyv*er*ed unto her g*r*ace at the co*ur*te … xxxix li. xvi s. viii d.

Money delyv*er*ed to my lady at div*er*s tymez for her offering*es* … xii li. xiii d.

A vestment and other stuff bought and yevon unto <the> Wymbo*ur*ne mynster this yere … xxviii s. vi d.

lix li. xv s. iiii d.[203]

Certen neccess*a*rie stuff as certen fresez and cottons of sondre colo*ur*s and bonett*es* w*ith* many other neccess*a*riez bought by Rob*er*t Hilton and other as well for my ladys almosse men and women as for my ladys mawndy and for many other pore folk*es* as nede requyreth this yere … xxiii li. xiii s.

Money delyv*er*ed to Jane Gower \xl s./ for her wagez for iii q*u*art*er*s and Henry Ludlowe \lx s./ for his fee for iii q*u*art*er*s … C s.

Certen wolen cloth bought for the warderope this yer*e* … lxiii s. vi d.

Money yeven to Elizabeth Merbury at her mariage … vi li. xiii s. iiii d.

[*p. 116*] Exhibicion of div*er*se scolers at my ladyes fyndyng at sondrie placez þ*a*t is to say for Thomas Pellett lxviii s. viii d. Thomas Bury lxxiiii s. iiii d. for the fawkneris sonn*e* xli s. vi d. ob. for m*aster* Colyngwode xl s. and for Stanbank at Parice xx s. In all … xii li. iiii s. vi d. ob.

Certen stuff bought for Herry the kyng*es* godd*es* sonn*e* \xvi s. iiii d./ and for Henry Baptist \iii s. viii d./ for this yer*e* … xx s.

li li. xiiii s. iiii d. ob.[204]

Cxi li. ix s. viii d. ob.[205]

Certen lynen cloth bought and also canvas … lxxiii s. ob.

Monye delyv*er*ed for a gowne for m*aster* Seynt Johns daughter therwyth to be bought … xx s.

iiii li. xiii s. ob.[206]

Money paijd by m*aster* Asheton my ladyes rec*eyver* unto Charles Brandon for the full payement of the maner of Gotehill for Wymbo*ur*ne mynster for the fyndyng of a prest to sing ther for my ladyes aunsyto*ur*z for ever*e* … C li.

Money paied for the tith of Coldeherburgh … liii s. iiii d.

[202] Bracketed in the margin to include all the items below, pp. 115–22 (first entry only).
[203] The total of the four items above, bracketed to the right of the items.
[204] The total of the two items above and the last four items on p. 115, bracketed to the right of the items; it occurs on p. 115 but is placed here as its most relevant position.
[205] The total of the items so far, bracketed to the right of the items and the two mid-page totals; it occurs on p. 115 but is placed here as its most relevant position.
[206] The total of the two items above, bracketed to the right of the items.

Exhibicion of div*er*se of my ladyes wardez þ*a*t is to say Henr*y* Lowe xxvi s. x d. Thomas Burgon iiii s. ii d. for young Stowell xv d. ob. and for the heirez of Herons xxxiii s. iiii d. In all … lxv s. vii d. ob.

Cxviii s. xi d. ob.[207]

[*p. 117*] Certen necc*essar*ie stuff bought by my lad*ys* co*m*maundement … Cxix s. ii d.

Certen stuff bought for the p*ro*pre use of my lad*ys* g*r*ace … iiii li. ii s. iii d.

A standyng bedd bought for my lad*ys* g*r*ace this yer*e* … xl s.

Certen furrez bought for my lad*ys* g*r*ace and other this yer … xi li. x s. vii d.

… xxxiii li. xii s.[208]

Div*er*se peces and yerd*es* of blake velvet \lxvi li. xviii s. v d./ certen yerd*es* of blake saten \xxi li. xi s. iii d./ i pece xv yerd*es* and i q*ua*rt*er* of russet damaske \xii li. xv s. v d./ and div*er*se yerd*es* of sersynet \xii li. vii s. i d. ob./ … Cxiii li. xii s. ii d. ob.

Nota. Certen necc*essar*ie spic*es* and other necc*essar*ie stuff bought by Will*i*am Hilmer for medysynes for my lad*ys* g*r*ace this yer … vii li. xiiii s. viii d.

Certen workyng gold of Venyce and flat gold and other gold and silver wyer \xxxiiii[209] li. xiii s. iiii d./ Certen raw silk*es* bought at sondry tymez \iiii li. iii s./ In all … xxxviii li. xvi s. iiii d.

Ciiii^{xx}iii li. xv s. ii d. ob.[210]

Certen stuff bought by m*aster* Cowp*er* þ*a*t was the lady of Norff[olkes] … xx s.

Certen small book*es* imprynted for my ladys g*r*ace withe the bynding of certen of them and for velom and p*ar*chement bought by Leonard of the chapell … xliiii s. viii d.

lxiiii s. viii d.[211]

[*p. 118*] Frontlett*es* of gold bought for the qwene of <Castell> Scott*es* and for the lady Elsabeth Stafford … lxxii s.

Bonett*es* and other necc*essar*ie stuff bought for mastres Yen and for m*astres* Perrot and other beyng at my lad*ys* fyndyng … Cxvi s. viii d.

Certen stuff bought for the exhibicion of yong master Souche this yer*e* … xxxviii s. i d. ob.

[207] The total of the two items above, bracketed to the right of the items.
[208] The total of the four items above, bracketed to the right of the items.
[209] MS 'xxxiijj'.
[210] The total of the three items above, plus the mid-page total, bracketed to the right of the items and mid-page total.
[211] The total of the two items above, bracketed to the right of the items.

Certen stuff bought for thexhibicion of master P*ar*ker and my m*astres* his wife their*e* childern and his servant w*ith* viii li. ii s. for velvet for a gowne for the same m*aster* P*ar*ker … xxxiii li. viii s. ii d. ob.

xliiii li. v s.[212]

Cost*es* of bote hier of my ladyes g*r*ace and her s*er*vant*es* … vi s. vi d.

Cost*es* of div*er*se of my ladys s*er*vant*es* ridyng unto sondrie placez apon her messagez … xviii li. v s. x d.

Cariage of stuff for my ladys g*r*ace at div*er*se tymes … lix s.

Cost*es* of the lady Shirley and other lyeng at the George þe tyme thei cam to se my ladyes g*r*ace … xxvi s.

Certen neccess*ar*iez bought for my ladyes fotemen … lix s.

Expens*e* of Edward Heven Geffrey Paynell w*ith* Humfrey Walcot and other syttyng by my ladyes co*m*mission to make inquerye and so to asserteigne her g*r*ace what s*er*vant*es* hur*e* g*r*ace may have to s*er*ve the kyng*es* g*r*ace out of the countie of Lincoln … vi li. xiii s. ii d.

xxxii li. ix s. vi d.[213]

[*p. 119*] Money yeven to my lord prince this yer*e* … xxxiii li. vi s. viii d.

Money paied unto mastres Denton for her fe … lxvi s. viii d.

Reward yeven to Piers Champion bringing the kyng*es* Newyers gift … C s.

Reward*es* yeven to div*er*se p*er*sones at sondry tymes w*ith*in the tyme of this accompt … iiii^{xx}xvii li. xix s. iiii d. ob.

Reward yeven unto m*aster* Morgan … vii li. vi s. viii d.

Reward yeven unto Walt*er* Cock*es* … lxiii s. iiii d.

Reward yeven to George Morgan the kyng*es* s*er*vant … xl s.

Reward unto m*aster* Seynt John the kyng*es* s*er*vant yeven this yer*e* … vi li. xiii s. iiii d.

Reward yeven unto m*aster* Scott of Crist*es* Colledge this yer*e* … l s.

Reward*es* yeven to the kyng*es* s*er*vant*es* at my ladys being at the co*ur*te … xxxiii li. xiii s. viii d.

Reward yeven unto Will*i*am Hilmer … lxvi s. viii d.

Reward yeven to mastres Massy \xx s./ and m*astres* Yen \v m*a*rc*el*[214] this yer*e* … iiii li. vi s. viii d.

Reward yeven unto m*aster* p*re*sident as v yerd*es* of skerlet bought by m*aster* rece*y*ver … l s.

Reward*es* yeven my lady being at m*aster* Lovell*es* … xl s.

[212] The total of the four items above, bracketed to the right of the items. It is 10s. short.
[213] The total of the six items above, bracketed to the right of the items.
[214] i.e. £3 6s. 8d.

[*p. 120*] Reward*es* yeven at my ladys beyng at Walsyngham … xl s.

Reward yeven to the kyng*es* offic*er*s the kyng beyng at Hatefeld this yer … xiii li. vi s. viii d.

<CCxvi li. x s. ob.> Clxxix li. xvi s. viii d. ob.[215]

CCxvi li. x s. ob.[216]

iii pec*es* of grene say bought this yer*e* … lxx s.

iii pec*es* of counterfett aras bought … xxxv li. xi s. ix d. qua.

ii pec*es* of verdurez bought this yer*e* … viii s.

xxxix li. ix s. ix d. qua.[217]

Certen pecez of black and tawney fustyan bought for div*er*se causes … vi li. xi s. iiii d.

iiii^or^ pecez of blake bokeram bought this yer*e* … xvi s. viii d.

iii superal[ta]riez[218] bought this yer*e* … x s.

vii li. xviii s.[219]

Certen so*m*mes of monye paied for certen land*es* bought of Richerd Chicheley in Malton for Cristis Colledge this yer*e* … xxxiii li. vi s. viii d.

Money paied for a subsidye dewe at Malton befor the p*ar*sonage was impropred … xl s.

Money paied for thapprop*ri*acion of the p*ar*sonage of the Maner of Bere and certen recov*er*yes of other land*es* w*ith* iiii li. x d. paied by my ladys solicito*ur* … xxxvi li. xvii d.

Expens*e* of the said solicito*ur* in ridyng by my ladyes co*m*maundement to þe abbey of Creke … xxiii s. iiii d.

Cost*es* of suet*es* bytwen the said colledge and the abbesse of Syon … iiii li. xvii s. vi d.

Money paied for iii \great/ antifeners bought … x li.

[*p. 121*] Money delyv*er*ed to James Morice for the accomplishement of the bildyng of Crist*es* College … Clxiiii li. ix s. v d.

Certen prynted book*es* bought for the said colledge … xxxviii li. iii s. ii d.

[215] The canc. and corrected totals are actually bracketed to the right on p. 119. The corrected total includes all the entries on that page (bar the first two) as well as the first two on p. 120.

[216] A second bracket on p. 119 includes the first two entries on p. 119 as well as the total of the pp. 119–20 entries, giving the total £216 10s. 0½d. (the sum of the canc. total within the first bracket).

[217] The correct total of the three items above, bracketed to the right of the items.

[218] MS 'superalettriez'.

[219] The correct total of the three items above, bracketed to the right of the items.

Money paied by Thomas Sop*er* my ladys solicit*our* for div*er*se sewt*es* and plees … lxxi s. ix d.

CCC li. xviii d.[220]

Money paijd by him for viii yerd*es* of scerlet for a robe yeven unto m*aster* Brutnell by my lad*ys* co*m*maundement … iiii li.

Cost*es* of the sewet ayenst Tempest for the maymyng of Cuff my ladys servant … ix li. xii s. iii d.

Money delyv*er*ed by the said Thomas unto John Castell my ladys att*our*ney in the eschequyer to pay for the p*ro*fers and other charges for to have my lad*ys* lib*er*tiez ther allowed … xl s.

xix li. iiii s.[221]

Money delyv*er*ed unto John Herryson lord of miserule for dyv*er*se disgisyng*es* and playes this Cristmas season … <xv li. x d. ob.> xv li. xd. ob.

Money paied for a paire of knyt gloves w*ith* roundes of gold set w*ith* ii safuers the whiche was yeven to the lord of Exceto*ur* … iiii li. x s. ii d.

Money delyv*er*ed to m*aster* Assheton for a cupp of gold for the kyng*es* New Yer*es* gift this yer*e* … C li.

Money delyv*er*ed unto my ladys g*r*ace apon New Yeres Day to yeve in New Yeres gift*es* … xiii li. vi s. viii d.

Cxiii li. vi s. viii d.[222]

[*p. 122*] Certen plate bought w*ith* xxxii li. ii s. vi d. for a chales of gold and xx li. v s. for a goblet of gold … lx<x>ix li. x s. x d.

Nota. So*m*me of all the hole allowancez befor said … MCClxxi li. vii s. xi d. qua.

And so he oweth yet … Diiii^{xx}viii li. viii s. ix d. ob. qua.[223] wherof ther is allowed him … xxvi s. of tharr*er*ag*es* of Thomas Sop*er* my ladys solicit*our* bycause the said Thomas is charged w*ith* þe same so*m*me in his accompt of my ladys sewt*es* and plees of this p*r*esent yer anno xxiiii^{to} as it doth mor*e* pleynly apper*e* in the same. And he is also discharged of … lx s. p*ar*cell of x li. of tharr*er*ag*es* of Ric*herd* Pynson <bycaus Ane> bicause the same Richerd hath delyv*er*ed certen printed book*es* to my ladys g*r*ace the xiiiith day of Januar*y* anno xxiiii^{to} to the value of the so*m*me befor said. And yet he owethe … Diiii^{xx}iiii li. ii s. ix d. ob. qua.

wherof resteth[224]

[220] The (incorrect) total of the last six items on p. 120 and the first three on p. 121, bracketed to the right of the items. The correct total is 293 13s. 3d.

[221] The correct total of the three items above (plus the Soper entry above them, already included in the previous total), bracketed to the right after the three items.

[222] The total of the two items above, bracketed to the right of the items.

[223] For this debt and the 'Somme' above see p. 114 above.

[224] Written small to the right at the foot of the page.

[*p. 123*] *upon*[225]

Richerd Conwey late of the chapell ov*er* and besid*es* xiii s. iiii d. paied unto Miles Worsley anno xxii^{do} and xx s. paied to the same Miles anno xxiii^{cio} … xlvi s. viii d.

George Henyngham my ladyes servant for money by my ladys g*r*ace payed to the lady Powes for a cheyne þ*at* he lost of hers … xxvii s. vi d.

Will*i*am Pole for money unto him lent over and besid*es* xx s. paied to Miles Worsley anno xxiii^{cio} … x li.

Thabbot of Croyland for money unto him lent … xl li.

Onerantur inter obligaciones.[226] S*ir* Henr*y* Willoughby knyght for money unto him lent over and besid*es* l li. paied unto my ladys <g*r*ace> coffers and l li. paied unto Miles Worsley … C li.

James Clarell for money unto him delyv*er*ed by the hand*es* of Henr*y* Salford iiii li. xv s. and by the hand*es* of Olyver Holand xlvi s. viii d. In all … vii li. xviii d.[227] wherof the said James hath delyv*er*ed xv yerd*es* of tawney medley lxxvii s. vi d. and also he hath delyv*er*ed unto Alexandre Thrognall xviii s. vi d. ob. And so yet resteth upon him … xlv s. v d. ob.

John Walter for money unto him prested to by stuff for the vestry … iii s. iiii d.

[*p. 124*] *yet apon*[228]

Allocaciones.[229] Thexecuto*ur*z of the testament of s*ir* Roger Urmyston knyght as apperith in the fote of acco*m*mpt by them made remaynyng in the kepyng of m*aster* Hugh Asheton … xvii li. vii s. ix d.

Rob*er*t Crathorn and his felowe expendito*ur*z of the slewse at Boston … lx li.

John Cann of Lynne m*er*chaunt for money unto him lent by an obligacion remainyng w*ith* Miles Worsley … xx li.

[*blank*] Rowle of the chapell for mony unto him lent and not yet paied … lxvi s. viii d.

The lady Jane for money unto her lent by James Morice … xvi li.

Will*i*am Ferthing late of my ladys chapell for money unto him lent and yet not paied … xiii li. vi s. viii d.

Oliver Holand yoman ussher of my ladys chamber*e* for money unto him lent and yet not paied … xiii li. vi s. viii d.

Allocaciones.[230] John Seynt John esquyer*e* for money unto him lent … lxvi s. viii d.

[225] Bracketed in the margin to include all the items on p. 123, most of which are repeated from pp. 61–3 above.
[226] See p. 61 above.
[227] The internal total is 2d. short.
[228] Bracketed in the margin to include all the items on pp. 124–5, most of which are repeated from p. 61 above.
[229] See p. 61 above.
[230] See p. 62 above.

Ingleberd bookebynder for mony unto him p*res*ted to by certen book*es* at Parice for my ladyes g*r*ace ... ov*er* and besid*es* Cxiii s. iiii d. paied to Miles Worsley this yer*e* ... xx s.[231]

My lord of Ely for mony unto him lent ... xx li.

Nicholas Aughton for money unto him lent ... vi s. viii d.

Thomas Ferthing for money unto him lent ... vii li.

[*p. 125*] <money> Nicholas Elneden for money unto him lent ... iiii li.

Richerd Pynson prynt*er* for money unto him lent ov*er* and besid*es* lx s. allowed befor*e* for certen book*es* delyv*er*ed to my ladys g*r*ace the xiiith day of Januar*y* anno xxiiii^{to} ... vii li.

The said lady Jane for money lent her by Miles W. ... lxvi s. viii d.

Som of all the money dewe and not payed of such þ*at* was prested the last yer*e* and in iiii o<r>ther yer*es* next befor ... CCCxxxix li. xviii d. ob. qua.[232]

The said lady Jane for money unto her lent this yer*e* ... xx s.

Will*i*am Hilmer for money to him lent this yer*e* ... xx li.

Nichil oneratur quia solvitur domine in una summa. M*aster* Conyngesby the kyng*es* s*er*jaunt for money unto him lent this yer*e* ... C li.

Rob*er*t Hilton for money remainyng in his hand*es* apon a prest for p*ro*vision of certen stuff this yer*e* ... xxxviii s. viii d.

Som*m*e of all the money lent and prested this yer*e* anno xxiiii^{to} ... Cxxii li. xviii s. viii d.

And ther restith yet in thand*es* of the said accomptaunt clerly ... 6Cxxii li. ii s. vii d.

<debet ... Cxx<iiii>\ii li./ ii s. vii d.>[233]

[*pp. 126–8 blank*]

[231] The sum is bracketed to the right of the Ingleberd entry, which is written as two entries.
[232] There is a dot calculation in the left margin.
[233] Written small to the left at the foot of the page and canc.; it is written out fair above.

D102.1 (SJLM/1/1/5/1) Account of Robert Fremingham treasurer of the chamber: [Hatfield], 20 January – 29 June 1509

Discussion See Introduction 4 and Plate 17.

Description Paper, bottom outer corner and lower edge of quire 2 once very damp but now conserved, written on both sides, approx. 305 x 220 mm. 22 ff. in two quires: 1^{14} 2^{8}.[1] Foliated recto 1–21 top right in pencil (MGU); ff. 1v, 3v, 19r–21v blank.[2] Left margins approx. 40–50 mm.; right margins variable; upper margins 15–30 mm.; lower margins variable. Bound into a modern brown/grey buckram cover ('SJLM/1/1/5/1' on a white pasted slip bottom left front cover, 'D102.1' altered to 'D102/1' and then cancelled to 'SJLM/1/1/5/1' top left inside cover). 'Drawer 102' (f. 1r, MGU in pencil), 'Summa … DCCCxv li. vi s. ii d. ob.' in the summary hand, with two scribbled calculations below ('ix^{C}ix ^{li} vj^{s} <j^{d}> \ij^{d}/ ob.' and 'Totalis … ix^{C}lxix ^{li} iiij ^{s} iiij ^{d}', cf. f. 16v). The summaries, i.e. initial and final material for the year[3] (ff. 2r–3r, 16r–18v), use a formal script (Bastard Anglicana, with a large decorated initial 'C' f. 2r, 'S' f. 3r) for the rubrics, infilled with either a smaller formal or a cursive script. The main body of the accounts is mostly in a current hand (Secretary with some Anglicana admixture), probably identifiable as the hand of Robert Fremingham himself ('the RF hand').[4] The 'sprawling hand' may be responsible for f. 16r-v and perhaps more of the work of the summary hand.[5] Folios 4r–15v are signed by the executors of Lady Margaret's estate, John Fisher ('Jo Roffensis'), Henry Hornby ('henry hornby'), and Hugh Ashton ('hugh assheton') (not noted in the edited text). Page totals are written in the summary hand; they are marked 'probatur' (^{P} in the edited text). Latin annotations occur occasionally, probably in the hand of the auditor.[6]

Summary
1509 (year 24) Rubric (Fremyngham, 20 January 1509–29 June 1509), arrears of last account, f. 2r; receipts, f. 2r-v; sum total of receipts, f. 3r; payments authorised by Lady Margaret, ff. 4r–16r; sum total of payments/expenses, debt of accountant, f. 16r-v; summary of expenses by item/person, ff. 17r–18r; sum total of payments/expenses and debt of accountant, f. 18r; loans/advances, sum total of loans/advances, debt of accountant, f. 18v.

[1] That is, ff. 1–14, 15–22.
[2] This is the only document edited here which has been foliated rather than paginated.
[3] Actually a quarter year and 67 days (see f. 2r).
[4] 'Computus Roberti Fremyngham', f. 2r.
[5] See footnote to f. 18r.
[6] Annotations to the text are indicated by double angle brackets. It may be this hand which is responsible for cancelling entries in a double zig-zag (noted as 'vigorously canc.' f. 18v).

Edited Text

[*f. 2r*] Computus Roberti Fremyngham <[...]> occupantis officium thesaurarii camere excellentissime principisse Margarete <mo> comitisse Richmond et Derbie ac matris nuper regis Henrici septimi anno xx^{o} die Januarii anno xxiiii^{to} nuper regis usque <a> festum appostolorum Petri et Pauli extunc proximo sequenti anno regni domini regis nunc Henrici viii^{mi} primo quo die prefata principessa obiit scilicet pro unum quarterium anni et lxvii dies.

Arreragia. Null[7]

Summa ... null

Recepta denariorum de Milone Worsley. First receyved the xii day of January by the hand*es* of Miles <wo> Worsley ... lxii li. ix s. iii d.

<Item receyved the xvith day of February by the hand*es* of foresaid Miles Worsley ... CCxlix li. vi s. vi d. ob.>

«cancellatur hic quia solvitur extra cofferum et oneratur ex altera parte folii»[8]

Summa ... <CCCxi li. xv s. ix d. ob.>[9]

lxii li. ix s. iii d.

[*f. 2v*] *Recepta denariorum extra cofferum prefate principesse*. Item receyved out of the said coffers att dyvers tymes that is to say the xvi day of February CCxlix li. vi s. vi d. ob. the vi day of Aprill xx li. the ix day of the same moneth CCiiii^{xx}xv li. the xxvii day of May anno primo regis H. viii^{mi} CCClix li. vi s. x d. and the xxviiith day of Junii the same yere Clx li. in all ... Miiii^{xx}iii li. xiii s. iiii d. ob.

Summa ... Miiii^{xx}iii li. xiii s. iiii d. ob.

[*f. 3r*]

MCxlvi li. ii s. vii d. ob.[10] Summa totalis recepte ... MCxlvi li. ii s. vii d. ob.

[*f. 3v blank*]

[*f. 4r*] [11]Paymentes made by the co*m*maundement of my ladies grace from the xiiiith day of January the xxiiiith yere of the reign of *our* souve*r*aigne lorde king Henry the viith unto the day of [*blank*] next after that immediatly ensuyng.

First the xvth day of January in reward yeven to a sust*er* of my lady Ryvers at the Mynuresse ... xx s.

[7] 'Null' written small in the tall thin hand of the summary below (see Description to D91.17). As in D91.16, it is left unexpanded because of the problems of properly recognising the referent.
[8] Add. below the canc. sum; see the verso, i.e. 'ex altera parte folii', f. 2v.
[9] The total of the two entries above (canc. because the second entry is canc.). The correct total is below it, perhaps in the same hand.
[10] The total of the receipts ff. 2r-v written small to the left of the 'Summa' which is written in a formal script.
[11] The RF hand begins here. See Plate 17.

Item in reward to maistresse Fitzherberd … xx s.

Item to Peter Oldall for his cost*es* to London by the space of thre dayes … iii s.

Item to Thomas Dod toward*es* his cost*es* to Ludlowe … xiii s. iiii d.

Item in reward yeven to the moder of doct*our* Metcalf … xx s.

Item the xxiith day of the said moneth delyv*er*ed to the hand*es* of my said ladies grace … xl s.

Item in reward yeven to the bargemen at Richemount … iii s. iiii d.

Item to the kep*er* of the great parc ther … xx d.

Item in reward to dame Margaret Wyndesore … vi s. viii d.

Item in reward to Lyonell Zouche … vi s. viii d.

Item in reward yeven to the princesse of Castiles footemen … xii d.

Item in reward to John Kyng somtyme cooke to my lord of Derby … iii s. iiii d.

Item in reward to a s*er*vant of a Boneho*mm*e<s s*er*vant > of Asshrige for bringing of wardens to my lad*ys* grace … viii d.

Item in reward to a poticary sometyme s*er*vant w*ith* my lord of Bedford … xx d.

Item the xxviiith day of January payed to John Vauntrix for a broche of gold havyng three p*er*sonnagies weying xxviii s. and for the faction of the same viii s. … xxxvi s.

Item for a tablet of gold w*ith* an ymaige of Saincte John baptist weying xxvi s. and for the faction therof viii s. … xxxiiii s.

Item for a broche of gold w*ith* an ymaige of o*ur* Lady of Pitie ponder*yng* xxix s. and for the faction therof viii s. … xxxvii s.

Summa partis … xii li. viii s. iiii d.[P]

[*f.* 4*v*] Item paid to William Hilm*er* for certayn medicynes for my ladies grace … xxi s. vi d.

Item delyv*er*ed to the hand*es* of my said ladies grace … vii li.

Regarda[12]

Item the xxixth day of January in reward to Rauf Jenet and Robert Hasilrig of the wardrobe of the king*es* bedd*es* … xx s.

Item to John Brent and Rauf Annesley of the seller … vi s. viii d.

Item to Gilmyn and Parker of the buttrye … vi s. viii d.

Item to Richard Brampton of the pantrye … v s.

Item to Lyvesay of the ewrye … iii s. iiii d.

Item to oon of the squillery whiche kept my lad*ys* silver vessell … iii s. iiii d.

[12] In the left margin, bracketed to include the rest of the entries on the page.

Item to Anthony clerc of the kechyn … vi s. viii d.

Item to Robert Joohns gentilman usshur … v s.

Item to the yeoman of the woodyerd … iii s. iiii d.

Item to him that bere wood into my ladies chambre … xx d.

Item by the hand*es* of my lad*ys* grace to my lord prince … <vi li. xiii s. iiii d.> xiii li. vi s. viii d.

Item to maistresse Denyce toward the rep*ara*c*i*on of a brydge at Chersey … xl s.

Item in reward to a s*er*vant of my lady princesse of Wales for bringing of div*er*se semes and work*es* … iii s. iiii d.

Item in reward to oon Patche being w*ith* my lord of London … iii s. iiii d.

Item in reward to the clerk*es* of the king*es* signet for a l*ett*re sent unto sir*e* Rauf Loungford conc*er*nyng maistres Yane … iii s. iiii d.

Item in reward to John Williams late footeman unto my lad*ys* grace … iii s. iiii d.

Item to oon of the prince*s* footemen … xx d.

Item in reward to the king*es* watche … x s.

Item in reward to my lady Boughan … vi s. viii d.

Item the last day of the said moneth yeven in reward to a s*er*vant of my lord of Sainct Johns whiche useth Gesting man*er* … vi s. viii d.

Item the same day in reward to twoo wayt*es* at Barnet … xii d.

Item in reward to my lady marquesse … xl s.

Summa … xliii li. xix s. ii d.[P]

[*f.* 5*r*] Item in reward to my [lady] Verney … xx s.

Item delyv*er*ed to the hand*es* of my lad*ys* grace <of> at Sainct Johns … xl s.

Item for my lad*ys* offering at the fest of Purifica*cion* of o*ur* Lady … xii s. vi d.

Item to Richard Aderton for ryding from Handworth to Bromley by the space of ii dayes … xvi d.

Item delyv*er*ed to maister Edward Booth the iii[d] day of February for p*er*fo*ur*myng of mariaige money for maistres Yan … xxxviii[13] li. vi s. viii d.

Item delyv*er*ed unto maister Horneby my ladies chanceller for the behouf of maister Nicholas Cooper in full payment of xxxi li. xii s. viii d. for stuff bought of the executo*ur*es of my lady of Norfolk … <C>Cxii s. viii d.

Item in reward to a frere whiche cam from doctour Standisshe \the/ frere … iii s. iiii d.

Item in reward to oon of the king*es* s*er*vant*es* whiche cam for maister Chambre … iii s. iiii d.

[13] MS 'xxxvjij'.

Item in reward to John Vauntrix … iii s. iiii d.

Item the vith day of February paid to Ric*hard* Aderton for riding from Hatfeld to London and from thens to Asshey by the space of iiii dayes … ii s. viii d.

Item the viiith day of the same moneth paid to Nicholas Aughton for riding from Hatfeld to Grenewich by the space of ii dayes w*ith* ii horses ii s. viii d. for riding to Hanworth at ii sundry tymes by the spaic*e* of vi dayes viii s. and for ryding to Asshey and Chersey by the space of iiii dayes iiii s. … xiiii s. viii d.

Item the xiith day of the said moneth paid to Olyv*er* Scales for the fee of Edward Mynskyp excheato*ur* in the countie of Cambrige for fynding of an office wherby Thomas Lymn*er* is warde unto my lad*ys* grace … xl s.

Item to the same for a writte direct unto the said excheato*ur* for fynding of the said office … ii s. vi d.

Summa … li li. iii s. v d.[P]

[*f. 5v*] Item in reward to a poore man whiche had his good*es* brent … xx d.

Item the xiiith day of the said moneth to Wynkyn de Woorde for vi book*es*[14] bounden cont*eynyng* the sermones of the vii psalmes … vi s.

Item to the same for vi book*es* unbounden … iii s.

Item for the Sheppard*es* Calender in a forell … xii d.

Item for a booke called Caton in prose … ii s.

Item for a book of fortune … xvi d.

Item for a dyall of tynne … xx d.

Item for ii psaulters bounden … xviii d.

Item for fifty dusseyn bullyons for bookes for Crist*es* Colleige in Cambrige … xvi s. viii d.

Item to the guylde of Sainct Bryde in Flete Strete for v yeres passed … v s.

Item to Nicholas Aughton for riding to Handworth by the space of iiii dayes … ii s. viii d.

Item paid for the emendyng of ii olde sensures of silv*er* for ii bolles of coper set in the same for emending of ii candelstikk*es* of silv*er* and for iii q*uarter* of an unc*e* of more silv*er* to the same … v s. iiii d.

Item to Thomas Sop*er* my lad*ys* solicito*ur* for c*er*tayn suyt*es* and other of my ladies causes … Cx s.

Item for vii peces of canvas cont*eynyng* CCiiii^{xx}vi ellnes at iii d. qua. the elne and in all vii d. ob. <ob.> ov*er* … lxxvi s. x d.

[14] 'book*es*' rep.

Item for metyng pakking threde for trussing[15] and for portaige of the said clouth … ix d.

Item for a salt of silv*er* and gilt bought of John Moundy yeven to my lord of London pondering viii unc*e* iii q*ua*rt*er*s at v s. the unc*e* … xliii s. ix d.

Summa … xiiii li. ii d.[P]

[*f. 6r*] Item to sir Andrue Fortscue knight in p*ar*te of payme*n*t of a more su*m*me for the man*our* called Bassingbo*ur*ne in the countie of Cambrige … vi li. xiii s. iiii d.

Item in reward to maister Parker … xx s.

Item to Robert Merbury for bringing of an hawke unto my lord prince by the space of ii dayes … xvi d.

Item the xxvth day of the said moneth to m*aister* Assheton for money paid unto sir Andrue Fortscue knight by the hand*es* of Thomas Sooper in p*ar*te of payment of a more su*m*me for the lordship of Bassingbo*ur*ne … C li.

Item to John Mundy goldesmyth for a potte of silv*er* and \p*ar*cell/ gilt ponder*yng* x unc*e* di. di. q*uar*t*er*.[16] Price the oz. iiii s. iiii d. … xlvi s. ob.

Item to the same John Mundy for making of a nue chalice of an old broken chalice and for di. q*uar*t*er* silv*er* put therunto … xxiiii s. x d.

Item the xxvth day of the said moneth in reward to doct*our* Fotherby for preching <f> bifore my lad*ys* grace … x s.

Item the xxvith day of the said moneth in reward to an heremyt of Graunthan … iii s. iiii d.

Item to maistres Fowler for c*er*tayn stuf bought by Peter browderer … xxx s.

Item in reward to the pri*our* of Hechyn … xx s.

Item the last day of the said moneth in reward to ii women of Southwik whiche were suyt*our*s unto my lad*ys* grace … iii s. iiii d.

Item the xith day of Marche to Thomas Maydewell for the boorde of Anne Heron by the space of <xviii> ii wek*es* aft*er* the \rate of/ xviii d. the weke … iii s.

Item in reward to a s*er*vant of m*aister* Dynous for bringing of a fowle … iii s. iiii d.

<Summa … xix li. xviii s. vi d. ob.> Summa … Cxiiii li. xviii s. vi d. ob.[P]

[*f. 6v*] Item for my ladies offering at oure Lady of Pue … ii s.

Item in reward to the king*es* mynstrell*es* at the bisshop of Londons place … xx s.

Item in reward to Gerard Osbo*ur*ne the king*es* s*er*vant … vi s. viii d.

Item in reward to Thomas Mery by m*aister* Morgan … iii s. iiii d.

[15] Vertical strokes indicate that three items are intended: 'metyng/pakking/threde for trussing/'.
[16] A vertical stroke between 'x unce di'. and 'di. quarter' indicates that the pot is 10½ oz. at 4s. 4d. the oz. (45s. 6d.) and the powder is ⅛ oz. at the same price (6½d.).

Item in reward to oon Thomas Spicer for comyng to my lad*ys* grace by hir co*m*maundement … viii d.

Item in reward to John Collop for emending of div*er*se clothes of arrasse and other by the space of iii wek*es* iii s. iiii d. and for a lib. of fyne yerne of crule rede and grene xvi d. … iiii s. viii d.

Item <f> in reward to John Sydington sometyme my lad*ys* fawken*er* … iii s. iiii d.

Item in reward to the cook*es* … xl s.

Item to Hugh Woorsley for his cost*es* at Ware by a night to cause the baillief ther to come to my lad*ys* grace … viii d.

Item to Leonard for dressing of v priksoung book*es* … xx d.

Item for dressing of a p*ar*chemyn booke for Crist*es* colleige … iiii d.

Item for brede and wyne <at> when my lady was in the cowrte … xxii d.

Item in reward to Thomas Dod for his cost*es* at Chesthunt being sick … iii s. iiii d.

Item in reward to a s*er*vant of the baillief of the Egle for bringing of a chest w*ith* oynetment*es* … vi s. viii d.

Item for the expens*es* of the said baillief and his s*er*vant*es* at Lowmans … xi s. iiii d.

Item paid to Henry Ludlowe for his wag*es* due at the feste of Annu*n*ciac*i*on of o*ur* Lady … xx s.

Summa … vi li. vi s. vi d.[P.]

[*f. 7r*] Item paid for ii pair*e* of shoes for Henry Baptist … xvi d.

Item paid for making of a shyrt for the same Henry … iiii d.

Item for pecyng of a bowe for the same Henry … iiii d.

Item for a pair*e* of shoes for John Stowell … vi d.

ii s. vi d.[17]

Item in reward to a frere for making of a s*er*mone bifore my ladies grace the ii^{de} Sonday of Lent … vi s. viii d.

Item to a s*er*vant of Edward Hevyn for expens*es* had aboute fisshing in takyng of xx breames and baking of the same at Tatteshall w*ith* the conveyaunce of the same breames from thens to Hatfeld … xlix s. vii d.

Item in reward to doctour Bokenham whiche preched before my ladies grace the iii^{de} Sonday of Lent … x s.

Item the xiith day of Marche in reward to the twoo anchoresses at Stampford … iii s. iiii d.

Item the xiiith day of Marche in reward to my lady Verney … xx s.

[17] The total of the four items above, written faint and bracketed to the right of the items.

Item the xvth day of the same moneth to Nicholas Aughton for riding from Hatfeld to Hanworth and Richemount at soundry tymes by the space of ii days by himsilf aft*er* viii d. a day xvi d. and for vi dayes w*ith* his s*er*vant after xvi d. a day viii s. … ix s. iiii d.

Item the same day to John Cat*ur* for conveying of breames to London for my lord of Ely m*ais*t*er* Dudley and m*ais*t*er* Empson by the space of ii dayes … xiiii d.

Item in reward to Thomas Porte lerned man … xx s.

Item the xviiith day of Marche to Wynkyn de Worde for ii portuouse … vi s. viii d.

Summa … vi li. ix s. iii d.[P]

[*f. 7v*] Item the xviiith day of Marche to Thomas <Sev> Senowe for vii lib. of rounde gold of Venyse cont*eynyng* xii oz. the lib. at iiii s. iii d. the oz. xvii li. xvii s. and for a lib. of flat gold conteynyng xii oz. at iiii s. x d. the unc*e* lviii s. … xx li. xv<i> s.

Item to Wynkyn de Worde for lxxvi dus[s]yn[18] bullyons t*o* be set upon book*es* apperteyning to Crist*es* colleige … xxv s. iiii d.

Item to John Nicholas for di. C pynkes xii lether skinnes ii lib. of white threde the hier of a workman by a day and a night for furring of my lad*ys* gown of saten and for the boordwag*es* of \the/ Saint John being sick by a fourtenyght … viii s. ii d.

Item to maister Hornby my lad*ys* chaunceller for money paide by him for seallyng of the acte <of the act> of app*ro*p*r*iac*i*on of the p*ar*sonnaige of Mano*ur*bere … xxvi s. viii d.

Item in reward to a s*er*vant of my lady princesse of Wales … x s.

Item the xxth day of Marche for my ladies offering at Sainct Albanes shryne … iii s. iiii d.

Item for my ladies offering at Asshrige at oon tyme xx d. the ii^{de} tyme xx d. and the iii^{de} tyme vi s. viii d. … x s.

Item in reward to the rect*our* of Assherige … iii s. iiii d.

Item in reward to my lorde of Derbyes suster … xx s.

Item to ii norisses of his childern … xiii s. iiii d.

Item for my lad*ys* offering at [B]ray[19] … iii s. iiii d.

Item to Hugh Worsley for his expens*es* going to London by my lad*ys* comaundment … xii d.

Item to the same Hugh for ii oz. of white lether patches bought of a glover at Sainct Albanes w*ith* ii d. p*ai*d for his expens*es* ther … x d.

[18] Awkwardly written so that it looks like 'dusbyn'..
[19] MS 'Pray'.

Item the xxiiii[th] day of the said moneth to John Mustyng and John Barnard Duchemen for emending of *cer*tayn pec*es* of arresse by the space of a moneth viii s. and for ii lib. and a q*u*art*er* of yerne for the same ii s. viii d. … x s. iiii d.[20]

Summa … xxvii li. xi s. viii d.[P]

[*f. 8r*] Item the xxvii[th] day of Marche in reward to docto*ur* Cooper for setting of div*er*se song*es* … xiii s. iiii d.

Item delyverd to the hand*es* of my ladies grace for hir almoys purse … xiii li. vi s. viii d.

Item to a s*er*vant of Edward Hevyns for al man*er* of charg*es* and expens*es* susteyned aboute taking baking and bringing of *cer*tain breames from Tatteshall to Hatfeld … xlvi s. xi s.

Item for my ladies offering at the feste of the Annu*n*ciacion of *our* Lady … v s.

Item to Thomas Bellingeham m*aister* comptroll*ours* s*er*vant for riding to Cambrige by the space of iiii dayes for *cer*tayn wryting*es* conc*er*nyng Sainct Johns house … iiii s.

Item to Rob*er*t Neswik for *cer*tayn spices to be bought for my lad*ys* grace … vi s. viii d.

Item in reward yeven to m*aister* Moore s*er*geaunt at lawe … xx s.

Item the xxviii[th] day of Marche to Nicholas Aughton for ryding to Richemount by the space of ii days … xvi d.

Item to the same for riding to the abbot of Sainct Albanes to my lord of Derby and Asshrige by the space of ii days to yeve knowleige of the co*m*myng of my ladies grace … xvi d.

Item to Richard Aderton for ridyng to Richemo*un*t by the space of ii days … xvi d.

Item to m*aister* Assheton comptroll*our* of my ladyes houshold for riding to London at iii dyv*er*se tymes and ther abiding in all by the space of viii dayes aboute the alteraci*on* of Sainctt Johns house in Cambrige into a colleige of secular student*es* and also to unyte the priory of Bromholme in Norffolk dissolved unto the same house … xxvi s. viii d.

Summa … xix li. xiii s. iii d.[P]

[*f. 8v*] Item to maistresse Fowler for viii unc*e* of we[bb]e[21] silk at xiiii d. the unc*e* … ix s. iiii d.

Item the first day of Aprill in reward to m*aister* Tanne whiche preched bifore my ladies grace … x s.

Item to maister Richard Wyot for <settin> money by him paide for setting bullyons upon div*er*se book*es* at London app*er*teynyng to Crist*es* colleige in Cambrige … xlix s.

[20] The total should be 10s. 8d.

[21] MS 'welle'.

Item to Reignald Stoughton joyn*our* for vi stoles wherof iii were wevyng stoles … v s.

Item the iii^{d} day of Aprill in reward to John Will*i*ams late foteman unto my lad*ys* g*r*ace … iii s. iiii d.

Item to maistresse Massy for brede \xii d./ ale \i d./ mylk \iiii d./ butt*er* \xiiii d./ and spices \v d./ bought for ii litill childer of Henry Parker with rybande*s* \viii d./ girdill*es* \vi d./ silke lac*es* \vi d./ hook*es* \iiii d./ pynnes \iii d./ combes \iii d./ bonett*es* \xi d./ knitting of iii p*ar* of hose \iii d./ lie pott*es* \ii d./ shoes \ii s. i d./ and watchyng candill*es* for the same childer \viii d./ makyng of ii kirtill*es* for Margaret Ludlowe \xviii d./ a p*ar* of hose for the same \iii d./ xii lib. of flax \ii s./ and spining of the same \xvi d./ w*ith* viii d. p*ai*d for spynn[y]ng of wollen … xv s. iiii d.

Item p*ai*d for xiii pair*e* of shoes for my lad*ys* almoysfolk and for underleying of so*m*me of the same … vi s. viii d.

Item in reward to dompn*e* John Woodhouse Bonehome of Asshrige for \rose water/ … iii s. iiii d.

Item to Richard Aderton for riding to Bugden to my lord of <london> Lincoln for sealling of a dede app*er*teynyng to Crist*es* colleige by the space of ii dayes … xvi d.

Item p*ai*d to Nicholas Aughton for conveying of breames to my lord of Wynchester my lady Gordon and maistres Dyonyce by the space of ii days w*ith* his s*er*vant … ii s. viii d.

Summa … Cvi s.[P]

[*f. 9r*] Item to the same Nycholas for riding to Richemount by the space of ii days … xvi d.

Item in reward to a s*er*vant of the provoust of the Kyng*es* Colleige in Cambrige for bringing of Reignald my ladies idyot … v s.

Item to Lowmans wief of Hatfeld for the hier of a p*ar*l*our* for Myles Worsley the tyme of the auditt having his stuff in the same by the space of xviii wek*es* … iiii s.

Item for my ladies offeryng upon Good Fryday … xxx s.

Item in reward to Laurence Bonde for keping of my ladies idyot … vi s. viii d.

Item to Warcop baillief of Hatfeld for the rent of my lad*ys* almoys house for di. yere ended at the Anunciac*i*on of *our* Lady last passed … xvi s.

Item to Laurence Bonde for ii pair*e* of shoes bought for John Assheton my lad*ys* idyot … xii d.

Item the last day of Marche in reward to a fotman of my lady princesse of England … v s.

Item to Will*i*am Hilm*er* for a lib. of fyne cast gyng*er* try dd. v s. and for emending of a loking glasse of pomaunder werk viii d. … v<i> s. viii d.

Item the vith day of Aprill in reward yeven to maistresse Bygod … xx s.

Item for my ladies offering on Ester morowe at the tyme of resurrecio*un* … ii s. vi d.

Item to Henry Baptist for taking of his right*es* the same day … iiii d.

Item for my ladies offeryng on Easter Day at high masse … v s.

Summa … Cii s. vi d.[P]

[*f. 9v*] Item in reward to the cook*es* … xxvi s. viii d.

Item to the squyllery and salsery … v s.

Item the vi day of Aprill to Nicholas Aughton for riding to Richmount by the space of ii days … xvi s.

Item the xth day of Aprill to Gerard Austen bargeman for conveying of my ladies grace and hir company from the blak freres to Coldherbergh in a barge w*ith* viii ores at viii d. the ore for the hier of the same barge viii d. and for the maistres wages xii d. … vii s.

Item to the same for the hier of ii barg*es* from London to Richemount xvi d. for xvi ores at viii d. the ore x s. viii d. and for ii maisteres wages ii s. … xiiii s.

Item to the same for the hier of a bote from Coldeberough to Putney w*ith* kechyn stuff … x d.

Item for the hier of a cart for Putney to Richem*ount* w*ith* the same stuff … vi d.

Item for my lad*ys* offering at Sainct Brygitt at Syon … xii d.

Item in reward to dame Margaret Poole … vi s. viii d.

Item in reward to dame Margaret Wyndesore … vi s. viii d.

Item to the awner of the house at Putney wherin my lad*ys* grace was at hir co*m*myng to Richemount … xx d.

Item in reward to Rob*er*t Deyes wief … v s.

Item to Richard Aderton for his horse standing at Hanworth by the space of iiii days … xii d.

Item in reward to Laurence Bonde for bringing of John Asshewell my lad*ys* ydiot to Barnet … xii d.

Item to maistresse Fowler for money by hir paied to the wief of Roger Notte of Hatfeld for expens*es* of <Roger> Reignald my ladies ydiot the first night of his co*m*myng … vi d.

Summa … lxxviii s. x d.[P]

[*f. 10r*] Item in reward to m*aister* Parker the xth day of Aprill … xl s.

Item to James Morice the xiiiith day of Ap*r*ill for buylding*es* to be made at Crist*es* Colleige in Cambrige … lxvi li. xiii s. iiii d.

Item the xxth day of Aprill in reward to my lady Daubeney … xl s.

Item to a suste*r* of the late lady Ryve*r*se at the Menuresses … xx s.

Item to John Vauntrix for emending of ii pair*e* of pott*es* silve*r* and gild whiche were broken and for ce*r*tayn more silve*r* put to the same … vi s. viii d.

Item for emending of another pair*e* of silv*er* pott*es* p*ar*cell gild … vi s.

Item for making of a new bosse of silv*er* in an old standing cuppe of silv*er* and emending of the same w*ith* iii q*uarter* of an unc*e* of silv*er* that was put therunto … vi s.

Item for emending and gilding of the hafte of a kerving knyfe … vi s.

Item for making of a newe handell of silv*er* to an holy wat*er* stok and for silv*er* that was occupied for the same … iiii s.

Item for a newe potenger of silv*er* w*ith* a cov*er* pondering x ounces iii q*uarter* at iii s. viii d. the oz. … xxxix s. v d.

Item for oon unc*e* of gold occupied in a poteng*er* pondering v unc*e* iii q*uarter* wherof iiii unc*e* iii q*uarter* d. of gold the said John Vauntrix rec*eyved* of my lad*ys* grace … xxx s.

Item for nue making of the same poteng*er* ponder*ing* v unc*e* iii q*uarter* d. as is bifor said aft*er* the rate of ii s. viii d. \for/ the oz. … xv s. viii d.

Summa … lxxvii<i> vii s. i d.[P]

[*f. 10v*] Item for ii newe spones of silv*er* pondering oon unc*e* q*uarter* di. at … v s. ob.

Item for a pair*e* of tirrett*es* for a greyhound*es* coller ponder*ing* ii unc*e* di. di. q*uarter* at v s. the oz. … xiii s. i d.

Item for emending of a crosse the mountayn nue enamelled and the crosse newe gilded … xxi s.

Item for a nue poteng*er* of silv*er* ponder*ing* x oz. di. q*uarter* at iii s. viii d. the oz. w*ith* the werkmanship[22] … xxxvii s. i d. ob.

Item the xxth day of Aprill to Laurence Bonde for conveying of Reignald my ladies idyot from Hatfeld to Richemount by the space of iii dayes for the hier of their*e* horses ii s. for their*e* mete by the same space xxii d. and for the diett*es* of the said Laurence the said idyot and a man whiche did help to convey him by ii dayes xii d. … iiii s. x d.

Item to Hugh Worsley for emending of a wevyng stole … viii d.

Item to the same for his expens*es* going t*o* London to cause maister Polido*ur* to come to Richemount … iiii d.

Item to Richard Aderton for his cost*es* going to London at iii soundry tymes to cause an instrument to be made of the yerely value of the late abbey of Creyke by the space of iiii dayes \ w*ith* his bote her*e*/ … ii s. iiii d.

Item the xxith day of Aprill to Thomas Senowe goldwire drawer for ii lib. of round gold of damask cont*eynyng* xii unc*e* the lib. at iiii s. iii d. the unc*e* … Cii s.

Item the xxiiiith day of Aprill in reward to my lady Kateryn … xx s.

Item to Ric*hard* Aderton for ryding to Hatfeld for my lady Jane and my lady Willoughby by the space of ii dayes … xvi d.

Summa … x li. vii s. ix d.[P]

[22] 'ship' add. later.

[*f. 11r*] Item p*ai*d to Nycholas Aughton for an holy water stok for my ladies grace … vii d.

Item to Laurence Bonde for conveying of a stonding bedde from Hatfeld to Richemount by the space of ii dayes … xvi d.

Item the xxviii[t] day of Aprill to Thomas Bury in full contentac*io*n of his tuto*ur* at Eton for suche as he had payd oute for hym … xiiii s. iii d.

Item to the freres at Richemount for emending of their*e* clok … iii s. iiii d.[23]

Item in reward to the king*es* wardrobers at London for the delyv*er*y of c*er*tain blak cloth for my lady and hir s*er*vant*es* aft*er* the death of king Henr*y* the vii[th]… ix s. iiii d.

Item for the hier of a cart from the Wardrobe to Coldherbergh w*ith* the said cloth … iiii d.

Item for the diet of Robert Fremyngham Rob*er*t Hilton and oon s*er*vant w*ith* theim by the space of vi days being at London for the said clothe … vi s. viii d.

Item for the hier of ii bot*es* whiche brought the said cloth from Coldherbergh to Richemount bank … ii s. viii d.

Item for bote hir*e* of the said Rob*er*t Fremyngham Rob*er*t Hilton and oon w*ith* theim in going to London for the said cloth … viii d.

Item for cristening of maister Lynches dought*er* wherof my lad*ys* grace is godmoder … liii s. iiii d.

Item to Peter Baldewyn for ii dd. p*ar*chemyn delyv*er*ed to the hand*es* of my lad*ys* chaunceller for the use of hir grace … iiii s.

Item for a dusseyn velome … v s.

Item for iii book*es* of paup*er* royall for the office of tresaurer of the chambre … ix s. iiii d.

Item for a lowe stole bought for my lad*ys* grace … x d.

Item the first day of May to Rob*er*t Merbury for riding to the bisshop of Lincoln to Walsingham Cambrige and to Lincoln for sealling of the anuytie g*r*aunted oute of the churche of Nave*n*by to Crist*es* Colleige by the space of xiii days at viii d. a day … viii s. viii d.

Summa … vi li. iiii d.[P]

[*f. 11v*] Item in reward to dompn*e* John Reymound vicair*e* of the charterhouse by the hand*es* of maist*er* confessour … vi s. viii d.

Item to William Hilm*er* for a panyo*ur* w*ith* a lok for syses and quarrio*urs* … vi d.

Item to a launder whiche wasshed al man*er* of lyn*n*en belonnging unto my ladies grace and hir gentilwomen at Richemound whiche ammounted to xiiii dd. at v d. the dd. … v s. x d.

[23] 'iiii d.' add, later.

Item to Hugh Worsley grome of my lad*ys* chambir for going to London of my lad*ys* message at ii soundry tymes from Richemount by ii days … viii d.

Item in reward to m*aister* Anthony keper of the king*es* galaries at Richemount … iii s. iiii d.

Item for the hier of iiii cart*es* from Richemount to the To*ur* w*ith* my lad*ys* stuf at xiiii d. the pece … iiii s. viii d.

Item the iii day of May in reward to Thomas Bury somtyme childe of my lad*ys* chapell … v s.

Item to the bargeman for conveying of my lad*ys* grace from Richemount to the To*ur* in a barge with viii ores at viii d. the ore. The hir*e* of the barge viii d. the maisters hier xii d. and for risshes ii d. … vii s. ii d.

Item the iiiith day of May to George Fraunceys for co*m*myng from Richemount to the To*ur* for the ordering of my lad*ys* lodgeyng by the space of ii days himsilf and his s*er*vant w*ith* the hier of his horses … iii s. x d.

Item to maistres Fowler for riding from Richemou*n*t to Hatfeld \again/ by the space of iiii days … vii s. ii d.

Item to the same for ale bought for my lad*ys* grace at Richemount … xviii d.

Summa … xlvi s. iiii d.[P]

[*f. 12r*] Item to the same for v elnes of blak ryband for my lad*ys* grace … v s.

Item for iii yerd*es* of cotton for my lad*ys* grace at xvi d. the yerd … iiii s.

Item for nedilles … vi d.

Item the vth day of May to maistres Parker for cristenyng of my lady Boughams childe in the name of my ladies grace … xl s.

Item in reward to m*aister* Cristofr Myddelton … x s.

Item the xith day of May in reward to m*ais*tres Massy by William Love … vi s. viii d.

Item to a smyth for emending of my lad*ys* clok at the Tour*e* … iiii d.

Item in reward to Tyler and Sharp … vi s. viii d.

Item to my lady Jane for hir cost*es* in goyng by wat*er* from Richemount to London to cristen in the name of my lad*ys* grace a child of m*aiste*r Lynches … ii s. vi d.

Item to Rob*er*t Neswik for a ryse to wynde silk on … iiii d.

Item to Rob*er*t Merbury for conveying of haulf a redd dere from the To*ur* to Richemou*n*t w*ith* his s*er*vant … xvi d.

Item to the same for going to Richemount to bring my lady knowledge of the honou*r*able s*er*vic*es* done about king Henry the viith in comeyng of his corps from thens to Westm*ynster* by the space of iii dayes … ii s.

Item to the same for tarying <of> bihinde my lad*ys* grace at Richemount aft*er* hir removing to the To*ur* for delyv*er*aunce of c*er*tayn stuf by ii days … viii d.

Item to John Madyson in like wise … viii d.

Summa … iiii li. viii d.[P]

[*f.* *12v*] Item to Nycholas Aughton for ryding to Wyndesore t*o* the princesses of England and Castill by the space of ii dayes … xvi d.

Item the xiii[th] day of May to maister Pexsall for his bote hir*e* from the Tower to my lord of Wynchest*ers* place in going of my lad*ys* message … ii d.

Item to George Frauncesse for his cost*es* in making of my ladies lodging at Grenewiche w*ith* his s*er*vant by the space of a day … xvi d.

Item to Hugh Worsley whiche was at Grenewiche with him for his diet by ii days … viii d.

Item the xv[th] day of May to Gerard bargeman for conveying of my lad*ys* grace from the Tower to Grenewiche in a barge w*ith* ix ores at viii d. the ore … vi s. For the hier of the barge viii d. For the m*aisters* hier xii d. For russhes … ii d. … vii s. x d.

Item for my lad*ys* offering at Grenewiche upon Assension Day … v s.

Item to John Mericok for going by wat*er* from Grenewich to London for m*aister* Assheton comptroll*our* of my lad*ys* houshold … viii d.

Item the xxi[th] day of May in reward to my lady Margaret Pole … xx s.

Item to Will*i*am Love for co*m*myng from Hatfeld to <Grenewiche> Richemount by my lad*ys* co*m*maundment … xii d.

Item to the same for ryding from Richemou*nt* t*o* Hatfeld for hanging*es* and other stuff to be brought to Coldherburgh by the space of ii dayes aft*er* xii d. a day biside iiii d. p*ai*d for his dyet at Hatfeld … ii s. iiii d.

Summa … xl s. iiii d.[P]

[*f.* *13r*] Item for riding from the To*ur* to Hatfeld for removing of my lad*ys* wardrobe stuf into the chambre of presence ther by the space of ii days goyng and comyng and for his dyet by a day habiding at Hatfeld … ii s. iiii d.

Item to the same for conveying of a bed for maistres Stanhop from Coldherbergh to the To*ur* … <xvi d.> ii d.

Item to the same William Love for trussing lyne … xvi d.[24]

Item in reward to c*er*tayn weders in the king*es* gardeyn at Grenewyche … xx d.

Item the xxii[th] day of May to Ric*hard* Aderton for riding for James Morice from Grenwyche to Cambrige by ii dayes … xvi d.

Item to maistres Linche for i \lib./ <di. lib.> of Venyce silv*er* … xxx s.

Item for vii unc*e* of other silv*er* … vi s. v d.

Item for a pece of <s> cotton of the middell assise … ii s. viii d.

[24] Entry originally om. but squeezed in here.

Item for a lib. q*uarter* of silv*er* … xviii s. x d.

Item for a lib. of Venyce silv*er* … xxiiii s.

Item for vi yerd*es* of ryband of ii peny brede … xii d.

Item for vi yerd*es* of ryband of iiii peny brede … ii s.

Item in reward to a s*er*vant of oon Pagnams of London for bringing of bake quyncesse … xx d.

Item for a penn*our* and inkhorn for my lad*ys* grace … iii d.

Item for setting in of m*aister* Parkers arme being oute of the joincte … iii s. iiii d.

Item in reward to a s*er*vant of my lord Burgevenyes for bringing of a salmon troute … xx d.

Item in reward yeven to the prioresse of Wilberfosse … vi s. viii d.

Summa … Cv s. v d.[P]

[*f. 13v*] Item to John Hasilby for going from Grenewiche to London to Wynkyn de Worde w*ith* a s*er*mone to be enp*r*inted and for bote hir*e* conveying of a federbed from Coldherb*ergh* to Grenewyche … ix d.

Item the xxv day of May for iiii pair*e* of gloves bought for my lad*ys* grace … xvi d.

Item to Rob*er*t Neswik for a weving stole … xvi d.

Item for my lad*ys* offering at Grenewiche upon Wyt Sonday … v s.

Item for the cost*es* of Rob*er*t Fremyngham being at London by ii days in receyving of money of maist*er* Assheton my lad*ys* receyvo*ur* generall … xx d.

Item for bote hyr*e* for conveying of the same from London to Grenewiche and for his going to London … x d.

item the xxviii[th] day of May to James Morice for the work*es* of the chapell in Crist*es* Colleige … xxvi li. xiii s. iiii d.

Item to the ii ancresses at Stampford in reward by the hand*es* of John Byrde … vi s. viii d.

Item delyv*er*ed to the hand*es* of my lad*ys* grace the xxix[th] day of May for reward*es* to be yeven at hir pleas*er* to dyv*er*se of the king*es* s*er*vant*es* nigh about his grace … xiii li. vi s. viii d.

Item the xxx[th] day of May to maistres Denton in reward … xx s.

Item to Rog*er* Ratclif for going of my lad*ys* message from Grenewiche to Handworth to the princesse of England by the space of ii days w*ith* his s*er*vant … iii s. x d.

Summa … xlii li. xvii d.[P]

[*f. 14r*] Item the first day of June to maistres Stanhop for ii pec*es* sypres of the myddell assise bought for my lad*ys* grace at ii s. vi d. the pece … v s.

Item for ii pec*es* of sypres of the lest sort at <u>xx d.</u> the pece … iii s. iiii d.

[25]Item to Will*i*am Lok of London mercer for a pece of tawny saten cont*eynyng* xli yerd*es* at viii s. the y*er*de … xvi li. xii s.

Item to Ric*hard* Clifford for a pece of tawny saten cont*eynyng* xxxii yerd*es* di. at vii s. viii d. the yerd … xii li. ix s. ii d.

Item to Lewes Harpesfeld for a pece of tawny damask cont*eynyng* xxix yerd*es* di. at vii s. iiii d. the yerd … x li. xvi s. iiii d.

Item to the same for a pece of tawny velwet cont*eynyng* xx y*er*d*es* di. at xiii s. iiii d. the yerd … xiii li. xiii s. iiii d.

Item to the same for a pece of blak velwet cont*eynyng* xxiiii y*er*d*es* at xi s. the yerd … xiii li. iiii s.

Item in reward to a s*er*vant of the prio*ur* of Lantony for bringing of chese … xx d.

Item to maistres Denton the vth day of June for hir fee due at the feste of Sainct Michaell last passed by the hand*es* of hir s*er*vant Will*i*am Morhand … lxvi s. viii d.

Item to Lewes Harpesfeld for v pec*es* of tawny chamblet at xxvi s. viii d. the pece … vi li. xiii s. iiii d.

Item to Will*i*am Lok for a pece of tawny damask cont*eynyng* xxv y*er*d*es* at vii s. iiii d. the yerd … ix li. vii s.

Item to maistres Stanhop for iiii playn bonett*es* of blak velwet at xiii s. the pece … lvi s.

Summa … iiii^{xx}ix li. vi s. x d.[P]

[*f. 14v*] Item for my ladies offering upon Corpus Chr*ist*i Day at Grenewiche … v s.

Item for the cost*es* of Rob*er*t Fremyngham in going from Grenewiche to London by iii soundry tymes for bying of div*er*se silk*es* … vii s. viii d.

Item to Will*i*am Hilm*er* for the hire of a bote from the To*ur* to Grenewiche for the conveyaunce of ii chayers and a basket w*ith* glasses … iiii d.

Item the viii day of June in reward to Margaret Redwoode of London for bringing of rose water to my lad*ys* grace … vi s. viii d.

Item in reward to Pellet husbond unto my lady Bougham … iii s. iiii d.

Item to John Henryson for co*m*myng from Hatfeld to Grenewiche by my lad*ys* co*m*maundeme*n*t by the space of iii days w*ith* his tarying ther … iii s. iiii d.

Item to John Grome in likewise … iii s. iiii d.

Item to Richard Aderton for ryding for m*ais*t*er* John Sainct John by i day … viii d.

Item to maistresse Fowler for a reward yeven to Will*i*am Thomas the king*es* s*er*vant … x s.

[25]This and the following four entries, together with the final three on the page, are each noted by a dot in the left margin.

Item the same day in reward to a woman whiche brought straberyes unto my lad*ys* grace … xx d.

Summa … xlii s. ^{P}

[*f. 15r*] Item paide to Thomas Senowe goldwyre drawer for vii lib. of rounde golde of damask the lib. cont*eynyng* xii unc*e* at iiii s. iii d. the unc*e* … <xvi li. xvi s.> xvii li. xvii s.

Item for iii unc*e* di. of piping flat golde at v s. iiii d. the unc*e* … xviii s. viii d.

Item for iiii unc*e* of rounde golde of damask delyv*er*ed to maistresse Odall at iiii s. iii d. the unc*e* … xvii s.

Item to John Vauntrix goldesmyth for making of an ymaige of Saincte George in golde garnisshed and sette w*ith* iii poynct*es* of dyamound*es* … xliii s. iiii d.

Item p*ai*d to the same John for an unc*e* q*ua*rt*er* iii penyweight di. of crowne golde for the same ymaige after xxxvi s. viii d. the unc*e* and xxii d. the penyweight … lii s. iii d.

Item paide to Henry Ludlowe for his wag*es* due at mydsom*er* last passed … xx s.

Item to John Merycok for certayn waters and pouders by him bought for my ladies grace in time of hir sekenesse … xvi d.

Item for iii yerd*es* of grene cloth bought to ley upon comptyng bourd*es* … vi s.

<Item the xxvi day of July to Nicholas Saunde for the use>

Item the xiiiith day of Ap*r*ill to John Leigh for a bill signed by m*ais*t*er* Assheton comptr*ollour* of houshold … ii s. iii d.

Item the iii^{de} day of May to John Leegh for the hier of a cart from Richemount to Putney w*ith* my lad*ys* kechin stuf … viii d. For brede \iii d./ ale \ii s./ butt*er* \v d./ fuell \viii d./ otemell \i d./ and salt \[…]/ floundres \iiii d./ egg*es* \ii d./ and house romth \viii d./ at the said Putney. Expens*es* of the said John ther iii d. egg*es* bought at Richemount xviii d. wasshing of the kechin stuf by the same space vi d. w*ith* the hier of a bote from the said Putney to the To*ur* for conveyaunce of the said kechin stuf viii d. … viii s. ii d.[26]

Summa … xxvi li. vi s. ^{P}

[*f. 15v*] Item p*ai*d to the same John Leigh the last day of May for bote hir*e* from the To*ur* to Grenewiche w*ith* the said kechin stuf … iiii d.

Item for butt*er* \vi d./ and egg*es* \xxii d./ … ii s. iiii d.

Item for a frying panne \xvi d./ and kechen pott*es* \iiii d./ … xx d.

Item for the hire of a labo*ur*er in my lad*ys* p*r*evy kechin by the space of vii wek*es* iii dayes aft*er* the rate of iiii d. a weke … ii s. vi d.

[26] The total is correct (even without the amount for salt, which is obscured by damp, like the -aunce of 'conveyaunce'). The whole entry and material below it is badly damaged by damp, including Fisher's signature.

Item p*ai*d to James Maurice the xiith day of M*ar*che anno regis Henrici viimi xxiiiito toward the buylding of the chapell in Cristes Colleige in the univ*er*sitie of Cambrige by the hand*es* of Nicholas Saunder ... lxxii li. vii d.

Item the vth day of Aprill deliv*er*ed to my lad*ys* g*r*ace for hir almoys yeven upon Shere Thursday to lxvii pore women to every of theim xiii d. ... lxvii s. vii d.[27]

Item to George Atcliff of London mercer for a mantelet of Parice for my lad*ys* grace ... xvi s.

Item paid the last day of August to Hugh Worsley by a bill assigned ... iiii s. viii d.

Item the same day to Nicholas Aughton by a bill signed ... iii s. x d.

Item to Henry Abney the first day of August by a bill signed ... ii s. iiii d.

Item in reward to my lady Pooll by the handes of my lad*ys* tr*esaur*are ... xl s.

Summa ... lxxx li. vi s. x d. P

[*f. 16r*] [28]Item payed to Rob*er*t Hilton att dyv*er*s tymes that ys to say the xxixth day of January xl s. The xxvti day of February xxi li. xvi s. xi d. The xvith day of Aprill ix li. The xxixti day of May lx s. The xix daye of Junn vi li. xiii s. iiii d. and the xxiiiti day of Juin xvi li. In all ... lviii li. x s. iii d.

Item paied to George Frauncez by my lad*ys* co*m*mandeme*n*t ... xxviii s.

Item payed to m*aster* doct*our* Bekensawe for the delyv*er*ance of certen prisoners ... xl li.

[*f. 16v*]

Summa omnium solucionum et expensarum predictarum ... <DCCCClxix li. iiii s. iiii d.> \Mix li. iiii s. iiii d./[29]

Et debet ... <Clxxvi li. xviii s. iii d. ob.> Cxxxvi li. xviii s. iii d. ob.[30]

[31]<DCCClxxv li. <iiii s. vi d. \v s. ob./> iiii s. vi d.

debet ... CClxx li. xviii s. i d.

Inde in denariis prestitis ... Cxvi li. xiii s. iiii d.[32]

Et debet ... Cliiii li. iiii s. ix d.>

Quere pro certo unde Super in secundo folio sequenti.[33]

[27] MS 'lxvjj' (i.e. altered from 66 to 67), 'lxxjj s. vjj d.' (i.e. alt. from 76s. 6d. to 77s. 7d.). However, Lady Margaret was not 67 on Maundy Thursday (5 April) 1509 but was approaching her 66th birthday, so that the alt. numbers are incorrect. Cf. 19/97I (65 in 1508).

[28] This page and the next are written in the 'sprawling' hand.

[29] The corrected sum adds the £40 from the final item on f. 16r.

[30] The corrected sum removes the £40 from the debt.

[31] All these canc. calculations (this line and the three below) are written small below each other to the left of 'Et debet', perhaps in the 'sprawling' hand.

[32] See f. 18v below.

[33] Written small mid-page in a neat hand. See f. 18v, i.e. the second folio following.

[34]<Summa omnium solucionum … DCCCClxix li. iiii s. iiii d.

debet … Clxxvi li. xviii s. iii d. ob.

Inde in denariis prestitis … Cxvi li. xiii s. <ix d.> iiii d.

debet … lx li. \iiii s. […] d. ob./>[35]

[*f. 17r*] *Wherof in*[36]

Money delyv*er*ed att sundry tymes and places for my lad*ys* offerying*es* … iiii li. ix s. viii s.

Money delyv*er*ed att dyv*er*s tymes unto my lad*ys* grace for her almos … lxxvii li. xvii s. iiii d.

Sundry medecynes bought att dyv*er*s tymes for my lady … xxix s. vi d.

Dyv*er*s necc*essar*y stuff bought for my lad*ys* grace … vi li. x s. x d.

Dyv*er*s necessary stuff bought for my lad*ys* almos folke with the rent of their*e* howse … xxiii s. viii d.

Money paied for certein stuff bought of the executo*ur*s of the lady of Norff*olk* … Cxii s. viii d.

Reward*es* yeven att the cristyng of dyv*er*s childer … iiii li. xiii s. iiii d.

Cost*es* of dyv*er*s of my lady s*er*vaunt*es* rydyng uppon sundry messagez … x li. xiiii s. xi d.

Money payed for barge hyre and bote hyre att dyv*er*s tymes … lxii s. iiii d.

Money paied for hyre of the howse in Chepesyde where my lad*ys* grace and the princesse of Castell stode whan þe kyng and the quene ca*m*me frome the Toure to Westm*ynster* to be crowned … xl s.

Dyv*er*s necessary stuff bought for John Stowell and John Baptist … ii s. x d.

Money payed by m*aister* Bekensawe for the delyv*er*aunce of certen prisoners … xl li.

[*f. 17v*] Exhibicion of maistres P*ar*ker childer leyng w*ith* m*aistr*es Massy … xv s. iiii d.

Cost*es* of the kepyng of a child that was geven to my lad*ys* grace … xl s.

Money payed for the mariage of m*aistr*es *Yan* … xxxviii li. vi s. viii d.

Money payed to the gild of Seynt Bride in Flete Strete … v s.

Money payed for workyng gold and sylver with silk and dyv*er*s other stuff bought by Peter the broderer … li li. viii s. iiii d.

[34] This second set of canc. calculations is written small to the left at the foot of the page in the same neat hand as those above; they form the basis for the calculations written fair higher up the page.
[35] Obscured by a mend in the page, but see the last entry f. 18v.
[36] Halfway down the left magin, bracketed to include all the items on ff. 17r–18r.

Dyv*er*s velvett*es* satens damask*es* sarcenett*es* and other silk*es* bought … Cxxxvi li. iiii s. xi d.

Certen bonett*es* frontlett*es* w*ith* the makyng bought and yeven to dyv*er*s gentilwomen … lxxi s. iiii d.

Certen plate broches and tablett*es* bought with mendyng of dyv*er*s pott*es* and flagons of sylver … xxv li. xii s. vii d. ob.

Dyv*er*s bok*es* bought of Wynkyn de Worde … xxxv s. vi d.

Bolyons bought for bok*es* of Crist*es* Colege w*ith* settyng on of the same … iiii li. xi s.

Money payed for fynding of an office wherby my lady was intitled to the wardship of Thomas Lyne … xlii s. vi d.

Money payed for parte of the cost*es* of the ap*ro*priacio*un* of the p*ar*sonage of Manorbere … xxvi s. viii d.

Money payed to m*aistr*es Denton for her fee … lxvi s. viii d.

Money delyv*er*ed to Rob*er*t Hilton att dyv*er*s tymes for the p*ro*vision of certen stuff … lxviii li. x s. iii d.

[*f. 18r*] Money payed for mendyng of old aras … x s. iiii d.

Money payed to George Fraunsez by my lad*ys* co*m*[m]a[n]d[m]e*nt*[37] … xxviii s.

Money delyv*er*t to James Mores for the rep*ar*acion doon att Crist*es* College in Cambrige … CCCxxv li. ii s. iii d.

Money payed to Thomas Sop*er* my lad*ys* solicito*ur* … Cx s.

Money payed to s*ir* Adrian Fortescu knyght for the mano*ur* off Bassyngbo*ur*n in Fordam … Cvi li. xiii s. iiii d.

Money payed for certen pecez of canvas bought with the cost*es* of the cariage of the same … lxxvii s. vii d.

Dyv*er*s reward*es* yeven unto sundry p*er*sones att dyv*er*s tymes … lxxvii li. xi .

[38]Summa omnium solucionum ut antea in secundo folio precedenti[39] … <DCCCClxix li. iiii s. iiii d.> \Mix li. iiii s. iiii d./

Et debet ut antea … <Clxxvi li. xviii s. iii d. ob.> Cxxxvi li. xviii s. iii d. ob. [40]

unde ut extra[41]

[37] MS 'co*m*naide*nt*', i.e. too few minims in –n- and –i-, and –m- om.

[38] From here through to f. 18v (certainly the rubric) appear to be written in the 'sprawling' hand.

[39] See f. 16v above for the same calculations of payments and debt.

[40] As noted, the two sums are exactly as at f. 16v above.

[41] Written small to the right of the page.

[*f. 18v*] *Super*

Georgium Hevenyngham ut pro tot denariis sibi per dominam infra tempus huius computi prestitis per obligacionem penes dominam remanentem … x li.

Thomam Sop*er* solicitarium domine ut pro tot denariis per ipsum receptis dicto computo per mandatum magistri contrarotulatoris … xiii li. vi s. viii d.

Wynkyn de Worde ut pro tot denariis sibi hoc anno prestitis per obligacionem penes dominam remanentem … xx li.

Philippum Morgan ut pro tot denariis sibi prestitis per consimilem obligacionem remanentem … xiii li. vi s. viii d.

magistrum Hugonem Asshton clericum ut pro tot denariis per ipsum receptis per manus Rogeri Radclyff … xx li.

<magistrum Robertum Bekinsawe ut pro tot denariis per[42] ipsum receptis super destribucionem elemosinarum … xl li.>[43] «cancellatur hic quia allocatur superius»[44]

Ipsum computatorem de propriis arreragiis … lx li. iiii s. xi d. ob.[45]

[46]*<Cxvi li. xiiii s. iiii d.>*

lxxvi li. xiiii s. iiii d.

[*ff. 19r–21v blank*]

[42] 'per' rep.

[43] Diagonal strokes of cancellation.

[44] See f. 16r above, last item.

[45] The accountant (cofferer) owes £60 4s. 11½ d. See the last entry f. 16v.

[46] Written small in the left margin above 'Ipsum … ', the canc. sum includes the (canc.) amount owed by Bekinsall.

D.102.2 (SJLM/1/1/4/1) and D102.6 (SJLM/1/1/4/2) Book of receipts and payments of Sir Roger Ormeston, chamberlain: 20 May - 18 December 1501 (D102.2), [January-February 1502][1] (D102.6)

Discussion See Introduction 4 and Plate 18.

Description D102.2 and D102.6 originally formed one volume,[2] but are now bound and identified separately.

D102.2 Paper, with some repair to flyleaf [i], written on both sides, approx. 260 x 180 mm. 20 ff. in a single quire, with an extra page sewn in (i.e. the fifth folio, pp. 5/6) and the twelfth folio cut out after pp. 19-20. First two folios unpaginated [blank], then paginated top right recto 1-35 in pencil (MGU); pp. [i-iv], 4, 19-20 blank. Left margins approx. 35-40 mm. (with some sub-headings); right margins variable; upper margins 20 mm.; lower margins variable. Bound into a modern brown/grey buckram cover ('D102.2' altered to 'SJLM/1/1/4/1' on a white pasted slip bottom left).

D102.6 Paper, in a good state, written on both sides, approx. 260 x 180 mm. 10 ff. in a single quire. Paginated 1-11 in pencil (MGU); [i-iv], 8, 10 and all pages thereafter blank. Margins as above. Binding as above (but 'D102.6' altered to 'SJLM/1/1/4/2' on a white pasted slip bottom left).

The summaries, i.e. initial and final material for the period of the account (D102.2/1-6, D102.6/2-6) use a formal script (Bastard Anglicana, with a large decorated initial 'S' D102.2/6, D102.6/2) for the rubrics, infilled with either a smaller formal hand (D102.2/1-2, D102.6/2-6), or the RO hand (D102.2/3-6).[3] The main body of the accounts and the page totals D102.2/21-35 are in a current hand (Anglicana, with Secretary influence),[4] seemingly identifiable as the hand of Roger Ormeston himself ('the RO hand').[5] 'Jh*esu*s m*er*cy lady hellp me Ame*n*' written sideways at the top outer edge D102.2, p. [i]r in the same hand; 'Jh*es*u' written in the upper margin D102.2, pp. 5, 7, 21 in the same hand. The 'sprawling hand' is responsible for the added note D102.6/2 (and perhaps more in D102.6). The auditor marks the page and summary

[1] 9 January is the first date given and 11 February the last (D102.6, pp. 2, 9).

[2] See, for example, D102.6, p. 5: 'Dyv*er*s necc*ess*ar*ie* stuff bought as threde tyke and other thyng*es* as apperith in dyv*er*s plac*es* of this boke'. These items are to be found in D102.2, e.g. tick p. 32.

[3] The blanket term, the 'summary' hand, is used for what may be one or more of the hands used in D91.20, D91.21, D91.19, D102.1, and D102.2 and D102.6. D102.6 consists only of final rubrics and end matter of the originally complete book; it is entirely written in a single summary hand, perhaps the 'sprawling' hand.

[4] The page totals D102.2/7-17, 36 are in the summary hand. The calculations of cloth in the entries D102.2/9-32 have been checked; footnotes detail only errors.

[5] 'I Roger Urmyston', D102.2/3, 5; 'by me Roger Urmyston', D102.6/7, 9, etc.

totals 'probatur' after the total ([P] in the edited text, but not D10.2.2/11, 15, 17, 18); Lady Margaret signs only D102.2/3, 18 ([M] in the edited text). Annotating marks similar to a sigma (σ) are sometimes added in the RO hand, e.g. D102.2/3, 5, 7, etc.

Summary

D102.2 [unpaginated first two ff. blank] statement of account (Ormeston, 20 May – 18 Dec. 1501), p. 1; receipts, pp. 1-3; sum total of receipts, p. 3 [p. 4 blank]; further receipts, p. 5; total of further receipts, p. 6; sum total of all the receipts, p. 6; payments, pp. 7-18; cancelled sum total of the payments and superplusage, p. 18 [pp. 19-20 blank]; 21-36 further payments.

D102.6 [unpaginated first f. blank] sum total of receipts and debt of Ormeston and repayment (9 Jan. 1502), p. 2; summary of payments made by RO, pp. 3-6 [pp. 7-8 blank]; memorandum of payment (11 Feb. 1502), p. 9 [all pages thereafter blank].

Edited Text

D102.2

[*unpaginated first folio verso and second folio recto and verso blank*[6]]

[*p. 1*] [7]Thaccompte of sir Roger Ormeston knyght as well of alle man*er* sommes of money by hym receyved as of alle man*er* payementes by hym made for the provysion of certeyn stuff bought for the most excellent princes Margaret countes of Richemond and Derby and moder unto oure sov*er*aine lord the kynge that nowe is that is to sey from the xxth day of Maye <Anno> the xvith yere of the raigne of oure seid sov*er*aigne lord \the kyng/ unto the xviiith day of Decemb*er* then next folowyng the xviith yere of the seid sov*er*aign lorde that is to sey by the space of xxxi wekys and v dayes.

London. First the seid sir Roger is charged with money by hym receyved of div*ers* tena*u*nt*es* there … vii li. ix s. vi d.

Lammersshe. Item receyved of <the Ba John mortym*er* Rev>[8] \hymselff by the hand*es* of his deupute/ there of the profit*es* of his office of this yere as apperith by the accompte of the said <John Mortym*er*> … xxxi li. xvi s. xi d.

[*p. 2*] *Colne Wake*. Item receyved of hymselff bayly there by the hand*es* of Thomas Mann his deputie of the p*ro*fit*es* of this office of this yere as apperith by his accompte … xxviii li. xiii s. iiii d. ob.

Hatfeld Peverell. Item receyved of hymselff bayly there by the hand*es* of Hugh Etton his deputie of the p*ro*fites of his office of this yere as apperith by his accompte … xxxiii li. vii s. viii d. ob.

[6] But see Description above.

[7] The summary hand begins the document.

[8] Alt. later in the same hand.

Deptford stronde. Item receyved of the fermer there of the p*ro*fit*es* of his ferme of this yere as apperith by his accompt ... xxviii li.

Mogdenhall. Item receyved of the fermer there of the p*ro*fit*es* of his ferme of this yere ... xxiii li.

Hengrave. Item receyved of the wiff of s*ir* William Carewe knyght late fermer there in p*ar*tye of payment of his ferme ... xv li.

Recepta foris.[9]

Item receyved of James Clarell by the hand*es* of Thomas Haselwode <s> in p*ar*te of his arrer*ag*es ... xxxiii li. vi s. viii d.

Item receyved of Edmond Mody for my lady Revers ... xx li.

Summa huius folii ... CCxx li. xiiii s. ii d.[P 10]

[*p. 3*] [11]Memorandum þ*at* I Rog*er* Urmyston haith resavyd off mast*er* Hewe Oldam chanselere w*ith* my lady the kyng*es* moder*e* <the> from the xx day of May the xvith ȝer*e* off the reyne off kyng Herr*y* the viith unt*o* the firste day off Auguste the next folowyng to my lady the kyng*es* mod*er* behove[12] ... C li.

Item off s*ir* Jon Schaa by the hond*es* off Jon Mondy the xxiiiith day off May the xvith ȝer*e* of the reyne of<f> kyng Herr*y* the viith \to my ladys behove/ ... ix^{xx} li.

Item mor*e* off the said s*ir* Jon Schaa by the hond*es* off Jon Mondy the xxvith day off Joly the xvith ȝer*e* off <of> the reyne of<... > kyng Herr*y* the viith t*o* my lady the kyng*es* mod*er* behove ... C li.

Item resavyd off mest*er* Hew Oldom chanseler*e* w*ith* my lad*ys* grasse the xxiiiith day off Jone the xvith ȝer*e* off the reyne off kyng Herr*y* the viith to my [lady] the kyng*es* mod*er* behove ... xxx li.

[M]Summa totalis recepte ut supra ... CCCCx li.[P 13]

[*p. 4 blank*]

[*p. 5*]

Memorandum þ*at* I Rog*er* Urmyston haith resavyd off syr John Schaa knyght by the hond*es* off John Mondy the xiith day off Auguste the xvith ȝer*e* off the reyne off kyng Herr*y* the viith to the behove off my lady the kyng*es* moth*er* ... xl li.

Item resavyd mor*e* off the said s*ir* John Schaa by the hond*es* off John Mondy the xiiith day off Auguste the xvith ȝer*e* off the reyne off kyng Herr*y* the viith ... lx li.

[9] Bracketed to include the next two items.

[10] The correct total of pp. 1-2.

[11] The RO hand starts here. See Plate 18.

[12] ‘to ... behoue’ add. on the next line in the hand of the corrections p. 1.

[13] The correct total of p. 3, written in the summary hand.

Item resavyd mor*e* off the said s*ir* Jon Schaa by the hond*es* off Jon Mondy the xxvth ȝer*e* off the reyne off kyng Herr*y* the viith *to* the behove off my lad*ys* grasse … xxvi li. xiii s. iiii d.

Item resavyd mor*e* off the said s*ir* Jon Schaa by the hond*es* off Jon Mondy the xxvth day off Auguste the xviith ȝer*e* off H. vii to my lady the kyng*es* moder behove … xl li.

Item resavyd mor*e* off the said s*ir* Jon Schaa by the hond*es* off Jon Mondy the viii day off Septe*m*ber*e* the xviith ȝer*e* off the reyne off H. viith … xx li.

[*p. 6*] Item resavyd mor*e* off the said s*ir* Jon Schaa by the hond*es* off Jon Mondy the xvth day off Septe*m*ber*e* the xviith ȝer*e* off H. viith to my lady the kyng*es* moder*e* behove … xl li.

Item resavyd mor*e* off the said s*ir* Jon Schaa by the hond*es* off Jon Mo*n*dy the xxiiith day off Septe*m*ber*e* the xviith ȝer*e* off the reyne off H. viith … xl li.

Item mor*e* off the said s*ir* Joh*n* Schaa by the hond*es* off Jon Mo*n*dy the[14] iith dey off Octob*e*r*e* the xviith ȝer*e* off the reyne off kyng*e* H. the viith … xl li.

Somma totalis … CCCvi li. xiii s. iiii d.[P] [15]

[16]Som*m*e totall of alle the receyt*es* afore written … DCCCCxxxvii li. vii s. vi d.[17]

Totalis recepte … DCCCCxxxvii li. vii s. vi d.[18]

[*p. 7*] [19]Memorandum þ*at* all these parcelles folowyng for*e* my lad*ys* grasse bowyght and paid for*e* by me Rog*er* Urmyston sy[n]*n*ys[20] the xxiiiith day off <may> Aprill anno xvito H. vii.

therof[21]

In primys paid to Palmer*e* the vth day off May at Coldherbar*e* … vi s.

Item paid the viith day off May unto Palmer*e* the sadeler*e* … xx s.

Item paid the viiith day off May to Will*ia*m Colverdeyne belfownder*e* off London for*e* makyng off a rame þ*at* went to Boston … iiii li. xviii s. i d.

Item paid the same day to mast*er* Browne cooke to my lad*ys* grasse for*e* oreg*es* sug*er* and honey … xxxiii s. iii d.

Item paid the same day to Wyll*ia*m Markus for c*er*tane stuff bowȝht by my lad*ys* comandeme*n*t for hir grasse … ix s. ii d.

[14] 'the' rep.

[15] The correct total of pp. 5-6.

[16] The summary hand returns here.

[17] The correct total of all the receipts written in the summary hand with a decorated initial 'S'.

[18] Written small to the left at the foot of the page in a summary hand, but with 'ixC', not 'DCCC' as the 'Somme totall' above.

[19] The RO hand returns here.

[20] MS 'sym*m*ys' (i.e. one minim too many).

[21] Written in the summary hand after the 'Somme totall' calculation but in the margin of the next p. (p. 7) to introduce the payments which begin after the 'Memorandum' p. 7 and continue to the end of the document.

Item paid the xth day off May to Palmer*e* the sadeler*e* … xxxiiii s.

Item the same day paid to Wato*ur* Ryffe for his cost*es* and is mens w*ith* hym from London to Boston … xxxvi s. viii d.

Item the same day to Will*ia*m Brayntt*es* bargeman … xl s.

Summa partis … xiii li. xvii s. iii d.[P][22]

[*p. 8*] Item paid the same day unto Jameys the mast*er* off Saynt Bartyllmewis s*erva*n*d* for rep*ar*acion*us* off Coldherbare … xx s.

Item paid the xi^th day off May to Richard Shurley for*e* makyng off my lad*ys* lytter*e* … xxxiii s. iiii d.

Item the same day paid to the glasiȝer*e* þ*at* glasid Coldherbar*e* … iii s. iiii d.

Item paid the xiii^th day off May unt*o* Richard Goght towardes the makyng off the owens at Coldherbar*e* … iii li.

Item paid the xv^th day off May unto the mast*er* off Saynt Bartyllmewis spyttyll for rep*ar*acion*us* at Coldherbar*e* … xx s.

Item the xvi^th day paid for*e* d. lib. off red thred … xvi d.

Item the same day for*e* a lib. off blake thred … xii d.

Item the same day for*e* one q*uarter* off tawne thred … vi d.

Item paid the same day to Palmer*e* the sadeler*e* one a prest for*e* makyng my lad*ys* ger*e* … viii li.

Item paid t*o* Colyngborne for wryttyng off act*e* off p*ar*leme*n*t for*e* maste*r* Saynt Jone … x s.

Item paid to Fizeherbar*e* for*e* enteryng th*er*off … v s.

Summa partis … xv li. xiiii s. vi d.[P]

[*p. 9*] Item paid the xvii^th day off May t*o* Benedyk Spynyall for*e* one peyce off right purpill velvet cont*enyng* xxviii ȝard*es*. P*r*ice the [ȝarde] xiiii s. … xix li. xii s.

Item the same day bowȝght off hym xxv ȝard*es* off black velvet. P*r*ice the yard viii s. … x li.

Item the same day bowȝght off hym xxv ȝard*es* q*uarter* off black velvet. P*r*ice the yard viii s. … x li. ii s.

Item bowȝght of the said Benedik Sppynoll the same day one peice off black velvet cont*enyng* xxi ȝard*es* iii q*uarter*. P*r*ice the yard viii s. … viii li. xv s.[23]

Item the same tyme of hym one peice off black velvet cont*enyng* xxv ȝard*es*. P*r*ice the[24] yard viii s. … x li.

[22] The total is 1d. over. Page totals pp. 7–17 are written in the summary hand.
[23] The correct total is £8 14s.
[24] 'the' rep.

Item bowȝght the same day off Mane Florentyne xxix yard*es* off black s*ar*cynet. P*r*ice the yard iii s. iiii d. … iiii li. xvi s. viii d.

Item the same tyme bowȝght off hym xxxi yard*es* off black s*ar*cynet. P*r*ice the yard iii s. iiii d. … v li. iii s. iiii d.

Item the xviii[th] day off May paid for*e* ii ownc*es* off crymson silke … ii s. viii d.

Summa partis … lxviii li. xi s. viii d.[P]

[*p. 10*] Item paid the same day for*e* ii pec*es* black chamelet … xl s.

Item paid the xix[th] day off May unt*o* the mast*er* off Saynt Bartylmews for*e* rep*ar*acio-n*us* at Coldherbar*e* … xx s.

Item unt*o* Robart Stonys þ*at* glasid Colherbar*e* … vi s. viii d.

Item unt*o* Palmer*e* the same day … x li.

Item paid the xxiiii[th] day off May t*o* Petour off Coldherbar*e* for*e* makyng off the garden as hit aperith by his bill*es* … iiii li. xviii s. iii d.

Item paid the same day t*o* Benedyk Spynall for*e* xxvii yard*es* off crymson vellvet and xxvi yard*es* di. P*r*ice the yard x s. vi d. … xxvii li. xix s.

Item paid the same day t*o* Richard Gogh for the rep*ar*acion*us* of the kechyn at Coldherbar*e* … iii li.

Item paid the xxv[th] day off May for*e* four*e* par*e* off pakkyng schettes … vi s. viii d.

Item paid the same day t*o* Clem*en*t clerk for iii comyssion*us* Kesten Le*n*sey and Holond … xxxvii s.

Summa partis … xliii li. vii s. vii d.[P]

[*p. 11*] Item paid the same day t*o* Clem*en*t clerk for writyng off the said comyssion*nus*. Thysse by mast*er* Bran comandem*en*t … vi s. viii d.

Item paid t*o* the lorymer the xxvi[th] day off May for ii dosen bett*es*. P*r*ic*e* … xxviii s.

Item paid the same tyme for*e* tynyng off vi bett*es* … xii d.

Item t*o* Palmer*e* the same day … xx s.

Item paid unt*o* Will[ia]m Whytyng for*e* payntyng of my lad*ys* scharis … liii s. iiii d.

Item paid the same day t*o* the mast*er* off Saynt Bartyllmews for rep*ar*acion*us* at Coldherbar … iiii li.

Item paid t*o* Palmer*e* the sadeler*e* the xxiii day off Jone by the hond*es* off Richard Schurley … xl s.

Item t*o* Robart Stonys the same day þ*at* glased Coldherbor*e* … x s.

Item paid the xxiv[th] day off Jone to Antone Savage f[o]r xxvii yard*es* off black cloth off gold. P*r*ice the yard xxvi s. viii d. … xxxvi li.

Item the same day t*o* Bartyllmew the Jewse for*e* xlvii ȝard*es* off blew s*ar*cynet. P*r*ic*e* the yard iii s. iiii d. … vii li. xvi s. viii d.

Summa partis … lv li. xv s. viii d.

[*p. 12*] Item paid the same day t*o* the cop*er*smyth for makyng off portkoles for my lad*ys* grasse … xx s.

Item t*o* the mast*er* off Saynt Bartylmew for rep*ar*acion*us* off Coldherbar*e* … iiii li. ix d.

Item \paid/ t*o* Nycolas Curtesse the xxviii*th* day off Jone for*e* xlvi yard*es* off whit*e* s*ar*cynet. P*r*ic*e* the yard iii s. iiii d. … vii li. xiii s. iiii d.

Item paid to Blagg off the exiekere for*e* c*er*chyng makyng and writyng of a p*ar*ley for master Saynt Jones lond*es* … xxvi s. viii d.

Item paid the last day off Jone t*o* Will*ia*m Bradschaa for xx yard*es* of crymyson saten. P*r*ice the yard vi s. viii d. … vi li. xiii s. iiii d.

Item paid the vith day off Joly t*o* the glasiȝer*e* þ*a*t glasid Coldherbar*e* … iii s. iiii d.

Item paid the same day t*o* mast*er*is Buck for one peice off tawne medly co*n*teny*ng* xxiii yard. P*r*ice the [yard] iii s. iii d. … iii li. xiiii s. ix d.

Item anoth*er* peice of medly co[n]tenyng xxiii yard*es*. P*r*ice the yard iii s. iii d. … iii li. xiiii s. ix d.

Item anoth*er* peice cont*enyng* xxiii yard*es*. P*r*ice the yard iii s. iii d. … iii li. xiiii s. ix d.

Summa partis … xxxii li. xx d.[P]

[*p. 13*] Item anoth*er* peice medly *contenyng* xxv yard*es*. P*r*ic*e* the yard iii s. iii d. … iiii li. iii d.[25]

Item anoth*er* peyce off medly *contenyng* xxiii yard*es*. P*r*ic*e* the yard iii s. iii d. … iii li. xiiii s. ix d.

Item ped t*o* Richard Bowden for xxiii yard*es* <off> iii q*uarter* off tawne medly. P*r*ic*e* the yard iii s. vi d. … iiii li. iii s.[26]

Item paid t*o* Wi*l*l*ia*m Baly for xxi yard*es* off tawne medly. P*r*ic*e* the yard iiii s. iiii d. … iiii li. xi s.

Item paid t*o* Thomas Spyght for xxx yard*es* off tawne medly. P*r*ice the yard iii s. vi d. … vi li. xvi s.[27]

Item paid to Bartylmew <siȝewill> Felbywill*ia*m for*e* xxvii yard*es* q*uarter* tawne medly. P*r*ic*e* the yard iii s. viii d. … iiii li. xix s. x d.[28]

Item paid t*o* Picketon by my lad*ys* co*m*mandeme*n*t for c*er*tan dyapur*e* … xxxvi li.

[25] The total is 1s.. short.
[26] The total is 1½d. short.
[27] The total should be £5 5s.
[28] The total is 1d. short.

Item t*o* Palmer*e* the ix day off Joly by the hond*es* off Richard Schurley … liii s. iiii d.

Item paid to the cop*er*smyth the same day by the hond*es* off Richard Schurley … xiii s. iiii d.

Summa partis … lxvii li. xi s. vi d.[P]

[*p. 14*] Item paid t*o* Penson the skynner*e* for thre thowzand poudryngis … xxx s.

Item t*o* Nycolas Curtes the same day for xlv yard*es* off black damask. P*ri*c*e* the yard … xviii li. vi s. viii d.

Item in reward to *sir* Sampson s*er*vand þ*a*t brow3ght qualis t*o* my lad*ys* grasse … vi s. viii d.

Item paid t*o* Robart glasi3or*e* þ*a*t glasid Coldherbar*e* … xiii s. iiii d.

Item paid t*o* Palmer*e* the sadyler*e* the v[th] day off Joly … iii li.

Item t*o* the glasi3er*e* the same day … iii s. iiii d.

Item paid to Porter*e* the viii day off Joly for*e* a writ callid Mandamo*us*[29] for mast*er* Saynt Jone … <iii> iii s. iiii d.

Item paid for vii yard*es* of tawne medly for*e* t[ow]elyn [and] lynn*es*.[30] P*ri*c*e* the yard v s. … xxxv s.

Item paid to Jamys Yetyll the xvi[th] day off Joly for one peice off purpull velvet *contenyng* xvii yard*es* iii q*uarter*. P*ri*c*e* the yard xi s. vi d. … x li. iiii s. i d.[31]

Item paid the same daie t*o* the mast*er* off Saynt Bertylmews for thyng*es* to be done at Coldherbar*e* … v li.

Summa partis … xli li. ii s. v d.[P]

[*p. 15*] Item paid to Palmer*e* the sadeler*e* the same day … xl s.

Item paid the same day t*o* the cop*er*smyth for makyng off portcoles … xiii s. iiii d.

Item delyv*er*yd to Richard Browther*e* the xixth day off Joly for is bordwag*es* and oth*er* thyng*es* þat he bow3ght for my lady … x s.[32]

Item bow3ght the same day ii yard*es* off skarlet. P*ri*c*e* the yard ix s. … xviii s.

Item paid to Herr*y* Dakers the same day for xxx yard*es* off tawne medly. P*ri*c*e* the yard iiii s. x d. … vii li. v s.

Item paid to mast*er*is Fynch the same day for ii li. di. off gold off Venys. P*ri*c*e* the pownd xlviii s. … vi li.

Item paid to mast*er*is Fynch for ii li. off sylk. P*ri*c*e* the ownce x d. … xxvi s. viii d.

[29] i.e. 'mandamus', we command. A writ (probably for the seizure of land, cf. *OED* **mandamus** *n.* (a)).

[30] A conjectural emendation, since the MS appears to read 'tamelyn melynn*es*'.

[31] The total is ½d. short.

[32] Blotted.

Item paid t*o* Robart Watt*es* for[33] xxix yard*es* off tawne medly. P*rice* the yard iiii s. iiii d. … vi li. v<i> s. viii d.

Item paid to Stevyn Dra*ver* for xxx yard*es* medly. P*rice* the yard iiii s. vi d. … vi li. xv s.[34]

Summa … xxxi li. xiii s. viii d.

[*p. 16*] Item paid to Kyrby the xxi day off Joly for xxviii yard*es* medly. P*rice* the yard iiii s. iii d. … <v li. xvi s. viii d.> <\Cxix s./> v li. xix s.[35]

Item paid to the said Kirkeby for anoth*er* peyse off medly. P*rice* the yard iii s. x d. contenyng xxv yard*es* di. … iiii li. xvii s. <vii d.> \ix d./

Item delyv*er*yd to Gogh the xxiith day off Joly for thyng*es* nessassair*e* t*o* be done at Coldherbar*e* in the kechyn and oth*er* offec*es* … iii li.

Item paid t*o* the cop*er*smyth the same day … xiii s. iiii d.

Item paid the same day to mast*er*is Fynch for halfe a pownd off gold off Venys … xxiiii s.

Item paid the xxvi day off Joly t*o* the cop*er*smyth for*e* makyng off portkolas … xiii s. iiii d.

Item paid t*o* Thomas Fzeyto*n* mers*er* for xxvii yard*es* off cremyson damaske. P*rice* the yard v s. x d. … <vii li. xvii s. vi d.> viii li. iii d.[36]

Item paid to Daker the same day for one peice medly *contenyng* xxxii yard*es*. P*rice* the yard iiii s. <v> viii d. … vii li. <v> ix s. iiii d.

Item paid to Palmer*e* the saidéler*e* the xxviith day off Joly … vi li. vi s. viii d.

Summa partis … xxxix li. x s. viii d.[P]

[*p. 17*] [37]Item paid to Wodward goldrawer*e* for*e* one pownd off gold off damask. P*rice* the pownd <v s.> iii li. … iii li.

Item paid to mast*er*is Fynch the xxviiith day off Joly for di. li. off gold off Venys … xxiiii s.

Item paid the xxixth day off Joly to mast*er*is Longton for working off xxxviii ownc*es* off gold off Venys. Pric*e* the ownc*e* ii d. … vi s. iiii d.

Item paid t*o* him the same day for workyng off xxxii ownc*es* off sylke for the frenge off the lytter. P*rice* the ownce … v s. iiii d.

[33] 'for' rep.

[34] -x- over er. in darker ink.

[35] The first sum (in the RO hand) has been corrected above the line in a different hand ('Cxix s.'); both these sums are canc. and the RO hand writes the correction v li. xix s.'); both canc. sums are in darker ink.

[36] The canc. calculation in dark ink seems to have been add. later than the uncanc. sum (in the RO hand) but is correct.

[37] The change to a thinner nib here improves legibility.

Item bowʒght off the said mast*er*is Longton off violet and whyt*e* sylk one pownd. P*r*ice the ownce x d. and the workma*n*schipe ii d. … Somma xvi s. ix d.[38]

Item bowʒght off hir violet and white sylk for the depe frenge xxxviiith ownc*es*. P*r*ic*e* the ownce x d. and the workma*n*schype th*er*off ii d. … xxxviii s.

Item t*o* Will*iam* Horne cop*er*smyth the same day for makyng off ii dosen portkeles and v. P*r*ice the peice xiii d. … xxxi s. v d.

Item t*o* the said smyth for gyltyng off ii boosses … ii s. viii d.

Summa partis … ix li. iiii s. vi d.

[*p. 18*] Item delyv*er*yd for Olyv*er*e Saynt Jons bed the xxixth day of Joly \and delyv*er*ed to hym into the Towre/[39] … xx s.

[40]<Summa totalis of all payment*es* aforsaid as p*ar*ticulr*e* apperth … <CCCCxvi li. x s. iii d.> CCCCxix li. vi s. vi d.

quia postea

*Sup*er*plus*. And so remaynyth dewe unt*o* the said Roger Ormeston the first day of August anno xvi° regis Henrici vii ovyr all suche money as by hym is receyved as sev*er*ally befor*e* in this boke apperith … vi li. x s. iii d.>

M

[*pp. 19, 20 blank*]

[*p. 21*]

[41]<Memorandum þ*at* I Rog*er* Urmyston haith <layd owte> bowʒght and paid for by me>

Memorandum þ*at* all these p*ar*celles folowyng for my lad*ys* grasse bowʒght and paid for by me Rog*er* Urmyston

In primys bowʒght the viith day off August the xvith ʒer*e* off the reyne off kyng Herr*y* the viith one peyse off purpull vellvet ryht off Jamys sadeler*e* conteny*n*g xxxii yard*es* di. P*r*ice the yard xi s. viii d. … xviii li. xviii s. x d.[42]

Item bowʒght off Herr*y* Brian the viii day off August one peyse damask black *contenyng* xvi ʒard*es* di. at v s. the yard … Somma iiii li. ii s. iiii d.[43]

[38] Assuming the workmanship cost 2d. per oz. (as in the next item, which is correct), the total should be 16s.

[39] Add. small, probably in the summary hand (which is responsible for the rest of the page).

[40] The total and the rest of the page is canc. (despite Lady Margaret's having signed the page) because there is a later 'Summa totalis … postea' (see D102.6/2), which adds the rest of the items in D102.2 and replaces RO's superplusage by a debt.

[41] The RO hand returns here.

[42] The total should be £18 19s. 2d.

[43] The total is 2d. short.

Item anoth*er* peyse damask black *contenyng* xxi ʒard*es* iii q*uarter* at v s. the yard … v li. viii s. ix d.

Item anoth*er* peyse damask black *contenyng* xxxv yerd*es* di. P*r*ice the yard v s. … viii li. xvii s. vi d.

Item anoth*er* peise off damask black *contenyng* xvi yard*es* q*uarter*. P*r*ice the yard v s. off the said Brian … iiii li. xv d.

Somma … li li. viii s. viii d.[P 44]

[*p. 22*] Item bowʒght the ix day off August the xvi[th] ʒer*e* off the reyne off kyng Herr*y* the vii[th] off Thomas Zeton one peysse damask black off Luk. P*r*ice the yard vi s. *contenyng* xxiii yard*es* di. … vii li. viii d.

Item payd the same day to the mast*er* off Saynt Bartylmew spytyll for rep*ar*acion*us* at Coldherbar*e* as hit aperis by his byll*es* … v li.

Item the xth day off August paid to mast*er*is Benyt for a hud off black velvet. P*r*ice xv s. for my lad*ys* grasse … xv s.

Item paid the same day to hir*e* for*e* ii frontelett*es*. P*r*ice xviii s. … xviii s.

Item paid t*o* Palmer*e* the sadeler*e* ii old nobill*es* by the hond*es* off Robart Laythu*n*s s*er*vand. P*r*ice the nobull ix s. … xviii s.

Item bowʒght the xii[th] day off August off John Fysier*e* one peyse tawne medly *contenyng* xiiii ʒard*es* iii q*uarter*. P*r*ice the yard v s. … iii li. xiii s. ix d.

So*m*ma … xviii li. v s. v d.[P]

[*p. 23*] Item bowʒght the same day off Richard Bradschaa iii peic*es* chamelet black. P*r*ice the peysse xxi s. viii d. … iii li. v s.

Item bowʒght the same day off Antone Savage fyve peic*es* chamelet black <p>. P*rice* the peysse xxi s. viii d. … v li. viii s. iiii d.

Item paid the same day to Wodward goldwyr drawer*e* for one pownd gold off damask. P*rice* the pownd iii li. … iii li.

Item paid the same day for ryng*es* for a travesse vi d. … vi d.

Item for ii helnys off kanvas to trusse the velvet in þ*at* was send to my lad*ys* grasse t*o* Bugdeyn. P*r*ice the helne iii d. ob. … vii d.

Item for serchyng off the owtlawre in the cownto*us* at London aʒanest Godfrey Darrold and the writyng th*er*off … xx d.

Item bowʒght \off Hobard/ the xiiii[th] day of August one peyse fyne black *contenyng* xxxiii yard*es* q*uarter*. P*r*ice the yard ii s. xi d. … iiii li. xvi s.[45]

Item paid to Palmer*e* the same day by the hond*es* off Pet*er* his s*er*vand … iii li. ii s.

[44] Page totals pp. 21-35 are in the RO hand.
[45] The total is 11¾d. short.

Item paid the same day for one helne off ca*n*vas to trusse the s*ar*cynettes in … iiii d.

Somma … xix li. xiiii s. v d.[P]

[*p. 24*] Item bowʒght the xiiiith day off August off Bartyllmew Fizewill*ia*m one peysse medly *contenyng* xxx yard*es* at iiii s. viii d. the yard … vii li.

Item bowʒght the same day off Will*ia*m Mellner*e* one peyse medly *contenyng* xxiii yard*es* iii q*uarter* at iiii s. the yard … iiii li. xv s.

Item bowʒght the same day off the said Will*ia*m Melner*e* anoth*er* peysse medly *contenyng* xxv yard*es* iii q*uarter* at iiii s. iiii d. the yard … v li. ix s. iiii d.

Item bowʒght off Dowget the xviith day off August one peice medly *contenyng* xxv yard*es*. P*r*ice the yard iiii s. x d. … vi li. x d.

Item bowʒght off Jon Wylkynson the same day one peyse medly *contenyng* xix yard*es* iii q*uarter*. P*r*ice the yard iiii s. iiii d. … iiii li. v s. iiii d.

Item bowʒght the same day one peyse medly *contenyng* xxiiii yard*es*. P*r*ice the yard iii s. iiii d. off Will*ia*m Meller*e* … iii li. xviii s.

Item paid the xixth day off August to Palmer by the hond*es* off is s*er*vant Pet*ur* … iii li.

item paid to Pet*our* off Goldherbar*e* for thyng*es* done th*er* as aperis by is bill the xxiiith day off August the xviith ʒ*ere* off the reyne off kyng Herr*y* the viith … xxvi s. viii d.

Somma … xxxv li. xv s. ii d.[P]

[*p. 25*] Item paid the same day for vii li. off lyr*e* <… > for a*n*ngiryns. P*r*ice the pou*n*d iiii d. … ii s. iiii d.

Item paid t*o* Peter off Coldherbar*e* the xxxth day off August for thyng*es* by hym done at Coldherbar*e* as peris by is bill*es* … xx s.

Item bowʒght the laste day off August thre <slok> skor*e* hellnys off ka*n*vas t*o* lyne the arras w*ith*. P*r*ice the elne iiii d. … xx s.

Item paid the xxviiith day off August t*o* Palmer*e* by the hond*es* off Jon Pereson … x li.

Item paid t*o* the mast*er* off Saynt Bartylmew the first day off Septe*m*ber*e* for thyng*es* done at Coldherbar*e* … iii li.

Item paid the thrid day off Septe*m*ber*e* for lynyng off viii peic*es* off verdur*e* … v s. viii d.

Item paid the same day for xliiii loodes off sownd browʒght t*o* Goldherbar*e*. P*r*ice the loyd iiii d. … xiiii s. viii d.

Item bowʒght for*e* Olyver*e* Saynt Jone the viii day off Septe*m*ber*e* one <bedd> feth*er* bed a bolst*our* ii blanket*es* one par*e* off chett*es*. P*r*ice … xx s.

Somma … xvii li. ii s. viii d.[P] [46]

[46] There is a dot calculation to the right at the foot of the page.

[*p. 26*] Item bowȝght off Franc*es* Gwyny the same day one peice damask black *contenyng* xxvi yard*es*. P*r*ice the yard vii s. … ix li. ii s.

Item paid for xviii ownc*es* off gold off Venys wich maid xxi doz*en* buttons for my lad*ys* horse hernys. P*r*ic*e* the pownd xl s. \to mast*er*is Longton/ … iii li.[47]

Item paid to the said mast*er*is Longton for xx ownc*es* off gold off damask þ*at* went to the tassell*es* off the said buttons. P*r*ice the pownd xl s. … iii li. iii s. iiii d.[48]

Item paid to hir*e* for*e* xxiiii ownc*es* and a q*uarter* off sylk*es* þ*at* went to the tassell*es*. P*r*ice the ownce xiiii d. … xxviii s. iiii d.[49]

Item for d. ou*n*ce off silk*es* and th*er* went a q*uar*tron off gold to the trenton reyne. P*r*ice … xviii d.

Item for makyng off xxi dosen buttons at vii d. the doz*en* … xxi s.

Item one ownce and iii q*uarter* off gold to p*er*forme the frenge w*ith*. P*r*ice the ou*n*ce iii s. iiii d. … v s. x d.

Somma … xviii li. xxiii d.[P]

[*p. 27*] Item one ownc*e* and iii q*uarter* off purpull and sylk*es* for the said freng*e* … ii s.

Item delyv*er*yd t*o* the sadeler*e* Palmer*e* ii ownc*es* off gold þ*at* went t*o* the freng*es*. P*r*ice the ownce iii s. iiii d. … vi s. viii d.

Item one ownce and iii q*uarter* and di. sylk*es*. P*r*ice the ownce xiiii d. … ii s. ii d.[50]

Item paid to mast*er*is Longton for iiii doz*en* silk pownt*es* … ii s.

Item paid to Palmer*e* the xvth day off Septe*m*ber*e* the xvii*th* ȝer*e* off the reyne off kyng Herr*y* the viith by the hond*es* off is s*er*vand Benet … iiii li.

Item paid to Jhon Brook off Fyncheley colyȝer for <[…]> lxxii quart*er*is off colis. P*r*ic*e* the q*uarter* iiii d. … xxiiii s.

Item paid to Palmer*e* the xviiith day off Septe*m*ber*e* by the hond*es* off Pereson is s*er*vand … vi li.

Item paid to Palmer*e* the xxiith day off Septe*m*ber*e* by the hond*es* off Pereson is s*er*vand … v li.

Item paid to Paule Gylis for xiii<th> yard*es* off crymyson velvet right the xxiiith day off Septe*m*ber*e*. P*r*ice the yard xxxiii s. iiii d. … xxiii li. vi s. viii d.

<Item bowȝght off Antone Savage one peice velvet blak *contenyng* xv yard*es*. P*r*ice the yard viii d. … vi li.>

Somma … xl li. iii s. vi d.[P]

[47] The total is correct, based on 12 oz. to the lb.

[48] The total should be £3 6s. 8d., based on 12 oz. to the lb.

[49] The total is ½d. over.

[50] The total is ¼d. short.

[*p. 28*] Item delyv*er*yd t*o* mast*er*is Wyndisowr*e* by my lad*ys* comandme*n*t the same day … v s.

Item bowȝght the same day for my lad*ys* grasse one helne s*ar*cynet tawne. P*r*ice … vi s.

Item bowȝght the same day off Will*ia*m Bradschaa one peyce damask black. P*r*ice the yard v s. *contenyng* xix yard*es* iii q*uarter* … iiii li. xviii s.

Item paid the same day to Penson the skynner*e* for ii furris off colabur for my ladys grasse. P*r*ice … lv s. x d.

Item paid t*o* the said Penson for x my*n*kis for my ladys grasse. P*r*ice the pece ii s. … xx s.

Item paid for thre kepe off white buge for mast*er* Saynt Jonys gowne and mast*er* P*ar*kers wich was delyv*er*yd to \Robart/ Hilton. P*r*ice the kepe xiii s. iiii d. … xl s.

Item paid to <s> Robart Hilton for xii bed strings for my lad*ys* grasse. P*r*ice xii d. … <xiii d.> xii d.

Item paid for iiii tavelyns off chaunkis for mast*er*is P*ar*kerys gowne. P*r*ice the tovely*n* iii d. … xii d.

Item paid t*o* Robart Thorne for dressyng off xxx yard*es* medly. P*r*ice the yard vi d. … xv s.

Somma … xii li. xviii d.[P]

[*p. 29*] Item paid for a heyge off schanks black for the said gowne *contenyng* in lenght iiii yard*es* q*uarter* … xx d.

Item paid t*o* Palmer*e* the xxivth day off Septe*m*ber*e* by the hond*es* off Pereson is s*er*vand … xl s.

Item paid the same day to the mast*er* off Saynt Bartylmews s*er*vand Jamys for rep*ar*acion*us* done at Coldherbar*e* … <xxx s.> xxv s.

Item delyv*er*yd the xxixth day off Septe*m*ber*e* by my lady the kyng*es* moder comandeme*n*t to doct*our* Jamys Westonys … xx li.

Item delyv*er*yd the vith day off Octob*er*e t*o* Palmer*e* hymselffe in my howsse[51] … xl s.

Item paid to Gray[52] the haburdasser*e* for*e* thr*e* rowlis off whit*e* bevo*ur*. P*r*ice the pece xx s. ev*er*y peice *contenyng* iiii^{xx}vi yard*es* … iii li.

Item paid to Robart Watt*es* for one peyse medly *contenyng* xxii yard*es*. P*r*ice the yard viii s. … ix li.

Item paid to Bradschaa the xiiiith day off Octob*er*e for*e* ii peic*es* chamelet black. P*r*ice the peice xxv s. … l s.

[51] Note 'my'.

[52] Not a certain reading of the name.

Item bowʒght off Thomas Tydmersh the xvith day off Octobere iiii peces chamel*e*t black. P*r*ice the peice xxv s. … v li.

Somma … xliiii li. xvi s. viii d.[P]

[*p. 30*] Item paid the xviith day off Octobe*re* to Kok*e* for dyeng off vi^{xx} yard*es* xii yard*es* off bevo*ur* blewe and wyte … xv s.

Item paid to Jamys Moris for c*er*tayn thyng*es* done at Coldherbar*e* the same day … xl s.

Item paid the same day at Coldherbar*e* to my ladis grasse hirselff in gold … xl li.

Item bowʒght the thrid day off Nove*m*ber*e* off Alderbornedyne iii yard*es* off cloth off gold off tyssue. P*r*ice the yard xxvi s. viii d. … iiii li.

Item paid t*o* the mast*er* off Saynt Bartyllmews spytyll for*e* thynges done at Goldherbar*e* the xiiiith day off Nove*m*bere … xl s.

Item paid for the vth day off Nove*m*bere to Bradschaa for ii pec*es* chamelet. P*r*ice the peice xxiiii s. … xlviii s.[53]

Item paid the same day t*o* Penson for xxxvii mynkis. P*r*ice the peice xvi d. … xlix s.[54]

Item paid the same day to the said Penson for x mynkis. P*r*ice the peice ii s. … xx s.

Item paid the same day to Wodward goldrawer*e* for one pownd off gold off damask wich mast*er* Bedyll send to my lad*ys* grasse. P*r*ice … iii li.

Item paid the same day t*o* Palmer*e* … xl s.

Somma … lix li. xii s.[P]

[*p. 31*] Item bawʒght the vith day off Nove*m*ber*e* off Herr*y* Lenʒel drap*er* xxxvi yard*es* di. tawne medly. P*r*ice the yard iii s. x d. … vi li. xix s. x d.[55]

Item paid to Wadward goldwyredrawʒer*e* the viiith day off Nove*m*ber*e* for iiii ownc*es* off gold off damask … xx s.

Item paid the same day to Olyver*e* Clem*en*t for ii <p> tapett*es* off ymager*y* work. P*r*ice the tapet xi s. … xxii s.

Item paid to the said Olyver*e* for anoth*er* tapet off ymager*y* work the same day … xiii s. iiii d.

Item paid the same day for thre yard*es* <d.> tyck in lenght i and in bred vii q*uar*ter … iiii s.

Item paid to Richard Lanon for ii paynys and a haff off whit*e* menever. P*r*ice the payne xv s. … xxxvii s. vi d.

Item for <ass sr> a p*er*se ryn[g][56] off a fur*e* off mynkis tal*es* … xx d.

[53] Written over an erasure.

[54] The total is 4d. under.

[55] The total is 1d. under.

[56] MS 'p*er*se rynh'. Emendation uncertain (see Glossary).

Item bowȝght and pa[i]d for the ix[th] day off Nove*m*ber off Jon*e* Saxse xii yard*es* \iii q*uarter*/ medly. P*r*ice the yard iiii s. … l s xi d.[57]

Item bowȝtht the[58] same day off Herr*y* Dakers one peice medly *contenyng* xxviii yard*es* di. P*r*ice the yard iiii s. … v li. xiii s. x d.[59]

Item bowȝght off Kyrkby the xth day off Nove*m*ber*e* one pec*e* medly *contenyng* xxv yard*es*. P*r*ic*e* the yard iiii s. viii d. … Somma v li. xvi s. viii d.

Somma … xxv li. xix s. ix d.[P]

[*p. 32*] Item bowȝght the same day off Will*ia*m Falworth xv yard*es* rede for the chariot men. P*r*ice the yard iii s. ii d. … xlvii s. vi d.

Item bowȝght the xth day off Nove*m*ber*e* off Jon Bownd xix yard*es* <l> di. tawne medly. P*r*ice the yard iiii s. vi d. … iiii li. vii s. viii d.[60]

Item bowȝght the same day off the said Bownd xxiii yard*es* di. off tawne medly. P*r*ice the yard iii s. viii d. … iiii li. vi s.[61]

Item bowȝght off Bradschaa the same day ii pec*es* chamelett. P*r*ice the peic*e* xxiiii s. … xlviii s.

Item bowȝght the same day off Will*ia*m Falworth xxv yard off tawne medly. P*r*ice the yard iiii s. vi d. … v li. xvi s. viii d.[62]

Item bowȝght the same day iiii yard*es* tikk. P*r*ice <iiii> … iiii s. viii d.

Item delyv*er*yd the xiii[th] day off Nove*m*ber*e* t*o* Jamys Morres for thyng*es* done at Coldherbar*e* … v li.

Item paid to Alderbornedyn the xiiii[th] day off Nove*m*ber*e* for a yard q*uarter* off cloth off gold off tyssue t*o* p*er*forme my lad*ys* cheris. P*r*ice the yard xxvi s. viii d. … xxxiii s. iiii d.

Item paid to Will*ia*m Joys for stondyng off my lad*ys* weme*n* in Poulis … vi s. viii d.

Item <… > for a yard di. of tyk … xx d.

Somma … xxvi li. xii s. ii d.[P]

[*p. 33*] Item paid in reward t*o* my lord off Northu*m*beland mynstrell*es* … xx s.

Item in reward to Herr*y* Glaseler*e* and is co*m*pany … xxvi s. viii d.

Item paid to mast*er*is Fynche for ii li. off gilt gold. P*r*ice the pownd xviii s. … xxxvi s.

Item delyv*er*yd t*o* Rog*er* Holond iiii yard*es* off tawne medly for is lever*e*. P*r*ice the yard v s. … xx s.

[57] The total is 1d. under.

[58] 'the' rep.

[59] The total is 2d. under.

[60] The total is 1d. under.

[61] The total is 2d. under.

[62] The total should be £5 12s. 6d.

Item in reward to the quenys mynstrell*es* … xx s.

Item in reward to Gyll*i*am and is company … xx s.

Item in reward to the prync*es* tromppett*es* … xx s.

Item in reward to Mathewe my lord off Oxynfforth jogeler*e* … x s.

Item paid for xx yard*es* off whyte and blew cloth for bargis mens leverey. P*r*ice the yard ii s. … xl s.

Item paid to Brenok <the> for bryngyng my lad*ys* wemen from Westmy*n*sto*ur* in a bote off vi oris t*o* Coldherbar*e* wen the first*e* justis was … ii s. iiii d.

Item for ix stone off fethurs for stuffyng off xiii question*us*. P*r*ice the stone xvi d. … xii s.

Item paid to ii men the spase off thre dayes for makyng off the said question*us* … ii s.

Item in reward to Mathew Bakers s*er*vand by my lad*ys* co*m*mandement … <x s.> v s.

Somma … xi li. xiiii d.[P]

[*p. 34*] Item paid for ii yard*es* iii q*uarter* off black cloth for hossis t*o* the fottem*en* … v s.

Item for ii bonett*es* for the said fottem*en*. P*r*ice … iii s. iiii d.

Item bowȝght for the said fottm*en* v yard*es* di. off saten off Brigg*es*. P*rice* the yard ii s. vi d. … xiii s. ix d.

Item bowȝght for the mynstrell*es* v yard*es* di. off saten off Brigg*es*. P*r*ice the yard ii s. vi d. … xiii s. ix d.

Item paid to Fowler*e* the xx day off Nove*m*ber*e* for xviii yard*es* saten. P*r*ice the yard <v> viii s. … vii li. iiii s.

Item delyv*er*yd to s*ir* Will*ia*m Knevet iiii yard*es* tawne for is lever*e*. P*r*ice the yard vii s. viii d. … xxx s. viii d.

Item paid the first day off Dese*m*ber*e* to the mast*er* off Saynt Bartylmew spetyll for rep*ar*acion*us* done at Coldherbar*e* by the hond*es* off Jamys Curline … v li. xiii d.

Item paid to Will*iam* Botr*e* in one yard velvet crymyson. P*r*ice the yard xxvi s. viii d. … xxvi s. viii d.

Item paid to the said Botre for one yard velvet black. P*r*ice the yard xiii s. iiii d. … xiii s. iiii d.

Item paid to mast*er*is Denton for a laysse for my lad*ys* ma*n*till … xxxi s. iiii d.

Item paid for thre yard*es* off tawne medly for Vynse*n*t <off *con*ont [… ..]> P*r*ice the yard iiii s. iiii d. … xiii s.

Somma … xix li. xv s. xi d.[P]

[*p. 35*] Item paid to mast*er*is Langton the <first> iiii day of Desember*e* for*e* bottons and freng*es* for my lad*ys* grasse … v li.

Item paid for thre yard*es* off tawne medly for Thomas Robartson lev*ere* gowne. P*r*ice the [yarde] v s. … xv s.

Item paid the iii day off Desember*e* t*o* the godman off the Kat*er*yn Well for iiii boltt*es* and iiii lynkis off yerne for the char*e* weyng[63] xvi li. P*r*ice the pownd i d. ob. … ii s.

Item for ii me*n*nys labur*e* halffe a day … vi d.

Item paid to hy*m* iii bolltt*es* and lynsy for anod*er* schar*e* weyng xiiii li. P*r*ice the pwnd i d. ob. … xxi d.

Item a stay for*e* the char*e* … ii d.

Item for ii wele keys for*e* the char*e* … viii d.

Item for*e* gresse t*o* the said char*e* … i d.

Item for*e* a pare off steppis t*o* the char*e* … xii d.

Item for*e* makyng cord and braystanys … ii d.

item for*e* iii mennys labur*e* iiii tymys comyng t*o* Coldherbar*e* for*e* dressyng off the scharis … xviii d.

Item paid to Palmer*e* the iiii day off Dese*m*ber*e* to is owne hond*es* at Saynt Jonis … viii li.

Somma … xiiii li. ii s. x d.[P]

[*p. 36*] Item paid t*o* Peto*ur* off Coldherbar*e* for*e* dyv*er*ce thyngk*es* done at Coldherbar*e* as apers by is bill*es* \the iiith day off Desember*e*/ … xix s. i d.

Item delyv*er*yd by my lad*ys* comandeme*n*t t*o* Mylis Worseley the vith day off Dese*m*ber*e* the xvii ȝer*e* off the reyne off kyng Herr*y* the viith … xxxv li.

Item paid the same day to Paule Gylis by my lad*ys* comandeme*n*t by the hond*es* off Jamys Moris … x li.

Item paid t*o* Jamys Moris the vith day off Desember*e* for*e* rep*ara*cion*us* done at Coldherbar*e* as aperis by is byll*es* … lvi s. iii d.

Item paid to Pynson for x mynk*es* wich Jon Skynner*e* tok off hym to the behove off my lad*ys* <s> grasse. P*r*ice the peic*e* xvi d. … xiii s. iiii d.

Item paid t*o* Watt*es* the same day for*e* iiii yard*es* di. off tawne medly for*e* mast*er* trerers lever*e*. P*r*ice the yard viii s. … xxxvi s.

Item paid to Penson for*e* xxxii ermyns wich my ladis skyn*n*er*e* toke for*e* my lad*ys* grasse. P*r*ice the peice <vii> d. vi d. … <xvii s. iiii d.> xix s.

Item paid t*o* the same Penson for*e* ii mynk*es* takyn by my lad*ys* skynner*e*. P*r*ice the pece xviii d. … iii s.

Somma … vii li. <xx d.> vi s. viii d.[P][64]

[63] 'weyng' rep.

[64] Written in the summary hand.

D102.6
[*p. 1 blank*]

[*p. 2*]

[65]Summa totall of alle the payment*es* aforseid … DCCCCxi li. xix s. v d.

And so the seide sir Roger owith to my ladyes grace … xxv li. viii s. i d. «quos liberavit ad i cofforum prefatis comitisse ix^{mo} die Januarii anno xvii^{mo} ex recognicione <[…]> ipsius comitisse. Et eque.»[66]

[*p. 3*] *As in*[67]

Velvet of div*er*s coloures and prises bought for my ladyes grace at dyv*er*s tymes … Cxli li. vii s. vi d.

Damaske of sondre coloures … lxix li. xvii s. v d.

Saten of div*er*s coloures and prises … xiii li. xvii s. iiii d.

Chamlet of dyv*er*s prises … xxii li. xix s. iiii d.

Sarsenet of div*er*s coloures and prises … xxx li. xii s.

Gold wire and gold of Venys and damaske bought … xxix li. xiii s. x d.

Diap*er* bought of Picton … xxxvi li.

Workyng silk*es* bought of mastres Langton and other … iiii li. ix s. iiii d.

Cloth of <Gold> gold of dyverse coloures … xli li. xiii s. iiii d.

Div*er*s furres bought for my ladyes grace and other … xxiii li. iii s.

ii olde nobles delyv*er*ed to Palmer sadeler for gildyng … xviii s.

Money paid to the seid Palmer at dyv*er*s tymes for makyng xii horse harnes xii sadell*es* and for the cov*er*yng and workemanship of a litter and chare and mendyng of another chare and many other harnesez and thyng*es* neccess*ar*ie <for> … iiii^{xx}viii li. iii s. iiii d.

Money paide to the cop*er*smyth for makyng of porcolyez for sadell*es* … Cvii s. v d.

[*p. 4*] Money payde to the joyner for my ladyes litter … xxxiii s. iiii d.

Money paid for payntyng of my ladyes chare of cloth of gold … liii s. iiii d.

Money paide to maistres Langton <for makyng of> for makyng of botons and freng*es* for my ladyes lytter … viii li. xiii s. iiii d.

Cvii li. viii s. ix d.[68]

[65] The summary hand is responsible for the document; it begins with a decorative initial ‘S’.
[66] Add. in the ‘sprawling’ hand. The transaction cannot be found in D102.10 but may have been recorded in William Bedell’s records.
[67] Midway down the page in the margin, bracketed to include all the rest of the document.
[68] The correct total of the last three items on p. 3 and the first three items on p. 4, bracketed to the right of the items.

Money paide to mistres Denton for a lase for my ladyes mantell … xxi s. iiii d.

Money paid for ii frontlett*es* … xviii s.

Money delyv*er*ed to docto*ur* Weston by <ma> my ladyes co*m*maundement … xx li.

M. Worsley.[69] Money delyv*er*ed to Miles Worsley … xxxv li.

Money delyv[er]ed to my ladyes grace … xl li.

Money lent to master Markam by my ladyes co*m*maundement for the which he is bounde to pay my ladyes grace ayen … xiii li xviii s.

J. Mores. Money delyv*er*ed to James Mores whiche he p*ro*mysed to pay to Paule Giles for my ladyes grace … x li.

Div*er*s stuf bought for my ladyes fotemen as hose clothes doblett*es* and bonett*es* … xxxv s. x d.

Dyv*er*se reward*es* yoven to dyv*er*s p*er*sones as to the kyng*es* mynstrell*es* the quenes and other … vi li. xix s.

[*p. 5*] Money payde for a ra*m*me of brasse by my ladyes co*m*maundement at London and delyv*er*ed to Boston for the makyng of slewse there … iiii li. xviii s. i d.

*Memorandum. My lady to have this mony ayen of the expendit*ours *of the slewse.*[70] Money paide to Water Reve m*aster* carpent*er* of the seid slewse for his cost*es* and his servant*es* from London to Boston … xxxvi s. viii d.

Money paide to William Jones for standyng of dyv*er*s of my ladyes gentilwomen in Poules churche to se the mariage of the prince … vi s. viii d.

A fetherbed and other stuff bought for Olyv*er* Seynt John with xx s. delyv*er*ed to hym in redy money in the Tower by my lad*ys* co*m*maundement … xl s.

Canvas bought as well for trussyng of dyv*er*s stuf as for lynyng of verdo*urs* … xxvii s. vii d.

Lynyng of the same verdour … v s.

Tapett*es* of ymagery warke bought for my ladyes litell parlo*ur* at Coldherber … xxxv s. iiii d.

Dyv*er*s necce*ssar*ie stuff bought as threde tyke and other thyng*es* as apperith in dyv*er*s plac*es* of this boke … l s. ix d.

DCClxvii yerd*es* i q*uarter* of tawney medley bought for my ladyes lyv*er*ey bought of dyv*er*s men of dyvers prices … Clx li. v s. vii d.

[*p. 6*] Money delyv*er*ed to div*er*s p*er*sones for their*e* levery gownes … ix li. xviii s. ii d.

ii yerdes of scarlet bought for my ladys g*r*ace … xviii s.

Rede cloth bought for the charet men … xlvii s. vi d.

[69] Each marginal heading on the page is preceded by a long-tailed <r> ('respice'?).
[70] Written in the 'sprawling' hand.

Money delyv*er*ed to mast*er* Broune m*aster* coke to my ladyes grace for orenges and … xxxiii s. iiii d.

Money paid to Richard browderer for his bordwag*es* … x s.

Money paide to the bargemen … xl s.

Money paide the master of Seint Bartilmewes for rep*ar*aci*o*ns doon at Coldherber … xxxii li. xix s. ix d.

Money paide to Peter [*blank*] for rep*ar*aci*o*nz \there/ … viii li. iiii s.

Money paide to James Mores \for rep*aracions* there/ … ix li. xvi s. iii d.

Money paide to Richard Gough \for rep*aracions* there/ … ix li.

Money paide for glasyng \there/ … xliiii s. iii d.

lxii li. iiii s. iii d.[71]

Money delyv*er*ed to Will*i*am Mark*us* … ix s. ii d.

Money paid to the comissione*rs* of Holand Kesten and Lyndesey … xliii s. viii d.

Money paide for \serchyng of/ the acte and other thyng*es* for master Seynt Johnz … xli s. viii d.

Charcoles bought … xxiiii s.

lxii li. iiii s. iii d.[72]

[*pp. 7–8 blank*]

[*p. 9*] [73]Memorandum payd by Roger Ormeston knight for div*ers* necessaries and implementt*es* to þe slewes att Boston of my lady þe king*es* moder money … xxvii li. viii s. vii d.

For the contentac*i*on of þe wiche money John Style hath payd unto Rob*er*t Pulv*er*tofte bailif of Tateschale þe xvi day of August xii li. þe xxiiii <day> day of Octobr*e* x li. and in þe moneth of Decembr*e* l s. by þe knowlege of þe said John Style … xxiiii li. x s.

And so þe*r* remaynes in þe handd*es* of þe sayd John Style … lviii s. vii d.

The whiche þe said John Style hath delyv*er*ed unto þe cofres of þe sayd lady þe xi day of Februar*y* þe xviith yere of kinge Herr*y* þe viith.

[*remaining pages blank*]

[71] The total of the five items above, bracketed to the right of the items.

[72] The total of the bracketed items above, written onto p. 7.

[73] The page is written in a neat cursive hand.

APPENDIX

D56.131 (SJLM/7/5/8)

A folio sheet folded in four, unfoliated/unpaginated. Headed 'Rewardes', it lists payments made to ninety-one of Lady Margaret's servants and contacts after her death. See D102.10/132 and Introduction 2.2, The Household. For details of the personnel listed see PEOPLE index (asterisks mark those not otherwise recorded in the edited accounts and not in the PEOPLE index).

[1] Rewardes
In primis to Anne Mounteney … xl s.
Item to Marget Bygott … xl s.
Item to Elen Massyngham … xl s.
Item to Marget Stukley … xx s.
Item to Jane Walter… xx s.
*Item to Elizabeth Colyns … xxvi s. viii d.
Item to master Pexsull … iii li. vi s. viii d.
Item to John Seint John the yonger … vi li. xiii s. iiii d.
Item to Lyonell Souche … xiii li. vi s. viii d.
Item to Henry my lad*ys* godsonne … x s.
Item to Thomas Mounteney … viii li.
Item to George Fraunces … xi li. vi s. viii d.
Item to Rob*er*t Fremyngham … v li.
Item to James Moris … v li.
Item to Nicholas Saunder … x li.
*Item to James Standish … xx s.

[2] *Item to George Marbury … iii li. vi s. viii d.
Item to Henry Clegg … xl s.
Item to John Lee … iii li. vi s. viii d.
Item to Rob*er*t Merbury … iiii li.
Item to Nicholas Aughton … vi li. xiii s. iiii d.
Item to Richard Stukley … xl s.
Item to Pet*ur* Baldewyn … xl s.
Item to Will*ia*m Love … v li.
Item to John Heryson … v li.
Item to John Madison … xl s.
Item to Rob*er*t Neswike … iii li. vi s. viii d.
Item to Richard Cotmont … xl s.
Item to John Ploffeld … xl s.
Item to Petur Oldale … xx s.

Item to Pety John … xx s.
Item to Henry Deye … xl s.
Item to Walter Cokkys … xl s.
Item to Reynold Daunpport … iii li. vi s. viii d.
Item to Edward Waus … iii li. vi s. viii d.
Item to Will*ia*m Kylner … xl s.

[3] Item to Cristofer Middilton … xl s.
Item to Rob*e*rt Deye … xx s.
Item to Thomas Hill … xl s.
*Item to John Talbot … x s.
Item to Thomas Flemyng … iii li. vi s. viii d.
Item to Leonard de la Fave … xx s.
Item to Rob*e*rt Ferro*ur* … x s.
Item to Hugh Care … xl s.
Item to Laur*ence* Bownde … xx s.
Item to Thomas Sympson … xl s.
Item to John Hasilby … xxvi s. viii d.
Item to John Ev*er*yngham … xl s.
*Item to Rob*e*rt Waterton … xl s.
Item to Hugh Asheton … vi s. viii d.
*Item to Henry Curtes … xxvi s. viii d.
Item to Rob*e*rt Edlyn … xl s.
Item to Will*ia*m Carleton … liii s. iiii d.
*Item to Rob*e*rt Goodwyn … xx s.
*Item to John Page … xx s.

[4] *Item to John Wright … xx s.
*Item to Nicholas Banckes … xiii s. iiii d.
*Item to Rob*e*rt Inkersall … xx s.
Item to Jaques Yerwell … xiii s. iiii d.
*Item to Rob*e*rt Clerk … xiii s. iiii d.
Item to John Carr … xl s.
Item to Thomas Richardson … vi s. viii d.
Item to Rob*e*rt Longe … x s.
Item to John Aps … xx s.
Item to the garden*er* … iii s. iiii d.
Item to the baile Nicholas Warcoppe … xx s.
*Item to John Foke … iii s. iiii d.
*Item to John Anderson … iii s. iiii d.
*Item to John Rice … iii s. iiii d.
*Item to Humfrey Basset … iii s. iiii d.
*Item to Henr*y* Baker … iii s. iiii d.
Item to Olyver Walcott … xl s.
*Item to John Walsheman … iii s. iiii d.

[5] *Item to the page of the catri … iii s. iiii d.
*Item to Thomas Waterton … vi s. viii d.

Item to Thomas Dodde … iii li. vi s. viii d.
Item to George Hevenyngham … v li.
Item to Henry Salfford … xl s.
Item to Rob*e*rt Hilton … xl s.
Item to Richard Aderton … xl s.
Item to John Grome … xl s.
Item to Laur*ence* Canwik … xl s.
*Item to John Und*e*rwood … xx s.
Item to Henr*y* Abney … xx s.
*Item to Rob*e*rt Fippownd … xx s.
Item to Edmu*n*d Norice … xx s.
Item to Hugh Ratcliff … xls.
Item to John Parker … vi s. viii d.
*Item to Thomas Osborne … iii s. iiii d.
Item to John Ormeston … xl s.
Item to Merycok … xxxiii s. iiii d.
Summa totalis … CC li. xvi s. viii d.

SELECT GLOSSARY

The Select Glossary is primarily of English words, although Latin (marked 'Lat.') and French ('Fr.') are included for the Latin roll (D91.16) or in order to explain Latin/French within an otherwise English document. Naturalised Latin/French words are taken as English ('Eng.' is only occasionally necessary, and 'Nth.' is used sometimes for northern dialect), although several are also found in D91.16 with *le(z)*, e.g. 'le unce', 'lez quarrye(r)s'. (For a discussion see Introduction 4.1.) Only an unusual spelling (not the usual spelling) is normally given for common words. When more than one spelling is given, the order is normally alphabetical, unless the first alphabetic spelling is rare . Since <i>/<y> were interchangeable at the time, <y> is always placed in <i> position, e.g. *cheverell*, *chyme*, *chippynges*, *cypers* in that order. Normally only four (or fewer) locations are cited, but more are given if many spelling variants are recorded. All definitions are from the *OED* (for English) or *DMLBS* (for Latin) unless otherwise indicated; the *OED*/*DMLBS* headword is not normally given, unless there might be difficulty in finding the entry or the specific definition. *MED* entries are only cited if the entry is not in the *OED* or less fully defined there. The Lexis of Cloth and Clothing Project (*LCCP*), which draws on the *OED* and *MED* as well as other sources, is preferred for definitions of fabrics when it differs from, or is more precise than, the *OED*/*MED* definition (see http://lexissearch.arts.manchester.ac.uk/). For the *Anglo-Norman Dictionary* (*AND*) see <http://www.anglo-norman.net/gate/>; for the *Dictionaries of the Scots Language* (*DSL*), see <http://www.dsl.ac.uk/>.

Grammatical abbreviations: *3sg.* 3rd person (present) singular, *3pl.* 3rd person (present) plural, *acc.* accusative case, *adj.* adjective, *adj.phr.* adjective phrase, *adv.* adverb, *n.* noun, *n.phr.* noun phrase, *n.pl* noun plural, *pa.sg.* past tense singular, *pass.* passive voice, *pp.* past participle, *ppl.adj.* participial adjective, *prep.* preposition, *pr.p.* present participle, *v.* verb, *vbl.adj.* verbal adjective (gerundive), *vbl.n.* verbal noun (gerund)

Abbreviamentum (Lat.) *n.* entry, brevement (see *OED* **brevement** f. med. L. *breviamentum*, by comparison with 'book of brevements'; the meaning is preferred to *DMLBS* **abbreviamentum** 2 account, record of expenses; **breviare** 2a to keep accounts of (expenses)) 16/20, 3d, 4d, 5d

accator (Lat.) *n.* buyer (*DMLBS*); **accatum (15)** purchase (cf. *DMLBS* 1) 16/15

aftur supper *n.* the time after supper; **at ~** in the period after supper 20/31

agistamentum (Lat.) *n.* agistment, (right of or payment for) pasturage (*DMLBS* 1) 16/3

agnes sede(s) (also **lez agnes sede**) *n.* the seeds of *agnus castus* (cf. *OED* **agnus castus** *n.* 2) 16/11, 26, 27d

ale salsia see **salsus**

aleacre, aleager *n.* vinegar produced by sour ale (*OED* **alegar** *n.*) 16/25, 4d

Alhaloutyd *n.* All Hallows tide, i.e. the period around 1 November, All Saints (Hallows) Day 20/122 (cf. **Al Halowe Day** 19/104 and see too **Hal(l)hallo(ez)**)

alkermes *n.* a medical preparation containing scale insects ('kermes') 20/47

allec (Lat.) *n.* herring (*DMLBS* 2) (extended as collective singular) 16/10, 17, 24, 14d

allocacio (Lat.) *n.* allowance in account (*DMLBS* **allocatio** 2a) 16/8, 16; 19/114

allocare (Lat.) *v.* to allow, to credit (a person with an expense) (*DMLBS* 3d) 16/7, 10, 14, 15; 10/4–6, 15–25, 83–6, 111, etc.

almer *n.* amber 19/56

almoigner *n.* almoner 20/83

almoys *n.pl.* alms 1/8r; ~ **folk** almsfolk 1/8v

amez, **amys** *n.* amice, vestment covering head and neck; also secular covering 19/43, 58

amigdala (Lat.) *n.* almond (*DMLBS* **amygdala, ~um**, **~us**) 16/26

amver grene *n.* ambergris 19/108

ancras, **ancry(e)s**, **ancrys(s)e**, **angcrys**, **ankeri(e)s**, **ankeryes** *n.* anchoress 20/30, 148, 179, 186, etc.; ~ **howse** 21/131; ~ **sister** 21/114; ~ **woman** 20/187; **thankorise** the anchoress 20/181

angelles, **angilles** *n.pl.* gold coins known as angels 20/57; 19/87

anglettes, **an(gel)lettes**, **anlyttes** *n.pl.* small rings, as in ring-mail (*OED* **anlet** *n.*) 20/54, 79; 21/55, 94; 19/97II, etc.

ankere, **ankure** *n.* anchorite 20/186

anngiryns *n.pl.* andirons 2/25

antyphaner, **antiphener** *n.*, **antefeners** *n.pl.* antiphoner, book of antiphons 19/34, 52, 88, 101

anuytie *n.* annual grant 1/11r

aperciare (Lat.) *v.* to open (form not recorded *DMLBS* but cf. **apertio** 1 '(act of) opening') 16/25

(ap)propriacion, **propreacion** *n.* appropriation, assignment of property (see *OED* **appropriation** *n.* 1, 2) 21/130; 19/92; 1/7v

approprie *v.*; **appropried** *p.p.* annexed (*OED* **appropre/approprie** *v.* 1, 3) 19/52

aqua vyte *n.* 'aqua vitae', distilled alcohol 21/91

arez, **arras(se)**, **arres(se)**, **arrow** *n.* figured tapestry (*LCCP* **arras**) 17/49; 1/6v, 7v; **counterfet(t)** ~ imitation arras, i.e. painted, not embroidered 20/25, 66; 19/120

armet(t) *n.* hermit 20/34, 61, 160; 19/87

armyn *n.* ermine 20/80

armletes *n.pl.* wristbands 20/125

arras(se), **arres(se)** see **arez**

arr(er)ages *n.pl.* arrears, debts, payment due (*OED* **arrearage** *n.* 4) 10/26, 123

arreragii (Lat.) *n.pl.* arrears 19/67

arreraz *n.pl.* arrears (*OED* **arrear** *n.* 7b) 20/135

arroez *n.pl.* arrows

arrow 17/49 see **arez**

artocria (Lat.) *n.* meat pie or tart (*DMLBS* **artocreas** a) 16/2d, 3d

as *conj.* like, for example 21/21/156

assigned *pp.* signed 21/21/7, etc.

assise, **assyse** *n.* size (*OED* **assize** *n.*[1] 6) 20/108; 1/13r, 14r

asurement *n.* agreement (to marry) 21/37

attingere (Lat.) *v.* to attain/reach 20/91, 99, 126c

auditor (Lat.), **audito(u)r** (Eng.) *n.* auditor (of an account) (*DMLBS* 3) 16/3d; 20/7, 11, 166; 19/109

avena (Lat.) *n.* oats (extended as collective singular, except 16/29d subheading where plural) 16/14, 23, 25, 29d

awyht *pa.sg.* owed 10/62

awndeyrnes *n.pl.* andirons 20/166

bacon *ppl.adj.* baked 19/81

bayle *n.* hoop or ring to support a canopy (*OED* **bail** *n.*[2]) 20/44

bayly, **baly(e)** *n.* bailiff (*OED* **bailie** *n.*) 10/29, 58; 20/42, 44, 88, 99, 113; **baylies** *n.pl.* 20/156

baytynges *n.pl.* food on a journey 21/43

bane *n.*; **raten** ~ ratsbane, rat poison 20/44

barbbe *n.* female covering for the chin and chest 20/80

bare hyde *n.* hide with the hairs removed, or undressed 21/18, 76

barell *n.* cask for, or measure of, liquids or solids, us. 30 gallons of ale, 36 gallons of beer, 30 gallons of fully packed herrings (*OED* **barrel** *n.*[1]) 16/4, 10, 12, 17

barys *n.pl.* the ornamental transverse bands on a girdle (*OED* **bar** *n.*[1] 4.) 19/29

barker *n.* tanner (*OED* **barker** *n.*[2] 1) 16/2, 19

barryng *vbl.n.* fastening with bars 21/26

basse *n.* baize (?) 20/81

baudkyn *n.* rich, silken textile of mixed silk and gold or silver thread (*LCCP* **baldachin** 1a) 20/126

baues, **bawes** *n.pl.* bows 20/15

bavyn *n.* bundle of brushwood, as used in bakers' ovens, bound with one withe or band (*OED* bavin *n.*) 16/30d

beara (Lat.) *n.* beer (cf. *DMLBS* **bera**) 16/5d

bedmen *n.pl.* almsfolk 19/103

bedstrings *n.pl.* strings for stretching the sacking of a bed (*OED* **bed** *n.* C1a)

bell *n.* bell, **bellez** *n.pl.* small bells for decoration (?) (cf. *OED* **bell** *n.*[1] 1b) 20/56; **wasshyng** ~ cauldron for doing the washing in (*MED* **belle** *n.*[1] 5b) 21/120

bettes *n.pl.* beds 19/82

bettes *n.pl.* horse bits (*OED* **bit** *n.*[1] 8a) 2/11

bichofe *n.* behalf 10/1

billa (Lat.) *n.* note of receipt (*DMLBS* **2 billa** 2c) (assumed to be singular unless other evidence) 16/2, 3d, 21d, 24d

bylles *n.pl.* printed pamphlets (?) (cf. *OED* **bill** *n.*[3] 1c, 8a) 20/21;

bylles *n.pl.*; **forest** ~ woodman's bill hooks (*OED* **bill** *n.*[1] 4; **forest** *n.* C2) 20/67

byllet *n.* wood for fuel (*OED* **billet** *n.*[2] 1b) 16/13

billettes *n.pl.* notes (*OED* **billet** *n.*[1]) 10/182

biry, **bure** (also *le biry*) (Fr.) *n.* strip of cloth (cf. *AND* **bure**, **bur**, **birre** strip of cloth, burel (coarse brown cloth) 20/98, 99

byttours *n.pl.* bitterns (*OED* **bittern** *n.*[1]) 16/4

by yen *prep.* beyond 19/99

blake, **blakk** *n.* a type of black cloth (*LCCP* **black** 2) 20/185, 191

blan(c)ket, **blonket**, **plonket** *n.*; **blanckettes** *n.pl.* material similar to blanket fabric; a blanket itself 20/126, 157; 21/31; 19/103, 111

blaunch(e) powder(e)/powdur (also **le blaunch(e) powder**) *n.* a preparation of sweet spices (cf. *MED* **blaunk** *adj.* 1b, **poudre** *n.* 5b b) 16/11, 26, 26d, 27d

blew *n.* blue cloth (*OED* **blue** B *n.* 2a) 20/13

blyne *adj.* blind 19/89

boche, **bodge**, **bodgy**, **bog(i)e**, **bug(g)e** *n.* lambskin with the wool dressed outward (*OED* **budge** *n.*[1]) 20/82; 21/38, 50, 51, 106; 19/106

bodying *vbl.n.* making up the body of a garment 19/98

bokeram, **bocrome** *n.* coarse (at an earlier date, fine) linen (*LCCP* **buckram**) 20/25, 54, 89, 97, 98, 153, etc.; 19/36

bol(l)yons, **bullyons** *n.pl.* metal knobs or bosses to decorate the covers of books (*OED* **bullion** *n.*[3] 1) 21/135; 1/5v, 7v, 8v, 17v

bolle *n.* bowl 20/82

boltyng cloth *n.* cloth used for sifting out bran 19/12

bombas *n.* cotton (down/fibre) (*LCCP* **bombace**, cf. *OED* **bombast** *n.* 1a) 20/16

bonnet *n.* brimless headgear for men (i.e. a cap) or women 19/87

bosse *n.* projecting ornament, knob 1/10r; **boosses** *n.pl.* 2/17

bourde *n.* board (*OED* **board** *n.*), **past ~** paste-board 19/41; **bourdes** *n.pl.*, **comptyng ~** counting boards, tables for counting money on 1/15r

bourdez *n.pl.* tilting, fencing with lances (*OED* **bourdis** *n.*) 20/23

bowys *n.pl.* boughs 19/17

braystanys *n.pl.* bridle or curb stones (?) (*OED* **break** *n.*5) 2/35

brasse *n.* brace 20/85

brauderer, **broderer**, **brotherar**, **brotherer(e)**, *n.*, **brotherers**, **browders** *n.pl.* embroiderer 17/20; 20/55; 20/89, 102, 115, 116; 21/47, 96, 98, 134; 19/13, 75, 88

bregynders, **brygynders**, **brygonders** *n.pl.* body-armour for foot-soldiers (*OED* **brigander** *n.*[1] 1) 20/27, 67; 21/52

brede *n.* breadth 1/13r (see too **tabell**)

breve *n.* a royal or papal brief (*OED* **breve** *n.* 1 a b) 10/23; 20/28

brevys *n.pl.* breviaries (not recorded *OED* or *MED*) 19/101

brygg(e) *n.* bridge (Nth.) 20/153

Brigges, **Brygges**, **Bryggez**, **Bruges**, **Brugez** *n.* Bruges; **sat(t)en of ~** a twill silk textile made in Bruges 17/20; 20/91; 19/6, 25; 2/34

brynyng *vbl.n.* burning 20/42

brochis, **brochys** *n.pl.* brooches, ornamental fastenings 19/29; **brothryng ~** fraternity brooches (cf. *OED* **brother** *n.* 4a, 5) 20/40

broderer see **brauderer**

brokyn wyne *n.* remains of drink (cf. *OED* **broken** *adj.* 1b. **~ ale, ~ beer**) 16/5d

broker *n.* middleman, agent (*OED* **broker** *n.* II 3a) 20/33

brother *v.* embroider 20/97

brotherar, **brotherer(e)**, **browders** see **brauderer**

Bruges, **Brugez** see **Brigges**

buce (also **le buce, lez buces)** (Fr.) *n.* bag, box (?) (cf. Anglo-Norman *buce*, var. *bouge*, *DMLBS* **2 bucca**) 16/11, 25, 26

bug(g)e see **boche**

bullyons see **bolyons**

bulwerkes *n.pl.* pads, padding (*LCCP* **bulwerk**, *OED* **bulwark** *n.* 2) 20/47, 175, 185

burdes *n.pl.*; ~ **of paste** pasteboards 20/177

bure see **biry**

buskynce, **buskyns** *n.pl.* high boots 20/45, 51, 54, 97, 156, 168, 169; 19/20, 109

(bus.) bussellus (Lat.) *n.* bushel, measure of 4 pecks/8 gallons (*DMLBS* 2) 16/2, 9, 12, 19

but(t), **but(t)e** (also **le butte**) *n.* a cask for wine or ale (*OED* **butt** *n.*[2] 1a) 16/9, 23, 6d

cade *n.* a barrel holding 500 herrings (*OED* **cade** *n.*[1] 2: see entry c.1503) 16/10, 17, 24, 15d

caibuls *n.pl.* horses (?) (cf. *OED* **caball** *n.*, *MED* **cabel** *n.*, but –ai- not recorded) 20/108

calabure, **callabor**, **colabur** *n.* grey squirrel fur from Calabria (*LCCP* **calabar**) 20/55; 19/35; 2/28

calle *n.* net(work) (*OED* **caul** *n.* 2); ~ **neldes** *n.pl.* netting needles (?) 19/27, 29

cameryk(e) (clothe) *n.* cambric, fine white linen from Cambrai 20/191, 196

cancellare (Lat.) *v.* to cancel/cross out 19/65

candyth *n.* crystallised cane sugar 19/92; **sewger** ~ 19/106

candle plates *n.pl.* plates for standing candles on (?) 21/101

canepe *n.* canopy over a throne, bed, etc. 20/44

caraweyes, **carewes** *n.pl.* sweetmeat containing caraway seeds (*OED* **caraway** *n.* 2) 16/11, 25, 24d

carbo silvestris (Lat.) *n.* wood charcoal (cf. *DMLBS* **carbo** 1d) 16/12

carcas, **carces** *n.* carcase (*OED* **carcass/carcase**) 16/11d

carcasium (Lat.) *n.* carcase 16/23, 9d–11d

card *n.* a combing implement (*OED* **card** *n.*[1] 1a) 20/174

cardynall see **whitte**

carecta (Lat.) *n.* cart-load (*DMLBS* **carretta** 3: see 16/12 for 1 carecta as 24 qr.) 16/2–4, 12

carre *v.* carry 20/108

carsay, **carsey** see **kersay**

carte taker *n.* the officer who impressed carts for the king's service 19/95

cassis *n.pl.* cases, containers 21/146

cast *n.* a couple (of hawks) (*OED* **cast** *n.* 14) 20/96, 156, 161, 165; 19/31

casualties *n.pl.* chance occurrences 10/139, 140

catri *n.* acatry, storehouse for provisions 56/5

catur *n.* the household officer responsible for purchase of the provisions ('cates') 21/18

celyster *n.* solicitor 20/147; 19/7

(C^{ma}) centum maius (Lat.) *n.* 'long hundred', i.e. 120 (*DMLBS* **centum** 1d) 16/11d

(C^{mi}) centum minus (Lat.) *n.* 'short hundred', i.e. 100 (*DMLBS* **centum** 1d) 16/11d

cepum (Lat.) *n.* suet (*DMLBS* **sebum**) 16/5

cerius (Lat.) *n.* wax candle (16d) (*DMLBS* **cereus** 2) 16/16d, 18d

cervisia (Lat.) *n.* ale 16/9

chaffur *n.* vessel for heating water 20/82

cham(b)let, chamelet *n.*, **chamlytez** *n.pl.* rich silken fabric (*LCCP* **camlet**) 20/17, 66, 82; 19/25, etc.

changeable see **reban**

chapplers *n.pl.* chaplains (*OED* **chapeler**) 20/94

chare *n.* chariot, car 17/20; ~ **clowtys** *n.pl.* metal plates to prevent excessive wear, as on an axletree (*MED* **clout** *n.*[1] 2a, cf. *OED* **clout** *n.*[1] I 2.) 17/30

chaund(e)re, chaundry *n.* chandlery, place where candles are kept (*OED* **chandry** *n.* 1, cf. **chandlery** *n.* 1) 16/24, 16d, 17d; 21/38

chaunkis see **shanke**

chauntour *n.* cantor, chorister, singing man 20/19

cheker see **eschequier**

chet(t)es (also **lez chetes**) *n.pl.* wheaten loaves of the second quality, more coarsely sifted than for **maunchettes** (*OED* **chet** *n.*[2] where the use is singular, 'bread') 16/6, 22, 2d, 4d

chettes *n.pl.* sheets 2/25

chevens *n.pl.* chubs (a fish) 21/115

cheverell *n.* kid 21/10

chyme *n.* set of bells in a church tower, etc. (*OED* **chime** *n.*[1] 3) 20/157

chippynges *n.pl.* parings of loaf-crusts (*OED* **chipping** *n.* 2a) 16/6

cypers, sypers, siper(u)s, syporis, sypres *n.* a light transparent fabric (lawn) (*OED* **cypress** *n.*[3] 1c, cf. *LCCP* **cypress**) 20/49; 21/20, 57, 120, 139, etc.; **saten/satyn of Cypres/ Sypres~** a twill silk textile made in Cyprus 21/136; 19/103

cyppe see **kepe**

cirop *n.* sweetener for confectionery (*OED* **syrup** *n.* 1b) 16/25

cirpus (Lat.) *n.* rush (*DMLBS* **scirpus**) 16/11

clapsys *n.pl.* clasps 19/90

clarycordes *n.pl.* clavichords 20/12

clausus (Lat.) *n.* close, enclosure 16/3, 10; end (of a document) 16/14, 10d, 12d

cleppyd, **clipped**, **clippid** *adj.* (coins) debased by clipping 10/77, 101, 102, 133, 199

clossed *n.* closet 19/111

cloth(e) *n.*, **~ sak(e)** *n.*, **~ sakkes** *n.pl.* sack(s) for clothes (*OED* **clothesack** *n.*) 20/126b; 21/18, 31, 76, 136; **clothis** *n.pl.*, **paynted/staned ~** *n.pl.* decorated hangings 20/179

cloves, **clowes**, **clowys** *n.pl.* cloves 16/11, 25, 21d

cluse see **slewes**

coawarante *n.* co-warrant (?) (not recorded, but cf. *OED* **warrant** *n.* 4b, pledge, guarantee) 20/62

coffyns *n.pl.* chests, caskets 19/96

colabur see **calabure**

coler *n.* collar 19/97 II

colyer, **colliar** *n.* coal-carrier, charcoal maker (*OED* **collier** *n.*) 16/13; 21/138; 19/99(?)

colletture *n.* collector of revenue due 21/121

comensement *n.* the ceremony of conferment of the full degree of Master or Doctor 17/9; 19/24

comfettes, **confettes** (also **lez comfettes**) *n.pl.* sweetmeats (*OED* **comfit** *n.* a, **confect** *n.*) 16/11, 25, 24d; **~ biskettes/byskettes** crisp sweetmeats, biscuits 16/11, 25, 24d; **~ carews** sweetmeats containing caraway seed 16/24d; **~ plates (24d)** flat sweetmeats 16/24d; **long ~** long sweetmeats 16/11, 24d

comyssary *n.* representative, deputy 19/28

comme *n.* comb 19/75

comptyng bourdes *n.pl.* counting boards, tables for counting money on (*OED* **board** *n.*) 1/15r

computabilis (Lat.) *adj.* involved in accounting (cf. *DMLBS* 2b) 16/3; **computare** *v.* to account (for), render account (for) (*DMLBS* 5) 16/7; **computant-** (nom. *computans* not recorded) *n.* accountant, person rendering account (cf. *DMLBS* **computare** 3, 5, **computator** 2b) 16/2, 4, 5, 7; **computus** *n.* computus/compotus, account (*DMLBS* **computus** a) 16/1–4, etc.; 20/93, 147, 194; 21/28, 35, 78, 161; 19/50; 1/2r, 18v

confeccions (also **lez confeccions**) *n.pl.* prepared sweetmeats (*OED* **confection** *n.* 5d) 16/11, 25, 26d

confectio (Lat.) *n.* confection, sweetmeat (*DMLBS* 2c) 16/25, 24d;

confectus (Lat.) *ppl.adj.* composed, compiled (of a document) (*DMLBS* **conficere** 4) 16/2, 16, 2d, 3d

conger (also **lez congres**) *n.pl.* conger, large eel (*OED* **conger** *n.*[1]) 16/10, 14d; **congra** (Lat.) conger-eel (cf. *DMLBS* **conger**) 16/2, 14d

content *v.* remunerate (*OED* **content** *v.* 4a) 19/48

contentacio(u)n *n.* confirmation by oath, legal dispute 10/50; 6/9

contrarotulator (Lat.) *n.* controller 1/18v

convincere (Lat.) *v.* to prove (a tally) (*DMLBS* 3c) 16/2d–4d, 7d

coolis *n.pl.* coals 20/175

cope *n.* cup; ~ **of assey** cup of assay, a cup used to taste and test wine 20/106

coperas (grene) *n.* copperas, ferrous sulphate, a mix of proto-sulphates used in making ink 19/13, 43

corans, **correynes**, **correnis** *n.pl.* currants (*OED* **currant** *n.* 1a, b) 16/11, 25, 21d

cordenar *n.* cordwainer, shoemaker 17/28

corperys, **corporas** *n.* corporal, the cloth on which the consecrated elements are put during mass 19/6, 56; ~ **casez** *n.pl.* cases to hold the corporal 10/19

corsse *n.*, **corsis** *n.pl.* ribbon for ornamentation with metalwork or embroidery (*OED* **corse** *n.* 5) 19/6, 109

cortex (Lat.) *n.* bark 16/30d

counterpeynt, **counterpoynt** *n.* counterpane 20/85, 126, 174

countiez *n.* countess 20/194

countria (Lat.) *n.* counting-house (form not recorded *DMLBS* but cf. Lat. **computatorium**, *OED* **counter** n[3] 5, var. sp. *countre*) 16/30d

co(u)rser men *n.pl.* men riding large, powerful horses (as used in battle or tournaments) (cf. *OED* **courser** *n.*[2], **horse-corser/courser** *n.*) 19/15, 33

coven *n.* convent, conventual college 21/62

Coventry threde *n.* blue embroidery thread made in Coventry (*OED* **Coventry** *n.* 4) 19/25

cowles *n.pl.* hooded garments (*OED* **cowl** *n.*[1]) 21/17

cowle *n.* a large tub for water (*OED* **cowl** *n.*[2]) 20/182

cowntous *n.pl.* accounts (?), counting house (?) 2/23

crane coleryd/collerd *adj.phr.* of an ashen-gray colour (*OED* **crane** *n.*[1] 6a) 19/106, 113

cremell *n.* openwork or fringe (*LCCP*) 20/108

cremys(s)yn, **crymysen** *adj.* dark red or purple (of expensive cloth) (*LCCP* **crimson**) 19/6

crest clothe *n.* a kind of linen cloth (*OED* **crest/cress** *n.*[3]) 20/185

crewettes *n.pl.* small vessels to hold wine or water at mass 19/108

crewle, **crule** *n.*, **crulys** *n.pl.* skein of yarn (*LCCP* **crewel**) 20/17, 21, 43, 82, 98, etc.

cruse *n.*, **crewsis** *n.pl.* small earthenware vessel for liquids (*OED* **cruse** *n.*, *MED* **crouse** *n.*, but 19/84 silver gilt) 20/127; 19/84

crisadoure *n.pl.* Portuguese gold coin with sign of cross (*OED* **crusado** *n.*[1]) 10/133

Cryshed *n.* Christ's head (?) (cf. 'Seynt Johens hed' 20/30) 20/31

crochettes *n.pl.* hooked implements (?) (cf. *MED* **crochet** *n.*); **hokes** ~ implements similar to crochet hooks (?) (cf. *OED* **crochet** *n.*) 17/26

currer *n.* courier 21/58

currss, **curse** *adj.* course 20/53, 55

curse *adj.* coarse 19/97 I; **curser** *comp.adj.* coarser 20/91

customer *n.* customs officer 19/105

custus (Lat.) *n.* cost, outlay, expense (*DMLBS* **costus** 1) 16/12

Cutbert foules *n.pl.* St Cuthbert ducks, eider ducks which breed on the Farne Islands (*OED* **Cuthbert** *n.*[1] 2) 20/163

dactulus (Lat.) *n.* date (*DMLBS* **dactylus** 3) 16/11; **dactus, dates** (also **lez dates**) *n.pl.* dates (for –ct-, cf. Middle French *datte*, Lat. *dactylus*, *dattilus*) 16/25, 23d

damask(e) *n.* silken fabric associated with Damascus and often woven with elaborate patterns (*LCCP* **damask**) 20/108; 21/8, 13, 32; 19/12, 77, 97 I; ~ **off Luk** damask from Lucca (Italy) 2/22; **Damask(e) gold(e)** 20/21; 21/101; 19/57; **gold of** ~ damask interwoven with gold thread (*LCCP* **gold damask**) 21/133; 19/7; 1/15r; 1/10v; 2/6

dampnare (Lat.) *v.* to cancel, annul (a tally) (*DMLBS* 4b) 16/2d–4d, 7d

debet(ur)/debentur (Lat.) *3sg.pass.* he owes/it is owed; *3pl.* (they) are owed 20/64, 134; 19/63

(d.) denarius (Lat.) *n.* penny (*DMLBS* 2b) 16/1, etc.; **in denariis rialles/riallis** coins called 'rials'/'ryals' (*OED* **rial** *n.*[1] I. 1b) 10/66, 78

desperatur, **disperatur** (Lat.) *3sg.pass.* it is despaired of (*DMLBS* **desperare** 2, cf. 'a desperate debt', *OED* **desperate** A *adj.* I 3a) 16/22; 21/79

dever *n.* appointed task (*OED* **devoir** *n.* 1) 20/191

dyall *n.* clock or sundial 21/109; 1/5r

diaper, **dyapur(e)** *n.* fabric woven with a geometric or lattice pattern (*LCCP* **diapur** 1) 20/113, 196; 19/23; 2/13; 6/3; ~ **tuell** *n.* a woven diaper (*LCCP* **toile** 1b) 21/62

dyesys *n.* diocese 19/105

dyet *n.* daily provisions 17/21

(di.) dimidium (Lat.) *n.* (a) half (*DMLBS* 1,2) 16/3, 9, 10, 11, etc.; ~ **quarter** one-eighth 16/31d, etc.

dymysey *n.* a kind of fabric (*MED* **dimesey** *n.*), perhaps a stout woven cotton (cf. *OED* **dimity**) 21/64

direccio (Lat.) *n.* dispatch (cf. *DMLBS* **directio** 2) 16/11

dirigere (Lat.) *v.* to dispatch (*DMLBS* 4) 16/11

disme *n.* a tithe (*OED* **dime** *n.* 1a) 10/160

dyspenciacion *n.* exemption from an ecclesiastical obligation (*OED* **dispensation** *n.* 8a)

disperatur see **desperatur**

dyteng *vbl.n.* preparing an animal for the kitchen 21/36

(dol.) dolium (Lat.) *n.* tun, cask, measure of liquid or dry goods (*DMLBS* 2) 16/9, 18, 23, 4d

dompne *n.* term of address for monastic superior (cf. *OED* **domine** *n.* 1) 1/11v

dowere *n.* dower, the portion of a dead husband's estate allowed to the widow for lif 10/55

dragges (lez dragges) *n.pl.* the sediment of beer, etc. (?) (cf. *OED* **dreg** *n.* 1a) 16/4d

draying(e) *vbl.n.* dragging, dredging (*OED* **draw** *v.* 43) 20/20; designing, modelling (*OED* **draw** *v.* 60a)

dreu, **drew** *pa.sg.* dragged 20/31, 21/30

drynk(k)ynge *n.*, **drynkyngez**, **drynkyns** *n.pl.* drinking, a snack on a journey 17/24, 29, 31, 35

D(o)uche (wo)man *n.*, **Duchemen** *n.pl.* Dutchmen/Germans 17/25, 30; 1/7v

(dd.) duodenarius (Lat.) *n.* dozen (*DMLBS* 1) 16/5, 6, 9, 12

dutie *n.* debt 10/31

egge, **heyge, negge** *n.* edging, border 19/97 II, 98, 111; 2/29

egge *v.* to edge 19/97 II

electrum (Lat.) *n.* gold/silver alloy, brass, pewter (?) (cf. *DMLBS* 2) 16/14

ell(e), **eln(e)**, **nell(e)**, **helne** *n.*, **elnes**, **elnez**, **helnys** *n.pl.* measurement of length (for English and Flemish ells, see *OED* **ell** *n.*[1] 1a) 10/19; 20/15, 16, 17, etc.; ~ **brode** ell-width 21/18

endent *v.* enter into a formal agreement 19/91

enrollyng, **inrollyng** *vbl.n.* copying or entering a document into an official roll or register (*MED* **enrollen** *v.* 1) 21/148–9; 19/45, 104

eque (Lat.) *adv.* in balance (*DMLBS* **aeque** d) 2/2

erynalles see **urenalles**

eschequier, **eschequyer**, **escheqwyere**, **exchekere**, **exiekere**, **cheker** *n.* the Court of Exchequer 20/126c, 170, 199; 19/55, 95, 121; 2/12

ever *n.* ewer, jug 20/12

every *n.* ivory 21/8; 19/9

evydance, **evydence** *n.* legal document 20/12; **evydences** *n.pl.* title-deeds 20/126b, 126c

ew(e)ry *n.* ewery, place in royal household for ewers, linen and towels 20/106; 19/97

excheatour, **excheter**, **exchetur(e)** *n.*, **escheters**, **eschetors** *n.pl.* escheator, officer for the certification of escheats 20/13, 128, 147, 160, etc.

exennium (Lat.) *n.* gift, payment 16/4

expenditores, **expenditours** *n.pl.* (Lat. but cf. *OED* **expenditor** *n.* person appointed to expend tax collected for the repair of sewers) 19/61, 124; 6/5

expenditus (Lat.) *ppl.adj.* spent (form not recorded *DMLBS* but used throughout D91.16 as pp. of *expendere*) 16/1, 7, 16, 22; **expendita** (Lat.) (used as *n.pl.*) expenses (form not recorded *DMLBS*) 16/7

facyon, **faction**, **fasshyn** *n.* fashioning, making, workmanship 20/50, 123; 19/29; 1/4r

fagottes *n.pl.* bundle of sticks, bound with two withes or bands 16/12, 13, 17, 24

fardell *n.* parcel of goods 20/29, 59, 166; 19/103

fardyng *n.* a gold coin (*OED* **farthing** *n.* 3a) 21/61

farina frumenti (Lat.) *n.phr.* wheatmeal (cf. *DMLBS* **farina** 2, **frumentum** 2, 3) 16/2d, 3d

fastenys *n.pl.* fastenings (?) (cf. *OED* **fastening** *n.* 3) 20/126

fee *n.* inherited estate 10/15; **knightes ~s** *n.pl.* estate sufficient to support a knight, held in homage to a feudal lord (*OED* **fee** *n.*[2] I 1a) 10/140

fee ferme *n.* rent paid by a tenant of land held in fee-simple 10/15

feffement *n.* feoffment, conveyance of freehold estate 19/55, 104

fellone *n.* felon, criminal 20/14

feman *n.* vassal (*OED* **feeman** *n.*) 20/163

fence *n.* defence; **cote of ~** coat of mail 20/59

fenum (Lat.) *n.* hay 16/3, 4, 14, 17

feodam *n.* feoffment 10/17

feodareship, **feodary** *n.* feudal tenancy (cf. *OED* **feudary/feodary** *n.*) 10/28; 20/27

feodum (Lat.) *n.* fee, payment (*DMLBS* 11) 16/5, 16; **feodi firma** (Lat.) *n.phr.* fee farm, i.e. rent paid by a tenant of land held in fee-simple 10/23

feofamentum (Lat.) *n.* feoffment (*DMLBS* **feoffamentum**) 10/23

ferme *n.* fixed annual rent 10/16, 21–2, 83, 181; 2/2; farm estate 10/181; 2/2; **fee ~** 10/4, 15, 23, 25 (see **feodum** above)

ferrore *n.* farrier 19/93

ferthyng *n.*, **~ (gold) weyght** one-twelfth of an ounce (*OED* **farthing** *n.* 3a (1530? ref.)) 20/188; 19/9, 84

fesanus (Lat.) *n.* pheasant (*DMLBS* **fasianus**) 16/4, 23

fet *v.* fetch 19/29, 72

figes *n.pl.* figs 20/17

fyndyng *vbl.n.* support, maintenance 20/40; **at …fyndyng** supported by 21/136; 19/111

fyre panne *n.* pan for carrying fire 20/82

fyrkyn *n.* a small cask for fish, liquids, etc. originally quarter of a barrel or half a kilderkin (*OED* **firkin** *n.* 1a) 16/10, 16d

fyveshillyngez *n.* a five-shilling coin (cf. *OED* **five** *adj.* and *n.* C1.a) 20/50

Flemych stikes see **stik**

flex *n.* flax 19/22, 89

focale (Lat.) *n.* fuel (*DMLBS* 3 **focalis** *n.*) 16/8, 12, 20, 24; for fuel (*DMLBS* 2 *adj.*) 16/12

foynes *n.pl.* furs of the beech-marten 19/97 I

foldes *n.pl.* folds of cloth (?) (cf. *OED* **fold** *n.*[3] 1d) 20/27

foller *n.* fuller, one who cleans cloth 20/98

fome floure *n.* fermented flour (?), as for sourdough (cf. *OED* **foam** *n.* 1a) 16/22

foryn, **furine** *adj.* foreign, i.e. outside the household 20/137, 185

forinsecus (Lat.) *adj.* from outside (the household), external 16/7, 13

forme *n.* bench 20/112

forrell *n.* covering for a book (*OED* **forel/forrel** *n.* 1c) 1/5v

forryng *vbl.n.* furring, covering with fur 20/81

fostyan see **fustian**

fote *n.*, **a** ~ on foot 19/102

fourme *n.* form, bench 20/82

fowne *pp.* found 19/97

frayles *n.pl.* rush baskets for figs and raisins; also weight of fruit therein (*OED* **frail** *n.*[1] 1) 16/19d

frankensense *n.* aromatic gum resin for use as incense (*OED* **frankincense** *n.* 1) 16/28d

frees, **fresez**, **frice**, **fryce**, **fryse** *n.* frieze, coarse woollen cloth (*LCCP* **frieze**) 20/43, 54, 167, 174, 195; 21/136; 19/51, 103

frenge *n.* fringe 2/17

frontelat *n.*, **fro(u)nt(e)lettes** *n.pl.* frontlet, covering for the forehead 20/67, 105; 19/80, 81, 105; 2/22

frumentum *n.* wheat 16/2, 6, 8, 9

frumentici- *adj.* produced from wheat (*DMLBS* **frumenticius**); **farina ~ie** n. frumenty (*DMLBS* b) 16/22, 2d, 3d

fungia (Lat.) *n.* dry cured fish, i.e. stockfish, or salt fish (*DMLBS* a, b) (extended as n.pl.) 16/10, 19, 23, 13d

furnire (Lat.) *v.* to bake (*DMLBS* **fornare**) 16/6, 2d

furre *n.* skin or hide (*LCCP* **fur** *n.* 1) 19/104, 111

fustian, **fusty(a)n**, **fostyan** *n.* fustian, coarse cloth made of cotton and flax 20/89, 108, 118; 19/31; **holmes** ~ a fustian made at Ulm, Germany 20/101; **tawney** ~ tawny-coloured fustian 19/102

fustik *n.* (wood for) yellow dye (*OED* **fustic** *n.* 1, 2) 20/40

gale pattes *n.pl.* sweet gale (bog myrtle) pasties (?) (cf. *MED* **gail(e)** *n.* + *OED* **patty** *n.*) 21/111

galyngale *n.* rhizome of the ginger family, used in cooking and medicine (*OED* **galangal** *n.* 1a) 16/27d

gallerys *n.pl.* covered space for walking in 20/127

galles, **gallis** *n.pl.* oak galls used in making ink 19/13, 43

gal(l)on, **gawne** *n.* 'gallon', liquid measure of eight pints 20/175; 21/36, 120; 19/96

garcions *n.pl.* serving-men, grooms (*OED* **garcion** *n.*) 16/14

gardevyan, **gardyvyan** *n.*, **gardevyans**, **gardyviance**, **gardyvyance**, **gardivians** *n.pl.* (travelling) trunk (*OED* **gardeviance** *n.*) 17/20; 20/108, 111; 21/18, etc.

gardyng *n.* trimming of braid or lace (*OED* **guarding** *n.* 2) 20/13

garnare *n.* granary (***OED*** **garnery** *n.*); **garnarium (11d)** granary 16/22

garnyshe *n.* a set of vessels for the table (*OED* **garnish** *n.*) 10/47

Gawde Flore *n.phr.* 'Gaude flore virginali', votive antiphon 20/97

geldyng amblyng *n.* a gelded horse trained to move at ambling pace 21/121

george *n.* a representation of St George, part of the insignia of the Order of the Garter 21/24, 29; ~ **weyt** the weight of a George (?) 21/29

gerth n. a belt fastened around a horse to secure a burden (*OED* **girth** *n.*[1] 1a) 21/43; ~ **webbe** *n.* woven material used for a girth or belt (*OED* **girth-web** *n.*) 20/127

gestare (Lat.) *v.* to assess (?) (cf. *DMLBS* **gistare**) 16/6

gilt, **gylt** *n.* gold leaf; gilded plate 20/184; ~ **gold(e)** 20/63, 98, 185; 21/133; 19/7 (*OED* **gilt** *n.*[2] 1, 2)

gynger *n.* ginger 16/23d; **grene** ~ undried ginger root, often preserved (*OED* **green** *adj.* and *n.* S3) 16/11, 25d

glasse *n.*; **glas(s)es**, **glassis** *n.pl.* articles made of glass, glass drinking vessels or phials 20/21, 27, 42, 85, 168, 199; 21/33, 43, 114, 116, 120; 19/6, 18, 56; ~ **of yvery** ivory drinking-vessels (*MED* **glas** *n.* 2) 20/35, 166

glyster pype *n.* clyster-pipe, i.e. tube for administering clysters, i.e. enemas 20/60, 90

gode *n.*, **godys** *n.pl.* item, commodity (cf. *OED* **good** *n.* B II 10c) 19/103, 106

godman *n.* host of an inn, landlord 21/125

gold(e) *n.* gold thread; **cloth of** ~ silk or wool interwoven with gold wire 20/196; 19/59; 6/3, 4; **crowne** ~ gold of the quality of crown coins 1/15r; **Damask(e)** ~ 20/21; 21/101; 19/57 (~ **of Damask** damask interwoven with gold thread (*LCCP* **gold damask**) 21/133; 19/7; 1/15r; 1/10v; 2/6); ~ **drawere/drayer** see below; **flat(te)** ~ flat (not round or twisted) gold wire 20/21; 19/57, 117; 1/15r; **gylt/gilt** ~ see **gilt**; **piping** ~ gold thread for piping a garment (?); error for 'pirling' (?) 1/15r; **pirle/pirling/purlyng** ~ gold thread made of twisted loops for embroidery and edging 20/183; 21/134, 141; **rounde/rownde** ~ round (not flat or twisted) gold wire 19/24, 57; 1/10v, 15r; **Veny(s)e** ~ 20/99; 21/101, 103; 19/82 (~ **of(f) Venys(e)/Vennes(e)/Venyes/Venyce** 17/19; 20/43, 63, 98, 185; 21/61, 73; 19/88, 104, 117; 2/3, 15–17, 26; ~ **of Wennes/Weness/Wenuth** gold thread from Venice 21/61, 96); ~ **(wyre) drawere/drayer** one who draws gold into wire 19/5, 46; 1/15r; 2/17

gomme, gumme *n.* gum 19/13; ~ **arabic** *n.* a gum used for glue 19/43

gonardes *n.pl.* gurnards (*OED* **gurnard** *n.*) 16/4

goode(s) *n.(pl.)* item of merchandise 21/51, 137

gossehalke, gossehauke *n.* goshawk 20/122, 124; 19/72, 96

goweges *n.pl.* gages, pledges (?) (cf. *OED* **gage** *n.*[1] 1a); chisels? (cf. *OED* **gouge** *n.*[1] 1a) 17/61

gray *n.* grey fur (*LCCP* **grey** 3) 20/53; 19/104, 111

grayll *n.* grail, gradual 19/90

graynes, greynes (also **lez greynes**) *n.pl.* 'grains of paradise, used as a spice and in medicine' (*OED* **grain** *n.*[1] 4a) 16/25, 21d

gra(y)ne *n.* an expensive red dyestuff (*LCCP* **grain** *n.*, see also *OED* **alkermes** *n.* 1) 20/47, 180; 19/108; **in** ~ cloth fast-dyed with alkermes (*LCCP* **grain**, *OED* **grain** *n.*[1] III 10a) 20/30; 21/74; 19/73

gravell *n.* a disease in a horse's hoof (cf. *OED* **gravelling** *n.* 2) 17/39

gravyng *vbl.n.* engraving 21/148

gresse *n.*, ~ **horsis** *n.pl.* horses kept at pasture (i.e. fed only on grass) 21/58

gresseld *adj.* grizzled, grey, roan-coloured 20/149

gres(s)om *n.* gersum, a premium paid to a feudal superior on entering a holding (*OED* **gersum** *n.*) 10/22, 27

gret(te) *n.*; **a** ~ altogether (*OED* **a great** *adv.*) 21/13; **in** ~ in total (*OED* **great** *n.* P2 b) 19/91

Greve place name (abl.) (?) 16/10d

grewhounde *n.* greyhound 19/90

grosse *n.*, **grossis** *n.pl.* foreign coin of various origins (*OED* **gross** *n.*[2]) 10/133; 20/184(?)

grot(t)es, grotez *n.pl.* coins worth 4d. 10/77, 101, 102, 199; **romayne** ~ large silver coins (*romanini/grossi*) 17/67 (also **romayn money** 17/27)

gussettes *n.pl.* flexible material protecting gaps between plates of armour (*OED* **gusset** *n.* 1) 20/27, 78

haberdeyne *n.*, **haberdenes, haberdeyns** *n.pl.* large cod, often salted or sun-dried (*OED* **haberdine** *n.* a) 16/10, 23, 13d

haffe *n.* half 19/14

hafte *n.* handle 1/10r

hakkenettes *n.pl.* hackneys, ordinary riding horses (often for hire) (cf. *AND* **hackeney**) 16/14

Hal(l)hallo(ez) *n.* All Saints (Hallows); (church) 19/16; ~ **Day** 1 November, All Saints' Day 19/34, 38; ~ **tyde** 19/46 (see too **Alhaloutyd**)

halyinge *vbl.n.* drag or pull from one place to another (*OED* hale *v.*[1] 1b) 17/30

halkys, howkes *n.pl.*. hawks 19/29; 20/96, 166

hamper *n.* hanaper, department of Chancery into which fees were paid for the sealing and enrolment of charters, etc. 19/39

hayndeyrne *n.* andiron, 'fire-dog' 21/43

hangelles *n.pl.* hangings (*MED* **hongel**) 17/22

hangyng lokk *n.* padlock 21/30; *n.pl.* 19/79

harbegure *n.* a purveyor of lodgings (*OED* **harbinger** *n.* 2) 17/33

harden, herden *n.* a coarse fabric made from the hards of flax or hemp (*OED* **harden/herden/hurden** *n.* and *adj.*) 20/15

hardes *n.*. the coarser part of flax or hemp (*OED* **hurds** *n.*) 19/106

hardware *n.* metalware; tools, utensils, fittings and other items for household use; ~ **man** seller of hardware 20/12, 35–6, etc., 21/8, 93, 145, etc., 19/20, 30 (both *hardward*), 43, etc.

hardwod, herdwod *n.* wood from deciduous trees (*OED* **hardwood** *n.* 1a) 16/12, 13, 24, 30d

harnesshe, harnys *n.* the metalwork of a girdle (*OED* **harness** *n.* 1) 19/29; horse harness 19/33, 34, 77

hassehokes *n.pl.* hassocks 21/134

hey(e) *n.* hay 21/33; rope made of hay (?) 21/131

heyge see **egge**

heirez *n.* heiress 19/116

helne/helnys see **ell**

hepes (lez hepes) *n.pl.* heaped (as opposed to struck or rased) measures (*MED* **hep** *n.* 2d; cf. **uphepen** *v.* 1) 16/1d

here *n.* haircloth used as an altar cloth (*LCCP* **haire** *n.* 1b) 19/108

herott *n.* herald 19/8

here lassys *n.pl.* hairbands 21/93

hevynge *vbl.n.* removing, conveying (*OED* **heave** *v.* 4) 17/20, 47

hobies, hobiez *n.pl.* a species of small falcon 20/107, 109

hob(b)y horsis *n.pl.* small horses, amblers, ponies 20/97, 105

hoddes *n.pl.* hoods 20/166

hog(e), **hogge** *n.* casks for, or measures of, liquids (cf. *OED* **hogshead** *n.*) 16/9, 18, 19, 23

hogyshedes *n.pl.* hogsheads, large barrels containing ale or wine of variable numbers of gallons (*OED* **hogshead** *n.* 1, 2a) 20/91

holland(e)/hollonde cloth(e) *n.* fine linen cloth made in Holland (*LCCP*) 20/104, 118, 156, etc.; 19/8

holy water styk *n.* aspergillum, branch or brush for sprinkling holy water 21/95; 19/9

homers *n.pl.* hammers(?) (*MED* **hamer** *n.* 1a) 21/18

hope *n.* hoop 17/20

hopying *vbl.n.* hooping, fastening with hoops 20/91

horse *n.*; ~ **hernys** *n.* horse harness 2/26; ~ **bred** *n.* provender 20/97; ~ **house** *n.*, ~ **howses** *n.pl.* horse rug, textile covering of a horse's back and flanks (*OED* **house** *n.*[2]) 20/13, 47; ~ **meyte** *n.* provender 20/22, 28, 34, 38, 53, etc.

hoselyng *vbl.n.* houselling, giving communion to 19/92

hossis see **howse**

house romth *n.* house-room, temporary space in a house (*OED* **house-roomth** *n.*) 1/15r

howkes see **halkys**

howse *n.*, **hossis** *n.pl.* hose, stockings 20/80, 93, 151; 2/34

hud(de) *n.* hood 19/97 I; 2/22

y(e)very *n.* ivory 20/35, 60

ymagery (warke/work) *n.* figured work, e.g. tapestry, embroidery (*OED* **imagery work** *n.* 1a) 19/17; 2/31; 6/5

impropred, **inproperyd** *pp.* appropriated 19/90, 120

impropriacioun *n.* appropriation of a benefice (see *OED* **impropriation** *n.* 1a(a)) 21/147

incrementum mensure (de incremento mensure) *n.phr.* the practice of using heaped measures 16/1d, 31d

indirittus (Lat.) *ppl.adj.* uncorrected, incorrect 17/48

inlonde *n.* environs of a large house not cultivated by tenants (*OED* **inland** *n.* A 1a) 17/26

inquessycion, **inquicioun** *n.* (record of a) judicial investigation (*MED* **inquisicioun** *n.* 1a, b) 21/149; 19/15

inrollyng see **enrollyng**

interyng *vbl.n.* entering an item into an official record (*MED* **entren** *v.* 12) 21/148

instrument *n.* authenticated record 1/10v

intrat (Lat.) *3sg.* he is answerable/accepts responsibility (for something)

ypacrace *n.* hippocras, spiced wine 19/28

irne see **yrne**

isshare *n.* usher 20/190

iter (Lat.) *n.* journey (abl. *itenere*) 16/13

jardyners *n.pl.* gardeners 20/20, 154

jelafers *n.pl.* gillyflowers, cloves 19/96

jonyd, **yonde** *adj.* joined, constructed by joining the parts (cf. *OED* joined *adj.*[1] 2); ~ **chayre** 21/120; ~ **stolis** 20/82

joinctour, **joyn(c)tour**, **joynter**, **jounyntour**, **juncture**, **junter** *n.* jointure 10/3, 31, 144; 20/126, etc.

jurnall *n.*, **jurnalles** *n.pl.* diurnal, service book of the day-hours 19/70

kendall, **kyndall** *n.* kendal, a type of fulled woollen cloth (green) (*OED*/*LCCP*) 20/93; 19/21, 102; **Kentisshe/Kyntyssh** ~ kendal from Kent 19/26

kennet *n.* heavy grey cloth of Welsh origin 19/37 (*LCCP*)

kepe, **kepp**, **kyp**, **kypp(e)**, **cyppe** *n.* the hide of a young animal (*OED* **kip** *n.*[1]) 20/25, 26, 167, 174; 21/31, 51, 100, 136; 19/40; 2/28

kersay, kersey, carsay, carsey *n.* coarse narrow cloth originally made at Kersey, Suffolk (*LCCP* kersey) 20/35, 112, 118, 123, etc.; tawny ~ tawny-coloured kersey cloth 20/80, 167

kynderkyn *n.*, **kylderkynnes (lez kylderkynnes)(9, 5d)** *n.pl.* cask for liquids, fish, etc. or measurement of such items (half a barrel) (*OED* **kilderkin** *n.*, cf. *OED* **firkin** *n.*) 16/9, 5d; 21/129

Kyntyssh *adj.* Kentish 20/93

kyrtill *n.* a gown or skirt/petticoat 21/32

kkottshyns *n.pl.* cushions 17/23

lac(c)agium (Lat.) *n.* ullage, i.e. (payment for) loss of transported liquor by leakage or absorption (*DMLBS*) 16/9, 4d

(lag.) lagena (Lat.) *n.* liquid measure, one gallon (*DMLBS* 2); (11) dry measure, one eighth of a bushel (*DMLBS* 3d) 16/9, 11, 23, 25

laysse, **lasshe** *n.*, **lacez**, **lasces**, **lasses**, **lassys** *n.pl.* lace, cord, tie 20/29; 21/93, 136; 19/75; 2/34; **Seynt Audrez** ~ *n.pl.* laces to wear round the neck (St Etheldreda died of a throat tumour) 17/36

lampe oyle *n.* oil for burning in lamps (*OED* **lamp oil** *n.*) 16/16d

lampre(ye)s (also **lez lampreyes)** *n.pl.* lampreys, i.e. fish similar to eels (*OED* **lamprey** *n.*) 16/10; 19/8, 77

lanars, **lan(n)ers** *n.pl.* a species of (female) falcon 20/96, 156, 165; 21/37 large *n.*; at ~ at length, in full (*OED* large *n.* P 1c) 10/62; 20/134

lassyng *vbl.n.* lacing 19/8

launde *n.* lawn, fine linen 20/171

la(u)nder(e) *n.* launderer, washer of linen 20/88, 168; 19/11, 46, 86, 95; 1/11v

laveret *n.* young hare (*OED* **leveret** *n.*) 20/162

lasshe *n.* flexible part of a whip (*OED* **lash** *n.*[1] 2a) 20/29

lectuary *n.* electuary, medicinal paste 20/94

leders *n.pl.* leathers 21/103

lenga *n.* (Lat.) *n.*, **linges**, **lynges** (Eng.) *n.pl.* ling, a fish usually salted, split and dried (*DMLBS* **linga**; *OED* **ling** *n.*[1]) 16/10, 15, 23, 13d

letter *n.* litter 21/8

let(t)ermen see **lytermen**

let(t)es, letice, letys(se), lettis, lettuys *n.pl.* white-grey fur used for trimming and lining garments (*OED*/*LCCP* lettice *n.*) 20/53, 146; 21/31, 54, 65, 149, 150; 19/12, 31, 75, 106, 110

lettres patens *n.pl.* letters patent 19/58

levere *n.* livery 2/33

Lewkes welvett see welvet(t)

lewtor *n.* lutenist 19/97

liberatura (Lat.) *n.* (*DMLBS* a, b) allowance 16/4d; livery 16/14, 30d

libertiez *n.pl.* privileges 19/121

(li.) libra (Lat.) *n.* one pound in currency (£) 16/1, 2, 3, 4

(lib.) libra (Lat.) *n.* one pound in weight (lb.) 16/6, 8, 9, 11

licoryse, **lucrise** *n.* liquorice (*OED* **liquorice/licorice** *n.*) 16/26; **powder of ~** ground liquorice root (*OED* C1 **liquorice powder**) 16/27d

lycoure *n.* lubricating oil (cf. *OED* **liquor** *n.*) 17/24

lye, **lie** *n.* alkaline solution for washing; urine (*OED* **lei(e** *n.*(1)); **~ pott** *n.* 19/42; **~ pottes** *n.pl.* pot(s) for holding washing water or urine 19/42; 1/8v

lyez (lez lyez) (Lat.) *n.pl.* dregs (?) (cf. *OED* **lye** *n.*[1]) 16/5d

lying *vbl.n.* treating with alkalised water or a similar cleaning substance (*OED* **lye** *v.*[2]) 19/6, 12, 21

lymyned *pp.* limned, i.e. illuminated, decorated 19/17; **lymmynge** *vbl.n.* 21/149

lymon(de)s *n.pl.* lemons (*OED* **lemon** *n.*[1]) 16/11, 25d

lynan, **lynam**, **lynnen**, **lynnyng** *n.* linen 20/15, 17; 21/136; 2/14 (?)

lyne *n.*flax (*OED* **line** *n.*[1]) 21/131; 1/13r

linguin aloes *n.* lign-aloes, a bitter drug, an aromatic wood 19/108

lynnes (?) *n.pl.* linen clothes (*MED* **lin** *n.* 3b)

lyns(e)y (wolseay) *n.* cloth of mixed wool and linen (*LCCP* **linsey-woolsey** *n.*) 20/192; 2/35

lyre *n.* textile associated with modern Lier, Belgium (*LCCP* **lire** 2) 20/56, 98, 108, 127; 21/18, 31, 76, 136, 149; 2/25

lyres *n.pl.* tapes, cords, binding (*OED* **lear** *n.*[2] 1) 20/58

lytermen, let(t)ermen *n.pl.* the men who carry a litter 20/80, 87; 19/97 I

lyverey *n.* the liveried household (*OED* **livery** *n.* 12b) 17/43

locram *n.* a type of linen fabric (*OED* **lockram** *n.*) 20/174

lodynge *vbl.n.* loading 17/47

loyd *n.*, **loodes** *n.pl.* load 2/25

lordshipp *n.* estate 10/15

lorymer *n.* maker of ironware, e.g. for horse bridles 2/11

lostes *n.pl.* losses 19/47

lottes *n.pl.*; **tymber** ~ sets (?) of fur (see **tymber** below) 20/82

lucrise see **licoryse**

lutere *n.* lutenist 21/110

ma(y)lyng cord *n.* cord for tying up things 20/93; 21/64

mairesale, mairesall *n.* marshalsea, stables 10/140

male *n.* travelling bag (*OED* **mail** *n.*[2]) 19/22 (see too pelyon)

malmessey, malves(e)y, malves(s)ey, mavessy *n.* malmsey, a sweet wine originally from Greece (*OED* **malmsey** *n.*, **malvoisie** *n.*) 16/9, 23, 6d; 10/18, 39; 20/83, 21/36

mantelet *n.* short cape 20/80; 1/15v

marchaunt(e) *n.* tradesman (*OED* **merchant** A *n.*1a), **de** ~ bought outside the household 16/11, 19d

marlyns see **merlyons**

marmelade *n.* a quince preserve (comparable to Spanish *membrillo*) (*OED* **marmalade** A *n.* 1a) 16/20d

marte *n.* market 19/108

martes *n.* mattresses (?) 17/24

Martilmasse *n.* Martlemass, i.e. Martinmass (feast of St Martin 11 November) 10/19

masys *n.pl.* maces, seed-coverings of nutmeg (*OED* **mace** *n.*[1]) 16/22d

maunchet(t)es *n.pl.* loaves of finest wheat flour 16/6, 22, 2d, 3d

maunde(y), maundy *n.* distribution of alms Maundy Thursday 20/16–17, 47, 88, 151–2; 19/12, 14, 97 I, 103; ~ **gowne** plain gown worn at the Maundy 20/23

meddeley, **medly** *n.* a type of cloth made of wools dyed and mixed before being spun (*OED* **medley** *n.* II 2; *LCCP* **medley**) 20/25, 47, 77, 111, etc.; **north(er)yn** ~ cloth from the north of England (?) 19/103, 104, 111; **tawn(en)y**, **tawne** ~ tawny-coloured medley cloth 20/167; 19/96, 97 II; 2/12, etc.

medelyng *n.* cloth made of different threads or pieces (*LCCP* **meddling**) 21/120

meytenge, **meytyng(e)** *vbl.n.* measuring (?) 20/98; 1/5v

menever see **mynyvere**

merlyons, **marlyns** *n.pl.* a species of small falcon, probably *Falco columbarius aesalon* 20/114, 165, 170; 19/31

mese *n.* messuage (*OED* **mese** *n.*[2]) 10/147

metsons *n.pl.* medicines 20/147; 19/72, 98

myndyng *vbl.n.* mending 20/187

mynet *n.*, **mynutes** *n.pl.* a summary or draft of a document or letter (*OED* **minut(e)** *n.* 3) 19/71–2

minutes *n.pl.* coins of small value (*OED* **minute** *n.*[1]); farthings or half farthings (*MED* **minut(e)** *n.*[1]) 10/133

mynyvere, **menever** *n.* white fur, typically the winter belly-fur (or the mixed grey and white fur) of the red squirrel (*LCCP* **miniver** 1a) 20/184; 2/31

mynsterlys, **mynstrles** *n.pl.* minstrels 20/42; 19/90

myture *n.* mitre 20/183

modiacio (Lat.) *n.* levy on grain or wine (*DMLBS* **modiatio**) 16/3

molendare (Lat.) *v.* to grind, mill (*DMLBS*) 16/2d

molendinarius (Lat.) *n.* miller (*DMLBS*) 16/2d

mollynges *n.pl.* foodstuffs (unknown) 19/81

mone(y) *n.* money 17/1–3, 26, etc.; 20/107, 169, etc.; **romayn** ~ see **grot(t)es**; **white** ~ silver coins (*OED* **white** *adj.* C1f) 17/31

monyht *n.* month 10/34, 61, 83

more *adj.* greater, further (*OED* **more** *adj.* II 4b) 10/32

morens, **moryns** *n.pl.* animals dead from disease 16/5, 20 (*OED* **murrain** A *n.* 1a, 3) 16/5, 20; **morina** (Lat.) *n.* murrein, any virulent disease of cattle (*DMLBS* **morina** b) 16/5, 18, 7d, 10d; **morinatus** *ppl.adj.* afflicted by or dead of cattle plague (*DMLBS*) 16/5, 17, 19, 8d

mores, **morez** *n.* morris dancing 21/159; 19/59

morrey *n.* purple-red cloth (*OED* **murrey** *n.*[1]) 20/54

morte(y)s *n.pl.* wax candles (*OED* **mort** *n.*[2]) 16/18d

mortes *v.* alienate in mortmain (*MED* **mortisen** *v.*, *OED* **amortize** *v.*) 21/77; **mortez** *n.* mortmain (?) (cf. *MED* **mortis(e)ment** *n.*, *OED* **amortizement** *n.*) 19/53

mortmayne *n.* mortmain, property held inalienably by an ecclesiastical or other organisation 10/127

moscadyne, **muskadyne**; **muscadell**, **muskadele**, **muskadell**; **mustadell**, **mustedell** *n.* muscatel, a sweet wine from muscat grapes (*OED* **muscadel** *n.* 1) 16/23; 21/20, 36; 19/56, 82

mountayn *n.* mounting 1/10v

nail(l), **nayle**, **nayll** *n.* a measure of length for cloth (2¼ i*n.*) (*LCCP* **nail** 1a) 20/148; 21/150; 19/40, 97 II, 106

napys *n.pl.* tablecloths 19/99

negge see **egge**

neldes *n.pl.* needles 20/26, 29, 42, 60, 89, etc.; 19/7, 10, 19, 27, etc.

nell(e) see **ell**

Neweres Day *n.* New Year's Day 20/189; 19/44; **Neweres Even** New Year's Eve 19/45; **Neuyerres/Newer(es)/Newyres gyf(f)t(es)** New Year gift(s) 20/57, 188, 189; 19/113

nonnage *n.* minority, under legal age (*OED* **nonage** *n.*[1]) 10/29

Normandy canvas/clothe *n.* cloth from Normandy (*OED* **Normandy** II 3) 20/37; 21/65; 19/25, 102

norshrye for **noryshe** *n.* nurse 10/9

northern dosyn *n.phr.* seventeen items 21/51

obligacio (Lat.) obligation, bond 1/18v; **obligacion** (Eng.) *n.* bond, written agreement 10/127, 158

(ob.) obolus (Lat.) *n.* halfpenny (½d.) 16/1, 2, 4, 5

olyves *n.pl.* olives 16/11, 23d

oneratur (Lat.) *3sg.pass.* it is charged (in/to/against) (*DMLBS* 4) 16/5, 6, 10; 10/33, 101–04, 107, 113, 114, 117–19, 123–6, 132, 133, 161

onus (Lat.) *n.* charge, debit side of an account (*DMLBS* 5a, b) 16/5, 6, 10

oragam, **organs**, **orgence** *n.pl.*; **a paire of ~** an organ 17/61, 64; 19/87

orages, **ore(n)g(es)**, **orygyns**, *n.pl.* oranges 21/12, 28; 19/74, 105, 110; 2/7; 6/6

or(i)ege, **oregen** *adj.* orange-coloured, tan (?) 20/169; **(of) ~ coller** orange-coloured 19/98, 110

ore tenus (Lat.) *n.phr.* verbally, orally 16/16

orritur *n.* orator (i.e. representative) 21/121

osey *n.* sweet Portuguese (or French) wine (*OED* **osey** *n.*) 16/4, 9

over *prep.* over and above 20/160

owens *n.pl.* ovens 2/8

ower *n.*, **owres** *n.pl.* oar 19/95

owtlawre *n.* outlawry; the legal process by which a person is declared outlaw 2/23

oying *pr.p.* owing 20/162

oz. see **unce**

pakkyng *vbl.n.* packing 1/5v; ~ **schettes** *n.pl.* sheets for packing goods (*OED* **packing** *n.*[1] C1.)

pakthred(d) *n.* strong cord or twine for tying packs 20/92, 94, 97; 21/7

palett *n.*, **pallattes** *n.pl.* straw beds or mattresses (*OED* **pallet** *n.*[3]) 19/78; ~ **case**, **cassis** (canvas) cases to hold them 20/81; 19/78

palffere(y)s, **palfreis** *n.pl.* palfrey, a small saddle horse for a woman 20/45, 49, 185

pampelyon *n.* pampilion, a kind of fur used for lining and trimming 19/73

pane *n.*, **paynys** *n.pl.* pelt of fur, esp. for lining or trimming a garment (*OED* **pane** *n.*[1] 1a) 21/64; 2/31

panell *n.* a saddle pad; a pillion (*OED* **panel** *n.*[1] I 1a, b) 21/43

panyour *n.* pannier, basket 19/82; 1/11v

panis (Lat.) *n.* bread; ~ **humanus** bread for human consumption 16/6; ~ **equinus** bread for horses 16/14 (form not recorded *DMLBS*, but cf. D91.17/30, 49: 'for horssemete & mannys mete')

pannum (Lat.) *n.* (piece of) cloth; ~ **laneum** woollen cloth (cf. *DMLBS* **pannus laneus** 1c, but here neuter gender) 16/4, 14, 21, 25

papire, **papure**, **pa(u)per**, **pa(w)per** *n.* paper 20/14, 55, 58, 175; 21/58, 135, 146; 19/7, 29, 91–2; ~ **de Gene**, ~ **Francie** varieties of paper (from Genoa, from France) 16/11, 26, 28d; **gold** ~ gold-leaf 20/56; ~ **regale/riall/r(o)yall** expensive, best quality paper of large size, cf. 'pawper of the larger syse' 19/29 (cf. **paper royal** in *OED* **royal** A. *adj.* 11a; **paper rial** in *OED* **rial** *adj.* 4; *DMLBS* **papirus re(g)alis** 2b) 16/28d; 19/7, 113; 1/11r; **sylver** ~ silver-leaf 20/56

par (Lat.) *n.* pair (*DMLBS* 5); ~ **organorum** pair of organs, i.e. an organ (cf. *OED* **pair** *n.*[1] 8) 16/14

parcella (Lat.) *n.* little part, portion (*DMLBS* 1); **(19d)** itemised or detailed part of an account (cf. *DMLBS* 3b) 16/20, 4d, 16d

parcell gild *adj.* partly gilded (*OED* **parcel-gilt** *adj.*) 1/10r

parley *n.* meeting for arbitration 2/11

Par(r)es, **Parice**, **Parys**, **Pariss** *n.* fabric made in Paris (*OED* **Paris** 2) 20/80, 177, 198; 1/15v; *adj.* 19/19

parres *n.* pairs (of) 20/48

past(e) *n.* paste 20/81, 177; ~ **bourde** paste-board 19/41

pasteria (Lat.) *n.* pastry house; **pastre (2d)** pastry house (*OED* **pastry** *n.* 3) 16/22, 3d

pastoron *n.* pastern, shackle attached to leg of a horse (*OED* **pastern** *n.* 1)

patlet *n.* bodice (*OED* **partlet** *n.*[2]) 19/102

patron *n.* model or design from which to make something (*OED* **pattern** *n.*) 21/31

pauper, **pawper** see **papire**

pax *n.*, ~ **bredes** *n.pl.* pax board kissed during the mass, osculatory 20/184; 21/146

(pec.) pecca (Lat.) *n.* peck, one quarter of a bushel 16/22, 1d, 2d

pechyr howse *n.* pitcher-house, room for storing ale and wine 19/86, 97

pecia (Lat.) *n.* piece, portion (*DMLBS* 1) 16/2, 4, 14, 24; item of tanned hide 16/5, 18, 19, 21 (*DMLBS* 1b)

pecyng *vbl.n.* assembling as one piece (*OED* **piece** *v.* 2a) 1/7r

peions *n.pl.* pigeons 20/117

pekelyng *n.* a coarse fabric (*OED* **pickling** *n.*[2]) 19/96

pelyon, **pylleon** *n.* pillion, a light saddle for women 20/98, 99; **male** ~ saddle with travelling bags 21/16

peloure *n.* pillow (?), seemingly not 'pelure', i.e. fur (cf. *OED* **pillow** *n.* β) 20/126

pendere (Lat.) *v.* to remain outstanding (*DMLBS* e) 16/1, 8, 21

pener, **pennard**, **pennour** *n.* pen-case (*OED* **penner** *n.*[1]) 19/20, 84; 1/13r

penes (Lat.) *prep.* + *acc.* with; in the possession of (*DMLBS* 1) 16/21, 3d, 19d; 1/18v

penyweight *n.* a unit of weight equivalent to a silver penny (for details see *OED* **penny-weight** *n.* 1) 19/94; 1/15r

pensons, **pynsons** *n.pl.* thin shoes, such as slippers or pumps (*LCCP* **pinson**) 20/45, 97; 21/12, 34, 93; 19/109

perdonare (Lat.) *v.* to excuse (someone of payment due) (*DMLBS* 2b) 16/18, 3d, 4d, 5d

performe *v.* to produce 19/97 I

perfourmyng *vbl.n.* finishing off 19/111

perlyng, **pyrlyng**, *vbl.n.* spinning; ~ **golde** spun gold thread (*OED* pirl *v.* 1) 20/183; ~ **well** *n.*, ~ **whelis** *n.pl.* spinning wheel(s) (*OED* **pirling** *adj.* 1) 21/49; 19/75; ~ **wyres** wires for spinning wheels (?) 19/27

perse rynk *n.* purse-ring (?) (*OED* **purse ring** *n.*) 2/31

pertrych *n.* partridge 20/42, 172

(pet.) petra (Lat.) *n.* one 'stone' in dry weight (*DMLBS* 6, and see 16/12d for 1 pet. of wool as 14lb., 16/19d for 1 pet. of wick as 8lb.) 16/18, 20, 21, 12d, 19d

petycote *n.* padded undercoat 20/124; 19/40, 47

pykell (le pykell) (Lat.) *n.* brine or vinegar (*OED* **pickle** A *n.*[1] I 1a) 16/11, 25, 23d, 25d

pykes *n.pl.* pointed tips 21/31

pylleon see **pelyon**

pyllydes, **pyllydys** *n.pl.* pullets (?) 19/106

pynkes *n.pl.* decorative holes/eyelets in gowns (*OED* **pink** *n.*[4]) 20/146; 19/47, 97 I; 1/7v

pynnesse *n.pl.* pins 20/84

pynsons see **pensons**

pynt(e) *n.* 'pint', liquid measure of one eighth of a gallon 21/33; 19/28

pip(e), **pype**, **pipp** *n.* cask, or liquid measure equivalent to two hogsheads (*OED* **pipe** *n.*[2] 2, cf. *DMLBS* **pipa** 4a, b) 16/9, 18, 23, 4d; 21/26; 19/10

pype of gold *n.phr.* gold wire used to decorate metalwork or garments (*OED* **pipe** *n.*[1] III 13) 21/34

pyppyns *n.* late-ripening sweet apples (*OED* **pippin** *n.*) 16/11

pyrlyng see **perlyng**

pissis (Lat.) *n.* fish (*DMLBS* **piscis**) (extended as plural) 16/8, 10, 15, 13d

placardes *n.pl.* proclamations, letters under seal (*OED* **placard** *n.* II 4a, b) 19/111

place *n.* palace 19/71

playth *n.* a twilled woollen cloth, a plaid (*DSL* **plaid**) 21/32

playttynge *vbl.n.* plaiting, strands plaited together 20/92

plates *n.pl.* flat cakes (*OED* **plate** *n.* II 10) 16/11, 25, 24d; **plattes** *n.pl.* flat plates of metal (*OED* **plate** *n.* I 2b) 20/59; 21/120

pleytt, **plyet(t)** *n.* fold or length of cloth; **plytes** *n.pl.* (*LCCP* **pleat**, cf. *OED* **pleat** *n.*, **plait** *n.* 2a, **plight** *n.*[3] 2a, b) 20/15, 125; 19/97 II

plonket see **blonket**

pointes, **poyntes**, **powntes** *n.pl.* tagged pieces of ribbon or cord used for attaching hose to a doublet, lacing a garment, fastening a shoe, etc. 20/125; 21/32; 2/27

polie *n.* pulley (?) (*OED* **puli** *n.*) 20/31

pomaunder werk *n.* perforated and filled with potpourri (cf. *OED* **pomander** *n.* 1a) 1/9r

pond *n.* pound (lib.) 16/24

pondyng, **pondering** *pr.p.* weighing 21/67; 1/10r, 10v

po(o)tes *n.pl.* paws, usually of squirrels (*LCCP* **pote**, cf. *OED* **pote** *n.*[2]) 20/174, 185; 21/31

popettes *n.pl.* dolls 19/111

popyngay *n.* the colour of a parrot, usu. blue/green (*OED* **popinjay** *n.*4) 20/112

porpasse *n.* porpoise 19/80

porcolyez, **portcoles**, **portkeles**, **portkolas**, **portkoles** *n.pl.* portcullises (livery badges displaying the Beaufort arms) 2/12, 15, 16, 17; 6/3; 2/

porthouse, **porthowse**, **portuys**, **portuous**, **portuse** *n.* porteous, portable breviary (*OED* **porteous** *n.*) 20/12, 17, 85, 126; 19/14, 79, 83; 1/7r

possnet *n.* a small three-legged metal pot (*OED* **posnet** *n.*) 20/179

potell *n.* unit of capacity for liquids (half a gallon) (*OED* **pottle** *n.* 1b) 16/23d

potenger *n.* bowl or pot (*OED* **pottinger** *n.*) 1/10r-v

poticar(y), **potycury** *n.* apothecary (cf. *OED* **potycaryar** *n.*) 21/28; 19/70; 1/4r

pot(t)ell *n.* half a gallon 17/35; vessel containing half a gallon 19/82 (*OED* **pottle** *n.*[1] 1a,b) 17/35; 19/82

poundes *n.pl.* ponds 20/20

poundgarnard, **pounde garnettes**, **pownegarnettes** *n.(pl.)* pomegranate(s) 21/23, 132, 134; 19/104–5

powdrynges, **poudryngis** *n.pl.* random (as if powdered or sprinkled) decorative motifs for textiles (cf. *OED* **powdering** *n.* II.4) 19/47; 2/14

power *adj.* poor 19/22, 92

preyse *v.* appraise, value; **preysyng** *pr.p.* 19/45; **praysed** *pp.* 10/141

pr(e)yser *n.*, **preysers** *n.pl.* valuer or appraiser 10/141; 21/118; 19/45

premer *n.* primer, book of hours 19/38, 109

prentes, **prentez**, **prentis(se)**, **pryntes** *n.* apprentice 20/173, 196; 21/91, 117, 155

presentacion *n.* presentation to a benefice 20/156

prest *n.* an advance of money, a loan 20/197; 21/111; 19/93, 125; *v.* to advance as a loan 10/104; 21/163; 19/95; 2/8; **prested** *pp.* 19/123, 125

prestitus (Lat.) *ppl.adj.* lent, advanced 1/16v, 18v

prewnes, prunes (also **lez prewnes**) *n.pl.* prunes (*OED* **prune** *n.*) 16/11, 25, 26d

prikettes, **prykettes** *n.pl.* candles to stick on spikes (*OED* **pricket** *n.* 1a) 16/16d, 18d

priksoung *n.* music sung from notes written or pricked 1/6v; **prykkyng** *vbl.n.* marking in musical notation (*OED* **prick** *v.* IV 20a) 21/39

prioris *n.* prioress 20/180

pryser see **pr(e)yser**

proc(a)tour *n.* proctor, agent, steward 19/71; administrator of a Carthusian house 20/86; *n.pl.* the two administrative officers running the University of Cambridge, i.e. syndics 20/79

procuracie *n.* letter of attourney 19/71

profers *n.pl.* provisional payments of dues to the exchequer 19/121

propreacion, **propriacion** see **(ap)propriacion**

provecioun *n.* provision 19/103, 108

proxies *n.pl.* letters of proxy 19/113

pukys *n.pl.* pouches (?) (*OED* **poke** *n.*[1], but see *LCCP* **poke** 1b) 21/31

pull *n.* young bird (*OED* **pull** *n.*[2]) 16/4

pullus (Lat.) *n.* chicken (*DMLBS* 2b) 16/15

pultys *n.pl.* animals' paws (*OED* **pote** *n.*[2]) 19/106

puppets *n.pl.* dolls 21/26

purcyvant, **pursyvant** *n.* pursuivant, attendant heraldic officer 20/127

purfell, **purffull**, **purfyll** *n.*, **purfells**, **purvillys** *n.pl.* decorative border or trim, chiefly of fur but also embroidered and decorated with pearls (*LCCP* **purfle** 1) 19/6, 47, 97 II, 103, 110

purpull *n.* costly purple cloth 2/27

purve *v.* purvey, purchase 10/20

puter *n.* pewter 20/112

(qua.) quadrans (Lat.) *n.* 'farthing' (¼d.) 16/2, 8, 9, 11

quarrears, **quarrye(r)s**, **quarriours** (also **lez quarrye(r)s**) *n.pl.* large square candles (*OED* **quarrier** *n.*[2]) 16/24, 16d; 1/11v

quart *n.* container or liquid measure of two pints, i.e. one quarter of a gallon (*OED* **quart** *n.*[1] 1b) 16/9, 26, 5d, 27d; 21/33; 19/17, 28; quarter of a pound in weight (*OED* **quart** *n.*[2] 2a) 20/21; 19/19; dry measure of two gallons, i.e. one peck, one quarter of a bushel (*DMLBS* **quartus** 4b) 10/120

quarter *n.* one-fourth (of a single unit), a quarter 16/4, 28d, 31d; 21/158; one-fourth of a year, i.e. three months 19/15, 17, 21, 108, etc.; one-fourth of a verge (cf. *DMLBS* **quartarius** 4) 16/24, 26, 6d, 9d; one-fourth of a linear measure 20/91; 19/24 (cf. *DMLBS* 5); **di.** ~ three-quarters 19/29; ~ **di.** three-eighths 16/26; 20/158

(qr.) quarterius (Lat.) *n.* a unit of dry measure, e.g. of corn (16/2, 9, 18, 22), sugar (16/11, 25, 19d, 20d), salt (16/12, 24, 15d), wick (16/12), charcoal (16/12), mustard seed (16/14, 25), oats (16/14, 23, 25, 29d), etc. (*DMLBS* **quartarius** 2a, d, h, i) (see **way(e)** below, and see 16/22 for 1 qr. as 8 bushels);

quartron *n.* quarter of an ounce (*OED* **quartern** *n.*[2] 3e) 20/164; 2/26

quene appollys *n.pl.* queen apples (?), red apples that ripen early 19/108

quessionus *n.pl.* cushions 2/33

quietus (Lat.) *ppl.adj.* quit (of debt, or charge) (*DMLBS* 6) 16/21

ram(e) *n.* ram, implement for ramming (for use in making a sluice) 2/7; 6/5 (see Jones, 'Lady Margaret Beaufort, the Royal Council')

rape *n.* a type of turnip used for oil (*OED* **rape** *n.*[5] 2b) 16/15d, 16d; ~ **oyle** rape-oil 16/12

rase *ppl.adj.* erased (see **vel(l)om**) 19/7, 29

rasoni *n.pl.* dried grape, raisin (*DMLBS* **racemus** 2) 16/11, 19d; **rasen correnis**, **rasoni/lez reson corans** (Eng./Lat.) *n.pl.* raisins from Corinth (currants) (*DMLBS* **racemus** 2c; *OED* **currant** *n.* 1a, **raisin** *n.* 2) 16/11, 25, 21d

reba(e)n *n.* ribbon, edging; **changeable/changeabull ~** ribbon that changes appearance in different contexts, 'shot', c.f. 'shot silk' (*OED* **changeable** *adj.* A. *adj.* 2a) 19/11, 23, 75

recens (Lat.) *adj.* fresh, unsalted (*DMLBS* 4) 16/15

recepta (Lat.) *n.* receipt(s), account of money received (*DMLBS* c) 10/3, 5, 6, 15

recognicio (Lat.) *n.* recognisance, legal document acknowledging debt or obligation (*OED* **recognizance** *n.* 1, 2, cf. *DMLBS* **recognitio**) 16/2, 5, 7, 8; 10/101

recury *n.* recovery, regaining of a right to property (*OED* **recovery** *n.* I 2a) 10/160; **recover(y)es** *n.pl.* 19/55

redde *n.* red cloth (of trappings) 20/176

reddere (Lat.) *v.* to render (account for) (*DMLBS* 2) 16/1d, 3d, 5d, 11d

redditus (Lat.) *n.* rent (*DMLBS* 3) 16/3

registre *n.* registration 19/71

relacio (Lat.) *n.* account related (by someone) (*DMLBS* 4) 16/5, 6, 20, 4d

relesses *n.pl.* legal documents of conveyancing property 21/93

remanent *n.* a remainder, a left-over portion 17/47

remanentia (Lat.) *n.* what is left over, remainder, residue (*DMLBS* 2, 3) 16/1, 8, 16, 1d

reme *n.* ream, i.e. 20 quires of paper (*OED* **ream** *n.*[3] 1a) 16/11, 26, 28d; 19/29

rere *adj.* hindmost, last 21/4

resyngnacion *n.* return of property to a superior 21/97

respectuare (Lat.) *v.* to grant respite or postponement (of a payment) (*DMLBS* a, b) 16/16

respondere (de) (Lat.) *v.* to be responsible for, to be chargeable for (*DMLBS* 12d) 16/3d, 5d, 11d, 12d

resorrecioun, resurreccio(u)n, resurrexson *n.* the stage in the Easter liturgy that marks the resurrection (?); a pictorial representation of the resurrection of Christ (?) (*MED* **resurrecioun** *n.* 1c) 21/15, 108; 19/14; 1/9r

retainers *n.pl.* authorisations to a creditor 19/105

retro (Lat.) *adv.*; **a ~** in arrears (*DMLBS* 5b) 16/18–19

revestry *n.* vestry 17/63

rybybe *n.* rebec, three-stringed instrument like a violin (*OED* **ribibe** *n.* 2) 19/97

ryghtes, **ryghtis** *n.pl.* first Eucharist (cf. *OED* **right** *n.* 15a) 20/20; 19/83, 86; 1/9r

ring *n.* a metal ring on a post which horsemen compete to take off with their lances (*OED* **ring** *n.*[1] 4a) 19/93

ryse *n.* winder for silk 1/12r

rivnews *n.pl.* revenues 10/127

roces *n.* woollen cloth (*LCCP* **russet** 2a, var. *rosas*) 20/13

roches *n.pl.* roaches (*OED* **roach** *n.*[1]) 16/4

romayn(e) Roman, i.e. Italian (see **grot(t)es**)

rom(e)ney, **rumney** *n.* rumney, a sweet red wine of Mediterranean origin (*MED* **romenei(e)** *n.* 1a, cf. *OED* **rumney** *n.* 1) 16/9, 23, 6d; 17/35; 21/36; 19/28

romth see **house romth**

rosyn *n.* rosin, a kind of resin (*OED* **rosin** *n.* 1a) 16/17d

roundes *n.pl.* rings (*OED* **round** *n.*[1] I1a) 19/79, 121

rubius (Lat.) *adj.* red (*DMLBS* **rubeus**) 16/9, 10, 17, 23

rumbus (Lat.) *n.* turbot (*DMLBS* **rhombus** 2a) 16/4, 10

Rumney *n.* a breed of sheep from Romney Marsh 21/150

runlet *n.* small cask; also, a measure for wine, varying from 15 to 18½ gallons (*MED* **roundelet** *n.* c) 21/26

russhers *n.pl.* those who strew rushes on the floor 19/95

russet(t), **rossett** *n.* coarse woollen cloth, red-brown cloth (*n.*); red-brown (*adj.*) 20/167, 185; 21/138; **Wynchester ~** russet cloth made in Winchester 19/106, 111

saf(f)er, **saffure**, **safuers** *n.* sapphire 20/30, 40; 21/95, 121

saff(e)ron (also **le saffron**) *n.* saffron (*OED* **saffron** A *n.* 1a) 16/26d; 20/90, 160, 172; 19/39; **~ inglyssh** English saffron 16/25d; **~ setter** planter of saffron (cf. *OED* **setter** *n.*[1] 2d) 20/160

say(e) *n.*, **saies**, **sayes** *n.pl.* say (*OED* **say** *n.*[1] A 1a), a fine serge or perhaps silk (cf. *LCCP* **say**[1] 1b, **say**[2]) 16/14; 17/19; 20/67, 199; 19/97, etc.

sakeryng bell *n.* sacring-bell, a small bell rung at the elevation of the Host 19/20

sal albus (Lat.) *n.* fine white salt (*DMLBS* 2b) 16/12, 15d; **~ de Bay** salt from Bayonne, or bay-salt (*DMLBS* 2g, cf. *OED* **bay-salt**) 16/2, 12, 15d

salet(t) oyle *n.* olive oil for dressing salads (*OED* **salad-oil** *n.*) 16/27d

sallettes *n.pl.* light armour-plated head-piece (*OED* **sallet/salade** *n.* 1a) 20/27, 78

salmo (Lat.) *n.* salmon (extended as plural) 16/4, 10, 17, 24

salsus (Lat.) *ppl.adj.* preserved or cured in salt 16/2, 7, 10, 17; **ale salsia** pickling ale (not recorded *DMLBS*, but cf. *OED* **souse** *n.*[1] 2 and **souse-ale**) 16/4d

salt *n.*, **saltez** *n.pl.* salt cellar 19/58; 20/50

sarcenett, **sarcynet**, **sars(y)net**, **sarssenyt**, **sersenett** *n.* a plain weave silk cloth (*LCCP* **sarsenet**) 20/20, 63, 89, 97, etc.

sarkett *n.* a garment worn next to the skin, e.g. a chemise (?) (cf. *OED* **sark** n.) 17/25

sat(t)en, **satyn** *n.* a twill silk textile often made in Italy (*LCCP* **satin**); **Brugez ~**, **~ of Bruges/Bryggez/Brygges/Brigges** the same textile made in Bruges 17/20; 20/91; 19/6, 25; 2/34; **~ of Cypres/Sypres~** the same textile made in Cyprus 21/136; 19/103

sau *v.* sow 20/17

saunders *n.pl.* sanders, powdered sandalwood (*OED* **sanders** *n.*[1]) 16/11, 25, 22d

saucere *n.* dish in which salt or sauces were kept 20/77

sa(w)cery, **salsery**, **saucery** *n.* department of a household which makes sauces 20/90; 19/85, 89; 1/9v

sawdyor *n.* soldier 20/97

sawdryng, **sowderyng** *vbl.n.* soldering 20/106, 124, 173

sawlyng *vbl.n.* soling 20/81; 21/13

scapelary *n.* scapular, short cloak 21/17

scarlet(t), **skarlett** *n.* an expensive woollen cloth (*LCCP* **scarlet**) 20/25; 19/25, 40, 102, etc.

schare *n.*, **scharis** *n.pl.* chair 2/11, 35

scleffes *n.pl.* sleeves (?) 19/75

scluse see **slewes**

scollery, **skollery** *n.* department concerned with crockery and utensils 19/85, 89

scowryng, **skowryng** *vbl.n.* scouring, cleaning 19/104

scurtes *n.pl.* skirts 20/78

seller *n.* cellar 20/86

senamom *n.* cinnamon 19/108

sengull *adj.* of one thickness of material; unlined (*OED* **single** *adj.* II 10) 19/111

sensures *n.pl.* censers 1/5r

senvy sed *n.* mustard seed (*OED* **senvy** *n.* 2) 16/25

sere clothe *n.* waxed cloth; winding sheet for a corpse (*OED* **cerecloth** *n.*) 20/168; 19/101

sergaunt *n.* sergeant at law 20/126b

serge *n.* large wax candle (*OED* **cierge** *n.*) 19/88

seryng *vbl.n.* waxing 21/16, 32

sester(ne) (also **le sesterne**, **lez sesternes**) *n.* sester, liquid measure for beer or wine (*OED* **sester** *n.* 2a, **sestern** *n.*, cf. *DMLBS* **sextarius**) 16/19, 5d

setwall *n.* the plant zedoary, or perhaps valerian 21/47

sewers *n.pl.* watercourses to drain fens 20/165

sewet, **sewte (of the lawe)** *n.*, **sewetes** *n.pl.* lawsuit, legal procedure 20/60, 67, 105; 19/121

sewger *n.* sugar 19/92; **~ candyth** see **candyth**

shanke *n.*, **chaunkis**, **s(c)hankes**, **shanckes** *n.pl.* animal leg fur 20/174; 21/45, 137, 150, etc.

shewed *pa.t.sg.* shoed 20/37

ship *n.* incense boat for a censer 21/131

shyrlynges *n.pl.* fleeces of once-shorn sheep (*OED* **shearling** *n.* 2) 16/5, 18, 19, 20

shreff *n.* sheriff 20/103

sices, **syses**, **sisez** *n.pl.* candles used esp. at court or in church (*OED* **size** *n.*[3]) 16/16d, 18d; 1/11v

syche *adj.* such 20/60

signum (Lat.) *n.* mark of recognition of a person, signature (*DMLBS* 3, 8b) 16/30d

signus (Lat.) *n.* swan 16/15, 23

sylk *n.*, **~ of Venys** 19/57; **open/opyn ~** loose silk (?) (*LCCP*) 20/98, 101; 19/80; **sat(t)en ~** silk textile with glossy surface 20/121; 19/80; **slevyd/slevyn ~** silk divided into filaments, cf. **sleved** below (*OED* **sleave** *v.*) 20/36; 19/19 (err. *slesid*), 31, 103; **twyne ~** twined/plied silk 20/101; **webbe ~** woven silk (*OED* **web** *n.*) 20/36; 1/8v; **Venysse/Venyes ~** silk from Venice 19/34, 38, 104

silver *n.* silver thread; **coper ~** copper-covered silver wire 19/31; **~ of Vennys** 21/8; **~ wiere** silver wire 19/57; **Venus/Vennez/Venysse/Venyce ~** silver thread from Venice 21/133, 134; 19/77; 1/13r

synamom(e) *n.* **~ large** large sticks of cinnamon 16/22d, 23d; **~ petit/petytte** small sticks of cinnamon 16/23d

syngyn(g) bred *n.* the wafer used in the Mass 20/14, 91; 19/8

sypers, **siper(u)s**, **syporis**, **sypres** see **cypers**

syses *n.pl.* large ceremonial candles (*OED* **size** *n.*[3]) 1/11v

sythen *adv.* afterwards 21/65

skarlett see **scarlett**

skowryng see **scowryng**

slaye *n.*, **slaies**, **slayes** *n.pl.* an instrument used to beat up the weft in weaving (*OED* **slay/sley** *n.*[1]) 19/29, 41, 74

slathe *n.* meaning unknown 91/96

sleffes *n.pl.* sleeves 19/75

slekyng stone *n.* polishing stone (*OED* **sleekstone** *n.*; *OED* **slike-ston** *n.*) 19/102

sleppers *n.pl.* slippers 20/169; 19/75, 109

sleved *adj.* ('silk' *sc.*) separated into filaments (*OED* **sleave** *v.*) 20/98, 109 (see too **sylk** above)

slevyng *vbl.n.* making up the sleeves of a garment 19/98

slewes, **slewse**, **(s)cluse** *n.* sluice; dam or embankment 10/18, 101; 20/32; 6/9; **slewcez** *n.pl.* sluices 19/124

slop(pe) loose mantle (*OED* **slop** *n.*[1] 2a) 20/81, 21/17

smigma, **smygma** (Lat.) *n.* soap (*DMLBS* **smigma**, **-atis**) 16/12, 26, 29d

snoffers *n.pl.* snuffers 20/61

sodering see **sowd(e)ryng**

sokkes *n.pl.* socks, light shoes 20/47, 175, 186

soluste *v.* solicit 19/52

solvitur (Lat.) *3sg.* it is paid 20/194

sooke *n.* district under local jurisdiction (*OED* **soke** *n.*[1] 2) 10/17

sortes, **sortez** (Lat.) *n.pl.* measures or weights of figs (*OED* **sort** *n.*[3]) 16/10, 19d

sownd *n.* sand (?) 2/25

sowd(e)ryng, **sodering** *vbl.n.* soldering 20/33, 47; 19/94

sparver *n.* canopy for a bed 20/179

speyres *n.pl.* soldiers armed with a long handled axe 21/23

splentes *n.pl.* armour-plated elbow protection (*OED* **splint** *n.* 1a) 20/27, 78; 21/57

sponyng *vbl.n.* securing wine from waste by tightening the cask with chips of wood (*OED* **spon** *v.*) 21/26

sprewse *n.* Prussian (*OED* **Spruce** *n.* CI) 19/97 II

sprynckyll *n.* sprinkler for holy water 19/103

sprottes *n.pl.* sprats or smelts (*OED* **sprot** *n.*[1] a, b) 16/10

squillery, **squyllery** *n.* scullery, the department of a household dealing with crockery and utensils 20/86, 90; 1/4v, 9v

stacionary *n.* bookdealer, esp. one licensed by a University; printer (*MED* **stacioner(e)** *n.* 1a) 21/40, 145(?)

stafes *n.pl.* sticks used for carrying torches (cf. *OED* **staff** *n.*[1] 8b, c) 16/24, 17d; **staff torches** *n.* tall thick torches for ceremonial purposes (*OED* **staff** *n.*[1] C4) 16/24, 17d

stayner *n.* one who stains wood or cloth 20/126c

stamen, **stamyn** *n.* woollen or worsted cloth (*OED* **stamin** *n.*) 20/174; 21/45

standarte, **stantarde** *n.*, **standardes**, **standardez** *n.pl.* large packing cases (*OED* **standard** *n.* 23) 17/20, 25, 28; a kind of collar of plate armour (*OED* **standard** *n.* 21) 20/27, 78

sta(u)ndyng, **stonding** *adj.*, **~ bedd(e)** high bedstead, not a truckle bed 19/82, 117; 1/11r; **~ cuppe** cup with a stem and base 1/10r; **~ tabull** a table with a stem and a base (cf. *OED* **standing** *adj.*) 20/66

startuppes *n.pl.* boots, as worn by rustics (*OED* **startup** *n.*) 21/42

staurum (Lat.) *n.* store, stock 16/16, 22, 16d, 21d

steyle *n.* flintlock (?) (*OED* **steel** *n.*[1] 8a) 20/82

stigacio (Lat.) *n.* driving (animals) (cf. *DMLBS* **stiga** 'point or spike', **stigare** 'to pierce or prick (with a stake)') 16/9

stik *n.* roll of textiles imported from Flanders; **stik(k)es/stykes** *n.pl.* (*OED* **stick** *n.*[3] 1) 20/63; **Flemych** ~ 20/63

stik *n.*, **holy water** ~ aspergillum, branch or brush for sprinkling holy water 20/187; 21/95; 19/9

styl hows *n.* distillery 20/47

styllyng *vbl.n.* extraction by distilling (*OED* **still** *v.*[2] 4a) 20/27, 40, 163

stocke, **stok** *n.*, **holy water** ~ holy-water stoup or basin 21/95; 19/84, 85, 103; 1/10r, 11r

stokkes *n.pl.* stockings 19/6

stokkes *n.pl.* logs (*OED* **stock** *n.*[1]) 19/80

stoles, **stollys** *n.pl.* stools 17/26; 1/8v; ~ **werk** *n.* embroidery of the kind made on a stool 21/103

stomacher *n.* ornamental covering under the lacing of a bodice 21/32

stonde *adj.* standing, upright 19/96

ston sleppere *n.* stone cutter (cf. *OED* **slip** *v.*[2] 1) 21/59

straungers *n.pl.* visitors, guests (*OED* **stranger** *n.* 3a) 21/66

streyneres, **streynours**, **strenors** *n.pl.* cloth used as strainers or sieves (cf. *OED* **strainer** *n.* 1a) 16/11, 26, 28d

subsedy, **subsidye** *n.* tax or donation to provide support (*OED* **subsidy** *n.*, cf. 3a and other definitions)

succad(e) *n.* fruit preserved in sugar (*OED* **succade** *n.* a) 20/180, 199; **succades** *n.pl.* candied fruit 16/11, 20d, 25d

suertie *n.* surety 19/70

suet(t)es *n.pl.* lawsuits 19/55, 120

suffrycan(s) *adj./n.* suffragan, deputy 20/59, 102, 106, 172, 185

suger *n.* sugar, ~ **candy** *n.* sugar from Crete (cf. *OED* **sugar-candian**) 16/11, 20d; ~ **course** unrefined sugar (cf. *OED* **coarse sugar**) 16/11, 20d; ~ **hole** 16/11, 25, 20d; ~ **powder** sugar granules (cf. *OED* **sugar-powder**) 16/25, 20d; ~ **valans** sugar from Valencia 16/11, 25, 21d

sumpter cloth *n.* cloth to cover the back of a sumpter or baggage horse 21/31

super (Lat.) *prep.* + *acc.* due from (someone) (*DMLBS* 23b) 16/2, 8, 17, 18; over and above (*DMLBS* 18a) 10/18; 1/18v; **oneratur** ~ it is charged upon (someone) 10/119, 133; **unde** ~ whence (it is charged) upon 16/16–17

superaltariez, **superaltarys** (both emended forms) *n.pl.* superaltars, portable altars 19/104, 120

superplus, **superplus(s)age**, **surplisage** *n.* surplus (*OED* **surplusage** *n.*) 10/50; 20/134; 19/52, 114; 2/18

supper lightes *n.* lights for use at suppers (*OED* **supper** *n.*1 C1.a) 16/18d

survayar, **survayer**, **survaier** *n.* one who has the oversight of a land and its boundaries and appurtenances (*OED* **surveyor** *n.* 1e) 20/115, 153, 159–60, 162, 175

tabell *n.*; **~ brede** table-width 21/8; **payer/peyer of (writtynge) tabellys/tabullys** portable writing tablet 17/19; 19/107

taberettour, **taborettes** *n.pl. n.* performer on a tabour 17/64; 19/99 (see too **Tabret** in the PEOPLE index)

tabure *n.* tabour, a small drum 17/33

takettes *n.pl.* tacks, small nails 21/60

tale fisshes *n.pl.* fish sold by number (*OED* **tale** *n.* **~-fish** C2 a fish to be sold 'by tale', i.e. by counting how many (II 6b, cf. 'by weight', 'by measure')) 16/13d

tal(le)wod *n.* wood for fuel (*OED* **talwood** *n.*) 16/12, 13, 24, 30d

tallia (Lat.) *n.* tally, originally a stick with notched debts divided in half and retained by debtor and debtee (*DMLBS* **talea** 2, 3; cf. *OED* **tally** *n.*[1] 1a; assumed to be singular unless other evidence) 16/2d, 3d, 4d, 7d

tapet *n.*, **tapettes** *n.pl.* figured cloth used as a cover or hanging or carpet 19/99; 2/31

tappenettes, **toppe(k)nottes** *n.pl.* rush baskets for figs (*OED* **tapnet/topnet** *n.*) 16/10, 19d

tarteryn, **tartren**, **tertren** *n.* silk, a type of sendal (*LCCP* **tartarin**) 20/126; 19/31, 57

tas(s)ell *n.* tercel, the male of the hawk 19/97, 101

tavelyn, **tovelyn** *n.*, **tavelynce**, **tavely(o)ns** *n.pl.* the board between which small skins were carried; the furs between these boards 20/62; 21/45, 137; 2/28

ta(w)ny *n.* cloth tawny in colour (*LCCP* **tawny** 1b) 20/15, 43, 48, 82, etc.; 21/31, 41, etc.; *adj.* tawny-coloured (*LCCP* 1a) 20/35; 19/111; **dark ~** darker coloured tawny 20/80; **diett ~** tawny cloth as part of a household allowance (?) (not rec. *OED* or *OED* or *LCCP*, but cf. *OED* **diet** *n.*[1] 6) 21/101, 137; **Frenche ~** tawny from France 19/25

tenne *n.* tin 21/146

tentyr hokes *n.pl.* metal hooks to hold cloth 20/21

tepet *n.* tippet, long narrow piece of cloth attached to sleeve or hood (*LCCP*) 19/97 II

tewke *n.* a kind of cloth, sometimes finer than canvas (*LCCP* **tuke**, cf. *OED* **tuke/tewke** *n.*) 20/20

thankorise see **ancras**

thembelys *n.pl.* thimbles 21/111

thenbassytor, **thenbassytur** *n.* the ambassador 20/31

threden *adj.* made of linen thread 20/21

tyk(k), **tyke**, **tikk** *n.* tikking, a fabric 20/174; 2/32; 6/5

tymber, **tymbre** *n.* package of 40 skins between wooden boards (*OED* **timber** *n.*[2]), cf. **tavelyn** above 20/53, 184; 21/54, 65, 149, 150; 19/12, 31, 104, 106, 111

tynyng *vbl.n.* fashioning (cf. *OED* **tine** *v.*[1], *v.*[3]) 2/11

typ(p)et(t) *n.* a flat tube of cloth attached to the crown of a hood (cf. *LCCP* **tippet**) 21/31; 19/111

tirrettes *n.pl.*; **paire of ~** two rings by which a leash is attached to a dog's collar (*OED* **terret/territ** *n.* cf. 1a, b) 1/10v

tisshew, **tyssue** *n.*; **cloth of (gold off) ~** rich cloth woven with gold or silver (*OED* **tissue** *n.* 1a) 10/127; 2/30, 32

tytell *n.* title or right to land or property 21/93

torta (Lat.) *n.* very large wax candle, distinct from a torch (*DMLBS* 4, cf. *OED* **tortis** *n.* 1) 16/24, 16d, 17d

tovelyn see **tavelyn**

towe *n.* rope of flax, hemp or jute 21/131

towelyn (?) *n.* towelling 2/14

travesse, **travyse** *n.* curtained space in a room (*OED* **travers** *n.* 2(b)) 19/71; 2/23

trede (for **threde**) *n.* thread 20/20, 89

tre(e)n *adj.* made of wood 20/174, 175

trencher *n.*, **~ bred** *n.* bread of unbolted flour used for trenchers, i.e. bread used as plates (*OED* **trencher** *n.*[1] 3) 16/6, 2d, 4d; **~ meyle** *n.* the unbolted flour used for trenchers 16/22; **trenchers** *n.pl.* wooden plates 20/175

trenton reyne *n.* turning rein (?) (*OED* **trend** *v.* 4a) 2/26

trerer *n.* treasurer 2/36

treveit *n.* trivet 20/175

tryakell, **tryakyll** *n.* uncrystallised syrup, often used as, or in, medicine (*OED* **treacle** *n.* 1, 4a) 19/92, 99, 106; **~ of Jene** treacle of Genoa (*OED* **treacle** *n.* 1c) 19/100

tryed *adj.* choice, excellent (*OED* **tried** *adj.* 2a) 19/99

trinyte *n.* image of the Trinity (?) 21/93

tukkyngyrdell *n.* a girdle worn with the alb (*OED* **tucking-girdle** *n.*)

turnesale (also **le turnsale**) *n.* turnsole, a purple colouring for confectionery (*OED* **turnsole** *n.* 1a) 16/11, 26d

twyne *adj.* twisted (?) (cf. *LCCP* **twine**[2] *v.*) 20/25

ultra (Lat.) *prep.* + *acc.* beyond, further, apart from 16/4, 6, 7, 16

unce (**le unce**) *n.*, **unc(e)z, unces** *n.pl.* ounce (oz.), dry measure of one-sixteenth of a pound (lb.) (*OED* **ounce** *n.*[1] I 1a) 16/11, 25, 21d, 22d; 20/12, 18, 20, 23, etc. (abbrev. as 'oz' except for **le unce** (16/22d), but D102.1 uses both 'unce' and 'oȝ', which are reproduced in the edited text as they occur, i.e. 'unce', e.g. 1/5v, 6r, 7v, 8v, etc. and 'oz.', e.g. 1/6r, 7v, 10r-v)

underleying *vbl.n.* supplying shoes with extra sole and heel pieces (*OED* **underlay** *v.* 1c) 1/8v

undicendus (Lat.) *adj.* unaccounted for (i.e. in this context, a customary allowance of a loaf a week to make up for the inevitable shortfall) 16/4d

urenalles, **urinalles**, **erynalles** *n.pl.* urinals, glass phials for collecting urine for medical examination 20/153, 199; 21/113

vacat (Lat.) *3sg.* it is void, it is missing (*DMLBS* 4e, f) 10/43

vas *n.* pledge, surety 16/11, 14

vel(l)om, **vellym**, **wellom** *n.* vellum, calfskin for writing on 21/40, 43, 74, 111, 118, 123, 135, 149, 156; 19/43, 46, 83, 92, 117; **rase** ~ scraped vellum, prepared for writing on 19/7, 29

Venyce, **Venyes**, **Venys(e)**, **Venys(s)e**, **Vennes(e)**, **Vennez**, **Venyes**, **Venus**; **Weness**, **Wennes**, **Wenuth** *n.* Venice; **gold of(f)** ~ gold thread from Venice 17/19; 20/43, 63, 98, 185; 21/61, 73, 96; 19/88, 104, 117; 2/3, 15–17, 26; ~ **gold** 20/99; 21/101, 103; 19/82; **silk(e)/silkes of** ~ silk from Venice 19/38, 57, 104; ~ **sylk** 19/34; ~ **silver/sylver** silver thread from Venice 21/133, 134; 19/77; 1/13r

verdour, **verdur(e)** *n.*, **verders**, **verdours**, **verdurez**, **werders** *n.pl.* hanging embroidered with depictions of vegetation (*LCCP* **verdure** 2) 20/50, 63, 174; 19/104, 120; 2/25; 6/5

vergus, **vertjuse** *n.* verjuice, a cooking liquid made from unripe fruit (*OED* **verjuice** *n.* 1a) 16/5; 17/36

vermyloun, **wermylyon** *n.* vermilion, a scarlet pigment 21/55; 19/13

vernys(she) *n.* varnish 20/171; 19/7

vice *n.*, **vices** *n.pl.* device, design, figure 20/79; 21/33

vice camerarius (Lat.) *n.* vice-chamberlain 21/87

vinacre *n.* vinegar (*OED* **vinegar** *n.* 1a) 16/25

vynet *n.* ornamental design 19/17

violett, **vyolett** *n.* cloth dyed violet (*LCCP* **violet** 1b) 20/29, 158, 167

(virg.) virga (Lat.) *n.* verge, a linear measure of one yard, i.e. three foot (*DMLBS* 6b) 16/4, 11, 14, 25

vokett, **woket(t)** *n.* advocate 20/35, 65

voyson, **voosen**, **vousen**, **vouson** *n.* advowson, the right of presentation to a benefice 20/175; 19/58, 69, 91

wacchyng candelles *n.pl.* candles burning before a shrine or on an altar (*OED* **watching** *n.* C2) 16/12, 16d; **wachyng candylstik** *n.* candlestick standing before a shrine or on an altar 20/118, 166

wachet *n.* light blue cloth (*OED* **watchet** *n.* A.1.a) 20/125

waffer *n.* wafer, thin biscuit 19/15

wafferer *n.* maker of wafers (q.v.) 19/15

way(e) (also **le way**) *n.* unit of weight of dry goods, 14 stone (16/12d) (*OED* **wey** *n.*[1] 1a cheese b wool c salt (for 5 quarters = 1 way, see 1533–4 entry), d corn (for 5 quarters = 40 bushels = 1 way, see 1891 entry) 16/12, 21, 12d, 15d

wayttes *n.pl.* waits, wind instrumentalists (*OED* **wait** *n.* 8a) 20/89; 19/28, 88

wardens, **wardons** *n.pl.* wardens, baking pears 20/51, 103, 175; 19/75; 1/4r

wardrop *n.* room for storing clothing 20/87, 174; 21/18, 136, 151; 19/37–8, 40; 1/11r (*OED* **wardrobe** *n.* 2b)

warke (Nth.) *n.* work 20/91

warpyng *vbl.n.* preparing a warp for weaving 9/106

weders *n.pl.* weeders 1/13r

we(e)ke (le weeke), **wyke** *n.* wick in a candle, twisted fibre in a torch (*OED* **wick** *n.*[1] a) 16/12; **taper** ~ *n.* wick in a wax candle (cf. *OED* **taper** *n.*[1] a, **wick** *n.*[1] a) 16/12, 18d; **torch** ~ *n.* fibre for burning in a torch (cf. *OED* **torch** *n.*[1] a, **wick** *n.*[1] a) 16/12, 18d

wefferer *n.* maker of wafers, i.e. thin, crisp cakes 19/15

weyffynge *ppl.adj.* weaving 17/26

wellom *see* **vel(l)om**

welvet(t) *n.* velvet 19/6; Lewkes ~ *n.* velvet from Lucca (*OED* Luke/Lukes *n.*[2]) 21/24

werders see **verdur(e)**

weryng *vbl.n.* wearing out, impairment (*OED* **wearing** *n.*[1] 14a) 20/125

wermylyon see **vermyloun**

wewe *v.* view 19/47

whytt, **whitte** *n.* white fabric (*OED* **white** *n.*[1] 9) 21/17, 137; **cardynall** ~ basic white (?) (cf. *OED* **cardinal** *adj.* 1a, **white** *n.*[1] 9, 'streyt white' 1503) 20/158

wyer *n.* gold or silver wire 20/175

Wynchester russet(t) see **russet(t)**

wynterfell *n.* sheepskin with winter fleece 16/5, 18, 19, 20

with(e) *n.* a customary payment to cooks at Easter (cf. *OED* withe/with *n.* 1c) 20/90, 152; 21/15, 107; 19/14, 89

woket(t) see **vokett**

wolle *n.* wool 20/180; **wol(l)efell**, **wulfell** *n.* sheepskin with unshorn fleece (*OED* **wool-fell** *n.*) 16/5, 20, 10d

wolstid, **wolstyd**, **worsted(e)** *n.* a woollen fabric, originally from Worstead in Norfolk 21/129, 133, 158; 19/26, 36, 103

wom(b)es *n.pl.* fur from the belly of an animal (*OED* **womb** *n.* 1d) 20/80, 186

wormesede *n.* medicinal plant (*OED n.* **wormseed**, *MED n.* **worm** 5) 21/128

yerne, **ȝerne** *n.* yarn 20/21, 159, 166, 169, 171; 19/7

yrne, **irne** *n.* iron 20/82, 175; 19/96

yonde see **ȝonyd**

ȝerne see **yerne**

zinziber (Lat.) *n.* ginger 16/25, 23d

INDEX OF PEOPLE

This comprehensive index of **PEOPLE** provides a prosopographical account of persons cited in the edited accounts about whom information exists; it also offers generic references, i.e. details of occupations, where known, e.g. **ABBOTS**; **ALMSFOLK, bedes(wo)men, and the poor**; **CARRIERS, carters, porters, and couriers**, etc.[1] The prosopographical relationship to Lady Margaret is usually made clear, with quotations from the texts where information is derived from them, e.g. **Hynkersall** ('grome de le scolery'), or **Stanley, Thomas** ('my lord(e) (of Derby)').[2]

The headword to each person uses a standardised modern spelling for the Christian name and for 'master'/'mistress' (also within the entry where there are multiple spellings). In order to facilitate search, a standardised form of the surname is used only where that form is familiar from scholarship (in relation to Lady Margaret Beaufort, the standard is that set by the usage of Jones and Underwood, *The King's Mother*); otherwise the most frequent document spelling is given (but the vowels <i>/<y>, which are interchangeable in the early modern period, are treated as the same, e.g. **Wynstanley** is followed by **Wittylbury**, etc.). If notably different from the headword, other forms of the name follow the headword in brackets, sometimes with a quotation from the text where that is useful: see, for example, **Ashton, Hugh**, where his roles as receiver (general) and controller are recorded as in the text with text references.[3] Women are cited under the surname of their most recent husband, with their birth surnames (and earlier married surnames where relevant) after their Christian name, e.g. **Parker, Alice St John**. References to the wife/sister/servant, etc. of a person are cited under that person without comment if no further information is known about them; the possessive case is normally removed where it occurs. Christian names are in brackets where not cited in the text. (?) before a description indicates that the identification is uncertain. Where the document spelling differs substantially from the standardised form of today, there is cross-reference, e.g. **Wauce/Waus** see **Vaux**. Superscript **R** and **W** before the headword indicate that the name occurs in the 'Rewardes' given after Lady Margaret's death (see Appendix (D56.131)) or in her will.[4]

Note: As throughout this edition D91.16 is cited as 16, D102.10 as 10, D91.17 as 17, D91.20 as 20, D91.21 as 21, D91.19 as 19, D102.1 as 1, D102.2 and D102.6 as 2 and 6 respectively, and D56.131 as 56, all in this order. A slant separates the page/folio number, e.g. 21/23 (D91.21, p. 23).

[1] For schoolchildren and students at University (at the time called 'scholars') see **STUDENTS**; for learned men (often with higher degrees and at the time called 'doctors') see **SCHOLARS**; for book dealers (at the time called 'stationers') see **BOOK DEALERS**.

[2] Additional information (where it exists) is mainly added from the usual reference works (cited in the Select Bibliography to this edition) and from Malcolm Underwood's record cards (on personal loan). The abbreviations for University degrees are those used by A.B. Emden in his *Biographical Registers*; only the highest degree is cited here, with a single date.

[3] Where 'etc.' is used, it means that other citations are recorded to the same effect.

[4] For the will: *Collegium Divi Johannis Evangelistae 1511–1911* (Cambridge: Cambridge University Press, 1911), Appendix: The Will of the Foundress (pp. 101–26). It is 'a composite document' (ibid., p. 103); for the versions: Jones and Underwood, *The King's Mother*, Appendix 4 (pp. 288–90).

ABBESSES
of Godstow see **Braynton**
of Syon see **Gibbs**
ABBOTS
of Chester see **Birkenshaw**
of Cirencester see **Aston**
of Crowland see **Bardney**, **Gedding**
of Gloucester see **Braunche**
of Kirkstall see **Stockdale**
of Leicester see **Penny**
of Peterborough see **Kirton**
of Pipewell 16/17 (see **Stamford**)
of Ramsey see **Huntingdon**
of St Alban's see **Ramryge**
of Waltham see **Rede**
of Westminster see **Islip**
R**Ab(e)ney, Henry** groom of the chamber to Lady Margaret 21/123; 19/78–9, 85; 1/15v; 56/5
Abseley, Beatrice 17/24
Adeys, Deygre 20/96
R**Aderton, Richard** ('Richard Atherton/Ad(d) erton', 'maister chamberlayns servande') yeoman of the chamber; servant of Roger Ormeston (q.v.) 10/104; 20/45, 78, 80, 102, 106, 117, 120–1, 147, 150, 152, 155, 159–60, 164–5, 167, 171–2, 176, 179, 185, 194; 21/8, 12, 14, 16–17, 19, 22, 26, 35–6, 38, 41, 43, 52, 95, 98, 109, 113, 118, 122, 124, 127, 140–1; 19/7, 22, 27–8, 34, 36–7, 40, 48, 72, 76, 78, 81, 85, 87–8, 97, 106–7, 113; 1/5r, 8r, 8v, 9v, 10v, 13r, 14v; 56/5
Aderton, Thomas servant of Lady Margaret 21/120
Aderton, William ('William Ad(d)erton/ Adrton', 'William Adthirton/ Adthyrton/Adtherton'; 'the grome') servant of Lady Margaret 10/11; 17/22, 34, 41, 44, 47, 53; 20/19, 22, 23, 29, 36, 39, 49–50, 81, 87, 105, 145, 171, 178, 187; 21/15
Adeson, Reynold 10/120
Alcok, Richard of Boston [Lincs.] 19/92
'Alderbornedyn(e)' 2/30, 32
ALDERMAN see **Baly**
Allen, Robert ('yssher of my lady Maries chambre') servant of Princess Mary (q.v.) 21/27
ALMONERS
to Lady Margaret (master almoner) 17/21, 33, 39, 43, 51; 20/65, 83, 96, 102, 151, 153, 173, 180; 21/44, 55, 57, 93, 123; 19/19–20 (see too **Bekinsall**, **Fell**, **Henry**)
to Henry VII see **Ednam**, **Mayhew**
ALMSFOLK, bedes(wo)men, and the poor 16/4d; 10/133; 17/22, 25–6, 38, 55; 20/15–16, 39, 41, 47, 54, 59, 88, 92, 95, 115, 122, 125, 126b, 127, 135, 152, 154, 158–60, 164, 167, 171, 181–2, 187–9, 195; 21/7, 14–15, 17, 20, 28, 34, 39–40, 42, 44–5, 54–5, 57, 63, 66, 71, 100, 107, 109, 117–18, 124, 128, 136–7, 150, 153; 19/5, 17, 22, 24–5, 27, 30, 37, 40, 46, 51, 75–6, 82, 97I, 103–4, 107–10, 112, 115; 1/5v, 7v–9r, 15v, 17r, 18v (see too **Alson**, **Davy**, **Dawson**, **Elyn**, **Kettell**, **Margaret**, **Marion**)
Alson ('moder Alson') almswoman 19/92
Alwen, Joan ('Jone Alwen') 20/189
AMBASSADOR 20/31
Ameas, Katherine ('dame Katherine Ameas') 10/83
Amias, Thomas ('Thomas Amias/ Amyas') 10/19; 17/57
Ancell, Andrew ('Andrew Ancell(e)') 21/108, 119; 19/35
ANCHORESSES and holy women 17/36; 20/148, 179, 181, 20/187; 21/20; 19/148
of (hospital of St Mary of) Bethlehem, London 21/21
(of St Mary) without Bishopsgate, London 20/186
of Boston 20/30
of Lynn 17/36; 20/154
of Pontefract 21/124
W**of St Alban's** 17/25; 21/132; 19/15, 30, 32, 80, 96
of Stamford (see Rogers, ed., *The Act Book of St Katherine's Gild*, pp. 10–12)
W**at the priory of St Michael (Benedictine nuns)** ('the anchoress at the nuns', i.e. Margaret White (q.v.)) 20/179, 183–6; 21/12, 19, 45, 48, 71, 91, 111, 114, 131; 19/13, 36, 51, 86, 89; 1/7r, 13v
W**at the church of St Paul** ('the anchoress (of Stamford/at St Katherine's)', i.e. Agnes Leche (q.v.), probably 'the old anchoress' 20/187; 21/20) 20/156, 181, 187; 21/10, 19, 30, 45, 48, 71, 91, 111, 154; 19/13, 36, 86, 89, 110; 1/7r, 13v
W**of Westminster** 20/186; 21/108
ANCHORITES
of Bury 17/31
of the London charterhouse 20/84; 21/23
W**of London Wall** 20/186; 19/18
of Lynn 17/36; 20/154, 157
of Sheen 20/186; 19/10 ('Syon' error for 'Sheen')
R**Anderson, John** 56/4
Andrew, Thomas 20/145

Annesley, Ralph ('of the seller') servant of Henry VII 19/95; 1/4v
Anthony, master ('keper of the kinges galaries at Richemount') 1/11v
Anthony ('clerc of the kechyn') servant of Henry VII 1/4v
Antwyssell, master 21/15
APOTHECARIES 21/28; 19/70, 89; 1/4r (see too **William**)
[R]**Ap(pli)s, John** 19/111; 56/4
APPRENTICES 20/173, 196; 21/117, 155 (see too **Davy**, **Sant**)
Appulton, Roger 21/87
Apt carrier 19/41
ARCHBISHOP of York see **Savage**
ARCHDEACONS, **of Bangor** 20/94; **of Richmond** 21/60
ARMOURERS 20/78; 21/57, 76 (see too **Beane**)
Arnold ('yssher of my lady Maries chambre') servant of Princess Mary (q.v.) 21/27
Arnold, John ('goldsmyth(e)') 19/8, 10
ARRAS MAKERS AND MENDERS 17/49 (see too **Barnard**, **Collop**, **Mustyng**)
Arthur, master ('master Arthur(e) (at London)') royal servant; (?) Arthur Somerset (q.v.) 20/64, 86, 189, 198; 21/59, 73
Arthur, prince of Wales ('the prince (Arthure)', 'my lord prince') (d. 1502) eldest son of Henry VII 10/62; 17/28, 31; 20/21; 6/5
Artwyk, Edward priest 19/39
Ashton, Henry ('Henry Assheton') 21/128
[R]**Ashton, Hugh** ('sir Hugh Asshton (my ladys) receyvour' 10/130, 149, 151, 20/184, 21/11, 145; '[master] Asshton my ladys/the (said) comptrollour' 10/133; 'sir Hugh Assheton (clerk) (our) generall receyvour'10/152;'Hugonis Assheton clerici receptoris' 20/147; 'the receyvour<S> Hughe Assheton' 20/176; 'the receyver syr Hughe Assheton' 21/8–9; '[master] receyver syr Hughe Assheton' 21/55–6, 146; '[master] Hughe Assheton receyver generall' 21/148; '[master] Assheton my ladis receivour'19/55, 116; '[master] Assheton receyver (to my ladys grace)' 19/8; '[master] Assheton comptrollour of (my ladyes) houshold' 1/8r, 12v, 15r; '[master] Assheton my ladys receyvour generall' 1/13v) (d. 1523) Lady Margaret's receiver general from at least 1502 (Jones and Underwood, *The King's Mother*, p. 268), but the term 'general' is not used here before 1506 (21/148); also called controller of Lady Margaret's household in 1509 (10/133 and 1/8r); an executor of Lady Margaret's will 16/10; 10/23, 24, 26–29, 31–34, 51, 67, 77, 83–86, 111–13, 130–33, 149, 151–3, 162, 179, 180;17/56, 61 ('[master] Hughe servante'); 20/5–7, 28, 37, 43, 46, 53, 57, 58, 60, 62, 79, 89, 105, 113, 126, 127–29, 142–44, 145, 147, 156, 163, 164, 166, 176, 182, 184–5, 191, 194; 21/8–9, 11, 15, 22–4, 53, 55–6, 67, 80, 95, 97, 100, 117, 119, 126, 138, 145–6, 148, 162, 163; 19/3, 7–9, 14, 16, 21–2, 37, 39, 48, 52, 55, 61, 65, 69, 73–4, 82–3, 116, 119, 121, 124; 1/6r, 8r, 12v, 13v, 15r, 18v; 56/3 (see too **CONTROLLERS** for references with no name)
Asse, Robert 20/153
Assheton/Asshewell, John ('John Assheton my ladys idyot' 1/9r, 'John Asshewell my ladys ydiot' 1/9v) Lady Margaret's fool 19/105;
1/9r–v
Asshewyn, Edward father of John Asshewyn (q.v.) 19/105
Asshewyn, John son of Edward Asshewyn (q.v.) 19/105
Aston, Thomas ('thabbot of Syscitour') abbot of Austin canons, Cirencester 1488–1504 10/4
Atcliff, George ('of London mercer') 1/15v
Atherton see **Aderton**
Atkyn, John of Louth [Lincs.] 19/91
Atkynson, James ('sadeller') 20/170; 2/21
Atkinson, William ('master/doctor Atkinson chaplain unto my lady Brey', etc.) D. Th. Cambridge 1497; fellow of Peterhouse and then Jesus College; chaplain to Katherine Bray (q.v.) 20/83, 127, 137; 21/49; 19/69
Atwode, John 10/62
AUDITORS, for Cecily Welles (q.v. sub **Kyme**) 19/33; **for Lady Margaret** 16/2d–3d (see too **Croke**, **Hobson**); **of the Exchequer** see **Southwell**
Aughton, George 16/22, 2d; 20/103
[R]**Aughton, Nicholas (of)** ('Nycholas/Nicholas (of) Aughton/Awg(h)ton', 'fotemen/ the gromes') footman/groom, later yeoman of the chamber to Lady Margaret 10/104; 17/22, 35, 41, 44, 47, 53, 55; 20/18, 38–9, 45, 78–9, 83, 100, 112, 113, 122, 145, 154, 156, 158–9, 168, 169, 175–6, 194; 21/11, 34–5, 44, 47–8, 52–3, 58, 97, 104, 143,

[R]**Aughton, Nicholas (of)** (*Cont.*) 147, 164; 19/24, 62, 74, 76, 85, 88, 93, 100, 104–5, 107–8, 124; 1/5r, 5v, 7r, 8r, 8v, 9r, 9v, 11r, 12v, 15v; 56/2

Austen, Gerard ('bargeman') 1/9v, 12v

Babyngton, (Henry) ('doctur Babyngton') (d. 1507) D.Th. Cambridge 1497–8; vice-chancellor 1500–1 21/92

Babyngton, Thomas 10/159; 19/70

BAGMAKER 20/48

BAILIFFS see too **REEVES**

bailiffs to Lady Margaret: of Bassingbourn 10/24; **of Bourne** 10/16; 16/3, 23, 8d; 20/26, 51, 121, 151, 156; **of Coleorton** (?) 20/99; **of Colston Basset** 10/24; **of Dalbury** 17/2; **of Droitwich** 10/23; 17/2; **of Elmdon** (?) 20/115; **of Enderby** 10/24; **of Easton Neston** 20/44; **of Fotheringhay** 21/37; **of Gayton** 10/17; **of Liddington** 20/113; **of Manorbier** 19/98; **of Overstone** 10/24; **of West Deeping** 16/3 (see too **Bothe** (Wykes and Frampton), **Butteller** (Sheldon and Great Wolford), **Calcott** (Collyweston), **Cowen** (Howden), **Etton** (Hatfield Peverel), **Heven** (Boston), **Hudilston** (Washingborough), **Mawdesley** (Deeping), **Mortymer** (Lamarsh), **Page** (Dartford), **Parker** (Tattershall), **Pulvertoft** (Tattershall), **Shirley** (Ware), **Stakhouse** (Cottingham), **Thornby** (Washingborough), **Warcop** (Hatfield), **Wyllyamson** (Maxey))

bailiff of Eagle commander of the preceptory of Eagle [Lincs.] 1/6v

BAKERS 16/6, 3d–4d; 20/145

Baker, (John) ('master Baker') (?) chaplain Oriel College, Oxford 1498–1507; D.Th. 1514 19/100

[R]**Baker, Henry** 56/4

Baker, Matthew esquire of the body to Henry VII 20/110; 2/33

Baker, Thomas 20/125

[R]**Baldwin, Peter** ('[Peter] Bald(e)wyn' 'Petrere of the Coldherbere', 'Perture keper of Coldherboro', '[Peter] of (the) Coldeherber(d)(e)/Coldherborogh/ Coldherboro(w)/Coldherbore/ Coldeharborght/Coldeharbor(o)gh/ Coldherbare/Goldherbare') keeper of Coldharbour; also scribe, limner and binder of books 10/20; 17/24, 28, 38; 19/59; 20/25, 163, 176, 182, 185; 21/60–1, 129; 19/5–7, 17, 23, 29–30, 36, 46, 70, 83, 104, 107, 110; 1/11r, 13v; 2/10, 24, 36; 6/6; 56/2

Baly, William (d. 1532) London alderman and draper, later sheriff and mayor of London 2/13

Balye, William ('(William) Bayly/Balye', 'Balye the quenys servante') servant of Elizabeth of York 10/20; 17/29

Banaster, William of Oxted [Sur.] 16/20

Banbridge, Christopher ('the maister of the Rolles') Master of the Rolls 1504–8 19/45

[R]**Banckes, Nicholas** 56/4

Baptist, Henry ('Henry Baptyst/ Baptist') 21/54, 55, 109; 19/111, 116; 1/7r, 9r

Baptist, Jerome ('maister (Jerowme) Baptist/ Baptyst oon of the kynges fecicions') physician to Henry VII 20/173; 21/25

Baptist, John 1/17r

Barbor, Piers ('Piers Barbon', 'Per(i)s/Perith Barbur', 'Perys Barbor') groom of the privy chamber to Henry VII; the king's barber 17/38; 20/84, 86, 109; 19/101

Bardney, Richard ('thabbot of Crowland') abbot of Crowland 1507–12 19/61, 123

Bardvyle ('mastres Bard(e)vyle/Bardwyle') widow of William Bardville of Chelmsford 17/29, 35

BARGEMEN, boatmen, watermen and ferrymen 20/81, 83, 85; 21/20, 28; 19/12, 18, 95; 1/4r, 9v, 11v; 2/33; 6/6 (see too **Austen**, **Braynttes**)

Barker, William 20/89

Barlow, Henry household servant of Thomas Stanley I (q.v.); perhaps then of Sir William Knyvett (q.v.) 20/114; 19/79

Barly, William of Ware 21/121

Barnard, John Dutch/German arras mender 1/7v

Baron, Stephen (d. 1513) studied at Cambridge; English Provincial of the Observant Franciscans; confessor to Henry VII from 1505 21/26; 19/36

Barons, William (d. 1505) bishop of London 1504–5 21/49

Bartholomew ('Bertylmew') clerk to master Croke 21/8

Bartholomew ('Bartyllmew the Jewse') see **Fitzwilliam**

[R]**Basset, Humfrey** 56/4

Batmanson, (John) ('docto(u)r Bat(e) manson') D.C.L. Cambridge 1493; legal adviser 20/115, 117, 119; 21/97, 142

Baughan/Baughyn see **Buchan**

Baxter, Nicholas 20/103

Beane, John ('armorer') 21/57

Beaufort, Jane ('the lady/dame Jane Bewford') daughter of Edmund Beaufort, duke of Somerset; cousin of Lady Margaret 10/158; 21/86
Beaumont, my lady see **Knyvett**
Beaupre, William ('sir William Beawpre/ Beaupray') priest 20/115; 21/13
Bedell, Cecily ('mastres Bedell') m. (3) William Bedell (q.v.) *c.*1506 19/101
Bedell, John deputy to William Bedell (q.v.) 16/17; 10/12, 24, 35–40, 50–52, 59–60, 70–1; 20/6, 49, 59, 64, 97, 102, 134, 157, 180
W**Bedell, William** (d. 1518) Lady Margaret's receiver general 1493–8 (Jones and Underwood, *The King's Mother*, p. 269); controller in January 1499 (D91.17/67); treasurer of the household from at least 14 January 1500 (D102.10/35) ('Willelmi Bedell thesauraurii hospicii' 16/1, 21, 1d, 7d; 'Wyllyam Bedell tresorere (of (my ladys/the) household)' 10/35,37, 38, 39, 59, 86, etc.; 20/64, 134;'William Bedell countrollere of my ladiez houshold' 17/67) 16/1, 21, 1d, 7d; 10/11–13, 17, 22, 35–40, 50–2, 59–62, 69–71, 78, 86–7, 91–3, 113–14, 117–20, 131, 134–7, 155–6, 165, 177; 17/26, 67; 20/20–2, 27, 46, 58, 64, 77, 79, 118, 121, 134, 172, 183, 194; 21/9, 30, 50, 55, 66, 92, 96, 105, 125; 19/3, 17, 20, 31, 33, 35–6, 43, 46, 72, 75, 98, 101–2, 105, 110; 1/15v; 2/30, 36 (see too **CONTROLLERS** for references with no name)
Bedford ('my lord of Bedford') see **Tudor**
Bedingfield, Edmund ('maister Benyfeld') probably the son and heir of Edmund and Margaret Bedingfield (q.v.) 21/37, 43
Bedingfield, (Margaret) ('my lady Benyffeld', 'my lady Beneffeld') (d. 1513) widow of Sir Edmund of Oxburgh Hall [Nfk] (d. 1496) 17/36
Beeke, Robert ('cariar of Kendall') 20/18
Bek, William servant of James Whitstones (q.v.) 20/119 (see too **Bekke**)
Bekensale, George 17/59
Bekinsall, Robert ('master Bekensale/ Bekynsall/Bekynsale/Beconsawe'; 'maister Bekynsall my ladys almener' 19/82; 'master doctour Bekensawe' 1/16r) supported by Lady Margaret at Cambridge; her almoner by April 1508, 19/82) 17/55; 20/18, 24, 34, 64, 115, 134, 164, 194; 21/21, 59, 133, 143; 19/10, 17–18, 20, 31, 43, 76, 82; 1/16r, 17r, 18v (see too **ALMONERS** for references with no name)
Bekke, Thomas ('of Kendall') 20/28 (see too **Beeke**)
Belamy, John ('sir John Belamy') priest 19/108
Bell, master ('maister Bell(e)', 'master of Fodringay') chaplain of Fotheringay maintained by Lady Margaret 10/75; 20/186; 21/39, 44, 59, 75, 96, 119, 147, 154; 19/15, 27, 35, 52
Belle, Roger Yorkshire yeoman 10/158
BELLFOUNDER see **Colverdeyne**
Bellingeham, Thomas ('maister comptrollours servant') servant of Hugh Ashton (q.v.) 1/8r
BELLRINGERS 20/125
Benet ('Palmere ...is servand') servant of Palmer, saddler (q.v.) 2/27
Benet, mistress ('ma(i)stres Benet(t)/Benat/ Benyt (the sylke woman)') silkwoman 20/53, 126; 19/72, 77; 2/22 (see too **SILKWOMEN**)
Benyfeld see **Bedingfield**
Benstid, master 19/40
Benstyd, mistress 19/22
Berell, Roger 17/57
Bergavenny, lord see **Neville, George**
Berkeley, Maurice ('(my)/the lord Barkley/ Berkeley', 'sir Morys Barkely') (d. 1506) 3rd baron Berkeley, or (d. 1523) fourth baron Berkeley 10/160; 21/93, 148, 160; 19/90
Bernard see **Flower**
Bertylmew see **Bartholomew**
Bess ('made Besse') 20/57
Bessaner, master 21/29
Bewley, Robert of Bristol 17/50
Bybe ('parson Bybe') priest 20/14, 28, 37, 52; 21/12
Bygge, John ('John Bigg/Bygg(e)') (?) groom of the chamber to Henry VII 17/53, 62; 20/50; 21/57
Bygge, Roger ('Roger Bygge') 10/158
Byggynsse, Christopher 20/87
Byggley singing man 17/63
Bigod, Elizabeth Scrope ('my lady Bygod/ Bygott') (d. 1503) m. (1) John Bigod, (2) Henry Rochford, (3) Oliver St John II (d. 1497); mother of master John St John (q.v.) 10/55; 20/5
Bigod, Henry ('Henry Bygot(t)', 'Harry Bygod', 'maister Bygot/Bygod') (d. 1527) son of Elizabeth Bigod (q.v.) 17/52; 20/37, 57, 135, 161
R**Bigod, Margaret** ('maistres(se)/Marget Bygott/Bygod') 21/8, 104; 1/9r; 56/1
Bigod, Ralph ('sir Rauffe Bygod') 20/175

Bygom, Christopher ('the grome') servant of Lady Margaret 17/22, 24, 26, 47, 60
Byllesby 20/44
Byrde, John see **Brydd**
Birkenshaw, John ('the abott of Chester') abbot of Chester 1493–1524 21/134
Byron, Nicholas (d. 1503) knight 20/6
BISHOPS
of Bath and Wells see **Castellesi**, **King**
of Carlisle see **Sever**
of Chester (i.e. Coventry and Lichfield) see **Blyth**
of Chichester see **Fitzjames**
of Durham see **Fox**, **Sever**, **Ruthall**
of Ely see **Redman, Stanley**
of Exeter see **Redman**, **Oldham**
of Hereford see **Castellesi**
of Lincoln see **Smith**
of London see **Barons**, **Fitzjames**
of Moray see **Stewart, Forman**
of Norwich see **Nix**
of Rochester see **Fitzjames, Fisher**
of St David's see **Sherbourne**
of Winchester see **Fox**
of Worcester see **de Gigli**
Bysshope, William 16/19
Blabe, William 20/107
Blagg(e), Robert (d. 1522) remembrancer of the Exchequer to Henry VII 20/25; 2/12
Blyth, Geoffrey ('episcopo Coventrie et Lichfeldie', 'the bysshop/my lord of Chester', 'the bysshop of vest Chester') bishop of Coventry and Lichfield 1503–31 10/158; 21/18, 125, 127
Blythe, (Margaret) ('my ladys goddowter') 19/31
Blot, John priest of Newport Pagnall 20/89, 92, 123
Blount, Edward 10/158
Boesse see **Bush**
Boyfeld, Thomas of Stilton 20/14
Boynton, Henry knight, son of Christopher Boynton and Agnes, daughter of Henry, Lord Scrope of Bolton 20/129, 140
Boynton, Isabel wife of Henry Boynton (q.v.) 20/129
Bokenham, (William) ('doctor Bokenham') D.Th. Cambridge 1506–7; vice-chancellor 1508–10 1/7r
Boleyn, William knight, of Blickling Hall [Nfk] (d. 1505) 17/33
Bolton, William ('the master of(f) Saynt/Seint Bartyl(l)mew(i)(s)/Bertylmews/ Bartilmewes (spytyll)') (d. 1532) Austin canon, later prior (1505) of St Bartholomew the Great, Smithfield, London 2/8, 10–12, 14, 22, 25, 29–30, 34; 6/6
[R]**Bo(w)nde, Laurence** 1/9r, 9v, 10v, 11r; 56/3
Bonehoure, Henry of Ashridge college 19/20
Bonet(t), Robert 20/32, 88, 153
Bonyface see Stanley, Boniface
BOOK BINDERS 21/21, 147 (see too **Baldwin**, **le Fevour**, **de la Haghe**, **Pynson**)
BOOK DEALERS 19/71 (see too **Garrett**, **de la Haghe**, **Pynson**, **Spierinck**, **Stacion**, **de Worde**)
Borton, Robert 19/47
Botery/Botre, William mercer of London 20/191; 2/34
Bothe, Edward ('sir Edward Bothe', 'master (Edward) Bothe/Booth') keeper of the jewel house to Lady Margaret 21/23, 25, 27, 33, 47, 60, 61, 93, 132, 135, 145; 19/30, 44, 70; 1/5r
Bothe, Richard ('Richard Bo(o)the/Both') bailiff of Lady Margaret's estates at Wykes and Frampton (Lincs.); feodary for the honour of Richmond 10/28, 83, 113; 20/11, 19, 52, 57, 61, 84, 104, 106, 115, 121; 21/37, 126
Botheby 20/19
Botteler, John 20/59
Botton ('my ladiez servand') servant of Lady Margaret 20/85
Bo(u)gh(h)am/Boughan/Boughyn/Bowghan see **Buchan**
Bowden, Richard clothman 2/13
Bowett ('Bowett/Bovet(t)') 20/32, 36, 51, 149; 'Bowettes landes' 20/51
Bowker, Hugh ('Hughe Bowkere') 20/13
Bownd, John 2/32
Bowrer, master priest 21/130; 19/31, 55
BOY BISHOPS 20/124, 148 (mitre), 183; 21/56, 143; **and St Nicholas clerks** 17/59; 21/56; 19/41
Bradley, John horse dealer 20/53, 146, 150, 163, 184, 189
Bradschaa, Richard ((?) for **William**) clothman 2/23
Bradschaa, William ((?) for **Richard**) clothman 2/12, 28–30, 32
Bray, Katherine Hussey('my lady(e) Bray(e)') (d. 1506) wife of Reginald Bray (q.v.); servant of Lady Margaret and then of Elizabeth of York 10/6; 17/37, 38, 45, 59, 63; 20/57, 68, 83, 137, 164, 188; 21/26, 59, 73, 76, 143, 156; 19/69
Bray, Reginald ('ma(i)ster Bray') (d. 1503) servant of Lady Margaret from 1465 (receiver-general of Henry, Lord

Stafford) and of Henry VII from 1485 (chancellor of the duchy of Lancaster) 10/158; 17/61, 63; 20/17, 25, 30, 54, 67–8, 95, 106
Braybroke, James page of the privy chamber to Henry VII 20/86
Braynton, Isabel ('the abbas of Godstow') 17/45
Braynttes, William bargeman 2/7
Brampton, Edward knight; ((?) d. 1508) soldier and merchant 10/7, 13
Bram(p)ton, Richard ('of the pantrye') yeoman of the pantry to Henry VII 19/95; 1/4v
Bran, master 2/11
Brandon, Charles (d. 1545) esquire of the body to Henry VII; close friend of future Henry VIII; 1st duke of Suffolk 1514 1/148; 19/73, 90, 116
Brandon, Margaret Neville Mortimer wife of Charles Brandon 1506–7 19/90
Brant(e) clerk of the privy cellar at Richmond ((?) same as John Brent (q.v.)) 21/27, 49; 19/11
Braunche, Thomas ('thabbott of Glawceter') abbot of Gloucester 1500–10 20/81; 19/8, 77
Bredd(e), John see **Brydd**
Bredenell see **Brudenell**
Bredkirke, Alice former servant to Alice Fitzhugh (q.v.) 19/99
Brenkley, (Richard) ('doctur Brenkley') D.Th. Cambridge 1493; Franciscan friar at Cambridge convent from 1489 17/27
Brenok 2/33
Brent, Ellen ('ma(i)stres Brent') gentlewoman to Elizabeth of York 17/49, 20/44
Brent, John ('Brent of the kynges seller') yeoman clerk of the cellar to Henry VII (see too **Brante**) 19/19, 86, 95; 1/4v
Bretane/Bretyn, John clothman 19/37, 91
Brewer, Robert ('syr Rob*ert* Brewer prest') 21/38
Brewster, Robert deputy to Edward Vavasour (q.v.) 10/15
Bre(w)tnell see **Brudenell**
Brian, Henry clothman 2/21
BRICKLAYER 21/119
Brydd, John ('John Bredd(e)/Byrd(e)/ Brydd(e)') servant of Lady Margaret 20/11, 12, 27, 40, 51, 103, 119, 126, 126b, 129, 149, 153, 179; 21/8, 28, 58, 103, 114, 121, 125, 146; 19/15, 19, 33, 110, 112; 1/13v
Brikenell/Bryknell/Brytnell see **Brudenell**
Briknet, Miles 10/15
Brysse, William ('of the kychen') yeoman of the kitchen to Henry VII 19/86
Brograve, John ('(John) Bro(w)grave') 20/94, 97, 107, 126, 129, 139, 159, 198
Broke ('yoman ussher') servant of Henry VII 19/97
Brook, John collier 2/27
Broune see **Browne**
Browne, master of Walcott 20/165
Browne, Christopher ('Crystofer Broune') (d. 1516) son of John Browne, merchant of Stamford [Lincs.], brother of William Browne (q.v.); alderman of Stamford; member of Lady Margaret's council 21/79
Browne, John ('grome of the beddes') groom of the beds to Elizabeth of York 20/61
Browne, John ('John Browne maister coke', 'master Browne/Broune (cooke to my ladys grasse)', 'master John my ladys coke') cook to Lady Margaret 17/52; 20/90, 175; 21/24, 52; 2/7; 6/6
Browne, Lucy Neville Fitzwilliam ('the lady Browne') (d. 1534) daughter of John Neville (d. 1471), marquess Montagu; sister of Elizabeth Neville Scrope (q.v. sub **Wentworth**); m. (1) Thomas Fitzwilliam (d. 1498), (2) Sir Anthony Browne (d. 1506), Henry VII's standard bearer and lieutenant of Calais castle 21/115
Browne, Maud ('Mawde Browne wedow presoner') prisoner at Newgate 19/10
Browne, William (?) (d. 1489) merchant of Stamford [Lincs.] 10/158
Brownyng, John ('John Brown(n)ynge', '(John) Brownyng', 'John Brownyng(e) of Burne', 'Brownyng of Burne my ladys almes man') Lady Margaret's almsman 17/46, 64; 20/22, 28, 45, 59, 65, 88, 100, 126, 138, 150, 160, 172, 182, 196; 21/12, 34
Brownyng, William son of John Brownyng (q.v.) 20/100
Brudenell, Robert ('maister Bryknell man of law', 'maister Brytnell man of law', '(maister) Bretnel(l)', 'ma(i)ster Brud(n)ell', 'master Brewtenell', 'master Brewtnell sergaunt of lawe' 20/148, 'maister Bred(e)nell/Brikenell/ Brudnelle/Brutnell/Brukenell') one of Lady Margaret's attorneys; *custos rotulorum* of Kesteven (20/156) 20/19, 33, 44, 62, 107, 118, 126, 126c, 128, 137, 148, 156, 175, 189, 197; 21/16, 39, 40, 56, 57, 63, 71, 74, 97, 126, 143, 154; 19/37, 121

de Bruxelles, Alexander goldsmith 21/24
Buchan, earl of see **Stewart, Alexander**
Buchan, lady see **Pellett, Jane Buchan**
Buckberd, John ('customer of London') London customs officer 19/105
Bucke, mistress ('[mistress] Buck(e)') clothwoman 20/20; 2/12
Buckingham, lord see **Stafford, Edward**
Bucknowre, Anne ('maistres Anne Buknowre the quenys gentylwoman') Anne Buckenham, gentlewoman to Elizabeth of York 20/57
Buk, William ('grome of the butre') (?) servant of Lady Margaret 19/114
Bulkeley, master ('master Bucley/Bokley/ Bulkeley') 19/31, 108; 20/50
Bulle, Stephen (?) vintner 17/47
Bulstrode, (William) 17/37
Burbage, William 16/17
Burgayne ('my lord of Bu\r/gayne', (?) for 'Bergavenny', q.v. sub **Neville**) 21/105
Burgon, Richard(e) ('(yonge) Burgon') ward of Lady Margaret; supported by her at Oxford 17/20, 49; **'Burgoyn(i)s landes'** 10/2–3
Burgon, Thomas ward of Lady Margaret 19/97, 116
Burne, mistress ('maistrez Burne') 21/22
Burnell, John Observant Franciscan; confessor to Henry VII before Baron (q.v.) 20/80
Burton (Davy) ('(litell)/maister Burton') child of Lady Margaret's chapel; perhaps later a gentleman of the Chapel Royal 20/25, 116, 120
Burton, Edith 20/87, 116
Burwell, master (mayster Burwell/ Burvell') 20/134, 172
Bury, Thomas ('somtyme childe of my ladys chapell') child of Lady Margaret's chapel; then scholar at Eton; later a gentleman of the Chapel Royal 20/159, 175, 181; 21/24–5; 19/83, 90, 116; 1/11r-v
Bush, Miles ('Mylez/Myles Busshe/[B]oesse ('my lady Scroppes servande)') servant to Elizabeth Scrope (q.v. sub **Wentworth**) 20/83, 119, 178
BUTCHERS 16/6, 3d–4d, 7d (see too **Davy**, **Unwyn**)
Butler, Thomas ('my lorde of Ormunnd') (d. 1515) seventh earl of Ormond; chamberlain to Elizabeth of York 17/29, 30; 20/109
BUTLERS 21/40; 19/19 (see too **Richard**)
Buttelare, Thomas 20/179
Butteller, John ('John Butteller(e) late bayly of Sheldon and Wolford Magna') former bailiff of Sheldon and Great Wolford 10/29, 58
Button, Robert 20/119

Calcott, Hugh ('Hugh Calkott', 'Calcott', 'the baillye of Colyweston') bailiff of Collyweston 16/3; 17/54, 67; 20/37, 122
Campynet ('of my ladys chappell') member of Lady Margaret's chapel 20/84, 89
Candysshe ('fryer Candysshe') friar named (?) Cavendish 17/27
Cann(e), John ('of Lynne merchaunt') 21/163; 19/124
CANONS, regular and secular 17/30
Austin 20/164 (see too Aston, Bolton)
Bonhommes 19/95, 102, 108, 110; 1/4r (see too **Bonehoure** and **Woodhouse**, and see **Ashridge** in the PLACES index)
CANTOR of Lincoln 20/19
[R]**Canwyk, Laurence** ('valettum promptuarii', 'Laurence/Laurencium Canwyk(e)/ Canwyck/Canwik') yeoman of the brewhouse to Lady Margaret 16/9, 4d; 17/27, 34, 40, 44, 46, 49, 52; 56/5
Carew, William ('sir William Karew/Carew(e) knyght (late fermer)') (d. 1501) of Hengrave (Sfk); m. (2) Margaret (q.v. sub **Carow**) 10/16, 21; 2/2
[R]**Carleton, William** 56/3
Carlisle, Christopher ('Norrey the harrowde') Norroy king of arms 1493–1510 17/57
Carow (for Carew (q.v.)), **Margaret** ('maistres Caro', 'maistres (Mergett) Carow') widow of William Carew (q.v.) 20/25; 21/95, 112
CARPENTERS see **JOINERS**
Carre, George ('Carre of Greenwich') 19/35, 37, 82
[R]**Carre, Hugh** ('Hugh(e) Car(r)e') groom of the chamber to Lady Margaret 20/88; 21/28, 98, 118, 124, 130; 19/6, 11, 18, 33, 41, 44, 75, 85–6, 95, 101, 104; 56/3
[R]**Carre, John** ('the post') courier, post-rider 19/88; 56/4
Carre, Ralph of Edinburgh 20/95 ('oon Carre'), 102, 123
Carre, Richard ('Richard(e) Carr(e)/Karre', 'Richard/Rychard Carre', 'fotemen/ the gromes') groom to Lady Margaret 17/20, 22, 26, 35, 41, 44, 46–7, 53; 20/17, 22, 49, 51–2, 58, 64, 79, 84, 88–9, 95–6, 105–6, 114, 121, 124, 134, 148, 150

CARRIERS, carters, porters, and couriers 17/38, 50; 20/24, 27, 36, 86, 101, 108, 158, 167; 21/44, 51–2, 56, 58, 61, 112, 137; 19/11–12, 18–19, 25, 75, 85–8, 93, 95, 97, 106 (see too **Apt**, **Beeke**, **John**, **Wyldebore**)

Carter, John ('[sir/master] (John) Carter(e) (of the chappell)', etc.; 'John Carter servand unto maister chaunceller', etc.; 'John Carter notary') servant of Henry Hornby; scribe and notary 20/146, 156, 168; 21/13, 37, 56, 92, 97, 99, 124, 142; 19/6, 17, 24, 28, 30, 39, 72, 89

Carter, John ('sir John Carter prest of the closse of Lycheffeld') priest of Lichfield, perhaps same as above 20/22, 43(?) ('a prest þat came from Lychfeld'), 59(?) ('a prest of Lechefeld'), 200

Cas(s)e, Thomas ('vallettum pasterie') yeoman of the pastry house 16/3d; 19/100, 112

Castell, John Lady Margaret's attourney at the Exchequer 20/170, 19; 21/1, 75, 108; 19/22, 121

Castell, Robert 17/25

Castellesi, Adriano ('popys collectour'; 'my lord of Bath') (d. 1521) papal collector in England; bishop of Hereford 1502–4; bishop of Bath and Wells 1504–18 (see Underwood, 'The Pope, the Queen and the King's Mother') 21/47, 56, 96; 19/20–1, 28, 77–8

Castile, king of see **Philip I**

Catherine, my lady see **Courtenay, Katherine Plantagenet**

Catysby, master servant of bishop of Lincoln (q.v. sub **Smith**) 20/161

Catysby, (Elizabeth) ('maistres Catysby') (?) wife of George Catesby and daughter of Richard Empson (q.v.) 21/27; 19/11

Catour, John 1/7r

Cecil, lady see **Kyme**

Cecyll, David ('Davy/David Cecell/Cecyll') landowner and burgess of Stamford; relative of David Philip(s) (q.v.)); grandfather of William Cecil, 1st baron Burghley 16/18; 21/20

Cellam, Robert 20/19

Chayne see **Cheney**

Chayne, Thomas ('of the chapell') gentleman of Lady Margaret's chapel; (?) same as 'master Chayne' 19/102 (see too **Cheney**) 19/107

Chambelett, John of Bletchingley 16/8d

Chamber, (John) ('maister John Chambers', 'master/doctur Chambre/Chamber') M.A. Oxford 1495, M.D. Padua 1505; physician to Henry VII from 1507 20/19; 19/69, 78–9, 88, 100; 1/5r

Chamber, John ('presoner') prisoner at Ludgate 19/10

Chamber, Thomas ('grome of my ladyes spycery') servant of Lady Margaret 19/9, 14, 58, 72, 96, 98

Chamberlayn, Ralph stepson to Roger Ormeston (q.v. sub **Urmeston**) 20/103

CHAMBERLAINS

of Elizabeth of York see **Butler**

of Henry VII see **Daubeney**, **de Vere**

of Lady Margaret's household (master/the/my lady's chamberlain) 10/28, 32–3, 67, 177–8; 20/7, 14, 16, 20, 25, 30–1, 33, 35, 40, 42, 44, 54–6, 58, 60, 74, 80–2, 85, 88–9, 98–9, 102, 104, 106, 108, 110, 115, 117, 121, 126, 126b, 126c, 128–9, 137; 21/19–20, 38; 19/27, 43, 76–7, 99, 101 (see too **Ormeston**, **John St John II of Bletsoe)**

of Margaret Tudor see **Verney**

Champion, Piers ('Pe(e)rs/Perith/Peris Champion/Champyon (the kynges servand)') esquire of the body to Henry VII 17/45; 20/34; 21/144, 154; 19/44, 54, 119

CHAPLAINS 20/13, 94; 21/37; 19/21 (see too **Atkinson**, **Bell**, **Ednam**, **Hatton**, **Mason**, **Metcalfe**, **Trafforth**, **Walles** and see **CHAPEL MEMBERS**)

CHANCELLORS

of the bishop of Ely see **Thorneboro**

of the bishop of Lincoln 17/42; 20/100

of Lady Margaret's household (master/my lady's chancellor) 10/30, 108; 20/6, 13, 17, 32, 42, 44, 56, 74, 87, 95, 104, 111, 127–9, 150, 156, 173; 21/14, 16, 19, 21–2, 25, 28, 30, 33, 37, 40, 44, 46, 48, 52, 55–6, 58–62, 66, 75, 92–3, 96, 97, 99–100, 102, 111, 117, 120, 122, 139, 144, 147; 19/13–14, 17, 21, 23–4, 28–9, 32, 34, 40, 42, 44–5, 71–2, 78, 82, 89, 92, 95, 99, 101, 107; 1/7v, 11r (see too **Oldham**, **Hornby)**

CHAPEL MEMBERS (see too SINGERS) 17/29 (Chapel Royal); 20/94 (Chapel Royal), 114, 125; 21/157; 19/30, 54, 101 (Chapel Royal) (see too **Crane** (Chapel Royal), **Crow**, **le Fevour**, **Fysher**, **Newton**, **Penter**)

chaplains see Carter, Clement, Crossley, Moldale

CHAPEL MEMBERS (*Cont.*)
children 16/14; 20/11, 15, 26, 29, 65, 88, 100, 103, 106, 111, 119, 122, 178; 21/42, 137; 19/21, 101 (see too **Burton**, **Bury**, **Erley**, **Freston**, **Moyne**, **Peper**, **Sherade**, **Watwod**)
clerks 17/59
gentlemen 17/29; 21/36 (see too **Campynet**, **Chayne**, **Conway**, **Elmeden**, **Ferthing**, **Fyssher**, **Prechet(t)**, **Rowley**, **Watson**)
master of the children, at Collyweston see **Couper**; **at Fotheringhay** see **Cotterell**
sub-dean see **Clerk**
Chappell, Robert ('doct(o)ur Chap(p)ell') D. Th. Cambridge 1507; fellow of Peterhouse, Cambridge 19/5, 24, 28, 53
CHARIOT MEN 2/32; 6/6 (see too **Daniel**)
Charles priest 20/109
Chattoke, Thomas 17/52
Chek(e), Richard servant of Lady Margaret 17/21, 34, 35, 40, 44, 47, 52, 53, 55
Cheney, my lady ('my lady Cheyney/Chayne') (?) (d. 1503) Margaret Chideock, widow of Sir John, baron Cheney (d. 1499) 10/142; (?) wife of Sir Thomas Cheney (q.v.) 19/89–90 (see too 'master Chayne' 19/102 and **Chayne, Thomas**)
Cheney, Thomas ('(sir) Thomas Chen(e)y (militem)') (d. 1558) knight; gentleman of Henry VII; nephew of John Cheney (q.v. sub **Cheney, my lady**) 16/19; 20/61
Chicheley, Henry ('Checheley/Chicheley/ Chychely') 19/66, 91, 100; **'Checheleys landes'** 10/160
Chicheley, Richard 19/120
Chicheley, William ('Checheley/Chicheley/ Chychely') 10/160; 19/66, 91, 100
Chymyngton, John falconer 21/129
Christian ('Madde Crystyan') 17/25
Christopher see **Crossley**
Chubbes, (William) ('[master/doctor] Chubbis/Chubbys', '[master/doctor] Jubbis/Jubbes/Jubbys/Jobbys') D.Th. Cambridge 1486; fellow of Pembroke College; first master of Jesus College 17/37, 54, 56–7; 20/20, 29, 95, 121, 124, 135, 147, 154, 195
Churche ('Churche/Chyrche'; 'thexchet*ur* ...of Lyncoln(shyre)', etc.) escheator of Lincolnshire 20/13, 16, 128, 160, 197; 21/19
Clarell, James ('Jamys/maister Clarrell', 'James (Clarell)') cofferer 1498–9 10/3–4; 17/1, 19, 66; 20/50, 158, 160, 194; 21/66, 79, 162; 19/61, 123; 2/2
[R]**Clegg, Henry** footman to Lady Margaret; shared a room at Collyweston with Wynstanley (q.v.) 17/46, 53; 20/152; 56/2
Clement ('sir Cleme[n]t (of the chapell)', 'Clement clerk') priest of Lady Margaret's chapel 19/89; 2/10, 11
Clement, Oliver supplier of tapestries 2/31
Clement, Richard ('grome of the kynges chamber', 'the kynges servant') groom of the privy chamber to Henry VII 17/50, 52; 20/190; 19/90
CLERK OF THE VESTRY (Syon) 21/113
CLERK OF WORKS (Syon) 21/113 (for Lady Margaret's clerk of works see **Morice**)
Clerk, Richard error for Richard Wyatt (q.v.)
[R]**Clerk, Robert** 56/4
Clerk, William sub-dean of Lady Margaret's chapel 21/11, 39, 108, 145, 154; 19/16, 70
Clyff, Nicholas ('of the pantre') yeoman(?) of the royal pantry 17/38; 20/109, 184; 21/48
Clifford, Anne St John ('my lady Clifford/ Clefford') (d. 1508) daughter of Sir John St John I; wife of Henry Clifford (q.v.); gentlewoman to Lady Margaret 10/138; 21/130
Clifford, Henry ('my lord Clefforth/Clyfford') (d. 1523) tenth Baron Clifford; m. Anne St John (q.v. sub **Clifford**) 20/177; 21/34
Clifford, Richard clothman 1/14r
Clifford, Robert ('syr Robert Clyfforth/ Clyfford/Clifford', 'maister Clyfforth', 'syr Robert/Roger Clyfford (his) wyff') knight 21/124 ((?) 'Roger' error), 126, 128, 139, 159
CLOCKMAKERS 21/141; 19/14, 32
Clowyle, John of the Isle of Purbeck 20/46
Cluer, Robert ('maister of the queristers in Stokelar') master of choristers at Stoke-by-Clare 20/119
Codde, Thomas 20/79, 118
COFFERERS, **to Henry VII** see **Cope**; **to Lady Margaret** (cofferer/clerk of the coffers) see **Clarell** and **Worsley**, and see too **TREASURERS of the chamber to Lady Margaret**
Coke, Henry see **Ludlow**
Coke, Thomas cook to Henry VII 20/86
Cokkes, John 16/5, 20, 10d
[R]**Cokkes, Walter** ('Walterum Cokkes valettum pistrine', 'Water Coke yoman of the bakhouse', 'Wa(l)ter/Watere Cokkes/

Cokkys (of the bakhowse)') yeoman of Lady Margaret's bakehouse 16/22, 2d, 4d; 17/61; 20/13, 41, 116, 134, 194 ; 21/79, 162; 19/61, 70, 119; 56/2
Coksey ('(Korse) my lady Chaynes fole', 'Coksey the fole') fool of lady Cheyney (q.v) 20/89–90; 19/90, 102
Cokworthy 10/139
Coles, Nicholas ('Nicholas Collis lerned man'; 'Nicholas Coles oon of the proctures of the Arches') a proctor of the Court of Arches 20/117; 21/25, 130, 154
Colet, Henry ('sir Henry/Herry Col(l)et(t)', 'maister Collett') (d. 1505) mercer of London and warden of Mercers' Company 1488, 1494, 1504; father of John Colet (q.v.) 21/3, 47, 67, 77, 93; 10/182
Colet, John ('doctor Collett', 'dean of Polles') (d. 1519) D.Th. Oxford (?)1504; dean of St Paul's 1505–19 20/101; 19/82
Colyngborne 2/8
[R]**Colyns, Elizabeth** 56/1
COLLIERS 21/138 (see too **Brook, Philip**)
Collyngwode, Roger ('maister Co(l) lyngwod(e)') M.A. 1499; fellow of Queens' College, Cambridge; maintained by Lady Margaret in study of canon law in Paris and abroad 19/35, 51, 94, 116
Collys, Agnes ('dame Agnes/Agnez Colles/ Collys', 'my lady Collys') nun at the Minories 17/24, 27; 19/37
Collop, John ('my ladys arrow mender', 'arres maker', 'John Collopp') arras maker and mender 17/48; 20/23, 39, 41, 46, 119, 145, 153, 159, 169, 171, 172, 176; 21/16, 20, 53, 103; 19/112; 1/6v
Colman, Thomas priest, supported at St Gregory's hostel, Cambridge, by Lady Margaret and Elizabeth of York 17/37
Colverdeyne, William London bellfounder 2/7
Colville, Robert ('the pryour of (the said) Ely') prior of the Benedictine abbey and cathedral priory of Ely 1500–10 21/91; 19/91
Compton, Nicholas/Nycholas ('one of my ladiez receyvourz') receiver until 16 January 1502 (10/40) 10/4, 5, 15–19, 21–24, 40; 17/2, 4
Compton, Walter deputy to Nicholas Compton (q.v.) 10/16, 19
Con(e)y see **Conway**
CONFESSOR GENERAL (of Syon) see **Sander**
CONFESSORS, to Henry VII see **Baron**, **Burnell**; **to Lady Margaret** (master confessor) 20/87, 124, 161, 168, 198; 21/21, 50, 62, 100, 126, 132; 19/20, 82, 99, 105; 1/11v (see too **Fitzjames**, **Fisher**, **Wilsford**); **to Mary Tudor** 19/92
Conyngsby, Humphrey ('ma(i)ster Cony(ng) sby/Conyngesby/Cony(e)sby(e)', 'Conysby sergant', 'Conysbe', '(Humfri) Connysby') (d. 1535) sergeant at law; justice of the King's Bench 1509 10/28, 32, 158, 160; 17/26; 20/18, 24, 33, 43, 59, 126c, 128, 137, 159, 173, 189, 197; 21/10, 14, 28, 34, 36 , 44, 49, 56, 58, 62, 71, 92, 97, 145, 154; 19/10, 15, 44–5, 54, 66, 92, 95, 99, 112, 125
CONTROLLERS (the/master controller) 10/11, 102–3, 108; 17/47, 49, 54; 20/7, 11, 13, 24, 28, 38–9, 43, 46, 79, 154–5, 163, 173, 177, 182, 188, 197; 21/3, 10, 18–19, 38, 47, 58, 63, 67, 112, 125, 135–6; 19/7, 29–31, 36, 66, 69, 88, 92, 100, 104; 1/8r, 18v (see too **Ashton**, **Bedell**, **Fothede**, **Merbury**)
Conway, Henry ('(Henry) Cony', 'Con(e)y my lordes/lord of Derbies servaunte/ servand') servant of Thomas Stanley I (q.v.) and II (q.v.); keeper of Hawarden (Flintshire) estate 17/59; 20/22, 48, 58, 128; 19/16
Conway, Richard ('yonge Coney', '(Richard) Con(we)y' 'Richard Conway/Convay of the chappell', 'Rychard/Richerd Conway/Conwey late of the chap(p) ell', 'Richard Conwey somme tyme on of the clerkes of my ladys chapell'; 'Richard <Goney> Coney my lordes servaunt') son of Henry Conway (q.v.); gentleman of Lady Margaret's chapel until 1502, after which servant of Thomas Stanley I and II (q.v.) 20/58, 64, 105, 120, 134, 194; 21/79, 134, 138, 139, 162; 19/61, 123
Conyers, Mary Scrope ('my lady Conyas/ Conyers') niece of the half-blood to Lady Margaret by her mother Elizabeth St John, half-sister of Lady Margaret Beaufort; m. William Conyers (q.v.) 20/163, 197
Conyers, William ('my lord Conyas') (d. 1524) 1st baron Conyers; husband of Mary Scrope (q.v. sub **Conyers**) 20/155, 164
COOKS 20/16, 90, 152, 160; 21/15, 107; 19/14, 89, 97; 1/6v, 9v (see too **Browne**, **Coke**, **Daye**, **Kynge**, **Ludlow**)

Cooper, Robert ('maister Couper/Co(w)per', 'sir Robert of the chappell', 'doctour Cooper') B.Mus., D.Mus. 1507; composer; master of the children of Lady Margaret's chapel 20/102, 160, 178, 198; 21/10, 55, 91, 145; 19/43, 117; 1/8r
Cope, William ('cofferere of the kyngez house') cofferer to Henry VII 17/48, 67
COPPERSMITH see **Horne**
Cordall, Thomas supplier of wood 10/75, 140; 20/142
Corhonde, William singing man 17/62
Corwell, Richard 20/59
Corwen servant of John Fisher (q.v.) 19/75
R**Cotemote, Richard** ('Richard Cot(e)mot(e)/ Cotmont (grome isshare of the haull)', 'Richard grome yssher of the hall') groom usher of the hall to Lady Margaret 20/57, 190; 19/40, 108; 56/2
Cotes of Grantham 20/46, 48, 106
Cotterell, master singing man; master of the children at Fotheringhay 20/104; 21/39, 59
Cotton, Henry ('Harry Cotton') household servant of Thomas Stanley I 20/91
Cotton, Laurence brother of Sir Robert Cotton (q.v.) 21/36
Cotton, (Margaret) ('maistres Cotton') (?) of the royal nursery 20/177
Cotton, Nicholas ('the grome') groom to Lady Margaret 17/44, 47, 53; 20/13
Cotton, Robert knight, landowner and supporter of Henry VII 17/36, 21/36
COUNCILS and groups, commissioners of sewers 20/165; 19/61, 124; 6/5–6; **Henry VII's council** 21/50, 60; 19/16, 91, 111; **Lady Margaret's council** 20/42, 61, 114, 120, 191; 21/14; 19/104 (see too **Broune**, **Hussey**, **Whitstones**)
countess of Spain see **Cabra**
Couper, Nicholas ('maister Nicholas Couper [servande]', 'Nicholas Couper stewarde of Saint Antones in London') steward of the hospital of St Anthony, London 19/24, 39, 69
Courtenay, Katherine Plantagenet ('my/the lady Kateryn(e)/Cateryn', 'my lady Katerin Courteney suster to the quenes grace decessed') (d. 1527) daughter of Edward IV; sister of Elizabeth of York; wife of Sir William Courtenay, earl of Devon (d. 1511) 17/29; 20/83; 21/25, 72; 1/10v
Cowen former bailiff of Howden, Yorks. 21/19
Crakenthorp, John 10/158
Crane, William gentleman of the Chapel Royal 21/110
Crathorne, Robert ('Robert Crathorn(e)/ Crathron') 20/171; 21/80, 163; 19/61, 124
Cressall, Richard ('syr Richard Cressall prior of the new hospitall of oure blessyd Lady withowte Bysshopyate in London') 21/24
Cretour, Thomas 10/158
Cristen, Mark ('my ladys servant') 17/47
Croke, master ('master Croke auditor' 20/166) auditor to Lady Margaret 20/145, 166; 21/8, 91–2
Crossley, Christopher ('sir Crystofer ...oon of the quenys chapleyns' 20/28, [sir/ master] (Crystof(f)er) Cros(se)ley (oon of my ladys chapplence)', etc., 'sir Crystofer clerk of the clossett', 'Crosley of the Kynges Haule', 'doctor Crystofer a physsicion in Cambrige') fellow of King's Hall, Cambridge; chaplain to Elizabeth of York and then to Lady Margaret 10/147; 20/28, 107, 112, 122 ('Crosby'), 126b, 161, 175; 21/9; 19/34
Crow, master ('maister Crow of the chappell') member of Lady Margaret's chapel by May 1503 20/95
Crowmeyre, Anne ('maistrez/maistres Cro(w) meyre', 'mastres Crowmer') mistress of the royal nursery 1503 21/25, 105 (note 'Cromers maners' 17/39)
Crowmeyre, William (former) gentleman usher of the chamber to Elizabeth of York 21/59
Cuff, Laurence ('(Laurence) Cuff (my ladys servant)') 19/40, 121
Curline, James 2/34
Curson, master ('maister Curson') 20/27
Curson, mistress ('ma(i)strez/maistres Curs(s) on', 'maistrez Corson') servant of Lady Margaret 17/23, 24; 20/88, 93, 134, 178; 21/16, 37, 71; 19/32, 88
Curson, Robert ('sir Robert Curson') 10/158
R**Curtes, Henry** ('(Henry Curtas/Curtes grome of the same' [i.e. bakehouse]) 17/61; 56/3
Curtes(se), Nicholas clothman 2/12, 14
CUSTOMS OFFICER see **Buckberd**
Cutler, William ('Wyllyam Cutler', 'maister Cutlerd (clerk)', '[master] Cuttyller/ Cuteler') clerk to Robert Brudenell (q.v.) 20/11, 32, 62, 92, 111–12, 126b, 137
Cutt(e), sir John receiver to Reginald Bray (q.v.) 21/126, 159

Daker(s), Henry 2/15, 16, 31
Dalaland see **Delaland**
Dalkyn(s), John receiver of Holderness 10/26, 31; 20/5
[W]**Dalton, Roger** household servant of Thomas Stanley I (q.v.) 20/116; 21/23
Dalton, Thomas 19/47
Daniell, William ('William/Wylliam Daniell/ Danyell (yoman of my ladys charyett)') yeoman of the chariot to Lady Margaret 10/2; 17/19, 24, 30, 51
Dantre, John 10/53
Darcy, sir Thomas ('sir Thomas Dassy') captain of Berwick; lieutenant of the east and middle Marches 20/59
Darley, (Brian) ('maister Derley', 'doctour Darley') B.A. Cambridge, D.Th. by 1505; studied at University of Turin 1503 20/38; 19/17
Darrold, Godfrey 2/23
Daubeney, Elizabeth Arundel ('my lady Dawbeney') wife of Giles Daubeney (q.v.) 21/43, 60, 92; 1/10r
Daubeney, Giles ('my lorde chamberlen (at Hampton Corte)') (d. 1508) 1st baron Daubeney; lord chamberlain to Henry VII 1496–1508 20/109; 21/25, 50, 62, 76, 118; 19/22
Daubeney, Henry ('my lord(e) chamberlayns son(ne)') heir to Giles Daubeney (q.v.) 21/50, 76, 118
[R]**Davenport, Reginald** ('Renold/Raynold Davempord/Davemport', 'Reynold/ Riginald Davenport (vallettum dicte panetrie)', 'Reynold Daunpport') yeoman of the pantry to Lady Margaret 16/3d–4d; 20/156, 176; 21/30, 46, 49, 53, 55, 63; 56/2
Davers, my lady (for **Danvers**?) 21/98
David see **Osbourne**
Davy, Nicholas ('Nicholas ...oon of the almez chyldren', 'Nycholas Davy my lad*ys* almes chyld') almschild of Lady Margaret, later apprenticed to a man from London 20/182; 21/117
Davy, Richard ('Ricardi/Ricardum Davy/ David nuper carnificem hospicii domine') former butcher to Lady Margaret's household 16/23, 8d
Davy, William 20/170
Dawson, mother ('moder Dawson') almswoman 21/51
Dawson, Richard servant of Lady Margaret 17/46, 58
Dawtre ('the quenez servante') servant of Elizabeth of York 17/56
[R]**Daye, Henry** 19/85; 56/1
[R]**Daye, Robert** ('Robertum Daye valettum pasterie', 'Rob(e)rt Dey/Day(e) (coke)') yeoman of the pastry house and master cook 16/3d; 20/116, 145, 152, 160, 170, 190; 21/35, 46, 73, 92, 105; 19/21; 1/9v; 56/3
DEANS
dean of chapel to John de Vere 21/8
dean of chapel to Lady Margaret (the/ master dean (of my (said) lady's chapel) 10/3, 9; 17/61, 65; 20/5, 13, 16, 23, 24, 28, 34, 36, 39, 43, 46, 48–50, 59–62, 77–81, 84, 86, 88, 94–5, 100, 103, 106, 111–21, 123, 126, 128, 146–51, 157, 159, 161–2, 165–6, 168, 170–1, 173, 175, 178–9, 182–3, 186–7, 189, Appendix; 21/9, 10, 12, 18, 23, 25, 36, 39, 56, 63, 99, 102, 104, 107, 118, 124, 130, 140–1, 143; 19/7, 10, 12–14, 16, 19–21, 28–9, 37, 39, 42, 71–2, 76, 82, 86–7, 90–1, 95, 100, 104 (see too **Hornby**)
dean of Lincoln see **Fitzhugh**
dean of St Paul's Cathedral see **Colet**
dean of St Stephen, Westminster 21/58
dean of Windsor see **Urswicke**
Debalbus, John goldsmith 20/22, 24, 50
Delaland, sir Thomas ('sir Thomas Dalaland/ Delaland') i.e. De la Launde; eldest son of attainted father; secured restitution of his lands in Lincs. 1485 20/27, 187
Deland, Edmund ('(maister Edmound Deland) oon of the fryour Austyns of Stampford') Austin friar of Stamford [Lincs.] 20/161
Delaware, lord see **West**
Delese, Leonard ('Lenard Delese') book dealer 20/171
van Delff, Robert ('Robert van Delff ston sleppere of London') London stone cutter 21/59
Democke, John clothman of Antwerp 19/99, 100
Denys, Hugh ('Hugh(e) Dennes/Denys(e)/ Denysse/Denyes', 'master Dynous') (d. 1508) groom of the stool, later esquire of the body, to Henry VII; husband of Mary Denys (q.v.) 20/82, 84, 86, 88, 109, 162, 184; 21/26, 102, 104; 19/11, 54; 1/6r
Denys, Mary Rouse ('Hughe Denys wyff', 'maistrez/maistres(se) (Mary) Denys(se)/Denyce/Dyonyce') royal servant; wife of Hugh Denys (q.v.) 20/84; 21/110; 19/11, 54; 1/4v, 8v

Denman, Thomas ('master Denman') (d. 1501) physician to Lady Margaret 1494; master of hospital of St Mary of Bethlehem 1494; master of Peterhouse, Cambridge 1500 17/21, 33, 39, 43, 46, 51

Denton, Elizabeth ('maisteresse/maistris/ma(i) stres/mistres Denton') mistress of the royal nursery, later attending on Margaret Tudor, Queen of Scots (q.v.) 20/81, 126, 138, 150, 191, 198; 21/24, 74, 140, 155; 19/13, 72, 119; 1/13v, 14r, 17v; 2/34, 6/4

Denton, James ('(maister) Jamys Denton', 'maister/James Denton my ladys scoller (at Orlyaunce') scholar at Orléans, supported by Lady Margaret (see Jones, 'Henry VII, Lady Margaret Beaufort and the Orléans ransom') 20/39, 78, 84, 146, 163, 189, 196; 21/125, 142, 144

Denton, William ('Willyam/Wyllyam Denton') one of Lady Margaret's receivers 10/4, 15, 23, 29; 20/7, 18

Derby, lord see **Stanley, Thomas (I/II)**; **Derby, lady** see **Stanley, Anne Hastings**

Derley see **Darley**

Deseney, Richard 21/87

Dyer, Thomas of Croydon 16/12d

Dykes, David/Dafydd ('David/Davyth/Davy Dykes (the kynges servant)', 'David now the kynges servaunt') servant of Henry VII 21/52, 57, 74, 97, 103, 106

Dymock, Elizabeth Arderne Skrene Harper ('the lady Skrene (late wyff unto Herper late my ladys receyvour of the duke of Bokynghams landes)') daughter of Sir Peter Arderne (d. 1467), baron of the Exchequer; m. (1) John Skrene, (2) Richard Harper (q.v.), (3) Andrew Dymock 10/103; 21/4

Dyse, William ('William Dyse a westment makere') 17/27

Dobbis, Robert of London 20/172

Docwra, Thomas ('my lord of Seynt/Sainct Joh(e)ns/Johnys') prior of the Knights Hospitallers of St John of Jerusalem, Clerkenwell 19/22, 100; 1/4v

[R]**Dod, Thomas** ('Thomas Dod(de)') (?) servant of Lady Margaret 21/115, 135, 147; 19/34, 85; 1/4r, 6v; 56/5

Dodly(e)/Dogley see **Dudley, Edmund** and **Sutton, Edward**

Donne, Gruffydd ('Greffeth/Gryffeth Donne') (d. 1503) son of Sir John Donne 21/30, 72

Dorset, marquess of see **Grey, Thomas**

Dowget clothman 2/24

Drace, master 19/108

Draver, Stephen 2/15

Drew, John ('Dru', '(John) Drew(e) my ladys ward') ward of Lady Margaret 19/20, 40, 51

DROVER 17/65

Dudley, lord see **Sutton**

Dudley, (Edmund) ('master/mastyr/maister Dudle(y)', 'maister Dodley') (ex. 1510) speaker of the House of Commons 1504; president of the council of Henry VII 1506 21/27, 49, 72, 124; 19/22, 27, 28, 52, 100; 1/7r

Dudley, (Elizabeth Grey) ('Dudleys wyff') wife of Edmund Dudley (q.v.); heir of John, fourth viscount Lisle 20/172

Duffeld, John 20/79

DUTCH/GERMANS 17/25, 30 (see too **Barnard** and **Mustyng**)

Duwes, Giles ('Gyles lewtor/lutere') lutenist in the Chapel Royal; French and lute teacher to the children of Henry VII; from September 1509 librarian to Henry VIII 21/110; 19/97

[R]**Edlyn, Robert** ('the grome') groom to Lady Margaret 17/26, 35, 41, 44, 53; 20/28, 30, 40, 88; 21/92, 96; 19/39; 56/3

Edmond, John 20/146

Edmund Tudor ('my lord Edmound') (d. 1500) son of Henry VII 10/9

Ednam, (John) ('doctour Ednam') D.Th. Cambridge 1488; chaplain to Henry VII and dean of Stoke-by-Clare college 1497; almoner and confessor to Prince Arthur (q.v.); almoner to Henry VII 1507–9 20/147

Edward, master ('master sir Edward') priest 17/60, 64

Egge see **Hegge**

Eland, Robert 10/140

Elyn ('mod(e)r Elyn') almswoman 20/15, 93, 111, 148, 188

Eline, John ('da[n]e John Eline') (d. 151) John Eliche/Ellis, monk of the Sheen charterhouse 20/85

Elys, Roger priest 19/111

[W]**Elizabeth of York** ('the quene') (d. 1503) wife of Henry VII (q.v.) 10/48; 17/37, 50, 56–7, 59, 62; 20/48, 57, 68, 83 ('the quenes grace decessed'), 87, 109, 191 (her midwife)

Elizabeth ('Gret Elyzabeth') 20/84; 21/27, 118

Elmeden, Nicholas ('Nicholas Elmeden/ Elneden (of the chappell') gentleman(?) of Lady Margaret's chapel 10/158; 19/28, 63, 125

Elmer(e) see **Hilmer**

Elmes, (William) ('maister Elmes/Elmez') (?) grandson of William Browne, merchant of Stamford (q.v.), but see too **Hilmer** 20/59, 104, 117

Elston, John 20/120

Elton, William Cambridge embroiderer 20/102

EMBROIDERERS 20/55, 79; 19/13, 75, 88, 102 (see too **Elton**, **Forster**, **Mussheka**, **Oldam**, **Paskall**, **Pety John**, **Rede**, **Richard**, **Thurstane**)

Empson, Richard ('ma(i)ster Em(p)son', 'the kynges attournay/solycitur') lawyer and attorney general; councillor to Henry VII; chancellor of the duchy of Lancaster 1505 (ex. 1510) 10/18; 20/25, 112, 126c, 137, 173; 21/104; 19/32; 1/7r

Engulbred see **de la Haghe, Ingelbert**

Enríquez de Velasco, Beatriz ('the counties of Spayne') (d. 1516) cousin of Ferdinand II of Aragon, father of Katherine of Aragon; wife of Diego Fernandez de Cordoba, 3rd count of Cabra (both accompanied Katherine of Aragon to England in 1501) 20/17

Erley/Ernelay child of Lady Margaret's chapel 20/39, 47

Essex, Alys 17/25

Etton, Hugh deputy bailiff at Hatfield Peverel 2/2

Everby, Guy ('Gye E(ve)rby') of Stilton 20/40, 42

[R]Everyngham, John 19/7; 56/3

Ewerby ('my lady Evarby') (?) mother of Joan Ewerby (q.v. sub **St John**) 19/81

EXECUTORS (of wills) 16/17–18; 10/1, 21; 20/107, 144; 19/39, 52, 58, 61, 124; 1/5r, 17r (see too **Hutton**, **Lovell**, **Marney**, **Ormeston**, **St John**, **Somerset**, **Waywyn**)

Exeter ('Exitur landes') lands forfeited by Henry Holland, 2nd duke of Exeter (d. 1475) 10/22 (see Jones and Underwood, *The King's Mother*, pp. 100, 105)

EXHIBITIONERS 17/67; 21/157 (see too **Frogenhall**, **Markham**, **Parker**, **St John (master John)**, **Skip**, and **STUDENTS**)

Fabbe, (John) ('maister Fabbe') M.A. Cambridge; fellow of God's House (later Christ's College 1492–1504 21/16, 25

Fairfax, Robert ('Robert Ferfax', 'Fayreffaxe/Feyreffax', 'master Fereffax', 'doctour Fayrefax') gentleman of the Chapel Royal; composer 17/27; 20/34, 178, 183; 19/31

Fairfax, William ((?) error for Robert Fairfax (q.v.)) 20/161

FALCONERS 19/29, 37, 75, 86, 92, 97, 101, 116 (see too **Chymyngton**, **Lowthe**, **Sydington**)

Falworth, William 2/32

Faques, William ('hym þat kepis the kynges lyberary') king's printer 1504–6; keeper of the king's library 1506–9 19/8 (see Payne, 'Quentin Poulet', pp. 145–6)

FARMERS 10/177; 2/2; see too **Carew**, **Masleyn**, **Walssh**

FARRIERS 17/24, 51

Farthing, Thomas ('Thomas Ferthyng') (d. 1520/1) 20/127; 19/7, 124 (see Ashbee and Lasocki, *Biographical Dictionary of English Court Musicians* for suggestion that Thomas and William (q.v.) are the same man; clear and separate references to both here suggest not, but it is Thomas who is elsewhere recorded as the singing man)

Farthing, William ('William Farthyng/Fertheng/Ferthyng(e)/Ferthing'; 'William Ferthynge late of my ladyes chappell', etc.) gentleman of Lady Margaret's chapel until at least 1504, after which probably gentleman of the Chapel Royal 20/13, 134, 194 ; 21/79, 147, 163; 19/62, 63, 124

Faughyn ('grome of the chambre') servant of Henry VII 19/97

Fauldrynge 17/38

Fawne, John ('(master) John Fawne', 'maister Fawne(e)', 'her precher in Cambryge') D.Th. Cambridge 1509–10; dean of chapel Queens' College 1498–9, 1501–2; junior and senior bursar 1499–1501; first Lady Margaret preacher 1504 17/26, 42, 61; 20/24, 79, 91, 119, 152, 188, 196; 21/56, 106; 19/112

Fawne, Ralph 20/152

Fawne, mistress ('maistris Fawne') 20/138

Fegarret, my lady see **Fitzgerald, Elizabeth St John**

Feherber see **Fitzherbert**

Felbywilliam see **Fitzwilliam**

Feldyng, sir Everard ('sir Everaude Feldyng', 'master Feldyng') 20/12, 22; 21/38

Fell, Robert ('Robert Fell', 'maister almeners brother', 'maister Felles/Fellis brother') brother of William Fell (q.v.) 19/19–20, 27, 40

Fell, William ('ma(i)ster/doct(o)ur Fell(e)', 'sir Wyllyam', 'doctour Felle (my ladyes) aumnour' 20/123, etc.; 'maister Fell amenere (to my ladys grace)' 21/124) (d. 1527/28) fellow of Magdalen College, Oxford; Lady Margaret's almoner from at least November 1503 (20/123) until at least May 1507 (19/19) when he was in Rome and was replaced by Bekinsall (q.v.) 17/21, 34, 40, 43, 51; 20/39, 40, 58, 102, 123; 21/124; 19/19, 27, 40, 54 (see too **ALMONERS** for references with no name)

FELONS see **PRISONERS and felons**

Fench(e) see **Fynch**

Fenton, John of Liddington 20/115

Fermor, Robert ('Robert Fermor my ladys sheppard') 20/35

Ferrers see **Grey, Thomas**

[R]**Ferror, Robert** ('Robert Fer(r)ore/ Ferrour') 21/129; 19/93, 95; 56/3

Fertheng/Ferthyng see **Farthing**

Fessher see **Fisher**

[R]**le Fevour, Leonard** ('Lenard/Leonarde (grome) of (the) vestry/vestre', 'Leonard (de la Fave', 'Lenard le Fevour') groom of the vestry; scribe and bookbinder 20/11, 14, 30, 39, 91, 102, 111, 122, 186–7; 21/16, 20, 38, 39, 75, 144; 19/23, 37–8, 70, 90, 105, 112–13, 117; 1/6v; 56/3

Fezaunt, Christopher 20/81

Fe(z)herber/Feharbour/Fyherberde see **Fitzherbert**

Fiyse, Richard 21/112

Fynch, mistress ('(mistress) Fynch(e)/ Fench(e)') silkwoman of London; wife of James Finch, freeman of London 17/23; 20/20, 25, 33, 42, 54–5, 82, 98–9; 21/109; 19/92; 2/15, 16, 17, 33

Fyndon, Richard 20/62

[R]**Fippownd, Robert** 56/5

Fisher, (Agnes) mother of John Fisher (q.v.) 20/178

Fysher, Henry ('Henry Fysher/Fessher', 'Fyssher of the chapell') member of Lady Margaret's chapel 20/122; 21/140; 19/45

[W]**Fisher, John** ('my lord(e) of Rochestre/ Rochester/Rochestour' 10/132; 'maister Fys(s)her' 20/24, 29, 124, 149; 19/31; 'maister Fyssher reder of my ladys lectures in divinitie in Cambryge' 20/37, 'maister Fessher my ladys reder in Cambryge' 20/46, etc., 'my lord suffrycan' (20/172 but without name), 'my lord of Rochester' 20/178, 179, etc.) (mart. 1535) D.Th. Cambridge 1501 (but styled master (corrected from doctor) as late as February 1504, 20/147); Lady Margaret divinity reader Cambridge 1502; confessor by 25 March 1504 (20/161154); bishop of Rochester by October 1504 (20/178); life-chancellor of Cambridge University 1504; an executor of Lady Margaret's will 10/132, 151, 153; 16/4; 20/24, 29, 37, 46, 128, 147, 172, 178–9; 21/11, 20, 24, 37, 44, 58–9, 63, 75, 99, 134–5, 141; 19/9, 12, 17, 21, 23, 29, 31–2, 35, 42, 55, 59, 70, 72, 75–6, 78, 88–9, 93, 101, 107, 110, 112

Fisher, (Robert) brother of John Fisher (q.v.); steward of his household 19/72

FISHERMEN 20/31–2; 21/30

FISH MERCHANT see **Burbage**

Fysiere, John 2/22

Fyssh, John ('Johannem Fissh valettum panetrie', 'John Fyssh(e)/Fissh(e)') yeoman of the pantry to Lady Margaret 16/21, 2d–4d; 17/21, 34–5, 40, 44, 52; 20/13, 83; 21/111

Fyssher, (John) ('maister Fessher sargant', 'maister Fyshhere the juge' 20/18; 'maister Fessher oon of the juges of the Comen Place' 20/129, 'maister Fyssher the jugge' 20/137) a justice of the Common Pleas 20/18, 24, 124, 129, 137, 129, 149(?)

Fyssher, John ('John Fyssher of Stampforth') pewterer 20/50

(?)**Fitzeton, Thomas** ('Thomas Fzeyton/Zeton (merser)') mercer 2/16, 22

Fitzgerald, Elizabeth St John ('my lady Fegarett') (d. 1516) daughter of Oliver St John II (d. 1497), m. Gerald Fitzgerald (q.v.) 20/161

Fitzgerald, Elizabeth Zouche ('maistres Sowche') granddaughter of Elizabeth St John (half-sister of Lady Margaret); m. Gerald Fitzgerald, heir of Gerald Fitzgerald (q.v.) 20/84

Fitzgerald, Gerald ('the erle of Kyldare', 'my lorde of Cyldare/Kyldare') (d. 1513) 8th earl of Kildare, m. Elizabeth St John (q.v. sub **Fitzgerald**) 1496 20/109, 124, 170

Fitzherbert, Anthony ('Fizeherbare') (d. 1538) a justice of the Common Pleas 2/8

Fitzherbert, (Elizabeth) ('[mistress] Feharbour/Fe(z)herber/ Fitzherberd/ Fyharber/ Fyherberde') (?) gentlewoman to Elizabeth of York;

sister (?) of Anthony Fitzherbert (q.v.) 17/23, 24; 20/43, 84; 21/108, 111; 19/79, 89, 90; 1/4r

Fitzhugh, Alice Neville ('the olde lady Fithughe') widow of Henry Fitzhugh, 5th baron Fitzhugh (d. 1472) 19/99

Fitzhugh, George ('the dean(e) of Lyncolne') (d. 1505) dean of Lincoln 1483–1505 10/127; 17/56; 20/32

Fitzjames, Richard ('my lord of London' 10/131, 1/4v; 'the busshop of Rochest(e)re' 17/3, 5; 'the bysshop of Chichester' 21/37, 'my lord of Chechestur' 21/59, etc.; 'my lord of London' 19/60, etc., 'bysshop of London' 19/72, etc.) (d. 1522) bishop of Rochester and Lady Margaret's confessor 1497–1503; bishop of Chichester 1503–6; bishop of London 1506–22 17/3, 5; 21/37, 59, 61, 96; 19/60, 62, 72; 1/4v, 6v (see too **CONFESSOR**)

Fitzwalter, lord/lady see **Radcliffe**

Fitzwilliam, Bartholomew ('Bartyllmew the Jewse', 'Bartyl(l)mew Felbywilliam/ Fizewilliam') clothman 2/11, 13, 24

Fitzwilliam, George 19/91

Fitzwilliam, William (?) gentleman usher to Henry VII 20/129

Flecher, Richard ('Richard/Richart Flec(c) her') 16/17; 20/126b, 147, 149–50, 157, 167, 173, 179, 189; 21/38

[R]**Flemyng, Thomas** ('Thomas Flemyng grome porter') servant of Lady Margaret 20/117, 159; 56/3

FLEMINGS 20/113 (see too **Stuard**)

Flewde see **Lloyd**

Fligh, John ('Flee yemon of the kynges wardrop') yeoman of the wardrobe of robes to Henry VII 20/114

Fligh, mistress ('ma(i)stres/maistrez Flee/ Flye') 20/52, 68, 84, 85, 115, 126, 136

Flyntte of Collyweston 20/120; 21/46

Flower, Bernard ('Bernard the kynges glassyer') glazier to Henry VII 19/37

Fod(e)rby see **Fotherby**

Fodyll, John ('John Fodyll of Croydon shomakere') 21/118

[R]**Foke, John** 56/4

Fol(l)er see **Fowler**

FOOLS 17/33; 20/45; 19/76, 105 (see too **Assheton**, **Coksey/Korse**, **Patche**, **Peter**, **Philip**, **Reginald**, **Skip**)

FOOTMEN 17/50; 20/87, 104, 110, 127; 21/30, 49; 19/12, 76, 95; 1/4r-v, 9r (see too **footmen** sub **SERVANTS of Lady Margaret**

Forman, Andrew ('the bysshop of Morrey') (d. 1521) Scottish diplomat and bishop of Moray 1501–16 20/13; 21/35

Forrest, Edmund prior of Lanthony 17/43; 19/11; 1/14r

Forsett, Edward 10/130

Forster(e), Adam 20/15, 16, 18, 19, 33, 121

Forster, John ('John (Forster) brotherer/ browderer') embroiderer 20/31, 33, 89, 126b; 21/96, 98

Forster, Thomas ('(Thomas) Forster ('fottmen', 'of the wardrop of beddes)') footman to Lady Margaret 20/116; 21/33–4; 19/32

Fortescue, Adrian ('maister Foskewe', 'sir Adrian Fortscue/Fortescu knight/ knyght') 21/127, 1/6r, 18r

Foske, John ('syngyng man') 20/22

[W]**Fothede, John** ('John Fothed comptroller' 10/101, 'maister Fotehede comptrollere of my ladys howsehold' 10/182, 'maister countroller maister John Fothed' 21/129; 'master John Fotehed master of Michaellhouse' 10/132) master of Michaelhouse, Cambridge 1497–1510 (so called 10/132, 12 July 1509); controller of the household 1504–6 (first so called by name 10/101, 27 January 1505, last so called by name 21/129, September 1506) 10/101, 126, 132, 182; 21/129 (see too **CONTROLLERS** for references with no name)

Fotherby, (Simon) ('master/docto(u)r Fod(e) rby/Fotherby (of Oxforth)') aka Simon Grene; D.Th. Oxford by 1501; rector of All Hallows, Honey Lane 1494–1503, succeeded by Yonge (q.v.); rector of St Peter, Cornhill 1503–36 21/98, 143; 19/14, 38; 1/6r

[W]**Fowler, Edith** ('maistres/maystres/maistrez (Edyth/Edithe) Fo(w)ler/Foller') (d. 1514) gentlewoman to Lady Margaret; wife of Thomas Fowler (q.v.) 16/25, 26d; 10/126; 20/13, 16, 40, 59, 62, 78, 113, 120, 122, 126b, 150, 161, 162, 168, 171, 178, 186, 188; 21/9, 12, 23, 25, 27, 28, 33, 36, 37, 39, 45, 46, 47, 49, 50, 56, 57, 58, 63, 92, 93, 95, 98, 99, 102, 104, 105, 106, 107, 108, 112, 117, 118, 119, 121, 123, 125, 127, 128, 130, 133, 134, 135, 140, 141, 142, 143, 144, 150; 19/16, 19, 20, 21, 22, 23, 24, 27, 28, 29, 32, 33, 35, 36, 37, 41, 42, 44, 46, 48, 58, 70, 74, 75, 80, 88, 89, 90, 92, 101, 102, 105, 107, 108, 109, 111, 114; 1/6r, 8v, 9v, 11v, 12r, 14v

Fowler, Thomas ('maister Fol(l)er') (d. 1506) squire of the body and gentleman usher of the chamber to Edward IV and Richard III; husband of Edith Fowler (q.v.) 20/37, 96; 21/98
Fowlere, (William) dyer of London 2/34
W**Fox, Richard** ('my lorde of Dyrham' 17/55; 'my lord prive sell' 20/25; 'my lord(e) of Wenchester/Wynchester/ Wynchestre/Wynchestour', 'the bysshop/bisshop of Wenchester/ Wynchestre') (d. 1528) Keeper of the Privy Seal 1487–1516; bishop of Durham 1494–1501; bishop of Winchester 1501–28; an executor of Lady Margaret's will 10/132; 17/55; 20/25, 110, 117–18, 121, 137–8; 21/54, 60, 114; 19/42, 72, 89, 93, 100, 104, 107; 1/8v, 12v
Fox, Thomas priest and singing man 20/106
Franke, Thomas 10/29
Frankyn, Joan ('dame Johne Frankyn a nonne') 20/145
Fraunces, Elizabeth ('Elizabeth Fraunicez') 17/49
R**Fraunces, George** ('George Frauncez/ Fraunsez/Frauncesse', '(George) Fraunce(y)s') gentleman of Lady Margaret 17/22, 34, 41, 44, 46, 53; 20/11, 34, 37, 41, 46, 57, 80, 81, 83–4, 86, 88, 94, 97, 100, 104, 112–14, 116, 127, 147, 150–1, 153–5, 158, 162, 165, 168, 179, 183, 187, 190; 21/13, 18–19, 23, 30, 40, 46, 48, 56, 59, 92–3, 99, 102, 112, 119, 132–3, 142; 19/8–10, 14, 18–19, 21, 70, 77, 83–5, 87, 90, 94–6, 98, 107, 109; 1/11v, 12v, 16r, 18r; 56/1
Fraunces, John 20/103
Fraunces, (Thomas) ('(maister) Fraunces (fissyssion/physicion)', etc., 'Fraunces oon of the kynges physsicions') (?) yeoman of the almonry to Henry VII 20/86, 168, 179; 19/10
Fredsham, William 20/21
Free, master 20/57, 128
Freman, Nicholas of Collyweston 20/90, 111, 187
Fremyngham, doctor ('doctur Fremyngham provinciall of the blake freris') Dominican Provincial 21/97, 114, 143; 19/90
R**Fremingham, Robert** ('Robert Fremyngham') gentleman of Lady Margaret, acting treasurer of the chamber 1509 10/151, 162, 169; 21/10, 34, 58, 97, 111, 120, 132, 134–5; 19/9, 16–17, 23, 80, 85–6, 89, 91, 100, 104–5; 1/2r, 11r, 13v, 14v; 56/1
the FRENCH 17/48; 20/20, 82 ('foreinge woman', but same woman as 84), 84, 123; 19/99 (see too **Doryn, John, Meautis, Mychyn, Mylner**)
Fresell, William ('the pryour of Benham') Benedictine prior of Binham [Nfk] 19/99
Freston, Thomas child of Lady Margaret's chapel; scholar at Winchester 19/48
Frevell, Anne see **Rede, Anne Freville**
FRIARS 17/36; 20/41, 124, 147, 166; 21/11, 21, 126; 19/13, 30, 42, 92, 104; 1/5r, 7r (see too **Baron, Brenkley, Burnell, Candysshe, Deland, Fremyngham, Langley, Robert, Standish, Thomson, Wotton**)
  of Bedford 19/98
  of Boston 20/30, 32, 158, 178; 21/37, 139
  of Caernarvon ((?) *recte* **Carmarthen**) 20/111
  of Cambridge 21/28; 19/27–8, 100
  of Canterbury see **Langley**
  of Denbigh see **Robert**
  of France 20/80
  of Grantham 20/31
  of Greenwich 20/78, 114; 21/21, 57
  of Hitchin 21/123
  of Ireland 20/14
  of King's Langley see **Thomson**
  of Lichfield 20/115
  of Lynn 20/154, 156
  of London 1/9v
  of Newcastle 20/39
  of Richmond [Sur.] 19/10; 1/9v, 11r
  of Richmond [Yorks.] 19/97
  of Stamford 20/12, 147, 150, 155, 164, 187, 195; 21/12, 37, 139 (see too **Deland** and **Wotton**)
  of Ware 20/155; 21/20, 40, 60; 19/31, 87
Frye ('Frye the kyngez servante') servant of Henry VII 17/55, 63; 20/140
W**Frogenhall, Alexander** ('Alexander (Thrognall)', 'Alexandre Thrognall', 'Alysander Frogoll', probably also '(master) Frognall' but see **Richard** below) son of Richard Frogenhall and Mary St John, daughter of Oliver St John I (d. 1437/8); carver to Elizabeth of York 10/179, 180; 20/64, 78, 115, 126, 134, 189, 192, 194, 199; 21/40, 47, 77, 79, 104, 162–3; 19/56, 61, 123; **'the landes of Frongnall*es* in Kent', 'Thrognalles/Frognalles landes'** 10/23, 179–80
Frogenhall, Elizabeth ('Elyzabeth Frognell/ Frogolles') 20/111; 21/20, 126
Frogenhall, Margaret ('Margaret Frognal' (20/126), 'maistres Frognoll/Frognell/ Frognall', 'mastres Thrognall') wife of

Alexander Frogenhall (q.v.) 20/83, 115, 126, 134, 137, 147, 157, 188, 194, 200; 21/45, 75, 77, 104, 105, 116, 120, 122, 127, 140, 142, 149, 150, 157; 19/6, 28, 56
Frogenhall, Richard ('Richard Frognall', 'Richard Frognall and Alexander his broder' 20/64) brother of Alexander Frogenhall (q.v.) 20/64; 21/104
Frowyk, Elizabeth Carnevyle ('maistrez Frowyk') second wife of Thomas Frowyk (q.v.) 21/134
Frowyk, sir Thomas ('(maister) Frowyk/Frawyk (the kynges servaunt)', 'Frawyk sargant of lawe', 'my/the lord(e) Frowyk/Frawyk', 'my lorde chefe jugg') (d. 1506) chief justice of the Common Pleas 20/24, 33, 42; 21/26, 124, 127, 148; 19/95
Fzeyton see **Fitzeyton**

Gabryell see **Silvester**
Gaynynsshe, John ('my lord of Burgavennes servaunt') servant of George Neville (q.v.) 19/96
Galee, Richard ('Richard Gal(i)e/Galy/Gal(l)ey/Gal(l)ee') a feodary of Lady Margaret 10/5, 17, 19, 24, 26, 28–9, 33, 83, 140; 20/7, 28
GARDENERS 17/42; 20/27, 32, 41, 47, 53, 124, 160 (saffron setter); 21/25, 49, 144, 154; 19/11, 52, 81, 83; 1/13r; 2/10; 56/4 (see too **Baldwin**, **Hegge**, **Hill**, **Leghe**)
Gardyner, John ('John Gardyner (syngyng man)') 20/106, 154; 21/133
Gardyner, (John) ('Gardener(e)', 'Gardyner') John Gardyner of London, former owner of land at Great and Little Chesterford, Essex 20/126, 126c, 139
Garter King of Arms see **Wriothesley**
Gasyon 19/105
Gedding, William ('thabbot of Crowland') abbot of Crowland 1504–7 21/162
Geny(n)son, Christopher ('oon Genynson of Gregoryes ostill in Cambryge', 'Crystofer Genyson of Penbroke Hall in Cambryge') fellow of Pembroke College, Cambridge from 1505 21/53, 106
Genowe, Thomas ('Lumberd') a Lombard from Genoa 20/148
Gentyll, James mercer 21/150; 19/34, 110
George see **Newton**
Gerard see **Austen**
Gerrade/Gerawde see **Osbourne**
Gere see **Gower**
Gerott, John 20/152
Gerson, master John (d. 1429) chancellor of the University of Paris, once thought to be author of *Imitatio Christi* 20/122
Gesson, John (?) supplier of furs 19/12
Gybbon, William ('(William) Gyb(b)on', 'lytell Gybon') a ward of Lady Margaret 20/58, 68, 115; 21/13
Gibbs, Elizabeth ('my lady of Syon', 'the abbesse of Syon') abbess of Syon 1497–1518 20/85; 19/8, 120
de Gigli, Paolo ('Paull/Pawle/Polles/Paule Gygles', 'Poule/Paule Gyles/Giles') kinsman of Silvestro de Gigli (q.v.) 10/19; 20/17, 67, 87, 139; 2/27, 36; 6/4
de Gigli, Silvestro ('the bysshop/my lord of Worsetur/Worsettor') papal legate; bishop of Worcester 1498–1521 19/9, 39, 56, 58
Gyles see **Duwes**
Gilles, Richard ('Richard Gillez') 20/23
Gylliam 2/33
Gilmyn ('of the buttrye') servant of Henry VII 1/4v
Glasebury, Henry ('Henry Glasebury/of Lasebury') marshal of the king's minstrels 20/96; 21/109
Glaselere, Henry 2/33
Glasse see **Nicholas(son)**
GLAZIERS see **Flower**, **Stones**
GLOVERS 1/7v
God, John fur tailor 19/97I
GODCHILDREN 21/102; 19/28; 1/11r, 12r (see too **Blythe**, **Henry** (x 3), **Windsor**)
Godfrey, Garrett ('Gerard Godfryde') Cambridge book dealer 19/110
Godson, John ('maister (John) Godson/Gotson notory of lawe') legal notary 21/135, 147
Godston, Elizabeth ('Ellissabeth Godestoun') ward of Lady Margaret with her sister Jane (q.v.) 20/64
Godston, Jane ('Godstons doughter', 'Jane Godston(ys)/Gostone') daughter of William Godston; ward of Lady Margaret with her sister Elizabeth (q.v.); sold (but not Elizabeth) to John Turney (q.v.) 10/32, 112; 17/25, 20/20, 147
Goldyng, Edward 20/155
Goldsmyth, Thomas 19/107
GOLDSMITHS 20/12, 28, 33, 47, 50, 65, 77, 79, 127; 21/37, 92, 110, 117, 127; 19/9, 41 (see too **Arnold**, **Bruxelles**, **Debalbus**, **Kleton**, **Mundy**, **Russell**, **Schaa**, **van Utrecht**, **Wylliams**, **Wreythe**)

GOLDWORKERS 20/126c, 145; 19/5, 46, 72;1/15r; 2/17 (see too **Seno(we)**, **Wodward**)
Golsell/Golson/Gonsell, Margaret ('Merget/ Marget Golsell/Golson/Gonsell'; 'Mergett oon of my ladys wardes') a ward of Lady Margaret 10/182; 20/57, 78, 93; 'landes of the said Margaret' 10/182
[R]**Goodwyn, Robert** 56/3
Gordon, Katherine ('my lady Gordon') daughter of George, earl of Huntly; wife of Perkin Warbeck 1/8v
Gore/Go(o)er see **Gower**
Gough, Richard ('Richard(e) Go(u)gh(t)/ Gowghe (clerke of my ladys kechyne)') clerk of the kitchen to Lady Margaret 17/26, 47, 57; 20/106, 146, 182, 188; 2/8, 10, 16; 6/6
Gough, William 17/67
Gower, Jane ('(mastrez/ma(i)stres) Jane Gower(e)' 'Jane Go(o)er/Ger(e)', 'Jan(n)e Go(w)re') servant of Lady Margaret until 1504. after which supported by her (20/195) 17/25, 27; 20/16, 40, 52, 56, 66, 89, 138, 147, 175, 195; 21/24, 55, 71, 108, 119, 125, 144, 155; 19/17, 21, 35, 45, 51, 87, 90, 101, 102, 115
(?)**Gray** ('the haburdassere') 2/29
Gray, Nicholas clerk of works to Henry VII 20/42, 86
a GREEK 20/11
Gremsby see **Grymosby**
Grendell see **Gryndell**
Grene, sir John knight 10/21, 32; 21/4
Greneway (?) servant of Henry VII 20/109
Greves, sir William ('sir Wyllyam Greves', 'the vyker of Maxsey') priest; vicar of Maxey [Lincs.] 17/57; 20/11, 65
Greville, William ('Willyam/William Grevell', 'Grewell') 20/48, 56, 86, 149, 168; 21/19, 24, 55, 115; 19/13
Greville, mistress ('mastres Grewell') 17/39, 45
Grey, Anne Herbert ('my lady Powes/Powez') (d. 1506), daughter of William Herbert (d. 1469), 1st earl of Pembroke, and Anne Devereux; wife of John Grey (d. 1497), 1st baron Grey of Powis; had a room at Collyweston 10/55, 138, 141–2, 151; 20/5; 21/79, 120, 121, 124, 159, 162; 19/61, 123
Grey, Cecily Bonville ('my ladye Harryngton', 'my ladye his [the 1st marquess's] wiffe', 'the lady Gray') (d. 1530) daughter of William Bonville, Lord Harington, and Katherine Neville; m. (1) Thomas Grey, 1st marquess of Dorset (q.v.), (2) Henry Stafford (q.v.) 17/42, 45; 21/48
Grey, Edmund ('my lord Grey Welton') (d. 1511) ninth baron Grey of Wilton 21/40
Grey, Eleanor St John ('my lady marques(se)/ markes') daughter of Oliver St John II (d. 1497); m. Thomas Grey, 2nd marquess of Dorset (q.v.) 20/35, 45, 51, 78, 95, 97, 126b, 157, 161, 198; 19/39, 72; 1/4v (cited here sub **Eleanor St John**, but note that Cecily Bonville Grey (q.v.) was suo jure 'marques Harrington and Bonvill': TNA PROB 11/23/364)
Grey, Richard ('my lord (of) Kent') (d. 1524) 3rd earl of Kent 21/129; 19/6
Grey I, Thomas ('my lord(e) marques') (d. 1501) 1st marquess of Dorset; half-brother of Elizabeth of York m. (2) Cecily Bonville Grey (q.v.) 17/38, 45
Grey II, Thomas ('my lord marques(se)', 'my lord marqueyes', 'lord Ferres/Ferrys' 21/129) (d. 1520) baron Ferrers of Groby, 2nd marquess of Dorset; third son of 1st marquess and Cecily Bonville; m. Eleanor St John (q.v.) 20/53, 161, 176 ('John'); 21/21, 129
Gryffeth ('Greffithe', 'Gryffeth maister deans servand') servant of Henry Hornby (q.v.) 20/16, 23; 19/39
Grymosby ('Gremsby', Grymosby') 20/45; 21/7
Grymston, William 10/182
Gryndell, John ('[master] (John) Gryndell/ Grendell/Grendyll/Grindel') (?) servant of Lady Margaret 16/19; 10/133; 20/12, 16, 24, 33, 41, 47, 52, 53, 77, 79, 90, 95, 106, 107, 122, 123, 124, 126b, 145, 173, 176, 187; 21/9, 12, 30, 37, 42, 45, 47, 59, 96, 97, 110, 117, 141
Gryse, John 17/45
GROCER see **Grove**
[R]**Grome, John** (but perhaps John Hodgeson q.v.) 21/125; 19/9, 22, 29, 85; 1/14v; 56/5
Grove, (Roger) ('groser of London') 19/14
GUARDS and watches 21/48; 1/4v
GUIDES 20/175; 21/48, 95
[W]**Guildford, Jane Vaux** ('(my/the lady) Jane') lady in waiting to Elizabeth of York and then to Lady Margaret; sister of Nicholas Vaux (q.v.); second wife of

Sir Richard Guildford (d. 1506), controller of the household of Henry VII) 10/48; 21/58, 121 ('Jane'), 163; 19/44, 62–3, 81, 124–5; 1/10v, 12r
Guylpyne, Guyberde horsekeeper at Woking [Sur.] 17/28
Gwyny, Francis 2/26

de la Haghe, Ingelbert ('Engulbred', 'Ingleberd bokebynder') bookbinder and book dealer 21/43, 164; 19/62, 124
Haye, Oliver servant to Ralph Langford (q.v.) 10/5, 22
Halley, John of Wittering [Northants] 20/153, 162, 171
Hallwell, Richard 21/87
Hamden 20/176
Hamer, doctor scholar (untraced) 21/15
Hamerton, George ('the kynges servande') groom porter to Elizabeth of York; royal servant 20/16; 21/8, 16
Hamerton, William yeoman of the wardrobe of beds to Elizabeth of York 20/16
Hanson, (Edmund) ('doctor Hanson') (d. 1511) D.Th. Cambridge (no date); precentor of Lincoln from 1506; warden of Tattershall college 1508–11 10/133; 17/60
HARDWARE MAN see **Nicholas(son)**
Harper, (Richard) ('Herper late my ladys receyvour of the duke of Bokynghams landes') (d. 1492) Lady Margaret's receiver for the lands of Edward Stafford, 3rd duke of Buckingham; m. Elizabeth Skrene (q.v. sub **Dymock**) 21/4
Harpesfeld, Lewis mercer of London 1/14r
Harington, lady see **Grey, Cecily Bonville**
Haryngton, (William) ('doctur/maister Har(r)yngton') D.C.L. Bologna 1499; canon of St Paul's 1497; rector of St Anne's, Aldgate 1506 20/37, 88, 117; 21/132, 144
R**Haryson, John** ('John Harison/Har(r)yson/Her(r)yson', 'lord of disportes') servant of Lady Margaret; lord of misrule at New Year festivities 20/22, 60–1, 67, 94, 105, 126, 137, 190; 21/23, 30, 61, 63, 77, 93, 98, 144–7, 159; 19/5, 8, 18, 24, 27–8, 47, 59, 74, 85, 111–12, 121; 56/2
Haryson, Richard 20/191
Harry see **Wynstanley**
Harris, John ('servand unto maister Curson') (q.v.) 20/27
Harvey, Davy ('Davy Hervy') servant of Thomas Stanley I (q.v.) 20/39, 171
Haselwode, Thomas 2/2
R**Hasilby, John** (?) servant of Lady Margaret 1/13v; 56/3
Hasulrygg, Robert ('Hasulryg(g) (grome of the beddes with the kyng)', 'Robert Hasilrig of the wardrobe of the kinges beddes') groom of the wardrobe of the beds to Henry VII 20/42, 86, 109–10, 163; 19/95; 1/4v
Hastings, Edward ('my lord Hastynges') (d. 1506) Edward, 2nd baron Hastings, son of William, 1st baron Hastings and Katherine Neville (q.v. sub **Hastings**) 20/11
Hastings, Katherine Neville ('my (old) lady(e) Hastynges/Hastinges') (d. 1504) daughter of Richard Neville, earl of Salisbury, and Alice Montagu; m. (1) William Bonville, Lord Harrington (d. 1460), (2) William Hastings, 1st baron Hastings (exec. 1483); mother of Cecily Bonville Grey (q.v.) 20/19, 41, 121
Hatton, Richard ('provoust of the Kynges Colleige in Cambrige') (d. 1509) provost of King's College, Cambridge 1507–9; chaplain to Henry VII 1/9r
Haute, Jacques servant of Elizabeth of York; esquire to Henry VII and organiser of court festivities 17/45
Haw, Joan ('domine Johanne Haw') nun 16/2
Haward, Edward priest 10/148; 19/3, 9, 59
Hawke, Thomas 10/158
Hechyn see **Hochyn**
Hede, master officer of John Fisher, bishop of Rochester (q.v.) 19/31
Hegge, William ('Wyllyam (H)egge (jardyner)') gardener to Lady Margaret 20/20, 44
Heymound see **Nicholas(son)**
Heyton, Roger ('maister chauncellers servande') servant of Hugh Oldham 20/44, 95, 128, 150
Henyngham, John 20/194
Henyngham see **Heveningham**
Henry VI ('king Henry') 19/94
W**Henry VII** ('the kyng(e)' 17/25, 'kyng(e) Harry (the viith)', 'the kynges grace') 10/20, 35, 39, 44, 55, 69, 75, 147–8, 152, 161; 17/1–2, 19, 25, 28–9, 31, 33, 38, 41–2, 48, 50, 53, 55, 63, 66–7; 20/11, 16, 19–20, 23–4, 34, 36, 38–40, 42, 46, 49, 53, 56–9, 61–2, 80, 91, 94, 96–7, 100, 105–6, 109–17, 121–3, 125–6, 126c, 127–8, 135, 137, 139–40, 145–6, 156, 162–3, 166, 169, 183, 189–91, 198; 21/8–9, 11, 14, 18–19, 23, 25–6, 30, 34, 40–1, 43–4,

[W]**Henry VII** (*Cont.*) 47–50, 52, 55, 57, 59–60, 62–3, 66–7, 71–4, 76, 79, 91, 93, 97, 99, 102–3, 106, 109–10, 112, 114, 117, 120, 122–3, 132, 144, 147, 150, 154–5; 19/3, 7–8, 11–12, 14–17, 21, 22–4, 27–9, 32–4, 36–7, 39, 44–5, 48, 52–5, 58–9, 66, 74, 76–7, 83, 85, 87, 89–102, 104–5, 109–11, 113, 116, 118–21, 125; 1/4v, 5r, 6v, 11r, 12r, 13r, 13v, 14v, 17r

Henry, duke of York/Prince of Wales (later Henry VIII) ('my lorde of Yorke' 17/25, 20/21; 'the prynce' 20/127, 'my lord prynce/prince' 21/25, 28) (d. 1547) second son of Henry VII; created duke of York 1494 (17/25, 20/21); Prince of Wales after the death 1502 of his brother Arthur (q.v.); Henry VIII 1509–47 17/25; 20/21, 127, 170; 21/25, 28, 100, 103, 155; 19/34, 57, 80, 90, 94, 97, 99, 119; 1/4v, 6r, 17r; 2/33

Henry ('Henry almoigner/amener (at Basse)', 'maister almoigner') almoner at Basse (see the PLACES index) 20/28, 83; 19/76

Henry ('Harry/Henry fotman') see **Wynstanley**

Henry servant of Mary Fitzlewis Rivers (q.v. sub **Neville**) 19/58, 69, 71

Henry ('Henry of Lasebury') see **Glasebury**

Henry ('the kynges olde godson', 'old(e) Herry/Henri the kynges godson') Henry VII's older godson (compared to 'yonge Henry' below); (?) Henry Pynago (rewarded in Nicolas, ed., *Privy Purse Expenses* for 1493, 1498, 1499) 21/23, 71, 154

Henry ('yonge Henry', '(Henry) the kynges godson', same as 'litell Henry' 21/101(?)) (?) Henry Guildford (born 1489), third son of Sir Richard Guildford and his second wife Jane Vaux Guildford (q.v.) 20/125–6; 21/14, 41, 62, 71, 101, 123, 132, 147; 19/29, 45, 83, 87, 110

[R]**Henry** ('Henry/Henri my ladys/ladis godson(ne)') (?) same as 'litell Henry' 21/101) Lady Margaret's godson; (?) Henry Guildford above 21/32, 41, 94, 100–1, 154; 56/1

Henryson, John 1/14v

HERALDS and pursuivants 17/64; 21/121; 19/90 (see too **Carlisle, Machado, Slacke, Videt, Wriothesley**)

Herbert, Henry ('sir Herry Erbet knyght') member of the Herbert family (see **Grey, Anne Herbert** and **Somerset, Charles**) 10/102

HERMITS 17/25; 20/34, 37, 39, 61, 92, 154, 160; 21/12; 19/87–8, 99; 1/6r

Heron, Anne ('maistres/Anne Heron') 19/110; 1/6r (perhaps 'the heirez of Herons' 19/116, but see too **Herons** in the PLACES index)

Heron, John ('on of the kyngez servantes') (d. 1522) knight; treasurer of the chamber to Henry VII and Henry VIII 1492–1521 17/1, 5, 20; 20/126, 139

Heron, Nicholas ('sir Nicholas Heron knight') 10/140

Herper see **Harper**

Hethe, Robert 20/179

Heven, Edward ('Edward(e) Heven/Hevyn(s)/He(y)von', 'Edward') bailiff of Boston; steward of Tattershall 10/24; 17/21, 22, 41, 52; 20/11, 23, 27, 32, 48–50, 157–8, 178; 21/139; 19/23, 32, 53, 79, 91–2, 118; 1/7r, 8r

[R]**Heveningham, George** ('maister/George Hev(en)yngham(e)', 'George Hen(n) yngham', 'Hevengham') gentleman of Lady Margaret 10/158; 20/6, 12, 64, 134, 166; 21/79, 162; 19/32, 41, 53, 61; 19/123; 56/5

Hyde ('the quenys servande') servant of Elizabeth of York 20/61

Hyde, Nicholas ('the kynges servand') servant of Henry VII 20/190

Hyggeson, John ('oon of the gromes of the stabell') servant of Lady Margaret 20/19

Hill, John servant of Thomas Stanley I (q.v.) 17/57; 20/150; 19/23

Hill, Thomas of Croydon 16/15d

[R]**Hill, Thomas** ('Thome Hyll', 'Thomam Hill valettum lardarii') yeoman of the dry larder 16/2, 11d, 13d; 56/3

[R]**Hyll, Thomas** ('Thomas Hyll ... jardyner') gardener to Lady Margaret 20/20, 44, 103, 154

[W]**Hilmer, William** ('William Hilmere/Hylmer'; 'Willelmum Elmer(e) (clericum spicerie)', etc. (called 'Elmer' in Lady Margaret's will); perhaps also 'master Elmes/Elmez' 20/59, 104, 117 but see **Elmes**) yeoman of the chamber; clerk of the spicery; physician to Lady Margaret 16/19d, 21d, 23d–8d; 10/29, 52, 104; 17/46, 55, 63; 20/17, 18; 20/23, 29, 32–3, 36, 38, 40, 47, 51, 57, 78, 82, 84, 94, 97, 107, 120, 128, 147, 153, 168, 175, 180, 188, 194; 21/7, 21, 25, 33, 57, 61, 75, 113, 117, 120–1; 19/6,

18, 33, 72–3, 75, 81, 88, 100–02, 108, 117, 119, 125; 1/4v, 9r, 11v, 14v

[R]**Hilton, Robert** ('Robart/Robert/Roberd(e) Hilton/Hylton', 'the grome') groom, later yeoman of the wardrobe, to Lady Margaret 17/35, 41, 44, 47, 53; 20/13, 23, 25, 35, 41, 47, 54, 80–1, 92–94, 112, 124–5, 148, 150–2, 158, 167, 169, 175, 177, 179, 181; 21/7, 13–14, 17, 31, 33–4, 41, 42, 50–1, 54, 64–5, 80, 94, 100–2, 105–6, 109, 111, 116, 122, 136–8, 149–50; 19/6, 12–13, 25–26, 34–8, 40–1, 43, 46–7, 51, 73–4, 93, 97–8, 102–3, 106, 111–13, 115, 125; 1/11r, 16r, 17v; 2/28; 56/5

Hynkersall ('grome de le scolery') servant of Lady Margaret 16/4d

Hobard clothman 2/23

Hobson, Thomas ('Thomas Hobsom auditour', 'Hobbson my ladys auditour', 'maister Hobson', '(master) audit(o)ur/awditur') master auditor to Lady Margaret 16/20; 10/22, 23, 62; 17/21; 20/7, 11–12, 194 (Appendix); 21/92; 19/69, 109

Hochyn, (John) ('[master] Hochyn/Hechyn', 'Thomas Pellettes tewtere (at Cambryge)', etc.) (d. 1521) B.Th. Cambridge (no date); fellow of Jesus College; junior proctor at University 1502–3; University preacher 1505–6; tutor to Thomas Pellett (q.v.) 20/22, 61, 120, 159, 178

Hodale, Thomas 21/91

Hodgeson, John ('John Ho(d)geson (oon of the gromes of the stabyll)', 'John Hodson grome of the stabyll') groom of the stable to Lady Margaret 20/172; 21/126

Holden, Thomas ('keper of the place at Westmester') keeper of the palace of Westminster 21/40, 112; 19/76

Holden, William of Southwark 16/19

Holland, John ('a servante of þe quenez ... John Hollonde') keeper of the council chamber to Elizabeth of York 17/57

Holland, Oliver ('Olyver Hol(l)and(e)', 'Oliver Holand yoman ussher of my ladys chambere') yeoman usher of the chamber to Lady Margaret 10/103; 20/116, 121, 146, 153, 155, 160, 166, 168, 177, 179, 194; 21/9, 18, 53, 65, 66, 79, 127, 128, 162, 163; 19/61, 62, 103, 123, 124

Holland, Roger ('Roger Hollande/Holond (of the west countre)') 21/58, 72; 2/33

Holt, John servant of Roger Ormeston 20/88, 152, 165, 177; 21/7, 11, 21, 23, 40, 49, 52–4, 60, 95, 108, 114, 121, 139, 147; 19/5, 9, 18, 27, 29, 32, 36, 43, 77, 85, 90, 99–100, 102, 107–8

Hoo, John ('John Hoo/How (late reve off Cheshunt)') former reeve of the estate of Cheshunt [Herts.] 10/29, 58; 19/15

Hopkyn, Robert 16/2

Hopwode, Ralph (?) scribe 21/143

Hopwode, Robert ('maister tresorers servande') servant of William Bedell (q.v.) 20/118

Horman, William fellow and vice-provost of Eton 1502–35 19/90

[W]**Hornby, (Henry)** ('master Horn(e)by(e)', 'maister Horneby my ladies chanceller' 1/5r, 7v) (d. 1518) Lady Margaret's secretary and dean of chapel; after Nov 1504/Jan 1505 chancellor of household after Oldham (q.v.); master of Peterhouse, Cambridge from 1501; master of Tattershall from 1502 10/77, 132, 182; 17/3, 24–5, 66–7; 1/5r, 7v (see too **SECRETARY** and **DEAN** for references which do not name Hornby; see too **CHANCELLOR** for references without a name attached)

Horne, William coppersmith 2/12–13, 15–17; 6/3

Hornywold, John 19/39

Hornywold, William ('maister deanes servand') servant of Henry Hornby (q.v.) 20/79

HORSE DEALERS see **Bradley**, **Penred**

HORSE KEEPERS 17/27–8, 43, 49; 20/39, 44, 53, 150, 161; 21/56, 97, 121; 19/89 (see too **Guylpyne**, **Penred**)

HORSEMEN 19/15, 33

HOSTS 20/85; 21/125

Houghton, William tanner of Cheshunt [Herts.] 16/19

Howard, Agnes Tilney ('my lady of Surraye', 'my lady Surre') (d. 1545) second wife (m. 1497) of Thomas Howard, earl of Surrey (d. 1524) 10/127; 19/79

[W]**Howard, Alice Lovell Parker** ('my lady Morley', 'his moder') sister and heir of Henry Lovell, 8th baron Morley; m. (1) Sir William Parker (q.v.) (2) Sir Edward Howard (q.v.); mother of Henry Parker (q.v.) 10/144; 19/35, 118

Howard, Edward knight, son of Thomas Howard, earl of Surrey; second husband (m. 1506) of Alice Lovell Parker Howard (q.v.) 19/41

ap Howel, John mercer of London 10/158

Hubbekes 21/20

Hudilston, Oliver ('baliff of Wasshingborogh') bailiff of Washingborough [Lincs.] 10/25
Hudleston, William 19/73
Hugh see **Ashton**
Humphrey ('Umfrey hir [lady Powis] servant') servant of Anne Herbert Grey (q.v.) 21/124
Hungerford, Jane Bulstrode ('my lady Hungerforth') wife of Sir Walter Hungerford (q.v.) 20/104, 169
Hungerford, Walter ('my lorde Hungerforth') (d. 1516) 20/116
Huntingdon, John ('thabbot of Ramesey') abbot of Ramsey 1489–1506 20/176
Hussey, John ('[sir] (John) Hus(s)y/Hus(i)e/Husye', 'maister Hussy') (exec. 1529) steward of the manors of Deeping and Maxey (and many other places in Lincs.); member of Lady Margaret's council; master of the king's wards 1503 10/2; 20/126c, 139, 165, 173; 21/11, 74, 124, 126, 159; 19/22, 99
Hussey, Robert ('Robert Hussy', '[sir Husie and] his broder') brother of Sir John Hussey (q.v.) 20/126c, 139
Hussey, Ursula Lovell ('maistres Husse') wife of William Hussey (q.v.); niece of Sir Thomas Lovell (q.v.) 19/86
Hussey, William ('William Hussy') son of Sir John Hussey (q.v.) 20/139(?); 21/109
Hutton, John (?) father of Thomas Hutton (q.v.) 10/1
Hutton, Thomas ('doctor Thomas Hutton') D.C.L. Cambridge 1474–5; prebendary of York and Lincoln; executor of will of John Hutton (q.v.) 10/1

Idyll, Thomas ('sir Thomas Idyll late parson of Malton', 'the parson late of Malton') former priest of Malton [Cambs.] 19/14, 47, 53
Yngellysby, Thomas ('grom of the stabell') servant of Lady Margaret 20/115
Ingleberd see **de la Haghe**
[R]**Inkersall, Robert** 56/4
Innez, John of Stamford [Lincs.] 20/64
INNKEEPERS 20/33; 19/39, 42 (see too **Loman** and see the PLACES index sub **Buntingford**, **Croydon**, **Hatfield**, **London**)
IRISHMEN 20/14, 36
Isabel, lady see **Lovell**
Islip, John ('thabbott of Vestmester', 'the abbott of Westmynster') abbot of Westminster 1500–32 20/151, 159; 21/27, 40, 59, 132, 139, 144, 149; 19/18, 44, 69, 71, 109

Jay, William of London 16/17
JAILERS 21/35
Jak of Lyddington 20/91
Jakes see **Yarwell**
Jakson ('Jakson/Jacson') shoemaker of Stamford [Lincs.] 20/15, 152; 21/15
Jakson of Windsor 17/25
Jakson, John ('master (John) Jakson (a skoller of my ladys in Oxfforde)', 'maister Jakson (of Cambryge)') supported by Lady Margaret at Oxford (1498) 17/50; 21/66, 92
James ('Jamys the kynges purcyvant') see **Videt**
James ('Jamys sadelere') see **Atkynson**
James ('sir James') see **Plowgh**
James servant of William Bolton (q.v.) 2/8, 29
Jan see **Yan**
Jane see **Guildford, Jane Vaux**
Jane, Elizabeth 20/15
Jenet, Ralph ('of the wardrobe of the kinges beddes') yeoman of the wardrobe of beds to Henry VII 1/4v
Jenson, Robert servant to Cecily Welles (q.v. sub **Kyme**) 20/156
JEW see **Bartholomew**
Jobourn, John prior of the charterhouse at Sheen 21/35
Jogeler, Matthew servant of John de Vere (q.v.) 20/119
John ('Johannis a Greve') 16/10d
John ('master John my ladys coke') cook to Lady Margaret (see **Browne**)
John ('John browderer/brotherer') embroiderer, prob. John Forster (q.v.)
John ('John cart takere') carter 19/12
John ('John fot(t)man/fo(o)teman') footman to Lady Margaret (see **Williams**)
John ('kyng John', perhaps jocular, cf. 'lord(e) John' below; perhaps John Kyng (q.v.)) 21/41, 45
John ('my lord John at Hatfeld', 'the lorde John [at Rychmond]', unidentified) 21/27, 72
John ('(John) the French(e) chyld') French child supported by Lady Margaret 20/20, 29, 64, 126
John ('John his [Hornby's] servande') servant of Henry Hornby (q.v.) 20/159
Johnson, Elizabeth 17/26
Johnson, Thomas prisoner at the Marshalsea 19/10
Joyner, John ('John Joyner/Joynes') of Stamford [Lincs.] 20/103, 134, 194

JOINERS 17/59; 20/32, 187; 19/24, 29, 80; 6/4; 1/8v; 6/3 (see too **Reve**, **Stoughton**)
Joys, William 2/32
Jok(e)/Jokye ('one of the gromes of the stabyll') groom of the stable to Lady Margaret 17/56; 20/97; 21/19, 121, 139
Jon see **Yan**
Jones, Eleanor ('[mistress] Alienor/Elnore (Johannes)', 'Elynour Jonys') gentlewoman to Elizabeth of York 17/49; 20/83; 19/72
Jones, Robert ('Robert Joohns/Jones/Jonys (gentilman usshur)') gentleman usher to Henry VII 20/109; 19/86, 97; 1/4v
Jones, William 6/5
Jubbes/Jubbis/Jubbys/Jobbys see **Chubbes**
Julius II Pope 1503–13 19/83, 104
Justice ('the quene of Skottes servande') servant of Margaret, Queen of Scots (q.v.) 20/173, 183; 21/60
Justyce, William ('supervisorem boscorum et focalis domine') supervisor of woods and fuel for Lady Margaret's household 16/8, 20

Kardon, Roger servant of Lady Margaret 17/22, 27, 34, 40, 44, 47, 52, 54
Karre see **Carr(e)**
Katherine, my lady see **Courtenay, Katherine Plantagenet**
Katherine of Aragon ('my lady princesse of Wales' 1/4v, 7v; 'my lady/the princesse of England' 1/9r, 12v, 13v) 1/4v, 7v, 9r, 12v, 13v
KEEPER of the camel 19/104
KEEPERS of palaces, parks, gardens, etc. 21/111
  of Benefield 20/117
  of Bletchingley 21/49
  of Bletsoe 21/38
  of Bromley 21/44; 19/31
  of Buckden 20/43
  of Cheshunt 19/32
  of Coldharbour see **Baldwin**
  of Collyweston 21/144, 154; 19/17
  of Derby House, London see **Wettnall**
  of Eltham see **Skelman**
  of Hampton Court 21/25
  of Harringworth 20/49, 116
  (?) **of Hatfield** 21/122; 19/17, 21
  of Henry Hornby's manor 19/101
  of jewel houses 20/159 (see too **Bothe**)
  of the king's galleries see **Anthony**
  of the king's garden 19/11
  of the king's library see **Faques**
  of the lion 19/97
  of the little park 19/17
  of Ludgate prison 19/10
  of Marshalsea prison 19/10
  of Maxey 20/170
  of Newgate prison 19/10
  of Richmond park 21/25, 38, 122; 19/11 (garden); 1/4r
  of Rockingham 20/114
  of Westminster abbey 21/40; **palace** see **Holden**
  of Windsor 21/23
Keham, master 20/194 ((?) see **Kyme**)
Kelke, Richard 20/66
Kelle, master 20/158
Kemy(a)s, John 20/59; 21/46
Kempe, William 19/89, 90
Kent, my lord (of) see **Grey, Richard**
Kettell, Agnes ('Annes Kettell won of the almeswomen') almswoman of Lady Margaret 19/24
Kildare, earl of see **Fitzgerald, Gerald**
Kylke, William servant of mistress Talbot (q.v.) 20/104, 138
[R]**Kylner, William** ('Willelmum Kylner(e)/ Kilnere (valettum chaundere)') yeoman of the chandlery 16/18, 20, 12d, 16d–17d; 56/2
Kylt(e), Richard servant of Lady Margaret 17/22, 34, 40, 44, 52; 20/27, 29
Kyme, Cecily Plantagenet Welles ('domina Cecilia', 'my lady Cessell/Cecill/Cicill/ Cycell/Cecell/Cecile/Cescell/Cissell') (d. 1507) daughter of Edward IV; m. (1) Ralph Scrope (annulled), (2) John Welles (q.v.), (3) 1502 Thomas Kyme (q.v.) 16/7; 10/60, 143, 147, 151; 20/14, 22, 88, 113, 126b, 147–8, 151, 156; 19/12, 23, 30, 32–5, 44–5, 59
Kyme, Thomas ('my lady Cicill and hir husbonde') husband of Cecily Welles (q.v. sub **Kyme**) 10/143 ((?) see too **Keham**)
Kyng, John ('John Kyng somtyme coke to my lord of Derby') former cook of Thomas Stanley I (q.v.) 1/4r
King, Oliver ('my lord of Bath') bishop of Bath and Wells 1495–1503 10/1
Kynge, John ('my ladys servante') servant of Lady Margaret 17/39, 47, 52
Kynge, John of Biggleswade 10/23(?); 20/42, 78
Kyngysland, John 20/35
Kynokes ('my ladys servand') servant of Lady Margaret 20/47
Kirkbye ('Kyrkbye/Kirkeby, Kyrbe/Kyrby') clothman 20/57, 111; 2/16, 31

Kirkham, George ('(George) Kyrk(h)am/ Kyrkeham(e)/Kirk(e)ham (clerk of the kynges hamper)') clerk of the hanaper to Henry VII 20/44, 77, 194 (Appendix), 200; 21/39, 72; 19/39, 45, 58

Kirton, Robert ('the abbot of Peturburgh', 'thabbott of Peturborogh') abbot of Peterborough 1496–1528 10/23, 132;20/148, 161, 172–3, 183; 21/9

KITCHEN BOYS 16/14

Kleton, John ('goldsmyth') 20/188

Knyvett, Joan Stafford Beaumont ('my lady(e) Bemownde/Beamount ') daughter of Humphrey Stafford (d. 1460), 1st duke of Buckingham; m. (1) William, 2nd viscount Beaumont (annulled), (2) Sir William Knyvett (q.v.) 17/33; 19/93

Knyvett, William ('sir William Knevet', 'maister stuard(e)') (d. 1515/16) steward of Lady Margaret's household by 1501–2 (TNA REQ 2/4/246); second husband of Joan Stafford (q.v. sub **Knyvett**) 2/34; 20/53, 170, 179; 21/30; 19/79

Knolles, (Robert) ('Knollez/Knolles/Knowles', 'Knowles gentilman ussher with the kinges grace') gentleman usher of the chamber to Henry VII 20/109; 21/27; 19/11, 94

Knott, Richard 16/2d

Knotte, Henry 16/22

Koke 2/30

Korse see **Coksey**

Laborer, Richard 20/15, 41, 53, 95, 169; 19/24, 106

Laborer, William ('Wyllyam Laborer (oon of the gromes of the stabyll)') servant of Lady Margaret 20/24, 50; 21/42, 132; 19/34, 93, 97I, 101, 108

LABOURERS 20/33, 53; 21/31, 49, 147; 19/6, 19, 83; 1/15v; 2/35

Lacy, master ('(maister) Laice/Lacy(e) (fesicion)') physician to Elizabeth of York 17/62; 20/84, 192

Lacy, mistress ('mastres/mastrez Lacye', 'maistres Layce/Lacy') 17/23, 49; 20/45–6, 100, 178; 21/28

LADY MARGARET PREACHERS AND READERS 20/65; see **Fawne**, **Fisher**, **Roper**, **Smyth**, **Wilsford**

Laghton, Richard of Stamford [Lincs.] 20/18

Laythun, Robert 2/22

Lake, Robert 16/18

Lambe, Walter ('Water Lambe of Wensor syngyng man') gentleman and composer of St George's chapel, Windsor 20/40

Langdale ward of Lady Margaret 21/128

Langford, Ralph ('sir Rauf(e) Langford/ Langforth/Lo(u)ngford') 10/4–5, 17, 22; 1/4v

Langley, friar ('frere Langley warden of the gray freris at Canturbury') warden of the Franciscan friars of Canterbury 21/93

Langlond, Thomas receiver to Sir William Parker (q.v.) 10/144

Langton 10/3

Langton, John 16/18 (perhaps same as above)

Langton, mistress 2/35; 6/3, 4

Lanon, Richard 2/31

Lathe, master 17/58

Lathom, Ralph ('Rauff(e) La(y)thum', 'Rauf Lathom') 20/42, 156, 194

Latymer, Hugh ('Hew/Hugh(e)/Heugh Latymer (my ladys servante)') servant of Lady Margaret 17/46, 47, 49, 60, 61(?); 20/13, 31, 44, 53, 90, 127, 157, 161, 163, 184

LAUNDERERS 17/46; 20/88, 168; 21/27; 19/11, 46, 86, 95; 1/11v

Laurence ('lytell Laurence grome of the chambre') groom of the chamber to Henry VII 19/86

Laurence, Thomas knight (see Jones and Underwood, *The King's Mother*, p. 134) 10/29

Lawe, Robert 19/39

LAWYERS
- **appraisers/valuers** 10/141; 19/45
- **attorneys** 20/20, 25 (see too **Brudenell**, **Castell**, **Empson**, **Mychyn**, **Mordaunt**, **Skipwith**)
- **beadle** 19/42
- **clerks** 17/21; 20/159, 175, 189, 197 (see too **Cutler**)
- **clerk of the privy seal** 17/42
- **clerks of the signet** 17/35; 20/156; 21/8; 19/8; 1/4v (see too **Meautis**)
- **doctors of the Arches** 20/122
- **escheators** 21/148–9; 19/42, 54 (see too **Churche**, **Mynkskyp**, **Molson**)
- **feodaries** see **Bothe**, **Galee**, **Morgan**
- **justices of the Common Pleas** 21/73 (see too **Fyssher**, **Fitzherbert**, **Frowyk**, **Mordaunt**)
- **king's remembrancer of the Exchequer** see **Blagge**
- **Lord Chancellor** see **Warham**
- **Master of the Rolls** see **Bainbridge**
- **notaries** see **Carter**, **Godson**, **Peter**, **Scales**
- **officer of the Court of Chancery** see **Malhame**

officer of the Exchequer see **Castell**
principal of Barnard's Inn 20/192
proctors of the Court of Arches see **Coles, Myddelton**
sergeants at law 20/118 (see too **Brudenell, Conyngsby, Fyssher, Frowyk, Leghe, Moore, Mordaunt, Nevell, Quttyler**)
sheriffs 20/103 (see too **Dudley, Nynes, Shore, Woodhull**)
solicitors see **Empson, Soper**
Laxam, Jane 21/37
Leche, Agnes (d. 1527–1531) anchoress at church of St Paul, Stamford [Lincs.]; admitted to St Katherine Guild 1496 (see **ANCHORESSES**)
Leche, John servant of Lady Margaret 17/34, 40, 41, 44, 46, 47, 52; 20/26
Leghe, Elizabeth ('Elyzabeth Leghe', 'mastres Lee') gentlewoman to Elizabeth of York 17/49; 20/86
[R]**Leghe, John** ('John Leghe/Leigh/Lee(gh) (jardyner)') 20/154; 19/80, 85; 1/15r, 15v; 56/2
[W]**Leghe, Robert** ('(Robert) Leghe', 'Leghe sergant') sergeant at law 20/57, 128
Leonard (of the vestry) see **le Fevor, Leonard**
Lenzel, Harry ('Herry Lenȝel draper') 2/31
Letton, master 19/41
Lewcie see **Lucy**
Lewis, Margaret ('dame Mergett/Margaret Lowes/Lewes'; 'my lady Ryverse suster (a nonne of the myneresse)', 'a suster of the late lady Ryverse at the Menuresses' 1/10r, etc.) Minoress nun; 'sister' (prob. cousin) of Mary Fitzlewis Rivers (q.v. sub **Neville**) 20/85–6, 105, 163, 184; 21/108, 146; 19/7, 18, 20, 82; 1/4r, 10r
Lybarde, John ('John Lybarde/Lyberde') goldsmith 17/20, 30, 37
LIBRARIAN of the king see **Duwes**
Lyllegrave, William ('(William/Wylliam) Lilgrave/Lellgrave/Lyl(l)egrave) servaunte unto my ladys receyvour', etc.) servant of Hugh Ashton 19/14, 22, 47, 52
Lymner, Thomas ('warde unto my ladys grace') ward of Lady Margaret 1/5r
Lynche, (William) physician to Elizabeth of York 20/84; 1/11r, 12r
Lynche, mistress ('maistrez/maistres Lenche/Lynche/Linche') 21/29, 57, 61, 80, 133, 134, 139; 19/7, 9, 15, 17, 19, 22, 33, 38, 88, 104; 1/13r
Lyne, Thomas ward of Lady Margaret 1/17v
Lyngam, Roger 10/158
Lynne, Alice ('m*aister* vichamberlayns wyffe', 'maistres/Alyse Lynne') wife of Richard Lynne (q.v.) 20/148; 21/39, 98
Lynne, Richard ('Richard(e) Lyn(ne)'; 'maister Lynne (vichamberlayn)' 21/40; 'ma(i)ster vichambirlain/vichamberlayn/vychamb(e)rlen', 'vice camerarii' 21/87) vice-chamberlain to Lady Margaret; steward of Bassingbourn manor 10/1, 144, 178; 17/65; 20/59, 119, 165; 21/28, 39–41, 43, 46, 57, 59, 61, 87, 92, 99, 102–3, 108, 110, 112–13, 125–6, 144, 147–8; 19/16–17, 27, 43–5, 48, 69, 76, 101, 108
Lynne, William brother of Richard Lynne (q.v.) 16/18
Lytchefeld, (William) ('maister Lytchefeld') D.C.L. Oxford 1485; vicar general to bishop of London and chaplain to Henry VII 1504 21/100
LITTERMEN 17/35, 41, 53; 20/80, 87; 21/31, 100; 19/25, 97I
Lyvesay, (Edmund) ('of the ewrye') former yeoman of the household to Elizabeth of York; yeoman(?) of the ewery 1/4v
Lloyd, John 10/158
Lloyd, Thomas ('Thomas Flewde a synger') 17/45
Lodlow(e) see **Ludlow**
Lok, William ('of London mercer') 1/14r
Lolle, master of Northampton 20/153
Loman, William ('(maister) Lo(w)man/Loman(de)', 'Lomons in Hatfeld') (?) Hatfield innkeeper 21/30, 125, 129, 134, 143; 19/15, 22, 37; 1/6v, 9r
a LOMBARD see **Genowe**
Lomley, John 10/158
London, dame Margaret ('(dame Mergaret London) a nonne of/in Camse abbey') Austin nun of Campsey Ash [Sfk] 20/79, 155
[R]**Long, Robert** ('Robert Long(e) (on of the gromes of the stabyll)') servant of Lady Margaret 19/27, 72, 94; 56/4
Long, William 20/156
Longland, Thomas 10/9
Longlond, John ('mastyr John Longlond of Magdalen Colege in Oxonford') (d. 1547) later almoner and confessor to Henry VIII 21/66
Longton, mistress silkwoman of London 2/17, 26–7
Lo(u)ngford, Ralph see **Langford**
Lord Chamberlain see **Daubeney**

Love, John ('the grome') groom to Lady Margaret 17/27, 41, 47, 53

[R]**Love, William** ('William Love/Luff(e)') yeoman of the chamber to Lady Margaret 20/125; 21/38, 50, 127; 19/40, 78, 81, 85, 94; 1/12r, 12v, 13r; 56/2

Lovell, Isabel Ros ('the lady Issebell') (d. 1508/9) daughter of Sir Thomas Ros, 9th baron Ros of Helmsley; wife of Sir Thomas Lovell (q.v.) 19/39

[W]**Lovell, Thomas** ('sir Thomas Lovell knyght', 'ma(i)ster Lovell') (d. 1524) treasurer of the household to Henry VII and Henry VIII 1502–22; an executor of Lady Margaret's will 17/1; 19/24, 86, 119

Lowe, Henry ward of Lady Margaret 19/87, 96, 116

Lowe, John ward of Lady Margaret 19/89, 96

Lowes see **Lewis**

Lowman see **Loman**

Lowthe, John ('(John) Lowth(e) (faukenere/ fokenere)'; prob. 'the fawkener', etc.) falconer 20/61, 164–5; 19/29, 37, 75, 86, 92, 97, 101, 116

Lowthe, Oliver ('Olyver Lowthe'; prob. 'the fawkeners son' 19/75, etc.) 20/147, 170, 185; 21/43, 49, 95, 105; 19/75, 86, 92, 97, 116

Lucy, (Thomas) ('maister Lewcie') (?) sewer of the chamber to Henry VII 21/112

[W]**Ludlow, Henry** ('Henry(e)/Harry Coke', 'Henry Lodlowe/Ludlowe') cook to Lady Margaret 17/22, 34, 37, 40, 43–4, 47, 52, 58; 20/122–3, 139; 19/96, 101, 108, 113, 115; 1/6v, 15r

Ludlow, Margaret ('Margaret/Mergaret Lodlow/Ludlow(e)') dependent/ servant of Lady Margaret 21/141; 19/16, 42, 106; 1/8v

Luff(e) see **Love**

Machado, Roger ('Richemonde') Richmond king of arms 1485–1510 17/42

Machell, doctor ('officer of the bysshop of Norwyche') officer of Richard Nix (q.v.) 19/15

Madde, master 17/25

[R]**Madison, John**('John Madyson/Madison/ Madeson') yeoman of the chamber 21/54, 62, 115, 118, 124, 150; 19/28, 77, 79, 85, 100, 104; 1/12r; 56/2

Maydwell, Thomas ('Thomas Ma(y)dwell/ Meydwell/Maidwell/Maydwall') shoemaker of Stamford, then (from 21/96, i.e. 1506) of Croydon 20/24, 94, 124; 21/12, 54, 96, 110, 122, 145; 19/20, 26, 39, 45, 75, 87, 109, 111; 1/6r

Mayhew, Richard ('the kyngez amner') president of Magdalen College, Oxford 1480–1507; almoner to Henry VII 1497–1507 17/42

Mayn, William (?) deputy to John Dalkyn (q.v.) 10/26–28, 31; 20/5, 14, 46

Makblythe, Richard ('Richard Makblythe procture of seynt Crystofers and seynt Jorge gyelde in Yorke', 'procter of Saint George gyld') proctor of the guild of St Christopher and St George, York 20/182; 19/84

Malhame, William ('maister William Malam on of the maistres of the chauncery', 'maister Malhame') 21/38, 149

Mane Florentyne clothman of Florence 2/9

Mann, Thomas deputy bailiff to John Mortimer (q.v.) 2/2

Manners, Anne St Leger ('my lady(e)/maistres Maner(e)s/Manneres') (d. 1526) niece of Elizabeth of York; m. George Manners (d. 1513) 17/27, 59; 21/43, 92; 19/86

Marbury see **Merbury**

Marcell ('Marcell[us wyff]' 19/30

Marcham see **Markham**

Marche ('Marche syngyng man') singing man 21/99

Marcus/Markus, William 2/7; 6/6

Margam see **Morgan**

Margaret ('moder Margarett') almswoman 21/7

Margaret, mistress see **Stukeley**

[W]**Margaret Tudor** ('my ladye Margerett', 'the quene of Skottes') (d. 1541) daughter of Henry VII; m. James IV of Scotland 1503 17/25; 20/84, 104, 113, 163, 168, 173, 183, 198; 21/23, 92, 135, 140; 19/16, 80, 82, 118

Marion ('Marion þat kepith the almes folkes', '(moder) Maryon (oon of the almes women)') 20/182, 189; 21/51

Markham, Anne Neville ('maistrez Markam', 'maistres Mark(h)am') (d. 1505) daughter of George Neville and Mary Fitzlewis Rivers (q.v. sub **Neville**); m. John Markham (q.v.) 1501 21/45, 47, 75, 77

Markham, John ('(sir John) Marcham') (d. 1508) father of John Markham (q.v.) 10/46; 20/19

Markham, John ('ma(i)ster Markehame/ Markam/Marcam/Margam') (d. 1559) son of John Markham (q.v.); husband of Anne Neville Markham (q.v) 10/46; 20/64, 103, 115, 116, 151,

161; 21/59, 62, 77, 91, 95, 152, 161; 19/17; 6/4
Marmyon 21/9
[W]**Marney, Henry** ('master/sir (Henry) Marney/Marner') (d. 1523) chancellor of the duchy of Lancaster; an executor of Lady Margaret's will 10/127–9
Marshall, John ('sir John Marshall') 19/13
Marten ('Philip and Marten the kinges fools') 21/119; 19/95
Martyn ('nuper de Croydon') 16/19
'Mary' 21/25
[W]**Mary Tudor** ('domina Maria filia domini regis' 16/13; 'my lady prynces' 20/123, 19/92; 'my lady Mar(i)e/Mary' 21/27, etc., 'the princesse of Castile' 1/4r, 12v, 17r) (d. 1533) daughter of Henry VII, betrothed to Charles of Ghent, duke of Castile, December 1508 16/13; 20/123; 21/27, 30, 41, 46, 110, 118; 19/11, 21, 76, 92; 1/4r, 12v, 17r
Maskam, John ('sir John Maskam') 20/121
Masleyn/Maslinge, Thomas farmer of Lydiard Tregoze [Wilts.] 10/176–7
MASONS 19/88
[W]**Massey, Elizabeth** ('[mistress] Masse(y)/ Massy(e)') servant of Lady Margaret 10/127; 17/24, 25; 20/12, 22, 57, 62, 122, 147, 154, 163, 178, 188; 21/20, 39, 45, 60, 75, 107, 122; 19/5, 17, 22, 30, 37, 41, 44, 46, 75, 79–80, 89–90, 92, 97, 102, 105, 110, 112, 119; 1/8v, 12r, 17v
[R]**Massyngham, Ellen** 19/108; 56/1
Masson, John ('(sir) John Mas(s)on') child of Lady Margaret's chapel; scholar and then chaplain at Tattershall 20/115, 162–3, 165, 175, 196; 21/9, 19, 40, 111, 130, 154; 19/13–14, 29, 32, 34–6, 51, 109
MASTERS, wardens, clerks, and brothers
of colleges, Ashridge 21/62; 19/33, 44; **Fotheringhay** 16/18; 21/60; **Manchester** 21/115 (see too **Hanson**); **St Laurence Pountney, London** 20/189
of friaries 20/111; 19/98 (see too **Langley**)
of Browne's hospital, Stamford 20/124
of Mercers' Company see **Colet**, **Picketon**
Mathew ('Mathew (my lord off Oxynfforth) jugler/jogelere') juggler to John de Vere (q.v.) 20/32; 21/27, 139; 2/33
Matthew, (Nicholas) ('Mathew a servand of the kynges') royal servant; (?) former yeoman of the chamber to Elizabeth of York 21/50
Mattok, Nicholas ('N(icholaum) Matick/ Mattok') 16/5d; 10/18
Mawdesley, James bailiff at Deeping [Lincs.] 17/2
Mawdesley, Thomas ('sir Thomas Maudysley/ Maudesley/Mawdislee/Mawdysle', 'sir Thomas Maudesley hir [Cecily Welles] confessour') nephew of Hugh Ashton; confessor to Cecily Welles (q.v. sub **Kyme**) 10/126, 127, 132, 147; 19/105
Mawdysley, (Thomas) ('doctur Mawdysley') D.Th. Cambridge by 1478 (d. 1505, i.e. earlier than references to Thomas Mawdesley *supra*) 21/10
MAY KING 20/23
Meautis, (John) ('Mewtys the kyngez Frensshe secretorye', 'Mewth') French secretary and clerk of the signet to Henry VII 17/42; 20/110
Meddelton see **Myddelton**
Mellere/Mel(l)nere, William clothman 2/24
Melton, Eleanor Zouche ('sir John Melton ... his wyff') granddaughter of Elizabeth St John (half-sister of Lady Margaret); m. Sir John Melton (q.v.) 21/162
Melton, John (d. 1545) Yorkshire knight; m. Eleanor Zouche (q.v. sub **Melton**) 20/134, 194; 21/12, 162
Merbury, Elizabeth ('mastres Merbury oon of my ladyes gentylwoman' 19/107; 'Elizabeth Merbury' 19/115) m. William Merbury (q.v.); sometime gentlewoman to Lady Margaret 20/57, 90, 160; 21/12, 19, 42–3, 47, 98; 19/107, 115
[R]**Merbury, George** ('George Marbury') 56/2
[R]**Merbury, Robert** ('Robert (Merbury/ Marbury)') yeoman usher of the chamber to Lady Margaret; (?) former groom of the chamber) 20/16(?), 36 (?), 42, 45; 21/ 20–1, 27, 34, 50, 53, 62, 93, 114–15, 123, 127, 135, 138, 147, 160; 19/9, 12, 16, 20, 23, 31, 35–6, 41–3, 82, 85, 89–90, 94, 98–9, 101, 107, 110; 1/6r, 11r, 12r; 56/2
Merbury, William ('Willyam Merbury countroller' 20/11) controller of the household in 1502 (20/11) until 1504 16/17; 20/11, 41 (see too **CONTROLLERS**)
MERCERS see **Atcliffe**, **Botery**, **Colet**, **Fitzeton**, **Gentyll**, **Harpesfeld**, **ap Howel**, **Lok**, **Pykton**
MERCHANTS 19/37 (see too **Nynes**, **Rede**, **Robertson**, **Spinola**, **Tanne**, **Ward**)
Mergett see **Golsell**

Mery, Thomas 1/6v
[R]**Merycok, John** ('(John) Mericok/Merycok(e) yemon of the chambre') yeoman of the chamber to Lady Margaret 19/88; 1/12v, 15r; 56/5
Meryman, William ('(Wylliam) Meryman/ Merymon/Mereman (of the (privey) kechen)') servant of Henry VII 21/49; 19/11, 86, 97
Merse, William ('Wyllyam Merse of Depyng') 20/77
Metcalfe, Nicholas ('(doctour) Met(t)calf', 'maister Maytcalf') chaplain to John Fisher (q.v.); later master of Michaelhouse and then St John's College, Cambridge 10/126–7; 21/37 ('a chappleyn of my lorde of Rochester'), 97; 1/4r
Mewtys see **Meautis**
Mychell, William ('William/Wyllyam Michell/ Mychell/Mochell') (?) servant of Lady Margaret 10/2, 7; 17/50, 58, 60, 63; 20/49
Mychyn, Piers ('Peris Mychon my ladys vokett in Parres', 'Peers Mychyn my ladis woket at Pares') Lady Margaret's Paris attorney 20/35, 65
[R]**Myddelton, Christopher** ('maister/Christofer Myd(d)elton of London (notarie)', 'maister/C(h)ristofer Myddelton/ Med(d)elton (oon of the proctours of the Arches)') proctor of the Court of Arches 20/102, 106; 21/140; 1/12r; 56/3
Middelton, John clothman 20/191
MIDWIVES see **NURSES**
Miklow, John ('clerk counttroller') clerk controller to Henry VII 19/85
MILLERS 16/2d
Mylner, William ('(William Mylner) a French prest') 20/123, 126b, 152
Mynskyp, Edward escheator of Cambridgeshire 1/5r
MISRULE, abbot of 17/63; 20/62, 126b (Prechet(t) (q.v.)); 19/47; **lord of** 20/126b; 19/59, 111, 121 (Haryson (q.v.)); **prior of** 17/63
Mody, Edward 2/2
Moyne, Richard ('Richard Moyn(e) (oon of the chyldren of the chappell)'; 'Richard Mowen my ladys skoller') child of Lady Margaret's chapel; scholar at London charterhouse 20/29, 30, 55, 65, 86
Moldale, William ('syr William Moldal(l)e (of the chappell)') chaplain to Lady Margaret 21/115, 118, 158
Molyne ('Molyne[s son]') 21/157
Molyneux, mistress ('maistres/maistrez Molynex/Molenars/Moleners') 20/48; 21/20; 19/89
Molson ('excheter of Lyncolnshere') escheator of Lincolnshire 20/128, 147, 160; 19/108
Moncaster/Monkester, James tailor 19/97 II, 98
Monde/Mondy see **Mundy**
MONKS
 of Ely 20/14
 of Eye 21/91
 of Faversham 21/62
 of London charterhouse 21/23; 19/18
 of Rochester 21/27
 of St Albans 19/15
 of St Catherine's, Mt Sinai, Egypt 21/100
 of Sempringham (monks and nuns) 20/94, 146
 of Sheen charterhouse see **Eline**, **Silvester**
 of Stamford 20/164
 of Vaudey 20/12
Moore, master sergeant at law 1/8r
Mordaunt, John/William ('maister Morda(u) nt') (?) John Mordaunt sergeant at law; (?) William Mordaunt attorney in the Court of Common Pleas 20/45, 48, 66
More, John (?) servant of Lady Margaret 20/13, 20
Moreton ('nuper de le Whytehorse') 16/19
Morgan, Eleanor ('maistres Morgan', 'Morgans wyff', 'his sister dame Elenour his late wiff' 19/53) wife of Philip Morgan (q.v.); professed as a vowess at Dartford after his ordination 1507 20/26, 30, 46, 122, 180; 21/106; 19/20, 53
Morgan, George ('George Morgan the kynges servant') servant of Henry VII 19/119
Morgan, Gregory ('Gregory Morgan feodary of Somersetshyre') 19/73
Morgan, (Philip) ('(ma(i)ster) Morgan/ Margam') fellow of King's College, Cambridge; physician to Lady Margaret; ordained 1507 10/132–3; 20/12, 31, 37, 46, 62, 85, 90, 94, 101, 122, 124, 128, 153, 157, 161, 163, 168–70, 175, 177, 179, 187–8; 21/11–12, 14, 17–18, 37, 39, 47, 52, 57, 63, 74, 97, 114, 121–2, 124, 127, 130, 143, 146–7; 19/9–11, 20–1, 23, 27, 53, 70, 72, 78–9, 86, 102, 119; 1/6v
Morhand, William servant of Elizabeth Denton (q.v.) 1/14r
[R]**Morice, James** ('James/Jamez/Jamys Moryce/Morice/ Moris(e)/Mo(r)res/ Morys/Mor(r)es/Morez/Maurice';

'Jacobum Morres clericum countrie' 16/31d; 'clerk of my ladiez warkez at Colyweston' 17/67) clerk of the counting house; clerk of works to Lady Margaret 16/31d; 10/69, 70, 76, 107, 109, 114, 127, 132–3, 136, 138, 147–8, 155, 159–60, 181–2; 17/54, 56, 58, 61, 64–5, 67; 20/5, 16, 42, 48, 62, 64, 66, 90, 116, 127, 134, 142, 148, 166, 174–5, 177, 185–6, 194; 21/ 2, 9, 28, 30, 33, 35, 37, 45, 48–9, 57, 86, 99–100, 107, 127, 134, 141, 163; 19/7, 8, 15–17, 28–9, 31, 33–7, 39–40, 44, 47, 53, 62, 65–6, 72, 88–91, 101, 110, 113–14, 121, 124; 1/10r, 13r, 13v, 15v, 18r; 2/30, 32, 36; 6/4, 6; 56/1

Morice, Morgan ('Morgan(e) Mores(s)') nephew of James Morice (q.v.); servant of John Fisher (q.v.) 10/127; 21/63, 99

Morley, lady, see **Howard, Alice Lovell Parker**

Morley, lord see **Parker, William**

Morrant, William servant of Elizabeth Denton (q.v.) 21/24, 140

Mortymer, John ('John Martymer/ Mortymer') deputy bailiff at Lamarsh [Ess.] 2/1

Morton, master 21/58

Moundy see **Mundy**

[R]**Mounteney, Anne** ('[mistress]/Anne Mounteney/Moynteney') servant of Lady Margaret 20/151, 162, 197; 56/1

[R]**Mount(e)ney, Thomas** servant of Lady Margaret 17/45, 52; 20/153, 182; 19/20; 56/1

Mouse, Richard ('Mouse my ladys servante', '(Richard) Mous(s)e/Mowse', 'the grome') groom to Lady Margaret 17/19, 35, 41, 44, 47, 53; 20/112

Mowbray, Elizabeth Talbot (('my lady(e)/the lady (o)f North(f)folk(e)/Norf(f) olk(e)) (d. 1507) widow of John Mowbray (VII), fourth duke of Norfolk 17/38; 20/116; 20/126; 21/21, 60, 108, 140; 19/39, 58, 69, 117; 1/5r, 17r

Mowen see **Moyne**

Mowre, Henry 19/37

Mundy, Joan ('a wedow at Hechyn oon Johan Mondy') 21/124

Mundy, John ('John Mundy(e)/Mundey/ Munde(e)/Mo(u)ndy/Monde') goldsmith; servant of Sir John Shaa (d. 1503) 10/126–8, 158; 17/20, 27; 20/82, 191; 21/23, 29, 41, 67, 110, 119, 128; 19/7, 21, 23, 66, 84, 113; 1/5v, 6r; 2/3, 5–6

MUSICIANS, minstrels, composers and waits 17/33, 64; 20/24, 39, 42, 46, 61, 89, 96, 100, 109–10, 115, 170; 21/9, 14, 19, 28, 43, 63, 109–10; 19/17, 21, 28, 36, 88–90, 97, 99, 107, 112; 1/4v, 6v; 2/33–4; 6/4 (see too **Cotterell**, **Couper**, **Fairfax**, **Gyles**, **Glasebury**, **Newton**, **Taberet**)

Mussheka/Musteka, Sebastian ('Bestyan Mussheka/Musteka broder(er)') Sebastian, embroiderer 17/20, 38

Mustyng, John Dutch/German arras mender 1/7v

Muswell bricklayer 21/119

Nelson, John horseman 20/154

[R]**Neswik, Robert** ('Rob(e)rt Nes(e)wyk(e)/ Neswik(e)') yeoman of the chamber to Lady Margaret 19/79, 82, 100, 108; 1/8r, 12r, 13v; 56/2

Neswik, Thomas 19/35

Nevell, master ('maister Nevell man of law') lawyer 20/100

Nevell, Robert 20/124

Neville, lady see **de Vere, Margaret Neville**

Neville, George ('George Nevill lord Burgevenny', 'my lord(e) (of) Burgeveny/Burgaveyn/Burgavenn') (d. 1535) George Neville, 3rd baron Bergavenny 10/158; 21/155; 19/90, 96; 1/13r (see too **Burgayne**)

Neville, Mary Fitzlewis Rivers ('my lady Revers(e)/Ryverse', 'the late lady Ryverse' 1/10r) daughter of Sir Henry Fitzlewis and Elizabeth Beaufort (daughter of Edmund Beaufort, 1st duke of Somerset); m.(1) Sir Anthony Woodville, 2nd Earl Rivers (d. 1483), (2) Sir George Neville, bastard son of Sir Thomas Neville; 'sister' (cousin) of Margaret Lewis (q.v.) 20/14, 51, 66, 85–6, 105, 123, 163, 184; 21/53, 134, 143–4, 146; 19/7, 18, 29, 71, 82; 1/4r, 10r; 2/2

Newby servant of Sir William Knyvett (q.v.) 20/170

Newport, master 20/39; 19/81

Newton, George ('George Newton that pleyth at oragam', 'George of the chapell', 'syr George Newton somtyme of my ladys chappell') musician and composer of Lady Margaret's chapel until January 1504 17/61; 20/12, 97, 145; 21/117

Nicholas see **Davy**

Nicholas ('Nicholas of the wardrop') groom of the wardrobe to Lady Margaret 20/104; 21/38; 19/16, 43

Nicholas, John skinner 20/146; 19/6; 1/7v
Nicholasse, Robert 19/19
Nicholas(son), Edmund ('(Edmond/Edward Nycholas (the) hardwar(e) man'; 'Heymounde/Haymo(u)nd Nichol(as) son hardware man', etc.; 'Heymound/ Heymonde Glasse (hardware man)', 'Heymunde/Haymound (hardware man)', 'the hardware man') 10/148; 20/12, 35–6, 48, 53, 60, 62, 67, 91, 95, 113–14, 160; 21/8, 93, 145; 19/20, 30, 43, 45, 69
Nic(h)olson, Henry 10/18, 46
Nynes, Nicholas member of Merchant Taylor's Company; sheriff of London 1502–3 17/67
Nix, Richard bishop of Norwich 1501–35 21/60, 100, 118, 139; 19/15
None, Robert of Hertford 16/5, 20, 8d
Norfolk, lady see **Mowbray, Elizabeth Talbot**
Norman, William ('sir William Norman') priest 20/183
Norrey see **Carlisle**
[R]**Nor(r)ice, Edmund** 19/88; 56/5
Norton, Elizabeth ('my lady (Elizabeth) Norton') wife of Sampson Norton (q.v.) 21/45, 53, 58, 99, 107, 130; 19/10, 33, 74, 105
Norton, Henry ('sir Harry/Henry/Herry Norman') 20/107, 138, 162, 194 (Appendix), 200
Norton, Sampson (d. 1517) knight; master porter and councillor at Calais 1500–5; master of the ordnance 20/84; 19/33**;** 2/14
Northumberland, lord of see **Percy**
Notman, William ('sir Wyllyam Notman') priest of Bourne [Lincs.] 20/51
Nott(e), Osmund ('Osm(o)unde/Ossemounde (Nott(e))') servant of Lady Margaret 17/22, 34, 40, 47; 20/23, 164
Notte, Roger of Hatfield 1/9v
Nun, Thomas ('maister Nun') M.Gram. Cambridge 1503–4; fellow of God's House (later Christ's College) 1505–13 21/25
NUNS 17/56; 20/145; 21/132 (see too **Haw**, **Frankyn**, **PRIORESSES**, and the PLACES index)
  of Campsey Ash see **London**
  of Catley 20/39, 90; 19/105
  of Cheshunt 21/132, 135
  of Dartford see **Morgan**
  of Ickleton 21/126
  of Ivinghoe 19/33
  of Kelsey 20/157
  of Lincoln 20/31
  of the Minories, London 20/105, 163, 184; 21/108; 19/20; 1/10r (see too **Collys, Lewis**)
  of Rothwell 20/153
  of Sempringham (monks and nuns) 20/13, 32, 39, 41, 71, 175; 21/11, 17, 19; 19/74, 105 (see too **Zouche**)
  of Sheppey ('the ancryse syster') 20/176, 184–6, 195; 21/114 (see **White**)
  of Stamford 20/22, 164, 179–80, 183–4, 187; 21/12, 19–20, 48, 91, 111, 114, 131
  of Swaffham Bulbeck 21/28
  of Syon see **Gibbs**, **Windsor**
  of Yorkshire 21/63
NURSES AND MIDWIVES 10/9; 20/48, 51, 111, 120, 126b, 145, 150, 161, 164, 170, 179, 191; 21/25, 33, 36–7, 41, 46–7, 75, 89, 95, 113, 126–7, 140; 19/10, 17, 20, 23, 29, 31, 37, 41, 75, 89, 92; 1/7v

Odall/Odell/Odoll see **Woodhull**
Ogyll from Prescot [Lancs.] 20/177
[R]**Oldall, Peter** ('Petour/Peter Oldeha(u)lle/ Oldall/Oldale') servant of Lady Margaret 19/31, 98, 103, 107; 1/4r; 56/2
Oldam, Peter ('Petur Oldam broderer'; 'Petur(e) bro(w)therer/bro(w)derer') embroiderer 19/5, 35, 41, 112, 114; 1/6r, 17v
Oldham, Hugh ('ma(i)ster Hugh/Hew (Oldom)', 'magistri Hugonis Oldom nunc episcopi Exoniensis' 16/5d; 'master Hugh Oldom at Excestre' 10/4; 'master Hugh Oldom my ladys chauncelere' 10/32; 'maister Hugh Oldom clerk' 17/67;'maister chaunceller maister Hughe Oldom' 20/5; 'maister chaunceller maister Hugh Oldom' 20/7; 'maister Hughe Oldom chaunceller' 20/30; 'maister Hugh Oldome my ladys chauncler' 20/138; 'master Hewe Oldam chanselere'2/3) (d. 1519) Lady Margaret's receiver for the Exeter lands until some time before 5 August 1503 (D102.10/1–31 passim); chancellor of the household from at least 20 May 1501 (D102.2/3) until November 1504 (last entry as such D91.20/138); bishop of Exeter 1505–19 (D91.21 and D91.19) 16/5d; 10/1, 3–5, 15–16, 18–20, 23, 27, 31–2, 67, 139;17/63, 67; 20/5, 7, 30, 138; 21/25, 103, 117, 131; 19/73, 121; 2/3

(see too **CHANCELLOR** and **BISHOPS** for references with no name)
Olyfe/Oliffe, John ('the baliffes deputie at Tateshall') deputy of Richard Parker (q.v.) 10/16–17
Olyver, Robert smith 21/49, 50
ORGAN MAKER 19/44
Orlow, Henry ('of Norwyche syngyng man') singing man 21/8
Ormeston, Roger ('Rogeri Urmeston militis' 16/18; 'Roger Ormyston/Ormysten' 10/18, 20, etc., '(sir) Roger(e) Urmeston/Urmyston' 10/31, 39, etc., 'syr Roger Urmyston knyght' 20/144, etc., 'sir Roger Urmeston my ladys chamberlyn' 20/137) (d. 1504) cousin of Hugh Oldham (q.v.); bailiff of various estates; knighted 1501; chamberlain to Lady Margaret from 1501 (only so named here 20/137, end of year 1503) 16/18; 10/18, 20, 31, 39; 17/20, 23, 30–1, 34, 40, 46, 52; 20/137, 144, 191, 194, 199; 21/80, 163; 19/61, 124; 2/1, 3, 5, 7, 18, 21; 6/9 (for his kin see **Urmeston**, his own preferred spelling) (see too **CHAMBERLAIN** for references with no name)
Ormond, lord see **Butler**
Orton, my lady ('my lady Orton') 21/53
Orton, Roger ('(Roger) Orton (my ladys servande)' servant of Lady Margaret 20/78, 159; 21/18
Osborne, Joan servant of Lady Margaret 17/49
R**Osborne, Thomas** 56/5
Osbourne, David ('David and Jerard Osbourne at theyr departynge to the kynges servyce', 'David now the kynges servant') 21/72, 74
Osbourne, Gerard (('Gerawde of Burne, 'Garrard/Ger(r)ade/Ger(r)awd(e)/ Jerard Osb(o)urne/Osborne/ Osseburne'; 'David and Jerard Osbourne at theyr departynge to the kynges servyce'; 'Garrard Osborne the kynges servant' 21/91, etc.) servant of Lady Margaret and then of Henry VII 21/52, 72, 91, 93, 106, 127; 19/11, 24, 48; 1/6v
Overton 20/119
Oxford, lord see **de Vere, John**

Page, Edmund ('the balyffe of Dertfforde') bailiff of Dartford [Kent] 10/20, 158; 17/25
R**Page, John** 56/3
Page, Richard 16/17
Pagnam 1/13r
Paynell, Geoffrey 19/91, 92, 118
Palmer, (Alexander) ('maister Palmer of the universite in Cambryge') B.A., M.A., B.D. by 1510/11; fellow of Peterhouse, Cambridge; parish chaplain of Little St Mary's (Peterhouse chapel) 17/37; 20/20, 49
Palmer(e), John saddler 17/27, 33; 20/89, 90, 99, 138; 21/102 , 103, 131, 157; 19/34, 59; 2/7, 8, 10, 11, 13, 14, 15, 16, 22, 23, 24, 25, 27, 29, 30, 35; 6/3
Palmer, Peter 20/33
PARDONERS 19/103, 105
PARISH CLERKS 19/17, 101
Parker ('of the buttrye') servant of Henry VII 1/4v
W**Parker, Alice St John** ('[mistress] (Alice) Parkar/Parker(e)'; '[maister Parker and] his wyff') gentlewoman to Lady Margaret; daughter of Sir John St John II (q.v.); wife of Henry Parker (q.v) 10/3, 9, 31, 144; 20/12, 51–2, 64, 145, 150, 154, 164, 179, 194; 21/42, 47, 53, 76, 126, 152, 161; 19/6, 10, 12, 26, 29, 32, 37, 56, 75, 79, 82, 83, 89, 91, 97 II, 98; 1/12r, 17v; 2/28
Parker, Henry ('(yonge) ma(i)ster Parker(e)/ Perker', 'Parker') (d. 1556) gentleman to Lady Margaret; m. Alice St John (q.v. sub **Parker**) 10/148; 17/20, 27–8, 49; 20/64, 90, 126, 134, 138, 148–9, 151, 192, 194, 199; 21/8, 71, 75, 77, 114, 152, 161; 19/3, 6, 12, 18, 21, 24–5, 27–8, 32, 35–6, 38, 41, 44, 46, 54, 56, 59, 70, 74, 76, 78, 83, 93, 95, 97 I, 97 II, 98, 100–2, 105–7, 109–11, 113, 118; 1/8v, 10r, 13r; 2/28; **'(master) Parkers landes'** 10/148; 19/3, 48, 59
Parker, Jane daughter of Henry and Alice Parker (q.v.) 19/89, 92, 97 II
R**Parker, John** ('of the buttrye') servant of Henry VII 1/4v; 56/5
Parker, Margaret ('litell/yonge maistres (Margett) Parker') daughter of Alice and Henry Parker (q.v.) 19/16, 41, 75, 111
Parker, Margaret ('the late wife of Richard Parkere late baylife of Tateshall') widow of Richard Parker bailiff (q.v.) 10/24; 19/26
Parker, Richard ('Richard Parker balife of Tateshall'; 'Richard Parkere late baylife of Tateshall' 10/24) (d. 1501) bailiff of Lady Margaret's Tattershall estates, succeeded by Pulvertoft (q.v.) 10/6, 16, 24
Parker, Richard of the Isle of Ely 20/61

Parker, William (d. 1504) knight; 9th baron Morley by right of his wife Alice Lovell Parker (q.v. sub **Howard**); father of Henry Parker (q.v.) 10/3, 144; 21/8, 40; **'the lord Morles landes'** 10/3

Parker, William ('William Parker/Parkar (of Hatfeld)') groom-porter at Hatfield 20/159, 161, 176, 185; 21/33, 35; 19/47

Parot(t) see **Doryn**

Parr, Thomas ('Thomas Par(r)e') (d. 1517) of the family formerly lords of Kendal 10/22, 27

Parres ('[a servand of] maister Parres [a safferon setter]'; 'sir Parres prest of Cambryge') priest of Cambridge 20/160; 21/41

Paskall ('Paskall brotherer/of Peturborogh') embroiderer of Peterborough 20/13, 102, 116

Passelaw, Robert (?) skinner 20/179

Paston servant of John de la Vere (q.v.) 20/117

Patche ('Pach(e)(e)', 'Passhe') (?) a fool 21/63, 117, 123; 1/4v

Patryk, Leonard ('Lenard Patryk syngyng man') 20/104

Peche, (Elizabeth) ('oon Peche the quenes servant') (?) gentlewoman to Elizabeth of York 20/45

R**Peksall, master** ('[master] Pecsall/Peksall/ Peckesall/Pex(s)all/Pexsull (clerk of my ladys/the clossett') clerk of the closet to Lady Margaret 10/126, 132; 19/7, 20, 22–3, 48, 71, 83, 85, 99; 1/12v; 56/1

Peynckeny/Pynckeneys servant of Wynkyn de Worde (q.v.) 19/95–6

Peyrepoynt, master ('maister Pe(y)r(e) poynt') 20/77, 79, 91

Peyton, John 20/126b

Pellett, Jane Buchan ('my ladye (Jane) Baughan/Baughyn/Bougham/ Bowghan/Boghham/Bougham/ Boughan/Boughyn') half-sister (illegitimate) of Alexander Stewart (q.v.); raised by Elizabeth of York; m. Thomas Pellett (q.v.) 17/45; 19/44, 54, 74, 77, 81, 89, 93, 95; 1/4v, 12r, 14v

Pellett, Robert 20/99

Pellett, Thomas ('(Thomas) Pelet/Pellet(t) (husbond unto my lady Bougham)') Cambridge scholar maintained by Lady Margaret; m. Jane Buchan (q.v. sub **Pellett**) 20/22, 38, 40, 61, 120, 125, 159, 170, 178, 196; 21/38, 99, 130; 19/13, 34, 44, 51, 113, 116; 1/14v

Pendant servant of John Fisher (q.v.) 10/127; 21/135; 19/70

Penny, John ('the abbot of Leceytour') abbot of St Mary, Leicester 1496–1505 20/145

Penred, John (?) horse dealer 19/102

Penser 21/49

Penson see **Pynson**

Penter, John ('of the chappell') member of Lady Margaret's chapel 20/60

Peper, Richard ('Richard Peper my ladyes scoler at Oxford') (?) error for Thomas Peper (q.v.) 19/14

Peper, Thomas ('(Thomas) Peper (oon of the chyldryn of the chappell)', 'exibucion of Pepure beyng in Oxforth', 'Pepire/ Pepur/Pepyr') child of Lady Margaret's chapel; scholar at Magdalen College, Oxford 20/146, 157, 172, 196; 21/66, 105–6, 125, 154; 19/14, 51

Percy, Henry ('my lord(e) of(f) Northumb(e) rland/Northhumbirlond') (d. 1527) 5th earl of Northumberland 20/31, 145, 152, 165; 2/33

Pereson, John ('Pereson ...is servand') servant of Palmer, saddler (q.v.) 2/25, 27, 29

PERFORMERS, players, dancers, morris men, and jugglers 20/61, 67, 115, 121, 126b, 190; 21/9, 43, 61, 63, 77, 92, 145–6; 19/6, 47, 59, 89, 112, 121; 2/33 (see too **Haryson**, **Mathew**)

Perpoynt see **Peyrepoynt**

Peter ('Blake Petur') 17/25

Peter ('Petur(e) bro(w)therer/bro(w)derer') see **Oldam**

Peter ('Petour the fole') 19/99

Peter ('Peter ...his servand') servant of Palmer, saddler (q.v.) 20/33; 2/23, 24

Peter ('the kynges secretary servant') (see **Ruthall**) 20/61

Peter, master ('maister Peter notarye') 19/71

Peter of Coldharbour see **Baldwin**

R**Pety John** ('browderer to my lady Dawbeney') embroiderer to Elizabeth, lady Daubeney (q.v.) 21/92; 19/5; 56/1

PEWTERER 20/50

Pex(s)all/Pexsull see **Peksall**

Philip I ('the kyng of Castell') (d. 1506) first Habsburg king of Castile (1506) (see 'The Meeting of Henry VII and the King of Castile') 21/99, 103, 108, 110

Philip the king's fool 19/95

Philip collier 16/13

Philip(s), David ('Davidum Philipp militem', '(maister/sir) Davy (Phyllyppes/ Phillippes)') knight; relative of David Cecyll (q.v.), also of Stamford; Lady

Margaret's bailiff at Collyweston and constable at Maxey; master of the king's swans in Lincs.; squire of the body to Henry VII 16/19; 20/37, 165, 170

Philip(s), Thomas ('Thomas Phylippes/ Philip(ps)/Philippe(s)/Phylippez/ Phillippez', 'the receptour of Kendal') bailiff/receiver of Kendall [Herts.] 16/19; 10/19, 21, 22, 25, 27, 29, 112; 17/22, 34, 39, 41, 47, 57; 20/51

PHYSICIANS and surgeons 17/28; 20/57; 21/55; 19/11, 29

to Elizabeth of York see **Crossley**, **Lacy**, **Lynche**

to Henry VII 20/110; 19/11, 54 (see too **Baptist**, **Chamber**, **Fraunces**, **Thomas**)

to Lady Margaret see **Denman**, **Hilmer**, **Morgan**

to Thomas Stanley see **Thomas Stanley I** and **Boniface Stanley**

Picketon, John ('(John) Pykton/Pic(ke)ton') warden of Mercers' Company (with Sir Henry Colet) 1488 17/26, 29; 6/3

Pyee, master 20/151

Pyk(e), John 21/131; 19/16, 36

Pykerell, William 20/37

Pykering, Christopher 10/158

Pykryng, John clerk at Tattershall college 1495–1504; singing man 20/105

Pynson, Richard ('Richard Pynson/Penson', 'Pynson (stacionary)', 'Penson bookeseller', 'Pynson the bokebynder', 'a prynter in London') London printer, bookbinder and book dealer; king's printer from 1506 20/104; 21/27, 30, 40, 123, 125, 133, 135, 142; 19/6, 21, 63

Pynson, Robert ('Robert Pynson of London skynner', 'Penson the skynnere') skinner of London 21/ 29; 2/14, 28, 30, 36

[R]**Plofeld, John** ('John Plofeld(e)/Ploffeld', '(John) Plo(w)feld') servant of James Morice (q.v.) 21/99, 107, 114, 115, 118, 119, 123, 133; 19/6, 13, 72, 83, 92, 105; 56/1

Plomer, Richard ('Richard Plomer(e)/ Plummer') servant of Lady Margaret 20/112, 123; 21/28, 33, 66, 96

Plowgh, James ('sir Jamys/James (Plo(w)gh) (parrech prest of Lydeȝard Tragose)') parish priest of Lydiard Tregoze [Wilts.] 10/176–7; 19/36

de la Pole, Edmund (d. 1513) 8th earl of Suffolk (see 'The Meeting of Henry VII and the King of Castile') 21/108

Pole, Hugh incumbent(?) of Manorbier [Pembs.] 19/105

Pole, John ('John Pole procatour unto doctur Owen Pole') steward to Owen Pole (q.v.) 19/71

Pole, Margaret Plantagenet ('dame Merg(ar) et/Margaret Po(o)le', 'the lady Pole', 'my lady (Margaret) Pole/Po(e)ll') (exec. 1541) daughter of George, duke of Clarence; m. Richard Pole (d. 1504), son of Geoffrey Pole and Edith St John (half-sister to Lady Margaret); suo jure countess of Salisbury 1514 21/22, 24, 35, 98, 113, 119, 128, 153; 19/10, 77, 96; 1/9v, 12v, 15v

Pole, Owen ('doctur Owen Pole') B.Cn. & B.C.L. Oxford by 1470, D.Cn.L. Cambridge 1477–8; treasurer of St David's [Pembs.] and Hereford 19/71

Pole, Ursula ('maistres Ursula (Pole)') daughter of Margaret Plantagenet Pole (q.v.) 21/105, 137, 141, 157; 19/26, 42, 56, 75, 98

Pole, William ('Wylliam/Willyam/Wyllyam/ maister Pole') gentleman usher of the chamber to Lady Margaret 17/21, 22, 34, 40, 44, 46, 52; 20/23, 24, 43, 44, 58, 107, 116, 128, 134, 151,164, 194; 21/8, 79, 126, 162; 19/18, 61, 69, 123

Pole, William ('Willyam Pole (the quenys servande)') groom of the chamber to Elizabeth of York (different from above) 20/44

Polydore Vergil ('maister Polidour') subcollector to Adriano Castellesi (q.v.) 1/10v

Pope 20/45

POPES see **Julius II**; **papal collector** see **Castellesi**; **papal legate** see **de Gigli**

(?)**Pormard, Thomas** 10/139

Porte, Thomas ('lerned man') D.Cn. L. Cambridge by 1515 1/7r

Porter, Thomas ('(Thomas) Porter') 19/85; 2/14(?)

PORTERS see **CARRIERS, carters, porters and couriers**

Portkullys see **Videt**

Pott, mistress ('maistres Pott(e)') 21/42, 100, 105, 110, 116

POTTER 19/21

Powdrell, Robert clothman 20/145

Powell, (Edward) ('maister Powell of Oryall college in Oxford') (mart. 1540) D.Th. Oxford 1506; rector, prebendary, court preacher 20/101

Powis, my lady see **Grey, Anne Herbert**

Prat, Davy ('yoman of the spycery') servant of Lady Margaret 19/84

PREACHERS see **SCHOLARS AND PREACHERS**

Prechet(t), Thomas ('Thomas Prechet (abbot of mysserowell' 20/126b; 'Prechett oon of the chappell at his departyng' 21/107) gentleman of the chapel (until 1502 (?)); abbot of misrule at Christmas festivities 20/39, 43, 47, 126b; 21/107; 19/16

PRESIDENT OF LADY MARGARET'S COUNCIL see **Whitstones**

Preston, Richard 10/158

PRIESTS, rectors, parsons and vicars 10/140; 16/10, 17; 17/27, 30, 35, 57, 63–4; 20/16, 31, 36, 38–40, 43, 87, 106, 115, 120, 123, 126b, 154, 163; 21/9, 19, 35, 39, 92, 111, 124; 19/13, 19, 21, 30, 38, 59, 93, 97, 116; 1/7v (see too **Artwyk, Beaupre, Belamy, Bell, Bybe, Blot, Bowrer, Brewer, Carter, Charles, Colet, Colman, Edward, Elys, Fotherby, Greves, Haward, Idyll, Longford, Marshall, Maskam, Norman, Norton, Notman, Parres, Plowgh, Reymounde, Royston, Shefeld, Stephyns, Thomas, Thomson, Urmeston, Verun, Whytelege, Yonge**)

PRINCESSES
- **of Castile** see **Mary Tudor**
- **of England** see **Katherine of Aragon**
- **of Wales** see **Katherine of Aragon**

PRINTERS 17/58; 20/166 (see too **Faques, Pynson, de Worde**)

PRIORS (see too the PLACES index)
- **of Binham** see **Fresell**
- **of Bisham** 21/128
- **of the Carmelites (prior general)** 21/21, 71
- **of the hospital of St John, Clerkenwell** see **Docwra**
- **of Coventry charterhouse** 19/70
- **of Crowland** 20/115, 134, 149, 194; 21/79
- **of Denbigh** see **Robert**
- **of Durham** 20/163
- **of Ely** see **Colville**
- **of Eye** 21/91
- **of Hinton charterhouse** 17/48
- **of Hitchin** 1/6r
- **of Langley** see **Thomson**
- **of Lanthony** see **Forrest**
- **of Leicester** 20/114
- **of St Katherine's, Lincoln** 20/78
- **of London charterhouse** see **Tynbygh**
- **of St Bartholomew, London** see **Bolton**
- **of St Mary without Bishopsgate, London** see **Cressall**
- **of Monmouth** 19/73
- **of St Andrew, Northampton** 20/38
- **of Ormsby** 20/62
- **of St Albans** 19/42
- **of Sempringham** 20/13, 90, 122, 139
- **of Sheen charterhouse** see **Jobourn**
- **of Spalding** 20/11, 102, 111;
- **of Thorney** 20/52, 90, 150, 166

PRIORESSES (see too the PLACES index)
- **of Catley** 19/105
- **of Dartford** 21/22
- **of the Minories, London** 21/108
- **of Margate** 17/62
- **of Sempringham** 21/19; 19/105
- **of Stamford** 20/180, 183; 21/19–20
- **of Wilberfoss** 1/13r

PRISONERS and felons 16/7d; 10/113, 140; 17/25; 20/14, 20, 36, 40, 85, 155, 159, 187; 21/21, 62, 66, 96; 19/10, 102; 1/16r, 17r; 2/23 (see too **Browne, Chamber, Johnson, Rhys, Savage, Shaw, Spencer**)

PROCTORS 17/45; 20/40, 79, 86, 182; 21/40, 187; 21/135; 19/18, 84 (see too **Coles, Makblythe, Middleton**)

PROVOSTS and vice-provosts see **Hatton** and **Horman**

Prowde, John clothman 21/97

Pudsey, Richard ('sir Richarde Pudsey') 17/42

Pulvertoft, Robert ('Robert Polvertoft/Pulvertoft') nephew of Henry Hornby (q.v.); bailiff of Lady Margaret's Tattershall estate by January 1502 10/19, 21–2, 26, 28; 20/11, 34, 59, 88; 21/11; 6/9

PURSER of ship 10/4

Quytyng see **Whytyng**

Quytston(e)s see **Whitstones, James**

Quttyler, William ((?) for **Whittyler**) sergeant at law 20/126b

[R]**Radclyff, Hugh** ('Hugh(e) Ratclyff/Tatcliff/Radclyff') of Collyweston 20/123, 139; 21/131; 56/5

Radclyff, Jane 19/75

Radclyff, Roger ('Roger(e) Radclyf(f)/Ratclif/Ratclyffe') gentleman of Lady Margaret 20/12, 18, 20, 23, 32, 48, 96, 120, 160, 178; 21/20, 98, 99, 139; 19/18, 27, 83, 84, 85, 86, 88, 104; 1/13v

Radclyff, William('William Radclyff/Ratclyff/Ratcliff (of Stampforth)', etc.) (?) builder 21/10, 20, 131; 19/36, 51, 89

Radcliffe, Elizabeth Stafford ('my lady Fitzwater', 'my/the lady [Elizabeth] Stafford/Stafforth') (d. 1532) gentlewoman to Lady Margaret; sister of Edward, 3rd duke of Buckingham;

m. Robert Radcliffe (q.v) 21/60; 19/80, 82, 118
Radcliffe, Robert ('my/the lord Fewater/ Fytzwater(e)') (d. 1542) 7th baron Fitzwalter (attainder raised November 1505) m. (before 1507) Elizabeth Stafford (q.v. sub **Radcliffe**) 10/103, 182; 21/58, 77
Ralph ('Rawffe', 'pore Rauff(e)') 21/20, 46, 138, 143) 20/167, 181; 21/20, 46, 65, 66, 138, 143
Ramryge, Thomas ('the abbot(t) of Seynt Abones/Albons/Albanes') abbot of St Albans 1492–1520 21/132; 19/15, 17; 1/8r
Randull, Elizabeth ('maistres Randull', 'Elyzabeth Raundull') 20/179; 21/20, 106
Rece see **Rhys**
RECEIVERS of Mountesdale and Hawarden 21/95 (see too **Compton**, **Cutte**, **Dalkyn**, **Denton**, **Harper**, **Langlond**, **Oldham**, **Philip(s)**, **Vavasour**, **Walles**, **Wren**)
receiver general to Henry VII see **Bray**
receiver (general) to Lady Margaret (the (said)/my lady's/our/master receiver (general)) see **Ashton**, **Bedell**, **Oldham**
receiver to John Fisher 21/44
Rede, Alan ('the <abb> abot of Waltham') abbot of Waltham Holy Cross1500–7 21/127
Rede, Anne Freville ('maistres (Anne) Frevell', 'Anne/maistrez/maistres Re(y)de'; 'the mariage of Rede and maistres Frevell' 20/23) m. William Rede (q.v.) 1502 20/23, 30, 32, 34, 60; 21/43, 122; 19/32
Rede, Robert ('maister Re(y)de (tresorer unto my lord prynce)', 'syr Robert Rede', 'maister Ride/Ryde oon of the kynges justice/justice of the kynges benche') (d. 1519) justice of the King's Bench; treasurer to Prince Henry 20/111; 21/28, 41, 98
Rede, Thomas embroiderer of London 20/115
Rede, William ('maister Rede') Boston merchant, m. Anne Freville (q.v. sub **Rede**) 1502 20/23
Redyng, (Mary) ('ma(i)stres Redyng(e)') (?) gentlewoman of Elizabeth of York (q.v.) and then Mary Tudor (q.v.) 21/72, 110
Redman, Richard ('the byshopp of Excester', 'the bysshop/my lord of Ely/Ele') (d. 1505) bishop of Exeter 1496–1501 (D91.17/63), bishop of Ely 1501–5 (D91.20 and D91.21) 17/63; 20/57, 163, 189, 198–9; 21/119, 133, 138, 140, 147, 164
Redwoode, Margaret ('of London') 1/14v
Re(e)s see **Rhys**
REEVES, of Cheshunt 16/3 (see too **Hoo**)
Reginald ('Reignald my ladies idyot') Lady Margaret's fool 1/9r-v, 10v
Reymound, John vicar of the Sheen charterhouse 1/11v
Reve, Walter ('(Water Reve) master carpenter of the (seid) slewse') maister carpenter of the sluice 20/32; 6/5
ap Rhys, Edward ('Edward ap Rees', (?) for **Owain**) (?) son of Sir Rhys ap Thomas (q.v.) 20/44
ap Rhys, Gruffydd ('Gruf ap Rees', '(syr) Gryffith/Griffith Rice') (d. 1521) son of Sir Rhys ap Thomas (q.v.); m. 1507 Catherine St John, daughter of Sir John St John II (q.v.) 10/158; 20/37, 95
[R] (?)**Rhys, John** ('John Res/Rice') 19/110; 56/4
(?)**Rhys, Richard** ('my lord Rece/ Richart') 21/129
(?)**Rhys, Robert** ('Robert Ryse') 19/101
(?)**Rhys, William** ('William Ryse presoner') prisoner at Newgate 19/10
Richard butler of the charterhouse at Sheen 20/85; 21/27
Richard caretaker of the king's household at Richmond 21/27
Richard ('Richard bro(w)derer/browtherer') embroiderer 20/15; 2/15; 6/6
ap Richard, Gruffydd ('Griffith/Gryffyth Richard(es)', 'Grefyth ap Rychard') 20/114, 119; 21/91
Richardson, Christopher ('Christoffer/ Crystofer R(i)chardson(e)/ Richartson') servant of Lady Margaret 17/19, 22, 34, 40, 47, 58, 149; 21/35, 65
[R]**Richardson, Thomas** 20/126; 56/4
Richmond see **Machado**
Ride/Ryde see **Rede**
Rider ('yssher of my lady Maries chambre') servant of Princess Mary (q.v.) 21/27
Ryffe, Walter 2/7
Rygecroft 19/29
Rygmaydon, George ('my lordes servande') servant of Thomas Stanley I (q.v.) 20/164
Rykells, Jane ('(Jane) Rikelles/Rykyls'; 'Rikills lande in Kent', 'Rikles/Rikels/ Rykyl(le)s' 10/44; 20/60, 64) a ward of Lady Margaret; daughter of Richard Rickells, London weaver 10/44; 20/64; **'Rikels/Rykyl(le)s/Rikills/Rikles lande(s)'** 10/17, 46, 178–80; 20/60
Ryse see **Rhys**

Rivers see **Neville, Mary Fitzlewis Rivers**
Robartson, Thomas (prob. not same as Thomas Robertson (q.v.)) 2/35
Roberde ('master Roberde surjoyne') surgeon 17/28
Roberde/Robert farrier 17/64; 19/93
Robert, John ('John Rober[t]') 20/111
Robert ('grome of the chambre') perhaps Robert Merbury (q.v.) 20/16, 36
Robert ('yssher of my lady Maries chambre') servant of Princess Mary (q.v.) 21/27
Robert ('Robert servaunt to master deane') 20/147
Robert ('frere Robert then prior of Denbeghe') Carmelite friar; prior of Denbigh friary 19/70
Robert ('sir Robert of the chapell') see **Couper**
Robertson, Thomas ('Thomas Robertson (of Boston)') merchant of Boston 20/37, 46, 48, 63, 67, 91, 102, 136, 149; 19/99, 108
Robynson, (William) ('doctur Robynson') D.Cn.L. Cambridge 1490; officer of bishop of Ely 20/117; 19/32, 39, 101
Robson, (William) ('doctur Robson') D.Th. Cambridge 1505–6; vice chancellor 1507–8 19/20
Roche, master 19/43
Rochester, bishops of see **Fitzjames, Richard** and **Fisher, John**
Royston, Richard ('maister/docture/sir Richard Ro(y)ston', 'doctor Rounston', '(docture Royston) (d. 1525) parson of Alhalowez (the litill)' 19/16, 59; 'doctur Royston parson of Coldherbore' 19/70) D.Cn.L. Cambridge 1488–9; master of St Laurence Pountney, London 1489–1525; rector of All Hallows the Less, London 20/58, 67, 189; 19/16, 59, 70
Romney 21/20
Roper, (John) ('doctor/doctur Roper(e)') D. Th. Oxford 1500–1; Lady Margaret divinity reader 1502; Oxford tutor of Peper (q.v.) 20/27, 58, 172; 21/62; 19/109
Rose, John ('Johannis Rose unius clericorum dicti hospicii', '(John Rose) the survayars servande') clerk in the household; servant to the surveyor of the estates 16/4d; 20/115, 153, 159; 19/89 (see too **Rosse** below and see **SURVEYORS**)
Rose servant to Elizabeth Neville Scrope (q.v. sub **Wentworth**) 10/1
Rosse, John (perhaps the same as **John Rose** above) 21/134
Rowlande ('my ladys cordenar') shoemaker to Lady Margaret 17/28
Rowley ('Ro(w)ley', 'Rowle') servant of master Edward (q.v.), after which gentleman of Lady Margaret's chapel 17/60; 21/10, 80, 107, 163; 19/62, 124
Rukley, master 20/97
Russell, John 10/158
Russell, Miles ('Myles Russell of London goldsmyth' 21/110
Ruthall, Thomas ('the kynges secretary') (d. 1523) secretary to Henry VII and Henry VIII (1500–16); bishop of Durham 1509 20/61

SADDLERS 17/28, 42, 49 (see too **Atkynson, Palmer**)
SAILORS 20/32
Saint John, my lord of see **Docwra**
St John, Anne see **Clifford**
St John, Eleanor see **Grey**
St John, Elizabeth see **Fitzgerald**
St John, Joan Ewerby ('[mistress] Seynt Joh(e)n', '[maister Seynt John] and his wyff') daughter of Sir John Ewerby; wife of John St John of Lydiard Tregoze (q.v.) 17/58; 20/64, 131, 134, 161, 194; 21/36, 41, 49–50, 56, 75, 77, 118; 19/41, 62
[W]**St John, John** ('sir John St John') (d. 1525) Sir John St John II of Bletsoe, son of Sir John St John I (d. after 1488, half-brother of Lady Margaret Beaufort); chamberlain of Lady Margaret's household from 1504 and an executor of her will; m. Sybil, daughter of Rhys ap Morgan 10/126; 20/49, 52, 113, 121 (see too **CHAMBERLAIN** for references with no name)
[R]**St John, master John** ('([master]) (John) St Jo(h)n', 'John St John the yonger', 'John St John esquier/esquyere' 21/164; 19/62, 124)) (d. 1512) John St John of Lydiard Tregoze; son of Oliver St John II (d. 1497), half-brother of Lady Margaret Beaufort); m. Joan Ewerby (q.v. sub **St John**) 1498; servant of Lady Margaret 10/55, 176–7, 179–80; 17/19–20, 22, 28, 38, 50, 52, 56, 63; 20/20, 25, 38, 51, 64, 66, 131, 134, 170, 179, 194, 199; 21/11, 49–50, 56, 75, 77, 164; 19/62, 81 ('maister Seynt Johnes doughtur'), 99, 116 ('maister Seynt Johns daughter'), 124; 1/7v, 14v; 2/8, 12, 28; 6/6; 56/1; '(master)

Saint Johnis landes 10/55, 176–7, 179–80; 20/60; 21/75
St John, Mary see **Frogenhall**
St John, Maurice ('(ma(i)ster) Morice/Morys/ Morris St John', 'master Seynt John the kynges servant' 19/119) son of Sir John St John II; servant of Henry VII 20/49, 162, 198; 21/28, 30, 72; 19/89, 95, 108, 119
St John, Oliver ('Olyver(e) Seynt John/ Sayntione') son of Sir John St John II 17/21, 27, 40, 49, 55; 20/20, 43, 89, 138; 2/18, 25; 6/5, 6
SAINTS 20/30–2 **Andrew** apostle 19/45; 20/123, 183; **Anne** mother of the Virgin Mary 20/35, 160; 19/88; **Bartholomew** apostle 21/125; 19/109; **Benedict** ('Benet') 19/13; **Bride** Irish saint 1/5v, 17v; **Bridget** ('Brygyt/ Bregett') Swedish saint, founder of order of Birgittine nuns 17/24; 20/81, 83; 21/46, 98; 19/77; **Christopher** patron saint of travellers 20/182; **David** ('Davi(e)') foremost Welsh saint 20/80; 19/8; **Edmund** ('Edmound') venerated at Bury St Edmunds 17/31–2; 21/108; **Edward** Edward the Confessor venerated at Westminster Abbey 21/108, 112 (both err. 'Edmound'); 19/76, 109; **Etheldreda** ('Audre') venerated at Ely 17/36; 19/22, 27; **George** patron saint of England 20/182; 19/84; 1/15r; **Guthlac** ('Gudlake/Goodlok') venerated at Crowland 20/154; 19/35; **James the Great** apostle venerated at Compostela (q.v. in the PLACES index) 19/33; **John** apostle 17/62; **John the Baptist** 17/1; 20/30; 1/4r; **Laurence** 20/154; **Margaret** 19/13; **Martin** of Tours 21/66; **Mary Magdalene** ('Mary Mawdeleyn') 20/36, 60; **Michael** archangel 20/126; 1/14r; **Nicholas** (the child taking the part of) St Nicholas 17/59; 20/52, 124, 148, 183; 21/56, 143; 19/41, 109 (see too **BOY BISHOPS**); **Oswald** venerated at Peterborough 20/37; **Peter** apostle 20/157; **Philip** apostle 20/157; **Robert of Knaresborough** ('Robert of Knavysborowe') Yorkshire hermit 19/72; **Saviour** Christ as Saviour 20/154; **Stephen** first martyr 17/62; **Thomas** apostle 17/62; 20/30; 21/142; 19/42, 109; **Thomas of Canterbury** venerated at Canterbury 20/182; **Thomas of Westacre** 20/157; **Ursula** 20/35(see too in the PLACES index)
[R]**Salford, Henry** ('Henry/Henri Salforth/Sal(f) ford') 10/143; 20/188, 194; 21/79, 162; 19/23, 61, 123; 56/5
Samson of Collyweston 21/65
Sand, mistress 17/37
Sander, Stephen ('the fader of the Syon') confessor general of Syon 1497–1513 21/60
Sanders ('Sanders ...maister Coles clerk') clerk to Nicholas Coles (q.v.) 21/130
Sander(s) see **Saunders, Nicholas**
Sandys, (Margery) ('my lady Sandez') (d. 1539) wife of Sir William Sandys (q.v.); niece and heir of Sir Reginald Bray (q.v.) 17/27
Sandys, William ('William Sandez/Sandes') (d. 1540), knight of the body to Henry VII, later 1st baron Sandys 1523 17/20, 49
Sant, Randoll apprentice of Boniface Stanley (q.v.) 21/91
Sapcott, master 21/35, 37
Saunder skinner 20/77
[R]**Saunders, Nicholas** ('([Nicholas]) Sa(u) nder(s)/Saunde/Saundr(e)/Sawnder') clerk of the kitchen 16/31d; 10/67, 70, 91–2, 102, 117–20, 132, 135–6, 148, 151, 155, 160, 165, 182; 20/26, 39, 119, 122–3, 152, 157, 171, 183; 21/2, 10, 44–5, 49, 53, 58, 65–6, 117, 127, 134, 143–4; 19/33, 35, 43, 66, 87–8, 94; 1/15r-v; 56/1
Savage, Antone 2/11, 23, 27
Savage, Edward ('Edward Sawage') (d. 1527) son of Sir John (VI) Savage 20/31
Savage, Elizabeth ('Elyzabeth Sawage') prisoner at Newgate 19/10
Savage, Thomas ('my lord of Yorke') (d. 1507) archbishop of York 1501–7, son of Sir John Savage and Katherine Stanley 21/34; 19/9
Saxse, John 2/31
Say, William ('master Say', 'sir William Sȝaye') (d. 1529) owner of Basse (see the PLACES index) 19/75, 77, 107
Scales, Oliver ('Olyver Scal(l)is/Scal(l)es') notary public 19/15, 89, 93, 113; 1/5r
Scasbryge 20/57
Schaa see **Shaa**
SCHOLARS AND PREACHERS 20/37, 78, 90, 113, 137, 150, 155, 156, 166, 175 (tutor to Bury); 21/11–12, 16 (fellows of God's House, viz. Edward Fowke, Thomas Nun, John Scott, and John Fabbe), 19, 24 (tutor to Bury), 35 (fellows of God's House), 56; 19/38,

SCHOLARS AND PREACHERS (*Cont.*) 42, 91, 100; 1/7r, 11r (tutor to Bury) (see too **FRIARS** passim, **LADY MARGARET PREACHERS AND READERS**, and **Atkinson**, **Babyngton**, **Baker**, **Batmanson**, **Bekinsall**, **Bokenham**, **Brenkley**, **Chamber**, **Chappell**, **Chubbes**, **Colet**, **Cooper**, **Crossley**, **Darley**, **Deland**, **Ednam**, **Fabbe**, **Fairfax**, **Fell**, **Fotherby**, **Fremyngham**, **Genynson**, **Hamer**, **Hanson**, **Haryngton**, **Hochyn**, **Hutton**, **Lytchefeld**, **Longlond**, **Mawdysley**, **Nun**, **Palmer**, **Porte**, **Powell**, **Robynson**, **Robson**, **Scott**, **Syclyng**, **Silvester**, **Tanne**, **Thompson**, **Vaughan**, **Weston**, **Wodrow**, **Yonge**)

SCHOOLMASTERS 20/86; 21/24, 40, 111; 19/86

Schurley see **Shirley**

SCOTS 17/24; 20/11, 31, 45; 21/19

Scott, John ('John/ma(i)ster Scot/Scott(e)/ Skott', 'Thomas Pellettes tewtere') M.A. Cambridge 1506–7; fellow of God's House (later Christ's College); junior proctor and university preacher 1510–11; tutor to Thomas Pellet (q.v.) after Hochyn (q.v.) 10/147; 19/13, 31, 34, 89, 92–3, 113–14, 119

SCRIBES and scriveners 17/37, 61; 19/71 (see too **Baldwin**, **Carter**, **le Fevour**, **Hopwode**)

Scrope, lady see **Wentworth, Elizabeth Neville Scrope**

Scrope, Margaret ('my ladye of Suthffolk') (d. 1515) countess of Suffolk, wife of Edmund de la Pole, 8th earl of Suffolk (q.v.) 17/35

SECRETARIES

- **French secretary to Henry VII** see **Meautis**
- **secretary to Lady Margaret** (the/master secretary) 10/2; 17/21, 40, 43, 51 (see too **Hornby**, to whom all these citations refer)

Sedyngton, John ('my ladyes scoler') supported by Lady Margaret (a man of the same name attended her funeral as a herald, D91.24.2, p. 58) 19/105

Seynt John see **St John**

Senowe, Thomas ('Thomas Seno(we my ladyes) goldewyer drauer', etc., 'Thomas Seno of London', 'Thomassyn gold drayer', 'Thomysyn of London (goldwyre drawer)') London worker in gold thread 19/5, 24, 46, 74, 96; 1/7v, 10v, 15r

SERVANTS of Lady Margaret (see too **ALMONERS**, **BAILIFFS**, **CARRIERS**, **CHAMBERLAINS**, **CHANCELLORS**, **CHAPEL MEMBERS**, **COFFERERS**, **CONFESSORS**, **CONTROLLERS**, **DEANS**, **FOOLS**, **HORSE KEEPERS**, **LAWYERS**, **PHYSICIANS**, **RECEIVERS**, **SECRETARIES**, **STEWARDS**, **TREASURERS**, **VICE-CHAMBERLAINS**)

servants (unspecified) 16/4, 8, 13–15, 21, 31d; 10/182; 17/31; 20/68, 136, 197; 21/74, 157; 19/55, 91–2, 101, 118; 1/17r; **servants, male** Aderton (Richard and Thomas), Botton, Brydd, Brownyng (John), Carre (Hugh), Cheke, Cristen, Cuff, Dawson, Haryson, Hasilby, Kardon, Kylte, Kynge (John), Kynokes, Latymer, Leche, Merbury (Robert and William), Mychell, More, Mounteney, Notte (Osmund), Oldall, Orton, Osbourne (David and Gerard), Plomer, Richardson (Christopher), St John (John II and master John), Sympson, Shirley (Ralph), Smyth (Robert), Stukeley, Urmeston (John), Walter (John), William, Wodd; **servants, female** Clifford, Curson, Doryn, Fowler, Gower, Guildford, Massey, Mounteney, Osborne, Parker, Radcliffe, Stanhope, Stukeley, Walter, Willoughby, Woodhull, Yan

- **butchers** 16/6; see **Davy**, **Unwyn**
- **chamberers** 20/17 (see too **Doryn**, **Walter**)
- **clerks** 16/20
  - **of the closet** see **Peksall**
  - **of the counting house/of the works** see **Morice**
  - **of the kitchen** see **Gough**
  - **of the signet** 17/35
  - **of the spicery** see **Hilmer**
  - **of the vestry** 21/113 (see too **le Fevour**)
- **cooks** 20/17, 90; 21/15, 107; 19/89 (see too **Browne**, **Daye**, **Ludlow**)
- **footmen** 17/22, 35, 41; 20/35, 45, 80–1, 87, 89, 152, 155, 158, 169, 179–80; 21/21, 31, 33, 42, 54, 64, 74, 94, 116, 122, 136, 157; 19/12, 25–6, 36, 56, 74, 76, 88, 97I, 113, 118; 1/4v, 8v; 2/34; 6/4 (see too **Aughton**, **Carre**, **Clegg**, **Forster**, **Whittyngton**, **Williams**, **Wynstanley**)
- **gentlemen** 17/24 (see too **Fraunces, George; Radclyff, Roger; Fremingham, Robert**); **gentleman usher of the chamber** see **Pole**

gentlewomen 20/17 (see too **Clifford, Fowler, Merbury, Parker, Radcliffe, Stanhope, Woodhull, Yan**)
grooms (unspecified roles) Aderton, William; Aughton, Nicholas (later groom); Bygom; Carre, Richard; Cotton; Edlyn; Hilton; Love, John; Mouse; Thom(a)son; **groom porter** see **Flemyng**; **groom usher of the hall** see **Cotemote**
of the bakehouse see **Curtes**
of the beds see **Browne**
of the buttery see **Buk**
of the chamber see **Abeney**; **Aughton, Nicholas** (later yeoman); **Merycok**; **Robert** ((?) **Merbury**); **Worsley, Hugh**
of the chariot 17/51
of the kitchen 16/14
of the scullery 19/15, 18 (see too **Hynkersall**)
of the spicery see **Chamber**
of the stable see **Hyggeson**, **Hodgeson**, **Yngellysby**, **Jokye**, **Laborer**, **Long**, **Thomas**, **White**
of the vestry 21/40 (see too **le Fevour**)
of the wardrobe see **Nicholas**; **of the wardrobe of beds** 21/34 (see too **Forster**); **of the wardrobe of robes** see **Sym(p)son**
keeper of the jewel house see **Bothe**
ladies see **Guildford**, **Willoughby**
page of the acatry 56/5
shepherd see **Fermor**
supervisor of woods and fuels see **Justyce**
surveyor see **SURVEYORS**
ushers
gentleman usher see **Pole**
groom usher see **Cotemote**
usher of the hall see **Grome**
yeoman ushers see **Holland**, **Merbury**
yeomen
of the bakehouse see **Cas(s)e**, **Coke**, **Cox**, **Daye**
of the brewhouse see **Canwyke**
of the cellar see Vaux
of the chamber see **Aderton, Richard**; **Aughton, Nicholas** (former groom); **Love, William**; **Merycok**, **Madison**; **yeoman usher of the chamber** see **Holland**, **Merbury**
of the chariot see **Daniell**
of the pantry see Bram(p)ton, **Clyff**, **Davenport**, **Fyssh**
of the spicery see **Prat**
Sever, William ('the bisshop of Carlisle elect to Duresme' 10/56, 'my lord Carlyle ellecte to be bysshop of Durham' 20/6; 'the bysshop of Carlile/Karlill' 20/26, 34; 'the bysshopp of Derram' 20/30, 'my lorde of Duresme/Durisme' 10/83, 20/64, etc.) (d. 1505) bishop of Carlisle 1495–1502, bishop of Durham 1502–5 ('elect' July 1502) 10/56, 83; 20/6, 26, 30, 34, 64, 134, 151, 186, 194; 21/34
SEXTON 20/30
Shaa, John ('sir Jo(h)n S(c)haa/Shawe/ Sha(ye)') goldsmith; mayor of London 1501 10/1, 158; 17/3, 19, 27; 20/4, 92, 108–9; 2/3, 5, 6
Sharow, John ('pastorem de Burne') shepherd of Bourne [Lincs.] 16/17
Sharow, Robert of Bourne 16/19
Sharp, (John) gentleman usher to Henry VII 1/12r
Shaw, John prisoner at the Marshalsea 19/10
Shaw ('maister Shaw') 20/54 (prob. not Shaa (q.v.))
Shawe/Shaye see **Shaa**
Shefeld, Thomas ('(sir Thomas Shefeld) tresourer of Seynt Johnes', 'maister Sheffeld') treasurer of the priory of the Knights of the Hospital of St John of Jerusalem 19/34, 45, 81
SHEPHERDS see **Fermor** and **Sharow**
Sherade, Thomas child of Lady Margaret's chapel 19/45
Sherborn, Robert ('my lord (bysshop) of Seynt/Saincte David') bishop of St David's 1505–8 19/71, 93–4, 96
Sherley, Thomas servant of Margaret, queen of Scots (q.v.) 19/16
Shirley, Anne Vernon ('the mariage betwix sir Rauf Shyrley and my lady his wyff' 20/19; 'my/the lady Shirley/Shyrley', 'dame Anne Sherley') wife of Sir Ralph Shirley (q.v.) 10/159; 20/19; 19/70, 90, 98, 107, 118
Shirley, John ('Shirley/Shyrley/Sherl(e)y', 'Sherley (maister) clerk of the (kynges) kychen', etc.) servant of Henry VII 20/86, 109; 21/48; 19/11, 85
Shirley, Ralph ('Raffe Schurley', 'Rauf Shyrley', 'sir Rauff Sherley[s]' 'the mariage betwix sir Rauf Shyrley and my lady his wyff') servant of Lady Margaret 17/22, 24, 34, 40, 44, 47, 52; 20/19; 19/112
Shirley, Richard ('Richard Shyrley bayle off Ware', 'Richard/Rcharde Schurley/ Sherl(e)y') bailiff of Lady Margaret's town and manor of Ware [Herts.] ; 16/3; 10/24, 120; 17/2, 27, 29–39, 46, 49, 51; 20/31; 21/28; 19/107; 1/6v; 2/8, 11, 13

Shirley, Robert ('Roberde Schurley') 17/39
SHOEMAKERS see **Fodyll**, **Jakson**, **Maydwell**, **Rowlande**, **Watson**
Shore, Richard (d. 1510) draper; sheriff of London 1505–6 21/96
Shottley, John 20/152, 162
Syclyng, John ('John Siclinge', 'Johannes Syclynge', 'the maister of Cristes college', 'maister Sekelyng/Syk(e)lyng/Sygelyn/Sykellyng/Sykelynge/Scykelyng/Sikleyng') master of God's House (later Christ's College), Cambridge 1501–6 10/108, 146, 182; 20/190; 21/12, 16, 26, 28, 35, 56, 71, 97, 99–100, 114, 123, 127, 160; 19/5, 52
Sydington, John falconer to Lady Margaret 1/6v
SILKWOMEN 19/81 (see too **Benet**, **Fynch**)
Silvester, Gabriel ('(doctur) Gabryell (Selvester)') D.Th. Cambridge 1500; master of Clare Hall, 1496–1506 20/13, 168
Silvester, Thomas ('dane Silvestre') (d. 1507) monk of the Sheen charterhouse 20/85
[R]**Sym(p)son, Thomas** ('grome of the wardrop of the robis') servant of Lady Margaret 20/21, 40; 21/23, 45, 54–5; 56/3
SINGERS, singing children 20/119, 124; 19/93, 97; **singing men** 20/19 (cantor), 105–6; 21/8, 59, 124, 140; 19/96–7 (see too **Byggley**, **Corhonde**, **Conway**, **Cotterell**, **Flewde**, **Foske**, **Fox**, **Gardyner**, **Lambe**, **Marche**, **Orlow**, **Patryk**, **Pykryng**, **Smyth**, **Sothewyk**, **Stephyns**, **Watson**)
Skelman ('keper of Eltham') keeper of Eltham Palace 21/25
Skynner, George 21/7
Skynner, John 21/13
SKINNERS 17/47; 20/80, 179; 21/32; 2/36 (see too **Nicholas**, **Passelaw**, **Pynson**, **Saunder**, **Skynner**)
Skip ('the/my ladys fole', 'Skypp(e)', 'Skippe', 'Skip(p)') Lady Margaret's fool (d. 1508) 17/29, 35; 20/13, 28, 41, 47, 54, 57, 65, 93–4, 112, 124, 127, 135, 155, 167, 169, 181, 187, 196; 21/ 14, 32, 42, 46, 71, 117, 121, 142, 149, 160; 19/26, 52, 75
Skipwith, Gregory ('Skipwith/Skypwith', 'Gregorye Skyppewith') one of Lady Margaret's attorneys 10/2–3, 6, 16, 21, 103, 177–8; 17/65, 67; 21/4
Skipwith, Margaret widow of Gregory Skipwith 10/177
Skrene, lady see **Dymock**
Slacke, Roger ('Wyndsore') Windsor herald 1486–1502 17/50
Slye, Robert of Luddington [Lincs.] 16/18
Smerte 21/108
Smyth, John 20/101, 162
Smyth, John ('John Smyth of Westmynster syngyng man') singing man of Westminster Abbey; gentleman of the Chapel Royal by 1509 20/105
Smyth, John ('doctur(e) Smyth(e) (vichaunceller of Cambrige') (d. 1509) D.Th. Cambridge (no date); first Cambridge divinity reader supported by Lady Margaret 1498; vice-chancellor of the University several times 1497–1505 17/37, 55, 60; 20/171, 182; 21/10; 19/12, 71, 100
Smyth, Robert ('Roberde Smyth', 'Robert Smythe') servant of Lady Margaret 17/22, 34, 40, 44, 47, 52; 20/18, 23, 35
Smyth, Thomas of Oakham 10/32
Smyth, William ('of the robes') page, later groom of the wardrobe of robes, to Henry VII 19/11
Smith, William ('the bysshop of Lyncoln', 'my lord (of) Lyncoln') (d. 1514) B.C.L. Oxford 1492; bishop of Coventry and Lichfield 1492–5; council member to Arthur, prince of Wales (q.v.) 1493–1502; bishop of Lincoln 1496–1514 20/43, 61, 100, 103, 107, 161; 21/27; 19/43, 100; 1/8v, 11r
Smythe, mistress 19/42
SMITHS 20/57; 21/109; 1/12r
Snow, Thomas of Croydon 16/2, 21
SOJOURNERS see **Cheney, Margaret**; **Clifford, Anne**; **Grey, Anne**; **Kyme, Cecily**; **Neville, Mary**; **Wentworth, Elizabeth**
Somerset, Arthur ('Arture Somersete') 20/83
Somerset, Charles ('sir Charles (Somerset)') (d. 1526) baron Herbert (earl of Worcester 1514); illegitimate son of Henry Beaufort, 2nd duke of Somerset; m. Elizabeth Herbert (d. 1507), granddaughter of William Herbert (d. 1469); vice-chamberlain to Henry VII; an executor of Lady Margaret's will 20/109, 137
Somerset ('Somersettes landes') lands originally held by Lady Margaret's father, John, duke of Somerset (see Jones and Underwood, *The King's Mother*, Appendix 2A, pp. 262–4) 10/22

Soper, Thomas ('Thomas Sooper', '(Thomas) Soper(e) (my ladys solyst(it)er/ celyster/solicit(o)ur/solicet(o)ur/ solister/solycetur(e)',) solicitor to Lady Margaret Beaufort 10/29, 58, 103, 131, 149, 152, 161; 20/7, 59–60, 67, 100, 128, 147, 173, 189; 21/4, 14, 44, 50, 62, 67, 73, 77, 80, 86, 87, 93, 123, 130, 145, 148, 149, 154, 160, 164; 19/3, 7, 17, 22, 42, 45, 48, 54, 55, 62, 66, 73, 94, 101 ('the selystour'), 104, 113, 120, 121; 1/5v, 6r, 18r
Sothewyk ('syngyng man') 20/39
Souche/Sowche/Swoche see **Zouche**
Southwell, Robert ('sir Robert Southwell/ Sothewell') auditor of the Exchequer 21/126, 159
SPANIARDS 20/121 (for 'the counties of Spayne' see **Enríquez de Velasco**; for 'the kyng of Castell' see **Philip I**)
SPEARMEN (King's Spears) 21/23, 72
Spencer, John ('presoner') prisoner at Ludgate 19/10
Spenser, mistress 20/13
Spicer, Thomas 1/6v
Spierinck, Nicholas ('Nicholas Spernig') Cambridge book dealer 19/110
Spyght, Thomas clothman 2/13
Spinola, Benedetto ('Benedyk Spyn(y)all', 'Benedik Sppynoll') Genoese merchant 2/9–10
Stacion (?) surname for an unknown book dealer; (?) *stacion[er]* (cf. *MED* **stacioner(e)** *n.* 1b) 21/145
Stafferton ('maister Stafferton') 21/110
Stafferton, Elizabeth 21/113; 19/5, 114
Stafford, Edward ('my lord(e) (of(f)) Bukyngham/Bokyngham') (d. 1521) 3rd duke of Buckingham, ward (with his brother Henry) of Lady Margaret 10/29; 20/176; 21/4, 25; 'the duke of Bokynghams landes' 21/4
Stafford, Elizabeth see **Radcliffe, Elizabeth Stafford**
Stafford, Henry ('lord Henry Stafforth') earl of Wiltshire, brother of Edward Stafford (q.v.); m. (1504) Cecily Bonville Grey (q.v.) 20/176
Stakhouse, John ('(John) Stak(e)house/ Stakhowse') bailiff of Cottingham 10/5; 17/2; 20/46, 66, 96, 149, 200; 21/8, 74, 127
Stamford, John abbot of Pipewell *c.*1504-*c.*1510 16/17
Stanbank ('Stanbancke my ladyes scoler at Parys') maintained in Paris by Lady Margaret 19/98, 116
Standish, (Henry) ('doct(o)ur Standych/ Standyshe/Standisshe') D.Th. Oxford by 1502; Franciscan friar; Provincial for the Order in England 1505; warden of London convent *c.*1508 20/146; 1/5r
[R]**Standish, James** 56/1
Stanhope, master ('maister Stannoppe') 19/63
[W]**Stanhope, Alice** ('([mistress]/Alyce Stannop(p)/Stan(e)hop') gentlewoman to Lady Margaret 20/145, 179–80, 187, 197; 21/22, 25, 27–8, 33, 38–9, 47, 57, 93, 100, 102–4, 108, 110–13, 117, 122, 126, 135, 146; 19/8, 23, 29, 31, 37, 40–1, 74, 76–8, 80–2, 84–6, 89, 104, 107, 109; 1/13r, 14r
Stanley, master of Staffordshire 20/119
Stanley, Anne Hastings ('my lady Derby') (d. 1550) wife of Thomas Stanley II (q.v.) 19/16, 87
Stanley, Boniface ('Bonyfface my lordes servand', 'Bonyf(f)ace/Boneface (Stanley)', 'Bonyface surgon') physician to Thomas Stanley I (q.v.) and after his death to Lady Margaret 20/117; 21/10, 12, 45, 47, 59, 75, 91, 117, 155
Stanley, Eleanor ('(mastres/maistrez) Elynor Stanley') (d. December 1503) daughter of George Stanley, Lord Strange (son of Thomas Stanley I (q.v.)) 20/125, 139, 146
Stanley, James ('my lord of Ely') bishop of Ely 1506–15, son of Thomas Stanley I (q.v.) and Eleanor Neville 10/158; 19/21, 28, 62, 80, 89, 91, 124; 1/7r
Stanley, Reynold ('Reynolde/Raynold', 'Stanley') household servant and kinsman of Thomas Stanley I (q.v.) 17/33, 62; 20/58
Stanley, Thomas ('my lord(e) (of Derby)') (d. 29 July 1504) Thomas Stanley I, 1st earl of Derby, constable of England, high steward of the duchy of Lancaster; m. (1) Eleanor Neville 1457, (2) Lady Margaret Beaufort 1472 17/33, 37–8, 59, 64; 20/22, 24, 36–7, 40, 52, 58, 66, 91, 100, 114, 116–17, 120, 128, 147–8, 150, 164, 171
Stanley, Thomas ('(maister) sir Thomas Stanley', 'my lord(e) (of) Derbye/ Derbie') (d. 1521) Thomas Stanley II, 2nd earl of Derby, grandson of Thomas Stanley I (q.v.) 20/36–7, 168; 21/23, 38–9, 92, 163, 168; 19/16, 87; 1/4r, 7v, 8r

Stark(e)y, Henry household servant of Thomas Stanley I (q.v.) 20/147; 21/143
Staunton, John ('John Stantons son', 'yong Staunton') (?) groom of the chamber to Elizabeth of York 17/24; 20/110
Stephyns, Thomas ('prest') Cambridge priest; singing man 20/105
Stevenson, John of Crowland 20/118
STEWARDS
of the abbot of Westminster 21/40 (see **Islip**)
of the hospital of St Anthony see **Couper**
of John Fisher's household see **Fisher, (Robert)**
of Lady Margaret's estates see **Heven**, **Hussey**, **Lynne**
of Lady Margaret's household see **Knyvett**
of Owen Pole see **Pole, John**
of Tattershall see **Heven**
Stewart, Alexander ('the erle of Boughen [son]') (d. 1505) 2nd earl of Buchan 20/95
Stewart, Andrew ('byschope of Murreyn', 'bysshop of morrey') (d. 1501) bishop of Moray 17/30; 20/100
Style, John 6/9
Stockdale, William ('thabbot of Cristall') abbot of Kirkstall 1501–9 10/25
Stok, Richard 21/12
Stoke, John 20/22
STONE CUTTER see **van Delff**
Stones, Robert glazier 2/8, 10–12, 14; 6/6
Stoughton, Reginald joiner 1/8v
Stowell, John ('yong Stowell') ward of Lady Margaret 1/7r, 17r; 19/112, 116
Strache 19/34
(?)**Strangways** ('Strangquysshe') 17/52
Stravarme, Nicholas 19/91
Strenger (?) personal name 19/46, 75
Stuard, Nicholas ('a Flemyng') 20/114
STUDENTS ((my lady's)/a scholar/scholars) supported at school/university 17/67; 20/30, 65, 186, 196; 21/11, 18, 71, 154, 159; 19/14, 21, 51, 98, 105, 116 (see **Burgon**, **Bury**, **Collyngwode**, **Colman**, **Denton**, **Fawne**, **Jakson**, **Lowthe**, **Masson**, **Moyne**, **Pellett**, **Peper**, **Sedyngton**, **Stanbank**, **Watwod**, **Wheteley**, **Wilsford**)
Stukeley ('Stukeley maister Hussy servande') 21/124
[RW]**Stukeley, Margaret** ('Merget(t)/Marg(ar)et Stuk(e)ley/Stewkely', 'maisteres Margaret') wife of Richard Stukeley; servant of Lady Margaret (q.v.) 20/120; 21/34, 157; 19/9, 34, 90; 56/1
[RW]**Stukeley, Richard** ('Richard(e) Stewk(e)ley/Stewkely', '(Richarde) Stukley/Stukel(e)y') servant of Lady Margaret 17/19, 26, 35, 46; 20/18, 24, 58, 94, 119, 127, 152, 165, 187, 189; 21/36, 46, 55, 102, 106, 118; 19/9, 46, 80, 105; 56/2
Suffolk, lady see **Scrope, Margaret**
SUFFRAGANS 20/59, 102, 106, 172, 185, 189, 198
SUITORS 1/6r
SUPPLIERS of furs see **Gesson**; **of wood** see **Cordall**
Surrey, lady see **Howard, Agnes Tilney**
SURVEYORS ('maister survayer' 20/160, 162 unnamed) 20/115, 153, 159–60, 162, 175
Sutton, Edward ('the baron(e) of Dudley', 'my lord Dudley/Dodlye', 'my lorde Dogley') (d. 1532) 2nd baron Dudley 10/141; 21/75, 120; 19/43

Tabret, Steven ('Steven Tab(e)ret') performer on a tabret, i.e. a small drum 20/38, 60, 128, 188; 21/61, 144; 19/45, 99(?), 109
Tayllebosse, Elizabeth Gascoigne ('a servand of the lady Taylebosse') wife of Sir George Tailboys of Lincs. (d. insane 1538) 20/42
Tayleor, Robert tailor 19/87
Taileour, William tailor 19/46
Tayllyour, Thomas ('Thomas Tayllyour servientis vice camerarii') servant of Richard Lynne (q.v.) 21/87
TAILORS 20/97, 181; 21/32; 19/6, 46; 21/32; 19/6 (see too **Dyse**, **God**, **Moncaster**, **Tayleor**, **Taileour**, **Tayllour**)
Talbot, mistress ('ma(i)stres Talbot(t)') 20/104, 138, 147
[R]**Talbot, John** ('master/John Talbot(t)' 17/39, 51, 62; 56/3
Tales, Robert of Stamford [Lincs.] 16/20, 16d
Tanne, John ('of Lynne merchaunt') 16/19; 20/122; 21/11, 80; 19/62
Tanne, (John) ('ma(i)ster Tanne') B.Th. Cambridge 1506–7; University preacher 1507–8 19/108; 1/8v
TANNERS see **Houghton** and **Thomson**
TAPESTRY WORKERS see **Collop**
Tempest 20/165; 19/121
Thomas ('blynde Thomas') 21/138
Thomas ('long Thomas') 21/31
Thomas ('sir Thomas of Cheston') priest of Cheshunt [Herts.] 19/29
Thomas ('grome of the stabyll') servant of Lady Margaret 20/61; 21/102

Thomas ('late servande unto maister Pyee') 20/151
Thomas servant of William Merbury (q.v.) 20/177
Thomas ('Long Thomas') 21/31
ap Thomas, Rhys ('sir Rice ap Thomas') (d. 1525) landowner and soldier; Henry VII's chief lieutenant in south Wales 19/81
Thomas, William ('the kinges servant') servant to Henry VII 1/14v
Thom(a)son, William ('the grome') groom to Lady Margaret 17/35, 41, 44, 47, 53
Thomassyn, Thomysyn see **Senowe**
Thomson, John tanner of Deeping 16/2, 21, 30d
Thomson, John priest of Windsor 17/25; 20/116
Thomson, (Robert) ('frere Thomson prior of the blak freris at Langley') B.Th. Cambridge 1496–7; prior of King's Langley; Dominican friar Cambridge convent 21/99
Thomson, (Thomas) ('master/doctor Tomson (master of Cristes college)') (d. 1540) D.Th. Cambridge 1506–7; third master of Christ's College 1508–17 10/132–3, 147
Thomson, William of St Alban's 16/21, 12d
Thornby, John ('baliff of Wasshingborogh') 10/25
Thorne, Robert 2/28
Thorneboro, (William) ('doctur Thorneboro chaunceller unto the bysshop of Ely') D.C.L. Cambridge 1494–5; chancellor of Ely diocese 1503 21/147
Thorp, John servant of the abbot of Pipewell (see **Stamford**) 16/17
Thrognall see **Frogenhall**
Thurstane, ((?) John) ('brotherar of London') London embroiderer 21/47
Thwaytes, John ('[master]/sir (John) (T) whayt(t)es/ Thwayt(t)es/Thwates/ Thwatis/Thawythis/Twa(yt)tes/Tw(h) aytes/Thayttes/Thawytez', 'Thawyttes sawdyor of Calles') scholar supported by Lady Margaret in Paris; thereafter in France on Lady Margaret's service 10/85, 87; 20/35, 54, 65, 82, 100, 107, 126c, 138, 156, 162, 194, 197; 21/28, 67, 77, 114, 128, 159
Thwaytes, Thomas ('Thomas Twhaytes') brother of John Thwaytes (q.v.) 10/85, 87; 21/67
Tydmersh, Thomas 2/29
Tiler, master 19/77
Tyler, (William) gentleman usher to Henry VII 1/12r
Tymes/Tymys, Edward 19/43, 104
Tynbygh, William (d. 1531) prior of the London charterhouse from 1500 21/104
Tyrrell, Thomas ('master Tyrell', 'sir Thomas Tyrell/Terell/Derrell') (?) of Heron, East Horndon, Essex (d. 1510); master of the horses to Elizabeth of York 17/29; 20/126, 126c
Todde, Thomas 21/58
Trafforth, Geoffrey ('sir Geffrey Trafforth') chaplain to Thomas Stanley I (q.v.) 20/171
TREASURERS
treasurer of the chamber to Henry VII see **Heron**
treasurer of the chamber to Lady Margaret 10/159; 21/83; 19/1, 65; 1/11r (see too **COFFERER** and **Worsley, Fremingham**)
treasurer of the household to Lady Margaret (the ((for)said)/(same)/my lady's/master) treasurer (of household)) see **Bedell**
treasurer of the Knights Hospitallers of St John of Jerusalem see **Shefeld**
treasurer to Prince Henry see **Rede, Robert**
Treglyston, John ('(John Treglyston) my lord chamberlayne servand') servant of Giles Daubeney (q.v.) 21/62, 118
Trevelyan ('Trevilian') 10/139
Treverne, Nicholas ('Nicholas Treverne/ Trevyrne') 21/37, 65; 19/113
Trygg, John of Peterborough 20/52
Trygge, Nicholas of Stamford [Lincs.] 20/118; (?) 21/20 ('Trygg'); 19/110
Trynam, master ('officer of the bysshop of Norwyche') officer of Richard Nix (q.v.) 19/15
Tudor, Jasper ('my lord of Bedford') (d. 1495) duke of Bedford; uncle of Henry VII 1/4r
Tuk, Agnes ('Annes Tuk of Dodyngton') 21/39
Turnar, Hugh 19/42
Turney, John 10/32, 112
Turner, John 20/51
Turpyn, Nicholas 20/126c, 139

Umfrey see **Humphrey**
[R]**Underwood, John** 56/5
Untryx see **van Utrecht**
Unwyn, Henry ('carnificem hospicii') butcher to Lady Margaret 16/8d, 10d
Urmeston, Elizabeth ('my lady Urmeston') m. (1) Roger Chamberlain, (2) Roger Ormeston (q.v.) 21/53

[R]**Urmeston, John** ('John Urmeston/ Ormeston') brother or nephew of Roger Ormeston (q.v. sub **Urmeston**); servant of Lady Margaret 20/30, 37, 87–8, 95, 117; 21/58, 118; 56/5
Urmeston, Roger see **Ormeston**
Urmeston, Thomas ('the vicare of Kendall', 'receyvor/receptour of Kendal(l)') brother of Roger Ormeston (q.v.) 10/31, 33, 83, 84, 112; 20/167
Urmeston, William ('sir William Urmeston clerke') priest; relative of Roger Ormeston 10/158
Urswick, Christopher ('the dean ... at Wynesowre') dean of Windsor 1496–1505 21/23
USHERS see **Allen**, **Arnold**, **Bulstrode**, **Crowmeyre**, **Fitzwilliam**, **Fowler**, **Jones**, **Knolles**, **Rider**, **Robert**, **Sharp**, **Tyler** (see too **USHERS** sub **SERVANTS of Lady Margaret**)
Utherby ('Utherby[is wyffe]') 20/125

(?)**van Utrecht, John** (('John Untryx/Utrike/ Utryth/Utryght/Utrysshe/Utrix/ Utryche (('my ladyes') gold(e) smyth)';'John Vanutaysshe/ Vanutrysshe/Vanutryk/Vanutrike/ Vauntrix**'**) goldsmith to Lady Margaret 21/146; 19/9, 11, 29, 36, 74, 79, 81, 89, 94, 96, 100, 102; 1/4r, 5r, 10r, 15r
Vayne, Geoffrey 19/73
Varnam see **Vernon**
Varney see **Verney**
Vaselay, mistress 19/36
Vatere see **Walter**
Vaughan, (Edward) ('maister/doctur Waghan') D.Cn.L. & D. C.L. Cambridge 1481–2; treasurer of St Paul's 1503–9; bishop of St David's 1509–22 20/104; 21/104
Vauntrix see **van Utrecht**
[R]**Vaux, Edward** ('Edward(um) Vauce/Vause/ Wauce/Waus(e) (valettum sellarii)', '(the yoman) of the seller') yeoman of the cellar to Lady Margaret 16/19, 5d; 17/30; 20/13, 39, 42, 175; 21/92, 124; 19/43, 82, 107; 56/2
Vaux, Katherine Peniston ('my lady Vause/ Wauce') mother of Nicholas Vaux (q.v.) and Jane Vaux Guildford (q.v.) 17/51; 20/13, 23
Vaux, Nicholas ('sir Nicholas Vaus') (d. 1523) knight; son of Sir William Vaux of Harrowden; brother of Lady Jane Guildford (q.v.) 17/62
Vavasour, Edward ('Edward Vavysere/ Vavesere') (?) receiver for Billingborough [Lincs.] 10/15, 23
Velles see **Welles**
de Vere, John ('my lord(e)(of) Ox(f)ford(e)/ Oxforth/Oxonford[es]') (d. 1513) 13th earl of Oxford; lord great chamberlain to Henry VII 1485–1513; m. (1) Margaret Neville (q.v. sub **de Vere**) 17/30–1; 20/32, 116–17, 119, 121, 146, 168; 21/8, 139; 19/9
de Vere, Margaret Neville ('my lady Nevell') daughter of Richard Neville, earl of Salisbury; wife of John de Vere, earl of Oxford (q.v.) 17/54
[W]**Verney, Eleanor Pole** ('[mistress]/my lady Varney//Verney/Werney'; 'dame Elynour Verney', 'my lady his [Ralph Verney] wyffe/wiff'; 'maistres Werney comyng from Skotland' 21/48, 'dame Alienor Werney with the quene of Skottes' 21/140,) daughter of Geoffrey Pole and Edith St John (half-sister of Lady Margaret); wife of Sir Ralph Verney (q.v.); gentlewoman to Margaret Tudor (q.v.) 17/49; 20/44, 86; 21/48, 140, 154; 19/21, 53; 1/5r, 7r
Verney, Ralph ('(sir) (Raff(e)/Rauffe) Verney/ Varney', 'sir Rauff Werney chamberlayn to the quene of Skottes' 20/177) m. Eleanor Pole (q.v. sub **Verney**) by 1503 (but see above 'mastres Varney' 17/49 (i.e. 1498)); chamberlain to Margaret Tudor (q.v.) 17/34, 40, 52; 20/177; 19/21, 53
Vernon ('Varnam/Wernam (of Baldok)') of Baldock [Herts.] 19/107, 110
Vertue, (Robert or **William)** master mason of the king's works at Westminster 21/40
Verun, Richard priest 20/186
VESTMENT MAKERS 17/27; 20/108–9 (see too **Rede**)
VICE-CHAMBERLAINS
vice-chamberlain of Henry VII's household see **Somerset**
vice-chamberlain of Lady Margaret's household (master vice-chamberlain) see **Lynne**
Videt, James/Jacques ('Portkullys' 17/21 47; 'Jamys the kynges purcyvant' 20/123, 127) Portcullis pursuivant 17/21, 47; 20/123, 127
Vincent ('Wensent/Wencent', 'Vynsent') 20/40, 170(?); 2/34
VINTNERS see **Bulle**, **Mattock**

Wadforth, Wyllyam 20/16
WAFER MAKER 19/15
Waghan see **Vaughan**
WAGONERS 17/48
Waynef(f)ord/Waynsforth see **Wentworth**
Waywyn ('executour to doctur Mawdysley' (q.v.) 21/10
Wake, master 20/58, 176
Walcot, Humfrey 19/105, 118
RWalcote/Walcott, Oliver 19/74; 56/4
Walker, Roger 19/73
Wall(es), William ('sir Willyam/William Wall(es) (of the lordship of Kendale)', etc.; 'maister Wallis/Walles (oon of the kynges chapplens)') receiver for Kendal *c.*1492–1501; chaplain to Thomas Stanley I (q.v.) and then to Henry VII 10/4, 5, 16–18; 20/94, 100, 104
Wallys, John of Stamford [Lincs.] 19/21
Walshe, Margaret 21/47
RWalsheman, John 56/4
Walssh, John farmer 17/2
RWalter, Jane chamberer of Lady Margaret 19/92; 56/1
Walter, John servant of Lady Margaret (d. 1506) 17/34, 37, 40, 46; 20/21, 103, 111, 168, 171, 173, 188, 194, 196; 21/16, 79, 115, 118, 121, 130, 159, 163; 19/61, 123
Walter, William 10/158; 21/136
Walter ('Vatere of the seller') servant of the privy cellar to Henry VII 21/49
RWarcop(pe), Nicholas bailiff of Hatfield 1/9r; 56/4
Ward, Hugh ('Hugh(e)/Hue Ward(e)') merchant of Boston 10/4, 5; 20/12, 38; 19/17
Warde, John servant of Reginald Bray (q.v.) 20/95
WARDROBERS OF THE KING 1/11r (see too **Fligh**, **Hasulrygg**, **Jenet**, **Smyth**)
WARDS of Lady Margaret 17/42; 20/57; 21/132 (see too **Burgon**, **Drew**, **Gybbon**, **Godston**, **Golsell**, **Heron**, **Langdale**, **Lymner**, **Lyne**, **Lowe**, **Rykyls**, **Stowell**)
Warham, William('my lorde of Canturburi[es]/Caunterbury[ez]/ Canterbury', 'my lord chauncellour') lord chancellor 1502–15; archbishop of Canterbury 1503–32 10/141; 21/49, 118; 19/45
Warre, William of Croydon 16/2; 21/92, 93
Warssop see **Wors(s)op**
RWaterton, Robert 56/3
RWaterton, Thomas 56/5
Watson shoemaker 21/135
Watson, Thomas ('(Thomas/maister) Watson (syngyng man of Westmynster)') master of the children at Westminster Abbey 1500–2; gentleman of Lady Margaret's chapel by January 1506 (21/94) 20/17, 25, 43, 45, 68, 106; 21/94
Wattes, Robert 2/15, 29, 36
Watwod, William ('Wyllyam Watwod chyld of the chappell') child of Lady Margaret's chapel; scholar at Eton 20/36
Wauce/Waus see **Vaux**
Webbe, Elizabeth/mistress see **Woodhall**
Webbe, William ('Willyam Webbe') of King's Cliffe [Northants] 20/41
Welby, Thomas ('maister Welby') of Moulton 20/107, 138, 162, 194 (Appendix), 200
Welles, Cecily see **Kyme**
Welles, John ('my lorde Welles/Wellis') Viscount Welles (d. 1499), half-brother to Lady Margaret 10/3; 17/38
Welles, Thomas ('Thomas Velles/Welles clerk of Eston') clerk of Easton Neston 20/187; 21/14
WELSHMEN 20/46, 80; 19/8, 19, 21 (see too **ap Howel**, **(ap) Rhys**, **ap Richard**, (?) **Walsheman**)
Welson, Margery 20/20
Wencent/Wensent see **Vincent**
Wentworth ('gentylman yssher with the kynges grace') servant of Henry VII 19/77
Wentworth, Elizabeth Neville Scrope ('my lady Waynef(f)ord/Waynsforth' 10/55, 142; 20/5; 'my lady Scro(o)pe/Scrop(p)') daughter of John Neville (d. 1471), marquess Montagu; sister of Lucy Neville Fitzwilliam Browne (q.v.); m. (1) Thomas, sixth Lord Scrope of Upsall and Masham (d. 1493), (2) Sir Henry Wentworth (d. 1500) 10/1, 55, 138, 142, 158; 20/5, 81; 21/16, 58; 19/36, 93, 105
Wentworth, Richard ('Richard Weyntworth') stepson of Elizabeth Neville Scrope (q.v. sub **Wentworth**) 10/158
Wernam see **Vernon**
Werney see **Verney**
West, Thomas ('my lord Delaware') (d. 1525) 8th baron de la Warr 21/95
Weston, (Anne) ('maistrez Weston') (?) former gentlewoman to Elizabeth of York; wife of Richard Weston (q.v.) 21/27
Weston, James ('doctour (Jamys) Weston') scholar (untraced) 2/29; 6/4

Weston, (Richard) ('(maister) Weston (the kynges servand)') groom of the privy chamber to Henry VII 20/42, 86, 88; 21/26, 48, 50; 19/11, 54, 85
Wettnall, Margaret ('Mergett Wettnall somtyme keper of my lordes place in London') former keeper of Derby House 21/23
Whayttes see **Thwaytes**
Whet(e)ley, Thomas ('a skoller of my ladys at Cambryge') supported by Lady Margaret at Cambridge 17/19, 61
Whytamore, Thomas ('Thomas Whytamore' 19/17
Whytamore, William ('[master]/William Whyt(a)more/W(h)itamore/Whitmore/ Quytmore', servant of Henry Parker (q.v.) 17/26, 67; 20/18; 21/47; 19/14, 24, 38, 44, 78, 95
[W]**White, Margaret** ('my ladyes ancrysse at the nunnys in Stampfort', etc.) anchoress at the Benedictine nuns of the priory of St Michael, Stamford [Lincs.]; admitted to the St Katherine guild of St Paul, Stamford 1504; (see **ANCHORESSES**; her sister was a Benedictine nun at Minster priory on the Isle of Sheppey (see **NUNS**)
White, Thomas ('oon of the gromys of the stabyll') servant of Lady Margaret 20/145
Whytelege, Robert priest 19/96
Whithed, John of Easton Neston 21/135
Whytyng, (John) ('Whitynge/Whytynge (gentylman ussher of the kyngez chamber)**'**, 'Quytyng') servant of Henry VII 17/38; 20/109; 21/27
Whytyng, William 2/11
Whitstones, James ('[master/doctor] Whitstones/Whetston', 'maister president/presyden(t)', 'the presydent of Stampforth', 'maister Quytstones presydent of my ladys councell', 'maister presydent doctur Quytstons') B.Cn.L. Cambridge 1492, D.Cn.L. Bologna 1494; president of Lady Margaret's council 20/20, 61, 94, 100, 104, 111, 113–14, 117, 119, 138–9, 183; 21/30, 49, 57, 73, 104, 109, 125, 130, 134, 140, 144; 19/48, 71–3, 83, 119
Whittyngton, William ('(William) Whittyngton/Whyt(t)yngton') footman to Lady Margaret; shared a room at Collyweston with Clegg (q.v.) 17/46, 52; 20/24, 77
Wyatt, Richard ('maister (Richard) Wyett(e)/ Wyat(t)/Wyot (maister of Crystes collage)'; 'master Richarde Clerke [sic] maister of the same college' 19/53, 'master Henry [sic] Wyat' 19/21) D. Th. Cambridge 1506–7; second master of Christ's College 1506–8 21/23(?); 19/5, 7, 14, 21, 34, 37, 53, 94; 1/8v
Wye servant of bishop of Lincoln (q.v. sub **Smith**) 19/100
Wyett, Henry 21/23 (perhaps also 21/23 but not 19/21)
Wyldebore, William ('Wyllyam/William Weldbore/Wyldebore/Wildebore') carrier 20/45, 126b, 162, 177, 183; 21/11
Wyle ('the kynges messenger') 20/16
Wylkyn see **de Worde**
Wylkynson, John 2/24
Wylles, William of Waltham Cross 21/139
William ('potyknar') apothecary 17/25, 27
William ('of the chaundry') servant of Lady Margaret 21/38; 19/87
Wylliams, Davy ('goldsmyth') 20/106
Williams, John ('John fot(t)man/fo(o)teman', 'John Williams/Wylliams (late footeman unto my ladys grace 1/4v, 8v)' footman to Lady Margaret 20/35, 45, 80–1, 87, 152–3, 155, 158, 169–70, 179–80; 21/21, 31, 127, 134; 19/37, 96, 102, 108, 112; 1/4v, 8v
Williams, John ('of the seller') servant of Henry VII 19/95
Williams, Thomas 21/46; 19/86
Willyamson, John 19/21
Williamson, Michael of Oakham 16/17
Wyllyamson, William ('þe bayly of Makesey', 'Wyllyam Wyllyamson baily of Maksey') bailiff of Maxey 10/131; 20/110
Wyllyn, William of Cheshunt 16/6, 21, 12d
Willoughby, Elizabeth Burgh Fitzhugh ('my lady Willoughby/Wylloughby') one of Lady Margaret's ladies; m. (1) Richard Fitzhugh, Baron Fitzhugh, (2) Sir Henry Willoughby (q.v) 19/97; 1/10v
Willoughby, Henry ('sir Harry Wellybe/ Wyllughby', 'sir Henry/Herry Wyllo(u)ghby/Willughby/Willoughbi/ Willoughby/Willyby (knyght)') (d. 1528) knight of the body to Henry VII 10/112, 114, 125, 158; 20/46, 134, 194; 21/79, 90, 153, 162; 19/61, 123
[W]**Wilsford, Edmund** ('doctur (Edmonde) Wylforde/Wilsforde my ladys reder in devenyte at Oxfforde'; 'doctor Willesford') D.Th. Oxford 1497; first Oxford divinity reader supported by Lady Margaret 1498; her confessor by

June 1508 (so called in her will) 10/133; 17/42, 46 (see too **CONFESSORS**)
Wilson, John 21/52
Winchester, bishop of see **Fox**
Windsor, Margaret ('[mistress] Wynd(y)sore/ Wynesowre/Wyndesor/Wyndisowre', 'maistres Wensoure/Wenysowre/ Wen(d)eso(w)re/Wendysore', 'lady Wynsour', 'dame Margaret Wyndesore') god-daughter of Lady Margaret; professed at Syon Abbey at Lady Margaret's expense 1506 10/104; 17/24; 20/29, 84–5, 127, 151, 154, 157, 186–7, 194; 21/16, 20, 23–4, 98, 113; 19/10, 35, 77; 1/4r, 9v; 2/28
Wyndsore see **Slacke**
Wynfeld, Robert ('Robert Wynfeld') 20/109
Wynslow ('on Wynslow doughtur') 21/126
Wynstanley, Henry ('Herry/Henry (Wynstanley fo(o)t(e)man)', 'Henry (Wenstanley (fottmen))', 'Harry/ Henry fotman') footman to Lady Margaret 20/35, 80, 94, 112, 123, 155, 158, 169, 188; 21/31, 33, 35, 46, 104, 117, 121, 142, 160; 19/48, 75
Wittylbury, master 21/39
Wodd, Randall (?) servant of Lady Margaret 17/53
Wodford, John 19/91
Wodforth, William 20/129
Wodrow, William ('doctour Woddrowe') D.Th. Cambridge 1506–7; master of Clare Hall from 1506 19/29
Wodward, William ('(Wyllyam) Wodward(e)', 'Wodward goldraw(ʒ)ere', 'Wadward goldwyredrawʒere') worker in gold thread 17/28; 20/20, 55, 89; 2/17, 23, 30–1
Wolverston, Thomas servant of Henry VII 20/86
Woodhouse, John ('dompne John Woodhouse Bonehome of Asshrige') member of the secular college of Bonhommes at Ashridge [Berks.] 1/8v
Woodhull, Elizabeth Webbe ('Elizabeth Webbe', '[mistress] Webb(e)', 'maistres Woldull/Odell/Odall') gentlewoman to Lady Margaret, m. Fulke Woodhull 1503 20/41, 52, 68, 87 (see SJCA D56.187, now SJLM/5/5), 115, 125, 126b, 127, 136, 153; 21/8, 77; 19/109; 'landes of maistres Woldull junter' 21/67, 77
Woodhull, Fulke ('Fouke/ma(i)ster O(w)dell/ Odall') (d. 1508) sheriff of Northants.; m. (2) Elizabeth Webbe (q.v. sub **Woodhull**) 20/157, 187; 21/20, 63, 146; 19/90
Woodhull, Henry ('Henry Odoll', also 'Henry Odall of the west countre') 20/109; 19/76
de Worde, Wynkyn ('Wynkyn de Ward/ Word(e)', 'Wylkyn prynter', 'the Word[yes]', 'Wyncke/Wynkyn the Worthy') (d. 1534/5) printer; successor to William Caxton (d. 1492) 19/70, 72, 80, 93, 95–6, 100, 104; 1/5v, 7r, 7v, 13v, 17v, 18v
Worsley, Hugh ('Hugh Wo(o)rsley (grome of my ladys chambir)') servant of Lady Margaret 1/7v, 10v, 11v, 12v, 15v
Worsley, Miles ('Myles/Mylez/Mylys/Miles/ Milys (Wors(e)ley/Wursley)', 'Miles/ Myles Worsley cof(f)erare' 20/4,71; 'Miles Worsley clerk (of þe coffers)' 20/141, 21/1; 'Myles Worsley tresowrer of chambre' 10/159, 21/83, 19/1, 65) cofferer to Lady Margaret (from 14 January 1506 treasurer of the chamber) in succession to James Clarell (q.v.) 10/4–6, 9–13, 15–24, 26, 27, 33, 43–48, 55–58, 65–67, 75–78, 83–85, 101–4, 107, 111–14, 123–5, 130–1, 135, 140, 143, 146–9, 151–3, 159–62, 169, 177–8, 180; 17/34, 40, 44, 47, 52; 20/4–5, 11, 64, 71, 77, 122, 134, 141, 145, 160–1, 177, 191, 194; 21/1–2, 7, 22–23, 79–80, 83, 91, 162–4; 19/1, 3, 5, 9–10, 61–3, 65, 69, 123–5; 1/2r, 9r; 2/36; 6/4
Worsop, William ('(Willelmum) Worshoppe/ Wors(s)op/Warshopp/Warssop (of Colyweston)') 16/17; 20/53, 56, 111, 159–60; 19/42, 54
Wotton, doctor ('doctur Wotton a frere of Stampforth') D.Th. (no date); friar of one of the four Stamford friaries 20/12
Wre(y)the, Hance ('Hance Wreythe of Croydon goldsmythe') goldsmith 21/107, 117, 120, 141
Wren, John receiver in Yorkshire 10/25, 26; 20/5
Wrenne, mistress 19/101
[R]**Wright, John** 56/4
Wriothesley, Thomas ('Garter the kyng of heroldes', 'Garter herott of armes') knight; Garter king of arms 1505–34 20/84; 19/8

Yan, Margaret ('Merget Yan/Jan', 'maistrez (Margaret/Merget) Jan', 'ma(i)stres Jan/Jon/Yon/Yan(e)/Yen; perhaps also '[mistress] Jane' 17/59, 21/157, cf. 'lady

Yan, Margaret (*Cont.*) Jane' for Jane Vaux Guildford) gentlewoman to Lady Margaret 21/64, 94, 105, 116, 119, 122, 142; 19/6, 10, 12, 26, 31, 56, 76, 97II (Yon *alt. from* Jan), 101, 106, 109, 118–19; 1/4v, 5r, 17v

Yarborogh, Charles 10/83

[R]**Yerwell, Jaques** ('Jakes/Jaques Yarwell/ Yerwell') of Fotheringay 21/14, 125, 130; 56/4

Yetyll, James 2/14

Yon, Richard 10/158 ((?) connected to **Yan** (q.v.))

Yonge, (John) ('Parson Yonge parson of Hony Lawne in London', 'doct(o)ur/ doctor Yong(e)') D.Th. Oxford 1504; rector of All Hallows, Honey Lane, London 1503–10, after Fotherby (q.v.) 21/102, 143; 19/42, 91

Youch see **Zouche**

Zeton see **Fitzeton**

Zouche, Agnes ('[mistress] Souche/Youch', 'maistrez Zouch of Sympryngham', 'Angues/Agnes/Angnce Swoche/ Souche/Sowche', 'mastres Anne Souche', 'a nonne of Sympryngham' 20/175, 'my ladyes kynneswoman at Sympryngham' 19/6, 'my lady Sowgh') granddaughter (?) of Elizabeth St John (half-sister to Lady Margaret); Gilbertine nun of Sempringham 20/40, 113, 122, 139, 146, 158, 160, 175, 198; 19/6, 74, 105

Zouche, Eleanor see **Melton**

Zouche, Elizabeth see **Fitzgerald**

Zouche, Florence ('maistres Flowrence Zouch') 19/80

Zouche, John ('(yong) ma(i)ster Souche') grandson of Elizabeth St John (half-sister to Lady Margaret); m. Margaret, daughter of Sir Henry Willoughby (q.v.) 21/79; 19/111, 118

[R]**Zouche, Lionel** ('Lyonell Zouche/ Souche') 1/4r; 56/1

INDEX OF PLACES

Places are given their present-day names and historic counties; the document spelling is in brackets (where there is no form in brackets, the document spelling is as today). Where a place cannot be securely identified, or refers to a field or farm or similar, only the document spelling is cited, in inverted commas. Places situated in historic London (i.e. as it was *c.*1500-20) are listed under London.[1] Estates inherited by Lady Margaret are marked * (for the source of the estate and further details: Jones and Underwood, *The King's Mother*, Appendix 2 (pp. 262-7)).

Note: As throughout this edition D91.16 is cited as 16, D102.10 as 10, D91.17 as 17, D91.20 as 20, D91.21 as 21, D91.19 as 19, D102.1 as 1, D102.2 and D102.6 as 2 and 6 respectively, and D56.131 as 56, all in this order. A slant separates the page/folio number, e.g. 21/23 (D91.21, p. 23).

Alford, Lincs. 19/91
Alwalton, Hunts. ('Alton') 20/96
Amersham, Bucks. ('Amersam') 20/79, 85
***Andover**, Hants. 21/52
Antwerp, Low Countries ('Andewarpe') 19/99
Ashby de la Zouch, Leics. ('Esby delasowche') 20/116
Ashey, Hants. ('Asshey') 1/5r
Ashridge, Bucks. ('Assh(e)rige ', 'Assery(n)ge', 'Assherygg', 'Assheryg(e)', 'Asryge'), **secular college of Bonhommes** 21/62, 91; 19/20, 33, 44, 95, 102, 108; 1/4r, 7v, 8r, 8v
Astley, Warks. ('Astlay') 20/121
Attleborough, Nfk ('Artelboro', '[A]telborowe', 'Attylberue') 21/100; 19/15, 51

Babraham, Cambs. ('Babram') 10/23; 19/87, 88
Baldock, Herts. ('Baldok') 19/110
Banbury, Oxon. ('Banbury(e)') 17/39, 50, 52, 54
Bangor, Wales ('Bangowr(e)') 20/94, 111 (see **Caernarvon**)
Barkway, Herts. 21/128
Barnet, Herts. ('Barnett(e)') 16/10, 24, 30d 1/4v, 9v
Barrington, Cambs. ('Barington', 'Baryngton') 10/160; 19/91
Barrowden, Rut. ('Barrodowne') 20/96
Barton on Humber, Lincs. ('Barton apon Umbere', 'Barton of Umbre') 20/96, 158
Barwick, Herts. ('Barwyke') preceptory of the Knights of St John of Jerusalem 19/100
Basse, Herts. ('(the) Bas(s)e (a plase of *maister* Sayes') manor of Baas, Broxbourne, Herts., house of Sir William Say (q.v. in the PEOPLE index) 10/159; 19/65, 75–6, 78
***Bassingbourn**, Cambs. ('Bassingb(o)urn', 'Bassyngburne') 10/24; 21/39, 40; 1/6r, 18r; **manor** 1/18r
'(the) Bayles' 20/34; 21/37 (cf. *OED* **bail/bayle** *n.*[3] 2. (the wall of) the outer court of a feudal castle)
Beaumaris, Anglesey, Wales ('Blewmaris') 20/50
Beddington, Sur. ('Bedyngton') manor of the Carews 19/105
Bedford, Beds. ('Bedforth') 20/176; **Franciscan friary** 19/98
Belvoir, Leics., **castle** ('Beauour castell') 16/23, 8d
Benefield, Northants. ('Benyfeld') 20/117
Berkeley, Gloucs. ('Bark(e)ley (castell)') 20/40; 21/30, 132
Berkshire ('Brukyshyre') 17/25
Berwick-on-Tweed, Northb. ('Berwyk') 20/95

[1] See *The British Atlas of Historic Towns*, ed. Mary D. Lobel and W. H. Johns, 3 vols (Oxford: Oxford University Press and Historic Towns Trust, 1969-89), iii (*The City of London from Prehistoric Times to c. 1520*): <http://www.historictownsatlas.org.uk/atlas/volume-iii/city-london-prehistoric-times-c1520-volume-iii/view-text-gazetteer-and-maps-early>

Bewdley, Worcs. ('Bewedeley') 21/52
Biggleswade, Beds. ('Bykelleswade', 'Bykellyswade') 20/19, 42, 78
***Billingborough**, Lincs. ('Billinge') 10/15
Bilsby, Lincs. ('Billesby', 'Byllysby', 'Byllesby') 10/130; 20/126c, 129, 139, 153, 157, 159
Binham, Nfk ('Benham'), **Benedictine priory** 19/99
Birmingham, Warks. ('Brymygam', 'Byrmyngham', 'Brymgham') 20/18, 21
Bisham, Berks., **priory of Austin canons** ('Byssam abbey') 21/128
Blackamoor, Yorks. ('Blakamore') 20/175
Bletchingley, Sur. ('Blechyngley', 'Blechyng Ley/Leghe') 16/8d; 21/49
Bletsoe, Beds. ('Bletsall', 'Bletso', 'maister chamberlayns place') principal manor of Sir John St John II 21/38; 19/99, 101
Bocking, Essex, **church of St Mary** ('the chyrche of Bokkyng') 19/89
***Boston**, Lincs. ('Boston(e)') 10/2, 4, 101; 20/11, 12, 30, 31, 34, 36, 37, 61, 63, 91, 102, 106, 111, 149, 155, 157–8; 21/80, 163; 19/19, 22, 61, 92, 124; 2/7; 6/5, 9
  Carmelite friary 20/30
  Franciscan friary 20/30, 158, 178; 21/37, 43, 139
  Our Lady of Boston 20/178
  Rood of Boston 20/178; 21/19 (also St Margaret altar (?) but see too **Ketsby** and **Roughton**)
Bottesford, Lincs. 21/19
***Bourne**, Lincs. ('Burn(e)') 16/3, 5, 10, 17, 19, 23, 8d; 10/16, 181; 17/65; 20/22, 26, 30, 51, 59, 65, 106, 121, 165, 168, 172, 182, 185, 187, 196; 21/12, 34, 52
  Bourne Fen ('Burne fenne') 16/7
  'seynt Johens hed besydes Burne' 20/30
Boxworth, Cambs.('Boxworth', 'Boxwith') 10/1, 6
(?)**Brancaster**, Nfk ('Bryncasterton') 20/112
Brandon, Sfk ('Brandon ferr(e)y') 17/36, 37; 19/87, 88
Bray, Berks. 1/7v
Brearton, Yorks. ('Brerton') 10/25
Brentford, Mx ('Braynforth') 19/33
(?)**Bretton**, Northants. ('Brettan') 20/46
Bristol, Gloucs. ('Brystow(e)') 17/50; 20/148
Bromholm, Nfk, **Cluniac priory** 1/8r
Bromley, Kent, **manor of John Fisher** 21/24, 44, 46, 58; 19/76, 96, 107; 1/5r
Brookwood, Sur. ('Brokwod') 20/39
Buckden, Hunts. ('Bukden', 'Bugde(y)n'), **episcopal palace** ('the bysshopp of Lyncolns place') palace and manor of the bishop of Lincoln,William Smith (q.v. in the PEOPLE index) 20/16, 17, 18, 43, 113; 1/8v; 2/23
Bulwick, Northants. ('Bulwy(c)k') 20/153
Buntingford, Herts. ('Bontyngforth'), **the Bell inn** 21/125
'Burymede' 16/3
Bury St Edmunds, Sfk ('Bur(r)y', 'Burye') 17/31–2, 35, 53, 61; 20/159
  Our Lady of Undercroft ('our Ladye of Undercrofte') 17/31
  St Edmund's shrine ('seynt Edmonde(s) schryne') 17/31–2 (see too **Westminster**)
Bytham (Little/Castle), Lincs. ('Byt(h) am') 20/45, 51

Calais, France ('Calice', 'Calyce', 'Calles', 'Callis', 'Calys') 20/50, 66, 97; 21/49; 19/108
Caldwell, Beds., **house of Austin canons** 20/176
Cambridge, Cambs. ('Cambryg(g)e', 'Cambrig(g)e', 'Cambrigg', 'Cambryche', 'Cambrigh', 'Chambrige') 16/8, 13, 16, 2d, 3d, 8d, 9d, 12d, 13d; 10/102, 107, 108, 124, 132, 160; 17/19, 26, 36–7, 41, 50, 53, 55, 61; 20/22, 37, 61, 65, 79, 91, 102–3, 105, 116, 120–1, 128, 135, 147, 152, 159, 161, 176, 178, 182, 186; 21/7, 11–12, 17, 28, 33, 40, 52, 56, 59, 60, 74, 92, 99, 108, 109, 124, 126–7, 130, 136, 143, 148, 159; 19/19, 23, 27, 28, 33, 35–6, 39, 41–2, 46, 65, 81, 93, 100–1, 108, 113; 1/11r, 13r
  Austin friary 21/28; 19/27
  Christ's College ('God's House') 10/107–8, 124, 132, 146–7, 160, 182; 20/190; 21/2, 16, 25–6, 28, 35, 37, 52, 56, 59, 67, 72, 97, 99, 114, 119, 123, 127, 129, 135, 138, 140, 145, 148, 158–60; 19/5, 7, 8, 13, 15, 17, 21, 22, 27–8, 31, 33–5, 37, 39, 43–5, 47, 52, 58, 65–6, 72–3, 88–90, 93, 96, 101, 110, 113–14, 119–21; 1/5v, 6v, 7v, 8v, 10r, 11r, 13v, 15v, 17v, 18r
  Clare Hall 20/13
  Dominican friary ('the blak frers') 19/27; 21/143
  Franciscan friary ('the gray freris') 19/28
  God's House see **Christ's College**
  Jesus College 20/95, 120, 135, 147, 154, 195; 21/27
  King's College 19/88; 1/9r
  King's Hall 19/34
  Michaelhouse 10/132

Our Lady of Grace 21/125
Pembroke Hall 21/106
Peterhouse ('Peturhowse') 19/5, 28
Queens' College 21/18, 126
St Anne's chapel ('seynt Anne chappell') hermitage chapel in Trumpington Street 20/160; 19/88
St Gregory's hostel ('Gregory hostell', 'Gregoryes ostill in Cambryge') student hall attached to Michaelhouse 17/37; 21/53
St John's hospital (later St John's College) ('Sainct Johns house') 1/8r
St Mary's church (now Great St Mary's) ('seynt Mary chirch/cherche/church') 20/155, 182, 195
Stourbridge common ('Stewrisbryge', 'Ste(w)rysbryge faire/fayre', 'Stirbyche', 'Stirbiche', 'Stirbridge', 'Sturbrigge') site of annual fair 10/7, 12; 20/66, 174, 177; 19/35, 46
University ('the universite/unyversite in/of Cambryge') 20/20, 38, 49, 155
Cambridgeshire ('Cambrygeshyre', 'the countie of Cambrige') 10/1; 20/103; 1/6r
Campsey Ash, Sfk, **priory of Austin nuns** ('Camse abbey') 20/79, 155
***Canford**, Dorset ('Canford', 'Canforth', 'Campforth') 21/47, 148, 160
Canterbury, Kent ('Canturbury', 'Cauntourbury') 20/115, 169; 19/102; **Franciscan friary** 21/93; **shrine of St Thomas Beckett** 21/117
Carlisle, Cum. ('Carlile') 19/113
(?)**Carmarthen**, Wales ('Carnerven' but no friary at Caernarvon), **friary** Franciscan; burial place of Edmund Tudor (d. 1456), first husband of Lady Margaret 20/111
Castle Acre, Nfk ('Castill Aker') 20/157
Castle Hedingham, Essex ('Hennyngham', 'Henynngham') home of John de Vere 17/30, 31, 35
Catley, Lincs. ('Cat(t)ley', 'Catle'), **Gilbertine priory** 20/39, 90; 19/105
Caxton, Cambs. ('Cakston') 21/11
'Chaldwell' 16/3
Chelsea, Mx ('Chelsey') manor of the abbot of Westminster 21/26; **the Neyte** the Neat, subsidiary house of the abbot of Westminster 19/71
Chertsey, Sur. ('Chartsey', 'Chersey') 21/26; 1/4v, 5r
Cheshire ('Cheysshere') 20/38
***Cheshunt**, Herts. ('Cheston(te)', 'Chestone', 'Chesth(o)unt/Chesthaunt', 'Chestham') 16/3, 6, 19, 21, 24, 12d, 30d; 10/7; 17/24; 21/15, 135; 19/29, 32, 98, 99, 101; 1/6v
guild of Our Lady 19/96
priory of Benedictine nuns 21/132, 135
'Seynt Gyles in the busshe besyde Cheston' 19/98
Chester, Chesh., **Benedictine abbey** 21/134
Chesterford, Essex ('Chesterforth', 'Chesterford', 'Chesterfeld' (error) 20/139) 20/116, 126, 139, 153; 21/62, 149
***Cirencester**, Gloucs. ('Siscitour') 10/4; **abbey of Austin canons** ('Syscitour') 10/4
Clerkenwell see **London**
(King's) Cliffe, Northants. ('Clyff', 'Cliff(e)') 16/17; 10/140; 20/41
Clopton, Northants 20/172; 21/65
'Closelaunde' 16/3
Codnor, Dbs. ('Cotnall, 'Coteno*ur*') 20/21, 21/79
Coldharbour see **London**
(?)**Coleorton**, Leics. ('Cold Horton') 20/99
***Collyweston**, Northants. ('Colyweston', 'Coleweston', 'Coliweston', 'Colywen', 'Colyveston', 'Colywyston') 16/2–3, 8, 11, 14, 16, 20, 23, 25, 5d, 7d, 8d, 29d, 30d; 10/3; 17/23, 30, 37–8, 41–2, 51–4, 58, 61, 65, [66], [67]; 20/4, 11, 14, 18–24, 28–9, 34–41, 45, 47, 49–51, 53, 56, 58–9, 62, 71, 77, 83, 85, 90–1, 94, 96–7, 99, 102, 104–6, 110–13, 115, 117,122, 124, 126b, 137–8, 146, 149, 151, 153, 155, 157–9, 162, 164, 167–8, 172, 175–7, 180–3, 185–6, 192, 194; 21/7–8, 12–13, 16, 17–21, 23, 30, 34, 37, 42, 46, 64–5, 75, 86, 118, 121, 144, 154; 19/39
Colne Wake see **Wakes Colne**
Colston Bassett, Northants. 10/24
Compostela, Galicia, Spain, **shrine of St James the Great** 19/33
'le Conynger' see **Hatfield**
Coningsby, Lincs. ('Conyngesby') 19/93
Cornbury, Oxon. ('Cornebury') 17/44
Cote, Oxon. 10/33
Coton, Cambs. 20/145
***Cottingham**, Northants. ('Cotingham', 'Cotyngham') 10/5, 15; 20/96, 114
the Court (wherever Henry VII was resident at the time) 17/49; 20/114; 21/7, 9, 49, 60, 113, 132, 135; 19/19, 21, 27, 34, 91, 115, 119; 1/6v
Coventry, Warks. ('Coventre', 'Coventr') 17/26; 20/77, 93, 95, 96, 101, 154, 167, 177, 181; 21/17; 19/74
charterhouse 19/70
Our Lady of Coventry 20/93
(?)**Cranborne**, Dorset ('Craneburne') 21/48

Creake, Nfk ('(the late abbey of) Creyke'), **abbey of Austin canons** 10/147; 19/14, 21, 22, 28, 47, 52, 120; 1/10v
(?)**Cromer**, Herts. 17/39 (but perhaps **Crowmer** (see the PEOPLE index)); **'oure Lady of Crome'** 21/41, 50
Crowland, Lincs. ('Croland(e)', 'Croyland') 20/45, 102, 103, 115, 117, 118, 120, 134, 154, 157, 159, 165, 173; 21/53; **shrine of St Guthlac** ('seynt Gudlake shryne') 20/154
Croydon, Sur. (most references are to the palace of the archbishop of Canterbury occupied by Lady Margaret 1505–6) 16/1–2, 10, 13–14, 19–21, 23, 1d, 2d, 4d, 5d, 7d, 12d, 15d, 29d; 10/141; 21/1, 40, 41, 43, 44, 45, 46, 47, 49, 50, 52, 56, 60, 63, 64, 67, 74, 75, 77, 91, 92, 93, 96, 97, 99, 100, 102, 104, 106, 107, 109, 110, 111, 114, 115, 117, 118, 119, 120, 121, 123, 124, 127, 156; 19/21
  the George inn 21/41, 56, 91, 98, 104, 132
  the Red Lion inn 21/96
  the Swan inn 21/100
***Curry Rivel** (Som.) ('Cory Ryver') 20/156

***Dalbury**, Derbs. ('Dalbur(le)y', 'Dalbery') 10/17, 22; 17/2; **Dalbury Lees** ('Dalburies lees', 'Dalbery/ Dalbury leys', 'Dalburleys') 10/17, 22; 17/2
***Dartford**, Kent ('Darford', 'Dertfforde') 10/20; 17/25; **house of Benedictine nuns** ('Detford', 'Depforth') 21/22; 19/20
***Deeping**, Lincs. ('Depyng(e)', 'Depinge') 16/2, 21, 24–5, 29d, 30d; 10/181; 17/49; 20/45, 77; 21/58, 75, 132; 19/76 (see too **West Deeping**)
Denbigh, Wales ('Denbeghe'), **Carmelite friary** 19/70
Deptford, Kent ('Dep(t)ford (stronde)') manor of the St Johns of Lydiard Tregoze 10/177; 2/2
Derbyshire ('Derbeshyre') 21/57
'Dere', near **Pennal** (q.v.) 17/2
Devon ('Devonshyre') 17/42
Diseworth, Leics. ('Dithesworth', 'Des(e) worth', 'Disworth', 'Dysworth') 10/160; 21/29, 67, 77, 93, 148, 160; 19/90
Doddington, Lincs. ('Dodington', 'Dodyngton') 10/28; 20/112; 21/39
Dogdyke ferry, Lincs. ('Dokedyke') 19/19
Dover, Kent 19/104
Drayton, Mx 20/30
***Droitwich**, Worcs. ('Dertwich', 'Dertwyche') 10/23; 17/2; 19/73
Dunstable, Kent ('Donstabyll') 20/24, 89

Eagle, Lincs. ('Egle') preceptory of St John of Jerusalem 1/6v
Easthampstead, Berks. ('Estamstede', 'Estamstyd') royal hunting lodge in Windsor Park 17/19, 21; 20/49
Easton Neston, Northants. ('Eston/ Estun') 10/140; 20/44–5, 187; 21/14, 20, 135 (some may refer to the Cistercian priory at Easton); **manor of Richard Empson** (q.v. in the PEOPLE index) 20/173; 19/32
Edgcote, Northants. ('Ochecott', 'Ochecote'), **manor of Reginald Bray** (q.v. in the PEOPLE index) 17/38, 39, 41
Edinburgh, Sc. ('Edynbore') 20/102
Eldernell, Cambs. ('Eldernall') 20/40, 45
(?)**Elmdon**, Essex ('Elmeton') 20/115
Elmswell, Sfk ('Emeswell') 20/160
Elsings, Enfield, Mx ('maister Lovelles', 'maister Lovels place') manor of Sir Thomas Lovell (q.v. in the PEOPLE index) 19/24, 86, 119
Eltham, Kent 21/52; **palace of Eltham** 19/93, 100; 21/25
Ely, Cambs. ('Ely', 'Ele') 17/36; 20/51, 145; 19/27–8, 53, 91; **Isle of Ely** ('Eyle/Yle of Ely') 20/61, 165
  abbey (Benedictine) 17/36; 20/14; 19/27; **Lady Chapel** 19/27; **St Etheldreda's shrine** 17/36; 19/27
***Enderby**, Leics. 10/24
Enfield, Mx ('Envyll') 19/98; **Enfield Chase**, Mx ('Endvyld Chasse') 21/53
'Eslyngham' see **Frindsbury**
Essex ('Exssexe') 21/148
Eton, Berks. ('E(y)ton') 17/25
  St Margaret's ('Seynt Mergettes besydes Eyton') (?) 20/16
  Eton school 20/36, 175; 21/23; 19/90; 1/11r
Exeter, Devon ('Excester', 'Excestre') 10/4, 5; 20/56; 21/131
  Exeter lands ('the duchye of Excestre', 'Exit*ur* landes') 10/4, 22 (see Jones and Underwood, *The King's Mother*, Appendix 2B (pp. 264–5)
  palace of the bishop of Exeter 20/194; 21/25
Eye, Sfk, **Benedictine priory** ('the monestory of Ey') 21/91

Faversham, Kent, **Benedictine abbey** ('Fethersam abbey') 21/62
Fen Drayton, Cambs. 21/147, 159

Fenny Stratford, Bucks. ('Fenne Stretford') 20/79
Finchley, Mx 2/27
Flanders 20/67
Fordham (Cambs.) 1/18r
Fordingbridge, Hants. ('Fournyng Brygges') 21/48
Fotheringhay, Northants. ('Foteringay', 'Fodring(h)ay', 'Fodryngay', 'Foderynghay', 'Fordynghay') collegiate church and castle 16/18; 10/69, 75; 17/63; 20/78, 104, 112, 158, 186; 21/12, 18, 19, 29, 30, 35, 36, 37, 38, 39, 41, 42, 43, 44, 46, 51, 59, 60, 75
France ('Fraunce') 17/21, 42; 20/80–1, 107, 126c, 138, 162; 21/159
Frindsbury, Kent ('Eslyngham', i.e. old name for Frindsbury) 10/62
Fulham, Mx ('Fullam') 21/58; 19/78
Fyfield, Essex ('Fyfeld'), **manor of the Scropes** 19/93

Gaddesden, Herts. ('Gaddysden') 19/87
'Garsey' see **Guernsey**
Garsington, Oxon. 10/177; **Garsington manor** ('Gesting maner') manor of the St Johns of Lydiard Tregoze 1/4v
***Gayton**, Northants. ('Gayton sooke') 10/17
Goathill, Som. ('Gotshyll', 'Gotehyll', 'Gotehill') 19/73, 90, 116
Godstow, Oxon. Benedictine nunnery 17/45
'Goldherbare' see **London (Coldharbour)**
Grainthorpe, Lincs. ('Garnethorp') 20/157
Grantham, Lincs. ('Grauntham') 17/64; 20/31, 36, 40, 43, 46, 48, 51, 61, 106, 129, 145, 149; 19/39; 1/6r; **Jesus guild** 21/135; 19/105
Great Harrowden, Northants. ('Harowdon/ Harowden') manor of Nicholas Vaux 17/37
Great Wolford, Warks. ('Wolford Magna') 10/29, 58
Greatford, Lincs. ('Gretford') 20/118
Greenwich, Kent ('Grenwych(e)', 'Grenewych(e)', 'Grenewich(e)', 'Greneweche') 10/3; 20/18, 19; 21/9, 18, 21, 29, 33, 35, 57, 62, 73, 114; 19/23, 27, 78, 79, 80, 81, 83, 84, 86, 88, 89, 92, 93, 96, 97i, 99, 100, 102, 104, 105, 107; 1/5r, 12v, 13v, 14v, 15v; **Observant friary** 20/78, 114; 21/21, 57; 1/14v
Guernsey ('Garsey') 17/61
Guildford, Sur. ('Gylford') 20/17
Haling, Sur. ('Haylyng', 'Halynge') manor near Croydon 21/48, 50, 52, 53, 73, 93
'Hal(l)ywell' see **Oakham**, but perhaps one of the three churches at Castle Bytham (for Dom William Jeralde as '(perpetual) vicar of Holywell' see Rogers (ed.), *The Act Book of St Katherine's Guild*, pp. 11, 82–3, etc.), or the chapel at Holywell-cum-Needingworth (see Page, Proby and Inskip Ladds (ed.), *A History of the County of Huntingdon*, ii, 175–8 at <http://www.british-history.ac.uk/vch/hunts/vol2/pp175–178>
Hampton Court, Mx ('Hampton Corte', 'my lord chambrlens playce', 'at my lord chamberlen at Hampton Corte') manor of Giles Daubeney 20/145; 21/25, 118; 19/22
Hanworth, Mx ('Han(d)worth', 'Hanwod') manor used by Henry VII from 1501 19/95, 96, 100; 1/5r, 7r, 9v, 13v
Harborough see **Market Harborough**
Harringworth, Northants. ('Harryngworth', 'Hor(r)yngworth') 20/49, 116
Harrow on the Hill, Mx ('Harowe upon the hill') 19/93
Hatfield, Herts. ('(Bysshop) Hat(e)feld', 'Hetfeld', 'Hatfeeld Episcopi') (most references are to the palace of the bishop of Ely occupied by Lady Margaret 1506–9) 16/1, 10, 13–14, 16, 22–5, 1d, 2d, 4d, 8d, 10d, 29d, 30d; 10/133; 21/27, 36, 83, 118, 119, 120, 121, 123, 124, 125, 127, 128, 129, 130, 131, 132, 133, 134, 135, 136, 139, 142, 144, 145, 150; 19/1, 5, 9, 12, 16, 20, 22, 23, 24, 27, 28, 29, 30, 32, 33, 34, 35, 37, 40, 42, 44, 47, 53, 55, 56, 69, 70, 72, 74, 75, 77, 78, 80, 81, 83, 84, 89, 90, 93, 96, 97i, 98, 99, 100, 101, 102, 104, 105, 107, 108, 110, 112, 113, 114, 120; 1/5r, 7r, 8r, 9r, 9v, 10v, 11r, 11v, 12v, 13r, 14v
  almshouse 1/9r, 17r
  Chequer inn ('the Chekkere') 21/129; 19/95
  church of St Etheldreda ('oure Lady of Lodwyke in the parysshe chyrche') 19/20
  'le Conynger' [i.e. rabbit warren] 16/10
  the George inn ('(at the syne of) the George (in Hatfeld)') 21/132, 138, 145; 19/39, 42, 90, 118; 1/9r
  Great Park 19/21
  Hatfield Chase ('Hatfeld chasse') 20/31
Hatfield Peverel, Essex ('Hatfeld Peverell') manor of the St Johns of Lydiard Tregoze 10/177; 2/2

Havering atte Bower, Essex ('Haveryng(e) (of þe boure/on the bower)') dower house of the Queen 17/29; 19/100
Hawarden, Flints. 21/95
Hawcross field ('Haucros feld') 16/10
'Helhow' 19/32
Helpston, Northants 21/130; 19/15, 52, 110
Hengrave, Sfk ('Hengrave', 'Ingrave') 10/16, 21; 2/2
Hennyngham/Henynngham see **Castle Hedingham**
Herons, Essex, **manor of the Tyrrell family** ('Herons', 'master Tyrelles') 17/29; 19/110
Hertford, Herts. ('Hertford', 'Herforth') 16/8d; 19/71
Higham Ferrers, Northants ('Heygham Ferres') 20/38, 103
Hinton, So., **charterhouse** 17/48
Hitchin, Herts. ('Hechyn'), **Carmelite friary** 21/123; 1/6r
Holderness, Yorks. ('Holdernes(se)', 'Haldernes') 10/26–28, 31; 20/5
Holland, Lincs. ('Holand/Holond') 20/28; 2/10; 6/6
Holywell see **Hal(l)ywell**
Horncastle, Lincs. ('Hornecastell') 20/20; 19/91, 92
Hor(r)yngworth see **Harringworth**
Howden, Yorks. ('Hoveden') 21/19
Humber (river), Yorks. ('Humbere', 'Hombere') 20/45, 175
Huntingdon, Cambs. ('Huntyngdon', 'Hyntyngdon', 'Huntyngton') 17/37, 41; 20/14, 42, 102, 177, 179; 21/16, 20, 42
Huntingdonshire ('Huntyngtonshyre') 20/145

Ickleton, Cambs. ('Ikylton'), **priory of Benedictine nuns** 21/126
Ingham, Nfk 19/41
Ipswich, Sfk ('Ipwhiche', 'Epsewich', 'Ypswyche') 17/35; 20/116; 19/47
Ireland ('Yerlande') 20/14
Irnham, Lincs. ('Irnam') 20/92
***Isle of Purbeck**, Dor. ('yle of Purbek') 20/46
Isle of Sheppey see **Sheppey**
Isleworth, Mx ('Thystelworthe') 19/95
Ivinghoe, Bucks., **Benedictine nunnery of St Margaret** 19/33

Kegworth, Leics. 21/29
Kelsey, Lincs. 20/157
***Kendal**, Westm. ('(the lordship of) Kendale/ Kendall') (for the lordship of Kendal: Jones and Underwood, *The King's Mother*, pp. 115–25) 10/4, 19, 21–2, 25, 27, 28, 31, 33, 83–6, 111–12, 130, 151; 20/18, 28, 95, 162, 167, 194 (Appendix)
***Kendall**, Herts. (Some/all of 20/18, 28, 95, 162, 167, 194 (Appendix) might refer to Kendall, but see too **Kendal** above.)
Kenilworth, Warks. ('Kyllyngworth') 20/117, 121
Kent 10/62; 20/83; 21/26, 114; **'Rikills lande in Kent'** 10/17; **'the landes of Frongnalles in Kent'** 10/23
Kesteven, Lincs. ('Keston/Kesten', 'Kestehevyn') 20/156, 157; 2/10; 6/6
Ketsby, Lincs. ('Ket(tel)esby', 'Kettysbe', 'Catesby'), **church of St Margaret** 20/79, 120; 21/19(?), 111; 19/13, 97 (see too **Tattershall**)
Kettering, Northants. ('Keterynge', 'Kettryng', 'Ketreng') 17/51; 20/85, 153, 183
(?)**Kilburn**, Mx ('Kylingburne') 21/55
Kirkstall, Yorks. ('Cristall'), **Cistercian abbey** 10/25
***Kirton in Holland**, Lincs. ('Kyrton in Holland') 21/22
Knaresborough, Yorks. ('Knavysborowe') 19/72
Kneesworth, Cambs. 20/153
Knole, Kent ('Knoll') 21/49
(South) Kyme, Lincs. 20/34; **Augustinian priory** 20/32

***Lamarsh**, Essex ('Lammersshe') 2/1
Lambeth, Sur. 21/40, 66
Lancashire ('Lankyschire', 'Lancashire', 'Lancashyre', 'Langkynshyre', 'Lanckeshere') 17/37; 20/123, 148, 164; 19/29, 73
(King's) Langley, Herts., **Dominican friary** 21/99
Langley, Oxon. ('Lang(e)ley') hunting lodge of Henry VII 17/43, 44, 53; 20/62, 118; 19/36
Launde, Leics., **Augustinian priory** ('Lawnd abbey') 20/106
Lavenham, Sfk ('Lan(eh)am') 17/31; 20/116
Leicester, Leics. ('Le(y(cetur', 'Leycester') 20/112, 114, 185; 21/21, 29, 148; 19/23, 52; **fair** 20/25; **college of the Annunciation of St Mary in the Newarke** ('the Newerke of Leycesture') 17/62
Leicestershire ('Leyceturshire') 21/15; 19/112
Lenton, Notts., **Cluniac priory** 17/61; **fair** 20/49, 122
'Levsted abbey' error for **Newstead**, q.v. (?) 20/113

Lichfield, Staffs. ('Lych(e)(f)feld') 20/22, 59, 115
Lincoln, Lincs. ('Lyncoln(e)') 20/11, 13, 31, 38–9, 114, 157, 165, 176; 21/35, 44; 19/91; 1/11r; **Gilbertine priory of St Katherine** ('Seynt Cattrens of Lyncoln') 20/31, 78
Lincolnshire ('Lyncolneschire', 'Lyncolnshire', 'Lyncolnshyre', 'Lyncolnshere', 'the countie of Lincoln') 17/39; 20/27 , 51, 128, 147, 165, 197; 21/14, 19; 19/42, 53, 105, 108, 118
Lindsey, Lincs. ('Lynd(e)sey', 'Lyndsay', 'Len(ys)sey', 'Lynce') 17/39; 20/16, 62, 79, 129; 19/92; 2/10; 6/6
Little Bytham, Lincs. ('Bytam') 20/45
(?)**Littlemore**, Oxon. ('Letyllmore'), **Our Lady of Littlemore** 19/98
Little Ponton, Lincs. ('Lytell Paunton') 20/177
Llanthony, Mon. or **Llanthony Secunda**, Gloucs. ('Lantony') 17/43; 19/11; 1/14r
London 16/13, 17; 10/39, 77, 102, 182; 17/26, 28, 33, 35, 46–7, 52; 20/5, 7, 11, 17, 23–4, 29, 37, 39–40, 45–8, 50, 56, 58, 64, 78–9, 81, 83–4, 90, 92, 94, 96–7, 99, 102, 106, 108, 111, 115–17, 121, 126–9, 138–9, 145, 147–8, 150–5, 158–9, 161–2, 165–8, 172, 176–8, 180, 182–4, 186, 192, 194, 196; 21/7–9, 16–18, 20, 26, 29, 36, 40, 45–7, 50, 52–5, 58, 63–6, 74, 96, 98, 100, 105–6, 109, 115, 117–19, 121, 123, 125, 128, 133, 141, 150, 156; 19/5, 7, 9, 10, 12, 13, 14, 15, 16, 18, 21–4, 28–30, 33–4, 37–8, 40–3, 46, 70–2, 74, 76–80, 83–4, 86, 92, 96–7, 97i, 98, 100–2, 104, 108, 112–14; 1/4r, 5r, 7v, 8v, 9v, 10v, 11r, 11v, 12v, 13r, 13v, 14v; 2/1, 23; 6/5
All Hallows (of) Barking ('oure Lady of Barkyng') church west of the Tower 21/21, 108
All Hallows, Honey Lane ('Hony Lawne in London') 21/102
All Hallows the Less ('Halhalloez', 'Alhalowez the litill') 19/16, 59
Barnard's Inn ('Barnardes ynne') Inn of Chancery on Holborn 20/192
Bath Place ('my lord of Bathes place in London') episcopal palace of Bishop of Bath on the Strand 19/77–8
Baynard's Castle ('Bernard(es castell)', 'Barnard') royal palace on the Thames south of St Paul's 19/18–19
Bethlehem see **St Mary of Bethlehem**
Billingsgate ('Byllyn(ges)gate') 20/184
Bishopsgate ('Bysshoppesgate') 20/186
Blackfriars Dominican friary south-west of St Paul's 1/9v
Blackwell Hall cloth market near the Guildhall 19/106
Chancery see **Westminster**
Charterhouse ('the charterhousse in London', 'charterhowse', 'cherterhowse') 17/45; 20/29, 30, 65, 86; 21/104; 19/8 (perhaps London), 18 (see too **Sheen**)
***Coldharbour**, London ('Coldeherber(de)', 'Coldherborow(e)', 'Coldherborogh(e)', 'Cold(e)herbore', 'Coldherboro', 'Coldharborogh(t)', 'Cold Horton' [error?] 20/99, 'Cold(e) herbur(o)gh', 'Coldherber(gh)', 'Coldberough', 'Coldherbare', 'Goldherbare') Lady Margaret's London house, granted her by the king in 1487 10/107; 17/24, 28, 38; 19/59; 20/17, 18, 25, 33, 58, 67, 91, 92, (99), 108, 126, 139, 172, 176, 182, 184, 185, 198, 199; 21/22, 33, 51, 60, 61, 107, 120, 129, 137; 19/5, 6, 7, 16, 17, 77, 78, 83, 84, 106,116; 1/9v, 11r, 12v, 13r, 13v; 2/7, 8, 10, 11, 12, 14, 16, 22, 24, 25, 29, 30, 32, 33, 34, 36; 6/5, 6
Court of Arches ('the Arches') ecclesiastical court of the province of Canterbury, meeting at St Mary le Bow 20/122
Derby House ('my lord*es* place in London') London house of the earls of Derby, between St Paul's and the Thames 21/23
Fleet Street 20/191; 1/5v, 17v
Gracechurch Street ('Gracious Strete'), **the Falcon** 20/33
Guild of the Holy Trinity ('the fraternite of the Trinite gylde in London') guild attached to St Botolph without Aldersgate 21/143, 153
Katherine Wheel ('Kateryn Well') tenement in the parish of St Nicholas Shambles 2/35
King's Head ('the Kynges Hed(e)') probably the large house with tavern owned by Canterbury Cathedral priory, on the south side of Cheapside near St Mary le Bow 20/126c, 192
London bridge 19/29
Ludgate prison 19/10
Minories ('Minory', 'Mynerez/ Myneres(se)', 'Mynorys/Mynores', 'the mynuresse', 'Menuresses') abbey of the Minoresses of the Order of St Clare without Aldgate (i.e. outside

London (*Cont.*)
Minories (*Cont.*) the city of London) 17/24; 20/85, 86, 163, 184; 21/21, 108, 146; 19/18, 20, 82; 1/4r, 10r
Newgate prison 19/10
the Riall ('(the) Riall/Ryall') London house of Margaret Beauchamp, Lady Margaret's mother, north of the Vintry 19/23, 30, 36, 46, 59
St Anthony ('Saint Antones in London') hospital, school, almshouses on Broad Street 19/39
St Bartholomew's hospital ('Saynt Bartyllmew[(i)s] (spytyll/spetyll)') hospital of St Bartholomew, Smithfield 2/8, 10–12, 14, 22, 25, 29–30, 34
St Bride, Fleet Street, guild of St Bride ('gild of seynt Bride in Flete Strete') 1/5v, 17v
St John of Jerusalem, Clerkenwell priory of the Knights Hospitallers 19/22, 45; 1/4v, 5r, 7v; 2/35
St Laurence Pountney (college of) ('seynt Laurence Pulteney') 20/189
St Magnus Martyr, guild of Our Lady and St Thomas of Canterbury 20/182
St Mary of Bethlehem, priory and hospital outside Bishopsgate ('oure Lady at/of Bethelem') 21/108; 19/18; (?) **anchorage** ('the ancryse besyd*es* Bethelem') 21/21
St Mary without Bishopsgate, priory and hospital ('the new hospitall of our*e* blessyd Lady w*i*thowte Bysshopyate in London') St Mary Spital north of St Mary of Bethlehem outside Bishopsgate 21/24; (?)**anchorage** ('the ankeryes w*i*thowte Bysshoppesgate') 20/186
St Nicholas Shambles ('seynt Nicholas Shamelles') church at corner of shambles on Newgate Street 19/69
St Paul's Cathedral ('Pawlis', 'Pawles', 'Powlis', 'Poulis/Poulys', 'Poules churche') 17/25; 20/30, 86; 21/21, 108; 2/32; 6/5; **Corpus Christi guild** 19/18; **palace of the bishop of London (north side of St Paul's)** 1/6v
St Peter, Cornhill ('Seynt Peturs in Cornell in London') 19/38
Steelyard ('Styllyard') Hanseatic Steelyard on Dowgate west of London Bridge 20/98
the Stocks ('the Stokes') ward of Cornhill with fish and flesh market on the north side of St Mary Woolchurch 19/59
the Tower of London ('Toure/Towre/Tower') 17/20, 28, 29; 19/18, 22, 24, 72, 104; 1/11v, 12r, 12v, 13r, 15v; 2/18; 6/5
the Wardrobe the King's, or Great, Wardrobe on Carter Lane 1/11r
the Wall ('the Valle/Wall') London Wall 20/186; 19/18
Long Marton, Westm. ('Marton') 10/3
Louth, Lincs. ('Lowthe') 19/91
Luddington, Lincs. ('Luthyngton'), but perhaps **Lyddington** (q.v.) 16/18
Ludlow, Shrop. ('Lodlow', 'Ludlow') 17/49; 20/18, 22, 35; 19/43; 1/4r
Lyddington, Rut. ('Lidington', 'Lyd(d)yngton', 'Lydington', 'Lyddengton', 'Liddyngton', 'Ledyngton', 'Lodyngton', 'Luthington') palace of the bishop of Lincoln, William Smith (q.v.) 10/44; 20/43, 91, 112–13, 115–21, 124, 127, 146, 155; 21/40, 74
Lydiard Tregoze, Wilts. ('Legdarde/Legeard Tregose', 'Lydeȝard Tragose') principal manor of master John St John 10/176, 177; 19/36
(King's) Lynn, Nfk ('Lyn(ne)') 17/35, 36; 20/33, 126b, 155–7; 21/11, 80; 19/62, 124
anchorage 20/154
friary 20/154; **Our Lady at the friars** 20/154
Our Lady of the Mount pilgrim chapel ('oure Ladye at/of the mounte/mownt') 17/36; 20/154
St Saviour 20/154
Lythe, Yorks. 20/175

Mablethorpe, Lincs. ('Mabilthorp') 19/91
Malton, Cambs. 10/160; 20/103, 126c, 139, 153, 159; 21/67, 77, 147, 148, 159; 19/14, 47, 66, 90, 91, 100, 120
Manchester, Lancs., **college of secular canons** 21/115
***Manorbier**, Wales ('Maner(e)bere', 'Meniburs', 'Manourbere', 'the Manour/Manere of Bere') 10/3, 83, 147; 19/28, 52, 89, 92, 96, 98, 105, 113, 120; 1/7v, 17v
'Marbures' 16/10
Margate, Kent 17/62
Market Harborough, Leics. ('Harbaro', 'Herberowe') 20/45; 21/18; 19/93
Marshalsea see **Southwark**
***Maxey**, Cambs. ('Maxsey' 17/57; 'Maksey(e)', 'Makes(s)ey' 20/11) 10/131; 16/25, 29d, 30d; 17/57;

20/11, 65, 110, 137; 19/47; **New Close** 20/11, 65; **the Park** 20/11, 65
***Medecroft**, Beds. ('Medcroft') 20/42
Melton Mowbray, Leics. ('Melton Molbrey') 19/45
Mitcham, Sur. ('Mycham') 21/113
'Mydroff' 21/95
Monmouth, Wales, **Benedictine priory of St Mary** ('the prior of the Monmouthe') 19/73
'Mountesdale' 21/95
Mount Sinai, Egypt, **St Catherine's monastery** ('Seynt Cattrens Mownte') 21/100
(?)**Much Pilton**, Devon ('Moche Petleng') 21/21
Mugdenhall, Essex 10/178; 2/2

Nassington, Lincs. ('Nasyngton') 19/101
Navenby, Lincs. 1/11r
Nettlestead, Sfk ('Nettelsted') 20/160
Newark, Northants. ('Newerk') 20/37, 96
Newcastle-under-Lyme, Staffs. ('New Castell'), **Observant friary** 20/39
the New Close, i.e. a field 20/11
New Forest 21/44
Newmarket, Sfk ('Newemarket') 19/99
Newport Pagnell, Bucks. ('Newporte paynell') 20/123
Newstead, near Stamford, Lincs. ('Newstyd'), **priory of Austin canons** 20/164 (see too **'Levsted abbey'**)
Neyte see **Chelsea**
Norfolk ('Norf(f)olk') 20/37; 19/9, 52; 1/8r
Northampton, Northants. 17/38, 50, 51; 20/80, 89, 103, 105, 153, 154, 159, 179; 21/10, 12; 19/52
  Austin friary (shrine to Our Lady of Grace) 20/86, 87
  church of St Gregory (guild of the Holy Rood in the Wall) ('rode of Walle') 20/87
  Cluniac priory of St Andrew 20/38
Northamptonshire 21/ 93
North Country ('the North Countre/ Country') north of the River Humber 20/81, 115, 175
Norwich, Nfk ('Norwhiche', 'Norwyche') 17/33, 35; 21/8; 19/15
Notley, Bucks. ('Not(t)ley') 10/44; **abbey of Arrouaisian canons** 17/53
Nottinghamshire ('Notinghamshire', 'Notynghamshire/shyre/shere') 20/19, 121, 124; 19/107

Oakham, Rut. ('Okeham', 'Ok(h)am') 16/17; 10/32; 20/19, 27
  (?)**All Saints church** ('Halywell', 'Holywell') (pardons on Marian feast days and the dedication day, cf. 20/23) 20/23, 165 (see Page (ed.), *A History of the County of Rutland,* ii, 5–27 at <http://www.british-history.ac.uk/vch/rutland/vol2/pp5–27>
  (?)**St Mary's well ('Lady Well')** ('(oure Lady of) Hal(l)ywell') (image of the Virgin, cf. 20/41, 123–4, 151, and pilgrimage, cf. 20/165) 20/41, 123–4, 151 (see *History of the County of Rutland*, ii, 5–27)
'Ochecott'/'Ochecote' see **Edgcote**
Old Buckenham, Nfk ('Buknam (Castell)') manor of Sir William Knyvett 17/32
Orléans, France ('Orlya(u)nce') 20/39, 84, 163, 196
Ormsby, Lincs. ('Urmesby in Lensey') 20/62
Overhall, Cambs. 10/1, 6
***Overstone**, Northants. ('Oveston') 10/24
Oxford, Oxon. ('Oxfforde', 'Oxforth', 'Oxenford') 17/20, 42, 46; 20/27, 65, 106, 135, 172; 21/98, 132, 146; 19/21
  Magdalen College 21/66
  Merton College ('Marton Colage') 21/40
  Oriel College ('Oryall College') 20/101
Oxted, Sur. ('Oxstede') 16/20

Paddington, Mx ('Padington', 'Padyngton') 20/30, 67
Paris ('Parise', 'Parres', 'Parice') 10/85; 20/156, 197; 21/128, 164; 19/62, 98, 124
Pembrokeshire, Wales ('Penbrokeshyre') 19/98
Pennal, Mer., Wales ('Pennale') 17/2
Peterborough, Cambs. ('Peturburgh', 'Peturborow(e)', 'Peturboro(u)gh', 'Peturboro', 'Peturbore', 'Peterborogh', 'Petorborogh') 10/23; 17/37, 39, 63; 20/13, 44, 100, 148, 176; 21/11; **Benedictine abbey** 20/37, 52, 157, 183
Pipewell, Northants. ('Pipwell'), **Cistercian abbey** 16/17
Pontefract, Yorks. ('Poumfrett'), **anchorage** 21/124
Poole, Dorset ('Pole') 21/148, 160
Porchester, Hants. 20/175
Potters Bar, Herts. ('Potters Barre') 19/21
Prescot, Lancs. 20/177
(?)**Pucknall**, Hants. ('Pyknall') 19/87
Putney, Sur. ('Potteney', 'Putney') 21/104; 1/9v, 15r

Raglan, Mon. ('Raglond') 20/39
Ramsey, Hunts. ('Rames(s)ey') 20/173, 176, 177
Ratcliff, Mx ('Ratclyffe') 19/86
Reading, Berks. ('Re(y)dyng') 21/50; 19/87
Reigate, Sur. ('Rygate') 21/55

Rhodes, Greece ('the Rodes') 19/46
Richmond, Sur. ('Rich(e)mount(e)', 'Richemound(e)', 'Richmound(e)', 'Rych(e)mond')
Observant friary 19/10; 1/11r
palace of Henry VII 16/13; 10/29, 31, 178; 20/17, 42, 78, 81–5, 92, 97; 21/27–30, 33, 35, 43, 46, 49, 52, 53–55, 60, 87–8; 21/7, 23, 25–30, 32–3, 43, 46, 49, 52–5, 60, 67, 71–2, 77, 91, 98, 104, 108–9, 113–15, 118, 121; 19/8–9, 12, 16–17, 40, 43, 53, 77, 95, 98–9, 110; 1/4r, 7r, 8r, 9r, 9v, 10v, 11r, 11v, 12r, 12v, 15r
Richmond bank 1/11r
Richmond Park 21/25; 19/7; 1/4r
Richmond, Yorks. ('Richmont') Franciscan friary 19/97
Richmond, honour of ('Rychmounte/ Richemond fee') lands of Lady Margaret in Cambs., Lincs., and Kendal (see **Kendal** above) 10/4, 15
Ripple, Worcs. ('Riple', 'Repull', 'Rypley') 19/39, 58, 105
Rochester, Kent ('Rochest(e)re', 'Rochester') 19/88, 93; **cathedral priory** 21/27
Rockingham, Northants. 20/114
'Rode of Walle' see **Northampton**
Rome, Italy 20/67; 21/56, 58, 66, 106, 119, 121, 122; 19/17, 19, 72, 92; **hospital of St John Lateran** 20/40; **hospital of St Thomas of Canterbury** 19/103
Romsey, Hants. ('Rumsey') 19/74
Rothwell, Northants. ('Ravell'), **priory of Austin canonesses** 20/153
(?)**Roughton**, Lincs., **church of St Margaret** ('seynt Merg(ar)ett*es* (besyd*es* Tatsall)') 20/31; 21/9, 19(?)
Roydon, Essex 21/3, 58, 62, 77, 148
Royston, Herts. 20/153; 21/66; 19/27
Rudham, Nfk ('Rudam') 20/159
Rutland 20/18; 21/126

Saffron Walden see **Walden**
St Albans, Herts. (('Sanctus Albanus', 'Seynt/ Saint Albon(e)s/Albonez', 'Syntalbonys', 'Senalbonis', 'Seynt Abones') 16/21, 12d; 17/25, 38, 52; 20/84, 87, 89; 19/15, 30, 32, 33, 75, 80, 86, 92, 96, 101, 105; **Benedictine abbey** 1/7v
St Anne's chapel see **Cambridge**
St Davids, Pembs., Wales ('Seynt Davis') 19/113; **cathedral** ('the churche of Saint David', 'Saincte David') 19/71, 93; **diocese** 19/105
St Johns see **London**
St Neots, Cambs. ('Seynt Nedes') 20/180
St Omer, France, **Observant friary** ('a howse of observauntes in Fraunce') 20/80
Santiago de Compostela, Spain ('Seynt Jamys') 19/33
Scotland ('Skot(t)land', 'Skotlonde', 'Scotlond') 20/31, 105, 115, 123, 126c; 21/18–19, 48; 19/40, 72
Scotterthorpe, Lincs. ('Stoterthorp') 21/7
***Scotton**, Yorks. 10/25
Sempringham, Lincs. ('Sympryngham', 'Sempryngham'), **Gilbertine priory** 20/13, 30, 32, 34, 41, 90, 94, 122, 139, 146, 158, 160, 175; 21/10–11, 17, 19, 71; 19/6, 74, 105
'le Serte' 16/3, 7
Sheen, Sur. ('Schene') 17/19, 21, 22, 28; **charterhouse** ('the charterhousse/auter at Schene', 'the (ankure at the) charterhous(s)e', '(the prior of) the charterhowse besyd*es* Richmound') 17/22, 24, 25; 20/84, 85; 21/27, 35; 19/8 (perhaps London), 10 ('Syon' but Sheen intended) (see too **London**)
Sheldon, Warks. 10/29, 58
Sheppey, Kent ('(ile of) Shep(p)ey/Shiphey'); **abbey of Benedictine nuns** 20/176, 184, 185, 186, 195
Shillingthorpe, Lincs. ('Shyllyngthorpe') 16/7, 10
Shrewsbury, Salop ('Scewresbryg'), **fair** 20/44
Skipwith, Yorks. ('Skyppwith') 17/22
Sleaford, Lincs. ('Slefford', 'Sleforth') 10/53; 20/36, 129, 173
Somerset ('Somursetshyre', 'Somersett', 'Somersetshyre') 19/42, 53, 73
Southampton, Hants. ('South Hamton', 'Sowthehampton') 10/53; 21/11, 44
South Holland, Lincs. ('Sowgh Holand') 20/157
***South Molton**, Devon ('Molton') 20/176
Southwark, Sur. ('Sothewark', 'Sowthewerk ') 16/19; 21/120; **Marshalsea** ('Marshalsee') prison, principally for poor debtors 19/10, 102
(?)**Southwick**, Northants. ('Southwik') 1/6r
Spalding, Lincs. ('Spaldyng') 20/11, 51, 62, 102, 111, 165
Staffordshire 20/119
Staines, Mx ('Stanes', 'Stany') 19/95, 96
Stamford, Lincs. ('S[t]ampford', 'Stampforth(e)', 'Stampfor(t) (towne)', 'Stanneford', 'Staunford') 16/20, 16d; 20/11, 12, 15, 18, 21, 22, 26, 28, 33, 39, 40, 47, 50, 57, 64, 65, 77, 79, 80, 103, 104, 118, 124, 147, 150, 152, 155, 156, 161, 164, 167, 168, 169, 171, 174, 179, 180, 182,

184, 185, 186, 187, 195, 197; 21/9, 12, 13, 15, 20–1, 30, 42, 46, 143; 19/13, 36, 51, 86; 1/7r
almshouse 20/164
anchorage see below and see too **ANCHORESSES** in the PEOPLE index
Browne's Hospital 20/124
church of St Paul, anchorage (see **ANCHORESSES** in the PEOPLE index); **(guild of) St Katherine** ('Seynte Katerynse') 21/71
church of St Stephen 20/163
fair 20/ 90
friaries 21/139
Augustinian 20/161, 164, 195; 21/28
Carmelite 20/164
Dominican 20/164
Franciscan 20/164, 195; 21/12, 37
priory of St Leonard (Benedictine monks) 20/164
priory of St Michael (Benedictine nuns) 20/164, 179–80, 183; 21/19–21, 39, 48, 71, 91, 111, 139; 19/13, 36; **anchorage** 21/131; 19/36, 51 (see too **ANCHORESSES** in the PEOPLE index)
Stapleford, Leics. ('Stapulforde') 19/45
Steelyard see **London**
Stilton, Hunts. ('Stelton') 20/14, 40; 21/11
Stoke-by-Clare, Sfk ('Stokelar') college of secular canons 20/119
Stony Stratford, Bucks. ('Stone in Stretforth') 20/80, 89
Stourbridge common see **Cambridge**
Stow Park, Lincs. deer park of the bishop of Lincoln 20/162
***Stratford**, Essex, **Cistercian abbey, i.e. Stratford Longthorne** ('Stratfforde abbey') 17/29
Stratton Audley, Oxon. ('Stratton Awd(e) ley') 17/43, 49
Stretton, Rutland ('Stretton in Strete') 21/14
Sudbury, Sfk, **Our Lady of Sudbury** ('oure Ladye Sudburye') 17/31
Sutterton, Lincs. 20/106
(?)**Suttons Chasse** 20/119
Swaffham Bulbeck, Cambs. ('Soffham'), **priory of Benedictine nuns** 21/27
Syon ('(the) Syon', '(the) Sion'), Mx; **Birgittine abbey** ('seynt Brygyt') ('seynt Brygyt(ez)/Bregett', '(Seynt Bregett at) Syon') 16/13; 17/24, 25; 20/81, 83, 85, 88; 21/22, 23, 24, 27, 30, 36, 46, 60, 61, 98, 113, 119, 128, 153; 19/8, 10 (but see **Sheen**), 12, 35 ('the Sion'), 77, 80, 94, 120; 1/9v; **Corpus Christi guild** ('Corpus Chr*ist*i gylde at Syon') (no such guild recorded, although there was a Guild of the Nine Orders of Holy Angels near Syon) 21/113

***Tattershall**, Lincs. ('Tateshale', 'Tat(t)eshall', 'Tatyshall', 'Tetersale', 'Tat(er)sall', 'Tater(sale)', 'Tatishald', 'Tatsall', 'Tatsull') castle with collegiate church, granted Lady Margaret by the King in 1487 10/6, 16, 17, 19, 21, 22, 24; 17/57; 20/31, 34, 35, 38, 88, 105; 21/9, 19, 40, 111, 121, 161, 165, 175, 196; 19/19, 23, 28, 34, 79, 91 ('Tater'); 1/7r, 8r
Thetford, Nfk ('Thettforde') 17/32, 33, 35
Thornall, Northants (home of David Phillips, constable at Maxey) 20/169–70
'Thornam' error for **Thorney** (q.v.) or Thornton, Lincs. (?) 20/96
Thorney, Cambs., **Benedictine abbey** ('the abbey of Thornaiy') 20/52, 90, 96
***Thorpe Waterville**, Northants. ('Throp Waterfeld') 20/41
Thurcaston, Leics 21/29
'Thystelworthe' see **Isleworth**
Tonbridge, Kent ('Tonnebryge') 21/92
Tongs, Herts. ('Tong(g)es') manor of Cecily Bedell (q.v. in the PEOPLE index) 19/99, 100, 101,
***Torrington**, Devon, **chapel** ('fre chappell in Torryngton') 21/97
Tutbury, Staffs. ('Tutbury', 'Tyddbery'), **Benedictine priory** 20/119, 122

Ulting, Essex ('Oultynge') 17/30

Vaudey, Lincs. ('Vaude', 'Vawde'), **Cistercian abbey** 20/12, 45

Wakerley, Northants. 20/175
***Wakes Colne**, Essex ('Colne Wake') 2/2
Walcott, Lincs. 20/165
Walden, Essex ('Wauldon') 17/35
Walderham Hall, Northants. ('Waldram Hall') farm and ferry crossing on the river Welland 20/102, 111
Wales ('Wal(l)es', 'Walez', 'Walis') 20/59, 111, 129; 19/19, 21, 73, 81, 98, 113
Walsingham, Nfk ('Waules(s)yngham', 'Waules(h)yngham', 'Walsyngham') 17/33, 34, 35, 39, 40, 41, 55; 20/155, 158; 19/41, 87, 88, 93, 97i, 120; 1/11r; **altar of St Laurence** 20/154; **Our Lady of Walsingham** 20/154; 21/12

***Waltham**, Essex 21/20, 126; **abbey of Austin canons** 10/15, 23; 21/127; 19/99
Waltham Cross, Herts. 21/55, 139; 19/39, 48, 100, 104
Wansford, Northants ('Walmesforth'), **Wansford bridge** 20/153, 162, 171, 195
Wanstead, Essex ('Waynstede') manor of Henry VII 21/150; 19/107
Wardrobe (see **London**)
***Ware**, Herts. ('War(r)e') 16/3, 5, 24–5, 7d, 29d, 30d; 10/120; 17/24, 28, 155; 21/26, 77, 102, 121, 129; 19/78, 93, 98; 1/6v; **friary** 21/20, 40, 60; 19/31, 87
***Washingborough**, Lincs. 10/25
Weldon, Northants ('Weldom') 20/87
'Welynge' near Grantham, Lincs. 17/64
'Wencent' altar of St Vincent at unknown church (?) 20/170
Westacre, Nfk ('Westacre'), **chapel of St Thomas Becket at Custhorpe** 20/157
West Country ('the west countre(e)', 'the west partiez')10/23, 84; 20/178; 19/40, 76
***West Deeping**, Lincs. ('West Depyng') 16/3, 14, 29d, 30d (see too **Deeping**)
Westhay, Som. 10/39
Westminster, Mx ('Westmy(n)ster', 'Vestmester', 'Vestmyster', 'Westmynstour') 16/13; 10/47; 17/19, 22, 24, 25, 26, 28; 20/43, 45, 105, 186; 21/28, 35, 41, 49, 55, 58, 66, 109, 112, 113, 115, 141; 19/18, 32, 76, 83; 2/33
  Benedictine abbey 21/22, 27, 40, 59, 108, 112, 132, 139, 144, 149, 160; 19/69, 71, 76
    St Edward the Confessor's shrine ('Seynt Edmoundes shryne', but with Westminster entries; seemingly an error for 'Edwardes') 21/108, 112
    St Stephen's Chapel 21/58
    Our Lady of Pew ('our(e) Lady of Pew(e)/Pue') oratory above St Stephen's Chapel, Westminster, OR chapel within the Abbey of Westminster (Matthew Payne, 'The first chantry chapel of Lady Margaret Beaufort at Westminster Abbey', in *Performance, Ceremony and Display in Late Medieval England*, ed. Julia Boffey (Donington: Shaun Tyas, 2020), pp. 273–83) 17/24, 27; 20/86; 21/40, 108, 112; 19/77; 1/6v
  Palace of Westminster 21/40, 112; 19/76, 91 ('the corte')
    Court of Chancery 21/38, 44, 67, 77, 148
    Court of Common Pleas ('the Comenplace') 20/129
    Court of Exchequer ('the chek(k)er(e)', 'the escheqwyere', 'the eschequ(i)er', 'the excekker(e)') 20/20, 126c, 164, 170, 198–9; 21/129; 19/55, 95
Whaddon, Cambs. 20/153
White Hill, Herts. ('Whithyll'), **our Lady of White Hill** 21/125
'(le) Whytehorse' 16/13, 19
Wilberfoss, Yorks., **Benedictine priory** 1/13r
Wimborne, Dorset ('Wynborn(e)', 'Wynbourne', 'Wynburne', 'Wymbourne'), **Wimborne minster** burial place of Lady Margaret's parents 10/148; 19/42, 53, 55, 73, 108, 115–16
Wymondham, Nfk ('Wemondan') 20/32
Winchester, Hants. ('Wenchester', 'Wynchester') 20/47, 162, 175; 21/48
Windsor, Berks. ('Wynd(e)sore', 'Wendesore', 'Wensor', 'Windsore', 'Wynesowre', 'Wenysowre') (most references are probably to the manor of Henry VII) 17/19, 21, 22, 24, 25, [67]; 20/38, 40, 121, 178, 183; 21/23, 25, 26, 50, 98; 19/94; 1/12v; **St George's chapel** 19/94; **deanery** 21/23;
Wingland, Lincs. ('Wilond') 20/62
Wisbech, Cambs. ('Wesbych', 'Wysbech') 20/155, 185; 19/91; **Our Lady of the Sea** 20/157; **St Peter's church** 20/157
Wittering, Northants ('Wittering/ Wettering') 20/162, 171
Wolford Magna see **Great Wolford**
Woodstock, Oxon. ('Wod(e)stok') hunting lodge of Henry VII 10/44; 17/39, 41, 42, 43, 44, 49, 50, 52, 53; 20/34, 126c; 19/32
***Woking**, Sur. ('Okyng(e)', 'Wokyng') 10/147; 17/24, 28, 32; 20/126, 139; 21/30; 19/3, 32, 59
Woolpit, Sfk, **Our Lady of Woolpit** ('our(e) Ladye of Wull(e)pitt') 17/31
Wothorpe, Northants. ('Worthorp') 20/122
***Wrestlingworth**, Beds. ('Wrastlingworth', 'Wrastlyngworth') 10/158; 20/78

York, guild of St Christopher and St George (at the Guildhall) 20/182
Yorkshire ('Yorkshyre') 20/45; 21/12, 63; 19/31; **the Wolds** ('Yorkes wold') 20/39

GENERAL INDEX

Note: As throughout this edition D91.16 is cited as 16, D102.10 as 10, D91.17 as 17, D91.20 as 20, D91.21 as 21, D91.19 as 19, D102.1 as 1, D102.2 and D102.6 as 2 and 6 respectively, and D56.131 as 56, all in this order. A slant separates the page/folio number, e.g. 21/23 (D91.21, p. 23).

ALE AND BEER 16/8–9, 19, 4d–5d; 17/20, 31; 20/91, 117; 21/37, 129; 19/9, 12, 75, 84, 92, 106; 1/8v, 11v, 15r; **ale vinegar** 16/25, 4d

ALMS 16/4d; 10/10, 133; 17/21, 25, 31, 35–6, 62, 67; 20/30, 39, 41, 54, 65, 92, 95, 115, 122–3, 127, 135, 151, 159–60, 178, 182, 188, 195; 21/20, 38–9, 44, 55, 57, 66, 71, 98, 100, 108, 111, 123–4, 128, 139, 153, 155; 19/17, 22, 25, 37, 40, 51, 82–3, 92–3, 107, 110, 115; 1/8r, 15v, 17r, 18v

ALMSHOUSES 20/164, 171

ANIMALS 16/10; **boar** 17/48; 20/56, 58; **camel** 19/104; **cattle and calves** 16/4–6, 8–10, 17, 19–20, 23, 7d, 8d–12d; 10/181; **dogs** 17/42; 20/85; 19/90; 1/10v; **goats** 16/4–5, 10; 19/81; **lion** 19/97; **oxen** 16/7d–8d; 10/114; 17/26; **pigs and piglets** 16/10, 15, 11d–12d; 20/117, 121; **sheep and lambs** 16/2, 4–6, 8–10, 17–21, 23, 9d–12d; 10/114

ANIMAL BY-PRODUCTS: **bacon** 19/81; **beef** 20/117; **carcases** 16/5, 9d–10d; **intestines** 16/6; **mutton** 20/117; **suet** 16/5–6, 18, 20–1, 12d

ARMOUR 20/27, 78; **briganders** 20/67; 21/52, 57; **(coat of) mail** 20/59; 21/57; **sallets** 21/57; **splints** 21/57

BAGS 20/48; 21/149; 19/8, 102; **money bags** 10/3, 36, 101, 126–7, 132–3, 159; 19/3, 63; **travelling bag** 19/22

BAKED GOODS and sweetmeats 16/11, 25, 3d, 24d, 26d; 21/25, 111; 19/15, 19, 27, 41

BEADS 17/48; 20/60, 88, 160, 176, 180; 21/8, 26, 59, 76; 19/23, 56, 92

BELLS 20/43, 56, 125

BEER see ALE AND BEER

BIRDS and fowl 16/15, 23; 1/6r; **bitterns** 16/4, 23; **capons** 16/4, 15, 23; 17/56; 21/129; 19/18, 46; **chickens** 16/4, 15; 20/30, 122; 19/18, 72, 106; **cignets** 16/4; **cockerels** 16/4, 15; 21/120; **cranes** 16/4, 15, 23; **doves** 20/43; **ducks** 16/4; **geese** 16/15; 20/117; **herons** 16/4; **partridges** 16/4, 23; 20/42, 172; **peacocks** 16/4, 23; **pheasants** 16/4, 15, 23; 17/56; 20/121; 21/52, 129, 132; **pigeons** 20/117; **quails** 16/4; 21/39; 2/14; **swans** 16/15, 23; **woodcock** 19/16

BOATS, barges, and boat hire 17/22, 24–5, 28; 20/17, 27, 45, 82, 87, 102, 175; 21/9, 18, 22, 33, 36, 111, 114, 120; 19/7–8, 12, 18–19, 76–8, 80–3, 89, 94–5, 104; 1/9v, 10v–12v, 13v, 14v–15v, 17r; 2/33

BOOKS (see too **SCRIBAL ACTIVITIES**, and for a discussion of the books see Powell, 'Lady Margaret Beaufort and her Books') 10/67; 20/42, 52, 163, 171, 187–8, 198; 21/18, 74, 99, 125, 141, 144–5, 156, 164; 19/8, 42, 48, 69–72, 93, 95–6, 100, 104–5, 110, 112; 1/5v, 6v, 7v, 8v, 17v

- **for accounts, inventories, official documents, etc.** 16/31d; 10/59; 17/22, 24, 28, 38; 20/11- 14, 24–5, 27, 67, 102, 134, 144, 194, 197; 21/17, 32, 44, 56, 58–9, 67, 75, 90, 130, 135–6, 148, 152; 19/3, 8, 18, 29, 50, 60, 72, 112, 124; 1/11r; 2/1–2, 18; 6/5
- **calendar** (see too ***Kalender of Shephardes*** below) 21/125
- **chapel and devotional books** 20/186, 198; 21/159
  - **antiphoners** 21/129, 159; 19/34, 52, 88, 101, 120;
  - **diurnal** 19/70
  - **graduals** 21/129, 159; 19/90
  - **missals** 20/14, 190; 21/40, 43, 74
  - **offices and mass settings (Name of Jesus, Transfiguration, 'Miserere')** 20/160, 171; 21/39; 19/31
  - **pontificals** 19/17
  - **porteous** 20/12, 17, 85, 126; 19/14, 79, 83; 1/7r
  - **prayer rolls** 17/51; 19/73 (?), 80
  - **pricksong books** 19/108; 1/6v

BOOKS (*Cont.*)
chapel and devotional books (*Cont.*)
primers 20/14, 28; 21/21, 40, 63, 135; 19/8, 38, 69, 81–2, 109
processional 20/14
psalters 20/173; 21/20, 71; 19/80; 1/5v
English books 19/71
French books 21/16; 19/38, 62, 124
grammar books 21/91
Lady Margaret authored books 20/42(?), 104
Latin books 19/89
manuscripts 17/37; 20/171
music books 19/108
named books (*STC* numbers cite first references to indentifiable printed books)
'A booke of fortune' 1/5v
The Canterbury Tales (*STC* 5083)19/70
'The coming of the king of Castile (and Edmund Pole)' (see **Select Bibliography** sub 'The Meeting') 21/103, 108
Eneydos compyled by Vyrgyle (*STC* 24796) 21/9
Festum dulcissimi nominis Jhesu (*STC* 15851, 15852) 20/160, 171
The Fruytfull Saynges of Davyd (*STC* 10902) 19/112; 1/5v
Horologium Sapiencie (*The Book of Diverse Ghostly Matters, STC* 3305) 19/13
Imitatio Christi (*STC* 23954.1, 23954.7) 20/122
Kalender of Shephardes (*STC* 22408) 19/13; 1/5v
Legenda Aurea (*STC* 24873) 20/111
Liber Cathonis (*STC* 4839.4) 1/5v
Meditationes Vitae Christi (*STC* 3259) 21/141
The Mirroure of Golde for the Synfull Soule (not named but identifiable as *STC* 6894.5) 21/142
'Miserere' (setting of Psalm 50) 20/171
'Rosary' 19/76
Scala Perfectionis (*STC* 14042) 21/10, 22; 19/9
This sermon folowynge (funeral sermon for Henry VII, *STC* 10900) 1/13v
De Transfiguratione Jhesu Cristi (STC 15855) 20/160
Vitas Patrum (*STC* 14507) 20/180
printed books (see too **named books** above and Powell, 'Lady Margaret Beaufort and her Books') 10/33; 20/17, 104, 122, 127, 129, 138, 160, 166, 171; 21/27, 30, 40, 43, 74, 123, 133, 135, 142, 156; 19/56, 117, 121–2, 125; 1/17v

BREAD, rolls, etc. 16/6, 22, 2d–4d; 17/20, 31; 20/117; 21/129; 19/12, 75, 92, 106; 1/6v, 8v, 15r
BRUSHES and combs (see too **HORSE SUNDRIES), brush** 20/87, 151, 174; 19/56; **combs** 20/60, 188; 19/42, 75; 1/8v
BUILDING WORKS
at Boston 20/158
at Cambridge
Christ's College 16/8, 16; 10/107–8, 124, 132, 146, 148, 160, 182 (paper slip); 21/2, 28, 35, 97, 99, 114, 123, 127, 135, 138, 160; 19/5, 7, 14–15, 17, 21, 28, 31, 33, 39, 53, 65, 89–90, 121; 1/10r, 18r; **chapel** 1/13v, 15v
Jesus College 20/94, 135, 154, 195
St Anne's chapel 19/88
St Mary's church (now Great St Mary's) 20/155, 182, 195
at Chertsey bridge 1/4v
at Coldharbour 10/107; 20/126, 139, 163, 185, 199; 21/129; 19/7, 59; 2/8, 10–12, 14, 16, 22, 29, 34, 36; 6/6
at Collyweston 17/54, 56, 59, 61, 64, 67; 20/41, 123, 139; **Worsop's house** 19/42, 54
at Fotheringhay 19/35
in France 20/80
at Hatfield 21/119
at Helpston 19/110
at Kelsey 20/157
at Kirton in Holland 21/22
at London, the Riall 19/23, 30, 36, 46, 59
at Richmond 21/43
at Stamford, anchorage at priory of St Michael 21/131, 154; 19/36, 51; **Austin friars** 20/161, 195
at Wansford bridge 20/153, 162, 171, 195
at Ware 20/155
at Westminster 10/47bo
at Windsor 17/25, 67
at Woking 20/126, 139
CANDLES, tapers, torches, lamps, wax, and wicks 16/6, 12, 20, 24, 16d–19d; 17/31, 35, 50–1, 53; 20/79, 83, 123–5, 154, 178; 21/7, 12, 18, 23, 32, 74, 111, 129; 19/13, 30, 75, 84, 87–8, 97, 106; 1/8v, 11v
CANDLESTICKS 20/47, 50–1, 118, 166, 173–4; 21/37, 92, 131, 159–60; 19/7, 38; 1/5v; **snuffers** 20/61
CARRIAGE of materials and people 16/3, 9–14; 17/47; 20/26, 33, 37, 45, 47, 66, 91–2, 102, 117, 127, 135, 138, 153, 160, 162, 167–8, 172, 177, 181, 183–4, 186, 192, 196, 200; 21/7, 9, 13, 16–17, 26–7, 35, 45, 61, 64–6, 74, 106, 120,

129, 136–8, 150; 19/12, 19, 35, 38, 41, 45, 47, 59, 74, 84, 87, 89–90, 94, 99, 102, 104, 106, 111; 1/5v, 7r, 9v, 10v, 12v, 15r, 18r
CEREALS: **bran** 16/6; **corn** 16/9; **grain** 20/47; **oats** 16/14, 23, 25, 29d; 1/15r; **wheat** 16/6, 8–9, 18–19, 21–2, 1d–2d, 4d; 10/62, 120; **wheatmeal** 16/18–19, 22, 2d–3d
CHAPEL FURNITURE **and equipment** (see too **chapel and devotional books** sub **BOOKS**) 20/66; 21/79
altars 17/24, 33; 19/104, 120; **altar cloths** 19/108
censers 21/131; 1/5v
chalices 10/130; 21/40, 67, 76, 115, 120; 19/84–5, 122; 1/6r; **chalice-cases** 19/85, 114
corporal 19/6; **corporal cases** 10/19; 19/56
cruet 17/64
crucifix 21/37
hassocks 21/134
holy water sprinklers 20/187; 21/95; 19/9, 85, 103
holy water stoups 20/106; 21/95, 146; 19/84–5, 103; 1/10r, 11r
mitre (for Boy Bishop) 20/148, 183
palms (for Palm Sunday) 20/30
pax 17/64; 20/184; 21/146; 19/20
pyx 20/12
sacring-bell 19/20
singing bread (i.e. wafers) 20/14, 91; 19/8
CHESTS 10/127; 20/184; 21/131; 19/29, 96; 1/6v
book press 17/63
coffers 10/126, 129, 132; 17/20, 35; 20/17, 67, 81, 92, 112–13, 118, 126b-c, 134, 166, 174; 19/16, 93
standards 10/133; 17/20, 25, 28
trunks 17/20; 20/108, 111; 21/18, 29, 76; 19/80, 95
CLOCKS **and dials** 17/24; 21/29, 47, 55, 76, 109, 118, 130, 141; 19/9, 32; 1/5v, 11r, 12v
CLOTHING (see too **HEADWEAR** and **FOOTWEAR**) 20/120, 146; 21/50, 61, 77, 106, 158; 19/59, 87; 6/4
armlet 20/125
chemise (?) 17/25
cloaks 21/17, 32
coats 20/13, 28, 61, 80, 92–3, 125, 190; 21/31–2, 41–2, 100, 136; 19/21, 25–6, 46, 48, 74, 87, 92, 96, 97I, 102, 113
doublets 20/53, 89; 21/41, 136; 19/6, 12, 41, 97I, 103; 6/4
garters 20/17, 21; 19/57
girdles 20/160, 188; 21/28, 31, 93, 137; 19/7, 29, 56; 1/8v
gloves 20/61, 166; 21/8, 93; 19/69, 73–4, 79–80, 93, 121; 1/13v
gowns, robes, and kirtles 10/143; 17/20, 64; 20/16, 23, 43, 52, 86, 89, 93, 95, 125, 148, 157–8, 181–2; 21/8, 13, 17, 31–2, 42, 101, 105–6, 116, 119, 136, 143; 19/10, 25–6, 36, 38, 40, 42, 46–7, 73, 81, 91, 97, 97I, 97II, 98, 102–3, 106, 110, 116, 118, 121; 1/7v, 8v; 2/28–9, 35; 6/6
hose 17/25; 20/15, 38, 41, 55, 58, 80, 86, 93–4, 112, 125, 148, 151, 155, 157–8, 167–8, 180–1; 21/7, 13, 17, 31–2, 41–2, 45–6, 54–5, 64, 94, 100–1, 109, 116, 136, 138, 142, 149–50; 19/6, 12, 25, 36, 41–2, 46, 48, 74, 87, 97, 97I, 97II, 102–3, 106, 111–13; 1/8v; 6/4
jackets 21/106; 19/75, 97I
kerchief 20/80
mantles and mantlets 20/80, 93, 148; 21/32; 1/15v; 2/34; 6/4
nightgowns 21/7, 17, 137
shirts 20/55; 21/32; 19/16; 1/6v
sleeves 21/31–2; 19/75 (?), 97I, 112
slop 20/81
smocks 20/93, 136
stockings 19/6
stomacher 21/32
surplice 19/90
tippets 19/97II, 111
undercoats 20/124; 19/40, 47
COAT OF ARMS 21/95
COINS **and currency**
angels 20/57; 19/87
cash 20/127, 162, 188, 199; 21/2, 112; 19/109; 6/5
clipped money 10/77, 101–02, 133 (in contrast to **good money** 10/133, cf. 20/191)
crusadoes 10/133
currency: **Flemish** 20/63; **sterling** 20/63
five-shillings gold 17/33; 20/50; 21/15; 19/15, 87
forty pence 19/15
gold (coins) 10/133; 20/50, 90, 127; 21/15, 22, 96, 99, 107, 123; 19/80, 84, 87, 109; 2/29 (see too **five-shillings gold** above, and **(gold) pence/shillings** and **thirty-pence (gold)** below)
groats 10/101; 20/191; 21/59, 112; **clipped groats** 10/77, 101; 20/143, 191, 199; 21/2, 9; 19/87; **Roman groats/money** 17/27, 67
grosses and minutes 10/133
(gold) pence 17/33; 19/15, 40, 70
(gold) shillings 19/14–15
nobles 2/22; 6/3
thirty-pence (gold) 17/31; 20/78; 19/15

COINS and currency (*Cont.*)
white money 17/31
CONTAINERS, including cooking and serving utensils (see too **GLASSES)** 10/47; 1/4v
barrels and other containers for beer, wine, fish, spices, etc. 16/4, 9–12, 17–19, 23–4, 6d, 14d–16d; 20/180, 199
basins 20/47, 50, 106, 112; 21/25, 107, 113, 120, 146; 19/97
baskets 16/10, 19d; 20/32, 36, 47, 53; 21/16, 30, 33–4, 57, 66, 120, 146; 19/29, 79, 81–2, 97I; 1/11v, 14v
bottles 17/35; 20/82; 21/33, 76, 92, 120, 147; 19/78
bowls 20/82, 104–5, 127, 153, 174–5, 182; 21/120; 19/80; 1/5v, 10r-v
boxes 10/19; 17/27; 20/54, 123; 21/56, 60, 111; 19/7, 78–9, 90, 94, 96, 110
bucket 20/182
cases 21/92, 107, 114, 146, 149; 19/78–9, 85
chafer 20/82
flagon 1/17v
hampers 20/82, 94, 166, 171; 21/33, 120; 19/7
jugs and ewers 17/51; 20/12, 57, 82; 21/42, 96, 120, 146
kettle 20/182
pans 20/13, 15, 58, 175; 19/73; 1/15v
parcels 20/184; 21/129
pincase 10/126
pots 10/127; 20/33, 77, 88, 94, 124, 173, 175, 179, 182, 191; 21/29, 96–7, 107, 146; 19/9, 42–3, 73, 84, 94, 99–100; 1/6r, 8v, 10r, 15v, 17v
CONVEYANCES
carts 20/122, 126b, 172; 21/42, 50, 120; 19/19; 1/9v, 11r-v, 15r
chair/chariot 17/20, 23–4, 27–8, 30, 67; 20/89, 99; 21/102–3, 157; 2/11, 32, 35; 6/3–4; **bolts and links** 2/35; **chariot nails** 17/30; 21/103; **stay and steps** 2/35; **wheel keys** 2/35
litter 17/30, 35, 37, 39, 41–3, 49–51; 20/170–1, 200; 21/17, 34, 76, 157; 19/15, 59, 77–8; 2/8, 17; 6/3–4; **nails and pins** 17/35, 42–3; 20/171; 21/26, 55, 60–1; **shafts** 19/78; **trimmings** 17/35; 20/13, 27

DAIRY PRODUCTS: **butter** 17/43; 20/85; 19/42, 72, 75, 92, 106; 1/8v, 15r-v; **cheese** 17/43; 20/117; 21/56, 63; 19/95, 109; 1/14r; **milk** 20/188; 21/20, 42; 19/42, 75, 92, 106; 1/8v
DECORATIONS and embroidery 17/67; 19/17; **embroidered eyelets** 20/146; 19/47, 97I; 1/7v; **embroidered flowers** 17/20; **(embroidered/copper) portcullises** 17/23, 38; 2/12, 15–17; 6/3; **embroidered rose branches** 17/38; **powderings** 17/27, 49; 20/99; 21/13; 19/47; 2/14
DEVOTIONAL ARTEFACTS: **brooches** 17/25, 33; 20/40, 62; 19/87; 1/4r, 17v; **St Audrey laces** 17/36
DIETS and commons 17/21–2, 29–40, 43–4, 49–53, 65; 20/22, 44, 53, 59, 62, 154, 159, 161, 176, 184, 192; 21/35, 41, 43, 56, 92, 96, 121, 125, 129; 19/13, 21, 34, 39, 75, 78, 83, 89, 101; 1/10v, 12v–13r
DOCUMENTS (i.e. 'writings'; see too **LEGAL AND FINANCIAL ARRANGEMENTS AND PROCESSES**) 20/12–13, 67, 126c (?); 21/44, 56, 135, 148; 19/47, 55, 92; 1/8r
acts of parliament 2/8
bills and billets 16/2, 2d–3d, 20d–21d, 23d–25d, 28d, 31d; 10/16, 26, 127, 132, 182 (paper slip); 17/19–21, 23–8, 30, 37–9, 42–3, 47, 49, 54–5, 60, 62, 65–7; 20/5–7, 11, 17–18, 21–2, 25, 32, 36, 48, 50–1, 58, 60, 74, 78–9, 81, 83, 91, 93–4, 98, 100, 105, 107–8, 113–14, 127, 142, 147, 150, 153, 155, 157–8, 160, 164–5, 167–70, 172, 180, 185, 187–8, 194; 21/7–8, 11, 13–14, 16–17, 20–1, 33–6, 38–9, 44, 46, 49, 55, 57, 60, 62–3, 65–6, 91, 94–5, 97–8, 100–5, 107–9, 113–7, 121–5, 129, 131, 133–4, 137, 139–42, 144, 147; 19/5–6, 8–9, 14, 22, 24–6, 30, 32–8, 40–3, 45, 47–8, 65, 69, 74–6, 78–9, 83–4, 88–9, 92–4, 110, 113; 1/15r-v; 2/10, 22, 24–5, 36
briefs 10/23; 20/28
letters (including papal and pardon letters) 17/38, 60; 20/18–19, 23, 28, 46, 67, 77, 88, 92, 94, 116, 119, 123, 146, 158, 164, 167–8, 179, 182–3, 187, 199; 21/14, 16, 33, 44, 48, 52, 59, 91, 118–20, 122; 19/20–1, 34–5, 39–40, 42, 72, 83, 91, 93–4, 100–4, 107; 1/4v; **letters of attorney** 19/71; **letters patent** 21/148, 160; 19/39, 45, 58; **letters under seal** 19/111
licences 17/42; 20/113; 21/77; 19/45
messages 17/21–2, 25, 35, 38, 42, 49, 53, 61, 65; 20/11–12, 14, 16, 18–19, 35, 38, 42, 68, 77–9, 87–8, 95, 102, 105, 107, 110–11, 115–8, 126, 151–2, 167–8, 170, 176–7, 180, 197; 21/52–3, 57, 66, 74, 92, 95, 97, 103–4, 108–9, 115, 118, 120–1, 123–4, 127, 131, 133, 138, 140, 143, 147, 157; 19/5, 23–4, 43, 53, 55, 80, 82, 113, 118; 1/11v, 12v, 13v, 17r
papal bulls 20/17, 67, 87, 139; 21/52, 56,

pardons 20/23, 28, 164, 182, 199; 21/12, 14, 16, 33; 19/10, 18, 72, 90, 93–4, 103
reckonings 20/172, 189; 21/50, 99, 111, 114, 141
subsidies 19/90, 120
tallies 16/2d–4d, 7d, 10d, 12d
DOLLS 19/111
DRINKINGS 17/24, 29, 31, 35, 41, 43, 53
DRINKS 17/27

EGGS 17/43; 19/42; 1/15r-v
ESTATES see **LAND and estates**
ENTERTAINMENTS 20/61; 19/5;
disguisings, morris and plays 20/60, 67, 126b, 190; 21/61, 63, 77, 93, 144–5, 159; 19/59, 112, 121
EXHIBITIONS (see too **WAGES, stipends and pensions)** 17/37, 42, 49, 55, 61, 67; 20/34, 63, 65, 84, 115, 120, 131, 134, 172, 175, 178, 194, 196, 199; 21/9, 19, 24, 38, 66, 71, 77, 99, 111, 117, 130, 152, 154, 157, 161; 19/14, 34–5, 51–2, 56, 90, 98, 116, 118; 1/17v

FAIRS 10/7, 12; 20/25, 44, 49, 66, 90, 122, 174, 177; 21/8, 51; 19/35, 46
FARRIER WORK 17/21–2, 33–4, 39–40, 43, 51, 67
FEASTS of the Christian calendar
All Saints (All Hallow Day/Eve/Tide), 1 November 17/54–5; 20/46, 120, 122, 178; 21/50, 135; 19/34, 37–8, 46, 59, 104
All Souls, 2 November 20/46
Annunciation of the Virgin (Our Lady Day/ Even (in Lent)), 25 March 20/22, 37, 84, 86, 88, 113, 150, 152; 21/12, 15, 30, 104–5, 108, 111; 19/13, 20, 78–9; 1/6v, 8r, 9r
Ascension Day (moveable) 20/155; 21/22, 112; 1/12v
Assumption of the Virgin (Our Lady('s) Day (the Assumption)), 15 August 17/31; 20/41, 165–6; 21/41, 124, 127; 19/29, 97
Candlemas (Day), (Purification of our Lady), 2 February 10/24, 160; 20/4, 11, 78, 146; 21/9, 34, 96; 19/70–1, 74–5, 95; 1/5r
Holy Innocents (Childermas Day), 28 December 17/62
Christmas (Eve/Day) (Nativity of Christ/the Lord), 24/25 December 17/62; 20/57, 59–61, 77, 111, 126, 126b, 127, 138, 145, 163, 182, 188, 190, 199; 21/13, 48, 59, 63, 92–3, 96, 142–7, 159; 19/5, 43, 45–7, 109–10, 113, 121
Conception of Our Lady (Our Lady Day), 8 December 17/59; 20/124, 183, 187; 21/56, 143; 19/41–2, 107
Corpus Christi Day (moveable) 20/101, 159; 21/23, 116; 19/20, 90–1; 1/14v
Dedication Day (of a church) (variable) 20/23, 118, 155; 21/115, 134
Easter (Day) (moveable) 10/16–17, 21; 20/16, 18, 20, 34, 39, 49, 90–1,126b, 152; 21/13, 15, 106–9, 111, 114; 19/14–17, 84, 89; 1/9r
Good Friday (moveable) 20/16, 90, 151; 21/15, 107; 19/14, 83; 1/8v
Lammas (St Peter ad Vincula), 1 August 21/94
Lent (moveable) 20/13–14, 83–4, 88, 147, 150; 21/10–12, 98–9, 102, 105, 108, 111; 19/8, 14, 53, 78; 1/7r
Maundy Thursday (the/my Lady's Maundy, 'Shere Thursday') (moveable) 20/16–17, 23, 88, 96, 151–2; 21/15, 101, 103, 107, 109, 153; 19/12, 14, 26, 51, 97I, 103, 106, 115; 1/15v
Michaelmas (St Michael (Day)), 29 September 10/26, 177; 17/43; 20/46, 126, 147, 170, 180; 21/44, 46; 19/38, 72, 94, 101; 1/14r
Midsummer (Nativity of St John the Baptist), 24 June 10/139; 17/19, 37; 20/24, 27–8, 37, 100, 160–1; 21/30, 34–5, 119; 19/24, 90, 95–6, 109; 1/15r
Nativity of the Virgin (Nativity of Our Lady, (Our) Lady Day (the Nativity)), 8 September 20/114, 171; 21/47; 19/32, 100
New Year (Day/Even), 1 January 10/1, 49–50, 148, 152, 161; 17/63, 67; 20/57–8, 60, 68, 128, 140, 148, 184, 188–9, 190–1, 198–9; 21/59, 61, 67, 73, 76, 144, 154–5; 19/3, 44–5, 58, 109, 121
Palm Sunday (moveable) 20/88; 21/106; 19/14
Relic Sunday (variable) 21/37
St Andrew (Day), 30 November 20/123, 183; 19/45
St Bartholomew (Day), 24 August 21/125
St David's Day, 1 March 19/75
St Etheldreda's Day, 23 June 19/21
St John's Day, 27 December 17/62
St Martin (Day) (Martinmas), 11 November 10/26; 21/66
St Nicholas (Day/Eve(n)), 6 December 17/59; 20/52, 124, 148, 183; 21/56, 143; 19/41, 109
St Stephen's Day, 26 December 17/62
St Thomas (Day), 29 December (Becket) 21/142; 19/109; **21 December (the Apostle)** 19/42

FEASTS of the Christian calendar (*Cont.*)
Twelfth Day (Epiphany), 6 January 17/65; 20/59, 126b, 155, 190; 21/62, 144; 19/45, 75, 110
Trinity Sunday (moveable) 20/31, 100, 158; 21/115; 19/20, 91
Whit Sunday (Pentecost) (moveable) 20/97, 155; 21/114; 19/19–20, 90; 1/13v
FISH and eels 16/2, 4, 8, 10, 15, 17, 19, 23–4, 13d–15d; 17/25, 42–3; 20/81; 21/18, 115; 19/8, 11, 77, 79–80; 1/7r, 8r-v, 13r, 15r
FLAX 21/131; 19/22, 75, 89, 92, 102, 106; 1/8v, 13r
FLOWERS 17/50; **roses** 20/162; 21/37, 119; 19/20, 22; **rose leaves** 17/27
FOOTWEAR
boots 20/24, 45, 51, 54, 97, 156, 168–9; 21/12, 21, 34, 42, 109, 122, 145; 19/20, 74, chees109
shoes 17/25, 28, 35, 44; 20/13, 15, 24, 28–9, 35, 38, 41, 47, 51, 53, 55, 58, 78, 80–1, 93–4, 103, 112, 120, 124–5, 148, 155, 158, 167–9, 181–2; 21/7, 13, 15, 21, 31–2, 34, 39, 41–2, 45–6, 51, 54–5, 64, 94, 96, 101, 109–10, 116, 118, 122, 135–6, 142, 145; 19/6, 12, 20, 25–6, 36, 42, 45–6, 48, 74–5, 87, 92, 97, 97I, 97II, 102, 106, 109, 111; 1/6v, 8v–9r
slippers and light shoes 17/28; 20/24, 45, 47, 93, 97, 103, 154, 158, 169, 175, 181, 186; 21/12, 34, 93, 96, 109, 122, 135; 19/6, 20, 39, 45, 75, 109
FRANKINCENSE 16/28d
FRATERNITIES and guilds 20/12, 32, 36, 40, 182, 187; 21/113, 135, 143, 153; 19/18, 39, 84, 96, 105; 1/5v, 17v
FRUIT
apples 16/11; 17/53; 20/32, 47, 87; 21/12, 21, 23, 129, 134; 19/81, 108
cherries 17/25
dates 16/11
dried, pickled and preserved fruit 16/11, 25, 19d–21d, 23d–26d; 20/180, 198=9
figs 16/11, 19d; 20/17
grapes 17/38; **verjuice** 16/25; 17/37
lemons 16/11, 25, 25d; 21/28
oranges 16/11, 25d; 20/103; 21/12, 28, 74; 19/105, 110; 2/7; 6/6
pears 17/25; 20/51, 103, 175; 21/129, 134; 19/29, 75
pomegranates 21/23, 132, 134; 19/104–5
prunes 16/11, 25, 26d
quinces 16/4, 25, 25d; 20/119, 175, 178, 188; 21/130; 19/33; 1/13r
strawberries 21/28; 19/22; 1/14v
FURNISHINGS, including bed furnishings (see too **TAPESTRIES and hangings** and for **beds** see **FURNITURE**) 20/106, 111
bedding 20/102, 106, 187; **(bed) canopies** 20/44, 179; **bed covers** 20/81; 21/32; **bed staves** 21/94; **bed strings** 2/28
blankets 20/126; 2/25
bolsters 10/14; 20/38, 126, 174; 21/65, 76; 2/25
carpets and mats 20/43, 127, 180; 21/7, 11, 16, 130; 19/7, 41, 71, 75, 112
coverlets 20/38, 85, 101, 126, 157, 174; 21/65–6, 76, 134
cushions 21/130; 2/33
mattresses 10/14; 17/24, 60; 20/38, 126, 127, 174; 21/65, 76, 94
pillows 20/126, 163; **feathers for pillows and cushions** 21/94; 2/33
sheets 20/38, 126, 157, 179; 21/26; 19/95; 2/25; **packing sheets** 2/10
FURNITURE
beds (see too **LODGINGS**) 17/22, 26, 60; 20/13, 61, 85, 89, 102, 113, 126, 136, 138, 177, 179, 188; 21/27, 32, 35, 49–50, 65, 76–7, 94, 126; 19/11, 77–8, 82, 94–5, 98, 117; 1/11r, 13r-v; 2/25; 6/5
benches 20/82, 112
boards and cupboards 17/59; 21/146; 19/41, 90, 111; 1/15r
chairs (see too **chair/chariot** sub **CONVEYANCES**) 21/101, 120; 1/14v
coffin 19/30
stools (see too **weaving stools** sub **SEWING, spinning, knitting and weaving**) 17/22; 21/33; 19/102; 1/8v, 11r; **footstools** 19/24
tables 17/59; 20/52, 66
FURS, skins, fleece, and hides 16/5–6, 17–20, 23, 8d–11d; 10/128; 17/27, 67; 20/25–6, 29, 48, 53, 55–6, 62, 66, 80–2, 118, 125, 136, 146, 167, 174, 177, 184–6, 198; 21/10, 13, 17–18, 26, 31–2, 34, 38, 45, 50–1, 54–5, 64–5, 73, 75–6, 94, 100, 106, 136–8, 149–50, 157; 19/6, 12, 31, 35, 38, 40, 47, 56, 73, 75, 83, 90, 97I, 103–4, 106, 110–11, 117; 1/7v; 2/28–31, 36; 6/3

GAME and hunted animals 16/23; **bucks** 20/40, 114, 120; 21/25, 30, 36, 38; 19/30; **deer** 17/55; 1/12r; **hares** 20/162, 165; **harts** 20/31, 44; 21/54, 112; **rabbits** 16/4; 20/170; 21/122
GAMES 20/17, 36–7, 126c; 21/30; 19/7, 94, 112; **jousts** 19/76; 2/33; **'the ring'** 19/93
GEMSTONES and stones: **amber** 21/121; 19/23, 56; **diamonds** 21/146; 1/15r; **pearls** 21/123, 128, 156; 19/108; **rubies**

21/119, 146; 19/10; **sapphires** 21/95; 19/79, 121
GIFTS 17/38; 21/58; **New Year gifts** 10/1, 48, 148, 152; 17/63, 67; 20/57–8, 60, 68, 128, 140, 148, 163, 184, 188–9, 191, 198–9; 21/59, 73, 76, 144, 154–5; 19/3, 44, 54, 58, 65, 109, 113, 121
GLASS 21/33, 76, 92; **glass windows** (see too **GLAZIERS** in the PEOPLE index) 19/37; 6/6; **looking glass** 1/9r
GLASSES (containers for various purposes, not all made of glass) 20/21, 27, 35 (ivory), 42, 85, 166 (ivory), 168, 199; 21/33, 43, 114, 116, 120; 19/6, 18, 56; 1/14v

HABERDASHERY
buttons 20/48, 171; 2/26, 35; 6/4
fringes 20/18, 33, 98–9, 171, 177; 21/16, 18, 36, 47, 65, 73, 94, 100–1; 19/38, 56; 2/17, 26–7, 35; 6/4
laces 20/48, 188; 21/93, 136, 149; 19/42, 75, 78, 92, 106; 1/8v; 2/34; 6/4
napkins 20/20, 54; 21/8, 62; 19/5, 23
points 20/27, 125, 188; 21/32; 2/27
ribbons 20/21, 47, 82, 98–9, 114, 135, 160, 164, 166, 171; 21/9, 11, 16, 18, 28, 31, 46, 73, 93, 101, 111–12, 115, 134, 141, 143–4, 156; 19/6, 8, 11, 20, 23, 36, 38, 56, 75–6, 81, 86, 92, 106–7, 109, 111; 1/8v, 12r, 13r
tapes 20/58
tassels 2/26
trims 19/6, 47, 82, 97II, 103, 110
HAWKS 20/26, 42, 44, 46, 50, 68, 96, 107, 114, 122, 124, 155–6, 164–5, 170; 21/37, 43, 49, 105, 122, 155; 19/29, 31, 41, 72, 96–7, 101, 108; 1/6r; **bells** 20/166; **hoods** 20/166
HAY 16/4, 14, 17, 24, 30d; 10/114; 17/49; 21/33; 19/31
HEADWEAR
bonnets 17/49, 53, 67, 92; 20/15–17, 26–7, 41, 82, 125–6, 127, 136, 156–7, 163, 185, 191–2; 21/13, 18, 41, 43, 53, 57, 76, 107, 120, 134, 136, 155; 19/12, 25, 36–7, 75–6, 82, 87, 92, 97I, 97II, 103, 106, 110–11, 115, 118; 1/8v, 14r, 17v; 2/34; 6/4
caps 20/92; 21/109, 137, 157; 19/106
frontlets 20/80–2; 19/105, 110, 118; 1/17v; 2/22; 6/4
hats 20/13; 21/26, 54, 128; 19/105, 110, 118
hoods 20/190; 19/97I; 2/22
HERBS 17/25; 20/32, 47, 168; 19/27
HIDES see **FURS, skins, and hides**
HONEY 16/10, 24, 16d, 27d; 19/18; 2/7
HOOPS 17/20
HORSES and horse hire 16/3, 13–14, 29d; 10/2, 7, 114; 17/21–2, 24, 27–44, 46–7, 49–53, 60, 65, 67; 20/11, 13, 17–19, 22, 28–9, 31, 35, 37, 39, 41, 44, 46, 48–50, 56, 61–2, 66, 81, 84, 90, 96–7, 103–5, 110, 114–15, 117, 120, 126, 136, 147, 149–50, 152, 154–5, 159–62, 168, 176–7, 185, 189, 197, 200; 21/15, 18, 26, 35, 38–9, 41, 43–4, 47, 49, 53, 57–9, 62, 66, 74–5, 91–2, 96, 100, 103–4, 114–15, 120–1, 125–6, 129, 131–2, 138, 141, 145–6, 155; 19/14–15, 17, 21, 23, 30, 32, 37, 39, 42, 47, 59, 71–2, 87, 89, 91–3, 95–6, 98, 100–2, 104–6, 108, 110, 114; 1/4v, 9v, 10v, 11v; 2/34
amblings 21/121
bay horses 21/8
geldings 20/172; 21/121
grass horses 21/58
hackneys 16/14; 17/29–33, 35–9, 43, 50–1
hobby horses 20/97, 105, 109
litter horses 17/39
mares 21/8
palfreys 16/14; 10/114; 20/45, 49, 185; 21/12; 19/27,
HORSE SUNDRIES
bits 20/29, 49; 21/103; 2/11
bosses 21/103; 2/17
bridles 20/29
collars 21/103; 19/78
harnesses 20/18, 27, 29, 90, 98–9, 138, 170; 21/17, 101, 103. 131, 157; 19/33–4, 57, 59, 77–8; 2/26; 6/3
horse nails 17/35–6, 51
horse rugs 20/13, 41, 47, 176
horseshoes 16/14; 17/21–2, 24, 32–6, 39–40, 43, 51–2;
pasterns (shackles) 17/36
reins 2/26
saddles 17/27–8, 32, 39, 67; 20/29, 98–9; 21/31, 100–1, 103, 157; 19/34, 59; 6/3; **saddle brushes** 17/32, 51; 20/29, 87, 151, 174; 21/32, 66, 137; **buckles** 17/27; 21/103; **girths** 17/36; 21/43, 103; **hair (for packing saddles)** 17/39; **pad** 21/43; **pendants** 17/27; 21/103
spurs 19/25, 74
stirrups 21/43, 103
sumpter cloth 21/31
HOUSEHOLD AND CHAMBER DEPARTMENTS (not restricted to Lady Margaret's household, for which see **SERVANTS** in the PEOPLE index)
acatry 56/5
bakehouse 16/22, 2d; 17/61; 20/41; 21/79, 162; 19/61, 70

HOUSEHOLD AND CHAMBER DEPARTMENTS (*Cont.*)
buttery 16/23; 20/86, 124; 21/27, 112; 19/11, 18, 76, 85–6, 97, 112, 114; 1/4v
cellar 16/23; 17/31; 20/86, 124; 21/21, 27, 49, 112; 19/11, 18–19, 76, 85–6, 95, 97; 1/4v
chamber 17/49; 21/24, 78–9; 19/86, 95, 124; 1/11v; **chamber of presence** 1/13r
chandlery 16/24, 16d–17d; 21/37
chapel 17/29, 42, 60; 20/12, 64–6, 87, 91, 111, 116, 119, 138–9, 194, 198; 21/79, 117, 140, 157, 162–3; 19/16–17, 30, 45, 54, 60, 62, 89, 101, 107–8, 117, 123–4; 19/28, 33, 37, 45, 47–8, 54, 62, 70, 73, 108, 124
closet 17/63, 65; 20/28, 52, 66, 112, 187; 21/60, 112–13; 19/22–3, 71, 111
coalhouse 20/86; 21/27
counting house 16/31d
ewery 20/106; 19/97; 1/4v
granary 16/22, 2d; 21/40
guardhouse 20/109
jewelhouse see **Bothe** in the PEOPLE index
kitchen 17/67; 20/86, 109; 21/21, 27, 49, 113; 19/11, 18, 76, 80, 85–6, 97; 1/4v, 9v, 15r-v; 2/10, 16; **privy kitchen** see **Meryman** in the PEOPLE index
larders, wet and dry 16/23–4, 7d, 13d
library 19/37
pantry 16/6, 22, 3d–4d; 20/86; 21/27, 48; 19/11, 18, 76, 85, 95, 97; 1/4v
parlour 6/5
pastry house 16/3d; 21/107**pitcher house** 19/86, 97
poultry house 16/6, 2d, 29d; 21/27**saucery** 20/16, 90, 152; 21/15, 107; 19/11, 15, 85, 89; 1/9v
scullery 16/25, 4d; 20/16, 86, 90, 152; 21/15, 27, 107; 19/11, 15, 85, 89, 97; 1/4v, 9v
spicery 16/25–6, 23d; 20/86; 21/27, 127; 19/9, 14, 58, 72, 84, 96, 98
stables 10/140; 17/59; 20/19, 50, 61, 97, 115, 145, 172; 21/19, 102, 121, 126, 139; 19/27
stillhouse 20/47
vestry 17/63; 21/79, 112, 163; 19/23, 38, 61, 69
wardrobe 16/4, 21, 25; 20/24, 87, 90, 104, 151, 174; 21/17–18, 32, 38, 42, 94, 118, 136, 141, 149–50, 159; 19/16, 25–6, 35, 37–8, 43, 51, 76, 86, 102–3, 107, 111; 1/11r (see PLACES index), 13r; **wardrobe of beds** 20/97, 104, 112, 116; 21/27, 31, 34, 112; 19/11, 18–19, 86, 95; 1/4v; **wardrobe of robes** 20/21; 19/40, 101
woodyard 20/86; 19/11, 85; 1/4v

IMAGES 17/25; 20/31, 35–6, 60, 113; 21/20, 93; 19/10, 69, 102; 1/4r, 15r
IRONMONGERY (see too **CONTAINERS**)
andirons 20/166; 21/43; 2/25
bellows 20/15, 81, 151, 174; 21/120; 19/7
bolts 2/35
fire pans 20/82, 174
hooks 20/55, 67; 21/55, 139; 19/94; 1/8v
keys 17/28; 20/17; 21/33, 92; 19/22, 95; 2/35
knives 20/188; 21/92; 19/30; 1/10r
links 2/35
locks 17/24, 28, 35; 20/17, 82, 94, 111–12, 171; 21/30, 33, 65, 120; 19/7, 22, 79; 1/11v
nails 20/33, 109, 131
ovens 2/8
rings (for furnishings, etc.) 20/25, 48, 55, 65, 171; 21/55, 94, 122, 136, 138, 150; 19/97II, 107; 2/23, 31
scissors 21/26
shears 20/15, 21, 93; 21/26; 19/13, 41, 96
shovels 20/81
tongs 20/151
trivet 20/175
IVORY (see too **GLASSES**) 20/35, 60, 88, 160, 166, 176, 180

JEWELLERY (see too **GEMSTONES and stones** and **METALWORK**) 10/127, 132, 141, 148, 151; 17/48, 67; 20/162; 21/119, 156

KITCHEN EQUIPMENT (see too **IRONMONGERY**), **ladle** 20/175; **sieve** 19/12; **strainers** 16/11, 26, 28d

LAND and estates 10/2–3, 6–7, 17, 22–3, 46, 55, 84, 102–3, 127, 130, 148, 159–60, 176–80, 182; 17/26, 67; 20/37, 51, 60, 65, 126, 126c, 129, 139, 147, 153, 156, 159, 198; 21/4, 11, 58, 67, 75, 77, 160; 19/3, 22, 34, 42, 45, 48, 52–3, 55, 59, 66, 91, 100, 107, 120; 2/12
enclosures 16/3, 10; 20/11, 65
farms 10/181; 2/2
fields 16/10; 19/17
gardens 16/10; 20/32, 41, 47, 53; 21/25, 49, 144, 154; 19/11, 52, 83; 2/10
honour of Richmond lands of Lady Margaret in Cambs., Lincs., and Kendal (see Jones and Underwood, *The King's Mother*, pp. 115–25) 10/4, 15
manors and palaces (see too **Bassingbourn, Beddington, Bromley, Buckden, Chelsea, Croydon, Deptford, Easton Neston, Edgcote, Eltham, Fyfield, Garsington, Haling, Hanworth,**

Herons, **Lyddington**, **Richmond**, **Tongs**, **Wanstead**, **Windsor** and asterisked items in the PLACES index) 17/39; 20/67; 21/58, 67, 77, 79, 93, 148, 160; 19/73, 90, 99, 116; 1/6r, 18r
orchards 19/52
parks see **Hatfield**, **Maxey**, **Richmond Park**, **Stow Park** in the PLACES index, and **KEEPERS** in the PEOPLE index
pastures and meadows 16/3, 6–7, 10, 14; 10/86, 114
woods 16/12, 17, 20
LEATHER 20/168; 21/10, 33–4, 103, 120, 137; 19/6, 25, 47, 90, 97II; 1/7v
LEGAL AND FINANCIAL ARRANGEMENTS AND PROCESSES (see too **DOCUMENTS**)
acquittances 19/9
actions 21/160
advowsons 20/175; 19/9, 39, 58, 69, 91, 93
allowances 20/140; 19/45, 65
annuities 20/88, 100, 138; 21/12; 19/71; 1/11r
appropriations of property or a benfice 21/130, 147, 159; 19/15, 52, 89, 90, 92, 96, 120; 1/7v, 17v
assizes 20/103, 114
bargains 20/129
benefices 20/156, 200; 21/100; 19/31, 53, 55, 69, 96, 105
charters 21/148
commissions 2/10–11
confirmations of legal agreements 19/39, 58
contentations 6/9
conveyances of property 21/93
covenants 10/158; 20/126b; 21/91
debts 10/4, 16, 23–4, 26–9, 32, 55, 61, 92, 101, 103, 109–11, 113–14, 120, 123, 125, 135, 143, 146, 158–9, 162; 17/1, 4–5; 20/4–6, 9, 71, 134, 138, 141–2, 144, 194 (see too Appendix to p. 194); 21/1–2, 5, 80, 83, 89, 120, 150, 165; 19/1–3, 60, 63, 65–7, 75, 98, 114, 122, 124 ; 1/18v; 2/2, 18; 6/2
deeds under seal 1/8v
dispensations 21/115, 158; 19/32
dowries 10/55; 1/5r
duties 20/129
evidences 20/20, 126b
examinations 20/61; 19/45
fee-farms 10/4, 15, 23, 25
fees 16/15; 17/65, 67; 20/60, 66, 67, 126, 138, 146; 21/11, 19, 74, 140, 155; 19/10, 42, 45, 52, 71–2, 115, 119; 1/14r, 17v; **knight's fees** 10/140
feodaries 10/28
feoffments 10/17, 23; 19/22, 55, 104
fines 10/22, 27, 138, 141; 20/147; 21/148; 19/90
grants 20/126b; 19/21
indentures 16/15; 10/107; 20/19, 32, 62, 126b, 128, 134, 194; 21/3, 135, 149, 152, 161; 19/14, 58
inquisitions 21/149; 19/15, 51,
instruments* 1/10v
jointures 10/3, 4, 15, 31, 144, 159; 20/126, 137, 147, 200; 21/67, 70, 77; 19/70, 107
judgments 19/7
lawsuits* 20/60, 67, 105; 21/67, 75, 77, 80, 87, 148, 160, 164; 19/55, 62, 105, 120–2; 1/5v
liberties 19/121
loans and advances 10/2, 56, 83, 85, 87, 101, 104, 112, 114, 125, 131, 147, 160; 17/1, 3; 20/134, 138, 192, 194, 197; 21/70, 79–80, 86, 162–5; 19/61–3, 65, 81, 93, 95, 123–5; 1/16v, 18v; 2/8; 6/4
lordships 10/3–4, 15, 17, 177; 17/1; 21/77; 1/6r
messuages 10/147
mortmains 10/127; 21/77; 19/53 (?)
nonage 10/29
obligations 10/2, 127–8, 158, 160; 21/79–80, 163; 19/28, 62, 71, 95, 124; 1/18v
outlawries 10/139; 2/23
parleys 2/12; 6/6
pleas 20/20, 25; 21/77, 121–2
pledges 17/61; 21/37, 79
probates 10/132
promises 20/129
ransoms 21/100
recovery and redemption of rights and property 10/160; 20/66, 147; 21/79, 148, 160; 19/3, 55, 59, 70, 90, 120
resignations of land or property 19/71, 113
seals 17/42; 20/129; 21/95, 107, 117, 146, 149; 19/8, 39, 73, 88
statutes 21/37, 56, 59, 119, 135–6, 159; 19/72
tithes 10/160; 20/11, 58, 65, 189, 198; 19/16, 59, 70, 116
titles to a property 21/93, 148
ullage 16/9, 4d
wardships 10/32, 44, 112, 139; 1/17v
(co-)warrants 20/62; 19/45
wills and testaments 10/132; 21/11
writs 21/148–9; 1/5r; 2/14
LEGUMES 16/30d; 21/23; 19/18
LIFE EVENTS
births 17/45; 20/52; 19/16, 87
burials/funerals 10/133, 147; 17/25; 20/125, 139, 164; 21/45, 75, 124, 159; 19/30, 59, 75, 101, 105, 130; 1/12r
christenings 10/9; 20/148, 151, 163, 180, 197; 21/9; 19/11, 54; 1/11r, 12r, 17r
commencements at University 17/19; 19/24, 27, 53

LIFE EVENTS (*Cont.*)
election of fellows and consecration of Christ's College 21/159
first mass of a new communicant 20/20; 19/83, 86; 1/9r; **first mass of a new priest** 21/118; 19/35, 79
marriages 10/46, 62; 17/19–20; 20/19, 23, 62, 78, 90, 126b, 127; 21/79, 106, 109, 111; 19/107, 115; 1/5r, 17v; 6/5
presentations 21/11
professions of nuns and solitaries 20/185; 21/71, 153; 19/20, 53

LITURGY: **dirige** 19/30; **mass** (see too **first mass** sub **LIFE EVENTS**) 17/31, 62–3, 65; 20/90 152, 164.; 21/15, 39, 108; 19/30–1, 84; 1/9r

LIVERY, **for horses** 16/14; 17/46–7, 49, 65; **for the household** 16/14, 4d, 31d; 20/92, 156, 182; 19/47; 2/33–5; 6/5–6 (see too **portcullises** sub **DECORATIONS and embroidery**)

LODGINGS and board 17/22, 28, 31, 34–7, 41, 44, 50, 53; 20/122, 139, 146, 184, 187, 192, 198; 21/14, 32, 39, 50, 65–6, 74–5, 91, 93–4, 96, 100, 121, 123, 129, 132, 139, 142–3, 160; 19/16, 21, 30, 37, 76, 84, 86, 89, 92, 101; 1/11v, 12v, 15r, 17v; 2/15

MASSES see **OFFERINGS** (see too **first mass** sub **LIFE EVENTS**)

MEAT 16/9d–11d; 20/117

MEDICAL EQUIPMENT: **clyster-pipes** 20/60, 90; **glass phials** see **GLASSES**; **urinals** 20/153, 168, 199; 21/33, 113; 19/6, 79

MEDICINES and beauty products 17/25; 20/47, 83, 117, 147, 172; 21/21, 57, 75, 155; 19/18, 72–3, 98, 108; 1/4v, 17r
ambergris 19/108
damask water 21/43
distilled waters 20/163; 21/36, 39; 1/15r
electuary 20/93
for a horse 17/39; 20/172
ointments 1/6v
powders 17/27; 1/15r
rose water 20/41–2, 85, 104, 169; 21/37, 62; 19/18, 44, 82–3, 96, 110; 1/8v, 14v
syrup 19/92, 99–100, 106
wormseed 21/128

METALS (see too **IRONMONGERY** and **TEXTILES**)
brass 19/7; 6/5
copper 21/131, 159; 1/5v (see too **(copper) portcullises** sub **METALWORK**); **copper gold** 19/73; **copper silver** 19/31
(silver/gold) foil 20/55–6
gilt(-gold) 20/33, 42, 53–5, 63, 67, 82, 97–8, 109, 173, 184–5, 188; 21/67, 76, 96–7, 101, 103, 107, 119–20, 131, 133, 139, 146, 159; 19/7, 41, 57, 81; 1/5v, 6r; 2/33
gold 17/67; 20/42, 53–5, 63, 66, 135, 185, 188; 21/26, 61, 67, 76, 146; 19/9, 11, 29, 57–8, 84, 94, 105, 118, 121–2; 1/4r, 10r, 15r, 17v; 2/26–7
pewter 20/112; 21/25, 113, 120; 19/97
plate (i.e. gold and silver) 10/113, 126–7; 20/65, 106, 108, 111, 135; 21/9, 23–4, 29, 76, 156; 19/11, 21, 57, 94, 122; 1/17v
silver 10/47; 20/42, 184; 21/29, 92, 96, 107, 119, 135, 139; 19/9, 84; 1/4v, 5v, 6r, 10r-v, 13r, 17v; **silver-gilt** 10/127; 20/55, 191; 21/84, 94; 1/10r
tin 10/29, 53; 21/76, 107, 120, 146; 19/99; 1/5v

METALWORK
buckles 21/119
bullions (for books) 21/135; 1/5v, 7v, 8v, 17v
(gold) chains 10/141; 17/20, 37; 21/79, 119, 162; 19/61, 123
(book) clasps 20/42, 52, 163; 21/149; 19/90, 109
crosses 20/335; 21/29, 119, 131, 149, 159; 1/10v (see too **crucifix** sub **CHAPEL FURNITURE and equipment**)
flowers (marguerites (?)) 21/146
Garter insignia 21/24, 29, 76; 19/9, 11
girdle metalwork 19/29
pendants 21/119
(gold) pomanders 19/29
(copper) portcullises 2/12, 15–17; 6/3
(gold) rings 17/48; 20/30, 35, 40, 79, 183; 21/24, 28–9, 67, 76, 95, 110, 119, 156; 19/14, 25
tablets 1/17v
wire (see too **gold and silver cloth/thread/wire** sub **TEXTILES**) 20/175; 21/26

MILL 20/116

MISCELLANEOUS MATERIALS: **chalk** 20/180; **paste** 20/177; **rat poison** 20/44; **sand** 2/25; **varnish** 20/171; 19/7; **white lead** 20/171

MUSIC; **antiphons** 17/61; 20/97; **ballads** 20/11, 100; **songs** 20/40, 160; 19/21, 108; 1/8r; **sonnets** 20/66

MUSICAL INSTRUMENTS: **claricord** 20/12; **organs** 16/14; 17/38, 61; 21/24, 75, 118; 19/15, 37, 44, 47, 59, 87; **tabour** 17/33

NUTS 16/11, 26, 26d; 20/87; 21/20; 19/92

OFFERINGS 17/19, 22, 24–5, 30–3, 35–6, 38, 50, 54, 59, 62–3, 65, 67; 20/11–12, 16, 23–5, 30–2, 37, 40–1, 44, 46, 57–9, 65,

78–9, 81, 83, 86–90, 93–4, 96–7, 100–1, 113–14, 118, 120, 124, 126b, 127–8, 135, 146, 150–5, 157–9, 165, 170–1, 178, 180, 183, 187–9, 195; 21/9, 15, 19–23, 28, 30, 37, 40–1, 46–7, 50, 56, 59, 62, 71, 96, 98, 104, 106–8, 110, 112, 114–18, 124–7, 135, 142–4; 19/7–8, 10, 13–16, 18–20, 22, 27, 29, 32–5, 41, 43, 45, 51, 70, 76–7, 79, 83–4, 88, 90, 93–4, 97, 98–100, 104, 107, 109–10, 115; 1/5r, 6v, 7v–8r, 9r-v, 12v, 13v, 14v, 17r

OFFICIAL GATHERINGS: **council meetings** 20/42–3, 61; **court of sessions** 20/11; **musters** 20/19, 27; 19/91–2, 105 (see too **COUNCILS and groups** in the PEOPLE index)

OILS 16/11–12, 24, 26, 15d–16d, 27d

PACKS and sacks 20/92–3, 126b, 167; 21/18, 31, 76, 136; 21/18, 31, 76, 136; 19/78

PILGRIMAGES 20/16, 165; 21/66; 19/102

PROVENDER 16/14; 17/24, 27, 29–40, 42–3, 49–52, 60; 20/22, 28, 34, 38, 53, 59, 78, 94, 97, 101, 106, 113, 122, 152, 157, 168, 173, 176, 185, 189, 192; 21/19, 27–8, 35, 37–8, 56, 58, 62, 91, 97, 128–9, 132, 145; 19/21, 23, 42, 89, 95; 1/10v

PROVISIONS 16 *passim*; 10/7, 12, 42; 17/26, 48

RENTS and revenues 10/2–6, 9, 15–17, 19, 21–8, 83, 86, 127, 130, 151, 176–9; 16/3, 7, 10, 14; 20/112; 21/94; 19/20, 101; 1/9r, 17r; 2/2

RICE 16/26, 26d

ROPE 20/21; 21/131

RUSHES 16/11; 19/95; 1/12v

SALT 16/12, 24, 15d; 1/15r

SCHOOL 17/20; 21/39, 71

SCRIBAL ACTIVITIES (see too **WRITING AND DRAWING MATERIALS**)
- **binding** 20/14, 111, 122, 186–7; 21/28, 38–9, 75, 136, 149; 19/13, 38, 69, 72, 112, 117
- **enrolling** 21/148–9; 19/45
- **limning** 21/149; 19/17
- **ruling** 21/123
- **sealing** 21/148; 1/8v, 11r
- **setting musical notation** 17/61; 20/97, 160; 21/10, 39; 1/8r
- **translating** 19/89
- **writing** 17/24, 30, 37, 61; 20/20, 24, 32, 62, 97, 126b, 126c (?), 128; 21/17, 56, 59, 99, 119, 130, 142–3, 148–9, 156, 159; 19/9, 15, 43, 45, 48, 58, 70–3, 83, 91, 94; 2/8, 11–12, 23

SEEDS 20/17, 58, 127; 21/55

SERMONS 20/13–14, 52, 78, 101, 124, 147, 150, 155–6, 166, 171–2, 182, 188; 21/10–12, 15, 19, 97–9, 102, 106, 143; 19/12–14, 20, 29, 38, 42, 71, 90–1, 100, 108–9, 112; 1/5v, 7r, 8v, 13v

SEWING, spinning, knitting, and weaving 17/20, 22–3, 27; 20/35, 41, 48, 51, 53, 80–1, 93, 95, 125, 157–8, 167, 169, 181, 190; 21/7, 14, 17, 31–2, 34, 41–2, 47, 54–5, 61, 64, 77, 93–4, 100, 106, 110, 116, 119, 136, 138, 150; 19/5, 7, 20–1, 36, 46, 48, 71, 74–5, 87, 92, 97, 97I, 97II, 98, 102, 106, 109–12; 1/8v, 12r
- **carpet frame** 21/130
- **crochet/needlework hooks** 17/26, 49; 20/108
- **needles** 20/26, 29, 42, 60, 85, 89, 93, 103, 113, 157, 171; 21/26, 55, 93, 106; 19/7, 10, 12–13, 27, 29, 41, 56, 96, 105; 1/12r
- **pins** 17/35, 42–3; 20/81, 84, 171, 191; 19/27, 79, 106; 1/8v
- **spinning wheels** 21/27, 49, 75
- **thimbles** 20/26, 29; 21/93, 111; 19/41, 56, 105
- **weaving frames and other implements** 21/26, 29; 19/29, 41, 74
- **weaving stools** 17/26; 21/26; 1/8v, 10v, 13v

SHRINES AND RELICS 17/36; 20/154, 157

SLAUGHTER HOUSE 16/10

SOAP 16/12, 26, 29d; 17/23; 20/27, 188; 19/7

SPECTACLES 20/95, 166; 21/60; 19/9, 57

SPICES 16/11, 14, 25–6, 21d–23d, 25d–28d; 10/29, 52; 20/32, 90, 146, 172–3; 21/34, 47, 75; 19/39, 79, 96, 99; 1/8r–9r

STRAW 19/78

SUGAR 16/10, 25, 20d–21d; 17/25; 21/129; 19/33, 92, 106; 2/7

TABLEWARE (see too **CONTAINERS**)
- **cups** 16/14; 10/1; 20/33, 79, 106, 166, 174–5; 21/67, 76, 116, 146; 19/84, 121; 1/10r
- **cutlery** 20/28
- **dishes** 20/81, 174, 182; 21/25, 92, 94, 96, 120
- **goblets** 20/182, 184, 188; 19/84, 122
- **platters** 20/174, 182
- **salt cellars** 20/50; 21/37, 67, 95; 19/58; 1/5v
- **saucers** 20/77, 182
- **spoons** 20/160, 175, 185; 1/10v
- **tablecloths** 20/179; 21/16; 19/34, 99
- **towels** 20/179; 19/23; 2/14 (?)
- **trenchers** 20/175
- **vessels** 16/14

TAPESTRIES and hangings 17/26; 20/63, 66, 91, 117; 1/12v; 6/5
arras 20/25, 172; 21/53; 19/99, 120; 1/6v, 7v, 18r; 2/25
canopies 20/44
cloths of estate 10/127; 21/102
(bed) hangings and curtains 10/127; 17/22; 20/43, 50, 136, 177; 2/23
painted/stained cloths 20/36, 179
Paris and Nebuchadnezzar hanging 10/127
verdures 20/50, 63, 174; 19/104, 120; 2/25; 6/5
TEXTILES and clothing materials (see too **LIVERY**) 20/13, 62; 19/96; 2/9–17, 21–36; 6/3–6
baize 20/81
blanket 20/157, 174; 21/31; 19/103, 111
bombast 20/16
buckram 17/20; 20/20, 25, 33, 54, 89, 97–9, 101, 111, 136, 150, 153, 164, 196; 21/13, 16, 31, 35–6, 47, 64, 66, 73, 98, 101, 116, 139, 149, 156; 19/25–6, 36, 97II, 102, 120
cambric 20/191, 196
canvas 20/26, 29, 33, 37, 49, 54–6, 81, 92–3, 98–9, 101, 103, 108, 118, 122, 125, 135, 153–4, 164, 167, 177, 186, 192, 196; 21/9–10, 18, 26, 34, 36, 41, 61, 64–5, 74, 134, 139, 141, 158; 19/19, 25, 57, 78, 97I, 97II, 102, 115–16; 1/5v, 18r; 2/23, 25; 6/5
cerecloth 20/168; 19/101
chamlet 17/54; 20/17, 66, 82, 136; 21/54, 73, 156; 19/25, 97II, 113; 1/14r; 2/10, 23, 29–30, 32; 6/3
cloth 10/61; 17/49, 51, 54, 61, 67; 20/13, 15, 29–30, 47, 93, 95, 99, 101, 118, 123, 157–8, 168, 170, 181, 185, 191, 197; 21/17–18, 23, 31–2, 42, 45, 54, 64–5, 74, 91, 94, 116, 137, 147; 19/12, 16, 43, 46, 57, 73–4, 78, 87, 97I, 102, 111, 113; 1/11r; 2/23, 27, 32–4; 6/6; **cloth of gold** 10/127, 143; 17/23, 26–8, 67; 20/33, 66, 163; 21/94, 97, 158; 19/8, 10, 12, 59, 108; 2/11, 30; 6/3; **cloth of (gold of) tissue** 10/127; 2/30, 32
cotton 20/23, 25–6, 54, 93, 103, 112, 118, 122–5, 148, 150, 171, 174, 177, 181, 195; 21/7, 13, 17, 31–2, 41, 45, 50–1, 64, 101, 105–6, 122, 137–8, 149, 158; 19/25–6, 51, 73, 87, 97, 97I, 97II, 98, 102–3, 106, 111, 115; 1/12r, 13r
damask 17/28; 20/17, 28, 55, 66, 108, 136, 156, 158, 191, 196; 21/8, 13, 32, 73, 116, 134, 138, 150, 156; 19/12, 76, 99, 103, 108, 117; 1/14r, 17v; 2/14, 16, 21–2, 26, 28; 6/3; **gold of ~** 20/20–1, 89, 96, 123, 126c, 145, 148, 196; 21/101, 133–4; 19/7, 15, 96; 2/17, 23, 26, 30–1; 6/3
diaper 20/113, 166, 196; 21/8, 62; 19/23, 57; 2/13; 6/3
down 20/108
frieze 20/43, 54, 135, 167, 174, 177, 195; 21/64, 74, 136–7, 158; 19/51, 103, 115
fustian 20/89, 95, 101, 108, 118, 125, 136, 181, 196; 21/64, 73, 136; 19/14, 37, 41, 97I, 98–9, 102, 106, 111–12, 120
gold and silver cloth/thread/wire 17/19, 28, 61, 67; 20/18, 21, 43, 63, 66, 78, 98–9, 136, 183, 185, 196; 21/8, 11, 26, 34, 36, 61, 73, 96–7, 101, 103, 133–4, 141, 158; 19/24, 46, 57, 76, 82, 88, 96, 104, 117; 1/7v, 10v, 13r, 15r; 2/15–17, 26; 6/3
'grain' 20/47, 180; 19/108
harden cloth 20/15
holland cloth 17/29; 20/104, 118, 156–7, 177; 21/18; 19/8
kendal 20/93; 19/97II, 102
kennet 19/37
kersey 20/35, 80, 112, 118, 123, 158, 167, 174, 182; 21/13, 31, 45, 50–1, 54, 136–7, 158; 19/12, 78, 87, 97, 103, 106
lawn 20/49, 55–6, 171; 21/20, 57, 61, 73, 120, 136, 139; 19/22, 38, 80–1, 88, 111; 1/14r
Lier (Belgium) cloth 20/56, 98, 108, 127; 21/18, 31, 76, 136, 149; 2/25
linen cloth 17/26, 28; 20/15, 17–18, 21, 56, 67, 89, 92, 118, 135, 157, 162, 172, 174, 177, 185, 195; 21/10, 16–17, 50, 109, 116, 122, 133, 136, 141, 158; 19/9, 19, 23–4, 28, 35, 37, 40, 43, 45, 57, 97II, 98, 105, 115–16; 1/11v; 2/14 (?); **linen mixed with wool** 20/192; 2/35
lining material 17/54, 64, 68; 20/124–5, 181, 190; 19/103
medley 20/20, 25–6, 68, 154, 158, 167, 191, 194; 21/13, 51, 79, 100, 105, 116, 136–7, 162; 19/12, 25, 37, 61, 96–7, 97I, 98, 103, 106, 111, 123; 2/12–16, 22, 24, 29, 31–4, 36; 6/5
murrey 20/54
padding 20/175, 186
Paris fabric 20/80, 177, 198; 19/19; 1/15v
russet 20/13; 19/106, 111
sarsenet 20/20, 49, 56, 63, 66, 89, 97–8, 136, 156, 196; 21/22, 29, 31, 54, 73, 102, 156; 19/57, 76, 97I, 98, 102, 111, 117; 1/17v; 2/9, 11–12, 23, 28; 6/3
satin 17/20; 20/55, 66, 82, 91, 108, 121, 136, 165, 182, 196; 21/22, 47, 50, 64, 73, 76, 138, 143, 150, 156; 19/6, 10, 17–19, 22,

25, 38, 43, 45, 57, 80, 97I, 99, 103, 106, 108, 110, 117; 1/7v, 14r, 17v; 2/12, 34; 6/3

say 10/14; 17/19; 20/33, 67, 166, 199; 21/76; 19/119

scarlet 20/25; 19/40–1, 74, 97II, 98, 102, 106, 119, 121; 2/15; 6/6

silk(s) 10/143; 17/23, 27, 61, 67; 20/17–18, 25, 33, 36, 46, 78, 82, 98, 101, 109, 126, 136, 156, 162, 164, 166, 180, 183, 196; 21/11–12, 26, 50, 61, 63, 65–6, 73, 93–4, 97, 101, 109, 133, 139, 158; 19/8, 10, 19–20, 28–9, 31, 34, 38, 57, 74, 80, 92, 103, 108, 117; 1/8v, 12r, 17v; 2/9, 15, 17, 26–7; 6/3

tawny 20/15–16, 35, 43, 48, 80, 118; 21/7, 41, 100–1, 105; 19/26, 40, 91, 102

ticking 20/174; 2/31–2, 34; 6/5

tuke 17/28; 20/20

velvet 10/127; 17/20; 20/55, 66, 98, 136, 146, 196; 21/9, 18, 22, 24, 32, 54, 57, 73, 76, 100–1, 103, 120, 133–4, 138, 149–50, 155–6; 19/6, 17, 19, 25, 33, 38, 57, 73–4, 76, 90, 97I, 97II, 99, 106, 108, 117–18; 1/14r, 17v; 2/9–10, 14, 21, 23, 27, 34; 6/3

violet (dyed cloth) 20/30, 158, 167; 21/17

watchet 20/125

wool and woollen cloth 16/4, 6, 14, 18, 21, 25, 12d, 31d; 17/27; 20/18, 21, 65, 67, 101, 127, 135, 174, 180, 195; 21/13, 45, 73–4, 105, 133, 137, 158; 19/11, 26, 36, 56, 97II, 98, 103, 106, 115; 1/8v

UNIVERSITY EDUCATION 20/24, 27, 37, 152

VERMILION 21/55

VESTMENTS 17/27; 20/21, 33; 20/108, 111, 115, 140, 153, 164, 168; 21/25, 47, 76, 134, 143; 19/24, 38, 73, 108, 115; **albs** 21/25; **amices** 19/43, 58; **copes** 20/21, 168; 21/115, 159; 19/24, 73

WAGES, stipends and pensions (see too **EXHIBITIONS** and **fees** sub **LEGAL AND FINANCIAL ARRANGEMENTS AND PROCESSES**) 16/15; 10/143; 17/24, 27, 35, 38, 46–7, 49, 55, 64–5, 67; 20/20, 24, 27, 39, 45–6, 49, 79, 91, 104, 152, 160–1, 170, 172, 182, 190, 192; 21/30, 33–5, 44, 46–9, 56, 91–2, 105–6, 108, 111, 119, 147; 19/14, 17, 21, 24, 27, 35, 38, 44–5, 56, 78, 89–90, 92, 94–6, 101, 108, 110, 113, 115; 1/7v, 9v, 15r; 6/6

WATER DEFENCES and management 10/2, 18, 101; 20/13, 20, 28, 32, 62, 80, 103, 165; 21/80, 163; 19/61, 124; 2/7; 6/5, 9

WAX AND WICKS see **CANDLES**

WEAPONS: **arrows (for children)** 20/88; 19/89; **bows (for children)** 17/56; 20/15; 19/89; 1/6v; **guns** 20/32

WINE 16/8–9, 18–19, 23, 5d–6d; 10/4, 18, 39; 17/20, 31, 41, 47, 51; 20/88; 21/26, 37, 57, 73, 129, 146 (from the Rhine); 19/10, 54, 95; 1/6v

aqua vitae 21/91; 19/33, 75

claret 16/23; 21/26; 19/10

hippocras 19/28

malmsey 16/9, 23, 6d; 10/18, 39; 17/47; 21/26, 36

muscatel 16/9, 23, 6d; 21/20, 36, 141; 19/8, 17, 56, 82

osey 16/4, 9

rumney 16/9, 23, 6d; 17/35, 53, 55; 21/36; 19/28

vinegar 16/11, 25; 17/37

WOOD and fuel 16/8, 12–13, 17, 20, 24, 30d–31d; 10/18, 39, 69, 75, 140; 17/37, 50, 54, 67; 20/142, 149, 172, 187; 21/61, 129; 19/80; 1/15r; **bark** 16/2, 8, 16–17, 21, 31d; 10/140; **charcoal** 6/8, 12, 20, 24, 31d; **coal** 20/175; 21/61, 66; 19/20; 2/27

WRITING AND DRAWING MATERIALS 17/24, 37

copperas 19/13, 43

galls 19/13, 43

gum arabic 19/13, 43

ink 20/58; 19/13, 43, 83, 92; **inkhorn** 19/20, 84; 1/13r; **pots (for mixing ink?)** 19/43

lead 20/58

paper 16/11, 26, 28d; 17/30; 20/35, 55–6, 58, 126b, 175; 21/58, 135; 19/7, 29, 38, 56, 71, 83, 91–2, 113; 1/11r; **wrapping paper** 20/99; 21/146

parchment 20/35, 113; 21/38, 55, 75, 114; 19/6, 56, 69, 83, 91–2, 101, 113, 117; 1/6v, 11r

pens 19/83, 92; 1/13r; **pencase** 19/20, 84; 1/13r; **penner** 19/20, 84; 1/13r

sealing wax 19/45, 83

vellom 21/40, 43, 74, 111, 115, 118, 123, 135, 149, 156; 19/7, 29, 43, 56, 83, 92, 117; 1/11r

writing tablets 17/19; 19/107

YARN 20/21, 159, 166, 169, 171; 21/36; 19/7, 41, 75, 112; 1/7v

YARN (*Cont.*)
cord and twine 20/92–4, 97, 99, 101, 107, 123, 126b, 167, 174, 186; 21/7, 9, 16, 31, 61, 64–6, 94, 146; 19/98, 103; 2/35
crewel 17/22; 20/17, 21, 43, 82, 98, 105, 108–9; 21/18, 92, 156; 19/22; 1/6v
thread (see too **gold and silver cloth/thread/wire** sub **TEXTILES**) 17/29, 49; 20/15, 20–1, 26, 43, 68, 89, 92–4, 97, 101, 118, 146, 153, 167, 171–2, 181; 21/11, 13, 16–17, 26, 31, 36, 53, 74, 105, 138, 149–50, 156; 19/6, 10, 13, 25, 36, 41, 56–7, 90, 96, 103, 107; 1/5v, 7v; 2/8; 6/5; **packthread** 20/92, 94, 97, 99; 21/7, 74; 1/5v

SELECT BIBLIOGRAPHY

The Select Bibliography lists web resources, manuscripts, archival documents, and printed sources cited in this edition and/or found to be of most value in the preparation of this edition. For a fuller bibliography of material relevant to the study of Lady Margaret (very full for publications before 1992): Jones and Underwood, *The King's Mother*, pp. 296–313.

WEB RESOURCES

Archival documents relating to Lady Margaret Beaufort: <https://www.sjcarchives.org.uk/institutional/index.php/the-records-of-lady-margaret-beaufort>

(*ACAD*) *A Cambridge Alumni Database*: <https://venn.lib.cam.ac.uk/> (see too Venn and Venn below)

(*AND*) *Anglo-Norman Dictionary*: <http://www.anglo-norman.net/gate/> (see too Stone, Rothwell, and Reid below)

Condon, Margaret, Samantha Harper, and James Ross, 'The Chamber Books of Henry VII and Henry VIII, 1485–1521: An Analysis of the Books and a Synopsis of Henry VII and his Life at Court': <https://www.tudorchamberbooks.org/chamber-books-analysis-and-synopsis–2/>

Condon, M. M., S. P. Harper, L. Liddy, and S. Cunningham and J. Ross (ed.), The Chamber Books of Henry VII and Henry VIII, 1485–1521: <https://www.tudorchamberbooks.org/>

(*DMLBS*) *Dictionary of Medieval Latin from British Sources* (and other Latin dictionaries): <https://logeion.uchicago.edu/> (see too Latham, Howlett, and Ashdowne below)

(*DSL*) *Dictionaries of the Scots Language*: <http://www.dsl.ac.uk/> (see too Craigie, Aitken, and Dareau below)

(*ESTC*) *English Short Title Catalogue*: <estc.bl.uk/> (see too Pollard, Redgrave, et al. below)

Gazeteer of British Place Names: <https://gazetteer.org.uk/>

(LCCP) Lexis of Cloth and Clothing Project (University of Manchester): <http://lexisproject.arts.manchester.ac.uk/>

Lobel, Mary D. and W. H. Johns (ed.), *The British Atlas of Historic Towns*, 3 vols (Oxford: Oxford University Press and Historic Towns Trust, 1969–89), iii (*The City of London from Prehistoric Times to c. 1520*): <http://www.historictownsatlas.org.uk/atlas/volume-iii/city-london-prehistoric-times-c1520-volume-iii/view-text-gazetteer-and-maps-early>

(*MED*) *Middle English Dictionary*: <https://quod.lib.umich.edu/m/middle-english-dictionary/dictionary>

(*ODNB*) *Oxford Dictionary of National Biography*: <https://www.oxforddnb.com/> (subscription only)

(*OED*) *Oxford English Dictionary*: <https://www.oed.com/> (subscription only)

(VCH) Victoria County History: <https://www.british-history.ac.uk/search/series/vch> (see too print volumes for each county)

MANUSCRIPTS

London, British Library: MS Add. 12060 (manuscript of Henry Parker); MSS Add. 59899 and 21480 (books of payments of Henry VII); MS Add. 7099 (antiquarian extracts from a lost chamber book of Henry VII); MS Lansdowne 441 (indenture of Lady Margaret and Westminster Abbey).

ARCHIVAL DOCUMENTS

Cambridge, St John's College, Institutional Archives: see **WEB RESOURCES** above. For archival documents edited or cited in this edition see CAMBRIDGE, ST JOHN'S COLLEGE, INSTITUTIONAL ARCHIVES: TABLES OF EQUIVALENCES 1 AND 2 (pp. 773–776).

London, The National Archives: TNA C 1/294/85; C 1/291/55; C 1/205/71; C 1/338/12; C 4/9/170 (documents relating to James Clarell); TNA C 1/309/39 (document relating to Robert Fremingham); TNA C 1/368/39 (document relating to Worsleys and Ormestons); TNA E 135/3/21 (cartulary of Wimborne chantry); TNA E 150/680/2; E 150/680/3; C 142/30/49–2; C 142/30/96; CP40/980 (documents relating to Miles Worsley); CP40/980 (document relating to Fremingham and Worsley); TNA LC 2/1 (Lord Chamberlain's Department, Record of Special Events, Accounts of Funerals and Mournings, Funeral of Henry VII); TNA SC 1/51/177 (document relating to Thomas Hobson); TNA SC 1/51/189 (letter signed by Lady Margaret Beaufort); TNA PROB 11/14/211 (will of Roger Ormeston); TNA PROB 11/16/179 (will of Richard Lynne); TNA PROB 11/19/69 (will of Henry Hornby); TNA PROB 11/19/116 (will of William Bedell); TNA PROB 11/21/58 (will of Hugh Ashton). TNA, E101/413/2/1; E101/413/2/2; E101/413/2/3 (three books of receipts of Henry VII); TNA, E36/210 (book of expenses of Elizabeth of York); TNA, E101/414/6; E101/414/16; E101/415/3; E36/210; E36/214 (books of payments of Henry VII).

London, Westminster Abbey Muniments: WAM 12181–90 (Stafford household accounts); WAM 19606 (1508–9 account roll of refectorer of Westminster Abbey); WAM 32364 (Stafford rental in hand of William Bedell)

PRINTED SOURCES

Antiquarian Communications: Being Papers Presented at the Meetings of the Cambridge Antiquarian Society, I (Cambridge: Cambridge University Press, 1859)

Ashbee, Andrew, and David Lasocki, *A Biographical Dictionary of English Court Musicians*, 1485–1714, 2 vols (Aldershot: Ashgate, 1998)

Baker, Thomas, *History of the College of St John the Evangelist, Cambridge*, ed. J. E. B. Mayor, 2 vols (Cambridge: Cambridge University Press, 1869)

Barron, Caroline M., and Matthew Davies (ed.), *The Religious Houses of London and Middlesex* (London: University of London, 2007)

Botfield, Beriah (ed.), *Manners and Household Expenses of England in the XIIIth and XVth Centuries*, Roxburghe Club 57 (1841)

Bowers, Roger, 'The musicians and liturgy of the Lady chapels of the monastery church, c.1235–1540', in *Westminster Abbey: The Lady Chapel of Henry VII*, ed. Tim Tatton-Brown and Richard Mortimer (Woodbridge: Boydell, 2003), pp. 33–57

Breverton, Terry, *Henry VII: The Maligned Tudor King* (Stroud: Amberley, 2016),

Brewer, J. S. (ed.), *Letters and Papers, Foreign and Domestic, Henry VIII*, I (London: HMSO, 1920)

Campbell, William, *Materials for a History of the Reign of Henry VII*, 2 vols (London: Longman, 1873–7)

Carley, James P., and Richard Rex, 'The Account of the Miracles of the Sacrament', in *Triumphs of English: Henry Parker, Lord Morley, Translator to the Tudor Court*, ed. Marie Axton and James P. Carley (London: British Library, 2000), Appendix 7 (pp. 253–69)

A Catalogue of the Lansdowne MSS in the British Museum, 2 vols (London: R. Taylor, 1812–19) [no author]

Cokayne, G. E., Vicary Gibbs, and Peter W. Hammond, *The Complete Peerage of England, Scotland, Ireland, Great Britain and the United Kingdom*, 14 vols in 15 (London: St. Catherine, 1910–98; vol. 14 Stroud: Sutton, 1998)

Collegium Divi Johannis Evangelistae 1511–1911 (Cambridge: Cambridge University Press, 1911) [no author]

Colvin, H. M., D. R. Ransome, and John Summerson, *The History of the King's Works*, III. I (London: HMSO, 1975)

Condon, M. M., 'Ruling Elites in the Reign of Henry VII', in *Patronage, Pedigree and Power in Late Medieval England*, ed. Charles Ross (Gloucester: Alan Sutton; Totowa NJ: Rowman and Littlefield, 1979), pp. 109–42

Condon, Margaret, 'God Save the King: Piety, Propaganda, and the Perpetual Memorial', in *Westminster Abbey: The Lady Chapel of Henry VII*, ed. Tim Tatton-Brown and Richard Mortimer (Woodbridge: Boydell, 2003), pp. 59–97

Cooper, C. H., 'On the Earlier High Stewards of the University of Cambridge', in *Antiquarian Communications: Being Papers Presented at the Meetings of the Cambridge Antiquarian Society*, I (Cambridge: Cambridge University Press, 1859), pp. 273–8

———, ed. by J. E. B. Mayor, *Memoir of Margaret Countess of Richmond and Derby* (Cambridge: Cambridge University Press, 1874)

Craigie, Sir William A., A. J. Aitken, and Margaret G. Dareau, *A Dictionary of the Older Scottish Tongue: From the Twelfth Century to the End of the Seventeenth*, 12 vols (London: Oxford University Press; Chicago: Chicago University Press, 1931–2002)

Crawford, Anne (ed.), *The Household Books of John Howard, Duke of Norfolk, 1462–1471, 1481–1483* (Stroud: Alan Sutton, 1992)

Cunningham, Sean, and James Ross, Kingship and Political Society in England, 1485–1529: The Projection and Reception of Royal Authority under Henry VII and Henry VIII (Oxford: Oxford University Press, forthcoming)

Dobie, Alisdair, *Accounting at Durham Cathedral Priory: Management and Control of a Major Ecclesiastical Corporation* , 1083- 1539 (Houndmills: Palgrave, 2015)

Earenfight, Theresa, 'A Precarious Household: Catherine of Aragon in England, 1501–1504', in *Royal and Elite Households in Medieval and Early Modern Europe: More than Just a Castle*, ed. Theresa Earenfight (Leiden/Boston: Brill, 2018), pp. 338–70

Emden, A. B., *A Biographical Register of the University of Oxford to A.D. 1500*, 3 vols (Oxford: Clarendon Press, 1957–9)

———, *A Biographical Register of the University of Cambridge to 1500* (Cambridge: Cambridge University Press, 1963)

Gunn, Steven, *Henry VII's New Men and the Making of Tudor England* (Oxford: Oxford University Press, 2016)

Harvey, Barbara, and C.M. Woolgar (ed.), The States of the Manors of Westminster Abbey c.1300–1422, 2 vols, British Academy, Records of Social and Economic History, n.s. 57–8 (Oxford: Oxford University Press for the British Academy, 2019)

Hatt, Cecilia A. (ed.), *John Fisher's Court Sermons: Preaching for Lady Margaret 1508–1509* (Oxford: Oxford University Press, 2021)

Hayward, Maria (ed.), *Dress at the Court of King Henry VII* (Leeds: Maney, 2007)

——, *The Great Wardrobe Accounts of Henry VII and Henry VIII* (Woodbridge: Brewer, 2012)

Heilpern, Anya, "'Souvent me souvient": Remembering Lady Margaret Beaufort's painted glass in Cambridge', in *Medieval Art, Architecture and Archaeology in Cambridge: College, Church and City*, ed. Gabriel Byng and Helen Lunnon, British Archaeological Association Conference Transactions, 43 (Abingdon and New York: Routledge, 2022), pp. 227–72

Hooker, R., 'Some Cautionary Notes on Henry VII's Household and Chamber "System"', *Speculum* 33 (1958), 69–75

Hosington, Brenda, 'Lady Margaret Beaufort's Translations as Mirrors of Practical Piety', in *English Women, Religion, and Textual Production, 1500–1625*, ed. Micheline White (Farnham: Ashgate, 2011), pp. 185–203

Jenkinson, C., *The Later Court Hands in England from the Fifteenth to the Seventeenth Century* (Cambridge: Cambridge University Press, 1927)

Jones, M. K., 'Lady Margaret Beaufort, the Royal Council, and an Early Fenland Drainage Scheme', *Lincolnshire Historical and Archaeological Society*, 21 (1986), 11–18

——, 'Henry VII, Lady Margaret Beaufort and the Orléans ransom', in *Kings and Nobles in the Later Middle Ages: A Tribute to Charles Ross*, ed. R. A. Griffiths and and J. Sherborne (Gloucester: Sutton, 1986), pp. 254–69

——, and Malcolm G. Underwood, *The King's Mother: Lady Margaret Beaufort, Countess of Richmond and Derby* (Cambridge: Cambridge University Press, 1992)

Kingsford, C. L., 'On some London Houses of the Early Tudor Period', *Archaeologia*, 71 (1921), 17–54

Kipling, Gordon (ed.), *The Receyt of the Ladie Katerine*, EETS OS 296 (1990)

Kisby, Fiona: 'The Early-Tudor Royal Household Chapel, 1485–1547' (unpub. doctoral thesis, University of London, 1996)

——, 'A Mirror for Monarchy: Music and Musicians in the Household Chapel of Lady Margaret Beaufort, Mother of Henry VII', *Early Music History*, 16 (1997) 203–34

Kleineke, Hannes, and Stephanie R. Hovland (ed.), *The Estate and Household Accounts of William Worsley Dean of St Paul's Cathedral 1479–1497*, Richard III and Yorkist History Trust, London Record Society Publications, 11 (Donington: Shaun Tyas, 2004)

Latham, R. E., D. R. Howlett, and Richard Ashdowne, *Dictionary of Medieval Latin from British Sources*, 17 fascicules in 3 vols (London: Oxford University Press for the British Academy, 1975–2013)

Lloyd, A. H., *The Early History of Christ's College, Cambridge: derived from contemporary documents* (Cambridge: Cambridge University Press, 1934)

Lobel, Mary D., and W. H. Johns (ed.), *The British Atlas of Historic Towns*, 3 vols (Oxford: Oxford University Press and Historic Towns Trust, 1969–89)

Martin, C. T., *The Record Interpreter* (London: Stevens & Sons, 2nd ed. 1910)

Mayor, J. E. B. (ed.), *The English Works of John Fisher now first Collected by John E. B. Mayor*, EETS ES 27 (1846)

McLean, N., 'Books given to the Library of Christ's College Cambridge by the Lady Margaret', *The Library* new series, 8 (1907), 218–23

'The Meeting of Henry VII and the King of Castile', *The Eagle*, 15 (March 1889), 1–4 [no author]

Mercator, G., and J. Hondius, *Atlas, or a geographicke description ...*, 2 vols (Amsterdam: Hondius-Janssonius, 1638)

Morgan, Nigel, 'The Scala Coeli Indulgence and the Royal Chapels', in *The Reign of Henry VII*, ed. Benjamin Thompson, Harlaxton Medieval Studies, 5 (Stamford: Paul Watkins, 1995), pp. 82–103

Myers, A. R., 'The Household of Queen Elizabeth Woodville 1466–7', *Bulletin of the John Rylands Library*, 50 (1968), 1–68

Nicolas, Nicholas Harris (ed.), *Privy Purse Expenses of Elizabeth of York* (London: William Pickering, 1830)

O'Mara, Veronica, 'Unearthing the History of an Early Printed Sermon: John Fisher and St John's College, Cambridge', in *Middle English Manuscripts and their Legacies: A Volume in Honour of Ian Doyle*, ed. Corinne Saunders and Richard Lawrie with Laurie Atkinson (Leiden and Boston: Brill, 2022), pp. 212–33

Page, William (ed.), A History of the County of Rutland, 2 vols, Victoria County History (London: Constable, 1908–35)

——, Granville Proby, and S. Inskip Ladds (ed.), *A History of the County of Huntingdon*, 3 vols, Victoria County History (London: St Catherine Press, 1926–36)

Payne, Matthew, 'The First Chantry Chapel of Lady Margaret Beaufort at Westminster Abbey', in *Performance, Ceremony and Display in Late Medieval England*, ed. Julia Boffey, Harlaxton Medieval Studies, 30 (Donington: Shaun Tyas, 2020), pp. 273–83

— (M. T. W.), 'Quentin Poulet, Royal Librarian to Henry VII', *Journal of the Early Book Society*, 24 (2021), 133–57

Payne Collier, J. (ed.), *Household Books of John Duke of Norfolk and Thomas Earl of Surrey; temp. 1481–90*, Roxburghe Club 61 (1844)

Petti, Anthony G., *English literary hands from Chaucer to Dryden* (London: Arnold, 1977)

Pollard, A. W. and G. R. Redgrave, (ed.), 2nd edn W. A. Jackson and F. S. Ferguson, completed Katharine F. Pantzer, *A Short Title Catalogue of Books Printed in England, Scotland and Ireland and of English Books Printed Abroad 1475–1640*, 3 vols (London: The Bibliographical Society, 1976–91)

Powell, Susan, 'Lady Margaret Beaufort and her Books', *The Library*, sixth series, 20 (1998), 197–240, rev. as Chapter 6 of Powell, *The Birgittines of Syon Abbey*, pp. 153–214 (see below)

——, 'Margaret Pole and Syon Abbey', *Historical Research*, 78 (2005), 563–7

——, 'Syon Abbey and the Mother of King Henry VII: The Relationship of Lady Margaret Beaufort with the English Birgittines', *Birgittiana*, 19 (2005), 211–24

——, 'Lady Margaret Beaufort as Patron of Scholars and Scholarship', in *Patrons and Professionals in the Middle Ages*, ed. Paul Binski and Elizabeth A. New, Harlaxton Medieval Studies, 22 (Donington: Shaun Tyas, 2012), pp. 100–21

——, 'Textiles and Dress in the Household Papers of Lady Margaret Beaufort (1443–1509), Mother of King Henry VII', in *Medieval Clothing and Textiles, 11*, ed. Robin Netherton and Gale R. Owen-Crocker (Woodbridge: Boydell, 2015), pp. 139–57

——, *The Birgittines of Syon Abbey: Preaching and Print* (Turnhout: Brepols, 2017) (chapters 6 and 7 include revised material from Powell 1998 and 2005a and b)

——, 'Lady Margaret Beaufort: a Progress through Essex and East Anglia, 1498', in *The Elite Household in England, 1100–1550*, ed. C. M. Woolgar, Harlaxton Medieval Studies, 28 (Donington: Shaun Tyas, 2018), pp. 295–316

——, 'Cambridge Commemorations of Lady Margaret Beaufort's Household', in *Commemoration in Medieval Cambridge*, ed. John S. Lee and Christian Steer (Woodbridge: Boydell, 2018), pp. 123–51

Rackham, H. (ed.), *Early Statutes of Christ's College, Cambridge* (Cambridge: Fabb and Tyler, 1927)

Rawcliffe, Carol, *The Staffords: Earls of Stafford and Dukes of Buckingham* (Cambridge: Cambridge University Press, 1978)

Rex, Richard, 'Lady Margaret and her Professorship 1502–1559', in *Lady Margaret Beaufort and her Professors of Divinity at Cambridge 1502 to 1649*, ed. P. Collinson, R. Rex, and G. Stanton (Cambridge: Cambridge University Press, 2003), pp. 19–56

——, 'The Sixteenth Century', in *St John's College Cambridge: A History*, ed. Peter Linehan (Woodbridge: Brewer, 2011), pp. 5–92

Rogers, Alan (ed.), *The Act Book of St Katherine's Gild, Stamford, 1480–1534* (Bury St Edmunds: Abramis, 2011)

Röhrkasten, Jens, *The Mendicant Houses of Medieval London, 1221–1539* (Münster and London: LIT Verlag, 2004)

S[cott], R. F., 'Notes from the College Records', *The Eagle*, 16 (December 1890), 341–57

Scott, R. F., 'On a List (preserved in the Treasury of St John's College) of the Plate, Books and Vestments Bequeathed by the Lady Margaret to Christ's College', *Proceedings of the Cambridge Antiquarian Society*, 9 (1896), 349–67

——, 'On the Contracts for the Tomb of Lady Margaret Beaufort', *Archaeologia*, 66 (1912–15), 365–76

Starkey, David (ed.), *The Inventory of King Henry VIII: The Transcript* (London: Harvey Miller for the Society of Antiquaries, 1998)

Stone, Louise W., William Rothwell, and T. B. W. Reid, *Anglo-Norman Dictionary*, 2 vols (London: MHRA, 1977–92)

Sutton, Anne F., *The Mercery of London: Trade, Goods and People, 1130–1578* (Aldershot and Vermont USA: Ashgate, 2005)

Underwood, Malcolm G., 'Records of the Foundress', *The Eagle*, 68 (Easter 1979), 7–23

——, 'The Lady Margaret and her Cambridge Connections', *The Sixteenth Century Journal*, 13 (1982), 67–82

——, 'Politics and Piety in the Household of Lady Margaret Beaufort', *Journal of Ecclesiastical History*, 38 (1987), 39–52

——, 'John Fisher and the Promotion of Learning', in *Humanism, Reform and the Reformation: The Career of Bishop John Fisher*, ed. B. Bradshaw and E. Duffy (Cambridge: Cambridge University Press, 1989), pp. 25–46

——, 'The Pope, the Queen and the King's Mother: or, the Rise and Fall of Adriano Castellesi', in *The Reign of Henry VII*, ed. Benjamin Thompson, Harlaxton Medieval Studies, 5 (Stamford: Paul Watkins, 1995), pp. 65–81

Venn, John, and J. A. Venn, *Alumni Cantabrigienses: A Biographical List of all known Students, Graduates and Holders of Office at the University of Cambridge from the Earliest Times to 1900*, 2 vols in 10 (Cambridge: Cambridge University Press, 1922–54)

Voigts, Linda Ehrsam, and Ann Payne, 'Medicine for a Great Household (ca. 1500): Berkeley Castle Muniments Select Book 89', in *Studies in medieval and renaissance history*, third series, 12 (AMS Press: New York), pp. 87–270

Ward, Jennifer (ed. and transl.), *Elizabeth de Burgh, Lady of Clare (1295–1360): Household and Other Records*, Suffolk Records Society, 57 (Woodbridge: Boydell, 2014)

Warnicke, R. M., 'The Lady Margaret Beaufort, Countess of Richmond (d. 1509) as seen by John Fisher and by Lord Morley', *Moreana*, 19 (1982), 47–55

'The Will of the Foundress', in *Collegium Divi Johannis Evangelistae*, pp. 101–26

Woolgar, C. M. (ed.), *Household Accounts from Medieval England*, RSEH n.s. 18, 2 vols (Oxford: Oxford University Press, 1992–3)

——, *The Great Household in Late Medieval England* (New Haven and London: Yale University Press, 1999)

CAMBRIDGE, ST JOHN'S COLLEGE, INSTITUTIONAL ARCHIVES: TABLE OF EQUIVALENCES 1

A list of documents, with catalogue equivalences, edited (marked *) or cited in this edition (SJCA references first, SJLM and other references second).

Old references	New references
D4.7, D4.6	SJLM/3/1/4, SJLM/3/1/5 (draft and probate copy of will of Lady Margaret)
D4.17	SJCR/SJGR/1/1 (Foundation Charter of St John's College, 1511)
D6.4	not yet re-catalogued (agreement to convert the hospital of St John into a college)
D56.12	SJLM/7/1/1 (bill of deposit, Hugh Ashton, 1514)
*D56.131	SJLM/7/5/8 ('Rewardes' to Lady Margaret's servants, 1509)
D56.148	SJLM/7/5/10 (bill of expenses, Thomas Symson, 1509)
D56.172	SJLM/7/5/11 (legal expenses, executors, 1512–13)
D57.17	SJLM/7/8/1 (John Fisher to William Bolton, 1512)
D57.18	SJLM/7/8/2 (John Fisher to Thomas Mawdesley, 1510-11)
D57.34	SJLM/1/3/6 (account of Henry Hornby, 1509–16)
D57.43	SJLM/8/2/3/1 (inventory of plate, etc. given Christ's College, 1509)
D57.160	SJLM/1/1/6/2 (bond of Roger Bell, 1503)
D57.172	SJLM/8/2/3/4 (injunctions of John Fisher, Visitor to Christ's College, 1510)
D91.1	SJLM/2/1/3 (inventory of domestic plate, 1509)
D91.2	SJLM/2/3/3/2 (inventory of wardrobe of robes, 1509)
D91.3	SJLM/3/2/5 (bequests of plate, some given Christ's College, 1509)
D91.4	SJLM/2/2/2 (inventory of Robert Hilton, Hatfield, 1509)
D91.5	SJLM/2/3/3/1 (inventory of robes, etc. in Lady Margaret's chamber and closet, 1509)
D91.6	SJLM/2/1/2 (inventory of goods delivered to Robert Hilton, Collyweston, 1500)
D91.7 and D91.8	SJLM/1/3/3 (draft accounts, executors, 1511–13)
D91.9	SJLM/1/3/2 (accounts of receipts and expenses, Nicholas Metcalfe, 1510)

Old references	New references
D91.10	SJLM/2/3/3/4 (list of jewels kept by Edith Fowler, 1509)
D91.11	SJLM/2/4/1 (inventory of small items kept in three coffers at St Paul's, 1509)
D91.12	SJLM/2/3/1/3 (inventory of wardrobe of beds, Hatfield, 1509)
D91.13	SJLM/1/2/2/2 (accounts of James Morice, 1504–5)
D91.14	SJLM/1/2/2/1 (accounts of James Morice, 1502–4)
D91.15	SJLM/2/3/2/1 (Book of the Revestrie, chapel stuff, 1509)
*D91.16	SJLM/1/1/1/1 (computus of William Bedell, 1506–7)
*D91.17	SJLM/1/1/2/1 (accounts of James Clarell, 1498–9)
*D91.19	SJLM/1/1/3/3 (accounts of Miles Worsley, 1507–9)
*D91.20	SJLM/1/1/3/1 (accounts of Miles Worsley, 1502–5)
*D91.21	SJLM/1/1/3/2 (accounts of Miles Worsley, 1505–7)
D91.22	SJLM/1/2/3 (accounts of James Morice, 1505–7)
D91.24.1	SJLM/2/3/1/5 (inventory of cloth stuff, 1505)
D91.24.2	SJLM/1/3/1 (accounts, executors, 1509–19)
*D102.1	SJLM/1/1/5/1 (accounts of Robert Fremingham, 1509)
*D102.2, D102.6	SJLM/1/1/4/1, SJLM/1/1/4/2 (accounts of Roger Ormeston, 1501–2)
D102.4	SJLM/2/3/1/2 (inventory of wardrobe of beds, 1509)
D102.9	SJLM/1/2/1 (accounts of James Morice, 1500–1)
*D102.10	SJLM/1/1/6/1 (book of receipts and payments of Henry Hornby, 1499-1509)
D102.11	SJLM/9/2/1 (draft of household of Elizabeth of York and Katherine of Aragon)
D102.12	SJLM/2/3/3/3 (jewels in the keeping of Edith Fowler)
D102.13	SJLM/2/3/2/2 (draft of Book of the Revestrie)
D102.14	SJLM/2/1/1 (inventory of goods of Henry Hornby, 1504)
D102.15	SJLM/2/3/1/1 (inventory of unsold stuff, wardrobe of beds, 1509)
D102.16	SJLM/2/3/5 (inventory of sold hangings, 1509)
D102.17	SJLM/3/2/3 (bequests, 1509)
D102.18	SJLM/2/3/1/4 (inventory of Lady Margaret's closet, 1509)
D102.19	SJLM/2/2/1 (inventory, Hatfield, 1509)
D105.89	SJLM/8/2/3/3 (letter Henry Hornby to John Fisher re Christ's College, 1510)
D105.162	SJLM/9/2/2 (record of meeting of Henry VII and Philip, King of Castile, 1505)
D106.1	SJLM/8/2/3/5 (account of expenses for Christ's College chapel, John Scott, 1510–11)

CAMBRIDGE, ST JOHN'S COLLEGE, INSTITUTIONAL ARCHIVES: TABLE OF EQUIVALENCES 2

A list of documents, with catalogue equivalences, edited (marked *) or cited in this edition (SJLM and other references first, SJCA references second).

Old references	New references
SJLM/1/1/1/1 (computus of William Bedell, 1506–7)	*D91.16
SJLM/1/1/2/1 (accounts of James Clarell, 1498–9)	*D91.17
SJLM/1/1/3/1 (accounts of Miles Worsley, 1502–5)	*D91.20
SJLM/1/1/3/2 (accounts of Miles Worsley, 1505–7)	*D91.21
SJLM/1/1/3/3 (accounts of Miles Worsley, 1507–9)	*D91.19
SJLM/1/1/4/1, SJLM/1/1/4/2 (accounts of Roger Ormeston, 1501–2)	*D102.2, D102.6
SJLM/1/1/5/1 (accounts of Robert Fremingham, 1509)	*D102.1
SJLM/1/1/6/1 (book of receipts and payments of Henry Hornby, 1499–1509)	*D102.10
SJLM/1/1/6/2 (bond of Roger Bell, 1503)	D57.160
SJLM/1/2/1 (accounts of James Morice, 1500–1)	D102.9
SJLM/1/2/2/1 (accounts of James Morice, 1502–4)	D91.14
SJLM/1/2/2/2 (accounts of James Morice, 1504–5)	D91.13
SJLM/1/2/3 (accounts of James Morice, 1505–7)	D91.22
SJLM/1/3/1 (accounts, executors, 1509–19)	D91.24.2
SJLM/1/3/2 (accounts of receipts and expenses, Nicholas Metcalfe, 1510)	D91.9
SJLM/1/3/3 (draft accounts, executors, 1511–13)	D91.7 and D91.8
SJLM/1/3/6 (account of Henry Hornby, 1509–16)	D57.34
SJLM/2/1/1 (inventory of goods of Henry Hornby, 1504)	D102.14
SJLM/2/1/2 (inventory of goods delivered to Robert Hilton, Collyweston, 1500)	D91.6
SJLM/2/1/3 (inventory of domestic plate, 1509)	D91.1
SJLM/2/2/1 (inventory, Hatfield, 1509)	D102.19
SJLM/2/2/2 (inventory of Robert Hilton, Hatfield, 1509)	D91.4
SJLM/2/3/1/1 (inventory of unsold stuff, wardrobe of beds, 1509)	D102.15
SJLM/2/3/1/2 (inventory of wardrobe of beds, 1509)	D102.4
SJLM/2/3/1/3 (inventory of wardrobe of beds, Hatfield, 1509)	D91.12

Old references	New references
SJLM/2/3/1/4 (inventory of Lady Margaret's closet, 1509)	D102.18
SJLM/2/3/1/5 (inventory of cloth stuff, 1505)	D91.24.1
SJLM/2/3/2/1 (Book of the Revestrie, chapel stuff, 1509)	D91.15
SJLM/2/3/2/2 (draft of Book of the Revestrie)	D102.13
SJLM/2/3/3/1 (inventory of robes, etc. in Lady Margaret's chamber and closet, 1509)	D91.5
SJLM/2/3/3/2 (inventory of wardrobe of robes, 1509)	D91.2
SJLM/2/3/3/3 (jewels in the keeping of Edith Fowler)	D102.12
SJLM/2/3/3/4 (list of jewels kept by Edith Fowler, 1509)	D91.10
SJLM/2/3/5 (inventory of sold hangings, 1509)	D102.16
SJLM/2/4/1 (inventory of small items kept in three coffers at St Paul's, 1509)	D91.11
SJLM/3/1/4, SJLM/3/1/5 (draft and probate copy of will of Lady Margaret)	D4.7, D4.6
SJLM/3/2/3 (bequests, 1509)	D102.17
SJLM/3/2/5 (bequests of plate, some given to Christ's College, 1509)	D91.3
SJLM/7/1/1 (bill of deposit, Hugh Ashton, 1514)	D56.12
SJLM/7/5/8 ('Rewardes' to Lady Margaret's servants, 1509)	*D56.131
SJLM/7/5/10 (bill of expenses, Thomas Symson, 1509)	D56.148
SJLM/7/5/11 (legal expenses, executors, 1512–13)	D56.172
SJLM/7/8/1 (John Fisher to William Bolton, 1512)	D57.17
SJLM/7/8/2 (John Fisher to Thomas Mawdesley, 1510–11)	D57.18
SJLM/8/2/3/1 (inventory of plate, etc. given Christ's College, 1509)	D57.43
SJLM/8/2/3/3 (letter Henry Hornby to John Fisher re Christ's College, 1510)	D105.89
SJLM/8/2/3/4 (injunctions of John Fisher, Visitor to Christ's College, 1510)	D57.172
SJLM/8/2/3/5 (account of expenses for Christ's College chapel, John Scott, 1510–11)	D106.1
SJLM/9/2/1 (draft of household of Elizabeth of York and Katherine of Aragon)	D102.11
SJLM/9/2/2 (record of meeting of Henry VII and Philip, King of Castile, 1505)	D105.162
SJCR/SJGR/1/1 (Foundation Charter of St John's College, 1511)	D4.17
not yet re-catalogued (agreement to convert the hospital of St John into a college)	D6.4